L203- Commercial Law I

Custom Edition

Frank B. Cross| Roger L. Miller

CENGAGE Learning

Australia • Brazil • Japan • Korea • Mexico • Singapore • Spain • United Kingdom • United States

L203- Commercial Law I, Custom Edition

Senior Manager, Student Engagement:
Linda deStefano

Manager, Student Engagement:
Julie Dierig

Marketing Manager:
Rachael Kloos

Manager, Premedia:
Kim Fry

Manager, Intellectual Property Project Manager:
Brian Methe

Senior Manager, Production:
Donna M. Brown

Manager, Production:
Terri Daley

The Legal Environment of Business: Text and Cases, 9th Edition
Frank B.Cross | Roger LeRoy Miller

The Legal Environment of Business: Text and Cases: Ethical, Regulatory, Global, and Corporate Issues, 8th Edition

Frank B.Cross | Roger LeRoy Miller

The Legal Environment of Business: Text and Cases -- Ethical, Regulatory, Global, and E-Commerce Issues, 7th Edition

Frank B.Cross | Roger LeRoy Miller

This book contains select works from existing Cengage Learning resources and was produced by Cengage Learning Custom Solutions for collegiate use. As such, those adopting and/or contributing to this work are responsible for editorial content accuracy, continuity and completeness.

ISBN: 9781305315280

WCN: 01-100-101

Cengage Learning
20 Channel Center Street
Boston, MA 02210
USA

Cengage Learning is a leading provider of customized learning solutions with office locations around the globe, including Singapore, the United Kingdom, Australia, Mexico, Brazil, and Japan. Locate your local office at:
www.international.cengage.com/region.

Cengage Learning products are represented in Canada by Nelson Education, Ltd.

For your lifelong learning solutions, visit **www.cengage.com/custom.**

Visit our corporate website at **www.cengage.com.**

BRIEF CONTENTS

APPENDICES

ADDITIONAL CASES

CONTENTS

APPENDICES

ADDITIONAL CASES

PREFACE

The study of the legal environment of business has universal applicability. A student entering any field of business must have at least a passing understanding of business law in order to function in the real world.

Additionally, students preparing for a career in accounting, government and political science, economics, and even medicine can use much of the information that they learn in a legal environment of business course. In fact, every individual throughout his or her lifetime can benefit from a knowledge of contracts, employment relationships, real property law, land-use control, and other legal topics. Consequently, we have fashioned this text as a useful "tool for living" for all of your students (including those taking the CPA exam).

For the Ninth Edition, we have spent a great deal of effort making this book more contemporary, exciting, and visually appealing than ever before. We have also added many new features and special pedagogical devices that focus on legal, ethical, global, and corporate issues, while addressing core curriculum requirements.

UNIQUE NEW DIGITAL LEARNING SYSTEMS

Before we discuss the many new aspects of this text, however, we wish to point out the exciting new digital products offered in conjunction with the text.

MindTap

New for *The Legal Environment of Business,* Ninth Edition, MindTap is a fully online, highly personalized learning experience built on Cengage Learning content. MindTap combines student learning tools—such as readings, multimedia, activities, and assessments from CengageNOW™—into a singular Learning Path that guides students through their course.

Instructors can personalize the experience by customizing authoritative Cengage Learning content and learning tools. MindTap offers instructors the ability to add their own content in the Learning Path with apps that integrate into the MindTap framework seamlessly with Learning Management Systems (LMS).

CengageNOW for *The Legal Environment of Business*: Interactive Assignment System

CengageNOW™ is a powerful course management tool that provides control and customization to optimize the student learning experience and produce desired outcomes. The application features a variety of question types to test simple reading comprehension, complex critical thinking, legal reasoning, and case analysis skills. CengageNOW includes:

- **An Interactive Book.**
- **Auto-graded Homework** with the following consistent question types:
    - Worksheets—Interactive worksheets prepare students for class by ensuring reading and comprehension.
    - Video Activities—Real-world video exercises make business law engaging and relevant.
    - Brief Hypotheticals—These applications provide students practice in spotting the issue and applying the law in the context of a short, factual scenario.
    - Case Problem Blueprints—Promote deeper critical thinking and legal reasoning by guiding students step-by-step through a case problem, building on acquired knowledge to truly assess their understanding of legal principles.
- **Personalized Student Plan** with multimedia study tools and videos.
- **Test Bank.**
- **Reporting and Assessment** options.

By using the optional CengageNOW system, students can complete the assignments online and can receive instant feedback on their answers.

Instructors can utilize CengageNOW to upload their course syllabi, create and customize homework assignments, and keep track of their students' progress. Instructors can also communicate with their students about assignments and due dates, and create reports summarizing the data for an individual student or for the whole class.

CourseMate

CourseMate for *The Legal Environment of Business* brings business law concepts to life with interactive learning, study, and exam preparation tools that support the printed textbook. Built-in engagement tracking tools allow you to assess the study activities of your students.

Additionally, *The Legal Environment of Business* CourseMate includes an interactive online textbook, which contains the complete content of the print textbook enhanced by the many advantages of a digital environment.

Cengage Learning Testing Powered by Cognero

Cengage Learning Testing Powered by Cognero is a flexible, online system that allows you to do the following:

- Author, edit, and manage *Test Bank* content from multiple Cengage Learning solutions.
- Create multiple test versions in an instant.
- Deliver tests from your LMS, your classroom, or wherever you want.

START RIGHT AWAY! *Cengage Learning Testing Powered by Cognero* works on any operating system or browser.

- No special installs or downloads are needed.
- Create tests from school, home, the coffee shop—anywhere with Internet access.

WHAT WILL YOU FIND

- ***Simplicity at every step.*** A desktop-inspired interface features drop-down menus and familiar intuitive tools that take you through content creation and management with ease.
- ***Full-featured test generator.*** Create ideal assessments with your choice of fifteen question types—including true/false, multiple choice, opinion scale/Likert, and essay. Multi-language support, an equation editor, and unlimited metadata help ensure your tests are complete and compliant.
- ***Cross-compatible capability.*** Import and export content into other systems.

WHAT IS NEW IN THE NINTH EDITION

Instructors have come to rely on the coverage, accuracy, and applicability of *The Legal Environment of Business.* To make sure that our text engages your students, solidifies their understanding of legal concepts, and provides the best teaching tools available, we now offer the following items in the text.

New Chapter on Internet Law, Social Media, and Privacy

For the Ninth Edition, we have included an entirely new chapter (Chapter 15) entitled **Internet Law, Social Media, and Privacy.** Social media have entered the mainstream and become a part of everyday life for many businesspersons. Throughout the text, we recognize this trend by incorporating the Internet and social media as they relate to the topics under discussion.

We also give the legal issues surrounding the Internet, social media, and privacy special emphasis in this new chapter. This chapter examines some of the laws pertaining to the Internet, intellectual property, and privacy. It also discusses recent legal developments concerning the protection of social media passwords and the use of social media by employers and law enforcement.

New *Managerial Strategy* Features

For the Ninth Edition, we have created a new feature entitled ***Managerial Strategy*** that focuses on the management aspects of business law. Special emphasis is given to sustainability, ethical trends, and changing managerial responsibilities.

Each feature includes a short section entitled ***Managerial Implications*** that provides concrete information for managers and connects the topic under discussion to operating a business. Each feature also concludes with two ***Business Questions*** that prompt students to further examine the issues discussed. **Suggested answers to all the *Business Questions* are included in both the *Instructor's Manual* and the *Answers Manual* for this text.**

Topics examined in these features include:

- Budget Cuts for State Courts Can Affect Businesses (Chapter 2).
- Many Companies Have to Revise Their Social Media Policies (Chapter 23).

New Appendix to Chapter 10 Focuses on Reading and Analyzing Contracts

Because reading and analyzing contracts is such a crucial skill for businesspersons, a special **new Appendix to Chapter 10** has been added. This appendix follows the second contracts chapter and explains how to read and analyze a contract. Then, it presents an example of an employee noncompetition and nondisclosure agreement. The sample contract is annotated so that students can quickly see what each contract provision means.

New Highlighted and Numbered *Examples* and *Case in Point* Illustrations

Many instructors use cases and examples to illustrate how the law applies to business. For this edition, we have expanded both our in-text examples and our discussion of case law by adding highlighted numbered ***Examples*** and ***Cases in Point*** in every chapter.

These two features are uniquely designed and consecutively numbered throughout each chapter for easy reference. *Examples* illustrate how the law applies in a specific situation. *Cases in Point* present the facts and issues of an actual case and then describe the court's decision and rationale. The numbered *Examples* and *Cases in Point* features are integrated throughout the text to help students better understand how courts apply the principles in the real world.

New *Spotlight Cases* and *Spotlight Case Problems*

For the Ninth Edition of *The Legal Environment of Business,* certain cases and case problems have been carefully chosen as exceptionally good teaching cases. ***Spotlight Cases*** and ***Spotlight Case Problems*** are labeled either by the name of one of the parties or by the subject involved. Some examples include *Spotlight on Amazon.com, Spotlight on Apple, Spotlight on Beer Labels, Spotlight on Macy's, Spotlight on the Seattle Mariners, and Spotlight on Verizon.*

Instructors will find these *Spotlight Cases* useful to illustrate the legal concepts under discussion. Students will enjoy studying these cases because the parties are often familiar and the cases involve interesting and memorable facts. **Suggested answers to all case-ending questions and case problems are included in both the *Instructor's Manual* and the *Answers Manual* for this text.**

New *ExamPrep* Section with Two *Issue Spotters*

For this edition, we have added a new section called *ExamPrep* at the conclusion of each chapter. The section includes **two new *Issue Spotters* related to the chapter's topics** that facilitate student learning and review of the materials. **Suggested answers to the *Issue Spotters* in every chapter are provided in Appendix E at the end of the text.**

New *Legal Reasoning Group Activities*

For instructors who want their students to engage in group projects, each chapter of the Ninth Edition includes a **special new *Legal Reasoning Group Activity.*** Each activity begins by describing a business scenario and then requires each group of students to answer a specific question pertaining to the scenario based on the information that they learned in the chapter. These projects may be used in class to spur discussion or as homework assignments. **Suggested answers to the *Legal Reasoning Group Activities* are included in both the *Instructor's Manual* and the *Answers Manual* for this text.**

New *Insight* Features

For the Ninth Edition, we have created **new *Insight into [E-Commerce, Ethics, the Global Environment, or Social Media]* features** that appear in selected chapters. These features provide valuable insights into how the courts and the law are dealing with specific issues. Each of these features ends with a **Legal Critical Thinking** question that explores some cultural, environmental, or technological aspect of the issue. The following are some of the topics explored in these features:

- ***Insight into E-Commerce***—Do Computers Have Free Speech Rights? (Chapter 5).
- ***Insight into Social Media***—"Catfishing": Is That Online "Friend" Who You Think It Is? (Chapter 10).
- ***Insight into Ethics***—Warning Labels for Video Games (Chapter 13).
- ***Insight into the Global Environment***—Is It Legal to Resell Textbooks Purchased Abroad? (Chapter 14).

Suggested answers to the *Legal Critical Thinking* questions are included in both the *Instructor's Manual* and the *Answers Manual* for this text.

New *Case Analysis Cases* with Four *Legal Reasoning Questions*

In every chapter of the Ninth Edition of *The Legal Environment of Business,* we have included one longer case excerpt—labeled ***Case Analysis Case***—followed by **four *Legal Reasoning Questions.*** The questions are designed to guide students' analysis of the case and build their legal reasoning skills.

These *Case Analysis Cases* may be used for case-briefing assignments and are also tied to the *Special Case Analysis* questions found in nearly every unit of the text (one per unit). **Suggested answers to the *Legal Reasoning Questions* are included in both the *Instructor's Manual* and the *Answers Manual* for this text.**

Improved Ethics Coverage

For the Ninth Edition of *The Legal Environment of Business,* we have significantly revised and updated the chapter on ethics and business decision making (Chapter 4). The chapter now presents a more practical, realistic, case-study approach to business ethics and the dilemmas facing businesspersons today. It also provides step-by-step guidance for making ethical business decisions.

The emphasis on ethics is reiterated in materials throughout the text, particularly the *Insight into Ethics* features, the *Focus on Ethics* features that conclude every unit, and the pedagogy that accompanies selected cases and features. We also discuss **corporate governance issues** in Chapter 28 and in the *Focus on Ethics* feature concluding Unit Four on the business environment. Finally, each chapter in the text includes ***A Question of Ethics*** case problem that provides a modern-day example of the kinds of ethical issues faced by businesspersons and explores the ways that courts can resolve them.

ADDITIONAL FEATURES OF THIS TEXT

The Legal Environment of Business, Ninth Edition, includes a number of pedagogical devices and special features, including those discussed here.

Emphasis on Business and on Critical Thinking

For the Ninth Edition, we have focused on making the text more business related. To that end, we have carefully chosen cases, features, and problems that are relevant to operating a business.

In addition, we recognize that today's business leaders must often think "outside the box" when making business decisions. For this reason, we have included numerous critical thinking and legal reasoning elements in this text. Almost all of the features and cases presented in the text conclude with some type of critical thinking question.

Cases may include one or more of the following critical thinking questions:

- *What If the Facts Were Different?*
- *The Ethical Dimension*
- *The E-Commerce Dimension*
- *The Global Dimension*
- *The Legal Environment Dimension*
- *The Social Dimension*

Suggested answers to all questions following cases can be found in both the *Instructor's Manual* and the *Answers Manual* for this text.

Managerial Implications in Selected Cases

In addition to the critical thinking questions, we have included special case pedagogy at the end of selected cases that have particular importance for business managers. This section, called *Managerial Implications,* points out the significance of the court's ruling in the case for business owners and managers.

Special Case Analysis Questions

For nearly every unit in the text, we also provide a *Special Case Analysis* question that is based on the *Case Analysis Case* excerpt in that chapter. The *Special Case Analysis* questions are designed to build students' analytical skills and appear in the *Business Case Problems* at the end of selected chapters.

The *Special Case Analysis* questions test students' ability to perform IRAC (which stands for Issue, Rule, Application, and Conclusion) case analysis. Students must identify the legal issue presented in the chapter's *Case Analysis Case,* understand the rule of law, determine how the rule applies to the facts of the case, and describe the court's conclusion. Instructors can assign these questions as homework or use them in class to elicit student participation and teach case analysis. **Suggested answers to the *Special Case Analysis* questions can be found in both the *Instructor's Manual* and the *Answers Manual* for this text.**

Reviewing Features in Every Chapter

In the Ninth Edition of *The Legal Environment of Business,* we continue to offer a *Reviewing* feature at the end of every chapter to help solidify students' understanding of the chapter materials. Each *Reviewing* feature presents a hypothetical scenario and then asks a series of questions that require students to identify the issues and apply the legal concepts discussed in the chapter.

These features are designed to help students review the chapter topics in a simple and interesting way and see how the legal principles discussed in the chapter affect the world in which they live. An instructor can use these features as the basis for in-class discussion or encourage students to use them for self-study prior to completing homework assignments. **Suggested answers to the questions posed in the *Reviewing* features can be found in both the *Instructor's Manual* and the *Answers Manual* for this text.**

Concept Summaries

When key areas of the law need additional emphasis, we provide a *Concept Summary.* These summaries have always been a popular pedagogical tool in this text. It now includes nineteen of these summaries, many of which have been expanded or revised.

Exhibits

When appropriate, we also illustrate important aspects of the law in graphic form in exhibits. In all, fifty exhibits are featured in *The Legal Environment of Business,* Ninth Edition. Several of these exhibits are new, and we have modified existing exhibits to achieve better clarity.

Case Problems

Every chapter includes a 2012 or 2013 case problem in the *Business Case Problems* that appear at the end of the chapter. These problems are designed to clarify how modern courts deal with the business issues discussed in the chapter.

At the request of instructors, we have given every business scenario and case problem a label that identifies the chapter topic to which the question relates. These labels make it easier for instructors who wish to assign only certain questions to their students. In addition, for this edition, we have added page references to the text where the problem's answer can be found.

We have also included two special problems—the *Spotlight Case Problems* (in selected chapters, as mentioned earlier), which are based on good teaching cases with interesting facts, and the *Business Case Problem with Sample Answer* (discussed next).

Suggested answers to all chapter-ending business scenarios and case problems are included in both the *Instructor's Manual* and the *Answers Manual* for this text.

Business Case Problem with Sample Answer in Each Chapter

In response to those instructors who would like students to have sample answers available for some of the questions and case problems, we include a *Business Case Problem with Sample Answer* in each chapter. The *Business Case Problem with Sample Answer* is based on an actual case, and students can access a sample answer in Appendix F at the end of the text.

THE LEGAL ENVIRONMENT OF BUSINESS ON THE WEB

The Web site for the Ninth Edition of *The Legal Environment of Business* can be found by going to www.cengagebrain.com and entering ISBN 9781285428949. The Web site offers a broad array of teaching/learning resources, including the following:

- ***Practice quizzes*** for every chapter in this text.
- ***Flashcards*** and a ***Glossary*** for every chapter in this text.
- ***Appendix A: How to Brief Cases and Analyze Case Problems*** that appears in the book is also posted on the Web site.
- ***Legal reference materials*** including a "Statutes" page that offers links to the full text of selected statutes referenced in the text, a Spanish glossary, and other important legal resources.
- ***CourseMate,*** which students can purchase access to, provides additional study tools, including an e-book, additional quizzes, flashcards, key terms, and PowerPoint slides.

THE MOST COMPLETE SUPPLEMENTS PACKAGE AVAILABLE TODAY

This edition of *The Legal Environment of Business* is accompanied by many teaching and learning supplements, which are available on the password-protected portion of the Instructor's Companion Web Site.

The complete teaching/learning package for the Ninth Edition includes the supplements listed next. For further information on *The Legal Environment of Business* teaching/learning package, contact your local sales representative or visit *The Legal Environment of Business* Web site.

Instructor's Companion Web Site

The Instructor's Companion Web Site contains the following supplements:

- ***Instructor's Manual.*** Includes sections entitled "Additional Cases Addressing This Issue" at the end of selected case synopses.
- ***Answers Manual.*** Provides answers to all questions presented in the text, including the questions in each case, feature, and unit-ending feature.
- ***Test Bank.*** A comprehensive test bank that contains multiple choice, true/false, and short essay questions.
- ***Case-Problem Cases.***
- ***Case Printouts.***
- ***PowerPoint slides.***
- ***Instructor's Manual*** for the *Drama of the Law* video series.

Software, Video, and Multimedia Supplements

- **Business Law Digital Video Library**—Provides access to ninety videos, including the *Drama of the Law* videos and video clips from actual Hollywood movies. Access to our Digital Library is available in an optional package with each new text at no additional cost. You can access the Business Law Digital Video Library, along with corresponding *Video Questions* that are related to specific chapters in the text, at www.cengagebrain.com.
- **CengageNow** (described on the first page of this preface).
- **MindTap** (described on the first page of this preface).
- **CourseMate** (described on the second page of this preface).

- **Westlaw®** (ten free hours for qualified adopters).

FOR USERS OF THE EIGHTH EDITION

First of all, we want to thank you for helping make *The Legal Environment of Business* the best-selling legal environment text in America today. Second, we want to make you aware of the numerous additions and changes that we have made in this edition—many in response to comments from reviewers.

New Chapter and Special Pedagogy

For this edition, we have added more material on Internet law and social media throughout the text. We have also created an entire chapter (Chapter 15) on Internet law, social media, and privacy.

We have also added the following entirely new elements for the Ninth Edition:

- New highlighted and numbered *Examples* and *Cases in Point.*
- New *Managerial Strategy* features.
- New *Insight into Social Media* features.
- New *Spotlight Cases and Spotlight Case Problems.*
- *Classic Cases.*
- Four *Legal Reasoning Questions* at the conclusion of *Case Analysis Cases.*
- *Appendix to Chapter 10: Reading and Analyzing Contracts.*
- *Issue Spotters* in every chapter.
- *Legal Reasoning Group Activities* in every chapter.
- *Appendix E* (Answers to the *Issue Spotters*), *Appendix F* (Sample Answers for *Business Case Problems with Sample Answer*).

Significantly Revised Chapters

Every chapter of the Ninth Edition has been revised as necessary to incorporate new developments in the law or to streamline the presentations. Other major changes and additions for this edition include the following:

- **Chapter 4 (Business Ethics)**—This chapter has been thoroughly revised with all new cases, business scenarios, and many new case problems. It includes a new section on business ethics and social media, as well as an in-depth discussion of stakeholders and corporate social responsibility. The chapter also provides step-by-step guidance on making ethical business decisions and includes materials on global business ethics. An *Insight into the Global Environment* feature examines bribery and the Foreign Corrupt Practices Act.
- **Chapter 5 (Business and the Constitution)**—The chapter has been revised and updated to be more business oriented. It has numerous new *Examples* and *Cases in Point,* many of which are based on United States Supreme Court decisions.
- **Chapter 8 (International Law in a Global Economy)**—This chapter has been thoroughly revised and updated. It now discusses international dispute resolution and includes a feature on border searches of electronic devices. All three cases presented in Chapter 8 are new, and an important 2013 United States Supreme Court decision has been selected as a *Spotlight on International Torts.*
- **Chapters 9 through 10 (the contracts materials)**—We have added many highlighted and numbered *Examples, Cases in Point,* and updates to clarify and enhance our already superb contract law coverage. The discussion of online contracting and electronic signatures has been merged with the coverage of traditional contracts. Chapter 9 presents a *Spotlight on Amazon.com* case and includes a *Spotlight on Taco Bell* case problem.
- **Chapter 11 (Sales and Lease Contracts)**—We have streamlined and simplified our coverage of the Uniform Commercial Code. We have added numerous new *Examples* and *Cases in Point* throughout the chapter to increase student comprehension. The chapter includes an *Insight into E-Commerce* on Taxing Web Purchases and a *Spotlight on Apple* case problem. It also contains a classic case and a 2013 *Case Analysis Case.*

- **Chapter 12 (Torts) and Chapter 13 (Strict Liability and Product Liability)**—Our torts coverage has been substantially revised, reorganized, and streamlined. The materials are up to date and business oriented. Intentional torts and negligence are covered in one chapter, and strict liability and product liability are covered in the next. Each chapter includes a *Spotlight Case,* and Chapter 13 presents an *Insight into Ethics* feature discussing warning labels for video games.
- **Chapter 14 (Intellectual Property Rights)**—The materials on intellectual property rights have been thoroughly revised and updated to reflect the most current laws and trends. There is a discussion of the dispute between Apple, Inc., and Samsung Electronics Company over smartphones. A feature discusses a 2013 United States Supreme Court decision on the resale on eBay of textbooks purchased abroad. The case problems include a *Spotlight on Macy's.*
- **Chapter 15 (Internet Law, Social Media, and Privacy)**—This chapter is all new and was created for the Ninth Edition to explore timely topics. It discusses legal issues that are unique to the Internet, such as spam, domain name disputes, cybersquatting, digital copyright laws, and file-sharing. It also discusses social media, company-wide social media networks, state legislation on social media, the Electronic Communications Privacy Act, and password protection. The chapter also covers online defamation, data collection and cookies, and online privacy.
- **Chapter 16 (Creditor-Debtor Relations and Bankruptcy)**—This chapter has been revised to be more up to date and comprehensible. We have streamlined the materials to focus on those concepts that students need to know, and included updated dollar amounts of various provisions of the Bankruptcy Code. An *Insight into Social Media* feature is included.
- **Chapters 17 through 19 (the Business Environment unit)**—This unit has been revised and updated to improve the flow and clarity. We provide more practical information and recent examples. Small-business organizational forms, including sole proprietorships and partnerships—as well as issues affecting owners of small businesses—are covered in Chapter 17. Limited liability forms of business are covered in Chapter 18, and corporations are discussed in Chapter 19. A new case and a new *Case Analysis Case* have been added in the corporate law chapter.
- **Chapter 21 (Employment Relationships)**—This chapter discusses many legal issues facing employers today and includes updated minimum wage figures and Social Security and Medicare percentages. We have also included a discussion of the Affordable Care Act (Obamacare).
- **Chapter 22 (Employment Discrimination)**—We have added *Examples* and *Cases in Point* throughout this chapter, as well as new numbered lists of elements, and two new cases. A new *Insight into Ethics* feature examines appearance-based discrimination. We discuss relevant United States Supreme Court decisions affecting employment issues throughout both Chapter 21 and this chapter.
- **Chapter 23 (Immigration and Labor Law)**—The materials on immigration law have been streamlined and updated and include a discussion of state immigration legislation and its constitutionality. A *Managerial Strategy* feature covers changing social media policies, and there is a new *Cases Analysis Case* on labor law.
- **Chapter 24 (Consumer Protection)**—This chapter has been streamlined and updated. The chapter also includes a *Spotlight on Honda* case and a *Spotlight on McDonald's* case problem.
- **Chapter 25 (Environmental Law)**—The materials on air pollution and water pollution have been updated, and a recent decision from the United States Supreme Court decision is presented.
- **Chapter 26 (Real Property and Land-Use Control)**—Parts of this chapter have been significantly revised. Several new terms were added. The discussion of eminent domain for economic development was updated. A *Spotlight Case* covers whether the buyer of an allegedly haunted house can seek rescission of the sale. The *Case Analysis Case* is on whether

a town can use a condemnation action to acquire rights-of-way for a natural gas pipeline that is not being built to furnish natural gas to the residents of that town. The discussion of zoning laws has been reworked, and several numbered lists explain permissible uses of land and requirements for variances.

- **Chapter 27 (Antitrust Law)**—We have added several new examples and expanded coverage of leading cases, including a discussion of price fixing and e-books. Updated thresholds for interlocking directorates have been incorporated.
- **Chapter 28 (Investor Protection and Corporate Governance)**—This chapter has been substantially revised, updated, and simplified. It includes new numbered lists of elements, two new cases, and a *Classic Case.*

ACKNOWLEDGMENTS FOR PREVIOUS EDITIONS

Since we began this project many years ago, a sizable number of legal environment of business professors and others have helped us in various phases of the undertaking. The following reviewers offered numerous constructive criticisms, comments, and suggestions during the preparation of the previous editions.

Peter W. Allan
Victor Valley College

William Dennis Ames
Indiana University of Pennsylvania

Thomas M. Apke
California State University, Fullerton

Linda Axelrod
Metropolitan State University

Jane Bennett
Orange Coast College

Robert C. Bird
University of Connecticut

Dean Bredeson
University of Texas at Austin

Sam Cassidy
University of Denver

Thomas D. Cavenagh
North Central College–Naperville, Illinois

Angela Cerino
Villanova University

Corey Ciocchetti
University of Denver

David Cooper
Fullerton College

Steven R. Donley
Cypress College

Paul F. Dwyer
Siena College

Joan Gabel
Florida State University

Gamewell Gant
Idaho State University

Arlene M. Hibschweiler
SUNY Fredonia

Barbara W. Kincaid
Southern Methodist University

Marty P. Ludlum
Oklahoma City Community College

Marty Salley McGee
South Carolina State University

Robert Mitchum
Arkansas State University, Beebe

Kathleen A. Phillips
University of Houston

David Redle
University of Akron

Larry A. Strate
University of Nevada–Las Vegas

Dawn Swink
Minnesota State University, Mankato

Brian Terry
Johnson and Wales University

John Theis
Mesa State College

Michael G. Walsh
Villanova University

Glynda White
Community College of Southern Nevada

LeVon E. Wilson
Western Carolina University

John A. Wrieden
Florida International University

Eric D. Yordy
Northern Arizona University

Mary-Kathryn Zachary
State University of West Georgia

We would also like to give credit to the following reviewers for their useful input during development of CengageNOW for *The Legal Environment of Business:* Interactive Assignment System:

Nena Ellison
Florida Atlantic University

Jacqueline Hagerott
Franklin University

Melanie Morris
Raritan Valley Community College

William H. Volz
Wayne State University

We also wish to extend special thanks to Diane May, Winona State University, for her contributions to the Ninth Edition, specifically for preparing the Blueprint Cases that are included in both CengageNOW and MindTap for this edition.

As in all past editions, we owe a debt of extreme gratitude to the numerous individuals who worked directly with us or at Cengage Learning. In particular, we wish to thank Vicky True-Baker, Rob Dewey, and Michael Worls for their helpful advice and guidance during all of the stages of this new edition. We extend our thanks to Jan Lamar, our longtime content developer, for her many useful suggestions and for her efforts in coordinating reviews and ensuring the timely and accurate publication of all supplemental materials. We are also indebted to Kristen Hurd for her excellent marketing advice and Mike Worls for his support.

Our content project manager, Ann Borman, and our art director, Michelle Kunkler, made sure that we came out with an error-free, visually attractive Ninth Edition. We appreciate their efforts. We are also indebted to the staff at Parkwood Composition, our compositor. Their ability to generate the pages for this text quickly and accurately made it possible for us to meet our ambitious printing schedule.

We especially wish to thank Katherine Marie Silsbee for her management of the entire project, as well as for the application of her superb research and editorial skills. We also wish to thank William Eric Hollowell, who co-authored the *Instructor's Manual* and the *Test Bank* for his excellent research efforts. We were fortunate enough to have the proofreading services of Pat Lewis. We are grateful for the efforts of Vickie Reierson and Roxanna Lee for their proofreading and other assistance, which helped to ensure an error-free text. Finally, we thank Suzanne Jasin of K & M Consulting for her many special efforts on this project.

In addition, we would like to give special thanks to all of the individuals who were instrumental in developing and implementing the new CengageNOW for *The Legal Environment of Business:* Interactive Assignment System. These include Rob Dewey, Vicky True-Baker, Jan Lamar, Kristen Hurd, and Kristen Meere at Cengage, and Katherine Marie Silsbee, Roger Meiners, Lavina Leed Miller, William Eric Hollowell, Kimberly Wallan, Kristi Wiswell, and Joseph Zavaleta who helped develop the content for this unique Web-based product.

Through the years, we have enjoyed an ongoing correspondence with many of you who have found points on which you wish to comment. We continue to welcome all comments and promise to respond promptly. By incorporating your ideas, we can continue to write a business law text that is best for you and best for your students.

F.B.C.
R.L.M.

UNIT ONE

THE FOUNDATIONS

CONTENTS

LAW AND LEGAL REASONING

One of the important functions of law in any society is to provide stability, predictability, and continuity so that people can know how to order their affairs. If any society is to survive, its citizens must be able to determine what is legally right and legally wrong. They must know what sanctions will be imposed on them if they commit wrongful acts. If they suffer harm as a result of others' wrongful acts, they must know how they can seek compensation. By setting forth the rights, obligations, and privileges of citizens, the law enables individuals to go about their business with confidence and a certain degree of predictability.

Although law has various definitions, they are all based on the general observation that **law** consists of *enforceable rules governing relationships among individuals and between individuals and their society.* These "enforceable rules" may consist of unwritten principles of behavior established by a nomadic tribe. They may be set forth in a law code, such as the Code of Hammurabi in ancient Babylon (c. 1780 B.C.E.) or the law code of one of today's European nations. They may consist of written laws and court decisions created by modern legislative and judicial bodies, as in the United States. Regardless of how such rules are created, they all have one thing in common: they establish rights, duties, and privileges that are consistent with the values and beliefs of their society or its ruling group.

In this introductory chapter, we first look at an important question for any student reading this text: How does the legal environment affect business decision making? We next describe the major sources of American law, the common law tradition, and some basic schools of legal thought. We conclude the chapter with sections offering practical guidance on several topics, including how to find the sources of law discussed in this chapter (and referred to throughout the text) and how to read and understand court opinions.

SECTION 1
BUSINESS ACTIVITIES AND THE LEGAL ENVIRONMENT

Laws and government regulations affect almost all business activities—from hiring and firing decisions to workplace safety, the manufacturing and marketing of products, business financing, and more. To make good business decisions, a basic knowledge of the laws and regulations governing these activities is beneficial—if not essential.

Realize also that in today's business world, a knowledge of "black-letter" law is not enough. Businesspersons are also pressured to make ethical decisions. Thus, the study of business law necessarily involves an ethical dimension.

Many Different Laws May Affect a Single Business Decision

As you will note, each chapter in this text covers specific areas of the law and shows how the legal rules in each area affect business activities. Though compartmentalizing the law in this fashion promotes conceptual clarity, it does not indicate the extent to which a number of different laws may apply to just one decision.

LESSONS FROM FACEBOOK When Mark Zuckerberg started Facebook as a Harvard student, he probably did not imagine all the legal challenges his company would face as a result of his business decisions.

- As you may know from the movie, *The Social Network,* shortly after Facebook was launched, others claimed that Zuckerberg had stolen their ideas for a social networking site. Their claims involved alleged theft of intellectual property (see Chapter 14), fraudulent misrepresentation (see Chapter 10), partnership law (see Chapter 17), and securities law (see Chapter 28). Facebook ultimately paid a significant amount ($65 million) to settle those claims out of court (see Chapter 3).

- Facebook has also been sued repeatedly for violating users' privacy (such as by disseminating private information to third parties for commercial purposes—see Chapters 5 and 15).
- In 2012, a *class-action* lawsuit was filed against Facebook that seeks damages of $15 billion for violating users' privacy (and federal wiretapping law) by tracking their Web site usage.
- Facebook's business decisions have also come under scrutiny by federal regulators, such as the Federal Trade Commission (FTC) and the Securities and Exchange Commission (SEC).
- In 2011, the company settled a complaint filed by the FTC alleging that Facebook failed to keep "friends" lists and other user information private.
- In 2012, Facebook conducted a much-anticipated initial public offering (IPO) of its stock. The IPO did not go well, however, and many investors suffered losses. Facebook is facing dozens of lawsuits (including class actions) related to business decisions made with regard to the IPO and alleged violations of securities laws (see Chapter 28).
- The SEC is also investigating whether Facebook engaged in any wrongdoing with regard to its IPO and trading of stock (see Chapter 28).

POINTS TO CONSIDER A key to avoiding business disputes is to think ahead when starting or running a business or entering a contract. Learn what you can about the laws pertaining to that specific enterprise or transaction. Have some idea of the legal ramifications of your business decisions and seek the advice of counsel when in doubt. Exhibit 1–1 on the following page illustrates the various areas of law that may influence business decision making.

Ethics and Business Decision Making

Merely knowing the areas of law that may affect a business decision is not sufficient in today's business world. Businesspersons must also take ethics into account. As you will learn in Chapter 4, *ethics* generally is defined as the principles governing what constitutes right or wrong behavior.

Today, business decision makers need to consider not just whether a decision is legal, but also whether it is ethical. Often, as in several of the claims against Facebook discussed above, disputes arise in business because one party feels that he or she has been treated unfairly. Thus, the underlying reason for bringing some lawsuits is a breach of ethical duties (such as when a partner or employee attempts to secretly take advantage of a business opportunity).

Throughout this text, you will learn about the relationship between the law and ethics, as well as about some of the types of ethical questions that often arise in business. For example, the unit-ending *Focus on Ethics* features are devoted solely to the exploration of ethical questions pertaining to topics treated within the unit. We have also included *Ethical Dimension* questions for selected cases that focus on ethical considerations in today's business climate and *Insight into Ethics* features that appear in selected chapters. A *Question of Ethics* case problem is included at the conclusion of every chapter to introduce you to the ethical aspects of specific cases involving real-life situations. Additionally, Chapter 4 offers a detailed look at the importance of business ethics.

SECTION 2

SOURCES OF AMERICAN LAW

There are numerous sources of American law. *Primary sources of law,* or sources that establish the law, include the following:

1. The U.S. Constitution and the constitutions of the various states.
2. Statutory law—including laws passed by Congress, state legislatures, or local governing bodies.
3. Regulations created by administrative agencies, such as the Food and Drug Administration.
4. Case law and common law doctrines.

We describe each of these important sources of law in the following pages.

Secondary sources of law are books and articles that summarize and clarify the primary sources of law. Examples include legal encyclopedias, treatises, articles in law reviews, and compilations of law, such as the *Restatements of the Law* (which will be discussed shortly). Courts often refer to secondary sources of law for guidance in interpreting and applying the primary sources of law discussed here.

EXHIBIT 1–1 Areas of the Law That May Affect Business Decision Making

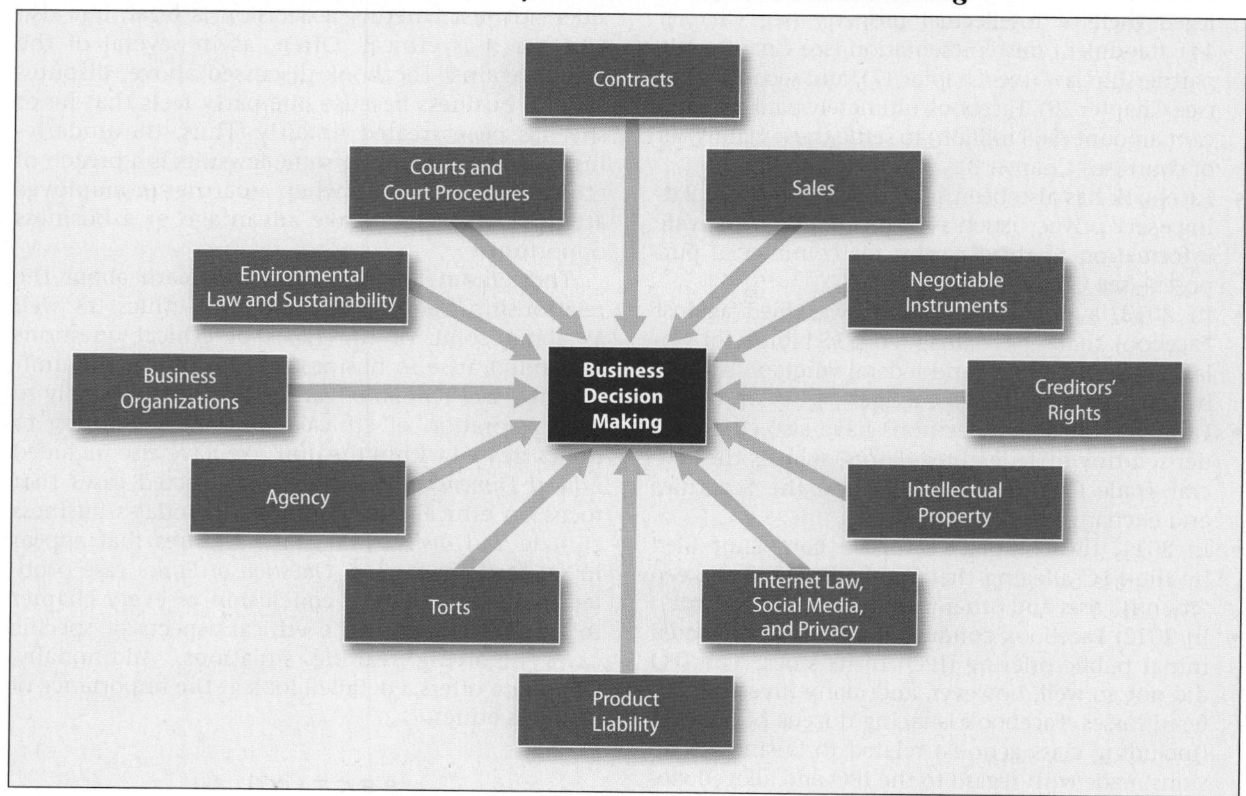

Constitutional Law

The federal government and the states have separate written constitutions that set forth the general organization, powers, and limits of their respective governments. **Constitutional law** is the law as expressed in these constitutions.

According to Article VI of the U.S. Constitution, the Constitution is the supreme law of the land. As such, it is the basis of all law in the United States. A law in violation of the Constitution, if challenged, will be declared unconstitutional and will not be enforced, no matter what its source. Because of its importance in the American legal system, we present the complete text of the U.S. Constitution in Appendix B and discuss it in depth in Chapter 5.

The Tenth Amendment to the U.S. Constitution reserves to the states all powers not granted to the federal government. Each state in the union has its own constitution. Unless it conflicts with the U.S. Constitution or a federal law, a state constitution is supreme within the state's borders.

Statutory Law

Laws enacted by legislative bodies at any level of government, such as statutes passed by Congress or by state legislatures, make up the body of law known as **statutory law.** When a legislature passes a statute, that statute ultimately is included in the federal code of laws or the relevant state code of laws (discussed later in this chapter).

Statutory law also includes local **ordinances**—statutes (laws, rules, or orders) passed by municipal or county governing units to govern matters not covered by federal or state law. Ordinances commonly have to do with city or county land use (zoning ordinances), building and safety codes, and other matters affecting the local community.

A federal statute, of course, applies to all states. A state statute, in contrast, applies only within the state's borders. State laws thus may vary from state to state. No federal statute may violate the U.S. Constitution, and no state statute or local ordinance may violate the U.S. Constitution or the relevant state constitution.

UNIFORM LAWS During the 1800s, the differences among state laws frequently created difficulties for businesspersons conducting trade and commerce among the states. To counter these problems, a group of legal scholars and lawyers formed the National Conference of Commissioners on Uniform State Laws (NCCUSL, **www.uniformlaws.org**) in 1892 to draft **uniform laws** (model statutes) for the states to consider adopting. The NCCUSL still exists today and continues to issue uniform laws.

Each state has the option of adopting or rejecting a uniform law. *Only if a state legislature adopts a uniform law does that law become part of the statutory law of that state.* Note that a state legislature may adopt all or part of a uniform law as it is written, or the legislature may rewrite the law however the legislature wishes. Hence, even though many states may have adopted a uniform law, those states' laws may not be entirely "uniform."

The earliest uniform law, the Uniform Negotiable Instruments Law, was completed by 1896 and adopted in every state by the 1920s (although not all states used exactly the same wording). Over the following decades, other acts were drawn up in a similar manner. In all, more than two hundred uniform acts have been issued by the NCCUSL since its inception. The most ambitious uniform act of all, however, is the Uniform Commercial Code.

THE UNIFORM COMMERCIAL CODE One of the most important uniform acts is the Uniform Commercial Code (UCC), which was created through the joint efforts of the NCCUSL and the American Law Institute.[1] The UCC was first issued in 1952 and has been adopted in all fifty states,[2] the District of Columbia, and the Virgin Islands.

The UCC facilitates commerce among the states by providing a uniform, yet flexible, set of rules governing commercial transactions. Because of its importance in the area of commercial law, we cite the UCC frequently in this text. We also present Article 2 of the UCC in Appendix C. From time to time, the NCCUSL revises the articles contained in the UCC and submits the revised versions to the states for adoption.

Administrative Law

Another important source of American law is **administrative law,** which consists of the rules, orders, and decisions of administrative agencies. An **administrative agency** is a federal, state, or local government agency established to perform a specific function. Administrative law and procedures constitute a dominant element in the regulatory environment of business.

Rules issued by various administrative agencies now affect almost every aspect of a business's operations. Regulations govern a business's capital structure and financing, its hiring and firing procedures, its relations with employees and unions, and the way it manufactures and markets its products. Regulations enacted to protect the environment also often play a significant role in business operations.

FEDERAL AGENCIES At the national level, the cabinet departments of the executive branch include numerous **executive agencies.** The U.S. Food and Drug Administration, for example, is an agency within the U.S. Department of Health and Human Services. Executive agencies are subject to the authority of the president, who has the power to appoint and remove their officers.

There are also major **independent regulatory agencies** at the federal level, such as the Federal Trade Commission, the Securities and Exchange Commission, and the Federal Communications Commission. The president's power is less pronounced in regard to independent agencies, whose officers serve for fixed terms and cannot be removed without just cause.

STATE AND LOCAL AGENCIES There are administrative agencies at the state and local levels as well. Commonly, a state agency (such as a state pollution-control agency) is created as a parallel to a federal agency (such as the Environmental Protection Agency). Just as federal statutes take precedence over conflicting state statutes, federal agency regulations take precedence over conflicting state regulations.

Case Law and Common Law Doctrines

The rules of law announced in court decisions constitute another basic source of American law. These rules include interpretations of constitutional provisions, of statutes enacted by legislatures, and of regulations created by administrative agencies.

Today, this body of judge-made law is referred to as **case law.** Case law—the doctrines and principles announced in cases—governs all areas not covered by

1. This institute was formed in the 1920s and consists of practicing attorneys, legal scholars, and judges.
2. Louisiana has not adopted Articles 2 and 2A (covering contracts for the sale and lease of goods), however.

statutory law or administrative law and is part of our common law tradition. We look at the origins and characteristics of the common law tradition in some detail in the pages that follow.

See *Concept Summary 1.1* below for a review of the sources of American law.

SECTION 3

THE COMMON LAW TRADITION

Because of our colonial heritage, much of American law is based on the English legal system, which originated in medieval England and continued to evolve in the following centuries. Knowledge of this system is necessary to understanding the American legal system today.

Early English Courts

The origins of the English legal system—and thus the U.S. legal system as well—date back to 1066, when the Normans conquered England. William the Conqueror and his successors began the process of unifying the country under their rule. One of the means they used to do this was the establishment of the king's courts, or *curiae regis*.

Before the Norman Conquest, disputes had been settled according to the local legal customs and traditions in various regions of the country. The king's courts sought to establish a uniform set of customs for the country as a whole. What evolved in these courts was the beginning of the **common law**—a body of general rules that applied throughout the entire English realm. Eventually, the common law tradition became part of the heritage of all nations that were once British colonies, including the United States.

COURTS OF LAW AND REMEDIES AT LAW The early English king's courts could grant only very limited kinds of **remedies** (the legal means to enforce a right or redress a wrong). If one person wronged another in some way, the king's courts could award as compensation one or more of the following: (1) land, (2) items of value, or (3) money.

The courts that awarded this compensation became known as **courts of law,** and the three remedies were called **remedies at law.** (Today, the remedy at law normally takes the form of monetary **damages**—an amount given to a party whose legal interests have been injured.) This system made the procedure for settling disputes more uniform. When a complaining party wanted a remedy other than economic compensation, however, the courts of law could do nothing, so "no remedy, no right."

COURTS OF EQUITY *Equity* is a branch of law—founded on notions of justice and fair dealing—that seeks to supply a remedy when no adequate remedy at law is available. When individuals could not obtain an adequate remedy in a court of law, they petitioned the king for relief. Most of these petitions were decided by an adviser to the king, called a **chancellor,** who had the power to grant new and unique remedies. Eventually, formal chancery courts, or **courts of equity,** were established.

CONCEPT SUMMARY 1.1

Sources of American Law

SOURCE	DESCRIPTION
Constitutional Law	The law as expressed in the U.S. Constitution and the state constitutions. The U.S. Constitution is the supreme law of the land. State constitutions are supreme within state borders to the extent that they do not violate a clause of the U.S. Constitution or a federal law.
Statutory Law	Laws (statutes and ordinances) enacted by federal, state, and local legislatures and governing bodies. None of these laws can violate the U.S. Constitution or the relevant state constitution. Uniform laws, when adopted by a state, become statutory law in that state.
Administrative Law	The rules, orders, and decisions of federal, state, and local government administrative agencies.
Case Law and Common Law Doctrines	Judge-made law, including interpretations of constitutional provisions, of statutes enacted by legislatures, and of regulations created by administrative agencies.

REMEDIES IN EQUITY The remedies granted by the equity courts became known as **remedies in equity,** or equitable remedies. These remedies include specific performance, an injunction, and rescission. *Specific performance* involves ordering a party to perform an agreement as promised. An *injunction* is an order to a party to cease engaging in a specific activity or to undo some wrong or injury. *Rescission* is the cancellation of a contractual obligation. We will discuss these and other equitable remedies in more detail at appropriate points in the chapters that follow, particularly in Chapter 10.

As a general rule, today's courts, like the early English courts, will not grant equitable remedies unless the remedy at law—monetary damages—is inadequate. ▶ **Example 1.1** Ted forms a contract (a legally binding agreement—see Chapter 9) to purchase a parcel of land that he thinks will be perfect for his future home. The seller **breaches,** or fails to fulfill, this agreement. Ted could sue the seller for the return of any deposits or down payment he might have made on the land, but this is not the remedy he really seeks. What Ted wants is to have the court order the seller to perform the contract. In other words, Ted wants the court to grant the equitable remedy of specific performance because monetary damages are inadequate in this situation. ◀

EQUITABLE MAXIMS In fashioning appropriate remedies, judges often were (and continue to be) guided by so-called **equitable maxims**—propositions or general statements of equitable rules. Exhibit 1–2 below lists some important equitable maxims.

The last maxim listed in that exhibit—"Equity aids the vigilant, not those who rest on their rights"—merits special attention. It has become known as the equitable doctrine of **laches** (a term derived from the Latin *laxus,* meaning "lax" or "negligent"), and it can be used as a defense. A **defense** is an argument raised by the **defendant** (the party being sued) indicating why the **plaintiff** (the suing party) should not obtain the remedy sought. (Note that in equity proceedings, the party bringing a lawsuit is called the **petitioner,** and the party being sued is referred to as the **respondent.**)

The doctrine of laches arose to encourage people to bring lawsuits while the evidence was fresh. What constitutes a reasonable time, of course, varies according to the circumstances of the case. Time periods for different types of cases are now usually fixed by **statutes of limitations.** After the time allowed under a statute of limitations has expired, no action (lawsuit) can be brought, no matter how strong the case was originally.

Legal and Equitable Remedies Today

The establishment of courts of equity in medieval England resulted in two distinct court systems: courts of law and courts of equity. The courts had different sets of judges and granted different types of remedies. During the nineteenth century, however, most states in the United States adopted rules of procedure that resulted in the combining of courts of law and equity. A party now may request both legal and equitable remedies in the same action, and the trial court judge may grant either or both forms of relief.

The distinction between legal and equitable remedies remains relevant to students of business law, however, because these remedies differ. To seek the proper remedy for a wrong, one must know what

EXHIBIT 1–2 Equitable Maxims

1. *Whoever seeks equity must do equity.* (Anyone who wishes to be treated fairly must treat others fairly.)
2. *Where there is equal equity, the law must prevail.* (The law will determine the outcome of a controversy in which the merits of both sides are equal.)
3. *One seeking the aid of an equity court must come to the court with clean hands.* (The plaintiff must have acted fairly and honestly.)
4. *Equity will not suffer a wrong to be without a remedy.* (Equitable relief will be awarded when there is a right to relief and there is no adequate remedy at law.)
5. *Equity regards substance rather than form.* (Equity is more concerned with fairness and justice than with legal technicalities.)
6. *Equity aids the vigilant, not those who rest on their rights.* (Equity will not help those who neglect their rights for an unreasonable period of time.)

remedies are available. Additionally, certain vestiges of the procedures used when there were separate courts of law and equity still exist. For example, a party has the right to demand a jury trial in an action at law, but not in an action in equity. Exhibit 1–3 below summarizes the procedural differences (applicable in most states) between an action at law and an action in equity.

The Doctrine of *Stare Decisis*

One of the unique features of the common law is that it is *judge-made* law. The body of principles and doctrines that form the common law emerged over time as judges decided legal controversies.

CASE PRECEDENTS AND CASE REPORTERS When possible, judges attempted to be consistent and to base their decisions on the principles suggested by earlier cases. They sought to decide similar cases in a similar way and considered new cases with care because they knew that their decisions would make new law. Each interpretation became part of the law on the subject and thus served as a legal **precedent.** A precedent is a decision that furnishes an example or authority for deciding subsequent cases involving identical or similar legal principles or facts.

In the early years of the common law, there was no single place or publication where court opinions, or written decisions, could be found. By the fourteenth century, portions of the most important decisions from each year were being gathered together and recorded in *Year Books,* which became useful references for lawyers and judges. In the sixteenth century, the *Year Books* were discontinued, and other forms of case publication became available. Today, cases are published, or "reported," in volumes called **reporters,** or *reports.* We describe today's case reporting system in detail later in this chapter.

STARE DECISIS* AND THE COMMON LAW TRADITION** The practice of deciding new cases with reference to former decisions, or precedents, became a cornerstone of the English and American judicial systems. The practice formed a doctrine known as ***stare decisis[3] (a Latin phrase meaning "to stand on decided cases"). Under this doctrine, judges are obligated to follow the precedents established within their jurisdictions. The term *jurisdiction* refers to a geographic area in which a court or courts have the power to apply the law—see Chapter 2.

Once a court has set forth a principle of law as being applicable to a certain set of facts, that court must apply the principle in future cases involving similar facts. Courts of lower rank (within the same jurisdiction) must do likewise. Thus, *stare decisis* has two aspects:

1. A court should not overturn its own precedents unless there is a compelling reason to do so.
2. Decisions made by a higher court are binding on lower courts.

CONTROLLING PRECEDENTS Controlling precedents in a jurisdiction are referred to as binding authorities. A **binding authority** is any source of law that a court must follow when deciding a case. Binding authorities include constitutions, statutes, and regulations that govern the issue being decided, as well as court decisions that are controlling precedents within the jurisdiction. United States Supreme Court case decisions, no matter how old, remain controlling until they are overruled by a subsequent decision of the Supreme Court or changed by further legislation or a constitutional amendment.

***STARE DECISIS* AND LEGAL STABILITY** The doctrine of *stare decisis* helps the courts to be more efficient because, if other courts have analyzed a similar case,

3. Pronounced *ster*-ay dih-*si*-ses.

EXHIBIT 1–3 Procedural Differences between an Action at Law and an Action in Equity

Procedure	Action at Law	Action in Equity
Initiation of lawsuit	By filing a complaint	By filing a petition
Parties	Plaintiff and defendant	Petitioner and respondent
Decision	By jury or judge	By judge (no jury)
Result	Judgment	Decree
Remedy	Monetary damages	Injunction, specific performance, or rescission

their legal reasoning and opinions can serve as guides. *Stare decisis* also makes the law more stable and predictable. If the law on a subject is well settled, someone bringing a case can usually rely on the court to rule based on what the law has been in the past.

DEPARTURES FROM PRECEDENT Although courts are obligated to follow precedents, sometimes a court will depart from the rule of precedent if it decides that the precedent should no longer be followed. If a court decides that a ruling precedent is simply incorrect or that technological or social changes have rendered the precedent inapplicable, the court might rule contrary to the precedent. Cases that overturn precedent often receive a great deal of publicity.

▶ **Case in Point 1.2** The United States Supreme Court expressly overturned precedent in the case of *Brown v. Board of Education of Topeka*.[4] The Court concluded that separate educational facilities for whites and blacks, which it had previously upheld as constitutional,[5] were inherently unequal. The Court's departure from precedent in this case received a tremendous amount of publicity as people began to realize the ramifications of this change in the law. ◀

Note that judges do have some flexibility in applying precedents. For instance, a lower court may avoid applying a precedent set by a higher court in its jurisdiction by distinguishing the two cases based on their facts. When this happens, the lower court's ruling stands unless it is appealed to a higher court and that court overturns the decision.

WHEN THERE IS NO PRECEDENT Occasionally, courts must decide cases for which no precedents exist, called cases of *first impression*. For instance, as you will read throughout this text, the extensive use of the Internet has presented many new and challenging issues for the courts to decide.

In deciding cases of first impression, courts often look at **persuasive authorities** (precedents from other jurisdictions) for guidance. A court may also consider legal principles and policies underlying previous court decisions or existing statutes. Other factors that courts look at include fairness, social values and customs, and **public policy** (governmental policy based on widely held societal values).

4. 347 U.S. 483, 74 S.Ct. 686, 98 L.Ed. 873 (1954). A later section in this chapter explains how to read legal citations.
5. See *Plessy v. Ferguson*, 163 U.S. 537, 16 S.Ct. 1138, 41 L.Ed. 256 (1896).

Stare Decisis and Legal Reasoning

In deciding what law applies to a given dispute and then applying that law to the facts or circumstances of the case, judges rely on the process of **legal reasoning.** Through the use of legal reasoning, judges harmonize their decisions with those that have been made before, as the doctrine of *stare decisis* requires.

Students of business law and the legal environment also engage in legal reasoning. For example, you may be asked to provide answers for some of the case problems that appear at the end of every chapter in this text. Each problem describes the facts of a particular dispute and the legal question at issue. If you are assigned a case problem, you will be asked to determine how a court would answer that question, and why. In other words, you will need to give legal reasons for whatever conclusion you reach.[6] We look here at the basic steps involved in legal reasoning and then describe some forms of reasoning commonly used by the courts in making their decisions.

BASIC STEPS IN LEGAL REASONING At times, the legal arguments set forth in court opinions are relatively simple and brief. At other times, the arguments are complex and lengthy. Regardless of the length of a legal argument, however, the basic steps of the legal reasoning process remain the same. These steps, which you can also follow when analyzing cases and case problems, form what is commonly referred to as the *IRAC method* of legal reasoning. IRAC is an acronym formed from the first letters of the following words: *Issue, Rule, Application,* and *Conclusion.* To apply the IRAC method, you would ask the following questions:

1. **Issue**—*What are the key facts and issues?* Suppose that a plaintiff comes before the court claiming *assault* (words or acts that wrongfully and intentionally make another person fearful of immediate physical harm—see Chapter 12). The plaintiff claims that the defendant threatened her while she was sleeping. Although the plaintiff was unaware that she was being threatened, her roommate heard the defendant make the threat. The legal issue is whether the defendant's action constitutes the tort (civil wrong) of assault, given that the plaintiff was unaware of that action at the time it occurred.

6. See Appendix A for further instructions on how to analyze case problems.

2. **Rule**—*What rules of law apply to the case?* A rule of law may be a rule stated by the courts in previous decisions, a state or federal statute, or a state or federal administrative agency regulation. In our hypothetical case, the plaintiff **alleges** (claims) that the defendant committed a tort. Therefore, the applicable law is the common law of torts—specifically, tort law governing assault (see Chapter 12). Case precedents involving similar facts and issues thus would be relevant. Often, more than one rule of law will be applicable to a case.
3. **Application**—*How do the rules of law apply to the particular facts and circumstances of this case?* This step is often the most difficult because each case presents a unique set of facts, circumstances, and parties. Although cases may be similar, no two cases are ever identical in all respects. Normally, judges (and lawyers and law students) try to find **cases on point**—previously decided cases that are as similar as possible to the one under consideration. (Because of the difficulty—and importance—of this step in the legal reasoning process, we discuss it in more detail in the next subsection.)
4. **Conclusion**—*What conclusion should be drawn?* This step normally presents few problems. Usually, the conclusion is evident if the previous three steps have been followed carefully.

There Is No One "Right" Answer

Many people believe that there is one "right" answer to every legal question. In most legal controversies, however, there is no single correct result. Good arguments can usually be made to support either side of a legal controversy. Quite often, a case does not involve a "good" person suing a "bad" person. In many cases, both parties have acted in good faith in some measure or in bad faith to some degree.

Additionally, each judge has her or his own personal beliefs and philosophy (see the discussion in the next section), which shape the legal reasoning process, at least to some extent. This means that the outcome of a particular lawsuit before a court cannot be predicted with absolute certainty. Sometimes, even though the law would seem to favor one party's position, judges, through creative legal reasoning, have found ways to rule for the other party to prevent injustice.

Legal reasoning and other aspects of the common law tradition are reviewed in *Concept Summary 1.2* below.

The Common Law Today

Today, the common law derived from judicial decisions continues to be applied throughout the United States. Common law doctrines and principles, how-

CONCEPT SUMMARY 1.2
The Common Law Tradition

ASPECT	DESCRIPTION
Origins of the Common Law	The American legal system is based on the common law tradition, which originated in medieval England. Following the conquest of England in 1066 by William the Conqueror, king's courts were established throughout England, and the common law was developed in these courts.
Legal and Equitable Remedies	Remedies at law (money or items of value, such as land) and remedies in equity (including specific performance, injunction, and rescission of a contractual obligation) originated in the early English courts of law and courts of equity, respectively.
Case Precedents and the Doctrine of *Stare Decisis*	In the king's courts, judges attempted to make their decisions consistent with previous decisions, called precedents. This practice gave rise to the doctrine of *stare decisis*. This doctrine, which became a cornerstone of the common law tradition, obligates judges to abide by precedents established in their jurisdictions.
***Stare Decisis* and Legal Reasoning**	Legal reasoning is the reasoning process used by judges in applying the law to the facts and issues of specific cases. Legal reasoning involves becoming familiar with the key facts of a case, identifying the relevant legal rules, applying those rules to the facts, and drawing a conclusion.

ever, govern only areas *not* covered by statutory or administrative law. In a dispute concerning a particular employment practice, for instance, if a statute regulates that practice, the statute will apply rather than the common law doctrine that applied before the statute was enacted.

COURTS INTERPRET STATUTES Even in areas governed by statutory law, though, judge-made law continues to be important because there is a significant interplay between statutory law and the common law. For instance, many statutes essentially codify existing common law rules, and regulations issued by various administrative agencies usually are based, at least in part, on common law principles. Additionally, the courts, in interpreting statutory law, often rely on the common law as a guide to what the legislators intended.

Furthermore, how the courts interpret a particular statute determines how that statute will be applied. If you wanted to learn about the coverage and applicability of a particular statute, for example, you would necessarily have to locate the statute and study it. You would also need to see how the courts in your jurisdiction have interpreted and applied the statute. In other words, you would have to learn what precedents have been established in your jurisdiction with respect to that statute. Often, the applicability of a newly enacted statute does not become clear until a body of case law develops to clarify how, when, and to whom the statute applies.

***RESTATEMENTS OF THE LAW* CLARIFY AND ILLUSTRATE THE COMMON LAW** The American Law Institute (ALI) has published compilations of the common law called *Restatements of the Law,* which generally summarize the common law rules followed by most states. There are *Restatements of the Law* in the areas of contracts, torts, agency, trusts, property, restitution, security, judgments, and conflict of laws. The *Restatements,* like other secondary sources of law, do not in themselves have the force of law, but they are an important source of legal analysis and opinion. Hence, judges often rely on them in making decisions.

Many of the *Restatements* are now in their second, third, or fourth editions. We refer to the *Restatements* frequently in subsequent chapters of this text, indicating in parentheses the edition to which we are referring. For example, we refer to the third edition of the *Restatement of the Law of Contracts* as simply the *Restatement (Third) of Contracts*.

SECTION 4
SCHOOLS OF LEGAL THOUGHT

How judges apply the law to specific cases, including disputes relating to the business world, depends in part on their philosophical approaches to law. Thus, the study of law, or **jurisprudence,** involves learning about different schools of legal thought and how the approaches to law characteristic of each school can affect judicial decision making.

Clearly, a judge's function is not to *make* the laws—that is the function of the legislative branch of government—but to interpret and apply them. From a practical point of view, however, the courts play a significant role in defining the laws enacted by legislative bodies, which tend to be expressed in general terms. Judges thus have some flexibility in interpreting and applying the law. It is because of this flexibility that different courts can, and often do, arrive at different conclusions in cases that involve nearly identical issues, facts, and applicable laws.

The Natural Law School

An age-old question about the nature of law has to do with the finality of a nation's laws at a given point in time. What if a particular law is deemed to be a "bad" law by a substantial number of that nation's citizens? According to the **natural law** theory, a higher or universal law exists that applies to all human beings, and written laws should imitate these inherent principles. If a written law is unjust, then it is not a true (natural) law and need not be obeyed.

The natural law tradition is one of the oldest and most significant schools of jurisprudence. It dates back to the days of the Greek philosopher Aristotle (384–322 B.C.E.), who distinguished between natural law and the laws governing a particular nation. According to Aristotle, natural law applies universally to all humankind.

The notion that people have "natural rights" stems from the natural law tradition. Those who claim that a specific foreign government is depriving certain citizens of their human rights are implicitly appealing to a higher law that has universal applicability. The question of the universality of basic human rights also comes into play in the context of international business operations. ▶ **Example 1.3** U.S. companies that have operations abroad often hire foreign workers as employees. Should the same laws that protect

U.S. employees apply to these foreign employees? This question is rooted implicitly in a concept of universal rights that has its origins in the natural law tradition. ◀

The Positivist School

In contrast to natural law, *positive,* or national, law (the written law of a given society at a particular time) applies only to the citizens of that nation or society. Those who adhere to **legal positivism** believe that there can be no higher law than a nation's positive law.

According to the positivist school, there are no "natural rights." Rather, human rights exist solely because of laws. If the laws are not enforced, anarchy will result. Thus, whether a law is "bad" or "good" is irrelevant. The law is the law and must be obeyed until it is changed—in an orderly manner through a legitimate lawmaking process.

A judge with positivist leanings probably would be more inclined to defer to an existing law than would a judge who adheres to the natural law tradition.

The Historical School

The **historical school** of legal thought emphasizes the evolutionary process of law by concentrating on the origin and history of the legal system. This school looks to the past to discover what the principles of contemporary law should be. The legal doctrines that have withstood the passage of time—those that have worked in the past—are deemed best suited for shaping present laws. Hence, law derives its legitimacy and authority from adhering to the standards that historical development has shown to be workable.

Adherents of the historical school are more likely than those of other schools to strictly follow decisions made in past cases.

Legal Realism

In the 1920s and 1930s, a number of jurists and scholars, known as *legal realists,* rebelled against the historical approach to law. **Legal realism** is based on the idea that law is just one of many institutions in society and that it is shaped by social forces and needs. The law is a human enterprise, and judges should take social and economic realities into account when deciding cases.

Legal realists also believe that the law can never be applied with total uniformity. Given that judges are human beings with unique personalities, value systems, and intellects, different judges will obviously bring different reasoning processes to the same case. Female judges, for instance, might be more inclined than male judges to consider whether a decision might have a negative impact on the employment of women or minorities.

Legal realism strongly influenced the growth of what is sometimes called the **sociological school,** which views law as a tool for promoting justice in society. In the 1960s, for example, the justices of the United States Supreme Court helped advance the civil rights movement by upholding long-neglected laws calling for equal treatment for all Americans, including African Americans and other minorities. Generally, jurists who adhere to this philosophy of law are more likely to depart from past decisions than are jurists who adhere to other schools of legal thought.

Concept Summary 1.3 on the following page reviews the schools of jurisprudential thought.

SECTION 5

CLASSIFICATIONS OF LAW

The law may be broken down according to several classification systems. For example, one classification system divides law into substantive law and procedural law. **Substantive law** consists of all laws that define, describe, regulate, and create legal rights and obligations. **Procedural law** consists of all laws that outline the methods of enforcing the rights established by substantive law.

Note that many statutes contain both substantive and procedural provisions. ▶ **Example 1.4** A state law that provides employees with the right to *workers' compensation benefits* for on-the-job injuries is a substantive law because it creates legal rights. Procedural laws establish the method by which an employee must notify the employer about an on-the-job injury, prove the injury, and periodically submit additional proof to continue receiving workers' compensation benefits. ◀

Other classification systems divide law into federal law and state law, private law (dealing with relationships between private entities) and public law (addressing the relationship between persons and their governments), and national law and international law. Here we look at still another classification

CONCEPT SUMMARY 1.3

Schools of Jurisprudential Thought

SCHOOL OF THOUGHT	DESCRIPTION
Natural Law School	One of the oldest and most significant schools of legal thought. Those who believe in natural law hold that there is a universal law applicable to all human beings.
Positivist School	A school of legal thought centered on the assumption that there is no law higher than the laws created by the government.
Historical School	A school of legal thought that stresses the evolutionary nature of law and looks to doctrines that have withstood the passage of time for guidance in shaping present laws.
Legal Realism	A school of legal thought that advocates a less abstract and more realistic and pragmatic approach to the law and takes into account customary practices and the circumstances surrounding the particular transaction.

system, which divides law into civil law and criminal law, as well as at what is meant by the term *cyberlaw.*

Civil Law and Criminal Law

Civil law spells out the rights and duties that exist between persons and between persons and their governments, as well as the relief available when a person's rights are violated. Typically, in a civil case, a private party sues another private party who has failed to comply with a duty (note that the government can also sue a party for a civil law violation). Much of the law that we discuss in this text is civil law. Contract law, for example, covered in Chapters 9 and 10, is civil law. The whole body of tort law (see Chapters 12 and 13) is also civil law.

Criminal law, in contrast, is concerned with wrongs committed *against the public as a whole.* Criminal acts are defined and prohibited by local, state, or federal government statutes. Criminal defendants are thus prosecuted by public officials, such as a district attorney (D.A.), on behalf of the state, not by their victims or other private parties. (See Chapter 7 for a further discussion of the distinction between civil law and criminal law.)

Cyberlaw

As mentioned, the use of the Internet to conduct business transactions has led to new types of legal issues. In response, courts have had to adapt traditional laws to situations that are unique to our age. Additionally, legislatures at both the federal and the state levels have created laws to deal specifically with such issues.

Frequently, people use the term **cyberlaw** to refer to the emerging body of law that governs transactions conducted via the Internet. Cyberlaw is not really a classification of law, nor is it a new *type* of law. Rather, it is an informal term used to refer to both new laws and modifications of traditional laws that relate to the online environment. Throughout this book, you will read how the law in a given area is evolving to govern specific legal issues that arise in the online context. We have also devoted Chapter 15 entirely to Internet law, social media, and privacy.

SECTION 6

HOW TO FIND PRIMARY SOURCES OF LAW

This text includes numerous references, or *citations,* to primary sources of law—federal and state statutes, the U.S. Constitution and state constitutions, regulations issued by administrative agencies, and court cases.

A **citation** identifies the publication in which a legal authority—such as a statute or a court decision or other source—can be found. In this section, we explain how you can use citations to find primary sources of law. Note that in addition to being published in sets of books, as described next, most federal and state laws and case decisions are available online.

Finding Statutory and Administrative Law

When Congress passes laws, they are collected in a publication titled *United States Statutes at Large.* When state legislatures pass laws, they are collected in similar state publications. Most frequently, however, laws are referred to in their codified form—that is, the form in which they appear in the federal and state codes. In these codes, laws are compiled by subject.

UNITED STATES CODE The *United States Code* (U.S.C.) arranges all existing federal laws by broad subject. Each of the fifty subjects is given a title and a title number. For instance, laws relating to commerce and trade are collected in Title 15, "Commerce and Trade." Titles are subdivided by sections.

A citation to the U.S.C. includes both title and section numbers. Thus, a reference to "15 U.S.C. Section 1" means that the statute can be found in Section 1 of Title 15. ("Section" may be designated by the symbol §, and "Sections," by §§.) In addition to the print publication, the federal government provides a searchable online database of the *United States Code* at **www.gpo.gov** (click on "Libraries" and then "Core Documents of Our Democracy" to find the U.S.C.).

Commercial publications of federal laws and regulations are also available. For instance, Legal Solutions from Thomson Reuters (formerly West Group) publishes the *United States Code Annotated* (U.S.C.A.). The U.S.C.A. contains the official text of the U.S.C., plus notes (annotations) on court decisions that interpret and apply specific sections of the statutes. The U.S.C.A. also includes additional research aids, such as cross-references to related statutes, historical notes, and library references. A citation to the U.S.C.A. is similar to a citation to the U.S.C.: "15 U.S.C.A. Section 1."

STATE CODES State codes follow the U.S.C. pattern of arranging law by subject. They may be called codes, revisions, compilations, consolidations, general statutes, or statutes, depending on the preferences of the states.

In some codes, subjects are designated by number. In others, they are designated by name. ▶ **Example 1.5** "13 Pennsylvania Consolidated Statutes Section 1101" means that the statute can be found in Title 13, Section 1101, of the Pennsylvania code. "California Commercial Code Section 1101" means that the statute can be found under the subject heading "Commercial Code" of the California code in Section 1101. Abbreviations are often used. For example, "13 Pennsylvania Consolidated Statutes Section 1101" is abbreviated "13 Pa. C.S. § 1101," and "California Commercial Code Section 1101" is abbreviated "Cal. Com. Code § 1101." ◀

ADMINISTRATIVE RULES Rules and regulations adopted by federal administrative agencies are initially published in the *Federal Register,* a daily publication of the U.S. government. Later, they are incorporated into the *Code of Federal Regulations* (C.F.R.).

Like the U.S.C., the C.F.R. is divided into fifty titles. Rules within each title are assigned section numbers. A full citation to the C.F.R. includes title and section numbers. ▶ **Example 1.6** A reference to "17 C.F.R. Section 230.504" means that the rule can be found in Section 230.504 of Title 17. ◀

Finding Case Law

Before discussing the case reporting system, we need to look briefly at the court system (which will be discussed in detail in Chapter 2). There are two types of courts in the United States, federal courts and state courts.

Both the federal and the state court systems consist of several levels, or tiers, of courts. *Trial courts,* in which evidence is presented and testimony given, are on the bottom tier (which also includes lower courts that handle specialized issues). Decisions from a trial court can be appealed to a higher court, which commonly is an intermediate *court of appeals,* or *appellate court.* Decisions from these intermediate courts of appeals may be appealed to an even higher court, such as a state supreme court or the United States Supreme Court.

STATE COURT DECISIONS Most state trial court decisions are not published in books (except in New York and a few other states, which publish selected trial court opinions). Decisions from state trial courts are typically filed in the office of the clerk of the court, where the decisions are available for public inspection. (Increasingly, they can be found online as well.)

Written decisions of the appellate, or reviewing, courts, however, are published and distributed (in print and online). As you will note, most of the state court cases presented in this textbook are from state appellate courts. The reported appellate decisions are published in volumes called *reports* or *reporters,* which are numbered consecutively. State appellate court decisions are found in the state reporters of that particular state. Official reports are published by the state, whereas unofficial reports are published by non-government entities.

Regional Reporters. State court opinions appear in regional units of the National Reporter System, published by West Group (now Thomson Reuters). Most lawyers and libraries have these reporters because they report cases more quickly and are distributed more widely than the state-published reporters. In fact, many states have eliminated their own reporters in favor of the National Reporter System.

The National Reporter System divides the states into the following geographic areas: *Atlantic* (A., A.2d, or A.3d), *North Eastern* (N.E. or N.E.2d), *North Western* (N.W. or N.W.2d), *Pacific* (P., P.2d, or P.3d), *South Eastern* (S.E. or S.E.2d), *South Western* (S.W., S.W.2d, or S.W.3d), and *Southern* (So., So.2d, or So.3d). (The *2d* and *3d* in the preceding abbreviations refer to *Second Series* and *Third Series,* respectively.) The states included in each of these regional divisions are indicated in Exhibit 1–4 on the following page, which illustrates the National Reporter System.

Case Citations. After appellate decisions have been published, they are normally referred to (cited) by the name of the case; the volume, name, and page number of the state's official reporter (if different from the National Reporter System); the volume, name, and page number of the National Reporter; and the volume, name, and page number of any other selected reporter. (Citing a reporter by volume number, name, and page number, in that order, is common to all citations. The year that the decision was issued is often included at the end in parentheses.) When more than one reporter is cited for the same case, each reference is called a *parallel citation.*

Note that some states have adopted a "public domain citation system" that uses a somewhat different format for the citation. For example, in Wisconsin, a Wisconsin Supreme Court decision might be designated "2013 WI 40," meaning that the case was decided in the year 2013 by the Wisconsin Supreme Court and was the fortieth decision issued by that court during that year. Parallel citations to the *Wisconsin Reports* and the *North Western Reporter* are still included after the public domain citation.

▶ **Example 1.7** Consider the following case citation: *Colbert v. Carr,* 140 Conn.App. 229, 57 A.3d. 878 (2013). We see that the opinion in this case can be found in Volume 140 of the official *Connecticut Appellate Court Reports,* on page 229. The parallel citation is to Volume 57 of the *Atlantic Reporter, Third Series,* page 878. ◀

When we present opinions in this text (starting in Chapter 2), in addition to the reporter, we give the name of the court hearing the case and the year of the court's decision. Sample citations to state court decisions are explained in Exhibit 1–5 on page 17.

FEDERAL COURT DECISIONS Federal district (trial) court decisions are published unofficially in the *Federal Supplement* (F.Supp. or F.Supp.2d), and opinions from the circuit courts of appeals (reviewing courts) are reported unofficially in the *Federal Reporter* (F., F.2d, or F.3d). Cases concerning federal bankruptcy law are published unofficially in the *Bankruptcy Reporter* (Bankr. or B.R.).

The official edition of the United States Supreme Court decisions is the *United States Reports* (U.S.), which is published by the federal government. Unofficial editions of Supreme Court cases include the *Supreme Court Reporter* (S.Ct.) and the *Lawyers' Edition of the Supreme Court Reports* (L.Ed. or L.Ed.2d). Sample citations for federal court decisions are also listed and explained in Exhibit 1–5 on pages 17–18.

UNPUBLISHED OPINIONS Many court opinions that are not yet published or that are not intended for publication can be accessed through Westlaw® (abbreviated in citations as "WL"). Westlaw® is an online legal database maintained by Thomson Reuters (formerly West Group). When no citation to a published reporter is available for cases cited in this text, we give the WL citation (see Exhibit 1–5 on page 19 for an example).

OLD CASE LAW On a few occasions, this text cites opinions from old, classic cases dating to the nineteenth century or earlier. Some of these are from the English courts. The citations to these cases may not conform to the descriptions just presented because the reporters in which they were originally published were often known by the names of the persons who compiled the reporters.

SECTION 7

HOW TO READ AND UNDERSTAND CASE LAW

The decisions made by the courts establish the boundaries of the law as it applies to almost all business relationships. It thus is essential that businesspersons know how to read and understand case law.

EXHIBIT 1-4 National Reporter System—Regional/Federal

Regional Reporters	Coverage Beginning	Coverage
Atlantic Reporter (A., A.2d, or A.3d)	1885	Connecticut, Delaware, District of Columbia, Maine, Maryland, New Hampshire, New Jersey, Pennsylvania, Rhode Island, and Vermont.
North Eastern Reporter (N.E. or N.E.2d)	1885	Illinois, Indiana, Massachusetts, New York, and Ohio.
North Western Reporter (N.W. or N.W.2d)	1879	Iowa, Michigan, Minnesota, Nebraska, North Dakota, South Dakota, and Wisconsin.
Pacific Reporter (P., P.2d, or P.3d)	1883	Alaska, Arizona, California, Colorado, Hawaii, Idaho, Kansas, Montana, Nevada, New Mexico, Oklahoma, Oregon, Utah, Washington, and Wyoming.
South Eastern Reporter (S.E. or S.E.2d)	1887	Georgia, North Carolina, South Carolina, Virginia, and West Virginia.
South Western Reporter (S.W., S.W.2d, or S.W.3d)	1886	Arkansas, Kentucky, Missouri, Tennessee, and Texas.
Southern Reporter (So., So.2d, or So.3d)	1887	Alabama, Florida, Louisiana, and Mississippi.
Federal Reporters		
Federal Reporter (F., F.2d, or F.3d)	1880	U.S. Circuit Courts from 1880 to 1912; U.S. Commerce Court from 1911 to 1913; U.S. District Courts from 1880 to 1932; U.S. Court of Claims (now called U.S. Court of Federal Claims) from 1929 to 1932 and since 1960; U.S. Courts of Appeals since 1891; U.S. Court of Customs and Patent Appeals since 1929; U.S. Emergency Court of Appeals since 1943.
Federal Supplement (F.Supp. or F.Supp.2d)	1932	U.S. Court of Claims from 1932 to 1960; U.S. District Courts since 1932; U.S. Customs Court since 1956.
Federal Rules Decisions (F.R.D.)	1939	U.S. District Courts involving the Federal Rules of Civil Procedure since 1939 and Federal Rules of Criminal Procedure since 1946.
Supreme Court Reporter (S.Ct.)	1882	United States Supreme Court since the October term of 1882.
Bankruptcy Reporter (Bankr.)	1980	Bankruptcy decisions of U.S. Bankruptcy Courts, U.S. District Courts, U.S. Courts of Appeals, and the United States Supreme Court.
Military Justice Reporter (M.J.)	1978	U.S. Court of Military Appeals and Courts of Military Review for the Army, Navy, Air Force, and Coast Guard.

NATIONAL REPORTER SYSTEM MAP

Pacific
North Western
South Western
North Eastern
Atlantic
South Eastern
Southern

EXHIBIT 1–5 How to Read Citations

STATE COURTS

285 Neb. 88, 825 N.W.2d 429 (2013)[a]

N.W. is the abbreviation for Thomson Reuters's publication of state court decisions rendered in the *North Western Reporter* of the National Reporter System. *2d* indicates that this case was included in the *Second Series* of that reporter. The number 825 refers to the volume number of the reporter; the number 429 refers to the page in that volume on which this case begins.

Neb. is an abbreviation for *Nebraska Reports,* Nebraska's official reports of the decisions of its highest court, the Nebraska Supreme Court.

213 Cal.App.4th 1, 152 Cal.Rptr.3d 30 (2013)

Cal.Rptr. is the abbreviation for the unofficial reports—titled *California Reporter*—of the decisions of California courts.

102 A.D.3d 774, 958 N.Y.S.2d 440 (2013)

N.Y.S. is the abbreviation for the unofficial reports—titled *New York Supplement*—of the decisions of New York courts.

A.D. is the abbreviation for *Appellate Division*, which hears appeals from the New York Supreme Court—the state's general trial court. The New York Court of Appeals is the state's highest court, analogous to other states' supreme courts.

319 Ga.App. 777, 736 S.E.2d 480 (2013)

Ga.App. is the abbreviation for *Georgia Appeals Reports,* Georgia's official reports of the decisions of its court of appeals.

FEDERAL COURTS

___ U.S. ___, 133 S.Ct. 721, 184 L.Ed.2d 553 (2013)

L.Ed. is an abbreviation for *Lawyers' Edition of the Supreme Court Reports*, an unofficial edition of decisions of the United States Supreme Court.

S.Ct. is the abbreviation for Thomson Reuters's unofficial reports—titled *Supreme Court Reporter*—of decisions of the United States Supreme Court.

U.S. is the abbreviation for *United States Reports*, the official edition of the decisions of the United States Supreme Court. The blank lines in this citation (or any other citation) indicate that the appropriate volume of the case reporter has not yet been published and no page number is available.

a. The case names have been deleted from these citations to emphasize the publications. It should be kept in mind, however, that the name of a case is as important as the specific page numbers in the volumes in which it is found. If a citation is incorrect, the correct citation may be found in a publication's index of case names. In addition to providing a check on errors in citations, the date of a case is important because the value of a recent case as an authority is likely to be greater than that of older cases from the same court.

Continued

EXHIBIT 1–5 How to Read Citations—Continued

FEDERAL COURTS (Continued)

705 F.3d 315 (8th Cir. 2013)

8th Cir. is an abbreviation denoting that this case was decided in the U.S. Court of Appeals for the Eighth Circuit.

___ F.Supp.2d ___ (D.D.C. 2013)

D.D.C. is an abbreviation indicating that the U.S. District Court for the District of Columbia decided this case.

ENGLISH COURTS

9 Exch. 341, 156 Eng.Rep. 145 (1854)

Eng.Rep. is an abbreviation for *English Reports, Full Reprint,* a series of reports containing selected decisions made in English courts between 1378 and 1865.

Exch. is an abbreviation for *English Exchequer Reports*, which includes the original reports of cases decided in England's Court of Exchequer.

STATUTORY AND OTHER CITATIONS

18 U.S.C. Section 1961(1)(A)

U.S.C. denotes *United States Code*, the codification of *United States Statutes at Large*. The number 18 refers to the statute's U.S.C. title number and 1961 to its section number within that title. The number 1 in parentheses refers to a subsection within the section, and the letter A in parentheses to a subsection within the subsection.

UCC 2–206(1)(b)

UCC is an abbreviation for *Uniform Commercial Code.* The first number 2 is a reference to an article of the UCC, and 206 to a section within that article. The number 1 in parentheses refers to a subsection within the section, and the letter b in parentheses to a subsection within the subsection.

***Restatement (Third) of Torts,* Section 6**

Restatement (Third) of Torts refers to the third edition of the American Law Institute's *Restatement of the Law of Torts.* The number 6 refers to a specific section.

17 C.F.R. Section 230.505

C.F.R. is an abbreviation for *Code of Federal Regulations*, a compilation of federal administrative regulations. The number 17 designates the regulation's title number, and 230.505 designates a specific section within that title.

EXHIBIT 1–5 How to Read Citations—Continued

WESTLAW® CITATIONS[b]

2013 WL 285688

WL is an abbreviation for Westlaw. The number 2013 is the year of the document that can be found with this citation in the Westlaw database. The number 285688 is a number assigned to a specific document. A higher number indicates that a document was added to the Westlaw database later in the year.

UNIFORM RESOURCE LOCATORS (URLs)

web2.westlaw.com[c]

The suffix *com* is the top-level domain (TLD) for this Web site. The TLD *com* is an abbreviation for "commercial," which usually means that a for-profit entity hosts (maintains or supports) this Web site.

westlaw is the host name—the part of the domain name selected by the organization that registered the name. In this case, West (now Thomson Reuters) registered the name. This Internet site is the Westlaw database on the Web.

web2 describes Web sites that use software allowing users to interact and collaborate with each other in a social media dialogue, rather than limiting users to the passive viewing of static content.

http://www.uscourts.gov

This is "The Federal Judiciary Home Page." The host is the Administrative Office of the U.S. Courts. The TLD *gov* is an abbreviation for "government." This Web site includes information and links from, and about, the federal courts.

www is an abbreviation for "World Wide Web." The Web is a system of Internet servers that support documents formatted in *HTML* (hypertext markup language) and other formats as well.

http://www.law.cornell.edu/index.html

This part of a URL points to a Web page or file at a specific location within the host's domain. This page is a menu with links to documents within the domain and to other Internet resources.

This is the host name for a Web site that contains the Internet publications of the Legal Information Institute (LII), which is a part of Cornell Law School. The LII site includes a variety of legal materials and links to other legal resources on the Internet. The TLD *edu* is an abbreviation for "educational institution" (a school or a university).

http://www.ipl.org/div/news

This part of the Web site points to a static *news* page at this Web site, which provides links to online newspapers from around the world.

ipl is an abbreviation for "Internet Public Library," which is an online service that provides reference resources and links to other information services on the Web. The IPL is supported chiefly by the School of Information at the University of Michigan. The TLD *org* is an abbreviation for "organization" (normally nonprofit).

div is an abbreviation for "division," which is the way that the Internet Public Library tags the content on its Web site as relating to a specific topic.

b. Many court decisions that are not yet published or that are not intended for publication can be accessed through Westlaw, an online legal database.

c. The basic form for a URL is "service://hostname/path." The Internet service for all of the URLs in this text is *http* (hypertext transfer protocol). Because most Web browsers add this prefix automatically when a user enters a host name or a hostname/path, we have generally omitted the *http://* from the URLs listed in this text.

The cases that we present in this text have been condensed from the full text of the courts' opinions and are presented in a special format. In approximately two-thirds of the cases (including the cases designated as Classic and Spotlight), we have summarized the background and facts, as well as the court's decision and remedy, in our own words. In those cases, we have included only selected portions of the court's opinion ("in the language of the court"). In the remaining one-third of the cases (labeled "Case Analysis Cases"), we have provided a longer excerpt from the court's opinion without summarizing the background and facts or decision and remedy.

The following sections will provide useful insights into how to read and understand case law.

Case Titles and Terminology

The title of a case, such as *Adams v. Jones,* indicates the names of the parties to the lawsuit. The *v.* in the case title stands for *versus,* which means "against." In the trial court, Adams was the plaintiff—the person who filed the suit. Jones was the defendant. If the case is appealed, however, the appellate court will sometimes place the name of the party appealing the decision first, so the case may be called *Jones v. Adams* if Jones is appealing.

Because some appellate courts retain the trial court order of names, it is often impossible to distinguish the plaintiff from the defendant in the title of a reported appellate court decision. You must carefully read the facts of each case to identify the parties. Otherwise, the discussion by the appellate court may be difficult to understand.

The following terms, phrases, and abbreviations are frequently encountered in court opinions and legal publications.

PARTIES TO LAWSUITS As mentioned previously, the party initiating a lawsuit is referred to as the *plaintiff* or *petitioner,* depending on the nature of the action. The party against whom a lawsuit is brought is the *defendant* or *respondent.* Lawsuits frequently involve more than one plaintiff and/or defendant.

When a case is appealed from the original court or jurisdiction to another court or jurisdiction, the party appealing the case is called the **appellant.** The **appellee** is the party against whom the appeal is taken. (In some appellate courts, the party appealing a case is referred to as the petitioner, and the party against whom the suit is brought or appealed is called the respondent.)

JUDGES AND JUSTICES The terms *judge* and *justice* are usually synonymous and represent two designations given to judges in various courts. All members of the United States Supreme Court, for instance, are referred to as justices, and justice is the formal title often given to judges of appellate courts, although this is not always the case. In New York, a *justice* is a judge of the trial court (called the Supreme Court), and a member of the Court of Appeals (the state's highest court) is called a *judge.*

The term *justice* is commonly abbreviated to J., and *justices,* to JJ. A United States Supreme Court case might refer to Justice Sotomayor as Sotomayor, J., or to Chief Justice Roberts as Roberts, C.J.

DECISIONS AND OPINIONS Most decisions reached by reviewing, or appellate, courts are explained in written **opinions.** The opinion contains the court's reasons for its decision, the rules of law that apply, and the judgment. You may encounter several types of opinions as you read appellate cases, including the following:

- When all the judges (or justices) agree, a *unanimous opinion* is written for the entire court.
- When there is not unanimous agreement, a **majority opinion** is generally written. It outlines the views of the majority of the judges deciding the case.
- A judge who agrees (concurs) with the majority opinion as to the result but not as to the legal reasoning often writes a **concurring opinion.** In it, the judge sets out the reasoning that he or she considers correct.
- A **dissenting opinion** presents the views of one or more judges who disagree with the majority view.
- Sometimes, no single position is fully supported by a majority of the judges deciding a case. In this situation, we may have a **plurality opinion.** This is the opinion that has the support of the largest number of judges, but the group in agreement is less than a majority.
- Finally, a court occasionally issues a ***per curiam* opinion** (*per curiam* is Latin for "of the court"), which does not indicate which judge wrote the opinion.

A Sample Court Case

To illustrate the various elements contained in a court opinion, we present an annotated court opinion in Exhibit 1–6 on page 22. The opinion is from an actual case decided by a federal trial court located in California.

BACKGROUND OF THE CASE. In 2011, Amazon.com launched an Appstore for viewing and downloading applications to Android devices, such as the Kindle Fire. Apple products (iPads, iPhones, iPods) use the term APP STORE. In this case, Apple claims that Amazon's use of the name "Appstore" constitutes false advertising and trademark infringement (discussed in Chapter 14). The issue before the court here is whether Amazon's use of "Appstore" might mislead the public into thinking that Amazon's Appstore is affiliated with Apple and offers the same content.

EDITORIAL PRACTICE. You will note that triple asterisks (* * *) and quadruple asterisks (* * * *) frequently appear in the opinion. The triple asterisks indicate that we have deleted a few words or sentences from the opinion for the sake of readability or brevity. Quadruple asterisks mean that an entire paragraph (or more) has been omitted.

Additionally, when the opinion cites another case or legal source, the citation to the case or source has been omitted to save space and to improve the flow of the text. These editorial practices are continued in the other court opinions presented in this book. In addition, whenever we present a court opinion that includes a term or phrase that may not be readily understandable, a bracketed definition or paraphrase has been added.

BRIEFING CASES. Knowing how to read and understand court opinions and the legal reasoning used by the courts is an essential step in undertaking accurate legal research. A further step is "briefing," or summarizing, the case.

Legal researchers routinely brief cases by reducing the texts of the opinions to their essential elements. Generally, when you brief a case, you first summarize the background and facts of the case, as the authors have done for the cases presented in this text. You then indicate the issue (or issues) before the court. An important element in the case brief is, of course, the court's decision on the issue and the legal reasoning used by the court in reaching that decision.

Detailed instructions on how to brief a case are given in Appendix A, which also includes a briefed version of the sample court case presented in Exhibit 1–6 on the following page.

THE SAMPLE COURT CASE STARTS ON THE FOLLOWING PAGE.

EXHIBIT 1–6 A Sample Court Case

This section contains the citation—the name of the case, the name of the court that heard the case, the year of the decision, and reporters in which the court's opinion can be found.

APPLE, INC. v. AMAZON.COM, INC.

United States District Court, Northern District of California,
__ F.Supp.2d __ , 2013 WL 11896 (2013).

This line provides the name of the judge (or justice) who authored the court's opinion.

Phyllis J. *HAMILTON*, District Judge.

* * * *

The court divides the opinion into three sections, each headed by an explanatory heading. The first section summarizes the factual background of the case.

BACKGROUND

To *allege* is to assert to be true as described.

This is a * * * false advertising case. Plaintiff Apple Inc. ("Apple") **alleges** that defendant Amazon.com Inc. ("Amazon") has been improperly using the term "APP STORE" in connection with sales of apps for Android devices and the Kindle Fire (Amazon's tablet computer).

Since July 2008, Apple has sold applications ("apps") for its mobile devices through its APP STORE service.

The Lanham Act is a federal statute enacted in 1946 that protects the owner of a trademark against the use of a similar mark if any consumer confusion might result.

* * * On March 22, 2011, Amazon launched the Amazon Appstore for Android.

Apple filed this action [in the same month, asserting] false advertising under Section 43(a) of the **Lanham Act.**

A *summary judgment* is a judgment that a court enters without beginning or continuing a trial. This judgment can be entered only if no facts are in dispute and the only question is how the law applies to the facts.

Amazon now seeks * * * **summary judgment,** as to the * * * cause of action for false advertising.

The second major section of the opinion responds to the defendant's motion.

DISCUSSION

* * * *

* * * A false advertising claim under Section 43(a) has five elements [including] a false statement of fact by the defendant in a commercial advertisement about its own or another's product.

To *grant* is to approve, warrant, or order a motion or some other request.

* * * Amazon argues that summary judgment should be **granted** as to this claim because Apple has not identified a single false statement that Amazon has made about the nature, characteristics, or quality of the Amazon Appstore for Android (or the Amazon Appstore, which allows viewing and downloading of apps for the Kindle Fire).

EXHIBIT 1–6 A Sample Court Case—Continued

Apple essentially alleges that by using the word "Appstore" in the name of Amazon's store, Amazon implies that its store is affiliated with or sponsored by Apple.

* * * *

Apple argues that * * * Amazon's service ("Appstore") does not possess the characteristics and qualities that the public has come to expect from the name APP STORE, based on their familiarity with Apple's service. For this reason, Apple argues, Amazon's use of "Appstore" misleads the public—in particular because (according to Apple) it "implies a false **equivalence** without cuing consumers to test this claim." Apple contends that because its APP STORE offers so many more apps than Amazon's Appstore, consumers will be misled into thinking that Amazon's Appstore will offer just as many.

An *equivalence* is a characteristic or quality corresponding in effect or function, or nearly equal or virtually identical, to another.

* * * The court finds no support for the proposition that Amazon has expressly or impliedly communicated that its Appstore for Android possesses the characteristics and qualities that the public has come to expect from the Apple APP STORE and/or Apple products.

That is, Apple has failed to establish that Amazon made any false statement (express or implied) of fact that actually deceived or had the tendency to deceive a substantial segment of its audience. The mere use of "Appstore" by Amazon to designate a site for viewing and downloading/purchasing apps cannot be **construed** as a representation that the nature, characteristics, or quality of the Amazon Appstore is the same as that of the Apple APP STORE. Apple has pointed to no advertisement by Amazon that qualifies as a false statement under Section 43(a) of the Lanham Act. Nor is there **sufficient evidence** to raise a **triable** issue.

To *construe* is to interpret or explain the sense of something according to judicial standards.

Sufficient evidence is evidence that is sufficient to satisfy an unprejudiced mind seeking the truth.

A *triable* issue is an issue that is subject to judicial examination and trial.

* * * If an advertisement is not false on its face (i.e., if there is no express or explicit false statement), the plaintiff must produce evidence, usually in the form of market research or consumer surveys, showing exactly what message was conveyed that was sufficient to constitute false advertising. Here, Apple has presented no evidence that

Continued

EXHIBIT 1–6 A Sample Court Case—Continued

In this context, *attribute* refers to the elements or properties of the App Store that are closely associated with Apple.

Here, *seamlessly integrated* means coordinated to operate without any awkward transitions or interruptions.

consumers or customers understand "app store" to include specific qualities or characteristics or **attributes** of the Apple APP STORE, or that any customers were misled by Amazon's use of the term.

Apple asserts that its APP STORE offers many more apps than Amazon's does, and that the apps are **"seamlessly integrated"** with all Apple devices. However, there is no evidence that a consumer who accesses the Amazon Appstore would expect that it would be identical to the Apple APP STORE, particularly given that the Apple APP STORE sells apps solely for Apple devices, while the Amazon Appstore sells apps solely for Android and Kindle devices. Further, the integration of Apple devices has more to do with Apple's technology than it does with the nature, characteristics, or qualities of the APP STORE.

Showing is the act of establishing through evidence and argument.

Apple fails to make clear how [Amazon's use of Appstore] constitutes a "statement" that implies something false about the nature, characteristics, or qualities of Apple's APP STORE, because it has made no **showing** that such (implied) statement deceived or had a tendency to deceive users of Amazon's Appstore.

In the third major section of the opinion, the court states its decision.

CONCLUSION

* * * Amazon's motion for summary judgment as to the * * * cause of action for false advertising is GRANTED.

Reviewing: Law and Legal Reasoning

Suppose that the California legislature passes a law that severely restricts carbon dioxide emissions from automobiles in that state. A group of automobile manufacturers files suit against the state of California to prevent the enforcement of the law. The automakers claim that a federal law already sets fuel economy standards nationwide and that fuel economy standards are essentially the same as carbon dioxide emission standards. According to the automobile manufacturers, it is unfair to allow California to impose more stringent regulations than those set by the federal law. Using the information presented in the chapter, answer the following questions.

1. Who are the parties (the plaintiffs and the defendant) in this lawsuit?
2. Are the plaintiffs seeking a legal remedy or an equitable remedy?
3. What is the primary source of the law that is at issue here?
4. Where would you look to find the relevant California and federal laws?

DEBATE THIS . . . *Under the doctrine of* stare decisis, *courts are obligated to follow the precedents established in their jurisdiction unless there is a compelling reason not to. Should U.S. courts continue to adhere to this common law principle, given that our government now regulates so many areas by statute?*

Terms and Concepts

ExamPrep

Issue Spotters

1. Under what circumstances might a judge rely on case law to determine the intent and purpose of a statute? **(See page 5.)**
2. After World War II, several Nazis were convicted of "crimes against humanity" by an international court. Assuming that these convicted war criminals had not disobeyed any law of their country and had merely been following their government's orders, what law had they violated? Explain. **(See page 11.)**

- **Check your answers to the Issue Spotters against the answers provided in Appendix E at the end of this text.**

Before the Test

Go to www.cengagebrain.com, enter the ISBN 9781285428949, and click on "Find" to locate this textbook's Web site. Then, click on "Access Now" under "Study Tools," and select Chapter 1 at the top. There, you will find an Interactive Quiz that you can take to assess your mastery of the concepts in this chapter, as well as Interactive Flashcards and a Glossary of important terms.

Business Scenarios

1–1. Binding versus Persuasive Authority. A county court in Illinois is deciding a case involving an issue that has never been addressed before in that state's courts. The Iowa Supreme Court, however, recently decided a case involving a very similar fact pattern. Is the Illinois court obligated to follow the Iowa Supreme Court's decision on the issue? If the United States Supreme Court had decided a similar case, would that decision be binding on the Illinois court? Explain. **(See page 8.)**

1–2. Sources of Law. This chapter discussed a number of sources of American law. Which source of law takes priority in the following situations, and why? **(See page 3.)**

(a) A federal statute conflicts with the U.S. Constitution.
(b) A federal statute conflicts with a state constitutional provision.
(c) A state statute conflicts with the common law of that state.
(d) A state constitutional amendment conflicts with the U.S. Constitution.

1–3. *Stare Decisis.* In the text of this chapter, we stated that the doctrine of *stare decisis* "became a cornerstone of the English and American judicial systems." What does *stare decisis* mean, and why has this doctrine been so fundamental to the development of our legal tradition? **(See page 8.)**

1–4. Remedies. Assume that Arthur Rabe is suing Xavier Sanchez for breaching a contract in which Sanchez promised to sell Rabe a painting by Vincent Van Gogh for $30 million. **(See page 7.)**

(a) In this lawsuit, who is the plaintiff and who is the defendant?
(b) Suppose that Rabe wants Sanchez to perform the contract as promised. What remedy would Rabe seek from the court?
(c) Now suppose that Rabe wants to cancel the contract because Sanchez fraudulently misrepresented the painting as an original Van Gogh when in fact it is a copy. What remedy would Rabe seek?
(d) Will the remedy Rabe seeks in either situation be a remedy at law or a remedy in equity? What is the difference between legal and equitable remedies?
(e) Suppose that the trial court finds in Rabe's favor and grants one of these remedies. Sanchez then appeals the decision to a higher court. On appeal, which party will be the appellant (or petitioner), and which party will be the appellee (or respondent)?

Business Case Problems

1–5. Spotlight on AOL—Common Law. AOL, LLC, mistakenly made public the personal information of 650,000 of its members. The members filed a suit, alleging violations of California law. AOL asked the court to dismiss the suit on the basis of a "forum-selection" clause in its member agreement that designates Virginia courts as the place where member disputes will be tried. Under a decision of the United States Supreme Court, a forum-selection clause is unenforceable "if enforcement would contravene a strong public policy of the forum in which suit is brought." California courts have declared in other cases that the AOL clause contravenes a strong public policy. If the court applies the doctrine of *stare decisis,* will it dismiss the suit?

Explain. [*Doe 1 v. AOL LLC,* 552 F.3d 1077 (9th Cir. 2009)] **(See page 8.)**

1–6. BUSINESS CASE PROBLEM WITH SAMPLE ANSWER—Reading Citations.

Assume that you want to read the entire court opinion in the case of United States v. Yi, *704 F.3d 800 (9th Cir. 2013). Refer to the subsection entitled "Finding Case Law" in this chapter, and then explain specifically where you would find the court's opinion.* **(See page 14.)**

- **For a sample answer to Problem 1–6, go to Appendix F at the end of this text.**

1–7. A QUESTION OF ETHICS—The Common Law Tradition.

*On July 5, 1884, Dudley, Stephens, and Brooks—"all able-bodied English seamen"—and a teenage English boy were cast adrift in a lifeboat following a storm at sea. They had no water with them in the boat, and all they had for sustenance were two one-pound tins of turnips. On July 24, Dudley proposed that one of the four in the lifeboat be sacrificed to save the others. Stephens agreed with Dudley, but Brooks refused to consent—and the boy was never asked for his opinion. On July 25, Dudley killed the boy, and the three men then fed on the boy's body and blood. Four days later, a passing vessel rescued the men. They were taken to England and tried for the murder of the boy. If the men had not fed on the boy's body, they would probably have died of starvation within the four-day period. The boy, who was in a much weaker condition, would likely have died before the rest. [*Regina v. Dudley and Stephens, *14 Q.B.D. (Queen's Bench Division, England) 273 (1884)]* **(See page 6.)**

(a) The basic question in this case is whether the survivors should be subject to penalties under English criminal law, given the men's unusual circumstances. Were the defendants' actions necessary but unethical? Explain your reasoning. What ethical issues might be involved here?

(b) Should judges ever have the power to look beyond the written "letter of the law" in making their decisions? Why or why not?

Legal Reasoning Group Activity

1–8. Court Opinions. Read through the subsection in this chapter entitled "Decisions and Opinions." **(See page 20.)**

(a) One group will explain the difference between a concurring opinion and a majority opinion.

(b) Another group will outline the difference between a concurring opinion and a dissenting opinion.

(c) A third group will explain why judges and justices write concurring and dissenting opinions, given that these opinions will not affect the outcome of the case at hand, which has already been decided by majority vote.

THE COURT SYSTEM

The United States has fifty-two court systems—one for each of the fifty states, one for the District of Columbia, and a federal system. Keep in mind that the federal courts are not superior to the state courts. They are simply an independent system of courts, which derives its authority from Article III, Section 2, of the U.S. Constitution. By the power given to it under the U.S. Constitution, Congress has extended the federal court system to U.S. territories such as Guam, Puerto Rico, and the Virgin Islands.[1]

As we shall see, the United States Supreme Court is the final controlling voice over all of these fifty-two systems, at least when questions of federal law are involved. The Supreme Court's decisions—whether on affirmative action, health-care reform, immigration, or same-sex marriage—represent the last word in the most controversial legal debates in our society.

Nevertheless, many of the legal issues that arise in our daily lives, such as the use of social media by courts, employers, and law enforcement, have not yet come before the nation's highest court. The lower courts usually resolve such pressing matters, making these courts equally important in our legal system.

Although an understanding of our nation's court systems is beneficial for anyone, it is particularly crucial for businesspersons, who will likely face a lawsuit at some time during their careers. Anyone involved in business should be familiar with the basic requirements that must be met before a party can bring a lawsuit before a particular court. We discuss these requirements in this chapter.

1. In Guam and the Virgin Islands, territorial courts serve as both federal courts and state courts. In Puerto Rico, they serve only as federal courts.

SECTION 1

THE JUDICIARY'S ROLE IN AMERICAN GOVERNMENT

As you learned in Chapter 1, the body of American law includes the federal and state constitutions, statutes passed by legislative bodies, administrative law, and the case decisions and legal principles that form the common law. These laws would be meaningless, however, without the courts to interpret and apply them. The essential role of the judiciary—the courts—in the American governmental system is to interpret the laws and apply them to specific situations.

Judicial Review

As the branch of government entrusted with interpreting the laws, the judiciary can decide, among other things, whether the laws or actions of the other two branches are constitutional. The process for making such a determination is known as **judicial review.** The power of judicial review enables the judicial branch to act as a check on the other two branches of government, in line with the system of checks and balances established by the U.S. Constitution.[2]

The Origins of Judicial Review in the United States

The power of judicial review is not mentioned in the U.S. Constitution (although many constitutional scholars believe that the founders intended the judi-

2. In a broad sense, judicial review occurs whenever a court "reviews" a case or legal proceeding—as when an appellate court reviews a lower court's decision. When discussing the judiciary's role in American government, however, the term *judicial review* refers to the power of the judiciary to decide whether the actions of the other two branches of government violate the U.S. Constitution.

ciary to have this power). The United States Supreme Court explicitly established this power in 1803 in the case *Marbury v. Madison.*[3] In that decision, the Court stated, "It is emphatically the province [authority] and duty of the Judicial Department to say what the law is. . . . If two laws conflict with each other, the courts must decide on the operation of each. . . . [I]f both [a] law and the Constitution apply to a particular case, . . . the Court must determine which of these conflicting rules governs the case. This is of the very essence of judicial duty." Since the *Marbury v. Madison* decision, the power of judicial review has remained unchallenged. Today, this power is exercised by both federal and state courts.

SECTION 2 BASIC JUDICIAL REQUIREMENTS

Before a lawsuit can be brought before a court, certain requirements must be met. These requirements relate to jurisdiction, venue, and standing to sue. We examine each of these important concepts here.

Jurisdiction

In Latin, *juris* means "law," and *diction* means "to speak." Thus, "the power to speak the law" is the literal meaning of the term **jurisdiction.** Before any court can hear a case, it must have jurisdiction over the person (or company) against whom the suit is brought (the defendant) or over the property involved in the suit. The court must also have jurisdiction over the subject matter of the dispute.

JURISDICTION OVER PERSONS OR PROPERTY A particular court usually can exercise ***in personam* jurisdiction** (personal jurisdiction) over any person or business that resides in a certain geographic area. A state trial court, for instance, normally has jurisdictional authority over residents (including businesses) of a particular area of the state, such as a county or district. A state's highest court (often called the state supreme court[4]) has jurisdictional authority over all residents within the state.

A court can also exercise jurisdiction over property that is located within its boundaries. This kind of jurisdiction is known as ***in rem* jurisdiction,** or "jurisdiction over the thing." ▶ **Example 2.1** A dispute arises over the ownership of a boat in dry dock in Fort Lauderdale, Florida. The boat is owned by an Ohio resident, over whom a Florida court normally cannot exercise personal jurisdiction. The other party to the dispute is a resident of Nebraska. In this situation, a lawsuit concerning the boat could be brought in a Florida state court on the basis of the court's *in rem* jurisdiction. ◀

Long Arm Statutes and Minimum Contacts. Under the authority of a state **long arm statute,** a court can exercise personal jurisdiction over certain out-of-state defendants based on activities that took place within the state. Before a court can exercise jurisdiction, though, it must be demonstrated that the defendant had sufficient contacts, or *minimum contacts,* with the state to justify the jurisdiction.[5]

Generally, the minimum-contacts requirement means that the defendant must have sufficient connection to the state for the judge to conclude that it is fair for the state to exercise power over the defendant. For instance, if an out-of-state defendant caused an automobile accident within the state or breached a contract formed there, a court will usually find that minimum contacts exist to exercise jurisdiction over that defendant. Similarly, a state may exercise personal jurisdiction over a nonresident defendant that is sued for selling defective goods within the state.

▶ **Case in Point 2.2** An Xbox game system caught fire in Bonnie Broquet's home in Texas and caused substantial personal injuries. Broquet filed a lawsuit in a Texas court against Ji-Haw Industrial Company, a nonresident company that made the Xbox components. Broquet alleged that Ji-Haw's components were defective and had caused the fire. Ji-Haw argued that the Texas court lacked jurisdiction over it, but a state appellate court held that the Texas long arm statute authorized the exercise of jurisdiction over the out-of-state defendant.[6] ◀

Corporate Contacts. Because corporations are considered legal persons, courts use the same principles to determine whether it is fair to exercise jurisdiction

3. 5 U.S. (1 Cranch) 137, 2 L.Ed. 60 (1803).
4. As will be discussed shortly, a state's highest court is often referred to as the state supreme court, but there are exceptions. For instance, in New York the supreme court is a trial court.
5. The minimum-contacts standard was first established in *International Shoe Co. v. State of Washington,* 326 U.S. 310, 66 S.Ct. 154, 90 L.Ed. 95 (1945).
6. *Ji-Haw Industrial Co. v. Broquet,* 2008 WL 441822 (Tex.App.—San Antonio 2008).

over a corporation.[7] A corporation normally is subject to personal jurisdiction in the state in which it is incorporated, has its principal office, and/or is doing business. Courts apply the minimum-contacts test to determine if they can exercise jurisdiction over out-of-state corporations.

The minimum-contacts requirement is usually met if the corporation advertises or sells its products within the state, or places its goods into the "stream of commerce" with the intent that the goods be sold in the state. ▶ **Example 2.3** A business is incorporated under the laws of Maine but has a branch office and manufacturing plant in Georgia. The corporation also advertises and sells its products in Georgia. These activities would likely constitute sufficient contacts with the state of Georgia to allow a Georgia court to exercise jurisdiction over the corporation. ◀

Some corporations do not sell or advertise products or place any goods in the stream of commerce. Determining what constitutes minimum contacts in these situations can be more difficult. ▶ **Case in Point 2.4** Independence Plating Corporation is a New Jersey corporation that provides metal-coating services. Its only office and all of its personnel are located in New Jersey, and it does not advertise out of state. Independence had a long-standing business relationship with Southern Prestige Industries, Inc., a North Carolina company. Eventually, Southern Prestige filed suit in North Carolina against Independence for defective workmanship. Independence argued that North Carolina did not have jurisdiction over it, but the court held that Independence had sufficient minimum contacts with the state to justify jurisdiction. The two parties had exchanged thirty-two separate purchase orders in a period of less than twelve months.[8] ◀

JURISDICTION OVER SUBJECT MATTER Subject-matter jurisdiction refers to the limitations on the types of cases a court can hear. Certain courts are empowered to hear certain kinds of disputes.

General and Limited Jurisdiction. In both the federal and the state court systems, there are courts of *general* (unlimited) *jurisdiction* and courts of *limited jurisdiction.* A court of general jurisdiction can decide cases involving a broad array of issues. An example of a court of general jurisdiction is a state trial court or a federal district court.

An example of a state court of limited jurisdiction is a probate court. **Probate courts** are state courts that handle only the disposition of a person's assets and obligations after that person's death, including issues relating to the custody and guardianship of children. An example of a federal court of limited subject-matter jurisdiction is a bankruptcy court. **Bankruptcy courts** handle only bankruptcy proceedings, which are governed by federal bankruptcy law.

A court's jurisdiction over subject matter is usually defined in the statute or constitution that created the court. In both the federal and the state court systems, a court's subject-matter jurisdiction can be limited by any of the following:

1. The subject of the lawsuit.
2. The sum in controversy.
3. Whether the case involves a felony (a more serious type of crime) or a misdemeanor (a less serious type of crime).
4. Whether the proceeding is a trial or an appeal.

Original and Appellate Jurisdiction. The distinction between courts of original jurisdiction and courts of appellate jurisdiction normally lies in whether the case is being heard for the first time. Courts having original jurisdiction are courts of the first instance, or trial courts. These are courts in which lawsuits begin, trials take place, and evidence is presented. In the federal court system, the *district courts* are trial courts. In the various state court systems, the trial courts are known by different names, as will be discussed shortly.

The key point here is that any court having original jurisdiction normally serves as a trial court. Courts having appellate jurisdiction act as reviewing, or appellate, courts. In general, cases can be brought before appellate courts only on appeal from an order or a judgment of a trial court or other lower courts.

JURISDICTION OF THE FEDERAL COURTS Because the federal government is a government of limited powers, the jurisdiction of the federal courts is limited. Federal courts have subject-matter jurisdiction in two situations: when a federal question is involved and when there is diversity of citizenship.

Federal Questions. Article III of the U.S. Constitution establishes the boundaries of federal judicial power. Section 2 of Article III states that "the judicial Power shall extend to all Cases, in Law and Equity, arising under this Constitution, the Laws of the United

7. In the eyes of the law, corporations are "legal persons"—entities that can sue and be sued.
8. *Southern Prestige Industries, Inc. v. Independence Plating Corp.,* 690 S.E.2d 768 (N.C. 2010).

States, and Treaties made, or which shall be made, under their Authority."

In effect, this clause means that whenever a plaintiff's cause of action is based, at least in part, on the U.S. Constitution, a treaty, or a federal law, a **federal question** arises. If a case involves a federal question, the case comes under the judicial power of the federal courts. A person who claims that her constitutional rights have been violated, for instance, can file the lawsuit in a federal court. Note that in a case based on a federal question, a federal court will apply federal law.

Diversity of Citizenship. Federal district courts can also exercise original jurisdiction over cases involving **diversity of citizenship.** The most common type of diversity jurisdiction[9] requires *both* of the following:

1. The plaintiff and defendant must be residents of different states.
2. The dollar amount in controversy must exceed $75,000.

9. Diversity jurisdiction also exists in cases between (1) a foreign country and citizens of a state or of different states and (2) citizens of a state and citizens or subjects of a foreign country. Cases based on these types of diversity jurisdiction occur infrequently.

For purposes of diversity jurisdiction, a corporation is a citizen of both the state in which it is incorporated and the state in which its principal place of business is located. A case involving diversity of citizenship can be filed in the appropriate federal district court. If the case starts in a state court, it can sometimes be transferred, or "removed," to a federal court.

A large percentage of the cases filed in federal courts each year are based on diversity of citizenship. As noted before, a federal court will apply federal law in cases involving federal questions. In a case based on diversity of citizenship, in contrast, a federal court will apply the relevant state law (which is often the law of the state in which the court sits).

The following dispute focused on whether diversity jurisdiction existed. A boat owner was severely burned when his boat exploded after being filled with excessive fuel at a marina in the U.S. Virgin Islands. The owner filed a suit in a federal district court against the marina and sought a jury trial.

The defendant argued that a plaintiff in an admiralty, or maritime (on the sea), case does not have a right to a jury trial unless the court has diversity jurisdiction. The defendant claimed that because it, like the plaintiff, was a citizen of the Virgin Islands, the court had no such jurisdiction.

CASE ANALYSIS

Case 2.1 Mala v. Crown Bay Marina, Inc.

United States Court of Appeals, Third Circuit, 704 F.3d 239 (2013).

IN THE LANGUAGE OF THE COURT

SMITH, Circuit Judge.

* * * *

Kelley Mala is a citizen of the United States Virgin Islands. * * * He went for a cruise in his powerboat near St. Thomas, Virgin Islands. When his boat ran low on gas, he entered Crown Bay Marina to refuel. Mala tied the boat to one of Crown Bay's eight fueling stations and began filling his tank with an automatic gas pump. Before walking to the cash register to buy oil, Mala asked a Crown Bay attendant to watch his boat.

By the time Mala returned, the boat's tank was overflowing and fuel was spilling into the boat and into the water. The attendant manually shut off the pump and acknowledged that the pump had been malfunctioning in recent days. Mala began cleaning up the fuel, and at some point, the attendant provided soap and water. Mala eventually departed the marina, but as he did so, the engine caught fire and exploded. Mala was thrown into the water and was severely burned. His boat was unsalvageable.

* * * Mala sued Crown Bay in the District Court of the Virgin Islands. Mala's * * * complaint asserted * * * that Crown Bay negligently maintained its gas pump. [Negligence is the failure to exercise the standard of care that a reasonable person would exercise in similar circumstances. Negligence is a tort—a breach of a legal duty that proximately causes harm or injury to another—that forms the basis for a claim subject to applicable state law.] The complaint also alleged that the District Court had admiralty and diversity jurisdiction over the case, and it requested a jury trial.

* * * *

* * * Crown Bay filed a motion to strike Mala's jury demand. Crown Bay argued that plaintiffs generally do not have a jury-trial right in admiralty cases—only when the court also has

CASE 2.1 CONTINUES

CASE 2.1 CONTINUED

diversity jurisdiction. And Crown Bay asserted that the parties were not diverse in this case * * * . In response to this motion, the District Court ruled that both Mala and Crown Bay were citizens of the Virgin Islands. The court therefore struck Mala's jury demand, but nevertheless opted to empanel an advisory jury. [The court could accept or reject the advisory jury's verdict.]

* * * At the end of the trial, the advisory jury returned a verdict of $460,000 for Mala—$400,000 for pain and suffering and $60,000 in compensatory damages. It concluded that Mala was 25 percent at fault and that Crown Bay was 75 percent at fault. The District Court ultimately rejected the verdict and entered judgment for Crown Bay.

* * * *

This appeal followed.

* * * *

Mala * * * argues that the District Court improperly refused to conduct a jury trial. This claim ultimately depends on whether the District Court had diversity jurisdiction.

The Seventh Amendment [to the U.S. Constitution] creates a right to civil jury trials in federal court: "In Suits at common law * * * the right of trial by jury shall be preserved." Admiralty suits are not "Suits at common law," which means that when a district court has only admiralty jurisdiction the plaintiff does not have a jury-trial right. But [a federal statute] allows plaintiffs to pursue state claims in admiralty cases as long as the district court also has diversity jurisdiction. In such cases [the statute] preserves whatever jury-trial right exists with respect to the underlying state claims.

Mala argues that the District Court had both admiralty and diversity jurisdiction. As a preliminary matter, the court certainly had admiralty jurisdiction. The alleged tort occurred on navigable water and bore a substantial connection to maritime activity.

The grounds for diversity jurisdiction are less certain. *District courts have jurisdiction only if the parties are completely diverse. This means that no plaintiff may have the same state or territorial citizenship as any defendant.* The parties agree that Mala was a citizen of the Virgin Islands. [Emphasis added.]

Unfortunately for Mala, the District Court concluded that Crown Bay also was a citizen of the Virgin Islands. Mala rejects this conclusion.

Mala bears the burden of proving that the District Court had diversity jurisdiction. Mala failed to meet that burden because he did not offer evidence that Crown Bay was anything other than a citizen of the Virgin Islands. Mala contends that Crown Bay admitted to being a citizen of Florida, but Crown Bay actually denied Mala's allegation.

Absent evidence that the parties were diverse, we are left with Mala's allegations. *Allegations are insufficient at trial. And they are especially insufficient on appeal,* where we review the District Court's underlying factual findings for clear error. Under this standard, we will not reverse unless we are left with the definite and firm conviction that Crown Bay was in fact a citizen of Florida. Mala has not presented any credible evidence that Crown Bay was a citizen of Florida—much less evidence that would leave us with the requisite firm conviction. [Emphasis added.]

* * * Accordingly, the parties were not diverse and Mala does not have a jury-trial right.

* * * *

* * * For these reasons we will affirm the District Court's judgment.

LEGAL REASONING QUESTIONS

1. What is "diversity of citizenship"?
2. How does the presence—or lack—of diversity of citizenship affect a lawsuit?
3. What did the court conclude with respect to the parties' "diversity of citizenship" in this case?
4. How did the court's conclusion affect the outcome?

EXCLUSIVE VERSUS CONCURRENT JURISDICTION When cases can be tried only in federal courts or only in state courts, exclusive jurisdiction exists. Federal courts have **exclusive jurisdiction** in the following types of cases:

1. Federal crimes.
2. Bankruptcy.
3. Most patent and copyright claims.
4. Any lawsuits against the United States.
5. Some areas of admiralty law (law governing seaborne transportation and ocean waters).

State courts also have exclusive jurisdiction over certain subjects—for example, divorce and adoption.

When both federal and state courts have the power to hear a case, as is true in suits involving diversity of citizenship, **concurrent jurisdiction** exists. When concurrent jurisdiction exists, a party may choose to bring a suit in either a federal court or a state court.

Many factors can affect a party's decision to litigate in a federal versus a state court. Examples include the availability of different remedies, the distance to the respective courthouses, or the experience or reputation of a particular judge.

For instance, if the dispute involves a trade secret, a party might conclude that a federal court—which has exclusive jurisdiction over copyrights and patents—would have more expertise in the matter. A party might also choose a federal court over a state court if a state court has a reputation for bias against certain types of cases or plaintiffs.

In contrast, a plaintiff might choose to litigate in a state court if the court has a reputation for awarding substantial amounts of damages or if the judge is perceived as being pro-plaintiff. The concepts of exclusive and concurrent jurisdiction are illustrated in Exhibit 2–1 below.

Jurisdiction in Cyberspace

The Internet's capacity to bypass political and geographic boundaries undercuts the traditional basis on which courts assert personal jurisdiction. This basis includes a party's contacts with a court's geographic jurisdiction.

As already discussed, for a court to compel a defendant to come before it, there must be at least minimum contacts—the presence of a salesperson within the state, for instance. When a defendant's only contacts with the state are through a Web site, however, it is more difficult to determine whether these contacts are sufficient for a court to exercise jurisdiction.

THE "SLIDING-SCALE" STANDARD The courts have developed a "sliding-scale" standard to determine when they can exercise personal jurisdiction over an out-of-state defendant based on the defendant's Web activities. The sliding-scale standard identifies three types of Internet business contacts and outlines the following rules for jurisdiction:

1. When the defendant conducts substantial business over the Internet (such as contracts and sales even using a smartphone), jurisdiction is proper.
2. When there is some interactivity through a Web site, jurisdiction may be proper, depending on the circumstances. Even a single contact can satisfy the minimum-contacts requirement in certain situations.
3. When a defendant merely engages in passive advertising on the Web, jurisdiction is never proper.[10] An Internet communication is typically considered passive if people have to voluntarily access it to read the message and active if it is sent to specific individuals.

Case in Point 2.5 A Louisiana resident, Daniel Crummey, purchased a used recreational vehicle (RV) from sellers in Texas after viewing photos of it on eBay. The sellers' statements on eBay claimed that "Everything works great on this RV and will provide comfort and dependability for years to come. This RV will go to Alaska and back without problems!"

10. For a leading case on this issue, see *Zippo Manufacturing Co. v. Zippo Dot Com, Inc.*, 952 F.Supp. 1119 (W.D.Pa. 1997).

EXHIBIT 2–1 Exclusive and Concurrent Jurisdiction

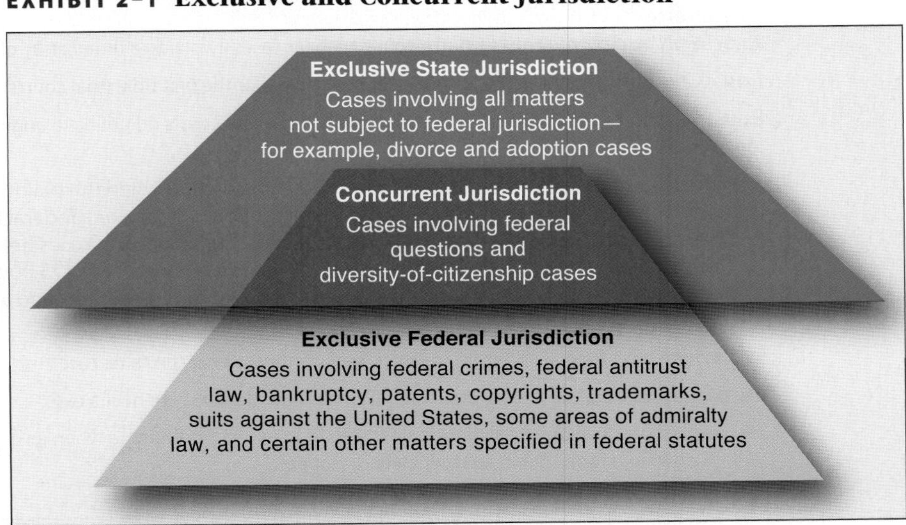

Crummey picked up the RV in Texas, but on the drive back to Louisiana, the RV quit working. He filed a suit in Louisiana against the sellers, alleging that the vehicle was defective. The sellers claimed that the Louisiana court lacked jurisdiction. The court found that Louisiana had jurisdiction because the sellers had used eBay to market and sell the RV to a Louisiana buyer—and had regularly used eBay to sell vehicles to remote parties in the past.[11] ◀

Concept Summary 2.1 reviews the various types of jurisdiction, including jurisdiction in cyberspace.

11. *Crummey v. Morgan,* 965 So.2d 497 (La.App. 1 Cir. 2007). But note that a single sale on eBay does not necessarily confer jurisdiction. Jurisdiction depends on whether the seller regularly uses eBay as a means for doing business with remote buyers. See *Boschetto v. Hansing,* 539 F.3d 1011 (9th Cir. 2008).

INTERNATIONAL JURISDICTIONAL ISSUES Because the Internet is international in scope, it obviously raises international jurisdictional issues. The world's courts seem to be developing a standard that echoes the requirement of minimum contacts applied by the U.S. courts.

Most courts are indicating that minimum contacts—doing business within the jurisdiction, for example—are enough to compel a defendant to appear and that a physical presence in the country is not necessary. The effect of this standard is that a business firm has to comply with the laws in any jurisdiction in which it targets customers for its products. This situation is complicated by the fact that many countries' laws on particular issues—free speech, for instance—are very different from U.S. laws.

CONCEPT SUMMARY 2.1
Jurisdiction

TYPE OF JURISDICTION	DESCRIPTION
Personal	Exists when a defendant is located in the territorial boundaries within which a court has the right and power to decide cases. Jurisdiction may be exercised over out-of-state defendants under state long arm statutes. Courts have jurisdiction over corporate defendants that do business within the state, as well as corporations that advertise, sell, or place goods into the stream of commerce in the state.
Property	Exists when the property that is subject to a lawsuit is located within the territorial boundaries within which a court has the right and power to decide cases.
Subject Matter	Limits the court's jurisdictional authority to particular types of cases. 1. *Limited jurisdiction*—Exists when a court is limited to a specific subject matter, such as probate or divorce. 2. *General jurisdiction*—Exists when a court can hear cases involving a broad array of issues.
Original	Exists with courts that have the authority to hear a case for the first time (trial courts).
Appellate	Exists with courts of appeal and review. Generally, appellate courts do not have original jurisdiction.
Federal	1. *Federal questions*—A federal court can exercise jurisdiction when the plaintiff's cause of action is based at least in part on the U.S. Constitution, a treaty, or a federal law. 2. *Diversity of citizenship*—A federal court can exercise jurisdiction in cases between citizens of different states when the amount in controversy exceeds $75,000 (or in cases between a foreign country and citizens of a state or of different states and in cases between citizens of a state and citizens or subjects of a foreign country).
Concurrent	Exists when both federal and state courts have authority to hear the same case.
Exclusive	Exists when only state courts or only federal courts have authority to hear a case.
Jurisdiction in Cyberspace	The courts have developed a sliding-scale standard to use in determining when jurisdiction over a Web site owner or operator in another state is proper.

The following case illustrates how federal courts apply a sliding-scale standard to determine if they can exercise jurisdiction over a foreign defendant whose only contact with the United States is through a Web site.

SPOTLIGHT on Gucci

Case 2.2 Gucci America, Inc. v. Wang Huoqing

United States District Court, Northern District of California, ___ F.Supp.2d ___ (2011).

BACKGROUND AND FACTS Gucci America, Inc., is a New York corporation headquartered in New York City. Gucci manufactures and distributes high-quality luxury goods, including footwear, belts, sunglasses, handbags, and wallets, which are sold worldwide. In connection with its products, Gucci uses twenty-one federally registered trademarks (trademark law will be discussed in Chapter 14). Gucci also operates a number of boutiques, some of which are located in California.

Wang Huoqing, a resident of the People's Republic of China, operates numerous Web sites. When Gucci discovered that Wang Huoqing's Web sites offered for sale counterfeit goods—products bearing Gucci's trademarks but not genuine Gucci articles—it hired a private investigator in San Jose, California, to buy goods from the Web sites. The investigator purchased a wallet that was labeled Gucci but was counterfeit. Gucci filed a trademark infringement lawsuit against Wang Huoqing in a federal district court in California seeking damages and an injunction to prevent further infringement. Wang Huoqing was notified of the lawsuit via e-mail (see the discussion of *service of process* on page 44) but did not appear in court. Gucci asked the court to enter a default judgment—that is, a judgment entered when the defendant fails to appear. First, however, the court had to determine whether it had personal jurisdiction over Wang Huoqing based on the Internet sales.

IN THE LANGUAGE OF THE COURT
Joseph C. *SPERO*, United States Magistrate Judge.

* * * *

* * * Under California's long-arm statute, federal courts in California may exercise jurisdiction to the extent permitted by the Due Process Clause of the Constitution. The Due Process Clause allows federal courts to exercise jurisdiction where * * * the defendant has had sufficient minimum contacts with the forum to subject him or her to the specific jurisdiction of the court. The courts apply a three-part test to determine whether specific jurisdiction exists:

> (1) The nonresident defendant must do some act or consummate some transaction with the forum or perform some act by which he purposefully avails himself of the privilege of conducting activities in the forum, thereby invoking the benefits and protections of its laws; (2) the claim must be one which arises out of or results from the defendant's forum-related activities; and (3) exercise of jurisdiction must be reasonable.

* * * *

In order to satisfy the first prong of the test for specific jurisdiction, a defendant must have either purposefully availed itself of [taken advantage of] the privilege of conducting business activities within the forum or purposefully directed activities toward the forum. *Purposeful availment typically consists of action taking place in the forum that invokes the benefits and protections of the laws of the forum, such as executing or performing a contract within the forum.* To show purposeful availment, a plaintiff must show that the defendant "engage[d] in some form of affirmative conduct allowing or promoting the transaction of business within the forum state." [Emphasis added.]

"In the Internet context, the Ninth Circuit utilizes a sliding scale analysis under which 'passive' websites do not create sufficient contacts to establish purposeful availment, whereas

CASE 2.2 CONTINUES ➧

CASE 2.2 CONTINUED

interactive websites may create sufficient contacts, depending on how interactive the website is." * * * *Personal jurisdiction is appropriate where an entity is conducting business over the Internet and has offered for sale and sold its products to forum [California] residents.* [Emphasis added.]

Here, the allegations and evidence presented by Plaintiffs in support of the Motion are sufficient to show purposeful availment on the part of Defendant Wang Huoqing. Plaintiffs have alleged that Defendant operates "fully interactive Internet websites operating under the Subject Domain Names" and have presented evidence in the form of copies of web pages showing that the websites are, in fact, interactive. * * * Additionally, Plaintiffs allege Defendant is conducting counterfeiting and infringing activities within this Judicial District and has advertised and sold his counterfeit goods in the State of California. * * * Plaintiffs have also presented evidence of one actual sale within this district, made by investigator Robert Holmes from the website bag2do.cn. * * * Finally, Plaintiffs have presented evidence that Defendant Wang Huoqing owns or controls the twenty-eight websites listed in the Motion for Default Judgment. * * * Such commercial activity in the forum amounts to purposeful availment of the privilege of conducting activities within the forum, thus invoking the benefits and protections of its laws. Accordingly, the Court concludes that Defendant's contacts with California are sufficient to show purposeful availment.

DECISION AND REMEDY *The U.S. District Court for the Northern District of California held that it had personal jurisdiction over the foreign defendant, Wang Huoqing. The court entered a default judgment against Wang Huoqing and granted Gucci an injunction.*

WHAT IF THE FACTS WERE DIFFERENT? *Suppose that Gucci had not presented evidence that Wang Huoqing had made one actual sale through his Web site to a resident (the private investigator) of the court's district. Would the court still have found that it had personal jurisdiction over Wang Huoqing? Why or why not?*

THE LEGAL ENVIRONMENT DIMENSION *Is it relevant to the analysis of jurisdiction that Gucci America's principal place of business is in New York rather than California? Explain.*

Venue

Jurisdiction has to do with whether a court has authority to hear a case involving specific persons, property, or subject matter. **Venue**[12] is concerned with the most appropriate location for a trial. For instance, two state courts (or two federal courts) may have the authority to exercise jurisdiction over a case. Nonetheless, it may be more appropriate or convenient to hear the case in one court than in the other.

The concept of venue reflects the policy that a court trying a case should be in the geographic neighborhood (usually the county) where the incident occurred or where the parties reside. Venue in a civil case typically is where the defendant resides, whereas venue in a criminal case normally is where the crime occurred. Pretrial publicity or other factors, though, may require a change of venue to another community, especially in criminal cases in which the defendant's right to a fair and impartial jury has been impaired.

12. Pronounced *ven*-yoo.

▶ **Example 2.6** Police raid a compound of religious polygamists in Texas and remove many children from the ranch. Authorities suspect that some of the girls were being sexually and physically abused. The raid receives a great deal of media attention, and people living in the nearby towns would likely be influenced by this publicity. If the government files criminal charges against a member of the religious sect, that individual may request a change of venue to another location. ◀

Note, though, that venue has lost some significance in today's world because of the Internet and 24/7 news reporting. Courts now rarely grant requests for a change of venue. Because everyone has instant access to all information about a purported crime, courts reason that no community is more or less informed or prejudiced for or against a defendant.

Standing to Sue

Before a party can bring a lawsuit to court, that party must have **standing to sue,** or a sufficient stake in a matter to justify seeking relief through the court system. Standing means that the party that filed the action in court has a legally protected interest at stake in the litigation. At times, a person can have standing to sue on behalf of another person, such as a minor (child) or a mentally incompetent person.

Standing can be broken down into three elements:

1. *Harm.* The party bringing the action must have suffered or will imminently suffer harm—an invasion of a legally protected interest. The controversy must be real and substantial rather than hypothetical.
2. *Causation.* There must be a causal connection between the conduct complained of and the injury.
3. *Remedy.* It must be likely, as opposed to merely speculative, that a favorable court decision will remedy, or make up for, the injury suffered.

▶ **Case in Point 2.7** The federal government's Legal Services Corporation (LSC) subsidizes legal services for people who cannot afford them. LSC restricts the use of its funds to certain purposes. In an attempt to cut costs, the state of Oregon tried to consolidate some of its legal assistance programs with similar programs provided by other organizations, including LSC. LSC did not approve, however, because Oregon's plan would integrate programs receiving federal funds with programs that engaged in restricted activities.

Oregon filed a suit against LSC, alleging that the state's ability to provide legal services to its citizens was frustrated, but the court dismissed the suit. Oregon had not accepted any federal funds and was not injured by the federal government's decision to subsidize certain private activities. The state had no standing to sue the federal government over federal subsidies to private parties.[13] ◀

SECTION 3

THE STATE AND FEDERAL COURT SYSTEMS

As mentioned earlier in this chapter, each state has its own court system. Additionally, there is a system of federal courts. Although no two state court systems are exactly the same, the right-hand side of Exhibit 2–2 below illustrates the basic organizational framework characteristic of the court systems in many states. The exhibit also shows how the federal court system is structured. We turn now to an examination of these court systems, beginning with the state courts.

The State Court Systems

Typically, a state court system includes several levels, or tiers, of courts, as shown in Exhibit 2–2. State courts may include (1) trial courts of limited jurisdiction, (2) trial courts of general jurisdiction, (3) appellate courts

13. *Oregon v. Legal Services Corp.*, 552 F.3d 965 (9th Cir. 2009).

EXHIBIT 2–2 The State and Federal Court Systems

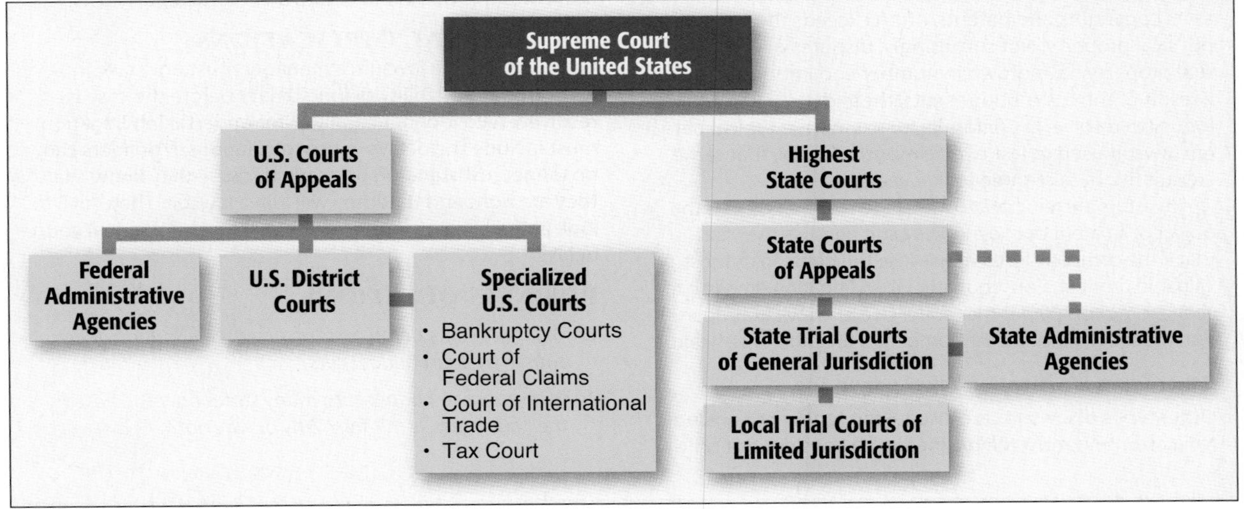

(intermediate appellate courts), and (4) the state's highest court (often called the state supreme court).

Generally, any person who is a party to a lawsuit has the opportunity to plead the case before a trial court and then, if he or she loses, before at least one level of appellate court. Finally, if the case involves a federal statute or federal constitutional issue, the decision of a state supreme court on that issue may be further appealed to the United States Supreme Court. (See this chapter's *Managerial Strategy* feature below for a discussion of how state budget cuts are making it more difficult to bring cases in some state courts.)

Budget Cuts for State Courts Can Affect Businesses

In the United States, businesses use the courts far more than anyone else. Most civil court cases involve a business suing another business for breach of contract or fraud, for instance. Additionally, when one company fails to pay another company for products or services, the unpaid company will often turn to the court system. If that firm does not have ready access to the courts, its financial stability can be put at risk.

Court Budgets Have Been Reduced

According to the National Center for State Courts, since 2008 forty-two state legislatures have reduced funding for their state courts. California's courts have experienced the steepest cuts—$844 million from their annual budget since 2011. Recently, the Alabama legislature cut its court funding by almost 9 percent. As a result, the state's chief justice ordered courthouses to close on Fridays. The number of weeks that jury trials are available to civil litigants in Alabama has been reduced by 50 percent.

Intellectual Property Cases Take Longer to Resolve

Today, the value of a company's intellectual property, such as its copyrights and patents, often exceeds the value of its physical property. Not surprisingly, disputes over intellectual property have grown in number and importance. As a result of the court budget cuts, these disputes also take longer to resolve. In California, for example, a typical patent lawsuit used to last twelve months. Today, that same lawsuit might take three to five years.

Investors are reluctant to invest in a company that is the object of a patent or copyright lawsuit because they fear that if the company loses, it may lose the rights to its most valuable product. Consequently, when litigation drags on for years, some companies may suffer because investors abandon them even though the companies are otherwise healthy.

Other Types of Litigation Take Longer, Too

Other types of lawsuits are also taking longer to conclude. Now attorneys must tell businesses to consider not only the cost of bringing a lawsuit, but also the length of time involved. The longer the litigation lasts, the larger the legal bills and the greater the drain on company employees' time. Roy Weinstein, managing director of Micronomics in California, argues that the economic impact of court delays on businesses is substantial. During the years that a lawsuit can take, some businesses find that they cannot expand or hire new employees, and they are reluctant to spend on additional marketing and advertising.

In fact, it is not unusual for a company to win its case but end up going out of business. As a result of putting its business on hold for years, the company becomes insolvent.

Some Meritorious Cases Are Never Filed

Facing long delays in litigation with potential negative effects on their companies, business managers are becoming reluctant to bring lawsuits, even when their cases clearly have merit. In Alabama, for instance, the number of civil cases filed has dropped by more than a third in the last few years. Judge J. Scott Vowell of Jefferson County attributes this decline to delays and higher court costs.

MANAGERIAL IMPLICATIONS

Before bringing a lawsuit, a manager must now take into account the possibility of long delays before the case is resolved. A cost-benefit analysis for undertaking litigation must include the delays in the calculations. Managers can no longer just stand on principle because they know that they are right and that they will win a lawsuit. They have to look at the bigger picture, which includes substantial court delays.

BUSINESS QUESTIONS

1. *What are some of the costs of increased litigation delays caused by court budget cuts?*
2. *In response to budget cuts, many states have increased their filing fees. Is this fair? Why or why not?*

The states use various methods to select judges for their courts. Usually, voters elect judges, but in some states judges are appointed. For instance, in Iowa, the governor appoints judges, and then the general population decides whether to confirm their appointment in the next general election. The states usually specify the number of years that judges will serve. In contrast, as you will read shortly, judges in the federal court system are appointed by the president of the United States and, if they are confirmed by the Senate, hold office for life—unless they engage in blatantly illegal conduct.

TRIAL COURTS Trial courts are exactly what their name implies—courts in which trials are held and testimony is taken. State trial courts have either general or limited jurisdiction.

General Jurisdiction. Trial courts that have general jurisdiction as to subject matter may be called county, district, superior, or circuit courts.[14] State trial courts of general jurisdiction have jurisdiction over a wide variety of subjects, including both civil disputes and criminal prosecutions. In some states, trial courts of general jurisdiction may hear appeals from courts of limited jurisdiction.

Limited Jurisdiction. Courts of limited jurisdiction as to subject matter are generally inferior trial courts or minor judiciary courts. Limited jurisdiction courts might include local municipal courts (which could also have separate traffic courts and drug courts) and domestic relations courts (which handle divorce and child-custody disputes).

Small claims courts are inferior trial courts that hear only civil cases involving claims of less than a certain amount, such as $5,000 (the amount varies from state to state). Procedures in small claims courts are generally informal, and lawyers are not required (in a few states, lawyers are not even allowed). Decisions of small claims courts and municipal courts may sometimes be appealed to a state trial court of general jurisdiction.

A few states have also established Islamic law courts, which are courts of limited jurisdiction that serve the American Muslim community. These courts decide cases with reference to the *sharia,* a system of law used in most Islamic countries that is derived from the Qur'an and the sayings and doings of Muhammad and his followers.

14. The name in Ohio and Pennsylvania is Court of Common Pleas. The name in New York is Supreme Court, Trial Division.

Appellate, or Reviewing, Courts. Every state has at least one court of appeals (appellate court, or reviewing court), which may be an intermediate appellate court or the state's highest court. About three-fourths of the states have intermediate appellate courts.

Generally, courts of appeals do not conduct new trials, in which evidence is submitted to the court and witnesses are examined. Rather, an appellate court panel of three or more judges reviews the record of the case on appeal, which includes a transcript of the trial proceedings. The appellate court hears arguments from attorneys and determines whether the trial court committed an error.

Reviewing courts focus on questions of law, not questions of fact. A **question of fact** deals with what really happened in regard to the dispute being tried—such as whether a party actually burned a flag. A **question of law** concerns the application or interpretation of the law—such as whether flag-burning is a form of speech protected by the First Amendment to the U.S. Constitution. Only a judge, not a jury, can rule on questions of law.

Appellate courts normally defer (or give weight) to the trial court's findings on questions of fact because the trial court judge and jury were in a better position to evaluate testimony. The trial court judge and jury can directly observe witnesses' gestures, demeanor, and other nonverbal behavior during the trial. An appellate court cannot.

HIGHEST STATE COURTS The highest appellate court in a state is usually called the supreme court but may be designated by some other name. For instance, in both New York and Maryland, the highest state court is called the Court of Appeals. The highest state court in Maine and Massachusetts is the Supreme Judicial Court, and in West Virginia, it is the Supreme Court of Appeals.

The decisions of each state's highest court on all questions of state law are final. Only when issues of federal law are involved can the United States Supreme Court overrule a decision made by a state's highest court. ▶ **Example 2.8** A city enacts an ordinance that prohibits citizens from engaging in door-to-door advocacy without first registering with the mayor's office and receiving a permit. A religious group then sues the city, arguing that the law violates the freedoms of speech and religion guaranteed by the First Amendment. If the state supreme court upholds the law, the group could appeal the decision to the United States Supreme Court—because a constitutional (federal) issue is involved. ◀

The Federal Court System

The federal court system is basically a three-tiered model consisting of (1) U.S. district courts (trial courts of general jurisdiction) and various courts of limited jurisdiction, (2) U.S. courts of appeals (intermediate courts of appeals), and (3) the United States Supreme Court.

Unlike state court judges, who are usually elected, federal court judges—including the justices of the Supreme Court—are appointed by the president of the United States, subject to confirmation by the U.S. Senate. All federal judges receive lifetime appointments under Article III of the U.S. Constitution, which states that federal judges "hold their offices during good Behaviour." In the entire history of the United States, only seven federal judges have been removed from office through impeachment proceedings.

U.S. DISTRICT COURTS At the federal level, the equivalent of a state trial court of general jurisdiction is the district court. U.S. district courts have original jurisdiction in matters involving a federal question and concurrent jurisdiction with state courts when diversity jurisdiction exists. Federal cases typically originate in district courts. There are other federal courts with original, but special (or limited), jurisdiction, such as the federal bankruptcy courts and others shown in Exhibit 2–2 on page 37.

There is at least one federal district court in every state. The number of judicial districts can vary over time, primarily owing to population changes and corresponding changes in caseloads. Today there are ninety-four federal judicial districts. Exhibit 2–3 below shows the boundaries of both the U.S. district courts and the U.S. courts of appeals (discussed next).

U.S. COURTS OF APPEALS In the federal court system, there are thirteen U.S. courts of appeals—referred to as U.S. circuit courts of appeals. Twelve of the federal courts of appeals (including the Court of Appeals for the D.C. Circuit) hear appeals from the federal district courts located within their respective judicial circuits, or geographic boundaries (shown in Exhibit 2–3 below).[15] The Court

15. Historically, judges were required to "ride the circuit" and hear appeals in different courts around the country, which is how the name "circuit court" came about.

EXHIBIT 2–3 Geographic Boundaries of the U.S. Courts of Appeals and U.S. District Courts

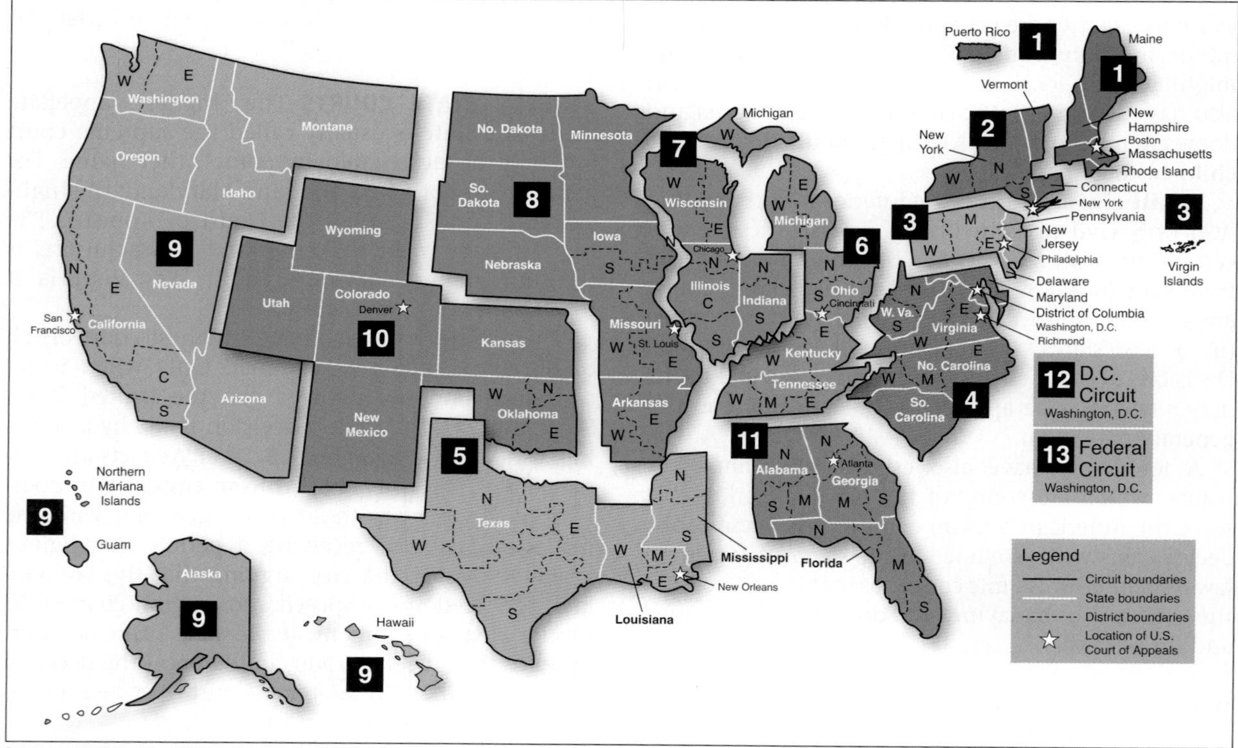

Source: Administrative Office of the United States Courts.

of Appeals for the Thirteenth Circuit, called the Federal Circuit, has national appellate jurisdiction over certain types of cases, such as those involving patent law and those in which the U.S. government is a defendant.

The decisions of a circuit court of appeals are binding on all courts within the circuit court's jurisdiction and are final in most cases, but appeal to the United States Supreme Court is possible.

THE UNITED STATES SUPREME COURT The highest level of the three-tiered federal court system is the United States Supreme Court. According to the U.S. Constitution, there is only one national Supreme Court. All other courts in the federal system are considered "inferior." Congress is empowered to create other inferior courts as it deems necessary. The inferior courts that Congress has created include the second tier in our model—the U.S. circuit courts of appeals—as well as the district courts and the various federal courts of limited, or specialized, jurisdiction.

The United States Supreme Court consists of nine justices. Although the Supreme Court has original, or trial, jurisdiction in rare instances (set forth in Article III, Sections 1 and 2), most of its work is as an appeals court. The Supreme Court can review any case decided by any of the federal courts of appeals. It also has appellate authority over cases involving federal questions that have been decided in the state courts. The Supreme Court is the final authority on the Constitution and federal law.

Appeals to the Supreme Court. To bring a case before the Supreme Court, a party requests the Court to issue a writ of *certiorari*.[16] A **writ of *certiorari*** is an order issued by the Supreme Court to a lower court requiring the latter to send it the record of the case for review. The Court will not issue a writ unless at least four of the nine justices approve of it. This is called the **rule of four.**

Whether the Court will issue a writ of *certiorari* is entirely within its discretion, and most petitions for writs are denied. (Although thousands of cases are filed with the Supreme Court each year, it hears, on average, fewer than one hundred of these cases.)[17] A denial of the request to issue a writ of *certiorari* is not a decision on the merits of the case, nor does it indicate agreement with the lower court's opinion. Also, denial of the writ has no value as a precedent. Denial simply means that the lower court's decision remains the law in that jurisdiction.

Petitions Granted by the Court. Typically, the Court grants petitions in cases that raise important constitutional questions or when the lower courts have issued conflicting decisions on a significant issue. The justices, however, never explain their reasons for hearing certain cases and not others, so it is difficult to predict which type of case the Court might select.

See *Concept Summary 2.2* on the next page to review the courts in the federal and state court systems.

SECTION 4

JUDICIAL PROCEDURES: FOLLOWING A CASE THROUGH THE COURTS

American and English courts follow the *adversarial system of justice*. Although parties are allowed to represent themselves in court (called *pro se* representation),[18] most parties to lawsuits hire attorneys to represent them. Each lawyer acts as his or her client's advocate, presenting the client's version of the facts in such a way as to convince the judge (or the judge and jury, in a jury trial) that this version is correct.

Procedural Rules

The parties to a lawsuit must comply with the procedural rules of the court in which the lawsuit is filed. Although people often think that substantive law determines the outcome of a case, procedural law can have a significant impact on a person's ability to pursue a legal claim. Procedural rules provide a framework for every dispute and specify what must be done at each stage of the litigation process.

Procedural rules are complex, and they vary from court to court and from state to state. There is a set of federal rules of procedure as well as various sets of rules for state courts. Additionally, the applicable procedures will depend on whether the case is a civil or criminal proceeding. All civil trials held in federal

16. Pronounced sur-shee-uh-*rah*-ree.

17. From the mid-1950s through the early 1990s, the Supreme Court reviewed more cases per year than it has since then. In the Court's 1982–1983 term, for example, the Court issued written opinions in 151 cases. In contrast, during the Court's 2012–2013 term, the Court issued written opinions in only 79 cases.

18. This right was definitively established in *Faretta v. California,* 422 U.S. 806, 95 S.Ct. 2525, 45 L.Ed.2d 562 (1975).

CONCEPT SUMMARY 2.2

Types of Courts

TYPE OF COURT	DESCRIPTION
Trial Courts	Trial courts are courts of original jurisdiction in which actions are initiated. 1. *State courts*—Courts of general jurisdiction can hear any case that has not been specifically designated for another court. Courts of limited jurisdiction include, among others, domestic relations courts, probate courts, municipal courts, and small claims courts. 2. *Federal courts*—The federal district court is the equivalent of the state trial court. Federal courts of limited jurisdiction include the bankruptcy courts and others shown in Exhibit 2–2 on page 37.
Intermediate Appellate Courts	Courts of appeals are reviewing courts. Generally, appellate courts do not have original jurisdiction. About three-fourths of the states have intermediate appellate courts. In the federal court system, the U.S. circuit courts of appeals are the intermediate appellate courts.
Supreme Courts	The highest state court is that state's supreme court, although it may be called by some other name. Appeal from state supreme courts to the United States Supreme Court is possible only if a federal question is involved. The United States Supreme Court is the highest court in the federal court system and the final authority on the Constitution and federal law.

district courts are governed by the **Federal Rules of Civil Procedure (FRCP).**[19]

Stages of Litigation

Broadly speaking, the litigation process has three phases: pretrial, trial, and posttrial. Each phase involves specific procedures, as discussed throughout this chapter. Although civil lawsuits may vary greatly in terms of complexity, cost, and detail, they typically progress through the specific stages charted in Exhibit 2–4 on the facing page.

To illustrate the procedures involved in a civil lawsuit, we will use a simple hypothetical case. The case arose from an automobile accident, which occurred when a car driven by Antonio Carvello, a resident of New Jersey, collided with a car driven by Jill Kirby, a resident of New York. The accident took place at an intersection in New York City. Kirby suffered personal injuries, which caused her to incur medical and hospital expenses as well as lost wages for four months. In all, she calculated that the cost to her of the accident was $100,000.[20] Carvello and Kirby have been unable to agree on a settlement, and Kirby now must decide whether to sue Carvello for the $100,000 compensation she feels she deserves.

19. The United States Supreme Court has authority to establish these rules, as spelled out in 28 U.S.C. Sections 2071–2077. Generally, though, the federal judiciary appoints committees that make recommendations to the Supreme Court. The Court then publishes any proposed changes in the rules and allows for public comment before finalizing the rules.

20. In this example, we are ignoring damages for pain and suffering and for permanent disabilities. Often, plaintiffs in personal-injury cases seek such damages.

Consulting with an Attorney

As mentioned, rules of procedure often affect the outcome of a dispute—a fact that highlights the importance of obtaining the advice of counsel. The first step taken by almost anyone contemplating a lawsuit is to seek the guidance of a qualified attorney.

In the hypothetical Kirby-Carvello case, assume that Kirby consults with a lawyer. The attorney will advise her regarding what she can expect in a lawsuit, her probability of success at trial, and the procedures that will be involved. If more than one court would have jurisdiction over the matter, the attorney will also discuss the advantages and disadvantages of filing in a particular court. In addition, the attorney will indicate how long it will take to resolve the dispute through litigation in a particular court and provide an estimate of the costs involved.

The attorney will also inform Kirby of the legal fees that she will have to pay in an attempt to collect damages from the defendant, Carvello. Attorneys base their fees on such factors as the difficulty of a matter, the amount of time involved, the experience and skill of the attorney in the particular area of the law, and the cost of doing business.

EXHIBIT 2–4 Stages in a Typical Lawsuit

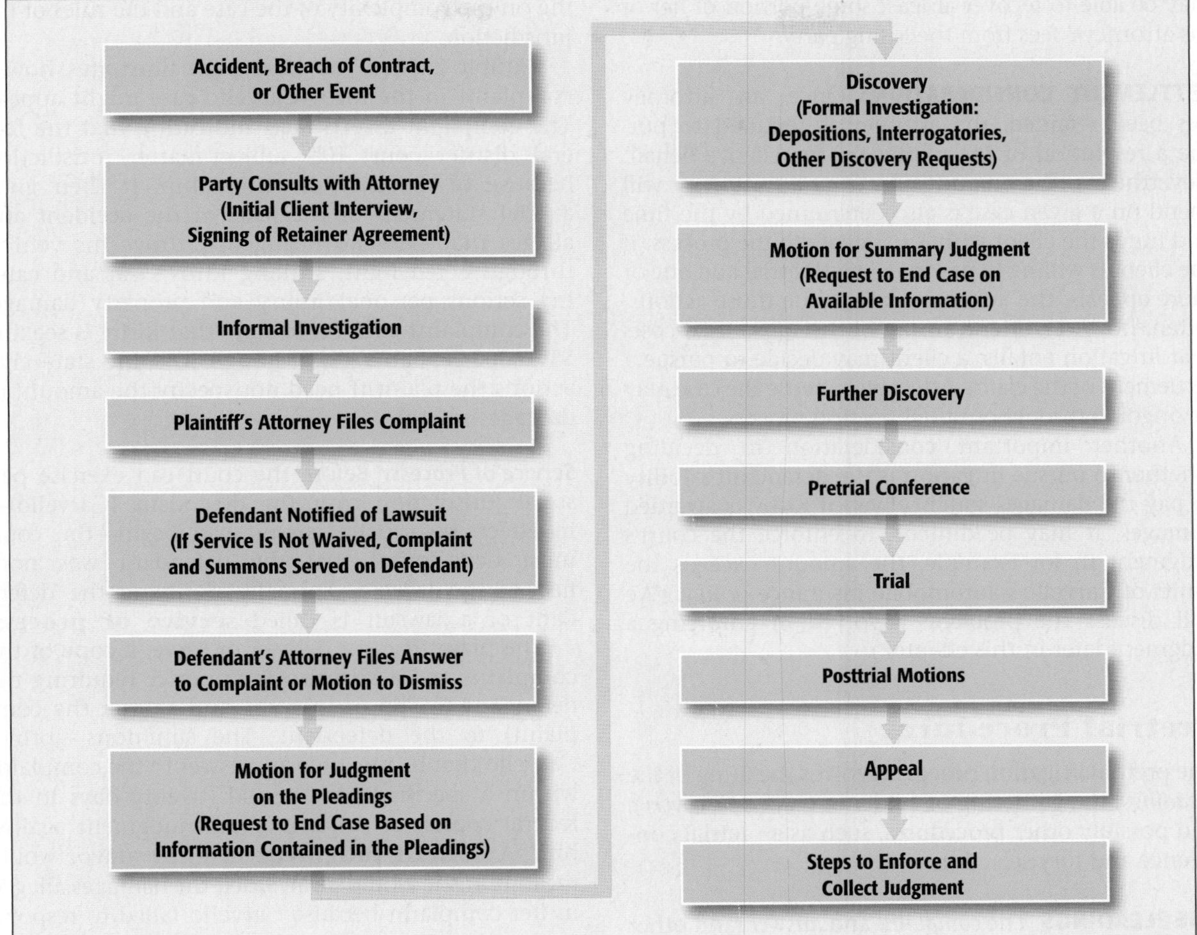

In the United States, legal fees range from $175 to $700 per hour or even higher (the average fee is between $200 and $425 per hour). In addition, the client must also pay various expenses related to the case (called "out-of-pocket" costs), such as court filing fees, travel expenses, and the cost of expert witnesses and investigators.

TYPES OF ATTORNEYS' FEES For a particular legal matter, an attorney may charge one type of fee or a combination of several types.

1. *Fixed fees* may be charged for the performance of such services as drafting a simple will.
2. *Hourly fees* may be charged for matters that will involve an indeterminate period of time. The amount of time required to bring a case to trial, for instance, probably cannot be precisely estimated in advance.
3. *Contingency fees* are fixed as a percentage (usually between 25 and 40 percent) of a client's recovery in certain types of lawsuits, such as a personal-injury lawsuit.[21] If the lawsuit is unsuccessful, the attorney receives no fee, but the client will have to reimburse the attorney for all out-of-pocket costs incurred.

Because Kirby's claim involves a personal injury, her lawyer will likely take the case on a contingency-fee

21. Note that attorneys may charge a contingency fee only in certain types of cases and are typically prohibited from entering into this type of fee arrangement in criminal cases, divorce cases, and cases involving the distribution of assets after death.

basis, but she may have to pay an amount up front to cover the court costs. In some cases, the winning party may be able to recover at least some portion of her or his attorneys' fees from the losing party.

SETTLEMENT CONSIDERATIONS Once an attorney has been retained, the attorney is required to pursue a resolution of the matter on the client's behalf. Nevertheless, the amount of energy an attorney will spend on a given case is also determined by the time and funds the client wishes to devote to the process. If the client is willing to pay for a lengthy trial and one or more appeals, the attorney may pursue those actions. Often, however, after learning of the substantial costs that litigation entails, a client may decide to pursue a settlement of the claim. Attempts to settle the case may be ongoing throughout the litigation process.

Another important consideration in deciding whether to pursue litigation is the defendant's ability to pay the damages sought. Even if Kirby is awarded damages, it may be difficult to enforce the court's judgment if, for example, the amount exceeds the limits of Carvello's automobile insurance policy. (We will discuss the problems involved in enforcing a judgment later in this chapter.)

Pretrial Procedures

The pretrial litigation process involves the filing of the *pleadings,* the gathering of evidence (called *discovery*), and possibly other procedures, such as a pretrial conference and jury selection.

THE PLEADINGS The *complaint* and *answer* (and other legal documents discussed below), taken together, are known as the **pleadings.** The pleadings inform each party of the other's claims and specify the issues (disputed questions) involved in the case. Because the rules of procedure vary depending on the jurisdiction of the court, the style and form of the pleadings may be different from those shown in this chapter.

The Plaintiff's Complaint. Kirby's action against Carvello commences when her lawyer files a **complaint**[22] with the clerk of the appropriate court. The complaint contains a statement alleging (1) the facts showing that the court has subject-matter and personal jurisdiction, (2) the facts establishing the plaintiff's basis for relief, and (3) the remedy the plaintiff is seeking. Complaints can be lengthy or brief, depending on the complexity of the case and the rules of the jurisdiction.

Exhibit 2–5 on the next page illustrates how a complaint in the Kirby-Carvello case might appear. The complaint asserts facts indicating that the federal district court has subject-matter jurisdiction because of diversity of citizenship. It then gives a brief statement of the facts of the accident and alleges that Carvello negligently drove his vehicle through a red light, striking Kirby's car and causing serious personal injury and property damage. The complaint goes on to state that Kirby is seeking $100,000 in damages, although in some state civil actions the plaintiff need not specify the amount of damages sought.

Service of Process. Before the court can exercise personal jurisdiction over the defendant (Carvello)—in effect, before the lawsuit can begin—the court must have proof that the defendant was notified of the lawsuit. Formally notifying the defendant of a lawsuit is called **service of process.**

The plaintiff must deliver, or serve, a copy of the complaint and a **summons** (a notice requiring the defendant to appear in court and answer the complaint) to the defendant. The summons notifies Carvello that he must file an answer to the complaint within a specified time period (twenty days in the federal courts) or suffer a default judgment against him. A **default judgment** in Kirby's favor would mean that she would be awarded the damages alleged in her complaint because Carvello failed to respond to the allegations.

Method of Service. How service of process occurs depends on the rules of the court or jurisdiction in which the lawsuit is brought. Under the Federal Rules of Civil Procedure, anyone who is at least eighteen years of age and is not a party to the lawsuit can serve process in federal court cases. In state courts, the process server is often a county sheriff or an employee of an independent company that provides process service in the local area.

Usually, the server hands the summons and complaint to the defendant personally or leaves it at the defendant's residence or place of business. In some states, process can be served by mail if the defendant consents (accepts service). When the defendant cannot be reached, special rules provide for alterna-

22. Sometimes, the document filed with the court is called a *petition* or a *declaration* instead of a complaint.

EXHIBIT 2–5 A Typical Complaint

IN THE UNITED STATES DISTRICT COURT
FOR THE SOUTHERN DISTRICT OF NEW YORK

JILL KIRBY Plaintiff, v. ANTONIO CARVELLO Defendant.	CIVIL NO. 9-1047 COMPLAINT

The plaintiff brings this cause of action against the defendant, alleging as follows:

1. This action is between the plaintiff, who is a resident of the State of New York, and the defendant, who is a resident of the State of New Jersey. There is diversity of citizenship between the parties.
2. The amount in controversy, exclusive of interest and costs, exceeds the sum of $75,000.
3. On September 10th, 2014, the plaintiff, Jill Kirby, was exercising good driving habits and reasonable care in driving her car through the intersection of Boardwalk and Pennsylvania Avenue, New York City, New York, when the defendant, Antonio Carvello, negligently drove his vehicle through a red light at the intersection and collided with the plaintiff's vehicle.
4. As a result of the collision, the plaintiff suffered severe physical injury, which prevented her from working, and property damage to her car.

WHEREFORE, the plaintiff demands judgment against the defendant for the sum of $100,000 plus interest at the maximum legal rate and the costs of this action.

By Joseph Roe
Joseph Roe
Attorney for Plaintiff
100 Main Street
New York, New York

1/3/15

tive means of service, such as publishing a notice in the local newspaper. In some situations, courts have allowed service of process via e-mail, as long as it is reasonably calculated to provide notice and an opportunity to respond.

In cases involving corporate defendants, the summons and complaint may be served on an officer or on a *registered agent* (representative) of the corporation. The name of a corporation's registered agent can usually be obtained from the secretary of state's office in the state where the company incorporated its business (and, frequently, from the secretary of state's office in any state where the corporation does business).

Waiver of Formal Service of Process. In many instances, the defendant is already aware that a lawsuit is being filed and is willing to waive (give up) her or his right to be served personally. The Federal Rules of Civil Procedure (FRCP) and many states' rules allow defendants to waive formal service of process, provided that certain procedures are followed. Kirby's attorney, for example, could mail to defendant Carvello a copy of the complaint, along with "Waiver of Service of Summons" forms for Carvello to sign. If Carvello signs and returns the forms within thirty days, formal service of process is waived.

Moreover, under the FRCP, defendants who agree to waive formal service of process receive additional time to respond to the complaint (sixty days, instead of twenty days). Some states provide similar incentives to encourage defendants to waive formal service of process and thereby reduce associated costs and foster cooperation between the parties.

The Defendant's Response. Typically, the defendant's response to the complaint takes the form of an **answer.** In an answer, the defendant either admits or denies each of the allegations in the plaintiff's complaint and may also set forth defenses to those allegations. Under the federal rules, any allegations that are not denied by the defendant will be deemed by the court to have been admitted. If Carvello admits to all of Kirby's allegations in his answer, a judgment will be entered for Kirby. If Carvello denies Kirby's allegations, the matter will proceed further.

Affirmative Defenses. Carvello can also admit the truth of Kirby's complaint but raise new facts to show that he should not be held liable for Kirby's damages. This is called raising an **affirmative defense.** As will be discussed in subsequent chapters, defendants in both civil and criminal cases can raise affirmative defenses. For example, Carvello could assert Kirby's own negligence as a defense by alleging that Kirby was driving negligently at the time of the accident. In some states, a plaintiff's contributory negligence operates as a complete defense. In most states, however, the plaintiff's own negligence constitutes only a partial defense (see Chapter 12).

Counterclaims. Carvello could also deny Kirby's allegations and set forth his own claim that the accident occurred as a result of Kirby's negligence and therefore she owes Carvello for damage to his car. This is appropriately called a counterclaim. If Carvello files a **counterclaim,** Kirby will have to submit an answer to the counterclaim.

DISMISSALS AND JUDGMENTS BEFORE TRIAL Many actions for which pleadings have been filed never come to trial. The parties may, for example, negotiate a settlement of the dispute at any stage of the litigation process. There are also numerous procedural avenues for disposing of a case without a trial. Many of them involve one or the other party's attempts to get the case dismissed through the use of various motions.

A **motion** is a procedural request submitted to the court by an attorney on behalf of her or his client. When a motion is filed with the court, the filing party must also send to, or personally serve, the opposing party a *notice of motion.* The notice of motion informs the opposing party that the motion has been filed. **Pretrial motions** include the motion to dismiss, the motion for judgment on the pleadings, and the motion for summary judgment, as well as the other motions listed in Exhibit 2–6 on page 48.

MOTION TO DISMISS Either party can file a **motion to dismiss** asking the court to dismiss the case for the reasons stated in the motion. Normally, though, it is the defendant who requests dismissal.

A defendant can file a motion to dismiss if the plaintiff's complaint fails to state a claim for which relief (a remedy) can be granted. Such a motion asserts that even if the facts alleged in the complaint are true, they do not give rise to any legal claim against the defendant. For example, if the allegations in Kirby's complaint do not constitute negligence on Carvello's part, Carvello can move to dismiss the case for failure to state a claim. Defendant Carvello could also file a motion to dismiss on the grounds that he was not properly served, that the court lacked jurisdiction, or that the venue was improper.

If the judge grants the motion to dismiss, the plaintiff generally is given time to file an amended complaint. If the judge denies the motion, the suit will go forward, and the defendant must then file an answer. Note that if Carvello wishes to discontinue the suit because, for example, an out-of-court settlement has been reached, he can likewise move for dismissal. The court can also dismiss a case on its own motion.

In the following case, one party filed a complaint against another, alleging a breach of contract. The defendant filed a motion to dismiss on the ground that the venue was improper. The court denied the motion, and the defendant appealed.

CASE 2.3

Espresso Disposition Corp. 1 v. Santana Sales & Marketing Group, Inc.

Florida Court of Appeal, Third District, 105 So.3d 592 (2013).

BACKGROUND AND FACTS Espresso Disposition Corporation 1 and Santana Sales & Marketing Group, Inc., entered into an agreement that included a mandatory *forum-selection clause*— that is, a provision in a contract designating the court or jurisdiction that will decide any disputes arising under the contract. This clause stated that, "the venue with respect to any action pertaining to this Agreement shall be the State of Illinois." When Santana Sales filed a lawsuit against Espresso in a Florida state court, Espresso filed a motion to dismiss based on the agreement's forum-selection clause. Santana responded to the motion to dismiss by claiming that the forum-selection clause had been a mistake. Specifically, Santana said that when the agreement was drafted, another agreement between different parties had been copied, and by mistake, the venue provision had not been changed from Illinois to Florida. The court denied Espresso's motion to dismiss. Espresso appealed.

IN THE LANGUAGE OF THE COURT
CORTIÑAS, J. [Judge]

* * * *

Florida courts have long recognized that forum selection clauses such as the one at issue here are presumptively valid. This is because *forum selection clauses provide a degree of certainty to business contracts by obviating [avoiding] jurisdictional struggles and by allowing parties to tailor the dispute resolution mechanism to their particular situation. Moreover, forum selection clauses reduce litigation over venue, thereby conserving judicial resources, reducing business expenses, and lowering consumer prices.* [Emphasis added.]

Because Florida law presumes that forum selection clauses are valid and enforceable, the party seeking to avoid enforcement of such a clause must establish that enforcement would be unjust or unreasonable. Under Florida law, the clause is only considered unjust or unreasonable if the party seeking avoidance establishes that enforcement would result in no forum at all. There is absolutely no set of facts that Appellee could plead and prove to demonstrate that Illinois state courts do not exist. Illinois became the twenty-first state in 1818, and has since established an extensive system of state trial and appellate courts. Clearly, Appellee failed to establish that enforcement would be unreasonable since the designated forum—Illinois—does not result in Appellee's having "no forum at all."

Further, as we have said on a number of occasions, if a forum selection clause unambiguously mandates that litigation be subject to an agreed upon forum, then it is [an] error for the trial court to ignore the clause. Generally, the clause is mandatory where the plain language used by the parties indicates exclusivity. Importantly, if the forum selection clause states or clearly indicates that any litigation must or shall be initiated in a specified forum, then it is mandatory. Here, the agreement's plain language provides that the venue for any action relating to a controversy under the agreement * * * "shall be the State of Illinois." The clear language unequivocally renders the forum selection clause mandatory.

Appellee would have us create an exception to our jurisprudence on mandatory forum selection clauses based on their error in cutting and pasting the clause from another agreement. Of course, the origin of "cutting and pasting" comes from the traditional practice of manuscript-editing whereby writers used to cut paragraphs from a page with editing scissors, that had blades long enough to cut an 8½ inch-wide page, and then physically pasted them onto another page. Today, the cut, copy, and paste functions contained in word processing software render unnecessary the use of scissors or glue. However, what has not been eliminated is the need to actually read and analyze the text being pasted, especially where it is to have legal significance. Thus, in reviewing the mandatory selection clause [that] Appellant

CASE 2.3 CONTINUES ➧

CASE 2.3 CONTINUED

seeks to enforce, we apply the legal maxim "be careful what you ask for" and enforce the pasted forum.

DECISION AND REMEDY *A state intermediate appellate court reversed the trial court's denial of Espresso's motion to dismiss and remanded the case to the lower court for the entry of an order of dismissal.*

THE LEGAL ENVIRONMENT DIMENSION *What is the effect of granting a motion to dismiss?*

THE ETHICAL DIMENSION *Why did the appellant in this case file a motion to dismiss? Explain.*

Motion for Judgment on the Pleadings. At the close of the pleadings, either party may make a **motion for judgment on the pleadings.** This motion asks the court to decide the issue solely on the pleadings without proceeding to trial. The judge will grant the motion only when there is no dispute over the facts of the case and the sole issue to be resolved is a question of law. For example, in the Kirby-Carvello case, if Carvello had admitted to all of Kirby's allegations in his answer and had raised no affirmative defenses, Kirby could file a motion for judgment on the pleadings.

In deciding a motion for judgment on the pleadings, the judge may consider only the evidence contained in the pleadings. In contrast, in a motion for summary judgment, discussed next, the court may consider evidence outside the pleadings, such as sworn statements and other materials that would be admissible as evidence at trial.

EXHIBIT 2–6 Pretrial Motions

MOTION TO DISMISS

A motion normally filed by the defendant in which the defendant asks the court to dismiss the case for a specified reason, such as improper service, lack of personal jurisdiction, or the plaintiff's failure to state a claim for which relief can be granted.

MOTION TO STRIKE

A motion filed by the defendant in which the defendant asks the court to strike (delete) certain paragraphs from the complaint. Motions to strike help to clarify the underlying issues that form the basis for the complaint by removing paragraphs that are redundant or irrelevant to the action.

MOTION TO MAKE MORE DEFINITE AND CERTAIN

A motion filed by the defendant to compel the plaintiff to clarify the basis of the plaintiff's cause of action. The motion is filed when the defendant believes that the complaint is too vague or ambiguous for the defendant to respond to it in a meaningful way.

MOTION FOR JUDGMENT ON THE PLEADINGS

A motion that may be filed by either party in which the party asks the court to enter a judgment in his or her favor based on information contained in the pleadings. A judgment on the pleadings will be made only if there are no facts in dispute and the only question is how the law applies to a set of undisputed facts.

MOTION TO COMPEL DISCOVERY

A motion that may be filed by either party in which the party asks the court to compel the other party to comply with a discovery request. If a party refuses to allow the opponent to inspect and copy certain documents, for instance, the party requesting the documents may make a motion to compel production of those documents.

MOTION FOR SUMMARY JUDGMENT

A motion that may be filed by either party in which the party asks the court to enter judgment in his or her favor without a trial. Unlike a motion for judgment on the pleadings, a motion for summary judgment can be supported by evidence outside the pleadings, such as witnesses' affidavits, answers to interrogatories, and other evidence obtained prior to or during discovery.

Motion for Summary Judgment. Either party can file a **motion for summary judgment,** which asks the court to grant a judgment in that party's favor without a trial. The motion can be made before or during the trial. As with a motion for judgment on the pleadings, a court will grant a motion for summary judgment only if no facts are in dispute and the only question is how the law applies to the facts. In determining whether no facts are in contention, the court considers the evidence in the light most favorable to the other party.

To support a motion for summary judgment, a party can submit evidence obtained at any point before the trial that refutes the other party's factual claim. The evidence may consist of **affidavits** (sworn statements by parties or witnesses) or copies of documents, such as contracts, e-mails, and letters obtained through the course of discovery (discussed next). Of course, the evidence must be *admissible* evidence—that is, evidence that the court would allow to be presented during the trial. As mentioned, the use of additional evidence is one feature that distinguishes the motion for summary judgment from the motion to dismiss and the motion for judgment on the pleadings.

DISCOVERY Before a trial begins, the parties can use a number of procedural devices to obtain information and gather evidence about the case. Kirby, for example, will want to know how fast Carvello was driving. She will also want to learn whether he had been drinking, was under the influence of medication, and was wearing corrective lenses if required by law to do so while driving.

The process of obtaining information from the opposing party or from witnesses prior to trial is known as **discovery.** Discovery includes gaining access to witnesses, documents, records, and other types of evidence. In federal courts, the parties are required to make initial disclosures of relevant evidence to the opposing party.

Discovery prevents surprises at trial by giving both parties access to evidence that might otherwise be hidden. This allows the litigants to learn as much as they can about what to expect at a trial before they reach the courtroom. Discovery also serves to narrow the issues so that trial time is spent on the main questions in the case. A court can impose sanctions on a party who fails to respond to discovery requests.

Discovery Rules. The FRCP and similar state rules set forth the guidelines for discovery activity. Generally, discovery is allowed regarding any matter that is relevant to the claim or defense of any party. Discovery rules also attempt to protect witnesses and parties from undue harassment, and to safeguard privileged or confidential material from being disclosed. Only information that is relevant to the case at hand—or likely to lead to the discovery of relevant information—is discoverable.

If a discovery request involves privileged or confidential business information, a court can deny the request and can limit the scope of discovery in a number of ways. For instance, a court can require the party to submit the materials to the judge in a sealed envelope so that the judge can decide if they should be disclosed to the opposing party.

Depositions. Discovery can involve the use of depositions. A **deposition** is sworn testimony by a party to the lawsuit or by any witness, recorded by an authorized court official. The person deposed gives testimony and answers questions asked by the attorneys from both sides. The questions and answers are recorded, sworn to, and signed. These answers, of course, will help the attorneys prepare their cases.

Depositions also give attorneys the opportunity to ask immediate follow-up questions and to evaluate how their witnesses will conduct themselves at trial. In addition, depositions can be employed in court to **impeach** (challenge the credibility of) a party or a witness who changes his or her testimony at the trial. A deposition can also be used as testimony if the witness is not available at trial.

Interrogatories. Discovery can also involve **interrogatories,** which are written questions for which written answers are prepared and then signed under oath. The main difference between interrogatories and written depositions is that interrogatories are directed to a party to the lawsuit (the plaintiff or the defendant), not to a witness. The party usually has thirty days to prepare answers.

The party's attorney often drafts the answers to interrogatories in a manner calculated to give away as little information as possible. Whereas depositions elicit candid answers not prepared in advance, interrogatories are designed to obtain accurate information about specific topics, such as how many contracts were signed and when. The scope of interrogatories is also broader because parties are obligated to answer questions, even if that means disclosing information from their records and files.

Note that, as with discovery requests, a court can impose sanctions on a party who fails to answer interrogatories.

▶ **Case in Point 2.9** Computer Task Group, Inc. (CTG), hired William Brotby as an information technology consultant. As a condition of his employment, Brotby signed an agreement that restricted his ability to work for CTG's customers if he left CTG. Less than two years later, Brotby left CTG and began working for Alyeska Pipeline Service Company, a CTG client, in breach of the agreement. CTG sued Brotby. During discovery, Brotby refused to respond fully to CTG's interrogatories. He gave contradictory answers, made frivolous objections, filed baseless motions, and never disclosed all the information that CTG sought. The court ordered Brotby to comply with discovery requests five times. Nevertheless, Brotby continued to make excuses and changed his story repeatedly, making it impossible for CTG to establish basic facts with any certainty. Eventually, CTG requested and the court granted a default judgment against Brotby based on his failure to cooperate.[23] ◀

Requests for Admissions. One party can serve the other party with a written request for an admission of the truth of matters relating to the trial. Any fact admitted under such a request is conclusively established as true for the trial. For example, Kirby can ask Carvello to admit that his driver's license was suspended at the time of the accident. A request for admission shortens the trial because the parties will not have to spend time proving facts on which they already agree.

Requests for Documents, Objects, and Entry Upon Land. A party can gain access to documents and other items not in her or his possession in order to inspect and examine them. Carvello, for example, can gain permission to inspect and copy Kirby's car repair bills. Likewise, a party can gain "entry upon land" to inspect the premises.

Requests for Examinations. When the physical or mental condition of one party is in question, the opposing party can ask the court to order a physical or mental examination by an independent examiner. If the court agrees to make the order, the opposing party can obtain the results of the examination. Note that the court will make such an order only when the need for the information outweighs the right to privacy of the person to be examined.

Electronic Discovery. Any relevant material, including information stored electronically, can be the object of a discovery request. The federal rules and most state rules (as well as court decisions) specifically allow individuals to obtain discovery of electronic "data compilations." Electronic evidence, or **e-evidence,** consists of all computer-generated or electronically recorded information, such as e-mail, voice mail, tweets, blogs, social media posts, spreadsheets, documents, and other data stored electronically.

E-evidence can reveal significant facts that are not discoverable by other means. Computers, smartphones, cameras, and other devices automatically record certain information about files—such as who created the file and when, and who accessed, modified, or transmitted it—on their hard drives. This information is called **metadata,** which can be thought of as "data about data." Metadata can be obtained only from the file in its electronic format—not from printed-out versions.

▶ **Example 2.10** In 2012, John McAfee, the programmer responsible for creating McAfee antivirus software, was wanted for questioning in the murder of his neighbor in Belize. McAfee left Belize and was on the run from police, but he allowed a journalist to come with him and photograph him. When the journalist posted photos of McAfee online, some metadata were attached to a photo. The police used the metadata to pinpoint the latitude and longitude of the image and subsequently arrested McAfee in Guatemala. ◀

E-Discovery Procedures. The Federal Rules of Civil Procedure deal specifically with the preservation, retrieval, and production of electronic data. Although traditional interrogatories and depositions are still used to find out whether e-evidence exists, a party usually must hire an expert to retrieve the evidence in its electronic format. The expert uses software to reconstruct e-mail, text, and other exchanges to establish who knew what and when they knew it. The expert can even recover computer files that the user thought had been deleted.

Advantages and Disadvantages of E-Discovery. Electronic discovery has significant advantages over paper discovery. Electronic versions of documents, e-mail, and text messages can provide useful—and often

23. *Computer Task Group, Inc. v. Brotby,* 364 F.3d 1112 (9th Cir. 2004).

quite damaging—information about how a particular matter progressed over several weeks or months. E-discovery can uncover the proverbial smoking gun that will win the lawsuit, but it is also time consuming and expensive, especially when lawsuits involve large firms with multiple offices. Also, many firms are finding it difficult to fulfill their duty to preserve electronic evidence from a vast number of sources.

A party that fails to preserve e-evidence may even find itself at such a disadvantage that it will settle a dispute rather than continue litigation. ▶ **Case in Point 2.11** Advanced Micro Devices, Inc. (AMD), sued Intel Corporation, one of the world's largest microprocessor suppliers, for violating antitrust laws. Immediately after the lawsuit was filed, Intel began collecting and preserving the electronic evidence on its servers and instructed its employees to retain documents and e-mails related to competition with AMD. Nevertheless, many employees saved only copies of the e-mails that they had received and not e-mails that they had sent. In addition, Intel did not stop its automatic e-mail deletion system, causing other information to be lost. In the end, although Intel produced data equivalent to "somewhere in the neighborhood of a pile 137 miles high" in paper, its failure to preserve e-discovery led it to settle the dispute.[24] ◀

PRETRIAL CONFERENCE After discovery has taken place and before the trial begins, the attorneys may meet with the trial judge in a **pretrial conference,** or hearing. Usually, the conference consists of an informal discussion between the judge and the opposing attorneys after discovery has taken place. The purpose is to explore the possibility of a settlement without trial and, if this is not possible, to identify the matters in dispute and to plan the course of the trial. In particular, the parties may attempt to establish ground rules to restrict the number of expert witnesses or discuss the admissibility or costs of certain types of evidence.

THE RIGHT TO A JURY TRIAL The Seventh Amendment to the U.S. Constitution guarantees the right to a jury trial for cases at law in *federal* courts when the amount in controversy exceeds $20. Most states have similar guarantees in their own constitutions (although the threshold dollar amount is higher than $20).

The right to a trial by jury need not be exercised, and many cases are tried without a jury. In most states and in federal courts, one of the parties must request a jury, or the judge presumes the parties waive this right. If there is no jury, the judge determines the truth of the facts alleged in the case.

JURY SELECTION Before a jury trial commences, a panel of jurors must be selected. Although some types of trials require twelve-person juries, most civil matters can be heard by six-person juries. The jury selection process is known as ***voir dire.***[25] In most jurisdictions, attorneys for the plaintiff and the defendant ask prospective jurors oral questions to determine whether they are biased or have any connection with a party to the action or with a prospective witness. In some jurisdictions, the judge may do all or part of the questioning based on written questions submitted by counsel for the parties.

During *voir dire,* a party may challenge a certain number of prospective jurors *peremptorily*—that is, ask that an individual not be sworn in as a juror without providing any reason. Alternatively, a party may challenge a prospective juror *for cause*—that is, provide a reason why an individual should not be sworn in as a juror. If the judge grants the challenge, the individual is asked to step down. A prospective juror, however, may not be excluded by the use of discriminatory challenges, such as those based on racial criteria or gender.

See *Concept Summary 2.3* on the following page for a review of pretrial procedures.

The Trial

Various rules and procedures govern the trial phase of the litigation process. There are rules governing what kind of evidence will or will not be admitted during the trial, as well as specific procedures that the participants in the lawsuit must follow. Today, some judges also have rules prohibiting or limiting the use of social media by jurors and others during trials.

OPENING STATEMENTS At the beginning of the trial, both attorneys are allowed to make **opening statements** setting forth the facts that they expect to prove during the trial. The opening statement provides an opportunity for each lawyer to give a brief version of the facts and the supporting evidence that

24. *In re Intel Corp. Microprocessor Antitrust Litigation,* 2008 WL 2310288 (D.Del. 2008).

25. Pronounced *vwahr deehr.* These verbs, based on Old French, mean "to speak the truth." In legal language, the phrase refers to the process of questioning jurors to learn about their backgrounds, attitudes, and similar attributes.

CONCEPT SUMMARY 2.3
Pretrial Procedures

PROCEDURE	DESCRIPTION
The Pleadings	1. *The plaintiff's complaint*—The plaintiff's statement of the cause of action and the parties involved, filed with the court by the plaintiff's attorney. After the filing, the defendant is notified of the suit through service of process. 2. *The defendant's response*—The defendant's response to the plaintiff's complaint may take the form of an answer, in which the defendant admits or denies the plaintiff's allegations. The defendant may raise an affirmative defense and/or assert a counterclaim.
Pretrial Motions	1. *Motion to dismiss*—May be made by either party to request that the judge dismiss the case for reasons stated in the motion (such as failure to state a claim for which relief can be granted). 2. *Motion for judgment* on the pleadings—May be made by either party and will be granted only if no facts are in dispute and only questions of law are at issue. 3. *Motion for summary judgment*—May be made by either party and will be granted only if no facts are in dispute and only questions of law are at issue. Unlike the motion for judgment on the pleadings, the motion for summary judgment may be supported by evidence outside the pleadings, such as testimony and other evidence obtained during discovery.
Discovery	The process of gathering evidence concerning the case, which may involve the following: 1. *Depositions* (sworn testimony by either party or any witness). 2. *Interrogatories* (in which parties to the action write answers to questions with the aid of their attorneys). 3. Requests for admissions, documents, examinations, or other information relating to the case. 4. Requests for electronically recorded information, such as e-mail, text messages, voice mail, and other data.
Pretrial Conference	A pretrial hearing, at the request of either party or the court, to identify the matters in dispute after discovery has taken place and to explore the possibility of settling the dispute without a trial. If no settlement is possible, the parties plan the course of the trial.
Jury Selection	In a jury trial, the selection of members of the jury from a pool of prospective jurors. During a process known as *voir dire,* the attorneys for both sides may challenge prospective jurors either for cause or peremptorily (for no cause).

will be used during the trial. Then the plaintiff's case is presented. In our hypothetical case, Kirby's lawyer would introduce evidence (relevant documents, exhibits, and the testimony of witnesses) to support Kirby's position.

RULES OF EVIDENCE Whether evidence will be admitted in court is determined by the **rules of evidence.** These are a series of rules that the courts have created to ensure that any evidence presented during a trial is fair and reliable. The Federal Rules of Evidence govern the admissibility of evidence in federal courts.

Evidence Must Be Relevant to the Issues. Evidence will not be admitted in court unless it is relevant to the matter in question. **Relevant evidence** is evidence that tends to prove or disprove a fact in question or to establish the degree of probability of a fact or action. For instance, evidence that the defendant was in another person's home when the victim was shot would be relevant—because it would tend to prove that the defendant was not the shooter.

Hearsay Evidence Not Admissible. Generally, hearsay is not admissible as evidence. **Hearsay** is testimony someone gives in court about a statement made by someone else who was not under oath at the time of the statement. Literally, it is what someone heard someone else say. For example, if a witness in the Kirby-Carvello case testified in court concerning what he or she heard another observer say about the accident, that testimony would be hearsay, or secondhand knowledge. Admitting hearsay into evidence carries many risks because, even though it may be relevant, there is no way to test its reliability.

EXAMINATION OF WITNESSES AND POTENTIAL MOTIONS Because Kirby is the plaintiff, she has the burden of proving that her allegations are true. Her attorney begins the presentation of Kirby's case by calling the first witness for the plaintiff and examining, or questioning, the witness. (For both attorneys, the types of questions and the manner of asking them are governed by the rules of evidence.) This questioning is called **direct examination.**

After Kirby's attorney is finished, the witness is subject to **cross-examination** by Carvello's attorney. Then Kirby's attorney has another opportunity to question the witness in *redirect examination,* and Carvello's attorney may follow the redirect examination with a *recross-examination.*

When both attorneys have finished with the first witness, Kirby's attorney calls the succeeding witnesses in the plaintiff's case, each of whom is subject to examination by the attorneys in the manner just described.

Expert Witnesses. As part of their cases, both the plaintiff and the defendant may present testimony from one or more expert witnesses, such as forensic scientists, physicians, and psychologists. An *expert witness* is a person who, by virtue of education, training, skill, or experience, has scientific, technical, or other specialized knowledge in a particular area beyond that of an average person. In Kirby's case, her attorney might hire an accident reconstruction specialist to establish Carvello's negligence or a physician to testify to the extent of Kirby's injuries.

Normally, witnesses can testify only about the facts of a case—that is, what they personally observed. When witnesses are qualified as experts in a particular field, however, they can offer their opinions and conclusions about the evidence in that field. Expert testimony is an important component of litigation today.

Because numerous experts are available for hire and expert testimony is powerful and effective with juries, there is tremendous potential for abuse. Therefore, in federal courts and most state courts, judges act as gatekeepers to ensure that the experts are qualified and that their opinions are based on scientific knowledge.[26]

If a party believes that the opponent's expert witness is not a qualified expert in the relevant field, that party can make a motion to prevent the witness from testifying.

Potential Motion and Judgment. At the conclusion of the plaintiff's case, the defendant's attorney may ask the judge to direct a verdict for the defendant on the ground that the plaintiff has presented no evidence to support her or his claim. This is called a **motion for a judgment as a matter of law** (or a **motion for a directed verdict** in state courts). In considering the motion, the judge looks at the evidence in the light most favorable to the plaintiff and grants the motion only if there is insufficient evidence to raise an issue of fact. (Motions for directed verdicts at this stage of a trial are seldom granted.)

Defendant's Evidence. The defendant's attorney then presents the evidence and witnesses for the defendant's case. Witnesses are called and examined by the defendant's attorney. The plaintiff's attorney has the right to cross-examine them, and there may be a redirect examination and possibly a recross-examination.

At the end of the defendant's case, either attorney can move for a directed verdict. Again, the test is whether the jury can, through any reasonable interpretation of the evidence, find for the party against whom the motion has been made. After the defendant's attorney has finished introducing evidence, the plaintiff's attorney can present a **rebuttal** by offering additional evidence that refutes the defendant's case. The defendant's attorney can, in turn, refute that evidence in a **rejoinder.**

CLOSING ARGUMENTS, JURY INSTRUCTIONS, AND VERDICT After both sides have rested their cases, each attorney presents a **closing argument.** In the closing argument, each attorney summarizes the facts and evidence presented during the trial and indicates why the facts and evidence support his or her client's claim. In addition to generally urging a verdict in favor of the client, the closing argument typically reveals the shortcomings of the points made by the opposing party during the trial.

Jury Instructions. Attorneys usually present closing arguments whether or not the trial was heard by

26. See Paul C. Giannelli and Edward J. Imwinkelried, *Scientific Evidence,* 4th ed. (Newark, N.J.: LexisNexis, 2007), Sections 1.06 and 1.16.

a jury. If it was a jury trial, the attorneys will have met with the judge before the closing arguments to determine how the jury will be instructed on the law. The attorneys can refer to these instructions in their closing arguments. After closing arguments are completed, the judge instructs the jury in the law that applies to the case (these instructions are often called *charges*). The jury then retires to the jury room to deliberate a verdict.

Juries are instructed on the standard of proof they must apply to the case. In most civil cases, the standard of proof is a *preponderance of the evidence.*[27] In other words, the plaintiff (Kirby in our hypothetical case) need only show that her factual claim is more likely to be true than the defendant's. (As you will read in Chapter 7, in a criminal trial the prosecution has a higher standard of proof to meet—it must prove its case *beyond a reasonable doubt.*)

27. Note that some civil claims must be proved by "clear and convincing evidence," meaning that the evidence must show that the truth of the party's claim is *highly* probable. This standard is often applied in situations that present a particular danger of deception, such as allegations of fraud.

Verdict. Once the jury has reached a decision, it issues a **verdict** in favor of one party. The verdict specifies the jury's factual findings. In some cases, the jury also decides on the amount of the *award* (the compensation to be paid to the prevailing party). After the announcement of the verdict, which marks the end of the trial itself, the jurors are dismissed.

See *Concept Summary 2.4* below for a review of trial procedures.

Posttrial Motions

After the jury has rendered its verdict, either party may make a posttrial motion. The prevailing party usually requests that the court enter a judgment in accordance with the verdict. The nonprevailing party frequently files one of the motions discussed next.

MOTION FOR A NEW TRIAL At the end of the trial, the losing party may make a motion to set aside the adverse verdict and any judgment and to hold a new trial. After looking at all the evidence, the judge will grant the **motion for a new trial** only if she or he

CONCEPT SUMMARY 2.4
Trial Procedures

PROCEDURE	DESCRIPTION
Opening Statements	Each party's attorney is allowed to present an opening statement indicating what the attorney will attempt to prove during the course of the trial.
Examination of Witnesses	1. Plaintiff's introduction and direct examination of witnesses, cross-examination by defendant's attorney, possible redirect examination by plaintiff's attorney, and possible recross-examination by defendant's attorney. 2. Both the plaintiff and the defendant may present testimony from one or more expert witnesses. 3. At the close of the plaintiff's case, the defendant may make a motion for a directed verdict (or for judgment as a matter of law), which, if granted by the court, will end the trial before the defendant presents witnesses. 4. Defendant's introduction and direct examination of witnesses, cross-examination by plaintiff's attorney, possible redirect examination by defendant's attorney, and possible recross-examination by plaintiff's attorney. 5. Possible rebuttal of defendant's argument by plaintiff's attorney, who presents more evidence. 6. Possible rejoinder by defendant's attorney to meet that evidence.
Closing Arguments, Jury Instructions, and Verdict	Each party's attorney argues in favor of a verdict for his or her client. The judge instructs (or charges) the jury as to how the law applies to the issue, and the jury retires to deliberate. When the jury renders its verdict, the trial comes to an end.

believes that the jury was in error and that it is not appropriate to grant judgment for the other side.

Usually, a new trial is granted only when the jury verdict is obviously the result of a misapplication of the law or a misunderstanding of the evidence presented at trial. A new trial can also be granted on the grounds of newly discovered evidence, misconduct by the participants during the trial (such as when a juror has made prejudicial and inflammatory remarks), or an error by the judge.

MOTION FOR JUDGMENT *N.O.V.* If Kirby wins and if Carvello's attorney has previously moved for a judgment as a matter of law, then Carvello's attorney can make a second *motion for a judgment as a matter of law* (the terminology used in federal courts). State courts may use different terms for these motions. In many state courts, if the defendant's attorney moved earlier for a directed verdict, he or she may now make a **motion for judgment *n.o.v.***—from the Latin *non obstante veredicto,* meaning "notwithstanding the verdict." Such a motion will be granted only if the jury's verdict was unreasonable and erroneous.

If the judge grants the motion, then the jury's verdict will be set aside, and a judgment will be entered in favor of the opposing party (Carvello). If the motion is denied, Carvello may then appeal the case. (Kirby may also appeal the case, even though she won at trial. She might appeal, for example, if she received a smaller monetary award than she had sought.)

The Appeal

Either party may appeal not only the jury's verdict but also the judge's ruling on any pretrial or posttrial motion. Many of the appellate court cases that appear in this text involve appeals of motions for summary judgment or other motions that were denied by trial court judges.

Note that a party must have legitimate grounds to file an appeal (some legal error) and that few trial court decisions are reversed on appeal. Moreover, the expenses associated with an appeal can be considerable.

FILING THE APPEAL If Carvello decides to appeal the verdict in Kirby's favor, then his attorney must file a *notice of appeal* with the clerk of the trial court within a prescribed period of time. Carvello then becomes the *appellant* or *petitioner*. The clerk of the trial court sends to the reviewing court (usually an intermediate court of appeals) the *record on appeal*. The record contains all the pleadings, motions, and other documents filed with the court and a complete written transcript of the proceedings, including testimony, arguments, jury instructions, and judicial rulings.

Carvello's attorney will file an appellate *brief* with the reviewing court. The **brief** is a formal legal document outlining the facts and issues of the case, the judge's rulings or jury's findings that should be reversed or modified, the applicable law, and arguments on Carvello's behalf (citing applicable statutes and relevant cases as precedents). The attorney for the *appellee* (Kirby, in our hypothetical case) usually files an answering brief. Carvello's attorney can file a reply, although it is not required. The reviewing court then considers the case.

APPELLATE REVIEW As mentioned, a court of appeals does not hear any evidence. Rather, it reviews the record for errors of law. Its decision concerning a case is based on the record on appeal and the briefs and arguments. The attorneys present oral arguments, after which the case is taken under advisement. The court then issues a written opinion. In general, appellate courts do not reverse findings of fact unless the findings are unsupported or contradicted by the evidence.

An appellate court has the following options after reviewing a case:

1. The court can *affirm* the trial court's decision. (Most decisions are affirmed.)
2. The court can *reverse* the trial court's judgment if it concludes that the trial court erred or that the jury did not receive proper instructions.
3. The appellate court can *remand* (send back) the case to the trial court for further proceedings consistent with its opinion on the matter.
4. The court might also affirm or reverse a decision *in part*. For example, the court might affirm the jury's finding that Carvello was negligent but remand the case for further proceedings on another issue (such as the extent of Kirby's damages).
5. An appellate court can also *modify* a lower court's decision. If the appellate court decides that the jury awarded an excessive amount in damages, for example, the court might reduce the award to a more appropriate, or fairer, amount.

HIGHER APPELLATE COURTS If the reviewing court is an intermediate appellate court, the losing party may decide to appeal the decision to the state's highest court, usually called its supreme court. Although the losing party has a right to ask (petition) a higher court to review the case, the party does not have a right to have the case heard by the higher appellate court. Appellate courts normally have discretionary power and can accept or reject an appeal. Like the United States Supreme Court, state supreme courts generally deny most petitions for appeal.

If the petition for review is granted, new briefs must be filed before the state supreme court, and the attorneys may be allowed or requested to present oral arguments. Like the intermediate appellate courts, the supreme court can reverse or affirm the lower appellate court's decision or remand the case. At this point, the case typically has reached its end (unless a federal question is at issue and one of the parties has legitimate grounds to seek review by a federal appellate court).

Enforcing the Judgment

The uncertainties of the litigation process are compounded by the lack of guarantees that any judgment will be enforceable. Even if the jury awards Kirby the full amount of damages requested ($100,000), for example, Carvello's auto insurance coverage might have lapsed. If so, the company would not pay any of the damages. Alternatively, Carvello's insurance policy might be limited to $50,000, meaning that Carvello personally would have to pay the remaining $50,000.

If the defendant does not have the funds available to pay the judgment, the plaintiff can go back to the court and request that the court issue a *writ of execution.* A **writ of execution** is an order directing the sheriff to seize and sell the defendant's nonexempt assets, or property (certain assets are exempted by law from creditors' actions). The proceeds of the sale are then used to pay the damages owed, and any excess proceeds are returned to the defendant. Alternatively, the nonexempt property itself could be transferred to the plaintiff in lieu of an outright payment.

The problem of collecting a judgment is less pronounced, of course, when a party is seeking to satisfy a judgment against a defendant with substantial assets that can be easily located, such as a major corporation. Usually, one of the factors considered by the plaintiff and his or her attorney before a lawsuit is initiated is whether the defendant has sufficient assets to cover the amount of damages sought. In addition, during the discovery process, attorneys routinely seek information about the location of the defendant's assets that might potentially be used to satisfy a judgment.

Reviewing: The Court System

Ronald Metzgar placed his fifteen-month-old son, Matthew, awake and healthy, in his playpen. Ronald left the room for five minutes and on his return found Matthew lifeless. A toy block had lodged in the boy's throat, causing him to choke to death. Ronald called 911, but efforts to revive Matthew were to no avail. There was no warning of a choking hazard on the box containing the block. Matthew's parents hired an attorney and sued Playskool, Inc., the manufacturer of the block, alleging that the manufacturer had been negligent in failing to warn of the block's hazard. Playskool filed a motion for summary judgment, arguing that the danger of a young child choking on a small block was obvious. Using the information presented in the chapter, answer the following questions.

1. Suppose that the attorney the Metzgars hired agreed to represent them on a contingency-fee basis. What does that mean?
2. How would the Metzgars' attorney likely have served process (the summons and complaint) on Playskool, Inc.?
3. Should Playskool's request for summary judgment be granted? Why or why not?
4. Suppose that the judge denied Playskool's motion and the case proceeded to trial. After hearing all the evidence, the jury found in favor of the defendant. What options do the plaintiffs have at this point if they are not satisfied with the verdict?

DEBATE THIS. . . *Some consumer advocates argue that attorneys' high contingency fees—sometimes reaching 40 percent—unfairly deprive winning plaintiffs of too much of their awards. Should the government cap contingency fees at, say, 20 percent of the award? Why or why not?*

Terms and Concepts

affidavit 49
affirmative defense 46
answer 46
bankruptcy court 30
brief 55
closing argument 53
complaint 44
concurrent jurisdiction 32
counterclaim 46
cross-examination 53
default judgment 44
deposition 49
direct examination 53
discovery 49
diversity of citizenship 31
e-evidence 50
exclusive jurisdiction 32
federal question 31
Federal Rules of Civil Procedure (FRCP) 42
hearsay 52
impeach 49
in personam jurisdiction 29
in rem jurisdiction 29
interrogatories 49
judicial review 28
jurisdiction 29
long arm statute 29
metadata 50
motion 46
motion for a directed verdict 53
motion for a judgment as a matter of law 53
motion for a new trial 54
motion for judgment *n.o.v.* 55
motion for judgment on the pleadings 48
motion for summary judgment 49
motion to dismiss 46
opening statement 51
pleadings 44
pretrial conference 51
pretrial motion 46
probate court 30
question of fact 39
question of law 39
rebuttal 53
rejoinder 53
relevant evidence 52
rule of four 41
rules of evidence 52
service of process 44
small claims court 39
standing to sue 36
summons 44
venue 36
verdict 54
voir dire 51
writ of *certiorari* 41
writ of execution 56

ExamPrep

Issue Spotters

1. Sue uses her smartphone to purchase a video security system for her architectural firm from Tipton, Inc., a company that is located in a different state. The system arrives a month after the projected delivery date, is of poor quality, and does not function as advertised. Sue files a suit against Tipton in a state court. Does the court in Sue's state have jurisdiction over Tipton? What factors will the court consider? **(See page 29.)**
2. At the trial, after Eve calls her witnesses, offers her evidence, and otherwise presents her side of the case, Tom has at least two choices between courses of actions. Tom can call his first witness. What else might he do? **(See page 53.)**

- **Check your answers to the Issue Spotters against the answers provided in Appendix E at the end of this text.**

Before the Test

Go to www.cengagebrain.com, enter the ISBN 9781285428949, and click on "Find" to locate this textbook's Web site. Then, click on "Access Now" under "Study Tools," and select Chapter 2 at the top. There, you will find an Interactive Quiz that you can take to assess your mastery of the concepts in this chapter, as well as Interactive Flashcards and a Glossary of important terms.

Business Scenarios

2–1. Standing. Jack and Maggie Turton bought a house in Jefferson County, Idaho, located directly across the street from a gravel pit. A few years later, the county converted the pit to a landfill. The landfill accepted many kinds of trash that cause harm to the environment, including major appliances, animal carcasses, containers with hazardous content warnings, leaking car batteries, and waste oil. The Turtons complained to the county, but the county did nothing. The Turtons then filed a lawsuit against the county alleging violations of federal environmental laws pertaining to groundwater contamination and other pollution. Do the Turtons have standing to sue? Why or why not? **(See page 37.)**

2–2. Jurisdiction. Marya Callais, a citizen of Florida, was walking along a busy street in Tallahassee, Florida, when a large crate flew off a passing truck and hit her, causing numerous injuries. She experienced a great deal of pain and suffering, incurred significant medical expenses, and could not work for six months. She wants to sue the trucking firm for $300,000 in damages. The firm's headquarters are in Georgia, although the company does business in Florida. In what court might Callais bring suit—a Florida state court, a Georgia state court, or a federal court? What factors might influence her decision? **(See page 29.)**

2–3. Motions. When and for what purpose is each of the following motions made? Which of them would be appropriate if a defendant claimed that the only issue between the parties was a question of law and that the law was favorable to the defendant's position? **(See page 48.)**

(a) A motion for judgment on the pleadings.

(b) A motion for a directed verdict.

(c) A motion for summary judgment.

(d) A motion for judgment *n.o.v.*

Business Case Problems

2–4. Venue. Brandy Austin used powdered infant formula to feed her infant daughter shortly after her birth. Austin claimed that a can of Nestlé Good Start Supreme Powder Infant Formula was contaminated with *Enterobacter sakazakii* bacteria. The bacteria can cause infections of the bloodstream and central nervous system, in particular, meningitis (inflammation of the tissue surrounding the brain or spinal cord). Austin filed an action against Nestlé in Hennepin County District Court in Minnesota. Nestlé argued for a change of venue because the alleged tortious action on the part of Nestlé occurred in South Carolina. Austin is a South Carolina resident and gave birth to her daughter in that state. Should the case be transferred to a South Carolina venue? Why or why not? [*Austin v. Nestlé USA, Inc.*, 677 F.Supp.2d 1134 (D.Minn. 2009)] **(See page 29.)**

2–5. Jury Misconduct. Michelle Fleshner worked for Pepose Vision Institute (PVI), a surgical practice. She was fired after she provided information to the U.S. Department of Labor about PVI's overtime pay policy. She sued for wrongful termination, and the jury awarded her $125,000. After the trial, a juror told PVI's attorneys that another juror had made anti-Semitic statements during jury deliberations. The comments concerned a witness who testified on PVI's behalf. According to the juror, the other juror said, about the witness: "She is a Jewish witch." "She is a penny-pinching Jew." "She was such a cheap Jew that she did not want to pay Plaintiff unemployment compensation." Another juror confirmed the remarks. PVI filed a motion for a new trial on the basis of juror misconduct. The trial judge held that the comments did not prevent a fair trial from occurring. PVI appealed. Do you think such comments are sufficient to require a new trial, or must a juror's bias be discovered during *voir dire* for it to matter? Explain. [*Fleshner v. Pepose Vision Institute*, 304 S.W.3d 81 (Mo. 2010)] **(See page 55.)**

2–6. Service of Process. Dr. Kevin Bardwell owns Northfield Urgent Care, LLC, a Minnesota medical clinic. Northfield ordered flu vaccine from Clint Pharmaceuticals, a licensed distributer of flu vaccine located in Tennessee. The parties signed a credit agreement that specified that any disputes would be litigated in the Tennessee state courts. When Northfield failed to pay what it owed for the vaccine, Clint Pharmaceuticals filed a lawsuit in Tennessee and served process on the clinic via registered mail to Dr. Bardwell, the registered agent of Northfield. Bardwell's wife, who worked as a receptionist at the clinic and handled inquiries on the clinic's Facebook site, signed for the letter. Bardwell did not appear on the trial date, however, and the Tennessee court entered a default judgment against Northfield. When Clint Pharmaceuticals attempted to collect on the judgment in Minnesota, Bardwell claimed that the judgment was unenforceable. He asserted that he had not been properly served because his wife was not a registered agent. Should the Minnesota court invalidate the Tennessee judgment? Was service of process proper when it was mailed to the defendant medical clinic and the wife of the physician who owned the clinic opened the letter? Explain. [*Clint Pharmaceuticals v. Northfield Urgent Care, LLC*, 2012 WL 3792546 (Minn.App. 2012).] **(See page 44.)**

2–7. Minimum Contacts. Seal Polymer Industries sold two freight containers of latex gloves to Med-Express, Inc., a company based in North Carolina. When Med-Express failed to pay the $104,000 owed for the gloves, Seal Polymer sued in an Illinois court and obtained a judgment against Med-Express. Med-Express argued that it did not have minimum contacts with Illinois and therefore the Illinois judgment based on personal jurisdiction was invalid. Med-Express stated that it was incorporated under North Carolina law, had its principal place of business in North Carolina, and therefore had no minimum contacts with Illinois. Was this statement alone sufficient to prevent the Illinois judgment from being collected against Med-Express in North Carolina? Why or why not? [*Seal Polymer Industries v. Med-Express, Inc.*, 725 S.E.2d 5 (N.C.App. 2012)] **(See page 29.)**

2–8. BUSINESS CASE PROBLEM WITH SAMPLE ANSWER: Discovery.

Jessica Lester died from injuries suffered in an auto accident caused by the driver of a truck owned by Allied Concrete Co. Jessica's widower, Isaiah, filed a suit against Allied for damages. The defendant requested copies of all of Isaiah's Facebook photos and other

postings. Before responding, Isaiah "cleaned up" his Facebook page. Allied suspected that some items had been deleted, including a photo of Isaiah holding a beer can while wearing a T-shirt that declared "I [heart] hotmoms." Can this material be recovered? If so, how? What effect might Isaiah's "postings" have on the result in this case? Discuss. [Allied Concrete Co. v. Lester, *736 S.E.2d 699 (2013)*] **(See page 49.)**

- **For a sample answer to Problem 2–8, go to Appendix F at the end of this text.**

2–9. A QUESTION OF ETHICS: Service of Process.

Narnia Investments, Ltd., filed a suit in a Texas state court against several defendants, including Harvestons Securities, Inc., a securities dealer. (Securities are documents evidencing the ownership of a corporation, in the form of stock, or debts owed by it, in the form of bonds.) Harvestons is registered with the state of Texas. Thus, a party may serve a summons and a copy of a complaint on Harvestons by serving the Texas Securities Commissioner. In this case, the return of service indicated that process was served on the commissioner "by delivering to JoAnn Kocerek defendant, in person, a true copy of this [summons] together with the accompanying copy(ies) of the [complaint]." Harvestons did not file an answer, and Narnia obtained a default judgment against the defendant for $365,000, plus attorneys' fees and interest. Five months after this judgment, Harvestons filed a motion for a new trial, which the court denied. Harvestons appealed to a state intermediate appellate court, claiming that it had not been served in strict compliance with the rules governing service of process. [Harvestons Securities, Inc. v. Narnia Investments, Ltd., *218 S.W.3d 126 (Tex.App.—Houston 2007)*] **(See page 44.)**

(a) Harvestons asserted that Narnia's service was invalid, in part, because "the return of service states that process was delivered to 'JoAnn Kocerek'" and did not show that she "had the authority to accept process on behalf of Harvestons or the Texas Securities Commissioner." Should such a detail, if it is required, be strictly construed and applied? Should it apply in this case? Explain.

(b) Who is responsible for ensuring that service of process is accomplished properly? Was it accomplished properly in this case? Why or why not?

Legal Reasoning Group Activity

2–10. Court Procedures. Bento Cuisine is a lunch-cart business. It occupies a street corner in Texarkana, a city that straddles the border of Arkansas and Texas. Across the street—and across the state line, which runs down the middle of the street—is Rico's Tacos. The two businesses compete for customers. Recently, Bento has begun to suspect that Rico's is engaging in competitive behavior that is illegal. Bento's manager overheard several of Rico's employees discussing these competitive tactics while on a break at a nearby Starbucks. Bento files a lawsuit against Rico's in a federal court based on diversity jurisdiction. **(See page 31.)**

(a) The first group will discuss whether Rico's could file a motion claiming that the federal court lacks jurisdiction over this dispute.

(b) The second group will assume that the case goes to trial. Bento believes that it has both the law and the facts on its side. Nevertheless, at the end of the trial, the jury decides against Bento, and the judge issues a ruling in favor of Rico's. If Bento is unwilling to accept this result, what are its options?

(c) As discussed in this chapter, hearsay is literally what a witness says he or she heard another person say. A third group will decide whether Bento's manager can testify about what he heard some of Rico's employees say to one another while at a coffee shop. This group will also discuss what makes the admissibility of hearsay evidence potentially unethical.

CHAPTER 3
ALTERNATIVE AND ONLINE DISPUTE RESOLUTION

Litigation—the process of resolving a dispute through the court system—is expensive and time consuming. Litigating even the simplest complaint is costly, and because of the backlog of cases pending in many courts, several years may pass before a case is actually tried. For these and other reasons, more and more businesspersons are turning to **alternative dispute resolution (ADR)** as a means of settling their disputes.

The great advantage of ADR is its flexibility. Methods of ADR range from the parties sitting down together and attempting to work out their differences to multinational corporations agreeing to resolve a dispute through a formal hearing before a panel of experts.

Normally with ADR, the parties themselves can control how they will attempt to settle their dispute. They can decide what procedures will be used, whether a neutral third party will be present or make a decision, and whether that decision will be legally binding or nonbinding. ADR also offers more privacy than court proceedings and allows disputes to be resolved relatively quickly.

Today, more than 90 percent of civil lawsuits are settled before trial using some form of ADR. Indeed, most states either require or encourage parties to undertake ADR prior to trial. Many federal courts have instituted ADR programs as well. In the following pages, we examine the basic forms of ADR.

SECTION 1
NEGOTIATION AND MEDIATION

Alternative dispute resolution methods differ in the degree of formality involved and the extent to which third parties participate in the process. Generally, negotiation is the least formal method and involves no third parties. Mediation may be similarly informal but does involve the participation of a third party.

Negotiation

The simplest form of ADR is **negotiation,** a process in which the parties attempt to settle their dispute informally, with or without attorneys to represent them. Attorneys frequently advise their clients to negotiate a settlement voluntarily before they proceed to trial. Parties may even try to negotiate a settlement during a trial or after the trial but before an appeal.

Negotiation traditionally involves just the parties themselves and (typically) their attorneys. The attorneys, though, are advocates—they are obligated to put their clients' interests first.

PREPARATION FOR NEGOTIATION In spite of the informality of negotiation, each party must carefully prepare his or her side of the case. The elements of the dispute should be considered, documents and other evidence should be collected, and witnesses should be prepared to testify.

Negotiating from a well-prepared position improves the odds of obtaining a favorable result. Even if a dispute is not resolved through negotiation, preparation for negotiation will reduce the effort required to prepare for the next step in the dispute-resolution process.

ASSISTED NEGOTIATION To facilitate negotiation, various forms of what might be called "assisted negotiation" have emerged in recent years. Assisted negotiation, as the term implies, involves the assistance of a third party. Forms of ADR associated with the negotiation process include *mini-trials, early neutral case evaluation,* and *facilitation.* Another form of assisted negotiation—the summary jury trial—will be discussed later in this chapter.

A **mini-trial** is a private proceeding in which each party's attorney briefly argues the party's case before the other party. Typically, a neutral third party, who acts as an adviser and an expert in the area being disputed, is also present. If the parties fail to reach an agreement, the adviser renders an opinion as to how a court would likely decide the issue. The proceeding assists the parties in determining whether they should negotiate a settlement of the dispute or take it to court.

In **early neutral case evaluation,** the parties select a neutral third party (generally an expert in the subject matter of the dispute) to evaluate their respective positions. The parties explain their positions to the case evaluator however they wish. The evaluator then assesses the strengths and weaknesses of the parties' positions, and this evaluation forms the basis for negotiating a settlement.

Disputes may also be resolved in a friendly, nonadversarial manner through **facilitation,** in which a third party assists disputing parties in reconciling their differences. The facilitator helps to schedule negotiating sessions and carries offers back and forth between the parties when they refuse to face each other in direct negotiations. Technically, facilitators are not to recommend solutions. (In practice, however, they often do.) In contrast, a mediator is expected to propose solutions.

Mediation

One of the oldest forms of ADR is mediation. In **mediation,** a neutral third party acts as a **mediator** and works with both sides in the dispute to facilitate a resolution. The mediator normally talks with the parties separately as well as jointly, emphasizes points of agreement, and helps the parties to evaluate their options.

Although the mediator may propose a solution (called a mediator's proposal), he or she does not make a decision resolving the matter. The mediator, who need not be a lawyer, usually charges a fee for his or her services (which can be split between the parties). States that require parties to undergo ADR before trial often offer mediation as one of the ADR options or (as in Florida) the only option.

Mediation is essentially a form of assisted negotiation. We treat it separately here because traditionally it has been viewed as an alternative to negotiation. Additionally, a mediator usually plays a more active role than the neutral third parties in negotiation-associated forms of ADR.

Today, characteristics of mediation are being combined with those of arbitration (to be discussed next). In *binding mediation,* for example, the parties agree that if they cannot resolve the dispute, the mediator can make a legally binding decision on the issue. In *mediation-arbitration,* or "med-arb," the parties first attempt to settle their dispute through mediation. If no settlement is reached, the dispute will be arbitrated.

ADVANTAGES OF MEDIATION Few procedural rules are involved in the mediation process—far fewer than in a courtroom setting. The proceedings can be tailored to fit the needs of the parties—the mediator can be told to maintain a diplomatic role or be asked to express an opinion about the dispute, lawyers can be excluded from the proceedings, and the exchange of a few documents can replace the more expensive and time-consuming process of pretrial discovery. Disputes are often settled far more quickly in mediation than in formal litigation.

Brings the Parties Together. One of the biggest advantages of mediation is that it is not as adversarial in nature as litigation. In mediation, the mediator takes an active role and attempts to bring the parties together so that they can come to a mutually satisfactory resolution.

The mediation process tends to reduce the antagonism between the disputants, allowing them to resume their former relationship while minimizing hostility. For this reason, mediation is often the preferred form of ADR for disputes involving business partners, employers and employees, or other parties involved in long-term relationships.

Parties Choose the Mediator. Another important benefit of mediation is that the mediator is selected by the parties. In litigation, the parties have no control over the selection of a judge. In mediation, the parties may select a mediator on the basis of expertise in a particular field as well as for fairness and impartiality. To the degree that the mediator has these attributes, he or she will more effectively aid the parties in reaching an agreement over their dispute.

DISADVANTAGES OF MEDIATION Mediation is not without disadvantages. A mediator is likely to charge a fee. (This can be split between the parties, though, as mentioned, and thus may represent less expense than would both sides' hiring lawyers.)

Informality and the absence of a third party referee can also be disadvantageous. (Remember that a mediator can only help the parties reach a decision, not make a decision for them.) Without a deadline hanging over the parties' heads, and without the threat of sanctions if they fail to negotiate in good faith, they may be less willing to make concessions or otherwise strive honestly and diligently to reach a settlement. This can slow the process or even cause it to fail.

SECTION 2 ARBITRATION

A more formal method of ADR is **arbitration,** in which an **arbitrator** (a neutral third party or a panel of experts) hears a dispute and imposes a resolution on the parties. Arbitration differs from other forms of ADR in that the third party hearing the dispute makes a decision for the parties. Exhibit 3–1 below outlines the basic differences among the three traditional forms of ADR.

The key difference between arbitration and the forms of ADR just discussed is that in arbitration, the third party's decision may be legally binding on the parties. Usually, the parties in arbitration agree that the third party's decision will be *legally binding,* although the parties can also agree to *nonbinding* arbitration.

When a dispute arises, the parties can agree to settle their differences informally through arbitration rather than formally through the court system. Alternatively, the parties may agree ahead of time that, if a dispute should arise, they will submit to arbitration rather than bring a lawsuit. If the parties agree that the arbitrator's decision will be legally binding, they are obligated to abide by the arbitrator's decision regardless of whether they agree with it.

Arbitration Clauses

Almost any commercial matter can be submitted to arbitration. Frequently, parties include an **arbitration clause** in a contract (a written agreement—see Chapter 9) specifying that any dispute arising under the contract will be resolved through arbitration rather than through the court system. Parties can also agree to arbitrate a dispute *after* it arises.

Arbitration Statutes

The federal government and many state governments favor arbitration over litigation. The federal

EXHIBIT 3–1 Basic Differences in the Traditional Forms of ADR

Type of ADR	Description	Neutral Third Party Present	Who Decides the Resolution
Negotiation	Parties meet informally with or without their attorneys and attempt to agree on a resolution. This is the simplest and least expensive method of ADR.	No	The parties themselves reach a resolution.
Mediation	A neutral third party meets with the parties and emphasizes points of agreement to bring them toward resolution of their dispute. 1. This method of ADR reduces hostility between the parties. 2. Mediation is preferred for resolving disputes between business partners, employers and employees, or others involved in long-term relationships.	Yes	The parties, but the mediator may suggest or propose a resolution.
Arbitration	The parties present their arguments and evidence before an arbitrator at a hearing, and the arbitrator renders a decision resolving the parties' dispute. 1. This ADR method is the most formal and resembles a court proceeding because some rules of evidence apply. 2. The parties are free to frame the issues and set the powers of the arbitrator. 3. If the parties agree that the arbitration is binding, then the parties' right to appeal the decision is limited.	Yes	The arbitrator imposes a resolution on the parties that may be either binding or nonbinding.

policy favoring arbitration is embodied in the Federal Arbitration Act (FAA),[1] enacted in 1925.

THE FEDERAL ARBITRATION ACT The Federal Arbitration Act does not establish a set arbitration procedure. The parties themselves must agree on the manner of resolving their dispute. The FAA provides the means for enforcing the arbitration procedure that the parties have established for themselves. Section 4 of the FAA allows a party to petition a federal district court for an order compelling (forcing) arbitration under an agreement to arbitrate a dispute. Under Section 9, the parties to the arbitration may agree to have the arbitrator's decision confirmed in a federal district court. Through confirmation, one party obtains a court order directing another party to comply with the terms of the arbitrator's decision.

The FAA enforces arbitration clauses in contracts involving maritime activity and interstate commerce. Because of the breadth of the commerce clause (see Chapter 5), arbitration agreements involving transactions only slightly connected to the flow of interstate commerce may fall under the FAA.

▶ **Case in Point 3.1** Buckeye Check Cashing, Inc., cashes personal checks for consumers in Florida. Buckeye would agree to delay submitting a consumer's check for payment if the consumer paid a "finance charge." For each transaction, the consumer signed an agreement that included an arbitration clause. A group of consumers filed a lawsuit claiming that Buckeye was charging an illegally high rate of interest in violation of state law. Buckeye filed a motion to compel arbitration, which the trial court denied, and the case was appealed. The plaintiffs argued that the entire contract—including the arbitration clause—was illegal and therefore arbitration was not required.

The United States Supreme Court found that the arbitration provision was *severable,* or capable of being separated, from the rest of the contract. The Court held that when the challenge is to the validity of a contract as a whole, and not specifically to an arbitration clause within the contract, an arbitrator must resolve the dispute. Even if the contract later proves to be unenforceable, this is true because the FAA established a national policy favoring arbitration and that policy extends to both federal and state courts.[2] ◀

STATE ARBITRATION STATUTES Nearly all states follow the federal approach to voluntary arbitration. Most of the states and the District of Columbia have adopted the Uniform Arbitration Act, which was drafted by the National Conference of Commissioners on Uniform State Laws in 1955. Those states that have not adopted the uniform act nonetheless follow many of the practices specified in it.

Under the uniform act, the basic approach is to give full effect to voluntary agreements to arbitrate disputes between private parties. The act supplements private arbitration agreements by providing explicit procedures and remedies for enforcing arbitration agreements. The uniform act does not, however, dictate the terms of the agreement. Moreover, under both federal and state statutes, the parties are afforded considerable latitude in deciding the subject matter of the arbitration and the methods for conducting the arbitration process. In the absence of a controlling statute, the rights and duties of the parties are established and limited by their agreement.

In the following case, the parties had agreed to arbitrate disputes involving their contract, but a state law allowed one party to void a contractual provision that required arbitration outside the state. The court had to decide if the FAA *preempted* (took priority over, or blocked—see Chapter 5) the state law.

1. 9 U.S.C. Sesctions 1–15.

2. *Buckeye Check Cashing, Inc. v. Cardegna,* 546 U.S. 440, 126 S.Ct. 1204, 163 L.Ed.2d 1038 (2006).

CASE 3.1

Cleveland Construction, Inc. v. Levco Construction, Inc.

Court of Appeals of Texas, First District, 359 S.W.3d 843 (2012).

BACKGROUND AND FACTS Cleveland Construction, Inc. (CCI), was the general contractor on a project to build a grocery store in Houston, Texas. CCI hired Levco Construction, Inc., as a subcontractor to perform excavation and grading. The contract included an arbitration provision stating that any disputes would be resolved by arbitration in Ohio. When a dispute arose between the parties, Levco filed a suit

CASE 3.1 CONTINUES ➧

CASE 3.1 CONTINUED

against CCI in a Texas state court. CCI sought to compel arbitration in Ohio under the Federal Arbitration Act (FAA), but a Texas statute allows a party to void a contractual provision that requires arbitration outside Texas. The Texas court granted an emergency motion preventing arbitration. CCI appealed.

IN THE LANGUAGE OF THE COURT
Evelyn N. *KEYES*, Justice.

* * * *

[Texas] Business and Commerce Code section 272.001 provides:

> If a contract contains a provision making * * * any conflict arising under the contract subject to * * * arbitration in another state, that provision is voidable by the party obligated by the contract to perform the construction * * * .

Levco argues * * * that it "exercised its option to void the requirement in the Contract to arbitrate in Lake County, Ohio."

*The FAA preempts all otherwise applicable inconsistent state laws * * * under the Supremacy Clause of the United States Constitution. The FAA declares written provisions for arbitration "valid, irrevocable, and enforceable, save upon such grounds as exist at law or in equity for the revocation of any contract."* [Emphasis added.]

* * * Applying section 272.001 as Levco asks us to do here would prevent us from enforcing a term of the parties' arbitration agreement—the venue—on a ground that is not recognized by the FAA or by general state-law contract principles. We hold that the FAA preempts application of this provision under the facts of this case. * * * By allowing a party to * * * declare void a previously bargained-for provision, application of section 272.001 would undermine the declared federal policy of rigorous enforcement of arbitration agreements.

DECISION AND REMEDY *The Texas appellate court reversed the trial court, holding that the FAA preempts the Texas statute. CCI could compel arbitration in Ohio.*

THE LEGAL ENVIRONMENT DIMENSION *How would business be affected if each state could pass a statute, like the one in Texas, allowing parties to void out-of-state arbitration?*

THE SOCIAL DIMENSION *Considering the relative bargaining power of the parties, was it fair to enforce the arbitration clause in this contract? Why or why not?*

The Arbitration Process

In some respects, formal arbitration resembles a trial, although usually the procedural rules are much less restrictive than those governing litigation. In a typical arbitration, the parties present opening arguments and ask for specific remedies. Both sides present evidence and may call and examine witnesses. The arbitrator then renders a decision.

SUBMISSION The arbitration process begins with a *submission.* **Submission** is the act of referring a dispute to an arbitrator. The parties may agree to submit questions of fact, questions of law, or both to the arbitrator. The parties may even agree to leave the interpretation of the arbitration agreement to the arbitrator. In the case of an existing agreement to arbitrate, the clause itself is the submission to arbitration.

The submission typically states the identities of the parties, the nature of the dispute to be resolved, the monetary amounts involved in the controversy, the location at which the arbitration is to take place, and the intention of the parties to be bound by the arbitrator's award. Exhibit 3–2 on the next page contains a sample submission form.

Most states require that an agreement to submit a dispute to arbitration be in writing. Moreover, because the goal of arbitration is speed and efficiency in resolving controversies, most states require that matters be submitted within a definite period of time. Generally, states require submission within six months from the date on which the dispute arises.

THE HEARING Because the parties are free to construct the method by which they want their dispute resolved, they must specify the issues that will be submitted and the powers that the arbitrator will exercise. The arbitrator may be given power at the outset of the process to establish rules that will govern the proceedings. Regardless of who establishes the rules, the

EXHIBIT 3-2 Sample Submission Form

American Arbitration Association
Dispute Resolution Services Worldwide

Please visit our website at www.adr.org if you would like to file this case online.
AAA Customer Service can be reached at 800-778-7879

SUBMISSION TO DISPUTE RESOLUTION

The named parties hereby submit the following dispute for resolution, under the rules of the American Arbitration Association.

To be completed and signed by all parties (attach additional sheets if necessary).

Rules Selected: ☐Commercial ☐Construction ☐Employment ☐Other (please specify) ____________

Procedure Selected: ☐Binding Arbitration ☐Mediation ☐Other (please specify)____________.

NATURE OF DISPUTE:

Dollar Amount of Claim $	Other Relief Sought: ☐Attorneys Fees ☐Interest ☐Arbitration Costs ☐Punitive/ Exemplary ☐Other ________

PLEASE DESCRIBE APPROPRIATE QUALIFICATIONS FOR ARBITRATOR(S) TO BE APPOINTED TO HEAR THIS DISPUTE:

Amount Enclosed $________ In accordance with Fee Schedule: ☐Flexible Fee Schedule ☐Standard Fee Schedule

HEARING LOCALE REQUESTED: ____________	Estimated time needed for hearings overall: ________ hours or ________days

We agree that, if arbitration is selected, we will abide by and perform any award rendered hereunder and that a judgment may be entered on the award.

Name of Party	Name of Party
Address:	Address:
City: / State / Zip Code	City: / State / Zip Code
Phone No. / Fax No.	Phone No. / Fax No.
Email Address:	Email Address:
Signature (required): / Date:	Signature (required): / Date:
Name of Representative:	Name of Representative:
Name of Firm (if applicable)	Name of Firm (if applicable)
Address (to be used in connection with this case)	Address (to be used in connection with this case)
City: / State / Zip Code	City: / State / Zip Code
Phone No. / Fax No.	Phone No. / Fax No.
Email Address:	Email Address:

To begin proceedings, please send a copy of this Demand and the Arbitration Agreement, along with the filing fee as provided for in the Rules, to: American Arbitration Association, Case Filing Services, 1101 Laurel Oak Road, Suite 100 Voorhees, NJ 08043. Send the original Demand to the Respondent.

arbitrator will apply them during the course of the hearing.

Restrictions on the kind of evidence and the manner in which it is presented may be less rigid in arbitration, partly because the arbitrator is likely to be an expert in the subject matter involved in the controversy. Restrictions may also be less stringent because there is less fear that the arbitrator will be swayed by improper evidence. In contrast, evidence in a jury trial must sometimes be presented twice: once to the judge, outside the presence of the jury, to determine if the evidence may be heard by the jury, and—depending on the judge's ruling—again, to the jury.

In the typical hearing format, the parties begin as they would at trial by presenting opening arguments to the arbitrator and stating what remedies should or should not be granted. After the opening statements have been made, evidence is presented. Witnesses may be called and examined by both sides. After all the evidence has been presented, the parties give their closing arguments. On completion of the closing arguments, the arbitrator closes the hearing.

THE ARBITRATOR'S DECISION After each side has had an opportunity to present evidence and to argue its case, the arbitrator reaches a decision. The arbitrator's decision is called an **award.** It is is usually the final word on the matter. Although the parties may appeal an arbitrator's decision, a court's review of the decision will be much more restricted in scope than an appellate court's review of a trial court's decision.

The general view is that because the parties were free to frame the issues and set the powers of the arbitrator at the outset, they cannot complain about the results. A court will set aside an award only in limited situations, such as if the award violates an established public policy. A court may also set aside the award if the arbitrator's conduct or "bad faith" substantially prejudiced the rights of one of the parties. (See the list on page 71 for more details on when a court will set aside an arbitrator's decision.)

Enforcement of Agreements to Submit to Arbitration

The role of the courts in the arbitration process is limited. One important role is played at the prearbitration stage. A court may be called on to order one party to an arbitration agreement to submit to arbitration under the terms of the agreement. The court in this role is essentially interpreting a contract. The court must determine what the parties have committed themselves to before ordering that they submit to arbitration.

THE ISSUE OF ARBITRABILITY The terms of an arbitration agreement can limit the types of disputes that the parties agree to arbitrate. Disputes can arise, however, when the parties do not specify limits or when the parties disagree on whether the particular matter is covered by their arbitration agreement.

When one party files a lawsuit to compel arbitration, it is up to the court to resolve the issue of *arbitrability.* That is, the court must decide whether the matter is one that must be resolved through arbitration.

If the court finds that the subject matter in controversy is covered by the agreement to arbitrate, then a party may be compelled to arbitrate the dispute. Usually, a court will allow the claim to be arbitrated if the court finds that the relevant statute (the state arbitration statute or the FAA) does not exclude such claims.

No party, however, will be ordered to submit a particular dispute to arbitration unless the court is convinced that the party has consented to do so. Additionally, the courts will not compel arbitration if it is clear that the arbitration rules and procedures are inherently unfair to one of the parties.

The terms of an arbitration agreement can limit the types of disputes that the parties agree to arbitrate. In the following case, the parties had previously agreed to arbitrate disputes involving their contract to develop software, but the dispute involved claims of copyright infringement (see Chapter 14). The question was whether the copyright infringement claims were beyond the scope of the arbitration clause.

CASE 3.2

NCR Corp. v. Korala Associates, Ltd.

United States Court of Appeals, Sixth Circuit, 512 F.3d 807 (2008).

COMPANY PROFILE In 1884, John H. Patterson founded the National Cash Register Company (NCR), maker of the first mechanical cash registers. In 1906, NCR created a cash register run by an electric motor. By 1914, the company had developed one of the first automated credit systems. By the 1950s, NCR had branched out into transistorized business computers, and later it expanded into liquid crystal displays

CASE 3.2 CONTINUED

and data warehousing. Today, NCR is a worldwide provider of automated teller machines (ATMs), integrated hardware and software systems, and related maintenance and support services. More than 300,000 NCR ATMs are installed throughout the world.

BACKGROUND AND FACTS To upgrade the security of its ATMs, NCR developed a software solution to install in all of its machines. At the same time, Korala Associates, Ltd. (KAL), claimed to have developed a similar security upgrade for NCR's ATMs. Indeed, KAL had entered into a contract with NCR in 1998 (the "1998 Agreement") to develop such software. To facilitate that process, NCR had loaned to KAL a proprietary ATM that contained copyrighted software called APTRA XFS. NCR alleged that KAL had "obtained access to, made unauthorized use of, and engaged in unauthorized copying of the APTRA XFS software." NCR further claimed that KAL had developed its version of the security upgrade only by engaging in this unauthorized activity. When NCR brought a suit claiming copyright infringement, KAL moved to compel arbitration under the terms of the 1998 Agreement. At trial, KAL prevailed. NCR appealed the order compelling arbitration.

IN THE LANGUAGE OF THE COURT
Chief Justice *BATCHELDER* delivered the opinion of the court.

* * * *

The arbitration clause contained within the 1998 Agreement provides that:

> Any controversy or claim arising out of or relating to this contract, or breach thereof, shall be settled by arbitration and judgment upon the award rendered by the arbitrator may be entered in any court having jurisdiction thereof. The arbitrator shall be appointed upon the mutual agreement of both parties failing which both parties will agree to be subject to any arbitrator that shall be chosen by the President of the Law Society.

The parties do not dispute that a valid agreement to arbitrate exists; rather the issue of contention is whether NCR's claims fall within the substantive scope of the agreement.

As a matter of federal law, any doubts concerning the scope of arbitrable issues should be resolved in favor of arbitration. Despite this strong presumption in favor of arbitration, "arbitration is a matter of contract between the parties, and one cannot be required to submit to arbitration a dispute which it has not agreed to submit to arbitration." *When faced with a broad arbitration clause, such as one covering any dispute arising out of an agreement, a court should follow the presumption of arbitration and resolve doubts in favor of arbitration. Indeed, in such a case, only an express provision excluding a specific dispute, or the most forceful evidence of a purpose to exclude the claim from arbitration, will remove the dispute from consideration by the arbitrators.* [Emphasis added.]

* * * It is sufficient that a court would have to reference the 1998 Agreement for part of NCR's direct [copyright] infringement claim. Under these circumstances, we find that the copyright infringement claim as to APTRA XFS falls within the scope of the arbitration agreement.

DECISION AND REMEDY *The U.S. Court of Appeals for the Sixth Circuit affirmed the part of the district court's decision compelling arbitration of NCR's claims of direct copyright infringement relating to the APTRA XFS software.*

THE LEGAL ENVIRONMENT DIMENSION *Why did NCR not want its claims decided by arbitration?*

THE ETHICAL DIMENSION *Could NCR have a claim that KAL engaged in unfair competition because KAL engaged in unethical business practices? (Hint: Unfair competition may occur when one party deceives the public into believing that its goods are the goods of another.) Why or why not?*

MANDATORY ARBITRATION IN THE EMPLOYMENT CONTEXT A significant question for businesspersons has concerned mandatory arbitration clauses in employment contracts. Many employees claim they are at a disadvantage when they are forced, as a condition of being hired, to agree to arbitrate all disputes and thus waive their rights under statutes designed to protect employees. The United States Supreme Court, however, has held that mandatory arbitration clauses in employment contracts are generally enforceable.

Case in Point 3.2 In a landmark decision, *Gilmer v. Interstate Johnson Lane Corp.*,[3] the Supreme Court held that a claim brought under a federal statute prohibiting age discrimination could be subject to arbitration. The Court concluded that the employee had waived his right to sue when he agreed, as part of a required application to be a securities representative, to arbitrate "any dispute, claim, or controversy" relating to his employment. ◀

Compulsory arbitration agreements often spell out the rules for a mandatory proceeding. For example, an agreement may address in detail the amount and payment of filing fees and other expenses. Employment-related agreements often require the parties to split the costs, but some courts have overturned those provisions when an individual worker lacked the ability to pay.[4]

MANDATORY ARBITRATION AND CLASS ACTION WAIVERS IN CREDIT-CARD CONTRACTS Many credit-card companies include mandatory arbitration clauses in their contracts that also contain class-action waivers. A class action occurs when a large group of plaintiffs files a lawsuit collectively for a larger amount of damages that they could claim individually (see Chapter 12). A *class action* waiver requires all disputes to be arbitrated on an individual basis, which provides an advantage to the credit card company.

The United States Supreme Court recently upheld an arbitration clause that included a class action waiver. **Case in Point 3.3** A group of retail merchants who accept American Express personal and corporate charge cards filed a lawsuit against the company. The suit alleged that American Express had used its market power to impose a policy requiring them to accept all American Express credit cards (not just one) in violation of antitrust laws (a tying agreement—see Chapter 27).

3. 500 U.S. 20, 111 S.Ct. 1647, 114 L.Ed.2d 26 (1991).

4. See, for example, *Davis v. O'Melveny & Myers, LLC*, 485 F.3d 1066 (9th Cir. 2007); and *Nagrampa v. MailCoups, Inc.*, 469 F.3d 1257 (9th Cir. 2006).

The retailers argued that the class-action waiver was unenforceable because the cost of pursuing individual actions would be prohibitively expensive in light of the relatively small potential recovery for any individual merchant. Thus, the retailers claimed they could not "effectively vindicate" their statutory rights. The federal district court and the United States Court of Appeals for the Second Circuit agreed with the plaintiffs, finding that the mandatory arbitration clause in the card acceptance agreement was unenforceable. The United States Supreme Court reversed the lower court's decision. The Supreme Court held the Federal Arbitration Act "reflects the overarching principle that arbitration is a matter of contract" and thus, "courts must rigorously enforce arbitration agreements according to their terms." The Court found the arbitration clause was valid regardless of the class action waiver.[5] ◀

CONSUMER ARBITRATION AGREEMENTS Arbitration clauses in contracts for consumer goods and services have also been a source of controversy. Generally, the criticism of compulsory arbitration in this context has to do with the parties' unequal bargaining power. As you will read in Chapter 9, a contract or clause drafted by one party (the dominant party) and presented to the other party on a take-it-or-leave-it basis is referred to as an *adhesion contract.* Although the courts normally enforce contractual agreements, when enforcement would be manifestly unfair or oppressive, a court may deem the contract *unconscionable*—that is, contrary to public policy—and refuse to enforce it.

In the following case, a travel agency included an arbitration clause in its contract with two clients who participated in an agency expedition to Mt. Kilimanjaro, the highest mountain in Africa. The court had to determine whether the agreement to arbitrate should be enforced.

5. *American Express Co. v. Italian Colors Restaurant*, ___ U.S. ___, 133 S.Ct. 2304, ___ L.Ed.2d ___ (2013).

CASE ANALYSIS

Case 3.3 Lhotka v. Geographic Expeditions, Inc.

California Court of Appeal, First District, 181 Cal.App.4th 816, 104 Cal.Rptr.3d 844 (2010).

IN THE LANGUAGE OF THE COURT

SIGGINS, J. [Judge]

* * * *

Jason Lhotka was thirty-seven years old when he died of an altitude-related illness while on a GeoEx [Geographic Expeditions, Inc.] expedition up Mount Kilimanjaro with his mother, plaintiff Sandra Menefee. GeoEx's limitation of liability and release form, which both Lhotka and Menefee signed as a requirement of participating in the expedition, provided that each of them released GeoEx from all liability in connection with the trek and waived any claims for liability "to the maximum extent permitted

CASE 3.3 CONTINUED

by law." The release * * * reads: "I understand that all Trip Applications are subject to acceptance by GeoEx in San Francisco, California, USA. I agree that in the unlikely event a dispute of any kind arises between me and GeoEx, the following conditions will apply: (a) the dispute will be submitted to a neutral third-party mediator in San Francisco, California, with both parties splitting equally the cost of such mediator. If the dispute cannot be resolved through mediation, then (b) the dispute will be submitted for binding arbitration to the American Arbitration Association in San Francisco, California; (c) the dispute will be governed by California law; and (d) the maximum amount of recovery to which I will be entitled under any and all circumstances will be the sum of the land and air cost of my trip with GeoEx. I agree that this is a fair and reasonable limitation on the damages, of any sort whatsoever, that I may suffer. I agree to fully indemnify [compensate] GeoEx for all of its costs (including attorneys' fees) if I commence an action or claim against GeoEx based upon claims I have previously released or waived by signing this release." Menefee paid $16,831 for herself and Lhotka to go on the trip.

A letter from GeoEx president James Sano that accompanied the limitation of liability and release explained that the form was mandatory and that, on this point, "our lawyers, insurance carriers and medical consultants give us no discretion. A signed, unmodified release form is required before any traveler may join one of our trips. * * * My review of other travel companies' release forms suggests that our forms are not a whole lot different from theirs."

After her son's death, Menefee sued GeoEx for wrongful death and alleged various theories of liability including fraud, gross negligence and recklessness, and intentional infliction of emotional distress. GeoEx moved to compel arbitration.

The trial court found the arbitration provision was unconscionable * * * and on that basis denied the motion. It ruled: "The agreement at issue is both procedurally and substantively unconscionable * * * ."

This appeal timely followed.

* * * *

We turn * * * to GeoEx's contention that the court erred when it found the arbitration agreement unconscionable. Although the issue arises here in a relatively novel setting, the basic legal framework is well established.

"Unconscionability has generally been recognized to include an absence of meaningful choice on the part of one of the parties together with contract terms which are unreasonably favorable to the other party. Phrased another way, *unconscionability has both a procedural and a substantive element. The procedural element requires oppression or surprise.* * * * *The substantive element concerns whether a contractual provision reallocates risks in an objectively unreasonable or unexpected manner.*" * * * [Emphasis added.]

GeoEx argues the arbitration agreement involved neither the oppression nor surprise aspects of procedural unconscionability. GeoEx argues the agreement was not oppressive because plaintiffs made no showing of an "industry-wide requirement that travel clients must accept an agreement's terms without modification" and "they fail[ed] even to attempt to negotiate" with GeoEx. We disagree. GeoEx's argument cannot reasonably be squared with its own statements advising participants that they must sign an *unmodified* release form to participate in the expedition; that GeoEx's "lawyers, insurance carriers and medical consultants give [it] no discretion" on that point; and *that other travel companies were no different.* In other words, GeoEx led the plaintiffs to understand not only that its terms and conditions were nonnegotiable, but that plaintiffs would encounter the same requirements with any other travel company. This is a sufficient basis for us to conclude the plaintiffs lacked bargaining power.

GeoEx also contends its terms were not oppressive, apparently as a matter of law, because Menefee and Lhotka could have simply decided not to trek up Mount Kilimanjaro. It argues that contracts for recreational activities can *never* be unconscionably oppressive because, unlike agreements for necessities such as medical care or employment, a consumer of recreational activities *always* has the option of [forgoing] the activity. The argument has some initial resonance [significance], but on closer inspection we reject it as unsound.

* * * *

Here, certainly, plaintiffs could have chosen not to sign on with the expedition. That option, like any availability of market alternatives, is relevant to the existence, and degree, of oppression. But we must also consider the other circumstances surrounding the execution of the agreement. GeoEx presented its limitation of liability and release form as mandatory and unmodifiable, and essentially told plaintiffs that any other travel provider would impose the same terms. "Oppression arises from an inequality of bargaining power which results in no real negotiation and an absence of meaningful choice * * * ." GeoEx presented its terms as both nonnegotiable and *no different than what plaintiffs would find with any other provider.* Under these circumstances, plaintiffs made a sufficient showing to establish at least a minimal level of oppression to justify a finding of procedural unconscionability. [Emphasis in original.]

* * * [We now] address whether the substantive unconscionability of the GeoEx contract warrants the trial court's ruling.

* * * *

The arbitration provision in GeoEx's release * * * guaranteed that plaintiffs could not possibly obtain anything approaching full recompense for their harm by limiting any recovery they could obtain to the amount they paid GeoEx for

CASE 3.3 CONTINUES ➧

CASE 3.3 CONTINUED

their trip. In addition to a limit on their recovery, plaintiffs, residents of Colorado, were required to mediate and arbitrate in San Francisco—all but guaranteeing both that GeoEx would never be out more than the amount plaintiffs had paid for their trip, and that any recovery plaintiffs might obtain would be devoured by the expense they incur in pursuing their remedy. The release also required plaintiffs to indemnify GeoEx for its costs and attorney fees for defending any claims covered by the release of liability form. Notably, there is no reciprocal limitation on damages or indemnification obligations imposed on GeoEx. Rather than providing a neutral forum for dispute resolution, GeoEx's arbitration scheme provides a potent disincentive for an aggrieved client to pursue any claim, in any forum—and may well guarantee that GeoEx wins even if it loses. Absent reasonable justification for this arrangement—and none is apparent—we agree with the trial court that the arbitration clause is so one-sided as to be substantively unconscionable.

* * * *

The order denying GeoEx's motion to compel arbitration is affirmed.

LEGAL REASONING QUESTIONS

1. What did the judge mean when he said that GeoEx's one-sided arbitration scheme "may well guarantee that GeoEx wins even if it loses"?
2. Did the fact that the terms of the release were nonnegotiable contribute to its unconscionability? Explain.
3. What two elements of unconscionability did the court identify? On which of these elements did the court base its ruling?
4. Did the court suggest any way that a travel company might create a valid release against injuries that occurred while participating in an expedition? Explain.

Setting Aside an Arbitration Award

After the arbitration has been concluded, the losing party may appeal the arbitrator's award to a court, or the winning party may seek a court order compelling the other party to comply with the award. As mentioned earlier, the scope of review in either situation is much more restricted than in an appellate court's review of a trial court decision. The court does not look at the merits of the underlying dispute, and the court will not add to or subtract from the remedies provided by the award.

The court's role is limited to determining whether there exists a valid award. If so, the court will order the parties to comply with the terms. The general view is that because the parties were free to frame the issues and set the powers of the arbitrator at the outset, they cannot complain about the result.

FACT FINDINGS AND LEGAL CONCLUSIONS The arbitrator's fact findings and legal conclusions are normally final. That the arbitrator may have erred in a ruling during the hearing or made an erroneous fact finding is normally no basis for setting aside an award: the parties agreed that the arbitrator would be the judge of the facts.

Similarly, no matter how obviously the arbitrator was mistaken in a conclusion of law, the award is normally nonetheless binding: the parties agreed to accept the arbitrator's interpretation of the law. A court will not look at the merits of the dispute, the sufficiency of the evidence presented, or the arbitrator's reasoning in reaching a particular decision.

This approach is consistent with the underlying view of all voluntary arbitration—that its basis is really contract law. If the parties freely contract with one another, courts will not interfere simply because one side feels that it received a bad bargain. Any party challenging an award must face the presumption that a final award is valid. But is an award final or binding if the parties did not agree that it would be?

PUBLIC POLICY AND ILLEGALITY In keeping with contract law principles, no award will be enforced if compliance with the award would result in the commission of a crime or would conflict with some greater social policy mandated by statute. A court will not overturn an award, however, simply because the arbitrator was called on to resolve a dispute involving a matter of significant public concern. For an award to be set aside, it must call for some action on the part of the parties that would conflict with or in some way undermine public policy.

DEFECTS IN THE ARBITRATION PROCESS There are some bases for setting aside an award when there is a defect in the arbitration process. These bases are typified by those set forth in the Federal Arbitration Act. Section 10 of the FAA provides four grounds on which an arbitration award may be set aside.

1. The award was the result of corruption, fraud, or other "undue means."
2. The arbitrator exhibited bias or corruption.
3. The arbitrator refused to postpone the hearing despite sufficient cause, refused to hear evidence pertinent and material to the dispute, or otherwise acted to substantially prejudice the rights of one of the parties.
4. The arbitrator exceeded his or her powers or failed to use them to make a mutual, final, and definite award.

WAIVER Although a defect in the arbitration process is sufficient grounds for setting aside an award, a party sometimes forfeits the right to challenge an award by failing to object to the defect in a timely manner. The party must object when he or she learns of the problem.

After making the objection, the party can proceed with the arbitration process and still challenge the award in court after the arbitration proceedings have concluded. If, however, a party makes no objection and proceeds with the arbitration process, then a later court challenge to the award may be denied on the ground that the party *waived* the right to challenge the award on the basis of the defect.

Frequently, this occurs when a party fails to object that an arbitrator is exceeding his or her powers in resolving a dispute because the subject matter is not arbitrable or because the party did not agree to arbitrate the dispute. The question of arbitrability is one for the courts to decide. If a party does not object on this issue at the first demand for arbitration, however, a court may consider the objection waived.

CONFLICTS OF LAW Parties are afforded wide latitude in establishing the manner in which their disputes will be resolved. Nevertheless, an agreement to arbitrate may be governed by the Federal Arbitration Act (FAA) or one of the many state arbitration acts, even though the parties do not refer to a statute in their agreement.

Recall that the FAA covers any arbitration clause in a contract that involves interstate commerce. Frequently, however, transactions involving interstate commerce also have substantial connections to particular states, which may in turn have their own arbitration acts. In such situations, unless the FAA and state arbitration law are nearly identical, the acts may conflict. How are these conflicts to be resolved?

As a general principle, the supremacy clause and the commerce clause of the U.S. Constitution are the bases for giving federal law preeminence. When there is a conflict, state law is preempted by federal law. Thus, in cases of arbitration, the strong federal policy favoring arbitration can override a state's laws that might be more favorable to normal litigation.

CHOICE OF LAW Notwithstanding federal preemption of conflicting state laws, the FAA has been interpreted as allowing the parties to choose a particular state law to govern their arbitration agreement. The parties may choose to have the laws of a specific state govern their agreement by including in the agreement a **choice-of-law clause.** The FAA does not mandate any particular set of rules that parties must follow in arbitration. The parties are free to agree on the manner best suited to their needs. Consistent with this view that arbitration is at heart a contractual matter between private parties, the United States Supreme Court has upheld arbitration agreements containing choice-of-law provisions.

Disadvantages of Arbitration

Arbitration has some disadvantages. The result in any particular dispute can be unpredictable, in part because arbitrators do not need to follow any previous cases in rendering their decisions. Unlike judges, arbitrators do not have to issue written opinions or facilitate a participant's appeal to a court. Arbitrators must decide disputes according to whatever rules have been provided by the parties, regardless of how unfair those rules may be.

In some disputes, arbitration can be nearly as expensive as litigation. In part, this is because both sides must prepare their cases for presentation before a third party decision maker, just as they would have to do to appear in court. Discovery usually is not available in arbitration, however, which means that during the hearing the parties must take the time to question witnesses whom, in a lawsuit, they would not need to call.

SECTION 3

THE INTEGRATION OF ADR AND FORMAL COURT PROCEDURES

Increasingly, courts are requiring that parties attempt to settle their differences through some form of ADR before proceeding to trial. For instance, a number of federal district courts encourage nonbinding arbitration for cases involving amounts less than $100,000. Less than 10 percent of the cases referred for arbitration ever go to trial. About half of all federal courts have adopted formal rules regarding the use of ADR, and many other courts without such rules use ADR procedures.

Most states have adopted programs that allow them to refer certain types of cases for negotiation, mediation, or arbitration. Typically—as in California and Hawaii—court systems have adopted mandatory mediation or nonbinding arbitration programs for certain types of disputes, usually involving less than a specified threshold dollar amount. Only if the parties fail to reach an agreement, or if one of the parties disagrees with the decision of a third party mediating or arbitrating the dispute, will the case be heard by a court. South Carolina was the first state to institute a voluntary arbitration program at the appellate court level. In the South Carolina system, litigants must waive a court hearing when requesting arbitration. All decisions by the arbitrators are final and binding.

Court-Annexed Arbitration

Court-annexed arbitration—that is, arbitration mandated by the court—differs significantly from the voluntary arbitration process discussed above. There are some disputes that courts will not allow to go to arbitration. Most states, for instance, do not allow court-annexed arbitration in disputes involving title to real estate or in cases in which a court's equity powers are involved.

DIFFERENT STANDARD OF COURT REVIEW A fundamental difference between voluntary arbitration and court-annexed arbitration is the finality and reviewability of the award. Because court-annexed arbitration is not voluntary, forcing an individual to accept the arbitrator's award would be the same as denying that person a right to have his or her "day in court." Therefore, either party may reject the award for any reason.

In the event that one of the parties does reject the award, the case will proceed to trial, and the court will hear the case *de novo* (meaning "from the beginning"). In other words, the court will reconsider all the evidence and legal questions as though no arbitration had occurred. This is much different from the limited review that courts typically give to arbitration awards (discussed earlier).

The party rejecting the award can be penalized, however. Many statutes that provide for court-annexed arbitration impose court costs and fees on a party who rejects an arbitration award but does not improve his or her position by going to trial. ▶ **Example 3.4** Mirrick Bobek rejects an arbitration award in a contract dispute. The award turns out to be more favorable to him than a subsequent jury verdict in the case. Under the court-annexed arbitration statute, the court can require Bobek to pay the costs of arbitration, or some fee for the costs of trial. ◀

DISCOVERY In court-annexed arbitration, discovery of evidence occurs before the hearing. After the hearing has commenced, a party seeking to discover new evidence must usually secure approval from the court that mandated the arbitration. This is intended to prevent the parties from using arbitration as a means of previewing each other's cases and then rejecting the arbitrator's award.

THE ROLE OF THE ARBITRATOR Notwithstanding the differences between voluntary and court-annexed arbitration, the role of the arbitrator is essentially the same in both types of proceedings. The arbitrator determines issues of both fact and law. The arbitrator also makes all decisions concerning applications of the rules of procedure and evidence during the hearing.

WHICH RULES APPLY Regarding the rules of evidence, there are differences among the states. Most states impose the same rules of evidence on an arbitration hearing as on a trial. Other states allow all evidence relevant to the dispute regardless of whether the evidence would be admissible at trial. Still other jurisdictions leave it to the arbitrator to decide what evidence is admissible.

WAIVER Once a court directs that a dispute is to be submitted to court-annexed arbitration, the parties must proceed to arbitration. As noted above, either side may reject the award that results from the arbitration for any reason. If a party fails to appear at, or participate in, the arbitration proceeding as directed by the court, however, that failure constitutes a waiver of the right to reject the award.

Court-Related Mediation

Mediation is proving to be more popular than arbitration as a court-related method of ADR, and mediation programs continue to increase in number in both federal and state courts. Today, more court systems offer or require mediation, rather than arbitration, as an alternative to litigation.

Mediation is often used in disputes relating to employment law, environmental law, product liability, or franchises. One of the most important business advantages of mediation is its lower cost, which can be 25 percent (or less) of the expense of litigation. Another advantage is the speed with which a dispute can go through mediation (possibly one or two days) compared with arbitration (possibly months) or litigation (possibly years).

Part of the popularity of mediation is that its goal, unlike that of litigation and some other forms of ADR, is for opponents to work out a resolution that benefits both sides. The rate of participants' satisfaction with the outcomes in mediated disputes is high.

Summary Jury Trials

Another means by which the courts have integrated alternative dispute-resolution methods into the traditional court process is through the use of summary jury trials. A **summary jury trial** is a mock trial that occurs in a courtroom before a judge and jury. Evidence is presented in an abbreviated form, along with each side's major contentions. The jury then presents a verdict.

The fundamental difference between a traditional trial and a summary jury trial is that in the latter, the jury's verdict is only advisory. A summary jury trial's goal is to give each side an idea of how it would fare in a full-blown jury trial with a more elaborate and detailed presentation of evidence and arguments. At the end of the summary jury trial, the presiding judge meets with the parties and may encourage them to settle their dispute without going through a standard jury trial.

SECTION 4
ADR FORUMS AND SERVICES

Services facilitating dispute resolution outside the courtroom are provided by both government agencies and private organizations, as well as by companies conducting business online.

Providers of ADR Services

Both government agencies and private organizations provide ADR services. A major provider of ADR services is the **American Arbitration Association (AAA).** The AAA was founded in 1926 and now handles more than 200,000 claims a year in its numerous offices worldwide.

Cases brought before the AAA are heard by an expert or a panel of experts in the area relating to the dispute and are usually settled quickly. Generally, about half of the panel members are lawyers. To cover its costs, the AAA charges a fee, paid by the party filing the claim. In addition, each party to the dispute pays a specified amount for each hearing day, as well as a special additional fee in cases involving personal injuries or property loss.

Hundreds of for-profit firms around the country also provide dispute-resolution services. Typically, these firms hire retired judges to conduct arbitration hearings or otherwise assist parties in settling their disputes. The judges follow procedures similar to those of the federal courts and use similar rules. Usually, each party to the dispute pays a filing fee and a designated fee for a hearing session or conference.

Online Dispute Resolution

An increasing number of companies and organizations are offering dispute-resolution services using the Internet. The settlement of disputes in these online forums is known as **online dispute resolution (ODR).** The disputes resolved in these forums have most commonly involved rights to domain names (Web site addresses—see Chapter 15) or the quality of goods sold via the Internet, including goods sold through Internet auction sites.

ODR may be best for resolving small- to medium-sized business liability claims, which may not be worth the expense of litigation or traditional ADR methods. Rules being developed in online forums may ultimately become a code of conduct for everyone who does business in cyberspace. Most online forums do not automatically apply the law of any specific jurisdiction. Instead, results are often based on general, more universal legal principles. As with offline methods of dispute resolution, any party may appeal to a court at any time if the ODR is nonbinding arbitration.

Some cities use ODR as a means of resolving claims against them. ▶ **Example 3.5** New York City uses Cybersettle.com to resolve auto accident, sidewalk, and other personal-injury claims made against the city. Parties with complaints submit their demands, and the city submits its offers confidentially online. If an offer exceeds a demand, the claimant keeps half the difference as a bonus, plus the original claim. ◀

SECTION 5

INTERNATIONAL DISPUTE RESOLUTION

Businesspersons who engage in international business transactions normally take special precautions to protect themselves in the event that a party with whom they are dealing in another country breaches an agreement. Often, parties to international contracts include special clauses in their contracts providing for how disputes arising under the contracts will be resolved.

Forum-Selection and Choice-of-Law Clauses

As you will read in Chapter 11, parties to international transactions often include forum-selection and choice-of-law clauses in their contracts. These clauses designate the jurisdiction (court or country) where any dispute arising under the contract will be litigated and which nation's law will be applied.

When an international contract does not include such clauses, any legal proceedings arising under the contract will be more complex and attended by much more uncertainty. For instance, litigation may take place in two or more countries, with each country applying its own national law to the particular transactions.

Furthermore, even if a plaintiff wins a favorable judgment in a lawsuit litigated in the plaintiff's country, the defendant's country could refuse to enforce the court's judgment. As will be discussed in Chapter 8, the judgment may be enforced in the defendant's country for reasons of courtesy. The United States, for example, will generally enforce a foreign court's decision if it is consistent with U.S. national law and policy. Other nations, however, may not be as accommodating as the United States, and the plaintiff may be left empty-handed.

Arbitration Clauses

International contracts also often include arbitration clauses that require a neutral third party to decide any contract disputes. In international arbitration proceedings, the third party may be a neutral entity (such as the International Chamber of Commerce), a panel of individuals representing both parties' interests, or some other group or organization.

The United Nations Convention on the Recognition and Enforcement of Foreign Arbitral Awards[6] has been implemented in more than 145 countries, including the United States. This convention assists in the enforcement of arbitration clauses, as do provisions in specific treaties among nations. The American Arbitration Association provides arbitration services for international as well as domestic disputes.

International Treaties and Arbitration

International treaties (formal agreements among several nations—see Chapter 8) sometimes also stipulate arbitration for resolving disputes. This is a tactic that has been used in the past to increase foreign investment. ▶ **Example 3.6** In the 1990s, Argentina encouraged foreign investment by forming bilateral investment treaties with other nations, including the United States and France. The treaties required Argentina to protect investors' property rights and provided that any grievances would be settled by arbitration at the International Centre for the Settlement of Investment Disputes (ICSID), which is part of the World Bank. Foreign investment in Argentina skyrocketed, in part, because companies had the security of knowing that disputes would be settled by the ICSID rather than by Argentina's courts.

After Argentina's economy collapsed in 2001, companies that had suffered significant losses filed claims against Argentina with the ICSID. The ICSID, however, resolved most claims in Argentina's favor. The few companies that won awards from the ICSID, such as Philip Morris International, then had to ask courts in Argentina to enforce the judgments. These problems have caused some nations to withdraw from the ICSID. Others, including Australia, have indicated that they will not enter any future trade agreements that require their domestic investors who invest in other countries to submit to arbitration. ◀

6. June 10, 1958, 21 U.S.T. 2517, T.I.A.S. No. 6997 (the "New York Convention").

Reviewing: Alternative and Online Dispute Resolution

Adrian Reese, a resident of New York, owned a strip mall located in Ohio, which he leased out to different businesses. The tenants in the building had complained that the two public restrooms were substandard and in need of repair. Reese therefore contracted with Lyle Copeland, a licensed contractor in Ohio, to remodel the bathrooms and fix the outdated plumbing. Copeland began the work on the date promised but progressed very slowly. Then, while ripping out the existing pipes, Copeland accidentally broke the main pipe, which caused flooding and water damage to the building. Several of the tenants immediately vacated the property after the incident. Reese claimed that Copeland was legally responsible for $300,000 in property damage because his actions were reckless and incompetent. Copeland maintained that it was an accident and refused to pay for the damage. Using the information presented in the chapter, answer the following questions.

1. What types of assisted negotiation might the parties use to settle this dispute?
2. Does the fact that the parties reside in different jurisdictions have any effect on whether they might try mediation or negotiation? Why or why not?
3. Why would the parties wish to use some method of alternative dispute resolution (ADR) rather than filing a traditional lawsuit?
4. Suppose that one of the parties rejects any attempt at using ADR and instead files a lawsuit in a federal district court. That court happens to require that this dispute be arbitrated prior to any trial on the matter. Explain whether this arbitration is likely to be legally binding on the parties.

DEBATE THIS . . . *Prior to all litigation, the opposing parties must submit to mediation or arbitration.*

Terms and Concepts

alternative dispute resolution (ADR) 60
American Arbitration Association 73
arbitration 62
arbitration clause 62
arbitrator 62
award 66
choice-of-law clause 71
early neutral case evaluation 61
facilitation 61
litigation 60
mediation 61
mediator 61
mini-trial 60
negotiation 60
online dispute resolution (ODR) 73
submission 64
summary jury trial 73

ExamPrep

Issue Spotters

1. Sue signs an agreement with her smartphone provider that includes an arbitration clause. Under the clause, Sue is required to pay two-thirds of the costs of arbitrating any dispute with the company. If a dispute arises, is the arbitration clause enforceable? Why or why not? **(See page 66.)**
2. The state in which Sue resides requires that her dispute with her smartphone provider be submitted to mediation or nonbinding arbitration. If the dispute is not resolved, or if either party disagrees with the decision of the mediator or arbitrator, will a court hear the case? Explain. **(See page 66.)**

- **Check your answers to the Issue Spotters against the answers provided in Appendix E at the end of this text.**

Before the Test

Go to **www.cengagebrain.com**, enter the ISBN 9781285428949, and click on "Find" to locate this textbook's Web site. Then, click on "Access Now" under "Study Tools," and select Chapter 3 at the top. There, you will find an Interactive Quiz that you can take to assess your mastery of the concepts in this chapter, as well as Flashcards and a Glossary of important terms.

Business Scenarios

3–1. Choice of Law. Two private U.S. corporations enter into an agreement to conduct mining operations in the newly formed Middle Eastern nation of Euphratia. As part of the agreement, the companies include an arbitration clause and a choice-of-law provision. The first states that any controversy arising out of the performance of the agreement will be settled by arbitration. The second states that the agreement is to be governed by the laws of the location of the venture, Euphratia. A dispute arises, and the parties discontinue operations. One of the parties claims sole ownership to the Euphratian mines and orders the other party to remove its equipment from the mines. The other party disputes the claim of sole ownership and seeks an order from a U.S. federal court compelling the parties to submit to arbitration over the ownership issue and alleged breaches of the agreement. How should the court rule if the laws of Euphratia state that, whereas arbitration agreements are to be enforced generally, matters of ownership of natural resources can only be resolved in a Euphratian court of law? Does it matter that two U.S. companies engaged in international commerce would be governed by the Federal Arbitration Act? Explain. **(See page 71.)**

3–2. Award. Two brothers, both of whom are certified public accountants (CPAs), form a professional association to provide tax-accounting services to the public. They also agree, in writing, that any disputes that arise between them over matters concerning the association will be submitted to an independent arbitrator, whom they designate to be their father, who is also a CPA. A dispute arises, and the matter is submitted to the father for arbitration. During the course of arbitration, which occurs over several weeks, the father asks the older brother, who is visiting one evening, to explain a certain entry in the brothers' association accounts. The younger brother learns of the discussion at the next meeting for arbitration. He says nothing about it, however. The arbitration is concluded in favor of the older brother, who seeks a court order compelling the younger brother to comply with the award. The younger brother seeks to set aside the award, claiming that the arbitration process was tainted by bias because "Dad always liked my older brother best." The younger brother also seeks to have the award set aside on the basis of improper conduct in that matters subject to arbitration were discussed between the father and older brother without the younger brother's being present. Should a court confirm the award or set it aside? Why or why not? **(See page 71.)**

3–3. Award. After resolving their dispute, the two brothers encountered in Question 3–2 decide to resume their tax-accounting practice according to the terms of their original agreement. Again a dispute arises, and again it is decided by the father (now retired except for numerous occasions on which he acts as an arbitrator) in favor of the older brother. The older brother files a petition to enforce the award. The younger brother seeks to set aside the award and offers evidence that the father, as arbitrator, made a gross error in calculating the accounts that were material to the dispute being arbitrated. If the court is convinced that the father erred in the calculations, should the award be set aside? Why or why not? **(See page 71.)**

Business Case Problems

3–4. BUSINESS CASE PROBLEM WITH SAMPLE ANSWER: Arbitration Clause.

Kathleen Lowden sued cellular phone company T-Mobile USA, Inc., contending that its service agreements were not enforceable under Washington state law. Lowden requested that the court allow a class-action suit, in which her claims would extend to similarly affected customers. She contended that T-Mobile had improperly charged her fees beyond the advertised price of service and charged her for roaming calls that should not have been classified as roaming.

*T-Mobile moved to force arbitration in accordance with the provisions that were clearly set forth in the service agreement. The agreement also specified that no class-action suit could be brought, so T-Mobile also asked the court to dismiss the request for a class-action suit. Was T-Mobile correct that Lowden's only course of action was to file for arbitration personally? Why or why not? [*Lowden v. T-Mobile USA, Inc.*, 512 F.3d 1213 (9th Cir. 2008)]* **(See page 66.)**

- **For a sample answer to Problem 3–4, go to Appendix F at the end of this text.**

3–5. Arbitration. PRM Energy Systems owned patents licensed to Primenergy to use in the United States. Their contract stated that "all disputes" would be settled by arbitration. Kobe Steel of Japan was interested in using the technology represented by PRM's patents. Primenergy agreed to let Kobe use the technology in Japan without telling PRM. When PRM learned about the secret deal, the firm filed a suit against Primenergy for fraud and theft. Does this dispute go to arbitration or to trial? Why? [*PRM Energy Systems v. Primenergy*, 592 F.3d 830 (8th Cir. 2010)] **(See page 66.)**

3–6. Spotlight on the National Football League—Arbitration.

Bruce Matthews played football for the Tennessee Titans. As part of his contract, he agreed to submit any dispute to arbitration. He also agreed that Tennessee law would determine all matters related to workers' compensation. After

Matthews retired, he filed a workers' compensation claim in California. The arbitrator ruled that Matthews could pursue his claim in California but only under Tennessee law. Should this award be set aside? Explain. [*National Football League Players Association v. National Football League Management Council*, 2011 WL 1137334 (S.D.Cal. 2011)] **(See page 62.)**

3–7. Arbitration. Horton Automatics and the Industrial Division of the Communications Workers of America, the union that represented Horton's workers, negotiated a collective bargaining agreement. If an employee's discharge for a workplace-rule violation was submitted to arbitration, the agreement limited the arbitrator to determining whether the rule was reasonable and whether the employee violated it. When Horton discharged employee Ruben de la Garza, the union appealed to arbitration. The arbitrator found that de la Garza had violated a reasonable safety rule, but "was not totally convinced" that Horton should have treated the violation more seriously than other rule violations. The arbitrator ordered de la Garza reinstated. Can a court set aside this order? Explain. *[Horton Automatics v. The Industrial Division of the Communications Workers of America, AFL-CIO*, 2013 WL 59204 (5th Cir. 2013)] **(See page 71.)**

3–8. A QUESTION OF ETHICS: Agreement to Arbitrate.

*Nellie Lumpkin, who suffered from various illnesses, including dementia, was admitted to the Picayune Convalescent Center, a nursing home. Because of her mental condition, her daughter, Beverly McDaniel, filled out the admissions paperwork and signed the admissions agreement. It included a clause requiring parties to submit to arbitration any disputes that arose. After Lumpkin left the center two years later, she sued, through her husband, for negligent treatment and malpractice during her stay. The center moved to force the matter to arbitration. The trial court held that the arbitration agreement was not enforceable. The center appealed. [*Covenant Health & Rehabilitation of Picayune, LP v. Lumpkin, *23 So.3d 1092 (Miss.App. 2009)]* **(See page 68.)**

(a) Should a dispute involving medical malpractice be forced into arbitration? This is a claim of negligent care, not a breach of a commercial contract. Is it ethical for medical facilities to impose such a requirement? Is there really any bargaining over such terms? Discuss fully.

(b) Should a person with limited mental capacity be held to the arbitration clause agreed to by the next-of-kin who signed on behalf of that person? Why or why not?

Legal Reasoning Group Activity

3–9. Access to Courts. Assume that a statute in your state requires that all civil lawsuits involving damages of less than $50,000 be arbitrated. Such a case can be tried in court only if a party is dissatisfied with the arbitrator's decision. The statute also provides that if a trial does not result in an improvement of more than 10 percent in the position of the party who demanded the trial, that party must pay the entire costs of the arbitration proceeding. **(See page 72.)**

(a) One group will argue that the state statute violates litigants' rights of access to the courts and to trial by jury.

(b) Another group will argue that the statute does not violate litigants' rights of access to the courts.

(c) A third group will evaluate how the determination on rights of access would be changed if the statute was part of a pilot program and affected only a few judicial districts in the state.

CHAPTER 4
BUSINESS ETHICS

One of the most complex issues businesspersons and corporations face is ethics. It is not as well defined as the law, and yet it can have tremendous impacts on a firm's finances and reputation. Consider, for instance, the experience of the Chick-fil-A restaurant chain in 2012 when its chief operating officer made several statements about the company's commitment to supporting traditional marriage.

After those comments were made, it became public knowledge that Chick-fil-A had made donations to Christian organizations perceived to be opposed to same-sex marriage. Opponents of same-sex marriage held support rallies and Chick-fil-A appreciation days. Supporters of same-sex marriage held "kiss-ins" at local Chick-fil-A restaurants. Some politicians denounced Chick-fil-A's position and said that they would block expansion of the company in their cities. Eventually, Chick-fil-A issued a statement saying that it had ceased donations to any organization that promotes discrimination in any way. Chick-fil-A no longer sponsors charities that discriminate against same-sex couples or those who identify as gay, lesbian, bisexual, or transgendered.

Chick-fil-A was not accused of violating any laws, but its actions raised questions about the role of corporations and the effect of corporate ethics on profit. This chapter addresses some of those same questions. First, we look at business ethics—its definitions, its importance, and its relationship to the law. Next, we examine the philosophical bases for making ethical decisions. Finally, we discuss the application of business ethics to global situations.

SECTION 1
BUSINESS ETHICS

At the most basic level, the study of **ethics** is the study of what constitutes right or wrong behavior. It is a branch of philosophy focusing on morality and the way moral principles are derived and implemented. Ethics has to do with the fairness, justness, rightness, or wrongness of an action.

The study of **business ethics** typically looks at the decisions businesses make or have to make and whether those decisions are right or wrong. It has to do with how businesspersons apply moral and ethical principles in making their decisions. Those who study business ethics also evaluate what duties and responsibilities exist or should exist for businesses.

At the end of every unit in this book, we present a series of ethical issues in features called *Focus on Ethics*. In each of these features, we expand on the concepts of business ethics discussed in this chapter.

Why Is Studying Business Ethics Important?

Over the last two hundred years, the public perception of the corporation has changed from an entity that primarily generates revenues for its owners to an entity that participates in society as a corporate citizen. Originally, the only goal or duty of a corporation was to maximize profits. Although many people today may view this idea as greedy or inhumane, the rationale for the profit-maximization theory is still valid.

PROFIT MAXIMIZATION In theory, if all firms strictly adhere to the goal of profit maximization, resources flow to where they are most highly valued by society. Corporations can focus on their strengths, and other entities that are better suited to deal with social problems and perform charitable acts can specialize in those activities. The government, through taxes and other financial allocations, can shift resources to those other entities to perform public services. Thus, in an ideal world, profit maximization leads to the most efficient allocation of scarce resources.

THE RISE OF CORPORATE CITIZENSHIP Over the years, as resources were not sufficiently reallocated to cover the costs of social needs, many people became dissatisfied with the profit-maximization theory. Investors and others began to look beyond profits and dividends and to consider the **triple bottom line**—a corporation's profits, its impact on people, and its impact on the planet. Magazines and Web sites began to rank companies based on their environmental impacts and their ethical decisions. The corporation came to be viewed as a "citizen" that was expected to participate in bettering communities and society.

Even so, many still believe that corporations are fundamentally money-making entities that should have no responsibility other than profit maximization.

The Importance of Ethics in Making Business Decisions

Whether one believes in the profit-maximization theory or corporate citizenship, ethics is important in making business decisions. Corporations should strive to be "good citizens." When making decisions, a business should evaluate:

1. The legal implications of each decision.
2. The public relations impact.
3. The safety risks for consumers and employees.
4. The financial implications.

This analysis will assist the firm in making decisions that not only maximize profits but also reflect good corporate citizenship.

LONG-RUN PROFIT MAXIMIZATION In attempting to maximize profits, however, corporate executives and employees have to distinguish between *short-run* and *long-run* profit maximization. In the short run, a company may increase its profits by continuing to sell a product, even though it knows that the product is defective. In the long run, though, because of lawsuits, large settlements, and bad publicity, such unethical conduct will cause profits to suffer. Thus, business ethics is consistent only with long-run profit maximization. An overemphasis on short-term profit maximization is the most common reason that ethical problems occur in business.

▶ **Case in Point 4.1** When the powerful narcotic painkiller OxyContin was first marketed, its manufacturer, Purdue Pharma, claimed that it was unlikely to lead to drug addiction or abuse. Internal company documents later showed that the company's executives knew that OxyContin could be addictive, but kept this risk a secret to boost sales and maximize short-term profits.

Subsequently, Purdue Pharma and three former executives pleaded guilty to criminal charges that they misled regulators, patients, and physicians about OxyContin's risks of addiction. Purdue Pharma agreed to pay $600 million in fines and other payments. The three former executives agreed to pay $34.5 million in fines and were barred from federal health programs for a period of fifteen years. Thus, the company's focus on maximizing profits in the short run led to unethical conduct that hurt profits in the long run.[1] ◀

THE INTERNET CAN RUIN REPUTATIONS In the past, negative information or opinions about a company might remain hidden. Now, however, cyberspace provides a forum where disgruntled employees, unhappy consumers, or special interest groups can post derogatory remarks. Thus, the Internet has increased the potential for a major corporation (or other business) to suffer damage to its reputation or loss of profits through negative publicity.

Wal-Mart and Nike in particular have been frequent targets for advocacy groups that believe that those corporations exploit their workers. Although some of these assertions may be unfounded or exaggerated, the courts generally have refused to consider them *defamatory* (the tort of defamation will be discussed in Chapter 12). Most courts regard online attacks as simply the expression of opinion and therefore a form of speech protected by the First Amendment. Even so, corporations often incur considerable expense in running marketing campaigns to thwart bad publicity and may even face legal costs (if the complaint leads to litigation).

IMAGE IS EVERYTHING The study of business ethics is concerned with the purposes of a business and how that business achieves those purposes. Thus, business ethics is concerned with the image of the business and the impacts that the business has on the environment, customers, suppliers, employees, and the global economy.

Unethical corporate decision making can negatively affect suppliers, consumers, the community, and society as a whole. It can also have a negative impact on the reputation of the company and the

1. *United States v. Purdue Frederick Co.,* 495 F.Supp.2d 569 (W.D.Va. 2007).

individuals who run that company. Hence, an in-depth understanding of business ethics is important to the long-run viability of any corporation today.

The Relationship of Law and Ethics

Because the law does not codify all ethical requirements of all persons, compliance with the law is not always sufficient to determine "right" behavior. Laws have to be general enough to apply in a variety of circumstances. Laws are broad in their purpose and their scope. They prohibit or require certain actions to avoid significant harm to society.

When two competing companies secretly agree to set prices on products, for instance, society suffers harm—typically, the companies will charge higher prices than they could if they continued to compete. This harm inflicted on consumers has negative consequences for the economy, and so colluding to set prices is an illegal activity. Similarly, when a company is preparing to issue stock, the law requires certain disclosures to potential investors. This requirement is meant to avoid harms that come with uninformed investing, such as occurred in the 1920s and contributed to the stock market crash and the Great Depression.

MORAL MINIMUM Compliance with the law is sometimes called the **moral minimum.** If people and entities merely comply with the law, they are acting at the lowest ethical level society will tolerate. The study of ethics goes beyond those legal requirements to evaluate what is right for society.

Businesspersons must remember that just because an action is legal does not mean it is ethical. For instance, no law specifies the salaries that publicly held corporations (companies that sell their shares to the public) can pay their officers (executive employees). Nevertheless, if a corporation pays its officers an excessive amount relative to other employees, or relative to what officers at other corporations are paid, the executives' compensation might be viewed as unethical.

In the following case, the court had to determine if a repair shop was entitled to receive full payment of an invoice or a lesser amount given its conduct in the matter.

CASE 4.1

Johnson Construction Co. v. Shaffer

Court of Appeal of Louisiana, Second Circuit, 87 So.3d 203 (2012).

BACKGROUND AND FACTS A truck owned by Johnson Construction Company needed repairs. John Robert Johnson, Jr., the company's president, took the truck with its attached fifteen-ton trailer to Bubba Shaffer, doing business as Shaffer's Auto and Diesel Repair. The truck was supposedly fixed, and Johnson paid the bill. The truck continued to leak oil and water. Johnson returned the truck to Shaffer, who again claimed to have fixed the problem. Johnson paid the second bill. The problems with the truck continued, however, so Johnson returned the truck and trailer a third time. Shaffer gave a verbal estimate of $1,000 for the repairs, but he ultimately sent an invoice for $5,863.49. Johnson offered to settle for $2,480, the amount of the initial estimate ($1,000), plus the costs of parts and shipping. Shaffer refused the offer and would not return Johnson's truck or trailer until full payment was made. Shaffer also charged Johnson a storage fee of $50 a day and 18 percent interest on the $5,863.49.

Johnson Construction filed a suit against Shaffer alleging unfair trade practices. The trial court determined that Shaffer had acted deceptively and wrongfully in maintaining possession of the trailer, on which no work had been performed. The trial court awarded Johnson $3,500 in general damages, plus $750 in attorneys' fees. Shaffer was awarded the initial estimate of $1,000 and appealed.

IN THE LANGUAGE OF THE COURT
LOLLEY, J. [Judge]

* * * *

* * * At the outset, we point out that Mr. Johnson maintained he had a verbal agreement with Bubba Shaffer, the owner of Shaffer's Auto Diesel and Repair, that the repairs to the truck would cost $1,000. Mr. Johnson also testified that he was not informed otherwise.

CASE 4.1 CONTINUED

The existence or nonexistence of a contract is a question of fact, and the finder of fact's determination may not be set aside unless it is clearly wrong.

* * * *

* * * At the trial of the matter, the trial court was presented with testimony from Mr. Johnson, Mr. Shaffer, and Michael Louton, a mechanic employed by Shaffer. * * * The trial court did not believe Mr. Johnson was informed of the cost for the additional work.

* * * We cannot say that the trial court was clearly wrong in its determination. * * * The trial court viewed Mr. Shaffer's testimony on the issue as "disingenuous" and we cannot see where that was an error.

As for the amount that Shaffer contends is due for storage, had it invoiced Mr. Johnson the amount of the original estimate in the first place, there would have been no need to store the truck or trailer. * * * We cannot see how Shaffer would be entitled to any payment for storage when it failed to return the truck and trailer where an offer of payment for the agreed upon price had been conveyed.

* * * *

* * * So considering, we see no error in the trial court's characterization of Shaffer's actions with the trailer as holding "hostage in an effort to force payment for unauthorized repairs." * * * Shaffer had no legal right to retain possession of the trailer * * * . *Thus, the trial court did not err in its determination that Shaffer's retention of Johnson Construction's trailer [for four years!] was a deceptive conversion of the trailer.* [Emphasis added.]

DECISION AND REMEDY *The state appellate court affirmed the judgment of the trial court in favor of Johnson Construction Company. It affirmed the award of $3,500, plus $750 in attorneys' fees, as well as Shaffer's original award of $1,000.*

WHAT IF THE FACTS WERE DIFFERENT? *Suppose that Shaffer had invoiced Johnson for only $1,500. Would the outcome have been different?*

THE ETHICAL DIMENSION *Would it have been ethical for Shaffer's mechanic to lie to support his employer's case? Discuss.*

ETHICS AND PRIVATE CODE OF ETHICS Most companies attempt to link ethics and law through the creation of internal codes of ethics. Company codes are not law. Instead, they are rules that the company sets forth that it can also enforce (by terminating an employee who does not follow them, for instance). Codes of conduct typically outline the company's policies on particular issues and indicate how employees are expected to act.

▶ **Example 4.2** Google's code of conduct starts with the motto "Don't be evil." The code then makes general statements about how Google promotes integrity, mutual respect, and the highest standard of ethical business conduct. Google's code also provides specific rules on a number of issues, such as privacy, drugs and alcohol, conflicts of interest, co-worker relationships, and confidentiality—it even has a dog policy. The company takes a stand against employment discrimination that goes further than the law requires. It prohibits discrimination based on sexual orientation, gender identity or expression, and veteran status. ◀

Numerous industries have also developed their own codes of ethics. The American Institute of Certified Public Accountants (AICPA) has a comprehensive Code of Professional Conduct for the ethical practicing of accounting. The American Bar Association has model rules of professional conduct for attorneys, and the American Nurses Association has a code of ethics that applies to nurses. These codes can give guidance to decision makers facing ethical questions. Violation of a code may result in discipline of an employee or sanctions against a company from the industry organization. Remember, though, that these internal codes are not laws, so their effectiveness is determined by the commitment of the industry or company leadership to enforcing the codes.

ETHICAL UNCERTAINTY Ethics can be a difficult subject for corporate officers to fully understand. Because it is often highly subjective and subject to change over time without any sort of formal process, ethics is less certain than law.

The law can also be uncertain, however, and contains numerous "gray areas" that make it difficult to predict with certainty how a court will apply a given law to a particular action. Uncertainty can make decision making difficult, especially when a law requires a court to determine what is "foreseeable" or "reasonable" in a particular situation. Because a business has no way of predicting how a specific court will decide these issues, decision makers need to proceed with caution and evaluate an action and its consequences from an ethical perspective.

Ethics is based more on judgment than research. A company that can show it acted ethically, responsibly, and in good faith (honestly) has a better chance of succeeding in a dispute than one that cannot make such a showing.

In the following case, the court concluded that the employer's response to complaints about a hostile work environment was so inadequate that it not only violated the employee's rights but was unethical enough to warrant a large penalty against the corporation. Notice the court's language about the company's behavior.

CASE 4.2

May v. Chrysler Group, LLC

United States Court of Appeals, Seventh Circuit, 692 F.3d 734 (2012).

COMPANY PROFILE Chrysler Group, LLC, is the parent company of Fiat, Chrysler, Dodge, Jeep, and several other automobile manufacturers. (An LLC is a limited liability company.) Chrysler Group was created in 2009 to manage the consolidation of the different automobile companies during the economic downturn of the late 2000s. The company employs more than 64,000 people at thirty-two manufacturing facilities. Its 2013 revenue was estimated to be $60 billion.

BACKGROUND AND FACTS Between 2002 and 2005, Otto May, Jr., a pipefitter at Chrysler's Belvedere Assembly Plant, was the target of more than fifty racist, homophobic, and anti-Semitic messages and graffiti. He found six death-threat notes in his toolbox, his bike and car tires were punctured, and someone poured sugar into the gas tank of his car twice. At one point, a dead bird wrapped in toilet paper to look like a member of the Ku Klux Klan (including the white pointed hat) was left at his work station. May complained to Chrysler. The director of human resources met with May, documented the complaints, and initiated an internal investigation. As part of that investigation, records were checked to determine who was in the building when the incidents occurred, and the handwriting on the notes and graffiti was analyzed.

The director held two meetings with about sixty employees (out of more than a thousand plant employees). At the meetings, the director reminded the workers that harassment was not acceptable. The harassers were never caught, and the harassment continued after the meetings. Chrysler's headquarters became involved only after the Anti-Defamation League wrote a letter on May's behalf. May sued Chrysler for hostile work environment harassment and was awarded $709,000 in compensatory damages and $3.5 million in punitive damages (or punishment). The judge overturned the punitive damages award, and May appealed.

IN THE LANGUAGE OF THE COURT
TINDER, Circuit Judge.

* * * *

May can recover punitive damages only if he presented sufficient evidence for the jury to conclude that Chrysler acted with "malice or with reckless indifference to [his] federally protected rights." * * * *No evidence of "egregious" or "outrageous" conduct by the employer is required, although, of course, such a showing could support a conclusion that the employer acted with the requisite mental state.* [Emphasis added.]

We have already explained why it was appropriate for Chrysler to be held responsible for the hostile work environment. Its response was shockingly thin as measured against the gravity of May's harassment.

CASE 4.2 CONTINUED

* * * *

* * *[A]lthough the district court did not rule on whether the jury's $3.5 million award of punitive damages is "grossly excessive" and therefore violates due process, * * * we asked the parties for supplemental briefing so that we might consider that question now. After reviewing the parties' submissions, we are convinced that the punitive damage award does not violate the Constitution and should therefore be reinstated in full. The award is substantial—five times the original compensatory damages and eleven times the remitted amount—but Chrysler's long-term recklessness in the face of repeated threats of violence against May and his family is sufficiently reprehensible [shameful] to support it.

DECISION AND REMEDY *The federal appellate court reinstated the punitive damages award based on the reprehensible and unethical nature of Chrysler's failure to sufficiently address the harassment.*

THE ETHICAL DIMENSION *Does an organization have an ethical obligation to secure a safe and harassment-free workplace for its employees? Why or why not? Discuss.*

MANAGERIAL IMPLICATIONS *It is clear from this opinion that employers have a significant duty to take complaints of harassment seriously. Even if Chrysler believed that May was harassing himself (perhaps in order to obtain compensation from the company), as the company implied at the trial, it had an obligation to do a serious investigation, to set up clear policies and procedures, and to follow those procedures when a complaint was made.*

SECTION 2

BUSINESS ETHICS AND SOCIAL MEDIA

Although most young people think of social media—Facebook, Twitter, Pinterest, Google+, MySpace, LinkedIn, and the like—as simply ways to communicate rapidly, businesses face ethical issues with respect to these same social media platforms.

Hiring Procedures

In the past, to learn about a prospective employee, the employer would ask the candidate's former employers for references. Today, employers are likely to also conduct Internet searches to discover what job candidates have posted on their Facebook pages, blogs, and tweets. Nevertheless, many people believe that judging a job candidate based on what she or he does outside the work environment is unethical.

Sometimes, too, the opposite situation occurs, and job candidates are rejected because they *do not* participate in any social media. Given that the vast majority of younger people do use social media, some employers have decided that the failure to do so raises a red flag. Some consider this employer behavior to be unethical as well.

The Use of Social Media to Discuss Work-Related Issues

Because so many Americans use social media many times a day, they often discuss work-related issues there. Numerous companies have provided strict guidelines about what is appropriate and inappropriate when making posts at one's own or others' social media accounts. A number of companies have fired employees for such activities as criticizing other employees or managers through social media outlets. Until recently, such disciplinary measures were considered ethical and legal.

Today, in contrast, a ruling by the National Labor Relations Board (NLRB—the federal agency that investigates unfair labor practices) has changed the legality of such actions. ▶ **Example 4.3** Costco's social media policy specified that its employees should not make statements that would damage the company, harm another person's reputation, or violate the company's policies. Employees who violated these rules were subject to discipline and could be fired.

In 2012, the NLRB ruled that Costco's social media policy violated federal labor law, which protects employees' right to engage in "concerted activities." Employees can freely associate with each other and have conversations about common workplace issues without employer interference. This right extends to social media posts. Therefore, Costco cannot broadly prohibit its employees from criticizing the company or co-workers, supervisors, or managers via social media. ◀

Ethics in Reverse

While most of the discussion in this chapter involves business ethics, employee ethics is also an important issue. For instance, is it ethical for employees to make negative posts in social media about other employees or, more commonly, about managers? After all, negative comments about managers reflect badly on those managers, who often are reluctant to respond via social media to such criticism. Disgruntled employees may exaggerate the negative qualities of managers whom they do not like.

Some may consider the latest decision by the National Labor Relations Board outlined in *Example 4.3* above to be too lenient toward employees and too stringent toward management. There is likely to be an ongoing debate about how to balance employees' right to free expression against employers' right to prevent inaccurate negative statements being spread across the Internet.

SECTION 3

ETHICAL PRINCIPLES AND PHILOSOPHIES

As Dean Krehmeyer, executive director of the Business Roundtable's Institute for Corporate Ethics, once said, "Evidence strongly suggests being ethical—doing the right thing—pays." Instilling ethical business decision making into the fabric of a business organization is no small task, even if ethics "pays." How do business decision makers decide whether a given action is the "right" one for their firms? What ethical standards should be applied?

Broadly speaking, **ethical reasoning**—the application of morals and ethics to a situation—applies to businesses just as it does to individuals. As businesses make decisions, they must analyze the alternatives in a variety of ways, one of which is the ethical implications.

Generally, the study of ethics is divided into two major categories—duty-based ethics and outcome-based ethics. **Duty-based ethics** is rooted in the idea that every person has certain duties to others, including both humans and the planet. Those duties may be derived from religious principles or from other philosophical reasoning. **Outcome-based ethics** focuses on the impacts of a decision on society or on key *stakeholders.*

Duty-Based Ethics

Duty-based ethics focuses on the obligations of the corporation. It deals with standards for behavior that traditionally were derived from revealed truths, religious authorities, or philosophical reasoning. These standards involve concepts of right and wrong, and duties owed and rights to be protected.

Corporations today often describe these values or duties in their mission statements or strategic plans. Some companies base their statements on a nonreligious rationale, but others still derive their values from religious doctrine (such as the statements of Chick-fil-A, discussed in the introduction to this chapter).

RELIGIOUS ETHICAL PRINCIPLES Nearly every religion has principles or beliefs about how one should treat others. In the Judeo-Christian tradition, which is the dominant religious tradition in the United States, the Ten Commandments of the Old Testament establish these fundamental rules for moral action. The principles of the Muslim faith are set out in the Qur'an, and Hindus find their principles in the four Vedas.

Religious rules generally are absolute with respect to the behavior of their adherents. ▶ **Example 4.4** The commandment "Thou shalt not steal" is an absolute mandate for a person who believes that the Ten Commandments reflect revealed truth. Even a benevolent motive for stealing (such as Robin Hood's) cannot justify the act because the act itself is inherently immoral and thus wrong. ◀

For businesses, religious principles can be a unifying force for employees or a rallying point to increase employee motivation. They can also be problematic, however, because different owners, suppliers, employees, and customers may all have different religious backgrounds. As the introduction to this chapter illustrated, taking an action based on religious principles, especially when those principles address socially or politically controversial topics, can lead to negative publicity and even to protests or boycotts.

PRINCIPLES OF RIGHTS Another view of duty-based ethics focuses on basic rights. The principle that human beings have certain fundamental rights (to life, freedom, and the pursuit of happiness, for example) is deeply embedded in Western culture. As discussed in Chapter 1, the natural law tradition embraces the concept that certain actions (such as killing another person) are morally wrong because they are contrary to nature (the natural desire to continue living).

Those who adhere to this **principle of rights,** or "rights theory," believe that a key factor in determining whether a business decision is ethical is how that decision affects the rights of others. These others include the firm's owners, its employees, the consumers of its products or services, its suppliers, the community in which it does business, and society as a whole.

Conflicting Rights. A potential dilemma for those who support rights theory, however, is that they may disagree on which rights are most important. When considering all those affected by a business decision to downsize a firm, for example, how much weight should be given to employees relative to shareholders? Which employees should be laid off first—those with the highest salaries or those who have worked there for less time (and have less seniority)? How should the firm weigh the rights of customers relative to the community, or employees relative to society as a whole?

Resolving Conflicts. In general, rights theorists believe that whichever right is stronger in a particular circumstance takes precedence. ▶ **Example 4.5** Murray Chemical Corporation has to decide whether to keep a chemical plant in Utah open, thereby saving the jobs of a hundred and fifty workers, or shut it down. Closing the plant will avoid contaminating a river with pollutants that would endanger the health of tens of thousands of people. In this situation, a rights theorist can easily choose which group to favor because the value of the right to health and well-being is obviously stronger than the basic right to work. (Not all choices are so clear-cut, however.) ◀

KANTIAN ETHICAL PRINCIPLES Duty-based ethical standards may also be derived solely from philosophical reasoning. The German philosopher Immanuel Kant (1724–1804) identified some general guiding principles for moral behavior based on what he thought to be the fundamental nature of human beings. Kant believed that human beings are qualitatively different from other physical objects and are endowed with moral integrity and the capacity to reason and conduct their affairs rationally.

People Are Not a Means to an End. Based on this view of human beings, Kant said that when people are treated merely as a means to an end, they are being treated as the equivalent of objects and are being denied their basic humanity. For instance, a manager who treats subordinates as mere profit-making tools is less likely to retain motivated and loyal employees than a manager who respects his or her employees. Management research has shown that employees who feel empowered to share their thoughts, opinions, and solutions to problems are happier and more productive.

Categorical Imperative. When a business makes unethical decisions, it often rationalizes its action by saying that the company is "just one small part" of the problem or that its decision would have "only a small impact." A central theme in Kantian ethics is that individuals should evaluate their actions in light of the consequences that would follow if everyone in society acted in the same way. This **categorical imperative** can be applied to any action.

▶ **Example 4.6** CHS Fertilizer is deciding whether to invest in expensive equipment that will decrease profits but will also reduce pollution from its factories. If CHS has adopted Kant's categorical imperative, the decision makers will consider the consequences if every company invested in the equipment (or if no company did so). If the result would make the world a better place (less polluted), CHS's decision would be clear. ◀

Outcome-Based Ethics: Utilitarianism

In contrast to duty-based ethics, outcome-based ethics focuses on the consequences of an action, not on the nature of the action itself or on any set of preestablished moral values or religious beliefs. Outcome-based ethics looks at the impacts of a decision in an attempt to maximize benefits and minimize harms. The premier philosophical theory for outcome-based decision making is **utilitarianism,** a philosophical theory developed by Jeremy Bentham (1748–1832) and modified by John Stuart Mill (1806–1873)—both British philosophers.

"The greatest good for the greatest number" is a paraphrase of the major premise of the utilitarian approach to ethics.

COST-BENEFIT ANALYSIS Under a utilitarian model of ethics, an action is morally correct, or "right," when, among the people it affects, it produces the greatest amount of good for the greatest number or creates the least amount of harm for the fewest people. When an action affects the majority adversely, it is morally wrong. Applying the utilitarian theory thus requires the following steps:

1. A determination of which individuals will be affected by the action in question.
2. A **cost-benefit analysis,** which involves an assessment of the negative and positive effects of alternative actions on these individuals.
3. A choice among alternative actions that will produce maximum societal utility (the greatest positive net benefits for the greatest number of individuals).

Thus, if expanding a factory would provide hundreds of jobs but generate pollution that could endanger the lives of thousands of people, a utilitarian analysis would find that saving the lives of thousands creates greater good than providing jobs for hundreds.

PROBLEMS WITH THE UTILITARIAN APPROACH There are problems with a strict utilitarian analysis. In some situations, an action that produces the greatest good for the most people may not seem to be the most ethical. ▶ **Example 4.7** Phazim Company is producing a drug that will cure a disease in 85 percent of patients, but the other 15 percent will experience agonizing side effects and a horrible, painful death. A quick utilitarian analysis would suggest that the drug should be produced and marketed because the majority of patients will benefit. Many people, however, have significant concerns about manufacturing a drug that will cause such harm to anyone. ◀

Corporate Social Responsibility

In pairing duty-based concepts with outcome-based concepts, strategists and theorists developed the idea of the corporate citizen. **Corporate social responsibility (CSR)** combines a commitment to good citizenship with a commitment to making ethical decisions, improving society, and minimizing environmental impact.

CSR is a relatively new concept in the history of business, but a concept that becomes more important every year. Although CSR is not imposed on corporations by law, it does involve a commitment to self-regulation in a way that attends to the text and intent of the law, ethical norms, and global standards. A survey of U.S. executives undertaken by the Boston College Center for Corporate Citizenship found that more than 70 percent of those polled agreed that corporate citizenship must be treated as a priority. More than 60 percent said that good corporate citizenship added to their companies' profits.

CSR can be an incredibly successful strategy for companies, but corporate decision makers must not lose track of the two descriptors in the title: *corporate* and *social*. The company must link the responsibility of citizenship with the strategy and key principles of the business. Incorporating both the social and the corporate components of CSR and making ethical decisions can help companies grow and prosper.

THE SOCIAL ASPECTS OF CSR First, the social aspect requires that corporations demonstrate that they are promoting goals that society deems worthwhile and are moving toward solutions to social problems. Because business controls so much of the wealth and power of this country, business, in turn, has a responsibility to society to use that wealth and power in socially beneficial ways. Companies may be judged on how much they donate to social causes, as well as how they conduct their operations with respect to employment discrimination, human rights, environmental concerns, and similar issues.

Some corporations publish annual social responsibility reports, which may also be called corporate sustainability (referring to the capacity to endure) or citizenship reports. ▶ **Example 4.8** The Hitachi Group has Web pages dedicated to its CSR initiatives and includes reports outlining its environmental strategies, its human rights policies, and its commitment to diversity. The software company Symantec Corporation issues corporate responsibility reports to demonstrate its focus on critical environmental, social, and governance issues. In its 2012 report, Symantec pointed out that 88 percent of facilities it owns or leases on a long-term basis are certified as environmentally friendly by the LEED program. LEED stands for Leadership in Energy and Environmental Design. Certification requires the achievement of high standards for energy efficiency, material usage in construction, and other environmental qualities. ◀

THE CORPORATE ASPECTS OF CSR Arguably, any socially responsible activity will benefit a corporation. The corporation may see an increase in goodwill from the local community for creating a park. Corporations may see increases in sales if they are viewed as good citizens.

At times, the benefit may not be immediate. Constructing a new plant that meets the high LEED standards may cost more initially. Nevertheless, over the life of the building, the savings in maintenance and utilities may more than make up for the extra cost of construction.

Surveys of college students about to enter the job market confirm that young people are looking for socially responsible employers. Socially responsible activities may cost a corporation now, but may lead to more impressive, and more committed employees. Corporations that engage in meaningful social activities retain workers longer, particularly younger ones.

Corporate responsibility is most successful when a company undertakes activities that are significant and related to its business operations. ▶ **Example 4.9** In 2012, the Walt Disney Company announced that in an effort to curb childhood obesity, it was issuing strict nutritional standards for all products advertised through its media outlets. In addition to focusing on a major social issue, the initiative was intended to clarify Disney's mission and values, as well as enhance its reputation as a trustworthy, family-friendly company. The initiative has been praised by commentators and politicians and is expected to increase Disney's revenue in the long term. ◀

STAKEHOLDERS One view of CSR stresses that corporations have a duty not just to shareholders, but also to other groups affected by corporate decisions—called **stakeholders.** The rationale for this "stakeholder view" is that, in some circumstances, one or more of these other groups may have a greater stake in company decisions than the shareholders do.

Under this approach, a corporation considers the impact of its decisions on its employees, customers, creditors, suppliers, and the community in which it operates. Stakeholders could also include advocacy groups such as environmental groups and animal rights groups. To avoid making a decision that may be perceived as unethical and result in negative publicity or protests, a corporation should consider the impact of its decision on the stakeholders. The most difficult aspect of the stakeholder analysis is determining which group's interests should receive greater weight if the interests conflict.

For instance, during the last few years, layoffs numbered in the millions. Nonetheless, some corporations succeeded in reducing labor costs without layoffs. To avoid slashing their workforces, these employers turned to alternatives such as (1) four-day workweeks, (2) unpaid vacations and voluntary furloughs, (3) wage freezes, (4) pension cuts, and (5) flexible work schedules. Some companies asked their workers to accept wage cuts to prevent layoffs, and the workers agreed. Companies finding alternatives to layoffs included Dell (extended unpaid holidays), Cisco Systems (four-day end-of-year shutdowns), Motorola (salary cuts), and Honda (voluntary unpaid vacation time).

SECTION 4

MAKING ETHICAL BUSINESS DECISIONS

Even if officers, directors, and others in a company want to make ethical decisions, it is not always clear what is ethical in a given situation. Thinking beyond things that are easily measured, such as profits, can be challenging. Although profit projections are not always accurate, they are more objective than considering the personal impacts of decisions on employees, shareholders, customers, and even the community. But this subjective component to decision making potentially has a great influence on a company's profits.

Companies once considered leaders in their industry, such as Enron and the worldwide accounting firm Arthur Andersen, were brought down by the unethical behavior of a few. A two-hundred-year-old British investment banking firm, Barings Bank, was destroyed by the actions of one employee and a few of his friends. Clearly, ensuring that all employees get on the ethical business decision-making "bandwagon" is crucial in today's fast-paced world.

Individuals entering the global corporate community, even in entry-level positions, must be prepared to make hard decisions. Sometimes, there is no "good" answer to the questions that arise. Therefore, it is important to have tools to help in the decision-making process and a framework for organizing those tools. Business decisions can be complex and may involve legal concerns, financial questions, possibly health and safety concerns, and ethical components.

A Systematic Approach

Organizing the ethical concerns and issues and approaching them systematically can help a businessperson eliminate various alternatives and identify the strengths and weaknesses of the remaining alternatives. Ethics consultant Leonard H. Bucklin of Corporate-Ethics.US™ has devised a procedure that he calls Business Process Pragmatism™. It involves five steps:

Step 1: Inquiry. First, the decision maker must understand the problem. To do this, one must identify the parties involved (the stakeholders) and collect the relevant facts. Once the ethical problem or problems are clarified, the decision maker lists any relevant legal and ethical principles that will guide the decision.

Step 2: Discussion. In this step, the decision maker lists possible actions. The ultimate goals for the decision are determined, and each option is evaluated using the laws and ethical principles listed in Step 1.

Step 3: Decision. In this step, those participating in the decision making work together to craft a consensus decision or consensus plan of action for the corporation.

Step 4: Justification. In this step, the decision maker articulates the reasons for the proposed action or series of actions. Generally these reasons should come from the analysis done in Step 3. This step essentially results in documentation to be shared with stakeholders explaining why the proposal is an ethical solution to the problem.

Step 5: Evaluation. This final step occurs once the decision has been made and implemented. The solution should be analyzed to determine if it was effective. The results of this evaluation may be used in making future decisions.

The Importance of Ethical Leadership

Talking about ethical business decision making is meaningless if management does not set standards. Furthermore, managers must apply the same standards to themselves as they do to the company's employees.

ATTITUDE OF TOP MANAGEMENT One of the most important ways to create and maintain an ethical workplace is for top management to demonstrate its commitment to ethical decision making. A manager who is not totally committed to an ethical workplace rarely succeeds in creating one. Management's behavior, more than anything else, sets the ethical tone of a firm. Employees take their cues from management. ▶ **Example 4.10** Devon, a BioTek employee, observes his manager cheating on her expense account. Later, when Devon is promoted to a managerial position, he "pads" his expense account as well, knowing that he is unlikely to face sanctions for doing so. ◀

Managers who set unrealistic production or sales goals increase the probability that employees will act unethically. If a sales quota can be met only through high-pressure, unethical sales tactics, employees will try to act "in the best interest of the company" and will continue to behave unethically.

A manager who looks the other way when she or he knows about an employee's unethical behavior also sets an example—one indicating that ethical transgressions will be accepted. Managers have found that discharging even one employee for ethical reasons has a tremendous impact as a deterrent to unethical behavior in the workplace. This is true even if the company has a written code of ethics. If management does not enforce the company code, the code is essentially nonexistent.

The following case demonstrates the types of situations that can occur when management demonstrates a lack of concern about ethics.

CASE ANALYSIS

Case 4.3 Moseley v. Pepco Energy Services, Inc.

United States District Court, District of New Jersey, 2011 WL 1584166 (2011).

IN THE LANGUAGE OF THE COURT

Joseph H. *RODRIGUEZ*, District Judge.

* * * Plaintiff Moseley is an employee of Defendant Pepco Energy Services, Inc. ("PES"). He has been employed by PES or its corporate predecessors for over twenty-five years. PES, a subsidiary of Defendant Pepco Holdings, Inc. ("PHI"), provides deregulated energy and energy-related services for residential, small business, and large commercial customers.

* * * *

In 1998, Thomas Herzog held the position of Vice President of CTS. * * * In or around 2002, CTS merged with Potomic Electric Power Company, Inc., and each company became a subsidiary of PHI. Following the merger, according to Plaintiff, he continued to work for PHI, still as

CASE 4.3 CONTINUED

Maintenance Manager at Midtown Thermal, until December 31, 2009.

* * * *

Following the 2002 merger with PHI, employees were required to complete an annual ethics survey. By March of 2007, Plaintiff and two co-workers had discussed their respective observations of Herzog's conduct, which they deemed questionable and possibly unethical. Specifically, they felt that Herzog improperly used company assets and improperly hired immediate family members and friends who did not appear on the payroll. The three decided to disclose this information on PHI's annual "Ethics Survey."

The three planned to reveal that Herzog employed his daughter, Laurie, as his secretary in the summer of 2005 and the beginning of 2006 without posting the position first and in violation of PHI's anti-nepotism policy.

* * * *

Next, Herzog hired his girlfriend's daughter as his secretary after his daughter had gone back to school. Plaintiff believed this was in violation of Company policy because the position again was not posted. Herzog also hired his son as a project manager, again through a third party independent contractor, Walter Ratai. Plaintiff thought this was wrong because (1) Herzog circumvented the Company's hiring process, (2) it violated Company policy, and (3) Herzog's son was being paid $75.00/hr, which was more than Plaintiff was making. * * * In addition, Plaintiff had learned that Herzog was improperly using the Company's Eagles' tickets for personal use. Finally, Herzog had leased a new SUV with Company funds, but which was not approved by the Company.

* * * *

[After the surveys were completed, an] investigation ensued. Following the investigation, effective on or about May 10, 2007, Herzog was escorted out of the building. * * * On March 8, 2008, Plaintiff received his annual performance evaluation * * * ; for the first time in twenty-three years, Plaintiff's performance review was negative. Plaintiff feels that this negative performance review was a further act of retaliation for his disclosure of Herzog's conduct.

* * * *

On or about June 11, 2008 the Plant/Operations Manager position was posted * * * . Plaintiff applied for the position, but it was offered to [another person]. Plaintiff alleges that he "was not promoted to the position of Plant/Operations Manager despite his experience performing the job for the previous two and a half years, qualifications for same and seniority, as a direct and proximate result of his prior complaints and/or disclosures regarding the Herzog illegal conduct and activities."

* * * *

The New Jersey Legislature enacted the Conscientious Employee Protection Act (CEPA) to "protect and encourage employees to report illegal or unethical workplace activities." * * * CEPA prohibits a New Jersey employer from taking "retaliatory action" against an employee who objects to "any activity, policy or practice which the employee reasonably believes" is in violation of applicable law. * * * "To prevail on a claim under this provision, a plaintiff must establish that: (1) he reasonably believed that [the complained-of] conduct was violating a law or rule or regulation promulgated pursuant to law; (2) he objected to the conduct; (3) an adverse employment action was taken against him; and (4) a causal connection exists between the whistleblowing activity and the adverse employment action.

* * * *

The first element of the prima facie case [a case sufficient to be sent to the jury] under CEPA is that the Plaintiff reasonably believed that the complained-of conduct (1) was violating a "law, rule, or regulation promulgated pursuant to law, including any violation involving deception of, or misrepresentation to, any shareholder, investor, client, patient, customer, employee, former employee, retiree or pensioner of the employer or any governmental entity"; or "(2) is fraudulent or criminal, including any activity, policy or practice of deception or misrepresentation which the employee reasonably believes may defraud any shareholder, investor, client, patient, customer, employee, former employee, retiree or pensioner of the employer or any governmental entity."

Although Defendants have argued that Plaintiff merely disclosed a violation of Company policy, Moseley has testified that in March 2007, he reported what he believed to be "unethical conduct, misappropriation of company funds, and theft" by his direct supervisor. * * * *Moreover, a plaintiff need not demonstrate that there was a violation of the law or fraud, but instead that he "reasonably believed" that to be the case.* The facts in this case support an objectively reasonable belief that a violation of law or fraudulent conduct was being committed by Plaintiff's supervisor. [Emphasis added.]

Regarding the causal connection between Plaintiff's whistleblowing activity and the negative adverse employment actions taken against him, Plaintiff stresses that he was employed by the Defendants for twenty-five years without a negative employment evaluation or any form of discipline until immediately after he disclosed the wrongful conduct of his supervisor. Not only did Plaintiff then receive a negative performance evaluation, but the posted position of Plant Manager was given to [another], despite [the other's] alleged past negative history and despite that Plaintiff asserts he had been acting in that job for over two years. Plaintiff contends that this is sufficient evidence of pretext.

The Court is unable to find as a matter of law that Defendants' inferences

CASE 4.3 CONTINUED

prevail or that a jury could not reasonably adopt a contrary inference of retaliation. There are questions of fact as to how much the individuals responsible for Plaintiff's negative performance evaluations knew about Plaintiff's complaints. "[A] finding of the required causal connection may be based solely on circumstantial evidence that the person ultimately responsible for an adverse employment action was aware of an employee's whistle-blowing activity." Because jurors may infer a causal connection from the surrounding circumstances, as well as temporal proximity, the Court will not grant summary judgment. [Emphasis added.]

* * * *

* * * Defendants' motion for summary judgment is hereby DENIED.

LEGAL REASONING QUESTIONS

1. Using duty-based ethical principles, what facts or circumstances in this case would lead Moseley to disclose Herzog's behavior?
2. Using outcome-based ethical principles, what issues would Moseley have to analyze in making the decision to report Herzog's behavior? What would be the risks to Moseley? The benefits?
3. Under the Business Process Pragmatism™ steps, what alternatives might Moseley have had in this situation?
4. Regardless of who wins this case at trial, in performing Step 5 (Evaluation) of the Business Process Pragmatism™ procedure, what changes should the company take with regard to the complaint process?

BEHAVIOR OF OWNERS AND MANAGERS Business owners and managers sometimes take more active roles in fostering unethical and illegal conduct. This may indicate to their co-owners, co-managers, employees, and others that unethical business behavior will be tolerated. Business owners' misbehavior can have negative consequences for themselves and their business. Not only can a court sanction the owners and managers, but it can also issue an injunction that prevents them from engaging in similar patterns of conduct in the future.

▶ **Example 4.11** Lawyer Samir Zia Chowhan posted a help-wanted ad on Craigslist seeking an "energetic woman" for the position of legal secretary. The ad stated that the position included secretarial and paralegal work, as well as "additional duties" for two lawyers in the firm. Applicants were asked to send pictures and describe their physical features.

When a woman applied for the job, Chowhan sent her an e-mail saying that "in addition to the legal work, you would be required to have sexual interaction with me and my partner, sometimes together sometimes separate." He also explained that she would need to perform sexual acts at the job interview so that he and his partner could determine whether she would be able to handle these duties. The woman filed a complaint with the Illinois Bar Association, which suspended Chowhan's law license for a year for making false statements about the ad. Because the bar association's ethics rules prohibited attorneys from having sex with their clients, but not with potential employees, Chowhan could only be disciplined for lying. ◀

THE SARBANES-OXLEY ACT The Sarbanes-Oxley Act of 2002[2] requires companies to set up confidential systems so that employees and others can "raise red flags" about suspected illegal or unethical auditing and accounting practices. (The Sarbanes-Oxley Act covers additional issues, and excerpts from and explanatory comments on this important law appear in Appendix D of this text.)

Some companies have implemented online reporting systems to accomplish this goal. In one such system, employees can click on an icon on their computers that anonymously links them with NAVEX Global, an organization based in Oregon. Through NAVEX, employees can report suspicious accounting practices, sexual harassment, and other possibly unethical behavior. NAVEX, in turn, alerts management personnel or the audit committee at the designated company to the possible problem. Those who have used the system say that it is less inhibiting than calling a company's toll-free number.

SECTION 5
GLOBAL BUSINESS ETHICS

Just as different religions have different moral codes, different countries, regions and even states have different ethical expectations and priorities. Some of

2. 15 U.S.C. Sections 7201 *et seq.*

these differences are based in religious values, whereas others are cultural in nature. As a result of the various cultures and religions throughout the world, making ethical business decisions can be even more difficult.

For instance, in certain countries the consumption of alcohol and specific foods is forbidden for religious reasons. It would be considered unethical for a U.S. business to build a factory to produce alcohol and employ local workers in a culture in which alcohol is forbidden.

International transactions often involve issues related to employment and financing. Congress has addressed some of these issues, not eliminating the ethical components but clarifying some of the conflicts between the ethics of the United States and the ethics of other nations. For example, the Civil Rights Act of 1964 and the Foreign Corrupt Practices Act (discussed in more detail below) have clarified the U.S. ethical position on employment issues and bribery in foreign nations. (Other nations, including Mexico, have also enacted laws that prohibit bribery, as discussed in this chapter's *Insight into the Global Environment* feature on the following page.)

Monitoring the Employment Practices of Foreign Suppliers

Many businesses contract with companies in developing nations to produce goods, such as shoes and clothing, because the wage rates in those nations are significantly lower than those in the United States. Yet what if a foreign company hires women and children at below-minimum-wage rates, for example, or requires its employees to work long hours in a workplace full of health hazards? What if the company's supervisors routinely engage in workplace conduct that is offensive to women? What if plants located abroad routinely violate labor and environmental standards?

▶ **Example 4.12** Apple, Inc., owns Pegatron Corporation, a subsidiary company based in China, which supplies parts for iPads and other Apple products. In December 2011, there was an explosion at a Pegatron factory in Shanghai. Dozens of employees were injured when aluminum dust from polishing cases for iPads caught fire and caused the explosion. Allegations surfaced that the conditions at the factory violated labor and environmental standards. California-based Apple did not comment on the issue. ◀

Given today's global communications network, few companies can assume that their actions in other nations will go unnoticed by "corporate watch" groups that discover and publicize unethical corporate behavior. As a result, U.S. businesses today usually take steps to avoid such adverse publicity—either by refusing to deal with certain suppliers or by arranging to monitor their suppliers' workplaces to make sure that the employees are not being mistreated.

The Foreign Corrupt Practices Act

Another ethical problem in international business dealings has to do with the legitimacy of certain side payments to government officials. In the United States, the majority of contracts are formed within the private sector. In many foreign countries, however, government officials make the decisions on most major construction and manufacturing contracts because of extensive government regulation and control over trade and industry.

Side payments to government officials in exchange for favorable business contracts are not unusual in such countries, nor are they considered to be unethical. In the past, U.S. corporations doing business in these nations largely followed the dictum "When in Rome, do as the Romans do."

In the 1970s, however, the U.S. media uncovered a number of business scandals involving large side payments by U.S. corporations to foreign representatives for the purpose of securing advantageous international trade contracts. In response to this unethical behavior, in 1977 Congress passed the Foreign Corrupt Practices Act[3] (FCPA), which prohibits U.S. businesspersons from bribing foreign officials to secure beneficial contracts.

PROHIBITION AGAINST THE BRIBERY OF FOREIGN OFFICIALS The first part of the FCPA applies to all U.S. companies and their directors, officers, shareholders, employees, and agents. This part prohibits the bribery of most officials of foreign governments if the purpose of the payment is to motivate the official to act in his or her official capacity to provide business opportunities.

The FCPA does not prohibit payment of substantial sums to minor officials whose duties are ministerial. A ministerial action is a routine activity such as the processing of paperwork with little or no discretion involved in the action. These payments are often referred to as "grease," or facilitating payments. They are meant to accelerate the performance of administrative services that might otherwise be carried out at a slow pace. Thus, for instance, if a firm makes a payment to a minor official to speed up an import licensing process, the firm has not violated the FCPA.

3. 15 U.S.C. Sections 78dd-1 *et seq.*

INSIGHT INTO THE GLOBAL ENVIRONMENT

Bribery and the Foreign Corrupt Practices Act

Many countries have followed in the footsteps of the United States by passing their own anticorruption laws, some of which are similar to our Foreign Corrupt Practices Act. Nevertheless, some countries are still not diligent in weeding out corruption—of government officials, for instance.

Mexico Faces a Corruption Issue

Recently, Mexico passed an anticorruption law that prevents hospital administrators from approving contracts. Medical device supplier Orthofix International NV, based in Texas, faced a problem after passage of the new law. It wanted to continue providing bone-repair products to Mexico. It therefore bribed regional government officials instead of hospital administrators. Over several years, Orthofix paid more than $300,000 in bribes to Mexican officials to retain government health-care contracts. Employees at Orthofix called these bribes "chocolates." The contracts generated almost $8.7 million in revenues for the company.

The Bribing Process

Before the anticorruption law was enacted, Orthofix's Mexican subsidiary, Promeca, regularly offered cash and gifts, such as vacation packages, televisions, and laptops, to hospital employees in order to secure sales contracts. These employees then submitted falsified receipts for imaginary expenses such as meals and new car tires. When the bribes became too large to hide in this manner, Promeca's employees falsely attributed the payments to promotional and training expenses. After the new law was passed, Mexico formed a special national committee to approve medical contracts. Promeca employees then simply bribed committee members to ensure that the company was awarded the contracts.

No Compliance Policy or Training to Prevent Violations

As it turned out, Orthofix did not provide any training in how to prevent violations of the Foreign Corrupt Practices Act or have a compliance policy in place in Mexico. Orthofix did create a code of ethics and antibribery training materials, but they were only distributed in English. When Orthofix managers found out about Promeca's overbudget expenses, they questioned the amounts, but initially took no further steps.

The U.S. Government Investigates

Sometime after Orthofix learned of the payments, it self-reported them to the U.S. Securities and Exchange Commission (SEC). After negotiations with the SEC, Orthofix agreed to terminate the Promeca executives who had engaged in the bribery and to end Promeca's operations. Orthofix required mandatory training for all employees and strengthened its auditing of company payments. In addition, the company paid more than $7 million in penalties.

LEGAL CRITICAL THINKING

INSIGHT INTO THE LEGAL ENVIRONMENT

Because managers are potentially responsible for all actions of their foreign subsidiaries whether or not they knew of the illegal conduct, what actions should Orthofix's upper management have taken before this corruption scandal came to light?

Generally, the act, as amended, permits payments to foreign officials if such payments are lawful within the foreign country. Payments to private foreign companies or other third parties are permissible—unless the U.S. firm knows that the payments will be passed on to a foreign government in violation of the FCPA. The U.S. Department of Justice also uses the FCPA to prosecute foreign companies suspected of bribing officials outside the United States.

ACCOUNTING REQUIREMENTS To prevent bribes from being concealed in the corporate financial records, the second part of the FCPA is directed toward accountants. All companies must keep detailed records that "accurately and fairly" reflect their financial activities. Their accounting systems must provide "reasonable assurance" that all transactions entered into by the companies are accounted for and legal. These requirements assist in detecting illegal bribes. The FCPA prohibits any person from making false statements to accountants or false entries in any record or account.

PENALTIES FOR VIOLATIONS The FCPA provides that business firms that violate the act may be fined up to $2 million. Individual officers or directors who violate the FCPA may be fined up to $100,000 (the fine cannot be paid by the company) and may be imprisoned for up to five years.

Reviewing: Business Ethics

James Stilton is the chief executive officer (CEO) of RightLiving, Inc., a company that buys life insurance policies at a discount from terminally ill persons and sells the policies to investors. RightLiving pays the terminally ill patients a percentage of the future death benefit (usually 65 percent) and then sells the policies to investors for 85 percent of the value of the future benefit. The patients receive the cash to use for medical and other expenses, the investors are "guaranteed" a positive return on their investment, and RightLiving profits on the difference between the purchase and sale prices. Stilton is aware that some sick patients might obtain insurance policies through fraud (by not revealing the illness on the insurance application). Insurance companies that discover this will cancel the policy and refuse to pay. Stilton believes that most of the policies he has purchased are legitimate, but he knows that some probably are not. Using the information presented in this chapter, answer the following questions.

1. Would a person who adheres to the principle of rights consider it ethical for Stilton not to disclose the potential risk of cancellation to investors? Why or why not?
2. Using Immanuel Kant's categorical imperative, are the actions of RightLiving, Inc., ethical? Why or why not?
3. Under utilitarianism, are Stilton's actions ethical? Why or why not? What difference does it make if most of the policies are legitimate and will be paid rather than being fraudulently procured and void?
4. Using the Business Process Pragmatism™ steps discussed in this chapter, discuss the decision process Stilton should use in deciding whether to disclose the risk of fraudulent policies to potential investors.

DEBATE THIS . . . *Executives in large corporations are ultimately rewarded if their companies do well, particularly as evidenced by rising stock prices. Consequently, should we let those who run corporations decide what level of negative side effects of their goods or services is "acceptable"?*

Terms and Concepts

business ethics 78
categorical imperative 85
corporate social responsibility (CSR) 86
cost-benefit analysis 86
duty-based ethics 84
ethical reasoning 84
ethics 78
moral minimum 80
outcome-based ethics 84
principle of rights 85
stakeholders 87
triple bottom line 79
utilitarianism 85

ExamPrep

Issue Spotters

1. News, Inc., is always looking for ways to increase the number of its viewers. Recently, it was the first network to interview surviving witnesses on location after a tragic school shooting. Are there ethical concerns about putting traumatized children on the news immediately after an event like this? Why or why not? **(See page 86.)**
2. Johnny Sport is a world-famous athlete. He is careful to avoid using any performance-enhancing drugs that are banned by his sport's oversight organization. Is it ethical for Johnny to take a performance-enhancing drug that has not been banned? Why or why not? **(See page 87.)**

- **Check your answers to the Issue Spotters against the answers provided in Appendix E at the end of this text.**

Before the Test

Go to **www.cengagebrain.com**, enter the ISBN 9781285428949, and click on "Find" to locate this textbook's Web site. Then, click on "Access Now" under

"Study Tools," and select Chapter 4 at the top. There, you will find an Interactive Quiz that you can take to assess your mastery of the concepts in this chapter, as well as Flashcards and a Glossary of important terms.

Business Scenarios

4–1. Business Ethics. Jason Trevor owns a commercial bakery in Blakely, Georgia, that produces a variety of goods sold in grocery stores. Trevor is required by law to perform internal tests on food produced at his plant to check for contamination. On three occasions, the tests of food products containing peanut butter were positive for salmonella contamination. Trevor was not required to report the results to U.S. Food and Drug Administration officials, however, so he did not. Instead, Trevor instructed his employees to simply repeat the tests until the results were negative. Meanwhile, the products that had originally tested positive for salmonella were eventually shipped out to retailers.

Five people who ate Trevor's baked goods that year became seriously ill, and one person died from a salmonella infection. Even though Trevor's conduct was legal, was it unethical for him to sell goods that had once tested positive for salmonella? Why or why not? **(See page 78.)**

4–2. Ethical Conduct. Internet giant Zoidle, a U.S. company, generated sales of £2.5 billion in the United Kingdom in 2013 (approximately $4 billion in U.S. dollars). Its net profits before taxes on these sales were £200 million, and it paid £6 million in corporate tax, resulting in a tax rate of 3 percent. The corporate tax rate in the United Kingdom is between 20 percent and 24 percent.

The CEO of Zoidle held a press conference stating that he was proud of his company for taking advantage of tax loopholes and for sheltering profits in other nations to avoid paying taxes. He called this practice "capitalism at its finest." He further stated that it would be unethical for Zoidle not to take advantage of loopholes and that it would be borderline illegal to tell shareholders that the company paid more taxes than it had to pay because it felt that it should. Zoidle receives significant benefits for doing business in the United Kingdom, including tremendous sales tax exemptions and some property tax breaks. The United Kingdom relies on the corporate income tax to provide services to the poor and to help run the agency that regulates corporations. Is it ethical for Zoidle to avoid paying taxes? Why or why not? **(See page 80.)**

Business Case Problems

4–3. Spotlight on Pfizer, Inc.—Corporate Social Responsibility. Methamphetamine (meth) is an addictive drug made chiefly in small toxic labs (STLs) in homes, tents, barns, or hotel rooms. The manufacturing process is dangerous and often results in explosions, burns, and toxic fumes. Government entities spend time and resources to find and destroy STLs, imprison meth dealers and users, treat addicts, and provide services for affected families. Meth cannot be made without ingredients that are also used in cold and allergy medications. Arkansas has one of the highest numbers of STLs in the United States. To recoup the costs of fighting the meth epidemic, twenty counties in Arkansas filed a suit against Pfizer, Inc., which makes cold and allergy medications. What is Pfizer's ethical responsibility here, and to whom is it owed? Why? [*Ashley County, Arkansas v. Pfizer, Inc.*, 552 F.3d. 659 (8th Cir. 2009)] **(See page 86.)**

4–4. Ethical Leadership. David Krasner, who worked for HSH Nordbank AG, complained that his supervisor, Roland Kiser, fostered an atmosphere of sexism that was demeaning to women. Among other things, Krasner claimed that career advancement was based on "sexual favoritism." He objected to Kiser's relationship with a female employee, Melissa Campfield, who was promoted before more qualified employees, including Krasner. How do a manager's attitudes and actions affect the workplace? [*Krasner v. HSH Nordbank AG*, 680 F.Supp.2d 502 (S.D.N.Y. 2010)] **(See page 88.)**

4–5. BUSINESS CASE PROBLEM WITH SAMPLE ANSWER: Online Privacy.

Facebook, Inc., launched a program called "Beacon" that automatically updated the profiles of users on Facebook's social networking site when those users had any activity on Beacon "partner" sites. For example, one partner site was Blockbuster.com. When a user rented or purchased a movie through Blockbuster.com, the user's Facebook profile would be updated to share the purchase. The Beacon program was set up as a default setting, so users never consented to the program, but they could opt out. What are the ethical implications of an opt-in program versus an opt-out program in social media? [Lane v. Facebook, Inc., *696 F.3d 811 (9th Cir. 2011)*] **(See page 84.)**

- **For a sample answer to Problem 4–5, go to Appendix F at the end of this text.**

4–6. Business Ethics on a Global Scale. After the fall of the Soviet Union, the new government of Azerbaijan began converting certain state-controlled industries to private ownership. Ownership in these companies could be purchased through a voucher program. Frederic Bourke, Jr., and Viktor Kozeny wanted to purchase the Azerbaijani oil company, SOCAR, but it was unclear whether the Azerbaijani president would allow SOCAR to be put up for sale. Kozeny met with one of the vice presidents of SOCAR (who was also the son of the president of Azerbaijan) and other Azerbaijani leaders to discuss the sale of SOCAR. To obtain their cooperation, Kozeny set up a series of parent and subsidiary companies through which the Azerbaijani leaders would eventually receive two-thirds of the SOCAR profits without ever investing any of their own funds. In return, the Azerbaijani leaders would attempt to use their influence to convince the president to put SOCAR up for sale. Assume that Bourke and Kozeny are operating out of a U.S. company. Discuss the ethics of this scheme, both in terms of the Foreign Corrupt Practices Act (FCPA) and as a general ethical issue. What duties did Kozeny have under the FCPA? [*United States v. Kozeny*, 667 F.3d 122 (2d Cir. 2011)] **(See page 90.)**

4–7. Business Ethics. Mark Ramun worked as a manager for Allied Erecting and Dismantling Co., where he had a tense relationship with his father, who was Allied's president. After more than ten years, Mark left Allied, taking 15,000 pages of Allied's documents on DVDs and CDs, which constituted trade secrets. Later, he joined Allied's competitor, Genesis Equipment & Manufacturing, Inc. Genesis soon developed a piece of equipment that incorporated elements of Allied equipment. How might business ethics have been violated in these circumstances? Discuss. [*Allied Erecting and Dismantling Co. v. Genesis Equipment & Manufacturing, Inc.*, 2013 WL 85907 (6th Cir. 2013)] **(See page 78.)**

4–8. A QUESTION OF ETHICS: Consumer Rights.

*Best Buy, a national electronics retailer, offered a credit card that allowed users to earn "reward points" that could be redeemed for discounts on Best Buy goods. After reading a newspaper advertisement for the card, Gary Davis applied for, and was given, a credit card. As part of the application process, he visited a Web page containing Frequently Asked Questions as well as terms and conditions for the card. He clicked on a button affirming that he understood the terms and conditions. When Davis received his card, it came with seven brochures about the card and the reward point program. As he read the brochures, he discovered that a $59 annual fee would be charged for the card. Davis went back to the Web pages he had visited and found a statement that the card "may" have an annual fee. Davis sued, claiming that the company did not adequately disclose the fee. [*Davis v. HSBC Bank Nevada, N.A., *691 F.3d 1152 (9th Cir. 2012)]* **(See page 79.)**

(a) Online applications frequently have click-on buttons or check boxes for consumers to acknowledge that they have read and understand the terms and conditions of applications or purchases. Often, the terms and conditions are so long that they cannot all be seen on one screen and users must scroll to view the entire document. Is it unethical for companies to put terms and conditions, especially terms that may cost the consumer, in an electronic document that is too long to read on one screen? Why or why not? Does this differ from having a consumer sign a hard-copy document with terms and conditions printed on it? Why or why not?

(b) The Truth-in-Lending Act requires that credit terms be clearly and conspicuously disclosed in application materials. Assuming that the Best Buy credit-card materials had sufficient legal disclosures, discuss the ethical aspects of businesses strictly following the language of the law as compared to following the intent of the law.

Legal Reasoning Group Activity

4–9. Global Business Ethics. Pfizer, Inc., developed a new antibiotic called Trovan (trovafloxacinmesylate). Tests showed that in animals Trovan had life-threatening side effects, including joint disease, abnormal cartilage growth, liver damage, and a degenerative bone condition. Several years later, an epidemic of bacterial meningitis swept across Nigeria. Pfizer sent three U.S. physicians to test Trovan on children who were patients in Nigeria's Infectious Disease Hospital. Pfizer did not obtain the patients' consent, alert them to the risks, or tell them that Médecins Sans Frontières (Doctors without Borders) was providing an effective conventional treatment at the same site. Eleven children died in the experiment, and others were left blind, deaf, paralyzed, or brain damaged. Rabi Abdullahi and other Nigerian children filed a suit in a U.S. federal court against Pfizer, alleging a violation of a customary international law norm prohibiting involuntary medical experimentation on humans. [*Abdullahi v. Pfizer, Inc.*, 562 F.3d 163 (2d Cir. 2009)] **(See page 84.)**

(a) One group should use the principles of ethical reasoning discussed in this chapter to develop three arguments that Pfizer's conduct was a violation of ethical standards.

(b) A second group should take a pro-Pfizer position and argue that the company did not violate any ethical standards (and counter the first group).

(c) A third group should come up with proposals for what Pfizer might have done differently to avert the consequences.

UNIT ONE Focus on Ethics

Ethics and the Legal Environment of Business

In Chapter 4, we examined the importance of ethical standards in the business context. We also offered suggestions on how business decision makers can create an ethical workplace. Certainly, it is not wrong for a businessperson to try to increase his or her firm's profits. But there are limits, both ethical and legal, to how far businesspersons can go. In preparing for a career in business, you will find that a background in business ethics and a commitment to ethical behavior are just as important as a knowledge of the specific laws that are covered in this text. Of course, no textbook can give an answer to each and every ethical question that arises in the business environment. Nor can it anticipate the types of ethical questions that will arise in the future, as technology and globalization continue to transform the workplace and business relationships.

The most we can do is examine the types of ethical issues that businesspersons have faced in the past and that they are facing today. In the *Focus on Ethics* sections in this book, we provide examples of specific ethical issues that have arisen in various areas of business activity.

In this initial *Focus on Ethics* feature, we look first at the relationship between business ethics and business law. We then examine various obstacles to ethical behavior in the business context. We conclude the feature by exploring the parameters of corporate social responsibility through a discussion of whether corporations have an ethical duty to the community or society at large.

Business Ethics and Business Law

Business ethics and business law are closely intertwined because ultimately the law rests on social beliefs about right and wrong behavior in the business world. Thus, businesspersons, by complying with the law, are acting ethically. Mere legal compliance (the "moral minimum" in terms of business ethics), however, is often not enough. This is because the law does not—and cannot—provide the answers for all ethical questions.

In the business world, numerous actions may be unethical but not necessarily illegal. Consider an example. Suppose that a pharmaceutical company is banned from marketing a particular drug in the United States because of the drug's possible adverse side effects. Yet no law prohibits the company from selling the drug in foreign markets—even though some consumers in those markets may suffer serious health problems as a result of using the drug. At issue here is not whether it would be legal to market the drug in other countries but whether it would be *ethical* to do so. In other words, the law has its limits—it cannot make all ethical decisions for us. Rather, the law assumes that those in business will behave ethically in their day-to-day dealings. If they do not, the courts will not come to their assistance.

LEGAL REASONING

1. *Can you think of a situation in which a business firm may be acting ethically but not in a socially responsible manner? Explain.*

Obstacles to Ethical Business Behavior

People sometimes behave unethically in the business context, just as they do in their private lives. Some businesspersons knowingly engage in unethical behavior because they think that they can "get away with it"—that is, no one will ever learn of their unethical actions.

Examples of this kind of unethical behavior include padding expense accounts, casting doubts on the integrity of a rival co-worker to gain a job promotion, and stealing company supplies or equipment. Obviously, these acts are unethical, and many of them are illegal as well. In some situations, however, businesspersons who would choose to act ethically may be deterred from doing so because of situational circumstances or external pressures.

Ethics and the Corporate Environment Individuals in their personal lives normally are free to decide ethical issues as they wish and to follow through on those decisions. In the business world, and particularly in the corporate environment, rarely is such a decision made by *one* person. If you are an officer or a manager of a large company, for example, you will find that the decision as to what is right or wrong for the company is not totally yours to make. Your input may weigh in the decision, but ultimately a corporate decision is a collective undertaking.

Additionally, collective decision making, because it places emphasis on consensus and unity of opinion, tends to hinder individual ethical assertiveness. For example, suppose that a director has ethical misgivings about a planned corporate venture that promises to be highly profitable. If the other directors have no such misgivings, the director who does may be swayed by the others' enthusiasm for the project and downplay her or his own criticisms.

Furthermore, just as no one person makes a collective decision, so no one person (normally) is held accountable for the decision. The corporate enterprise thus tends to shield corporate personnel from both individual exposure to the consequences of their decisions (such as direct contact with someone who suffers harm from a corporate product) and personal accountability for those decisions.

Ethics and Management Much unethical business behavior occurs simply because management does not always make clear what ethical standards and behaviors are expected of the firm's employees. Although most firms now issue ethical policies or codes of conduct, these policies and codes are not always effective in creating an ethical workplace. At times, this is because the firm's ethical policies are not communicated clearly to employees or do not bear on the real ethical issues confronting decision makers. Additionally, particularly in a large corporation, unethical behavior in one corporate department may simply escape the attention of those in control of the corporation or the corporate officials respon-

sible for implementing and monitoring the company's ethics program.

Unethical behavior may also occur when corporate management, by its own conduct, indicates that ethical considerations take a second seat. If management makes no attempt to deter unethical behavior—through reprimands or employment terminations, for example—it will be obvious to employees that management is not very serious about ethics. Likewise, if a company gives promotions or salary increases to those who clearly use unethical tactics to increase the firm's profits, then employees who do not resort to such tactics will be at a disadvantage. An employee in this situation may decide that because "everyone else does it," he or she might as well do it too.

Of course, an even stronger encouragement of unethical behavior occurs when employers engage in blatantly unethical or illegal conduct and expect their employees to do so as well. An employee in this situation faces two options, neither of which is satisfactory: participate in the conduct or "blow the whistle" on (inform authorities of) the employer's actions—and, of course, risk being fired. (Whistleblowing is a controversial issue because it is sometimes difficult to prove employers' motivations for dismissals.)

LEGAL REASONING

2. *What might be some other deterrents to ethical behavior in the business context, besides those discussed in this* Focus on Ethics *feature?*

Corporate Social Responsibility

As discussed in Chapter 4, just what constitutes corporate social responsibility has been debated for some time. In particular, questions arise concerning a corporation's ethical obligations to its community and to society as a whole.

A Corporation's Duty to the Community In some circumstances, the community in which a business enterprise is located is greatly affected by corporate decisions and therefore may be considered a stakeholder. Assume, for example, that a company employs two thousand workers at one of its plants. If the company decides that it would be profitable to close the plant, the employees—and the community—would suffer as a result. To be considered ethical in that situation (and, in some circumstances, to comply with laws governing plant shutdowns), a corporation must take both the employees' needs and the community's needs into consideration when making its decision.

Another ethical question sometimes arises when a firm moves into a community. Does the company have an obligation to evaluate first how its presence will affect that community (even though the community is not a stakeholder yet)? This question has surfaced in regard to the expansion of Wal-Mart Stores, Inc., into smaller communities. Generally, most people in such communities welcome the lower prices and wider array of goods that Wal-Mart offers relative to other, smaller stores in the area. A vocal minority of people in some communities, however, claim that smaller stores often find it impossible to compete with Wal-Mart's prices and thus are forced to go out of business. Many of these smaller stores have existed for years and, according to Wal-Mart's critics, enhance the quality of community life. These critics claim that it is unethical of Wal-Mart to disregard a town's interest in the quality and character of its community life.

In addition to expanding, Wal-Mart has been consolidating some of its smaller stores into large "superstores." As it consolidates, Wal-Mart is closing stores in some of the very towns in which it drove its smaller competitors out of business. This development raises yet another ethical question: Does a store such as Wal-Mart have an obligation to continue operations in a community once it has driven its competitors out of business?

LEGAL REASONING

3. *Why are consumers and the public generally more concerned with ethical and socially responsible business behavior today than they were, say, fifty years ago?*

A Corporation's Duty to Society Perhaps the most disputed area of corporate social responsibility is the nature of a corporation's duty to society at large. Those who contend that corporations should first and foremost attend to the goal of profit maximization would argue that it is by generating profits that a firm can best contribute to society. Society benefits from profit-making activities because profits can only be realized when a firm markets products or services that are desired by society. These products and services enhance the standard of living, and the profits accumulated by successful business firms generate national wealth. Our laws and court decisions promoting trade and commerce reflect the public policy that the fruits of commerce (wealth) are desirable and good. Because our society values wealth as an ethical goal, corporations, by contributing to that wealth, automatically are acting ethically.

Those arguing for profit maximization as a corporate goal also point out that it would be inappropriate to use the power of the corporate business world to further society's goals by promoting social causes. Determinations as to what exactly is in society's best interest involve questions that are essentially political. Therefore the public, through the political process, should have a say in making those determinations. Thus, the legislature—not the corporate boardroom—is the appropriate forum for making such decisions.

FOCUS ON ETHICS CONTINUES ➧

Critics of the profit-maximization view believe that corporations should become actively engaged in seeking and furthering solutions to social problems. Because business controls so much of the wealth and power of this country, business has a responsibility to use its resources in socially beneficial ways. Corporations should therefore promote human rights, strive for equal treatment of minorities and women in the workplace, take steps to preserve the environment, and generally not profit from activities that society has deemed unethical. The critics also point out that it is ethically irresponsible to leave decisions concerning social welfare up to the government, because many social needs are not being met sufficiently through the political process.

LEGAL REASONING

4. *Suppose that an automobile manufacturing company has to choose between two alternatives: contributing $1 million annually to the United Way or reinvesting the $1 million in the company. In terms of ethics and social responsibility, which is the better choice? Why?*

It Pays to Be Ethical

Most corporations today have learned that it pays to be ethically responsible—even if this means less profit in the short run (and it often does). Today's corporations are subject to more intensive scrutiny—by both government agencies and the public—than corporations of the past. "Corporate watch" groups monitor the activities of U.S. corporations, including activities conducted in foreign countries. Through the Internet, complaints about a corporation's practices can easily be disseminated to a worldwide audience. Similarly, dissatisfied customers and employees can voice their complaints about corporate policies, products, or services in Internet chat rooms and other online forums. Thus, if a corporation fails to conduct its operations ethically or to respond quickly to an ethical crisis, its goodwill and reputation (and future profits) will likely suffer as a result.

There are other reasons as well for a corporation to behave ethically. For example, companies that demonstrate a commitment to ethical behavior—by implementing ethical programs, complying with environmental regulations, and promptly investigating product complaints, for example—often receive more lenient treatment from government agencies and the courts. Additionally, investors may shy away from a corporation's stock if the corporation is perceived to be socially irresponsible. Finally, unethical (and/or illegal) corporate behavior may result in government action, such as new laws imposing further requirements on corporate entities.

LEGAL REASONING

5. *Have Internet chat rooms and online forums affected corporate decision makers' willingness to consider the community and public interest when making choices? Are corporate decision makers more apt to make ethical choices in the cyber age?*

Unit Two

The Public and International Environment

Contents

CHAPTER 5
BUSINESS AND THE CONSTITUTION

Laws that govern business have their origin in the lawmaking authority granted by the U.S. Constitution, which is the supreme law in this country.[1] As mentioned in Chapter 1, neither Congress nor any state may pass a law that is in conflict with the Constitution.

Constitutional disputes frequently come before the courts. For instance, numerous states challenged the Obama administration's Affordable Care Act on constitutional grounds. The United States Supreme Court decided in 2012 that the provisions of this law, which require most Americans to have health insurance by 2014, did not exceed the constitutional authority of the federal government. The Court's decision in the matter continues to have a significant impact on the business environment.

In this chapter, we examine some basic constitutional concepts and clauses and their significance for businesspersons. We then look at certain freedoms guaranteed by the first ten amendments to the Constitution—the Bill of Rights—and discuss how these freedoms affect business activities.

1. See Appendix B for the full text of the U.S. Constitution.

SECTION 1
THE CONSTITUTIONAL POWERS OF GOVERNMENT

Following the Revolutionary War, the states adopted the Articles of Confederation. The Articles created a *confederal form of government* in which the states had the authority to govern themselves and the national government could exercise only limited powers. When problems arose because the nation was facing an economic crisis and state laws interfered with the free flow of commerce, a national convention was called, and the delegates drafted the U.S. Constitution. This document, after its ratification by the states in 1789, became the basis for an entirely new form of government.

A Federal Form of Government

The new government created by the U.S. Constitution reflected a series of compromises made by the convention delegates on various issues. Some delegates wanted sovereign power to remain with the states. Others wanted the national government alone to exercise sovereign power. The end result was a compromise—a **federal form of government** in which the national government and the states *share* sovereign power.

FEDERAL POWERS The Constitution sets forth specific powers that can be exercised by the national government. It further provides that the national government has the implied power to undertake actions necessary to carry out its expressly designated powers (or *enumerated powers*). All other powers are expressly "reserved" to the states under the Tenth Amendment to the U.S. Constitution.

REGULATORY POWERS OF THE STATES As part of their inherent **sovereignty** (independence), state governments have the authority to regulate affairs within their borders. As mentioned, this authority stems, in part, from the Tenth Amendment, which reserves all powers not delegated to the national government to the states or to the people.

State regulatory powers are often referred to as **police powers.** The term encompasses more than just the enforcement of criminal laws. Police powers also give state governments broad rights to regulate private activities to protect or promote the public order, health, safety, morals, and general welfare. Fire and building codes, antidiscrimination laws, parking regulations, zoning restrictions, licensing requirements, and thousands of other state statutes have been enacted pursuant to states' police powers.

Local governments, including cities, also exercise police powers.[2] Generally, state laws enacted pursuant to a state's police powers carry a strong presumption of validity.

Relations among the States

The U.S. Constitution also includes provisions concerning relations among the states in our federal system. Particularly important are the *privileges and immunities clause* and the *full faith and credit clause.*

THE PRIVILEGES AND IMMUNITIES CLAUSE Article IV, Section 2, of the Constitution provides that the "Citizens of each State shall be entitled to all Privileges and Immunities of Citizens in the several States." This clause is often referred to as the interstate **privileges and immunities clause.**[3] It prevents a state from imposing unreasonable burdens on citizens of another state—particularly with regard to means of livelihood or doing business.

When a citizen of one state engages in basic and essential activities in another state (the "foreign state"), the foreign state must have a *substantial reason* for treating the nonresident differently from its own residents. Basic activities include transferring property, seeking employment, or accessing the court system. The foreign state must also establish that its reason for the discrimination is *substantially related* to the state's ultimate purpose in adopting the legislation or regulating the activity.[4]

THE FULL FAITH AND CREDIT CLAUSE Article IV, Section 1, of the U.S. Constitution provides that "Full Faith and Credit shall be given in each State to the public Acts, Records, and judicial Proceedings of every other State." This clause, which is referred to as the **full faith and credit clause,** applies only to civil matters. It ensures that rights established under deeds, wills, contracts, and similar instruments in one state will be honored by other states. It also ensures that any judicial decision with respect to such property rights will be honored and enforced in all states.

▶ **Example 5.1** The legal issues raised by same-sex marriage involve, among other things, the full faith and credit clause because that clause requires each state to honor marriage decrees issued by another state. Therefore, if same-sex partners marry in Washington, which legalized same-sex marriage in 2012, and the couple later moves to another state, that state would be required to recognize the validity of their marriage. ◀

The full faith and credit clause has contributed to the unity of American citizens because it protects their legal rights as they move about from state to state. It also protects the rights of those to whom they owe obligations, such as a person who is awarded monetary damages by a court. The ability to enforce such rights is extremely important for the conduct of business in a country with a very mobile citizenry.

The Separation of Powers

To make it difficult for the national government to use its power arbitrarily, the Constitution provided for three branches of government. The legislative branch makes the laws, the executive branch enforces the laws, and the judicial branch interprets the laws. Each branch performs a separate function, and no branch may exercise the authority of another branch.

Additionally, a system of **checks and balances** allows each branch to limit the actions of the other two branches, thus preventing any one branch from exercising too much power. Some examples of these checks and balances include the following:

1. The legislative branch (Congress) can enact a law, but the executive branch (the president) has the constitutional authority to veto that law.
2. The executive branch is responsible for foreign affairs, but treaties with foreign governments require the advice and consent of the Senate.
3. Congress determines the jurisdiction of the federal courts, and the president appoints federal judges, with the advice and consent of the Senate. The judicial branch has the power to hold actions of the other two branches unconstitutional.[5]

---

2. Local governments derive their authority to regulate their communities from the state, because they are creatures of the state. In other words, they cannot come into existence unless authorized by the state to do so.
3. Interpretations of this clause commonly use the terms *privilege* and *immunity* synonymously. Generally, the terms refer to certain rights, benefits, or advantages enjoyed by individuals.
4. This test was first announced in *Supreme Court of New Hampshire v. Piper,* 470 U.S. 274, 105 S.Ct. 1272, 84 L.Ed.2d 205 (1985). For another example, see *Lee v. Miner,* 369 F.Supp.2d 527 (D.Del. 2005).
5. As discussed in Chapter 2, the power of judicial review was established by the United States Supreme Court in *Marbury v. Madison,* 5 U.S. (1 Cranch) 137, 2 L.Ed. 60 (1803).

The Commerce Clause

To prevent states from establishing laws and regulations that would interfere with trade and commerce among the states, the Constitution expressly delegated to the national government the power to regulate interstate commerce. Article I, Section 8, of the U.S. Constitution explicitly permits Congress "[t]o regulate Commerce with foreign Nations, and among the several States, and with the Indian Tribes." This clause, referred to as the **commerce clause,** has had a greater impact on business than any other provision in the Constitution. The commerce clause provides the basis for the national government's extensive regulation of state and even local affairs.

Initially, the courts interpreted the commerce clause to apply only to commerce between the states (*interstate* commerce) and not commerce within the states (*intrastate* commerce). In 1824, however, the United States Supreme Court decided the landmark case of *Gibbons v. Ogden.*[6] The Court held that commerce within the states could also be regulated by the national government as long as the commerce *substantially affected* commerce involving more than one state.

THE EXPANSION OF NATIONAL POWERS UNDER THE COMMERCE CLAUSE As the nation grew and faced new kinds of problems, the commerce clause became a vehicle for the additional expansion of the national government's regulatory powers. Even activities that seemed purely local in nature came under the regulatory reach of the national government if those activities were deemed to substantially affect interstate commerce. In 1942, the Supreme Court held that wheat production by an individual farmer intended wholly for consumption on his own farm was subject to federal regulation.[7]

▶ **Case in Point 5.2** In *Heart of Atlanta Motel v. United States,*[8] a landmark case decided in 1964, the Supreme Court upheld the federal government's authority under the commerce clause to prohibit racial discrimination nationwide in public facilities. The case was brought by an Atlanta motel owner who refused to rent rooms to African Americans, in violation of the Civil Rights Act of 1964. The Court concluded that local motels and restaurants do affect interstate commerce. The Court stated that "if it is interstate commerce that feels the pinch, it does not matter how local the operation that applies the squeeze." ◀

THE COMMERCE CLAUSE TODAY Today, at least theoretically, the power over commerce authorizes the national government to regulate almost every commercial enterprise in the United States. The breadth of the commerce clause permits the national government to legislate in areas in which Congress has not explicitly been granted power.

In the last twenty years, the Supreme Court has on occasion curbed the national government's regulatory authority under the commerce clause. In 1995, the Court held—for the first time in sixty years—that Congress had exceeded its regulatory authority under the commerce clause. The Court struck down an act that banned the possession of guns within one thousand feet of any school because the act attempted to regulate an area that had "nothing to do with commerce."[9] Subsequently, the Court invalidated key portions of two other federal acts on the ground that they exceeded Congress's commerce clause authority.[10]

MEDICAL MARIJUANA AND THE COMMERCE CLAUSE In one notable case, however, the Supreme Court did allow the federal government to regulate noncommercial activities taking place wholly within a state's borders. ▶ **Case in Point 5.3** More than a dozen states, including California, have adopted laws that legalize marijuana for medical purposes. Marijuana possession, however, is illegal under the federal Controlled Substances Act (CSA).[11] After the federal government seized the marijuana that two seriously ill California women were using on the advice of their physicians, the women filed a lawsuit. They argued that it was unconstitutional for the federal statute to prohibit them from using marijuana for medical purposes that were legal within the state.

The Supreme Court, though, held that Congress has the authority to prohibit the *intrastate* possession and noncommercial cultivation of marijuana as part of a larger regulatory scheme (the CSA).[12] In other

6. 22 U.S. (9 Wheat.) 1, 6 L.Ed. 23 (1824).
7. *Wickard v. Filburn,* 317 U.S. 111, 63 S.Ct. 82, 87 L.Ed. 122 (1942).
8. 379 U.S. 241, 85 S.Ct. 348, 13 L.Ed.2d 258 (1964).
9. The Court held the Gun-Free School Zones Act of 1990 to be unconstitutional in *United States v. Lopez,* 514 U.S. 549, 115 S.Ct. 1624, 131 L.Ed.2d 626 (1995).
10. *Printz v. United States,* 521 U.S. 898, 117 S.Ct. 2365, 138 L.Ed.2d 914 (1997), involving the Brady Handgun Violence Prevention Act of 1993; and *United States v. Morrison,* 529 U.S. 598, 120 S.Ct. 1740, 146 L.Ed.2d 658 (2000), concerning the federal Violence Against Women Act of 1994.
11. 21 U.S.C. Sections 801 *et seq.*
12. *Gonzales v. Raich,* 545 U.S. 1, 125 S.Ct. 2195, 162 L.Ed.2d 1 (2005).

words, state medical marijuana laws do not insulate the users from federal prosecution. ◀

THE "DORMANT" COMMERCE CLAUSE The Supreme Court has interpreted the commerce clause to mean that the national government has the *exclusive* authority to regulate commerce that substantially affects trade and commerce among the states. This express grant of authority to the national government is often referred to as the "positive" aspect of the commerce clause. But this positive aspect also implies a negative aspect—that the states do *not* have the authority to regulate interstate commerce. This negative aspect of the commerce clause is often referred to as the "dormant" (implied) commerce clause.

The dormant commerce clause comes into play when state regulations affect interstate commerce. In this situation, the courts weigh the state's interest in regulating a certain matter against the burden that the state's regulation places on interstate commerce. Because courts balance the interests involved, it is difficult to predict the outcome in a particular case.

In the following case, the plaintiffs—a group of California wineries and others—contended that a Massachusetts statute discriminated against out-of-state wineries in violation of the dormant commerce clause. A federal district court agreed and enjoined (prevented) the enforcement of the statute. The commonwealth of Massachusetts appealed the trial court's decision.

CASE ANALYSIS

Case 5.1 Family Winemakers of California v. Jenkins[a]

United States Court of Appeals, First Circuit, 592 F.3d 1 (2010).

IN THE LANGUAGE OF THE COURT

LYNCH, Chief Judge.

* * * *

The ratification of the Twenty-first Amendment ended Prohibition[b] and gave states substantial control over the regulation of alcoholic beverages. Most states, including Massachusetts, then imposed a three-tier system to control the sale of alcoholic beverages within their territories. The hallmark of the three-tier system is a rigid, tightly regulated separation between producers, wholesalers, and retailers of alcoholic beverages. Producers can ordinarily sell alcoholic beverages only to licensed in-state wholesalers. Wholesalers then must obtain licenses to sell to retailers. Retailers, which include stores, taverns, restaurants, and bars, must in turn obtain licenses to sell to consumers or to serve alcohol on their premises. Recently, as to wine, Massachusetts has adjusted the separation between these three tiers * * * .

* * * *

Wineries have heralded direct shipping as a supplemental avenue of distribution because of its economic advantages, especially for wineries that do not rank among the fifty to one hundred largest producers. Direct shipping lets consumers directly order wines from the winery, with access to their full range of wines, not just those a wholesaler is willing to distribute. Direct shipping also avoids added steps in the distribution chain, eliminating wholesaler and retailer price markups.

Before 2005, Massachusetts's * * * winery licensing law * * * allowed only in-state wineries to obtain licenses to combine distribution methods through wholesalers, retailers, and direct shipping to consumers. [After the United States Supreme Court] invalidated similar facially discriminatory state laws, [the 2005 Massachusetts law] was held to be invalid under the Commerce Clause.

In 2006, the Massachusetts legislature enacted [a new law regulating wineries, which] does not distinguish on its face between in-state and out-of-state wineries' eligibility for direct shipping licenses, but instead distinguishes between "small" or "large" wineries through [a] 30,000 gallon cap.

* * * *

* * * All wineries producing over 30,000 gallons of wine—all of which are located outside Massachusetts—can apply for a "large winery shipment license[.]" * * * "Large" wineries can either choose to remain completely within the three-tier system and distribute their wines solely through wholesalers, or they can completely opt out of the three-tier system and sell their wines in Massachusetts exclusively through direct shipping [to consumers]. They cannot do both. * * * By contrast, "small" wineries can simultaneously use the traditional

CASE 5.1 CONTINUES ➧

a. The case was brought against Eddie J. Jenkins, the chair of the Massachusetts Alcoholic Beverages Control Commission, in his official capacity.

b. The Eighteenth Amendment to the U.S. Constitution, adopted in 1919, prohibited the sale of alcoholic beverages, giving rise to the so-called Prohibition Era. The Twenty-first Amendment, ratified in 1933, repealed the Eighteenth Amendment.

CASE 5.1 CONTINUED

wholesaler distribution method, direct distribution to retailers, and direct shipping to reach consumers.

* * * *

* * * *Discrimination under the Commerce Clause "means differential treatment of in-state and out-of-state economic interests that benefits the former and burdens the latter," as opposed to state laws that "regulate * * * evenhandedly with only incidental effects on interstate commerce[.]"* [Emphasis added.]

* * * Plaintiffs argue that Massachusetts's choice of 30,000 gallons as the demarcation [separation] point between "small" and "large" wineries, along with [a] production exception for fruit wine, has both a discriminatory effect and [a] purpose. The discriminatory effect is because [the law's] definition of "large" wineries encompasses the wineries which produce 98 percent of all wine in the United States, all of which are located out-of-state and all of which are deprived of the benefits of combining distribution methods. All wines produced in Massachusetts, on the other hand, are from "small" wineries that can use multiple distribution methods. Plaintiffs also say that [the law] is discriminatory in purpose because the gallonage cap's particular features, along with legislators' statements and [the law's] process of enactment, show that [the law's] true purpose was to ensure that Massachusetts's wineries obtained advantages over their out-of-state counterparts.

* * * *

* * * State laws that alter conditions of competition to favor in-state interests over out-of-state competitors in a market have long been subject to invalidation.

* * * Here, the totality of the evidence introduced by plaintiffs demonstrates that [the law's] preferential treatment of "small" wineries that produce 30,000 gallons or less of grape wine is discriminatory. Its effect is to significantly alter the terms of competition between in-state and out-of-state wineries to the detriment of the out-of-state wineries that produce 98 percent of the country's wine.

[The 2006 law] confers a clear competitive advantage to "small" wineries, which include all Massachusetts's wineries, and creates a comparative disadvantage for "large" wineries, none of which are in Massachusetts. "Small" wineries that obtain a * * * license can use direct shipping to consumers, retailer distribution, and wholesaler distribution simultaneously. Combining these distribution methods allows "small" wineries to sell their full range of wines at maximum efficiency because they serve complementary markets. "Small" wineries that produce higher-volume wines can continue distributing those wines through wholesaler relationships. They can obtain new markets for all their wines by distributing their wines directly to retailers, including individual bars, restaurants, and stores. They can also use direct shipping to offer their full range of wines directly to Massachusetts consumers, resulting in greater overall sales.

* * * *

We conclude that [the 2006 law] altered the competitive balance to favor Massachusetts's wineries and disfavor out-of-state competition by design.

* * * *

We *affirm* the judgment of the district court.

LEGAL REASONING QUESTIONS

1. The court held that the Massachusetts statute discriminated against out-of-state wineries "by design" (intentionally). How can a court determine legislative intent?
2. Suppose that most "small" wineries, as defined by the 2006 Massachusetts law, were located out of state. How could the law be discriminatory in that situation?
3. Suppose that the state had only required the out-of-state wineries to obtain a special license that was readily available. Would this have affected the outcome of the case? Explain.
4. When it is difficult to predict how the law might be applied—as in cases arising under the dormant commerce clause—what is the best course of conduct for a business?

The Supremacy Clause and Federal Preemption

Article VI of the U.S. Constitution, commonly referred to as the **supremacy clause,** provides that the Constitution, laws, and treaties of the United States are "the supreme Law of the Land." When there is a direct conflict between a federal law and a state law, the state law is rendered invalid. Because some powers are *concurrent* (shared by the federal government and the states), however, it is necessary to determine which law governs in a particular circumstance.

When Congress chooses to act (legislate) exclusively in an area in which the federal government and the states have concurrent powers, **preemption** occurs. A valid federal statute or regulation will take precedence over a conflicting state or local law or regulation on the same general subject.

FEDERAL STATUTES MAY SPECIFY PREEMPTION Sometimes, the federal statute will include a preemption provision to make it clear that Congress intends the legislation to preempt any state laws on the matter. ▶ **Case in Point 5.4** A man who alleged that he had been injured by a faulty medical device (a balloon catheter that was inserted into his artery following a heart attack) sued the manufacturer.

The case ultimately came before the United States Supreme Court, which noted that the Medical Device Amendments of 1976 had included a preemption provision. The medical device had passed the U.S. Food and Drug Administration's rigorous premarket approval process. Therefore, the Court concluded that the federal regulation of medical devices preempted the injured party's state common law claims for negligence, strict liability, and implied warranty (see Chapters 11 through 13).[13] ◀

WHEN THE STATUTE DOES NOT EXPRESSLY MENTION PREEMPTION Often, it is not clear whether Congress, in passing a law, intended to preempt an entire subject area against state regulation. In those situations, the courts determine whether Congress intended to exercise exclusive power over a given area.

No single factor is decisive as to whether a court will find preemption. Generally, congressional intent to preempt will be found if a federal law regulating an activity is so pervasive, comprehensive, or detailed that the states have no room to regulate in that area. Also, when a federal statute creates an agency—such as the National Labor Relations Board—to enforce the law, matters that come within the agency's jurisdiction will likely preempt state laws.

The Taxing and Spending Powers

Article I, Section 8, of the U.S. Constitution provides that Congress has the "Power to lay and collect Taxes, Duties, Imposts, and Excises." Section 8 further requires uniformity in taxation among the states, and thus Congress may not tax some states while exempting others.

In the distant past, if Congress attempted to regulate indirectly, by taxation, an area over which it had no authority, the courts would invalidate the tax. Today, however, if a tax measure is reasonable, it generally is held to be within the national taxing power. Moreover, the expansive interpretation of the commerce clause almost always provides a basis for sustaining a federal tax.

Article I, Section 8, also gives Congress its spending power—the power "to pay the Debts and provide for the common Defence and general Welfare of the United States." Congress can spend revenues not only to carry out its expressed powers but also to promote any objective it deems worthwhile, so long as it does not violate the Bill of Rights. The spending power necessarily involves policy choices, with which taxpayers (and politicians) may disagree.

SECTION 2

BUSINESS AND THE BILL OF RIGHTS

The importance of a written declaration of the rights of individuals caused the first Congress of the United States to submit twelve amendments to the U.S. Constitution to the states for approval. Ten of these amendments, known as the **Bill of Rights,** were adopted in 1791 and embody a series of protections for the individual against various types of interference by the federal government.[14]

The protections guaranteed by these ten amendments are summarized in Exhibit 5–1 on the following page.[15] Some of these constitutional protections apply to business entities as well. For example, corporations exist as separate legal entities, or *legal persons,* and enjoy many of the same rights and privileges as *natural persons* do.

Limits on Federal and State Governmental Actions

As originally intended, the Bill of Rights limited only the powers of the national government. Over time, however, the United States Supreme Court "incorporated" most of these rights into the protections against state actions afforded by the Fourteenth Amendment to the Constitution.

13. *Riegel v. Medtronic, Inc.,* 552 U.S. 312, 128 S.Ct. 999, 169 L.Ed.2d 892 (2008).

14. Another of these proposed amendments was ratified more than two hundred years later (in 1992) and became the Twenty-seventh Amendment to the Constitution. See Appendix B.

15. See the Constitution in Appendix B for the complete text of each amendment.

EXHIBIT 5–1 Protections Guaranteed by the Bill of Rights

First Amendment: Guarantees the freedoms of religion, speech, and the press and the rights to assemble peaceably and to petition the government.

Second Amendment: States that the right of the people to keep and bear arms shall not be infringed.

Third Amendment: Prohibits, in peacetime, the lodging of soldiers in any house without the owner's consent.

Fourth Amendment: Prohibits unreasonable searches and seizures of persons or property.

Fifth Amendment: Guarantees the rights to indictment by a grand jury, to due process of law, and to fair payment when private property is taken for public use. Prohibits compulsory self-incrimination and double jeopardy (being tried again for an alleged crime for which one has already stood trial).

Sixth Amendment: Guarantees the accused in a criminal case the right to a speedy and public trial by an impartial jury and with counsel. The accused has the right to cross-examine witnesses against him or her and to solicit testimony from witnesses in his or her favor.

Seventh Amendment: Guarantees the right to a trial by jury in a civil case involving at least twenty dollars.[a]

Eighth Amendment: Prohibits excessive bail and fines, as well as cruel and unusual punishment.

Ninth Amendment: Establishes that the people have rights in addition to those specified in the Constitution.

Tenth Amendment: Establishes that those powers neither delegated to the federal government nor denied to the states are reserved to the states and to the people.

a. Twenty dollars was forty days' pay for the average person when the Bill of Rights was written.

THE FOURTEENTH AMENDMENT The Fourteenth Amendment, passed in 1868 after the Civil War, provides, in part, that "[n]o State shall . . . deprive any person of life, liberty, or property, without due process of law." Starting in 1925, the Supreme Court began to define various rights and liberties guaranteed in the U.S. Constitution as constituting "due process of law," which was required of state governments under that amendment.

Today, most of the rights and liberties set forth in the Bill of Rights apply to state governments as well as the national government. In other words, neither the federal government nor state governments can deprive persons of those rights and liberties.

JUDICIAL INTERPRETATION The rights secured by the Bill of Rights are not absolute. Many of the rights guaranteed by the first ten amendments are set forth in very general terms. The Second Amendment states that people have a right to keep and bear arms, but it does not explain the extent of this right. As the Supreme Court noted in 2008, this does not mean that people can "keep and carry any weapon whatsoever in any manner whatsoever and for whatever purpose."[16] Legislatures can prohibit the carrying of concealed weapons or certain types of weapons, such as machine guns.

Ultimately, it is the United States Supreme Court, as the final interpreter of the Constitution, that gives meaning to these rights and determines their boundaries. Changing public views on controversial topics, such as privacy in an era of terrorist threats or the rights of gay men and lesbians, may affect the way the Supreme Court decides a case. On several occasions, justices on the Supreme Court have even mentioned that they have considered foreign laws in reaching a decision.

Freedom of Speech

A democratic form of government cannot survive unless people can freely voice their political opinions and criticize government actions or policies. Freedom of speech, particularly political speech, is thus a prized right, and traditionally the courts have protected this right to the fullest extent possible.

Symbolic speech—gestures, movements, articles of clothing, and other forms of expressive conduct—is also given substantial protection by the courts. The Supreme Court has held that the burning of the American flag as part of a peaceful protest is a constitutionally protected form of expression.[17] Similarly, wearing a T-shirt with a photo of a presidential candidate is a constitutionally protected form of expression. ▶ **Example 5.5** As a form of expression, Nate

16. *District of Columbia v. Heller,* 554 U.S. 570, 128 S.Ct. 2783, 171 L.Ed.2d 637 (2008).

17. *Texas v. Johnson,* 491 U.S. 397, 109 S.Ct. 2533, 105 L.Ed.2d 342 (1989).

has gang signs tattooed on his torso, arms, neck, and legs. If a reasonable person would interpret this conduct as conveying a message, then it might be a protected form of symbolic speech. ◀

An interesting topic in today's legal environment is whether computers should have free speech rights. For a discussion of this issue, see this chapter's *Insight into E-Commerce* feature below.

REASONABLE RESTRICTIONS Expression—oral, written, or symbolized by conduct—is subject to reasonable restrictions. A balance must be struck between

INSIGHT INTO E-COMMERCE
Do Computers Have Free Speech Rights?

When you do a Web search using Bing, Google, or any other search engine, the program inherent in the engine gives you a list of results. When you use a document-creation program, such as Microsoft Word, it often guesses what you intend and corrects your misspellings automatically. Do computers that make such choices engage in "speech," and if so, do they enjoy First Amendment protection? This question is not as absurd as it may seem at first.

Are Google's Search Results "Speech"?

More than a decade ago, a company dissatisfied with its rankings in Google's search results sued. Google argued that its search results were constitutionally protected speech. The plaintiff, Search King, Inc., sought an injunction against Google, but a federal district court decided in Google's favor. The court ruled that the ranking of results when a search is undertaken "constitutes opinions protected by the First Amendment. . . . *Page Ranks* are opinions—opinions are the significance of particular Web sites as they correspond to a search query." Therefore, the First Amendment applied to the search results.[a]

Google versus the Federal Trade Commission

For the last few years, Google has been the dominant search engine. Yet in the 1990s, the federal government was worried that Microsoft's search engine was too dominant and was crushing the search engines of Yahoo!, AltaVista, and Lycos. Today, of course, AltaVista and Lycos no longer exist, and Microsoft's new search engine, Bing, is a relatively minor player in the field.

Fast-forward to 2011. The Federal Trade Commission (FTC) contemplated bringing charges against Google for favoring its own offerings, such as restaurant reviews, in its search results. Now it was Microsoft that was encouraging the FTC to proceed. After a nineteen-month investigation, in early 2013 the FTC announced that it would *not* prosecute Google. The FTC's decision was a blow to search engines that compete with Google, including Microsoft's Bing.

The First Amendment Protection Argument

Google commissioned Eugene Volokh and Donald Falk, two legal experts in this field, to research the issue of whether search engine results are protected by the First Amendment.[b] The researchers concluded that search engine results are the same as the editorial judgments that a newspaper makes in deciding which wire service stories to run and which op-ed and business columnists to feature. The authors further claim that free speech applies to editorial choices no matter what their format. Search engines are protected even when they are "unfair" in ranking search results. Whether the search engine uses a computerized algorithm to compile its rankings is irrelevant.

Columbia Law professor Tim Wu disagrees. He argues that the First Amendment was intended to protect humans against the evils of state censorship and that protecting a computer's speech is not related to that purpose. At best, he says, search engine results are *commercial speech,* which has always received limited protection under the First Amendment. After all, computers make trillions of invisible decisions each day. Is each of those decisions protected speech?

LEGAL CRITICAL THINKING

INSIGHT INTO SOCIAL MEDIA

Facebook has numerous computers, all programmed by humans, of course. If Facebook's computers make decisions that allow your private information to be shared without your knowledge, should the First Amendment protect Facebook? Why or why not?

a. *Search King, Inc. v. Google Technology, Inc.,* 2003 WL 21464568 (W.D.Okla. 2003). See also *Langdon v. Google, Inc.,* 474 F.Supp.2d 622 (D.Del. 2007).

b. Eugene Volokh and Donald Falk, "First Amendment Protection for Search Engine Search Results: White Paper Commissioned by Google" (UCLA School of Law Research Paper No. 12-22, April 20, 2012).

a government's obligation to protect its citizens and those citizens' exercise of their rights. Reasonableness is analyzed on a case-by-case basis.

Content-Neutral Laws. Laws that regulate the time, manner, and place, but not the content, of speech receive less scrutiny by the courts than do laws that restrict the content of expression. If a restriction imposed by the government is content neutral, then a court may allow it. To be content neutral, the restriction must be aimed at combatting some societal problem, such as crime or drug abuse, and not be aimed at suppressing the expressive conduct or its message. Courts have often protected nude dancing as a form of symbolic expression but typically allow content-neutral laws that ban all public nudity.

▶ **Case in Point 5.6** Ria Ora was charged with dancing nude at an annual "anti-Christmas" protest in Harvard Square in Cambridge, Massachusetts, under a statute banning public displays of open and gross lewdness. Ora argued that the statute was overbroad and unconstitutional, and a trial court agreed. On appeal, however, a state appellate court upheld the statute as constitutional in situations in which there was an unsuspecting or unwilling audience.[18] ◀

Laws That Restrict the Content of Speech. If a law regulates the content of the expression, it must serve a compelling state interest and must be narrowly written to achieve that interest. Under the **compelling government interest** test, the government's interest is balanced against the individual's constitutional right to free expression. For the statute to be valid, there must be a compelling government interest that can be furthered only by the law in question.

The United States Supreme Court has held that schools may restrict students' speech at school events. ▶ **Case in Point 5.7** Some high school students held up a banner saying "Bong Hits 4 Jesus" at an off-campus but school-sanctioned event. The Supreme Court ruled that the school did not violate the students' free speech rights when school officials confiscated the banner and suspended the students for ten days. Because the banner could reasonably be interpreted as promoting drugs, the Court concluded that the school's actions were justified. Several justices disagreed, however, noting that the majority's holding creates an exception that will allow schools to censor any student speech that mentions drugs.[19] ◀

At issue in the following case was an Indiana state law that barred most sex offenders from using social networking sites such as Facebook, instant messaging services such as Twitter, and chat programs that the offenders knew were accessible to minors. Was this law unconstitutional under the First Amendment?

18. *Commonwealth v. Ora,* 451 Mass. 125, 883 N.E.2d 1217 (2008).

19. *Morse v. Frederick,* 551 U.S. 393, 127 S.Ct. 2618, 168 L.Ed.2d 290 (2007).

CASE 5.2

Doe[a] v. Prosecutor, Marion County, Indiana

United States Court of Appeals, Seventh Circuit, 705 F.3d 694 (2013).

BACKGROUND AND FACTS John Doe was convicted of child exploitation in Marion County, Indiana. After his release from prison, he was not subject to court supervision, but was required to register as a sex offender with the state. Under an Indiana statute that covered child exploitation and other sex offenses, Doe could not use certain Web sites and programs. Doe filed a suit in a federal district court against the Marion County prosecutor, alleging that the statute violated his right to freedom of speech under the First Amendment. Doe asked the court to issue an injunction to block enforcement of the law. The court held that "the regulation is narrowly tailored to serve a significant state interest" and entered a judgment for the defendant. Doe appealed to the U.S. Court of Appeals for the Seventh Circuit.

IN THE LANGUAGE OF THE COURT
FLAUM, Circuit Judge.

* * * *

Indiana Code Section 35-42-4-12 prohibits certain sex offenders from "knowingly or intentionally using: a social networking Web site" or "an instant messaging or chat room program"

a. The names *John Doe* and *Jane Doe* are used as placeholders in litigation to represent a party whose true identity is either unknown or being withheld for some reason.

CASE 5.2 CONTINUED

that "the offender knows allows a person who is less than eighteen (18) years of age to access or use the Web site or program." The law applies broadly to all individuals required to register as sex offenders.

* * * *

This case presents a single legal question * * * . The statute clearly implicates Doe's First Amendment rights * * * . It not only precludes [prohibits] expression through the medium of social media, it also limits his right to receive information and ideas. The Indiana law, however, is content neutral because it restricts speech without reference to the expression's content. As such, it may impose reasonable time, place, or manner restrictions. To do so, the law * * * must be narrowly tailored to serve a significant governmental interest.

The state initially asserts an interest in "protecting public safety, and specifically in protecting minors from harmful online communications." Indiana is certainly justified in shielding its children from improper sexual communication.

* * * *

* * * The state agrees there is nothing dangerous about Doe's use of social media as long as he does not improperly communicate with minors. Further, there is no disagreement that illicit communication comprises a minuscule subset of the universe of social network activity. As such, *the Indiana law targets substantially more activity than the evil it seeks to redress.* * * * *Indiana has other methods to combat unwanted and inappropriate communication between minors and sex offenders.* For instance, [under Indiana Code Section 35-42-4-6] it is a felony in Indiana for persons over twenty-one to "solicit" children under sixteen "to engage in: (1) sexual intercourse; (2) deviate sexual conduct; or (3) any fondling intended to arouse or satisfy the sexual desires of either the child or the older person." A separate statute goes further. [Indiana Code Section 35-42-4-13] punishes mere "inappropriate communication with a child" and communication "with the intent to gratify the sexual desires of the person or the individual." Significantly, both statutes have enhanced penalties for using a computer network and better advance Indiana's interest in preventing harmful interaction with children (by going beyond social networks). They also accomplish that end more narrowly (by refusing to burden benign Internet activity). That is, they are neither over nor under-inclusive like the statute at issue here. [Emphasis added.]

* * * *

For the foregoing reasons, we REVERSE the district court's decision, and REMAND with instructions to enter judgment in favor of Doe and issue the injunction.

DECISION AND REMEDY *The U.S. Court of Appeals for the Seventh Circuit reversed the lower court's judgment in the defendant's favor and remanded the case for the entry of a judgment for Doe. A law that concerns rights under the First Amendment must be narrowly tailored to accomplish its objective. The blanket ban on social media in this case did not pass this test.*

THE LEGAL ENVIRONMENT DIMENSION *What is an injunction? What did the plaintiff in this case hope to gain by seeking an injunction?*

THE SOCIAL DIMENSION *Could a state effectively enforce a law that banned all communication between minors and sex offenders through social media sites? Why or why not?*

CORPORATE POLITICAL SPEECH Political speech by corporations also falls within the protection of the First Amendment. Many years ago, the United States Supreme Court struck down as unconstitutional a Massachusetts statute that prohibited corporations from making political contributions or expenditures that individuals were permitted to make.[20] The Court has also held that a law forbidding a corporation from including inserts with its bills to express its views on controversial issues violates the First Amendment.[21]

Corporate political speech continues to be given significant protection under the First Amendment. ▶ **Case in Point 5.8** In *Citizens United v. Federal*

20. *First National Bank of Boston v. Bellotti,* 435 U.S. 765, 98 S.Ct. 1407, 55 L.Ed.2d 707 (1978).

21. *Consolidated Edison Co. v. Public Service Commission,* 447 U.S. 530, 100 S.Ct. 2326, 65 L.Ed.2d 319 (1980).

Election Commission,[22] the Supreme Court issued a landmark decision that overturned a twenty-year-old precedent on campaign financing. The case involved Citizens United, a nonprofit corporation that has a *political action committee* (an organization that registers with the government and campaigns for or against political candidates).

Citizens United had produced a film called *Hillary: The Movie* that was critical of Hillary Clinton, who was seeking the Democratic nomination for presidential candidate. Campaign-finance law restricted Citizens United from broadcasting the movie, however. The Court ruled that the restrictions were unconstitutional and that the First Amendment prevents limits from being placed on independent political expenditures by corporations. ◀

COMMERCIAL SPEECH The courts also give substantial protection to *commercial speech,* which consists of communications—primarily advertising and marketing—made by business firms that involve only their commercial interests. The protection given to commercial speech under the First Amendment is less extensive than that afforded to noncommercial speech, however.

22. 558 U.S. 310, 130 S.Ct. 876, 175 L.Ed.2d 753 (2010).

A state may restrict certain kinds of advertising, for instance, in the interest of preventing consumers from being misled. States also have a legitimate interest in roadside beautification and therefore may impose restraints on billboard advertising. ▶ **Case in Point 5.9** Café Erotica, a nude dancing establishment, sued the state after being denied a permit to erect a billboard along an interstate highway in Florida. The state appellate court decided that because the law directly advanced a substantial government interest in highway beautification and safety, it was not an unconstitutional restraint on commercial speech.[23] ◀

Generally, a restriction on commercial speech will be considered valid as long as it meets three criteria:

1. It must seek to implement a substantial government interest.
2. It must directly advance that interest.
3. It must go no further than necessary to accomplish its objective.

At issue in the following case was whether a government agency had unconstitutionally restricted commercial speech when it prohibited the inclusion of a certain illustration on beer labels.

23. *Café Erotica v. Florida Department of Transportation,* 830 So.2d 181 (Fla.App. 1 Dist. 2002); review denied by *Café Erotica We Dare to Bare v. Florida Department of Transportation,* 845 So.2d 888 (Fla. 2003).

SPOTLIGHT on Beer Labels

Case 5.3 Bad Frog Brewery, Inc. v. New York State Liquor Authority

United States Court of Appeals, Second Circuit, 134 F.3d 87 (1998).

BACKGROUND AND FACTS Bad Frog Brewery, Inc., makes and sells alcoholic beverages. Some of the beverages feature labels that display a drawing of a frog making the gesture generally known as "giving the finger." Bad Frog's authorized New York distributor, Renaissance Beer Company, applied to the New York State Liquor Authority (NYSLA) for brand label approval, as required by state law before the beer could be sold in New York.

The NYSLA denied the application, in part, because "the label could appear in grocery and convenience stores, with obvious exposure on the shelf to children of tender age." Bad Frog filed a suit in a federal district court against the NYSLA, asking for, among other things, an injunction against the denial of the application. The court granted summary judgment in favor of the NYSLA. Bad Frog appealed to the U.S. Court of Appeals for the Second Circuit.

IN THE LANGUAGE OF THE COURT
Jon O. *NEWMAN,* Circuit Judge:

* * * *

* * * To support its asserted power to ban Bad Frog's labels [NYSLA advances] * * * the State's interest in "protecting children from vulgar and profane advertising" * * * .

CASE 5.3 CONTINUED

[This interest is] substantial * * * . *States have a compelling interest in protecting the physical and psychological wellbeing of minors* * * * . [Emphasis added.]

* * * *

* * * NYSLA endeavors to advance the state interest in preventing exposure of children to vulgar displays by taking only the limited step of barring such displays from the labels of alcoholic beverages. *In view of the wide currency of vulgar displays throughout contemporary society, including comic books targeted directly at children, barring such displays from labels for alcoholic beverages cannot realistically be expected to reduce children's exposure to such displays to any significant degree.* [Emphasis added.]

* * * If New York decides to make a substantial effort to insulate children from vulgar displays in some significant sphere of activity, at least with respect to materials likely to be seen by children, NYSLA's label prohibition might well be found to make a justifiable contribution to the material advancement of such an effort, but its currently isolated response to the perceived problem, applicable only to labels on a product that children cannot purchase, does not suffice. * * * A state must demonstrate that its commercial speech limitation is part of a substantial effort to advance a valid state interest, not merely the removal of a few grains of offensive sand from a beach of vulgarity.

* * * *

* * * Even if we were to assume that the state materially advances its asserted interest by shielding children from viewing the Bad Frog labels, it is plainly excessive to prohibit the labels from all use, including placement on bottles displayed in bars and taverns where parental supervision of children is to be expected. Moreover, to whatever extent NYSLA is concerned that children will be harmfully exposed to the Bad Frog labels when wandering without parental supervision around grocery and convenience stores where beer is sold, that concern could be less intrusively dealt with by placing restrictions on the permissible locations where the appellant's products may be displayed within such stores.

DECISION AND REMEDY *The U.S. Court of Appeals for the Second Circuit reversed the judgment of the district court and remanded the case for the entry of a judgment in favor of Bad Frog. The NYSLA's ban on the use of the labels lacked a "reasonable fit" with the state's interest in shielding minors from vulgarity. In addition, the NYSLA had not adequately considered alternatives to the ban.*

WHAT IF THE FACTS WERE DIFFERENT? *If Bad Frog had sought to use the offensive label to market toys instead of beer, would the court's ruling likely have been the same? Why or why not?*

THE LEGAL ENVIRONMENT DIMENSION *Whose interests are advanced by the banning of certain types of advertising?*

UNPROTECTED SPEECH The United States Supreme Court has made it clear that certain types of speech will not be protected under the First Amendment. Speech that violates criminal laws (threatening speech and pornography, for example) is not constitutionally protected. Other unprotected speech includes fighting words, or words that are likely to incite others to respond violently. Speech that harms the good reputation of another, or defamatory speech (see Chapter 12), also is not protected under the First Amendment.

Obscene Speech. The First Amendment, as interpreted by the Supreme Court, also does not protect obscene speech. Establishing an objective definition of obscene speech has proved difficult, however, and the Court has grappled from time to time with this problem. In *Miller v. California*,[24] the Supreme Court created a test for legal obscenity, including a set of requirements that must be met for material to be legally obscene. Under this test, material is obscene if all of the following are true:

1. The average person finds that it violates contemporary community standards.
2. The work taken as a whole appeals to a prurient (arousing or obsessive) interest in sex.
3. The work shows patently offensive sexual conduct.
4. The work lacks serious redeeming literary, artistic, political, or scientific merit.

24. 413 U.S. 15, 93 S.Ct. 2607, 37 L.Ed.2d 419 (1973).

Because community standards vary widely, the *Miller* test has had inconsistent applications, and obscenity remains a constitutionally unsettled issue. Numerous state and federal statutes make it a crime to disseminate obscene materials, including child pornography.

Online Obscenity. Congress's first two attempts at protecting minors from pornographic materials on the Internet—the Communications Decency Act (CDA) of 1996[25] and the Child Online Protection Act (COPA) of 1998[26]—failed. Ultimately, the United States Supreme Court struck down both the CDA and COPA as unconstitutional restraints on speech, largely because the wording of these acts was overbroad and would restrict nonpornographic materials.

In 2000, Congress enacted the Children's Internet Protection Act (CIPA),[27] which requires public schools and libraries to install **filtering software** on computers to keep children from accessing adult content. Such software is designed to prevent persons from viewing certain Web sites based on a site's Internet address or its **meta tags,** or key words. The CIPA was challenged on constitutional grounds, but in 2003 the Supreme Court held that the act does not violate the First Amendment. The Court concluded that because libraries can disable the filters for any patrons who ask, the system is reasonably flexible and does not burden free speech to an unconstitutional extent.[28]

Virtual Pornography. In 2003, Congress enacted the Prosecutorial Remedies and Other Tools to end the Exploitation of Children Today Act (Protect Act).[29] The act makes it a crime to knowingly advertise, present, distribute, or solicit "any material or purported material in a manner that reflects the belief, or that is intended to cause another to believe, that the material or purported material" depicts actual child pornography.

Thus, it is a crime to intentionally distribute virtual child pornography—which uses computer-generated images, not actual people—without indicating that it is computer-generated. In a case challenging the constitutionality of the Protect Act, the Supreme Court held that the statute was valid because it does not prohibit a substantial amount of protected speech.[30] Rather, the act generally prohibits offers to provide, and requests to obtain, child pornography—both of which are unprotected speech. Nevertheless, because of the difficulties of policing the Internet, as well as the constitutional complexities of prohibiting online obscenity through legislation, it remains a problem worldwide.

Freedom of Religion

The First Amendment states that the government may neither establish any religion nor prohibit the free exercise of religious practices. The first part of this constitutional provision is referred to as the **establishment clause,** and the second part is known as the **free exercise clause.** Government action, both federal and state, must be consistent with this constitutional mandate.

THE ESTABLISHMENT CLAUSE The establishment clause prohibits the government from establishing a state-sponsored religion, as well as from passing laws that promote (aid or endorse) religion or show a preference for one religion over another. Although the establishment clause involves the separation of church and state, it does not require a complete separation.

Applicable Standard. Establishment clause cases often involve such issues as the legality of allowing or requiring school prayers, using state-issued vouchers to pay tuition at religious schools, and teaching creation theories versus evolution. Federal or state laws that do not promote or place a significant burden on religion are constitutional even if they have some impact on religion. For a government law or policy to be constitutional, it must not have the primary effect of promoting or inhibiting religion.

Religious Displays. Religious displays on public property have often been challenged as violating the establishment clause, and the United States Supreme Court has ruled on a number of such cases. Generally, the Court has focused on the proximity of the religious display to nonreligious symbols, such as reindeer and candy canes, or to symbols from different religions, such as a menorah (a nine-branched candelabrum used in celebrating Hanukkah). The Supreme Court

25. 47 U.S.C. Section 223(a)(1)(B)(ii).
26. 47 U.S.C. Section 231.
27. 17 U.S.C. Sections 1701–1741.
28. *United States v. American Library Association,* 539 U.S. 194, 123 S.Ct. 2297, 156 L.Ed.2d 221 (2003).
29. 18 U.S.C. Section 2252A(a)(5)(B).
30. *United States v. Williams,* 553 U.S. 285, 128 S.Ct. 1830, 170 L.Ed.2d 650 (2008).

took a slightly different approach when it held that public displays having historical, as well as religious, significance do not necessarily violate the establishment clause.[31]

▶ **Case in Point 5.10** Mount Soledad is a prominent hill near San Diego. There has been a forty-foot cross on top of Mount Soledad since 1913. In the 1990s, a war memorial with six walls listing the names of veterans was constructed next to the cross. The site was privately owned until 2006, when Congress authorized the property's transfer to the federal government "to preserve a historically significant war memorial."

Steve Trunk and the Jewish War Veterans filed lawsuits claiming that the cross violated the establishment clause because it endorsed the Christian religion. A federal appellate court agreed, finding that the primary effect of the memorial as a whole sent a strong message of endorsement of Christianity and exclusion (of non-Christian veterans). Although the inclusion of a cross in a war memorial does not always violate the establishment clause, the cross in this case physically dominated the site. Also, the cross was originally dedicated to religious purposes, had a long history of religious use, and was the only portion visible to drivers on the freeway below.[32] ◀

THE FREE EXERCISE CLAUSE The free exercise clause guarantees that a person can hold any religious belief that she or he wants, or a person can have no religious belief. The constitutional guarantee of personal freedom restricts only the actions of the government and not those of individuals or private businesses.

Restrictions Must Be Necessary. The government must have a compelling state interest for restricting the free exercise of religion, and the restriction must be the only way to further that interest. ▶ **Case in Point 5.11** Members of a particular Mennonite church must use horses and buggies for transportation, but they can use tractors to take their agricultural products to market. Their religion requires the tractors to have steel cleats on the tires, and they drove tractors with cleats on county roads for many years. Then the county passed an ordinance that prohibited the use of steel cleats because the cleats tend to damage newly surfaced roads.

When a member of the church received a citation for driving a tractor with cleats, he claimed that the ordinance violated the church's right to freely exercise its religion. Ultimately, the court ruled in his favor. The county had not met its burden of showing that the ordinance served a compelling state interest and was the least restrictive means of attaining that interest. There was no evidence of how much the cleats harmed the roads, other events also harmed the roads, and the county had allowed the cleats to be used for many years. Therefore, the ordinance was not carefully tailored to achieve the stated objective of road preservation.[33] ◀

Public Welfare Exception. When religious *practices* work against public policy and the public welfare, though, the government can act. For instance, the government can require that a child receive certain types of vaccinations or medical treatment if his or her life is in danger—regardless of the child's or parent's religious beliefs. When public safety is an issue, an individual's religious beliefs often have to give way to the government's interest in protecting the public.

▶ **Example 5.12** In the Muslim faith, it is a religious violation for a woman to appear in public without a scarf over her head. Due to public safety concerns, many courts today do not allow any headgear to be worn in courtrooms. A courthouse in Georgia prevented a Muslim woman from entering because she refused to remove her scarf. As she left, she uttered an expletive at the court official and was arrested and brought before the judge, who ordered her to serve ten days in jail. ◀

Searches and Seizures

The Fourth Amendment protects the "right of the people to be secure in their persons, houses, papers, and effects." Before searching or seizing private property, law enforcement officers must usually obtain a **search warrant**—an order from a judge or other public official authorizing the search or seizure.

SEARCH WARRANTS AND PROBABLE CAUSE To obtain a search warrant, law enforcement officers must convince a judge that they have reasonable grounds, or probable cause, to believe a search will reveal evidence of a specific illegality. To establish **probable cause,** the officers must have trustworthy evidence that would convince a reasonable person that the proposed search or seizure is more likely justified than not.

31. *Van Orden v. Perry,* 545 U.S. 677, 125 S.Ct. 2854, 162 L.Ed.2d 607 (2005).
32. *Trunk v. City of San Diego,* 629 F.3d 1099 (9th Cir. 2011).
33. *Mitchell County v. Zimmerman,* 810 N.W.2d 1 (Iowa Sup.Ct. 2012).

Furthermore, the Fourth Amendment prohibits *general* warrants. It requires warrants to include a particular description of whatever is to be searched or seized. General searches through a person's belongings are impermissible. The search cannot extend beyond what is described in the warrant. Although search warrants must be specific, if a warrant is issued for a person's residence, officers may search items found in that residence even though they belong to other individuals.

▶ **Case in Point 5.13** Paycom Billing Services, Inc., an online payment service, stores vast amounts of customer credit-card information. Christopher Adjani, a former Paycom employee, threatened to sell Paycom's confidential client information if the company did not pay him $3 million. Pursuant to an investigation, the Federal Bureau of Investigation (FBI) obtained a search warrant to search Adjani's person, automobile, and residence, including computer equipment. When the FBI agents served the warrant, they discovered evidence of the criminal scheme in the e-mail communications on a computer in Adjani's residence that belonged to Adjani's live-in girlfriend. The court held that the search of the computer was proper given the involvement of computers in the alleged crime.[34] ◀

SEARCHES AND SEIZURES IN THE BUSINESS CONTEXT Because of the strong government interest in protecting the public, a warrant normally is not required for seizures of spoiled or contaminated food. Nor are warrants required for searches of businesses in such highly regulated industries as liquor, guns, and strip mining.

The standard used for highly regulated industries is sometimes applied in other contexts as well, such as screening for airline travel. ▶ **Case in Point 5.14** Christian Hartwell was attempting to board a flight from Philadelphia to Phoenix. When he walked through the security checkpoint, he set off the alarm. Airport security took him aside and eventually discovered that he had two packages of crack cocaine in his pocket. When Hartwell was convicted of possession of drugs, he appealed, claiming that the airport search was suspicionless and violated his Fourth Amendment rights. A federal appellate court held that airports can be treated as highly regulated industries and that suspicionless checkpoint screening of airline passengers is constitutional.[35] ◀

34. *United States v. Adjani,* 452 F.3d 1140 (9th Cir. 2006); *cert.* denied, 549 U.S. 1025, 127 S.Ct. 568, 166 L.Ed.2d 420 (2006).

35. *United States v. Hartwell,* 436 F.3d 174 (3d Cir. 2006).

Generally, however, government inspectors do not have the right to enter business premises without a warrant, although the standard of probable cause is not the same as that required in nonbusiness contexts. The existence of a general and neutral enforcement plan will normally justify issuance of the warrant. Lawyers and accountants frequently possess the business records of their clients, and inspecting these documents while they are out of the hands of their true owners also requires a warrant.

Self-Incrimination

The Fifth Amendment guarantees that no person "shall be compelled in any criminal case to be a witness against himself." Thus, in any court proceeding, an accused person cannot be forced to give testimony that might subject him or her to any criminal prosecution. The guarantee applies to both federal and state proceedings because the due process clause of the Fourteenth Amendment extends the protection to state courts.

The Fifth Amendment's guarantee against self-incrimination extends only to natural persons. Therefore, neither corporations nor partnerships receive Fifth Amendment protection. When a partnership is required to produce business records, it must do so even if the information provided incriminates the individual partners of the firm. In contrast, sole proprietors and sole practitioners (those who fully own their businesses) cannot be compelled to produce their business records. These individuals have full protection against self-incrimination because they function in only one capacity, and there is no separate business entity.

SECTION 3

DUE PROCESS AND EQUAL PROTECTION

Other constitutional guarantees of great significance to Americans are mandated by the *due process clauses* of the Fifth and Fourteenth Amendments and the *equal protection clause* of the Fourteenth Amendment.

Due Process

Both the Fifth and Fourteenth Amendments provide that no person shall be deprived "of life, liberty, or property, without due process of law." The

due process clause of these constitutional amendments has two aspects—procedural and substantive. Note that the due process clause applies to "legal persons" (that is, corporations), as well as to individuals.

PROCEDURAL DUE PROCESS *Procedural* due process requires that any government decision to take life, liberty, or property must be made equitably. In other words, the government must give a person proper notice and an opportunity to be heard. Fair procedures must be used in determining whether a person will be subjected to punishment or have some burden imposed on her or him.

Fair procedure has been interpreted as requiring that the person have at least an opportunity to object to a proposed action before an impartial, neutral decision maker (which need not be a judge). ▶ **Example 5.15** Doyle Burns, a nursing student in Kansas, poses for a photograph standing next to a placenta used as a lab specimen. Although she quickly deletes the photo from her library, it ends up on Facebook. When the director of nursing sees the photo, Burns is expelled. She sues for reinstatement and wins. The school violated Burns's due process rights by expelling her from the nursing program for taking a photo without giving her an opportunity to present her side to school authorities. ◀

SUBSTANTIVE DUE PROCESS *Substantive* due process focuses on the content of legislation rather than the fairness of procedures. Substantive due process limits what the government may do in its legislative and executive capacities. Legislation must be fair and reasonable in content and must further a legitimate governmental objective. A city cannot, for instance, pass an ordinance that allows police officers to break up any group of two or more persons who are standing together if one of those persons is believed to be a gang member.

If a law or other governmental action limits a fundamental right, the state must have a legitimate and compelling interest to justify its action. Fundamental rights include interstate travel, privacy, voting, marriage and family, and all First Amendment rights. Thus, a state must have a substantial reason for taking any action that infringes on a person's free speech rights.

In situations not involving fundamental rights, a law or action does not violate substantive due process if it rationally relates to any legitimate government purpose. In these circumstances, only state conduct that is arbitrary or shocks the conscience will violate substantive due process. Under this test, almost any business regulation will be upheld as reasonable.

Equal Protection

Under the Fourteenth Amendment, a state may not "deny to any person within its jurisdiction the equal protection of the laws." The United States Supreme Court has interpreted the due process clause of the Fifth Amendment to make the **equal protection clause** applicable to the federal government as well. Equal protection means that the government cannot enact laws that treat similarly situated individuals differently.

Equal protection, like substantive due process, relates to the substance of a law or other governmental action. When a law or action limits the liberty of *all* persons, it may violate substantive due process. When a law or action limits the liberty of *some* persons but not others, it may violate the equal protection clause. ▶ **Example 5.16** If a law prohibits all persons from buying contraceptive devices, it raises a substantive due process question. If it prohibits only unmarried persons from buying the same devices, it raises an equal protection issue. ◀

In an equal protection inquiry, when a law or action distinguishes between or among individuals, the basis for the distinction—that is, its classification—is examined. Depending on the classification, the courts apply different levels of scrutiny, or "tests," to determine whether the law or action violates the equal protection clause. The courts use one of three standards: strict scrutiny, intermediate scrutiny, or the "rational basis" test.

STRICT SCRUTINY If a law or action prohibits or inhibits some persons from exercising a fundamental right, the law or action will be subject to "strict scrutiny" by the courts. Under this standard, the classification must be necessary to promote a *compelling state interest.* Also, if the classification is based on a *suspect trait*—such as race, national origin, or citizenship status—it must be necessary to promote a compelling government interest.[36]

Compelling state interests include remedying past unconstitutional or illegal discrimination but do not include correcting the general effects of "society's discrimination." ▶ **Example 5.17** For a city to give

36. See *Johnson v. California,* 543 U.S. 499, 125 S.Ct. 1141, 160 L.Ed.2d 949 (2005).

preference to minority applicants in awarding construction contracts, it normally must identify past unconstitutional or illegal discrimination against minority construction firms. Because the policy is based on suspect traits (race and national origin), it will violate the equal protection clause *unless* it is necessary to promote a compelling state interest. ◀ Generally, few laws or actions survive strict-scrutiny analysis by the courts.

INTERMEDIATE SCRUTINY Another standard, that of *intermediate scrutiny,* is applied in cases involving discrimination based on gender or discrimination against illegitimate children (children born out of wedlock). Laws using these classifications must be *substantially related to important government objectives.* For instance, an important government objective is preventing illegitimate teenage pregnancies. Because males and females are not similarly situated in this regard, a law that punishes men but not women for statutory rape will be upheld, even though it treats men and women unequally.

The state also has an important objective in establishing time limits (called *statutes of limitation*) for how long after an event a particular type of action can be brought. Nevertheless, the limitation period must be substantially related to the important objective of preventing fraudulent or outdated claims. ▶ **Example 5.18** A state law requires illegitimate children to bring paternity suits within six years of their births in order to seek support from their fathers. A court will strike down this law if legitimate children are allowed to seek support from their parents at any time. Distinguishing between support claims on the basis of legitimacy is not related to the important government objective of preventing fraudulent or outdated claims. ◀

THE "RATIONAL BASIS" TEST In matters of economic or social welfare, a classification will be considered valid if there is any conceivable *rational basis* on which the classification might relate to a legitimate government interest. It is almost impossible for a law or action to fail the rational basis test.

▶ **Example 5.19** A city ordinance prohibits all pushcart vendors, except a specific few, from operating in a particular area of the city. It will be upheld under the equal protection clause if the city provides a rational basis—such as reducing the traffic in the particular area—for the ordinance. ◀ In contrast, a law that provides unemployment benefits only to people over six feet tall would clearly fail the rational basis test because it could not further any legitimate government objective.

SECTION 4
PRIVACY RIGHTS

The U.S. Constitution does not explicitly mention a general right to privacy. In a 1928 Supreme Court case, *Olmstead v. United States,*[37] Justice Louis Brandeis stated in his dissent that the right to privacy is "the most comprehensive of rights and the right most valued by civilized men." The majority of the justices at that time, however, did not agree with Brandeis.

It was not until the 1960s that the Supreme Court endorsed the view that the Constitution protects individual privacy rights. In a landmark 1965 case, *Griswold v. Connecticut,*[38] the Supreme Court held that a constitutional right to privacy was implied by the First, Third, Fourth, Fifth, and Ninth Amendments.

Federal Statutes Affecting Privacy Rights

In the 1960s, Americans were sufficiently alarmed by the accumulation of personal information in government files that they pressured Congress to pass laws permitting individuals to access their files. Congress responded in 1966 with the Freedom of Information Act, which allows any person to request copies of any information on her or him contained in federal government files.

In 1974, Congress passed the Privacy Act, which also gives persons the right to access such information. Since then, Congress has passed numerous other laws protecting individuals' privacy rights with respect to financial transactions, electronic communications, and other activities in which personal information may be gathered and stored by organizations.

Since the 1990s, one of the major concerns of individuals has been how to protect privacy rights in cyberspace and to safeguard private information that may be revealed online. The increasing value of personal information for online marketers has exacerbated the situation. Chapter 15 discusses online privacy in more detail.

PRETEXTING A *pretext* is a false motive put forth to hide the real motive, and *pretexting* is the process of

37. 277 U.S. 438, 48 S.Ct. 564, 72 L.Ed. 944 (1928).
38. 381 U.S. 479, 85 S.Ct. 1678, 14 L.Ed.2d 510 (1965).

obtaining information by false means. Pretexters may try to obtain personal data by claiming that they are taking a survey for a research firm, a political party, or even a charity. The Gramm-Leach-Bliley Act[39] makes pretexting to obtain financial information illegal, but it does not mention lying to obtain *nonfinancial* information (for purposes other than identity theft).

▶ **Example 5.20** To find out who had leaked confidential company information to the press, Patricia C. Dunn, the chair of Hewlett-Packard, hired private investigators. They used false pretenses to access individuals' personal cell phone records. Dunn claimed that she had not been aware of the investigators' methods and had assumed that they had obtained the information from a public record. Criminal charges were filed but later dropped. Nevertheless, the scandal was highly publicized, and several civil lawsuits followed. Hewlett-Packard wound up paying millions to settle these lawsuits, including $14.5 million in fines to settle a claim filed by the California attorney general. ◀

To clarify the law on pretexting to gain access to phone records, Congress enacted the Telephone Records and Privacy Protection Act.[40] This act makes it a federal crime to pretend to be someone else or to make false representations for the purpose of obtaining another person's confidential phone records. The Federal Trade Commission investigates and prosecutes violators, who can be fined and sentenced to up to ten years in prison.

MEDICAL INFORMATION Responding to the growing need to protect the privacy of individuals' health records—particularly computerized records—Congress passed the Health Insurance Portability and Accountability Act (HIPAA).[41] This act defines and limits the circumstances in which an individual's "protected health information" may be used or disclosed.

HIPAA also requires health-care providers and health-care plans, including certain employers who sponsor health plans, to inform patients of their privacy rights and of how their personal medical information may be used. The act also states that a person's medical records generally may not be used for purposes unrelated to health care—such as marketing, for example—or disclosed to others without the individual's permission. Congress later expanded HIPAA's provisions to apply to vendors (those who maintain personal health records for health-care providers) and to electronic records shared by multiple medical providers. Congress also authorized the Federal Trade Commission to enforce HIPAA and pursue violators.

THE USA PATRIOT ACT The USA Patriot Act was passed by Congress in the wake of the terrorist attacks of September 11, 2001, and then reauthorized in 2006.[42] The Patriot Act has given government officials increased authority to monitor Internet activities (such as e-mail and Web site visits) and to gain access to personal financial information and student information. Law enforcement officials can now track the telephone and e-mail communications of one party to find out the identity of the other party or parties. Privacy advocates argue that this law adversely affects the constitutional rights of all Americans, and it has been widely criticized in the media.

To gain access to these communications, the government must certify that the information likely to be obtained by such monitoring is relevant to an ongoing criminal investigation. The government need not provide proof of any wrongdoing.[43]

▶ **Example 5.21** In 2012, General David Petraeus, who ran the wars in Iraq and Afghanistan, resigned as director of the Central Intelligence Agency after his extramarital affair with Paula Broadwell, his biographer, became public. Apparently, after Petraeus broke off the affair with Broadwell, she sent harassing e-mails to another woman. When she reported the harassment, the FBI investigated, accessed Petraeus's e-mail accounts, and discovered that he had communicated with Broadwell via messages left in a draft folder on his e-mail account. Although there was no evidence that Petraeus did anything illegal, he was urged to resign and did so. ◀

Other Laws Affecting Privacy

State constitutions and statutes also protect individuals' privacy rights, often to a significant degree. Privacy rights are also protected to some extent under tort law

39. Also known as the Financial Services Modernization Act, Pub. L. No. 106-102 (1999), 113 Stat. 1338, codified in numerous sections of 12 U.S.C.A.
40. 18 U.S.C. Section 1039.
41. HIPAA was enacted as Pub. L. No. 104-191 (1996) and is codified in 29 U.S.C.A. Sections 1181 *et seq.*
42. The Uniting and Strengthening America by Providing Appropriate Tools Required to Intercept and Obstruct Terrorism Act of 2001, also known as the USA Patriot Act, was enacted as Pub. L. No. 107-56 (2001) and reauthorized by Pub. L. No. 109-173 (2006).
43. See, for example, *American Civil Liberties Union v. National Security Agency,* 493 F.3d 644 (6th Cir. 2007), in which a federal appellate court upheld the government's warrantless monitoring of electronic communications.

(see Chapter 12), Internet law (see Chapter 15), and employment law (see Chapter 21). Additionally, the Federal Trade Commission has played an active role in protecting the privacy rights of online consumers.

Reviewing: Business and the Constitution

A state legislature enacted a statute that required any motorcycle operator or passenger on the state's highways to wear a protective helmet. Jim Alderman, a licensed motorcycle operator, sued the state to block enforcement of the law. Alderman asserted that the statute violated the equal protection clause because it placed requirements on motorcyclists that were not imposed on other motorists. Using the information presented in the chapter, answer the following questions.

1. Why does this statute raise equal protection issues instead of substantive due process concerns?
2. What are the three levels of scrutiny that the courts use in determining whether a law violates the equal protection clause?
3. Which standard of scrutiny, or test, would apply to this situation? Why?
4. Applying this standard, or test, is the helmet statute constitutional? Why or why not?

DEBATE THIS . . . *Legislation aimed at "protecting people from themselves" concerns the individual as well as the public in general. Protective helmet laws are just one example of such legislation. Should individuals be allowed to engage in unsafe activities if they choose to do so?*

Terms and Concepts

Bill of Rights 105
checks and balances 101
commerce clause 102
compelling government interest 108
due process clause 115
equal protection clause 115
establishment clause 112
federal form of government 100
filtering software 112
free exercise clause 112
full faith and credit clause 101
meta tags 112
police powers 100
preemption 105
privileges and immunities clause 101
probable cause 113
search warrant 113
sovereignty 100
supremacy clause 104
symbolic speech 106

ExamPrep

Issue Spotters

1. Can a state, in the interest of energy conservation, ban all advertising by power utilities if conservation could be accomplished by less restrictive means? Why or why not? **(See page 110.)**
2. Suppose that a state imposes a higher tax on out-of-state companies doing business in the state than it imposes on in-state companies. Is this a violation of equal protection if the only reason for the tax is to protect the local firms from out-of-state competition? Explain. **(See page 103.)**

- **Check your answers to the Issue Spotters against the answers provided in Appendix E at the end of this text.**

Before the Test

Go to **www.cengagebrain.com**, enter the ISBN 9781285428949, and click on "Find" to locate this textbook's Web site. Then, click on "Access Now" under "Study Tools," and select Chapter 5 at the top. There, you will find an Interactive Quiz that you can take to assess your mastery of the concepts in this chapter, as well as Flashcards and a Glossary of important terms.

Business Scenarios

5–1. Commerce Clause. A Georgia state law requires the use of contoured rear-fender mudguards on trucks and trailers operating within Georgia state lines. The statute further makes it illegal for trucks and trailers to use straight mudguards. In approximately thirty-five other states, straight mudguards are legal. Moreover, in Florida, straight mudguards are explicitly required by law. There is some evidence suggesting that contoured mudguards might be a little safer than straight mudguards. Discuss whether this Georgia statute violates any constitutional provisions. **(See page 102.)**

5–2. Freedom of Religion. Thomas worked in the nonmilitary operations of a large firm that produced both military and nonmilitary goods. When the company discontinued the production of nonmilitary goods, Thomas was transferred to a plant producing military equipment. Thomas left his job, claiming that it violated his religious principles to participate in the manufacture of goods to be used in destroying life. In effect, he argued, the transfer to the military equipment plant forced him to quit his job. He was denied unemployment compensation by the state because he had not been effectively "discharged" by the employer but had voluntarily terminated his employment. Did the state's denial of unemployment benefits to Thomas violate the free exercise clause of the First Amendment? Explain. **(See page 112.)**

5–3. Equal Protection. With the objectives of preventing crime, maintaining property values, and preserving the quality of urban life, New York City enacted an ordinance to regulate the locations of commercial establishments that featured adult entertainment. The ordinance expressly applied to female, but not male, topless entertainment. Adele Buzzetti owned the Cozy Cabin, a New York City cabaret that featured female topless dancers. Buzzetti and an anonymous dancer filed a suit in a federal district court against the city, asking the court to block the enforcement of the ordinance. The plaintiffs argued, in part, that the ordinance violated the equal protection clause. Under the equal protection clause, what standard applies to the court's consideration of this ordinance? Under this test, how should the court rule? Why? **(See page 115.)**

Business Case Problems

5–4. Spotlight on Plagiarism—Due Process. The Russ College of

Engineering and Technology of Ohio University announced in a press conference that it had found "rampant and flagrant plagiarism" in the theses of mechanical engineering graduate students. Faculty singled out for "ignoring their ethical responsibilities" included Jay Gunasekera, chair of the department. Gunasekera was prohibited from advising students. He filed a suit against Dennis Irwin, the dean of Russ College, for violating his due process rights. What does due process require in these circumstances? Why? [*Gunasekera v. Irwin,* 551 F.3d 461 (6th Cir. 2009)] **(See page 114.)**

5–5. Commerce Clause. Under the federal Sex Offender Registration and Notification Act (SORNA), sex offenders must register and update their registration as sex offenders when they travel from one state to another. David Hall, a convicted sex offender in New York, moved to Virginia, where he did not update his registration. He was charged with violating SORNA. He claimed that the statute is unconstitutional, arguing that Congress cannot criminalize interstate travel if no commerce is involved. Is that reasonable? Why or why not? [*United States v. Guzman,* 591 F.3d 83 (2d Cir. 2010)] **(See page 102.)**

5–6. BUSINESS CASE PROBLEM WITH SAMPLE ANSWER: Establishment Clause.

Judge James DeWeese hung a poster in his courtroom showing the Ten Commandments. The American Civil Liberties Union (ACLU) filed a suit, alleging that the poster violated the establishment clause. DeWeese responded that his purpose was not to promote religion but to express his view about "warring" legal philosophies—moral relativism and moral absolutism. "Our legal system is based on moral absolutes from divine law handed down by God through the Ten Commandments." Does this poster violate the establishment clause? Why or why not? [American Civil Liberties Union of Ohio Foundation, Inc. v. DeWeese, *633 F.3d 424 (6th Cir. 2011)*] **(See page 112.)**

- **For a sample answer to Problem 5–6, go to Appendix F at the end of this text.**

5–7. The Dormant Commerce Clause. In 2001, Puerto Rico enacted a law that requires specific labels on cement sold in Puerto Rico and imposes fines for any violations of these requirements. The law prohibits the sale or distribution of cement manufactured outside Puerto Rico that does not carry a required label warning that the cement may not be used in government-financed construction projects. Antilles Cement Corp., a Puerto Rican firm that imports foreign cement, filed a complaint in federal court, claiming that this law violated the dormant commerce clause. (The dormant commerce clause doctrine applies not only to commerce among the states and U.S. territories, but also to international commerce.) Did the 2001 Puerto Rican law violate the dormant commerce clause? Why or why not? [*Antilles Cement Corp. v. Fortuno,* 670 F.3d 310 (1st Cir. 2012)] **(See page 103.)**

5–8. Freedom of Speech. Mark Wooden sent an e-mail to an alderwoman for the city of St. Louis. Attached was a nineteen-minute audio file that compared her to the biblical character Jezebel. The audio said she was a "bitch in the Sixth Ward," spending too much time with the rich and powerful and too little time with the poor. In a menacing, maniacal tone, Wooden said that he was "dusting off a sawed-off shotgun," called himself a "domestic terrorist," and referred to the assassination of President John Kennedy, the murder of federal judge John Roll, and the shooting of Representative Gabrielle Giffords. Feeling threatened, the alderwoman called the police. Wooden was convicted of harassment under a state criminal statute. Was this conviction unconstitutional under the First Amendment? Discuss. [*State v. Wooden,* 388 S.W.3d 522 (Mo. 2013)] **(See page 106.)**

5–9. A QUESTION OF ETHICS: Defamation.

*Aric Toll owns and manages the Balboa Island Village Inn, a restaurant and bar in Newport Beach, California. Anne Lemen lives across from the inn. Lemen complained to the authorities about the inn's customers, whom she called "drunks" and "whores." She referred to Aric's wife as "Madam Whore" and told neighbors that the owners were involved in illegal drugs and prostitution. Lemen told the inn's bartender Ewa Cook that Cook "worked for Satan." She repeated her statements to potential customers, and the inn's sales dropped more than 20 percent. The inn filed a suit against Lemen. [*Balboa Island Village Inn, Inc. v. Lemen, *40 Cal.4th 1141, 156 P.3d 339 (2007)]* **(See page 111.)**

(a) Are Lemen's statements about the inn's owners, customers, and activities protected by the U.S. Constitution? Should such statements be protected? In whose favor should the court rule? Why?

(b) Did Lemen behave unethically in the circumstances of this case? Explain.

Legal Reasoning Group Activity

5–10. Free Speech and Equal Protection. For many years, New York City has had to deal with the vandalism and defacement of public property caused by unauthorized graffiti. In an effort to stop the damage, the city banned the sale of aerosol spray-paint cans and broad-tipped indelible markers to persons under twenty-one years of age. The new rules also prohibited people from possessing these items on property other than their own. Within a year, five people under age twenty-one were cited for violations of these regulations, and 871 individuals were arrested for actually making graffiti.

Lindsey Vincenty and other artists wished to create graffiti on legal surfaces, such as canvas, wood, and clothing. Unable to buy her supplies in the city or to carry them in the city if she bought them elsewhere, Vincenty and others filed a lawsuit on behalf of themselves and other young artists against Michael Bloomberg, the city's mayor, and others. The plaintiffs claimed that, among other things, the new rules violated their right to freedom of speech. **(See page 106.)**

(a) One group will argue in favor of the plaintiffs and provide several reasons why the court should hold that the city's new rules violate the plaintiffs' freedom of speech.

(b) Another group will develop a counterargument that outlines the reasons why the new rules do not violate free speech rights.

(c) A third group will argue that the city's ban violates the equal protection clause because it applies only to persons under age twenty-one.

CHAPTER 7
CRIMINAL LAW AND CYBER CRIME

Criminal law is an important part of the legal environment of business. Various sanctions are used to bring about a society in which individuals engaging in business can compete and flourish. These sanctions include damages for various types of tortious conduct (see Chapters 12 and 13), damages for breach of contract (to be discussed in Chapter 10), and the equitable remedies discussed in Chapter 1. Additional sanctions are imposed under criminal law. Indeed, many statutes regulating business provide for criminal as well as civil penalties.

In this chapter, after explaining some essential differences between criminal law and civil law, we look at how crimes are classified and at the elements that must be present for criminal liability to exist. We then examine the various categories of crimes, the defenses that can be raised to avoid criminal liability, and the rules of criminal procedure.

We conclude the chapter with a discussion of crimes that occur in cyberspace, which are often called *cyber crimes*. Cyber attacks are becoming all too common—even e-mail and data of government agencies and former U.S. presidents have been hacked. Smartphones are being infected by malicious software, which puts users' data at risk, as you will read in a feature later in this chapter.

SECTION 1
CIVIL LAW AND CRIMINAL LAW

Recall from Chapter 1 that *civil law* pertains to the duties that exist between persons or between persons and their governments. Criminal law, in contrast, has to do with crime. A **crime** can be defined as a wrong against society set forth in a statute and punishable by a fine and/or imprisonment—or, in some cases, death.

As mentioned in Chapter 1, because crimes are *offenses against society as a whole,* they are prosecuted by a public official, such as a district attorney (D.A.) or an attorney general (A.G.), not by the victims. Once a crime has been reported, the D.A.'s office decides whether to file criminal charges and to what extent to pursue the prosecution or carry out additional investigation.

Key Differences between Civil Law and Criminal Law

Because the state has extensive resources at its disposal when prosecuting criminal cases, there are numerous procedural safeguards to protect the rights of defendants. We look here at one of these safeguards—the higher burden of proof that applies in a criminal case—as well as the harsher sanctions for criminal acts compared with those for civil wrongs (torts—see Chapter 12). Exhibit 7–1 on the facing page summarizes these and other key differences between civil law and criminal law.

BURDEN OF PROOF In a civil case, the plaintiff usually must prove his or her case by a *preponderance of the evidence*. Under this standard, the plaintiff must convince the court that based on the evidence presented by both parties, it is more likely than not that the plaintiff's allegation is true.

In a criminal case, in contrast, the state must prove its case **beyond a reasonable doubt.** If the jury views the evidence in the case as reasonably permitting either a guilty or a not guilty verdict, then the jury's verdict must be not guilty. In other words, the government (prosecutor) must prove beyond a reasonable doubt that the defendant has committed every essential element of the offense with which she or he is charged.

If the jurors are not convinced of the defendant's guilt beyond a reasonable doubt, they must find

EXHIBIT 7–1 Key Differences between Civil Law and Criminal Law

Issue	Civil Law	Criminal Law
Party who brings suit	The person who suffered harm.	The state.
Wrongful act	Causing harm to a person or to a person's property.	Violating a statute that prohibits some type of activity.
Burden of proof	Preponderance of the evidence.	Beyond a reasonable doubt.
Verdict	Three-fourths majority (typically).	Unanimous (almost always).
Remedy	Damages to compensate for the harm or a decree to achieve an equitable result.	Punishment (fine, imprisonment, or death).

the defendant not guilty. Note also that in a criminal case, the jury's verdict normally must be unanimous—agreed to by all members of the jury—to convict the defendant.[1] (In a civil trial by jury, in contrast, typically only three-fourths of the jurors need to agree.)

CRIMINAL SANCTIONS The sanctions imposed on criminal wrongdoers are also harsher than those applied in civil cases. As we will see in Chapter 12, the purpose of tort law is to enable a person harmed by a wrongful act to obtain compensation from the wrongdoer, rather than to punish the wrongdoer. In contrast, criminal sanctions are designed to punish those who commit crimes and to deter others from committing similar acts in the future.

Criminal sanctions include fines as well as the much harsher penalty of the loss of one's liberty by incarceration in a jail or prison. Most criminal sanctions also involve probation and sometimes require performance of community service, completion of an educational or treatment program, or payment of restitution. The harshest criminal sanction is, of course, the death penalty.

Civil Liability for Criminal Acts

Some torts, such as assault and battery, provide a basis for a criminal prosecution as well as a civil action in tort. ▶ **Example 7.1** Jonas is walking down the street, minding his own business, when a person attacks him. In the ensuing struggle, the attacker stabs Jonas several times, seriously injuring him. A police officer restrains and arrests the assailant. In this situation, the attacker may be subject both to criminal prosecution by the state and to a tort lawsuit brought by Jonas to obtain compensation for his injuries. ◀

Exhibit 7–2 on the following page illustrates how the same wrongful act can result in both a civil (tort) action and a criminal action against the wrongdoer.

Classification of Crimes

Depending on their degree of seriousness, crimes are classified as felonies or misdemeanors. **Felonies** are serious crimes punishable by death or by imprisonment for more than one year.[2] Many states also define different degrees of felony offenses and vary the punishment according to the degree.[3] For instance, most jurisdictions punish a burglary that involves forced entry into a home at night more harshly than a burglary that involves breaking into a nonresidential building during the day.

Misdemeanors are less serious crimes, punishable by a fine or by confinement for up to a year. **Petty offenses** are minor violations, such as jaywalking or violations of building codes, considered to be a subset of misdemeanors. Even for petty offenses, however, a guilty party can be put in jail for a few days, fined, or both, depending on state or local law. Whether a crime is a felony or a misdemeanor can determine in which court the case is

1. A few states allow jury verdicts that are not unanimous. Arizona, for example, allows six of eight jurors to reach a verdict in criminal cases. Louisiana and Oregon have also relaxed the requirement of unanimous jury verdicts.

2. Some states, such as North Carolina, consider felonies to be punishable by incarceration for at least two years.

3. Although the American Law Institute issued the Model Penal Code in 1962, it is not a uniform code, and each state has developed its own set of laws governing criminal acts. Thus, types of crimes and prescribed punishments may differ from one jurisdiction to another.

EXHIBIT 7–2 Civil (Tort) Lawsuit and Criminal Prosecution for the Same Act

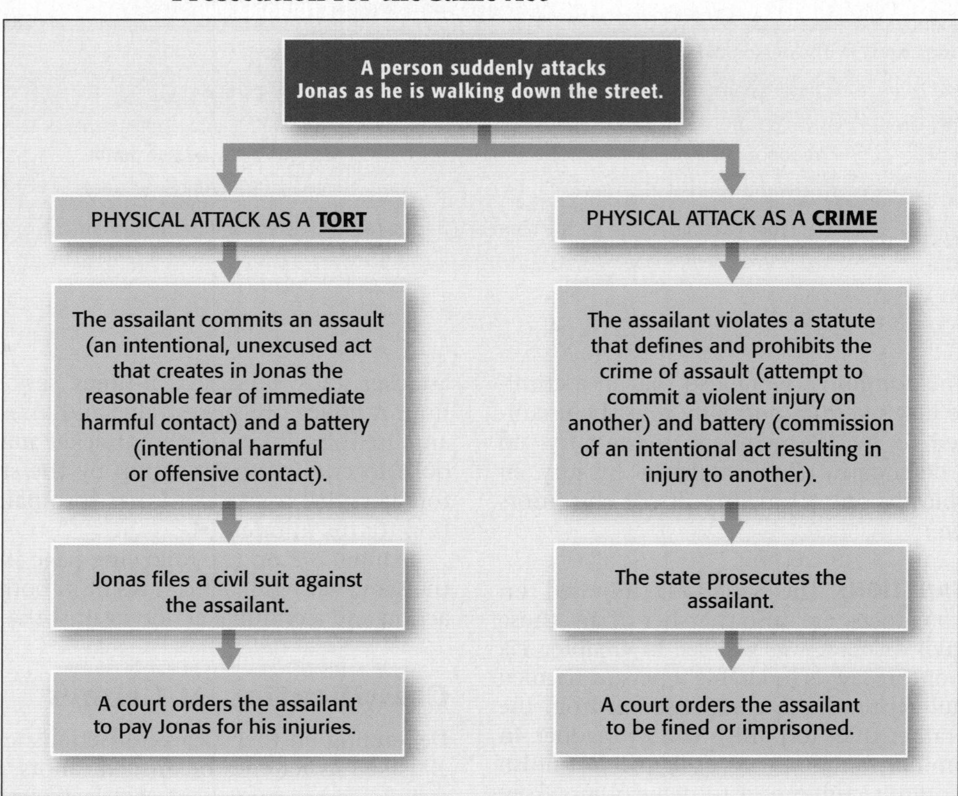

tried and, in some states, whether the defendant has a right to a jury trial.

SECTION 2 CRIMINAL LIABILITY

The following two elements normally must exist *simultaneously* for a person to be convicted of a crime:

1. The performance of a prohibited act *(actus reus).*
2. A specified state of mind, or intent, on the part of the actor *(mens rea).*

The Criminal Act

Every criminal statute prohibits certain behavior. Most crimes require an act of *commission*—that is, a person must *do* something in order to be accused of a crime. In criminal law, a prohibited act is referred to as the ***actus reus,***[4] or guilty act. In some instances, an act of omission can be a crime, but only when a person has a legal duty to perform the omitted act, such as filing a tax return.

The *guilty act* requirement is based on one of the premises of criminal law—that a person should be punished for harm done to society. For a crime to exist, the guilty act must cause some harm to a person or to property. Thinking about killing someone or about stealing a car may be morally wrong, but the thoughts do no harm until they are translated into action.

Of course, a person can be punished for *attempting* murder or robbery, but normally only if he or she has taken substantial steps toward the criminal objective. Additionally, the person must have specifically

4. Pronounced *ak*-tuhs *ray*-uhs.

intended to commit the crime to be convicted of an attempt.

State of Mind

A wrongful mental state, or ***mens rea,***[5] also is typically required to establish criminal liability. The required mental state, or intent, is indicated in the applicable statute or law. Murder, for example, involves the guilty act of killing another human being, and the guilty mental state is the desire, or intent, to take another's life. For theft, the guilty act is the taking of another person's property. The mental state involves both the awareness that the property belongs to another and the desire to deprive the owner of it.

RECKLESSNESS A court can also find that the required mental state is present when a defendant's acts are reckless or criminally negligent. A defendant is *criminally reckless* if he or she consciously disregards a substantial and unjustifiable risk.

▶ Example 7.2 A fourteen-year-old New Jersey girl posts a Facebook message saying that she is going to launch a terrorist attack on her high school and asking if anyone wants to help. The police arrest the girl for the crime of making a terrorist threat. The statute requires the intent to commit an act of violence with "the intent to terrorize" or "in reckless disregard of the risk of causing" terror or inconvenience. Although the girl argues that she had no intent to cause harm, the police can prosecute her under the "reckless disregard" part of the statute. ◀

CRIMINAL NEGLIGENCE *Criminal negligence* involves the mental state in which the defendant takes an unjustified, substantial, and foreseeable risk that results in harm. A defendant can negligent even if she or he was not actually aware of the risk but *should have been aware* of it.[6]

A homicide is classified as *involuntary manslaughter* when it results from an act of criminal negligence and there is no intent to kill. **▶ Example 7.3** Dr. Conrad Murray, the personal physician of pop star Michael Jackson, was convicted of involuntary manslaughter in 2011 for prescribing the drug that led to Jackson's sudden death in 2009. Murray had given Jackson propofol, a powerful anesthetic normally used in surgery, as a sleep aid on the night of his death, even though he knew that Jackson had already taken other sedatives. ◀

STRICT LIABILITY AND OVERCRIMINALIZATION An increasing number of laws and regulations impose criminal sanctions for strict liability crimes. Strict liability crimes are offenses that do not require a wrongful mental state to establish criminal liability.

Federal Crimes. The federal criminal code now lists more than four thousand criminal offenses, many of which do not require a specific mental state. There are also at least ten thousand federal rules that can be enforced through criminal sanctions, and many of these rules do not require intent.

▶ Example 7.4 Eddie Leroy Anderson, a retired logger and former science teacher, and his son went digging for arrowheads near a campground in Idaho. They did not realize that they were on federal land and that it is a felony to remove artifacts from federal land without a permit. Although the crime carries as much as two years in prison, father and son pleaded guilty, and each received a sentence of probation and a $1,500 fine. ◀

Strict liability crimes are particularly common in environmental laws, laws aimed at combatting illegal drugs, and other laws affecting public health, safety, and welfare. Under federal law, for example, tenants can be evicted from public housing if a member of the household or a guest used illegal drugs. The eviction can occur regardless of whether the tenant knew or should have known about the drug activity.[7]

State Crimes. Many states have also enacted laws that punish behavior as criminal without the need to show criminal intent. **▶ Example 7.5** In Arizona, a hunter who shoots an elk outside the area specified by the hunting permit has committed a crime. The hunter can be convicted of the crime regardless of her or his intent or knowledge of the law. ◀

Overcriminalization. Proponents of strict liability criminal laws argue that they are necessary to protect the public and the environment. Critics say laws that criminalize conduct without any required intent have led to *overcriminalization,* or the use of criminal law as

5. Pronounced *mehns ray*-uh.
6. Model Penal Code Section 2.02(2)(d).
7. See, for example, *Department of Housing and Urban Development v. Rucker,* 535 U.S. 125, 122 S.Ct. 1230, 152 L.Ed.2d 258 (2002).

the main tool to solve social problems, such as illegal drug use. They argue that when the requirement of intent is removed, people are more likely to commit crimes unknowingly—and perhaps even innocently. When an honest mistake can lead to a criminal conviction, the idea that crimes are a wrong against society is undermined.

Corporate Criminal Liability

A corporation is a legal entity created under the laws of a state. At one time, it was thought that a corporation could not incur criminal liability because, although a corporation is a legal person, it can act only through its agents (corporate directors, officers, and employees). Therefore, the corporate entity itself could not "intend" to commit a crime. Over time, this view has changed. Obviously, corporations cannot be imprisoned, but they can be fined or denied certain legal privileges (such as necessary licenses).

LIABILITY OF THE CORPORATE ENTITY Today, corporations normally are liable for the crimes committed by their agents and employees within the course and scope of their employment.[8] For liability to be imposed, the prosecutor generally must show that the corporation could have prevented the act or that a supervisor authorized or had knowledge of the act. In addition, corporations can be criminally liable for failing to perform specific duties imposed by law (such as duties under environmental laws or securities laws).

▶ **Case in Point 7.6** A prostitution ring, the Gold Club, was operating out of some motels in West Virginia. A motel manager, who was also a corporate officer, gave discounted rates to Gold Club prostitutes, and they paid him in cash. The corporation received a portion of the funds generated by the Gold Club's illegal operations. A jury found that the corporation was criminally liable because a supervisor within the corporation—the motel manager—had knowledge of the prostitution and the corporation had allowed it to continue.[9] ◀

LIABILITY OF THE CORPORATE OFFICERS AND DIRECTORS Corporate directors and officers are personally liable for the crimes they commit, regardless of whether the crimes were committed for their private benefit or on the corporation's behalf. Additionally, corporate directors and officers may be held liable for the actions of employees under their supervision. Under the *responsible corporate officer* doctrine, a court may impose criminal liability on a corporate officer who participated in, directed, or merely knew about a given criminal violation.

▶ **Case in Point 7.7** The Roscoe family owned the Customer Company, which operated an underground storage tank that leaked gasoline. An employee, John Johnson, reported the leak to the state environmental agency, and the Roscoes hired an environmental services firm to clean up the spill. The clean-up did not occur immediately, however. The state sent many notices to John Roscoe, a corporate officer, warning him that the company was violating federal and state environmental laws. Roscoe gave the letters to Johnson, who passed them on to the environmental services firm, but the spill was not cleaned up.

The state eventually filed criminal charges against the corporation and the Roscoes individually. They were convicted under the responsible corporate officer doctrine. The Roscoes were in positions of responsibility, they had influence over the corporation's actions, and their failure to act constituted a violation of environmental laws.[10] ◀

SECTION 3

TYPES OF CRIMES

Federal, state, and local laws provide for the classification and punishment of hundreds of thousands of different criminal acts. Generally, though, criminal acts can be grouped into five broad categories: violent crime (crimes against persons), property crime, public order crime, white-collar crime, and organized crime. Note also that many crimes may be committed in cyberspace, as well as the physical world. When they occur in the virtual world, we

8. See Model Penal Code Section 2.07.

9. As a result of the convictions, the motel manager was sentenced to fifteen months in prison, and the corporation was ordered to forfeit the motel property. *United States v. Singh,* 518 F.3d 236 (4th Cir. 2008).

10. The Roscoes and the corporation were sentenced to pay penalties of $2,493,250. *People v. Roscoe,* 169 Cal.App.4th 829, 87 Cal.Rptr.3d 187 (3 Dist. 2008).

refer to them as cyber crimes, as discussed later in the chapter.

Violent Crime

Certain crimes are called *violent crimes,* or crimes against persons, because they cause others to suffer harm or death. Murder is a violent crime. So is sexual assault, or rape. **Robbery**—defined as the taking of money, personal property, or any other article of value from a person by means of force or fear—is also a violent crime. Typically, states have more severe penalties for *aggravated robbery*—robbery with the use of a deadly weapon.

Assault and battery, which will be discussed in Chapter 12 in the context of tort law, are also classified as violent crimes. ▶ **Example 7.8** Former rap star Flavor Flav (whose real name is William Drayton) was arrested in Las Vegas in 2012 on assault and battery charges. During an argument with his fiancée, Drayton allegedly threw her to the ground and then grabbed two kitchen knives and chased her son. ◀

Each violent crime is further classified by degree, depending on the circumstances surrounding the criminal act. These circumstances include the intent of the person committing the crime and whether a weapon was used. For crimes other than murder, the level of pain and suffering experienced by the victim is also a factor.

Property Crime

The most common type of criminal activity is property crime, in which the goal of the offender is some form of economic gain or the damaging of property. Robbery is a form of property crime, as well as a violent crime, because the offender seeks to gain the property of another. We look here at a number of other crimes that fall within the general category of property crime. (Note also that many types of cyber crime, discussed later in this chapter, are forms of property crime as well.)

BURGLARY Traditionally, **burglary** was defined as breaking and entering the dwelling of another at night with the intent to commit a felony. This definition was aimed at protecting an individual's home and its occupants. Most state statutes have eliminated some of the requirements found in the common law definition. The time of day at which the breaking and entering occurs, for example, is usually immaterial. State statutes frequently omit the element of breaking, and some states do not require that the building be a dwelling. When a deadly weapon is used in a burglary, the perpetrator can be charged with *aggravated burglary* and punished more severely.

LARCENY Under the common law, the crime of **larceny** involved the unlawful taking and carrying away of someone else's personal property with the intent to permanently deprive the owner of possession. Put simply, larceny is stealing, or theft. Whereas robbery involves force or fear, larceny does not. Therefore, picking pockets is larceny, not robbery. Similarly, taking company products and supplies home for personal use without permission is larceny. (Note that a person who commits larceny generally can also be sued under tort law because the act of taking possession of another's property involves the tort of trespass to personal property—see Chapter 12.)

Most states have expanded the definition of property that is subject to larceny statutes. Stealing computer programs may constitute larceny even though the "property" is not physical (see the discussion of computer crime later in this chapter). So, too, can the theft of natural gas or Internet and television cable service.

OBTAINING GOODS BY FALSE PRETENSES Obtaining goods by means of false pretenses is a form of theft that involves trickery or fraud, such as using someone else's credit-card number without permission to purchase an iPad. Statutes dealing with such illegal activities vary widely from state to state. They often apply not only to property, but also to services and cash.

Sometimes, a statute consolidates the crime of obtaining goods by false pretenses with other property offenses, such as larceny and embezzlement, into a single crime called simply "theft." Under such a statute, it is not necessary for a defendant to be charged specifically with larceny, embezzlement, or obtaining goods by false pretenses. *Petty theft* is the theft of a small quantity of cash or low-value goods. *Grand theft* is the theft of a larger amount of cash or higher-value property. In the following case, the sales manager of a sports vehicle dealership was charged under a state statute with grand theft.

CASE ANALYSIS

Case 7.1 People v. Whitmer

Court of Appeal of California, Second District, Division 4, 213 Cal.App.4th 122, 152 Cal.Rptr.3d 216 (2013).

IN THE LANGUAGE OF THE COURT

MANELLA, J. [Judge]

* * * *

Jerome Gilding owned Temple City Power Sports, a business located in San Gabriel [California] that sold and serviced motorcycles, motorized dirt bikes [all terrain vehicles (ATVs)], and jet skis.

Customers of the dealership negotiated purchases with salespersons. The dealership made sales to customers who entered into financing agreements or paid with credit cards. In such cases, after the salesperson reached an agreement with the customer regarding an item and the manner of payment, the transaction was referred to the sales manager for approval. If approved, the transaction was sent to the dealership finance department, which collected the information necessary to process the financing agreement or credit card sale. When the dealership sold an item to a customer who failed to make the loan payments or used a bad credit card, the dealership incurred a "charge back," that is, took responsibility for the loss on the transaction. * * * To prevent charge backs, the dealership's policy was to require customers to make purchases in person and to present two forms of identification.

Ordinarily, when credit card purchases were made, the card was swiped through a credit card machine, which instantaneously sent information regarding the purchase to the pertinent bank. An approval or denial was received from the bank within a few seconds. In contrast, if the machine was set for an "offline" * * * sale, the machine recorded the transaction but sent no information to the bank. As a result, no immediate credit approval or denial was generated; instead, information regarding the transaction was transmitted to the bank at the end of the business day. Gilding did not permit offline sales.

Associated with each vehicle sold by the dealership is a document known as the "manufacturer certificate of origin" (MSO). The vehicle's original MSO can be used to establish title to the vehicle in other states and countries. The dealership retained the original MSO after a sale unless the vehicle was sold to an out-of-state purchaser or transferred to another dealer. The dealership had contractual obligations to several manufacturers not to sell vehicles for exportation outside the United States.

In 2009 [Jeffrey Whitmer] was the dealership's sales manager, and Alex Barrera was employed as a salesperson. Eric Van Hek worked in the financial department until August or September 2009, when he was replaced by Richard Carlos. In late August or early September 2009, Gilding told [Whitmer] not to deal with Mordichi Mor, who had engaged in a fraudulent transaction at the dealership in 2008.

* * * *

* * * In the fall of 2009, * * * after meeting with Mordichi [Whitmer] directed Carlos to process sales transactions involving customers Carlos had never met * * * . Whenever the transaction involved a credit card [Whitmer] told Carlos to process it as an offline sale. Carlos prepared the paperwork for each transaction and gave it to [Whitmer] who returned the documents to him with the customer's signature. [Whitmer] directed other employees to deliver the purchased vehicles to Mordichi's home.

* * * *

[At Whitmer's request] Angela Wilcox, a dealership employee, * * * gave [Whitmer] original MSOs from the dealership's files related to deals [Whitmer] arranged with Mor.

* * * In mid-December 2009, a credit card company told [Gilding] that credit card usage had increased at the dealership, and that he should expect charge backs. He initiated an inquiry that uncovered 20 potentially fraudulent sales of motorcycles, motorized dirt bikes, ATVs, and recreational vehicles at the dealership from August 4 to December 8, 2009. Barrera was the salesperson in all the sales, each of which involved one of seven purported buyers. * * * The dealership incurred a charge back on each sale ranging from $9,100 to $21,479.80, resulting in losses exceeding $250,000. In addition, the original MSOs for the vehicles in the dealership's files had been replaced by copies, even though the transactions were not of the type that required the dealership to transfer the original MSO to the purchaser.

Shortly after Gilding discovered the potential fraud, Barrera stopped appearing for work.

Later, [local] Police Department Detective Armando Valenzuela determined that the identification information provided for the buyers on the sales documents was false, and that the existence of the buyers could not be established. He also discovered that several of the vehicles had been shipped to Israel.

On February 16, 2010, Detective Valenzuela * * * arrested [Whitmer, who was charged with twenty counts of grand theft. A jury in a California state court convicted him on all counts. He appealed to a state intermediate appellate court, contending that he was unlawfully convicted.]

* * * We will affirm the convictions if there is substantial evidence to support a finding that each act of grand theft qualified as an independent offense.

CASE 7.1 CONTINUED

We conclude that the record discloses evidence sufficient to establish that appellant was properly convicted of 20 counts of grand theft. Each transaction involved a different vehicle. The 20 transactions occurred on 13 different dates. With the exception of two dates, whenever more than one transaction occurred on a single date, the transactions involved distinct fictitious buyers. On the two dates a fictitious buyer purportedly bought more than one vehicle, the transactions involved separate paperwork and documentation. This constituted substantial evidence that the 20 transactions constitute distinct offenses.

* * * In sum, appellant was properly convicted under the 20 counts of grand theft.

* * * *

* * * Appellant argues there was no direct evidence that he intentionally participated in the fraud activities related to the taking of each vehicle.

Appellant's argument misapprehends our role in reviewing the record for substantial evidence. We do not engage in independent factfinding, but instead affirm the jury's determinations if they are supported by any logical inferences grounded in the evidence. [Emphasis added.]

There was ample evidence that appellant directly perpetrated the thefts. * * * Appellant authorized the offline credit card sales and other violations of dealership policies, obtained the false signatures from the fictitious buyers on the sales documents, and arranged for the delivery of the vehicles. Furthermore, * * * appellant admitted that Mor had "gotten the ball rolling" on the thefts, that Van Hek had instructed appellant how to do offline transactions, and that appellant had participated for "personal gain." This evidence was sufficient to establish that appellant supervised and directed the thefts within the dealership.

* * * *

* * * The judgment is affirmed.

LEGAL REASONING QUESTIONS

1. What is the definition of the crime of obtaining goods by false pretenses? Do the facts in this case satisfy that definition? Explain.
2. Besides the defendant, who may have committed a crime in this case?
3. How might the dealership have prevented the crimes in this case?
4. Why do some states combine larceny, embezzlement, and obtaining goods by false pretenses into a single crime called theft? Discuss.

RECEIVING STOLEN GOODS It is a crime to receive goods that a person knows or should have known were stolen or illegally obtained. To be convicted, the recipient of such goods need not know the true identity of the owner or the thief, and need not have paid for the goods. All that is necessary is that the recipient knows or should know that the goods are stolen, which implies an intent to deprive the true owner of those goods.

ARSON The willful and malicious burning of a building (and, in some states, vehicles and other items of personal property) is the crime of **arson.** At common law, arson applied only to burning down another person's house. The law was designed to protect human life. Today, arson statutes have been extended to cover the destruction of any building, regardless of ownership, by fire or explosion.

Every state has a special statute that covers the act of burning a building for the purpose of collecting insurance. (Of course, the insurer need not pay the claim when insurance fraud is proved.)

FORGERY The fraudulent making or altering of any writing (including electronic records) in a way that changes the legal rights and liabilities of another is **forgery.** ▶ **Example 7.9** Without authorization, Severson signs Bennett's name to the back of a check made out to Bennett and attempts to cash it. Severson is committing forgery. ◀ Forgery also includes changing trademarks, falsifying public records, counterfeiting, and altering a legal document.

Public Order Crime

Historically, societies have always outlawed activities that are considered contrary to public values and morals. Today, the most common public order crimes include public drunkenness, prostitution, gambling, and illegal drug use. These crimes are sometimes referred to as *victimless crimes* because they normally harm only the offender. From a broader perspective, however, they are deemed detrimental to society as a whole because they may create an environment that gives rise to property and violent crimes.

▶ **Example 7.10** A man flying from Texas to California on a commercial airliner becomes angry and yells obscenities at a flight attendant when a beverage cart strikes his knee. After the pilot diverts the plane and makes an unscheduled landing at a nearby airport, police remove the passenger and arrest him. If the man is later found guilty of the public order crime of interfering with a flight crew, he may be sentenced to more than two years in prison. ◀

White-Collar Crime

Crimes occurring in the business context are popularly referred to as *white-collar crimes,* although this is not an official legal term. Ordinarily, **white-collar crime** involves an illegal act or series of acts committed by an individual or business entity using some nonviolent means to obtain a personal or business advantage.

Usually, this kind of crime takes place in the course of a legitimate business occupation. Corporate crimes fall into this category. Certain property crimes, such as larceny and forgery, may also be white-collar crimes if they occur within the business context. The crimes discussed next normally occur only in the business context.

EMBEZZLEMENT When a person who is entrusted with another person's property fraudulently appropriates it, **embezzlement** occurs. Typically, embezzlement is carried out by an employee who steals funds. Banks are particularly prone to this problem, but embezzlement can occur in any firm. Embezzlement is not larceny because the wrongdoer does not *physically* take the property from the possession of another, and it is not robbery because no force or fear is used. The intent to return the embezzled property—or its actual return—is not a defense to the crime of embezzlement.

Embezzlement occurs whether the embezzler takes the funds directly from the victim or from a third person. If the financial officer of a large corporation pockets checks from third parties that were given to her to deposit into the corporate account, she is embezzling.

Frequently, an embezzler takes a relatively small amount at one time but does so repeatedly over a long period. This might be done by underreporting income or deposits and embezzling the remaining amount or by creating fictitious persons or accounts and writing checks to them from the corporate account. Even an employer's failure to remit state withholding taxes that were collected from employee wages can constitute embezzlement.

MAIL AND WIRE FRAUD Among the most potent weapons against white-collar criminals are the federal laws that prohibit mail fraud[11] and wire fraud.[12] These laws make it a federal crime to devise any scheme that uses U.S. mail, commercial carriers (FedEx, UPS), or wire (telegraph, telephone, television, the Internet, e-mail) with the intent to defraud the public. These laws are often applied when persons send out advertisements or e-mails with the intent to fraudulently obtain cash or property by false pretenses.

▶ **Case in Point 7.11** Cisco Systems, Inc., offers a warranty program to authorized resellers of Cisco parts. Iheanyi Frank Chinasa and Robert Kendrick Chambliss devised a scheme to intentionally defraud Cisco with respect to this program and obtain replacement parts to which they were not entitled. The two men planned and used specific language in numerous e-mails and Internet service requests that they sent to Cisco to convince Cisco to ship them new parts via commercial carriers. Ultimately, Chinasa and Chambliss were convicted of mail and wire fraud, and conspiracy to commit mail and wire fraud.[13] ◀

The maximum penalty under these statutes is substantial. Persons convicted of mail, wire, and Internet fraud may be imprisoned for up to twenty years and/or fined. If the violation affects a financial institution or involves fraud in connection with emergency disaster-relief funds, the violator may be fined up to $1 million, imprisoned for up to thirty years, or both.

BRIBERY The crime of bribery involves offering to give something of value to a person in an attempt to influence that person, who is usually, but not always, a public official, to act in a way that serves a private interest. Three types of bribery are considered crimes: bribery of public officials, commercial bribery, and bribery of foreign officials. As an element of the crime of bribery, intent must be present and proved. The bribe itself can be anything the recipient considers to be valuable. Realize that the *crime of bribery occurs when the bribe is offered*—it is not required that the bribe be accepted. *Accepting a bribe* is a separate crime.

Commercial bribery involves corrupt dealings between private persons or businesses. Typically, people make commercial bribes to obtain proprietary information, cover up an inferior product, or secure

11. The Mail Fraud Act of 1990, 18 U.S.C. Sections 1341–1342.
12. 18 U.S.C. Section 1343.
13. *United States v. Chinasa,* 789 F.Supp.2d 691 (E.D.Va. 2011). See also *United States v. Lyons,* 569 F.3d 995 (9th Cir. 2009).

new business. Industrial espionage sometimes involves commercial bribes. ▶ **Example 7.12** Kent Peterson works at the firm of Jacoby & Meyers. He offers to pay Laurel, an employee in a competing firm, to give him that firm's trade secrets and pricing schedules. Peterson has committed commercial bribery. ◀ So-called kickbacks, or payoffs for special favors or services, are a form of commercial bribery in some situations.

BANKRUPTCY FRAUD Federal bankruptcy law allows individuals and businesses to be relieved of oppressive debt through bankruptcy proceedings. Numerous white-collar crimes may be committed during the many phases of a bankruptcy action. A creditor may file a false claim against the debtor, which is a crime. Also, a debtor may fraudulently transfer assets to favored parties before or after the petition for bankruptcy is filed. For instance, a company-owned automobile may be "sold" at a bargain price to a trusted friend or relative. Closely related to the crime of fraudulent transfer of property is the crime of fraudulent concealment of property, such as the hiding of gold coins.

INSIDER TRADING An individual who obtains "inside information" about the plans of a publicly listed corporation can often make stock-trading profits by purchasing or selling corporate securities based on this information. *Insider trading* is a violation of securities law. Basically, securities law prohibits a person who possesses inside information and has a duty not to disclose it to outsiders from trading on that information. A person may not profit from the purchase or sale of securities based on inside information until the information is made available to the public.

THEFT OF TRADE SECRETS AND OTHER INTELLECTUAL PROPERTY As will be discussed in Chapter 14, trade secrets constitute a form of intellectual property that for many businesses can be extremely valuable. The Economic Espionage Act[14] makes the theft of trade secrets a federal crime. The act also makes it a federal crime to buy or possess another person's trade secrets, knowing that the trade secrets were stolen or otherwise acquired without the owner's authorization.

Violations of the Economic Espionage Act can result in steep penalties: imprisonment for up to ten years and a fine of up to $500,000. A corporation or other organization can be fined up to $5 million. Additionally, the law provides that any property acquired as a result of the violation, such as airplanes and automobiles, is subject to criminal forfeiture, or seizure by the government. Similarly, any property used in the commission of the violation, such as servers and other electronic devices, is subject to forfeiture. A theft of trade secrets conducted via the Internet, for instance, could result in the forfeiture of every computer or other device used to commit or facilitate the violation as well as any assets gained.

Organized Crime

White-collar crime takes place within the confines of the legitimate business world. *Organized crime,* in contrast, operates *illegitimately* by, among other things, providing illegal goods and services. Traditionally, the preferred markets for organized crime have been gambling, prostitution, illegal narcotics, and loan sharking (lending funds at higher-than-legal interest rates), along with more recent ventures into counterfeiting and credit-card scams.

MONEY LAUNDERING The profits from organized crime and illegal activities amount to billions of dollars a year. These profits come from illegal drug transactions and, to a lesser extent, from racketeering, prostitution, and gambling. Under federal law, banks, savings and loan associations, and other financial institutions are required to report currency transactions involving more than $10,000. Consequently, those who engage in illegal activities face difficulties in depositing their cash profits from illegal transactions.

As an alternative to storing cash from illegal transactions in a safe-deposit box, wrongdoers and racketeers launder "dirty" money through legitimate business to make it "clean." **Money laundering** is engaging in financial transactions to conceal the identity, source, or destination of illegally gained funds.

▶ **Example 7.13** Leo Harris, a successful drug dealer, becomes a partner with a restaurateur. Little by little, the restaurant shows increasing profits. As a partner in the restaurant, Harris is able to report the "profits" of the restaurant as legitimate income on which he pays federal and state taxes. He can then spend those funds without worrying that his lifestyle may exceed the level possible with his reported income. ◀

RACKETEERING To curb the entry of organized crime into the legitimate business world, Congress enacted the Racketeer Influenced and Corrupt

14. 18 U.S.C. Sections 1831–1839.

Organizations Act (RICO).[15] The statute makes it a federal crime to:

1. Use income obtained from racketeering activity to purchase any interest in an enterprise.
2. Acquire or maintain an interest in an enterprise through racketeering activity.
3. Conduct or participate in the affairs of an enterprise through racketeering activity.
4. Conspire to do any of the preceding activities.

Broad Application of RICO. The broad language of RICO has allowed it to be applied in cases that have little or nothing to do with organized crime. RICO incorporates by reference twenty-six separate types of federal crimes and nine types of state felonies.[16] If a person commits two of these offenses, he or she is guilty of "racketeering activity."

Under the criminal provisions of RICO, any individual found guilty is subject to a fine of up to $25,000 per violation, imprisonment for up to twenty years, or both. Additionally, any assets (property or cash) that were acquired as a result of the illegal activity or that were "involved in" or an "instrumentality of" the activity are subject to government forfeiture.

Civil Liability. In the event of a RICO violation, the government can seek civil penalties. The government can seek the divestiture of a defendant's interest in a business or the dissolution of the business. (Divestiture refers to the taking of possession—or forfeiture—of the defendant's interest and its subsequent sale.)

Moreover, in some cases, the statute allows private individuals to sue violators and potentially recover three times their actual losses (treble damages), plus attorneys' fees, for business injuries caused by a RICO violation. This is perhaps the most controversial aspect of RICO and one that continues to cause debate in the nation's federal courts. The prospect of receiving treble damages in civil RICO lawsuits has given plaintiffs a financial incentive to pursue businesses and employers for violations.

See *Concept Summary 7.1* on the facing page for a review of the different types of crimes.

15. 18 U.S.C. Sections 1961–1968.
16. See 18 U.S.C. Section 1961(1)(A). The crimes listed in this section include murder, kidnapping, gambling, arson, robbery, bribery, extortion, money laundering, securities fraud, counterfeiting, dealing in obscene matter, dealing in controlled substances (illegal drugs), and a number of others.

SECTION 4
DEFENSES TO CRIMINAL LIABILITY

Persons charged with crimes may be relieved of criminal liability if they can show that their criminal actions were justified under the circumstances. In certain situations, the law may also allow a person to be excused from criminal liability because she or he lacks the required mental state. We look at several defenses to criminal liability here.

Note that procedural violations (such as obtaining evidence without a valid search warrant) may also operate as defenses. Evidence obtained in violation of a defendant's constitutional rights may not be admitted in court. If the evidence is suppressed, then there may be no basis for prosecuting the defendant.

Justifiable Use of Force

Probably the best-known defense to criminal liability is **self-defense.** Other situations, however, also justify the use of force: the defense of one's dwelling, the defense of other property, and the prevention of a crime. In all of these situations, it is important to distinguish between deadly and nondeadly force. *Deadly force* is likely to result in death or serious bodily harm. *Nondeadly force* is force that reasonably appears necessary to prevent the imminent use of criminal force.

Generally speaking, people can use the amount of nondeadly force that seems necessary to protect themselves, their dwellings, or other property, or to prevent the commission of a crime. Deadly force can be used in self-defense only when the defender *reasonably believes* that imminent death or grievous bodily harm will otherwise result. In addition, normally the attacker must be using unlawful force, and the defender must not have initiated or provoked the attack.

Many states are expanding the situations in which the use of deadly force can be justified. Florida, for instance, allows the use of deadly force to prevent the commission of a "forcible felony," including robbery, carjacking, and sexual battery.

Necessity

Sometimes, criminal defendants can be relieved of liability by showing **necessity**—that a criminal act was necessary to prevent an even greater harm. ▶ **Example 7.14** Jake Trevor is a convicted felon and, as such, is legally prohibited from possessing a

CONCEPT SUMMARY 7.1
Types of Crimes

CRIME CATEGORY	DEFINITION AND EXAMPLES
Violent Crime	1. *Definition*—Crime that causes others to suffer harm or death. 2. *Examples*—Murder, assault and battery, sexual assault (rape), and robbery.
Property Crime	1. *Definition*—Crime in which the goal of the offender is some form of economic gain or the damaging of property; the most common form of crime. 2. *Examples*—Burglary, larceny, arson, receiving stolen goods, forgery, and obtaining goods by false pretenses.
Public Order Crime	1. *Definition*—Crime that is contrary to public values and morals. 2. *Examples*—Public drunkenness, prostitution, gambling, and illegal drug use.
White-Collar Crime	1. *Definition*—An illegal act or series of acts committed by an individual or business entity using some nonviolent means to obtain a personal or business advantage; usually committed in the course of a legitimate occupation. 2. *Examples*—Embezzlement, mail and wire fraud, bribery, bankruptcy fraud, insider trading, and the theft of intellectual property.
Organized Crime	1. *Definition*—A form of crime conducted by groups operating illegitimately to satisfy the public's demand for illegal goods and services (such as gambling and illegal narcotics). 2. *Money laundering*—Passing "dirty" money (obtained through criminal activities, such as illegal drug trafficking) through legitimate enterprises so as to "launder" it (make it appear to be legitimate income). 3. *RICO*—The Racketeer Influenced and Corrupt Organizations Act (RICO) makes it a federal crime to (a) use income obtained from racketeering activity to purchase any interest in an enterprise, (b) acquire or maintain an interest in an enterprise through racketeering activity, (c) conduct or participate in the affairs of an enterprise through racketeering activity, or (d) conspire to do any of the preceding activities. RICO provides for both civil and criminal liability.

firearm. While he and his wife are in a convenience store, a man draws a gun, points it at the cashier, and demands all the cash in the register. Afraid that the man will start shooting, Trevor grabs the gun and holds onto it until police arrive. In this situation, if Trevor is charged with possession of a firearm, he can assert the defense of necessity. ◀

Insanity

A person who suffers from a mental illness may be incapable of the state of mind required to commit a crime. Thus, insanity may be a defense to a criminal charge. Note that an insanity defense does not enable a person to avoid imprisonment. It simply means that if the defendant successfully proves insanity, she or he will be placed in a mental institution.

▶ **Example 7.15** James Holmes opened fire with an automatic weapon in a crowded Colorado movie theater during the screening of *The Dark Knight Rises,* killing twelve people and injuring more than fifty. Holmes had been a graduate student until he suffered from mental health problems. Before the incident, he had no criminal history. Holmes's attorneys have asserted the defense of insanity to try to avoid a possible death penalty. If the defense is successful, Holmes will be confined to a mental institution, rather than a prison. ◀

MODEL PENAL CODE The courts have had difficulty deciding what the test for legal insanity should be. Federal courts and some states use the substantial-capacity test set forth in the Model Penal Code:

> A person is not responsible for criminal conduct if at the time of such conduct as a result of mental

> disease or defect he or she lacks substantial capacity either to appreciate the wrongfulness of his [or her] conduct or to conform his [or her] conduct to the requirements of the law.

***M'NAGHTEN* AND OTHER STATE RULES** Some states use the *M'Naghten* test.[17] Under this test, a person is not responsible if, at the time of the offense, he or she did not know the nature and quality of the act or did not know that the act was wrong. Other states use the irresistible-impulse test. A person operating under an irresistible impulse may know an act is wrong but cannot refrain from doing it. Under any of these tests, proving insanity is extremely difficult. For this reason, the insanity defense is rarely used and usually is not successful. Four states have abolished the insanity defense.

Mistake

Everyone has heard the saying "Ignorance of the law is no excuse." Ordinarily, ignorance of the law or a mistaken idea about what the law requires is not a valid defense. A *mistake of fact,* however, as opposed to a *mistake of law,* can excuse criminal responsibility if it negates the mental state necessary to commit a crime.

▶ **Example 7.16** Oliver Wheaton mistakenly walks off with Julie Tyson's briefcase. If Wheaton genuinely thought that the case was his, there is no theft. Theft requires knowledge that the property belongs to another. (If Wheaton's act causes Tyson to incur damages, however, she may sue him in a civil action for trespass to personal property or conversion—torts that will be discussed in Chapter 12.) ◀

Duress

Duress exists when the *wrongful threat* of one person induces another person to perform an act that he or she would not otherwise have performed. In such a situation, duress is said to negate the mental state necessary to commit a crime because the defendant was forced or compelled to commit the act.

Duress can be used as a defense to most crimes except murder. Both the definition of duress and the types of crimes that it can excuse vary among the states, however. Generally, to successfully assert duress as a defense, the defendant must reasonably have believed that he or she was in immediate danger, and the jury (or judge) must conclude that the defendant's belief was reasonable.

Entrapment

Entrapment is a defense designed to prevent police officers or other government agents from enticing persons to commit crimes in order to later prosecute them for those crimes. In the typical entrapment case, an undercover agent *suggests* that a crime be committed and somehow pressures or induces an individual to commit it. The agent then arrests the individual for the crime.

For entrapment to be considered a defense, both the suggestion and the inducement must take place. The defense is not intended to prevent law enforcement agents from setting a trap for an unwary criminal. Rather, its purpose is to prevent them from pushing the individual into a criminal act. The crucial issue is whether the person who committed a crime was predisposed to commit the illegal act or did so only because the agent induced it.

Statute of Limitations

With some exceptions, such as the crime of murder, statutes of limitations apply to crimes just as they do to civil wrongs. In other words, the state must initiate criminal prosecution within a certain number of years. If a criminal action is brought after the statutory time period has expired, the accused person can raise the statute of limitations as a defense.

The running of the time period in a statute of limitations may be *tolled*—that is, suspended or stopped temporarily—if the defendant is a minor or is not in the jurisdiction. When the defendant reaches the age of majority or returns to the jurisdiction, the statutory time period begins to run again.

Immunity

Accused persons are understandably reluctant to give information if it will be used to prosecute them, and they cannot be forced to do so. The privilege against **self-incrimination** is guaranteed by a clause in the Fifth Amendment to the U.S. Constitution. The clause reads "nor shall [any person] be compelled in any criminal case to be a witness against himself."

When the state wishes to obtain information from a person accused of a crime, the state can grant

---

17. A rule derived from *M'Naghten's* Case, 8 Eng.Rep. 718 (1843).

immunity from prosecution. Alternatively, the state can agree to prosecute the accused for a less serious offense in exchange for the information. Once immunity is given, the person has an absolute privilege against self-incrimination and therefore can no longer refuse to testify on Fifth Amendment grounds.

Often, a grant of immunity from prosecution for a serious crime is part of the **plea bargaining** between the defending and prosecuting attorneys. The defendant may be convicted of a lesser offense, while the state uses the defendant's testimony to prosecute accomplices for serious crimes carrying heavy penalties.

SECTION 5 CRIMINAL PROCEDURES

Criminal law brings the force of the state, with all of its resources, to bear against the individual. Criminal procedures are designed to protect the constitutional rights of individuals and to prevent the arbitrary use of power on the part of the government.

The U.S. Constitution provides specific safeguards for those accused of crimes. The United States Supreme Court has ruled that most of these safeguards apply not only in federal court but also in state courts by virtue of the due process clause of the Fourteenth Amendment. These protections include the following:

1. The Fourth Amendment protection from unreasonable searches and seizures.
2. The Fourth Amendment requirement that no warrant for a search or an arrest be issued without probable cause.
3. The Fifth Amendment requirement that no one be deprived of "life, liberty, or property without due process of law."
4. The Fifth Amendment prohibition against **double jeopardy** (trying someone twice for the same criminal offense).[18]
5. The Fifth Amendment requirement that no person be required to be a witness against (incriminate) himself or herself.
6. The Sixth Amendment guarantees of a speedy trial, a trial by jury, a public trial, the right to confront witnesses, and the right to a lawyer at various stages in some proceedings.
7. The Eighth Amendment prohibitions against excessive bail and fines and against cruel and unusual punishment.

Fourth Amendment Protections

The Fourth Amendment protects the "right of the people to be secure in their persons, houses, papers, and effects." Before searching or seizing private property, normally law enforcement officers must obtain a **search warrant**—an order from a judge or other public official authorizing the search or seizure.

Advances in technology allow the authorities to track phone calls and vehicle movements with greater ease and precision. Nevertheless, the use of such technology can still constitute a search within the meaning of the Fourth Amendment. ▶ **Case in Point 7.17** Antoine Jones owned and operated a nightclub. Police suspected that he was also trafficking in narcotics. As part of their investigation, police obtained a warrant to attach a Global Positioning System (GPS) device to his wife's car. Although the warrant specified that the GPS device had to be attached within ten days, officers did not attach it until eleven days later.

Law enforcement then tracked the vehicle's movement for about a month, eventually arresting Jones for possession and intent to distribute cocaine. Jones was convicted. He appealed, arguing that police did not have a warrant for the GPS tracking. The United States Supreme Court held that the attachment of a GPS tracking device to a suspect's vehicle constitutes a Fourth Amendment search. The Court did not rule on whether the search in this case was unreasonable and required a warrant, however, and allowed Jones's conviction to stand.[19] ◀

PROBABLE CAUSE To obtain a search warrant, law enforcement officers must convince a judge that they have reasonable grounds, or **probable cause,** to believe a search will reveal a specific illegality. Probable cause requires the officers to have trustworthy evidence that would convince a reasonable person that the proposed search or seizure is more likely justified than not.

18. The prohibition against double jeopardy means that once a criminal defendant is found not guilty of a particular crime, the government may not indict that person again and retry him or her for the same crime. The prohibition does not preclude the crime victim from bringing a *civil* suit against that same person to recover damages, however. Additionally, a state's prosecution of a crime will not prevent a separate federal prosecution of the same crime, and vice versa.

19. *United States v. Jones,* __ U.S. __, 132 S.Ct. 945, 181 L.Ed.2d 911 (2012).

SCOPE OF WARRANT The Fourth Amendment prohibits general warrants. It requires a particular description of what is to be searched or seized. General searches through a person's belongings are impermissible. The search cannot extend beyond what is described in the warrant. Although search warrants require specificity, if a warrant is issued for a person's residence, items in that residence may be searched even if they do not belong to that individual.

In the following case, police officers obtained a search warrant and conducted a search for weapons in the home of a suspect's foster mother. A judge later ruled that the warrant was not supported by probable cause, and the homeowners sued individual police officers for executing an illegal search warrant.

CASE 7.2

Messerschmidt v. Millender

Supreme Court of the United States, ___ U.S. ___, 132 S.Ct. 1235, 182 L.Ed.2d 47 (2012).

BACKGROUND AND FACTS The Los Angeles County Sheriff's Department was protecting a woman from Jerry Ray Bowen, when he tried to kill her with a shotgun. The woman told the police that she and Bowen used to date, that Bowen was a gang member, and that she thought Bowen was staying at the home of Augusta Millender, his former foster mother. After investigating the incident further, the police prepared a warrant to search the home for all guns and gang-related material, and a magistrate approved it.

When the police, including Curt Messerschmidt, served the search warrant, they discovered that Bowen was not at the home, but they searched it anyway. The homeowners sued individual police officers in federal court for subjecting them to an illegal search. A federal appellate court held that the police lacked probable cause for such a broad search and that the police officers could be held personally liable. The police officers appealed. The United States Supreme Court granted *certiorari* to determine whether the police officers were immune from personal liability.

IN THE LANGUAGE OF THE COURT
Chief Justice *ROBERTS* delivered the opinion of the Court.

* * * *

The validity of the warrant is not before us. The question instead is whether Messerschmidt and [the other officers] are entitled to immunity from damages, even assuming that the warrant should not have been issued.

"The doctrine of qualified immunity protects government officials 'from liability for civil damages insofar as their conduct does not violate clearly established statutory or constitutional rights of which a reasonable person would have known.'" * * * "Whether an official protected by qualified immunity may be held personally liable for an allegedly unlawful official action generally turns on the 'objective legal reasonableness' of the action * * *."

Where the alleged Fourth Amendment violation involves a search or seizure pursuant to a warrant, the fact that a neutral magistrate has issued a warrant is the clearest indication that the officers acted in an objectively reasonable manner * * *. "Nonetheless, * * * we have recognized an exception allowing suit when 'it is obvious that no reasonably competent officer would have concluded that a warrant should issue.'" [Emphasis added.]

Our precedents make clear, however, that the threshold for establishing this exception is a high one, and it should be. * * * As we explained in [another case], "in the ordinary case, an officer cannot be expected to question the magistrate's probable-cause determination" because "it is the magistrate's responsibility to determine whether the officer's allegations establish probable cause and, if so, to issue a warrant comporting in form with the requirements of the Fourth Amendment."

DECISION AND REMEDY *The United States Supreme Court reversed the decision of the federal appellate court. It held that Messerschmidt and the other police officers were immune from personal liability.*

THE LEGAL ENVIRONMENT DIMENSION *How would police officers behave if they could always be held personally liable for executing unconstitutional warrants? Would they be more or less inclined to apply for and execute search warrants? Explain.*

CASE 7.2 CONTINUED

MANAGERIAL IMPLICATIONS *The principles of this case would also apply in the context of searches of businesses. Businesses may be subject to warrantless administrative searches. Evidence gleaned from a search conducted in reasonable reliance on information that later proves to have been false may still be admissible in court in a case against the business.*

The Exclusionary Rule

Under what is known as the **exclusionary rule,** any evidence obtained in violation of the constitutional rights spelled out in the Fourth, Fifth, and Sixth Amendments generally is not admissible at trial. All evidence derived from the illegally obtained evidence is known as the "fruit of the poisonous tree," and such evidence normally must also be excluded from the trial proceedings. For instance, if a confession is obtained after an illegal arrest, the arrest is the "poisonous tree," and the confession, if "tainted" by the arrest, is the "fruit."

The purpose of the exclusionary rule is to deter police from conducting warrantless searches and engaging in other misconduct. The rule can sometimes lead to injustice, however. If the evidence of a defendant's guilt was obtained improperly (without a valid search warrant, for instance), it normally cannot be used against the defendant in court.

The *Miranda* Rule

An important question many courts faced in the 1950s and 1960s was not whether suspects had constitutional rights—that was not in doubt—but how and when those rights could be exercised. Could the right to be silent (under the Fifth Amendment's protection against self-incrimination) be exercised during pretrial interrogation proceedings or only during the trial? Were confessions obtained from suspects admissible in court if the suspects had not been advised of their right to remain silent and other constitutional rights?

To clarify these issues, the United States Supreme Court issued a landmark decision in 1966 in *Miranda v. Arizona,* which we present here. Today, the procedural rights required by the Court in this case are familiar to almost every American.

CLASSIC CASE 7.3

Miranda v. Arizona

Supreme Court of the United States, 384 U.S. 436, 86 S.Ct. 1602, 16 L.Ed.2d 694 (1966).

BACKGROUND AND FACTS On March 13, 1963, Ernesto Miranda was arrested at his home for the kidnapping and rape of an eighteen-year-old woman. Miranda was taken to a Phoenix, Arizona, police station and questioned by two officers. Two hours later, the officers emerged from the interrogation room with a written confession signed by Miranda. A paragraph at the top of the confession stated that the confession had been made voluntarily, without threats or promises of immunity, and "with full knowledge of my legal rights, understanding any statement I make may be used against me."

Miranda was never advised that he had a right to remain silent and a right to have a lawyer present. The confession was admitted into evidence at his trial, and Miranda was convicted and sentenced to prison for twenty to thirty years. Miranda appealed, claiming that he had not been informed of his constitutional rights. The Supreme Court of Arizona held that Miranda's constitutional rights had not been violated and affirmed his conviction. The *Miranda* case was subsequently reviewed by the United States Supreme Court.

IN THE LANGUAGE OF THE COURT

Mr. Chief Justice *WARREN* delivered the opinion of the Court.

The cases before us raise questions which go to the roots of our concepts of American criminal jurisprudence; the restraints society must observe consistent with the Federal Constitution in prosecuting individuals for crime.

CASE 7.3 CONTINUES ➧

CASE 7.3 CONTINUED

* * * *

At the outset, if a person in custody is to be subjected to interrogation, he must first be informed in clear and unequivocal terms that he has the right to remain silent.

* * * *

The warning of the right to remain silent must be accompanied by the explanation that anything said can and will be used against the individual in court. This warning is needed in order to make him aware not only of the privilege, *but also of the consequences of forgoing it.* [Emphasis added.]

The circumstances surrounding in-custody interrogation can operate very quickly to overbear the will of one merely made aware of his privilege by his interrogators. Therefore the right to have counsel present at the interrogation is indispensable to the protection of the Fifth Amendment privilege under the system we delineate today.

* * * *

In order fully to apprise a person interrogated of the extent of his rights under this system then, it is necessary to warn him not only that he has the right to consult with an attorney, but also that if he is indigent [without funds] a lawyer will be appointed to represent him. * * * The warning of a right to counsel would be hollow if not couched in terms that would convey to the indigent—the person most often subjected to interrogation—the knowledge that he too has a right to have counsel present.

DECISION AND REMEDY *The United States Supreme Court held that Miranda could not be convicted of the crime on the basis of his confession because his confession was inadmissible as evidence. For any statement made by a defendant to be admissible, the defendant must be informed of certain constitutional rights prior to police interrogation. If the accused waives his or her rights to remain silent and to have counsel present, the government must demonstrate that the waiver was made knowingly, voluntarily, and intelligently.*

IMPACT OF THIS CASE ON TODAY'S LAW *Despite considerable criticism and later attempts to overrule the* Miranda *decision through legislation, the requirements stated in this case continue to provide the benchmark by which criminal procedures are judged today. Police officers routinely advise suspects of their "*Miranda *rights" on arrest. When Ernesto Miranda himself was later murdered, the suspected murderer was "read his* Miranda *rights."*

THE GLOBAL DIMENSION *The right to remain silent has long been a legal hallmark in Great Britain as well as in the United States. In 1994, however, the British Parliament passed an act that provides that a criminal defendant's silence may be interpreted as evidence of his or her guilt. British police officers are now required, when making an arrest, to inform the suspect, "You do not have to say anything. But if you do not mention now something which you later use in your defense, the court may decide that your failure to mention it now strengthens the case against you. A record will be made of everything you say, and it may be given in evidence if you are brought to trial." Should U.S. law also be changed to allow a defendant's silence during questioning to be considered as an indication of guilt? Why or why not?*

Exceptions to the *Miranda* Rule

Although the Supreme Court's decision in the *Miranda* case was controversial, it has survived several attempts by Congress to overrule it. Over time, however, the Supreme Court has made a number of exceptions to the *Miranda* ruling. For instance, the Court has recognized a "public safety" exception that allows certain statements to be admitted even if the defendant was not given *Miranda* warnings. A defendant's statements that reveal the location of a weapon would be admissible under this exception.

Additionally, a suspect must unequivocally and assertively ask to exercise her or his right to counsel in order to stop police questioning. Saying, "Maybe I should talk to a lawyer" during an interrogation after being taken into custody is not enough.

Criminal Process

As mentioned earlier in this chapter, a criminal prosecution differs significantly from a civil case in several respects. These differences reflect the desire to safeguard the rights of the individual against the state. Exhibit 7–3 below summarizes the major steps in processing a criminal case. We now discuss three phases of the criminal process—arrest, indictment or information, and trial—in more detail.

ARREST Before a warrant for arrest can be issued, there must be probable cause to believe that the individual in question has committed a crime. As discussed earlier in this chapter, *probable cause* can be defined as a substantial likelihood that the person has committed or is about to commit a crime. Note that probable cause involves a likelihood, not just a possibility. Arrests can be made without a warrant if there is no time to get one, but the action of the arresting officer is still judged by the standard of probable cause.

INDICTMENT OR INFORMATION Individuals must be formally charged with having committed specific

EXHIBIT 7–3 Major Procedural Steps in a Criminal Case

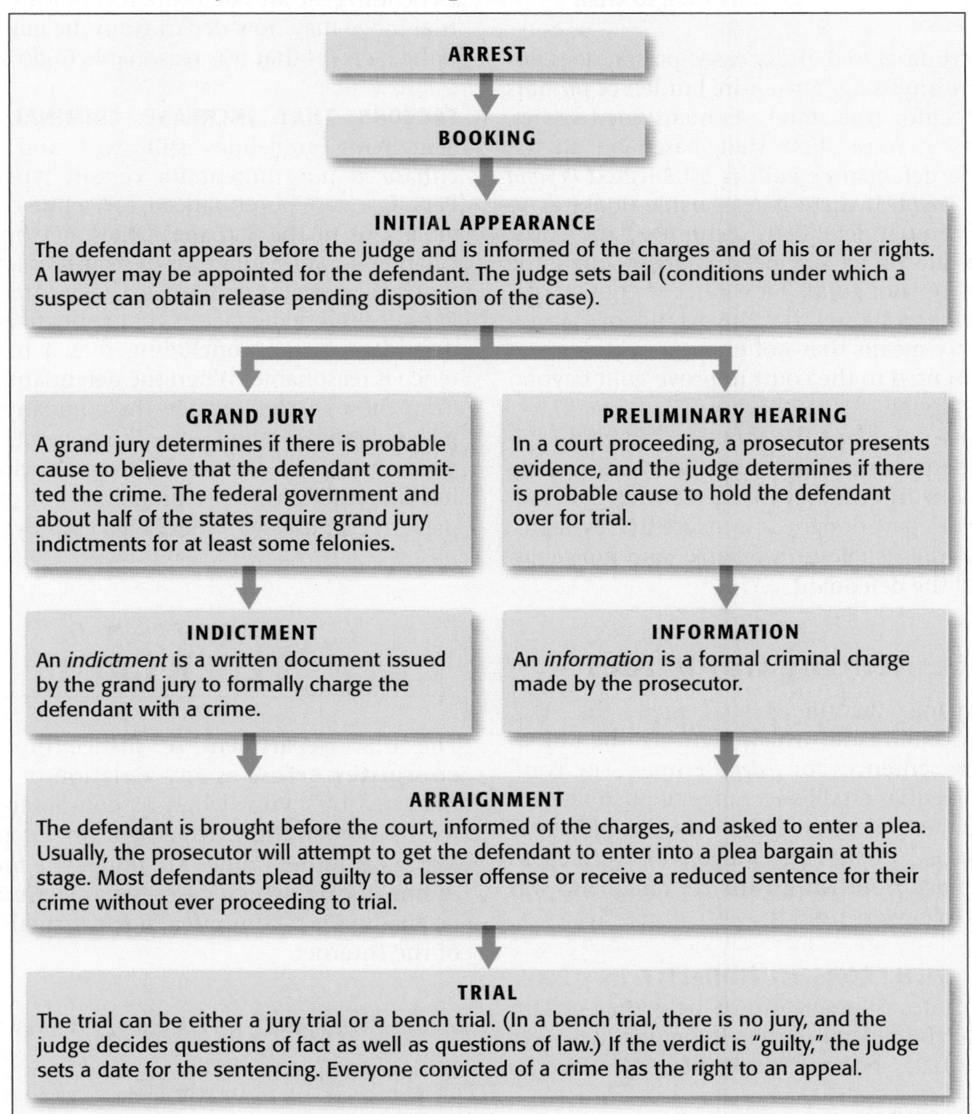

crimes before they can be brought to trial. If issued by a grand jury, such a charge is called an **indictment.**[20] A **grand jury** does not determine the guilt or innocence of an accused party. Rather, its function is to hear the state's evidence and to determine whether a reasonable basis (probable cause) exists for believing that a crime has been committed and that a trial ought to be held.

Usually, grand juries are called in cases involving serious crimes, such as murder. For lesser crimes, an individual may be formally charged with a crime by an **information,** or criminal complaint. An information will be issued by a government prosecutor if the prosecutor determines that there is sufficient evidence to justify bringing the individual to trial.

TRIAL At a criminal trial, the accused person does not have to prove anything. The entire burden of proof is on the prosecutor (the state). As mentioned earlier, the prosecution must show that, based on all the evidence, the defendant's guilt is established *beyond a reasonable doubt.* If there is reasonable doubt as to whether a criminal defendant committed the crime with which she or he has been charged, then the verdict must be "not guilty." A verdict of "not guilty" is not the same as stating that the defendant is innocent. It merely means that not enough evidence was properly presented to the court to prove guilt beyond a reasonable doubt.

Courts have complex rules about what types of evidence may be presented and how the evidence may be brought out in criminal cases, especially in jury trials. These rules are designed to ensure that evidence presented at trials is relevant, reliable, and not prejudicial toward the defendant.

Federal Sentencing Guidelines

The Sentencing Reform Act created the U.S. Sentencing Commission, which performs the task of standardizing sentences for *federal* crimes. The commission's guidelines establish a range of possible penalties for each federal crime. Originally, the guidelines were mandatory, in that the judge was required to select a sentence from within the set range and was not allowed to deviate from it.

PROBLEMS WITH CONSTITUTIONALITY In 2005, the United States Supreme Court held that certain provisions of the federal sentencing guidelines were unconstitutional. ▶ **Case in Point 7.18** Freddie Booker was arrested with 92.5 grams of crack cocaine in his possession. Booker admitted to police that he had sold an additional 566 grams of crack cocaine, but he was never charged with, or tried for, possession of this additional quantity. Nevertheless, under the federal sentencing guidelines the judge was required to sentence Booker to twenty-two years in prison. The Court ruled that this sentence was unconstitutional because a jury did not find beyond a reasonable doubt that Booker had possessed the additional 566 grams of crack.[21] ◀

Essentially, the Court's ruling changed the federal sentencing guidelines from mandatory to advisory. Depending on the circumstances of the case, a federal trial judge may now depart from the guidelines if she or he believes that it is reasonable to do so.

FACTORS THAT INCREASE CRIMINAL PENALTIES Sentencing guidelines still exist and provide for enhanced punishment for certain types of crimes. Penalties can be enhanced for white-collar crimes, violations of the Sarbanes-Oxley Act (mentioned in Chapter 4), and violations of securities laws.[22]

The sentencing judge must take into account the various sentencing factors that apply to an individual defendant before concluding that a particular sentence is reasonable. When the defendant is a business firm, these factors include the company's history of past violations, management's cooperation with federal investigators, and the extent to which the firm has undertaken specific programs and procedures to prevent criminal activities by its employees.

SECTION 6
CYBER CRIME

The U.S. Department of Justice broadly defines **computer crime** as any violation of criminal law that involves knowledge of computer technology for its perpetration, investigation, or prosecution. Many computer crimes fall under the broad label of **cyber crime,** which describes any criminal activity occurring via a computer in the virtual community of the Internet.

20. Pronounced in-*dyte*-ment.

21. *United States v. Booker,* 543 U.S. 220, 125 S.Ct. 738, 160 L.Ed.2d 621 (2005).

22. The sentencing guidelines were amended in 2003, as required under the Sarbanes-Oxley Act of 2002, to impose stiffer penalties for corporate securities fraud.

Most cyber crimes are simply existing crimes, such as fraud and theft of intellectual property, in which the Internet is the instrument of wrongdoing. ▶ **Example 7.19** Richard O'Dwyer ran TVShack.net, a Web site with links directing users to copyrighted TV shows and movies. U.S. authorities seized his .net domain name, claiming that the site was nothing more than a search engine for pirated content. O'Dwyer simply moved the site to a .cc domain over which the United States apparently has no authority. ◀

Here we look at several types of activities that constitute cyber crimes against persons or property. (Of course, just as computers and the Internet have expanded the scope of crime, they have also provided new ways of detecting and combatting crime. For instance, police are using social media as an investigative tool, as discussed in Chapter 15.)

Cyber Fraud

As you will read in Chapter 12, fraud is any misrepresentation knowingly made with the intention of deceiving another and on which a reasonable person would and does rely to her or his detriment. **Cyber fraud** is fraud committed over the Internet.

ONLINE AUCTION FRAUD Online auction fraud, in its most basic form, is a simple process. A person puts up an expensive item for auction, on either a legitimate or a fake auction site, and then refuses to send the product after receiving payment. Or, as a variation, the wrongdoer may send the purchaser an item that is worth less than the one offered in the auction.

The larger online auction sites, such as eBay, try to protect consumers against such schemes by providing warnings about deceptive sellers or offering various forms of insurance. It is nearly impossible to completely block fraudulent auction activity on the Internet, however. Because users can assume multiple identities, it is very difficult to pinpoint fraudulent sellers—they will simply change their screen names with each auction.

ONLINE RETAIL FRAUD Somewhat similar to online auction fraud is online retail fraud, in which consumers pay directly (without bidding) for items that are never delivered. As with other forms of online fraud, it is difficult to determine the actual extent of online sales fraud, but anecdotal evidence suggests that it is a substantial problem.

▶ **Case in Point 7.20** Jeremy Jaynes grossed more than $750,000 per week selling nonexistent or worthless products such as "penny stock pickers" and "Internet history erasers." By the time he was arrested, he had amassed an estimated $24 million from his various fraudulent schemes.[23] ◀

Cyber Theft

In cyberspace, thieves are not subject to the physical limitations of the "real" world. A thief can steal data stored in a networked computer with Internet access from anywhere on the globe. Only the speed of the connection and the thief's computer equipment limit the quantity of data that can be stolen.

IDENTITY THEFT Not surprisingly, there has been a marked increase in identity theft in recent years. **Identity theft** occurs when the wrongdoer steals a form of identification—such as a name, date of birth, or Social Security number—and uses the information to access the victim's financial resources.

The Internet has provided even easier access to private data, as we will discuss further in Chapter 15. Frequent Web surfers surrender a wealth of information about themselves without knowing it. Most Web sites use "cookies" to collect data on those who visit their sites. Web browsers often store information such as the consumer's name and e-mail address. Finally, every time a purchase is made online, the item is linked to the purchaser's name.

PHISHING A distinct form of identity theft known as **phishing** has added a different wrinkle to the practice. In a phishing attack, the perpetrator "fishes" for financial data and passwords from consumers by posing as a legitimate business, such as a bank or credit-card company. The "phisher" sends an e-mail asking the recipient to update or confirm vital information, often with the threat that an account or some other service will be discontinued if the information is not provided. Once the unsuspecting individual enters the information, the phisher can use it to masquerade as that person or to drain his or her bank or credit account.

▶ **Example 7.21** Customers of Wachovia Bank (now owned by Wells Fargo) received official-looking e-mails telling them to type in personal information on a Web form to complete a mandatory installation of a new Internet security certificate. But the Web site was bogus. When people filled out the forms, their

23. *Jaynes v. Commonwealth of Virginia,* 276 Va.App. 443, 666 S.E.2d 303 (2008).

computers were infected and funneled their data to a computer server. The cyber criminals then sold the data. ◀

EMPLOYMENT FRAUD Cyber criminals also look for victims at online job-posting sites. Claiming to be an employment officer in a well-known company, the criminal sends bogus e-mail messages to job seekers. The messages ask the unsuspecting job seekers to reveal enough information to allow for identity theft. As the unemployment rate has remained high, cyber criminals have found many opportunities for employment fraud.

▶ **Example 7.22** The job site Monster.com once asked 4.5 million users to change their passwords. Cyber thieves had broken into its databases and stolen user identities, passwords, and other data in one of Britain's largest cyber theft cases. ◀

CREDIT-CARD NUMBERS Companies take risks by storing their online customers' credit-card numbers. Although the consumer can make a purchase more quickly without entering a lengthy card number, the electronic warehouses that store the numbers are targets for cyber thieves. Stolen credit-card numbers are much more likely to hurt merchants and credit-card issuers (such as banks) than consumers. In most situations, the legitimate holders of credit cards are not held responsible for the costs of purchases made with a stolen number.

Hacking

A **hacker** is someone who uses one computer to break into another. The danger posed by hackers has increased significantly because of **botnets,** or networks of computers that have been appropriated by hackers without the knowledge of their owners. A hacker may secretly install a program on thousands, if not millions, of personal computer "robots," or "bots," that allows him or her to forward transmissions to an even larger number of systems.

▶ **Example 7.23** When a hacker broke into Sony Corporation's PlayStation 3 video gaming and entertainment networks, the company had to temporarily shut down its online services. This single hacking incident affected more than 100 million online accounts that provide gaming, chat, and music streaming services. ◀

MALWARE Botnets are one of the latest forms of **malware,** a term that refers to any program that is harmful to a computer or, by extension, a computer user. A **worm,** for example, is a software program that is capable of reproducing itself as it spreads from one computer to the next.

▶ **Example 7.24** Within three weeks, the computer worm called "Conflicker" spread to more than a million personal computers around the world. It was transmitted to some computers through the use of Facebook and Twitter. This worm also infected servers and devices plugged into infected computers, via USB ports, such as iPads, iPhones, and flash drives. ◀

A **virus,** another form of malware, is also able to reproduce itself, but must be attached to an "infested" host file to travel from one computer network to another. For instance, hackers are now capable of corrupting banner ads that use Adobe's Flash Player. When an Internet user clicks on the banner ad, a virus is installed. Worms and viruses can be programmed to perform a number of functions, such as prompting host computers to continually "crash" and reboot, or otherwise infect the system. (For a discussion of how malware is now affecting smartphones, see this chapter's *Insight into the Global Environment* feature on the facing page.)

SERVICE-BASED HACKING Today, many companies offer "software as a service." Instead of buying software to install on a computer, the user connects to Web-based software. The user can write e-mails, edit spreadsheets, or perform other tasks using his or her Web browser. Cyber criminals have adapted this distribution method to provide "crimeware as a service."

A would-be thief no longer has to be a computer hacker to create a botnet or steal banking information and credit-card numbers. He or she can rent the online services of cyber criminals to do the work for a small price. Fake security software (also known as scareware) is a common example. The thief can even target individual groups, such as U.S. physicians or British attorneys.

CYBERTERRORISM Cyberterrorists, as well as hackers, may target businesses. The goals of a hacking operation might include a wholesale theft of data, such as a merchant's customer files, or the monitoring of a computer to discover a business firm's plans and transactions. A cyberterrorist might also want to insert false codes or data. For instance, the processing control

INSIGHT INTO THE GLOBAL ENVIRONMENT
Even Smartphones Are Vulnerable to International Cyber Attacks

Recent statistics show that the number of bank robberies occurring annually is on the decline. Criminals have learned that it is easier, less risky, and more profitable to steal via the Internet. Advances in the speed and use of the Internet have fostered the growth of a relatively new criminal industry that uses malware to conduct espionage and profit from crime.

Who Are the Creators of Malware?

While any smart teenager can buy prepackaged hacking software on the Internet, the malware that businesses and governments are worried about is much more sophisticated. There is evidence that malware that can be used for international diplomatic espionage as well as industrial espionage is most often developed by so-called cyber mercenaries. According to Steve Sachs of the cyber security firm FireEye, "There are entire little villages dedicated to malware in Russia, villages in China, very sophisticated, very organized, very well-funded."

Flame Malware

The most sophisticated globally created and propagated malware has been labeled Flame. Flame was discovered in 2012, although experts believe that it was lying dormant in thousands of computers worldwide for at least five years.

Flame can record screen shots, keyboard strokes, network traffic, and audio. It can also record Skype conversations. It can even turn infected computers into Bluetooth beacons, which can then attempt to download contact information from nearby Bluetooth-enabled devices.

The Malware Can Infect Smartphones

Many smartphone owners are unaware that their Apple, Nokia, and Microsoft Windows mobile phones can be infected with Flame malware or variants of it without their knowledge. The information that is hacked from smartphones can then be sent on to a series of command-and-control servers and ultimately to members of international criminal gangs.

Once a computer or smartphone is infected with this malware, all information in the device can be transferred. Additionally, files can be deleted, and furthermore, files that have been erased on hard drives can be resurrected. This malware has been responsible for stealing e-mail databases from Microsoft's e-mail program Outlook and has even been able to capture e-mail from remote servers.[a]

Until recently, most attacks involved diplomatic espionage, but cyber technicians at large business enterprises are now worried that industrial espionage may be taking place. In fact, an extensive hacking operation was uncovered in 2013 that was linked to a Chinese military unit (the "Comment Crew"). The wide-ranging cyber attacks involved the theft of hundreds of terabytes of data and intellectual property of more than 140 corporations in twenty different industries. The goal of the attacks was to help Chinese companies better compete against U.S. and foreign firms.[b]

LEGAL CRITICAL THINKING

INSIGHT INTO THE TECHNOLOGICAL ENVIRONMENT

What entities might pay "cyber mercenaries" to create some of the malware described in this feature?

a. Mark Stevens, "CWI Cryptanalyst Discovers New Cryptographic Attack Variant in Flame Spy Malware," June 7, 2012, **www.cwi.nl/news/2012.**

b. David E. Sanger, David Barboza, and Nicole Perlroth, "Chinese Army Unit Is Seen as Tied to Hacking Against U.S.," **www.nytimes.com/2013.**

system of a food manufacturer could be changed to alter the levels of ingredients so that consumers of the food would become ill.

A cyberterrorist attack on a major financial institution, such as the New York Stock Exchange or a large bank, could leave securities or money markets in flux and seriously affect the daily lives of millions of citizens. Similarly, any prolonged disruption of computer, cable, satellite, or telecommunications systems due to the actions of expert hackers would have serious repercussions on business operations—and national security—on a global level.

Prosecuting Cyber Crime

Cyber crime has raised new issues in the investigation of crimes and the prosecution of offenders. Determining the "location" of a cyber crime and identifying a criminal in cyberspace present significant challenges for law enforcement.

JURISDICTION AND IDENTIFICATION CHALLENGES A threshold issue is, of course, jurisdiction. Jurisdiction is normally based on physical geography, as discussed in Chapter 2. Each state and nation has jurisdiction, or authority, over crimes committed within its boundaries. But geographic boundaries simply do not apply in cyberspace. A person who commits an act against a business in California, where the act is a cyber crime, might never have set foot in California but might instead reside in New York, or even in Canada, where the act may not be a crime.

Identifying the wrongdoer can also be difficult. Cyber criminals do not leave physical traces, such as fingerprints or DNA samples, as evidence of their crimes. Even electronic "footprints" can be hard to find and follow. For instance, e-mail may be sent through a remailer, an online service that guarantees that a message cannot be traced to its source.

For these reasons, laws written to protect physical property are often difficult to apply in cyberspace. Nonetheless, governments at both the state and the federal level have taken significant steps toward controlling cyber crime. California, for instance, which has the highest identity theft rate in the nation, has established a new eCrime unit to investigate and prosecute cyber crimes. Other states, including Florida, Louisiana, and Texas, also have special law enforcement units that focus solely on Internet crimes.

THE COMPUTER FRAUD AND ABUSE ACT Perhaps the most significant federal statute specifically addressing cyber crime is the Counterfeit Access Device and Computer Fraud and Abuse Act.[24] This act is commonly known as the Computer Fraud and Abuse Act (CFAA).

Among other things, the CFAA provides that a person who accesses a computer online, without authority, to obtain classified, restricted, or protected data (or attempts to do so) is subject to criminal prosecution. Such data could include financial and credit records, medical records, legal files, military and national security files, and other confidential information. The data can be located in government or private computers. The crime has two elements: accessing a computer without authority and taking the data.

This theft is a felony if it is committed for a commercial purpose or for private financial gain, or if the value of the stolen data (or computer time) exceeds $5,000. Penalties include fines and imprisonment for up to twenty years. A victim of computer theft can also bring a civil suit against the violator to obtain damages, an injunction, and other relief.

24. 18 U.S.C. Section 1030.

Reviewing: Criminal Law and Cyber Crime

Edward Hanousek worked for Pacific & Arctic Railway and Navigation Company (P&A) as a roadmaster of the White Pass & Yukon Railroad in Alaska. Hanousek was responsible "for every detail of the safe and efficient maintenance and construction of track, structures and marine facilities of the entire railroad," including special projects. One project was a rock quarry, known as "6-mile," above the Skagway River. Next to the quarry, and just beneath the surface, ran a high-pressure oil pipeline owned by Pacific & Arctic Pipeline, Inc., P&A's sister company. When the quarry's backhoe operator punctured the pipeline, an estimated 1,000 to 5,000 gallons of oil were discharged into the river. Hanousek was charged with negligently discharging a harmful quantity of oil into a navigable water of the United States in violation of the criminal provisions of the Clean Water Act (CWA). Using the information presented in the chapter, answer the following questions.

1. Did Hanousek have the required mental state *(mens rea)* to be convicted of a crime? Why or why not?
2. Which theory discussed in the chapter would enable a court to hold Hanousek criminally liable for violating the statute if he participated in, directed, or merely knew about the specific violation?
3. Could the backhoe operator who punctured the pipeline also be charged with a crime in this situation? Explain.

4. Suppose that at trial, Hanousek argued that he should not be convicted because he was not aware of the requirements of the CWA. Would this defense be successful? Why or why not?

DEBATE THIS . . . *Because of overcriminalization, particularly by the federal government, Americans may be breaking the law regularly without knowing it. Should Congress rescind many of the more than four thousand federal crimes now on the books?*

Terms and Concepts

actus reus 142
arson 147
beyond a reasonable doubt 140
botnet 160
burglary 145
computer crime 158
crime 140
cyber crime 158
cyber fraud 159
double jeopardy 153
duress 152
embezzlement 148
entrapment 152
exclusionary rule 155
felony 141
forgery 147
grand jury 158
hacker 160
identity theft 159
indictment 158
information 158
larceny 145
malware 160
mens rea 143
misdemeanor 141
money laundering 149
necessity 150
petty offense 141
phishing 159
plea bargaining 153
probable cause 153
robbery 145
search warrant 153
self-defense 150
self-incrimination 152
virus 160
white-collar crime 148
worm 160

ExamPrep

Issue Spotters

1. Dana takes her roommate's credit card without permission, intending to charge expenses that she incurs on a vacation. Her first stop is a gas station, where she uses the card to pay for gas. With respect to the gas station, has she committed a crime? If so, what is it? **(See page 145.)**
2. Without permission, Ben downloads consumer credit files from a computer belonging to Consumer Credit Agency. He then sells the data to Dawn. Has Ben committed a crime? If so, what is it? **(See page 162.)**

- **Check your answers to the Issue Spotters against the answers provided in Appendix E at the end of this text.**

Before the Test

Go to **www.cengagebrain.com**, enter the ISBN 9781285428949, and click on "Find" to locate this textbook's Web site. Then, click on "Access Now" under "Study Tools," and select Chapter 7 at the top. There, you will find an Interactive Quiz that you can take to assess your mastery of the concepts in this chapter, as well as Flashcards and a Glossary of important terms.

Business Scenarios

7–1. Types of Cyber Crimes. The following situations are similar, but each represents a variation of a particular crime. Identify the crime and point out the differences in the variations. **(See page 159.)**

(a) Chen, posing fraudulently as Diamond Credit Card Co., sends an e-mail to Emily, stating that the company has observed suspicious activity in her account and has frozen the account. The e-mail asks her to reregister her credit-card number and password to reopen the account.

(b) Claiming falsely to be Big Buy Retail Finance Co., Conner sends an e-mail to Dino, asking him to confirm or update his personal security information to prevent his Big Buy account from being discontinued.

(c) Felicia posts her résumé on GotWork.com, an online job-posting site, seeking a position in business and managerial finance and accounting. Hayden, who misrepresents himself as an employment officer with International Bank & Commerce Corp., sends her an e-mail asking for more personal information.

7–2. Property Crimes. Which, if any, of the following crimes necessarily involves illegal activity on the part of more than one person? **(See page 145.)**

(a) Bribery.

(b) Forgery.

(c) Embezzlement.

(d) Larceny.

(e) Receiving stolen property.

7–3. Cyber Scam. Kayla, a student at Learnwell University, owes $20,000 in unpaid tuition. If Kayla does not pay the tuition, Learnwell will not allow her to graduate. To obtain the funds to pay the debt, she sends e-mails to people that she does not personally know asking for financial help to send Milo, her disabled child, to a special school. In reality, Kayla has no children. Is this a crime? If so, which one? **(See page 159.)**

Business Case Problems

7–4. Cyber Crime. Jiri Klimecek was a member of a group that overrode copyright protection in movies, video games, and software, and made them available for download online. Klimecek bought and installed hardware and software to set up a computer server and paid half of the monthly service charges to connect the server to the Internet. He knew that users around the world could access the server to upload and download copyrighted works. He obtained access to Czech movies and music to make them available. Klimecek was indicted in a federal district court for copyright infringement. He claimed that he did not understand the full scope of the operation. Did Klimecek commit a crime? If so, was he a "minor participant" entitled to a reduced sentence? Explain. [*United States v. Klimecek,* ___F.3d ___ (7th Cir. 2009)] **(See page 158.)**

7–5. Fourth Amendment. Three police officers, including Maria Trevizo, were on patrol in Tucson, Arizona, near a neighborhood associated with the Crips gang, when they pulled over a car with suspended registration. Each officer talked to one of the three occupants. Trevizo spoke with Lemon Johnson, who was wearing clothing consistent with Crips membership. Visible in his jacket pocket was a police scanner, and he said that he had served time in prison for burglary. Trevizo asked him to get out of the car and patted him down "for officer safety." She found a gun. Johnson was charged in an Arizona state court with illegal possession of a weapon. What standard should apply to an officer's patdown of a passenger during a traffic stop? Should a search warrant be required? Could a search proceed solely on the basis of probable cause? Would a reasonable suspicion short of probable cause be sufficient? Discuss. [*Arizona v. Johnson,* 555 U.S. 323, 129 S.Ct. 781, 172 L.Ed.2d 694 (2009)] **(See page 153.)**

7–6. Searches. Charles Byrd was in a minimum-security jail awaiting trial. A team of sheriff's deputies took several inmates into a room for a strip search without any apparent justification. Byrd was ordered to remove all of his clothing except his boxer shorts. A female deputy searched Byrd while several male deputies watched. One of the male deputies videotaped the search. Byrd filed a suit against the sheriff's department. Did the search violate Byrd's rights? Discuss. [*Byrd v. Maricopa County Sheriff's Department,* 629 F.3d. 1135 (9th Cir. 2011)] **(See page 153.)**

7–7. Credit-Card Theft. Jacqueline Barden was shopping for school clothes with her children when her purse and automobile were taken. In Barden's purse were her car keys, credit and debit cards for herself and her children, as well as the children's Social Security cards and birth certificates needed for enrollment at school. Immediately after the purse and car were stolen, Rebecca Mary Turner attempted to use Barden's credit card at a local Exxon gas station, but the card was declined. The gas station attendant recognized Turner because she had previously written bad checks and used credit cards that did not belong to her.

Turner was later arrested while attempting to use one of Barden's checks to pay for merchandise at a Wal-Mart—where the clerk also recognized Turner from prior criminal activity. Turner claimed that she had not stolen Barden's purse or car, and that a friend had told her he had some checks and credit cards and asked her to try using them at Wal-Mart. Turner was convicted at trial. She appealed, claiming that there was insufficient evidence that she committed credit- and debit-card theft. Was the evidence sufficient to uphold her conviction? Why or why not? [*Turner v. State of Arkansas,* 2012 Ark.App. 150 (2012)] **(See page 145.)**

7–8. BUSINESS CASE PROBLEM WITH SAMPLE ANSWER: Criminal Liability.

During the morning rush hour, David Green threw bottles and plates from a twenty-sixth-floor hotel balcony overlooking Seventh Avenue in New York City. A video of the incident also showed him doing cartwheels while holding a beer bottle and sprinting toward the balcony while holding a glass steadily in his hand. When he saw police on the street below and on the roof of the building across the street, he suspended his antics but resumed tossing objects off the balcony after the police left. He later admitted that he could recall what he had done, but claimed to have been intoxicated and said his only purpose was to amuse himself and his friends. Did Green have the mental state required to establish criminal liability? Discuss. [State of New York v. Green, *104 A.D.3d 126, 958 N.Y.S.2d 138 (1 Dept. 2013)]* **(See page 143.)**

- **For a sample answer to Problem 7–8, go to Appendix F at the end of this text.**

7–9. A QUESTION OF ETHICS: Identity Theft.

*Twenty-year-old Davis Omole had good grades in high school, where he played on the football and chess teams, and went on to college. Omole worked at a cell phone store where he stole customers' personal information. He used the stolen identities to create a hundred different accounts on eBay, and held more than three hundred auctions listing for sale items that he did not own (including cell phones, plasma televisions, and stereos). From these auctions, he collected $90,000. To avoid getting caught, he continuously closed and opened the eBay accounts, activated and deactivated cell phone and e-mail accounts, and changed mailing addresses and post office boxes. Omole, who had previously been convicted in a state court for Internet fraud, was convicted in a federal district court of identity theft and wire fraud. [*United States v. Omole, *523 F.3d 691 (7th Cir. 2008)]* **(See page 159.)**

(a) Omole displayed contempt for the court and ridiculed his victims, calling them stupid for having been cheated. What does this behavior suggest about Omole's ethics?

(b) Under federal sentencing guidelines, Omole could have been imprisoned for more than eight years. He received only three years, however, two of which comprised the mandatory sentence for identity theft. Was this sentence too lenient? Explain.

Legal Reasoning Group Activity

7–10. Cyber Crime. Cyber crime costs consumers millions of dollars per year, and it costs businesses, including banks and other credit-card issuers, even more. Nonetheless, when cyber criminals are caught and convicted, they are rarely ordered to pay restitution or sentenced to long prison terms. **(See page 158.)**

(a) One group should argue that stiffer sentences would reduce the amount of cyber crime.

(b) A second group should determine how businesspersons can best protect themselves from cyber crime and avoid the associated costs.

CHAPTER 8
INTERNATIONAL LAW IN A GLOBAL ECONOMY

International business transactions are not unique to the modern world. Commerce has always crossed national borders. What is new in our day is the dramatic growth in world trade and the emergence of a global business community. Exchanges of goods, services, and ideas (intellectual property) on a global level are now routine. Therefore, students of business law and the legal environment should be familiar with the laws pertaining to international business transactions.

Laws affecting the international legal environment of business include both international law and national law. **International law** can be defined as a body of law—formed as a result of international customs, treaties, and organizations—that governs relations among or between nations.

International law may be public, creating standards for the nations themselves. It may also be private, establishing international standards for private transactions that cross national borders. (Can officials legally search electronic devices, including laptops and smartphones, of persons who cross national borders? See this chapter's *Insight into the Global Environment* feature on the facing page for the answer.) **National law** is the law of a particular nation, such as Brazil, Germany, Japan, or the United States. In this chapter, we examine how both international law and national law frame business operations in the global context.

SECTION 1
INTERNATIONAL LAW

The major difference between international law and national law is that government authorities can enforce national law. What government, however, can enforce international law? By definition, a *nation* is a sovereign entity—which means that there is no higher authority to which that nation must submit. ▶ **Example 8.1** In February 2013, North Korea performed its third underground nuclear weapons test in violation of United Nations Security Council resolutions. Although world leaders uniformly condemned North Korea's action, the United Nations had no ready means of enforcing its resolutions. ◀

If a nation violates an international law and persuasive tactics fail, other countries or international organizations have no recourse except to take coercive actions. Coercive actions might include economic sanctions, severance of diplomatic relations, boycotts, and, as a last resort, war against the violating nation.

International law attempts to reconcile each country's need to be the final authority over its own affairs with the desire of nations to benefit economically from trade and harmonious relations with one another. Sovereign nations can, and do, voluntarily agree to be governed in certain respects by international law, usually for the purpose of facilitating international trade and commerce. As a result, a body of international law has evolved.

Sources of International Law

Basically, there are three sources of international law: international customs, treaties and international agreements, and international organizations and conferences. We look at each of these sources here.

INTERNATIONAL CUSTOMS One important source of international law consists of the international customs that have evolved among nations in their relations with one another. Article 38(1) of the Statute of the International Court of Justice refers to an international custom as "evidence of a general practice accepted as law." The legal principles and doctrines that you will read about shortly are rooted in international customs and traditions that have evolved over time in the international arena.

INSIGHT INTO THE GLOBAL ENVIRONMENT
Border Searches of Your Electronic Devices

Every year, tens of millions of travelers arrive at U.S. borders where they are subject to a search. Of these travelers, about 12 million undergo a secondary screening, and approximately five thousand of these screenings involve an electronic device. About three hundred devices—computers, BlackBerrys, tablets, and smartphones—are sent to the Immigration and Customs Enforcement forensics laboratory in Fairfax, Virginia, for further examination.

The U.S. government has historically had a broad power to search travelers and their property when they enter this country. That power includes the right to inspect papers and other physical documents in the possession of anyone entering the United States, including U.S. citizens.

A Legal Challenge to Extensive Searches of Electronic Devices

Increasingly, however, instead of being carried in physical form, documents are carried on the hard drives of laptop computers, in tablets, or in smartphones. Indeed, a person might have thousands and thousands of photos, e-mails, video clips, and documents on the hard drive of a laptop. Does the government's power to conduct border searches give it the right to rummage through all of the data on an electronic device? Several recent lawsuits have raised this issue.

When Pascal Abidor, a Ph.D. student who has dual U.S. and French citizenship, traveled by train from Canada to New York, U.S. Customs and Border Control agents pulled him aside and required him to log on to his computer. They then examined much of its contents. Abidor was released after a few hours, but the Department of Homeland Security kept his laptop for eleven days. Abidor challenged the search. His complaint alleged:

> [A government policy that authorizes] the suspicionless search of the contents of Americans' laptops, cell phones, cameras, and other electronic devices at the international border . . . violates the constitutional rights of American citizens to keep the private and expressive details of their lives, as well as sensitive information obtained or created in the course of their work, free from unwarranted government scrutiny.

Although the lawsuit was filed several years ago, as we go to press, there is no information available on the verdict.[a]

Protecting Attorney-Client Privilege

Border searches present a special problem for attorneys because they have a duty to protect the attorney-client privilege by preventing anyone, including the government, from accessing client communications. To avoid this problem, attorneys should never keep client files on a digital device that they are taking abroad. If the attorneys will need the files during the trip abroad, they can be put on a server in the "cloud."

LEGAL CRITICAL THINKING

INSIGHT INTO THE TECHNOLOGICAL ENVIRONMENT

What are some steps that businesspersons can take to avoid any issues at the border with respect to the contents of their electronic devices?

a. *Abidor v. Napolitano,* 10-cv-04059-ERK (E.D.N.Y.).

TREATIES AND INTERNATIONAL AGREEMENTS Treaties and other explicit agreements between or among foreign nations provide another important source of international law. A **treaty** is an agreement or contract between two or more nations that must be authorized and ratified by the supreme power of each nation. Under Article II, Section 2, of the U.S. Constitution, the president has the power "by and with the Advice and Consent of the Senate, to make Treaties, provided two-thirds of the Senators present concur."

A *bilateral* agreement, as the term implies, is an agreement formed by two nations to govern their commercial exchanges or other relations with one another. A *multilateral* agreement is formed by several nations. For instance, regional trade associations such as the Andean Community, the Association of Southeast Asian Nations, and the European Union are the result of multilateral trade agreements.

INTERNATIONAL ORGANIZATIONS The term **international organization** generally refers to an organization composed mainly of officials of member nations and usually established by treaty. The United States is a member of more than one hundred multilateral and bilateral organizations, including at least twenty through the United Nations.

Adopt Resolutions. These organizations adopt resolutions, declarations, and other types of standards that often require nations to behave in a particular manner. The General Assembly of the United Nations, for instance, has adopted numerous nonbinding resolutions and declarations that embody principles of international law. Disputes with respect to these resolutions and declarations may be brought before the International Court of Justice. That court, however, normally has authority to settle legal disputes only when nations voluntarily submit to its jurisdiction.

Create Uniform Rules. The United Nations Commission on International Trade Law has made considerable progress in establishing uniformity in international law as it relates to trade and commerce. One of the commission's most significant creations to date is the 1980 Convention on Contracts for the International Sale of Goods (CISG).

As you will read in Chapter 11, the CISG is similar to Article 2 of the Uniform Commercial Code in that it is designed to settle disputes between parties to sales contracts. It spells out the duties of international buyers and sellers that will apply if the parties have not agreed otherwise in their contracts. The CISG governs only sales contracts between trading partners in nations that have ratified the CISG, however.

Common Law and Civil Law Systems

Companies operating in foreign nations are subject to the laws of those nations. In addition, international disputes are often resolved through the court systems of foreign nations.

Businesspersons should understand that legal systems around the globe generally are divided into *common law* and *civil law* systems. Exhibit 8–1 below indicates some of the nations that use civil law systems and some that use common law systems.

EXHIBIT 8–1 The Legal Systems of Selected Nations

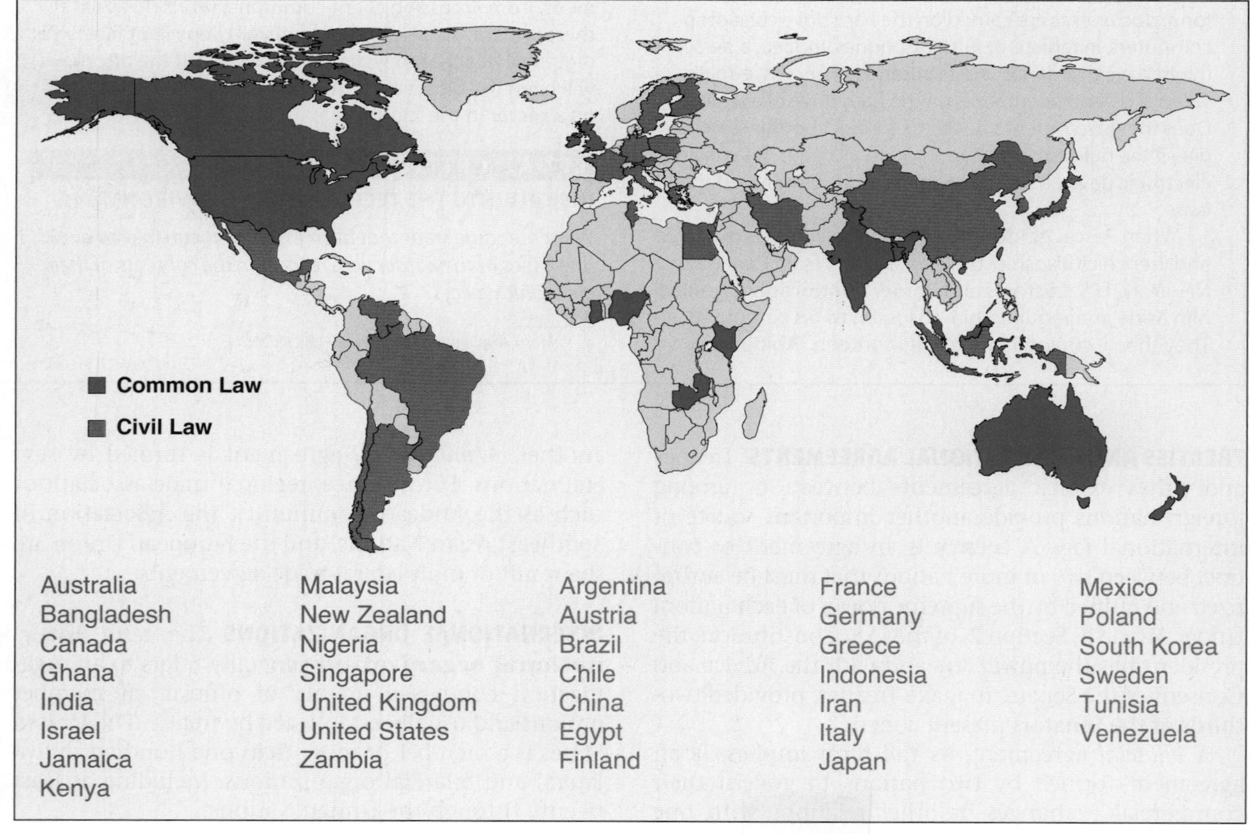

COMMON LAW SYSTEMS As discussed in Chapter 1, in a common law system, the courts independently develop the rules governing certain areas of law, such as torts and contracts. These common law rules apply to all areas not covered by statutory law. Although the common law doctrine of *stare decisis* obligates judges to follow precedential decisions in their jurisdictions, courts may modify or even overturn precedents when deemed necessary.

CIVIL LAW SYSTEMS In contrast to common law countries, most European nations, as well as nations in Latin America, Africa, and Asia, base their legal systems on Roman civil law, or "code law." The term *civil law,* as used here, refers not to civil as opposed to criminal law but to *codified* law—an ordered grouping of legal principles enacted into law by a legislature or other governing body.

In a **civil law system,** the primary source of law is a statutory code. Courts interpret the code and apply the rules to individual cases, but courts may not depart from the code and develop their own laws. Judicial precedents are not binding, as they are in a common law system. In theory, the law code sets forth all of the principles needed for the legal system. Trial procedures also differ in civil law systems. Unlike judges in common law systems, judges in civil systems often actively question witnesses.

ISLAMIC LEGAL SYSTEMS A third, less prevalent, legal system is common in Islamic countries, where the law is often influenced by *sharia,* the religious law of Islam. *Sharia* is a comprehensive code of principles that governs both the public and the private lives of persons of the Islamic faith. *Sharia* directs many aspects of day-to-day life, including politics, economics, banking, business law, contract law, and social issues.

Although *sharia* affects the legal codes of many Muslim countries, the extent of its impact and its interpretation vary widely. In some Middle Eastern nations, aspects of *sharia* have been codified and are enforced by national judicial systems.

International Principles and Doctrines

Over time, a number of legal principles and doctrines have evolved and are employed—to a greater or lesser extent—by the courts of various nations to resolve or reduce conflicts that involve a foreign element. The three important legal principles discussed below are based primarily on courtesy and respect, and are applied in the interests of maintaining harmonious relations among nations.

One way to understand two of these principles—*comity* and the *act of state doctrine*—is to consider the relationships among the states in our federal form of government. Each state honors (gives "full faith and credit" to) the contracts, property deeds, wills, and other legal obligations formed in other states, as well as judicial decisions with respect to such obligations.

On a global basis, nations similarly attempt to honor judgments rendered in other countries when it is feasible to do so. Of course, in the United States the states are constitutionally required to honor other states' actions, whereas international law does not *require* nations to honor the actions of other nations.

THE PRINCIPLE OF COMITY The principle of **comity** basically refers to legal reciprocity. One nation will defer and give effect to the executive, legislative, and judicial acts of another country, as long as the acts are consistent with the law and public policy of the accommodating nation. For instance, a U.S. court ordinarily will recognize and enforce a default judgment (see Chapter 2) from an Australian court because the legal procedures in Australia are compatible with those in the United States. Nearly all nations recognize the validity of marriage decrees (at least those between a man and a woman) issued in another country.

▶ **Case in Point 8.2** Karen Goldberg's husband was killed in a terrorist bombing in Israel. She filed a lawsuit in a federal court in New York against UBS AG, a Switzerland-based global financial services company with many offices in the United States. Goldberg claimed that UBS was liable under the U.S. Anti-Terrorism Act for aiding and abetting the murder of her husband. She argued that UBS was liable because it provided financial services to the international terrorist organizations responsible for his murder.

UBS requested that the case be transferred to a court in Israel, which would offer a remedy "substantially the same" as the one available in the United States. The court refused, however. Transferring the case would require an Israeli court to take evidence and judge the emotional damage suffered by Goldberg, "raising distinct concerns of comity and enforceability."[1] ◀

In the following case, the court was asked to balance interests that were significant and serious to all of the parties. The defendant wanted the court to give particular weight to the principle of comity.

1. *Goldberg v. UBS AG,* 690 F.Supp.2d 92 (E.D.N.Y. 2010).

CASE ANALYSIS

Case 8.1 Linde v. Arab Bank, PLC[a]

United States Court of Appeals, Second Circuit, 706 F.3d 92 (2013).

IN THE LANGUAGE OF THE COURT

Susan L. *CARNEY*, Circuit Judge:

This case concerns claims brought by victims and families of victims of terrorist attacks committed in Israel between 1995 and 2004 [during a period commonly referred to as the Second Intifada]. Proceeding under the Anti-Terrorism Act [ATA] and the Alien Tort Claims Act, plaintiffs [filed a suit in a federal district court to] seek monetary damages from Arab Bank, PLC ("Arab Bank" or the "Bank"), a large bank headquartered in Jordan, with branches in New York, throughout the Middle East, and around the world. According to plaintiffs, Arab Bank provided financial services and support to terrorists during this period, facilitating the attacks that caused them grave harm.

* * * *

This appeal is brought by defendant Arab Bank from the District Court's orders imposing sanctions.

That order was entered following the Bank's repeated failures, over several years and despite multiple discovery orders, to produce certain documents relevant to plaintiffs' case. The Bank argues that the documents are covered by foreign bank secrecy laws such that their disclosure would subject the Bank to criminal prosecution and other penalties in several foreign jurisdictions. The sanctions order takes the form of a jury instruction that would permit—but not require—the jury to infer from the Bank's failure to produce these documents that the Bank provided financial services to designated foreign terrorist organizations, and did so knowingly.

* * * *

The District Court carefully explained its decision to impose this sanction. It noted that many of the documents that plaintiffs had already obtained tended to support the inference that Arab Bank knew that its services benefited terrorists. According to the District Court, these documents included * * * documents from Arab Bank's Lebanon branch that suggested * * * Arab Bank officials approved the transfer of funds into an account at that branch despite the fact that the transfers listed known terrorists as beneficiaries. As a consequence of the evidentiary gap created by Arab Bank's non-disclosure, the court reasoned, plaintiffs would be "hard-pressed to show that * * * these transfers were not approved by mistake, but instead are representative of numerous other transfers to terrorists." The permissive inference instruction will, according to the District Court, help to rectify this evidentiary imbalance.

* * * *

* * * Arab Bank * * * filed [a] petition for mandamus [an order from a federal appellate court to a district court correcting an erroneous order under circumstances amounting to a clear abuse of discretion by the district court].

* * * *

Arab Bank argues that the District Court's decisions ordering production and imposing sanctions should be vacated because they offend international comity. This argument derives from the notion that the sanctions force foreign authorities either to waive enforcement of their bank secrecy laws or to enforce those laws, and in so doing create an allegedly devastating financial liability for the leading financial institution in their region. The Bank asserts, further, that international comity principles merit special weight here because the District Court's decisions affect the United States' interests in combating terrorism and pertain to a region of the world pivotal to United States foreign policy.

* * * The [District] Court expressly noted that it had "considered the interests of the United States and the foreign jurisdictions whose foreign bank secrecy laws are at issue."

Additionally, international comity calls for more than an examination of only some of the interests of some foreign states. Rather, the concept of international comity requires a particularized analysis of the respective interests of the foreign nation and the requesting nation. In other words, the analysis invites a weighing of all of the relevant interests of all of the nations affected by the court's decision. * * * The District Court recognized the legal conflict faced by Arab Bank and the comity interests implicated by the bank secrecy laws. But [the Court] also observed—and properly so—that Jordan and Lebanon have expressed a strong interest in deterring the financial support of terrorism, and that these interests have often outweighed the enforcement of bank secrecy laws, even in the view of the foreign states. Moreover, * * * the District Court took into account the United States' interests in the effective prosecution of civil claims under the ATA [Anti-Terrorism Act]. This type of holistic, multi-factored analysis does not so obviously offend international comity so as to support issuance of a writ of mandamus. [Emphasis added.]

* * * *

* * * We find no clear abuse of discretion in the District Court's

---

a. *PLC* stands for "public liability company," which is a publicly traded company in England and Ireland. This business form is the equivalent to a publicly traded corporation in the United States.

CASE 8.1 CONTINUED

conclusion that the interests of other sovereigns in enforcing bank secrecy laws are outweighed by the need to impede terrorism financing as embodied in the tort remedies provided by U.S. civil law and the stated commitments of the foreign nations.

* * * *

* * * The Bank's petition for a writ of *mandamus* is DENIED.

LEGAL REASONING QUESTIONS

1. How is the principle of comity applied?
2. What considerations can take precedence over comity?
3. What interests were at stake in the dispute at the heart of this case?
4. Did this court apply the principle of comity? Why or why not?

THE ACT OF STATE DOCTRINE The **act of state doctrine** provides that the judicial branch of one country will not examine the validity of public acts committed by a recognized foreign government within the latter's own territory.

▶ **Case in Point 8.3** Spectrum Stores, Inc., a gasoline retailer in the United States, filed a lawsuit in a U.S. court against Citgo Petroleum Corporation, which is owned by the government of Venezuela. Spectrum alleged that Citgo had conspired with other oil companies in Venezuela and Saudi Arabia to limit production of crude oil and thereby fix the prices of petroleum products sold in the United States.

Because Citgo is owned by a foreign government, the U.S. court dismissed the case under the act of state doctrine. A government controls the natural resources, such as oil reserves, within its territory. A U.S. court will not rule on the validity of a foreign government's acts within its own territory.[2] ◀

When a Foreign Government Takes Private Property. The act of state doctrine can have important consequences for individuals and firms doing business with, and investing in, other countries. This doctrine is frequently employed in cases involving expropriation or confiscation.

Expropriation occurs when a government seizes a privately owned business or privately owned goods for a proper public purpose and awards just compensation. When a government seizes private property for an illegal purpose and without just compensation, the taking is referred to as a **confiscation.** The line between these two forms of taking is sometimes blurred because of differing interpretations of what is illegal and what constitutes just compensation.

▶ **Example 8.4** Flaherty, Inc., a U.S. company, owns a mine in Brazil. The government of Brazil seizes the mine for public use and claims that the profits Flaherty has already realized from the mine constitute just compensation. Flaherty disagrees, but the act of state doctrine may prevent the company's recovery in a U.S. court. ◀ Note that in a case alleging that a foreign government has wrongfully taken the plaintiff's property, the defendant government has the burden of proving that the taking was an expropriation, not a confiscation.

Doctrine May Immunize a Foreign Government's Actions. When applicable, both the act of state doctrine and the doctrine of *sovereign immunity,* which we discuss next, tend to shield foreign nations from the jurisdiction of U.S. courts. As a result, firms or individuals who own property overseas generally have little legal protection against government actions in the countries where they operate.

THE DOCTRINE OF SOVEREIGN IMMUNITY When certain conditions are satisfied, the doctrine of **sovereign immunity** exempts foreign nations from the jurisdiction of the U.S. courts. In 1976, Congress codified this rule in the Foreign Sovereign Immunities Act (FSIA).[3]

The FSIA exclusively governs the circumstances in which an action may be brought in the United States against a foreign nation, including attempts to attach a foreign nation's property. Because the law is jurisdictional in nature, a plaintiff generally has the burden of showing that a defendant is not entitled to sovereign immunity.

When a Foreign State Will Not Be Immune. Section 1605 of the FSIA sets forth the major exceptions to the jurisdictional immunity of a foreign state. A foreign state is not immune from the jurisdiction of U.S. courts in the following situations:

2. *Spectrum Stores, Inc. v. Citgo Petroleum Corp.,* 632 F.3d 938 (5th Cir. 2011).

3. 28 U.S.C. Sections 1602–1611.

1. When the foreign state has waived its immunity either explicitly or by implication.
2. When the foreign state has engaged in commercial activity within the United States or in commercial activity outside the United States that has "a direct effect in the United States."
3. When the foreign state has committed a tort in the United States or has violated certain international laws.

Application of the Act. When courts apply the FSIA, questions frequently arise as to whether an entity is a "foreign state" and what constitutes a "commercial activity." Under Section 1603 of the FSIA, a *foreign state* includes both a political subdivision of a foreign state and an instrumentality (department or agency of any branch of a government) of a foreign state.

Section 1603 broadly defines a *commercial activity* as a regular course of commercial conduct, transaction, or act that is carried out by a foreign state within the United States. Section 1603, however, does not describe the particulars of what constitutes a commercial activity. Thus, the courts are left to decide whether a particular activity is governmental or commercial in nature.

SECTION 2 DOING BUSINESS INTERNATIONALLY

A U.S. domestic firm can engage in international business transactions in a number of ways. The simplest way is for U.S. firms to **export** their goods and services to foreign markets. Alternatively, a U.S. firm can establish foreign production facilities to be closer to the foreign market or markets in which its products are sold. The advantages may include lower labor costs, fewer government regulations, and lower taxes and trade barriers. A domestic firm can also obtain revenues by licensing its technology to an existing foreign company or by selling franchises to overseas entities.

Exporting

Exporting can take two forms: direct exporting and indirect exporting. In *direct exporting,* a U.S. company signs a sales contract with a foreign purchaser that provides for the conditions of shipment and payment for the goods. (International contracts for the purchase and sale of goods, as well as the use of letters of credit to make payments, will be discussed in Chapter 11.)

If sufficient business develops in a foreign country, a U.S. company may establish a specialized marketing organization there by appointing a foreign agent or a foreign distributor. This is called *indirect exporting.*

When a U.S. firm wishes to limit its involvement in an international market, it will typically establish an *agency relationship* with a foreign firm. The foreign firm then acts as the U.S. firm's agent and can enter contracts in the foreign location on behalf of the principal (the U.S. company).

DISTRIBUTORSHIPS When a foreign country represents a substantial market, a U.S. firm may wish to appoint a distributor located in that country. The U.S. firm and the distributor enter into a **distribution agreement.** This is a contract setting out the terms and conditions of the distributorship, such as price, currency of payment, guarantee of supply availability, and method of payment. Disputes concerning distribution agreements may involve jurisdictional or other issues, as well as contract law.

THE NATIONAL EXPORT INITIATIVE Although the United States is one of the world's major exporters, exports make up a much smaller share of annual output in the United States than they do in our most important trading partners. In the past, the United States has not promoted exports as actively as many other nations have.

In an effort to increase U.S. exports, the Obama administration created the National Export Initiative (NEI) with a goal of doubling U.S. exports by 2015. Some commentators believe that another goal of the NEI is to reduce outsourcing—the practice of having manufacturing or other activities performed in lower-wage countries such as China and India.

Export Promotion. An important component of the NEI is the Export Promotion Cabinet, which includes officials from sixteen government agencies and departments. All cabinet members must submit detailed plans to the president, outlining the steps that they will take to increase U.S. exports.

The U.S. Commerce Department plays a leading role in the NEI, and hundreds of its trade experts serve as advocates to help some twenty thousand U.S. companies increase their export sales. In addition, the Commerce Department and other Export Promotion Cabinet members work to promote U.S. exports in the high-growth developing markets of Brazil, China, and India. The members also identify market opportunities in fast-growing sectors, such as environmental goods and services, biotechnology, and renewable energy.

Increased Export Financing. Under the NEI, the Export-Import Bank of the United States increased the financing that it makes available to small and medium-sized businesses by 50 percent. In the initial phase, the bank added hundreds of new small-business clients that sell a wide variety of products, from sophisticated polymers to date palm trees and nanotechnology-based cosmetics.

Manufacturing Abroad

An alternative to direct or indirect exporting is the establishment of foreign manufacturing facilities. Typically, U.S. firms establish manufacturing plants abroad when they believe that by doing so they will reduce costs. Costs for labor, shipping, and raw materials may be lower in foreign nations, which can enable the business to compete more effectively in foreign markets.

Foreign firms have done the same in the United States. Sony, Nissan, and other Japanese manufacturers have established U.S. plants to avoid import duties that the U.S. Congress may impose on Japanese products entering this country.

LICENSING A U.S. firm may license a foreign manufacturing company to use its copyrighted, patented, or trademarked intellectual property or trade secrets. Basically, licensing allows the foreign firm to use an established brand name for a fee. A licensing agreement with a foreign-based firm is much the same as any other licensing agreement (see Chapters 9, 14, and 15). Its terms require a payment of royalties on some basis—such as so many cents per unit produced or a certain percentage of profits from units sold in a particular geographic territory.

▶ **Example 8.5** The Coca-Cola Bottling Company licenses firms worldwide to use (and keep confidential) its secret formula for the syrup used in its soft drink. In return, the company receives a percentage of the income gained from the sale of Coca-Cola by those firms. ◀

The firm that receives the license can take advantage of an established reputation for quality. The firm that grants the license receives income from the foreign sales of its products and also establishes a global reputation. Once a firm's trademark is known worldwide, the demand for other products manufactured or sold by that firm may increase—obviously, an important consideration.

FRANCHISING Franchising is a well-known form of licensing and is evident the world over. The owner of a trademark, trade name, or copyright (the franchisor) licenses another (the franchisee) to use the mark, name, or copyright, under certain conditions or limitations, in the selling of goods or services.

Franchising allows the franchisor to maintain greater control over the business operation than is possible with most other licensing agreements. In return, the franchisee pays a fee, usually based on a monthly percentage of gross or net sales. Examples of international franchises include Holiday Inn and Hertz.

INVESTING IN A WHOLLY OWNED SUBSIDIARY OR A JOINT VENTURE Another way to expand into a foreign market is to establish a wholly owned subsidiary firm in a foreign country. In many European countries, a subsidiary would likely take the form of a *société anonyme* (S.A.), which is similar to a U.S. corporation. In German-speaking nations, it would be called an *Aktiengesellschaft* (A.G.).

When a wholly owned subsidiary is established, the parent company remains in the United States. The parent maintains complete ownership of all of the facilities in the foreign country, as well as total authority and control over all phases of the operation.

A U.S. firm can also expand into international markets through a *joint venture*. In a joint venture, the U.S. company owns only part of the operation. The rest is owned either by local owners in the foreign country or by another foreign entity. All of the firms involved in a joint venture share responsibilities, as well as profits and liabilities.

SECTION 3

REGULATION OF SPECIFIC BUSINESS ACTIVITIES

Doing business abroad can affect the economies, foreign policies, domestic politics, and other national interests of the countries involved. For this reason, nations impose laws to restrict or facilitate international business. Controls may also be imposed by international agreements.

Investment Protections

Firms that invest in foreign nations face the risk that the foreign government may expropriate the investment property. Expropriation, as mentioned earlier in this chapter, occurs when property is taken and the owner is paid just compensation for what is taken. This generally does not violate accepted principles of international law.

Confiscating property without compensation (or without adequate compensation), in contrast, normally violates international law. Few remedies are available for confiscation of property by a foreign government. Claims are often resolved by lump-sum settlements after negotiations between the United States and the taking nation.

Because the possibility of confiscation may deter potential investors, many countries guarantee compensation to foreign investors if their property is taken. A guaranty can be in the form of national constitutional or statutory laws or provisions in international treaties. As further protection for foreign investments, some countries provide insurance for their citizens' investments abroad.

Export Controls

Article I, Section 9, of the U.S. Constitution provides that "No Tax or Duty shall be laid on Articles exported from any State." Thus, Congress cannot impose any export taxes.

Congress can, however, use a variety of other devices to restrict or encourage exports, including the following:

1. *Export quotas.* Congress sets export quotas on various items, such as grain being sold abroad.
2. *Restrictions on technology exports.* Under the Export Administration Act,[4] the flow of technologically advanced products and technical data can be restricted.
3. *Incentives and subsidies.* The United States (and other nations) also uses incentives and subsidies to stimulate other exports and thereby aid domestic businesses. ▶ **Example 8.6** Under the Export Trading Company Act,[5] U.S. banks are encouraged to invest in export trading companies, which are formed when exporting firms join together to export a line of goods. The Export-Import Bank of the United States provides financial assistance, primarily in the form of credit guaranties given to commercial banks that in turn lend funds to U.S. exporting companies. ◀

Import Controls

All nations have restrictions on imports, and the United States is no exception. Restrictions include strict prohibitions, quotas, and tariffs.

PROHIBITED GOODS Under the Trading with the Enemy Act,[6] no goods may be imported from nations that have been designated enemies of the United States. Other laws prohibit the importation of illegal drugs, books that urge insurrection against the United States,[7] and agricultural products that pose dangers to domestic crops or animals.

The importation of goods that infringe U.S. patents is also prohibited. The International Trade Commission is the government agency that investigates allegations that imported goods infringe U.S. patents and imposes penalties if necessary.

▶ **Case in Point 8.7** Fuji Photo Film Company owned numerous patents for disposable cameras, including the plastic shell covering. Jazz Photo Corporation collected used plastic shells in the United States, shipped them abroad to have new film inserted, and imported the refurbished shells back into the United States for sale. The International Trade Commission (ITC) determined that Jazz's resale of shells originally sold outside the United States infringed Fuji's patents. The ITC ordered Jazz to stop the imports. When Jazz imported and sold 27 million more refurbished shells, Fuji complained to the ITC, which fined Jazz more than $13.5 million.[8] ◀

QUOTAS AND TARIFFS Limits on the amounts of goods that can be imported are known as **quotas.** At one time, the United States had legal quotas on the number of automobiles that could be imported from Japan. Today, Japan "voluntarily" restricts the number of automobiles exported to the United States.

4. 50 U.S.C. Sections 2401–2420.
5. 15 U.S.C. Sections 4001, 4003.
6. 12 U.S.C. Section 95a.
7. Because numerous resources that advocate the overthrow of the U.S. government are available on the Internet, this prohibition against importing books that urge insurrection is rather meaningless.
8. *Fuji Photo Film Co. v. International Trade Commission,* 474 F.3d 1281 (Fed.Cir. 2007).

Tariffs are taxes on imports. A tariff is usually a percentage of the value of the import, but it can be a flat rate per unit (such as per barrel of oil). Tariffs raise the prices of imported goods, causing some consumers to purchase domestically manufactured goods instead of imports.

POLITICAL FACTORS Sometimes, countries impose tariffs on goods from a particular nation in retaliation for political acts. ▶ **Example 8.8** In 2009, Mexico imposed tariffs of 10 to 20 percent on ninety products exported from the United States in retaliation for the Obama administration's cancellation of a cross-border trucking program. The program had been instituted to comply with a provision in the North American Free Trade Agreement (to be discussed shortly) that called for Mexican trucks to eventually be granted full access to U.S. highways.

U.S. truck drivers opposed the program, however, and consumer protection groups claimed that the Mexican trucks posed safety issues. Because the Mexican tariffs were imposed on $2.4 billion of U.S. goods annually, in 2011 President Barack Obama negotiated a deal that allowed Mexican truckers to enter the United States. In exchange, Mexico agreed to suspend half of the tariffs immediately and the remainder when the first Mexican hauler complied with the new U.S. requirements. ◀

ANTIDUMPING DUTIES The United States has laws specifically directed at what it sees as unfair international trade practices. **Dumping,** for example, is the sale of imported goods at "less than fair value." *Fair value* is usually determined by the price of the goods in the exporting country. Foreign firms that engage in dumping in the United States hope to undersell U.S. businesses and obtain a larger share of the U.S. market. To prevent this, an extra tariff—known as an *antidumping duty*—may be assessed on the imports.

Two U.S. government agencies are instrumental in imposing antidumping duties: the International Trade Commission (ITC) and the International Trade Administration (ITA). The ITC assesses the effects of dumping on domestic businesses and then makes recommendations to the president concerning temporary import restrictions.

The ITA, which is part of the Department of Commerce, decides whether imports were sold at less than fair value. The ITA's determination establishes the amount of antidumping duties, which are set to equal the difference between the price charged in the United States and the price charged in the exporting country. A duty may be retroactive to cover past dumping.

Minimizing Trade Barriers

Restrictions on imports are also known as *trade barriers*. The elimination of trade barriers is sometimes seen as essential to the world's economic well-being. Most of the world's leading trading nations are members of the World Trade Organization (WTO), which was established in 1995 to minimize trade barriers among nations.

Each member country of the WTO is required to grant **normal trade relations (NTR) status** (formerly known as *most-favored-nation status*) to other member countries. This means that each member is obligated to treat other members at least as well as it treats the country that receives its most favorable treatment with regard to imports or exports. Various regional trade agreements and associations also help to minimize trade barriers between nations.

THE EUROPEAN UNION (EU) The European Union (EU) arose out of the 1957 Treaty of Rome, which created the Common Market, a free trade zone comprising the nations of Belgium, France, Italy, Luxembourg, the Netherlands, and West Germany. Today, the EU is a single integrated trading unit made up of twenty-eight European nations.

The EU has gone a long way toward creating a new body of law to govern all of the member nations—although some of its efforts to create uniform laws have been confounded by nationalism. Its governing authorities issue regulations, or directives, that define EU law in various areas, such as environmental law, product liability, anticompetitive practices, and corporations. The directives normally are binding on all member countries.

THE NORTH AMERICAN FREE TRADE AGREEMENT (NAFTA) The North American Free Trade Agreement (NAFTA) created a regional trading unit consisting of Canada, Mexico, and the United States. The goal of NAFTA was to eliminate tariffs among these three nations on substantially all goods by reducing the tariffs incrementally over a period of time.

NAFTA gives the three countries a competitive advantage by retaining tariffs on goods imported from countries outside the NAFTA trading unit. Additionally, NAFTA provides for the elimination of barriers that traditionally have prevented the cross-border movement of services, such as financial and transportation services. NAFTA also attempts to eliminate citizenship requirements for the licensing of accountants, attorneys, physicians, and other professionals.

THE CENTRAL AMERICA–DOMINICAN REPUBLIC–UNITED STATES FREE TRADE AGREEMENT (CAFTA-DR) The Central America–Dominican Republic–United States Free Trade Agreement (CAFTA-DR) was formed by Costa Rica, the Dominican Republic, El Salvador, Guatemala, Honduras, Nicaragua, and the United States. Its purpose is to reduce trade tariffs and improve market access among all of the signatory nations, including the United States. Legislatures from all seven countries have approved the CAFTA-DR, despite significant opposition in certain nations.

THE REPUBLIC OF KOREA–UNITED STATES FREE TRADE AGREEMENT (KORUS FTA) In 2011, the United States ratified its first free trade agreement with South Korea—the Republic of Korea–United States Free Trade Agreement (KORUS FTA). The treaty's provisions will eliminate 95 percent of each nation's tariffs on industrial and consumer exports within five years.

KORUS is the largest free trade agreement that the United States has entered into since NAFTA. It is expected to boost U.S. exports by more than $10 billion a year and will benefit U.S. automakers, farmers, ranchers, and manufacturers by enabling them to compete in new markets.

Also in 2011, Congress ratified free trade agreements with Colombia and Panama. The Colombian trade agreement includes a provision requiring an exchange of tax information, and the Panama bill incorporates assurances on labor rights. The treaties are expected to increase U.S. exports and reduce prices for consumers. The Obama administration hopes that the agreements will also provide impetus for negotiations of the trans-Pacific trade initiative, aimed at increasing exports to Japan and other Asian nations.

SECTION 4

INTERNATIONAL DISPUTE RESOLUTION

International contracts frequently include arbitration clauses. By means of such clauses, the parties agree in advance to be bound by the decision of a specified third party in the event of a dispute, as discussed in Chapter 3.

The New York Convention

The United Nations Convention on the Recognition and Enforcement of Foreign Arbitral Awards (often referred to as the New York Convention) assists in the enforcement of arbitration clauses, as do provisions in specific treaties among nations. Basically, the convention requires courts in nations that have signed it to honor private agreements to arbitrate and recognize arbitration awards made in other contracting states. The New York Convention has been implemented in nearly one hundred countries, including the United States.

Under the New York Convention, a court will compel the parties to arbitrate their dispute if all of the following are true:

1. There is a written (or recorded) agreement to arbitrate the matter.
2. The agreement provides for arbitration in a convention signatory nation.
3. The agreement arises out of a commercial legal relationship.
4. One party to the agreement is not a U.S. citizen. In other words, both parties cannot be U.S. citizens.

In the following case, the parties had agreed to arbitrate any disputes in Guernsey, which is a British Crown dependency in the English Channel. The court had to decide whether the agreement was enforceable even though one party was a U.S. company and the other party may have had its principal place of business in the United States.

CASE 8.2

S & T Oil Equipment & Machinery, Ltd. v. Juridica Investments, Ltd.

United States Court of Appeals, Fifth Circuit, 2012 WL 28242 (2012).

BACKGROUND AND FACTS Juridica Investments, Ltd. (JIL), entered into a financing contract with S & T Oil Equipment & Machinery, Ltd., a U.S. company. The contract included an arbitration provision stating that any disputes would be arbitrated "in St. Peter Port, Guernsey, Channel Islands." The contract

CASE 8.2 CONTINUED

also stated that it was executed in Guernsey and would be fully performed there. When a dispute arose between the parties, JIL initiated arbitration in Guernsey. Nevertheless, S & T filed a suit in federal district court in the United States. When JIL filed a motion to dismiss in favor of arbitration, the court granted the motion and compelled arbitration under the Convention on the Recognition and Enforcement of Foreign Arbitral Awards. S & T appealed.

IN THE LANGUAGE OF THE COURT
PER CURIAM: [By the Whole Court]

* * * *

The parties dispute whether the fourth * * * factor [that one party is not an American citizen] is satisfied in this case. In considering this fourth factor, courts must ask the following: Is a party to the agreement not an American citizen or does the commercial relationship have some reasonable relation with one or more foreign states? If either question is answered in the affirmative, then the fourth * * * factor is satisfied.

* * * *

*Although it is not absolutely clear where JIL has its principal place of business, it is evident that the commercial relationship between S & T and JIL has some reasonable relation with one or more foreign states. Even if JIL's principal place of business is in the United States, the * * * agreement's arbitral clause can still be enforceable under the Convention if the legal relationship between JIL and S & T involved "property abroad, envisages performance or enforcement abroad, or has some other reasonable relation with one or more foreign states." As we stated in [another case], this reasonable relation with a foreign state must be "independent of the arbitral clause itself."* [Emphasis added.]

Here, it is evident that the legal relationship between JIL and S & T envisaged performance abroad. The * * * agreement specifically states that it was executed in Guernsey and would be performed by JIL "exclusively and wholly in and from Guernsey." Indeed, pursuant to the terms of the * * * agreement, JIL performed part of the agreement abroad when it wired funds from Guernsey to cover * * * legal fees and costs * * * .

Given these facts, it is evident that the commercial relationship between S & T and JIL has some reasonable relation with one or more foreign states that is independent of the arbitral clause itself. As such, the fourth * * * factor is satisfied in this case. The district court therefore did not err in compelling arbitration.

DECISION AND REMEDY *The U.S. Court of Appeals for the Fifth Circuit held that arbitration was required under the Convention on the Recognition and Enforcement of Foreign Arbitral Awards. It therefore affirmed the district court's judgment compelling arbitration.*

THE GLOBAL DIMENSION *What would happen if Congress did not require a reasonable relationship with a foreign state for arbitration agreements between U.S. citizens doing business abroad? Would there be more or fewer agreements to arbitrate disputes abroad?*

THE TECHNOLOGICAL DIMENSION *How might these parties have avoided the time and expense of settling their dispute in a foreign jurisdiction?*

Effect of Choice-of-Law and Choice-of-Forum Clauses

If a sales contract does not include an arbitration clause, litigation may occur. When the contract contains forum-selection and choice-of-law clauses (see Chapter 11), the lawsuit will be heard by a court in the specified forum and decided according to that forum's law.

Case in Point 8.9 Intermax Trading Corporation, a New York firm, contracted to act as the North American sales agent for Garware Polyester, Ltd., based in Mumbai, India. The parties executed a series of contracts with provisions stating that the courts of Mumbai, India, would have exclusive jurisdiction over any disputes relating to the agreements. When Intermax fell behind in its payments to Garware, Garware filed a lawsuit in a U.S. court to collect the balance due. Garware claimed that the forum-selection clause did not apply to sales of warehoused goods, but the court sided with Intermax. Because the forum-selection clause was valid and enforceable, Garware had to bring its complaints against Intermax in a court in India.[9] ◀

If the contract does not specify a forum and choice of law, proceedings will be more complex and legally uncertain. Litigation may take place in two or more countries, with each country applying its own choice-of-law rules to determine the substantive law that will be applied to the particular transactions. Even if a plaintiff wins a favorable judgment in its own country, there is no way to predict whether courts in the defendant's country will enforce the judgment.

SECTION 5

U.S. LAWS IN A GLOBAL CONTEXT

The globalization of business raises questions about the extraterritorial application of a nation's laws—that is, the effect of the country's laws outside its boundaries. To what extent do U.S. domestic laws apply to other nations' businesses? To what extent do U.S. domestic laws apply to U.S. firms doing business abroad? Here, we discuss the extraterritorial application of certain U.S. laws, including antitrust laws, tort laws, and laws prohibiting employment discrimination.

U.S. Antitrust Laws

U.S. antitrust laws have a wide application. They may *subject* firms in foreign nations to their provisions, as well as *protect* foreign consumers and competitors from violations committed by U.S. citizens. Section 1 of the Sherman Act—the most important U.S. antitrust law—provides for the extraterritorial effect of the U.S. antitrust laws.

The United States is a major proponent of free competition in the global economy. Thus, any conspiracy that has a *substantial effect* on U.S. commerce is within the reach of the Sherman Act. The law applies even if the violation occurs outside the United States, and foreign governments as well as businesses can be sued for violations. Before U.S. courts will exercise jurisdiction and apply antitrust laws, however, it must be shown that the alleged violation had a substantial effect on U.S. commerce.

▶ **Example 8.10** An investigation by the U.S. government revealed that a Tokyo-based auto-parts supplier, Furukawa Electric Company, and its executives conspired with competitors in an international price-fixing agreement (an agreement to set prices). The agreement lasted more than ten years and resulted in automobile manufacturers paying noncompetitive higher prices for parts in cars sold to U.S. consumers.

Because the conspiracy had a substantial effect on U.S. commerce, the United States had jurisdiction to prosecute the case. In 2011, Furukawa agreed to plead guilty and pay a $200 million fine. The Furukawa executives from Japan also agreed to serve up to eighteen months in a U.S. prison and to cooperate fully with the ongoing investigation. ◀

International Tort Claims

The international application of tort liability is growing in significance and controversy. An increasing number of U.S. plaintiffs are suing foreign (or U.S.) entities for torts that these entities have allegedly committed overseas. Often, these cases involve human rights violations by foreign governments. The Alien Tort Claims Act (ATCA),[10] allows even foreign citizens to bring civil suits in U.S. courts for injuries caused by violations of the law of nations or a treaty of the United States.

Since 1980, foreign plaintiffs have increasingly used this act to bring actions against companies operating in nations such as Colombia, Ecuador, Egypt, Guatemala, India, Indonesia, Nigeria, and Saudi Arabia. Some of these cases have involved alleged environmental destruction. Others have involved human rights violations.[11] In addition, mineral companies in Southeast Asia have been sued for collaborating with oppressive government regimes.

In the following *Spotlight Case,* the United States Supreme Court considers the parameters of the ATCA (which the Court refers to as the Alien Tort Statute, or ATS). The question is whether the statute allows courts to recognize a cause of action for violations of the law of nations occurring within the territory of a sovereign other than the United States.

9. *Garware Polyester, Ltd. v. Intermax Trading Corp.,* 2001 WL 1035134 (S.D.N.Y. 2001).

10. 28 U.S.C. Section 1350.

11. See, for example, *Khulumani v. Barclay National Bank, Ltd.,* 504 F.3d 254 (2007), in which plaintiffs claimed that hundreds of corporations "aided and abetted" the government of South Africa in maintaining its apartheid (racially discriminatory) regime.

SPOTLIGHT on International Torts

Case 8.3 Kiobel v. Royal Dutch Petroleum Co.

Supreme Court of the United States, __ U.S. __, 133 S.Ct. 1659, __ L.Ed. __ (2013).

BACKGROUND AND FACTS Shell Petroleum Development Company of Nigeria, Ltd. (SPDC), a Nigerian firm, engaged in oil exploration and production in Ogoniland, Nigeria. When some Ogoni residents protested the environmental effects of SPDC's practices, the Nigerian government violently suppressed the demonstrations. Some protesters who were granted political asylum in the United States filed a suit in a federal district court against Royal Dutch Petroleum Company (a Dutch firm and one of SPDC's parent companies) under the Alien Tort Statute (ATS). The petitioners alleged that the respondents aided and abetted Nigerian military and police atrocities, which violated the law of nations. The court dismissed parts of the complaint. On appeal, the U.S. Court of Appeals for the Second Circuit dismissed the entire complaint. The petitioners appealed.

IN THE LANGUAGE OF THE COURT

Chief Justice *ROBERTS* delivered the opinion of the Court.

* * * *

* * * A canon of statutory interpretation known as the presumption against extraterritorial application * * * provides that when a statute gives no clear indication of an extraterritorial application, it has none and reflects *the presumption that United States law governs domestically but does not rule the world.* [Emphasis added.]

This presumption serves to protect against unintended clashes between our laws and those of other nations [that] could result in international discord.

* * * *

Petitioners contend that even if the presumption applies, the text, history, and purposes of the ATS rebut it for causes of action brought under that statute.

[But] nothing in the text of the statute suggests that Congress intended causes of action recognized under it to have extraterritorial reach. *The ATS covers actions by aliens for violations of the law of nations, but that does not imply extraterritorial reach—such violations affecting aliens can occur either within or outside the United States.* [Emphasis added.]

* * * *

Nor does the historical background against which the ATS was enacted overcome the presumption * * * . When Congress passed the ATS, three principal offenses against the law of nations had been identified * * * : violation of safe conducts, infringement of the rights of ambassadors, and piracy.

* * * *

* * * Prominent contemporary examples [of the first two offenses that occurred in the United States] provide no support for the proposition that Congress expected causes of action to be brought under the statute for violations of the law of nations occurring abroad.

* * * Piracy typically occurs on the high seas, beyond the territorial jurisdiction of the United States or any other country.

Applying U.S. law to pirates, however, does not typically impose the sovereign will of the United States onto conduct occurring within the territorial jurisdiction of another sovereign, and therefore carries less direct foreign policy consequences.

* * * *

Finally, there is no indication that the ATS was passed to make the United States a uniquely hospitable forum for the enforcement of international norms. * * * Indeed, the parties offer no evidence that any nation, meek or mighty, presumed to do such a thing.

DECISION AND REMEDY *The United States Supreme Court affirmed the lower court's judgment. The presumption against extraterritoriality applies to claims under the ATS, nothing in the statute rebuts that presumption, and all the conduct about which the petitioners complained took place outside the United States.*

CASE 8.3 CONTINUES ➧

CASE 8.3 CONTINUED

THE LEGAL ENVIRONMENT DIMENSION *What are the ramifications of the ruling in this case for the respondents?*

THE GLOBAL DIMENSION *If the Court had adopted the petitioners' view, how might U.S. citizens have been affected?*

Antidiscrimination Laws

As you probably already know, federal laws in the United States prohibit discrimination on the basis of race, color, national origin, religion, gender, age, and disability. These laws, as they affect employment relationships, generally apply extraterritorially.

▶ **Example 8.11** The Age Discrimination in Employment Act (see Chapter 22) protects U.S. employees working abroad for U.S. employers. The Americans with Disabilities Act, which requires employers to accommodate the needs of workers with disabilities, also applies to U.S. nationals working abroad for U.S. firms. ◀

In addition, the major U.S. law regulating employment discrimination—Title VII of the Civil Rights Act—also applies extraterritorially to all U.S. employees working for U.S. employers abroad. Generally, U.S. employers must abide by U.S. discrimination laws unless to do so would violate the laws of the country where their workplaces are located. This "foreign laws exception" allows employers to avoid being subjected to conflicting laws.

Reviewing: International Law in a Global Economy

Robco, Inc., was a Florida arms dealer. The armed forces of Honduras contracted to purchase weapons from Robco over a six-year period. After the government was replaced and a democracy installed, the Honduran government sought to reduce the size of its military, and its relationship with Robco deteriorated. Honduras refused to honor the contract and purchase the inventory of arms, which Robco could sell only at a much lower price. Robco filed a suit in a federal district court in the United States to recover damages for this breach of contract by the government of Honduras. Using the information presented in the chapter, answer the following questions.

1. Should the Foreign Sovereign Immunities Act (FSIA) preclude this lawsuit? Why or why not?
2. Does the act of state doctrine bar Robco from seeking to enforce the contract? Explain.
3. Suppose that prior to this lawsuit, the new government of Honduras had enacted a law making it illegal to purchase weapons from foreign arms dealers. What doctrine of deference might lead a U.S. court to dismiss Robco's case in that situation?
4. Now suppose that the U.S. court hears the case and awards damages to Robco, but the government of Honduras has no assets in the United States that can be used to satisfy the judgment. Under which doctrine might Robco be able to collect the damages by asking another nation's court to enforce the U.S. judgment?

DEBATE THIS . . . *The U.S. federal courts are accepting too many lawsuits initiated by foreigners that concern matters not relevant to this country.*

Terms and Concepts

act of state doctrine 171
civil law system 169
comity 169
confiscation 171
distribution agreement 172
dumping 175

ExamPrep

Issue Spotters

1. Café Rojo, Ltd., an Ecuadoran firm, agrees to sell coffee beans to Dark Roast Coffee Company, a U.S. firm. Dark Roast accepts the beans but refuses to pay. Café Rojo sues Dark Roast in an Ecuadoran court and is awarded damages, but Dark Roast's assets are in the United States. Under what circumstances would a U.S. court enforce the judgment of the Ecuadoran court? **(See page 169.)**
2. Gems International, Ltd., is a foreign firm that has a 12 percent share of the U.S. market for diamonds. To capture a larger share, Gems offers its products at a below-cost discount to U.S. buyers (and inflates the prices in its own country to make up the difference). How can this attempt to undersell U.S. businesses be defeated? **(See page 175.)**

- **Check your answers to the Issue Spotters against the answers provided in Appendix E at the end of this text.**

Before the Test

Go to **www.cengagebrain.com**, enter the ISBN 9781285428949, and click on "Find" to locate this textbook's Web site. Then, click on "Access Now" under "Study Tools," and select Chapter 8 at the top. There, you will find an Interactive Quiz that you can take to assess your mastery of the concepts in this chapter, as well as Flashcards and a Glossary of important terms.

Business Scenarios

8–1. Doing Business Internationally. Macrotech, Inc., develops an innovative computer chip and obtains a patent on it. The firm markets the chip under the trade-marked brand name "Flash." Macrotech wants to sell the chip to Nitron, Ltd., in Pacifica, a foreign country. Macrotech is concerned, however, that after an initial purchase, Nitron will duplicate the chip, pirate it, and sell the pirated version to computer manufacturers in Pacifica. To avoid this possibility, Macrotech could establish its own manufacturing facility in Pacifica, but it does not want to do this. How can Macrotech, without establishing a manufacturing facility in Pacifica, protect Flash from being pirated by Nitron? **(See page 172.)**

8–2. Dumping. The U.S. pineapple industry alleged that producers of canned pineapple from the Philippines were selling their canned pineapple in the United States for less than its fair market value (dumping). The Philippine producers also exported other products, such as pineapple juice and juice concentrate. These products used separate parts of the same fresh pineapple, so they shared raw material costs with the canned fruit, according to the producers' own financial records. To determine fair value and antidumping duties, the pineapple industry argued that a court should calculate the Philippine producers' cost of production and allocate a portion of the shared fruit costs to the canned fruit. The result of this allocation showed that more than 90 percent of the canned fruit sales were below the cost of production. Is this a reasonable approach to determining the production costs and fair market value of canned pineapple in the United States? Why or why not? **(See page 175.)**

8–3. Sovereign Immunity. Taconic Plastics, Ltd., is a manufacturer incorporated in Ireland with its principal place of business in New York. Taconic enters into a contract with a German firm, Werner Voss Architects and Engineers, acting as an agent for the government of Saudi Arabia. The contract calls for Taconic to supply special material for tents designed to shelter religious pilgrims visiting holy sites in Saudi Arabia. Most of the material is made in, and shipped from, New York. The German company does not pay Taconic and files for bankruptcy. Taconic files a suit in a U.S. court against the government of Saudi Arabia, seeking to collect $3 million. The defendant files a motion to dismiss the suit based on the doctrine of sovereign immunity. Under what circumstances does this doctrine apply? What are its exceptions? Should this suit be dismissed? Explain. **(See page 171.)**

Business Case Problems

8–4. Dumping. Nuclear power plants use low-enriched uranium (LEU) as a fuel. LEU consists of feed uranium enriched by energy to a certain assay—the percentage of the isotope necessary for a nuclear reaction. The amount of energy required is described by an industry standard as a "separative work unit" (SWU). A nuclear utility may buy LEU from an enricher, or the utility may provide an enricher with feed uranium and pay for the SWUs necessary to produce LEU. Under an SWU contract, the LEU returned to the utility may not be exactly the uranium the utility provided. This is because feed uranium is fungible and trades like a commodity (such as wheat or corn), and profitable enrichment requires the constant processing of undifferentiated stock. Foreign enrichers, including Eurodif, S.A., allegedly exported LEU to the United States and sold it for "less than fair value." Did this constitute dumping? Explain. If so, what could be done to prevent it? [*United States v. Eurodif, S.A.*, 555 U.S. 305, 129 S.Ct. 878, 172 L.Ed.2d 679 (2009)] **(See page 175.)**

8–5. International Agreements and Jurisdiction. U.S. citizens who were descendants of victims of the Holocaust (the mass murder of 6 million Jews by the Nazis during World War II) in Europe filed a claim for breach of contract in the United States against an Italian insurance company, Assicurazioni Generali, S.P.A. (Generali). Before the Holocaust, the plaintiffs' ancestors had purchased insurance policies from Generali, but Generali refused to pay them benefits under the policies. Due to certain agreements among nations after World War II, such lawsuits could not be filed for many years. In 2000, however, the United States agreed that Germany could establish a foundation—the International Commission on Holocaust-Era Insurance Claims, or ICHEIC—that would compensate victims who had suffered losses at the hands of the Germans during the war. Whenever a German company was sued in a U.S. court based on a Holocaust-era claim, the U.S. government would inform the court that the matter should be referred to the ICHEIC as the exclusive forum and remedy for the resolution. There was no such agreement with Italy, however, so the federal district court dismissed the suit. The plaintiffs appealed. Did the plaintiffs have to take their claim to the ICHEIC rather than sue in a U.S. court? Why or why not? [*In re Assicurazioni Generali, S.P.A.*, 592 F.3d 113 (2d Cir. 2010)] **(See page 171.)**

8–6. BUSINESS CASE PROBLEM WITH SAMPLE ANSWER: Sovereign Immunity.

Bell Helicopter Textron, Inc., designs, makes, and sells helicopters with distinctive and famous trade dress that identifies them as Bell aircraft. Bell also owns the helicopters' design patents. Bell's Model 206 Series includes the Jet Ranger. Thirty-six years after Bell developed the Jet Ranger, the Islamic Republic of Iran began to make and sell counterfeit Model 206 Series helicopters and parts. Iran's counterfeit versions—the Shahed 278 and the Shahed 285—used Bell's trade dress *(see Chapter 14). The Shahed aircraft was promoted at an international air show in Iran to aircraft customers. Bell filed a suit in a U.S. district court against Iran, alleging violations of trademark and patent laws. Is Iran—a foreign nation—exempt in these circumstances from the jurisdiction of U.S. courts? Explain. [*Bell Helicopter Textron, Inc. v. Islamic Republic of Iran, *764 F.Supp.2d 122 (D.D.C. 2011)]* **(See page 171.)**

- **For a sample answer to Problem 8–6, go to Appendix F at the end of this text.**

8–7. Commercial Activity Exception. Technology Incubation and Entrepreneurship Training Society (TIETS) entered into a joint-venture agreement with Mandana Farhang and M.A. Mobile to develop and market certain technology for commercial purposes. Farhang and M.A. Mobile filed a suit in a federal district court in California, where they both were based, alleging claims under the joint-venture agreement and a related nondisclosure agreement. The parties agreed that TIETS was a "foreign state" covered by the Foreign Sovereign Immunities Act (FSIA) because it was a part of the Indian government. Nevertheless, Farhang and M.A. Mobile argued that TIETS did not enjoy sovereign immunity because it had engaged in a commercial activity that has a direct effect in the United States. Could TIETS still be subject to the jurisdiction of U.S. courts under the commercial activities exception even though the joint venture was to take place outside the United States? If so, how? [*Farhang v. Indian Institute of Technology*, 2012 WL113739 (N.D.Cal. 2012)] **(See page 171.)**

8–8. Sovereign Immunity. In 1954, the government of Bolivia began expropriating land from Francisco Loza for public projects, including an international airport. The government directed the payment of compensation in exchange for at least some of his land. But the government never paid the full amount. Decades later, his heirs, Genoveva and Marcel Loza, who were both U.S. citizens, filed a suit in a federal district court in the United States against the government of Bolivia, seeking damages for the taking. Can the court exercise jurisdiction? Explain. [*Santivanez v. Estado Plurinacional de Bolivia*, 2013 WL 879983 (11th Cir. 2013)] **(See page 171.)**

8–9. A QUESTION OF ETHICS: Terrorism.

On December 21, 1988, Pan Am Flight 103 exploded 31,000 feet in the air over Lockerbie, Scotland, killing all 259 passengers and crew on board and 11 people on the ground. Among those killed was Roger Hurst, a U.S. citizen. An investigation determined that a portable radio-cassette player packed in a brown Samsonite suitcase smuggled onto the plane was the source of the explosion. The explosive device was constructed with a digital timer specially made for, and bought by, Libya.

*Abdel Basset Ali Al-Megrahi, a Libyan government official and an employee of the Libyan Arab Airline (LAA), was convicted by the Scottish High Court of Justiciary on criminal charges that he planned and executed the bombing in association with members of the Jamahiriya Security Organization (JSO) (an agency of the Libyan government that performed security and intelligence functions) or the Libyan military. Members of the victims' families filed a suit in a U.S. district court against the JSO, the LAA, Al-Megrahi, and others. The plaintiffs claimed violations of U.S. federal law, including the Anti-Terrorism Act, and state law, including the intentional infliction of emotional distress. [*Hurst v. Socialist People's Libyan Arab Jamahiriya, *474 F.Supp.2d 19 (D.D.C. 2007)]* **(See page 171.)**

(a) Under what doctrine, codified in which federal statute, might the defendants claim to be immune from the jurisdiction of a U.S. court? Should this law include an exception for "state-sponsored terrorism"? Why or why not?

(b) The defendants agreed to pay $2.7 billion, or $10 million per victim, to settle all claims for "compensatory death damages." The families of eleven victims, including Hurst, were excluded from the settlement because they were "not wrongful death beneficiaries under applicable state law." These plaintiffs continued the suit. The defendants filed a motion to dismiss. Should the motion be granted on the ground that the settlement bars the plaintiffs' claims? Explain.

Legal Reasoning Group Activity

8–10. Globalization. Assume that you are manufacturing iPad accessories and that your business is becoming more successful. You are now considering expanding operations into another country. **(See page 172.)**

(a) One group will explore the costs and benefits of advertising on the Internet.

(b) Another group will consider whether to take in a partner from a foreign nation and will explain the benefits and risks of having a foreign partner.

(c) A third group will discuss what problems may arise if you want to manufacture in a foreign location.

UNIT TWO Focus on Ethics

Ethics and the Public and International Environment

No other areas of law are as dynamic and engender as much controversy as those relating to the public and international environment. All areas of law touch on ethical considerations. But many laws have as their basis practical necessity or commercial need. The law of the public environment, however, concerns issues such as the protection of freedom of speech, privacy, the promotion of equality, and government regulation of behavior for the public welfare versus individual rights.

The law in the international environment involves such questions as the influence of foreign and international laws, the impact of divergent cultures, and the effect of different legal, political, and economic systems. These issues are in large measure purely ethical in nature. In resolving them, one must rely on basic notions of fairness and justice. Yet conceptions of fairness, justice, and equality differ among individuals and change over time.

Ethical and legal concepts are often closely intertwined. This is because the common law, as it evolved in England and then in America, reflects society's values and customs. This connection between law and ethics is clearly evident in the area of criminal law, which is founded on concepts of right and wrong behavior—although common law concepts governing criminal acts are now expressed in, or replaced by, federal, state, and local criminal statutes. The number of crimes has continued to expand as new ways to commit wrongs have been discovered. In this *Focus on Ethics* feature, we look at the ethical dimensions of selected topics discussed in the preceding chapters, including some issues that are unique to the cyber age.

Free Speech and the Corporation

Free speech is regarded as one of the basic rights of a democratic society. Yet it has never been considered an absolute right. The right of free speech must be balanced against other important rights and the advancement of other important social goals. In that sense, the proper extent of freedom of speech, in its many forms, involves ethical considerations.

Because freedom of speech is not absolute, not all forms of expression are protected. Pornography, for example, is not protected by the First Amendment. Nor are utterances protected that would induce an immediate threat of violence or injury. Even within the context of protected speech, the United States Supreme Court has historically looked to the nature of the speech involved in determining the extent of the protection afforded.

As mentioned in Chapter 5, for example, commercial speech is afforded less protection from government restriction than is noncommercial speech. The lesser degree of protection means in practical terms that it is easier for government to show that the interest it seeks to promote by regulating the speech is more important than protecting the right of speech. But in balancing such conflicting rights and goals, value judgments must be made. For instance, should it make a difference that the speaker is a corporation? Or should the only issue be whether the speech is of a political nature? Is it fair to allow corporations to use their superior economic resources and marketing skills to influence politics? Although it is legal, some argue that it is unethical, particularly when a corporation's decision to allocate funds and influence legislation is motivated by self-interest (profit maximization) rather than by a concern for public welfare.

Privacy Rights in an Online World

Privacy rights are protected under constitutional law, tort law, and various federal and state statutes. How to protect privacy rights in the online world, though, has been a recurring problem over the past decade. One difficulty is that individuals today often are not even aware that information about their personal lives and preferences is being collected by Internet companies and other online users. Nor do they know how that information will be used. Today, "cookies" installed in computers may allow users' Web movements to be tracked. Many e-mail services, such as Google's Gmail, automatically scan and save information about users. Persons who purchase goods from online merchants or auctions inevitably must reveal some personal information, often including their credit-card numbers.

In addition, many goods purchased today use radio-frequency identification (RFID) tags to transmit information. Such tags are frequently included in automobiles, clothing, and cell phones. For instance, clothing manufacturers may use RFID tags to track merchandise and see which products are being sold through which retailers. Health-care facilities, hospitals, libraries, museums, and schools may also use RFID tags. The possibility that these tags may be used to read information linked to a person without her or his consent raises privacy concerns.

The Increased Value of Personal Information

One of the major concerns of consumers in recent years has been the collection and sale of their personal information—sometimes even by third parties with whom the consumers have never had dealings. This information has become increasingly valuable to online marketers, who are willing to pay a high price to those who collect and sell it.

Because of consumers' concerns—and the possibility of lawsuits based on privacy laws—businesses marketing goods online need to exercise care. Today, many online businesses create and post on their Web sites a privacy policy disclosing how any information obtained from their customers will be used.

Privacy Rights in the Workplace

Another area of concern is the extent to which employees' privacy rights should be protected in the workplace. Traditionally, employees have been afforded a certain "zone of privacy" in the workplace. For example, the courts have concluded that

employees have a reasonable expectation of privacy with respect to personal items contained in their desks or in their lockers. Should this zone of privacy extend to personal e-mail sent via the employer's server or social media posts made via a smartphone that the employer provided? This question and others relating to employee privacy rights should be considered by employers today given the increased use of the Internet and social media by employees.

LEGAL REASONING

1. *Some observers maintain that privacy rights are quickly becoming a thing of the past. In your opinion, is it possible to protect privacy rights in today's online world? Why or why not?*

Should Civil Liberties Be Sacrificed to Control Crime and Terrorist Activities in the Cyber Age?

The very real and substantial threat posed by criminal conspirators and terrorists today has raised some important questions about what methods should be used to combat them. In 2012, for instance, the movie *Zero Dark Thirty* raised the question of whether it is ever acceptable for the United States to use torture to obtain information about terrorists.

Similarly, as criminals and terrorists use the Internet to communicate and even to recruit new members, the question arises as to whether it is possible to control many types of crime and terrorist activities without sacrificing some civil liberties. Should the U.S. government actively monitor e-mail, social media, and other electronic communications of particular users or groups?

Traditionally, Americans rejected any attempt by the government to monitor Internet use to detect criminal conspiracies or terrorist activities. Immediately after the terrorist attacks of 2001, however, Americans seemed more willing to trade off some of their civil liberties for greater national security. The USA Patriot Act (see Chapter 5) gave law enforcement personnel more authority to conduct electronic surveillance, such as monitoring Web sites and e-mail exchanges. Today, though, many complain that this legislation has gone too far in curbing traditional civil liberties guaranteed by the U.S. Constitution.

LEGAL REASONING

2. *Many believe that the federal government should not be allowed to monitor the Internet activities and e-mail exchanges of its citizens without obtaining a warrant. Yet others maintain that in some situations, when time is of the essence, such monitoring may be necessary to keep Americans safe from terrorists. Where should the line be drawn between justifiable and unjustifiable governmental interference with American citizens' civil liberties? Discuss fully.*

Global Companies and Censorship Issues—Google China

Doing business on a global level can sometimes involve serious ethical challenges. Consider the ethical firestorm that erupted when Google, Inc., decided to market "Google China" (Google.cn) in 2006. This version of Google's widely used search engine was tailored to the Chinese government's censorship requirements.

In China, Web sites that offer pornography, criticism of the government, or information on sensitive topics, such as the Tiananmen Square massacre in 1989, are censored—that is, they cannot be accessed by Web users. Government agencies enforce the censorship and encourage citizens to inform on one another. Thousands of Web sites are shut down each year, and the sites' operators are subject to potential imprisonment.

The Chinese government insists that in restricting access to certain Web sites, it is merely following the lead of other national governments, which also impose controls on information access. As an example, it cites France, which bans access to any Web sites selling or displaying Nazi paraphernalia. The United States itself prohibits the dissemination of certain types of materials, such as child pornography, over the Internet. Furthermore, the U.S. government monitors Web sites and e-mail communications to protect against terrorist threats. How, ask Chinese officials, can other nations point their fingers at China for engaging in a common international practice?

Censorship—The Lesser of Two Evils?

Human rights groups came out strongly against Google's decision, maintaining that the company was seeking profits in a lucrative marketplace at the expense of assisting the Chinese Communist Party in suppressing free speech. Google defended its actions by pointing out that its Chinese search engine at least lets users know which sites are being censored. Google China includes the links to censored sites, but when a user tries to access a link, the program states that it is not accessible.

Google claimed that its approach was essentially the "lesser of two evils": if U.S. companies did not cooperate with the Chinese government, Chinese residents would have less user-friendly Internet access. Moreover, Google asserted that providing Internet access, even if censored, is a step toward more open access in the future because technology is, in itself, a revolutionary force.

China's Cyberattack and Google's Response

Google's attitude changed when it discovered that its software had been the target of a cyberattack that apparently originated in China. David Drummond, senior vice president of corporate development and Google's chief legal officer, informed the public about the attack in an article on the official Google blog on January 12, 2010. Drummond described the attack

FOCUS ON ETHICS CONTINUES ➧

UNIT TWO Focus on Ethics

Ethics and the Public and International Environment, *Continued*

as "highly sophisticated" and said that it was not limited to Google—some twenty other large companies were similarly targeted. Drummond believed the goal of the attackers was to access the Gmail accounts of Chinese human rights activists. Google also discovered that the accounts of dozens of human rights advocates in the United States, China, and Europe had routinely been accessed by third parties.

Drummond said that the attacks and the surveillance that the investigation uncovered led Google to announce a change in its China policy: "We have decided we are no longer willing to continue censoring our results on **Google.cn** . . . . We recognize that this may well mean having to shut down **Google.cn**."[1] In 2010, Google stopped operating **Google.cn** and automatically redirected users to its Hong Kong servers at **Google.com.hk** for search services in Chinese.

Although the Chinese government censors results on Google's Hong Kong servers, it nonetheless found Google's auto-redirect policy unacceptable and threatened to revoke Google's license. Then Google again revised its policy so that it no longer auto-redirects Chinese users to the Hong Kong servers. Instead, Google directs Chinese users to a Web page at which they must elect to use the Hong Kong servers. In addition, Google reopened Google China to host minimal searches for content that does not require censorship, such as for maps, music, and translation services.

Proponents of human rights applauded Google's efforts to avoid censorship of its search content, but others are not so sure. If Google and similar companies refuse to cooperate with governments that engage in censorship, will this transform the World Wide Web? Will the information highway of the future be forced to stop at national borders?

LEGAL REASONING

3. *Do companies that do business on a global level, such as Google, have an ethical duty to foreign citizens not to suppress free speech? Is it ever acceptable for these companies to censor the information that they provide in other nations at the request of a foreign government? Explain your answer.*

1. David Drummond, "A New Approach to China," *The Official Google Blog,* January 12, 2010.

International Transactions

Conducting business internationally presents unique challenges including, at times, ethical challenges. This is understandable, given that laws and cultures vary from one country to another. Consider the role of women.

In the United States, equal employment opportunity is a fundamental public policy. This policy is clearly expressed in Title VII of the Civil Rights Act, which prohibits discrimination against women in the employment context. Some other countries, however, largely reject any professional role for women. Consequently, U.S. women conducting business transactions in those countries may encounter difficulties. For example, when the World Bank sent a delegation that included women to negotiate with the Central Bank of Korea, the Koreans were surprised and offended. They thought that the presence of women meant that the negotiations were not being taken seriously.

There are also some important ethical differences among nations. In Islamic countries, for example, the consumption of alcohol and certain foods is forbidden by the Islamic religion. Thus, it would be thoughtless and imprudent to invite a Saudi Arabian business contact out for a drink.

Additionally, in many foreign nations, gift giving is a common practice between contracting companies or between companies and government officials. To Americans, such gift giving may look suspiciously like an unethical (and possibly illegal) bribe. This cultural difference has been an important source of friction in international business, particularly since the U.S. Congress passed the Foreign Corrupt Practices Act in 1977 (discussed in Chapters 4 and 7). This act prohibits U.S. business firms from offering certain side payments to foreign officials to secure favorable contracts.

LEGAL REASONING

4. *Should U.S. firms doing business internationally send female employees to foreign nations that reject any role for women in business? Why or why not? How can a U.S. company accommodate the culture of foreign nations and still treat its own employees equally?*

UNIT THREE

THE COMMERCIAL ENVIRONMENT

CONTENTS

CHAPTER 9

FORMATION OF TRADITIONAL AND E-CONTRACTS

No aspect of modern life is entirely free of contractual relationships. You acquire rights and obligations, for example, when you borrow funds, buy or lease a house, obtain insurance, and purchase goods or services. Contract law is designed to provide stability and predictability.

Contract law deals with, among other things, the formation and keeping of promises. A **promise** is a declaration by a person (the *promisor*) to do or not to do a certain act. As a result, the person to whom the promise is made (the *promisee*) has a right to expect or demand that something either will or will not happen in the future.

Like other types of law, contract law reflects our social values, interests, and expectations at a given point in time. It shows, for instance, to what extent our society allows people to make promises or commitments that are legally binding. It distinguishes between promises that create only *moral* obligations (such as a promise to take a friend to lunch) and promises that are legally binding (such as a promise to pay for merchandise purchased).

Contract law also demonstrates which excuses our society accepts for breaking certain types of promises. In addition, it indicates which promises are considered to be contrary to public policy—against the interests of society as a whole—and therefore legally invalid. When the person making a promise is a child or is mentally incompetent, for example, a question will arise as to whether the promise should be enforced. Resolving such questions is the essence of contract law.

SECTION 1 AN OVERVIEW OF CONTRACT LAW

Before we look at the numerous rules that courts use to determine whether a particular promise will be enforced, it is necessary to understand some fundamental concepts of contract law. In this section, we describe the sources and general function of contract law and introduce the objective theory of contracts.

Sources of Contract Law

The common law governs all contracts except when it has been modified or replaced by statutory law, such as the Uniform Commercial Code (UCC),[1] or by administrative agency regulations. Contracts relating to services, real estate, employment, and insurance, for instance, generally are governed by the common law of contracts. (For a sample contract with an explanation of its terms, see the *Appendix to Chapter 10: Reading and Analyzing Contracts.*)

Contracts for the sale and lease of goods, however, are governed by the UCC—to the extent that the UCC has modified general contract law. The relationship between general contract law and the law governing sales and leases of goods will be explored in detail in Chapter 11. In the discussion of general contract law that follows, we indicate in footnotes the areas in which the UCC has significantly altered common law contract principles.

The Definition of a Contract

A **contract** is "a promise or a set of promises for the breach of which the law gives a remedy, or the performance of which the law in some way recognizes as a duty."[2] Put simply, a contract is an agreement that can be enforced in court. It is formed by two or more par-

1. See Chapters 1 and 11 for further discussions of the significance and coverage of the UCC. The UCC is presented in Appendix C at the end of this book.

2. *Restatement (Second) of Contracts,* Section 1. As mentioned in Chapter 1, *Restatements of the Law* are scholarly books that restate the existing common law principles distilled from court opinions as a set of rules on a particular topic. Courts often refer to the *Restatements* for guidance.

ties who agree to perform or to refrain from performing some act now or in the future.

Generally, contract disputes arise when there is a promise of future performance. If the contractual promise is not fulfilled, the party who made it is subject to the sanctions of a court (see Chapter 10). That party may be required to pay damages for failing to perform the contractual promise. In a few instances, the party may be required to perform the promised act.

The Objective Theory of Contracts

In determining whether a contract has been formed, the element of intent is of prime importance. In contract law, intent is determined by what is called the **objective theory of contracts,** not by the personal or subjective intent, or belief, of a party. The theory is that a party's intention to enter into a legally binding agreement, or contract, is judged by outward, objective facts. The facts are as interpreted by a *reasonable* person, rather than by the party's own secret, subjective intentions. Objective facts may include:

1. What the party said when entering into the contract.
2. How the party acted or appeared (intent may be manifested by conduct as well as by oral or written words).
3. The circumstances surrounding the transaction.

A party may have many reasons for entering into an agreement—obtaining real property, goods, or services, for example, and profiting from the deal. Any of these purposes may provide a motivation for performing the contract. In the following case, however, one party failed to perform and claimed that he had not intended to enter into the contract when he signed it.

CASE ANALYSIS

Case 9.1 Pan Handle Realty, LLC v. Olins

Appellate Court of Connecticut, 140 Conn.App. 556, 59 A.3d 842 (2013).

IN THE LANGUAGE OF THE COURT
SHELDON, J. [Judge]

* * * *

* * * The plaintiff is a Connecticut limited liability company [a form of business organization—see Chapter 17] * * *, which constructed a luxury home at 4 Pan Handle Lane in Westport [Connecticut] (the property). * * * The defendant [Robert Olins] expressed an interest in leasing the property from the plaintiff for a period of one year. In pursuit of that interest, he submitted an application proposing to rent the property from the plaintiff at the rate of $12,000 per month, together with an accompanying financial statement. The plaintiff responded to the defendant's proposal by preparing a draft lease for his review, which the defendant promptly forwarded to his attorney.

On January 17, 2009, the defendant and his real estate agent, Laura Sydney, met with Irwin Stillman, then acting as the plaintiff's representative, to discuss the draft lease (January 17 meeting). At that meeting, the defendant and Irwin Stillman agreed to several revisions to the draft lease that had been proposed by the defendant's attorney, then incorporated the revisions into the lease and signed it. The resulting lease, which was dated January 19, 2009, specified a lump sum annual rent of $138,000. At the time of the signing, the defendant gave the plaintiff a postdated check for $138,000 * * *. The lease agreement required the plaintiff to make certain modifications to the property prior to the occupancy date, including the removal of all of the furnishings from the leased premises.

On January 21, 2009, the plaintiff's real estate broker informed it that, according to Sydney, the defendant planned to move into the property on January 28, 2009. The next day, the defendant requested information from the plaintiff for his renter's insurance policy, which the plaintiff duly provided. By that time, the plaintiff had also completed the modifications requested by the defendant at the January 17 meeting and agreed to in the lease agreement, including the removal of the furniture. The defendant's check, which was postdated January 26, 2009, was deposited by the plaintiff on that date.

The following day, however, Citibank advised the plaintiff that the defendant had issued a stop payment order on his postdated rental check and explained that the check would not be honored. The plaintiff subsequently received a letter from the defendant's attorney stating that "[the defendant] is unable to pursue any further interest in the property."

CASE 9.1 CONTINUES ➧

CASE 9.1 CONTINUED

Thereafter, the plaintiff made substantial efforts to secure a new tenant for the property, listing the property with a real estate broker, advertising its availability and expending $80,000 to restage it. Although, by these efforts, the plaintiff generated several offers to lease the property, it was never able to find a qualified tenant, or, for that reason, to enter into an acceptable lease agreement with anyone for all or any part of the one year period of the defendant's January 19, 2009 lease.

Thereafter, on March 6, 2009, the plaintiff filed this action [in a Connecticut state court], alleging that the defendant had breached an enforceable lease agreement. The plaintiff further alleged that, despite its efforts to mitigate [lessen] its damages, it had sustained damages as a result of the defendant's breach, including unpaid rental payments it was to have received under the lease, brokerage commissions it incurred to rent the property again and the cost of modifications to the property that were completed at the defendant's request.

* * * The court issued a memorandum of decision resolving the merits of the case in favor of the plaintiff (May 11 decision). In that decision, the court found, more particularly, that the plaintiff had met its burden of proving that the parties had entered into an enforceable lease agreement, that the defendant had breached that agreement, and that the breach had caused the plaintiff damages in lost rent and utility bills incurred during the lease period * * * . On the basis of these findings, the court awarded the plaintiff compensatory damages in the amount of $146,000—$138,000 in unpaid rent for the term of the lease and $8,000 in utility fees incurred by the plaintiff during the lease period—plus interest, and attorney's fees.

* * * This appeal followed.

* * * *

The defendant's * * * claim on appeal is that the court improperly determined that the parties entered into a valid lease agreement. The defendant contends that because "material terms were still being negotiated and various issues were unresolved," there was no meeting of the minds, which is required to form a contract.

* * * *

In order for an enforceable contract to exist, the court must find that the parties' minds had truly met. * * * *If there has been a misunderstanding between the parties, or a misapprehension by one or both so that their minds have never met, no contract has been entered into by them and the court will not make for them a contract which they themselves did not make.* [Emphasis added.]

There was evidence in the record to support the court's finding that the parties entered into a valid lease agreement because there was a true meeting of the parties' minds as to the essential terms of the agreement. Prior to the January 17 meeting, the plaintiff had provided the defendant with a draft lease agreement, which the defendant had forwarded to his attorney for review. The defendant testified that at the January 17 meeting, he and the plaintiff's representative discussed the revisions proposed by the defendant's attorney, made the revisions and signed the lease. It was then that the defendant tendered a check, postdated to the start of the lease period, on which he noted payment for a one-year lease of the premises.

There is no evidence in the record to support the defendant's contention that he did not intend to be bound by the lease when he signed it or that terms of the lease were still being negotiated at that time. Pursuant to the lease, the plaintiff was obligated to make modifications to the premises and the defendant was required to tender a security deposit [and] procure renter's insurance * * * . The defendant's apparent unilateral change of heart regarding the lease agreement does not negate the parties' prior meeting of the minds that occurred at the time the lease was executed. There is ample evidence in the record evincing [showing] the intent of the parties to be bound by the lease when they signed it and, thus, to support the court's finding that "the lease agreement was a valid and binding contract which the defendant * * * has breached."

* * * *

* * * As in any other contract action the measure of damages is that the award should place the injured party in the same position as he would have been in had the contract been fully performed. * * * As a consequence, the unpaid rent * * * may be used by the court in computing the losses suffered by the plaintiff by reason of the defendant's breach of contract of lease.

* * * *

The judgment is affirmed.

LEGAL REASONING QUESTIONS

1. What is the objective theory of contracts?
2. How did the objective theory of contracts affect the result in this case? Explain.
3. The defendant never moved into the house. Why then did the court find that he breached the lease?
4. On finding that the defendant breached the lease, what did the court impose as a sanction? How was this determined?

Requirements of a Valid Contract

The following list briefly describes the four requirements that must be met before a valid contract exists. If any of these elements is lacking, no contract will have been formed. (Each requirement will be explained more fully later in this chapter.)

1. *Agreement.* An agreement to form a contract includes an *offer* and an *acceptance.* One party must offer to enter into a legal agreement, and another party must accept the terms of the offer.
2. *Consideration.* Any promises made by the parties to the contract must be supported by legally sufficient and bargained-for *consideration* (something of value received or promised, such as money, to convince a person to make a deal).
3. *Contractual capacity.* Both parties entering into the contract must have the contractual *capacity* to do so. The law must recognize them as possessing characteristics that qualify them as competent parties.
4. *Legality.* The contract's purpose must be to accomplish some goal that is legal and not against public policy.

Defenses to the Enforceability of a Contract

Even if all of the requirements listed above are satisfied, a contract may be unenforceable if the following requirements are not met. These requirements typically are raised as *defenses* to the enforceability of an otherwise valid contract.

1. *Voluntary consent.* The consent of both parties must be voluntary. For instance, if a contract was formed as a result of fraud, undue influence, mistake, or duress, the contract may not be enforceable (see Chapter 10).
2. *Form.* The contract must be in whatever form the law requires. Some contracts must be in writing to be enforceable, as discussed later in this chapter.

SECTION 2 TYPES OF CONTRACTS

There are many types of contracts. They are categorized based on legal distinctions as to their formation, performance, and enforceability.

Contract Formation

Contracts can be classified according to how and when they are formed. Exhibit 9–1 below shows three such classifications, and the following subsections explain them in greater detail.

BILATERAL VERSUS UNILATERAL CONTRACTS Every contract involves at least two parties. The *offeror* is the party making the offer. The *offeree* is the party to whom the offer is made. Whether the contract is classified as *bilateral* or *unilateral* depends on what the offeree must do to accept the offer and bind the offeror to a contract.

Bilateral Contracts. If the offeree can accept simply by promising to perform, the contract is a **bilateral contract.** Hence, a bilateral contract is a "promise for a promise." No performance, such as payment of

EXHIBIT 9–1 Classifications Based on Contract Formation

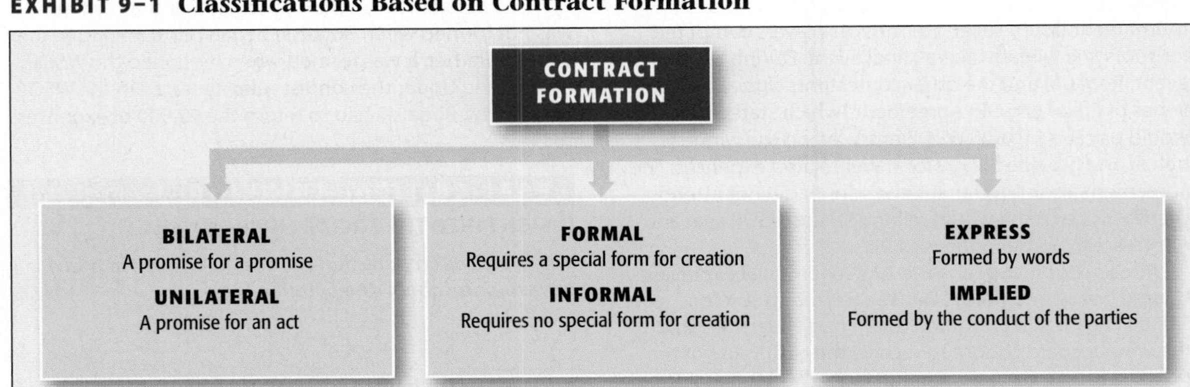

funds or delivery of goods, need take place for a bilateral contract to be formed. The contract comes into existence at the moment the promises are exchanged. (An example of a bilateral contract appears in the *Appendix to Chapter 10.*)

▶ **Example 9.1** Javier offers to buy Ann's smartphone for $200. Javier tells Ann that he will give her the $200 for the smartphone next Friday, when he gets paid. Ann accepts Javier's offer and promises to give him the smartphone when he pays her on Friday. Javier and Ann have formed a bilateral contract. ◀

Unilateral Contracts. If the offer is phrased so that the offeree can accept the offer only by completing the contract performance, the contract is a **unilateral contract.** Hence, a unilateral contract is a "promise for an act."[3] In other words, a unilateral contract is formed not at the moment when promises are exchanged but at the moment when the contract is *performed.* ▶ **Example 9.2** Reese says to Celia, "If you drive my car from New York to Los Angeles, I'll give you $1,000." Only on Celia's completion of the act—bringing the car to Los Angeles—does she fully accept Reese's offer to pay $1,000. If she chooses not to accept the offer to drive the car to Los Angeles, there are no legal consequences. ◀

Contests, lotteries, and other competitions involving prizes are examples of offers to form unilateral contracts. If a person complies with the rules of the contest—such as by submitting the right lottery number at the right place and time—a unilateral contract is formed. The organization offering the prize is then bound to a contract to perform as promised in the offer. If the person fails to comply with the contest rules, however, no binding contract is formed. (See this chapter's *Insight into Ethics* feature below for a discussion of whether a company can change a contest prize from what it originally advertised.)

Revocation of Offers for Unilateral Contracts. A problem arises in unilateral contracts when the promisor

3. The phrase *unilateral contract,* if read literally, is a contradiction in terms. A contract cannot be one sided because, by definition, an agreement implies the existence of two or more parties.

INSIGHT INTO ETHICS

Can a Company That Sponsors a Contest Change the Prize from What It Originally Offered?

Courts have historically treated contests as unilateral contracts, which typically cannot be modified by the offeror after the offeree has begun to perform. But this principle may not always apply to contest terms or advertisements.

John Rogalski entered a poker tournament conducted by Little Poker League, LLC (LPL).The tournament lasted several months as players competed for spots in a winner-take-all final event. During the final event, Rogalski and the other contestants signed a "World Series of Poker (WSOP) Agreement," which stated that LPL would pay the $10,000 WSOP entry fee on the winner's behalf and provide $2,500 for travel-related expenses. The agreement also stated that if the winner did not attend the WSOP, he or she would relinquish the WSOP seat and return the expense money to LPL.

Rogalski won and took the $2,500 for travel expenses, but did not attend the WSOP. He then filed a suit for $10,000 against LPL, arguing that it had advertised that the winner could choose to receive the cash value of the prizes ($12,500) instead of going to the WSOP. Rogalski claimed that, by participating in the tournament, he had accepted the advertised offer to take the cash in lieu of entering the WSOP. He further claimed that the later agreement was an invalid contract modification. LPL filed a counterclaim to recover the $2,500 in expenses. The court ruled in favor of LPL, finding that the contract was not formed when Rogalski began participating in the contest. Rather, it was formed when he signed the WSOP agreement. Under the contest rules as stated in the WSOP agreement, Rogalski had to return the $2,500 of expenses to LPL.[a]

LEGAL CRITICAL THINKING

INSIGHT INTO THE SOCIAL ENVIRONMENT

Why would a company that changes its advertised prizes have to worry about its reputation?

a. *Rogalski v. Little Poker League, LLC,* 2011 WL 589636 (Minn.App. 2011).

attempts to *revoke* (cancel) the offer after the promisee has begun performance but before the act has been completed. ▶ **Example 9.3** Seiko offers to buy Jin's sailboat, moored in San Francisco, on delivery of the boat to Seiko's dock in Newport Beach, three hundred miles south of San Francisco. Jin rigs the boat and sets sail. Shortly before his arrival at Newport Beach, Jin receives a message from Seiko withdrawing her offer. Seiko's offer was for a unilateral contract, which could be accepted only by Jin's delivery of the sailboat at her dock. ◀

In contract law, offers are normally *revocable* (capable of being taken back, or canceled) until accepted. Under the traditional view of unilateral contracts, Seiko's revocation would terminate the offer. Because of the harsh effect on the offeree of the revocation of an offer to form a unilateral contract, the modern-day view is different.

Today, once performance has been *substantially* undertaken, the offeror cannot revoke the offer. Thus, in *Example 9.3*, even though Jin has not yet accepted the offer by complete performance, Seiko is normally prohibited from revoking it. Jin can deliver the boat and bind Seiko to the contract.

FORMAL VERSUS INFORMAL CONTRACTS Another classification system divides contracts into formal contracts and informal contracts. **Formal contracts** are contracts that require a special form or method of creation (formation) to be enforceable.[4] One example is *negotiable instruments,* which include checks, drafts, promissory notes, bills of exchange, and certificates of deposit. Negotiable instruments are formal contracts because, under the Uniform Commercial Code (UCC), a special form and language are required to create them.

Letters of credit, which are frequently used in international sales contracts (see Chapter 8), are another type of formal contract. Letters of credit are agreements to pay contingent on the purchaser's receipt of invoices and *bills of lading* (documents evidencing receipt of, and title to, goods shipped).

Informal contracts (also called *simple contracts*) include all other contracts. No special form is required (except for certain types of contracts that must be in writing), as the contracts are usually based on their substance rather than their form. Typically, businesspersons put their contracts in writing to ensure that there is some proof of a contract's existence should disputes arise.

EXPRESS VERSUS IMPLIED CONTRACTS Contracts may also be categorized as *express* or *implied.* In an **express contract,** the terms of the agreement are fully and explicitly stated in words, oral or written. A signed lease for an apartment or a house is an express written contract. If one classmate calls another on the phone and agrees to buy her textbooks from last semester for $300, an express oral contract has been made.

A contract that is implied from the conduct of the parties is called an **implied contract** (or sometimes an *implied-in-fact contract*). This type of contract differs from an express contract in that the conduct of the parties, rather than their words, creates and defines the terms of the contract.

Requirements for Implied Contracts. For an implied contract to arise, certain requirements must be met. Normally, if the following conditions exist, a court will hold that an implied contract was formed:

1. The plaintiff furnished some service or property.
2. The plaintiff expected to be paid for that service or property, and the defendant knew or should have known that payment was expected.
3. The defendant had a chance to reject the services or property and did not.

▶ **Example 9.4** Oleg, a small-business owner, needs an accountant to complete his tax return. He drops by a local accountant's office, explains his situation to the accountant, and learns what fees she charges. The next day, he returns and gives the receptionist all of the necessary documents to complete his return. Then he walks out without saying anything further to the accountant. In this situation, Oleg has entered into an implied contract to pay the accountant the usual fees for her services. The contract is implied because of Oleg's conduct and hers. She expects to be paid for completing the tax return, and by bringing in the records she will need to do the job, Oleg has implied an intent to pay her. ◀

Contracts with Express and Implied Terms. Note that a contract may be a mixture of an express contract and an implied contract. In other words, a contract may contain some express terms, while others are implied. During the constructions of a home, for instance, the homeowner often asks the builder to make changes in the original specifications.

4. See *Restatement (Second) of Contracts,* Section 6, which explains that formal contracts include (1) contracts under seal, (2) recognizances, (3) negotiable instruments, and (4) letters of credit.

Case in Point 9.5 Lamar Hopkins hired Uhrhahn Construction & Design, Inc., for several projects in building his home. For each project, the parties signed a written contract that was based on a cost estimate and specifications and that required changes to the agreement to be in writing. While the work was in progress, however, Hopkins repeatedly asked Uhrhahn to deviate from the contract specifications, which Uhrhahn did. None of these requests was made in writing.

One day, Hopkins asked Uhrhahn to use Durisol blocks instead of the cinder blocks specified in the original contract, indicating that the cost would be the same. Uhrhahn used the Durisol blocks but demanded extra payment when it became clear that the Durisol blocks were more complicated to install. Although Hopkins had paid for the other deviations from the contract that he had orally requested, he refused to pay Uhrhahn for the substitution of the Durisol blocks. Uhrhahn sued for breach of contract. The court found that Hopkins, through his conduct, had waived the provision requiring written contract modification and created an implied contract to pay the extra cost of installing the Durisol blocks.[5] ◀

Contract Performance

Contracts are also classified according to the degree to which they have been performed. A contract that has been fully performed on both sides is called an **executed contract.** A contract that has not been fully performed by the parties is called an **executory contract.** If one party has fully performed but the other has not, the contract is said to be executed on the one side and executory on the other, but the contract is still classified as executory.

Example 9.6 Jackson, Inc., agreed to buy ten tons of coal from the Northern Coal Company. Northern delivered the coal to Jackson's steel mill, where it is being burned. At this point, the contract is executed on the part of Northern and executory on Jackson's part. After Jackson pays Northern, the contract will be executed on both sides. ◀

Contract Enforceability

A **valid contract** has the elements necessary to entitle at least one of the parties to enforce it in court. In other words, it meets the four basic requirements listed on page 000. As you can see in Exhibit 9–2 below, valid contracts may be enforceable, voidable, or unenforceable. Additionally, a contract may be referred to as a *void contract.* We look next at the meaning of the terms *voidable, unenforceable,* and *void* in relation to contract enforceability.

VOIDABLE CONTRACTS A **voidable contract** is a valid contract but one that can be avoided at the

5. *Uhrhahn Construction & Design, Inc. v. Hopkins,* 179 P.3d 808 (Utah App. 2008).

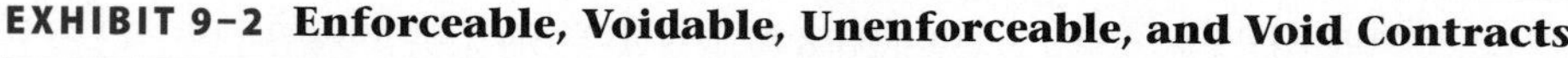

EXHIBIT 9–2 Enforceable, Voidable, Unenforceable, and Void Contracts

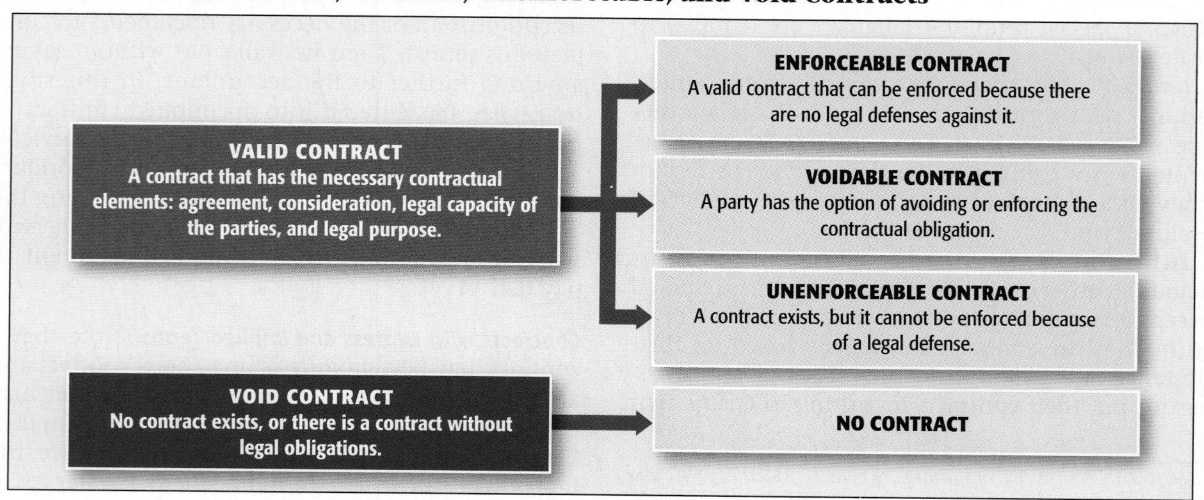

option of one or both of the parties. The party having the option can elect either to avoid any duty to perform or to *ratify* (make valid) the contract. If the contract is avoided, both parties are released from it. If it is ratified, both parties must fully perform their respective legal obligations.

As you will read later in this chapter, contracts made by minors generally are voidable at the option of the minor (with certain exceptions). Contracts made by mentally incompetent persons and intoxicated persons may also be voidable. Additionally, contracts entered into under duress, fraudulent conditions, or undue influence are also voidable.

UNENFORCEABLE CONTRACTS An **unenforceable contract** is one that cannot be enforced because of certain legal defenses against it. It is not unenforceable because a party failed to satisfy a legal requirement of the contract. Rather, it is a valid contract rendered unenforceable by some statute or law. For instance, certain contracts must be in writing, and if they are not, they will not be enforceable except in certain exceptional circumstances.

VOID CONTRACTS A **void contract** is no contract at all. The terms *void* and *contract* are contradictory. None of the parties have any legal obligations if a contract is void. A contract can be void because one of the parties was determined by a court to be mentally incompetent, for instance, or because the purpose of the contract was illegal (as you will read later in this chapter).

To review the various types of contracts, see *Concept Summary 9.1* below.

SECTION 3
AGREEMENT

Whether a contract is formed in the traditional way (on paper) or online, an essential element for contract formation is **agreement**—the parties must agree on the terms of the contract and manifest to each other their *mutual assent* (agreement) to the same bargain. Ordinarily, agreement is evidenced by two events: an *offer* and an *acceptance*. One party offers a certain bargain to another party, who then accepts that bargain.

The agreement does not necessarily have to be in writing. Both parties, however, must manifest their assent, or voluntary consent, to the same bargain. Once an agreement is reached, if the other elements of a contract (consideration, capacity, and legality—discussed later in this chapter) are present, a valid contract is formed. Generally, the contract creates enforceable rights and duties between the parties.

CONCEPT SUMMARY 9.1
Types of Contracts

ASPECT	DEFINITION
Formation	1. *Bilateral*—A promise for a promise. 2. *Unilateral*—A promise for an act (acceptance is the completed performance of the act). 3. *Formal*—Requires a special form for creation. 4. *Informal*—Requires no special form for creation. 5. *Express*—Formed by words (oral, written, or a combination). 6. *Implied*—Formed by the conduct of the parties.
Performance	1. *Executed*—A fully performed contract. 2. *Executory*—A contract not fully performed.
Enforceability	1. *Valid*—The contract has the necessary contractual elements: agreement (offer and acceptance), consideration, legal capacity of the parties, and legal purpose. 2. *Voidable*—One party has the option of avoiding or enforcing the contractual obligation. 3. *Unenforceable*—A contract exists, but it cannot be enforced because of a legal defense. 4. *Void*—No contract exists, or there is a contract without legal obligations.

Requirements of the Offer

An **offer** is a promise or commitment to do or refrain from doing some specified action in the future. As mentioned, the parties to a contract are the *offeror,* the one who makes an offer or proposal to another party, and the *offeree,* the one to whom the offer or proposal is made. Under the common law, three elements are necessary for an offer to be effective:

1. The offeror must have a serious intention to become bound by the offer.
2. The terms of the offer must be reasonably certain, or definite, so that the parties and the court can ascertain the terms of the contract.
3. The offer must be communicated to the offeree.

Once an effective offer has been made, the offeree's acceptance of that offer creates a legally binding contract (providing the other essential elements for a valid and enforceable contract are present).

INTENTION The first requirement for an effective offer is a serious intent on the part of the offeror. Serious intent is not determined by the subjective intentions, beliefs, and assumptions of the offeror. Rather, it is determined by what a reasonable person in the offeree's position would conclude that the offeror's words and actions meant. Offers made in obvious anger, jest, or undue excitement do not meet the serious-and-objective-intent test because a reasonable person would realize that a serious offer was not being made. Because these offers are not effective, an offeree's acceptance does not create an agreement.

A classic contracts case from 1954 illustrates the serious-and-objective-intent requirement in the context of an offer made "after a few drinks." ▶ **Case in Point 9.7** W. O. Lucy had known A. H. Zehmer more than fifteen years and had offered to buy the Ferguson Farm from him many times. One night, Lucy stopped to visit the Zehmers at the restaurant and gas station they operated and tried to buy the Ferguson Farm once again. Lucy said to Zehmer, "I bet you wouldn't take $50,000 for that place." Zehmer replied, "Yes, I would too; you wouldn't give fifty." Throughout the evening, both men continued to drink whiskey while talking, and the conversation returned to the sale of the Ferguson Farm for $50,000.

Eventually, Lucy enticed Zehmer to write up an agreement to the effect that the Zehmers would sell the Ferguson Farm to Lucy for $50,000 complete. Later, Lucy sued Zehmer to compel him to go through with the sale. Zehmer argued that he had been drunk and that the offer had been made in jest and hence was unenforceable. The trial court agreed with Zehmer, and Lucy appealed. The Virginia Supreme Court looked at the parties' outward expressions of intent and held in favor of Lucy. The parties had discussed the terms of the sale for at least forty minutes and had done two drafts of the contract before both men agreed to sign it. Therefore, the serious-intent requirement had been met, and the contract was binding.[6] ◀

SITUATIONS WHEN INTENT MAY BE LACKING The concept of intention can be further clarified through an examination of types of statements that are *not* offers. We look at these expressions and statements in the subsections that follow.

Expressions of Opinion. An expression of opinion is not an offer. It does not indicate an intention to enter into a binding agreement.

▶ **Case in Point 9.8** George Hawkins took his son to McGee, a physician, and asked McGee to operate on the son's hand. McGee said that the boy would be in the hospital three or four days and that the hand would *probably* heal a few days later. The son's hand did not heal for a month, but the father did not win a suit for breach of contract. The court held that McGee had not made an offer to heal the son's hand in a few days. He had merely expressed an opinion as to when the hand would heal.[7] ◀

Statements of Future Intent. A statement of an intention to do something in the future is not an offer. ▶ **Example 9.9** Samir says, "I *plan* to sell my stock in Novation, Inc., for $150 per share." If John "accepts" and tenders the $150 per share for the stock, no contract is created. Samir has merely expressed his intention to enter into a future contract for the sale of the stock. No contract is formed because a reasonable person would conclude that Samir was only *thinking about* selling his stock, not *promising* to sell it. ◀

Preliminary Negotiations. A request or invitation to negotiate is not an offer. It only expresses a willingness to discuss the possibility of entering into a contract. Statements such as "Will you sell Blythe Estate?" or "I wouldn't sell my car for less than $5,000" are examples. A reasonable person in the offeree's position would not conclude that these statements indicated an intention to enter into a binding obligation.

6. *Lucy v. Zehmer,* 196 Va. 493, 84 S.E.2d 516 (1954).
7. *Hawkins v. McGee,* 84 N.H. 114, 146 A. 641 (1929).

Likewise, when the government or private firms require construction work, they invite contractors to submit bids. The *invitation* to submit bids is not an offer, and a contractor does not bind the government or private firm by submitting a bid. (The bids that the contractors submit are offers, however, and the government or private firm can bind the contractor by accepting the bid.)

Advertisements. In general, advertisements (including representations made in catalogues, price lists, circulars, and Web sites) are treated not as offers to contract but as invitations to negotiate.

Price lists are another form of invitation to negotiate or trade. A seller's price list is not an offer to sell at that price. It merely invites the buyer to offer to buy at that price. In fact, the seller usually puts "prices subject to change" on the price list. Only in rare circumstances will a price quotation be construed as an offer.

Although most advertisements and price lists are treated as invitations to negotiate, this does not mean that they can never be an offer. On some occasions, courts have construed advertisements to be offers because the ads contained definite terms that invited acceptance (such as an ad offering a reward for the return of a lost dog).

Preliminary Agreements. Increasingly, the courts are holding that a preliminary agreement constitutes a binding contract if the parties have agreed on all essential terms and no disputed issues remain to be resolved. In contrast, if the parties agree on certain major terms but leave other terms open for further negotiation, a preliminary agreement is not binding. The parties are bound only in the sense that they have committed themselves to negotiate the undecided terms in good faith in an effort to reach a final agreement.

In the following *Spotlight Case,* the dispute was over an agreement to settle a case during the trial. One party claimed that the agreement formed via e-mail was binding. The other party claimed the e-mail exchange was merely an agreement to work out the terms of a settlement in the future. Can an exchange of e-mails create a complete and unambiguous agreement?

Case 9.2 Basis Technology Corp. v. Amazon.com, Inc.

Appeals Court of Massachusetts, 71 Mass.App.Ct. 29, 878 N.E.2d 952 (2008).

BACKGROUND AND FACTS Basis Technology Corporation created software and provided technical services for a Japanese-language Web site belonging to Amazon.com, Inc. The agreement between the two companies allowed for separately negotiated contracts for additional services that Basis might provide to Amazon. At the end of 1999, Basis and Amazon entered into stock-purchase agreements. Later, Amazon objected to certain actions related to the securities that Basis sold. Basis sued Amazon for various claims involving these securities and for failing to pay for services performed by Basis that were not included in the original agreement. During the trial, the two parties appeared to reach an agreement to settle out of court via a series of e-mail exchanges outlining the settlement. When Amazon reneged, Basis served a motion to enforce the proposed settlement. The trial judge entered a judgment against Amazon, which appealed.

IN THE LANGUAGE OF THE COURT

SIKORA, J. [Judge]

* * * *

* * * On the evening of March 23, after the third day of evidence and after settlement discussions, Basis counsel sent an e-mail with the following text to Amazon counsel:

> [Amazon counsel]—This e-mail confirms the essential business terms of the settlement between our respective clients * * *. Basis and Amazon agree that they promptly will take all reasonable steps to memorialize in a written agreement, to be signed by individuals authorized by each party, the terms set forth below, as well as such other terms that are reasonably necessary to make these terms effective.

CASE 9.2 CONTINUES ➧

CASE 9.2 CONTINUED

* * * *

[Amazon counsel], please contact me first thing tomorrow morning if this e-mail does not accurately summarize the settlement terms reached earlier this evening.
See you tomorrow morning when we report this matter settled to the Court.

At 7:26 A.M. on March 24, Amazon counsel sent an e-mail with a one-word reply: "correct." Later in the morning, in open court and on the record, both counsel reported the result of a settlement without specification of the terms.

On March 25, Amazon's counsel sent a facsimile of the first draft of a settlement agreement to Basis's counsel. The draft comported with all the terms of the e-mail exchange, and added some implementing and boilerplate [standard contract provisions] terms.

* * * *

[Within a few days, though,] the parties were deadlocked. On April 21, Basis served its motion to enforce the settlement agreement. Amazon opposed. * * * The motion and opposition presented the issues whether the e-mail terms were sufficiently complete and definite to form an agreement and whether Amazon had intended to be bound by them.

* * * *

We examine the text of the terms for the incompleteness and indefiniteness charged by Amazon. *Provisions are not ambiguous simply because the parties have developed different interpretations of them.* [Emphasis added.]

* * * *

We must interpret the document as a whole. In the preface to the enumerated terms, Basis counsel stated that the "e-mail confirms the essential business terms of the settlement between our respective clients," and that the parties "agree that they promptly will take all reasonable steps to memorialize" those terms. Amazon counsel concisely responded, "correct." Thus the "essential business terms" were resolved. The parties were proceeding to "memorialize" or record the settlement terms, not to create them.

* * * *

To ascertain intent, a court considers the words used by the parties, the agreement taken as a whole, and surrounding facts and circumstances. The essential circumstance of this disputed agreement is that it concluded a trial.

* * * As the trial judge explained in her memorandum of decision, she "terminated" the trial; she did not suspend it for exploratory negotiations. She did so in reliance upon the parties' report of an accomplished agreement for the settlement of their dispute.

* * * *

In sum, the deliberateness and the gravity attributable to a report of a settlement, especially during the progress of a trial, weigh heavily as circumstantial evidence of the intention of a party such as Amazon to be bound by its communication to the opposing party and to the court.

DECISION AND REMEDY *The Appeals Court of Massachusetts affirmed the trial court's finding that Amazon intended to be bound by the terms of the March 23 e-mail. That e-mail constituted a complete and unambiguous statement of the parties' desire to be bound by the settlement terms.*

WHAT IF THE FACTS WERE DIFFERENT? *Suppose that the attorneys for both sides had simply had a phone conversation that included all of the terms to which they actually agreed in their e-mail exchanges. Would the court have ruled differently? Why or why not?*

THE LEGAL ENVIRONMENT DIMENSION *What does the result in this case suggest that a businessperson should do before agreeing to a settlement of a legal dispute?*

DEFINITENESS OF TERMS The second requirement for an effective offer involves the definiteness of its terms. An offer must have reasonably definite terms so that a court can determine if a breach has occurred and give an appropriate remedy.[8] The specific terms required depend, of course, on the type of contract.

8. *Restatement (Second) of Contracts,* Section 33.

Generally, a contract must include the following terms, either expressed in the contract or capable of being reasonably inferred from it:

1. The identification of the parties.
2. The identification of the object or subject matter of the contract (also the quantity, when appropriate), including the work to be performed, with specific identification of such items as goods, services, and land.
3. The consideration to be paid.
4. The time of payment, delivery, or performance.

An offer may invite an acceptance to be worded in such specific terms that the contract is made definite. ▶ **Example 9.10** Nintendo of America, Inc., contacts your Play 2 Win Games store and offers to sell "from one to twenty-five Nintendo 3DS gaming systems for $75 each. State number desired in acceptance." You agree to buy twenty systems. Because the quantity is specified in the acceptance, the terms are definite, and the contract is enforceable. ◀

When the parties have clearly manifested an intent to form a contract, courts sometimes are willing to supply a missing term in a contract, especially a sales contract.[9] But a court will not rewrite a contract if the parties' expression of intent is too vague or uncertain to be given any precise meaning.

COMMUNICATION The third requirement for an effective offer is communication—the offer must be communicated to the offeree. Ordinarily, one cannot agree to a bargain without knowing that it exists. ▶ **Example 9.11** Tolson advertises a reward for the return of her lost cat. Dirk, not knowing of the reward, finds the cat and returns it to Tolson. Usually, Dirk cannot recover the reward because an essential element of a reward contract is that the one who claims the reward must have known it was offered. ◀

Termination of the Offer

The communication of an effective offer to an offeree gives the offeree the power to transform the offer into a binding, legal obligation (a contract) by an acceptance. This power of acceptance does not continue forever, though. It can be terminated either by action of the parties or by operation of law.

TERMINATION BY ACTION OF THE PARTIES An offer can be terminated by action of the parties in any of three ways: by revocation, by rejection, or by counteroffer.

Revocation. The offeror's act of withdrawing (revoking) an offer is known as **revocation.** Unless an offer is irrevocable, the offeror usually can revoke the offer, as long as the revocation is communicated to the offeree before the offeree accepts. Revocation may be accomplished by either of the following:

1. Express repudiation of the offer (such as "I withdraw my previous offer of October 17").
2. Performance of acts that are inconsistent with the existence of the offer and are made known to the offeree (for instance, selling the offered property to another person in the presence of the offeree).

In most states, a revocation becomes effective when the offeree or the offeree's *agent* (a person acting on behalf of the offeree) actually receives it. Therefore, a revocation sent via FedEx on April 1 and delivered at the offeree's residence or place of business on April 3 becomes effective on April 3. An offer made to the general public can be revoked in the same manner that the offer was originally communicated, such as by being broadcast over a local television news program.

Irrevocable Offers. Although most offers are revocable, some can be made irrevocable—that is, they cannot be revoked. Increasingly, courts refuse to allow an offeror to revoke an offer when the offeree has changed position because of justifiable reliance on the offer. In some circumstances, "firm offers" made by merchants may also be considered irrevocable—see the discussion of a "merchant's firm offer" in Chapter 11.

Another form of irrevocable offer is an **option contract.** An option contract is created when an offeror promises to hold an offer open for a specified period of time in return for a payment (consideration) given by the offeree. An option contract takes away the offeror's power to revoke the offer for the period of time specified in the option.

Option contracts are frequently used in conjunction with the sale or lease of real estate. ▶ **Example 9.12** Tyrell agrees to lease a house from Jackson, the property owner. The lease contract includes a clause stating that Tyrell is paying an additional $15,000 for an option to purchase the property within a specified period of time. If Tyrell decides not to purchase the house after the specified period has lapsed, he loses

9. See UCC 2–204, discussed in Chapter 11. Article 2 modifies general contract law by requiring *less* specificity.

the $15,000, and Jackson is free to sell the property to another buyer. ◀

Rejection. If the offeree rejects the offer—by words or by conduct—the offer is terminated. Any subsequent attempt by the offeree to accept will be construed as a new offer, giving the original offeror (now the offeree) the power of acceptance. Like a revocation, a rejection of an offer is effective only when it is actually received by the offeror or the offeror's agent.

Merely inquiring about an offer does not constitute rejection. When the offeree merely inquires as to the "firmness" of the offer, there is no reason to presume that he or she intends to reject it.

▶ **Example 9.13** Raymond offers to buy Francie's iPhone 5 for $200, and Francie responds, "Is that your best offer?" or "Will you pay me $275 for it?" A reasonable person would conclude that Francie did not reject the offer but merely made an inquiry about it. She can still accept and bind Raymond to the $200 purchase price. ◀

Counteroffer. A **counteroffer** is a rejection of the original offer and the simultaneous making of a new offer. ▶ **Example 9.14** Burke offers to sell his home to Lang for $270,000. Lang responds, "Your price is too high. I'll offer to purchase your house for $250,000." Lang's response is called a counteroffer because it rejects Burke's offer to sell at $270,000 and creates a new offer by Lang to purchase the home at a price of $250,000. ◀

At common law, the **mirror image rule** requires the offeree's acceptance to match the offeror's offer exactly—to mirror the offer. Any change in, or addition to, the terms of the original offer automatically terminates that offer and substitutes the counteroffer. The counteroffer, of course, need not be accepted, but if the original offeror does accept the terms of the counteroffer, a valid contract is created.[10]

TERMINATION BY OPERATION OF LAW The power of the offeree to transform the offer into a binding, legal obligation can be terminated by operation of law through the occurrence of any of the following events:

1. Lapse of time.
2. Destruction of the specific subject matter of the offer (such as a smartphone or a house).
3. Death or incompetence of the offeror or the offeree.
4. Supervening illegality of the proposed contract. (A statute or court decision that makes an offer illegal automatically terminates the offer.)

Lapse of Time. An offer terminates automatically by law when the period of time *specified in the offer* has passed. If the offer states that it will be left open until a particular date, then the offer will terminate at midnight on that day. If the offer states that it will be open for a number of days, this time period normally begins to run when the offeree *receives* the offer (not when it is formed or sent).

If the offer does not specify a time for acceptance, the offer terminates at the end of a *reasonable* period of time. What constitutes a reasonable period of time depends on the subject matter of the contract, business and market conditions, and other relevant circumstances. An offer to sell farm produce, for example, will terminate sooner than an offer to sell farm equipment because farm produce is perishable. Produce is also subject to greater fluctuations in market value.

Supervening Illegality of the Proposed Contract. A statute or court decision that makes an offer illegal automatically terminates the offer.[11] ▶ **Example 9.15** Lee offers to lend Kim $10,000 at an annual interest rate of 15 percent. Before Kim can accept the offer, a law is enacted that prohibits interest rates higher than 12 percent. Lee's offer is automatically terminated. (If the statute is enacted after Kim accepts the offer, a valid contract is formed, but the contract may still be unenforceable.) ◀

Concept Summary 9.2 on the next page provides a review of the ways in which an offer can be terminated.

Acceptance

Acceptance is a voluntary act by the offeree that shows assent (agreement) to the terms of an offer. The offeree's act may consist of words or conduct. The acceptance must be unequivocal and must be communicated to the offeror. Generally, only the person to whom the offer is made or that person's agent can accept the offer and create a binding contract.

UNEQUIVOCAL ACCEPTANCE To exercise the power of acceptance effectively, the offeree must accept unequivocally. This is the *mirror image rule* previously

10. The mirror image rule has been greatly modified in regard to sales contracts. Section 2–207 of the UCC provides that a contract is formed if the offeree makes a definite expression of acceptance (such as signing the form in the appropriate location), even though the terms of the acceptance modify or add to the terms of the original offer (see Chapter 11).

11. *Restatement (Second) of Contracts,* Section 36.

CONCEPT SUMMARY 9.2

Methods by Which an Offer Can Be Terminated

BY ACTION OF THE PARTIES—

1. *Revocation*—Unless the offer is irrevocable, it can be revoked at any time before acceptance without liability. Revocation is not effective until received by the offeree or the offeree's agent. Some offers, such as a merchant's firm offer and option contracts, are irrevocable. Also, in some situations, an offeree's detrimental reliance or partial performance will cause a court to rule that the offeror cannot revoke the offer.
2. *Rejection*—Accomplished by words or actions that demonstrate a clear intent not to accept the offer; not effective until received by the offeror or the offeror's agent.
3. *Counteroffer*—A rejection of the original offer and the making of a new offer.

BY OPERATION OF LAW—

1. *Lapse of time*—The offer terminates at the end of the time period specified in the offer or, if no time period is stated in the offer, at the end of a reasonable time period.
2. *Destruction of the subject matter*—When the specific subject matter of the offer is destroyed before the offer is accepted, the offer automatically terminates.
3. *Death or incompetence of the offeror or offeree*—If the offeror or offeree dies or becomes incompetent, the offer terminates (unless the offer is irrevocable).
4. *Supervening illegality*—When a statute or court decision makes the proposed contract illegal, the offer automatically terminates.

discussed. An acceptance may be unequivocal even though the offeree expresses dissatisfaction with the contract. For instance, "I accept the offer, but can you give me a better price?" is an effective acceptance.

An acceptance cannot impose new conditions or change the terms of the original offer. If it does, the acceptance may be considered a counteroffer, which is a rejection of the original offer. For instance, the statement "I accept the offer but only if I can pay on ninety days' credit" is a counteroffer and not an unequivocal acceptance.

Certain terms, when included in an acceptance, will not change the offer sufficiently to constitute rejection. ▶ **Example 9.16** In response to an art dealer's offer to sell a painting, the offeree, Ashton Gibbs, replies, "I accept. Please send a written contract." Gibbs is requesting a written contract but is not making it a condition for acceptance. Therefore, the acceptance is effective without the written contract. In contrast, if Gibbs replies, "I accept *if* you send a written contract," the acceptance is expressly conditioned on the request for a writing, and the statement is not an acceptance but a counteroffer. (Notice how important each word is!)[12] ◀

12. As noted in footnote 10, in regard to sales contracts, the UCC provides that an acceptance may still be valid even if some terms are added. The new terms are simply treated as proposed additions to the contract.

SILENCE AS ACCEPTANCE Ordinarily, silence cannot constitute acceptance, even if the offeror states, "By your silence and inaction, you will be deemed to have accepted this offer." An offeree should not be obligated to act affirmatively to reject an offer when no consideration (nothing of value) has passed to the offeree to impose such a duty.

In some instances, however, the offeree does have a duty to speak and her or his silence or inaction will operate as an acceptance. Silence may constitute an acceptance in the following circumstances:

1. When an offeree takes the benefit of offered services even though he or she had an opportunity to reject them and knew that they were offered with the expectation of compensation.
2. When the offeree has had prior dealings with the offeror. For instance, a merchant routinely receives shipments from a certain supplier and always notifies that supplier when defective goods are rejected. The merchant's silence regarding a particular shipment (failure to reject the goods) will constitute acceptance.

COMMUNICATION OF ACCEPTANCE In a bilateral contract, acceptance is in the form of a promise (not performance). Because bilateral contracts are formed when the promise is made (rather than when the act is performed), communication of acceptance is necessary. Communication of acceptance may not be necessary if the offer dispenses with the requirement, however, or if the offer can be accepted by silence.

▶ **Case in Point 9.17** Powerhouse Custom Homes, Inc., owed $95,260.42 to 84 Lumber Company under a credit agreement. When Powerhouse failed to pay, 84 Lumber filed a suit to collect. During mediation, the parties agreed to a deadline for objections to whatever agreement they might reach. If there were no objections, the agreement would be binding.

Powerhouse then offered to pay less than the amount owed, and 84 Lumber did not respond. Powerhouse argued that 84 Lumber accepted the offer by not objecting to it within the deadline. The court, however, held that for a contract to be formed, an offer must be accepted unequivocally. Although Powerhouse had made an offer of a proposed settlement, 84 Lumber did not communicate its acceptance. Thus, the court reasoned that the parties did not reach an agreement on the proposed settlement.[13] ◀

Because a unilateral contract calls for the full performance of some act, acceptance is usually evident, and notification is therefore unnecessary. Nevertheless, exceptions do exist, such as when the offeror requests notice of acceptance or has no way of determining whether the requested act has been performed.

MODE AND TIMELINESS OF ACCEPTANCE In bilateral contracts, acceptance must be timely. The general rule is that acceptance in a bilateral contract is timely if it is made before the offer is terminated. Problems may arise, though, when the parties involved are not dealing face to face. In such situations, the offeree should use an authorized mode of communication.

The Mailbox Rule. Acceptance takes effect, thus completing formation of the contract, at the time the offeree sends or delivers the communication via the mode expressly or impliedly authorized by the offeror. This is the so-called **mailbox rule,** also called the *deposited acceptance rule,* which the majority of courts follow. Under this rule, if the authorized mode of communication is the mail, then an acceptance becomes valid when it is dispatched (placed in the control of the U.S. Postal Service)—*not* when it is received by the offeror. (Note, however, that if the offer stipulates when acceptance will be effective, then the offer will not be effective until the time specified.)

The mailbox rule does not apply to instantaneous forms of communication, such as when the parties are dealing face to face, by telephone, by fax, and usually by e-mail. Under the law of most states (based on the Uniform Electronic Transactions Act), e-mail is considered sent when it either leaves the control of the sender or is received by the recipient. This rule takes the place of the mailbox rule when the parties have agreed to conduct transactions electronically and allows an e-mail acceptance to become effective when sent.

Authorized Means of Acceptance. A means of communicating acceptance can be expressly authorized by the offeror or impliedly authorized by the facts and circumstances of the situation. An acceptance sent by means not expressly or impliedly authorized normally is not effective until it is received by the offeror.

When an offeror specifies how acceptance should be made (for example, by overnight delivery), *express authorization* is said to exist. The contract is not formed unless the offeree uses that specified mode of acceptance. Moreover, both offeror and offeree are bound in contract the moment this means of acceptance is employed. ▶ **Example 9.18** Motorola Mobility, Inc., offers to sell 144 Atrix 4G smartphones and 72 Lapdocks to Call Me Plus phone stores. The offer states that Call Me Plus must accept the offer via FedEx overnight delivery. The acceptance is effective (and a binding contract is formed) the moment that Call Me Plus gives the overnight envelope containing the acceptance to the FedEx driver. ◀

If the offeror does not expressly authorize a certain mode of acceptance, then acceptance can be made by *any reasonable means.*[14] Courts look at the prevailing business usages and the surrounding circumstances to determine whether the mode of acceptance used was reasonable. Usually, the offeror's choice of a particular means in making the offer implies that the offeree can use the *same or a faster means* for acceptance. Thus, if the offer is made via Priority U.S. mail, it would be reasonable to accept the offer via Priority mail or by a faster method, such as signed scanned documents sent as attachments via e-mail or overnight delivery.

Substitute Method of Acceptance. Sometimes, the offeror authorizes a particular method of acceptance, but the offeree accepts by a different means. In that situation, the acceptance may still be effective if the substituted method serves the same purpose as the authorized means.

13. *Powerhouse Custom Homes, Inc. v. 84 Lumber Co.,* 307 Ga.App. 605, 705 S.E.2d 704 (2011).

14. *Restatement (Second) of Contracts,* Section 30. This is also the rule under UCC 2–206(1)(a).

The acceptance by a substitute method is not effective on dispatch, though, and no contract will be formed until the acceptance is received by the offeror. For instance, an offer specifies acceptance by FedEx overnight delivery, but the offeree instead accepts by overnight delivery from another carrier. The substitute method of acceptance will still be effective, but the contract will not be formed until the offeror receives it.

SECTION 4

E-CONTRACTS

Numerous contracts are formed online. Electronic contracts, or **e-contracts,** must meet the same basic requirements (agreement, consideration, contractual capacity, and legality) as paper contracts. Disputes concerning e-contracts, however, tend to center on contract terms and whether the parties voluntarily agreed to those terms.

Online contracts may be formed not only for the sale of goods and services but also for *licensing*. As you will read in Chapter 15, the purchase of software generally involves a license, or a right to use the software, rather than the passage of title (ownership rights) from the seller to the buyer. ▶ **Example 9.19** Lynn downloads an app on her iPad that enables her to work on spreadsheets. During the transaction, she has to select "I agree" several times to indicate that she understands that she is purchasing only the right to use the software under specific terms. After she agrees to these terms (the licensing agreement), she can use the application. ◀

Online Offers

Sellers doing business via the Internet can protect themselves against contract disputes and legal liability by creating offers that clearly spell out the terms that will govern their transactions if the offers are accepted. All important terms should be conspicuous and easy to view.

The seller's Web site should include a hypertext link to a page containing the full contract so that potential buyers are made aware of the terms to which they are assenting. The contract generally must be displayed online in a readable format, such as a twelve-point typeface.

PROVISIONS TO INCLUDE An important rule to keep in mind is that the offeror (the seller) controls the offer and thus the resulting contract. The seller should therefore anticipate the terms he or she wants to include in a contract and provide for them in the offer. At a minimum, an online offer should include the following provisions:

1. *Acceptance of terms*. A clause that clearly indicates what constitutes the buyer's agreement to the terms of the offer, such as a box containing the words "I accept" that the buyer can click.
2. *Payment*. A provision specifying how payment for the goods (including any applicable taxes) must be made.
3. *Return policy*. A statement of the seller's refund and return policies.
4. *Disclaimer*. Disclaimers of liability for certain uses of the goods. For instance, an online seller of business forms may add a disclaimer that the seller does not accept responsibility for the buyer's reliance on the forms rather than on an attorney's advice.
5. *Limitation on remedies*. A provision specifying the remedies available to the buyer if the goods are found to be defective or if the contract is otherwise breached. Any limitation of remedies should be clearly spelled out.
6. *Privacy policy*. A statement indicating how the seller will use the information gathered about the buyer.
7. *Dispute resolution*. Provisions relating to dispute settlement, such as an arbitration clause or a *forum-selection clause* (discussed next).

DISPUTE-SETTLEMENT PROVISIONS Online offers frequently include provisions relating to dispute settlement. For instance, the offer might include an arbitration clause specifying that any dispute arising under the contract will be arbitrated in a designated forum.

Forum-Selection Clause. Many online contracts contain a **forum-selection clause** indicating the forum, or location (such as a court or jurisdiction), in which contract disputes will be resolved. As discussed in Chapter 2, significant jurisdictional issues may arise when parties are at a great distance, as they often are when they form contracts via the Internet. A forum-selection clause will help to avert future jurisdictional problems and also help to ensure that the seller will not be required to appear in court in a distant state.

▶ **Case in Point 9.20** Before advertisers can place ads through Google, Inc., they must agree to certain terms that are displayed in an online window. These terms include a forum-selection clause, which provides that any dispute is to be "adjudicated in Santa Clara County, California." Lawrence Feldman, who advertised through Google, complained that he was overcharged and filed a lawsuit against Google in a federal district court in Pennsylvania. The court held that Feldman had agreed to the forum-selection clause in Google's online contract and transferred the case to a court in Santa Clara County.[15] ◄

Choice-of-Law Clause. Some online contracts may also include a *choice-of-law clause* specifying that any contract dispute will be settled according to the law of a particular jurisdiction, such as a state or country. As discussed in Chapter 8, choice-of-law clauses are particularly common in international contracts, but they may also appear in e-contracts to specify which state's laws will govern in the United States.

Online Acceptances

The *Restatement (Second) of Contracts,* which, as noted earlier, is a compilation of common law contract principles, states that parties may agree to a contract "by written or spoken words or by other action or by failure to act."[16] The Uniform Commercial Code (UCC), which governs sales contracts, has a similar provision. Section 2–204 of the UCC states that any contract for the sale of goods "may be made in any manner sufficient to show agreement, including conduct by both parties which recognizes the existence of such a contract."

CLICK-ON AGREEMENTS The courts have used the *Restatement* and UCC provisions to conclude that a binding contract can be created by conduct. This includes the act of clicking on a box indicating "I accept" or "I agree" to accept an online offer. The agreement resulting from such an acceptance is often called a **click-on agreement** (sometimes referred to as a *click-on license* or *click-wrap agreement*). Exhibit 9–3 alongside shows a portion of a typical click-on agreement that accompanies a software package.

Generally, the law does not require that the parties have read all of the terms in a contract for it to be effective. Therefore, clicking on a box that states "I agree" to certain terms can be enough. The terms may be contained on a Web site through which the buyer is obtaining goods or services. They may also appear on a screen when software is loaded from a CD-ROM or DVD or downloaded from the Internet.

► **Case in Point 9.21** The "Terms of Use" that govern Facebook users' accounts include a forum-selection clause that provides for the resolution of all disputes in a court in Santa Clara County, California. To sign up for a Facebook account, a person must click on a box indicating that he or she has agreed to this term.

Mustafa Fteja was an active user of facebook.com when his account was disabled. He sued Facebook in a federal court in New York, claiming that it had disabled his Facebook page without justification and for discriminatory reasons. Facebook filed a motion to transfer the case to California under the forum-selection clause. The court found that the clause in Facebook's online contract was binding and transferred the case. When Fteja clicked on the button to accept the "Terms of Use" and become a Facebook user, he agreed to resolve all disputes with Facebook in Santa Clara County, California.[17] ◄

SHRINK-WRAP AGREEMENTS With a **shrink-wrap agreement** (or *shrink-wrap license*), the terms are expressed inside the box in which the goods are packaged. (The term *shrink-wrap* refers to the plastic that covers the box.) Usually, the party who opens the box

EXHIBIT 9–3 A Sample Click-On Agreement

This exhibit illustrates an online offer to form a contract. To accept the offer, the user simply scrolls down the page and clicks on the "I Accept" button.

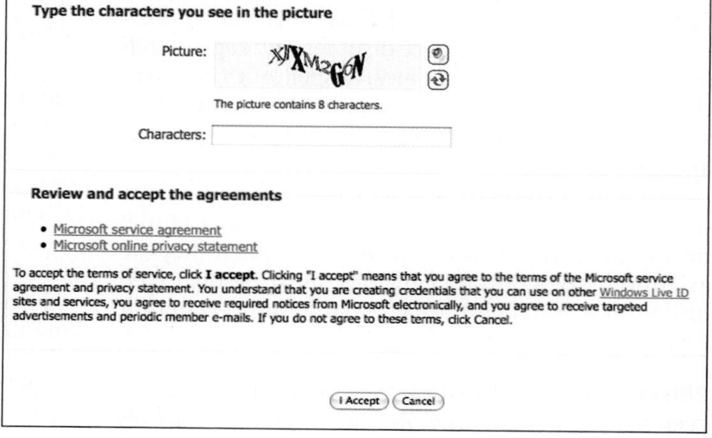

15. *Feldman v. Google, Inc.,* 513 F.Supp.2d 229 (E.D.Pa. 2007).
16. *Restatement (Second) of Contracts,* Section 19.
17. *Fteja v. Facebook, Inc.,* 841 F.Supp.2d 829 (S.D.N.Y. 2012).

is told that she or he agrees to the terms by keeping whatever is in the box. Similarly, when a purchaser opens a software package, he or she agrees to abide by the terms of the limited license agreement.

▶ **Example 9.22** Ava orders a new iMac from Big Dog Electronics, which ships it to her. Along with the iMac, the box contains an agreement setting forth the terms of the sale, including what remedies are available. The document also states that Ava's retention of the iMac for longer than thirty days will be construed as an acceptance of the terms. ◀

In most instances, a shrink-wrap agreement is not between a retailer and a buyer, but between the manufacturer of the hardware or software and the ultimate buyer-user of the product. The terms generally concern warranties, remedies, and other issues associated with the use of the product.

Shrink-Wrap Agreements and Enforceable Contract Terms. In some cases, the courts have enforced the terms of shrink-wrap agreements in the same way as the terms of other contracts. These courts have reasoned that by including the terms with the product, the seller proposed a contract. The buyer could accept this contract by using the product after having an opportunity to read the terms. Thus, a buyer's failure to object to terms contained within a shrink-wrapped software package may constitute an acceptance of the terms by conduct.

Shrink-Wrap Terms That May Not Be Enforced. Sometimes, however, the courts have refused to enforce certain terms included in shrink-wrap agreements because the buyer did not expressly consent to them. An important factor is when the parties formed their contract.

If a buyer orders a product over the telephone, for instance, and is not informed of an arbitration clause or forum-selection clause at that time, the buyer clearly has not expressly agreed to these terms. If the buyer discovers the clauses *after* the parties entered into a contract, a court may conclude that those terms were proposals for additional terms and were not part of the contract.

BROWSE-WRAP TERMS Like the terms of click-on agreements, **browse-wrap terms** can occur in transactions conducted over the Internet. Unlike click-on agreements, however, browse-wrap terms do not require Internet users to assent to the terms before downloading or using certain software. In other words, a person can install the software without clicking "I agree" to the terms of a license. Browse-wrap terms are often unenforceable because they do not satisfy the agreement requirement of contract formation.[18]

▶ **Example 9.23** BrowseNet Corporation provides free downloadable software called "QuickLoad" on its Web site. Users must indicate, by clicking on a designated box, that they wish to obtain it. On the Web site's download page is a reference to a license agreement that users can view only by scrolling to the next screen. In other words, the user does not have to agree to the terms of the license before downloading the software. One of the license terms requires all disputes to be submitted to arbitration in California. If a user sues BrowseNet in Washington state, the arbitration clause might not be enforceable because users were not required to indicate their assent to the agreement. ◀

E-Signature Technologies

Today, numerous technologies allow electronic documents to be signed. An **e-signature** has been defined as "an electronic sound, symbol, or process attached to or logically associated with a record and executed or adopted by a person with the intent to sign the record."[19] Thus, e-signatures include encrypted digital signatures, names (intended as signatures) at the end of e-mail messages, and clicks on a Web page if the click includes some means of identification.

Federal Law on E-Signatures and E-Documents

In 2000, Congress enacted the Electronic Signatures in Global and National Commerce Act (E-SIGN Act),[20] which provides that no contract, record, or signature may be "denied legal effect" solely because it is in electronic form. In other words, under this law, an electronic signature is as valid as a signature on paper, and an e-document can be as enforceable as a paper one.

For an e-signature to be enforceable, the contracting parties must have agreed to use electronic signatures. For an electronic document to be valid, it must be in a form that can be retained and accurately reproduced.

The E-SIGN Act does not apply to all types of documents. Contracts and documents that are exempt include court papers, divorce decrees, evictions, foreclosures, health-insurance terminations, prenuptial

18. See, for example, *Jesmer v. Retail Magic, Inc.*, 863 N.Y.S.2d 737 (2008).
19. This definition is from the Uniform Electronic Transactions Act, which will be discussed shortly.
20. 15 U.S.C. Sections 7001 *et seq.*

agreements, and wills. Also, the only agreements governed by the UCC that fall under this law are those covered by Articles 2 and 2A (sales and lease contracts) and UCC 1–107 and 1–206. Despite these limitations, the E-SIGN Act significantly expanded the possibilities for contracting online.

The Uniform Electronic Transactions Act

Although most states have laws governing e-signatures and other aspects of electronic transactions, these laws vary. In an attempt to create more uniformity among the states, in 1999 the National Conference of Commissioners on Uniform State Laws and the American Law Institute promulgated the Uniform Electronic Transactions Act (UETA). The UETA has been adopted, at least in part, by forty-eight states. Among other things, the UETA declares that a signature may not be denied legal effect or enforceability solely because it is in electronic form.

The primary purpose of the UETA is to remove barriers to e-commerce by giving the same legal effect to electronic records and signatures as is given to paper documents and signatures. As mentioned earlier, the UETA broadly defines an *e-signature* as "an electronic sound, symbol, or process attached to or logically associated with a record and executed or adopted by a person with the intent to sign the record."[21] A **record** is "information that is inscribed on a tangible medium or that is stored in an electronic or other medium and is retrievable in perceivable [visual] form."[22]

SCOPE AND APPLICABILITY The UETA does not create new rules for electronic contracts but rather establishes that records, signatures, and contracts may not be denied enforceability solely due to their electronic form. The UETA does not apply to all writings and signatures. It covers only electronic records and electronic signatures *relating to a transaction* between two or more people in a business, commercial, or governmental context.

The act specifically does not apply to wills or testamentary trusts or to transactions governed by the UCC (other than those covered by Articles 2 and 2A).[23] In addition, the provisions of the UETA allow the states to exclude its application to other areas of law.

The UETA does not apply to a transaction unless each of the parties has previously agreed to conduct transactions by electronic means. The agreement need not be explicit, however. It can be implied by the conduct of the parties and the surrounding circumstances, such as negotiating a contract via e-mail. The parties can agree to opt out of all or some of the terms of the UETA, but if they do not, then the UETA terms will govern their electronic transactions.

THE FEDERAL E-SIGN ACT AND THE UETA Congress passed the E-SIGN Act in 2000, a year after the UETA was presented to the states for adoption. The E-SIGN Act refers explicitly to the UETA and provides that if a state has enacted the uniform version of the UETA, it is not preempted by the E-SIGN Act.[24]

In other words, if the state has enacted the UETA without modification, state law will govern. The problem is that many states have enacted nonuniform (modified) versions of the UETA, usually to exclude other areas of state law from the UETA's terms. The E-SIGN Act specifies that those exclusions will be preempted to the extent that they are inconsistent with the E-SIGN Act's provisions.

The E-SIGN Act explicitly allows the states to enact alternative requirements for the use of electronic records or electronic signatures. Generally, however, the requirements must be consistent with the provisions of the E-SIGN Act, and the state must not give greater legal status or effect to one specific type of technology. Additionally, if a state enacts alternative requirements after the E-SIGN Act was adopted, the state law must specifically refer to the E-SIGN Act. The relationship between the UETA and the E-SIGN Act is illustrated in Exhibit 9–4 on the following page.

SIGNATURES ON ELECTRONIC RECORDS Under the UETA, if an electronic record or signature is the act of a particular person, the record or signature may be attributed to that person. If a person types her or his name at the bottom of an e-mail purchase order, for instance, that name would qualify as a "signature." The signature would therefore be attributed to the person whose name appeared.

The UETA does not contain any express provisions about what constitutes fraud or whether an agent is authorized to enter a contract. Other state laws control if any issues relating to agency, authority, forgery, or contract formation arise.

21. UETA 102(8).
22. UETA 102(15).
23. UETA 3(b).
24. 15 U.S.C. Section 7002(2)(A)(i).

EXHIBIT 9–4 The E-SIGN Act and the UETA

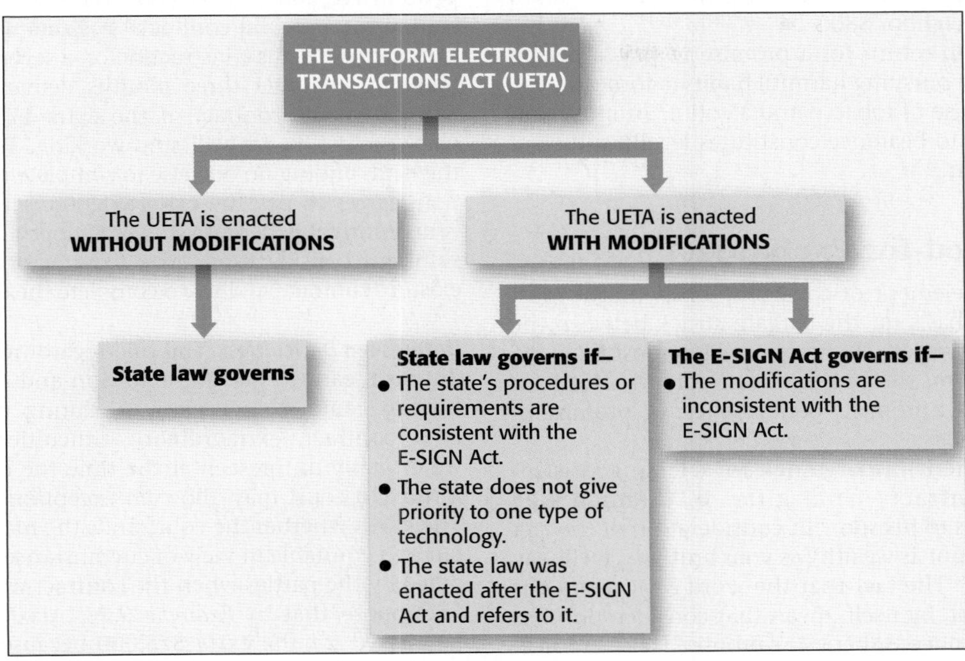

Under the UETA, an electronic record is considered *sent* when it is properly directed to the intended recipient in a form readable by the recipient's computer system. Once the electronic record leaves the control of the sender or comes under the control of the recipient, the UETA deems it to have been sent. An electronic record is considered *received* when it enters the recipient's processing system in a readable form—*even if no individual is aware of its receipt.*

SECTION 5 CONSIDERATION

The fact that a promise has been made does not mean the promise can or will be enforced. Under the common law, a primary basis for the enforcement of promises is consideration. **Consideration** usually is defined as the value (such as cash) given in return for a promise (in a bilateral contract) or in return for a performance (in a unilateral contract). As long as consideration is present, the courts generally do not interfere with contracts based on the amount of consideration paid.

Often, consideration is broken down into two parts: (1) something of *legally sufficient value* must be given in exchange for the promise, and (2) there must be a *bargained-for* exchange.

Legally Sufficient Value

To be legally sufficient, consideration must be something of value in the eyes of the law. The "something of legally sufficient value" may consist of the following:

1. A promise to do something that one has no prior legal duty to do.
2. The performance of an action that one is otherwise not obligated to undertake.
3. The refraining from an action that one has a legal right to undertake (called a **forbearance**).

Consideration in bilateral contracts normally consists of a promise in return for a promise, as explained earlier. In a contract for the sale of goods, for instance, the seller promises to ship specific goods to the buyer, and the buyer promises to pay for those goods. Each of these promises constitutes consideration for the contract.

In contrast, unilateral contracts involve a promise in return for a performance. ▶ **Example 9.24** Anita says to her neighbor, "When you finish painting the garage, I will pay you $800." Anita's neighbor paints the garage. The act of painting the garage is the consideration that creates Anita's contractual obligation to pay her neighbor $800. ◀

What if, in return for a promise to pay, a person refrains from pursuing harmful habits (a forbearance), such as the use of tobacco and alcohol? In most situations, such forbearance constitutes legally sufficient consideration.[25]

Bargained-for Exchange

The second element of consideration is that it must provide the basis for the bargain struck between the contracting parties. The item of value must be given or promised by the promisor (offeror) in return for the promisee's promise, performance, or promise of performance.

This element of bargained-for exchange distinguishes contracts from gifts. **▶ Example 9.25** Sheng-Li says to his son, "In consideration of the fact that you are not as wealthy as your brothers, I will pay you $5,000." The fact that the word *consideration* is used does not, by itself, mean that consideration has been given. Indeed, Sheng-Li's promise is not enforceable because the son does not have to do anything in order to receive the $5,000 promised. Because the son does not need to give Sheng-Li something of legal value in return for his promise, there is no bargained-for exchange. Rather, Sheng-Li has simply stated his motive for giving his son a gift. ◀

Agreements That Lack Consideration

Sometimes, one of the parties (or both parties) to an agreement may think that consideration has been exchanged when in fact it has not. Here, we look at some situations in which the parties' promises or actions do not qualify as contractual consideration.

PREEXISTING DUTY Under most circumstances, a promise to do what one already has a legal duty to do does not constitute legally sufficient consideration. The preexisting legal duty may be imposed by law or may arise out of a previous contract. A sheriff, for instance, has a duty to investigate crime and to arrest criminals. Hence, a sheriff cannot collect a reward for providing information leading to the capture of a criminal.

Likewise, if a party is already bound by contract to perform a certain duty, that duty cannot serve as consideration for a second contract. **▶ Example 9.26** Ajax Contractors begins construction on a seven-story office building and after three months demands an extra $75,000 on its contract. If the extra $75,000 is not paid, the contractor will stop working. The owner of the land, finding no one else to complete the construction, agrees to pay the extra $75,000. The agreement is unenforceable because it is not supported by legally sufficient consideration. Ajax Contractors had a preexisting contractual duty to complete the building. ◀

Unforeseen Difficulties. The rule regarding preexisting duty is meant to prevent extortion and the so-called holdup game. Nonetheless, if, during performance of a contract, extraordinary difficulties arise that were totally unforeseen at the time the contract was formed, a court may allow an exception to the rule. The key is whether the court finds the modification is fair and equitable in view of circumstances not anticipated by the parties when the contract was made.

Suppose that in *Example 9.26,* Ajax Contractors had asked for the extra $75,000 because it encountered a rock formation that no one knew existed. If the landowner agrees to pay the extra $75,000 to excavate the rock and the court finds that it is fair to do so, Ajax Contractors can enforce the agreement. If rock formations are common in the area, however, the court may determine that the contractor should have known of the risk. In that situation, the court may choose to apply the preexisting duty rule and prevent Ajax Contractors from obtaining the extra $75,000.

Rescission and New Contract. The law recognizes that two parties can mutually agree to rescind, or cancel, their contract, at least to the extent that it is *executory* (still to be carried out). **Rescission**[26] is the unmaking of a contract so as to return the parties to the positions they occupied before the contract was made.

Sometimes, parties rescind a contract and make a new contract at the same time. When this occurs, it is often difficult to determine whether there was consideration for the new contract, or whether the parties had a preexisting duty under the previous contract. If a court finds there was a preexisting duty, then the new contract will be invalid because there was no consideration.

25. For a classic case holding that a person's promise to refrain from using alcohol and tobacco was sufficient consideration, see *Hamer v. Sidway,* 124 N.Y. 538, 27 N.E. 256 (1891).

26. Pronounced reh-*sih*-zhen.

PAST CONSIDERATION Promises made in return for actions or events that have already taken place are unenforceable. These promises lack consideration in that the element of bargained-for exchange is missing. In short, you can bargain for something to take place now or in the future but not for something that has already taken place. Therefore, **past consideration** is no consideration.

Case in Point 9.27 Jamil Blackmon became friends with Allen Iverson when Iverson was a high school student who showed tremendous promise as an athlete. One evening, Blackmon suggested that Iverson use "The Answer" as a nickname in the summer league basketball tournaments. Blackmon said that Iverson would be "The Answer" to all of the National Basketball Association's woes. Later that night, Iverson said that he would give Blackmon 25 percent of any proceeds from the merchandising of products that used "The Answer" as a logo or a slogan. Because Iverson's promise was made in return for past consideration, it was unenforceable. In effect, Iverson stated his intention to give Blackmon a gift.[27]

In a variety of situations, an employer will often ask an employee to sign a **covenant to compete,** also called a *noncompete agreement.* Under such an agreement, the employee agrees not to compete with the employer for a certain period of time after the employment relationship ends. When a current employee is required to sign a noncompete agreement, his or her employment is not sufficient consideration for the agreement because the individual is already employed. To be valid, the agreement requires new consideration.

In the following case, the court had to decide if new consideration supported a noncompete agreement between physicians and a medical clinic.

27. *Blackmon v. Iverson,* 324 F.Supp.2d 602 (E.D.Pa. 2003).

CASE 9.3

Baugh v. Columbia Heart Clinic, P.A.[a]

Court of Appeals of South Carolina, 2013 WL 163955 (2013).

BACKGROUND AND FACTS Columbia Heart Clinic, P.A., in Columbia, South Carolina, provides comprehensive cardiology services. Its physicians are all cardiologists. When Kevin Baugh, M.D., and Barry Feldman, M.D., became employees and shareholders of Columbia Heart, and again several years later, they signed noncompete agreements. Under these agreements, Baugh and Feldman would forfeit certain payments if they competed with Columbia Heart within a year after their employment ended. Specifically, they were not to practice cardiology "within a twenty (20) mile radius of any Columbia Heart office at which [they] routinely provided services." Later, Baugh and Feldman left Columbia Heart and opened a new cardiology practice near one of Columbia Heart's offices. They then filed a suit in a South Carolina state court against Columbia Heart, seeking a ruling that their noncompete agreements were unenforceable. From a judgment in favor of Baugh and Feldman, Columbia Heart appealed.

IN THE LANGUAGE OF THE COURT
THOMAS, J. [Judge]

* * * *

* * * Article 5 [of the agreements] says the following:

> Physician, in the event of termination * * * for any reason, during the twelve (12) month period immediately following the date of termination * * * shall not Compete * * * with Columbia Heart * * * within a twenty (20) mile radius of any Columbia Heart office at which Physician routinely provided services during the year prior to the date of termination.

No separate monetary consideration was paid to any shareholder-physician to sign the Agreements, nor did the Agreements change the [established] compensation system.

* * * *

[Baugh and Feldman] contend * * * that the Agreements are unenforceable because they are not supported by new consideration. We disagree.

a. *P.A.* means "professional association."

CASE 9.3 CONTINUES

CASE 9.3 CONTINUED

When a covenant not to compete is entered into after the inception of employment, separate consideration, in addition to continued at-will employment, is necessary in order for the covenant to be enforceable. There is no consideration when the contract containing the covenant is exacted after several years' employment and the employee's duties and position are left unchanged. [Emphasis added.]

[Baugh and Feldman] executed the Agreements after they became employed by Columbia Heart, and the Agreements did not change the general compensation system agreed to by the parties under their prior employment contracts. However, * * * Article 4 of the Agreements provides the following:

> Physician shall be paid Five Thousand and No/100 Dollars ($5,000.00) per month for each of the twelve (12) months following termination, so long as the Physician is not in violation of Article 5 of this Agreement.

This language established that Columbia Heart promised to pay [Baugh and Feldman] each * * * a total of $60,000 over twelve months after termination so long as they did not violate the non-competition provision in Article 5. * * * Consequently, the Agreements are supported by new consideration.

DECISION AND REMEDY *A state intermediate appellate court reversed the lower court's finding that the noncompete provisions were unenforceable. The agreements were supported by new consideration because they provided for compensation to physicians who left Columbia Heart so long as they did not compete with the clinic's cardiology practice.*

THE LEGAL ENVIRONMENT DIMENSION *Did the court hold that the noncompete agreement at the heart of the dispute was supported by consideration? Why or why not?*

THE ETHICAL DIMENSION *When a noncompete agreement is entered into after employment has begun, is continued employment sufficient consideration for the agreement? Explain.*

SECTION 6

CONTRACTUAL CAPACITY

In addition to agreement and consideration, for a contract to be deemed valid, the parties to the contract must have **contractual capacity**—the legal ability to enter into a contractual relationship. Courts generally presume the existence of contractual capacity, but in some situations, as when a person is young or mentally incompetent, capacity may be lacking or questionable.

Minors

Today, in almost all states, the *age of majority* (when a person is no longer a minor) for contractual purposes is eighteen years.[28] In addition, some states provide for the termination of minority on marriage. Minority status may also be terminated by a minor's *emancipation,* which occurs when a child's parent or legal guardian relinquishes the legal right to exercise control over the child. Normally, minors who leave home to support themselves are considered emancipated.

The general rule is that a minor can enter into any contract that an adult can, except contracts prohibited by law for minors (for instance, the purchase of tobacco or alcoholic beverages). A contract entered into by a minor, however, is voidable at the option of that minor, subject to certain exceptions.

The legal avoidance, or setting aside, of a contractual obligation is referred to as **disaffirmance.** To disaffirm, a minor must express his or her intent, through words or conduct, not to be bound to the contract.

Case in Point 9.28 Fifteen-year-old Morgan Kelly was a cadet in her high school's Navy Junior Reserve Officer Training Corps. As part of the program, she visited a U.S. Marine Corps training facility. To enter the camp, she was required to sign a waiver that exempted the Marines from all liability for any injuries arising from her visit. While participating in activities on the camp's confidence-building course, Kelly fell from the "Slide for Life" and suffered serious injuries. She filed a suit to recover her medical costs.

28. The age of majority may still be twenty-one for other purposes, such as the purchase and consumption of alcohol.

The Marines asserted that she had signed their waiver of liability. Kelly claimed that she had disaffirmed the waiver when she filed suit. The court ruled in Kelly's favor. Liability waivers are generally enforceable contracts, but a minor can avoid a contract by disaffirming it.[29] ◀

Note that an adult who enters into a contract with a minor cannot avoid his or her contractual duties on the ground that the minor can do so. Unless the minor exercises the option to disaffirm the contract, the adult party normally is bound by it.

Intoxication

Intoxication is a condition in which a person's normal capacity to act or think is inhibited by alcohol or some other drug. A contract entered into by an intoxicated person can be either voidable or valid (and thus enforceable).

If the person was sufficiently intoxicated to lack mental capacity, then the agreement may be voidable even if the intoxication was purely voluntary. If a contract is voidable because one party was intoxicated, that person has the option of disaffirming it while intoxicated and for a reasonable time after becoming sober. If, despite intoxication, the person understood the legal consequences of the agreement, the contract will be enforceable.

Courts look at objective indications of the intoxicated person's condition to determine if he or she possessed or lacked the required capacity. It is difficult to prove that a person's judgment was so severely impaired that he or she could not comprehend the legal consequences of entering into a contract. Therefore, courts rarely permit contracts to be avoided due to intoxication.

Mental Incompetence

Contracts made by mentally incompetent persons can be void, voidable, or valid. If a court has previously determined that a person is mentally incompetent, any contract made by that person is *void*—no contract exists. Only a guardian appointed by the court to represent a mentally incompetent person can enter into binding legal obligations on that person's behalf.

If a court has not previously judged a person to be mentally incompetent but the person was incompetent at the time the contract was formed, the contract may be voidable.[30] A contract is *voidable* if the person did not know he or she was entering into the contract or lacked the mental capacity to comprehend its nature, purpose, and consequences.

▶ **Example 9.29** Larry agrees to sell his stock in Google, Inc., to Sergey for substantially less than its market value. At the time of the deal, Larry is confused about the purpose and details of the transaction, but he has not been declared incompetent. Nonetheless, if a court finds that Larry did not understand the nature and consequences of the contract due to a lack of mental capacity, he can avoid the sale. ◀

A contract entered into by a mentally incompetent person (whom a court has not previously declared incompetent) may also be *valid* if the person had capacity *at the time the contract was formed.* Some people who are incompetent due to age or illness have *lucid intervals*—temporary periods of sufficient intelligence, judgment, and will. During such intervals, they will be considered to have legal capacity to enter into contracts.

SECTION 7 LEGALITY

Legality is the fourth requirement for a valid contract to exist. For a contract to be valid and enforceable, it must be formed for a legal purpose. A contract to do something that is prohibited by federal or state statutory law is illegal and, as such, void from the outset and thus unenforceable. Additionally, a contract to commit a tortious act—such as an agreement to engage in fraudulent misrepresentation (see Chapter 12)—is contrary to public policy and therefore illegal and unenforceable.

Contracts Contrary to Statute

Statutes often set forth rules specifying which terms and clauses may be included in contracts and which are prohibited. We now examine several ways in which contracts may be contrary to statute and thus illegal.

CONTRACTS TO COMMIT A CRIME Any contract to commit a crime is in violation of a statute. Thus, a contract to sell illegal drugs in violation of criminal laws is unenforceable, as is a contract to cover up a corporation's violation of the Dodd-Frank Wall Street Reform and Consumer Protection Act.

29. *Kelly v. United States,* 809 F.Supp.2d 429 (E.D.N.C. 2011).

30. This is the rule in the majority of states. See, for example, *Hernandez v. Banks,* 65 A.3d 59 (D.C. 2013).

Sometimes, the object or performance of a contract is rendered illegal by a statute *after* the parties entered into the contract. In that situation, the contract is considered to be discharged by law. (See the discussion of impossibility or impracticability of performance in Chapter 10.)

USURY Almost every state has a statute that sets the maximum rate of interest that can be charged for different types of transactions, including ordinary loans. A lender who makes a loan at an interest rate above the lawful maximum commits **usury.**

Although usurious contracts are illegal, most states simply limit the interest that the lender may collect on the contract to the lawful maximum interest rate in that state. In a few states, the lender can recover the principal amount of the loan but no interest. In addition, states can make exceptions to facilitate business transactions. For instance, many states exempt corporate loans from the usury laws, and nearly all states allow higher interest rate loans for borrowers who could not otherwise obtain funds.

GAMBLING Gambling is the creation of risk for the purpose of assuming it. Traditionally, the states have deemed gambling contracts illegal and thus void. It is sometimes difficult, however, to distinguish a gambling contract from the risk sharing inherent in almost all contracts.

All states have statutes that regulate gambling, and many states allow certain forms of gambling, such as betting on horse races, poker machines, and charity-sponsored bingo. In addition, nearly all states allow state-operated lotteries as well as gambling on Native American reservations. Even in states that permit certain types of gambling, though, courts often find that gambling contracts are illegal.

▶ **Case in Point 9.30** Video poker machines are legal in Louisiana, but their use requires the approval of the state video gaming commission. Gaming Venture, Inc., did not obtain this approval before agreeing with Tastee Restaurant Corporation to install poker machines in some of its restaurants. For this reason, when Tastee allegedly reneged on the deal by refusing to install the machines, a state court held that their agreement was an illegal gambling contract and therefore void.[31] ◀

LICENSING STATUTES All states require members of certain professions—including physicians, lawyers, real estate brokers, accountants, architects, electricians, and stockbrokers—to have licenses. Some licenses are obtained only after extensive schooling and examinations, which indicate to the public that a special skill has been acquired. Others require only that the applicant be of good moral character and pay a fee.

Whether a contract with an unlicensed person is legal and enforceable depends on the purpose of the licensing statute. If the statute's purpose is to protect the public from unauthorized practitioners (such as unlicensed architects, attorneys, and electricians), then a contract involving an unlicensed practitioner is generally illegal and unenforceable. If the statute's purpose is merely to raise government revenues, however, a court may enforce the contract and fine the unlicensed person.

Contracts Contrary to Public Policy

Although contracts involve private parties, some are not enforceable because of the negative impact they would have on society. These contracts are said to be *contrary to public policy.* Examples include a contract to commit an immoral act, such as selling a child, and a contract that prohibits marriage. We look here at certain types of business contracts that are often found to be against public policy.

CONTRACTS IN RESTRAINT OF TRADE Contracts in restraint of trade (anticompetitive agreements) usually adversely affect the public policy that favors competition in the economy. Typically, such contracts also violate one or more federal or state antitrust statutes (see Chapter 27).

An exception is recognized when the restraint is reasonable and is contained in an ancillary (secondary or subordinate) clause in a contract. Restraints called covenants not to compete are often included in contracts for the sale of an ongoing business and employment contracts, as we saw in Case 9.3 presented earlier.

Covenants Not to Compete and the Sale of an Ongoing Business. A covenant not to compete or a restrictive covenant (promise) may be created when a seller of a store agrees not to open a new store in a certain geographic area surrounding the old business. The agreement enables the purchaser to buy, and the seller to sell, the goodwill and reputation of an ongoing business without having to worry that the seller will open a competing business a block away.

31. *Gaming Venture, Inc. v. Tastee Restaurant Corp.*, 996 So.2d 515 (La.App. 5 Cir. 2008).

Provided the restrictive covenant is reasonable and is an ancillary part of the sale of an ongoing business, it is enforceable.

Covenants Not to Compete in Employment Contracts. As explained earlier, agreements not to compete (*noncompete agreements*) are sometimes included in employment contracts. People in middle- or upper-level management positions commonly agree not to work for competitors or not to start competing businesses for a specified period of time after termination of employment. (For an example of such a noncompete clause, see paragraph 9 of the sample contract in the appendix following Chapter 10.)

Such agreements are legal in most states so long as the specified period of time (of restraint) is not excessive in duration and the geographic restriction is reasonable. What constitutes a reasonable time period may be shorter in the online environment than in conventional employment contracts because the restrictions apply worldwide.

To be reasonable, a restriction on competition must protect a legitimate business interest and must not be any greater than necessary to protect that interest. ▶ **Case in Point 9.31** Safety and Compliance Management, Inc. (SCMI), provides drug- and alcohol-testing services. When SCMI hired Angela to pick up test specimens, she signed a covenant not to compete "in any area of SCMI business." Angela later quit SCMI's employ to work in a hospital where she sometimes collected patient specimens. SCMI claimed this was a breach of their noncompete agreement. A court ruled that the covenant was unreasonable because it imposed a greater restriction on Angela than necessary to protect SCMI.[32] ◀

Enforcement Problems. The laws governing the enforceability of covenants not to compete vary significantly from state to state. In some states, including Texas, such a covenant will not be enforced unless the employee has received some benefit in return for signing the noncompete agreement. This is true even if the covenant is reasonable as to time and area. If the employee receives no benefit, the covenant will be deemed void. California prohibits altogether the enforcement of covenants not to compete.

Occasionally, depending on the jurisdiction, courts will *reform* covenants not to compete. If a covenant is found to be unreasonable in time or geographic area, the court may convert the terms into reasonable ones and then enforce the reformed covenant. Such court actions present a problem, though, in that the judge implicitly becomes a party to the contract. Consequently, courts usually resort to contract **reformation** only when necessary to prevent undue burdens or hardships.

UNCONSCIONABLE CONTRACTS OR CLAUSES A court ordinarily does not look at the fairness or equity of a contract. Persons are assumed to be reasonably intelligent, and the courts will not come to their aid just because they have made an unwise or foolish bargain.

In certain circumstances, however, bargains are so oppressive that the courts relieve innocent parties of part or all of their duties. Such bargains are deemed **unconscionable**[33] because they are so unscrupulous or grossly unfair as to be "void of conscience."

The Uniform Commercial Code incorporates the concept of unconscionability in its provisions with regard to the sale and lease of goods.[34] A contract can be unconscionable on either procedural or substantive grounds. *Procedural* unconscionability often involves inconspicuous print, unintelligible language ("legalese"), or the lack of an opportunity to read the contract or ask questions about its meaning. *Substantive* unconscionability occurs when contracts, or portions of contracts, are oppressive or overly harsh. For instance, a contract clause that gives the business entity free access to the courts but requires the other party to arbitrate any dispute with the firm may be unconscionable.

EXCULPATORY CLAUSES Often closely related to the concept of unconscionability are **exculpatory clauses,** which release a party from liability in the event of monetary or physical injury *no matter who is at fault.* Indeed, courts sometimes refuse to enforce such clauses on the ground that they are unconscionable.

Most courts view exculpatory clauses with disfavor. Exculpatory clauses found in rental agreements for commercial property are frequently held to be contrary to public policy, and such clauses are almost always unenforceable in residential property leases. Courts also usually hold that exculpatory clauses are against public policy in the employment context.

Courts do enforce exculpatory clauses if they are reasonable, do not violate public policy, and do not

32. *Stultz v. Safety and Compliance Management, Inc.,* 285 Ga.App.799, 648 S.E.2d 129 (2007).

33. Pronounced un-*kon*-shun-uh-bul.

34. See UCC 2–302 and 2A–719.

protect parties from liability for intentional misconduct. The language used must not be ambiguous, and the parties must have been in relatively equal bargaining positions.

Businesses such as health clubs, racetracks, amusement parks, skiing facilities, horse-rental operations, golf-cart concessions, and skydiving organizations frequently use exculpatory clauses to limit their liability for patrons' injuries. ▶ **Case in Point 9.32** Colleen Holmes participated in the Susan G. Komen Race for the Cure in St. Louis, Missouri. Her signed entry form included an exculpatory clause under which Holmes agreed to release the event sponsors from liability "for any injury or damages I might suffer in connection with my participation in this Event." During the race, Holmes sustained injuries when she tripped and fell over an audiovisual box left on the ground by one of the sponsors. She filed a negligence suit against the sponsor whose employees had placed the box on the ground without barricades or warnings of its presence. The court held that the language used in the exculpatory clause clearly released all sponsors and their agents and employees from liability for future negligence. Holmes could not sue for the injuries she sustained during the race.[35] ◀

SECTION 8
FORM: THE WRITING REQUIREMENT AND ELECTRONIC RECORDS

A contract that is otherwise valid may still be unenforceable if it is not in the proper form. Certain types of contracts are required to be in writing or evidenced by a memorandum or electronic record. The writing requirement does not mean that an agreement must be a formal written contract. An exchange of e-mails that evidences the parties' agreement usually is sufficient, provided that they are "signed," or agreed to, by the party against whom enforcement is sought.

Every state has a statute that stipulates what types of contracts must be in writing. We refer to such a statute as the **Statute of Frauds.** The actual name of the Statute of Frauds is misleading because the statute does not apply to fraud. Rather, it denies enforceability to certain contracts that do not comply with its writing requirements.

35. *Holmes v. Multimedia KSDK, Inc.*, __ S.W.3d __, 2013 WL 150809 (2013).

The following types of contracts are generally required to be in writing or evidenced by a written memorandum or electronic record:

1. Contracts involving interests in land.
2. Contracts that cannot *by their terms* be performed within *one year from the day after* the date of formation.
3. Collateral, or secondary, contracts, such as promises to answer for the debt or duty of another and promises by the administrator or executor of an estate to pay a debt of the estate personally—that is, out of her or his own pocket.
4. Promises made in consideration of marriage.
5. Under the Uniform Commercial Code, contracts for the sale of goods priced at $500 or more (see Chapter 11).

A contract that is oral when it is required to be evidenced by a writing or an electronic record is voidable by a party who does not wish to follow through with the agreement.

SECTION 9
THIRD PARTY RIGHTS

Once it has been determined that a valid and legally enforceable contract exists, attention can turn to the rights and duties of the parties to the contract. A contract is a private agreement between the parties who have entered into it, and traditionally these parties alone have rights and liabilities under the contract. This principle is referred to as **privity of contract** (see Chapter 13). A *third party*—one who is not a direct party to a particular contract—normally does not have rights under that contract.

There are exceptions to the rule of privity of contract. One exception allows a party to a contract to transfer the rights or duties arising from the contract to another person through an *assignment* (of rights) or a *delegation* (of duties). Another exception involves a *third party beneficiary contract*—a contract in which the parties to the contract intend that the contract benefit a third party.

In a bilateral contract, the two parties have corresponding rights and duties. One party has a *right* to require the other to perform some task, and the other has a *duty* to perform it. The transfer of contractual *rights* to a third party is known as an **assignment.** The transfer of contractual *duties* to a third party is known as a **delegation.** An assignment or a delegation occurs *after* the original contract was made.

Assignments

In an assignment, the party assigning the rights to a third party is known as the *assignor,*[36] and the party receiving the rights is the *assignee.*[37] When rights under a contract are assigned unconditionally, the rights of the assignor are extinguished. The third party (the assignee) has a right to demand performance from the other original party to the contract. The assignee takes only those rights that the assignor originally had, however.

Assignments are important because they are used in many types of business financing. Banks, for instance, frequently assign their rights to receive payments under their loan contracts to other firms, which pay for those rights.

Case in Point 9.33 Edward Hosch entered into four loan agreements with Citicapital Commercial Corporation to finance the purchase of heavy construction equipment. A few months later, Citicapital merged into Citicorp Leasing, Inc., which was then renamed GE Capital Commercial, Inc. One year later, GE Capital assigned the loans to Colonial Pacific Leasing Corporation. When Hosch defaulted on the loans, Colonial provided a notice of default and demanded payment. Hosch failed to repay the loans, so Colonial sued to collect the amount due. The trial court granted summary judgment to Colonial and the appellate court affirmed. There was sufficient evidence that the loans had been assigned to Colonial.[38]

As a general rule, all rights can be assigned. Exceptions are made, however, under certain circumstances, including the following:

1. The assignment is prohibited by statute.
2. The contract is personal.
3. The assignment significantly changes the risk or duties of the obligor.
4. The contract prohibits assignment.

Delegations

Just as a party can transfer rights through an assignment, a party can also transfer duties. Duties are not assigned, however, they are *delegated.* The party delegating the duties is the *delegator,* and the party to whom the duties are delegated is the *delegatee.* Normally, a delegation of duties does not relieve the delegator of the obligation to perform in the event that the delegatee fails to do so.

No special form is required to create a valid delegation of duties. As long as the delegator expresses an intention to make the delegation, it is effective. The delegator need not even use the word *delegate.*

As a general rule, any duty can be delegated. There are, however, some exceptions to this rule. Delegation is prohibited in the following circumstances:

1. When special trust has been placed in the *obligor* (the person contractually obligated to perform).
2. When performance depends on the personal skill or talents of the obligor.
3. When performance by a third party will vary materially from that expected by the *obligee* (the person to whom an obligation is owed) under the contract.
4. When the contract expressly prohibits delegation by including an *antidelegation clause.*

If a delegation of duties is enforceable, the obligee must accept performance from the delegatee. As noted, a valid delegation of duties does not relieve the delegator of obligations under the contract. Although there are many exceptions, the general rule today is that the obligee can sue both the delegatee and the delegator if the duties are not performed.

Third Party Beneficiaries

Another exception to the doctrine of privity of contract arises when the contract is intended to benefit a third party. When the original parties to the contract agree that the contract performance should be rendered to or directly benefit a third person, the third person becomes an *intended* **third party beneficiary** of the contract. As the **intended beneficiary** of the contract, the third party has legal rights and can sue the promisor directly for breach of the contract.

Case in Point 9.34 The classic case that gave third party beneficiaries the right to bring a suit directly against a promisor was decided in 1859. The case involved three parties—Holly, Lawrence, and Fox. Holly had borrowed $300 from Lawrence. Shortly thereafter, Holly loaned $300 to Fox, who in return promised Holly that he would pay Holly's debt to Lawrence on the following day. When Lawrence failed to obtain the $300 from Fox, he sued Fox to recover the funds. The court had to decide whether Lawrence could sue Fox directly (rather than suing Holly). The court held that when

36. Pronounced uh-*sye*-nore.
37. Pronounced uh-*sye*-nee.
38. *Hosch v. Colonial Pacific Leasing Corp.,* 313 Ga.App. 873, 722 S.E.2d 778 (2012).

"a promise [is] made for the benefit of another, he for whose benefit it is made may bring an action for its breach."[39] ◀

The law distinguishes between *intended* beneficiaries and *incidental* beneficiaries. An incidental beneficiary is a third person who receives a benefit from a contract even though that person's benefit is not the reason the contract was made. Because the benefit is unintentional, an incidental beneficiary cannot sue to enforce the contract. Only intended beneficiaries acquire legal rights in a contract.

39. *Lawrence v. Fox,* 20 N.Y. 268 (1859).

Reviewing: Formation of Traditional and E-Contracts

Shane Durbin wanted to have a recording studio custom-built in his home. He sent invitations to a number of local contractors to submit bids on the project. Rory Amstel submitted the lowest bid, which was $20,000 less than any of the other bids Durbin received. Durbin called Amstel to ascertain the type and quality of the materials that were included in the bid and to find out if he could substitute a superior brand of acoustic tiles for the same bid price. Amstel said he would have to check into the price difference. The parties also discussed a possible start date for construction. Two weeks later, Durbin changed his mind and decided not to go forward with his plan to build a recording studio. Amstel filed a suit against Durbin for breach of contract. Using the information presented in the chapter, answer the following questions.

1. Did Amstel's bid meet the requirements of an offer? Explain.
2. Was there an acceptance of the offer? Why or why not?
3. How is an offer terminated? Assuming that Durbin did not inform Amstel that he was rejecting the offer, was the offer terminated at any time described here? Explain.

DEBATE THIS . . . *The terms and conditions in click-on agreements are so long and detailed that no one ever reads the agreements. Therefore, the act of clicking on "I agree" is not really an acceptance.*

Terms and Concepts

ExamPrep

Issue Spotters

1. Joli receives a letter from Kerin saying that he has a book at a certain price. Joli signs and returns the letter to Kerin. When Kerin delivers the book, Joli sends it back, claiming that they do not have a contract. Kerin claims they do. What standard determines whether these parties have a contract? **(See page 189.)**
2. Dyna tells Ed that she will pay him $1,000 to set fire to her store so that she can collect under a fire insurance policy. Ed sets fire to the store, but Dyna refuses to pay. Can Ed recover? Why or why not? **(See page 195.)**

- **Check your answers to the Issue Spotters against the answers provided in Appendix E at the end of this text.**

Before the Test

Go to **www.cengagebrain.com**, enter the ISBN 97812851428949, and click on "Find" to locate this textbook's Web site. Then, click on "Access Now" under "Study Tools," and select Chapter 9 at the top. There, you will find an Interactive Quiz that you can take to assess your mastery of the concepts in this chapter, as well as Flashcards and a Glossary of important terms.

Business Scenarios

9–1. Unilateral Contract. Rocky Mountain Races, Inc., sponsors the "Pioneer Trail Ultramarathon" with an advertised first prize of $10,000. The rules require the competitors to run 100 miles from the floor of Blackwater Canyon to the top of Pinnacle Mountain. The rules also provide that Rocky reserves the right to change the terms of the race at any time. Monica enters the race and is declared the winner. Rocky offers her a prize of $1,000 instead of $10,000. Did Rocky and Monica have a contract? Explain. **(See page 192.)**

9–2. Online Acceptance. Anne is a reporter for *Daily Business Journal,* a print publication consulted by investors and other businesspersons. She often uses the Internet to perform research for the articles that she writes for the publication. While visiting the Web site of Cyberspace Investments Corp., Anne reads a pop-up window that states, "Our business newsletter, *E-Commerce Weekly,* is available at a one-year subscription rate of $5 per issue. To subscribe, enter your e-mail address below and click 'SUBSCRIBE.' By subscribing, you agree to the terms of the subscriber's agreement. To read this agreement, click 'AGREEMENT.' " Anne enters her e-mail address, but does not click on "AGREEMENT" to read the terms. Has Anne entered into an enforceable contract to pay for *E-Commerce Weekly?* Explain. **(See page 204.)**

Business Case Problems

9–3. Spotlight on Taco Bell—Implied Contract. Thomas Rinks and Joseph Shields developed Psycho Chihuahua, a caricature of a Chihuahua dog with a "do-not-back-down" attitude. They promoted and marketed the character through their company, Wrench, L.L.C. Ed Alfaro and Rudy Pollak, representatives of Taco Bell Corp., learned of Psycho Chihuahua and met with Rinks and Shields to talk about using the character as a Taco Bell "icon." Wrench sent artwork, merchandise, and marketing ideas to Alfaro, who promoted the character within Taco Bell. Alfaro asked Wrench to propose terms for Taco Bell's use of Psycho Chihuahua. Taco Bell did not accept Wrench's terms, but Alfaro continued to promote the character within the company. Meanwhile, Taco Bell hired a new advertising agency, which proposed an advertising campaign involving a Chihuahua. When Alfaro learned of this proposal, he sent the Psycho Chihuahua materials to the agency. Taco Bell made a Chihuahua the focus of its marketing but paid nothing to Wrench. Wrench filed a suit against Taco Bell in a federal court claiming that it had an implied contract with Taco Bell and that Taco Bell breached that contract. Do these facts satisfy the requirements for an implied contract? Why or why not? [*Wrench, L.L.C. v. Taco Bell Corp.,* 256 F.3d 446 (6th Cir. 2001), *cert.* denied, 534 U.S. 1114, 122 S.Ct. 921, 151 L.Ed.2d 805 (2002)] **(See page 193.)**

9–4. BUSINESS CASE PROBLEM WITH SAMPLE ANSWER: Offer and Acceptance.

*While gambling at Prairie Meadows Casino, Troy Blackford became angry and smashed a slot machine. He was banned from the premises. Despite the ban, he later gambled at the casino and won $9,387. When he tried to collect his winnings, the casino refused to pay. Blackford filed a suit for breach of contract, arguing that he and the casino had a contract because he had accepted its offer to gamble. Did the casino and Blackford have a contract? Discuss. [*Blackford v. Prairie Meadows Racetrack and Casino, *778 N.W.2d 184 (Sup.Ct. Iowa 2010)]* **(See page 195.)**

- **For a sample answer to Problem 9–4, go to Appendix F at the end of this text.**

9–5. Consideration. On Brenda Sniezek's first day of work for the Kansas City Chiefs Football Club, she signed a document that purported to compel arbitration of any disputes that she might have with the Chiefs. In the document, Sniezek agreed to comply at all times with and be bound by the constitution and bylaws of the National Football League (NFL). She agreed to refer all disputes to the NFL Commissioner for a binding decision. On the Commissioner's decision, she agreed to release the Chiefs and others from any related claims. Nowhere in the document did the Chiefs agree to do anything. Was there consideration for the arbitration provision? Explain. [*Sniezek v. Kansas City Chiefs Football Club,* __ S.W.3d __, 2013 WL 661632 (Mo.App. W.D. 2013)] **(See page 207.)**

9–6. Implied Contracts. Ralph Ramsey insured his car with Allstate Insurance Co. He also owned a house on which he maintained a homeowner's insurance policy with Allstate. Bank of America had a mortgage on the house and paid the insurance premiums on the homeowner's policy from Ralph's account. After Ralph died, Allstate canceled the car insurance. Ralph's son Douglas inherited the house. The bank continued to pay the premiums on the homeowner's policy, but from Douglas's account, and Allstate continued to renew the insurance. When a fire destroyed the house, Allstate denied coverage, however, claiming that the policy was still in Ralph's name. Douglas filed a suit in a federal district court against the insurer. Was Allstate liable under the homeowner's policy? Explain. [*Ramsey v. Allstate Insurance Co.,* 2013 WL 467327 (6th Cir. 2013)] **(See page 193.)**

9–7. Acceptance. Judy Olsen, Kristy Johnston, and their mother, Joyce Johnston, owned seventy-eight acres of real property on Eagle Creek in Meagher County, Montana. When Joyce died, she left her interest in the property to Kristy. Kristy wrote to Judy, offering to buy Judy's interest or to sell her own interest to Judy. The letter said to "please respond to Bruce Townsend." In a letter to Kristy—not to Bruce—Judy accepted Kristy's offer to sell her interest. By that time, however, Kristy had made the same offer to sell her interest to their brother Dave, and he had accepted. Did Judy and Kristy have an enforceable binding contract? Or did Kristy's offer specifying one exclusive mode of acceptance mean that Judy's reply was not effective? Discuss. [*Olsen v. Johnston,* 368 Mont. 347, __ P.3d __, (2013)] **(See page 200.)**

9–8. Minors. D.V.G. (a minor) was injured in a one-car auto accident in Hoover, Alabama. The vehicle was covered by an insurance policy issued by Nationwide Mutual Insurance Co. Stan Brobston, D.V.G.'s attorney, accepted Nationwide's offer of $50,000 on D.V.G.'s behalf. Before the settlement could be submitted to an Alabama state court for approval, D.V.G. died from injuries received in a second, unrelated auto accident. Nationwide argued that it was not bound to the settlement because a minor lacks the capacity to contract and so cannot enter into a binding settlement without court approval. Should Nationwide be bound to the settlement? Why or why not? [*Nationwide Mutual Insurance Co. v. Wood,* 402 So.3d 580 (Ala. 2013)] **(See page 210.)**

9–9. A QUESTION OF ETHICS: Covenants Not to Compete.

Brendan Coleman created and marketed Clinex, a software billing program. Later, Retina Consultants, P.C., a medical practice, hired Coleman as a software engineer. Together, they modified the Clinex program to create Clinex-RE. Coleman signed an agreement to the effect that he owned Clinex, Retina owned Clinex-RE, and he would not market Clinex in competition with Clinex-RE. After Coleman quit Retina, he withdrew funds from a Retina bank account and marketed both forms of the software to other medical practices. At trial, the court entered a judgment enjoining (preventing) Coleman from marketing the software that was in competition with the software he had developed for Retina Consultants. The court also obligated Coleman to return the funds taken from the company's bank account. Coleman appealed. [Coleman v. Retina Consultants, P.C., *286 Ga. 317, 687 S.E.2d 457 (2009)*] **(See page 209.)**

(a) Should the court uphold the noncompete clause? If so, why? If not, why not?

(b) Should the court require Coleman to return the funds he withdrew from the company's accounts? Discuss fully.

Legal Reasoning Group Activity

9–10. E-Contracts. To download a specific application (app) to your smartphone or tablet device, usually you have to check a box indicating that you agree to the company's terms and conditions. Most individuals do so without ever reading those terms and conditions. Print out a specific set of terms and conditions from a downloaded app to use in this assignment. **(See page 203.)**

(a) One group will determine which of these terms and conditions are favorable to the company.

(b) Another group will determine which of these terms and conditions conceivably will be favorable to the individual.

(c) A third group will determine which terms and conditions, on net, favor the company too much.

CHAPTER 10
CONTRACT PERFORMANCE, BREACH, AND REMEDIES

Just as rules are necessary to determine when a legally enforceable contract exists, so also are they required to determine when one of the parties can justifiably say, "I have fully performed, so I am now discharged from my obligations under this contract." The legal environment of business requires the identification of some point at which the parties can reasonably know that their duties have ended.

Additionally, the parties to a contract need to know what remedies are available to them if one party decides that he or she does not want to, or cannot, perform as promised. A *remedy* is the relief provided for an innocent party when the other party has breached the contract. Remedies may include monetary damages, rescission and restitution, specific performance, and reformation.

In this chapter, we first look at several defenses to performance of a contract based on a lack of voluntary consent. Next, we examine performance obligations, including conditions of performance, the degree of performance required, and what constitutes a breach of contract. We also discuss some other ways in which a contract can be discharged (or terminated). Finally, we outline the various remedies available to the nonbreaching party.

SECTION 1
VOLUNTARY CONSENT

An otherwise valid contract may still be unenforceable if the parties have not genuinely agreed to its terms. As mentioned in Chapter 9, a lack of *voluntary consent* (assent) can be used as a defense to the contract's enforceability.

Voluntary consent may be lacking because of a mistake, misrepresentation, undue influence, or duress—in other words, because there is no true "meeting of the minds." Generally, a party who demonstrates that he or she did not truly agree to the terms of a contract has a choice. The party can choose either to carry out the contract or to rescind (cancel) it and thus avoid the entire transaction.

Mistakes

We all make mistakes, so it is not surprising that mistakes are made when contracts are formed. In certain circumstances, contract law allows a contract to be avoided on the basis of mistake. It is important to distinguish between *mistakes of fact* and *mistakes of value or quality.*

Only a mistake of fact makes a contract voidable. Also, the mistake must involve some *material fact*—a fact that a reasonable person would consider important when determining his or her course of action.

▶ **Example 10.1** Sung buys a violin from Bev for $250. Although the violin is very old, neither party believes that it is valuable. Later, however, an antiques dealer informs the parties that the violin is rare and worth thousands of dollars. Here, both parties were mistaken, but the mistake is a mistake of *value* rather than a mistake of *fact* that warrants contract rescission. Therefore, Bev cannot rescind the contract. ◀

Mistakes of fact occur in two forms—*bilateral* and *unilateral,* as shown in Exhibit 10–1 on the following page. A unilateral mistake is made by only *one* of the parties. A bilateral, or mutual, mistake is made by *both* of the contracting parties. We look next at these two types of mistakes.

UNILATERAL MISTAKES OF FACT A **unilateral mistake** is made by only one of the parties. In general, a unilateral mistake does not give the mistaken party any right to relief from the contract. Normally, the contract is enforceable.

▶ **Example 10.2** Elena intends to sell her jet ski for $2,500. When she learns that Chin is interested in buying a used jet ski, she sends him an e-mail offering to sell the jet ski to him. When typing the e-mail, however, she mistakenly keys in the price of $1,500. Chin immediately sends Elena an e-mail reply accepting her

EXHIBIT 10–1 Mistakes of Fact

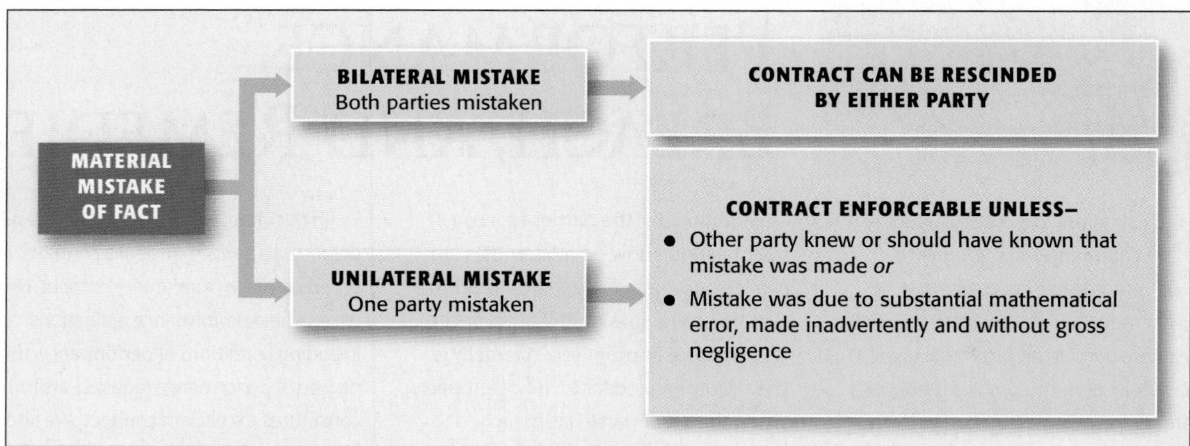

offer. Even though Elena intended to sell her personal jet ski for $2,500, she has made a unilateral mistake and is bound by the contract to sell it to Chin for $1,500. ◀

This general rule has at least two exceptions.[1] The contract may be enforceable if:

1. The *other* party to the contract knows or should have known that a mistake of fact was made.
2. The error was due to a substantial mathematical mistake in addition, subtraction, division, or multiplication and was made inadvertently and without gross (extreme) negligence. If, for instance, a contractor's bid was significantly low because he or she made a mistake in addition when totaling the estimated costs, any contract resulting from the bid normally may be rescinded.

Of course, in both situations, the mistake must still involve some material fact.

BILATERAL (MUTUAL) MISTAKES OF FACT A **bilateral mistake** is a "mutual misunderstanding concerning a basic assumption on which the contract was made."[2] When both parties are mistaken about the same material fact, the contract can be rescinded by either party.

A word or term in a contract may be subject to more than one reasonable interpretation. If the parties to the contract attach materially different meanings to the term, a court may allow the contract to be rescinded because there has been no true "meeting of the minds."

▶ **Case in Point 10.3** L&H Construction Company contracted with Circle Redmont, Inc., to make a staircase and flooring system. Circle Redmont's original proposal was to "engineer, fabricate, and install" the system. Installation was later cut from the deal. In the final agreement, payment was due on Circle Redmont's "supervision" instead of "completion" of installation. But the final contract still included the wording, "engineer, fabricate, and install." Later, Circle Redmont claimed that this wording was a mistake. L&H insisted that installation was included and filed a suit against Circle Redmont.

The court held that the use of the word *install* in the contract was a mutual mistake. Circle Redmont's witnesses stated that the parties had agreed that Circle Redmont would only supervise the installation, not perform it. The court found the witnesses were credible, and ruled that installation was not included.[3] ◀

MISTAKES OF VALUE If a mistake concerns the future market value or quality of the object of the contract, the mistake is one of *value*, and the contract normally is enforceable. The reason for this is that value is variable. Depending on the time, place, and other circumstances, the same item may be worth considerably different amounts.

When parties form a contract, their agreement establishes the value of the object of their transaction—for the moment. Each party is considered to have assumed the risk that the value will change in the future or prove to be different from what he or she thought. Without this rule, almost any party who did not receive what she or he considered a fair bargain could argue mistake.

1. *Restatement (Second) of Contracts,* Section 153.
2. *Restatement (Second) of Contracts,* Section 152.
3. *L&H Construction Co. v. Circle Redmont, Inc.,* 55 So.3d 630 (Fla.App. 2011).

Fraudulent Misrepresentation

Although fraud is a tort (see Chapter 12), it also affects the authenticity of the innocent party's consent to the contract. When an innocent party is fraudulently induced to enter into a contract, the contract normally can be avoided because that party has not *voluntarily* consented to its terms. Ordinarily, the innocent party can either rescind the contract and be restored to her or his original position or enforce the contract and seek damages for any harms resulting from the fraud.

Generally, fraudulent misrepresentation refers only to misrepresentation that is consciously false and is intended to mislead another. The person making the fraudulent misrepresentation knows or believes that the assertion is false or knows that she or he does not have a basis (stated or implied) for the assertion. Typically, fraudulent misrepresentation consists of the following elements:

1. A misrepresentation of a material fact must occur.
2. There must be an intent to deceive.
3. The innocent party must justifiably rely on the misrepresentation.
4. To collect damages, a party must have been harmed as a result of the misrepresentation.

MISREPRESENTATION BY WORDS OR ACTIONS The misrepresentation can occur by words or actions. For instance, the statement "This sculpture was created by Michelangelo" is a misrepresentation of fact if another artist sculpted the statue. Similarly, if a customer asks to see only paintings by the decorative artist Paul Wright and the gallery owner immediately leads the customer over to paintings that were not done by Wright, the owner's actions can be a misrepresentation.

Misrepresentation also occurs when a party takes specific action to conceal a fact that is material to the contract. ▶ **Case in Point 10.4** Actor Tom Selleck contracted to purchase a horse named Zorro for his daughter from Dolores Cuenca. Cuenca acted as though Zorro was fit to ride in competitions, when in reality the horse suffered from a medical condition. Selleck filed a lawsuit against Cuenca for wrongfully concealing the horse's condition and won. A jury awarded Selleck more than $187,000 for Cuenca's misrepresentation by conduct.[4] ◀

INJURY TO THE INNOCENT PARTY Most courts do not require a showing of injury when the action is to rescind the contract. These courts hold that because rescission returns the parties to the positions they held before the contract was made, a showing of injury to the innocent party is unnecessary.

In contrast, to recover damages caused by fraud, proof of harm is universally required. The measure of damages is ordinarily equal to the property's value had it been delivered as represented, less the actual price paid for the property. (What if someone pretends to be someone else online? Can the victim of the hoax prove injury sufficient to recover for fraudulent misrepresentation? See this chapter's *Insight into Social Media* feature on the following page for a discussion of this topic.)

Undue Influence

Undue influence arises from relationships in which one party can greatly influence another party, thus overcoming that party's free will. A contract entered into under excessive or undue influence lacks voluntary consent and is therefore voidable.

In various types of relationships, one party may have the opportunity to dominate and unfairly influence another party. Minors and elderly people, for instance, are often under the influence of guardians (persons who are legally responsible for another). If a guardian induces a young or elderly ward (a person whom the guardian looks after) to enter into a contract that benefits the guardian, the guardian may have exerted undue influence.

Undue influence can arise from a number of fiduciary relationships, such as physician-patient, parent-child, husband-wife, or guardian-ward situations. When a contract enriches the dominant party in a fiduciary relationship (such as an attorney), the court will often *presume* that the contract was made under undue influence.

The essential feature of undue influence is that the party being taken advantage of does not, in reality, exercise free will in entering into a contract. It is not enough that a person is elderly or suffers from some physical or mental impairment. There must be clear and convincing evidence that the person did not act out of her or his free will. Similarly, the existence of a fiduciary relationship alone is insufficient to prove undue influence.

Duress

Agreement to the terms of a contract is not voluntary if one of the parties is *forced* into the agreement. The use of threats to force a party to enter into a contract is referred to as *duress*. In addition, blackmail or

4. *Selleck v. Cuenca,* Case No. GIN056909, North County of San Diego, California, decided September 9, 2009.

INSIGHT INTO SOCIAL MEDIA

"Catfishing": Is That Online "Friend" Who You Think It Is?

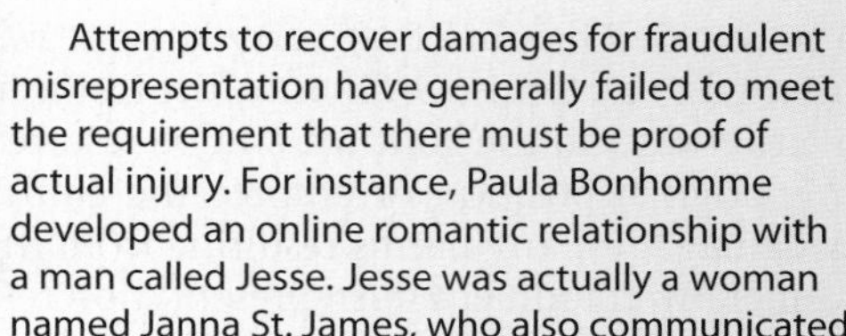

When you are communicating with a person you have met only online, how do you know that person is who she or he purports to be? After all, the person could turn out to be a "catfish." The term comes from *Catfish,* a 2010 film about a fake online persona.

According to a story told in the film, when live cod were shipped long distances, they were inactive and their flesh became mushy. When catfish were added to the tanks, the cod swam around and stayed in good condition. At the end of the film, a character says of the creator of the fake persona, "There are those people who are catfish in life. And they keep you on your toes. They keep you guessing, they keep you thinking, they keep you fresh."

Catfishing Makes National Headlines

Catfishing made headlines in 2012 when a popular Notre Dame football star supposedly fell victim to it. Linebacker Manti Te'o said that his girlfriend Lennay Kekua, a student at Stanford, had died of leukemia after a near-fatal car accident. Although Kekua had Facebook and Twitter accounts and Te'o had communicated with her online and by telephone for several years, reporters could find no evidence of her existence. Te'o later claimed that he had been a victim of a catfishing hoax. Others suggested that his friends created the persona and her tragic death to provide an inspirational story what would increase Te'o's chances of winning the Heisman trophy.

Is Online Fraudulent Misrepresentation Actionable?

Some victims of catfishing have turned to the courts, but they have had little success. A few have attempted to sue Internet service providers for allowing fake personas, but the courts have generally dismissed these suits.[a] Laws in some states make it a crime to impersonate someone online, but these laws generally do not apply to those who create totally fake personas.

Attempts to recover damages for fraudulent misrepresentation have generally failed to meet the requirement that there must be proof of actual injury. For instance, Paula Bonhomme developed an online romantic relationship with a man called Jesse. Jesse was actually a woman named Janna St. James, who also communicated with Bonhomme using her own name and pretending to be a friend of Jesse's.

St. James created a host of fictional characters, including an ex-wife and a son for Jesse. Bonhomme in turn sent gifts totaling more than $10,000 to Jesse and the other characters. After being told by St. James that Jesse had attempted suicide, Bonhomme suffered such emotional distress that she incurred more than $5,000 in bills for a therapist. Eventually, she was told that Jesse had died of liver cancer. When Bonhomme finally learned the truth, she suffered additional emotional distress, resulting in more expenses for a therapist and lost earnings due to her "affected mental state."

Although Bonhomme had incurred considerable expenses, the Illinois Supreme Court ruled that she could not bring a suit for fraudulent misrepresentation. The case involved only a "purely personal relationship" without any "commercial, transactional, or regulatory component." Bonhomme and St. James "were not engaged in any kind of business dealings or bargaining." Therefore, the truth of representations "made in the context of purely private personal relationships is simply not something the state regulates or in which the state possesses any kind of valid public policy interest."[b]

LEGAL CRITICAL THINKING

INSIGHT INTO THE LEGAL ENVIRONMENT

So far, victims of catfishing have had little success in the courts. Under what circumstances might a person be able to collect damages for fraudulent misrepresentation involving online impersonation?

a. See, for example, *Robinson v. Match.com, LLC,* 2012 WL 3263992 (N.D.Tex. 2012).

b. *Bonhomme v. St. James,* 970 N.E.2d 1 (Ill. 2012).

extortion to induce consent to a contract constitutes duress. Duress is both a defense to the enforcement of a contract and a ground for the rescission of a contract.

To establish duress, there must be proof of a threat to do something that the threatening party has no right to do. Generally, for duress to occur, the threatened act must be wrongful or illegal, and it must render the person incapable of exercising free will. A threat to exercise a legal right, such as the right to sue someone, ordinarily does not constitute duress.

SECTION 2

PERFORMANCE AND DISCHARGE

The most common way to **discharge,** or terminate, one's contractual duties is by the **performance** of those duties. For example, a buyer and seller enter into an agreement via e-mail for the sale of a 2014 Lexus for $42,000. This contract will be discharged by performance when the buyer pays $42,000 to the seller and the seller transfers possession of the Lexus to the buyer.

The duty to perform under any contract (including e-contracts) may be *conditioned* on the occurrence or nonoccurrence of a certain event, or the duty may be *absolute.* In this section, we look at conditions of performance and the degree of performance required. We then examine some other ways in which a contract can be discharged, including discharge by agreement of the parties and discharge by operation of law.

Conditions of Performance

In most contracts, promises of performance are not expressly conditioned or qualified. Instead, they are *absolute promises.* They must be performed, or the parties promising the acts will be in breach of contract. ▶ **Example 10.5** Paloma Enterprises contracts to sell a truckload of organic produce to Tran for $10,000. The parties' promises are unconditional: Paloma will deliver the produce to Tran, and Tran will pay $10,000 to Paloma. The payment does not have to be made if the produce is not delivered. ◀

In some situations, however, performance is contingent on the occurrence or nonoccurrence of a certain event. A **condition** is a qualification in a contract based on a possible future event. The occurrence or nonoccurrence of the event will trigger the performance of a legal obligation or terminate an existing obligation under a contract.[5] If the condition is not satisfied, the obligations of the parties are discharged.

A condition that must be fulfilled before a party's performance can be required is called a **condition precedent.** The condition precedes the absolute duty to perform. Life insurance contracts frequently specify that certain conditions, such as passing a physical examination, must be met before the insurance company will be obligated to perform under the contract.

In addition, many contracts are conditioned on an independent appraisal of value. ▶ **Example 10.6** Restoration Motors offers to buy Charlie's 1960 Cadillac limousine only if an expert appraiser estimates that it can be restored for less than a certain price. Thus, the parties' obligations are conditioned on the outcome of the appraisal. If the condition is not satisfied—that is, if the appraiser deems the cost to be above that price—their obligations are discharged. ◀

Discharge by Performance

The great majority of contracts are discharged by performance. The contract comes to an end when both parties fulfill their respective duties by performing the acts they have promised.

Performance can also be accomplished by *tender.* **Tender** is an unconditional offer to perform by a person who is ready, willing, and able to do so. Therefore, a seller who places goods at the disposal of a buyer has tendered delivery and can demand payment. A buyer who offers to pay for goods has tendered payment and can demand delivery of the goods.

Once performance has been tendered, the party making the tender has done everything possible to carry out the terms of the contract. If the other party then refuses to perform, the party making the tender can sue for breach of contract. There are two basic types of performance—*complete performance* and *substantial performance.*

COMPLETE PERFORMANCE When a party performs exactly as agreed, there is no question as to whether the contract has been performed. When a party's performance is perfect, it is said to be complete. Normally, conditions expressly stated in a contract must fully occur in all respects for complete performance (strict performance) of the contract to take place. Any deviation breaches the contract and discharges the other party's obligations to perform.

Most construction contracts, for instance, require the builder to meet certain specifications. If the specifications are conditions, complete performance is required to avoid material breach (*material breach* will be discussed shortly). If the conditions are met, the other party to the contract must then fulfill her or his obligation to pay the builder.

If the parties to the contract did not expressly make the specifications a condition, however, and the

5. The *Restatement (Second) of Contracts,* Section 224, defines a condition as "an event, not certain to occur, which must occur, unless its nonoccurrence is excused, before performance under a contract becomes due."

builder fails to meet the specifications, performance is not complete. What effect does such a failure have on the other party's obligation to pay? The answer is part of the doctrine of *substantial performance.*

SUBSTANTIAL PERFORMANCE A party who in good faith performs substantially all of the terms of a contract can enforce the contract against the other party under the doctrine of substantial performance. The basic requirements for performance to qualify as substantial performance are as follows:

1. The party must have performed in good faith. Intentional failure to comply with the contract terms is a breach of the contract.
2. The performance must not vary greatly from the performance promised in the contract. An omission, variance, or defect in performance is considered minor if it can easily be remedied by compensation (monetary damages).
3. The performance must create substantially the same benefits as those promised in the contract.

Courts decide whether the performance was substantial on a case-by-case basis, examining all of the facts of the particular situation. ▶ **Case in Point 10.7** Wisconsin Electric Power Company (WEPCO) contracted with Union Pacific Railroad to transport coal to WEPCO from mines in Colorado. The contract required WEPCO to notify Union Pacific monthly of how many tons of coal (below a specified maximum) it wanted to have shipped the next month. Union Pacific was to make "good faith reasonable efforts" to meet the schedule.

The contract also required WEPCO to supply the railcars. When WEPCO did not supply the railcars, Union Pacific used its own railcars and delivered 84 percent of the requested coal. In this situation, a federal court held that the delivery of 84 percent of the contracted amount constituted substantial performance.[6] ◀

Effect on Duty to Perform. If performance is substantial, the other party's duty to perform remains absolute (except that the party can sue for damages due to the minor deviations). In other words, the parties must continue performing under the contract (for instance, making payment to the party who substantially performed). If performance is not substantial, there is a *material breach* (to be discussed shortly), and the nonbreaching party is excused from further performance.

Measure of Damages. Because substantial performance is not perfect, the other party is entitled to damages to compensate for the failure to comply with the contract. The measure of the damages is the cost to bring the object of the contract into compliance with its terms, if that cost is reasonable under the circumstances.

If the cost is unreasonable, the measure of damages is the difference in value between the performance that was rendered and the performance that would have been rendered if the contract had been performed completely.

The following case is a classic illustration that there is no exact formula for deciding when a contract has been substantially performed.

6. *Wisconsin Electric Power Co. v. Union Pacific Railroad Co.,* 557 F.3d 504 (7th Cir. 2009).

CLASSIC CASE 10.1

Jacob & Youngs v. Kent

Court of Appeals of New York, 230 N.Y. 239, 129 N.E. 889 (1921).

BACKGROUND AND FACTS The plaintiff, Jacob & Youngs, Inc., was a builder that had contracted with George Kent to construct a country residence for him. A specification in the building contract required that "all wrought-iron pipe must be well galvanized, lap welded pipe of the grade known as 'standard pipe' of Reading manufacture." Jacob & Youngs installed substantially similar pipe that was not of Reading manufacture. When Kent became aware of the difference, he ordered the builder to remove all of the plumbing and replace it with the Reading type. To do so would have required removing finished walls that encased the plumbing—an expensive and difficult task. The builder explained that the plumbing was of the same quality, appearance, value, and cost as Reading pipe. When Kent refused to pay the $3,483.46 still owed for the work, Jacob & Youngs sued to compel payment. The trial court ruled in favor of Kent. The plaintiff appealed, and the appellate court reversed the trial court's decision. Kent then appealed to the Court of Appeals of New York, the state's highest court.

CASE 10.1 CONTINUED

IN THE LANGUAGE OF THE COURT
CARDOZO, Justice.

* * * *

* * * The courts never say that one who makes a contract fills the measure of his duty by less than full performance. They do say, however, that *an omission, both trivial and innocent, will sometimes be atoned [compensated] for by allowance of the resulting damage, and will not always be the breach of a condition[.]* [Emphasis added.]

* * * Where the line is to be drawn between the important and the trivial cannot be settled by a formula. * * * *We must weigh the purpose to be served, the desire to be gratified, the excuse for deviation from the letter, [and] the cruelty of enforced adherence. Then only can we tell whether literal fulfillment is to be implied by law as a condition.* [Emphasis added.]

* * * We think the measure of the allowance is not the cost of replacement, which would be great, but the difference in value, which would be either nominal or nothing. * * * The owner is entitled to the money which will permit him to complete, unless the cost of completion is grossly and unfairly out of proportion to the good to be attained.

DECISION AND REMEDY *New York's highest court affirmed the appellate court's decision, holding that Jacob & Youngs had substantially performed the contract.*

IMPACT OF THIS CASE ON TODAY'S LAW *At the time of the* Jacob & Youngs *case, some courts did not apply the doctrine of substantial performance to disputes involving breaches of contract. This landmark decision contributed to a developing trend toward equity and fairness in those circumstances. Today, an unintentional and trivial deviation from the terms of a contract will not prevent its enforcement but will permit an adjustment in the value of its performance.*

THE LEGAL ENVIRONMENT DIMENSION *The New York Court of Appeals found that Jacob & Youngs had substantially performed the contract. To what, if any, remedy was Kent entitled?*

PERFORMANCE TO THE SATISFACTION OF ANOTHER Contracts often state that completed work must personally satisfy one of the parties or a third person. When the subject matter of the contract is *personal,* the obligation is conditional, and performance must actually satisfy the party specified in the contract. For instance, contracts for portraits, works of art, and tailoring are considered personal because they involve matters of personal taste. Therefore, only the personal satisfaction of the party fulfills the condition—unless a court finds that the party is expressing dissatisfaction simply to avoid payment or otherwise is not acting in good faith.

Most other contracts need to be performed only to the satisfaction of a reasonable person unless they *expressly state otherwise.* When the subject matter of the contract is mechanical, courts are more likely to find that the performing party has performed satisfactorily if a reasonable person would be satisfied with what was done. ▶ **Example 10.8** Mason signs a contract with Jen to mount a new heat pump on a concrete platform to her satisfaction. Such a contract normally need only be performed to the satisfaction of a reasonable person. ◀

MATERIAL BREACH OF CONTRACT A **breach of contract** is the nonperformance of a contractual duty. The breach is *material* when performance is not at least substantial.[7] As mentioned earlier, when there is a material breach, the nonbreaching party is excused from the performance of contractual duties. That party can also sue the breaching party for damages resulting from the breach.

▶ **Example 10.9** When country singer Garth Brooks's mother died, he donated $500,000 to a hospital in his hometown to build a new women's health center named after his mother. After several years passed and the health center was not built, Brooks demanded a refund. The hospital refused, claiming that while it had promised to honor his mother in some way, it did not promise to build a women's health center. Brooks sued for breach of contract. A jury determined that the hospital's failure to build a women's health center and name it after Brooks's mother was a material breach of the contract. The jury awarded Brooks damages. ◀

7. *Restatement (Second) of Contracts,* Section 241.

Material versus Minor Breach. If the breach is *minor* (not material), the nonbreaching party's duty to perform can sometimes be suspended until the breach has been remedied, but the duty to perform is not entirely excused. Once the minor breach has been cured, the nonbreaching party must resume performance of the contractual obligations.

Both parties in the following case were arguably in breach of their contract. Which party's breach was material?

CASE ANALYSIS

Case 10.2 Kohel v. Bergen Auto Enterprises, L.L.C.

Superior Court of New Jersey, Appellate Division, 2013 WL 439970 (2013).

IN THE LANGUAGE OF THE COURT

PER CURIAM.

* * * *

On May 24, 2010, plaintiffs Marc and Bree Kohel entered into a sales contract with defendant Bergen Auto Enterprises, L.L.C. d/b/a Wayne Mazda Inc. (Wayne Mazda), for the purchase of a used 2009 Mazda. Plaintiffs agreed to pay $26,430.22 for the Mazda and were credited $7,000 as a trade-in, for their 2005 Nissan Altima. As plaintiffs still owed $8,118.28 on the Nissan, Wayne Mazda assessed plaintiffs a net pay-off of this amount and agreed to remit the balance due to satisfy the outstanding lien.

Plaintiffs took possession of the Mazda with temporary plates and left the Nissan with defendant. A few days later, a representative of defendant advised plaintiffs that the Nissan's vehicle identification tag (VIN tag) was missing. The representative claimed it was unable to sell the car and offered to rescind the transaction. Plaintiffs refused.

When the temporary plates on the Mazda expired on June 24, 2010, defendant refused to provide plaintiffs with the permanent plates they had paid for. In addition, defendant refused to pay off plaintiffs' outstanding loan on the Nissan, as they had agreed. As a result, plaintiffs were required to continue to make monthly payments on both the Nissan and the Mazda.

On July 28, 2010, plaintiffs filed a complaint in [a New Jersey state court] against Wayne Mazda * * * . Plaintiffs alleged breach of contract.

* * * *

On February 2, 2012, the court rendered an oral decision finding that there was a breach of contract by Wayne Mazda * * * . On February 17, 2012, the court entered judgment in the amount of $5,405.17 in favor of plaintiffs against Wayne Mazda. [The defendant appealed to a state intermediate appellate court.]

* * * *

Defendant argues that plaintiffs' delivery of the Nissan without a VIN tag was, itself, a breach of the contract of sale and precludes a finding that defendant breached the contract. However, the trial court found that plaintiffs were not aware that the Nissan lacked a VIN tag when they offered it in trade. Moreover, defendant's representatives examined the car twice before accepting it in trade and did not notice the missing VIN until they took the car to an auction where they tried to sell it. *There is a material distinction in plaintiffs' conduct, which the court found unintentional, and defendant's refusal to release the permanent plates for which the plaintiffs had paid, an action the court concluded was done to maintain "leverage."* [Emphasis added.]

* * * The evidence * * * indicated that * * * the problem with the missing VIN tag could be rectified. Marc Kohel applied and paid for a replacement VIN tag at Meadowlands [Nissan for $35.31]. While he initially made some calls to Meadowlands, he did not follow up in obtaining the VIN tag after the personnel at Wayne Mazda began refusing to take his calls.

* * * The court concluded that "Wayne Mazda didn't handle this as—as adroitly [skillfully] as they could * * * ." Kevin DiPiano, identified in the complaint as the owner and/or CEO of Wayne Mazda, would not even take [the plaintiffs'] calls to discuss this matter. The court found:

> Mr. DiPiano could have been a better businessman, could have been a little bit more compassionate or at least responsive, you know? He was not. He acted like he didn't care. That obviously went a long way to infuriate the plaintiffs. I don't blame them for being infuriated.

* * * *

* * * Here, plaintiffs attempted to remedy the VIN tag issue but this resolution was frustrated by defendant's unreasonable conduct. We thus reject defendant's argument that plaintiffs' failure to obtain the replacement VIN tag amounted to a repudiation of the contract.

* * * *

Affirmed.

CASE 10.2 CONTINUED

LEGAL REASONING QUESTIONS

1. What is a *material* breach of contract? When a material breach occurs, what are the nonbreaching party's options?
2. What is a *minor* breach of contract? When a minor breach occurs, is the nonbreaching party excused from performance? Explain.
3. In this case, what were the defendant's main arguments that the plaintiffs should not have been granted relief for Wayne Mazda's breach?
4. Was there a difference in the degree to which the plaintiffs and the defendant failed to perform the contract? Explain. Which party was in material breach?

Discharges Nonbreaching Party from Further Performance. Any breach entitles the nonbreaching party to sue for damages, but only a material breach discharges the nonbreaching party from the contract. The policy underlying these rules allows a contract to go forward when only minor problems occur but allows it to be terminated if major difficulties arise.

Case in Point 10.10 Su Yong Kim sold an apartment building with substandard plumbing that violated the city's housing code. The contract stated that Kim would have the plumbing fixed (brought up to code) within eight months. A year later, Kim still had not made the necessary repairs, so the buyers stopped making the payments due under the contract. A court found that Kim's failure to make the required repairs was a material breach because it defeated the purpose of the contract—to lease the building to tenants. Because Kim's breach was material, the buyers were no longer obligated to continue making payments under the contract.[8]

ANTICIPATORY REPUDIATION Before either party to a contract has a duty to perform, one of the parties may refuse to carry out his or her contractual obligations. This is called **anticipatory repudiation** of the contract.

When an anticipatory repudiation occurs, it is treated as a material breach of the contract, and the nonbreaching party is permitted to bring an action for damages immediately. The nonbreaching party can file suit even though the scheduled time for performance under the contract may still be in the future. Until the nonbreaching party treats an early repudiation as a breach, however, the repudiating party can retract her or his anticipatory repudiation by proper notice and restore the parties to their original obligations.[9]

An anticipatory repudiation is treated as a present, material breach for two reasons. First, the nonbreaching party should not be required to remain ready and willing to perform when the other party has already repudiated the contract. Second, the nonbreaching party should have the opportunity to seek a similar contract elsewhere and may have a duty to do so to minimize his or her loss.

TIME FOR PERFORMANCE If no time for performance is stated in the contract, a *reasonable time* is implied.[10] If a specific time is stated, the parties must usually perform by that time. Unless time is expressly stated to be vital, though, a delay in performance will not destroy the performing party's right to payment.

When time is expressly stated to be "of the essence" or vital, the parties normally must perform within the stated time period because the time element becomes a condition. Even when the contract states that time is of the essence, a court may find that a party who fails to complain about the other party's delay has waived the breach of the time provision.

Discharge by Agreement

Any contract can be discharged by agreement of the parties. The agreement can be contained in the original contract, or the parties can form a new contract for the express purpose of discharging the original contract.

DISCHARGE BY MUTUAL RESCISSION As mentioned in Chapter 9, *rescission* is the process by which a

8. *Kim v. Park,* 192 Or.App. 365, 86 P.3d 63 (2004).

9. See Uniform Commercial Code (UCC) 2–611.

10. See UCC 2–204.

contract is canceled or terminated and the parties are returned to the positions they occupied prior to forming it. For **mutual rescission** to take place, the parties must make another agreement that also satisfies the legal requirements for a contract. There must be an *offer*, an *acceptance*, and *consideration*. Ordinarily, if the parties agree to rescind the original contract, their promises not to perform the acts stipulated in the original contract will be legal consideration for the second contract (the rescission).

Agreements to rescind most executory contracts (in which neither party has performed) are enforceable, even if the agreement is made orally and even if the original agreement was in writing. Under the Uniform Commercial Code (UCC), however, agreements to rescind a sales contract must be in writing (or contained in an electronic record) when the contract requires a written rescission.[11] Agreements to rescind contracts involving transfers of realty also must be evidenced by a writing or record.

When one party has fully performed, an agreement to cancel the original contract normally will *not* be enforceable unless there is additional consideration. Because the performing party has received no consideration for the promise to call off the original bargain, additional consideration is necessary to support a rescission contract.

DISCHARGE BY NOVATION A contractual obligation may also be discharged through novation. A **novation** occurs when both of the parties to a contract agree to substitute a third party for one of the original parties. The requirements of a novation are as follows:

1. A previous valid obligation.
2. An agreement by all parties to a new contract.
3. The extinguishing of the old obligation (discharge of the prior party).
4. A new contract that is valid.

▶ **Example 10.11** Union Corporation enters into a contract to sell its pharmaceutical division to British Pharmaceuticals, Ltd. Before the transfer is completed, Union, British Pharmaceuticals, and a third company, Otis Chemicals, execute a new agreement to transfer all of British Pharmaceuticals' rights and duties in the transaction to Otis Chemicals. As long as the new contract is supported by consideration, the novation will discharge the original contract (between Union and British Pharmaceuticals) and replace it with the new contract (between Union and Otis Chemicals). ◀

11. UCC 2–209(2), (4).

A novation expressly or impliedly revokes and discharges a prior contract. The parties involved may expressly state in the new contract that the old contract is now discharged. If the parties do not expressly discharge the old contract, it will be impliedly discharged if the new contract's terms are inconsistent with the old contract's terms. It is this immediate discharge of the prior contract that distinguishes a novation from both an accord and satisfaction, which will be discussed shortly, and an assignment of all rights, discussed in Chapter 9.

DISCHARGE BY SETTLEMENT AGREEMENT A compromise, or settlement agreement, that arises out of a genuine dispute over the obligations under an existing contract will be recognized at law. The agreement will be substituted as a new contract and will either expressly or impliedly revoke and discharge the obligations under the prior contract. In contrast to a novation, a substituted agreement does not involve a third party. Rather, the two original parties to the contract form a different agreement to substitute for the original one.

DISCHARGE BY ACCORD AND SATISFACTION In an *accord and satisfaction*, the parties agree to accept performance that is different from the performance originally promised. An *accord* is a contract to perform some act to satisfy an existing contractual duty that is not yet discharged. A *satisfaction* is the performance of the accord agreement. An accord and its satisfaction discharge the original contractual obligation.

Once the accord has been made, the original obligation is merely suspended until the accord agreement is fully performed. If it is not performed, the obligee (the one to whom performance is owed) can file a lawsuit based on the original obligation or the accord. ▶ **Example 10.12** Fahreed has a judgment against Ling for $8,000. Later, both parties agree that the judgment can be satisfied by Ling's transfer of his automobile to Fahreed. This agreement to accept the auto in lieu of $8,000 in cash is the accord. If Ling transfers the car to Fahreed, the accord is fully performed, and the debt is discharged. If Ling refuses to transfer the car, the accord is breached. Because the original obligation was merely suspended, Fahreed can sue Ling to enforce the original judgment for $8,000 in cash or bring an action for breach of the accord. ◀

Discharge by Operation of Law

Under specified circumstances, contractual duties may be discharged by operation of law. These circumstances include material alteration of the contract, the running of the statute of limitations, bankruptcy, and the impossibility or impracticability of performance.

MATERIAL ALTERATION OF THE CONTRACT To discourage parties from altering written contracts, the law allows an innocent party to be discharged when the other party has materially altered a written contract without consent. For instance, a party alters a material term of a contract, such as the stated quantity or price, without the knowledge or consent of the other party. In this situation, the party who was unaware of the alteration can treat the contract as discharged or terminated.

STATUTES OF LIMITATIONS As mentioned earlier in this text, statutes of limitations restrict the period during which a party can sue on a particular cause of action. After the applicable limitations period has passed, a suit can no longer be brought. The limitations period for bringing suits for breach of oral contracts usually is two to three years, and for written or otherwise recorded contracts, four to five years. Parties generally have ten to twenty years to file for recovery of amounts awarded in judgments, depending on state law.

Lawsuits for breach of a contract for the sale of goods generally must be brought within four years after the cause of action has accrued. By their original agreement, the parties can reduce this four-year period to not less than one year, but they cannot agree to extend it.

BANKRUPTCY A proceeding in bankruptcy (see Chapter 16) attempts to allocate the debtor's assets to the creditors in a fair and equitable fashion. Once the assets have been allocated, the debtor receives a **discharge in bankruptcy.** A discharge in bankruptcy ordinarily prevents the creditors from enforcing most of the debtor's contracts. Partial payment of a debt *after* discharge in bankruptcy will not revive the debt.

IMPOSSIBILITY OF PERFORMANCE After a contract has been made, supervening events (such as a fire) may make performance impossible in an objective sense. This is known as **impossibility of performance** and can discharge a contract. The doctrine of impossibility of performance applies only when the parties could not have reasonably foreseen, at the time the contract was formed, the event that rendered performance impossible. Performance may also become so difficult or costly due to some unforeseen event that a court will consider it commercially unfeasible, or impracticable, as will be discussed later in the chapter.

Objective impossibility ("It can't be done") must be distinguished from *subjective impossibility* ("I'm sorry, I simply can't do it"). An example of subjective impossibility occurs when a party cannot deliver goods on time because of freight car shortages or cannot make payment on time because the bank is closed. In effect, in each of these situations the party is saying, "It is impossible for *me* to perform," not "It is impossible for *anyone* to perform." Accordingly, such excuses do not discharge a contract, and the nonperforming party is normally held in breach of contract.

When Performance Is Impossible. Three basic types of situations may qualify as grounds for the discharge of contractual obligations based on impossibility of performance:[12]

1. *When one of the parties to a personal contract dies or becomes incapacitated prior to performance.*
   ▶ **Example 10.13** Frederic, a famous dancer, contracts with Ethereal Dancing Guild to play a leading role in its new ballet. Before the ballet can be performed, Frederic becomes ill and dies. His personal performance was essential to the completion of the contract. Thus, his death discharges the contract and his estate's liability for his nonperformance. ◀
2. *When the specific subject matter of the contract is destroyed.*
   ▶ **Example 10.14** A-1 Farm Equipment agrees to sell Gunther the green tractor on its lot and promises to have the tractor ready for Gunther to pick up on Saturday. On Friday night, however, a truck veers off the nearby highway and smashes into the tractor, destroying it beyond repair. Because the contract was for this specific tractor, A-1's performance is rendered impossible owing to the accident. ◀
3. *When a change in law renders performance illegal.*
   ▶ **Example 10.15** Hopper contracts with Playlist, Inc., to create a Web site through which users can post and share movies, music, and other forms of digital entertainment. Hopper goes to work. Before the site is operational, however, Congress passes the No Online Piracy in Entertainment (NOPE) Act. The NOPE Act makes it illegal to operate a Web site on which copyrighted works

12. *Restatement (Second) of Contracts,* Sections 261–266; UCC 2–615.

are posted without the copyright owners' consent. In this situation, the contract is discharged by operation of law. The purpose of the contract has been rendered illegal, and contract performance is objectively impossible. ◀

Temporary Impossibility. An occurrence or event that makes performance temporarily impossible operates to suspend performance until the impossibility ceases. Once the temporary event ends, the parties ordinarily must perform the contract as originally planned.

▶ **Case in Point 10.16** Keefe Hurwitz contracted to sell his home in Louisiana to Wesley and Gwendolyn Payne for $241,500. Four days later, Hurricane Katrina made landfall and caused extensive damage to the house. Hurwitz refused to pay the cost ($60,000) for the necessary repairs before the deal closed. The Paynes filed a lawsuit to enforce the contract at the agreed-on price. Hurwitz argued that Hurricane Katrina had made it impossible for him to perform and had discharged his duties under the contract. The court, however, ruled that Hurricane Katrina had caused only a temporary impossibility. Hurwitz was required to pay for the necessary repairs and to perform the contract as written. He could not obtain a higher purchase price to offset the cost of the repairs.[13] ◀

Sometimes, the lapse of time and the change in circumstances surrounding the contract make it substantially more burdensome for the parties to perform the promised acts. In that situation, the contract is discharged. ▶ **Case in Point 10.17** In 1942, actor Gene Autry was drafted into the U.S. Army. Being drafted rendered his contract with a Hollywood movie company temporarily impossible to perform, and it was suspended until the end of World War II in 1945. When Autry got out of the army, the purchasing power of the dollar had declined so much that performance of the contract would have been substantially burdensome to him. Therefore, the contract was discharged.[14] ◀

COMMERCIAL IMPRACTICABILITY Courts may also excuse parties from their performance when it becomes much more difficult or expensive than the parties originally contemplated at the time the contract was formed. For someone to invoke the doctrine of **commercial impracticability** successfully, however, the anticipated performance must become *significantly* difficult or costly.[15] The added burden of performing not only must be extreme but also *must not have been known by the parties when the contract was made.*

FRUSTRATION OF PURPOSE Closely allied with the doctrine of commercial impracticability is the doctrine of **frustration of purpose.** In principle, a contract will be discharged if supervening circumstances make it impossible to attain the purpose both parties had in mind when they made the contract. As with commercial impracticability and impossibility, the supervening event must not have been reasonably foreseeable at the time the contract was formed.

There are some differences between the doctrines, however. Commercial impracticability usually involves an event that increases the cost or difficulty of performance. In contrast, frustration of purpose typically involves an event that decreases the value of what a party receives under the contract.

See Exhibit 10–2 on the following page for a summary of the ways in which a contract can be discharged.

SECTION 3

DAMAGES FOR BREACH OF CONTRACT

A breach of contract entitles the nonbreaching party to sue for monetary damages. Damages are designed to compensate a party for harm suffered as a result of another's wrongful act. In the context of contract law, damages compensate the nonbreaching party for the loss of the bargain. Often, courts say that innocent parties are to be placed in the position they would have occupied had the contract been fully performed.

Types of Damages

There are four broad categories of damages:

1. Compensatory (to cover direct losses and costs).
2. Consequential (to cover indirect and foreseeable losses).
3. Punitive (to punish and deter wrongdoing).
4. Nominal (to recognize wrongdoing when no monetary loss is shown).

COMPENSATORY DAMAGES Damages that compensate the nonbreaching party for the *loss of the bargain* are known as *compensatory damages.* These damages compensate the injured party only for damages actu-

13. *Payne v. Hurwitz,* 978 So.2d 1000 (La.App. 1st Cir. 2008).
14. *Autry v. Republic Productions,* 30 Cal.2d 144, 180 P.2d 888 (1947).
15. *Restatement (Second) of Contracts,* Section 264.

EXHIBIT 10–2 Contract Discharge

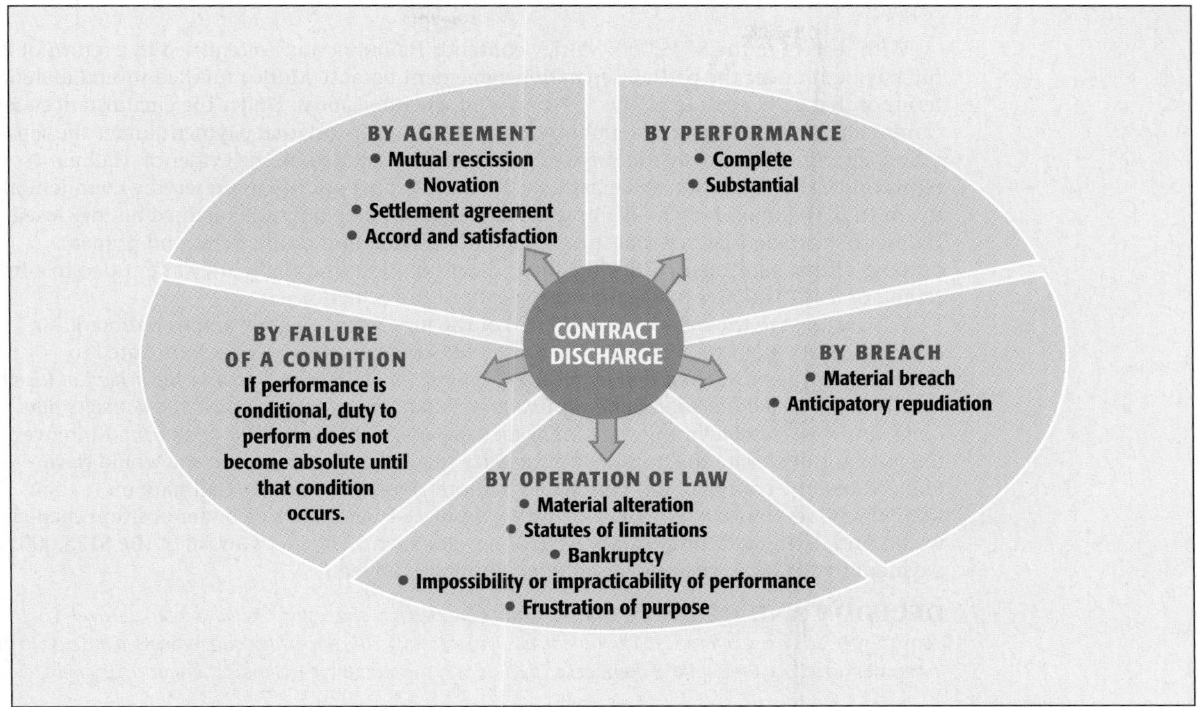

ally sustained and proved to have arisen directly from the loss of the bargain caused by the breach of contract. They simply replace what was lost because of the wrong or damage and, for this reason, are often said to "make the person whole."

Can an award of damages for a breach of contract elevate the nonbreaching party to a better position than he or she would have been in if the contract had not been breached? That was the question in the following case.

CASE 10.3

Hallmark Cards, Inc. v. Murley

United States Court of Appeals, Eighth Circuit, 703 F.3d 456 (2013).

BACKGROUND AND FACTS Janet Murley served as Hallmark Cards, Inc.'s, vice president of marketing. In 2002, Hallmark eliminated her position as part of a corporate restructuring. Murley and Hallmark entered into a separation agreement under which she agreed not to work in the greeting card industry for eighteen months, disclose or use any confidential information, or retain any business records relating to Hallmark. In exchange, Hallmark offered Murley a $735,000 severance payment. After the *noncompete agreement* (see Chapter 9) expired, Murley accepted a consulting assignment with Recycled Paper Greetings (RPG) for $125,000. Murley disclosed confidential Hallmark information to RPG. On learning of the disclosure, Hallmark filed a suit in a federal district court against Murley, alleging breach of contract. A jury returned a verdict in Hallmark's favor and awarded $860,000 in damages, consisting of the $735,000 severance payment and the $125,000 Murley received from RPG. Murley appealed.

CASE 10.3 CONTINUES ➧

CASE 10.3 CONTINUED

IN THE LANGUAGE OF THE COURT
BYE, Circuit Judge.

* * * *

With respect to the $735,000, Murley contends Hallmark was not entitled to a return of its full payment under the parties' separation agreement because Murley fulfilled several material terms of that agreement (e.g., the * * * non-compete provisions). Under the circumstances, we cannot characterize the jury's reimbursement of Hallmark's original payment under the separation agreement as grossly excessive or glaringly unwarranted by the evidence. Hallmark's terms under the separation agreement clearly indicated its priority in preserving confidentiality. At trial, Hallmark presented ample evidence that Murley not only retained but disclosed Hallmark's confidential materials to a competitor in violation of the terms and primary purpose of that agreement. Thus, the jury's determination that Hallmark was entitled to a full refund of its $735,000 is not against the weight of the evidence.

With respect to the remaining $125,000 of the jury award, Murley argues Hallmark can claim no entitlement to her compensation by RPG for consulting services unrelated to Hallmark. We agree. *In an action for breach of contract, a plaintiff may recover the benefit of his or her bargain as well as damages naturally and proximately caused by the breach and damages that could have been reasonably contemplated by the defendant at the time of the agreement.* Moreover, the law cannot elevate the non-breaching party to a better position than she would have enjoyed had the contract been completed on both sides. By awarding Hallmark more than its $735,000 severance payment, the jury award placed Hallmark in a better position than it would find itself had Murley not breached the agreement. The jury's award of the $125,000 payment by RPG was, therefore, improper. [Emphasis added.]

DECISION AND REMEDY *The U.S. Court of Appeals for the Eighth Circuit vacated the award of damages but otherwise affirmed the judgment in Hallmark's favor. The appellate court remanded the case to the lower court to reduce the award of damages to include only the amount of Hallmark's severance payment.*

THE LEGAL ENVIRONMENT DIMENSION *What are compensatory damages? What is the standard measure of compensatory damages?*

THE E-COMMERCE DIMENSION *Murley retained Hallmark-related documents on her private computer for five years after her termination but deleted them forty-eight hours before an inspection of her hard drive. How might Hallmark have discovered these facts?*

Standard Measure. The standard measure of compensatory damages is the difference between the value of the breaching party's promised performance under the contract and the value of her or his actual performance. This amount is reduced by any loss that the injured party has avoided, however.

▶ **Example 10.18** Randall contracts to perform certain services exclusively for Hernandez during the month of March for $4,000. Hernandez cancels the contract and is in breach. Randall is able to find another job during March but can earn only $3,000. He can sue Hernandez for breach and recover $1,000 as compensatory damages. Randall can also recover from Hernandez the amount that he spent to find the other job. ◀

Expenses that are caused directly by a breach of contract—such as those incurred to obtain performance from another source—are known as **incidental damages.** Note that the measure of compensatory damages often varies by type of contract. Certain types of contracts deserve special mention.

Sale of Goods. In a contract for the sale of goods, the usual measure of compensatory damages is an amount equal to the difference between the contract price and the market price.[16] ▶ **Example 10.19** Medik Laboratories contracts to buy ten model UTS network servers from Cal Industries for $4,000 each. Cal Industries, however, fails to deliver the ten servers to Medik. The market price of the servers at the time

16. More specifically, the amount is the difference between the contract price and the market price at the time and place at which the goods were to be delivered or tendered. See Sections 2–708 and 2–713 of the Uniform Commercial Code (UCC).

Medik learns of the breach is $4,500. Therefore, Medik's measure of damages is $5,000 (10 × $500), plus any incidental damages (expenses) caused by the breach. ◀

When the buyer breaches and the seller has not yet produced the goods, compensatory damages normally equal lost profits on the sale, not the difference between the contract price and the market price.

Sale of Land. Ordinarily, because each parcel of land is unique, the remedy for a seller's breach of a contract for a sale of real estate is specific performance. The buyer is awarded the parcel of property for which she or he bargained (*specific performance* will be discussed more fully later in this chapter). When the buyer is the party in breach, the measure of damages is typically the difference between the contract price and the market price of the land. The same measure is used when specific performance is not available (because the seller has sold the property to someone else, for example). The majority of states follow this rule.

A minority of states follow a different rule when the seller breaches the contract and the breach is not deliberate (intentional). These states limit the prospective buyer's damages to a refund of any down payment made plus any expenses incurred (such as fees for title searches, attorneys, and escrows). Thus, the minority rule effectively returns purchasers to the positions they occupied prior to the sale, rather than giving them the benefit of the bargain.

Construction Contracts. The measure of damages in a building or construction contract varies depending on which party breaches and when the breach occurs.

1. *Breach by owner.* The owner may breach at three different stages—before performance has begun, during performance, or after performance has been completed. If the owner breaches *before performance has begun,* the contractor can recover only the profits that would have been made on the contract (that is, the total contract price less the cost of materials and labor).

   If the owner breaches *during performance,* the contractor can recover the profits plus the costs incurred in partially constructing the building. If the owner breaches *after the construction has been completed,* the contractor can recover the entire contract price, plus interest.
2. *Breach by contractor.* When the construction contractor breaches the contract—either by failing to begin construction or by stopping work partway through the project—the measure of damages is the cost of completion. The cost of completion includes reasonable compensation for any delay in performance. If the contractor finishes late, the measure of damages is the loss of use.
3. *Breach by both owner and contractor.* When the performance of both parties—the construction contractor and the owner—falls short of what their contract required, the courts attempt to strike a fair balance in awarding damages.

▶ **Case in Point 10.20** Jamison Well Drilling, Inc., contracted to drill a well for Ed Pfeifer for $4,130. Jamison drilled the well and installed a storage tank. The well did not comply with state health department requirements, however, and failed repeated tests for bacteria. The health department ordered the well to be abandoned and sealed. Pfeifer used the storage tank but paid Jamison nothing. Jamison filed a suit to recover. The court held that Jamison was entitled to $970 for the storage tank but was not entitled to the full contract price because the well was not usable.[17] ◀

The rules concerning the measurement of damages in breached construction contracts are summarized in Exhibit 10–3 below.

17. *Jamison Well Drilling, Inc. v. Pfeifer,* 2011 Ohio 521 (2011).

EXHIBIT 10–3 Measurement of Damages—Breach of Construction Contracts

Party in Breach	Time of Breach	Measurement of Damages
Owner	Before construction has begun.	Profits (contract price less cost of materials and labor).
Owner	During construction.	Profits, plus costs incurred up to time of breach.
Owner	After construction is completed.	Full contract price, plus interest.
Contractor	Before construction has begun.	Cost in excess of contract price to complete work.
Contractor	Before construction is completed.	Generally, all costs incurred by owner to complete.

CONSEQUENTIAL DAMAGES Foreseeable damages that result from a party's breach of contract are called **consequential damages,** or *special damages.* They differ from compensatory damages in that they are caused by special circumstances beyond the contract itself. They flow from the consequences, or results, of a breach. When a seller fails to deliver goods, knowing that the buyer is planning to use or resell those goods immediately, a court may award consequential damages for the loss of profits from the planned resale.

▶ **Example 10.21** Marty contracts to buy a certain quantity of Quench, a specialty sports drink, from Nathan. Nathan knows that Marty has contracted with Ruthie to resell and ship the Quench within hours of its receipt. The beverage will then be sold to fans attending the Super Bowl. Nathan fails to timely deliver the Quench. Marty can recover the consequential damages—the loss of profits from the planned resale to Ruthie—caused by the nondelivery. (If Marty purchases Quench from another vender, he can also recover compensatory damages for the difference between the contract wholesale price and the market wholesale price.) ◀

For the nonbreaching party to recover consequential damages, the breaching party must have known (or had reason to know) that special circumstances would cause the nonbreaching party to suffer an additional loss.

PUNITIVE DAMAGES Punitive damages generally are not awarded in lawsuits for breach of contract. Because punitive damages are designed to punish a wrongdoer and set an example to deter similar conduct in the future, they have no legitimate place in contract law. A contract is simply a civil relationship between the parties. The law may compensate one party for the loss of the bargain—no more and no less. When a person's actions cause both a breach of contract and a tort (such as fraud), punitive damages may be available. Overall, though, punitive damages are almost never available in contract disputes.

NOMINAL DAMAGES When no actual damage or financial loss results from a breach of contract and only a technical injury is involved, the court may award **nominal damages** to the innocent party. Awards of nominal damages are often small, such as one dollar, but they do establish that the defendant acted wrongfully. Most lawsuits for nominal damages are brought as a matter of principle under the theory that a breach has occurred and some damages must be imposed regardless of actual loss.

Mitigation of Damages

In most situations, when a breach of contract occurs, the innocent injured party is held to a duty to mitigate, or reduce, the damages that he or she suffers. Under this doctrine of **mitigation of damages,** the duty owed depends on the nature of the contract.

For instance, some states require a landlord to use reasonable means to find a new tenant if a tenant abandons the premises and fails to pay rent. If an acceptable tenant is found, the landlord is required to lease the premises to this tenant to mitigate the damages recoverable from the former tenant.

The former tenant is still liable for the difference between the amount of the rent under the original lease and the rent received from the new tenant. If the landlord has not taken reasonable steps to find a new tenant, a court will likely reduce any award made by the amount of rent the landlord could have received had he or she done so.

Liquidated Damages versus Penalties

A **liquidated damages** provision in a contract specifies that a certain dollar amount is to be paid in the event of a *future* default or breach of contract. (*Liquidated* means determined, settled, or fixed.)

Liquidated damages differ from penalties. Although a **penalty** also specifies a certain amount to be paid in the event of a default or breach of contract, it is designed to penalize the breaching party, not to make the innocent party whole. Liquidated damages provisions usually are enforceable. In contrast, if a court finds that a provision calls for a penalty, the agreement as to the amount will not be enforced, and recovery will be limited to actual damages.

ENFORCEABILITY To determine if a particular provision is for liquidated damages or for a penalty, a court must answer two questions:

1. When the contract was entered into, was it apparent that damages would be difficult to estimate in the event of a breach?
2. Was the amount set as damages a reasonable estimate and not excessive?

If the answers to both questions are yes, the provision normally will be enforced. If either answer is no, the provision usually will not be enforced.

▶ **Case in Point 10.22** James Haber contracted with B-Sharp Musical Productions, Inc., to provide a particular band to perform at his son's bar mitzvah for $30,000. The contract contained a liquidated damages clause under which if Haber canceled within ninety days of the date of the bar mitzvah, he would still owe $30,000 to B-Sharp. If he canceled more than ninety days beforehand, Haber would owe B-Sharp half of that amount ($15,000).

Haber canceled less than ninety days before the bar mitzvah and refused to pay B-Sharp the $25,000 balance due under the contract. B-Sharp sued. The court held that the liquidated damages clause was enforceable. The court reasoned that the expense and possibility of rebooking a canceled performance could not be determined at the time of contracting and that the clause provided a reasonable amount of damages.[18] ◀

LIQUIDATED DAMAGES COMMON IN CERTAIN CONTRACTS Liquidated damages provisions are frequently used in construction contracts. For instance, a provision requiring a construction contractor to pay $300 for every day he or she is late in completing the project is a liquidated damages provision.

Such provisions are also common in contracts for the sale of goods. In addition, contracts with entertainers and professional athletes often include liquidated damages provisions. ▶ **Example 10.23** A television network settled its contract dispute with *Tonight Show* host Conan O'Brien for $33 million. The amount of the settlement was somewhat less than the $40 million O'Brien could have received under a liquidated damages clause in his contract. ◀

SECTION 4
EQUITABLE REMEDIES

Sometimes, damages are an inadequate remedy for a breach of contract. In these situations, the nonbreaching party may ask the court for an equitable remedy. Equitable remedies include rescission and restitution, specific performance, and reformation.

Rescission and Restitution

Rescission is essentially an action to undo, or terminate, a contract—to return the contracting parties to the positions they occupied prior to the transaction.[19] When fraud, a mistake, duress, undue influence, misrepresentation, or lack of capacity to contract is present, unilateral rescission is available. Rescission may also be available by statute. The failure of one party to perform entitles the other party to rescind the contract. The rescinding party must give prompt notice to the breaching party.

Generally, to rescind a contract, both parties must make **restitution** to each other by returning goods, property, or funds previously conveyed. If the property or goods can be returned, they must be. If the goods or property have been consumed, restitution must be made in an equivalent dollar amount.

Essentially, restitution involves the plaintiff's recapture of a benefit conferred on the defendant that has unjustly enriched her or him. ▶ **Example 10.24** Katie contracts with Mikhail to design a house for her. Katie pays Mikhail $9,000 and agrees to make two more payments of $9,000 (for a total of $27,000) as the design progresses. The next day, Mikhail calls Katie and tells her that he has taken a position with a large architectural firm in another state and cannot design the house. Katie decides to hire another architect that afternoon. Katie can obtain restitution of the $9,000. ◀

Restitution may be appropriate when a contract is rescinded, but the right to restitution is not limited to rescission cases. Because an award of restitution basically returns something to its rightful owner, a party can seek restitution in actions for breach of contract, tort actions, and other types of actions.

Specific Performance

The equitable remedy of **specific performance** calls for the performance of the act promised in the contract. This remedy is attractive to a nonbreaching party because it provides the exact bargain promised in the contract. It also avoids some of the problems inherent in a suit for damages, such as collecting a judgment and arranging another contract. In addition, the actual performance may be more valuable than the monetary damages.

Normally, however, specific performance will not be granted unless the party's legal remedy (monetary damages) is inadequate.[20] For this reason, contracts for

18. *B-Sharp Musical Productions, Inc. v. Haber,* 27 Misc.3d 41, 899 N.Y.S.2d 792 (2010).

19. The rescission discussed here is *unilateral* rescission, in which only one party wants to undo the contract. In mutual rescission, which was discussed in Chapter 9, both parties agree to undo the contract. Mutual rescission discharges the contract. Unilateral rescission generally is available as a remedy for breach of contract.

20. *Restatement (Second) of Contracts,* Section 359.

the sale of goods rarely qualify for specific performance. The legal remedy—monetary damages—is ordinarily adequate in such situations because substantially identical goods can be bought or sold in the market. Only if the goods are unique will a court grant specific performance. For instance, paintings, sculptures, or rare books or coins are so unique that monetary damages will not enable a buyer to obtain substantially identical substitutes in the market.

SALE OF LAND A court may grant specific performance to a buyer in an action for a breach of contract involving the sale of land. In this situation, the legal remedy of monetary damages may not compensate the buyer adequately because every parcel of land is unique: the same land in the same location obviously cannot be obtained elsewhere. Only when specific performance is unavailable (such as when the seller has sold the property to someone else) will monetary damages be awarded instead.

▶ **Case in Point 10.25** Howard Stainbrook entered into a contract to sell Trent Low forty acres of mostly timbered land for $45,000. Low agreed to pay for a survey of the property and other costs in addition to the price. He gave Stainbrook a check for $1,000 to show his intent to fulfill the contract. One month later, Stainbrook died. His son David became the executor of the estate. After he discovered that the timber on the property was worth more than $100,000, David asked Low to withdraw his offer to buy the forty acres. Low refused and filed a suit against David seeking specific performance of the contract. The court found that because Low had substantially performed his obligations under the contract and offered to perform the rest, he was entitled to specific performance.[21] ◀

21. *Stainbrook v. Low*, 842 N.E.2d 386 (Ind.App. 2006).

CONTRACTS FOR PERSONAL SERVICES Contracts for personal services require one party to work personally for another party. Courts generally refuse to grant specific performance of personal-service contracts because to order a party to perform personal services against his or her will amounts to a type of involuntary servitude.[22]

Moreover, the courts do not want to monitor contracts for personal services, which usually require the exercise of personal judgment or talent. ▶ **Example 10.26** Nicole contracts with a surgeon to perform surgery to remove a tumor on her brain. If he refuses, the court would not compel (nor would Nicole want) the surgeon to perform under those circumstances. A court cannot ensure meaningful performance in such a situation. ◀

If a contract is not deemed personal, the remedy at law of monetary damages may be adequate if substantially identical service (such as lawn mowing) is available from other persons.

Reformation

As noted in Chapter 9, **reformation** is an equitable remedy used when the parties have *imperfectly* expressed their agreement in writing. Reformation allows a court to rewrite the contract to reflect the parties' true intentions.

Exhibit 10–4 below graphically summarizes the remedies, including reformation, that are available to the nonbreaching party.

WHEN FRAUD OR MUTUAL MISTAKE IS PRESENT Courts order reformation most often when fraud or mutual mistake (for example, a clerical error) is present. Typically, a party seeks reformation so that some other remedy may then be pursued.

22. Involuntary servitude, or slavery, is contrary to the public policy expressed in the Thirteenth Amendment to the U.S. Constitution.

EXHIBIT 10–4 Remedies for Breach of Contract

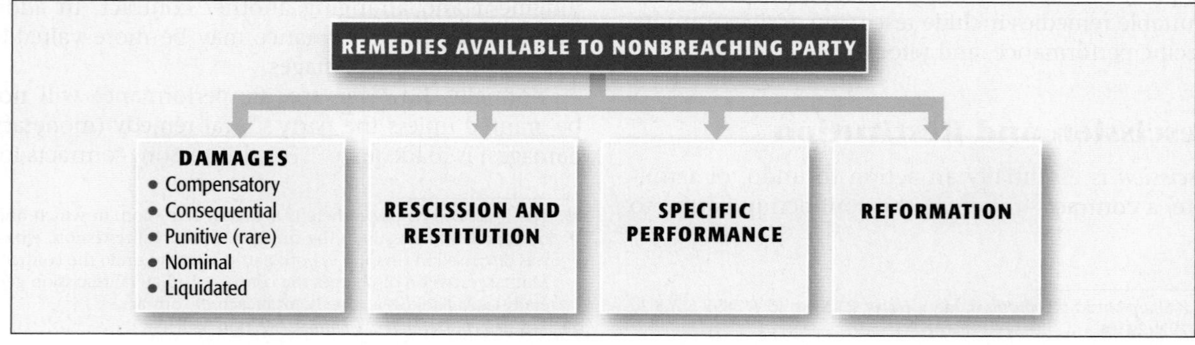

▶ **Example 10.27** If Carson contracts to buy a forklift from Yoshie but their contract mistakenly refers to a crane, a mutual mistake has occurred. Accordingly, a court can reform the contract so that it conforms to the parties' intentions and accurately refers to the forklift being sold. ◀

WRITTEN CONTRACT INCORRECTLY STATES THE PARTIES' ORAL AGREEMENT A court will also reform a contract when two parties enter into a binding oral contract but later make an error when they attempt to put the terms into writing. Normally, a court will allow into evidence the correct terms of the oral contract, thereby reforming the written contract.

COVENANTS NOT TO COMPETE Courts also may reform contracts when the parties have executed a written covenant not to compete (discussed in Chapter 9). If the covenant is for a valid and legitimate purpose (such as the sale of a business) but the area or time restraints of the covenant are unreasonable, reformation may occur. Some courts will reform the restraints by making them reasonable and then will enforce the entire contract as reformed. Other courts, however, will throw out the entire restrictive covenant as illegal.

SECTION 5

WAIVER OF BREACH

Under certain circumstances, a nonbreaching party may be willing to accept a defective performance of the contract. This knowing relinquishment of a legal right (that is, the right to require satisfactory and full performance) is called a **waiver.**

Consequences of a Waiver of Breach

When a waiver of a breach of contract occurs, the party waiving the breach cannot take any later action on it. In effect, the waiver erases the past breach, and the contract continues as if the breach had never occurred. Of course, the waiver of breach of contract extends only to the matter waived and not to the whole contract.

Reasons for Waiving a Breach

Businesspersons often waive breaches of contract to obtain whatever benefit is still possible out of the contract. For instance, a seller contracts with a buyer to deliver to the buyer ten thousand tons of coal on or before November 1. The contract calls for the buyer to pay by November 10 for coal delivered. Because of a coal miners' strike, coal is hard to find. The seller breaches the contract by not tendering delivery until November 5. The buyer will likely choose to waive the seller's breach, accept delivery of the coal, and pay as contracted.

Waiver of Breach and Subsequent Breaches

Ordinarily, a waiver by a contracting party will not operate to waive subsequent, additional, or future breaches of contract. This is always true when the subsequent breaches are unrelated to the first breach. ▶ **Example 10.28** Ashton owns a multimillion-dollar apartment complex that is under construction. Ashton allows the contractor to complete a stage of construction late. By doing so, Ashton waives his right to sue for the delay. Ashton does not, however, waive the right to sue for failure to comply with engineering specifications on the same job. ◀

PATTERN-OF-CONDUCT EXCEPTION A waiver can extend to subsequent defective performance if a reasonable person would conclude that similar defective performance in the future will be acceptable. Therefore, a *pattern of conduct* that waives a number of successive breaches will operate as a continued waiver. To change this result, the nonbreaching party should give notice to the breaching party that full performance will be required in the future.

EFFECT ON THE CONTRACT The party who has rendered defective or less-than-full performance remains liable for the damages caused by the breach of contract. In effect, the waiver operates to keep the contract going. The waiver prevents the nonbreaching party from declaring the contract at an end or rescinding the contract. The contract continues, but the nonbreaching party can recover damages caused by the defective or less-than-full performance.

SECTION 6

CONTRACT PROVISIONS LIMITING REMEDIES

A contract may include provisions stating that no damages can be recovered for certain types of breaches or that damages will be limited to a maximum amount.

The contract may also provide that the only remedy for breach is replacement, repair, or refund of the purchase price. The contract may also provide that one party can seek injunctive relief if the other party breaches the contract (for an example, see Paragraph 11 in *Appendix to Chapter 10: Reading and Analyzing Contracts,* following this chapter). Provisions stating that no damages can be recovered are called *exculpatory clauses* (see Chapter 9). Provisions that affect the availability of certain remedies are called *limitation-of-liability clauses.*

The UCC Allows Sales Contracts to Limit Remedies

The Uniform Commercial Code (UCC) provides that in a contract for the sale of goods, remedies can be limited. We will examine the UCC provisions on limited remedies in Chapter 11.

Enforceability of Limitation-of-Liability Clauses

Whether a limitation-of-liability clause in a contract will be enforced depends on the type of breach that is excused by the provision. Normally, a provision excluding liability for fraudulent or intentional injury will not be enforced. Likewise, a clause excluding liability for illegal acts, acts that are contrary to public policy, or violations of law will not be enforced. A clause that excludes liability for negligence may be enforced in some situations when the parties have roughly equal bargaining positions.

▶ **Case in Point 10.29** Engineering Consulting Services, Ltd. (ECS), contracted with RSN Properties, Inc, a real estate developer. ECS was to perform soil studies for $2,200 and render an opinion on the use of septic systems in a particular subdivision being developed. A clause in the contract limited ECS's liability to RSN to the value of the engineering services or the sum of $50,000, whichever was greater.

ECS concluded that most of the lots were suitable for septic systems, so RSN proceeded with the development. RSN constructed the roads and water lines to the subdivision in reliance on ECS's conclusions, which turned out to be incorrect. RSN sued ECS for breach of contract and argued that the limitation of liability was against public policy and unenforceable. The court, however, enforced the limitation-of-liability clause as "a reasonable allocation of risks in an arm's-length business transaction."[23] ◀

23. *RSN Properties, Inc. v. Engineering Consulting Services, Ltd.,* 301 Ga.App. 52, 686 S.E.2d 853 (2009).

Reviewing: Contract Performance, Breach, and Remedies

Val's Foods signs a contract to buy 1,500 pounds of basil from Sun Farms, a small organic herb grower, as long as an independent organization inspects the crop and certifies that it contains no pesticide or herbicide residue. Val's has a contract with several restaurant chains to supply pesto and intends to use Sun Farms' basil in the pesto to fulfill these contracts. While Sun Farms is preparing to harvest the basil, an unexpected hailstorm destroys half the crop. Sun Farms attempts to purchase additional basil from other farms, but it is late in the season and the price is twice the normal market price. Sun Farms is too small to absorb this cost and immediately notifies Val's that it will not fulfill the contract. Using the information presented in the chapter, answer the following questions.

1. Suppose that the basil does not pass the chemical-residue inspection. Which concept discussed in the chapter might allow Val's to refuse to perform the contract in this situation?
2. Under which legal theory or theories might Sun Farms claim that its obligation under the contract has been discharged by operation of law? Discuss fully.
3. Suppose that Sun Farms contacts every basil grower in the country and buys the last remaining chemical-free basil anywhere. Nevertheless, Sun Farms is able to ship only 1,475 pounds to Val's. Would this fulfill Sun Farms' obligations to Val's? Why or why not?

4. Now suppose that Sun Farms sells its operations to Happy Valley Farms. As a part of the sale, all three parties agree that Happy Valley will provide the basil as stated under the original contract. What is this type of agreement called?

DEBATE THIS . . . *The doctrine of commercial impracticability should be abolished.*

Terms and Concepts

anticipatory repudiation 227
bilateral mistake 220
breach of contract 225
commercial impracticability 230
condition 223
condition precedent 223
consequential damages 234
discharge 223
discharge in bankruptcy 229
frustration of purpose 230
impossibility of performance 229
incidental damages 232
liquidated damages 234
mitigation of damages 234
mutual rescission 228
nominal damages 234
novation 228
penalty 234
performance 223
reformation 236
restitution 235
specific performance 235
tender 223
unilateral mistake 219
voluntary consent 219
waiver 237

ExamPrep

Issue Spotters

1. Simmons finds a stone in his pasture that he believes to be quartz. Jenson, who also believes that the stone is quartz, contracts to purchase it for $10. Just before delivery, the stone is discovered to be a diamond worth $1,000. Is the contract enforceable? Why or why not? **(See page 220.)**
2. Greg contracts to build a storage shed for Haney, who pays Greg in advance, but Greg completes only half the work. Haney pays Ipswich $500 to finish the shed. If Haney sues Greg, what would be the measure of recovery? **(See page 230.)**

- **Check your answers to the Issue Spotters against the answers provided in Appendix E at the end of this text.**

Before the Test

Go to **www.cengagebrain.com**, enter the ISBN 9781285428949, and click on "Find" to locate this textbook's Web site. Then, click on "Access Now" under "Study Tools," and select Chapter 10 at the top. There, you will find an Interactive Quiz that you can take to assess your mastery of the concepts in this chapter, as well as Flashcards and a Glossary of important terms.

Business Scenarios

10–1. Conditions of Performance. The Caplans contract with Faithful Construction, Inc., to build a house for them for $360,000. The specifications state "all plumbing bowls and fixtures . . . to be Crane brand." The Caplans leave on vacation, and during their absence, Faithful is unable to buy and install Crane plumbing fixtures. Instead, Faithful installs Kohler brand fixtures, an equivalent in the industry. On completion of the building contract, the Caplans inspect the work, discover the substitution, and refuse to accept the house, claiming Faithful has breached the conditions set forth in the specifications. Discuss fully the Caplans' claim. **(See page 223.)**

10–2. Impossibility of Performance. In the following situations, certain events take place after the contracts are formed. Discuss which of these contracts are discharged because the events render the contracts impossible to perform. **(See page 229.)**

(a) Jimenez, a famous singer, contracts to perform in your nightclub. He dies prior to performance.

(b) Raglione contracts to sell you her land. Just before title is to be transferred, she dies.

(c) Oppenheim contracts to sell you one thousand bushels of apples from her orchard in the state of Washington. Because of a severe frost, she is unable to deliver the apples.

(d) Maxwell contracts to lease a service station for ten years. His principal income is from the sale of gasoline. Because of an oil embargo by foreign oil-producing nations, gasoline is rationed, cutting sharply into Maxwell's gasoline sales. He cannot make his lease payments.

10–3. Liquidated Damages. Cohen contracts to sell his house and lot to Windsor for $100,000. The terms of the contract call for Windsor to pay 10 percent of the purchase price as a deposit toward the purchase price, or a down payment. The terms further stipulate that if the buyer breaches the contract, Cohen will retain the deposit as liquidated damages. Windsor pays the deposit, but because her expected financing of the $90,000 balance falls through, she breaches the contract. Two weeks later Cohen sells the house and lot to Ballard for $105,000. Windsor demands her $10,000 back, but Cohen refuses, claiming that Windsor's breach and the contract terms entitle him to keep the deposit. Discuss who is correct. **(See page 234.)**

Business Case Problems

10–4. Fraudulent Misrepresentation. Ricky and Sherry Wilcox hired Esprit Log and Timber Frame Homes to build a log house, which the Wilcoxes intended to sell. They paid Esprit $125,260 for materials and services. They eventually sold the home for $1,620,000 but sued Esprit due to construction delays. The logs were supposed to arrive at the construction site precut and predrilled, but that did not happen. So it took five extra months to build the house while the logs were cut and drilled one by one. The Wilcoxes claimed that the interest they paid on a loan for the extra construction time cost them about $200,000. The jury agreed and awarded them that much in damages, plus $250,000 in punitive damages and $20,000 in attorneys' fees. Esprit appealed, claiming that the evidence did not support the verdict because the Wilcoxes had sold the house for a good price. Is Esprit's argument credible? Why or why not? How should the court rule? [*Esprit Log and Timber Frame Homes, Inc. v. Wilcox,* 302 Ga. App. 550, 691 S.E.2d 344 (2010)] **(See page 221.)**

10–5. BUSINESS CASE PROBLEM WITH SAMPLE ANSWER: Consequential Damages.

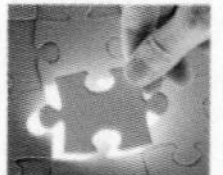

*After submitting the high bid at a foreclosure sale, David Simard entered into a contract to purchase real property in Maryland for $192,000. Simard defaulted (failed to pay) on the contract. A state court ordered the property to be resold at Simard's expense, as required by state law. The property was then resold for $163,000, but the second purchaser also defaulted on his contract. The court then ordered a second resale, resulting in a final price of $130,000. Assuming that Simard is liable for consequential damages, what is the extent of his liability? Is he liable for losses and expenses related to the first resale? If so, is he also liable for losses and expenses related to the second resale? Why or why not? [*Burson v. Simard, *35 A.3d 1154 (Md. 2012)]* **(See page 234.)**

- **For a sample answer to Problem 10–5, go to Appendix F at the end of this text.**

10–6. Liquidated Damages. Cuesport Properties, LLC, sold a condominium in Anne Arundel County, Maryland, to Critical Developments, LLC. As part of the sale, Cuesport agreed to build a wall between Critical Developments' unit and an adjacent unit within thirty days of closing. If Cuesport failed to do so, it was to pay $126 per day until completion. This was an estimate of the amount of rent that Critical Developments would lose until the wall was finished and the unit could be rented. Actual damages were otherwise difficult to estimate at the time of the contract. The wall was built on time, but without a county permit, and it did not comply with the county building code. Critical Developments did not modify the wall to comply with the code until 260 days after the date of the contract deadline for completion of the wall. Does Cuesport have to pay Critical Developments $126 for each of the 260 days? Explain. [*Cuesport Properties, LLC v. Critical Developments, LLC,* 209 Md.App. 607, 61 A.3d 91 (2013)] **(See page 234.)**

10–7. Material Breach. The Northeast Independent School District in Bexar County, Texas, hired STR Constructors, Ltd., to renovate a middle school. STR subcontracted the tile work in the school's kitchen to Newman Tile, Inc. (NTI). The project had already fallen behind schedule. As a result, STR allowed other workers to walk over and damage the newly installed tile before it had cured, forcing NTI to constantly redo its work. Despite NTI's requests for payment, STR remitted only half the amount due under their contract. When the school district refused to accept the kitchen, including the tile work, STR told NTI to quickly make the repairs. A week later, STR terminated their contract. Did STR breach the contract with NTI? Explain. [*STR Constructors, Ltd. v. Newman Tile, Inc.,* __ S.W.3d __, 2013 WL 632969 (Tex.App.—El Paso 2013)] **(See page 225.)**

10–8. A QUESTION OF ETHICS: Remedies.

On a weekday, Tamara Cohen, a real estate broker, showed a townhouse owned by Ray and Harriet Mayer to Jessica Seinfeld, the wife of comedian Jerry Seinfeld. On the weekend, when

Cohen was unavailable because her religious beliefs prevented her from working, the Seinfelds revisited the townhouse on their own and agreed to buy it. The contract stated that the "buyers will pay buyer's real estate broker's fees." [Cohen v. Seinfeld, *15 Misc.3d 1118(A), 839 N.Y.S.2d 432 (Sup. 2007)*] **(See page 235.)**

(a) Is Cohen entitled to payment even though she was not available to show the townhouse to the Seinfelds on the weekend? Explain.

(b) What obligation do parties involved in business deals owe to each other with respect to their religious beliefs? How might the situation in this case have been avoided?

10–9. SPECIAL CASE ANALYSIS: Material Breach.

Go to Case Analysis Case 10.2, *Kohel v. Bergen Auto Enterprises, L.L.C.*, on pages 226 and 227. Read the excerpt and answer the following questions.

(a) **Issue:** This case involved allegations of breach of contract involving which parties and for what actions?

(b) **Rule of Law:** What is the difference between a *material* breach and a *minor* breach of contract?

(c) **Applying the Rule of Law:** How did the court determine which party was in material breach of the contract in this case?

(d) **Conclusion:** Was the defendant liable for breach? Why or why not?

Legal Reasoning Group Activity

10–10. Breach and Remedies. Frances Morelli agreed to sell Judith Bucklin a house in Rhode Island for $177,000. The sale was supposed to be closed by September 1, when the parties were to exchange the deed for the price. The contract included a provision that "if Seller is unable to convey good, clear, insurable, and marketable title, Buyer shall have the option to: (a) accept such title as Seller is able to convey without reduction of the Purchase Price, or (b) cancel this Agreement and receive a return of all Deposits."

An examination of the public records revealed that the house did not have marketable title. Bucklin offered Morelli additional time to resolve the problem, and the closing did not occur as scheduled. Morelli decided "the deal is over" and offered to return the deposit. Bucklin refused and, in mid-October, decided to exercise her option to accept the house without marketable title. She notified Morelli, who did not respond. She then filed a lawsuit against Morelli in a state court. **(See page 225.)**

(a) One group will discuss whether Morelli breached the contract and will decide in whose favor the court should rule.

(b) A second group will assume that Morelli did breach the contract and will determine what the appropriate remedy is in this situation.

APPENDIX TO CHAPTER 10

READING AND ANALYZING CONTRACTS

As the text and cases in this unit have indicated, businesses use contracts to make their transactions more predictable. Contracts allow parties to clarify their obligations in great detail. Businesses also use contracts to resolve anticipated problems or conflicts and to clarify responsibility in the event of a breach. An understanding of what is in a typical contract is crucial to using contracts effectively.

Being able to read and understand a contract takes some practice, however. Contract terms often are highly technical and complex, and sometimes the vocabulary and phrasing can be unfamiliar. Nevertheless, businesspersons need to be able to understand the meaning of various contract provisions so that they will know what their business's obligations and rights are under the contract.

Reading a Contract

A contract is generally intended to serve two purposes:

1. To achieve some commercial purpose—such as, a sale of goods, a lease of property, or an employment agreement.
2. To prevent future conflict by clarifying the obligations and rights of the parties.

Parties should address the details of the business agreement and also should think strategically about how a conflict should be resolved if something goes awry.

Different types of contracts will have different provisions. Sales contracts should contain information on the products being sold, the quantity, the price, and delivery terms. Employment contracts may contain information on the term of employment, employment duties, confidentiality and nondisclosure of the employer's documents and information, and restrictions on competing with the employer after leaving the position.

Although standard forms exist for many types of contracts, the parties to a particular contract may have specific requirements and thus may need to tailor the contract to fit their transaction. A larger transaction or more specialized goods or real estate will require a more specific and probably a longer contract. For example, a sales contract between Airbus and American Airlines for the sale of an Airbus S.A.S. plane was more than 109 pages, not counting the eleven exhibits that followed the main contract.[1]

Regardless of the specificity of the contract provisions, it is important for a businessperson to read and evaluate the responsibilities or commitments of both parties to the contract. Sometimes, a single word or phrase can make an enormous difference. For example, a rental contract for a house may state that the owner is responsible for any plumbing issues, or it may specify that the renter is the responsible party. If a plumber has to be called to deal with clogged pipes on a holiday, that single phrase in the contract will determine who has to pay the plumber's very high holiday rates.

1. "Sample Business Contracts," *Onecle.com,* July 14, 2012.

(Denis Opolja/Shutterstock.com)

Contract Analysis Exercise

The sample contract on pages 244–247 is based on an actual employment-related contract between a company called Boulder Dry and its chief financial officer (CFO). As you read the contract, think about the following questions:

1. Which party seems to have had the stronger bargaining position, and why?
2. Which specific provisions favor the employer?
3. Which specific provisions favor the employee?
4. The parties' main intentions in signing this contract were to protect the firm's confidential information and to explain how the CFO could use that information. Which provisions are related to those two purposes?
5. Which provisions seem entirely unrelated to the main purposes? Why are these other provisions included in the contract? What do they do for the parties?
6. What terms in the contract do you find difficult to understand?
7. As a potential employee being asked to sign this agreement, what concerns might you have?
8. If after one year the employee resigns from Boulder Dry, what provisions of this contract should the employee have reviewed before resigning because they would affect his or her future? When leaving the company, what actions would the employee take to ensure that he or she was in compliance with all obligations?

SEE SAMPLE CONTRACT ON THE FOLLOWING PAGES.

EMPLOYEE NONCOMPETITION AND NONDISCLOSURE AGREEMENT

In consideration of my employment or continued employment, with Boulder Dry (the "Company"), and the compensation received from the Company, I hereby agree as follows:

1. ***Proprietary Information and Inventions:*** I understand and acknowledge that:
   - **A.** The Company is engaged in research, development, production, marketing, and servicing. I am expected to make new contributions and inventions of value to the Company as part of my employment.
   - **B.** My employment creates a relationship of trust between the Company and me with respect to information that may be made known to me or learned by me during my employment.
   - **C.** The Company possesses information that has been discovered or developed by the Company that has commercial value to the Company and is treated by the Company as confidential. All such information is hereinafter called "Proprietary Information," which term shall include, but shall not be limited to, systems, processes, data, computer programs, discoveries, marketing plans, strategies, forecasts, new products, unpublished financial statements, licenses, and customer and supplier lists. The term "Proprietary Information" shall not include any of the foregoing that is in the public domain.
   - **D.** All existing confidential lists of customers of the Company, and all confidential lists of customers developed during my employment, are the sole and exclusive property of the Company and I shall not have any right, title, or interest therein.
2. ***Ownership of Proprietary Information:*** All Proprietary Information shall be the sole property of the Company, including patents, copyrights, and trademarks. I hereby assign to the Company any rights I may have or acquire in such Proprietary Information. Both during and after my employment, I will keep in strictest confidence and trust all Proprietary Information. I will not use or disclose any Proprietary Information without the written consent of the Company, except as may be necessary in performing my duties as a Company employee.
3. ***Commitment to Company and Other Employment:*** During my employment, I will devote substantially all of my time to the Company, and I will not, without the Company's prior written consent, engage in any employment or business other than for the Company.
4. ***Documentation:*** Upon the termination of my employment, I will deliver to the Company all documents, computer programs, data, and other materials of any nature pertaining to my work with the Company. I will not take any originals or reproductions of the foregoing that are embodied in a tangible medium of expression.
5. ***Disclosure of Inventions:*** I will promptly disclose to the Company all discoveries, designs, inventions, blueprints, computer programs, and data ("Inventions") made by me, either alone or jointly with others, during my employment. Inventions include by definition those things that are related to the business of the Company or that result from the use of property owned, leased, or contracted for by the Company.
6. ***Ownership of Inventions:*** All Inventions shall be the sole property of the Company, and the Company shall be the sole owner of all patents, copyrights, trademarks, and other rights. I assign to the Company any rights I may have or acquire in such Inventions. I shall assist the Company to obtain and enforce patents, copyrights, trademarks, and other rights and protections relating to Inventions. This obligation shall continue beyond the termination of my employment, but the Company shall compensate me at a reasonable rate after my termination.
7. ***Other Agreements:*** I represent and warrant that this Agreement and the performance of it do not breach any other agreement to which I am a party. I have not entered into and shall not enter into any agreement in conflict with this Agreement.
8. ***Use of Confidential Information of Other Persons:*** I have not brought and will not bring with me to the Company any materials or documents of an employer or a former employer that are not generally available to the public. If I desire or need to use any materials from a prior employer, I will obtain express written authorization from such employer.
9. ***Restrictive Covenant:*** I hereby acknowledge my possession of Proprietary Information and the highly competitive nature of the business of the Company. I will not, during my employment and for three (3) years following my termination, directly or indirectly engage in any competitive business or assist others in engaging in any competitive business. I understand that this Section is not meant to prevent me from earning a living. It does intend to prevent any competitive business from gaining any unfair advantage from my knowledge of Proprietary Information. I understand that by making my new employer aware of the provisions of this Section 9, that employer can take such action as to avoid my breaching the provisions hereof and to indemnify me in the event of a breach.

COMMENTS TO CONTRACT PARAGRAPHS

Paragraph 1A. This is essentially a broad description of the employee's role at the company and explains why this agreement is necessary. Often, a clause like this precedes a statement indicating that the employer gets to keep any value that the employee adds to the firm.

Paragraph 1B. This paragraph establishes that a relationship of trust and confidence exists between employer and employee. Through this clause, both parties are agreeing they owe duties to each other related to information that benefits the company. The clause implies that that there will be negative consequences for the employee if he or she breaks that relationship.

Paragraph 1C. This paragraph establishes what the term "Proprietary Information" means. In contracts, terms that are capitalized and placed in quotation marks (sometimes in parentheses as well) are called "defined terms." Whenever the term "Proprietary Information" appears throughout the rest of the contract, it will have the definition set out in this paragraph. The definition is extremely broad and captures almost any intellectual property, data, and similar items. The contract asserts that this information is important to the business and gives the company some strategic advantage.

Paragraph 1D. This clause clarifies that customer lists belong to the employer even if the employee develops or expands the lists in some way. This may become important if the employee leaves the company because the clause clarifies that the employee may not recruit or "steal" customers.

Paragraph 2. Here, we see the defined term "Proprietary Information" again. This paragraph documents that the employer owns all Proprietary Information, as defined, even if it was created by the employee. Further, the employee agrees to give the employer any legal rights that the employee may obtain to any Proprietary Information.

Paragraph 3. In this clause, the employee promises that he or she will work full time for the employer and will not take any additional employment without the employer's permission.

Paragraph 4. This clause further asserts that the company takes the confidential nature of the Proprietary Information seriously. Here, the employee promises that if he or she leaves the company's employment, he or she will turn over any work-related material to the company.

Paragraph 5. If the employee creates something of any kind at work, he or she must tell the employer about it, and the employer will receive any disclosures confidentially. The contract goes out of its way to ensure that almost anything the employee invents at work or that is related to work fits under this paragraph. Such items are given a new term called "Inventions." Note that the definition of inventions includes the same items that are in the definition of Proprietary Information as well as some additional ones. The paragraphs discussing Proprietary Information deal with information that the company already possesses and will continue to possess and that the employee will access or need. This paragraph expands the obligations of the employee to what could be called new proprietary information, defined as "Inventions."

Paragraph 6. Just as the employee agreed to give any right in already existing information (such as a modified customer list) to the employer, here the employee promises to give all legal rights to inventions to the employer. In addition, because the rights may originally belong to the employee, the employee promises to help the employer secure any rights or protections necessary to increase the value of the invention. This obligation to help the employer continues to exist after the employee leaves the firm, and the employer agrees to pay for the work required in that situation. The employer is making sure that it can keep anything the employee invents during work time or with company resources.

Paragraph 7. The employer wants to ensure that this contract does not conflict with any others the employee may have already signed. Here, the employee affirms that he or she has made no conflicting agreements. The clause implies that the employee will be responsible for any consequences that arise from such conflicts.

Paragraph 8. The employer does not want to become involved in a dispute with another company by hiring this employee. In this clause, the employee states that he or she is not bringing the employer any confidential information belonging to someone else.

Paragraph 9. This paragraph is a covenant not to compete, one of the most important provisions from the perspective of the employee. Employers worry that former employees will join a rival company and take their information and expertise with them. A covenant not to compete helps prevent that from happening. In short, a covenant not to compete prohibits an employee from working for a competing business for a specified time. This covenant applies regardless of whether the employee leaves the company or is terminated. Covenants not to compete have to be carefully drafted. A court will not enforce a covenant that is too broad in its coverage or that lasts for too long. Three years, the length of this covenant not to compete, is not unduly long. If the covenant is challenged, however, the employer will have to show that this length of time was necessary to protect its business interests. Employees do not appreciate covenants not to compete, but find that they are an inevitable part of employment in information-sensitive industries.

10. ***Agreement Not to Solicit Customers:*** During the course of my employment and for a period of three (3) years following my termination, I will not attempt to solicit any person, firm, or corporation that has been a customer account of the Company.
11. ***Remedies:*** I acknowledge that a remedy at law for any breach or threatened breach of the provisions of this Agreement would be inadequate. I therefore agree that the Company shall be entitled to injunctive relief in addition to any other available rights and remedies in case of any such breach or threatened breach. Nothing contained herein shall be construed as prohibiting the Company from pursuing any other remedies available for any such breach or threatened breach.
12. ***Assignment:*** This Agreement and the rights and obligations of the parties hereto shall bind and inure to the benefit of any successor(s) of the Company, whether by reorganization, merger, consolidation, sale of assets, or otherwise. Neither this Agreement nor any rights or benefits hereunder may be assigned by me.
13. ***Interpretation:*** It is the desire and intent of the parties hereto that the provisions of this Agreement shall be enforced to the fullest extent permissible. Accordingly, if any provision of this Agreement shall be adjudicated to be invalid or unenforceable, such provision shall be deemed deleted. Such deletion will apply only to the deleted provision in the particular jurisdiction in which such adjudication is made. If any provision contained herein shall be held to be excessively broad as to duration, geographical scope, activity, or subject, it shall be construed by limiting and reducing it so as to be enforceable.
14. ***Notices:*** All notices pursuant to this Agreement shall be given by personal delivery or by certified mail, return receipt requested. Notices to the Employee shall be addressed to the Employee at the address of record with the Company. Notices to the Company shall be addressed to its principal office. The date of personal delivery or the date of mailing any such notice shall be deemed to be the date of delivery thereof.
15. ***Waivers:*** Any waiver of breach of any provision of this Agreement shall not thereby be deemed a waiver of any preceding or succeeding breach of the same or any other provision of this Agreement.
16. ***Headings:*** The headings of the sections hereof are inserted for convenience only and shall not be deemed to constitute a part hereof nor to affect the meaning hereof.
17. ***Governing Law:*** This Agreement shall be governed by and construed and enforced in accordance with the laws of the State of New Hampshire.
18. ***No Employment Agreement:*** I acknowledge that this Agreement does not constitute an employment agreement. This Agreement shall be binding upon me regardless of whether my employment shall continue for any length of time and whether my employment is terminated for any reason whatsoever. This is true whether my employment is terminated by the Company or by me.
19. ***Complete Agreement, Amendments, and Prior Agreements:*** The foregoing is the entire agreement of the parties with respect to the subject matter hereof and may not be amended, supplemented, canceled, or discharged except by written instrument executed by both parties hereto. This Agreement supersedes any and all prior agreements between the parties hereto with respect to the matters covered hereby.

Date: ____________ Employee: ____________________

Accepted and agreed to as of this date by Company:

Date: ____________ By: ____________________

Name: ____________________

Title: ____________________

Paragraph 10. Similar to a covenant not to compete, this clause prohibits an employee from soliciting the company's customers during his or her employment or for up to three years afterward. Without such protection, an employer would be vulnerable to any former employee taking customer lists and using them to solicit customers at a new employer or at his or her own business.

Paragraph 11. This paragraph allows the employer to seek injunctive relief against the employee, should it be necessary. Here, the employee agrees that the employer not only may seek monetary damages from the employee in the event that this agreement is breached but may also prohibit him or her from engaging in whatever behavior violates the contract. Recall that typically the first line of remedies is damages to compensate for injury. Here the parties are acknowledging in advance (for the benefit of any court that later is involved) that the harm caused by a breach of the contract cannot be compensated or corrected with monetary damages.

Paragraph 12. Companies change, and so do their owners. This paragraph states that the contract will survive even if ownership of the company changes due to a merger, reorganization, or other reason. The employee cannot avoid this contract simply because the owner that signed the agreement later sells the company to someone else. This paragraph and many of the subsequent paragraphs are often referred to as "boilerplate language," meaning provisions that appear in some form in many contracts. They are included because conflicts have arisen over these points in the past and courts have interpreted contracts without this language in a way that the parties want to avoid. Boilerplate language can be very dangerous because parties may see the headings and not read further because the language is similar from contract to contract. But boilerplate language can make a difference in which party later wins a dispute (because the language spells out the law that will be used to interpret the contract, where a case must be brought, the proper way to give notice of changes, and the like).

Paragraph 13. Employers know that even the most carefully drafted agreements can sometimes be rendered unenforceable by a reviewing court. Laws change over time, and so do attitudes toward contract terms. This paragraph states that if part of this contract is rendered unenforceable for some reason, the rest of the contract will survive intact (that is, the unenforceable part of the contract is severable). The paragraph specifically references the covenant not to compete and the prohibition against solicitation. If a court rejects those terms as too broad in scope or too lengthy, the parties agree that the court should adjust the clause in order to make it enforceable under the law.

Paragraph 14. This paragraph deals with notices. If the employer or the employee wants to communicate about the contract, the communication must be sent by personal delivery or registered/certified mail. Note that this means that an e-mail is not sufficient notice under this agreeement.

Paragraph 15. This paragraph is meant to protect the employer. Sometimes, through generosity or neglect, employers fail to enforce every clause of a contract. For example, an employer may allow a former employee to start a competing business earlier than the contract states or permit an employee to take a second job. This paragraph ensures that if the employer allows some action that is prohibited in the contract, that does not mean that the contract term is waived forever. Just because the employer does not fully enforce the contract every time does not necessarily mean the employer is barred from doing so in the future.

Paragraph 16. This clause is meant to clarify that the headings are just headings and do not change the interpretation of the language in the paragraphs or the overall meaning of the contract.

Paragraph 17. This contract will be interpreted using the law of the state of New Hampshire. It is likely that the employer selected New Hampshire for some particular reason. Typically, an employer chooses a state where the law provides the most benefits for the employer. For example, employers typically choose the law of a particular state because it is their geographic home state and the employer's lawyers are familiar with its law. Employers may also choose a legal jurisdiction because its laws create a climate that is more favorable to the employer than the employee.

Paragraph 18. In this paragraph, the employee acknowledges that this contract is about nondisclosure of information and does not constitute an employment agreement that promises any length of service or any promise of continued employment.

Paragraph 19. This paragraph states that this contract is the complete agreement between the employer and the employee. Any other side agreements, e-mails, conversations, or other communications are irrelevant. The employee cannot rely on a manager's promise of a particular salary or terms of a covenant not to compete. This agreement is the final statement of the relationship between the employer and the employee.

CHAPTER 12
TORTS

Part of doing business today—and, indeed, part of everyday life—is the risk of being involved in a lawsuit. The list of circumstances in which businesspersons can be sued is long and varied. A customer who is injured by a security guard at a business establishment, for instance, may sue the business owner, claiming that the security guard's conduct was intentionally wrongful. The parents of a young girl who is bitten while feeding a dolphin may file a suit against Sea World, alleging *negligence* (to be explained later in this chapter).

Any time that one party's allegedly wrongful conduct causes injury to another, an action may arise under the law of *torts* (the word *tort* is French for "wrong"). Through tort law, society compensates those who have suffered injuries as a result of the wrongful conduct of others.

Many of the lawsuits brought by or against business firms are based on the tort theories discussed in this chapter and the next chapter, which covers strict liability and product liability. In addition, Chapter 15 discusses how tort law applies to wrongful actions in the online environment.

SECTION 1
THE BASIS OF TORT LAW

Two notions serve as the basis of all **torts:** wrongs and compensation. Tort law is designed to compensate those who have suffered a loss or injury due to another person's wrongful act. In a tort action, one person or group brings a lawsuit against another person or group to obtain compensation (monetary damages) or other relief for the harm suffered.

The Purpose of Tort Law

Generally, the purpose of tort law is to provide remedies for the violation of various *protected interests.* Society recognizes an interest in personal physical safety. Thus, tort law provides remedies for acts that cause physical injury or that interfere with physical security and freedom of movement.

Society recognizes an interest in protecting property, and tort law provides remedies for acts that cause destruction of or damage to property. Note that in legal usage, the singular *damage* is used to refer to harm or injury to persons or property, and the plural *damages* is used to refer to monetary compensation for such harm or injury.

Damages Available in Tort Actions

Because the purpose of tort law is to compensate the injured party for the damage suffered, you need to have an understanding of the types of damages that plaintiffs seek in tort actions.

COMPENSATORY DAMAGES A plaintiff is awarded **compensatory damages** to compensate or reimburse the plaintiff for actual losses. Thus, the goal is to make the plaintiff whole and put her or him in the same position that she or he would have been in had the tort not occurred. Compensatory damages awards are often broken down into *special damages* and *general damages.*

Special damages compensate the plaintiff for quantifiable monetary losses. Such losses might include medical expenses, lost wages and benefits (now and in the future), extra costs, the loss of irreplaceable items, and the costs of repairing or replacing damaged property.

▶ **Case in Point 12.1** Seaway Marine Transport operates the *Enterprise,* a large cargo ship, which has twenty-two hatches for storing coal. When the *Enterprise* positioned itself to receive a load of coal on the shores of Lake Erie, in Ohio, it struck a land-based coal-loading machine operated by Bessemer & Lake Erie Railroad Company. A federal court found

Seaway liable and awarded $522,000 in special damages to compensate Bessemer for the cost of repairing the damage to the loading boom.[1] ◀

General damages compensate individuals (not companies) for the nonmonetary aspects of the harm suffered, such as pain and suffering. A court might award general damages for physical or emotional pain and suffering, loss of companionship, loss of consortium (losing the emotional and physical benefits of a spousal relationship), disfigurement, loss of reputation, or loss or impairment of mental or physical capacity.

PUNITIVE DAMAGES Occasionally, the courts also award **punitive damages** in tort cases to punish the wrongdoer and deter others from similar wrongdoing. Punitive damages are appropriate only when the defendant's conduct was particularly egregious (reprehensible).

Usually, this means that punitive damages are available in *intentional* tort actions and only rarely in negligence lawsuits (negligence actions will be discussed later in this chapter). They may be awarded, however, in suits involving *gross negligence.* Gross negligence can be defined as an intentional failure to perform a manifest duty in reckless disregard of the consequences of such a failure for the life or property of another.

Courts exercise great restraint in granting punitive damages to plaintiffs in tort actions because punitive damages are subject to limitations under the due process clause of the U.S. Constitution (see Chapter 5). The United States Supreme Court has held that to the extent an award of punitive damages is grossly excessive, it furthers no legitimate purpose and violates due process requirements.[2] Consequently, an appellate court will sometimes reduce the amount of punitive damages awarded to a plaintiff on the ground that it is excessive and thereby violates the due process clause.[3]

Tort Reform

Tort law performs a valuable function by enabling injured parties to obtain compensation. Nevertheless, critics contend that certain aspects of today's tort law encourage too many trivial and unfounded lawsuits, which clog the courts and add unnecessary costs. They say that damages awards are often excessive and bear little relationship to the actual damage suffered, which inspires more plaintiffs to file lawsuits. The result, in the critics' view, is a system that disproportionately rewards a few plaintiffs while imposing a "tort tax" on business and society as a whole. For instance, to avoid *medical malpractice* (see page 296) suits, physicians and hospitals often order more tests than necessary.

TYPES OF REFORMS The federal government and a number of states have begun to take some steps toward tort reform. Measures to reduce the number of tort cases can include any of the following:

1. Limiting the amount of both punitive damages and general damages that can be awarded.
2. Capping the amount that attorneys can collect in *contingency fees* (attorneys' fees that are based on a percentage of the damages awarded to the client—see Chapter 2).
3. Requiring the losing party to pay both the plaintiff's and the defendant's expenses.

FEDERAL REFORM At the federal level, the Class Action Fairness Act (CAFA) of 2005[4] shifted jurisdiction over large interstate tort and product liability class-action lawsuits from the state courts to the federal courts. (A *class action* is a lawsuit in which a large number of plaintiffs bring the suit as a group. *Product liability* suits involve the manufacture, sale, and distribution of dangerous and defective goods—see Chapter 13 for details.)

The CAFA prevents plaintiffs' attorneys from *forum shopping*—looking for a state court known to be sympathetic to their clients' cause. Previously, some state courts had been predisposed to award large damages in class-action suits, even when the case had only a weak connection to that jurisdiction. State courts no longer have jurisdiction over class actions under the CAFA.

STATE REFORMS At the state level, more than half of the states have placed caps ranging from $250,000 to $750,000 on noneconomic general damages (for example, pain and suffering), especially in medical malpractice suits. More than thirty states have limited punitive damages, with some imposing outright bans.

Note that the supreme courts in about half a dozen states have declared their state's damages caps to be unconstitutional. ▶ **Case in Point 12.2** Naython

1. *Bessemer & Lake Erie Railroad Co. v. Seaway Marine Transport,* 357 F.3d 596 (6th Cir. 2010).
2. *State Farm Mutual Automobile Insurance Co. v. Campbell,* 538 U.S. 408, 123 S.Ct. 1513, 155 L.Ed.2d 585 (2003).
3. See, for example, *Buell-Wilson v. Ford Motor Co.,* 160 Cal.App.4th 1107, 73 Cal.Rptr.3d 277 (2008).
4. 28 U.S.C. Sections 1711–1715, 1453.

Watts was born with disabling brain injuries because Cox Medical Centers in Missouri, and its associated physicians, were negligent in providing health-care services. At the age of six, Naython cannot walk, talk, or feed himself; has the mental capacity of a two-year-old; suffers from seizures; and needs around-the-clock care. His mother, Deborah Watts, sued the medical center on his behalf. Watts won a $1.45 million jury award for noneconomic damages, plus $3.37 million for future medical damages.

The trial court reduced the noneconomic damages award to $350,000—the statutory cap under Missouri's law. State law also required the trial court to split the future damages award into two parts, with half the amount payable in yearly installments for fifty years (Naython's life expectancy). Watts appealed. Missouri's highest court struck down the state's damages cap, holding that it had violated the state constitution's right to trial by jury. The court reasoned that the amount of damages is a fact for the jury to determine, and the legislature cannot place caps on jury awards independent of the facts of a case.[5] ◀

Classification of Torts

There are two broad classifications of torts: *intentional torts* and *unintentional torts* (torts involving negligence). The classification of a particular tort depends largely on how the tort occurs (intentionally or negligently) and the surrounding circumstances. Intentional torts result from the intentional violation of person or property (fault plus intent). Negligence results from the breach of a duty to act reasonably (fault without intent).

Defenses

Even if a plaintiff proves all the elements of a tort, the defendant can raise a number of legally recognized *defenses* (reasons why the plaintiff should not obtain damages). The defenses available may vary depending on the specific tort involved. A common defense to intentional torts against persons, for instance, is *consent*. When a person consents to the act that damages her or him, there is generally no liability. The most widely used defense in negligence actions is *comparative negligence* (see page 301). A successful defense releases the defendant from partial or full liability for the tortious act.

5. *Watts v. Lester E. Cox Medical Centers,* 376 S.W.3d 633 (Mo. 2012).

SECTION 2

INTENTIONAL TORTS AGAINST PERSONS

An **intentional tort,** as the term implies, requires intent. The **tortfeasor** (the one committing the tort) must intend to commit an act, the consequences of which interfere with another's personal or business interests in a way not permitted by law. An evil or harmful motive is not required—in fact, the person committing the action may even have a beneficial motive for doing what turns out to be a tortious act.

In tort law, *intent* means only that the person intended the consequences of his or her act or knew with substantial certainty that specific consequences would result from the act. The law generally assumes that individuals intend the *normal* consequences of their actions. Thus, forcefully pushing another—even if done in jest—is an intentional tort (if injury results), because the object of a strong push can ordinarily be expected to fall down.

In addition, intent can be transferred when a defendant intends to harm one individual, but unintentionally harms a second person. This is called **transferred intent.** ▶ **Example 12.3** Alex swings a bat intending to hit Blake but misses and hits Carson instead. Carson can sue Alex for the tort of battery (discussed shortly) because Alex's intent to harm Blake can be transferred to Carson. ◀

Assault

An **assault** is any intentional and unexcused threat of immediate harmful or offensive contact—words or acts that create a reasonably believable threat. An assault can occur even if there is no actual contact with the plaintiff, provided that the defendant's conduct creates a reasonable apprehension of imminent harm in the plaintiff. Tort law aims to protect individuals from having to expect harmful or offensive contact.

Battery

If the act that created the apprehension is *completed* and results in harm to the plaintiff, it is a **battery**—an unexcused and harmful or offensive physical contact *intentionally* performed. ▶ **Example 12.4** Ivan threatens Jean with a gun and then shoots her. The pointing of the gun at Jean is an assault. The firing of the gun (if the bullet hits Jean) is a battery. ◀

The contact can be harmful, or it can be merely offensive (such as an unwelcome kiss). Physical injury need not occur. The contact can involve any part of the body or anything attached to it—for instance, a hat, a purse, or a jacket. The contact can be made by the defendant or by some force set in motion by the defendant, such as by throwing a rock. Whether the contact is offensive is determined by the *reasonable person standard.*[6]

If the plaintiff shows that there was contact, and the jury (or judge, if there is no jury) agrees that the contact was offensive, then the plaintiff has a right to compensation. A plaintiff may be compensated for the emotional harm or loss of reputation resulting from a battery, as well as for physical harm. A defendant may assert self-defense or defense of others in an attempt to justify his or her conduct.

False Imprisonment

False imprisonment is the intentional confinement or restraint of another person's activities without justification. False imprisonment interferes with the freedom to move without restraint. The confinement can be accomplished through the use of physical barriers, physical restraint, or threats of physical force. Moral pressure does not constitute false imprisonment. It is essential that the person being restrained does not wish to be restrained. (The plaintiff's consent to the restraint bars any liability.)

Businesspersons often face suits for false imprisonment after they have attempted to confine a suspected shoplifter for questioning. Under the "privilege to detain" granted to merchants in most states, a merchant can use *reasonable force* to detain or delay persons suspected of shoplifting and hold them for the police. Although laws pertaining to this privilege vary from state to state, generally any detention must be conducted in a *reasonable* manner and for only a *reasonable* length of time. Undue force or unreasonable detention can lead to liability for the business.

Cities and counties may also face lawsuits for false imprisonment if they detain individuals without reason. ▶ **Case in Point 12.5** Police arrested Adetokunbo Shoyoye for an unpaid subway ticket and for a theft that had been committed by someone who had stolen his identity. A court ordered him to be released, but a county employee mistakenly confused Shoyoye's paperwork with that of another person—who was scheduled to be sent to state prison. As a result, instead of being released, Shoyoye was held in county jail for more than two weeks. Shoyoye later sued the county for false imprisonment and won.[7] ◀

Intentional Infliction of Emotional Distress

The tort of *intentional infliction of emotional distress* involves an intentional act that amounts to extreme and outrageous conduct resulting in severe emotional distress to another. To be **actionable** (capable of serving as the ground for a lawsuit), the act must be extreme and outrageous to the point that it exceeds the bounds of decency accepted by society.

OUTRAGEOUS CONDUCT Courts in most jurisdictions are wary of emotional distress claims and confine them to situations involving truly outrageous behavior. Generally, repeated annoyances (such as those experienced by a person who is being stalked), coupled with threats, are enough. Acts that cause indignity or annoyance alone usually are not sufficient.

▶ **Example 12.6** A father attacks a man who has had consensual sexual relations with the father's nineteen-year-old daughter. The father handcuffs the man to a steel pole and threatens to kill him unless he leaves town immediately. The father's conduct may be sufficiently extreme and outrageous to be actionable as an intentional infliction of emotional distress. ◀

LIMITED BY THE FIRST AMENDMENT When the outrageous conduct consists of speech about a public figure, the First Amendment's guarantee of freedom of speech also limits emotional distress claims.

▶ **Case in Point 12.7** *Hustler* magazine once printed a false advertisement that showed a picture of the late Reverend Jerry Falwell and described him as having lost his virginity to his mother in an outhouse while he was drunk. Falwell sued the magazine for intentional infliction of emotional distress and won, but the United States Supreme Court overturned the decision. The Court held that creators of parodies of public figures are protected under the First Amendment from intentional infliction of emotional distress claims. (The Court used the same standards that apply to public figures in defamation lawsuits, discussed next.)[8] ◀

---

6. The *reasonable person standard* is an "objective" test of how a reasonable person would have acted under the same circumstances. See "The Duty of Care and Its Breach" later in this chapter.

7. *Shoyoye v. County of Los Angeles,* 203 Cal.App.4th 947, 137 Cal.Rptr.3d 839 (2012).

8. *Hustler Magazine, Inc. v. Falwell,* 485 U.S. 46, 108 S.Ct. 876, 99 L.Ed.2d 41 (1988). For another example of how the courts protect parody, see *Busch v. Viacom International, Inc.,* 477 F.Supp.2d 764 (N.D.Tex. 2007), involving a false endorsement of televangelist Pat Robertson's diet shake.

Defamation

As discussed in Chapter 5, the freedom of speech guaranteed by the First Amendment is not absolute. The courts are required to balance the vital guarantee of free speech against other pervasive and strong social interests, including society's interest in preventing and redressing attacks on reputation.

Defamation of character involves wrongfully hurting a person's good reputation. The law imposes a general duty on all persons to refrain from making false, defamatory *statements of fact* about others. Breaching this duty in writing or in another permanent form (such as a digital recording) involves the tort of **libel.** Breaching this duty orally involves the tort of **slander.** The tort of defamation also arises when a false statement of fact is made about a person's product, business, or legal ownership rights to property.

To establish defamation, a plaintiff normally must prove the following:

1. The defendant made a false statement of fact.
2. The statement was understood as being about the plaintiff and tended to harm the plaintiff's reputation.
3. The statement was published to at least one person other than the plaintiff.
4. If the plaintiff is a public figure, she or he must prove *actual malice* (discussed on page 289).

STATEMENT-OF-FACT REQUIREMENT Often at issue in defamation lawsuits (including online defamation, which will be discussed later in this chapter) is whether the defendant made a statement of fact or a *statement of opinion*. Statements of opinion normally are not actionable because they are protected under the First Amendment.

In other words, making a negative statement about another person is not defamation unless the statement is false and represents something as a fact rather than a personal opinion. ▶ **Example 12.8** The statement "Lane cheats on his taxes," if false, can lead to liability for defamation. The statement "Lane is a jerk," however, cannot constitute defamation because it is an opinion. ◀

THE PUBLICATION REQUIREMENT The basis of the tort of defamation is the publication of a statement or statements that hold an individual up to contempt, ridicule, or hatred. *Publication* here means that the defamatory statements are communicated (either intentionally or accidentally) to persons other than the defamed party. ▶ **Example 12.9** If Rodriques sends Andrews a private handwritten letter falsely accusing him of embezzling funds, the action does not constitute libel. If Peters falsely states that Gordon is dishonest and incompetent when no one else is around, the action does not constitute slander. In neither instance was the message communicated to a third party. ◀

The courts have generally held that even dictating a letter to a secretary constitutes publication, although the publication may be privileged (a concept that will be explained shortly). Moreover, if a third party merely overhears defamatory statements by chance, the courts usually hold that this also constitutes publication. Defamatory statements made via the Internet are actionable as well. Note also that any individual who repeats or republishes defamatory statements normally is liable even if that person reveals the source of the statements.

DAMAGES FOR LIBEL Once a defendant's liability for libel is established, general damages are presumed as a matter of law. General damages are designed to compensate the plaintiff for nonspecific harms such as disgrace or dishonor in the eyes of the community, humiliation, injured reputation, and emotional distress—harms that are difficult to measure. In other words, to recover damages, the plaintiff need not prove that he or she was actually harmed in any specific way as a result of the libelous statement.

DAMAGES FOR SLANDER In contrast to cases alleging libel, in a case alleging slander, the plaintiff must prove *special damages* to establish the defendant's liability. The plaintiff must show that the slanderous statement caused her or him to suffer actual economic or monetary losses.

Unless this initial hurdle of proving special damages is overcome, a plaintiff alleging slander normally cannot go forward with the suit and recover any damages. This requirement is imposed in slander cases because oral statements have a temporary quality. In contrast, a libelous (written) statement has the quality of permanence and can be circulated widely, especially through tweets and blogs. Also, libel usually results from some degree of deliberation by the author.

SLANDER *PER SE* Exceptions to the burden of proving special damages in cases alleging slander are made for certain types of slanderous statements. If a false statement constitutes "slander *per se*," it is actionable with no proof of special damages required. In most states, the following four types of declarations are considered to be slander *per se:*

1. A statement that another has a particular type of disease (such as a sexually transmitted disease or mental illness).
2. A statement that another has committed improprieties while engaging in a profession or trade.
3. A statement that another has committed or has been imprisoned for a serious crime.
4. A statement that a person (usually only unmarried persons and sometimes only women) is unchaste or has engaged in serious sexual misconduct.

DEFENSES TO DEFAMATION Truth is normally an absolute defense against a defamation charge. In other words, if a defendant in a defamation case can prove that the allegedly defamatory statements of fact were true, normally no tort has been committed.

Other defenses to defamation may exist if the speech is *privileged* or concerns a public figure. Note that the majority of defamation actions are filed in state courts, and state laws differ somewhat in the defenses they allow, such as privilege (discussed shortly).

At the heart of the following case were allegedly defamatory statements posted online that criticized a doctor for what the son of one of the doctor's patients perceived as rude and insensitive behavior.

CASE ANALYSIS

Case 12.1 McKee v. Laurion

Supreme Court of Minnesota, 825 N.W.2d 725 (2013).

IN THE LANGUAGE OF THE COURT

PAGE, Justice.

* * * *

On April 17, 2010, Kenneth Laurion, the father of Dennis Laurion (Laurion), was admitted to St. Luke's Hospital in Duluth [Minnesota] after suffering a hemorrhagic stroke. On April 19, Kenneth Laurion was transferred from the intensive care unit (ICU) of St. Luke's to a private room. The attending physician arranged for Dr. [David] McKee, a neurologist, to examine Kenneth Laurion. Dr. McKee had never met Kenneth Laurion before he examined him on April 19.

Three family members were present in Kenneth Laurion's hospital room when Dr. McKee's examination began: Laurion, his mother, and his wife. The examination lasted no longer than 20 minutes, during which time Dr. McKee made certain statements and acted in a manner that, as a whole, the Laurions perceived as rude and insensitive. After Kenneth Laurion had been discharged from the hospital, Laurion posted the following statements regarding Dr. McKee on various "rate-your-doctor" websites:

> My father spent 2 days in ICU after a hemorrhagic stroke. He saw a speech therapist and a physical therapist for evaluation. About 10 minutes after my father transferred from ICU to a ward room, Dr. McKee walked into a family visit with my dad. He seemed upset that my father had been moved. Never having met my father or his family, Dr. McKee said, "When you weren't in ICU, I had to spend time finding out if you transferred or died." When we gaped at him, he said, "Well, 44 percent of hemorrhagic strokes die within 30 days. I guess this is the better option." * * * When my father said his gown was just hanging from his neck without a back, Dr. McKee said, "That doesn't matter." My wife said, "It matters to us; let us go into the hall."

* * * *

After learning of Laurion's online postings from another patient, Dr. McKee commenced this action [in a Minnesota state court] against Laurion, asserting claims for defamation * * * . Laurion moved for summary judgment seeking dismissal of Dr. McKee's lawsuit. The * * * court granted Laurion's motion * * * , concluding that * * * the statements were * * * substantially true.

The court of appeals * * * reversed the [lower] court * * * . The [appellate] court concluded that * * * there were genuine issues of material fact as to the statements' falsity.

* * * *

Truth is a complete defense to a defamation action and true statements, however disparaging, are not actionable. * * * *If the statement is true in substance, minor inaccuracies of expression or detail are immaterial. Minor inaccuracies do not amount to falsity so long as the substance, the gist, the sting, of the libelous charge is justified.* A statement is substantially true if it would have the same effect on the mind of the reader or listener as that which the pleaded truth would have produced.

CASE 12.1 CONTINUES ➧

CASE 12.1 CONTINUED

The plaintiff has the burden of proving falsity in order to establish a successful defamation claim. [Emphasis added.]

Viewing the evidence here in a light most favorable to Dr. McKee, we conclude that there is no genuine issue of material fact as to the falsity of [the] statements * * *. As to Statement 1 (Dr. McKee said he had to "spend time finding out if you transferred or died."), Dr. McKee described his account of the statement in his deposition testimony:

> I made a jocular [funny] comment * * * to the effect of I had looked for Kenneth Laurion up in the intensive care unit and was glad to find that, when he wasn't there, that he had been moved to a regular hospital bed, because you only go one of two ways when you leave the intensive care unit; you either have improved to the point where you're someplace like this or you leave because you've died.

In light of the substantial similarity between Statement 1 and Dr. McKee's account, we conclude that any differences between the two versions are nothing more than minor inaccuracies that cannot serve as a basis for satisfying the falsity element of a defamation claim. Here, the gist or sting of Laurion's and Dr. McKee's versions are the same. Both communicate the notion that patients in the intensive care unit who have suffered a hemorrhagic stroke leave the intensive care unit either because they have been transferred to a regular room or they have died. Therefore, the substance of Statement 1 is justified given the similarity of the two versions. In other words, Dr. McKee's account of what he said would produce the same effect on the mind of the reader as Statement 1. The minor inaccuracies of expression in Statement 1 as compared to Dr. McKee's version of what he said do not give rise to a genuine issue as to falsity. For these reasons, we conclude that there is no genuine issue of material fact as to the falsity of Statement 1.

As to Statement 2 (Dr. McKee said, "Well, 44 percent of hemorrhagic strokes die within 30 days. I guess this is the better option."), Dr. McKee acknowledged in his deposition that during the examination of Kenneth Laurion, he communicated to those present that some ICU patients die. However, he denies referencing a specific percentage. Thus, Dr. McKee posits that Statement 2 is false, or that, at the least, there is a genuine issue of material fact as to the falsity of Statement 2 because he never stated a specific percentage. The problem for Dr. McKee with respect to Statement 2 is that the gist or sting of Statement 2 is the mention of hemorrhagic stroke patients dying and not the percentage referenced. Statement 2 squarely satisfies the test for substantial truth because it would have the same effect on the reader regardless of whether a specific percentage is referenced (or whether the percentage is accurate). The presence or absence of a specific percentage within Statement 2, without more, has no bearing on how a reader would perceive the statement because the gist or sting of Dr. McKee's reference to death does not change based on the statistical reference. Nor does the presence, absence, or inaccuracy of the stated percentage, without more, cast Dr. McKee in a more negative light than does his discussion of patients dying. That is especially true when the reader is given no context for the statistics. Therefore, we conclude that there is no genuine issue of material fact as to the falsity of Statement 2.

As to Statement [3] (Dr. McKee said, "That doesn't matter" that the patient's gown did not cover his backside), Dr. McKee testified that he told the patient that the gown "looks like it's okay" because it did not appear that the gown was at risk of falling off. We are not persuaded that there is any meaningful difference between the two versions of the statements sufficient to create a genuine issue as to the falsity of Statement [3]. The substance or gist of the two versions is the same. Commenting that the gown "looks like it's okay" is another way of communicating that "it didn't matter" that the gown was not tied in the back. Thus, any inaccuracy of expression does not change the meaning of what Dr. McKee admits to having said. For these reasons, we conclude that Statement [3] is not actionable.

* * * *

Because the [three] statements at issue, viewed individually or in the context of the entire posting, are not actionable, we conclude that the [lower] court properly granted summary judgment in favor of Laurion.

Reversed.

LEGAL REASONING QUESTIONS

1. What are the required elements to establish a claim of defamation? Which party has to plead and prove these elements?
2. Which element of the claim is undercut by the "truth"?
3. How did the court's interpretation of the "truth" affect its decision in this case?
4. Suppose that Laurion had posted online, "When I mentioned Dr. McKee's name to a friend who is a nurse, she said, 'Dr. McKee is a real tool!' " Would this statement have been defamatory? Explain.

Privileged Communications. In some circumstances, a person will not be liable for defamatory statements because she or he enjoys a **privilege,** or immunity. Privileged communications are of two types: absolute and qualified.[9] Only in judicial proceedings and certain government proceedings is an *absolute privilege* granted. Thus, statements made by attorneys and judges in the courtroom during a trial are absolutely privileged, as are statements made by government officials during legislative debate.

In other situations, a person will not be liable for defamatory statements because he or she has a *qualified,* or *conditional, privilege.* An employer's statements in written evaluations of employees, for instance, are protected by a qualified privilege. Generally, if the statements are made in good faith and the publication is limited to those who have a legitimate interest in the communication, the statements fall within the area of qualified privilege.

▶ Example 12.10 Jorge has worked at Sony Corporation for five years and is being considered for a management position. His supervisor, Lydia, writes a memo about Jorge's performance to those evaluating him for the position. The memo contains certain negative statements, which Lydia honestly believes are true. If Lydia limits the disclosure of the memo to company representatives, her statements will likely be protected by a qualified privilege. ◀

Public Figures. Politicians, entertainers, professional athletes, and others in the public eye are considered **public figures.** In general, public figures are considered "fair game," and false and defamatory statements about them that are published in the media will not constitute defamation unless the statements are made with **actual malice.**

To be made with actual malice, a statement must be made *with either knowledge of its falsity or a reckless disregard of the truth.*[10] Statements made about public figures, especially when they are communicated via a public medium, usually are related to matters of general public interest. Public figures generally have some access to a public medium for answering belittling falsehoods about themselves. For these reasons, public figures have a greater burden of proof in defamation cases (to show actual malice) than do private individuals.

Invasion of Privacy

A person has a right to solitude and freedom from prying public eyes—in other words, to privacy. As mentioned in Chapter 5, the courts have held that certain amendments to the U.S. Constitution imply a right to privacy. Some state constitutions explicitly provide for privacy rights, as do a number of federal and state statutes. Tort law also safeguards these rights through the tort of *invasion of privacy.* Generally, to sue successfully for an invasion of privacy, a person must have a reasonable expectation of privacy, and the invasion must be highly offensive.

INVASION OF PRIVACY UNDER THE COMMON LAW

The following four acts qualify as an invasion of privacy under the common law:

1. *Intrusion into an individual's affairs or seclusion.* Invading someone's home or searching someone's briefcase or laptop without authorization is an invasion of privacy. This tort has been held to extend to eavesdropping by wiretap, unauthorized scanning of a bank account, compulsory blood testing, and window peeping. **▶ Example 12.11** A female sports reporter for ESPN is digitally videoed while naked through the peephole in the door of her hotel room. She will probably win a lawsuit against the man who took the video and posted it on the Internet. ◀
2. *False light.* Publication of information that places a person in a false light is also an invasion of privacy. For instance, it is an invasion of privacy to write a story about a person that attributes ideas and opinions not held by that person. (Publishing such a story could involve the tort of defamation as well.) **▶ Example 12.12** An Arkansas newspaper prints an article with the headline "Special Delivery: World's oldest newspaper carrier, 101, quits because she's pregnant!" Next to the article is a picture of a ninety-six-year-old woman who is not the subject of the article (and not pregnant). She sues the paper for placing her in a false light and probably will prevail. ◀
3. *Public disclosure of private facts.* This type of invasion of privacy occurs when a person publicly discloses private facts about an individual that an ordinary person would find objectionable or embarrassing. A newspaper account of a private

9. Note that the term *privileged communication* in this context is not the same as privileged communication between a professional, such as an attorney, and his or her client.

10. *New York Times Co. v. Sullivan,* 376 U.S. 254, 84 S.Ct. 710, 11 L.Ed.2d 686 (1964). As mentioned earlier, the First Amendment also protects the creator of a parody from liability for defamation of a public figure.

citizen's sex life or financial affairs could be an actionable invasion of privacy. This is so even if the information revealed is true, because it should not be a matter of public concern.

Note, however, that news reports about public figures' personal lives are often not actionable because a public figure's behavior *is* a legitimate public concern. For instance, when U.S. Congressman Anthony Weiner posted partially nude photos of himself on Twitter, his action was a matter of legitimate public concern. In contrast, the same online communications by a neighbor would likely not be a matter of public concern.

4. *Appropriation of identity.* Using a person's name, picture, likeness, or other identifiable characteristic for commercial purposes without permission is also an invasion of privacy. An individual's right to privacy normally includes the right to the exclusive use of her or his identity. ▶ **Example 12.13** An advertising agency asks a singer with a distinctive voice and stage presence to do a marketing campaign for a new automobile. The singer rejects the offer. If the agency then uses someone who imitates the singer's voice and dance moves in the ad, it would be actionable as an appropriation of identity. ◀

APPROPRIATION STATUTES Most states today have codified the common law tort of appropriation of identity in statutes that establish the distinct tort of appropriation or right of publicity. States differ as to the degree of likeness that is required to impose liability for appropriation, however.

Some courts have held that even when an animated character in a video or a video game is made to look like an actual person, there are not enough similarities to constitute appropriation. ▶ **Case in Point 12.14** The Naked Cowboy, Robert Burck, is a street entertainer in New York City who performs for tourists wearing only a white cowboy hat, white cowboy boots, and white underwear. He carries a guitar strategically placed to give the illusion of nudity and has become famous. Burck sued Mars, Inc., the maker of M&Ms candy, over a video it showed on billboards in Times Square that depicted a blue M&M dressed exactly like The Naked Cowboy. The court, however, held that the use of Burck's signature costume did not amount to appropriation.[11] ◀

11. *Burck v. Mars, Inc.*, 571 F.Supp.2d 446 (S.D.N.Y. 2008).

Fraudulent Misrepresentation

A misrepresentation leads another to believe in a condition that is different from the condition that actually exists. Although persons sometimes make misrepresentations accidentally because they are unaware of the existing facts, the tort of **fraudulent misrepresentation,** or *fraud,* involves *intentional* deceit for personal gain. The tort includes several elements:

1. A misrepresentation of material facts or conditions with knowledge that they are false or with reckless disregard for the truth.
2. An intent to induce another party to rely on the misrepresentation.
3. A justifiable reliance on the misrepresentation by the deceived party.
4. Damages suffered as a result of that reliance.
5. A causal connection between the misrepresentation and the injury suffered.

For fraud to occur, more than mere **puffery,** or *seller's talk,* must be involved. Fraud exists only when a person represents as a fact something he or she knows is untrue. For instance, it is fraud to claim that the roof of a building does not leak when one knows that it does. Facts are objectively ascertainable, whereas seller's talk (such as "I am the best accountant in town") is not.

Normally, the tort of fraudulent misrepresentation occurs only when there is reliance on a *statement of fact.* Sometimes, however, reliance on a *statement of opinion* may involve the tort of fraudulent misrepresentation if the individual making the statement of opinion has superior knowledge of the subject matter. For instance, when a lawyer makes a statement of opinion about the law in a state in which the lawyer is licensed to practice, a court might treat it as a statement of fact.

Abusive or Frivolous Litigation

Tort law recognizes that people have a right not to be sued without a legally just and proper reason. It therefore protects individuals from the misuse of litigation. If the party that initiated a lawsuit did so out of malice and without a legitimate legal reason, and ended up losing that suit, the party can be sued for *malicious prosecution.*

Abuse of process can apply to any person using a legal process against another in an improper manner or to accomplish a purpose for which the process was not designed. The key difference between the torts of abuse of process and malicious prosecution is the level of proof. Abuse of process is not limited to prior litigation and does not require the plaintiff to prove malice. It can be based on the wrongful use of subpoenas, court orders to attach or seize real property, or other types of formal legal process.

Concept Summary 12.1 below reviews intentional torts against persons.

SECTION 3

BUSINESS TORTS

The torts known as *business torts* generally involve wrongful interference with another's business rights. Business torts involving wrongful interference generally fall into two categories: interference with a contractual relationship and interference with a business relationship.

Wrongful Interference with a Contractual Relationship

Three elements are necessary for wrongful interference with a contractual relationship to occur:

1. A valid, enforceable contract must exist between two parties.
2. A third party must know that this contract exists.
3. This third party must *intentionally induce* a party to the contract to breach the contract.

Case in Point 12.15 A landmark case in this area involved an opera singer, Joanna Wagner, who was under contract to sing for a man named Lumley for a specified period of years. A man named Gye, who knew of this contract, nonetheless "enticed" Wagner to refuse to carry out the agreement, and Wagner began to sing for Gye. Gye's action constituted a tort because it interfered with the contractual relationship between Wagner and Lumley. (Of course, Wagner's refusal to carry out the agreement also entitled Lumley to sue Wagner for breach of contract.)[12] ◀

The body of tort law relating to wrongful interference with a contractual relationship has increased greatly in recent years. In principle, any lawful contract can be the basis for an action of this type. The contract could be between a firm and its employees or a firm and its customers. Sometimes, a competitor of a firm draws away one of the firm's key employees. Only if the original employer can show that the competitor knew of the contract's existence, and intentionally

12. *Lumley v. Gye*, 118 Eng.Rep. 749 (1853).

CONCEPT SUMMARY 12.1
Intentional Torts against Persons

NAME OF TORT	DESCRIPTION
Assault and Battery	Any unexcused and intentional act that causes another person to be apprehensive of immediate harm is an assault. An assault resulting in physical contact is a battery.
False Imprisonment	An intentional confinement or restraint of another person's movement without justification.
Intentional Infliction of Emotional Distress	An intentional act that amounts to extreme and outrageous conduct resulting in severe emotional distress to another.
Defamation (Libel or Slander)	A false statement of fact, not made under privilege, that is communicated to a third person and that causes damage to a person's reputation. For public figures, the plaintiff must also prove that the statement was made with actual malice.
Invasion of Privacy	Publishing or otherwise making known or using information relating to a person's private life and affairs, with which the public has no legitimate concern, without that person's permission or approval.
Fraudulent Misrepresentation (Fraud)	A false representation made by one party, through misstatement of facts or through conduct, with the intention of deceiving another and on which the other reasonably relies to his or her detriment.
Abusive or Frivolous Litigation	The filing of a lawsuit without legitimate grounds and with malice. Alternatively, the use of a legal process in an improper manner.

induced the breach, can damages be recovered from the competitor.

Wrongful Interference with a Business Relationship

Businesspersons devise countless schemes to attract customers. They are prohibited, however, from unreasonably interfering with another's business in their attempts to gain a greater share of the market.

There is a difference between *competitive practices* and *predatory behavior*—actions undertaken with the intention of unlawfully driving competitors completely out of the market. Attempting to attract customers in general is a legitimate business practice, whereas specifically targeting the customers of a competitor is more likely to be predatory.

▶ **Example 12.16** A shopping mall contains two athletic shoe stores: Joe's and Zappato's. Joe's cannot station an employee at the entrance of Zappato's to divert customers to Joe's by telling them that Joe's will beat Zappato's prices. Doing this would constitute the tort of wrongful interference with a business relationship because it would interfere with a prospective economic advantage. Such behavior is commonly considered to be an unfair trade practice. If this type of activity were permitted, Joe's would reap the benefits of Zappato's advertising. ◀

Generally, a plaintiff must prove that the defendant used predatory methods to intentionally harm an established business relationship or prospective economic advantage. The plaintiff must also prove that the defendant's interference caused the plaintiff to suffer economic harm.

Defenses to Wrongful Interference

A person will not be liable for the tort of wrongful interference with a contractual or business relationship if it can be shown that the interference was justified or permissible. Bona fide competitive behavior—through aggressive marketing and advertising strategies, for instance—is a permissible interference even if it results in the breaking of a contract.

▶ **Example 12.17** Taylor Meats advertises so effectively that it induces Sam's Restaurant to break its contract with Burke's Meat Company. In that situation, Burke's Meat Company will be unable to recover against Taylor Meats on a wrongful interference theory. The public policy that favors free competition through advertising outweighs any possible instability that such competitive activity might cause in contractual relations. ◀

SECTION 4

INTENTIONAL TORTS AGAINST PROPERTY

Intentional torts against property include trespass to land, trespass to personal property, conversion, and disparagement of property. These torts are wrongful actions that interfere with individuals' legally recognized rights with regard to their land or personal property.

The law distinguishes real property from personal property (see Chapter 26). *Real property* is land and things permanently attached to the land, such as a house. *Personal property* consists of all other items, including cash and securities (stocks, bonds, and other ownership interests in companies).

Trespass to Land

A **trespass to land** occurs when a person, without permission, does any of the following:

1. Enters onto, above, or below the surface of land that is owned by another.
2. Causes anything to enter onto land owned by another.
3. Remains on land owned by another or permits anything to remain on it.

Actual harm to the land is not an essential element of this tort because the tort is designed to protect the right of an owner to exclusive possession.

Common types of trespass to land include walking or driving on another's land, shooting a gun over another's land, and throwing rocks at a building that belongs to someone else. Another common form of trespass involves constructing a building so that part of it extends onto an adjoining landowner's property.

ESTABLISHING TRESPASS Before a person can be a trespasser, the real property owner (or another person in actual and exclusive possession of the property, such as a renter) must establish that person as a trespasser. For instance, "posted" trespass signs expressly establish as a trespasser a person who ignores these signs and enters onto the property. A guest in your home is not a trespasser—unless he or she has been asked to leave and refuses. Any person who enters onto another's property to commit an illegal act (such as a thief entering a lumberyard at night to steal lumber) is established impliedly as a trespasser, without posted signs.

DAMAGES At common law, a trespasser is liable for any damage caused to the property and generally cannot hold the owner liable for injuries that the trespasser sustains on the premises. This common law rule is being abandoned in many jurisdictions, however, in favor of a *reasonable duty of care* rule that varies depending on the status of the parties.

For instance, a landowner may have a duty to post a notice that guard dogs patrol the property. Also, if young children were attracted to the property by some object, such a swimming pool or a sand pile, and were injured, the landowner may be held liable for their injuries. This is the so-called *attractive nuisance doctrine*. An owner can normally use reasonable force, however, to remove a trespasser from the premises—or detain the trespasser for a reasonable time—without liability for damages.

DEFENSES AGAINST TRESPASS TO LAND One defense to a claim of trespass is to show that the trespass was warranted—such as when a trespasser enters a building to assist someone in danger. Another defense exists when the trespasser can show that she or he had a *license* to come onto the land.

A **licensee** is one who is invited (or allowed to enter) onto the property of another for the licensee's benefit. A person who enters another's property to read an electric meter, for example, is a licensee. When you purchase a ticket to attend a movie or sporting event, you are licensed to go onto the property of another to view that movie or event.

Note that licenses to enter onto another's property are *revocable* by the property owner. If a property owner asks an electric meter reader to leave and she or he refuses to do so, the meter reader at that point becomes a trespasser.

Trespass to Personal Property

Whenever any individual wrongfully takes or harms the personal property of another or otherwise interferes with the lawful owner's possession and enjoyment of personal property, **trespass to personal property** occurs. This tort may also be called *trespass to chattels* or *trespass to personalty*.[13] In this context, harm means not only destruction of the property, but also anything that diminishes its value, condition, or quality.

Trespass to personal property involves intentional meddling with a possessory interest (one arising from possession), including barring an owner's access to personal property. ▶ **Example 12.18** Kelly takes Ryan's business law book as a practical joke and hides it so that Ryan is unable to find it for several days before the final examination. Here, Kelly has engaged in a trespass to personal property (and also *conversion*, the tort discussed next). ◀

If it can be shown that trespass to personal property was warranted, then a complete defense exists. Most states, for instance, allow automobile repair shops to hold a customer's car (under what is called an *artisan's lien*) when the customer refuses to pay for repairs already completed.

Conversion

Any act that deprives an owner of personal property or of the use of that property without the owner's permission and without just cause can constitute **conversion.** Even the taking of electronic records and data may form the basis of a conversion claim. Often, when conversion occurs, a trespass to personal property also occurs because the original taking of the personal property from the owner was a trespass. Wrongfully retaining the property is conversion.

Conversion is the civil side of crimes related to theft, but it is not limited to theft. Even when the rightful owner consented to the initial taking of the property, so no theft or trespass occurred, a failure to return the property may still be conversion. ▶ **Example 12.19** Chen borrows Mark's iPad mini to use while traveling home from school for the holidays. When Chen returns to school, Mark asks for his iPad back, but Chen says that he gave it to his little brother for Christmas. In this situation, Mark can sue Chen for conversion, and Chen will have to either return the iPad or pay damages equal to its replacement value. ◀

Conversion can occur even when a person mistakenly believed that she or he was entitled to the goods. In other words, good intentions are not a defense against conversion. Someone who buys stolen goods, for instance, may be sued for conversion even if he or she did not know the goods were stolen. If the true owner brings a tort action against the buyer, the buyer must either return the property to the owner or pay the owner the full value of the property (despite having already paid the purchase price to the thief).

13. Pronounced *per*-sun-ul-tee.

Disparagement of Property

Disparagement of property occurs when economically injurious falsehoods are made about another's product or property rather than about another's reputation (as in the tort of defamation). *Disparagement of property* is a general term for torts that can be more specifically referred to as *slander of quality* or *slander of title*.

SLANDER OF QUALITY The publication of false information about another's product, alleging that it is not what its seller claims, constitutes the tort of **slander of quality,** or **trade libel.** To establish trade libel, the plaintiff must prove that the improper publication caused a third person to refrain from dealing with the plaintiff and that the plaintiff sustained economic damages (such as lost profits) as a result.

An improper publication may be both a slander of quality and a defamation of character. For instance, a statement that disparages the quality of a product may also, by implication, disparage the character of a person who would sell such a product.

SLANDER OF TITLE When a publication falsely denies or casts doubt on another's legal ownership of property, resulting in financial loss to the property's owner, the tort of **slander of title** occurs. Usually, this is an intentional tort in which someone knowingly publishes an untrue statement about another's ownership of certain property with the intent of discouraging a third person from dealing with the person slandered. For instance, it would be difficult for a car dealer to attract customers after competitors published a notice that the dealer's stock consisted of stolen automobiles.

See *Concept Summary 12.2* below for a review of intentional torts against property.

SECTION 5

UNINTENTIONAL TORTS (NEGLIGENCE)

The tort of **negligence** occurs when someone suffers injury because of another's failure to live up to a required *duty of care*. In contrast to intentional torts, in torts involving negligence, the tortfeasor neither wishes to bring about the consequences of the act nor believes that they will occur. The person's conduct merely creates a risk of such consequences. If no risk is created, there is no negligence. Moreover, the risk must be foreseeable. In other words, it must be such that a reasonable person engaging in the same activity would anticipate the risk and guard against it. In determining what is reasonable conduct, courts consider the nature of the possible harm.

Many of the actions giving rise to the intentional torts discussed earlier in the chapter constitute negligence if the element of intent is missing (or cannot be proved). ▶ **Example 12.20** Juan walks up to Maya and intentionally shoves her. Maya falls and breaks her arm as a result. In this situation, Juan is liable for the intentional tort of battery. If Juan carelessly bumps into Maya, however, and she falls and breaks her arm as a result, Juan's action constitutes

CONCEPT SUMMARY 12.2
Intentional Torts against Property

NAME OF TORT	DESCRIPTION
Trespass to Land	The invasion of another's real property without consent or privilege. Once a person is expressly or impliedly established as a trespasser, the property owner has specific rights, which may include the right to detain or remove the trespasser.
Trespass to Personal Property	The intentional interference with an owner's right to use, possess, or enjoy his or her personal property without the owner's consent.
Conversion	The wrongful possession or use of another person's personal property without just cause.
Disparagement of Property	Any economically injurious falsehood that is made about another's product or property; an inclusive term for the torts of *slander of quality* and *slander of title*.

negligence. In either situation, Juan has committed a tort. ◀

To succeed in a negligence action, the plaintiff must prove each of the following:

1. *Duty.* The defendant owed a duty of care to the plaintiff.
2. *Breach.* The defendant breached that duty.
3. *Causation.* The defendant's breach caused the plaintiff's injury.
4. *Damages.* The plaintiff suffered a legally recognizable injury.

The Duty of Care and Its Breach

Central to the tort of negligence is the concept of a **duty of care.** The basic principle underlying the duty of care is that people are free to act as they please so long as their actions do not infringe on the interests of others. When someone fails to comply with the duty to exercise reasonable care, a potentially tortious act may have been committed.

Failure to live up to a standard of care may be an act (accidentally setting fire to a building) or an omission (neglecting to put out a campfire). It may be a careless act or a carefully performed but, nevertheless, dangerous act that results in injury. Courts consider the nature of the act (whether it is outrageous or commonplace) and the manner in which the act is performed (carelessly versus cautiously). In addition, courts look at the nature of the injury (whether it is serious or slight) in determining whether the duty of care has been breached. Creating a very slight risk of a dangerous explosion might be unreasonable, whereas creating a distinct possibility of someone's burning his or her fingers on a stove might be reasonable.

THE REASONABLE PERSON STANDARD Tort law measures duty by the **reasonable person standard.** In determining whether a duty of care has been breached, the courts ask how a reasonable person would have acted in the same circumstances. The reasonable person standard is said to be objective. It is not necessarily how a particular person *would* act. It is society's judgment of how an ordinarily prudent person *should* act. If the so-called reasonable person existed, he or she would be careful, conscientious, even tempered, and honest.

The courts frequently use the hypothetical reasonable person standard in other areas of law as well. That individuals are required to exercise a reasonable standard of care in their activities is a pervasive concept in business law. Many of the issues discussed in subsequent chapters of this text have to do with the duty of reasonable care.

In negligence cases, the degree of care to be exercised varies, depending on the defendant's occupation or profession, her or his relationship with the plaintiff, and other factors. Generally, whether an action constitutes a breach of the duty of care is determined on a case-by-case basis. The outcome depends on how the judge (or jury, if it is a jury trial) decides a reasonable person in the position of the defendant would have acted in the particular circumstances of the case.

THE DUTY OF LANDOWNERS Landowners are expected to exercise reasonable care to protect individuals coming onto their property from harm. In some jurisdictions, as mentioned earlier, landowners may even have a duty to protect trespassers against certain risks. Landowners who rent or lease premises to tenants are expected to exercise reasonable care to ensure that the tenants and their guests are not harmed in common areas, such as stairways, entryways, and laundry rooms.

The Duty to Warn Business Invitees of Risks. Retailers and other companies that explicitly or implicitly invite persons to come onto their premises have a duty to exercise reasonable care to protect these **business invitees.** The duty normally requires storeowners to warn business invitees of foreseeable risks, such as construction zones or wet floors, about which the owners knew or *should have known.*

▶ Example 12.21 Liz enters a supermarket, slips on a wet floor, and sustains injuries as a result. If there was no sign or other warning that the floor was wet at the time Liz slipped, the supermarket owner would be liable for damages. A court would hold that the owner was negligent by failing to exercise a reasonable degree of care to protect customers against the foreseeable risk of injury from slipping on the wet floor. The owner should have taken care to avoid this risk and warned the customer of it (by posting a sign or setting out orange cones, for example). ◀

The landowner also has a duty to discover and remove any hidden dangers that might injure a customer or other invitee. Hidden dangers might include uneven surfaces or defects in the pavement of a parking lot or a walkway. Store owners also have a duty to protect customers from slipping and injuring themselves on merchandise that has fallen off the shelves, for example. Thus, the owners of business premises should evaluate and frequently reassess potential hazards on the property to ensure the safety of business invitees.

Obvious Risks Provide an Exception. Some risks, of course, are so obvious that an owner need not warn of them. For example, a business owner does not need to warn customers to open a door before attempting to walk through it. Other risks, however, even though they may seem obvious to a business owner, may not be so in the eyes of another, such as a child. In addition, even if a risk is obvious, that does not necessarily excuse a business owner from the duty to protect its customers from foreseeable harm.

▶ **Case in Point 12.22** Giorgio's Grill is a restaurant in Florida that becomes a nightclub after hours. At those times, traditionally, as the manager of Giorgio's knew, the staff and customers throw paper napkins into the air as the music plays. The napkins land on the floor, but no one picks them up. One night, Jane Izquierdo went to Giorgio's. Although she had been to the club on prior occasions and knew about the napkin-throwing tradition, she slipped and fell, breaking her leg. She sued Giorgio's for negligence, but lost at trial because a jury found that the risk of slipping on the napkins was obvious. A state appellate court reversed, however, holding that the obviousness of a risk does not discharge a business owner's duty to its invitees to maintain the premises in a safe condition.[14] ◀

THE DUTY OF PROFESSIONALS If an individual has knowledge or skill superior to that of an ordinary person, the individual's conduct must be consistent with that status. Professionals—including physicians, dentists, architects, engineers, accountants, and lawyers, among others—are required to have a standard minimum level of special knowledge and ability. Therefore, in determining what constitutes reasonable care in the case of professionals, the law takes their training and expertise into account. Thus, an accountant's conduct is judged not by the reasonable person standard, but by the reasonable accountant standard.

If a professional violates his or her duty of care toward a client, the client may bring a suit against the professional, alleging **malpractice,** which is essentially professional negligence. For instance, a patient might sue a physician for *medical malpractice.* A client might sue an attorney for *legal malpractice.*

14. *Izquierdo v. Gyroscope, Inc.,* 946 So.2d 115 (Fla.App. 2007).

Causation

Another element necessary to a negligence action is *causation.* If a person breaches a duty of care and someone suffers injury, the person's act must have caused the harm for it to constitute the tort of negligence.

COURTS ASK TWO QUESTIONS In deciding whether the requirement of causation is met, the court must address two questions:

1. *Is there causation in fact?* Did the injury occur because of the defendant's act, or would it have occurred anyway? If the injury would not have occurred without the defendant's act, then there is causation in fact.

   Causation in fact usually can be determined by use of the *but for* test: "but for" the wrongful act, the injury would not have occurred. This test determines whether there was an actual cause-and-effect relationship between the act and the injury suffered. In theory, causation in fact is limitless. One could claim, for example, that "but for" the creation of the world, a particular injury would not have occurred. Thus, as a practical matter, the law has to establish limits, and it does so through the concept of proximate cause.
2. *Was the act the proximate, or legal, cause of the injury?* **Proximate cause,** or *legal cause,* exists when the connection between an act and an injury is strong enough to justify imposing liability. Proximate cause asks whether the injuries sustained were foreseeable or were too remotely connected to the incident to trigger liability. Judges use proximate cause to limit the scope of the defendant's liability to a subset of the total number of potential plaintiffs that might have been harmed by the defendant's actions.

   ▶ **Example 12.23** Ackerman carelessly leaves a campfire burning. The fire not only burns down the forest but also sets off an explosion in a nearby chemical plant that spills chemicals into a river, killing all the fish for a hundred miles downstream and ruining the economy of a tourist resort. Should Ackerman be liable to the resort owners? To the tourists whose vacations were ruined? These are questions of proximate cause that a court must decide. ◀

Both of these causation questions must be answered in the affirmative for liability in tort to arise. If there is causation in fact but a court decides that the defendant's action is not the proximate cause of the plaintiff's injury, the causation requirement has not been met. Therefore, the defendant normally will not be liable to the plaintiff.

FORESEEABILITY Questions of proximate cause are linked to the concept of foreseeability because it would be unfair to impose liability on a defendant unless the defendant's actions created a foreseeable risk of injury.

Probably the most cited case on the concept of foreseeability and proximate cause is the *Palsgraf* case, which is presented next. In determining the issue of proximate cause, the court addressed the following question: Does a defendant's duty of care extend only to those who may be injured as a result of a foreseeable risk, or does it also extend to a person whose injury could not reasonably have been foreseen?

CLASSIC CASE 12.2

Palsgraf v. Long Island Railroad Co.

Court of Appeals of New York, 248 N.Y. 339, 162 N.E. 99 (1928).

BACKGROUND AND FACTS The plaintiff, Helen Palsgraf, was waiting for a train on a station platform. A man carrying a package was rushing to catch a train that was moving away from a platform across the tracks from Palsgraf. As the man attempted to jump aboard the moving train, he seemed unsteady and about to fall. A railroad guard on the car reached forward to grab him, and another guard on the platform pushed him from behind to help him board the train.

In the process, the man's package, which (unknown to the railroad guards) contained fireworks, fell on the railroad tracks and exploded. There was nothing about the package to indicate its contents. The repercussions of the explosion caused scales at the other end of the train platform to fall on Palsgraf, causing injuries for which she sued the railroad company. At the trial, the jury found that the railroad guards had been negligent in their conduct. The railroad company appealed. The appellate court affirmed the trial court's judgment, and the railroad company appealed to New York's highest state court.

IN THE LANGUAGE OF THE COURT
CARDOZO, C.J. [Chief Justice]

* * * *

The conduct of the defendant's guard, if a wrong in its relation to the holder of the package, was not a wrong in its relation to the plaintiff, standing far away. Relatively to her it was not negligence at all.

* * * *

* * * What the plaintiff must show is "a wrong" to herself; i.e., a violation of her own right, and not merely a wrong to someone else[.] * * * *The risk reasonably to be perceived defines the duty to be obeyed[.]* * * * Here, by concession, there was nothing in the situation to suggest to the most cautious mind that the parcel wrapped in newspaper would spread wreckage through the station. If the guard had thrown it down knowingly and willfully, he would not have threatened the plaintiff's safety, so far as appearances could warn him. His conduct would not have involved, even then, an unreasonable probability of invasion of her bodily security. Liability can be no greater where the act is inadvertent. [Emphasis added.]

* * * One who seeks redress at law does not make out a cause of action by showing without more that there has been damage to his person. If the harm was not willful, he must show that the act as to him had possibilities of danger so many and apparent as to entitle him to be protected against the doing of it though the harm was unintended. * * * The victim does not sue * * * to vindicate an interest invaded in the person of another. * * * He sues for breach of a duty owing to himself.

* * * [To rule otherwise] would entail liability for any and all consequences, however novel or extraordinary.

CASE 12.2 CONTINUES ➧

CASE 12.2 CONTINUED

DECISION AND REMEDY *Palsgraf's complaint was dismissed. The railroad had not been negligent toward her because injury to her was not foreseeable. Had the owner of the fireworks been harmed, and had he filed suit, there could well have been a different result.*

IMPACT OF THIS CASE ON TODAY'S LAW *The* Palsgraf *case established foreseeability as the test for proximate cause. Today, the courts continue to apply this test in determining proximate cause—and thus tort liability for injuries. Generally, if the victim or the consequences of a harm done were unforeseeable, there is no proximate cause. Note, though, that in the online environment, distinctions based on physical proximity, such as that used by the court in this case, are largely inapplicable.*

THE GLOBAL DIMENSION *What would be the advantages and disadvantages of a universal principle of proximate cause applied everywhere by all courts in all relevant cases? Discuss.*

The Injury Requirement and Damages

For a tort to have been committed, the plaintiff must have suffered a *legally recognizable* injury. To recover damages (receive compensation), the plaintiff must have suffered some loss, harm, wrong, or invasion of a protected interest. Essentially, the purpose of tort law is to compensate for legally recognized harms and injuries resulting from wrongful acts. If no harm or injury results from a given negligent action, there is nothing to compensate—and no tort exists.

For instance, if you carelessly bump into a passerby, who stumbles and falls as a result, you may be liable in tort if the passerby is injured in the fall. If the person is unharmed, however, there normally can be no suit for damages because no injury was suffered.

As mentioned at the start of this chapter, compensatory damages are the norm in negligence cases. Occasionally, though, a court will award punitive damages if the defendant's conduct was *grossly negligent,* meaning that the defendant intentionally failed to perform a duty with reckless disregard of the consequences to others.

Negligence *Per Se*

Certain conduct, whether it consists of an action or a failure to act, may be treated as **negligence *per se*** ("in or of itself"). Negligence *per se* may occur if an individual violates a statute or an ordinance providing for a criminal penalty and that violation causes another to be injured. The statute must be designed to prevent the type of injury that the plaintiff suffered and must clearly set out what standard of conduct is expected. The statute must also indicate when, where, and of whom that conduct is expected. The standard of conduct required by the statute is the duty that the defendant owes to the plaintiff, and a violation of the statute is the breach of that duty.

▶ Case in Point 12.24 A Delaware statute states that anyone "who operates a motor vehicle and who fails to give full time and attention to the operation of the vehicle" is guilty of inattentive driving. Michael Moore was cited for inattentive driving after he collided with Debra Wright's car when he backed a truck out of a parking space. Moore paid the ticket, which meant that he pleaded guilty to violating the statute.

The day after the accident, Wright began having back pain, which eventually required surgery. She sued Moore for damages, alleging negligence *per se.* The court ruled that the inattentive driving statute sets forth a sufficiently specific standard of conduct to warrant application of negligence *per se.*[15] ◀

Good Samaritan Statutes

Most states now have laws that are called **Good Samaritan statutes.**[16] Under these statutes, someone who is aided voluntarily by another cannot turn around and sue the "Good Samaritan" for negligence.

These laws were passed largely to protect physicians and medical personnel who volunteer their services in emergency situations to those in need, such as individuals hurt in car accidents.[17] Indeed, the California Supreme Court has interpreted that state's Good Samaritan statute to mean that a person who

15. *Wright v. Moore,* 931 A.2d 405 (Del.Supr. 2007).

16. These laws derive their name from the Good Samaritan story in the Bible. In the story, a traveler who had been robbed and beaten lay along the roadside, ignored by those passing by. Eventually, a man from the region of Samaria (the "Good Samaritan") stopped to render assistance to the injured person.

17. See, for example, the discussions of various state statutes in *Chamley v. Khokha,* 730 N.W.2d 864 (N.D. 2007), and *Mueller v. McMillian Warner Insurance Co.,* 2006 WI 54, 290 Wis.2d 571, 714 N.W.2d 183 (2006).

renders nonmedical aid is not immune from liability.[18] Thus, only medical personnel and persons rendering medical aid in emergencies are protected in California.

Dram Shop Acts

Many states have also passed **dram shop acts,**[19] under which a bar's owner or bartender may be held liable for injuries caused by a person who became intoxicated while drinking at the bar. The owner or bartender may also be held responsible for continuing to serve a person who was already intoxicated.

Some states' statutes also impose liability on *social hosts* (persons hosting parties) for injuries caused by guests who became intoxicated at the hosts' homes. Under these statutes, it is unnecessary to prove that the bar owner, bartender, or social host was negligent. ▶ **Example 12.25** Jane hosts a Super Bowl party at which Brett, a minor, sneaks alcoholic drinks. Jane is potentially liable for damages resulting from Brett's drunk driving after the party. ◀

SECTION 6
DEFENSES TO NEGLIGENCE

Defendants often defend against negligence claims by asserting that the plaintiffs have failed to prove the existence of one or more of the required elements for negligence. Additionally, there are three basic *affirmative* defenses in negligence cases (defenses that a defendant can use to avoid liability even if the facts are as the plaintiff states): *assumption of risk, superseding cause,* and *contributory and comparative negligence.*

Assumption of Risk

A plaintiff who voluntarily enters into a risky situation, knowing the risk involved, will not be allowed to recover. This is the defense of **assumption of risk,** which requires:

1. Knowledge of the risk.
2. Voluntary assumption of the risk.

The defense of assumption of risk is frequently asserted when the plaintiff was injured during recreational activities that involve known risk, such as skiing and skydiving. Courts do not apply the assumption of risk doctrine in emergency situations. Note that assumption of risk can apply not only to participants in sporting events, but also to spectators and bystanders who are injured while attending those events.

In the following *Spotlight Case,* the issue was whether a spectator at a baseball game voluntarily assumed the risk of being hit by an errant ball thrown while the players were warming up before the game.

18. *Van Horn v. Watson,* 45 Cal.4th 322, 197 P.3d 164, 86 Cal.Rptr.3d 350 (2008).
19. Historically, a dram was a small unit of liquid, and distilled spirits (strong alcoholic liquor) were sold in drams. Thus, a dram shop was a place where liquor was sold in drams.

SPOTLIGHT on the Seattle Mariners

Case 12.3 Taylor v. Baseball Club of Seattle, LP

Court of Appeals of Washington, 132 Wash.App. 32, 130 P.3d 835 (2006).

BACKGROUND AND FACTS Delinda Taylor went to a Seattle Mariners baseball game at Safeco Field with her boyfriend and two minor sons. Their seats were four rows up from the field along the right field foul line. They arrived more than an hour before the game so that they could see the players warm up and get their autographs. When she walked in, Taylor saw that Mariners pitcher Freddy Garcia was throwing a ball back and forth with José Mesa right in front of their seats.

As Taylor stood in front of her seat, she looked away from the field, and a ball thrown by Mesa got past Garcia and struck her in the face, causing serious injuries. Taylor sued the Mariners for the allegedly

CASE 12.3 CONTINUES ➧

CASE 12.3 CONTINUED

negligent warm-up throw. The Mariners filed a motion for summary judgment in which they argued that Taylor, a longtime Mariners fan, was familiar with baseball and the inherent risk of balls entering the stands. Thus, the motion asserted, Taylor had assumed the risk of her injury. The trial court granted the motion and dismissed Taylor's case. Taylor appealed.

IN THE LANGUAGE OF THE COURT
DWYER, J. [Judge]

* * * *

* * * For many decades, courts have required baseball stadiums to screen some seats—generally those behind home plate—to provide protection to spectators who choose it.

A sport spectator's assumption of risk and a defendant sports team's duty of care are accordingly discerned under the doctrine of primary assumption of risk. * * * "Implied *primary* assumption of risk arises where a plaintiff has impliedly consented (often in advance of any negligence by defendant) to relieve defendant of a duty to plaintiff regarding specific *known* and appreciated risks." [Emphasis in original.]

* * * *

Under this implied primary assumption of risk, defendant must show that plaintiff had full subjective understanding of the specific risk, both its nature and presence, and that he or she voluntarily chose to encounter the risk.

* * * It is undisputed that the warm-up is part of the sport, that spectators such as Taylor purposely attend that portion of the event, and that the Mariners permit ticket-holders to view the warm-up.

* * * We find the fact that Taylor was injured during warm-up is not legally significant because that portion of the event is necessarily incident to the game.

* * * *

Here, there is no evidence that the circumstances leading to Taylor's injury constituted an unusual danger. It is undisputed that it is the normal, every-day practice at all levels of baseball for pitchers to warm up in the manner that led to this incident. *The risk of injuries such as Taylor's are within the normal comprehension of a spectator who is familiar with the game.* Indeed, the possibility of an errant ball entering the stands is part of the game's attraction for many spectators. [Emphasis added.]

* * * The record contains substantial evidence regarding Taylor's familiarity with the game. She attended many of her sons' baseball games, she witnessed balls entering the stands, she had watched Mariners' games both at the Kingdome and on television, and she knew that there was no screen protecting her seats, which were close to the field. In fact, as she walked to her seat she saw the players warming up and was excited about being in an unscreened area where her party might get autographs from the players and catch balls.

DECISION AND REMEDY *The state intermediate appellate court affirmed the lower court's judgment. As a spectator who chose to sit in an unprotected area of seats, Taylor voluntarily undertook the risk associated with being hit by an errant baseball thrown during the warm-up before the game.*

WHAT IF THE FACTS WERE DIFFERENT? *Would the result in this case have been different if it had been Taylor's minor son, rather than Taylor herself, who had been struck by the ball? Should courts apply the doctrine of assumption of risk to children? Discuss.*

THE LEGAL ENVIRONMENT DIMENSION *What is the basis underlying the defense of assumption of risk? How does that basis support the court's decision in this case?*

Superseding Cause

An unforeseeable intervening event may break the causal connection between a wrongful act and an injury to another. If so, the intervening event acts as a **superseding cause**—that is, it relieves the defendant of liability for injuries caused by the intervening event.

▶ **Example 12.26** While riding his bicycle, Derrick negligently hits Julie, who is walking on the sidewalk. As a result of the impact, Julie falls and fractures her hip. While she is waiting for help to arrive, a small aircraft crashes nearby and explodes, and some of the fiery debris hits her, causing her to sustain severe burns. Derrick will be liable for the damages related to Julie's fractured hip, because the risk of injuring her with his bicycle was foreseeable. Normally, Derrick will not be liable for the burns caused by the plane crash—because the risk of a plane crashing nearby and injuring Julie was not foreseeable. ◀

Contributory Negligence

All individuals are expected to exercise a reasonable degree of care in looking out for themselves. In the past, under the common law doctrine of **contributory negligence,** a plaintiff who was also negligent (failed to exercise a reasonable degree of care) could not recover anything from the defendant. Under this rule, no matter how insignificant the plaintiff's negligence was relative to the defendant's negligence, the plaintiff would be precluded from recovering any damages. Today, only a few jurisdictions still hold to this doctrine.

Comparative Negligence

In most states, the doctrine of contributory negligence has been replaced by a **comparative negligence** standard. Under this standard, both the plaintiff's and the defendant's negligence are computed, and the liability for damages is distributed accordingly. Some jurisdictions have adopted a "pure" form of comparative negligence that allows the plaintiff to recover, even if the extent of his or her fault is greater than that of the defendant. Under pure comparative negligence, if the plaintiff was 80 percent at fault and the defendant 20 percent at fault, the plaintiff may recover 20 percent of his or her damages.

Many states' comparative negligence statutes, however, contain a "50 percent" rule that prevents the plaintiff from recovering any damages if she or he was more than 50 percent at fault. Under this rule, a plaintiff who is 35 percent at fault could recover 65 percent of his or her damages, but a plaintiff who is 65 percent (more than 50 percent) at fault could recover nothing.

Reviewing: Torts

Elaine Sweeney went to Ragged Mountain Ski Resort in New Hampshire with a friend. Elaine went snow tubing down a snow-tube run designed exclusively for snow tubers. There were no Ragged Mountain employees present in the snow-tube area to instruct Elaine on the proper use of a snow tube. On her fourth run down the trail, Elaine crossed over the center line between snow-tube lanes, collided with another snow tuber, and was injured. Elaine filed a negligence action against Ragged Mountain seeking compensation for the injuries that she sustained. Two years earlier, the New Hampshire state legislature had enacted a statute that prohibited a person who participates in the sport of skiing from suing a ski-area operator for injuries caused by the risks inherent in skiing. Using the information presented in the chapter, answer the following questions.

1. What defense will Ragged Mountain probably assert?
2. The central question in this case is whether the state statute establishing that skiers assume the risks inherent in the sport bars Elaine's suit. What would your decision be on this issue? Why?
3. Suppose that the court concludes that the statute applies only to skiing and not to snow tubing. Will Elaine's lawsuit be successful? Explain.
4. Now suppose that the jury concludes that Elaine was partly at fault for the accident. Under what theory might her damages be reduced in proportion to the degree to which her actions contributed to the accident and her resulting injuries?

DEBATE THIS . . . *Each time a state legislature enacts a law that applies the assumption of risk doctrine to a particular sport, participants in that sport suffer.*

Terms and Concepts

ExamPrep

Issue Spotters

1. Jana leaves her truck's motor running while she enters a Kwik-Pik Store. The truck's transmission engages, and the vehicle crashes into a gas pump, starting a fire that spreads to a warehouse on the next block. The warehouse collapses, causing its billboard to fall and injure Lou, a bystander. Can Lou recover from Jana? Why or why not? **(See page 296.)**
2. A water pipe bursts, flooding a Metal Fabrication Company utility room and tripping the circuit breakers on a panel in the room. Metal Fabrication contacts Nouri, a licensed electrician with five years' experience, to check the damage and turn the breakers back on. Without testing for short circuits, which Nouri knows that he should do, he tries to switch on a breaker. He is electrocuted, and his wife sues Metal Fabrication for damages, alleging negligence. What might the firm successfully claim in defense? **(See page 299.)**

- **Check your answers to the Issue Spotters against the answers provided in Appendix E at the end of this text.**

Before the Test

Go to **www.cengagebrain.com**, enter the ISBN 9781285428949, and click on "Find" to locate this textbook's Web site. Then, click on "Access Now" under "Study Tools," and select Chapter 12 at the top. There, you will find an Interactive Quiz that you can take to assess your mastery of the concepts in this chapter, as well as Flashcards and a Glossary of important terms.

Business Scenarios

12–1. Defamation. Richard is an employee of the Dun Construction Corp. While delivering materials to a construction site, he carelessly backs Dun's truck into a passenger vehicle driven by Green. This is Richard's second accident in six months. When the company owner, Dun, learns of this latest accident, a heated discussion ensues, and Dun fires Richard. Dun is so angry that he immediately writes a letter to the union of which Richard is a member and to all other construction companies in the community, stating that Richard is the "worst driver in the city" and that "anyone who hires him is asking for legal liability." Richard files a suit against Dun, alleging libel on the basis of the statements made in the letters. Discuss the results. **(See page 286.)**

12–2. Wrongful Interference. Lothar owns a bakery. He has been trying to obtain a long-term contract with the owner of Martha's Tea Salons for some time. Lothar starts a local advertising campaign on radio and television and in the newspaper. This advertising campaign is so persuasive that Martha decides to break the contract she has had with Harley's Bakery so that she can patronize Lothar's bakery. Is Lothar liable to Harley's Bakery for the tort of wrongful interference with a contractual relationship? Is Martha liable for this tort? Why or why not? **(See page 291.)**

12–3. Liability to Business Invitees. Kim went to Ling's Market to pick up a few items for dinner. It was a stormy day, and the wind had blown water through the market's door each time it opened. As Kim entered through the door, she slipped and fell in the rainwater that had accumulated on the floor. The manager knew of the weather conditions but had not posted any sign to warn customers of the water hazard. Kim injured her back as a result of the fall and sued Ling's for damages. Can Ling's be held liable for negligence? Discuss. **(See page 295.)**

Business Case Problems

12–4. Spotlight on Intentional Torts—Defamation. Sharon Yeagle was an assistant to the vice president of student affairs at Virginia Polytechnic Institute and State University (Virginia Tech). As part of her duties, Yeagle helped students participate in the Governor's Fellows Program. The *Collegiate Times,* Virginia Tech's student newspaper, published an article about the university's success in placing students in the program. The article's text surrounded a block quotation attributed to Yeagle with the phrase "Director of Butt Licking" under her name. Yeagle sued the *Collegiate Times* for defamation. She argued that the phrase implied the commission of sodomy and was therefore actionable. What is *Collegiate Times's* defense to this claim? [*Yeagle v. Collegiate Times,* 497 S.E.2d 136 (Va. 1998)] **(See page 287.)**

12–5. Proximate Cause. Galen Stoller was killed at a railroad crossing when an AMTRAK train hit his car. The crossing was marked with a stop sign and a railroad-crossing symbol, but there were no flashing lights. Galen's parents filed a suit against National Railroad Passenger Corp. (AMTRAK) and Burlington Northern & Santa Fe Railroad Corp., alleging negligence in the design and maintenance of the crossing. The defendants argued that Galen had not stopped at the stop sign. Was AMTRAK negligent? What was the proximate cause of the accident? Discuss. [*Henderson v. National Railroad Passenger Corp.,* __ F.3d __ (10th Cir. 2011)] **(See page 296.)**

12–6. Business Torts. Medtronic, Inc., is a medical technology company that competes for customers with St. Jude Medical S.C., Inc. James Hughes worked for Medtronic as a sales manager. His contract prohibited him from working for a competitor for one year after leaving Medtronic. Hughes sought a position as a sales director for St. Jude. St. Jude told Hughes that his contract with Medtronic was unenforceable and offered him a job. Hughes accepted. Medtronic filed a suit, alleging wrongful interference. Which type of interference was most likely the basis for this suit? Did it occur here? Explain. [*Medtronic, Inc. v. Hughes,* __ N.W.2d __ (Minn.App. 2011)] **(See page 291.)**

12–7. Intentional Infliction of Emotional Distress. While living in her home country of Tanzania, Sophia Kiwanuka signed an employment contract with Anne Margareth Bakilana, a Tanzanian living in Washington, D.C. Kiwanuka traveled to the United States to work as a babysitter and maid in Bakilana's house. When Kiwanuka arrived, Bakilana confiscated her passport, held her in isolation, and forced her to work long hours under threat of having her deported. Kiwanuka worked seven days a week without breaks and was subjected to regular verbal and psychological abuse by Bakilana. Kiwanuka filed a complaint against Bakilana for intentional infliction of emotional distress, among other claims. Bakilana argued that Kiwanuka's complaint should be dismissed because the allegations were insufficient to show outrageous intentional conduct that resulted in severe emotional distress. If you were the judge, in whose favor would you rule? Why? [*Kiwanuka v. Bakilana,* 844 F.Supp.2d 107 (D.D.C. 2012)] **(See page 285.)**

12–8. BUSINESS CASE PROBLEM WITH SAMPLE ANSWER: Negligence.

At the Weatherford Hotel in Flagstaff, Arizona, in Room 59, a balcony extends across thirty inches of the room's only window, leaving a twelve-inch gap with a three-story drop to the concrete below. A sign prohibits smoking in the room but invites guests to "step out onto the balcony" to smoke. Toni Lucario was a guest in Room 59 when she climbed out of the window and fell to her death. Patrick McMurtry, her estate's personal representative, filed a suit against the Weatherford. Did the hotel breach a duty of care to Locario? What might the Weatherford assert in its defense? Explain. [McMurtry v. Weatherford Hotel, Inc., *293 P.3d 520 (Ariz.App. 2013)]* **(See page 294.)**

- **For a sample answer to Problem 12–8, go to Appendix F at the end of this text.**

12–9. A QUESTION OF ETHICS: Wrongful Interference with a Contractual Relationship.

*White Plains Coat & Apron Co. is a New York–based linen rental business. Cintas Corp. is a competitor. White Plains had five-year exclusive contracts with some of its customers. As a result of Cintas's soliciting of business, dozens of White Plains' customers breached their contracts and entered into rental agreements with Cintas. White Plains filed a suit against Cintas, alleging wrongful interference. [*White Plains Coat & Apron Co. v. Cintas Corp., *8 N.Y.3d 422, 867 N.E.2d 381 (2007)]* **(See page 291.)**

(a) What are the two important policy interests at odds in wrongful interference cases? Which of these interests should be accorded priority?

(b) The U.S. Court of Appeals for the Second Circuit asked the New York Court of Appeals to answer a question: Is a general interest in soliciting business for profit a sufficient defense to a claim of wrongful interference with a contractual relationship? What do you think? Why?

Legal Reasoning Group Activity

12–10. Negligence. Donald and Gloria Bowden hosted a cookout at their home in South Carolina, inviting mostly business acquaintances. Justin Parks, who was nineteen years old, attended the party. Alcoholic beverages were available to all of the guests, even those like Parks, who were between the ages of eighteen and twenty-one. Parks consumed alcohol at the party and left with other guests. One of these guests detained Parks at the guest's home to give Parks time to "sober up." Parks then drove himself from this guest's home and was killed in a one-car accident. At the time of death, he had a blood alcohol content of 0.291 percent, which exceeded the state's limit for driving a motor vehicle. Linda Marcum, Parks's mother, filed a suit in a South Carolina state court against the Bowdens and others, alleging that they were negligent. **(See page 294.)**

(a) The first group will present arguments in favor of holding the social hosts liable in this situation.

(b) The second group will formulate arguments against holding the social hosts liable based on principles in this chapter.

(c) The states vary widely in assessing liability and imposing sanctions in the circumstances described in this problem. The third group will determine the reasons why courts do not treat social hosts the same as parents who serve alcoholic beverages to their underage children.

CHAPTER 13

STRICT LIABILITY AND PRODUCT LIABILITY

In this chapter, we look at a category of tort called **strict liability,** or *liability without fault.* Under the doctrine of strict liability, a person who engages in certain activities can be held responsible for any harm that results to others, even if the person used the utmost care.

We open this chapter with an examination of this doctrine and then look at an area of tort law of particular importance to businesspersons—product liability. The manufacturers and sellers of products may incur **product liability** when product defects cause injury or property damage to consumers, users, or bystanders (people in the vicinity of the product when it fails).

Although multimillion-dollar product liability claims often involve big automakers, pharmaceutical companies, or tobacco companies, many businesses face potential liability. For instance, in the last few years, there have been numerous reports of energy drinks, such as Monster, Red Bull, Rockstar, and 5-hour Energy, having serious adverse effects—especially on young people. Several individuals have been hospitalized, and some have even died after consuming energy drinks. In 2012, the federal government issued a report concerning the adverse effects of these products and launched an investigation into their safety. Parents of a teenage girl who died after consuming two Monster energy drinks then filed a lawsuit against Monster Beverage Corporation in California—perhaps the first case in a wave of lawsuits against makers of energy drinks.

SECTION 1 STRICT LIABILITY

The modern concept of strict liability traces its origins, in part, to an English case decided in 1868. ▶ **Case in Point 13.1** In the coal-mining area of Lancashire, England, the Rylands, who were mill owners, had constructed a reservoir on their land. Water from the reservoir broke through a filled-in shaft of an abandoned coal mine nearby and flooded the connecting passageways in an active coal mine owned by Fletcher.

Fletcher sued the Rylands, and the court held that the defendants (the Rylands) were liable, even though the circumstances did not fit within existing tort liability theories. The court held that a "person who for his own purposes brings on his land and collects and keeps there anything likely to do mischief if it escapes . . . is *prima facie*[1] answerable for all the damage which is the natural consequence of its escape."[2] ◀ British courts liberally applied the doctrine that emerged from the case.

Initially, few U.S. courts accepted this doctrine, presumably because the courts were worried about its effect on the expansion of American business. Today, however, the doctrine of strict liability is the norm rather than the exception.

Abnormally Dangerous Activities

Strict liability for damages proximately caused by an abnormally dangerous, or ultrahazardous, activity is one application of strict liability. Courts apply the doctrine of strict liability in these situations because of the extreme risk of the activity. Abnormally dangerous activities are those that involve a high risk of serious harm to persons or property that cannot be completely guarded against by the exercise of reasonable care.

1. *Prima facie* is Latin for "at first sight." Legally, it refers to a fact that is presumed to be true unless contradicted by evidence.

2. *Rylands v. Fletcher,* 3 L.R.–E & I App. [Law Reports, English & Irish Appeal Cases] (H.L. [House of Lords] 1868).

Activities such as blasting or storing explosives qualify as abnormally dangerous. Even if blasting with dynamite is performed with all reasonable care, there is still a risk of injury. Considering the potential for harm, it seems reasonable to ask the person engaged in the activity to pay for injuries caused by that activity. Although there is no fault, there is still responsibility because of the dangerous nature of the undertaking.

Other Applications of Strict Liability

Persons who keep wild animals are strictly liable for any harm inflicted by the animals. The basis for applying strict liability is that wild animals, should they escape from confinement, pose a serious risk of harm to people in the vicinity. An owner of domestic animals (such as dogs, cats, cows, or sheep) may be strictly liable for harm caused by those animals if the owner knew, or should have known, that the animals were dangerous or had a propensity to harm others.

A significant application of strict liability is in the area of product liability—liability of manufacturers and sellers for harmful or defective products. Liability here is a matter of social policy and is based on two factors:

1. The manufacturer can better bear the cost of injury because it can spread the cost throughout society by increasing the prices of its goods.
2. The manufacturer is making a profit from its activities and therefore should bear the cost of injury as an operating expense.

We will discuss product liability in greater detail next. Strict liability is also applied in certain types of *bailments* (a bailment exists when goods are transferred temporarily into the care of another).

SECTION 2

PRODUCT LIABILITY

Those who make, sell, or lease goods can be held liable for physical harm or property damage caused by those goods to a consumer, user, or bystander. This is called *product liability*. Product liability may be based on the theories of negligence, misrepresentation, strict liability, and warranties (see Chapter 11). Multiple theories of liability can be, and often are, asserted in the same case. We look here at product liability based on negligence and on misrepresentation.

Based on Negligence

In Chapter 12, *negligence* was defined as the failure to exercise the degree of care that a reasonable, prudent person would have exercised under the circumstances. If a manufacturer fails to exercise "due care" to make a product safe, a person who is injured by the product may sue the manufacturer for negligence.

DUE CARE MUST BE EXERCISED Manufacturers must use due care in all of the following areas:

1. Designing the product.
2. Selecting the materials.
3. Using the appropriate production process.
4. Assembling and testing the product.
5. Placing adequate warnings on the label to inform the user of dangers of which an ordinary person might not be aware.
6. Inspecting and testing any purchased components used in the product.

PRIVITY OF CONTRACT NOT REQUIRED A product liability action based on negligence does not require *privity of contract* between the injured plaintiff and the defendant-manufacturer. As explained in Chapter 9, *privity of contract* refers to the relationship that exists between the parties to a contract. Privity is the reason that normally only the parties to a contract can enforce that contract.

In the context of product liability law, privity is not required. A person who is injured by a defective product may bring a negligence suit even though he or she was not the one who actually purchased the product—and thus is not in privity. A manufacturer, seller, or lessor is liable for failure to exercise due care to *any person* who sustains an injury proximately caused by a negligently made (defective) product. Relative to the long history of the common law, this exception to the privity requirement is a fairly recent development—it dates to the early part of the twentieth century.[3]

Based on Misrepresentation

When a user or consumer is injured as a result of a manufacturer's or seller's fraudulent misrepresentation, the basis of liability may be the tort of fraud. In

3. A landmark case in this respect is *MacPherson v. Buick Motor Co.*, 217 N.Y. 382, 111 N.E. 1050 (1916).

this situation, the misrepresentation must have been made knowingly or with reckless disregard for the facts. The intentional mislabeling of packaged cosmetics, for instance, or the intentional concealment of a product's defects would constitute fraudulent misrepresentation.

The misrepresentation must be of a material fact, and the seller must have intended to induce the buyer's reliance on the misrepresentation. Misrepresentation on a label or advertisement is enough to show an intent to induce the reliance of anyone who may use the product. In addition, the buyer must have relied on the misrepresentation.

SECTION 3

STRICT PRODUCT LIABILITY

As discussed at the beginning of this chapter, under the doctrine of strict liability, people may be liable for the results of their acts regardless of their intentions or their exercise of reasonable care. In addition, liability does not depend on privity of contract. Thus, the injured party does not have to be the buyer, as required under contract warranty theory (see Chapter 23). In the 1960s, courts applied the doctrine of strict liability in several landmark cases involving manufactured goods, and it has since become a common method of holding manufacturers liable.

Strict Product Liability and Public Policy

The law imposes strict product liability as a matter of public policy. This public policy rests on the threefold assumption that:

1. Consumers should be protected against unsafe products.
2. Manufacturers and distributors should not escape liability for faulty products simply because they are not in privity of contract with the ultimate user of those products.
3. Manufacturers and distributors can better bear the costs associated with injuries caused by their products—because they can ultimately pass the costs on to all consumers in the form of higher prices.

DEVELOPMENT OF THE DOCTRINE California was the first state to impose strict product liability in tort on manufacturers. ▶ **Case in Point 13.2** William Greenman was injured when his Shopsmith combination power tool threw off a piece of wood that struck him in the head. He sued the manufacturer, claiming that he had followed the product's instructions and the product must be defective. In a landmark decision, *Greenman v. Yuba Power Products, Inc.,*[4] the California Supreme Court set out the reason for applying tort law rather than contract law (including laws governing warranties) in cases involving consumers who were injured by defective products.

According to the *Greenman* court, the "purpose of such liability is to [e]nsure that the costs of injuries resulting from defective products are borne by the manufacturers . . . rather than by the injured persons who are powerless to protect themselves." ◀ Today, the majority of states recognize strict product liability, although some state courts limit its application to situations involving personal injuries (rather than property damage).

STATED PUBLIC POLICY Public policy may be expressed in a statute or in the common law. Sometimes, public policy may be revealed in a court's interpretation of a statute, as in the following case.

4. 59 Cal.2d 57, 377 P.2d 897, 27 Cal.Rptr. 697 (1962).

SPOTLIGHT on Injuries from Vaccines

Case 13.1 Bruesewitz v. Wyeth, LLC

Supreme Court of the United States, __ U.S. __, 131 S.Ct. 1068, 179 L.Ed.2d 1 (2011).

COMPANY PROFILE Wyeth, LLC—a subsidiary of Pfizer, Inc.—is an international pharmaceutical and health-care company with its corporate headquarters in Madison, New Jersey. Wyeth develops, makes, and markets medical therapies, clinical programs, nutritional supplements, prescription drugs, and other health-care products, including over-the-counter medications. Wyeth was incorporated in 1926. In 1994, the

CASE 13.1 CONTINUES ➧

CASE 13.1 CONTINUED

company bought Lederle Laboratories. Since 1948, Lederle had been making the diphtheria, tetanus, and pertussis (DTP) vaccine for children.

BACKGROUND AND FACTS When Hannah Bruesewitz was six months old, her pediatrician administered a dose of the DTP vaccine according to the Centers for Disease Control's recommended childhood immunization schedule. Within twenty-four hours, Hannah began to experience seizures. She suffered more than one hundred seizures during the next month. Her doctors diagnosed her with "residual seizure disorder" and "developmental delay." Hannah's parents, Russell and Robalee Bruesewitz, filed a claim for relief in the U.S. Court of Federal Claims under the National Childhood Vaccine Injury Act (NCVIA) of 1986, which set up a no-fault compensation program for persons injured by vaccines. The claim was denied. The Bruesewitzes then filed a suit in a state court against Wyeth, LLC, the maker of the vaccine, alleging strict product liability. The suit was moved to a federal district court, which held that the claim was preempted by the NCVIA, which includes provisions protecting manufacturers from liability for "a vaccine's unavoidable, adverse side effects." The U.S. Court of Appeals for the Third Circuit affirmed the district court's judgment. The Bruesewitzes appealed to the United States Supreme Court.

IN THE LANGUAGE OF THE COURT

Justice *SCALIA* delivered the opinion of the Court.

* * * *

In the 1970's and 1980's vaccines became, one might say, victims of their own success. They had been so effective in preventing infectious diseases that the public became much less alarmed at the threat of those diseases, and much more concerned with the risk of injury from the vaccines themselves.

Much of the concern centered around vaccines against * * * DTP, which were blamed for children's disabilities * * * . This led to a massive increase in vaccine-related tort litigation. * * * This destabilized the DTP vaccine market, causing two of the three domestic manufacturers to withdraw.

* * * *

To stabilize the vaccine market and facilitate compensation, Congress enacted the NCVIA in 1986. The Act establishes a no-fault compensation program designed to work faster and with greater ease than the civil tort system. A person injured by a vaccine, or his legal guardian, may file a petition for compensation in the United States Court of Federal Claims.

* * * *

Successful claimants receive compensation for medical, rehabilitation, counseling, special education, and vocational training expenses; diminished earning capacity; pain and suffering; and $250,000 for vaccine-related deaths. Attorney's fees are provided * * * . These awards are paid out of a fund created by a * * * tax on each vaccine dose.

The *quid pro quo* [something done in exchange] for this, designed to stabilize the vaccine market, was the provision of significant tort-liability protections for vaccine manufacturers. * * * *Manufacturers are generally immunized from liability * * * if they have complied with all regulatory requirements * * * . * * * And most relevant to the present case, the Act expressly eliminates liability for a vaccine's unavoidable, adverse side effects.* [Emphasis added.]

* * * *

The Act's structural *quid pro quo* leads to the * * * conclusion: The vaccine manufacturers fund from their sales an informal, efficient compensation program for vaccine injuries; in exchange they avoid costly tort litigation.

DECISION AND REMEDY *The United States Supreme Court affirmed the lower court's judgment. The NCVIA preempted the Bruesewitzes' claim against Wyeth for compensation for the injury to their daughter caused by the DTP vaccine's side effects. The Court found that the NCVIA's compensation program strikes a balance between paying victims harmed by vaccines and protecting the vaccine industry from collapsing under the costs of tort liability.*

THE ECONOMIC DIMENSION *What is the public policy expressed by the provisions of the NCVIA?*

THE POLITICAL DIMENSION *If the public wants to change the policy outlined in this case, which branch of the government—and at what level—should be lobbied to make the change? Explain.*

The Requirements for Strict Product Liability

After the *Restatement (Second) of Torts* was issued in 1964, Section 402A became a widely accepted statement of how the doctrine of strict liability should be applied to sellers of goods (including manufacturers, processors, assemblers, packagers, bottlers, wholesalers, distributors, retailers, and lessors).

The bases for an action in strict liability that are set forth in Section 402A of the *Restatement (Second) of Torts* can be summarized as a set of six requirements, which are listed here. Depending on the jurisdiction, if these requirements are met, a manufacturer's liability to an injured party can be almost unlimited.

1. The product must be in a *defective condition* when the defendant sells it.
2. The defendant must normally be engaged in the *business of selling* (or otherwise distributing) that product.
3. The product must be *unreasonably dangerous* to the user or consumer because of its defective condition (in most states).
4. The plaintiff must incur *physical harm* to self or property by use or consumption of the product.
5. The defective condition must be the *proximate cause* of the injury or damage.
6. The *goods must not have been substantially changed* from the time the product was sold to the time the injury was sustained.

PROVING A DEFECTIVE CONDITION Under these requirements, in any action against a manufacturer, seller, or lessor, the plaintiff need not show why or in what manner the product became defective. The plaintiff does, however, have to prove that the product was defective at the time it left the hands of the seller or lessor. The plaintiff must also show that this defective condition made the product "unreasonably dangerous" to the user or consumer.

Unless evidence can be presented to support the conclusion that the product was defective when it was sold or leased, the plaintiff will not succeed. If the product was delivered in a safe condition and subsequent mishandling made it harmful to the user, the seller or lessor normally is not strictly liable.

UNREASONABLY DANGEROUS PRODUCTS The *Restatement* recognizes that many products cannot be made entirely safe for all uses. Thus, sellers or lessors are liable only for products that are *unreasonably* dangerous. A court could consider a product so defective as to be an **unreasonably dangerous product** in either of the following situations:

1. The product was dangerous beyond the expectation of the ordinary consumer.
2. A less dangerous alternative was *economically* feasible for the manufacturer, but the manufacturer failed to produce it.

As will be discussed next, a product may be unreasonably dangerous due to a flaw in the manufacturing process, a design defect, or an inadequate warning.

Product Defects

The *Restatement (Third) of Torts: Products Liability* defines the three types of product defects that have traditionally been recognized in product liability law—manufacturing defects, design defects, and inadequate warnings.

MANUFACTURING DEFECTS According to Section 2(a) of the *Restatement (Third) of Torts,* a product "contains a manufacturing defect when the product departs from its intended design even though all possible care was exercised in the preparation and marketing of the product." Basically, a manufacturing defect is a departure from a product unit's design specifications that results in products that are physically flawed, damaged, or incorrectly assembled. A glass bottle that is made too thin and explodes in a consumer's face is an example of a product with a manufacturing defect.

Quality Control. Usually, such defects occur when a manufacturer fails to assemble, test, or adequately check the quality of a product. Liability is imposed on the manufacturer (and on the wholesaler and retailer) regardless of whether the manufacturer's quality control efforts were "reasonable." The idea behind holding defendants strictly liable for manufacturing defects is to encourage greater investment in product safety and stringent quality control standards.

Expert Testimony. Cases involving allegations of a manufacturing defect are often decided based on the opinions and testimony of experts. ▶ **Case in Point 13.3** Kevin Schmude purchased an eight-foot stepladder and used it to install radio-frequency shielding in a hospital room. While Schmude was standing on the ladder, it collapsed, and he was seriously injured. He filed a lawsuit against the ladder's maker, Tricam Industries, Inc., based on a manufacturing defect.

An expert testified that in the manufacturing process, a rivet securing one of the rear legs to the ladder's platform had been misaligned with the hole through which is was supposed to pass. As a result, the rivet had not securely fastened the leg in place, causing the ladder to fail. A jury concluded that this manufacturing defect made the ladder unreasonably dangerous and awarded Schmude more than $677,000 in damages.[5] ◀

DESIGN DEFECTS Unlike a product with a manufacturing defect, a product with a design defect is made in conformity with the manufacturer's design specifications. Nevertheless, the product results in injury to the user because the design itself was faulty. A product "is defective in design when the foreseeable risks of harm posed by the product could have been reduced or avoided by the adoption of a reasonable alternative design by the seller or other distributor, or a predecessor in the commercial chain of distribution, and the omission of the alternative design renders the product not reasonably safe."[6]

To successfully assert a design defect, a plaintiff has to show that:

1. A reasonable alternative design was available.
2. The defendant's failure to adopt the alternative design rendered the product not reasonably safe.

In other words, a manufacturer or other defendant is liable only when the harm was reasonably preventable.

According to the *Restatement,* a court can consider a broad range of factors. These include the magnitude and probability of the foreseeable risks as well as the relative advantages and disadvantages of the product as it was designed and as it could have been designed.

Risk-Utility Analysis. Most courts engage in a risk-utility analysis to determine whether the risk of harm from the product as designed outweighs its utility to the user and to the public. ▶ **Case in Point 13.4** Jodie Bullock smoked cigarettes manufactured by Philip Morris for forty-five years. When she was diagnosed with lung cancer, Bullock brought a product liability suit against Philip Morris. She presented evidence that by the late 1950s, scientists had proved that smoking caused lung cancer. Nonetheless, Philip Morris had issued full-page announcements stating that there was no proof that cigarette smoking caused cancer and that "numerous scientists" questioned "the validity of the statistics." At trial, the judge instructed the jury to consider the gravity of the danger posed by the design, as well as the likelihood that the danger would cause injury.

The jury found that there was a defect in the design of the cigarettes and that they had been negligently designed. It awarded Bullock $850,000 in compensatory damages and $28 million in punitive damages. Philip Morris appealed, claiming that no evidence had been offered to show that there was a safer design for cigarettes. Nonetheless, the reviewing court found that the jury had been properly instructed. The court affirmed the award but remanded the case for a reconsideration of the proper amount of punitive damages.[7] ◀

Consumer-Expectation Test. Other courts apply the consumer-expectation test to determine whether a product's design was defective. Under this test, a product is unreasonably dangerous when it fails to perform in the manner that would reasonably be expected by an ordinary consumer. The court applied this test in the following case.

5. *Schmude v. Tricam Industries, Inc.,* 550 F.Supp.2d 846 (E.D.Wis. 2008).
6. *Restatement (Third) of Torts: Products Liability,* Section 2(b).
7. *Bullock v. Philip Morris USA, Inc.,*159 Cal.App.4th 655, 71 Cal.Rptr.3d 775 (2008).

CASE ANALYSIS

Case 13.2 Wilson Sporting Goods Co. v. Hickox

District of Columbia Court of Appeals, 59 A.3d 1267 (2013).

IN THE LANGUAGE OF THE COURT

McLEESE, Associate Judge.

* * * *

* * * At an annual retreat for Major League Baseball umpires, a Wilson [Sporting Goods Company] representative gave [Edwin] Hickox an umpire's mask with what the representative claimed was a new, safer design. Several months later, Mr. Hickox wore the mask while working behind home plate as an umpire during a game in Washington, D.C. In the top of the ninth inning, a foul-tipped ball struck the mask. The impact of the ball gave Mr. Hickox a concussion and damaged a joint between the bones in Mr. Hickox's inner ear. As a result, Mr. Hickox suffered permanent hearing loss of mild to moderate severity.

CASE 13.2 CONTINUED

The mask was a traditional umpire's mask, but had a newly designed throat guard that angled forward instead of extending straight down. According to the Hickoxes, the throat guard should have had a center wire and should have extended straight down with no forward angle. Because the mask lacked these features, when the ball hit the throat guard, the mask did not deflect the ball but rather temporarily trapped the ball, concentrating the ball's energy at the point of impact. As a result, the mask was driven into Mr. Hickox's jaw with great force.

* * * *

In contrast to the Hickoxes' version of events, Wilson contended the following at trial. The ball hit the mask above the throat guard, not on it, and so the same injury would have occurred even if the mask had not had a throat guard at all. Wilson intended the mask to provide protection by deflecting balls away from the wearer's head, and the mask accomplished this objective during the incident.

* * * *

[Hickox and his wife filed a suit in a District of Columbia court against Wilson, claiming product liability based on a design defect.] The jury rendered verdict for the Hickoxes * * *, awarding $750,000 to Mr. Hickox and $25,000 to his wife. [Wilson appealed, arguing that the evidence was insufficient to support the verdict.]

* * * *

There are two tests commonly used to determine whether a product's design was defective: the consumer-expectation test and the risk-utility test.

Wilson explicitly assented at trial to jury instructions that required the jury to make findings under a consumer-expectation test. Specifically, the jury was told that "a design is defective if the product fails to perform as safely as an ordinary customer would expect when the product is used in an intended or reasonably foreseeable manner."

* * * Accordingly, we employ the consumer-expectation test to evaluate the sufficiency of the evidence in this case.

* * * The evidence indicated that the mask at issue was more dangerous than comparable masks sold at the time, such as hockey-style masks, because the mask could concentrate energy at the point of impact, rather than distribute energy evenly throughout the padded area of the mask. Because the energy possessed by a pitched baseball is adequate to cause severe injury, the jury could reasonably have concluded that a mask that concentrated energy would increase the risk of severe injury.

The jury could also have relied on the existence of safer, commercially available alternatives to draw inferences about the level of safety an ordinary user would expect. There was evidence that alternative masks with detachable throat guards and no forward angle work well and do not excessively restrict the umpire's movement. There also was evidence that Mr. Hickox would not have suffered injury to his ear had he been wearing a hockey-style mask or a mask with a center wire and no forward angle.

In addition, the jury could have concluded that the statements made by Wilson's representative to Mr. Hickox about the mask reflected Wilson's standard marketing approach, and that an ordinary consumer therefore would have expected the mask to perform more safely than other models. There was evidence that Wilson's representative told Mr. Hickox that the mask would disperse energy and protect against concussion, and that the mask was the best and safest technology. Mr. Hickox also testified that he believed that companies like Wilson tested new products and did not sell them unless they were safe to use. Jurors could consider such testimony in combination with their own reasonable inferences to determine an ordinary consumer's expectations. [Emphasis added.]

Evidence of industry practice can also be relevant to reasonable consumer expectations. Wilson's objective in designing the mask was to disperse energy, not to concentrate it. At the time of the incident, Wilson tested its hockey-style masks to determine if they met impact-intensity standards, but did not perform such testing on its baseball masks. At a time when Wilson used energy dispersal as a design objective for its baseball masks and when impact-intensity standards existed for football helmets, *a reasonable juror could infer that an ordinary consumer would have expected baseball masks to disperse rather than concentrate energy.* In sum, considering all the evidence, a reasonable juror could conclude that an ordinary consumer would have expected the mask to perform more safely than it did. [Emphasis added.]

* * * *

The judgment of the trial court is therefore

Affirmed.

LEGAL REASONING QUESTIONS

1. What is the "consumer-expectation test"?
2. What factors did the court consider in determining whether the evidence in this case was sufficient to establish reasonable consumer expectations?
3. Can a jury make "inferences" to arrive at a verdict? Explain.
4. How did the appellate court's conclusion in this case affect the parties?

INADEQUATE WARNINGS A product may also be deemed defective because of inadequate instructions or warnings. A product will be considered defective "when the foreseeable risks of harm posed by the product could have been reduced or avoided by the provision of reasonable instructions or warnings by the seller or other distributor . . . and the omission of the instructions or warnings renders the product not reasonably safe."[8]

Content of Warnings. Important factors for a court to consider include the risks of a product, the "content and comprehensibility" and "intensity of expression" of warnings and instructions, and the "characteristics of expected user groups."[9] Courts apply a "reasonableness" test to determine if the warnings adequately alert consumers to the product's risks. For instance, children will likely respond readily to bright, bold, simple warning labels, whereas educated adults might need more detailed information.

An action alleging that a product is defective due to an inadequate label can be based on state law. (For a discussion of a case involving a state law that required warning labels on violent video games, see this chapter's *Insight into Ethics* feature on page 314.)

In the following case, the court had to decide whether the plaintiff could pursue a theory of recovery alleging both a design defect and inadequate warnings.

8. *Restatement (Third) of Torts: Products Liability,* Section 2(c).

9. *Restatement (Third) of Torts: Products Liability,* Section 2, Comment h.

CASE 13.3

Johnson v. Medtronic, Inc.

Missouri Court of Appeals, 365 S.W.3d 226 (2012).

BACKGROUND AND FACTS In 2005, Jeffrey Johnson was taken to the emergency room for an episode of atrial fibrillation, a heart rhythm disorder. Dr. David Hahn used a defibrillator manufactured by Medtronic, Inc., to deliver electric shocks to Johnson's heart. The defibrillator had synchronous and asynchronous modes, and it reverted to the asynchronous mode after each use. Dr. Hahn intended to deliver synchronized shocks, which required him to select the synchronous mode for each shock.

Unfortunately, Dr. Hahn did not read the device's instructions, which Medtronic provided both in a manual and on the device itself. As a result, he delivered a synchronized shock, followed by twelve asynchronous shocks that endangered Johnson's life. Johnson and his wife filed a product liability suit against Medtronic, asserting both that Medtronic had provided inadequate warnings about the defibrillator and that the device had a design defect. The trial court found for Medtronic under both product liability theories. The Johnsons appealed.

IN THE LANGUAGE OF THE COURT
James Edward *WELSH,* Judge.

* * * *

Jeffrey Johnson was not damaged as a result of the [defibrillator] being sold without an adequate warning, at least as described by the Johnsons. The undisputed facts established that Dr. Hahn failed to read or in any way follow the instructions * * * , and the Johnsons have not contended that the manner in which the instructions were provided failed to effectively communicate to users * * * .

* * * *

* * * We nevertheless conclude that [the Johnsons] have raised [enough evidence about] whether the [defibrillator] was * * * in a defective condition and unreasonably dangerous when put to a reasonably anticipated use and whether Dr. Hahn's actions constituted a "reasonably anticipated use" of the device.

* * * *

We recognize that Dr. Hahn's actions in this case were contrary to the instructions provided by Medtronic, both on a label on the defibrillator and in its instruction manual. However, *the fact that a particular use of a product is contrary to the manufacturer's instructions does not, per se, establish that the use could not be anticipated.* [Emphasis added.]

CASE 13.3 CONTINUED

The fact that we have rejected the Johnsons' failure to warn claim does not mandate a similar result as to the product defect claim. As the Missouri Supreme Court emphasized recently, "Design defect and failure to warn theories constitute distinct theories aimed at protecting consumers from dangers that arise in different ways."

In other words, in certain instances, a manufacturer may be held liable where it chooses to warn of the danger (even admittedly adequately warn) rather than preclude the danger by design.

DECISION AND REMEDY *The Missouri appellate court held that the Johnsons could not pursue a claim based on the inadequacy of Medtronic's warnings, but that they could pursue a claim alleging a design defect. The court therefore affirmed the trial court's decision in part and reversed it in part.*

THE LEGAL ENVIRONMENT DIMENSION *What could Medtronic have done to avoid possible liability to plaintiffs like the Johnsons? Was there a reasonable alternative design for the defibrillator?*

THE ECONOMIC DIMENSION *Could Hahn or the hospital be held liable for Johnson's injury on a product liability theory? Explain.*

Obvious Risks. There is no duty to warn about risks that are obvious or commonly known. Warnings about such risks do not add to the safety of a product and could even detract from it by making other warnings seem less significant. As will be discussed later in the chapter, the obviousness of a risk and a user's decision to proceed in the face of that risk may be a defense in a product liability suit based on an inadequate warning.

▶ **Case in Point 13.5** Sixteen-year-old Gary Crosswhite failed in an attempt to do a back flip on a trampoline and was paralyzed as a result. There were nine warning labels affixed to the trampoline, an instruction manual with safety warnings, and a placard attached to the entrance that advised users not to do flips. Crosswhite sued the manufacturer for inadequate warnings. The court found that the warnings were sufficient to make the risks obvious and insulate the manufacturer from liability for Crosswhite's injuries.[10] ◀

Risks that may seem obvious to some users, though, will not be obvious to all users, especially when the users are likely to be children. A young child may not be able to read or understand warning labels or comprehend the risk of certain activities. To avoid liability, the manufacturer would have to prove that the warnings it provided were adequate to make the risk of injury obvious to a young child.[11]

Foreseeable Misuses. Generally, a seller must warn those who purchase its product of the harm that can result from the foreseeable misuse of the product as well. The key is the foreseeability of the misuse. Sellers are not required to take precautions against every conceivable misuse of a product, just those that are foreseeable.

10. *Crosswhite v. Jumpking, Inc.*, 411 F.Supp.2d 1228 (D.Or. 2006).

11. See, for example, *Bunch v. Hoffinger Industries, Inc.*,123 Cal.App.4th 1278, 20 Cal.Rptr.3d 780 (2004).

Market-Share Liability

Ordinarily, in all product liability claims, a plaintiff must prove that the defective product that caused his or her injury was the product of a specific defendant. In a few situations, however, courts have dropped this requirement when plaintiffs could not prove which of many distributors of a harmful product supplied the particular product that caused the injuries. Under a theory of **market-share liability,** a court can hold each manufacturer responsible for a percentage of the plaintiff's damages that is equal to the percentage of its market share.

▶ **Case in Point 13.6** John Smith suffered from hemophilia (a blood-clotting disorder). Because of his condition, Smith received injections of a blood protein known as antihemophiliac factor (AHF) concentrate. Smith later tested positive for the acquired immune deficiency syndrome (AIDS) virus. Because there was no way to determine which manufacturer was responsible for the particular AHF received by Smith, the court held that all of the manufacturers of AHF could be held liable.[12] ◀

Many jurisdictions do not recognize this theory of liability because they believe that it deviates too significantly from traditional legal principles.

12. *Smith v. Cutter Biological, Inc.*, 72 Haw. 416, 823 P.2d 717 (1991). See also *Sutowski v. Eli Lilly & Co.*, 82 Ohio St.3d 347, 696 N.E.2d 187 (1998); and *In re Methyl Tertiary Butyl Ether ("MTBE") Products Liability Litigation*, 447 F.Supp.2d 289 (S.D.N.Y. 2006).

INSIGHT INTO ETHICS
Warning Labels for Video Games

Almost every product that you purchase in the physical world has one or more warning labels. Indeed, some critics argue that these labels have become so long and ubiquitous that consumers ignore them. In other words, putting warnings on just about everything defeats their original purpose.

Until recently, video games have largely escaped mandated warning labels, although the video game industry has instituted a voluntary rating system to provide information about a video game's content. Each video game is assigned one of six age-specific ratings, ranging from "Early Childhood" to "Adults Only."

Should video games, whether downloaded or bought on a CD-ROM or DVD, have additional warnings to advise potential users (or their parents) that the games might be overly violent? When the California legislature enacted a law imposing restrictions and a labeling requirement on the sale or rental of "violent video games" to minors, this issue became paramount.[a]

Video Software Dealers Sue the State

The Video Software Dealers Association, along with the Entertainment Software Association, immediately brought a suit in federal district court seeking to invalidate the law. The court granted summary judgment in favor of the plaintiffs.

The act defined a violent video game as one in which "the range of options available to a player includes killing, maiming, dismembering, or sexually assaulting an image of a human being." While agreeing that some video games are unquestionably violent by everyday standards, the trial court pointed out that many video games are based on popular novels or motion pictures and have extensive plot lines.

Accordingly, the court found that the definition of a violent video game was unconstitutionally vague and thus violated the First Amendment's guarantee of freedom of speech. The court also noted the existence of the voluntary rating system. The U.S. Court of Appeals for the Ninth Circuit affirmed the district court's decision.[b]

The United States Supreme Court's Decision

The state of California appealed to the United States Supreme Court, but in 2011 the Court affirmed the decision in favor of the video game and software industries. The Court noted that video games are entitled to First Amendment protection. Because California had failed to show that the statute was justified by a compelling government interest and that the law was narrowly tailored to serve that interest, the Court ruled that the statute was unconstitutional.[c]

LEGAL CRITICAL THINKING

INSIGHT INTO THE SOCIAL ENVIRONMENT

Should victims of a mass shooting be able to sue the manufacturer of a violent video game for a design defect if the shooter had been a devoted player of that game? Discuss.

a. California Civil Code Sections 1746–1746.5.

b. *Video Software Dealers Association v. Schwarzenegger*, 556 F.3d 950 (9th Cir. 2009).

c. *Brown v. Entertainment Merchants Association*, ___ U.S. ___, 131 S.Ct. 2729, 180 L.Ed.2d 708 (2011).

Jurisdictions that do recognize market-share liability apply it only when it is difficult to determine which company made a particular product. Cases usually involve drugs or chemicals.

Other Applications of Strict Product Liability

Almost all courts extend the strict liability of manufacturers and other sellers to injured bystanders. Thus, if a defective forklift that will not go into reverse injures a passerby, that individual can sue the manufacturer for product liability (and possibly bring a negligence action against the forklift operator as well).

Strict product liability also applies to suppliers of component parts. ▶ **Example 13.7** Toyota buys brake pads from a subcontractor and puts them in Corollas without changing their composition. If those pads are defective, both the supplier of the brake pads and Toyota will be held strictly liable for the injuries caused by the defects. ◀

SECTION 4

DEFENSES TO PRODUCT LIABILITY

Defendants in product liability suits can raise a number of defenses. One defense, of course, is to show that there is no basis for the plaintiff's claim. If a defendant can show that the plaintiff has *not* met the requirements (such as causation) for an action in negligence, for instance, generally the defendant will not be liable.

Similarly, in a case involving strict product liability, a defendant can claim that the plaintiff failed to meet one of the requirements. For instance, if the defendant shows that the goods were altered after they were sold, normally the defendant will not be held liable. Defendants may also assert the defenses discussed next.

Preemption

A defense that has been successfully raised by defendants in recent years is preemption—that government regulations preempt claims for product liability (see *Spotlight Case* 13.1 on page 307, for example). An injured party may not be able to sue the manufacturer of defective products that are subject to comprehensive federal regulatory schemes. Medical devices, for instance, are subject to extensive government regulation and undergo a rigorous premarket approval process.

Assumption of Risk

Assumption of risk can sometimes be used as a defense in a product liability action. To establish assumption of risk, the defendant must show the following:

1. The plaintiff knew and appreciated the risk created by the product defect.
2. The plaintiff voluntarily assumed the risk—by express agreement or by words or conduct—even though it was unreasonable to do so.

For instance, if a buyer failed to heed a seller's product recall, the buyer may be deemed to have assumed the risk of the product defect that the seller had offered to repair. (See Chapter 12 for a more detailed discussion of assumption of risk.)

Some states do not allow the defense of assumption of risk in strict product liability claims, however.

▶ **Case in Point 13.8** When Savannah Boles became a customer of Executive Tans, she signed a contract that included a clause stating that she was using a tanning booth at her own risk. The clause also stated that she released the manufacturer and others from any liability for any injuries. Later, Boles's fingers were partially amputated when they came into contact with a tanning booth's fan. Boles sued the manufacturer for strict product liability. The Colorado Supreme Court held that assumption of risk was not applicable because strict product liability is driven by public-policy considerations. The theory focuses on the nature of the product rather than the conduct of either the manufacturer or the person injured.[13] ◀

Product Misuse

Similar to the defense of voluntary assumption of risk is that of **product misuse,** which occurs when a product is used for a purpose for which it was not intended. The courts have severely limited this defense, however, and it is now recognized as a defense *only when the particular use was not foreseeable.* If the misuse is reasonably foreseeable, the seller must take measures to guard against it.

Comparative Negligence (Fault)

Comparative negligence or fault (see Chapter 12) can also affect strict liability claims. Today, courts in many jurisdictions consider the negligent or intentional actions of both the plaintiff and the defendant when apportioning liability and damages. A defendant may be able to limit some of its liability if it can show that the plaintiff's misuse of the product contributed to his or her injuries.

When proved, comparative negligence differs from other defenses in that it does not completely absolve the defendant of liability, but it can reduce the total amount of damages that will be awarded to the plaintiff. Note that some jurisdictions allow only intentional conduct to affect a plaintiff's recovery, whereas other states allow ordinary negligence to be used as a defense to product liability.

▶ **Case in Point 13.9** Dan Smith, a mechanic, was not wearing a hard hat at work when he was asked to start the diesel engine of an air compressor. Because the compressor was an older model, he had to prop open a door to start it. When the engine started, the door fell from its position and hit Smith's head. The injury caused him to suffer from seizures. Smith sued the

13. *Boles v. Sun Ergoline, Inc.*, 223 P.3d 724 (Col.Sup.Ct. 2010).

manufacturer, claiming that the engine was defectively designed. The manufacturer contended that Smith had been negligent by failing to wear a hard hat and propping open the door in an unsafe manner. Smith argued that ordinary negligence could not be used as a defense in product liability cases. The court ruled that defendants can use the plaintiff's ordinary negligence to reduce their liability proportionately.[14] ◀

Commonly Known Dangers

The dangers associated with certain products (such as matches and sharp knives) are so commonly known that, as mentioned, manufacturers need not warn users of those dangers. If a defendant succeeds in convincing the court that a plaintiff's injury resulted from a *commonly known danger,* the defendant will not be liable.

▶ **Case in Point 13.10** In a classic example from 1957, Marguerite Jamieson was injured when an elastic exercise rope slipped off her foot and struck her in the eye, causing a detachment of the retina. Jamieson claimed that the manufacturer should be liable because it had failed to warn users that the exerciser might slip off a foot in such a manner. The court stated that to hold the manufacturer liable in these circumstances "would go beyond the reasonable dictates of justice in fixing the liabilities of manufacturers." After all, stated the court, "almost every physical object can be inherently dangerous or potentially dangerous in a sense. . . . A manufacturer cannot manufacture a knife that will not cut or a hammer that will not mash a thumb or a stove that will not burn a finger. The law does not require [manufacturers] to warn of such common dangers."[15] ◀

Knowledgeable User

A related defense is the *knowledgeable user* defense. If a particular danger (such as electrical shock) is or should be commonly known by particular users of a product (such as electricians), the manufacturer need not warn these users of the danger.

▶ **Case in Point 13.11** The parents of teenagers who had become overweight and developed health problems filed a product liability suit against McDonald's. The teenagers claimed that the fast-food chain had failed to warn customers of the adverse health effects of eating its food. The court rejected this claim, however, based on the knowledgeable user defense.

The court found that it is well known that the food at McDonald's contains high levels of cholesterol, fat, salt, and sugar and is therefore unhealthful. The court's opinion, which thwarted future lawsuits against fast-food restaurants, stated: "If consumers know (or reasonably should know) the potential ill health effects of eating at McDonald's, they cannot blame McDonald's if they, nonetheless, choose to satiate their appetite with a surfeit [excess] of super-sized McDonald's products."[16] ◀

Statutes of Limitations and Repose

As noted in Chapter 1, statutes of limitations restrict the time within which an action may be brought. The statute of limitations for product liability cases varies according to state law. Usually, the injured party must bring a product liability claim within two to four years. Often, the running of the prescribed period is **tolled** (that is, suspended) until the party suffering an injury has discovered it or should have discovered it.

To ensure that sellers and manufacturers will not be left vulnerable to lawsuits indefinitely, many states have passed **statutes of repose,** which place *outer* time limits on product liability actions. For instance, a statute of repose may require that claims be brought within twelve years from the date of sale or manufacture of the defective product. If the plaintiff does not bring an action before the prescribed period expires, the seller cannot be held liable.

14. *Smith v. Ingersoll-Rand Co.,* 14 P.3d 990 (Alaska 2000).
15. *Jamieson v. Woodward & Lothrop,* 247 F.2d 23 (D.C.Cir. 1957).
16. *Pelman v. McDonald's Corp.,* 237 F.Supp.2d 512 (S.D.N.Y. 2003).

Reviewing: Strict Liability and Product Liability

Shalene Kolchek bought a Great Lakes Spa from Val Porter, a dealer who was selling spas at the state fair. Kolchek signed an installment contract. Porter then handed her the manufacturer's paperwork and arranged for the spa to be delivered and installed for her. Three months later, Kolchek left her six-year-old daughter, Litisha, alone in the spa. While exploring the spa's hydromassage jets, Litisha stuck her index finger into one of the jet holes and was unable to remove her finger from the jet.

Litisha yanked hard, injuring her finger, then panicked and screamed for help. Kolchek was unable to remove Litisha's finger, and the local police and rescue team were called to assist. After a three-hour operation that included draining the spa, sawing out a section of the spa's plastic molding, and slicing the jet casing, Litisha's finger was freed. Following this procedure, the spa was no longer functional. Litisha was taken to the local emergency room, where she was told that a bone in her finger was broken in two places. Using the information presented in the chapter, answer the following questions.

1. Under which theories of product liability can Kolchek sue Porter to recover for Litisha's injuries?
2. Would privity of contract be required for Kolchek to succeed in a product liability action against Great Lakes? Explain.
3. For an action in strict product liability against Great Lakes, what six requirements must Kolchek meet?
4. What defenses to product liability might Porter or Great Lakes be able to assert?

DEBATE THIS . . . *All liability suits against tobacco companies for lung cancer should be thrown out of court now and forever.*

Terms and Concepts

market-share liability 313
product liability 305
product misuse 315
statute of repose 316
strict liability 305
tolling 316
unreasonably dangerous product 309

ExamPrep

Issue Spotters

1. Rim Corporation makes tire rims that it sells to Superior Vehicles, Inc., which installs them on cars. One set of rims is defective, which an inspection would reveal. Superior does not inspect the rims. The car with the defective rims is sold to Town Auto Sales, which sells the car to Uri. Soon, the car is in an accident caused by the defective rims, and Uri is injured. Is Superior Vehicles liable? Explain your answer. **(See page 306.)**
2. Real Chocolate Company makes a box of candy and sells it to Sweet Things, Inc., a distributor. Sweet sells the box to a Tasty Candy store, where Jill buys it. Jill gives it to Ken, who breaks a tooth on a stone the same size and color as a piece of the candy. If Real, Sweet, and Tasty were not negligent, can they be liable for the injury? Why or why not? **(See page 307.)**

- **Check your answers to the Issue Spotters against the answers provided in Appendix E at the end of this text.**

Before the Test

Go to **www.cengagebrain.com**, enter the ISBN 9781285428949, and click on "Find" to locate this textbook's Web site. Then, click on "Access Now" under "Study Tools," and select Chapter 13 at the top. There, you will find an Interactive Quiz that you can take to assess your mastery of the concepts in this chapter, as well as Flashcards and a Glossary of important terms.

Business Scenarios

13–1. Strict Liability. Danny and Marion Klein were injured when part of a fireworks display went astray and exploded near them. They sued Pyrodyne Corp., the pyrotechnic company that was hired to set up and discharge the fireworks. The Kleins alleged, among other things, that the company should be strictly liable for damages caused by the fireworks display. Will the court agree with the Kleins? What factors will the court consider in making its decision? Discuss fully. **(See page 305.)**

13–2. Product Liability. Jason Clark, an experienced hunter, bought a paintball gun. Clark practiced with the gun and knew how to screw in the carbon dioxide cartridge, pump the gun, and use its safety and trigger. Although Clark was aware that he could purchase protective eyewear, he chose not to buy it. Clark had taken gun safety courses and understood that it was "common sense" not to shoot anyone in the face. Clark's friend, Chris Wright, also owned a paintball gun and was similarly familiar with the gun's use and its risks.

Clark, Wright, and their friends played a game that involved shooting paintballs at cars whose occupants also had the guns. One night, while Clark and Wright were cruising with their guns, Wright shot at Clark's car, but hit Clark in the eye. Clark filed a product liability lawsuit against the manufacturer of Wright's paintball gun to recover for the injury. Clark claimed that the gun was defectively designed. During the trial, Wright testified that his gun "never malfunctioned." In whose favor should the court rule? Why? **(See page 306.)**

13–3. Defenses to Product Liability. Baxter manufactures electric hair dryers. Julie purchases a Baxter dryer from her local Ace Drugstore. Cox, a friend and guest in Julie's home, has taken a shower and wants to dry her hair. Julie tells Cox to use the new Baxter hair dryer that she has just purchased. As Cox plugs in the dryer, sparks fly out from the motor, and sparks continue to fly as she operates it. Despite this, Cox begins drying her hair. Suddenly, the entire dryer ignites into flames, severely burning Cox's scalp. Cox sues Baxter on the basis of negligence and strict liability in tort. Baxter admits that the dryer was defective but denies liability, particularly because Cox was not the person who purchased the dryer. In other words, Cox had no contractual relationship with Baxter. Discuss the validity of Baxter's defense. Are there any other defenses that Baxter might assert to avoid liability? Discuss fully. **(See page 315.)**

Business Case Problems

13–4. Defenses to Product Liability. Brandon Stroud was driving a golf car made by Textron, Inc., to transport guests at Christmas party. The golf car did not have lights, but Textron did not warn against using it on public roads at night. When Stroud attempted to cross a road at 8:30 P.M., his golf car was struck by a vehicle driven by Joseph Thornley. Stroud was killed. His estate filed a suit against Textron, alleging strict product liability and product liability based on negligence. The charge was that the golf car was defective and unreasonably dangerous. What defense might Textron assert? Explain. [*Moore v. Barony House Restaurant, LLC,* 382 S.C. 35, 674 S.E.2d 500 (S.C.App. 2009)] **(See page 315.)**

13–5. Product Misuse. Five-year-old Cheyenne Stark was riding in the backseat of her parents' Ford Taurus. Cheyenne was not sitting in a booster seat. Instead, she was using a seatbelt designed by Ford, but was wearing the shoulder belt behind her back. The car was involved in a collision. As a result, Cheyenne suffered a spinal cord injury and was paralyzed from the waist down. The family filed a suit against Ford Motor Co., alleging that the seatbelt was defectively designed. Could Ford successfully claim that Cheyenne had misused the seatbelt? Why or why not? [*Stark v. Ford Motor Co.,* 693 S.E.2d 253 (N.C.App. 2010)] **(See page 315.)**

13–6. Design Defects. Yun Tung Chow tried to unclog a floor drain in the kitchen of the restaurant where he worked. He used a drain cleaner called Lewis Red Devil Lye that contained crystalline sodium hydroxide. The product label said to wear eye protection, to put one tablespoon of lye directly into the drain, and to keep one's face away from the drain because there could be dangerous backsplash. Without eye protection, Chow mixed three tablespoons of lye in a can and poured that mixture down the drain while bending over it. Liquid splashed back into his face, causing injury. He brought a product liability suit based on inadequate warnings and design defect. The trial court granted summary judgment to the manufacturer, and Chow appealed. An expert for Chow stated that the product was defective because it had a tendency to backsplash. Is that a convincing argument? Why or why not? [*Yun Tung Chow v. Reckitt & Coleman, Inc.,* 69 A.D.3d 413, 891 N.Y.S.2d 402 (N.Y.A.D. 1 Dept. 2010)] **(See page 310.)**

13–7. Strict Product Liability. David Dobrovolny bought a new Ford F-350 pickup truck. A year later, the truck spontaneously caught fire in Dobrovolny's driveway. The truck was destroyed, but no other property was damaged, and no one was injured. Dobrovolny filed a suit in a Nebraska state court against Ford Motor Co. on a theory of strict product liability to recover the cost of the truck. Nebraska limits the application of strict product liability to situations involving personal injuries. Is Dobrovolny's claim likely to succeed? Why or why not? Is there another basis for liability on which he might recover? Explain. [*Dobrovolny v. Ford Motor Co.,* 281 Neb. 86, 793 N.W.2d 445 (2011)] **(See page 307.)**

13–8. BUSINESS CASE PROBLEM WITH SAMPLE ANSWER: Product Liability.

While driving on Interstate 40 in North Carolina, Carroll Jett became distracted by a texting system in the cab of his tractor-trailer truck. He smashed into several vehicles that were slowed or stopped in

front of him, injuring Barbara and Michael Durkee and others. The injured motorists filed a suit in a federal district court against Geologic Solutions, Inc., the maker of the texting system, alleging product liability. Was the accident caused by Jett's inattention or the texting device? Should a manufacturer be required to design a product that is incapable of distracting a driver? Discuss. [Durkee v. Geologic Solutions, Inc., *2013 WL 14717 (4th Cir. 2013)*] **(See page 306.)**

- **For a sample answer to Problem 13–8, go to Appendix F at the end of this text.**

13–9. A QUESTION OF ETHICS: Dangerous Products.

Susan Calles lived with her four daughters—Amanda, age eleven; Victoria, age five; and Jenna and Jillian, age three. In March 1998, Calles bought an Aim N Flame utility lighter, which she stored on the top shelf of her kitchen cabinet. A trigger can ignite the Aim N Flame after an "ON/OFF" switch is slid to the "on" position. On the night of March 31, Calles and Victoria left to get videos. Jenna and Jillian were in bed, and Amanda was watching television. Calles returned to find fire trucks and emergency vehicles around her home. Robert Finn, a fire investigator, determined that Jenna had started a fire using the lighter. Jillian suffered smoke inhalation, was hospitalized, and died on April 21. Calles filed a suit in an Illinois state court against Scripto-Tokai Corp., which distributed the Aim N Flame, and others. In her suit, which was grounded, in part, in strict liability claims, Calles alleged that the lighter was an "unreasonably dangerous product." Scripto filed a motion for summary judgment. [Calles v. Scripto-Tokai Corp., *224 Ill.2d 247, 864 N.E.2d 249, 309 Ill. Dec. 383 (2007)*] **(See page 309.)**

(a) A product is "unreasonably dangerous" when it is dangerous beyond the expectation of the ordinary consumer. Whose expectation—Calles's or Jenna's—applies? Does the lighter pass this test? Explain.

(b) Calles presented evidence as to the likelihood and seriousness of injury from lighters that do not have child-safety devices. Scripto argued that the Aim N Flame is an alternative source of fire and is safer than a match. Calles admitted that she knew the dangers presented by lighters in the hands of children. Scripto admitted that it had been a defendant in several suits for injuries under similar circumstances. How should the court rule? Why?

Legal Reasoning Group Activity

13–10. Product Liability. Bret D'Auguste was an experienced skier when he rented equipment to ski at Hunter Mountain Ski Bowl in New York. When D'Auguste entered an extremely difficult trail, he noticed immediately that the surface consisted of ice with almost no snow. He tried to exit the steeply declining trail by making a sharp right turn, but in the attempt, his left ski snapped off. D'Auguste lost his balance, fell, and slid down the mountain, striking his face and head against a fence along the trail. According to a report by a rental shop employee, one of the bindings on D'Auguste's skis had a "cracked heel housing." D'Auguste filed a lawsuit against the bindings' manufacturer on a theory of strict product liability. The manufacturer filed a motion for summary judgment. **(See page 307.)**

(a) The first group will take the position of the manufacturer and develop an argument why the court should *grant* the summary judgment motion and dismiss the strict product liability claim.

(b) The second group will take the position of D'Auguste and formulate a basis for why the court should *deny* the motion and allow the strict product liability claim.

CHAPTER 14

INTELLECTUAL PROPERTY RIGHTS

Intellectual property is any property that results from intellectual, creative processes—that is to say, the products of an individual's mind. Although it is an abstract term for an abstract concept, intellectual property is nonetheless familiar to almost everyone. The apps for your iPhone and iPad, the movies you see, and the music you listen to are all forms of intellectual property.

More than two hundred years ago, the framers of the U.S. Constitution recognized the importance of protecting creative works in Article I, Section 8 (see Appendix B). Statutory protection of these rights began in the 1940s and continues to evolve to meet the needs of modern society.

Of significant concern to businesspersons is the need to protect their rights in intellectual property, which in today's world may exceed the value of physical property, such as machines and buildings. Consider, for instance, the importance of intellectual property rights to technology companies, such as Apple, Inc. Intellectual property rights can be a company's most valuable assets, which is why Apple sued rival Samsung Electronics Company. Apple claimed that Samsung's Galaxy line of mobile phones and tablets (those that run Google's Android software) copied the look, design, and user interface of Apple's iPhone and iPad. Although Apple is one of Samsung's biggest customers and buys many of its components from Samsung, Apple must also protect its iPhone and iPad revenues from competing Android products. You will read about the verdict in this case on page 327.

SECTION 1

TRADEMARKS AND RELATED PROPERTY

A **trademark** is a distinctive mark, motto, device, or implement that a manufacturer stamps, prints, or otherwise affixes to the goods it produces so that they can be identified on the market and their origins made known. In other words, a trademark is a source indicator. At common law, the person who used a symbol or mark to identify a business or product was protected in the use of that trademark. Clearly, by using another's trademark, a business could lead consumers to believe that its goods were made by the other business. The law seeks to avoid this kind of confusion. In this section, we examine various aspects of the law governing trademarks.

In the following classic case concerning Coca-Cola, the defendants argued that the Coca-Cola trademark was entitled to no protection under the law because the term did not accurately represent the product.

CLASSIC CASE 14.1

The Coca-Cola Co. v. The Koke Co. of America

Supreme Court of the United States, 254 U.S. 143, 41 S.Ct. 113, 65 L.Ed.189 (1920).

COMPANY PROFILE John Pemberton, an Atlanta pharmacist, invented a caramel-colored, carbonated soft drink in 1886. His bookkeeper, Frank Robinson, named the beverage Coca-Cola after two of the ingredients, coca leaves and kola nuts. Asa Candler bought the Coca-Cola Company (**www.coca-colacompany.com**) in 1891, and within seven years, he had made the soft drink available throughout the United States, as well as in parts of Canada and Mexico. Candler continued to sell Coke aggressively and to open up new markets, reaching Europe before 1910. In doing so, however, he attracted numerous competitors, some of which tried to capitalize directly on the Coke name.

BACKGROUND AND FACTS The Coca-Cola Company sought to enjoin (prevent) the Koke Company of America and other beverage companies from, among other things, using the word *Koke* for their products. The Koke Company of America and other beverage companies contended that the Coca-Cola trademark was a fraudulent representation and that Coca-Cola was therefore not entitled to any help from the courts. The Koke Company and the other defendants alleged that the Coca-Cola Company, by its use of the Coca-Cola name, represented that the beverage contained cocaine (from coca leaves), which it no longer did. The trial court granted the injunction against the Koke Company, but the appellate court reversed the lower court's ruling. Coca-Cola then appealed to the United States Supreme Court.

IN THE LANGUAGE OF THE COURT
Mr. Justice *HOLMES* delivered the opinion of the Court.

* * * *

* * * Before 1900 the beginning of [Coca-Cola's] good will was more or less helped by the presence of cocaine, a drug that, like alcohol or caffeine or opium, may be described as a deadly poison or as a valuable [pharmaceutical item, depending on the speaker's purposes]. The amount seems to have been very small,[a] but it may have been enough to begin a bad habit and after the Food and Drug Act of June 30, 1906, if not earlier, long before this suit was brought, it was eliminated from the plaintiff's compound.

* * * Since 1900 the sales have increased at a very great rate corresponding to a like increase in advertising. The name now characterizes a beverage to be had at almost any soda fountain. It means a single thing coming from a single source, and well known to the community. It hardly would be too much to say that the drink characterizes the name as much as the name the drink. In other words *Coca-Cola probably means to most persons the plaintiff's familiar product to be had everywhere rather than a compound of particular substances.* * * * Before this suit was brought the plaintiff had advertised to the public that it must not expect and would not find cocaine, and had eliminated everything tending to suggest cocaine effects except the name and the picture of [coca] leaves and nuts, which probably conveyed little or nothing to most who saw it. It appears to us that it would be going too far to deny the plaintiff relief against a palpable [readily evident] fraud because possibly here and there an ignorant person might call for the drink with the hope for incipient cocaine intoxication. The plaintiff's position must be judged by the facts as they were when the suit was begun, not by the facts of a different condition and an earlier time. [Emphasis added.]

DECISION AND REMEDY *The district court's injunction was allowed to stand. The competing beverage companies were enjoined from calling their products* Koke.

IMPACT OF THIS CASE ON TODAY'S LAW *In this early case, the United States Supreme Court made it clear that trademarks and trade names (and nicknames for those marks and names, such as the nickname "Coke" for "Coca-Cola") that are in common use receive protection under the common law. This holding is significant historically because it is the predecessor to the federal statute later passed to protect trademark rights—the Lanham Act of 1946, to be discussed next. In many ways, this act represented a codification of common law principles governing trademarks.*

WHAT IF THE FACTS WERE DIFFERENT? *Suppose that Coca-Cola had been trying to make the public believe that its product contained cocaine. Would the result in this case likely have been different? Why or why not?*

a. In reality, until 1903 the amount of active cocaine in each bottle of Coke was equivalent to one "line" of cocaine.

Statutory Protection of Trademarks

Statutory protection of trademarks and related property is provided at the federal level by the Lanham Act of 1946.[1] The Lanham Act was enacted, in part, to protect manufacturers from losing business to rival companies that used confusingly similar trademarks.

The Lanham Act incorporates the common law of trademarks and provides remedies for owners of trademarks who wish to enforce their claims in federal court. Many states also have trademark statutes.

TRADEMARK DILUTION In 1995, Congress amended the Lanham Act by passing the Federal Trademark Dilution Act,[2] which allowed trademark owners to bring suits in federal court for trademark **dilution.** In 2006, Congress further amended the law on trademark dilution by passing the Trademark Dilution Revision Act (TDRA).[3]

Under the TDRA, to state a claim for trademark dilution, a plaintiff must prove the following:

1. The plaintiff owns a famous mark that is distinctive.
2. The defendant has begun using a mark in commerce that allegedly is diluting the famous mark.
3. The similarity between the defendant's mark and the famous mark gives rise to an *association* between the marks.
4. The association is likely to impair the distinctiveness of the famous mark or harm its reputation.

Trademark dilution laws protect "distinctive" or "famous" trademarks (such as Rolls Royce, McDonald's, and Apple) from certain unauthorized uses even when the use is on noncompeting goods or is unlikely to confuse. More than half of the states have also enacted trademark dilution laws.

SIMILAR MARKS MAY CONSTITUTE TRADEMARK DILUTION Note that a famous mark may be diluted by the use of an *identical* mark or by the use of a *similar* mark.[4] A similar mark is more likely to lessen the value of a famous mark when the companies using the marks provide related goods or compete against each other in the same market.

Case in Point 14.1 Samantha Lundberg opened "Sambuck's Coffeehouse," in Astoria, Oregon, even though she knew that "Starbucks" is one of the largest coffee chains in the nation. When Starbucks Corporation filed a dilution lawsuit, the federal court ruled that use of the "Sambuck's" mark constituted trademark dilution because it created confusion for consumers. Not only was there a "high degree" of similarity between the marks, but also both companies provided coffee-related services and marketed their services through "stand-alone" retail stores. Therefore, the use of the similar mark (Sambuck's) reduced the value of the famous mark (Starbucks).[5] ◀

Trademark Registration

Trademarks may be registered with the state or with the federal government. To register for protection under federal trademark law, a person must file an application with the U.S. Patent and Trademark Office in Washington, D.C. Under current law, a mark can be registered (1) if it is currently in commerce or (2) if the applicant intends to put it into commerce within six months.

In special circumstances, the six-month period can be extended by thirty months. Thus, the applicant would have a total of three years from the date of notice of trademark approval to make use of the mark and file the required use statement. Registration is postponed until the mark is actually used.

During this waiting period, any applicant can legally protect his or her trademark against a third party who previously has neither used the mark nor filed an application for it. Registration is renewable between the fifth and sixth years after the initial registration and every ten years thereafter (every twenty years for those trademarks registered before 1990).

Trademark Infringement

Registration of a trademark with the U.S. Patent and Trademark Office gives notice on a nationwide basis that the trademark belongs exclusively to the registrant. The registrant is also allowed to use the symbol ® to indicate that the mark has been registered. Whenever that trademark is copied to a substantial degree or used in its entirety by another, intentionally or unintentionally, the trademark has been *infringed* (used without authorization).

1. 15 U.S.C. Sections 1051–1128.
2. 15 U.S.C. Section 1125.
3. Pub. L. No. 103-312, 120 Stat. 1730 (2006).
4. See *Louis Vuitton Malletier S.A. v. Haute Diggity Dog, LLC,* 507 F.3d 252 (4th Cir. 2007); and *Moseley v. V Secret Catalogue, Inc.,* 537 U.S. 418, 123 S.Ct. 1115, 155 L.Ed.2d 1 (2003).
5. *Starbucks Corp. v. Lundberg,* 2005 WL 3183858 (D.Or. 2005).

When a trademark has been infringed, the owner of the mark has a cause of action against the infringer. To succeed in a trademark infringement action, the owner must show that the defendant's use of the mark created a likelihood of confusion about the origin of the defendant's goods or services. The owner need not prove that the infringer acted intentionally or that the trademark was registered (although registration does provide proof of the date of inception of the trademark's use).

The most commonly granted remedy for trademark infringement is an *injunction* to prevent further infringement. Under the Lanham Act, a trademark owner that successfully proves infringement can recover actual damages, plus the profits that the infringer wrongfully received from the unauthorized use of the mark. A court can also order the destruction of any goods bearing the unauthorized trademark. In some situations, the trademark owner may also be able to recover attorneys' fees.

Distinctiveness of the Mark

A trademark must be sufficiently distinctive to enable consumers to identify the manufacturer of the goods easily and to distinguish between those goods and competing products.

STRONG MARKS Fanciful, arbitrary, or suggestive trademarks are generally considered to be the most distinctive (strongest) trademarks. Marks that are fanciful, arbitrary, or suggestive are protected as inherently distinctive without demonstrating secondary meaning. These marks receive automatic protection because they serve to identify a particular product's source, as opposed to describing the product itself.

Fanciful and Arbitrary Trademarks. Fanciful trademarks are inherently distinctive and include invented words, such as "Xerox" for one manufacturer's copiers and "Google" for search engines. Arbitrary trademarks are those that use common words in an uncommon way that is nondescriptive, such as "Dutch Boy" as a name for paint.

Even a single letter used in a particular style can be an arbitrary trademark. ▶ **Case in Point 14.2** Sports entertainment company ESPN sued Quiksilver, Inc., a maker of youth-oriented clothing, alleging trademark infringement. ESPN claimed that Quiksilver's clothing had used the stylized "X" mark that ESPN uses in connection with the "X Games" (extreme action sports competitions). Quiksilver filed counterclaims for trademark infringement and dilution, arguing that it had a long history of using the stylized X on its products.

ESPN created the X Games in the mid-1990s, and Quiksilver has been using the X mark since 1994. ESPN asked the court to dismiss Quiksilver's counterclaims, but the court refused, holding that the X on Quiksilver's clothing is clearly an arbitrary mark. The court found that the two Xs are "similar enough that a consumer might well confuse them."[6] ◀

Suggestive Trademarks. Suggestive trademarks indicate something about a product's nature, quality, or characteristics, without describing the product directly. These marks require imagination on the part of the consumer to identify the characteristic. For example, "Dairy Queen" suggests an association between its products and milk, but it does not directly describe ice cream.

"Blu-ray" is a suggestive mark that is associated with the high-quality, high-definition video contained on a particular optical data storage disc. Although blue-violet lasers are used to read *blu-ray* discs, the term *blu-ray* does not directly describe the disc.

SECONDARY MEANING Descriptive terms, geographic terms, and personal names are not inherently distinctive and do not receive protection under the law until they acquire a secondary meaning. A secondary meaning may arise when customers begin to associate a specific term or phrase (such as *London Fog*) with specific trademarked items (coats with "London Fog" labels) made by a particular company.

▶ **Case in Point 14.3** Frosty Treats, Inc., sells frozen desserts out of ice cream trucks. The video game series Twisted Metal depicts an ice cream truck with a clown character on it that is similar to the clowns on Frosty Treats' trucks. In the last game of the series, the truck bears the label "Frosty Treats." Frosty sued the video game maker for trademark infringement. The court, however, held that "Frosty Treats" is a descriptive term and is not protected by trademark law unless it has acquired a secondary meaning.

To establish secondary meaning, Frosty Treats would have had to show that the public recognized its trademark and associated it with a single source. Because Frosty Treats failed to do so, the court entered a judgment in favor of the video game producer.[7] ◀

6. *ESPN, Inc. v. Quiksilver, Inc.*, 586 F.Supp.2d 219 (S.D.N.Y. 2008).
7. *Frosty Treats, Inc., v. Sony Computer Entertainment America, Inc.*, 426 F.3d 1001 (8th Cir. 2005).

Once a secondary meaning is attached to a term or name, a trademark is considered distinctive and is protected. Even a color can qualify for trademark protection, as did the color schemes used by some state university sports teams, including Ohio State University and Louisiana State University.[8]

GENERIC TERMS Generic terms that refer to an entire class of products, such as *bicycle* and *computer,* receive no protection, even if they acquire secondary meanings. A particularly thorny problem arises when a trademark acquires generic use. For instance, *aspirin* and *thermos* were originally the names of trademarked products, but today the words are used generically. Other trademarks that have acquired generic use are *escalator, trampoline, raisin bran, dry ice, lanolin, linoleum, nylon,* and *cornflakes.*

Service, Certification, and Collective marks

A **service mark** is essentially a trademark that is used to distinguish the *services* (rather than the products) of one person or company from those of another. For example, each airline has a particular mark or symbol associated with its name. Titles and character names used in radio and television are frequently registered as service marks.

Other marks protected by law include certification marks and collective marks. A **certification mark** is used by one or more persons, other than the owner, to certify the region, materials, mode of manufacture, quality, or other characteristic of specific goods or services. Certification marks include "Good Housekeeping Seal of Approval" and "UL Tested."

When used by members of a cooperative, association, or other organization, a certification mark is referred to as a **collective mark.** Collective marks appear at the ends of motion picture credits to indicate the various associations and organizations that participated in the making of the films. The union marks found on the tags of certain products are also collective marks.

Trade Dress

The term **trade dress** refers to the image and overall appearance of a product. Trade dress is a broad concept and can include either all or part of the total image or overall impression created by a product or its packaging.

▶ **Example 14.4** The distinctive decor, menu, layout, and style of service of a particular restaurant may be regarded as trade dress. Trade dress can also include the layout and appearance of a catalogue, the use of a lighthouse as part of the design of a golf hole, the fish shape of a cracker, or the G-shaped design of a Gucci watch. ◀

Basically, trade dress is subject to the same protection as trademarks. In cases involving trade dress infringement, as in trademark infringement cases, a major consideration is whether consumers are likely to be confused by the allegedly infringing use.

Counterfeit Goods

Counterfeit goods copy or otherwise imitate trademarked goods, but they are not the genuine trademarked goods. The importation of goods that bear counterfeit (fake) trademarks poses a growing problem for U.S. businesses, consumers, and law enforcement. In addition to the negative financial effects on legitimate businesses, certain counterfeit goods, such as pharmaceuticals and nutritional supplements, can present serious public health risks.

Although Congress has enacted statutes against counterfeit goods (discussed next), the United States cannot prosecute foreign counterfeiters because our national laws do not apply to them. Instead, one effective tool that U.S. officials use to combat online sales of counterfeit goods is to obtain a court order to close down the domain names of Web sites that sell such goods.

▶ **Example 14.5** In 2012, U.S. agents shut down 101 domain names on the Monday after Thanksgiving ("Cyber Monday," the online version of "Black Friday," the day after Thanksgiving when the holiday shopping season begins). Although the criminal enterprises may continue selling counterfeit versions of brand-name products under different domain names, shutting down the Web sites, particularly on key shopping days, prevents some counterfeit goods from entering the United States. ◀

THE STOP COUNTERFEITING IN MANUFACTURED GOODS ACT The Stop Counterfeiting in Manufactured Goods Act[9] (SCMGA) was enacted to combat counterfeit goods. The act makes it a crime to traffic inten-

8. *Board of Supervisors of Louisiana State University v. Smack Apparel Co.,* 438 F.Supp.2d 653 (E.D.La. 2006). See also *Abraham v. Alpha Chi Omega,* 781 F.Supp.2d 396 (N.D.Tex. 2011).

9. Pub. L. No. 109-181 (2006), which amended 18 U.S.C. Sections 2318–2320.

tionally in or attempt to traffic in counterfeit goods or services, or to knowingly use a counterfeit mark on or in connection with goods or services.

Before this act, the law did not prohibit the creation or shipment of counterfeit labels that were not attached to any product. Therefore, counterfeiters would make labels and packaging bearing another's trademark, ship the labels to another location, and then affix them to an inferior product to deceive buyers. The SCMGA closed this loophole by making it a crime to knowingly traffic in counterfeit labels, stickers, packaging, and the like, regardless of whether the items are attached to any goods.

PENALTIES FOR COUNTERFEITING Persons found guilty of violating the SCMGA may be fined up to $2 million or imprisoned for up to ten years (or more if they are repeat offenders). If a court finds that the statute was violated, it must order the defendant to forfeit the counterfeit products (which are then destroyed), as well as any property used in the commission of the crime. The defendant must also pay restitution to the trademark holder or victim in an amount equal to the victim's actual loss.

▶ **Case in Point 14.6** Wajdi Beydoun pleaded guilty to conspiring to import cigarette-rolling papers from Mexico that were falsely marked as "Zig-Zags" and selling them in the United States. The court sentenced Beydoun to prison and ordered him to pay $566,267 in restitution. On appeal, the court affirmed the prison sentence but reversed the restitution because the amount exceeded the actual loss suffered by the legitimate sellers of Zig-Zag rolling papers.[10] ◀

The United States has also joined with other nations in a new international agreement aimed at combatting counterfeiting (see the discussion on page 337).

Trade Names

Trademarks apply to *products*. A **trade name** indicates part or all of a business's name, whether the business is a sole proprietorship, a partnership, or a corporation. Generally, a trade name is directly related to a business and its goodwill.

A trade name may be protected as a trademark if the trade name is also the name of the company's trademarked product—for example, Coca-Cola. Unless it is also used as a trademark or service mark, a trade name cannot be registered with the federal government. Trade names are protected under the common law, but only if they are unusual or fancifully used. The word *Safeway,* for example, was sufficiently fanciful to obtain protection as a trade name for a grocery chain.

Licensing

One way to avoid litigation and still make use of another's trademark or other form of intellectual property is to obtain a license to do so. A **license** in this context is an agreement, or contract, permitting the use of a trademark, copyright, patent, or trade secret for certain purposes. The party that owns the intellectual property rights and issues the license is the *licensor,* and the party obtaining the license is the *licensee.*

A license grants only the rights expressly described in the license agreement. A licensor might, for example, allow the licensee to use the trademark as part of its company or domain name, but not otherwise use the mark on any products or services. Disputes frequently arise over licensing agreements, particularly when the license involves Internet uses.

▶ **Case in Point 14.7** George V Restauration S.A. and others owned and operated the Buddha Bar Paris, a restaurant with an Asian theme in Paris, France. One of the owners allowed Little Rest Twelve, Inc., to use the Buddha Bar trademark and its associated concept in New York City under the name *Buddha Bar NYC.* Little Rest paid royalties for its use of the Buddha Bar mark and advertised Buddha Bar NYC's affiliation with Buddha Bar Paris, a connection also noted on its Web site and in the media.

When a dispute arose, the owners of Buddha Bar Paris withdrew their permission for Buddha Bar NYC's use of their mark, but Little Rest continued to use it. The owners of the mark filed a suit in a New York state court against Little Rest. The court granted an injunction to prevent Little Rest from using the mark.[11] ◀

SECTION 2

PATENTS

A **patent** is a grant from the government that gives an inventor the exclusive right to make, use, or sell his or her invention for a period of twenty years. Patents for designs, as opposed to those for inventions, are given for a fourteen-year period. The applicant must

10. *United States v. Beydoun,* 469 F.3d 102 (5th Cir. 2006).

11. *George V Restauration S.A. v. Little Rest Twelve, Inc.,* 58 A.D.3d 428, 871 N.Y.S.2d 65 (2009).

demonstrate to the satisfaction of the U.S. Patent and Trademark Office that the invention, discovery, process, or design is novel, useful, and not obvious in light of current technology.

Until recently, U.S. patent law differed from the laws of many other countries because the first person to invent a product obtained the patent rights rather than the first person to file for a patent. It was often difficult to prove who invented an item first, however, which prompted Congress to change the system in 2011 by passing the America Invents Act.[12] Now the first person to file an application for a patent on a product or process will receive patent protection. In addition, the new law established a nine-month limit for challenging a patent on any ground.

The period of patent protection begins on the date the patent application is filed, rather than when the patent is issued, which may sometimes be years later. After the patent period ends (either fourteen or twenty years later), the product or process enters the public domain, and anyone can make, sell, or use the invention without paying the patent holder.

Searchable Patent Databases

A significant development relating to patents is the availability online of the world's patent databases. The Web site of the U.S. Patent and Trademark Office (**www.uspto.gov**) provides searchable databases covering U.S. patents granted since 1976. The Web site of the European Patent Office (**www.epo.org**) provides online access to 50 million patent documents in more than seventy nations through a searchable network of databases.

Businesses use these searchable databases in many ways. Because patents are valuable assets, businesses may need to perform patent searches to list or inventory their assets. Patent searches may also be conducted to study trends and patterns in a specific technology or to gather information about competitors in the industry.

What Is Patentable?

Under federal law, "[w]hoever invents or discovers any new and useful process, machine, manufacture, or composition of matter, or any new and useful improvement thereof, may obtain a patent therefor, subject to the conditions and requirements of this title."[13] Thus, to be patentable, the applicant must prove that the invention, discovery, process, or design is *novel, useful,* and *not obvious* (in light of current technology).

In sum, almost anything is patentable, except the laws of nature, natural phenomena, and abstract ideas (including algorithms[14]). Even artistic methods and works of art, certain business processes, and the structures of storylines are patentable, provided that they are novel and not obvious.[15]

Plants that are reproduced asexually (by means other than from seed), such as hybrid or genetically engineered plants, are patentable in the United States, as are genetically engineered (or cloned) microorganisms and animals. ▶ **Case in Point 14.8** Monsanto, Inc., sells its patented genetically modified (GM) seeds to farmers as a way to achieve higher yields from crops using fewer pesticides. It requires farmers who buy GM seeds to sign licensing agreements promising to plant the seeds for only one crop and to pay a technology fee for each acre planted. To ensure compliance, Monsanto has many full-time employees whose job is to investigate and prosecute farmers who use the GM seeds illegally. Monsanto has filed nearly 150 lawsuits against farmers in the United States and has been awarded more than $15 million in damages (not including out-of-court settlement amounts).[16] ◀

Patent Infringement

If a firm makes, uses, or sells another's patented design, product, or process without the patent owner's permission, that firm commits the tort of patent infringement. Patent infringement may occur even though the patent owner has not put the patented product into commerce. Patent infringement may also occur even though not all features or parts of a product are copied. (To infringe the patent on a process, however, all steps or their equivalent must be copied.)

12. The full title of this law is the Leahy-Smith America Invents Act, Pub. L. No. 112-29 (2011), which amended 35 U.S.C. Sections 1, 41, and 321.

13. 35 U.S.C. Section 101.

14. An *algorithm* is a step-by-step procedure, formula, or set of instructions for accomplishing a specific task. An example is the set of rules used by a search engine to rank the listings contained within its index in response to a query.

15. For a United States Supreme Court case discussing the obviousness requirement, see *KSR International Co. v. Teleflex, Inc.,* 550 U.S. 398, 127 S.Ct. 1727, 167 L.Ed.2d 705 (2007).

16. See, for example, *Monsanto Co. v. Bowman,* 657 F.3d 1341 (Fed.Cir. 2011); and *Monsanto Co. v. Scruggs,* 2009 WL 1228318 (Fed.Cir. 2009).

PATENT INFRINGEMENT SUITS AND HIGH-TECH COMPANIES Obviously, companies that specialize in developing new technology stand to lose significant profits if someone "makes, uses, or sells" devices that incorporate their patented inventions. Because these firms are the holders of numerous patents, they are frequently involved in patent infringement lawsuits (as well as other types of intellectual property disputes).

Many companies that make and sell electronics and computer software and hardware are based in foreign nations (for example, Samsung Electronics Company is a Korean firm). Foreign firms can apply for and obtain U.S. patent protection on items that they sell within the United States. Similarly, U.S. firms can obtain protection in foreign nations where they sell goods.

LIMITATIONS ON EXPORTED SOFTWARE The United States Supreme Court has narrowly construed patent infringement as it applies to exported software. As a general rule, under U.S. law, no patent infringement occurs when a patented product is made and sold in another country.

▶ **Case in Point 14.9** AT&T Corporation holds a patent on a device used to digitally encode, compress, and process recorded speech. AT&T brought an infringement case against Microsoft Corporation, which admitted that its Windows operating system incorporated software code that infringed on AT&T's patent.

The case reached the United States Supreme Court on the question of whether Microsoft's liability extended to computers made in another country. The Court held that it did not. Microsoft was liable only for infringement in the United States and not for the Windows-based computers produced in foreign locations. The Court reasoned that Microsoft had not "supplied" the software for the computers but had only electronically transmitted a master copy, which the foreign manufacturers copied and loaded onto the computers.[17] ◀

APPLE, INC. V. SAMSUNG ELECTRONICS COMPANY As mentioned in the chapter introduction, Apple sued Samsung alleging that Samsung's Galaxy mobile phones and tablets that use Google's HTC Android operating system infringe on Apple's patents. Apple has design patents that cover the graphical user interface (the display of icons on the home screen), the device's shell, and the screen and button design. Apple also has patents that cover the way information is displayed on iPhones and other devices, the way windows pop open, and the way information is scaled and rotated.

In 2012, a jury issued a verdict in favor of Apple and awarded more than $1 billion in damages—one of the largest awards ever made in a patent case (a judge later ruled that part of the damages had been incorrectly calculated, however).[18] The jury found that Samsung had willfully infringed five of Apple's patents. The case provides an important precedent for Apple in its legal battles against Android devices made by other companies worldwide. Nevertheless, litigation between the two companies has continued.

Remedies for Patent Infringement

If a patent is infringed, the patent holder may sue for relief in federal court. The patent holder can seek an injunction against the infringer and can also request damages for royalties and lost profits. In some cases, the court may grant the winning party reimbursement for attorneys' fees and costs. If the court determines that the infringement was willful, the court can triple the amount of damages awarded (treble damages).

In the past, permanent injunctions were routinely granted to prevent future infringement. In 2006, however, the United States Supreme Court ruled that patent holders are not automatically entitled to a permanent injunction against future infringing activities. The courts have discretion to decide whether equity requires it. According to the Court, a patent holder must prove that it has suffered irreparable injury and that the public interest would not be disserved by a permanent injunction.[19] This decision gives courts discretion to decide what is equitable in the circumstances and allows them to consider what is in the public interest rather than just the interests of the parties.

▶ **Case in Point 14.10** In the first case applying this rule, a court found that although Microsoft had infringed on the patent of a small software company, the latter was not entitled to an injunction. According to the court, the small company was not irreparably harmed and could be adequately compensated by monetary damages. Also, the public might suffer negative effects from an injunction because the

17. *Microsoft Corp. v. AT&T Corp.*, 550 U.S. 437, 127 S.Ct. 1746, 167 L.Ed.2d 737 (2007).

18. *Apple, Inc. v. Samsung Electronics Co.*, CV 11-1846 and CV 12-0630 (N.D.Cal. August 24, 2012). In 2013, a judge ruled that part of the damages awarded were incorrectly calculated and excessive, invalidating approximately $450.5 million of the jury's award. The judge ordered a new trial to determine the appropriate amount of damages. *Apple, Inc. v. Samsung Electronics Co.*, ___ F.Supp.2d ___, 2013 WL 772525 (N.D.Cal. 2013).

19. *eBay, Inc. v. MercExchange, LLC*, 547 U.S. 388, 126 S.Ct. 1837, 164 L.Ed.2d 641 (2006).

infringement involved part of Microsoft's widely used Office Suite software.[20] ◀

SECTION 3 COPYRIGHTS

A **copyright** is an intangible property right granted by federal statute to the author or originator of a literary or artistic production of a specified type. The Copyright Act of 1976,[21] as amended, governs copyrights. Works created after January 1, 1978, are automatically given statutory copyright protection for the life of the author plus 70 years. For copyrights owned by publishing houses, the copyright expires 95 years from the date of publication or 120 years from the date of creation, whichever comes first. For works by more than one author, the copyright expires 70 years after the death of the last surviving author.[22]

Copyrights can be registered with the U.S. Copyright Office (**www.copyright.gov**) in Washington, D.C. A copyright owner no longer needs to place the symbol © or the term *Copr.* or *Copyright* on the work to have the work protected against infringement. Chances are that if somebody created it, somebody owns it.

Generally, copyright owners are protected against the following:

1. Reproduction of the work.
2. Development of derivative works.
3. Distribution of the work.
4. Public display of the work.

What Is Protected Expression?

Works that are copyrightable include books, records, films, artworks, architectural plans, menus, music videos, product packaging, and computer software. To be protected, a work must be "fixed in a durable medium" from which it can be perceived, reproduced, or communicated. Protection is automatic. Registration is not required.

Section 102 of the Copyright Act explicitly states that it protects original works that fall into one of the following categories:

1. Literary works (including newspaper and magazine articles, computer and training manuals, catalogues, brochures, and print advertisements).
2. Musical works and accompanying words (including advertising jingles).
3. Dramatic works and accompanying music.
4. Pantomimes and choreographic works (including ballets and other forms of dance).
5. Pictorial, graphic, and sculptural works (including cartoons, maps, posters, statues, and even stuffed animals).
6. Motion pictures and other audiovisual works (including multimedia works).
7. Sound recordings.
8. Architectural works.

SECTION 102 EXCLUSIONS It is not possible to copyright an *idea*. Section 102 of the Copyright Act specifically excludes copyright protection for any "idea, procedure, process, system, method of operation, concept, principle, or discovery, regardless of the form in which it is described, explained, illustrated, or embodied." Thus, anyone can freely use the underlying ideas or principles embodied in a work.

What is copyrightable is the particular way in which an idea is *expressed*. Whenever an idea and an expression are inseparable, the expression cannot be copyrighted. Generally, anything that is not an original expression will not qualify for copyright protection. Facts widely known to the public are not copyrightable. Page numbers are not copyrightable because they follow a sequence known to everyone. Mathematical calculations are not copyrightable.

COMPILATIONS OF FACTS Unlike ideas, *compilations* of facts are copyrightable. Under Section 103 of the Copyright Act, a compilation is "a work formed by the collection and assembling of preexisting materials or data that are selected, coordinated, or arranged in such a way that the resulting work as a whole constitutes an original work of authorship."

The key requirement in the copyrightability of a compilation is originality. If the facts are selected, coordinated, or arranged in an original way, they can qualify for copyright protection. Therefore, the White Pages of a telephone directory do not qualify for copyright protection because they simply list alphabetically names and telephone numbers. The Yellow Pages of a directory can be copyrightable, provided the information is selected, coordinated, or arranged in an original way. Similarly, a compilation of infor-

20. *Z4 Technologies, Inc. v. Microsoft Corp.*, 434 F.Supp.2d 437 (E.D.Tex. 2006).
21. 17 U.S.C. Sections 101 *et seq.*
22. These time periods reflect the extensions of the length of copyright protection enacted by Congress in the Copyright Term Extension Act of 1998, 17 U.S.C. Section 302. The United States Supreme Court upheld the constitutionality of the act in 2003. See *Eldred v. Ashcroft*, 537 U.S. 186, 123 S.Ct. 769, 154 L.Ed.2d 683 (2003).

mation about yachts listed for sale has qualified for copyright protection.[23]

Copyright Infringement

Whenever the form or expression of an idea is copied, an infringement of copyright has occurred. The reproduction does not have to be exactly the same as the original, nor does it have to reproduce the original in its entirety. If a substantial part of the original is reproduced, the copyright has been infringed.

In the following case, rapper Curtis Jackson—better known as "50 Cent"—was the defendant in a suit that claimed his album *Before I Self-Destruct,* and the companion film of the same name, infringed the copyright of Shadrach Winstead's book, *The Preacher's Son—But the Streets Turned Me into a Gangster.*

23. *BUC International Corp. v. International Yacht Council, Ltd.,* 489 F.3d 1129 (11th Cir. 2007).

CASE ANALYSIS

Case 14.2 Winstead v. Jackson

United States Court of Appeals, Third Circuit, 2013 WL 139622 (2013).

IN THE LANGUAGE OF THE COURT

PER CURIAM. [By the Whole Court]

* * * *

* * * Winstead filed his * * * complaint in the United States District Court for the District of New Jersey, claiming that Jackson's album/CD and film derived their contents from, and infringed the copyright of, his book.

* * * *

* * * The District Court dismissed Winstead's * * * complaint * * * , concluding that Jackson * * * did not improperly copy protected aspects of Winstead's book.

* * * *

Winstead appeals.

* * * *

Here, it is not disputed that Winstead is the owner of the copyrighted property * * * . However, *not all copying is copyright infringement, so even if actual copying is proven, the court must decide, by comparing the allegedly infringing work with the original work, whether the copying was unlawful. Copying may be proved inferentially by showing that the allegedly infringing work is substantially similar to the copyrighted work.* A court compares the allegedly infringing work with the original work, and considers whether a "lay-observer" would believe that the copying was of protectable aspects of the copyrighted work. The inquiry involves distinguishing between the author's expression and the idea or theme that he or she seeks to convey or explore, because the former is protected and the latter is not. The court must determine whether the allegedly infringing work is similar because it appropriates the unique expressions of the original work, or merely because it contains elements that would be expected when two works express the same idea or explore the same theme. [Emphasis added.]

* * * A lay observer would not believe that Jackson's album/CD and film copied protectable aspects of Winstead's book. Jackson's album/CD is comprised of 16 individual songs, which explore drug-dealing, guns and money, vengeance, and other similar clichés of hip hop gangsterism. Jackson's fictional film is the story of a young man who turns to violence when his mother is killed in a drive-by shooting. The young man takes revenge by killing the man who killed his mother, and then gets rich by becoming an "enforcer" for a powerful criminal. He takes up with a woman who eventually betrays him, and is shot to death by her boyfriend, who has just been released from prison. The movie ends with his younger brother vowing to seek vengeance. Winstead's book purports to be autobiographical and tells the story of a young man whose beloved father was a Bishop in the church. The protagonist was angry as a child because his stepmother abused him, but he found acceptance and self-esteem on the streets of Newark because he was physically powerful. He earned money robbing and beating people, went to jail, returned to crime upon his release, and then made even more money. The protagonist discusses his time at Rahway State Prison in great and compelling detail. The story ends when the protagonist learns that his father has passed away; he conveys his belief that this tragedy has led to his redemption, and he hopes that others might learn from his mistakes.

* * * Although Winstead's book and Jackson's works share similar themes and setting, the story of an angry and wronged protagonist who turns to a life of violence and crime

CASE 14.2 CONTINUES ➧

CASE 14.2 CONTINUED

has long been a part of the public domain [and is therefore not protected by copyright law]. Winstead argues * * * that a protagonist asking for God's help when his father dies, cutting drugs with mixing agents to maximize profits, and complaining about relatives who are addicts and steal the product, are protectable, but these things are not unique. To the extent that Jackson's works contain these elements, they are to be expected when two works express the same idea about "the streets" or explore the same theme. Winstead argues that not every protagonist whose story concerns guns, drugs, and violence in an urban setting winds up in prison or loses a parent, but this argument only serves to illustrate an important difference between his book and Jackson's film. Jackson's protagonist never spends any time in prison, whereas Winstead's protagonist devotes a considerable part of his story to his incarcerations.

In addition, Winstead's book and Jackson's works are different with respect to character, plot, mood, and sequence of events. Winstead's protagonist embarks on a life of crime at a very young age, but is redeemed by the death of his beloved father. Jackson's protagonist turns to crime when he is much older and only after his mother is murdered. He winds up dead at a young age, unredeemed. Winstead's book is hopeful; Jackson's film is characterized * * * by moral apathy. It is true that both works involve the loss of a parent and the protagonist's recognition of the parent's importance in his life, but nowhere does Jackson appropriate anything unique about Winstead's expression of this generic topic.

Winstead contends that direct phrases from his book appear in Jackson's film. * * * He emphasizes these phrases: "Yo, where is my money at," "I would never have done no shit like that to you," "my father, my strength was gone," "he was everything to me," and "I did not know what to do," but, like the phrases "putting the work in," "get the dope, cut the dope," "let's keep it popping," and "the strong take from the weak but the smart take from everybody," they are either common in general or common with respect to hip hop culture, and do not enjoy copyright protection. The average person reading or listening to these phrases in the context of an overall story or song would not regard them as unique and protectable. Moreover, words and short phrases do not enjoy copyright protection. The similarity between Winstead's book and the lyrics to Jackson's songs on the album/CD is even more tenuous. "Stretching the dope" and "bloodshot red eyes" are common phrases that do not enjoy copyright protection. A side-by-side comparison of Winstead's book and the lyrics from Jackson's album/CD do not support a claim of copyright infringement.

For the foregoing reasons, we will affirm the order of the District Court dismissing [Winstead's] complaint.

LEGAL REASONING QUESTIONS

1. Which expressions of an original work are protected by copyright law?
2. Is all copying copyright infringement? If not, what is the test for determining whether a creative work has been unlawfully copied?
3. How did the court in this case determine whether the defendant's work infringed on the plaintiff's copyright?
4. Is a claim of copyright infringement supported if two works share similar themes and setting, as well as words and short phrases? Explain.

REMEDIES FOR COPYRIGHT INFRINGEMENT Those who infringe copyrights may be liable for damages or criminal penalties. These range from actual damages or statutory damages, imposed at the court's discretion, to criminal proceedings for willful violations.

Actual damages are based on the harm caused to the copyright holder by the infringement, while statutory damages, not to exceed $150,000, are provided for under the Copyright Act. Criminal proceedings may result in fines and/or imprisonment. A court can also issue a permanent injunction against a defendant when the court deems it necessary to prevent future copyright infringement.

▶ **Case in Point 14.11** Rusty Carroll operated an online term paper business, R2C2, Inc., that offered up to 300,000 research papers for sale at nine Web sites. Individuals whose work was posted on these Web sites without their permission filed a lawsuit against Carroll for copyright infringement. Because Carroll had repeatedly failed to comply with court orders regarding discovery, the court found that the copyright infringement was likely to continue unless an injunction was issued. The court therefore issued a permanent injunction prohibiting Carroll and R2C2 from selling any term paper without sworn documentary evidence that the paper's author had given permission.[24] ◀

THE "FAIR USE" EXCEPTION An exception to liability for copyright infringement is made under the "fair use" doctrine. In certain circumstances, a person or organization can reproduce copyrighted material without paying royalties (fees paid to the copyright holder for the privilege of reproducing the copyrighted material). Section 107 of the Copyright Act provides as follows:

> [T]he fair use of a copyrighted work, including such use by reproduction in copies or phonorecords or by any other means specified by [Section 106 of the Copyright Act], for purposes such as criticism, comment, news reporting, teaching (including multiple copies for classroom use), scholarship, or research, is not an infringement of copyright. In determining whether the use made of a work in any particular case is a fair use the factors to be considered shall include—
>
> (1) the purpose and character of the use, including whether such use is of a commercial nature or is for nonprofit educational purposes;
> (2) the nature of the copyrighted work;
> (3) the amount and substantiality of the portion used in relation to the copyrighted work as a whole; and
> (4) the effect of the use upon the potential market for or value of the copyrighted work.

WHAT IS FAIR USE? Because these guidelines are very broad, the courts determine whether a particular use is fair on a case-by-case basis. Thus, anyone who reproduces copyrighted material may be committing a violation. In determining whether a use is fair, courts have often considered the fourth factor to be the most important.

▶ **Case in Point 14.12** BMG Music Publishing, an owner of copyrighted music, granted a license to Leadsinger, Inc., a manufacturer of karaoke devices. The license gave Leadsinger permission to reproduce the sound recordings, but not to reprint the song lyrics, which appeared at the bottom of a TV screen when the karaoke device was used.

BMG demanded that Leadsinger pay a "lyric reprint" fee and a "synchronization" fee. Leadsinger refused to pay, claiming that its use of the lyrics was educational and thus did not constitute copyright infringement under the fair use exception. A federal appellate court disagreed. The court held that Leadsinger's display of the lyrics was not a fair use because it would have a negative effect on the value of the copyrighted work.[25] ◀

The First Sale Doctrine

Section 109(a) of the Copyright Act provides that "the owner of a particular copy or phonorecord lawfully made under [the Copyright Act], or any person authorized by such owner, is entitled, without the authority of the copyright owner, to sell or otherwise dispose of the possession of that copy or phonorecord." This rule is known as the first sale doctrine.

Under this doctrine, once a copyright owner sells or gives away a particular copy of a work, the copyright owner no longer has the right to control the distribution of that copy. Thus, for example, a person who buys a copyrighted book can sell it to someone else.

In 2011, a court held that the first sale doctrine also applies to a person who receives promotional CDs, such as a music critic or radio programmer. ▶ **Case in Point 14.13** Universal Music Group (UMG) regularly ships promotional CDs to people in the music industry. Troy Augusto obtained some of these promotional CDs from various sources and sold them through online auction sites. UMG filed a copyright infringement lawsuit. Augusto argued that the music company had given up its right to control further distribution of the CDs under the first sale doctrine. Ultimately, a federal appellate court held in favor of Augusto. The promotional CDs were dispatched to the recipients without any prior arrangement as to those particular copies. Therefore, the court concluded that UMG had conveyed title of the copyrighted promotional CDs to the recipients.[26] ◀

In 2012, the United States Supreme Court heard the appeal of a case involving the resale of textbooks on eBay. To read about the Court's decision in this important case, see this chapter's *Insight into the Global Environment* feature on the following page.

Copyright Protection for Software

In 1980, Congress passed the Computer Software Copyright Act, which amended the Copyright Act of 1976 to include computer programs in the list of

24. *Weidner v. Carroll,* 2010 WL 310310 (S.D.Ill. 2010).

25. *Leadsinger, Inc. v. BMG Music Publishing,* 512 F.3d 522 (9th Cir. 2008).

26. *UMG Recordings, Inc. v. Augusto,* 628 F.3d 1175 (9th Cir. 2011).

INSIGHT INTO THE GLOBAL ENVIRONMENT
Is It Legal to Resell Textbooks Purchased Abroad?

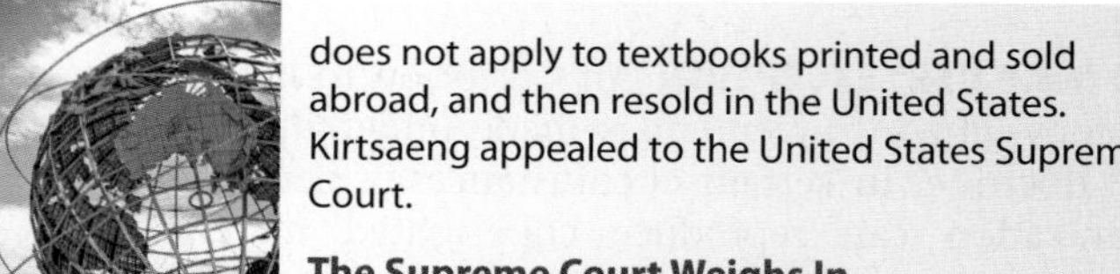

Students and professors alike complain about the high price of college textbooks. Some enterprising students have found that if they purchase textbooks printed abroad, they can sometimes save enough to justify the shipping charges. Textbook prices are lower in other countries because (1) production costs are lower there and (2) average incomes are also lower, so students are unable to pay the higher prices that U.S. students face. (Also, neither students nor professors abroad have the full range of paper and digital supplements that are offered with most textbooks in the United States.)

A Cornell University Student Starts a Side Business

Supap Kirtsaeng, a citizen of Thailand, started his studies at Cornell University in 1997 and then went on to a Ph.D. program at the University of Southern California. He enlisted friends and family in Thailand to buy copies of textbooks there and ship them to him in the United States. To pay for his education, Kirtsaeng resold the textbooks on eBay, where he eventually made about $100,000. John Wiley & Sons, Inc., which had printed eight of those textbooks in Asia, sued Kirtsaeng in federal district court for copyright infringement under Section 602(a)(1) of the Copyright Act. Wiley claimed that it is impermissible to import a work "without the authority of the owner." Kirtsaeng's defense was that Section 109(a) of the Copyright Act allows the first purchaser-owner of a book to sell or otherwise dispose of it without the copyright owner's permission. Kirtsaeng did not prevail.[a]

Kirtsaeng Appeals the Verdict

Kirtsaeng appealed to the U.S. Court of Appeals for the Second Circuit, but the court upheld the lower court's judgment.[b] The majority held that the first sale doctrine of the Copyright Act refers specifically to works that are manufactured in the United States. Therefore, the doctrine does not apply to textbooks printed and sold abroad, and then resold in the United States. Kirtsaeng appealed to the United States Supreme Court.

The Supreme Court Weighs In

The Supreme Court had to decide this question: Can any copy of a book or CD or DVD that was legally produced abroad, acquired abroad, and then imported into the United States be resold in the United States without the copyright owner's permission? The answer to this question has implications for discount sellers, such as Costco, and online businesses, such as eBay and Google, all of which offer "good" prices on many products that were made abroad.

The Supreme Court ruled that in Kirtsaeng's favor, reversing the appellate court's decision.[c] The majority of the Court ruled that the first sale doctrine applies, even when the good was purchased abroad: " [T]he common-law history of the 'first-sale' doctrine . . . favors a non-geographical interpretation. We . . . doubt that Congress would have intended to create the practical copyright-related harms with which a geographical interpretation would threaten ordinary scholarly, artistic, commercial activities." As it turned out, much of the Court's decision concerned the potential consequences of what might occur if the Court did not reverse the appellate court's decision. Allowing that decision to stand would have meant that one "could prevent a buyer from domestically selling or even giving away copies of a video game made in Japan, a film made in Germany or a dress (with a design copyright) made in China."

LEGAL CRITICAL THINKING

INSIGHT INTO THE SOCIAL ENVIRONMENT

What options do textbook publishers face given this Supreme Court decision?

a. *John Wiley & Sons, Inc. v. Kirtsaeng*, 93 U.S.P.Q.2d 1432 (S.D.N.Y. 2009).
b. *John Wiley & Sons, Inc. v. Kirtsaeng*, 654 F.3d 210 (2d Cir. 2011).
c. *Kirtsaeng v. John Wiley & Sons, Inc.*, ___ U.S. ___, 133 S.Ct. 1351, ___ L.Ed.2d ___ (2013).

creative works protected by federal copyright law.[27] Generally, copyright protection extends to those parts of a computer program that can be read by humans, such as the "high-level" language of a source code. Protection also extends to the binary-language object code, which is readable only by the computer, and to such elements as the overall structure, sequence, and organization of a program.

Not all aspects of software are protected, however. Courts typically have not extended copyright protec-

27. Pub. L. No. 96-517 (1980), amending 17 U.S.C. Sections 101, 117.

tion to the "look and feel"—the general appearance, command structure, video images, menus, windows, and other screen displays—of computer programs. ▶ **Example 14.14** MiTek develops a software program for laying out wood trusses (used in construction). Another company comes out with a different program that includes similar elements, such as the menu and submenu command tree-structures. MiTek cannot successfully sue for copyright infringement because the command structure of software is not protected. ◀ (Note that copying the "look and feel" of another's product may be a violation of trade dress or trademark laws, however.)

As will be explored in Chapter 15, technology has vastly increased the potential for copyright infringement via the Internet.

SECTION 4

TRADE SECRETS

The law of trade secrets protects some business processes and information that are not, or cannot be, patented, copyrighted, or trademarked against appropriation by competitors. A **trade secret** is basically information of commercial value, such as customer lists, plans, and research and development. Trade secrets may also include pricing information, marketing methods, production techniques, and generally anything that makes an individual company unique and that would have value to a competitor.

Unlike copyright and trademark protection, protection of trade secrets extends both to ideas and to their expression. (For this reason, and because there are no registration or filing requirements for trade secrets, trade secret protection may be well suited for software.) Of course, the secret formula, method, or other information must be disclosed to some persons, particularly to key employees. Businesses generally attempt to protect their trade secrets by having all employees who use a process or information agree in their contracts, or in confidentiality agreements, never to divulge it.

State and Federal Law on Trade Secrets

Under Section 757 of the *Restatement of Torts,* those who disclose or use another's trade secret, without authorization, are liable to that other party if:

1. They discovered the secret by improper means, or
2. Their disclosure or use constitutes a breach of a duty owed to the other party.

Stealing confidential business data by industrial espionage, such as by tapping into a competitor's computer, is a theft of trade secrets without any contractual violation and is actionable in itself.

Although trade secrets have long been protected under the common law, today most states' laws are based on the Uniform Trade Secrets Act,[28] which has been adopted in forty-seven states. Additionally, the Economic Espionage Act[29] (discussed in Chapter 7) makes the theft of trade secrets a federal crime.

Trade Secrets in Cyberspace

Computer technology is undercutting many business firms' ability to protect their confidential information, including trade secrets. For example, a dishonest employee could e-mail trade secrets in a company's computer to a competitor or a future employer. If e-mail is not an option, the employee might walk out with the information on a flash drive.

A former employee's continued use of a Twitter account after leaving the company may provide grounds for a suit alleging misappropriation of trade secrets. ▶ **Case in Point 14.15** Noah Kravitz worked for a company called PhoneDog for four years as a product reviewer and video blogger. PhoneDog provided him with the Twitter account "@PhoneDog_Noah." Kravitz's popularity grew, and he had approximately 17,000 followers by the time he quit. PhoneDog requested that Kravitz stop using the Twitter account.

Although Kravitz changed his handle to "@noah kravitz," he continued to use the account. PhoneDog subsequently sued Kravitz for misappropriation of trade secrets, among other things. Kravitz moved for a dismissal, but the court found that the complaint adequately stated a cause of action for misappropriation of trade secrets and allowed the suit to continue.[30] ◀

For a comprehensive summary of trade secrets and the other forms of intellectual property discussed in this chapter, see Exhibit 14–1 on the following page.

28. The Uniform Trade Secrets Act, as drafted by the National Conference of Commissioners on Uniform State Laws (NCCUSL), can be found at **uniformlaws.org**.
29. 18 U.S.C. Sections 1831–1839.
30. *PhoneDog v. Kravitz,* 2011 WL 5415612 (N.D.Cal. 2011). See also *Mintel Learning Technology, Inc. v. Ambrow Education Holding Ltd.,* 2012 WL 762126 (N.D.Cal. 2012).

EXHIBIT 14–1 Forms of Intellectual Property

Form	Definition	How Acquired	Duration	Remedy for Infringement
Patent	A grant from the government that gives an inventor exclusive rights to an invention.	By filing a patent application with the U.S. Patent and Trademark Office and receiving its approval.	Twenty years from the date of the application; for design patents, fourteen years.	Monetary damages, including royalties and lost profits, *plus* attorneys' fees. Damages may be tripled for intentional infringements.
Copyright	The right of an author or originator of a literary or artistic work, or other production that falls within a specified category, to have the exclusive use of that work for a given period of time.	Automatic (once the work or creation is put in tangible form). Only the *expression* of an idea (and not the idea itself) can be protected by copyright.	For authors: the life of the author, plus 70 years. For publishers: 95 years after the date of publication or 120 years after creation.	Actual damages plus profits received by the party who infringed *or* statutory damages under the Copyright Act, *plus* costs and attorneys' fees in either situation.
Trademark (service mark and trade dress)	Any distinctive word, name, symbol, or device (image or appearance), or combination thereof, that an entity uses to distinguish its goods or services from those of others. The owner has the exclusive right to use that mark or trade dress.	1. At common law, ownership created by use of the mark. 2. Registration with the appropriate federal or state office gives notice and is permitted if the mark is currently in use or will be within the next six months.	Unlimited, as long as it is in use. To continue notice by registration, the owner must renew by filing between the fifth and sixth years, and thereafter, every ten years.	1. Injunction prohibiting the future use of the mark. 2. Actual damages plus profits received by the party who infringed (can be increased under the Lanham Act). 3. Destruction of articles that infringed. 4. *Plus* costs and attorneys' fees.
Trade Secret	Any information that a business possesses and that gives the business an advantage over competitors (including formulas, lists, patterns, plans, processes, and programs).	Through the originality and development of the information and processes that constitute the business secret and are unknown to others.	Unlimited, so long as not revealed to others. Once revealed to others, it is no longer a trade secret.	Monetary damages for misappropriation (the Uniform Trade Secrets Act also permits punitive damages if willful), *plus* costs and attorneys' fees.

SECTION 5

INTERNATIONAL PROTECTION FOR INTELLECTUAL PROPERTY

For many years, the United States has been a party to various international agreements relating to intellectual property rights. For instance, the Paris Convention of 1883, to which about 173 countries are signatory, allows parties in one country to file for patent and trademark protection in any of the other member countries. Other international agreements in this area include the Berne Convention, the Trade-Related Aspects of Intellectual Property Rights (known as the TRIPS agreement), the Madrid Protocol, and the Anti-Counterfeiting Trade Agreement.

The Berne Convention

Under the Berne Convention of 1886, if a U.S. citizen writes a book, every country that has signed the convention must recognize the U.S. author's copyright in the book. Also, if a citizen of a country that has not signed the convention first publishes a book in one of the 165 countries that have signed, all other countries that have signed the convention must recognize that author's copyright. Copyright notice is not needed to gain protection under the Berne Convention for works published after March 1, 1989.

This convention and other international agreements have given some protection to intellectual property on a worldwide level. None of them, however, has been as significant and far reaching in scope as the TRIPS agreement, discussed in the next subsection.

In 2011, the European Union agreed to extend the period of royalty protection for musicians from fifty years to seventy years. This decision aids major record labels as well as performers and musicians who previously faced losing royalties from sales of their older recordings. The profits of musicians and record companies have been shrinking in recent years because of the sharp decline in sales of compact discs and the rise in illegal downloads.

In the following case, the United States Supreme Court had to decide if Congress had exceeded its authority under the U.S. Constitution when it enacted a law that restored copyright protection to many foreign works that were already in the public domain. (*Public domain* means that rights to certain intellectual property, such as songs and other published works, belong to everyone and are not protected by copyright or patent laws.)

CASE 14.3

Golan v. Holder

Supreme Court of the United States, ___ U.S. ___, 132 S.Ct. 873, 181 L.Ed.2d 835 (2012).

BACKGROUND AND FACTS The United States joined the Berne Convention in 1989, but it failed to give foreign copyright holders the same protections enjoyed by U.S. authors. Contrary to the Berne Convention, the United States did not protect any foreign work that had already entered the public domain.

In 1994, Congress enacted the Uruguay Round Agreements Act (URAA), which "restored" copyright protection for many foreign works that were already in the public domain. The URAA put foreign and domestic works on the same footing, allowing their copyrights to extend for the same number of years. Lawrence Golan, along with a group of musicians, conductors, and publishers, filed a suit against Eric Holder, in his capacity as the U.S. attorney general. These individuals had enjoyed free access to foreign works in the public domain before the URAA's enactment. They claimed that the URAA violated the copyright clause of the U.S. Constitution and thus that Congress had exceeded its constitutional authority in passing the URAA.

A federal appellate court held that Congress did not violate the copyright clause by passing the URAA. The petitioners appealed. The United States Supreme Court granted *certiorari* to resolve the matter.

IN THE LANGUAGE OF THE COURT
Justice *GINSBURG* delivered the opinion of the Court.

* * * *

* * * The Constitution states that "Congress shall have Power . . . to promote the Progress of Science . . . by securing for limited Times to Authors . . . the exclusive Right to their . . . Writings." Petitioners [Golan and others] find in this grant of authority an impenetrable [impassable] barrier to the extension of copyright protection to authors whose writings, for whatever reason, are in the public domain. We see no such barrier in the text of the Copyright Clause * * * .

* * * *

The text of the Copyright Clause does not exclude application of copyright protection to works in the public domain. * * * Petitioners' contrary argument relies primarily on the Constitution's confinement of a copyright's lifespan to a "limited Tim[e]." "Removing works from the public domain," they contend, "violates the 'limited times' restriction by turning a

CASE 14.3 CONTINUES ➧

CASE 14.3 CONTINUED

fixed and predictable period into one that can be reset or resurrected at any time, even after it expires."

Our decision in [a prior case] is largely dispositive [capable of settling a dispute] of petitioners' limited-time argument.[a] There we addressed the question of whether Congress violated the Copyright Clause when it extended, by 20 years, the terms of existing copyrights. Ruling that Congress acted within constitutional bounds, we declined to infer from the text of the Copyright Clause "the command that a time prescription, once set, becomes forever 'fixed' or 'inalterable.'" *"The word 'limited,' we observed, "does not convey a meaning so constricted." Rather, the term is best understood to mean "confine[d] within certain bounds," "restrain[ed]," or "circumscribed."* The construction petitioners tender closely resembles the definition rejected in *Eldred* [the prior case] and is similarly infirm [weak]. [Emphasis added.]

* * * *

* * * In aligning the United States with other nations bound by the Berne Convention, and thereby according equitable treatment to once disfavored foreign authors, Congress can hardly be charged with a design to move stealthily toward a regime of perpetual copyrights.

DECISION AND REMEDY *The United States Supreme Court affirmed the federal appellate court's ruling that the URAA does not violate the U.S. Constitution's copyright clause. Thus, Golan and the others could no longer use, without permission, any of the foreign works that were previously in the public domain. By passing the URAA in the United States, Congress, in effect, took those works out of the public domain and extended copyright protection to them. Henceforth, U.S. copyright and patent laws cover all such foreign intellectual property.*

THE GLOBAL DIMENSION *What does the Court's decision in this case mean for copyright holders in the United States who want copyright protection in other countries? Will other nations be more or less inclined to protect U.S. authors? Explain.*

THE ECONOMIC DIMENSION *Why did a group of musicians, conductors, publishers, and others file this suit? What did they hope to gain by a decision in their favor?*

a. See *Eldred v. Ashcroft,* 537 U.S. 186, 123 S.Ct. 769, 154 L.Ed.2d 683 (2003).

The TRIPS Agreement

Representatives from more than one hundred nations signed the TRIPS agreement in 1994. The agreement established, for the first time, standards for the international protection of intellectual property rights, including patents, trademarks, and copyrights for movies, computer programs, books, and music. The TRIPS agreement provides that each member country of the World Trade Organization must include in its domestic laws broad intellectual property rights and effective remedies (including civil and criminal penalties) for violations of those rights.

Generally, the TRIPS agreement forbids member nations from discriminating against foreign owners of intellectual property rights (in the administration, regulation, or adjudication of such rights). In other words, a member nation cannot give its own nationals (citizens) favorable treatment without offering the same treatment to nationals of all other member countries. ▶ **Example 14.16** A U.S. software manufacturer brings a suit for the infringement of intellectual property rights under Germany's national laws. Because Germany is a member of the TRIPS agreement, the U.S. manufacturer is entitled to receive the same treatment as a German manufacturer. ◀

Each member nation must also ensure that legal procedures are available for parties who wish to bring actions for infringement of intellectual property rights. Additionally, a related document established a mechanism for settling disputes among member nations.

The Madrid Protocol

In the past, one of the difficulties in protecting U.S. trademarks internationally was the time and expense required to apply for trademark registration in foreign countries. The filing fees and procedures for trademark registration vary significantly among individual countries. The Madrid Protocol, which was signed into law in 2003, may help to resolve these problems.

The Madrid Protocol is an international treaty that has been signed by eighty-six countries. Under its provisions, a U.S. company wishing to register its trademark abroad can submit a single application and designate other member countries in which the company would like to register its mark. The treaty was designed to reduce the costs of international trademark protection by more than 60 percent.

Although the Madrid Protocol may simplify and reduce the cost of trademark registration in foreign countries, it remains to be seen whether it will provide significant benefits to trademark owners. Even with an easier registration process, there are still questions as to whether all member countries will enforce the law and protect the mark.

The Anti-Counterfeiting Trade Agreement

In 2011 Australia, Canada, Japan, Korea, Morocco, New Zealand, Singapore, and the United States signed the Anti-Counterfeiting Trade Agreement (ACTA), an international treaty to combat global counterfeiting and piracy. The members of the European Union, Mexico, Switzerland, and other nations that support ACTA are still developing domestic procedures to comply with its provisions. Once a nation has adopted appropriate procedures, it can ratify the treaty.

PROVISIONS AND GOALS The goals of the treaty are to increase international cooperation, facilitate the best law enforcement practices, and provide a legal framework to combat counterfeiting. The treaty will have its own governing body.

ACTA applies not only to counterfeit physical goods, such as medications, but also to pirated copyrighted works being distributed via the Internet. The idea is to create a new standard of enforcement for intellectual property rights that goes beyond the TRIPS agreement and encourages international cooperation and information sharing among signatory countries.

BORDER SEARCHES Under ACTA, member nations are required to establish border measures that allow officials, on their own initiative, to search commercial shipments of imports and exports for counterfeit goods. The treaty neither requires nor prohibits random border searches of electronic devices, such as laptops, tablet devices, and smartphones, for infringing content. If border authorities reasonably believe that any goods in transit are counterfeit, the treaty allows them to keep the suspect goods unless the owner proves that the items are authentic and noninfringing.

The treaty allows member nations, in accordance with their own laws, to order online service providers to furnish information about (including the identity of) suspected trademark and copyright infringers.

Reviewing: Intellectual Property Rights

Two computer science majors, Trent and Xavier, have an idea for a new video game, which they propose to call "Hallowed." They form a business and begin developing their idea. Several months later, Trent and Xavier run into a problem with their design and consult a friend, Brad, who is an expert in designing computer source codes. After the software is completed but before Hallowed is marketed, a video game called Halo 2 is released for both the Xbox and the Playstation systems. Halo 2 uses source codes similar to those of Hallowed and imitates Hallowed's overall look and feel, although not all the features are alike. Using the information presented in the chapter, answer the following questions.

1. Would the name *Hallowed* receive protection as a trademark or as trade dress? Explain.
2. If Trent and Xavier had obtained a patent on Hallowed, would the release of Halo 2 have infringed on their patent? Why or why not?
3. Based only on the facts described above, could Trent and Xavier sue the makers of Halo 2 for copyright infringement? Why or why not?
4. Suppose that Trent and Xavier discover that Brad took the idea of Hallowed and sold it to the company that produced Halo 2. Which type of intellectual property issue does this raise?

DEBATE THIS . . . *Congress has impeded the spread of ideas by amending copyright law several times to give copyright holders protection for many decades.*

Terms and Concepts

certification mark 324
collective mark 324
copyright 328
dilution 322
intellectual property 320
license 325
patent 325
service mark 324
trade dress 324
trade name 325
trade secret 333
trademark 320

ExamPrep

Issue Spotters

1. Roslyn is a food buyer for Organic Cornucopia Food Company when she decides to go into business for herself as Roslyn's Kitchen. She contacts Organic's suppliers, offering to buy their entire harvest for the next year, and Organic's customers, offering to sell her products for less than her ex-employer. Has Roslyn violated any of the intellectual property rights discussed in this chapter? Explain. **(See page 333.)**
2. Global Products develops, patents, and markets software. World Copies, Inc., sells Global's software without the maker's permission. Is this patent infringement? If so, how might Global save the cost of suing World for infringement and at the same time profit from World's sales? **(See page 326.)**

- **Check your answers to the Issue Spotters against the answers provided in Appendix E at the end of this text.**

Before the Test

Go to **www.cengagebrain.com**, enter the ISBN 9781285428949, and click on "Find" to locate this textbook's Web site. Then, click on "Access Now" under "Study Tools," and select Chapter 14 at the top. There, you will find an Interactive Quiz that you can take to assess your mastery of the concepts in this chapter, as well as Flashcards and a Glossary of important terms.

Business Scenarios

14–1. Fair Use. Professor Wise is teaching a summer seminar in business torts at State University. Several times during the course, he makes copies of relevant sections from business law texts and distributes them to his students. Wise does not realize that the daughter of one of the textbook authors is a member of his seminar. She tells her father about Wise's copying activities, which have taken place without her father's or his publisher's permission. Her father sues Wise for copyright infringement. Wise claims protection under the fair use doctrine. Who will prevail? Explain. **(See page 331.)**

14–2. Patent Infringement. John and Andrew Doney invented a hard-bearing device for balancing rotors. Although they obtained a patent for their invention from the U.S. Patent and Trademark Office, it was never used as an automobile wheel balancer. Some time later, Exetron Corp. produced an automobile wheel balancer that used a hard-bearing device with a support plate similar to that of the Doneys' device. Given that the Doneys had not used their device for automobile wheel balancing, does Exetron's use of a similar device infringe on the Doneys' patent? Why or why not? **(See page 326.)**

Business Case Problems

14–3. Trade Secrets. Briefing.com offers Internet-based analyses of investment opportunities to investors. Richard Green is the company's president. One of Briefing.com's competitors is StreetAccount, LLC (limited liability company), whose owners include Gregory Jones and Cynthia Dietzmann. Jones worked for Briefing.com for six years until he quit in March 2003 and was a member of its board of directors until April 2003. Dietzmann worked for Briefing.com for seven years until she quit in March 2003. As Briefing.com employees, Jones and Dietzmann had access to confidential business data. For instance, Dietzmann developed a list of contacts through which Briefing.com obtained market information to display online. When Dietzmann quit, she did not return all of the contact information to the company. Briefing.com and Green filed a suit in a federal district court against Jones, Dietzmann, and StreetAccount, alleging that they had appropriated these data and other "trade secrets" to form a competing business. What are trade secrets? Why are they protected? Under what circumstances is a party liable at common law for their appropriation? How should these principles apply in this case? [*Briefing.com v. Jones,* 2006 WY 16, 126 P.3d 928 (2006)] **(See page 333.)**

14–4. Licensing. Redwin Wilchcombe composed, performed, and recorded a song called *Tha Weedman* at the request of Lil Jon, a member of Lil Jon & the East Side Boyz (LJESB), for LJESB's album *Kings of Crunk.* Wilchcombe was not paid, but was given credit on the album as a producer. After the album had sold 2 million copies, Wilchcombe filed a suit against LJESB, alleging copyright infringement. The defendants claimed that they had a license to use the song. Do the facts support this claim? Explain. [*Wilchcombe v. TeeVee Toons, Inc.,* 555 F.3d 949 (11th Cir. 2009)] **(See page 325.)**

14–5. BUSINESS CASE PROBLEM WITH SAMPLE ANSWER: Trade Secrets.

Jesse Edwards, an employee of Carbon Processing and Reclamation, LLC (CPR), put unmarked boxes of company records in his car. Edwards's wife, Channon, who suspected him of hiding financial information from her, gained access to the documents. William Jones, the owner of CPR, filed a suit, contending that Channon's unauthorized access to the files was a theft of trade secrets. Could the information in the documents be trade secrets? Should liability be imposed? Why or why not? [Jones v. Hamilton, *53 So.3d 134 (Ala.Civ.App. 2010)]* **(See page 333.)**

- **For a sample answer to Problem 14–5, go to Appendix F at the end of this text.**

14–6. Spotlight on Macy's—Copyright Infringement. United

Fabrics International, Inc., bought a fabric design from an Italian designer and registered a copyright to it with the U.S. Copyright Office. When Macy's, Inc., began selling garments with a similar design, United filed a copyright infringement suit against Macy's. Macy's argued that United did not own a valid copyright to the design and so could not claim infringement. Does United have to prove that the copyright is valid to establish infringement? Explain. [*United Fabrics International, Inc. v. C&J Wear, Inc.,* 630 F.3d 1255 (9th Cir. 2011)] **(See page 329.)**

14–7. Theft of Trade Secrets. Hanjuan Jin, a citizen of the People's Republic of China, began working at Motorola in 1998. She worked as a software engineer in a division that created proprietary standards for cellular communications. In 2004 and 2005, contrary to Motorola's policies, Jin also began working as a consultant for Lemko Corp. Lemko introduced Jin to Sun Kaisens, a Chinese software company. During 2005, Jin returned to Beijing on several occasions and began working with Sun Kaisens and with the Chinese military. The following year, she started corresponding with Sun Kaisens's management about a possible full-time job in China. During this period, she took several medical leaves of absence from Motorola. In February 2007, after one of these medical leaves, she returned to Motorola.

During the next several days at Motorola, she accessed and downloaded thousands of documents on her personal laptop as well as on pen drives. On the following day, she attempted to board a flight to China but was randomly searched by U.S. Customs and Border Protection officials at Chicago's O'Hare International Airport. Ultimately, U.S. officials discovered the downloaded Motorola documents. Are there any circumstances under which Jin could avoid being prosecuted for theft of trade secrets? If so, what are these circumstances? Discuss fully. [*United States v. Hanjuan Jin,* 833 F.Supp.2d 977 (N.D.Ill. 2012)] **(See page 333.)**

14–8. Copyright Infringement. SilverEdge Systems Software hired Catherine Conrad to perform a singing telegram. SilverEdge arranged for James Bendewald to record Conrad's performance of her copyrighted song to post on its Web site. Conrad agreed to wear a microphone to assist in the recording, told Bendewald what to film, and asked for an additional fee only if SilverEdge used the video for a commercial purpose. Later, the company chose to post a video of a different performer's singing telegram instead. Conrad filed a suit in a federal district court against SilverEdge and Bendewald for copyright infringement. Are the defendants liable? Explain. [*Conrad v. Bendewald,* 2013 WL 310194 (7th Cir. 2013)] **(See page 329.)**

14–9. A QUESTION OF ETHICS: Copyright Infringement.

Custom Copies, Inc., prepares and sells coursepacks, which contain compilations of readings for college courses. A teacher selects the readings and delivers a syllabus to the copy shop, which obtains the materials from a library, copies them, and binds the copies. Blackwell Publishing, Inc., which owns the copyright to some of the materials, filed a suit, alleging copyright infringement. [Blackwell Publishing, Inc. v. Custom Copies, Inc., *2006 WL 1529503 (N.D.Fla. 2006)]* **(See page 329.)**

(a) Custom Copies argued, in part, that creating and selling did not "distribute" the coursepacks. Does a copy shop violate copyright law if it only copies materials for coursepacks? Does the copying fall under the "fair use" exception? Should the court grant the defendant's motion? Why or why not?

(b) What is the potential impact if copies of a book or journal are created and sold without the permission of, and the payment of royalties or a fee to, the copyright owner? Explain.

14–10. SPECIAL CASE ANALYSIS: Copyright Infringement.

Go to Case Analysis Case 14.2, *Winstead v. Jackson,* on pages 329 and 330. Read the excerpt and answer the following questions.

(a) Issue: This case focused on an allegation of copyright infringement involving what parties and which creative works?

(b) **Rule of Law:** What is the test for determining whether a creative work infringes the copyright of another work?

(c) **Applying the Rule of Law:** How did the court determine whether the claim of copyright infringement was supported in this case?

(d) **Conclusion:** Was the defendant liable for copyright infringement? Why or why not?

Legal Reasoning Group Activity

14–11. Patents. After years of research, your company develops a product that might revolutionize the green (environmentally conscious) building industry. The product is made from relatively inexpensive and widely available materials combined in a unique way that can substantially lower the heating and cooling costs of residential and commercial buildings. The company has registered the trademark it intends to use on the product, and has filed a patent application with the U.S. Patent and Trademark Office. **(See page 325.)**

(a) One group should provide three reasons why this product does or does not qualify for patent protection.

(b) Another group should develop a four-step procedure for how your company can best protect its intellectual property rights (trademark, trade secret, and patent) and prevent domestic and foreign competitors from producing counterfeit goods or cheap knockoffs.

(c) Another group should list and explain three ways your company can utilize licensing.

CHAPTER 15

INTERNET LAW, SOCIAL MEDIA, AND PRIVACY

The Internet has changed our lives and our laws. Technology has put the world at our fingertips and now allows even the smallest business to reach customers around the globe. At the same time, the Internet presents a variety of challenges for the law. Courts are often in uncharted waters when deciding disputes that involve the Internet, social media, and online privacy. There may not be any common law precedents for judges to rely on when resolving a case. Long-standing principles of justice may be inapplicable. New rules are evolving, as we discuss in this chapter, but often not as quickly as technology.

SECTION 1 INTERNET LAW

A number of laws specifically address issues that arise only on the Internet. Three such issues are unsolicited e-mail, domain names, and cybersquatting, as we discuss here. We also discuss how the law is dealing with problems of trademark infringement and dilution online.

Spam

Businesses and individuals alike are targets of **spam.**[1] Spam is the unsolicited "junk e-mail" that floods virtual mailboxes with advertisements, solicitations, and other messages. Considered relatively harmless in the early days of the Internet, by 2013 spam accounted for roughly 75 percent of all e-mails.

STATE REGULATION OF SPAM In an attempt to combat spam, thirty-six states have enacted laws that prohibit or regulate its use. Many state laws that regulate spam require the senders of e-mail ads to instruct the recipients on how they can "opt out" of further e-mail ads from the same sources. For instance, in some states, an unsolicited e-mail must include a toll-free phone number or return e-mail address that the recipient can use to ask the sender to send no more unsolicited e-mails.

1. The term *spam* is said to come from the lyrics of a Monty Python song that repeats the word *spam* over and over.

THE FEDERAL CAN-SPAM ACT In 2003, Congress enacted the Controlling the Assault of Non-Solicited Pornography and Marketing (CAN-SPAM) Act.[2] The legislation applies to any "commercial electronic mail messages" that are sent to promote a commercial product or service. Significantly, the statute preempts state antispam laws except for those provisions in state laws that prohibit false and deceptive e-mailing practices.

Generally, the act permits the sending of unsolicited commercial e-mail but prohibits certain types of spamming activities. Prohibited activities include the use of a false return address and the use of false, misleading, or deceptive information when sending e-mail. The statute also prohibits the use of "dictionary attacks"—sending messages to randomly generated e-mail addresses—and the "harvesting" of e-mail addresses from Web sites through the use of specialized software.

▶ **Example 15.1** Federal officials arrested Robert Alan Soloway, considered to be one of the world's most prolific spammers. Soloway, known as the "Spam King," had been using *botnets* (automated spamming networks) to send out hundreds of millions of unwanted e-mails. In 2008, Soloway pleaded guilty to mail fraud, spam, and failure to pay taxes. ◀

Arresting prolific spammers, however, has done little to curb spam, which continues to flow at a rate of 70 billion messages per day.

THE U.S. SAFE WEB ACT After the CAN-SPAM Act of 2003 prohibited false and deceptive e-mails originating in the United States, spamming from servers

2. 15 U.S.C. Sections 7701 *et seq.*

located in other nations increased. These cross-border spammers generally were able to escape detection and legal sanctions because the Federal Trade Commission (FTC) lacked the authority to investigate foreign spamming.

Congress sought to rectify the situation by enacting the U.S. Safe Web Act (also known as the Undertaking Spam, Spyware, and Fraud Enforcement with Enforcers Beyond Borders Act).[3] The act allows the FTC to cooperate and share information with foreign agencies in investigating and prosecuting those involved in spamming, spyware, and various Internet frauds and deceptions.

The Safe Web Act also provides a "safe harbor" for **Internet service providers (ISPs)**—that is, organizations that provide access to the Internet. The safe harbor gives ISPs immunity from liability for supplying information to the FTC concerning possible unfair or deceptive conduct in foreign jurisdictions.

Domain Names

As e-commerce expanded worldwide, one issue that emerged involved the rights of a trademark owner to use the mark as part of a domain name. A **domain name** is part of an Internet address, such as "**cengage.com**."

STRUCTURE OF DOMAIN NAMES Every domain name ends with a generic top-level domain (TLD), which is the part of the name to the right of the period that often indicates the type of entity that operates the site. For instance, *com* is an abbreviation for *commercial,* and *edu* is short for *education.*

The second-level domain (SLD)—the part of the name to the left of the period—is chosen by the business entity or individual registering the domain name. Competition for SLDs among firms with similar names and products has led to numerous disputes. By using an identical or similar domain name, parties have attempted to profit from a competitor's **goodwill** (the nontangible value of a business). For instance, a party might use a similar domain name to sell pornography, offer for sale another party's domain name, or otherwise infringe on others' trademarks.

DISTRIBUTION SYSTEM The Internet Corporation for Assigned Names and Numbers (ICANN), a nonprofit corporation, oversees the distribution of domain names and operates an online arbitration system. Due to numerous complaints, ICANN completely overhauled the domain name distribution system.

In 2012, ICANN started selling new generic top-level domain names (gTLDs) for an initial price of $185,000 plus an annual fee of $25,000. Whereas TLDs were limited to only a few terms (such as "com," "net," and "org"), gTLDs can take any form. By 2013, many companies and corporations had acquired gTLDs based on their brands, such as .aol, .bmw, .canon, .gap, .target, .toyota, and .walmart. Some companies have numerous gTLDs. Google's gTLDs, for instance, include .android, .chrome, .gmail, .goog, and .YouTube.

Cybersquatting

One of the goals of the new gTLD system is to alleviate the problem of *cybersquatting.* **Cybersquatting** occurs when a person registers a domain name that is the same as, or confusingly similar to, the trademark of another and then offers to sell the domain name back to the trademark owner.

▶ **Case in Point 15.2** Apple, Inc., has repeatedly sued cybersquatters that registered domain names similar to its products, such as iphone4s.com and ipods.com. In 2012, Apple won a judgment in litigation at the World Intellectual Property Organization (WIPO) against a company that was squatting on the domain name iPhone5.com.[4] ◀

ANTICYBERSQUATTING LEGISLATION Because cybersquatting has led to so much litigation, Congress enacted the Anticybersquatting Consumer Protection Act (ACPA),[5] which amended the Lanham Act—the federal law protecting trademarks, discussed in Chapter 14. The ACPA makes cybersquatting illegal when both of the following are true:

1. The name is identical or confusingly similar to the trademark of another.
2. The one registering, trafficking in, or using the domain name has a "bad faith intent" to profit from that trademark.

THE ONGOING PROBLEM OF CYBERSQUATTING Despite the ACPA, cybersquatting continues to present a problem for businesses, largely because more TLDs and gTLDs are now available and many more companies are registering domain names. Indeed, domain name registrars have proliferated. Registrar compa-

3. Pub. L. No. 109-455, 120 Stat. 3372 (2006), codified in various sections of 15 U.S.C. and 12 U.S.C. Section 3412.

4. WIPO Case No. D2012-0951.

5. 15 U.S.C. Section 1129.

nies charge a fee to businesses and individuals to register new names and to renew annual registrations (often through automated software). Many of these companies also buy and sell expired domain names.

All domain name registrars are supposed to relay information about these transactions to ICANN and other companies that keep a master list of domain names, but this does not always occur. The speed at which domain names change hands and the difficulty in tracking mass automated registrations have created an environment where cybersquatting can flourish.

▶ **Case in Point 15.3** OnNet USA, Inc., owns the English-language rights to 9Dragons, a game with a martial arts theme, and operates a Web site for its promotion. When a party known as "Warv0x" began to operate a pirated version of the game at Play9D.com, OnNet filed an action under the ACPA in a federal court. OnNet was unable to obtain contact information for the owner of Play9D.com through its Australian domain name registrar, however, and thus could not complete service of process (see Chapter 2). Therefore, the federal court allowed OnNet to serve the defendant by publishing a notice of the suit in a newspaper in Gold Coast, Australia.[6] ◀

TYPOSQUATTING Cybersquatters have also developed new tactics, such as **typosquatting,** or registering a name that is a misspelling of a popular brand, such as googl.com or appple.com. Because many Internet users are not perfect typists, Web pages using these misspelled names receive a lot of traffic.

More traffic generally means increased profit (advertisers often pay Web sites based on the number of unique visits, or hits), which in turn provides incentive for more cybersquatters. Also, if the misspelling is significant, the trademark owner may have difficulty proving that the name is identical or confusingly similar to the trademark of another as the ACPA requires.

Cybersquatting is costly for businesses, which must attempt to register all variations of a name to protect their domain name rights from would-be cybersquatters and typosquatters. Large corporations may have to register thousands of domain names across the globe just to protect their basic brands and trademarks.

APPLICABILITY AND SANCTIONS OF THE ACPA The ACPA applies to all domain name registrations of trademarks. Successful plaintiffs in suits brought under the act can collect actual damages and profits, or they can elect to receive statutory damages ranging from $1,000 to $100,000.

Although some companies have been successful suing under the ACPA, there are roadblocks to pursuing such lawsuits. Some domain name registrars offer privacy services that hide the true owners of Web sites, making it difficult for trademark owners to identify cybersquatters. Thus, before bringing a suit, a trademark owner has to ask the court for a subpoena to discover the identity of the owner of the infringing Web site. Because of the high costs of court proceedings, discovery, and even arbitration, many disputes over cybersquatting are settled out of court.

Meta Tags

Search engines compile their results by looking through a Web site's key-word field. As noted in Chapter 5, *meta tags* are key words that are inserted into the HTML (hypertext markup language) code to tell Internet browsers specific information about a Web page. Meta tags increase the likelihood that a site will be included in search engine results, even though the site may have nothing to do with the key words. Using this same technique, one site may appropriate the key words of other sites with more frequent hits so that the appropriating site will appear in the same search engine results as the more popular sites.

Using another's trademark in a meta tag without the owner's permission, however, normally constitutes trademark infringement. Some uses of another's trademark as a meta tag may be permissible if the use is reasonably necessary and does not suggest that the owner authorized or sponsored the use.

▶ **Case in Point 15.4** Farzad and Lisa Tabari are auto brokers—the personal shoppers of the automotive world. They contact authorized dealers, solicit bids, and arrange for customers to buy from the dealer offering the best combination of location, availability, and price. The Tabaris offered this service at the Web sites **buy-a-lexus.com** and **buyorleaselexus.com.**

Toyota Motor Sales U.S.A., Inc., the exclusive distributor of Lexus vehicles and the owner of the Lexus mark, objected to the Tabaris' practices. The Tabaris removed Toyota's photographs and logo from their site and added a disclaimer in large type at the top, but they refused to give up their domain names. Toyota sued for infringement. The court forced the Tabaris to stop using any "domain name, service mark, trademark,

6. *OnNet USA, Inc. v. Play9D.com,* ___ F.Supp.2d ___, 2013 WL 120319 (N.D.Cal. 2013).

trade name, meta tag or other commercial indication of origin that includes the mark LEXUS."[7] ◀

Trademark Dilution in the Online World

As discussed in Chapter 14, trademark *dilution* occurs when a trademark is used, without authorization, in a way that diminishes the distinctive quality of the mark.

Unlike trademark infringement, a claim of dilution does not require proof that consumers are likely to be confused by a connection between the unauthorized use and the mark. For this reason, the products involved need not be similar, as the following *Spotlight Case* illustrates.

7. *Toyota Motor Sales, U.S.A., Inc. v. Tabari*, 610 F.3d 171 (9th Cir. 2011).

SPOTLIGHT on Internet Porn

Case 15.1 Hasbro, Inc. v. Internet Entertainment Group, Ltd.

United States District Court, Western District of Washington, ___ F.Supp.2d ___ (1996).

BACKGROUND AND FACTS In 1949, Hasbro, Inc.—then known as the Milton Bradley Company—published its first version of Candy Land, a children's board game. Hasbro is the owner of the trademark "Candy Land," which has been registered with the U.S. Patent and Trademark Office since 1951. Over the years, Hasbro has produced several versions of the game, including Candy Land puzzles, a travel version, a computer game, and a handheld electronic version. In the mid-1990s, Brian Cartmell and his employer, the Internet Entertainment Group, Ltd., used the term *candyland.com* as a domain name for a sexually explicit Internet site. Anyone who performed an online search using the word *candyland* was directed to this adult Web site. Hasbro filed a trademark dilution claim in a federal court, seeking a permanent injunction to prevent the defendants from using the Candy Land trademark.

IN THE LANGUAGE OF THE COURT
DWYER, U.S. District Judge

* * * *

2. Hasbro has demonstrated a probability of proving that defendants Internet Entertainment Group, Ltd., Brian Cartmell and Internet Entertainment Group, Inc. (collectively referred to as "defendants") have been diluting the value of Hasbro's CANDY LAND mark by using the name CANDYLAND to identify a sexually explicit Internet site, and by using the name string "candyland.com" as an Internet domain name which, when typed into an Internet-connected computer, provides Internet users with access to that site.

* * * *

4. Hasbro has shown that defendants' use of the CANDY LAND name and the domain name candyland.com in connection with their Internet site is causing irreparable injury to Hasbro.

5. *The probable harm to Hasbro from defendants' conduct outweighs any inconvenience that defendants will experience if they are required to stop using the CANDYLAND name.* [Emphasis added.]

* * * *

THEREFORE, IT IS HEREBY ORDERED that Hasbro's motion for preliminary injunction is granted.

DECISION AND REMEDY *The federal district court granted Hasbro an injunction against the defendants, agreeing that the domain name* candyland *was "causing irreparable injury to Hasbro." The judge ordered the defendants to immediately remove all content from the* candyland.com *Web site and to stop using the Candy Land mark.*

CASE 15.1 CONTINUED

THE ECONOMIC DIMENSION *How can companies protect themselves from others who create Web sites that have similar domain names, and what limits each company's ability to be fully protected?*

WHAT IF THE FACTS WERE DIFFERENT? *Suppose that the site using* candyland.com *had not been sexually explicit but had sold candy. Would the result have been the same? Explain.*

Licensing

Recall from Chapter 14 that a company may permit another party to use a trademark (or other intellectual property) under a license. A licensor might grant a license allowing its trademark to be used as part of a domain name, for example.

Indeed, licensing is ubiquitous in the online world. When you download an application on your smartphone, tablet, or other mobile device, for instance, you are typically entering into to a license agreement. You are obtaining only a *license* to use that app and not ownership rights in it. Apps published on Google Play, for instance, may use its licensing service to prompt users to agree to a license at the time of installation and use.

Licensing agreements frequently include restrictions that prohibit licensees from sharing the file and using it to create similar software applications. The license may also limit the use of the application to a specific device or give permission to the user for a certain time period. For further discussion of licensing and e-contracts, see Chapter 9.

SECTION 2

COPYRIGHTS IN DIGITAL INFORMATION

Copyright law is probably the most important form of intellectual property protection on the Internet. This is because much of the material on the Internet (including software and database information) is copyrighted, and in order to transfer that material online, it must be "copied." Generally, whenever a party downloads software or music into a computer's random access memory, or RAM, without authorization, a copyright is infringed. Technology has vastly increased the potential for copyright infringement.

▶ **Case in Point 15.5** In one case, a rap song that was included in the sound track of a movie had used only a few seconds from the guitar solo of another's copyrighted sound recording without permission. Nevertheless, a federal court held that digitally sampling a copyrighted sound recording of any length constitutes copyright infringement.[8] ◀

Some other federal courts have not found that digital sampling is always illegal. Some courts have allowed the defense of fair use (see Chapter 14), while others have not. ▶ **Example 15.6** Hip hop stars Jay-Z and Kanye West were sued for digitally sampling music by soul musician Syl Johnson. Given the uncertain outcome of the litigation, they ended up settling the suit in 2012 for an undisclosed amount. ◀

Initially, criminal penalties for copyright violations could be imposed only if unauthorized copies were exchanged for financial gain. Yet much piracy of copyrighted materials online was "altruistic" in nature—unauthorized copies were made simply to be shared with others. Then, Congress amended the law and extended criminal liability for the piracy of copyrighted materials to persons who exchange unauthorized copies of copyrighted works without realizing a profit.

Digital Millennium Copyright Act

In 1998, Congress passed further legislation to protect copyright holders—the Digital Millennium Copyright Act (DMCA).[9] The DMCA gave significant protection to owners of copyrights in digital information. Among other things, the act established civil and criminal penalties for anyone who circumvents (bypasses) encryption software or other technological antipiracy protection. Also prohibited are the manufacture, import, sale, and distribution of devices or services for circumvention.

The DMCA provides for exceptions to fit the needs of libraries, scientists, universities, and others. In general, the law does not restrict the "fair use" of circumvention methods for educational and other noncommercial purposes. For instance, circumvention is allowed to test computer security, to conduct

8. *Bridgeport Music, Inc. v. Dimension Films,* 410 F.3d 792 (6th Cir. 2005).
9. 17 U.S.C. Sections 512, 1201–1205, 1301–1332; and 28 U.S.C. Section 4001.

encryption research, to protect personal privacy, and to enable parents to monitor their children's use of the Internet. The exceptions are to be reconsidered every three years.

The DMCA also limits the liability of Internet service providers (ISPs). Under the act, an ISP is not liable for copyright infringement by its customer *unless* the ISP is aware of the subscriber's violation. An ISP may be held liable only if it fails to take action to shut down the subscriber after learning of the violation. A copyright holder must act promptly, however, by pursuing a claim in court, or the subscriber has the right to be restored to online access.

MP3 and File-Sharing Technology

Soon after the Internet became popular, a few enterprising programmers created software to compress large data files, particularly those associated with music. The best-known compression and decompression system is MP3, which enables music fans to download songs or entire CDs onto their computers or onto portable listening devices, such as iPods. The MP3 system also made it possible for music fans to access other fans' files by engaging in file-sharing via the Internet.

METHODS OF FILE-SHARING File-sharing is accomplished through **peer-to-peer (P2P) networking.** The concept is simple. Rather than going through a central Web server, P2P networking uses numerous personal computers (PCs) that are connected to the Internet. Individuals on the same network can access files stored on one another's PCs through a **distributed network.** Parts of the network may be distributed all over the country or the world, which offers an unlimited number of uses. Persons scattered throughout the country or the world can work together on the same project by using file-sharing programs.

A newer method of sharing files via the Internet is **cloud computing,** which is essentially a subscription-based or pay-per-use service that extends a computer's software or storage capabilities. Cloud computing can deliver a single application through a browser to multiple users. Alternatively, cloud computing might be a utility program to pool resources and provide data storage and virtual servers that can be accessed on demand. Amazon, Facebook, Google, IBM, and Sun Microsystems are using and developing more cloud computing services.

SHARING STORED MUSIC FILES When file-sharing is used to download others' stored music files, copyright issues arise. Recording artists and their labels stand to lose large amounts of royalties and revenues if relatively few digital downloads or CDs are purchased and then made available on distributed networks. Anyone can get the music for free on these networks.

▶ **Case in Point 15.7** The issue of file-sharing infringement has been the subject of an ongoing debate since the highly publicized cases against two companies (Napster, Inc. and Grokster, Ltd.) that created software used for copyright infringement. In the first case, Napster operated a Web site with free software that enabled users to copy and transfer MP3 files via the Internet. Firms in the recording industry sued Napster. Ultimately, the court held that Napster was liable for contributory and vicarious[10] (indirect) copyright infringement.

As technology evolved, Grokster, Ltd., and several other companies created and distributed new types of file-sharing software. This software did not maintain a central index of content, but allowed P2P network users to share stored music files. The court held that because the companies distributed file-sharing software "with the object of promoting its use to infringe the copyright," they were liable for the resulting acts of infringement by the software's users.[11] ◀

In the following case, a group of recording companies sued an Internet user who had downloaded a number of copyrighted songs from the Internet. The user then shared the audio files with others via a P2P network. One of the issues before the court was whether the user was an "innocent infringer." In other words, was she innocent of copyright infringement because she was unaware that the works were copyrighted?

---

10. *Vicarious (indirect) liability* exists when one person is subject to liability for another's actions. A common example occurs in the employment context, when an employer is held vicariously liable by third parties for torts committed by employees in the course of their employment.

11. *A&M Records, Inc. v. Napster, Inc.,* 239 F.3d 1004 (9th Cir. 2001); and *Metro-Goldwyn-Mayer Studios, Inc. v. Grokster, Ltd.,* 545 U.S. 913, 125 S.Ct. 2764, 162 L.Ed.2d 781 (2005). Grokster, Ltd., later settled this dispute out of court and stopped distributing its software.

CASE 15.2

Maverick Recording Co. v. Harper

United States Court of Appeals, Fifth Circuit, 598 F.3d 193 (2010).

COMPANY PROFILE Recording star Madonna, others in the music business, and Time Warner created Maverick Records in 1992. Initially, the company saw great success with Alanis Morissette, The Prodigy, Candlebox, and the Deftones. It also created the sound track for the movie *The Matrix*. In a dispute over management of the company, Madonna and another co-owner were bought out. Today, Maverick is a wholly owned subsidiary of Warner Music Group.

BACKGROUND AND FACTS Maverick Recording Company and several other music-recording firms (the plaintiffs) hired MediaSentry to investigate the infringement of their copyrights over the Internet. During its investigation, MediaSentry discovered that Whitney Harper was using a file-sharing program to share digital audio files with other users of a peer-to-peer network. The shared audio files included a number of the plaintiffs' copyrighted works. The plaintiffs brought an action in a federal court against Harper for copyright infringement. They sought $750 per infringed work, the minimum amount of damages set forth in Section 504(c)(1) of the Copyright Act.

Harper asserted that her infringement was "innocent" and that therefore Section 504(c)(2) of the Copyright Act should apply. That section provides that when an infringer was not aware, and had no reason to believe, that his or her acts constituted copyright infringement, "the court in its discretion may reduce the award of statutory damages to a sum of not less than $200. "The trial court granted summary judgment for the plaintiffs on the issue of copyright infringement and enjoined Harper from further downloading and sharing of copyrighted works. The court, however, awarded the plaintiffs only $200 for each infringed work. Both parties appealed. Harper claimed that there was insufficient evidence of copyright infringement. The plaintiffs argued that the district court had erred by failing to rule out the innocent infringer defense as a matter of law.

IN THE LANGUAGE OF THE COURT

Edith *BROWN CLEMENT,* Circuit Judge:

* * * *

The uncontroverted [undisputed] evidence is more than sufficient to compel a finding that Harper had downloaded the files: there was no evidence from which a fact-finder could draw a reasonable inference that Harper had *not* downloaded them or that they were something other than audio files. * * * The district court properly rejected Harper's argument that the evidence of infringement was insufficient.

* * * *

* * * The district court held that there was a genuine issue of material fact as to whether Harper was an innocent infringer. * * * Harper averred [asserted] in an affidavit that she did not understand the nature of file-sharing programs and that she believed that listening to music from file-sharing networks was akin to listening to a noninfringing Internet radio station. The district court ruled that this assertion created a triable [capable of being tried before a judge or a jury] issue as to whether Harper's infringement was "innocent" under [Section 504(c)(2) of the Copyright Act].

* * * We hold that the defense was unavailable to her as a matter of law. *The innocent infringer defense is limited by [Section 402(d) of the Copyright Act]: with one exception not relevant here, when a proper copyright notice "appears on the published * * * phonorecords to which a defendant * * * had access, then no weight shall be given to such a defendant's interposition of a defense based on innocent infringement in mitigation of actual or statutory damages."* [Emphasis added.]

CASE 15.2 CONTINUES ➧

CASE 15.2 CONTINUED

The district court acknowledged that Plaintiffs provided proper notice on each of the published phonorecords from which the audio files were taken. * * * Harper contended only that she was too young and naive to understand that the copyrights on published music applied to downloaded music.

These arguments are insufficient to defeat the interposition [interference] of the [Section 402(d)] limitation on the innocent infringer defense. Harper's reliance on her own understanding of copyright law—or lack thereof—is irrelevant in the context of [Section 402(d)]. *The plain language of the statute shows that the infringer's knowledge or intent does not affect its application. Lack of legal sophistication cannot overcome a properly asserted [Section 402(d)] limitation to the innocent infringer defense.* [Emphasis added.]

* * * *

In short, the district court found a genuine issue of fact as to whether Harper intended to infringe Plaintiffs' copyrights, but that issue was not material: [Section 402(d)] forecloses, as a matter of law, Harper's innocent infringer defense. Because the defense does not apply, Plaintiffs are entitled to statutory damages. And because Plaintiffs requested the minimum statutory damages under [Section 504(c)(1)], Harper's culpability is not an issue and there are no issues left for trial. Plaintiffs must be awarded statutory damages of $750 per infringed work.

DECISION AND REMEDY *The U.S. Court of Appeals for the Fifth Circuit affirmed the trial court's finding of copyright liability, reversed its finding that the innocent infringer defense presented an issue for trial, and remanded the case for further proceedings consistent with the court's opinion. The appellate court concluded that the district court had erred by awarding damages of $200 per infringement because Harper was not an innocent infringer.*

THE ETHICAL DIMENSION *In this and other cases involving similar rulings, the courts have held that when the published phonorecordings from which audio files were taken contained copyright notices, the innocent infringer defense does not apply. It is irrelevant that the notice is not provided in the online file. Is this fair? Explain.*

MANAGERIAL IMPLICATIONS *Owners and managers of firms in the business of recording and distributing music face a constant challenge in protecting their copyrights. This is particularly true for audio files in the online environment, where Internet users can easily download a copyrighted song and make it available to P2P file-sharing networks. Among other things, this means that recording companies must be ever vigilant in searching the Web to find infringing uses of any works distributed online. Today, it is not uncommon for companies to hire antipiracy firms to investigate the illegal downloading of their copyrighted materials.*

DVDs AND FILE-SHARING File-sharing also creates problems for the motion picture industry, which loses significant amounts of revenue annually as a result of pirated DVDs. Numerous Web sites offer software that facilitates the illegal copying of movies, such as BitTorrent, which enables users to download high-quality files from the Internet.

▶ **Case in Point 15.8** TorrentSpy, a popular BitTorrent indexing Web site, enabled users to locate and exchange files. The Motion Picture Association of America (MPAA) and Columbia Pictures, Inc., brought a lawsuit against the operators of TorrentSpy for facilitating copyright infringement. The MPAA also claimed that the operators had destroyed evidence that would reveal the identity of individual infringers. The operators had ignored a court order to keep server logs of the Internet addresses of people who facilitated the trading of files via the site. Because TorrentSpy's operators had willfully destroyed evidence, a federal court found in favor of the MPAA and ordered the defendants to pay a judgment of $111 million.[12] ◀

SECTION 3
SOCIAL MEDIA

Social media provide a means by which people can create, share, and exchange ideas and comments via the Internet. Social networking sites, such as Facebook, Google+, MySpace, LinkedIn, Pinterest, and Tumblr, have become ubiquitous. Studies show that Internet users spend more time on social networks than at any other sites. The amount of time people spend accessing social networks on their smartphones and other

12. *Columbia Pictures Industries, v. Bunnell,* 2007 WL 4877701 (C.D.Cal. 2007).

mobile devices has increased every year (by nearly 37 percent in 2012 alone).

▶ **Example 15.9** Facebook, which was launched in 2004, had more than a billion active users by 2013. Individuals of all ages use Facebook to maintain social contacts, update friends on events, and distribute images to others. Facebook members often share common interests based on their school, location, or recreational affiliation, such as a sports team. ◀

Legal Issues

The emergence of Facebook and other social networking sites has created a number of legal and ethical issues for businesses. For instance, a firm's rights in valuable intellectual property may be infringed if users post trademarked images or copyrighted materials on these sites without permission.

Social media posts now are routinely included in discovery in litigation (see Chapter 2) because they can provide damaging information that establishes a person's intent or what she or he knew at a particular time. Like e-mail, posts on social networks can be the smoking gun that leads to liability.

Tweets and other social media posts can also be used to reduce damages awards. ▶ **Example 15.10** Omeisha Daniels sued for injuries she sustained in a car accident. She claimed that her injuries made it impossible for her to continue working as a hairstylist. The jury originally awarded her $237,000, but when the jurors saw Daniels's tweets and photographs of her partying in New Orleans and vacationing on the beach, they reduced the damages to $142,000. ◀

CRIMINAL INVESTIGATIONS Law enforcement uses social media to detect and prosecute criminals. ▶ **Example 15.11** A nineteen-year-old posts a message on Facebook bragging about how drunk he was on New Year's Eve and apologizing to the owner of the parked car that he hit. The next day, police officers arrest him for drunk driving and leaving the scene of an accident. ◀

ADMINISTRATIVE AGENCIES Federal regulators also use social media posts in their investigations into illegal activities. ▶ **Example 15.12** Reed Hastings, the top executive of Netflix, stated on Facebook that Netflix subscribers had watched a billion hours of video the previous month. As a result, Netflix's stock price rose, which prompted a federal agency investigation. Because such a statement is considered to be material information to investors, it must be disclosed to all investors under securities law (see Chapter 28). The agency ultimately concluded that it could not hold Hastings responsible for any wrongdoing because the agency's policy on social media use was not clear. The agency then issued new guidelines that allow companies to disclose material information through social media if investors have been notified in advance. ◀

The decision in a hearing before an administrative law judge can turn on the content of two Facebook posts, as occurred in the following case.

CASE ANALYSIS

Case 15.3 In re O'Brien

Superior Court of New Jersey, Appellate Division, 2013 WL 132508 (2013).

IN THE LANGUAGE OF THE COURT

PER CURIAM.

* * * *

[Jennifer] O'Brien has been employed as a teacher in the [City of Paterson, New Jersey] schools since March 1998. She has a master's degree in education, and certifications as an elementary school teacher and supervisor.

* * * In December 2010, O'Brien was assigned to teach the first grade [at School No. 21].

* * * There were twenty-three students in O'Brien's first-grade class. Almost all were six years old. All were either Latino or African-American.

On March 28, 2011, O'Brien posted two statements on Facebook, an Internet social-networking site. The first statement was, "I'm not a teacher—I'm a warden for future criminals!" The second statement was, "They had a scared straight program in school—why couldn't I bring first graders?"

* * * *

On March 30, 2011, [Frank Puglise, the principal of School No. 21] confronted O'Brien about the postings. According to Puglise, O'Brien insisted that she did not intend her comments to be offensive, but she was otherwise unrepentant [unapologetic]. O'Brien was suspended * * *, pending a complete investigation.

News of O'Brien's Facebook postings spread quickly throughout the district. * * * Two angry parents went

CASE 15.3 CONTINUES ➧

CASE 15.3 CONTINUED

to Puglise's office to express their outrage. One parent threatened to remove her child from the school. According to Puglise, the school received at least a dozen irate phone calls. * * * There was a protest outside the school, attended by twenty to twenty-five persons.

The following day, reporters and camera crews from major news organizations descended upon the school and remained there until late in the afternoon. A larger-than-usual crowd attended the Home-School Council meeting that evening, and the meeting was principally devoted to the Facebook postings. Parents expressed their outrage concerning the postings, and Puglise reassured the attendees that O'Brien had been removed from the classroom.

On April 14, 2011, the deputy superintendent of schools filed a complaint against O'Brien, charging her with conduct unbecoming a teacher.

The charges were filed with the Commissioner of Education * * *, and the matter was referred to the Office of Administrative Law for a hearing before an Administrative Law Judge (ALJ).

* * * *

On October 31, 2011, the ALJ issued her initial decision. The ALJ rejected O'Brien's contention that her comments were protected by the First Amendment to the United States Constitution. The ALJ wrote that O'Brien's remarks were not addressing a matter of public concern, but were "a personal expression" of dissatisfaction with her job.

The ALJ also wrote that * * * her right to express her views was outweighed by the district's need to operate its schools efficiently. The ALJ stated that:

> An Internet social-networking site such as Facebook is a questionable place to begin an earnest conversation about an important school issue such as classroom discipline. More to the point, a description of first-grade children as criminals with their teacher as their warden is intemperate and vituperative [insulting]. It becomes impossible for parents to cooperate with or have faith in a teacher who insults their children and trivializes legitimate educational concerns on the internet.

The ALJ added that, while First Amendment protections do not generally rise or fall on the public reactions to a person's statements, "in a public school setting thoughtless words can destroy the partnership between home and school that is essential to the mission of the schools."

The ALJ found that evidence supported the charges of conduct unbecoming a teacher. The ALJ determined that the evidence established that O'Brien failed to maintain a safe, caring, nurturing, educational environment * * *. The ALJ additionally determined that O'Brien breached her duty as a professional teacher * * *. In addition, the ALJ found that O'Brien's conduct endangered the mental well-being of the students.

The ALJ also determined O'Brien's actions warranted her removal * * *. The ALJ wrote,

> If this was an aberrational [not normal] lapse in judgment, a reaction to an unusually bad day, I would have expected to have heard more genuine and passionate contrition in O'Brien's testimony. I needed to hear that she was terribly sorry she had insulted her young students; that she loved being their teacher; and that she wanted desperately to return to the classroom. I heard nothing of the sort. Rather, I came away with the impression that O'Brien remained somewhat befuddled by the commotion she had created, and that while she continued to maintain that her conduct was not inappropriate, she was sorry others thought differently.

The ALJ observed that, with some sensitivity training, and after some time to "reflect," O'Brien might successfully return to the classroom. The ALJ concluded, however, that O'Brien's relationship with the Paterson school community had been irreparably damaged, "not because the community thinks so, but because O'Brien fails to understand why it does." The ALJ ordered O'Brien's removal from her tenured position.

* * * The Acting Commissioner issued a final decision * * *. *The Acting Commissioner concluded that O'Brien's Facebook postings were not constitutionally protected; the evidence established that O'Brien engaged in conduct unbecoming a teacher; and removal was the appropriate penalty.* This appeal followed. [Emphasis added.]

* * * *

We * * * affirm the Acting Commissioner's final determination substantially for the reasons stated by the ALJ and the Acting Commissioner in their decisions.

* * * *

* * * We are satisfied that, in determining the appropriate penalty, the ALJ and Acting Commissioner considered all relevant factors and reasonably concluded that the seriousness of O'Brien's conduct warranted her removal from her tenured position in the district.

Affirmed.

LEGAL REASONING QUESTIONS

1. Certain interests of public employees and their employer are balanced to determine whether the First Amendment protects an employee's Facebook posts. What are those interests?
2. What did O'Brien do that constituted conduct unbecoming a tenured teacher?
3. What penalty did the administrative law judge impose? Why?
4. Would the outcome have been different if O'Brien had apologized? Discuss.

EMPLOYERS' SOCIAL MEDIA POLICIES Employees who use social media in a way that violates their employer's stated policies may be disciplined or fired from their jobs. (Many large corporations have established specific guidelines on creating a social media policy in the workplace.) Courts and administrative agencies usually uphold an employer's right to terminate a person based on his or her violation of a social media policy.

▶ **Case in Point 15.13** Virginia Rodriquez worked for Wal-Mart Stores, Inc., for almost twenty years and had been promoted to management. Then she was disciplined for violating the company's policies by having a fellow employee use Rodriquez's password to alter the price of an item that she purchased. Under Wal-Mart's rules, another violation within a year would mean termination. Nine months later, on Facebook, Rodriquez publicly chastised employees under her supervision for calling in sick to go to a party. The posting violated Wal-Mart's "Social Media Policy," which was "to avoid public comment that adversely affects employees." Wal-Mart terminated Rodriquez. She filed a lawsuit, alleging discrimination, but the court issued a summary judgment in Wal-Mart's favor.[13] ◀ Note, however, that employees' posts on social media may be protected under labor law, as discussed in *Example 4.3* in Chapter 4.

The Electronic Communications Privacy Act

The Electronic Communications Privacy Act (ECPA)[14] amended federal wiretapping law to cover electronic forms of communications. Although Congress enacted the ECPA many years before social media networks existed, it nevertheless applies to communications through social media.

The ECPA prohibits the intentional interception of any wire, oral, or electronic communication. It also prohibits the intentional disclosure or use of the information obtained by the interception.

EXCLUSIONS Excluded from the ECPA's coverage are any electronic communications through devices that an employer provides for its employee to use "in the ordinary course of its business." Consequently, if a company provides the electronic device (cell phone, laptop, tablet) to the employee for ordinary business use, the company is not prohibited from intercepting business communications made on it.

This "business-extension exception" to the ECPA permits employers to monitor employees' electronic communications made in the ordinary course of business. It does not, however, permit employers to monitor employees' personal communications. Another exception allows an employer to avoid liability under the act if the employees consent to having their electronic communications monitored by the employer.

STORED COMMUNICATIONS Part of the ECPA is known as the Stored Communications Act (SCA).[15] The SCA prohibits intentional and unauthorized access to *stored* electronic communications and sets forth criminal and civil sanctions for violators. A person can violate the SCA by intentionally accessing a stored electronic communication. The SCA also prevents "providers" of communication services (such as cell phone companies and social media networks) from divulging private communications to certain entities and individuals.

▶ **Case in Point 15.14** Two restaurant employees, Brian Pietrylo and Doreen Marino, were fired after their manager uncovered their password-protected MySpace group. The group's communications, stored on MySpace's Web site, contained sexual remarks about customers and management, and comments about illegal drug use and violent behavior. One employee said the group's purpose was to "vent about any BS we deal with out of work without any outside eyes spying on us." The restaurant learned about the private MySpace group when a hostess showed it to a manager who requested access. The hostess was not explicitly threatened with termination but feared she would lose her job if she did not comply. The court allowed the employees' SCA claim, and the jury awarded them $17,003 in compensatory and punitive damages.[16] ◀

Protection of Social Media Passwords

In recent years, employees and applicants for jobs or colleges have sometimes been asked to divulge their social media passwords. Employers and schools have sometimes looked at an individual's Facebook or other account to see if it included controversial postings such as racially discriminatory remarks or photos of drug parties. Such postings can have a negative effect on a person's prospects even though they were made years earlier or have been taken out of context.

13. *Rodriquez v. Wal-Mart Stores, Inc.*, ___ F.Supp.2d ___, 2013 WL 102674 (N.D.Tex. 2013).
14. 18 U.S.C. Sections 2510–2521.
15. 18 U.S.C. Sections 2701–2711.
16. *Pietrylo v. Hillstone Restaurant Group*, 2009 WL 3128420 (D.N.J. 2009).

By 2013, four states (California, Illinois, Maryland, and Michigan) had enacted legislation to protect individuals from having to disclose their social media passwords. Each state's law is slightly different. Some states, such as Michigan, prohibit employers from taking adverse action against an employee or job applicant based on what the person has posted online. Michigan's law also applies to e-mail and cloud storage accounts. The federal government is also considering legislation that would prohibit employers and schools from demanding passwords to social media accounts.

Even if legislation is passed, however, it will not completely prevent employers and others from taking actions against a person based on his or her social network postings. Management and human resources personnel are unlikely to admit that they looked at someone's Facebook page and that it influenced their decision. How would a person who does not get a job be able to prove that she or he was rejected because the employer accessed social media? Also, the employer or school may use private browsing, which enables people to keep their Web browsing activities confidential.

Company-wide Social Media Networks

Many companies, including Dell, Inc., and Nikon Instruments, form their own internal social media networks. Software companies offer a variety of systems, including Salesforce.com's Chatter, Microsoft's Yammer, and Cisco Systems' WebEx Social. Posts on these internal networks are quite different from the typical posts on Facebook, LinkedIn, and Twitter. Employees use these intranets to exchange messages about topics related to their work such as deals that are closing, new products, production flaws, how a team is solving a problem, and the details of customer orders. Thus, the tone is businesslike.

PROTECTION OF TRADE SECRETS An important advantage to using an internal system for employee communications is that the company can better protect its trade secrets. The company usually decides which employees can see particular intranet files and which employees will belong to each specific "social" group within the company. Companies providing internal social media networks often keep the resulting data on their own servers in secure "clouds."

OTHER ADVANTAGES Internal social media systems also offer additional benefits such as real-time information about important issues, such as production glitches. Additionally, posts can include tips on how to best sell new products or deal with difficult customers, as well as information about competitors' products and services.

Another major benefit of intranets is a significant reduction in the use of e-mail. Rather than wasting fellow employees' time reading mass e-mailings, workers can post messages or collaborate on presentations via the company's social network.

SECTION 4 ONLINE DEFAMATION

Cyber torts are torts that arise from online conduct. One of the most prevalent cyber torts is online defamation. Recall from Chapter 12 that defamation is wrongfully hurting a person's reputation by communicating false statements about that person to others. Because the Internet enables individuals to communicate with large numbers of people simultaneously (via a blog or tweet, for instance), online defamation has become a problem in today's legal environment.

▶ **Example 15.15** Courtney Love was sued for defamation based on remarks she posted about fashion designer Dawn Simorangkir on Twitter. Love claimed that her statements were opinion (rather than statements of fact, as required) and therefore were not actionable as defamation. Nevertheless, Love ended up paying $430,000 to settle the case out of court. ◀

Identifying the Author of Online Defamation

An initial issue raised by online defamation is simply discovering who is committing it. In the real world, identifying the author of a defamatory remark generally is an easy matter. Suppose, though, that a business firm has discovered that defamatory statements about its policies and products are being posted in an online forum. Such forums allow anyone—customers, employees, or crackpots—to complain about a firm that they dislike while remaining anonymous.

Therefore, a threshold barrier to anyone who seeks to bring an action for online defamation is discovering the identity of the person who posted the defamatory message. An Internet service provider (ISP) can disclose personal information about its customers only when ordered to do so by a court. Consequently, businesses and individuals are increasingly bringing lawsuits against "John Does" (John Doe, Jane Doe, and the like are fictitious names used in lawsuits when the identity of a party is not known or when a party wishes to conceal his or her name for privacy reasons). Then, using the authority of the courts, the plaintiffs can obtain from the ISPs the identity of the persons responsible for the defamatory messages.

Liability of Internet Service Providers

Recall from the discussion of defamation in Chapter 12 that normally one who repeats or otherwise republishes a defamatory statement is subject to liability as if he or she had originally published it. Thus, newspapers, magazines, and television and radio stations are subject to liability for defamatory content that they publish or broadcast, even though the content was prepared or created by others.

Applying this rule to cyberspace, however, raises an important issue: Should ISPs be regarded as publishers and therefore be held liable for defamatory messages that are posted by their users in online forums or other arenas?

GENERAL RULE The Communications Decency Act (CDA) states that "[n]o provider or user of an interactive computer service shall be treated as the publisher or speaker of any information provided by another information content provider."[17] Thus, under the CDA, ISPs usually are treated differently from publishers in print and other media and are not liable for publishing defamatory statements that come from a third party.

EXCEPTIONS Although the courts generally have construed the CDA as providing a broad shield to protect ISPs from liability for third party content, some courts have started establishing some limits to this immunity. ▶ **Case in Point 15.16** Roommate.com, LLC, operates an online roommate-matching Web site that helps individuals find roommates based on their descriptions of themselves and their roommate preferences. Users respond to a series of online questions, choosing from answers in drop-down and select-a-box menus.

Some of the questions asked users to disclose their sex, family status, and sexual orientation—which is not permitted under the federal Fair Housing Act. When a nonprofit housing organization sued Roommate.com, the company claimed it was immune from liability under the CDA. A federal appellate court disagreed and ruled that Roommate.com was not immune from liability. Roommate.com was ordered to pay nearly $500,000 for prompting discriminatory preferences from users and matching users based on these criteria in violation of federal law.[18] ◀

17. 47 U.S.C. Section 230.

SECTION 5 PRIVACY

Facebook, Google, and Yahoo have all been accused of violating users' privacy rights. As discussed in Chapter 5, the courts have held that the right to privacy is guaranteed by the Bill of Rights, and some state constitutions guarantee it as well. To maintain a suit for the invasion of privacy, though, a person must have a reasonable expectation of privacy in the particular situation (see Chapter 12). People clearly have a reasonable expectation of privacy when they enter their personal banking or credit-card information online. They also have a reasonable expectation that online companies will follow their own privacy policies. But it is probably not reasonable to expect privacy in statements made on Twitter.

Sometimes, people are confused and mistakenly believe that they are making statements or posting photos in a private forum. ▶ **Example 15.17** Randi Zuckerberg, the older sister of Mark Zuckerberg (the founder of Facebook), used a mobile app called "Poke" to post a "private" photo on Facebook of their family gathering during the holidays. Poke allows the sender to decide how long the photo can be seen by others. Facebook allows users to configure their privacy settings to limit access to photos, which Randi thought she had done. Nonetheless, the photo showed up in the Facebook feed of Callie Schweitzer, who then put it on Twitter where it eventually went viral. Schweitzer apologized and removed the photo, but it had already gone public for the world to see. ◀

Data Collection and Cookies

Whenever a consumer purchases items from an online retailer, such as Amazon.com, or a retailer that sells

18. *Fair Housing Council of San Fernando Valley v. Roommate.com, LLC*, 666 F.3d 1216 (9th Cir. 2012).

both offline and online, such as Best Buy, the retailer collects information about the consumer. **Cookies** are invisible files that computers, smartphones, and other mobile devices create to track a user's Web browsing activities. Cookies provide detailed information to marketers about an individual's behavior and preferences, which is then used to personalize online services.

Over time, the retailer can amass considerable data about a person's shopping habits. Does collecting this information violate a consumer's right to privacy? Should retailers be able to pass on the data they have collected to their affiliates? Should they be able to use the information to predict what a consumer might want and then create online "coupons" customized to fit the person's buying history?

▶ **Example 15.18** Facebook, Inc., recently settled a lawsuit over its use of a targeted advertising technique called "Sponsored Stories." An ad would display a Facebook friend's name, profile picture, and a statement that the friend "likes" the company sponsoring the advertisement, alongside the company's logo. A group of plaintiffs filed suit, claiming that Facebook had used their pictures for advertising without their permission. When a federal court refused to dismiss the case, Facebook agreed to settle. ◀

Internet Companies' Privacy Policies

The Federal Trade Commission (FTC) investigates consumer complaints of privacy violations. The FTC has forced many companies, including Google, Facebook, Twitter, and MySpace, to enter a consent decree that gives the FTC broad power to review their privacy and data practices. It can then sue companies that violate the terms of the decree.

▶ **Example 15.19** In 2012, Google settled a suit brought by the FTC alleging that it had misused data from Apple's Safari users. Google allegedly had used cookies to trick the Safari browser on iPhones and iPads so that Google could monitor users who had blocked such tracking. This violated the consent decree with the FTC. Google agreed to pay $22.5 million to settle the suit without admitting liability. ◀

Facebook has faced a number of complaints about its privacy policy and has changed its policy several times to satisfy its critics and ward off potential government investigations. Other companies, including mobile app developers, have also changed their privacy policies to provide more information to consumers. Consequently, it is frequently the companies, rather than courts or legislatures, that are defining the privacy rights of their online users.

The Consumer Privacy Bill of Rights

To protect consumers' personal information, the Obama administration has proposed a consumer privacy bill of rights (see Exhibit 15–1 below). The goal is to ensure that personal information is safe online.

If this proposed privacy bill of rights becomes law, retailers will have to change some of their procedures. Retailers will have to give customers better choices about what data are collected and how the data are used for marketing. They may also have to take into account consumers' expectations about how their information will be used once it is collected.

EXHIBIT 15–1 The Proposed Consumer Privacy Bill of Rights

1. Individual Control—Consumers have a right to exercise control over what personal data organizations collect from them and how they use it.
2. Transparency—Consumers have the right to easily understandable information about privacy and security practices.
3. Respect for Context—Consumers have a right to expect that organizations will collect, use, and disclose personal data in ways that are consistent with the context in which consumers provide the data.
4. Security—Consumers have the right to secure and responsible handling of personal data.
5. Access and Accuracy—Consumers have a right to access and correct personal data in usable formats, in a manner that is appropriate to the sensitivity of the data and the risk of adverse consequences to consumers if the data are inaccurate.
6. Focus Collection—Consumers have a right to reasonable limits on the personal data that companies collect and retain.
7. Accountability—Consumers have a right to have personal data handled by companies with appropriate measures in place to assure that they adhere to the Consumer Privacy Bill of Rights.

Reviewing: Internet Law, Social Media, and Privacy

While he was in high school, Joel Gibb downloaded numerous songs to his smartphone from an unlicensed file-sharing service. He used portions of the copyrighted songs when he recorded his own band and posted videos on YouTube and Facebook. Gibb also used BitTorrent to download several movies from the Internet. Now he has applied to Boston University. The admissions office has requested access to his Facebook password, and he has complied. Using the information presented in the chapter, answer the following questions.

1. What laws, if any, did Gibb violate by downloading the music and videos from the Internet?
2. Was Gibb's use of portions of copyrighted songs in his own music illegal? Explain.
3. Can individuals legally post copyrighted content on their Facebook pages? Why or why not?
4. Did Boston University violate any laws when it asked Joel to provide his Facebook password? Explain.

DEBATE THIS . . . *Internet service providers should be subject to the same defamation laws as newspapers, magazines, and television and radio stations.*

Terms and Concepts

ExamPrep

Issue Spotters

1. Karl self-publishes a cookbook titled *Hole Foods,* in which he sets out recipes for donuts, Bundt cakes, tortellini, and other foods with holes. To publicize the book, Karl designs the Web site **holefoods.com**. Karl appropriates the key words of other cooking and cookbook sites with more frequent hits so that **holefoods.com** will appear in the same search engine results as the more popular sites. Has Karl done anything wrong? Explain. **(See page 343.)**
2. Eagle Corporation began marketing software in 2001 under the mark "Eagle." In 2013, Eagle.com, Inc., a different company selling different products, begins to use *eagle* as part of its URL and registers it as a domain name. Can Eagle Corporation stop this use of *eagle?* If so, what must the company show? **(See page 342.)**

- **Check your answers to the Issue Spotters against the answers provided in Appendix E at the end of this text.**

Before the Test

Go to **www.cengagebrain.com**, enter the ISBN 9781285428949, and click on "Find" to locate this textbook's Web site. Then, click on "Access Now" under "Study Tools," and select Chapter 15 at the top. There, you will find an Interactive Quiz that you can take to assess your mastery of the concepts in this chapter, as well as Flashcards and a Glossary of important terms.

Business Scenarios

15–1. Domain Names. Tony owns Antonio's, a pub in a small town in Iowa. Universal Dining, Inc., opens a chain of pizza parlors in California called "Antonio's." Without Tony's consent, Universal uses "antoniosincalifornia" as part of the domain name for the chain's Web site. Has Universal committed trademark dilution or any other violation of the law? Explain. **(See page 342.)**

15–2. Internet Service Providers. CyberConnect, Inc., is an Internet service provider (ISP). Pepper is a CyberConnect subscriber. Market Reach, Inc., is an online advertising company. Using sophisticated software, Market Reach directs its ads to those users most likely to be interested in a particular product. When Pepper receives one of the ads, she objects to the content. Further, she claims that CyberConnect should pay damages for "publishing" the ad. Is the ISP regarded as a publisher and therefore liable for the content of Market Reach's ad? Why or why not? **(See page 353.)**

15–3. Privacy. SeeYou, Inc., is an online social network. SeeYou's members develop personalized profiles to interact and share information—photos, videos, stories, activity updates, and other items—with other members. Members post the information that they want to share and decide with whom they want to share it. SeeYou launched a program to allow members to share with others what they do elsewhere online. For example, if a member rents a movie through Netflix, SeeYou will broadcast that information to everyone in the member's online network. How can SeeYou avoid complaints that this program violates its members' privacy? **(See page 353.)**

Business Case Problems

15–4. Copyrights in Digital Information. When she was in college, Jammie Thomas-Rasset wrote a case study on Napster, the online peer-to-peer (P2P) file-sharing network, and knew that it was shut down because it was illegal. Later, Capitol Records, Inc., which owns the copyrights to a large number of music recordings, discovered that "tereastarr"—a user name associated with Thomas-Rasset's Internet protocol address—had made twenty-four songs available for distribution on KaZaA, another P2P network. Capitol notified Thomas-Rasset that she had been identified as engaging in the unauthorized trading of music. She replaced the hard drive on her computer with a new drive that did not contain the songs in dispute. Is Thomas-Rasset liable for copyright infringement? Explain. [*Capitol Records, Inc. v. Thomas-Rasset,* 692 F.3d 899 (8th Cir. 2012)] **(See page 346.)**

15–5. Domain Names. Austin Rare Coins, Inc., buys and sells rare coins, bullion, and other precious metals through eight Web sites with different domain names. An unknown individual took control of Austin's servers and transferred the domain names to another registrant without Austin's permission. The new registrant began using the domain names to host malicious content—including hate letters to customers and fraudulent contact information—and to post customers' credit-card numbers and other private information, thereby tarnishing Austin's goodwill. Austin filed a suit in a federal district court against the new registrant under the Anticybersquatting Consumer Protection Act. Is Austin entitled to a transfer of the domain names? Explain. [*Austin Rare Coins, Inc. v. Acoins.com,* __ F.Supp.2d __, 2013 WL 85142 (E.D.Va. 2013)] **(See page 342.)**

15–6. BUSINESS CASE PROBLEM WITH SAMPLE ANSWER: Privacy.

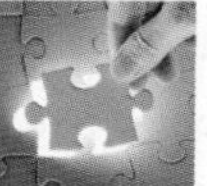

*Using special software, South Dakota law enforcement officers found a person who appeared to possess child pornography at a specific Internet protocol address. The officers subpoenaed Midcontinent Communications, the service that assigned the address, for the personal information of its subscriber. With this information, the officers obtained a search warrant for the residence of John Rolfe, where they found a laptop that contained child pornography. Rolfe argued that the subpoenas violated his "expectation of privacy." Did Rolfe have a privacy interest in the information obtained by the subpoenas issued to Midcontinent? Discuss. [*State of South Dakota v. Rolfe, *825 N.W.2d 901 (S.Dak. 2013)]* **(See page 353.)**

- **For a sample answer to Problem 15–6, go to Appendix F at the end of this text.**

15–7. File-Sharing. Dartmouth College professor M. Eric Johnson, in collaboration with Tiversa, Inc., a company that monitors peer-to-peer networks to provide security services, wrote an article titled "Data Hemorrhages in the Health-Care Sector." In preparing the article, Johnson and Tiversa searched the networks for data that could be used to commit medical or financial identity theft. They found a document that contained the Social Security numbers, insurance information, and treatment codes for patients of LabMD, Inc. Tiversa notified LabMD of the find in order to solicit its business. Instead of hiring Tiversa, however, LabMD filed a suit in a federal district court against the company, alleging trespass, conversion, and violations of federal statutes. What do these facts indicate about the security of private information? Explain. How should the court rule? [*LabMD, Inc. v. Tiversa, Inc.*, 2013 WL 425983 (11th Cir. 2013)] **(See page 345.)**

15–8. A QUESTION OF ETHICS: Criminal Investigations.

*After the unauthorized release and posting of classified U.S. government documents to WikiLeaks.org, involving Bradley Manning, a U.S. Army private first class, the U.S. government began a criminal investigation. The government obtained a court order to require Twitter, Inc., to turn over subscriber information and communications to and from the e-mail addresses of Birgitta Jonsdottir and others. The court sealed the order and the other documents in the case, reasoning that "there exists no right to public notice of all the types of documents filed in a . . . case." Jonsdottir and the others appealed this decision. [*In re Application of the United States of America for an Order Pursuant to 18 U.S.C. Section 2703(d), *707 F.3d 283 (4th Cir. 2013)]* **(See page 349.)**

(a) Why would the government want to "seal" the documents of an investigation? Why would the individuals under investigation want those documents to be "unsealed"? What factors should be considered in striking a balance between these competing interests?

(b) How does law enforcement use social media to detect and prosecute criminals? Is this use of social media an unethical invasion of individuals' privacy? Discuss.

Legal Reasoning Group Activity

15–9. File-Sharing. James, Chang, and Sixta are roommates. They are music fans and frequently listen to the same artists and songs. They regularly exchange MP3 music files that contain songs from their favorite artists. **(See page 346.)**

(a) One group of students will decide whether the fact that the roommates are transferring files among themselves for no monetary benefit precludes them from being subject to copyright law.

(b) The second group will consider an additional fact. Each roommate regularly buys CDs and rips them to his or her hard drive. Then the roommate gives the CDs to the other roommates to do the same.

CHAPTER 16

CREDITOR-DEBTOR RELATIONS AND BANKRUPTCY

Many people in today's economy are struggling to pay their monthly debts. Although in the old days, debtors were punished and sometimes even sent to jail for failing to pay their debts, people today rarely go to jail. They have many other options. In this chapter, we discuss some basic laws that assist the debtor and creditor in resolving disputes.

We then turn to the topic of bankruptcy—a last resort in resolving debtor-creditor problems. The right to petition for bankruptcy relief is an essential aspect of our capitalistic society. Hence, every businessperson should have some understanding of the bankruptcy process that is outlined in this chapter. We also discuss in a feature on page 369 how some bankruptcy courts are using the Web and social media to communicate with the public.

SECTION 1
LAWS ASSISTING CREDITORS

Normally, creditors have no problem collecting the debts owed to them. When disputes arise over the amount owed, however, or when the debtor simply cannot or will not pay, what happens? Both the common law and statutory laws create various rights and remedies for creditors when a debtor **defaults** (fails to pay as promised). We discuss here some of these rights and remedies.

Liens

A **lien** is an encumbrance on (claim against) property to satisfy a debt or protect a claim for the payment of a debt. Liens may arise under the common law (usually by possession of the property) or under statutory law. Statutory liens include *mechanic's liens,* whereas *artisan's liens* were recognized at common law. *Judicial liens* may be used by a creditor to collect on a debt before or after a judgment is entered by a court.

Liens can be an important tool for creditors because they generally take priority over other claims, except those of creditors who have a *perfected security interest* in the same property. (A *security interest* is an interest in a debtor's personal property—called *collateral*—that a seller, lender, or other creditor takes to secure payment of an obligation. *Perfection,* which is generally accomplished by filing a financing statement with a state official, is the legal process by which a creditor protects its security interest from the claims of others.) In fact, unless a statute provides otherwise, the holders of mechanic's and artisan's liens normally take priority even over creditors who have a perfected security interest in the property.

For liens other than mechanic's and artisan's liens, priority depends on whether the lien was obtained before the other creditor perfected its security interest. If the lien was obtained first, the lienholder has priority, but if the security interest was perfected first, the party with the perfected security interest has priority.

MECHANIC'S LIENS Sometimes, a person who has contracted for labor, services, or materials to be furnished for making improvements on real property does not immediately pay for the improvements. When that happens, the creditor can place a **mechanic's lien** on the property. A mechanic's lien creates a special type of debtor-creditor relationship in which the real estate itself becomes security for the debt.

▶ **Example 16.1** Kirk contracts to paint Tanya's house for an agreed-on price to cover labor and materials. If Tanya refuses to pay or pays only a portion of the charges after the work is completed, a mechanic's lien against the property can be created. Kirk is then a lienholder, and the real property is encumbered (burdened) with the mechanic's lien for the amount owed.

If Tanya does not pay the lien, the property can be sold to satisfy the debt. Tanya must be given notice of the *foreclosure* (the process by which the creditor legally takes the debtor's property to satisfy a debt, discussed later in this chapter) and sale in advance, however. ◀

State law governs the procedures that must be followed to create a mechanic's (or other statutory) lien. Generally, the lienholder must file a written notice of lien within a specific time period (usually within 60 to 120 days) from the last date that material or labor was provided. If the property owner fails to pay the debt, the lienholder is entitled to foreclose on the real estate and to sell it to satisfy the debt. The sale proceeds are used to pay the debt and the costs of the legal proceedings. The surplus, if any, is paid to the former owner.

ARTISAN'S LIENS When a debtor fails to pay for labor and materials furnished for the repair or improvement of personal property, a creditor can recover payment through an **artisan's lien.**

Lienholder Must Retain Possession. In contrast to a mechanic's lien, an artisan's lien is *possessory.* The lienholder ordinarily must have retained possession of the property and have expressly or impliedly agreed to provide the services on a cash, not a credit, basis. The lien remains in existence as long as the lienholder maintains possession, and the lien is terminated once possession is *voluntarily* surrendered—unless the surrender is only temporary.

▶ **Example 16.2** Kenzie takes a sapphire necklace that she inherited to a jewelry store to have it made into a ring and set of earrings. The store's owner agrees to reset the sapphires into custom jewelry for $4,000. Kenzie comes to pick up the jewelry but refuses to pay the $4,000 she owes. The jeweler can assert an artisan's lien on the jewelry in his possession until Kenzie pays. If the jeweler gives the jewelry to Kenzie (without requiring full payment), the lien disappears. ◀ As mentioned, artisan's liens usually take priority over other creditors' claims to the same property.

Foreclosure on Personal Property Possible. Modern statutes permit the holder of an artisan's lien to foreclose and sell the property subject to the lien to satisfy the debt. As with a mechanic's lien, the lienholder is required to give notice to the owner of the property before the foreclosure and sale. The sale proceeds are used to pay the debt and the costs of the legal proceedings, and the surplus, if any, is paid to the former owner.

JUDICIAL LIENS When a debt is past due, a creditor can bring a legal action against the debtor to collect the debt. If the creditor is successful in the action, the court awards the creditor a judgment against the debtor (usually for the amount of the debt plus any interest and legal costs incurred in obtaining the judgment). Frequently, however, the creditor is unable to collect the awarded amount.

To ensure that a judgment in the creditor's favor will be collectible, the creditor may request that certain nonexempt property of the debtor be seized to satisfy the debt. (As will be discussed later in this chapter, under state or federal statutes, some kinds of property are exempt from attachment by creditors.) A court's order to seize the debtor's property is known as a *writ of attachment* if it is issued prior to a judgment in the creditor's favor. If the order is issued after a judgment, it is referred to as a *writ of execution.*

Writ of Attachment. In the context of judicial liens, **attachment** refers to a court-ordered seizure and taking into custody of property before a judgment is obtained on a past-due debt. Because attachment is a *prejudgment* remedy, it occurs either at the time a lawsuit is filed or immediately afterward.

A creditor must comply with the specific state's statutory restrictions and requirements. Under the due process clause of the Fourteenth Amendment to the U.S. Constitution, the debtor must be given notice and an opportunity to be heard (see Chapter 5). The creditor must have an enforceable right to payment of the debt under law and must follow certain procedures. Otherwise, the creditor can be liable for damages for wrongful attachment.

The typical procedure for attachment is as follows:

1. The creditor files with the court an *affidavit* (a written statement, made under oath) stating that the debtor has failed to pay and indicating the statutory grounds under which attachment is sought.
2. The creditor must post a bond to cover at least the court costs, the value of the property attached, and the value of the loss of use of that property suffered by the debtor.
3. When the court is satisfied that all the requirements have been met, it issues a **writ of attachment,** which directs the sheriff or other officer to seize the debtor's nonexempt property.

If the creditor prevails at trial, the seized property can be sold to satisfy the judgment.

Writ of Execution. If a creditor wins a judgment against a debtor and the debtor will not or cannot pay the amount due, the creditor can request a **writ of execution** from the court. A writ of execution is an order that directs the sheriff to seize (levy) and sell any of the debtor's nonexempt real or personal property. The writ applies only to property that is within the court's geographic jurisdiction (usually the county in which the courthouse is located).

The proceeds of the sale are used to pay the judgment, accrued interest, and costs of the sale. Any excess is paid to the debtor. The debtor can pay the judgment and redeem the nonexempt property at any time before the sale takes place. (Because of exemption laws and bankruptcy laws, however, many judgments are practically uncollectible.)

Garnishment

An order for **garnishment** permits a creditor to collect a debt by seizing property of the debtor (such as wages or funds in a bank account) that is being held by a third party. As a result of a garnishment proceeding, the debtor's employer may be ordered by the court to turn over a portion of the debtor's wages to pay the debt.

▶ **Case in Point 16.3** Helen Griffin failed to pay a debt she owed to Indiana Surgical Specialists. When Indiana Surgical filed a lawsuit to collect, the court issued a judgment in favor of Indiana Surgical and a garnishment order to withhold the appropriate amount from Griffin's earnings until her debt was paid. At the time, Griffin was working as an independent contractor (see Chapter 21 for a discussion of independent-contractor status) driving for a courier service. She claimed that her wages could not be garnished because she was not an employee. The court held that payments for the services of an independent contractor fall within the definition of earnings and can be garnished.[1] ◀

Many types of property can be garnished, including tax refunds, pensions, and trust funds—so long as the property is not exempt from garnishment and is in the possession of a third party.

PROCEDURES Garnishment can be a prejudgment remedy, requiring a hearing before a court, but it is most often a postjudgment remedy. State law governs garnishment actions, so the specific procedures vary from state to state. According to the laws in many states, the judgment creditor needs to obtain only one order of garnishment, which will then apply continuously to the judgment debtor's wages until the entire debt is paid. In other states, the judgment creditor must go back to court for a separate order of garnishment for each pay period.

LAWS LIMITING THE AMOUNT OF WAGES SUBJECT TO GARNISHMENT Both federal and state laws limit the amount that can be taken from a debtor's weekly take-home pay through garnishment proceedings.[2] Federal law provides a minimal framework to protect debtors from losing all their income to pay judgment debts.[3] State laws also provide dollar exemptions, and these amounts are often larger than those provided by federal law.

Under federal law, an employer cannot dismiss an employee because his or her wages are being garnished.

Creditors' Composition Agreements

Creditors may contract with the debtor for discharge of the debtor's liquidated debts (debts that are definite, or fixed, in amount) on payment of a sum less than that owed. These agreements are referred to as **creditors' composition agreements** (or *composition agreements*) and usually are held to be enforceable unless they are formed under duress.

SECTION 2

MORTGAGES

When individuals purchase real property, they typically borrow from a financial institution part or all of the funds needed to pay the purchase price. A **mortgage** is a written instrument that gives the creditor an interest in, or lien on, the debtor's real property as security for payment of a debt. The creditor is the *mortgagee,* and the debtor is the *mortgagor.*

Typically, as part of the mortgage loan, borrowers make a **down payment** (the part of the purchase price that is paid up front in cash). Lenders offer vari-

1. *Indiana Surgical Specialists v. Griffin,* 867 N.E.2d 260 (Ind.App. 2007).

2. A few states (for example, Texas) do not permit garnishment of wages by private parties except under a child-support order.

3. For example, the federal Consumer Credit Protection Act, 15 U.S.C. Sections 1601–1693r, provides that a debtor can retain either 75 percent of his or her disposable earnings per week or an amount equivalent to thirty hours of work paid at federal minimum wage rates, whichever is greater.

ous types of mortgages to meet the needs of different borrowers, but a basic distinction is whether the interest rate is fixed or variable.

Fixed-Rate Mortgages

A *fixed-rate mortgage* has a fixed, or unchanging, rate of interest, so the payments remain the same for the duration of the loan. Lenders determine the interest rate for a standard fixed-rate mortgage loan based on a variety of factors, including the borrower's credit history, credit score, income, and debts. For a borrower to qualify, lenders typically require that the monthly mortgage payment (including principal, interest, taxes, and insurance) not exceed 28 percent of the person's monthly gross income.

Adjustable-Rate Mortgages

The rate of interest paid by the borrower changes periodically with an *adjustable-rate mortgage (ARM).* Typically, the initial interest rate for an ARM is set at a relatively low fixed rate for a specified period, such as a year or three years. After that time, the interest rate adjusts annually or by some other period, such as biannually or monthly. The interest rate adjustment is calculated by adding a certain number of percentage points (called the margin) to an index rate (one of various government interest rates).

ARMs contractually shift the risk that the interest rate will change from the lender to the borrower. Borrowers will have lower initial payments if they are willing to assume the risk of interest rate changes.

Creditor Protection

When creditors extend mortgages, they are advancing a significant amount of funds for a number of years. Consequently, creditors take a number of steps to protect their interest, including the following:

1. *Requiring mortgage insurance.* One precaution is to require debtors to obtain private mortgage insurance if they do not make a down payment of at least 20 percent of the purchase price. For instance, if a borrower makes a down payment of only 5 percent of the purchase price, the creditor might require insurance covering 15 percent of the cost. Then, if the debtor defaults, the creditor repossesses the house and receives reimbursement from the insurer for the covered portion of the loan.
2. *Recording the mortgage.* The creditor will record the mortgage with the appropriate office in the county where the property is located. Recording ensures that the creditor is officially on record as holding an interest in the property. In essence, recording a mortgage perfects the lender's security interest in the property. A lender that fails to record a mortgage could find itself in the position of an unsecured creditor.
3. *Including contract provisions.* Creditors also include provisions in the mortgage contract that are aimed at protecting their investment. For instance, many lenders include a **prepayment penalty** clause, which requires the borrower to pay a penalty if the mortgage is repaid in full within a certain period. A prepayment penalty helps to protect the lender should the borrower refinance within a short time after obtaining a mortgage.

Mortgage Foreclosure

If the homeowner *defaults,* or fails to make the mortgage payments, the lender has the right to foreclose on the mortgaged property. **Foreclosure** is the legal process by which the lender repossesses and auctions off the property that has secured the loan.

Foreclosure is expensive and time consuming, though. It generally benefits neither the borrowers, who lose their homes, nor the lenders, which face the prospect of losses on their loans. Therefore, both lenders and borrowers are motivated to avoid foreclosure proceedings if possible.

WAYS TO AVOID FORECLOSURE There are several possible methods of avoiding foreclosure. If the borrower might be able to make payments in the future, the lender may grant a **forbearance,** which is a postponement of part or all of the payments on a loan for a limited time. This option works well when the debtor can solve the problem by securing a new job, selling the property, or finding another acceptable solution.

The borrower and the lender may also enter into a **workout agreement**—a contract that describes their respective rights and responsibilities as they try to resolve the default without proceeding to foreclosure. Usually, the lender agrees to delay seeking foreclosure in exchange for the borrower providing additional financial information that might be used to modify the mortgage.

When a borrower is unable to make mortgage payments, a lender may agree to a **short sale**—that is, a sale of the property for less than the balance due on the mortgage loan. Typically, the borrower has to show some hardship, such as the loss of job, a decline in the value of the home, a divorce, or a death in the household. The lender often has approval rights in a short sale, so the sale process may take much longer than an ordinary real estate transaction.

FORECLOSURE PROCEDURE If all efforts to find another solution fail, the lender will proceed to foreclosure. The lender must strictly comply with the state statute governing foreclosures. Many problems arose in the last ten years because lenders, facing a record number of foreclosures during the recession, had difficulty complying with the required statutory formalities.

To bring a foreclosure action, a bank must have standing to sue (see Chapter 2). In the following case, the court had to decide whether a bank could foreclose a mortgage even though the bank could not prove when it became the owner of the borrower's promissory note.

CASE 16.1

McLean v. JPMorgan Chase Bank, N.A.

District Court of Appeal of Florida, Fourth District, 79 So.2d 170 (2012).

BACKGROUND AND FACTS On May 11, 2009, JPMorgan Chase Bank (Chase) filed a foreclosure action against Robert McLean. The complaint alleged that Chase was entitled to enforce the mortgage and promissory note on which McLean had defaulted. Nevertheless, the attached mortgage identified a different mortgagee and lender, and Chase claimed that the note had been "lost, stolen, or destroyed." When McLean filed a motion to dismiss, Chase produced a mortgage assignment dated May 14, 2009, which was three days after it had filed the lawsuit. Eventually, Chase also filed the original note. Although the indorsement to Chase was undated, Chase then filed a motion for summary judgment. The trial court granted Chase's motion even though the accompanying affidavit failed to show that Chase owned the mortgage or note when it had filed the complaint. McLean appealed.

IN THE LANUGAGE OF THE COURT
PER CURIAM. [By the Whole Court]

* * * *

A crucial element in any mortgage foreclosure proceeding is that the party seeking foreclosure must demonstrate that it has standing to foreclose.

* * * *

* * * A party's standing is determined at the time the lawsuit was filed. Stated another way, *"the plaintiff's lack of standing at the inception of the case is not a defect that may be cured by the acquisition of standing after the case is filed." Thus,* a party *is not permitted to establish the right to maintain an action retroactively by acquiring standing to file a lawsuit after the fact.* [Emphasis added.]

* * * *

In the present case, as is common in recent foreclosure cases, Chase did not attach a copy of the original note to its complaint, but instead [filed a claim] to re-establish a lost note. Later, however, Chase filed * * * the original promissory note, which bore a special endorsement in favor of Chase. [Thus,] * * * it obtained standing to foreclose, at least at some point.

Nonetheless, the record evidence is insufficient to demonstrate that Chase had standing to foreclose *at the time the lawsuit was filed.* [Emphasis in original.] The mortgage was assigned to Chase three days after Chase filed the instant foreclosure complaint. While the original note contained an undated special endorsement in Chase's favor, the affidavit filed in support of summary judgment did not state when the endorsement was made to Chase. Furthermore, the affidavit, which was dated after the lawsuit was filed, did not specifically state when Chase became the owner of the note, nor did the affidavit indicate that Chase was the owner of the note before suit was filed.

We therefore reverse the summary judgment and corresponding final judgment of foreclosure. On remand, in order for Chase to be entitled to summary judgment, it must show * * *

CASE 16.1 CONTINUED

that it was the holder of the note on the date the complaint was filed ([meaning] that the note was endorsed to Chase on or before the date the lawsuit was filed). By contrast, if the evidence shows that the note was endorsed to Chase after the lawsuit was filed, then Chase had no standing at the time the complaint was filed, in which case the trial court should dismiss the instant lawsuit and Chase must file a new complaint.

DECISION AND REMEDY *The Florida appellate court held that Chase did not prove it had standing to foreclose against McLean. The court therefore reversed the trial court's grant of summary judgment.*

THE LEGAL ENVIRONMENT DIMENSION *If Chase cannot prove that it had owned the note at the time of its complaint, what will happen next? Will Chase prevail? Why or why not?*

THE ETHICAL DIMENSION *Why do states require strict compliance with the provisions of their foreclosure laws, such as the requirement in this case that the lender own the note at the time of the complaint?*

REDEMPTION RIGHTS Every state allows a defaulting borrower to redeem the property before the foreclosure sale by paying the full amount of the debt, plus any interest and costs that have accrued. This is known as the **right of redemption.** The idea behind this right is that it is only fair for the borrower to have a chance to regain possession after default.

Some states even allow a borrower to repurchase property *after* a judicial foreclosure—called a *statutory right of redemption*. Generally, the borrower may exercise this right for up to one year from the time the house is sold at a foreclosure sale.[4] The borrower may retain possession of the property after the foreclosure sale until the statutory redemption period ends. If the borrower does not exercise the right of redemption, the new buyer receives title to and possession of the property.

Concept Summary 16.1 below provides a synopsis of the remedies available to creditors.

4. Some states do not allow a borrower to waive the statutory right of redemption. This means that a buyer at auction must wait one year to obtain title to, and possession of, a foreclosed property.

CONCEPT SUMMARY 16.1

Remedies Available to Creditors

REMEDY	DESCRIPTION
Liens	1. *Mechanic's lien*—A lien placed on an owner's real estate for labor, services, or materials furnished for improvements made to the realty. 2. *Artisan's lien*—A lien placed on an owner's personal property for labor performed or value added to that property. 3. *Judicial liens*— a. Writ of attachment—A court-ordered seizure of property prior to a court's final determination of the creditor's rights to the property. Creditors must strictly comply with applicable state statutes to obtain a writ of attachment. b. Writ of execution—A court order directing the sheriff to seize (levy) and sell a debtor's nonexempt real or personal property to satisfy a court's judgment in the creditor's favor.
Garnishment	A collection remedy that allows the creditor to attach a debtor's funds (such as wages owed or bank accounts) and property that are held by a third person.
Creditors' Composition Agreement	A contract between a debtor and her or his creditors by which the debtor's debts are discharged by payment of a sum less than the amount that is actually owed.
Mortgage Foreclosure	On the debtor's default, the entire mortgage debt is due and payable, allowing the creditor to foreclose on the realty by selling it to satisfy the debt.

SECTION 3

SURETYSHIP AND GUARANTY

When a third person promises to pay a debt owed by another in the event that the debtor does not pay, either a *suretyship* or a *guaranty* relationship is created. Exhibit 16–1 below illustrates these relationships. The third person's creditworthiness becomes the security for the debt owed.

Suretyship and guaranty provide creditors with the right to seek payment from the third party if the primary debtor, or *principal,* defaults on her or his obligations. At common law, there were significant differences in the liability of a surety and a guarantor, as discussed in the following subsections. Today, however, the distinctions outlined here have been abolished in some states.

Suretyship

A contract of strict **suretyship** is a promise made by a third person to be responsible for the debtor's obligation. It is an express contract between the **surety** (the third party) and the creditor.

In the strictest sense, the surety is primarily liable for the debt of the principal. The creditor can demand payment from the surety from the moment the debt is due. Moreover, the creditor need not exhaust all legal remedies against the principal debtor before holding the surety responsible for payment.

▶ **Example 16.4** Roberto Delmar wants to obtain a loan from the bank to buy a used car. Because Roberto is still in college, the bank will not lend him the funds without a cosigner. Roberto's father, José Delmar, who has dealt with the bank before, agrees to cosign (add his signature to) the note, thereby becoming a surety and thus jointly liable for payment of the debt. When José Delmar cosigns the note, he becomes primarily liable to the bank. On the note's due date, the bank can seek payment from either Roberto or José Delmar, or both jointly. ◀

EXHIBIT 16–1 Suretyship and Guaranty Parties

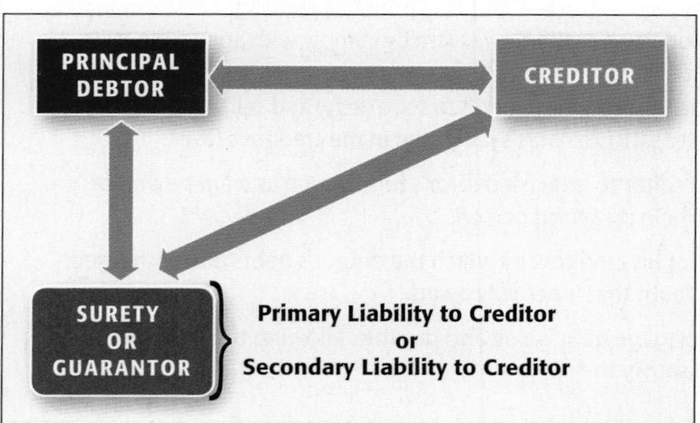

Guaranty

With a suretyship arrangement, the surety is *primarily* liable for the debtor's obligation. With a guaranty arrangement, the **guarantor**—the third person making the guaranty—is *secondarily* liable.

LIABILITY ARISES WHEN DEBTOR DEFAULTS The guarantor can be required to pay the obligation *only after the principal debtor defaults,* and usually only after the creditor has made an attempt to collect from the debtor. The guaranty contract terms determine the extent and time of the guarantor's liability.

▶ **Example 16.5** BX Enterprises, a small corporation, needs to borrow funds to meet its payroll. BX's president is Dawson, a wealthy businessperson who owns 70 percent of the company. The bank is skeptical about the creditworthiness of BX and requires Dawson to sign an agreement making herself personally liable for payment if BX does not pay off the loan. As a guarantor of the loan, Dawson cannot be held liable until BX is in default. ◀

WRITING OR RECORD REQUIRED Under the Statute of Frauds (see Chapter 9), a guaranty contract between the guarantor and the creditor must be in writing (or electronically recorded) to be enforceable unless the *main purpose* exception applies. The main purpose exception provides that if the main purpose of the guaranty agreement is to benefit the guarantor, then the contract need not be in writing to be enforceable. Under the common law, a suretyship agreement did not need to be in writing to be enforceable, and oral surety agreements were sufficient. Today, however, some states require a writing (or electronic record) to enforce a suretyship.

In the following *Spotlight Case,* the issue was whether a guaranty of a lease signed by the president of a corporation was enforceable against the officer personally, although he claimed to have signed the guaranty only as a representative of the corporation.

SPOTLIGHT on Personal Guaranties

Case 16.2 Wilson Court Limited Partnership v. Tony Maroni's, Inc.

Supreme Court of Washington, 134 Wash.2d 692, 952 P.2d 590 (1998).

BACKGROUND AND FACTS Tony Riviera founded Tony Maroni's, Inc., to sell Tony Maroni's Famous Gourmet Pizza in Seattle, Washington. Tony Maroni's, Inc., agreed to lease retail space owned by Wilson Court Limited Partnership. Riviera, Tony Maroni's president, signed the lease for 1,676 square feet of space for a sixty-month term. When he signed the lease, Riviera also signed a guaranty agreement that was incorporated by reference into the lease.

On the signature line of the guaranty, Riviera wrote "President" after his name. The guaranty did not specifically identify who was bound, referring only to "the undersigned" or "Guarantor." Riviera also signed the lease in a representative capacity, but the lease clearly indicated that only Tony Maroni's was bound by its terms. When Tony Maroni's defaulted on the lease, Wilson filed a suit in a Washington state court against Tony Maroni's, Riviera, and others. Riviera asserted, in part, that he was not personally liable on the guaranty because he signed only in his capacity as a corporate officer. The court issued a summary judgment in favor of Wilson. Riviera appealed to the Washington Supreme Court.

IN THE LANGUAGE OF THE COURT
TALMADGE, Justice.

* * * *

* * * [The] combination of circumstances [in this case] renders the Guaranty ambiguous.

In construing the Guaranty in light of this ambiguity, we acknowledge contracts to answer for the debt of another must be explicit and are strictly construed, but we must also recognize the commercial context in which this Guaranty was signed. Where two commercial entities sign a commercial agreement, we will give such an agreement a commercially reasonable construction. In this case, such a construction leads us to the conclusion Riviera is personally liable on the Guaranty as a matter of law.

First, any ambiguity in the Guaranty was created by Riviera himself in adding the descriptive language to his signature. *Such ambiguity will be construed against Riviera as the party who drafted this language.* [Emphasis added.]

Second, the language of the Guaranty itself compels the view Riviera is personally liable. We must interpret the Lease and Guaranty as a whole, giving reasonable effect to each of its parts. The plain language of the Guaranty clearly contemplates three separate entities, the Landlord, the Tenant and the Guarantor, and so designates them. It identifies Wilson as the Landlord, Tony Maroni's as the Tenant, and addresses the obligations of a separate third party, referred to interchangeably as the undersigned or Guarantor. * * * The only reasonable interpretation of these provisions is that the Landlord, Tenant and undersigned/Guarantor are three separate and distinct entities. If Riviera signed the Guaranty only in his representative capacity, Tony Maroni's would be both Tenant and Guarantor, rendering the Guaranty provisions absurd.

Moreover, the Guaranty language stands in stark contrast to the language of the Lease where a corporate obligation was unambiguously contemplated. Riviera signed the Lease as president of Tony Maroni's to bind the company. No such intent can be gleaned from the Guaranty.

Third, the very nature of a guaranty is such that Riviera created personal liability by his signature.

* * * *

Riviera is an experienced businessperson with prior experience in commercial leasing who dealt directly with Wilson in securing the Lease. There is no evidence or assertion of any improper conduct by Wilson. Given the commercial sophistication of the parties, the

CASE 16.2 CONTINUES ➧

CASE 16.2 CONTINUED

circumstances under which the Guaranty was entered into, and the nature of the Guaranty, a commercially reasonable approach to this case requires us * * * to hold Riviera personally liable under the Guaranty.

DECISION AND REMEDY *The Washington Supreme Court affirmed the judgment of the lower court. The president was personally liable because otherwise the corporation would be the guarantor of its own lease. This would be commercially unreasonable because, as a matter of law, a party cannot be the guarantor of its own contract.*

WHAT IF THE FACTS WERE DIFFERENT? *Suppose that the parties had carefully read the contract before they signed it. If they had been sure that the agreement stated what they intended and if everything discussed was in writing, how might the outcome of this case have been different?*

THE ECONOMIC DIMENSION *Why would a landlord, a lender, or any creditor require a guaranty?*

Actions That Release the Surety and the Guarantor

Basically, the same actions will release a surety or a guarantor from an obligation. In general, the following rules apply to both sureties and guarantors, but for simplicity, we refer just to sureties:

1. *Material modification.* Making any material modification to the terms of the original contract—without the surety's consent—will discharge the surety's obligation. (The extent to which the surety is discharged depends on whether he or she was compensated and to what extent he or she suffered a loss from the modification. For example, a father who receives no consideration in return for acting as a surety on his daughter's loan will be completely discharged if the loan contract is modified without his consent.)
2. *Surrender of property.* If a creditor surrenders the collateral to the debtor or impairs the collateral without the surety's consent, these acts can reduce the obligation of the surety. If the creditor's actions reduce the value of the property used as collateral, the surety is released to the extent of any loss suffered.
3. *Payment or tender of payment.* Naturally, any payment of the principal obligation by the debtor or by another person on the debtor's behalf will discharge the surety from the obligation. Even if the creditor refused to accept payment of the principal debt when it was tendered, the obligation of the surety can be discharged (if the creditor knew about the suretyship).

Defenses of the Surety and the Guarantor

Generally, the surety or guarantor can also assert any of the defenses available to the principal debtor to avoid liability on the obligation to the creditor. A few exceptions do exist, however. They apply to both sureties and guarantors, although we refer just to sureties.

INCAPACITY AND BANKRUPTCY Incapacity and bankruptcy are personal defenses, which can be asserted only by the person who is affected. Therefore, the surety cannot assert the principal debtor's incapacity or bankruptcy as a defense. A surety may assert his or her own incapacity or bankruptcy as a defense, however.

STATUTE OF LIMITATIONS The surety cannot assert the statute of limitations as a defense. (In contrast, the principal debtor can claim the statute of limitations as a defense to payment.)

FRAUD If the creditor fraudulently induced the person to act as a surety on the debt, the surety can assert fraud as a defense. In most states, the creditor has a legal duty to inform the surety, before the formation of the suretyship contract, of material facts known by the creditor that would substantially increase the surety's risk. Failure to so inform may constitute fraud and renders the suretyship obligation voidable.

Rights of the Surety and the Guarantor

When the surety or guarantor pays the debt owed to the creditor, he or she acquires certain rights, as discussed next. Again, for simplicity, the discussion refers just to sureties.

THE RIGHT OF SUBROGATION The surety has the legal **right of subrogation.** Simply stated, this means that any right that the creditor had against the debtor now becomes the right of the surety. Included are creditor rights in bankruptcy, rights to collateral possessed by the creditor, and rights to judgments obtained by the creditor. In short, the surety now stands in the shoes of the creditor and may pursue any remedies that were available to the creditor against the debtor.

▶ **Case in Point 16.6** Guerrero Brothers, Inc. (GBI), contracted with the Public School System (PSS) to build a high school. Century Insurance Company (CIC) agreed to provide GBI with the required payment and performance bonds on the project. Thus, CIC acted as a surety of GBI's performance and promised to finish the project if GBI defaulted.

Four years after construction began, PSS canceled GBI's contract, and CIC fulfilled GBI's obligations by finishing construction of the school. Numerous disputes arose, and litigation ensued. Ultimately, PSS agreed to pay GBI $500,000 in contract funds. CIC then filed an action against GBI and PSS to recover the $867,000 it claimed PSS owed it for finishing the school. The court found that CIC, as a performing surety, was entitled to the remaining contract funds through the right of subrogation. It had performed GBI's obligations and therefore stepped into GBI's shoes and had the right to obtain payment from PSS.[5] ◀

THE RIGHT OF REIMBURSEMENT The surety has a **right of reimbursement** from the debtor. Basically, the surety is entitled to receive from the debtor all outlays made on behalf of the suretyship arrangement. Such outlays can include expenses incurred as well as the actual amount of the debt paid to the creditor.

THE RIGHT OF CONTRIBUTION Two or more sureties are called **co-sureties.** When a co-surety pays more than her or his proportionate share on a debtor's default, she or he is entitled to recover from the other co-sureties the amount paid above that surety's obligation. This is the **right of contribution.** Generally, a co-surety's liability either is determined by agreement or, in the absence of agreement, is set at the maximum liability under the suretyship contract.

▶ **Example 16.7** Yasser and Itzhak, two co-sureties, are obligated under a suretyship contract to guarantee Jules's debt. Itzhak's maximum liability is $15,000, and Yasser's is $10,000. Jules owes $10,000 and is in default. Itzhak pays the creditor the entire $10,000.

In the absence of an agreement to the contrary, Itzhak can recover $4,000 from Yasser. The amount of the debt that Yasser agreed to cover ($10,000) is divided by the total amount that he and Itzhak together agreed to cover ($25,000). The result is multiplied by the amount of the default, yielding the amount that Yasser owes—$10,000 ÷ $25,000 × $10,000 = $4,000. ◀

5. *Century Insurance Co. v. Guerrero Brothers, Inc.*, 2010 WL 997112 (N.Mariana Islands 2010).

SECTION 4

PROTECTION FOR DEBTORS

The law protects debtors as well as creditors. Certain property of the debtor, for example, is exempt under state law from creditors' actions. Consumer protection statutes (see Chapter 24) also protect debtors' rights. Of course, bankruptcy laws, which will be discussed shortly, are designed specifically to assist debtors in need of help.

In most states, certain types of real and personal property are exempt from execution or attachment. State exemption statutes usually include both real and personal property.

Exempted Real Property

Probably the most familiar exemption is the **homestead exemption.** Each state permits the debtor to retain the family home, either in its entirety or up to a specified dollar amount, free from the claims of unsecured creditors or trustees in bankruptcy.

The purpose of the homestead exemption is to ensure that the debtor will retain some form of shelter. (Note that federal bankruptcy law places a cap on the amount that debtors filing bankruptcy can claim is exempt under their states' homestead exemption—see page 375 for details.)

In a few states, statutes allow the homestead exemption only if the judgment debtor has a family. If a judgment debtor does not have a family, a creditor may be entitled to collect the full amount realized from the sale of the debtor's home. In addition, the homestead exemption interacts with other areas of law and can sometimes operate to cancel out a portion of a lien on a debtor's real property.

▶ **Case in Point 16.8** Antonio Stanley purchased a modular home from Yates Mobile Services Corporation. When Stanley failed to pay the purchase price of the modular home, Yates obtained a judicial lien against Stanley's property in the amount of $165,138. Stanley then filed for bankruptcy and asserted the homestead exemption. The court found that Stanley was entitled to avoid the lien to the extent that it impaired his exemption. Using a bankruptcy law formula, the court determined that the total impairment was $143,639 and that Stanley could avoid paying this amount to Yates. Thus, Yates was left with a judicial lien on Stanley's home in the amount of $21,499.[6] ◀

Exempted Personal Property

Personal property that is most often exempt from satisfaction of judgment debts includes the following:

1. Household furniture up to a specified dollar amount.
2. Clothing and certain personal possessions, such as family pictures or a Bible.
3. A vehicle (or vehicles) for transportation (at least up to a specified dollar amount).
4. Certain classified animals, usually livestock but including pets.
5. Equipment that the debtor uses in a business or trade, such as tools or professional instruments, up to a specified dollar amount.

SECTION 5

BANKRUPTCY LAW

Bankruptcy law in the United States has two goals—to protect a debtor by giving him or her a fresh start, free from creditors' claims, and to ensure equitable treatment to creditors who are competing for the debtor's assets. Bankruptcy law is federal law, but state laws on security interests, liens, judgments, and exemptions also play a role in federal bankruptcy proceedings.

Article I, Section 8, of the U.S. Constitution gave Congress the power to establish "uniform laws on the subject of bankruptcies throughout the United States." Federal bankruptcy legislation was first enacted in 1898 and since then has undergone several modifications, most recently in the 2005 Bankruptcy Reform Act.[7] Federal bankruptcy laws (as amended) are called the Bankruptcy Code or, more simply, the Code.

6 *In re Stanley*, 2010 WL 2103441 (M.D.N.C. 2010).

7. The full title of the act was the Bankruptcy Abuse Prevention and Consumer Protection Act of 2005, Pub. L. No. 109-8, 119 Stat. 23 (April 20, 2005).

Bankruptcy Courts

Bankruptcy proceedings are held in federal bankruptcy courts, which are under the authority of U.S. district courts. Rulings from bankruptcy courts can be appealed to the district courts. The bankruptcy court holds the proceedings required to administer the estate of the debtor in bankruptcy (the *estate* consists of the debtor's assets, as will be discussed shortly). For a discussion of how bankruptcy courts are adapting to the use of social media, see this chapter's *Insight into Social Media* feature on the facing page.

Bankruptcy court judges are appointed for terms of fourteen years. A bankruptcy court can conduct a jury trial if the appropriate district court has authorized it and the parties to the bankruptcy consent. Bankruptcy courts follow the Federal Rules of Bankruptcy Procedure rather than the Federal Rules of Civil Procedure (discussed in Chapter 2).

Types of Bankruptcy Relief

The Bankruptcy Code is contained in Title 11 of the *United States Code* and has eight chapters. Chapters 1, 3, and 5 of the Code contain general definitional provisions, as well as provisions governing case administration, creditors, the debtor, and the estate. These three chapters normally apply to all kinds of bankruptcies.

Four chapters of the Code set forth the most important types of relief that debtors can seek:

1. Chapter 7 provides for **liquidation** proceedings (the selling of all nonexempt assets and the distribution of the proceeds to the debtor's creditors).
2. Chapter 11 governs reorganizations.
3. Chapter 12 (for family farmers and family fishermen) and 13 (for individuals) provide for the adjustment of debts by persons with regular incomes.[8]

Note that a debtor (except for a municipality) need not be insolvent[9] to file for bankruptcy relief under

8. There are no Chapters 2, 4, 6, 8, or 10 in Title 11. Such "gaps" are not uncommon in the *United States Code*. They occur because chapter numbers (or other subdivisional unit numbers) are sometimes reserved for future use when a statute is enacted. (A gap may also appear if a law has been repealed.)

9. The inability to pay debts as they become due is known as *equitable* insolvency. *Balance sheet* insolvency, which exists when a debtor's liabilities exceed assets, is not the test. Thus, debtors whose cash-flow problems become severe may petition for bankruptcy voluntarily or be forced into involuntary bankruptcy even though their assets far exceed their liabilities.

INSIGHT INTO SOCIAL MEDIA

Live Chatting with Your State's Bankruptcy Court

Chatting on social media has become a way of life for most younger people in this country and elsewhere. Online chats preceded social media and are still used at retail Web sites. Today, some tech-savvy employees at bankruptcy courts are using the retail online chat model to answer questions about bankruptcy.

Arizona Was First to Use Live Chats

The U.S. Bankruptcy Court for the District of Arizona started live chatting several years ago. It added live chat to its Web site as part of a strategic initiative to educate the public about bankruptcy. Rather than leaving voice messages, people who access the court's Web site can send and receive text messages via an easy-to-use chat box. The court's goal is to respond to a live chat request within thirty seconds.

In 2011, New Mexico became the second state to add online chatting to its bankruptcy court's Web site. Nevada followed with its live chat in 2012.

The courts that have adopted online chatting average about ten chats a day. Most chats last less than ten minutes.

Who Uses Bankruptcy Court Chat Rooms?

At first, only individuals interested in filing for bankruptcy without an attorney used the live chat services. When paralegals learned that they could get quick answers to their questions online, they also began to use the services.

Then, during the real estate meltdown of the last few years, many real estate lawyers expanded into the area of bankruptcy law, often as a way to help their clients avoid foreclosure through bankruptcy filings. Many of these lawyers also have used live chat to expand their knowledge of bankruptcy law.

The Courts and Facebook

In this age of expanding social media, many courts have created their own Facebook pages. For example, the New Jersey Supreme Court, Superior Court, and Tax Court have a Facebook page that covers all three courts.

Increasingly, bankruptcy courts are posting announcements on their Facebook pages. Anyone who has signed up for Facebook can readily find announcements from the U.S. Bankruptcy Court for the Southern District of Mississippi. Information from the bankruptcy courts for Hawaii, New Mexico, Rhode Island, and Riverside, California, also is available on Facebook.

LEGAL CRITICAL THINKING

INSIGHT INTO TECHNOLOGY

Are there any downsides to live chats with bankruptcy courts? If so, what are they?

the Bankruptcy Code. Anyone obligated to a creditor can declare bankruptcy.

Special Requirements for Consumer-Debtors

A **consumer-debtor** is a debtor whose debts result primarily from the purchase of goods for personal, family, or household use. The Bankruptcy Code requires that the clerk of the court give all consumer-debtors written notice of the general purpose, benefits, and costs of each chapter under which they might proceed. In addition, the clerk must provide consumer-debtors with information on the types of services available from credit counseling agencies.

SECTION 6

LIQUIDATION PROCEEDINGS

Liquidation under Chapter 7 of the Bankruptcy Code is probably the most familiar type of bankruptcy proceeding and is often referred to as an *ordinary,* or *straight, bankruptcy.* Put simply, a debtor in a liquidation bankruptcy turns all assets over to a **bankruptcy trustee,** a person appointed by the court to manage the debtor's funds. The trustee sells the nonexempt assets and distributes the proceeds to creditors. With certain exceptions, the remaining debts are then **discharged** (extinguished), and the debtor is relieved of the obligation to pay the debts.

Any "person"—defined as including individuals, partnerships, companies, corporations, and labor unions—may be a debtor in a liquidation proceeding. A husband and wife may file jointly for bankruptcy under a single petition. Railroads, insurance companies, banks, savings and loan associations, investment companies licensed by the Small Business Administration, and credit unions *cannot* be debtors in a liquidation bankruptcy, however. Other chapters of the Bankruptcy Code or other federal or state statutes apply to them.

A straight bankruptcy can be commenced by the filing of either a voluntary or an involuntary **petition in bankruptcy**—the document that is filed with a bankruptcy court to initiate bankruptcy proceedings. If a debtor files the petition, the bankruptcy is voluntary. If one or more creditors file a petition to force the debtor into bankruptcy, the bankruptcy is involuntary. We discuss both voluntary and involuntary bankruptcy proceedings under Chapter 7 in the following subsections.

Voluntary Bankruptcy

To bring a voluntary petition in bankruptcy, the debtor files official forms designated for that purpose in the bankruptcy court. The law now requires that *before* debtors can file a petition, they must receive credit counseling from an approved nonprofit agency within the 180-day period preceding the date of filing. Debtors filing a Chapter 7 petition must include a certificate proving that they have received individual or group counseling from an approved agency within the last 180 days (roughly six months).

A consumer-debtor who is filing for liquidation bankruptcy must confirm the accuracy of the petition's contents. The debtor must also state in the petition, at the time of filing, that he or she understands the relief available under other chapters of the Code and has chosen to proceed under Chapter 7.

Attorneys representing the consumer-debtors must file an affidavit stating that they have informed the debtors of the relief available under each chapter of the Bankruptcy Code. In addition, the attorneys must reasonably attempt to verify the accuracy of the consumer-debtors' petitions and schedules (described below). Failure to do so is considered perjury.

CHAPTER 7 SCHEDULES The voluntary petition must contain the following schedules:

1. A list of both secured and unsecured creditors, their addresses, and the amount of debt owed to each.
2. A statement of the financial affairs of the debtor.
3. A list of all property owned by the debtor, including property that the debtor claims is exempt.
4. A list of current income and expenses.
5. A certificate of credit counseling (as discussed previously).
6. Proof of payments received from employers within sixty days prior to the filing of the petition.
7. A statement of the amount of monthly income, itemized to show how the amount is calculated.
8. A copy of the debtor's federal income tax return for the most recent year ending immediately before the filing of the petition.

The official forms must be completed accurately, sworn to under oath, and signed by the debtor. To conceal assets or knowingly supply false information on these schedules is a crime under the bankruptcy laws.

With the exception of tax returns, failure to file the required schedules within forty-five days after the filing of the petition (unless an extension is granted) will result in an automatic dismissal of the petition. The debtor has up to seven days before the date of the first creditors' meeting to provide a copy of the most recent tax returns to the trustee.

TAX RETURNS DURING BANKRUPTCY In addition, a debtor may be required to file a tax return at the end of each tax year while the case is pending and to provide a copy to the court. This may be done at the request of the court or of the **U.S. trustee**—a government official who performs administrative tasks that a bankruptcy judge would otherwise have to perform.

Any *party in interest* (a party, such as a creditor, who has a valid interest in the outcome of the proceedings) may make this request as well. Debtors may also be required to file tax returns during Chapter 11 and 13 bankruptcies.

SUBSTANTIAL ABUSE—MEANS TEST In the past, a bankruptcy court could dismiss a Chapter 7 petition for relief (discharge of debts) if the use of Chapter 7 would constitute a "substantial abuse" of bankruptcy law. Today, the law provides a *means test* to determine a debtor's eligibility for Chapter 7.

The purpose of the test is to keep upper-income people from abusing the bankruptcy process by filing for Chapter 7, as was thought to have happened in the past. The test forces more people to file for Chapter 13 bankruptcy rather than have their debts discharged under Chapter 7.

The Basic Formula. A debtor wishing to file for bankruptcy must complete the means test to determine whether she or he qualifies for Chapter 7. The debtor's average monthly income in recent months is compared with the median income in the geographic area in which the person lives. (The U.S. Trustee Program provides these data at its Web site.) If the debtor's income is below the median income, the debtor usually is allowed to file for Chapter 7 bankruptcy, as there is no presumption of bankruptcy abuse.

Applying the Means Test to Future Disposable Income. If the debtor's income is above the median income, then further calculations must be made to determine whether the person will have sufficient disposable income in the future to repay at least some of his or her unsecured debts. *Disposable income* is calculated by subtracting living expenses and secured debt payments, such as mortgage payments, from monthly income.

In making this calculation, the debtor's recent monthly income is presumed to continue for the next sixty months. Living expenses are the amounts allowed under formulas used by the Internal Revenue Service (IRS). The IRS allowances include modest allocations for food, clothing, housing, utilities, transportation (including a car payment), health care, and other necessities. (The U.S. Trustee Program's Web site also provides these amounts.) The allowances do not include expenditures for items such as cell phones and cable television service.

Can the Debtor Afford to Pay Unsecured Debts? Once future disposable income has been estimated, that amount is used to determine whether the debtor will have income that could be applied to unsecured debts. The courts may also consider the debtor's bad faith or other circumstances indicating abuse.

► **Case in Point 16.9** At thirty-three years old, Lisa Hebbring owned a home and a car, but had $11,124 in credit-card debt. Hebbring was earning $49,000 per year when she filed for Chapter 7 bankruptcy. Her petition listed monthly net income of $2,813 and expenditures of $2,897, for a deficit of $84.

In calculating her income, Hebbring excluded a $313 monthly deduction for contributions to retirement plans. The U.S. trustee filed a motion to dismiss Hebbring's petition due to substantial abuse, claiming that the retirement contributions should be disallowed. The court agreed and dismissed the Chapter 7 petition. Because Hebbring's retirement contributions were not reasonably necessary based on her age and financial circumstances, the court found that she was capable of paying her unsecured debts.[10] ◄

ADDITIONAL GROUNDS FOR DISMISSAL As already noted, a court can dismiss a debtor's voluntary petition for Chapter 7 relief for substantial abuse or for failing to provide the necessary documents within the specified time.

In addition, a court might dismiss a Chapter 7 in two other situations. First, if the debtor has been convicted of a violent crime or a drug-trafficking offense, the victim can file a motion to dismiss the voluntary petition.[11] Second, if the debtor fails to pay postpetition domestic-support obligations (which include child and spousal support), the court may dismiss the debtor's petition.

ORDER FOR RELIEF If the voluntary petition for bankruptcy is found to be proper, the filing of the petition will itself constitute an **order for relief.** (An order for relief is a court's grant of assistance to a petitioner.) Once a consumer-debtor's voluntary petition has been filed, the trustee and creditors must be given notice of the order for relief by mail not more than twenty days after entry of the order.

Involuntary Bankruptcy

An involuntary bankruptcy occurs when the debtor's creditors force the debtor into bankruptcy proceedings. An involuntary case cannot be filed against a charitable institution or a farmer (an individual or business that receives more than 50 percent of gross income from farming operations).

An involuntary petition should not be used as an everyday debt-collection device, and the Code provides penalties for the filing of frivolous petitions against debtors. If the court dismisses an involuntary petition, the petitioning creditors may be required to pay the costs and attorneys' fees incurred by the debtor in defending against the petition. If the petition was filed in bad faith, damages can be awarded for injury to the debtor's reputation. Punitive damages may also be awarded.

---

10. *Hebbring v. U.S. Trustee,* 463 F.3d 902 (9th Cir. 2006).

11. Note that the court may not dismiss a case on this ground if the debtor's bankruptcy is necessary to satisfy a claim for a domestic-support obligation.

REQUIREMENTS For an involuntary action to be filed, the following requirements must be met:

1. If the debtor has twelve or more creditors, three or more of these creditors having unsecured claims totaling at least $15,325 must join in the petition.
2. If a debtor has fewer than twelve creditors, one or more creditors having a claim totaling $15,325 or more may file.[12]

ORDER FOR RELIEF If the debtor challenges the involuntary petition, a hearing will be held, and the bankruptcy court will enter an order for relief if it finds either of the following:

1. The debtor is not paying debts as they come due.
2. A general receiver, assignee, or custodian took possession of, or was appointed to take charge of, substantially all of the debtor's property within 120 days before the filing of the petition.

If the court grants an order for relief, the debtor will be required to supply the same information in the bankruptcy schedules as in a voluntary bankruptcy.

Automatic Stay

The moment a petition, either voluntary or involuntary, is filed, an **automatic stay,** or suspension, of all actions by creditors against the debtor or the debtor's property normally goes into effect. In other words, once a petition has been filed, creditors cannot contact the debtor by phone or mail or start any legal proceedings to recover debts or to repossess property. (In some circumstances, a secured creditor or other party in interest may petition the bankruptcy court for relief from the automatic stay, as will be discussed shortly.)

If a creditor *knowingly* violates the automatic stay (a willful violation), any injured party, including the debtor, is entitled to recover actual damages, costs, and attorneys' fees, and may be awarded punitive damages as well. Until the bankruptcy proceeding is closed or dismissed, the automatic stay prohibits a creditor from taking any act to collect, assess, or recover a claim against the debtor that arose before the filing of the petition.

▶ **Case in Point 16.10** Stefanie Kuehn filed for bankruptcy. When she requested a transcript from the university at which she obtained her master's degree, the university refused because she owed more than $6,000 in tuition. Kuehn complained to the court. The court ruled that the university violated the automatic stay by refusing to provide a transcript because it was attempting to collect an unpaid tuition debt.[13] ◀

THE ADEQUATE PROTECTION DOCTRINE Underlying the Code's automatic-stay provision for a secured creditor is a concept known as *adequate protection.* The **adequate protection doctrine,** among other things, protects secured creditors from losing their security as a result of the automatic stay.

The bankruptcy court can provide adequate protection by requiring the debtor or trustee to make periodic cash payments or a one-time cash payment. The court can also require the debtor or trustee to provide additional collateral or replacement liens to the extent that the stay may actually cause the value of the property to decrease.

EXCEPTIONS TO THE AUTOMATIC STAY The Code provides the following exceptions to the automatic stay:

1. Collection efforts can continue for domestic-support obligations, which include any debt owed to or recoverable by a spouse, a former spouse, a child of the debtor, that child's parent or guardian, or a governmental unit.
2. Proceedings against the debtor related to divorce, child custody or visitation, domestic violence, and support enforcement are not stayed.
3. Investigations by a securities regulatory agency (see Chapter 28) can continue.
4. Certain statutory liens for property taxes are not stayed.

REQUESTS FOR RELIEF FROM THE AUTOMATIC STAY A secured creditor or other party in interest can petition the bankruptcy court for relief from the automatic stay. If a creditor or other party requests relief from the stay, the stay will automatically terminate sixty days after the request, unless the court grants an extension or the parties agree otherwise.

SECURED PROPERTY The automatic stay on secured property terminates forty-five days after the creditors' meeting (to be discussed shortly). The stay terminates unless the debtor redeems or reaffirms certain debts (*reaffirmation* will be discussed later in this chapter).

In other words, the debtor cannot keep the secured property (such as a financed automobile), even if she or

12. 11 U.S.C. Section 303. The amounts stated in this chapter are in accordance with those computed on April 1, 2013.

13. *In re Kuehn,* 563 F.3d 289 (7th Cir. 2009).

he continues to make payments on it, without reinstating the rights of the secured party to collect on the debt.

BAD FAITH If the debtor had two or more bankruptcy petitions dismissed during the prior year, the Code presumes bad faith. In such a situation, the automatic stay does *not* go into effect until the court determines that the petition was filed in good faith.

Estate in Bankruptcy

On the commencement of a liquidation proceeding under Chapter 7, an *estate in bankruptcy* (sometimes called an *estate in property*) is created. The estate consists of all the debtor's interests in property currently held, wherever located. The estate in bankruptcy includes all of the following:

1. *Community property* (property jointly owned by a husband and wife in certain states—see Chapter 26).
2. Property transferred in a transaction voidable by the trustee.
3. Proceeds and profits from the property of the estate.

Certain after-acquired property—such as gifts, inheritances, property settlements (from divorce), and life insurance death proceeds—to which the debtor becomes entitled *within 180 days after filing* may also become part of the estate.

Generally, though, the filing of a bankruptcy petition fixes a dividing line. Property acquired prior to the filing of the petition becomes property of the estate, and property acquired after the filing of the petition, except as just noted, remains the debtor's.

The Bankruptcy Trustee

Promptly after the order for relief in the liquidation proceeding has been entered, a trustee is appointed. The basic duty of the trustee is to collect the debtor's available estate and reduce it to cash for distribution, preserving the interests of both the debtor and the unsecured creditors. The trustee is held accountable for administering the debtor's estate.

To enable the trustee to accomplish this duty, the Code gives the trustee certain powers, stated in both general and specific terms. These powers must be exercised within two years of the order for relief.

DUTIES FOR MEANS TESTING The trustee is required to promptly review all materials filed by the debtor to determine if there is substantial abuse. Within ten days after the first meeting of the creditors (discussed shortly), the trustee must file a statement indicating whether the case is presumed to be an abuse under the means test. The trustee must provide a copy of this statement to all creditors within five days.

When there is a presumption of abuse, the trustee must either file a motion to dismiss the petition (or convert it to a Chapter 13 case) or file a statement explaining why a motion would not be appropriate. If the debtor owes a domestic-support obligation (such as child support), the trustee must provide written notice of the bankruptcy to the claim holder (a former spouse, for instance).

THE TRUSTEE'S POWERS The trustee has the power to require persons holding the debtor's property at the time the petition is filed to deliver the property to the trustee.[14] To enable the trustee to implement this power, the Code provides that the trustee has rights *equivalent* to those of certain other parties, such as a creditor who has a judicial lien. This power of a trustee, which is equivalent to that of a lien creditor, is known as *strong-arm power.*

In addition, the trustee has specific *powers of avoidance*. They enable the trustee to set aside (avoid) a sale or other transfer of the debtor's property and take the property back for the debtor's estate. These powers apply to voidable rights available to the debtor, preferences, and fraudulent transfers by the debtor. Each power is discussed in more detail below. In addition, a trustee can avoid certain statutory liens (creditors' claims against the debtor's property).

The debtor shares most of the trustee's avoidance powers. Thus, if the trustee does not take action to enforce one of the rights just mentioned, the debtor in a liquidation bankruptcy can enforce that right.

VOIDABLE RIGHTS A trustee steps into the shoes of the debtor. Thus, any reason that a debtor can use to obtain the return of her or his property can be used by the trustee as well. These grounds include fraud, duress, incapacity, and mutual mistake.

▶ **Example 16.11** Ben sells his boat to Tara. Tara gives Ben a check, knowing that she has insufficient funds in her bank account to cover the check. Tara has committed fraud. Ben has the right to avoid that transfer and recover the boat from Tara. If Ben files for bankruptcy relief under Chapter 7, the trustee can

14. Usually, though, the trustee takes constructive, rather than actual, possession of the debtor's property. For example, to obtain control of a debtor's business inventory, a trustee might change the locks on the doors to the business and hire a security guard.

exercise the same right to recover the boat from Tara, and the boat becomes a part of the debtor's estate. ◀

PREFERENCES A debtor is not permitted to transfer property or to make a payment that favors—or gives a **preference** to—one creditor over others. The trustee is allowed to recover payments made both voluntarily and involuntarily to one creditor in preference over another.

To have made a recoverable preferential payment, an *insolvent* debtor must have transferred property, for a *preexisting* debt, within *ninety days* before the filing of the bankruptcy petition. The transfer must have given the creditor more than the creditor would have received as a result of the bankruptcy proceedings. The Code presumes that a debtor is insolvent during the ninety-day period before filing a petition.

If a **preferred creditor** (one who has received a preferential transfer from the debtor) has sold the property to an innocent third party, the trustee cannot recover the property from the innocent party. The preferred creditor, however, generally *can* be held accountable for the value of the property.

Preferences to Insiders. Sometimes, the creditor receiving the preference is an insider. An **insider** is an individual, partner, partnership, corporation, or officer or director of a corporation (or a relative of one of these) who has a close relationship with the debtor. In this situation, the avoidance power of the trustee extends to transfers made within *one year* before filing. (If the transfer was fraudulent, as will be discussed shortly, the trustee can avoid transfers made within *two years* before filing.)

If the transfer occurred before the ninety-day period, however, the trustee must prove that the debtor was insolvent when the transfer occurred or that it was made to or for the benefit of an insider.

Transfers That Do Not Constitute Preferences. Not all transfers are preferences. To be a preference, the transfer must be made for something other than current consideration.

Most courts generally assume that payment for services rendered *within fifteen days* before the payment is not a preference. If a creditor receives payment in the ordinary course of business from an individual or business debtor, such as payment of last month's cell phone bill, the bankruptcy trustee cannot recover the payment.

To be recoverable, a preference must be a transfer for an antecedent (preexisting) debt, such as a year-old landscaping bill. In addition, the Code permits a consumer-debtor to transfer any property to a creditor up to a total value of $6,225 without the transfer's constituting a preference. Payment of domestic-support debts does not constitute a preference.

FRAUDULENT TRANSFERS The trustee may avoid fraudulent transfers or obligations if they (1) were made within two years prior to the filing of the petition or (2) were made with actual intent to hinder, delay, or defraud a creditor. ▶ **Example 16.12** April is planning to petition for bankruptcy, so she sells her gold jewelry, worth $10,000, to a friend for $500. The friend agrees that in the future he will "sell" the jewelry back to April for the same amount. This is a fraudulent transfer that the trustee can undo. ◀

Transfers made for less than reasonably equivalent consideration are also vulnerable if the debtor thereby became insolvent or was left engaged in business with an unreasonably small amount of capital. When a fraudulent transfer is made outside the Code's two-year limit, creditors may seek alternative relief under state laws. Some state laws may allow creditors to recover transfers made up to three years before the filing of a petition.

Exemptions

As just described, the trustee takes control of the debtor's property in a Chapter 7 bankruptcy, but an individual debtor is entitled to exempt (exclude) certain property from the bankruptcy. The Bankruptcy Code exempts the following property:[15]

1. Up to $22,975 in equity in the debtor's residence and burial plot (the homestead exemption).
2. Interest in a motor vehicle up to $3,675.
3. Interest, up to $550 for a particular item, in household goods and furnishings, wearing apparel, appliances, books, animals, crops, and musical instruments (the aggregate total of all items is limited, however, to $12,250).
4. Interest in jewelry up to $1,550.
5. Interest in any other property up to $1,225, plus any unused part of the $22,975 homestead exemption up to $11,500.

15. The dollar amounts stated in the Bankruptcy Code are adjusted automatically every three years on April 1 based on changes in the Consumer Price Index. The adjusted amounts are rounded to the nearest $25. The amounts stated in this chapter are in accordance with those computed on April 1, 2013.

6. Interest in any tools of the debtor's trade up to $2,300.
7. A life insurance contract owned by the debtor (other than a credit life insurance contract).
8. Certain interests in accrued dividends and interest under, or loan value of, life insurance contracts owned by the debtor, not to exceed $12,250.
9. Professionally prescribed health aids.
10. The right to receive Social Security and certain welfare benefits, alimony and support, certain retirement funds and pensions, and education savings accounts held for specific periods of time.
11. The right to receive certain personal-injury and other awards up to $22,975.

Individual states have the power to pass legislation precluding debtors from using the federal exemptions within the state. A majority of the states have done this. In those states, debtors may use only state, not federal, exemptions. In the rest of the states, an individual debtor (or a husband and wife filing jointly) may choose either the exemptions provided under state law or the federal exemptions.

The Homestead Exemption

The Bankruptcy Code limits the amount of equity that can be claimed under the homestead exemption. In general, if the debtor acquired the homestead within three and a half years preceding the date of filing, the maximum equity exempted is $155,675, even if state law would permit a higher amount.

In addition, the state homestead exemption is available only if the debtor has lived in a state for two years before filing the bankruptcy petition. Furthermore, a debtor who has violated securities laws, been convicted of a felony, or engaged in certain other intentional misconduct may not be permitted to claim the homestead exemption.

Creditors' Meeting

Within a reasonable time after the order for relief has been granted (not more than forty days), the trustee must call a meeting of the creditors listed in the schedules filed by the debtor. The bankruptcy judge does not attend this meeting. The debtor is required to attend (unless excused by the court) and to submit to examination under oath by the creditors and the trustee. At the meeting, the trustee ensures that the debtor is aware of the potential consequences of bankruptcy and of his or her ability to file for bankruptcy under a different chapter of the Bankruptcy Code.

Creditors' Claims

To be entitled to receive a portion of the debtor's estate, each creditor normally files a *proof of claim* with the bankruptcy court clerk within ninety days of the creditors' meeting.[16] A proof of claim is necessary if there is any dispute concerning the claim. The proof of claim lists the creditor's name and address, as well as the amount that the creditor asserts is owed to the creditor by the debtor.

When the debtor has no assets—called a "no-asset case"—creditors are notified of the debtor's petition for bankruptcy but are instructed not to file a claim. In no-asset cases, the unsecured creditors will receive no payment, and most, if not all, of these debts will be discharged.

Distribution of Property

The Code provides specific rules for the distribution of the debtor's property to secured and unsecured creditors. If any amount remains after the priority classes of creditors have been satisfied, it is turned over to the debtor. Exhibit 16–2 on the following page illustrates the collection and distribution of property in most voluntary bankruptcies.

DISTRIBUTION TO SECURED CREDITORS As noted earlier, secured creditors are creditors who received an interest in collateral to secure a debtor's payment or performance. The Code requires that consumer-debtors file a statement of intention with respect to the secured collateral. They can choose to pay off the debt and redeem the collateral, claim it is exempt, reaffirm the debt and continue making payments, or surrender the property to the secured party.

If the collateral is surrendered to the secured party, the secured creditor can enforce the security interest. The secured party can either (1) accept the property in full satisfaction of the debt or (2) sell the collateral and use the proceeds to pay off the debt. Thus, the secured party has priority over unsecured parties as to the proceeds from the disposition of the collateral. Should the collateral be insufficient to cover the secured debt owed, the secured creditor becomes an unsecured creditor for the difference.

DISTRIBUTION TO UNSECURED CREDITORS Bankruptcy law establishes an order of priority for classes of

16. This ninety-day rule applies in Chapter 12 and Chapter 13 bankruptcies as well.

EXHIBIT 16–2 Collection and Distribution of Property in Most Voluntary Bankruptcies

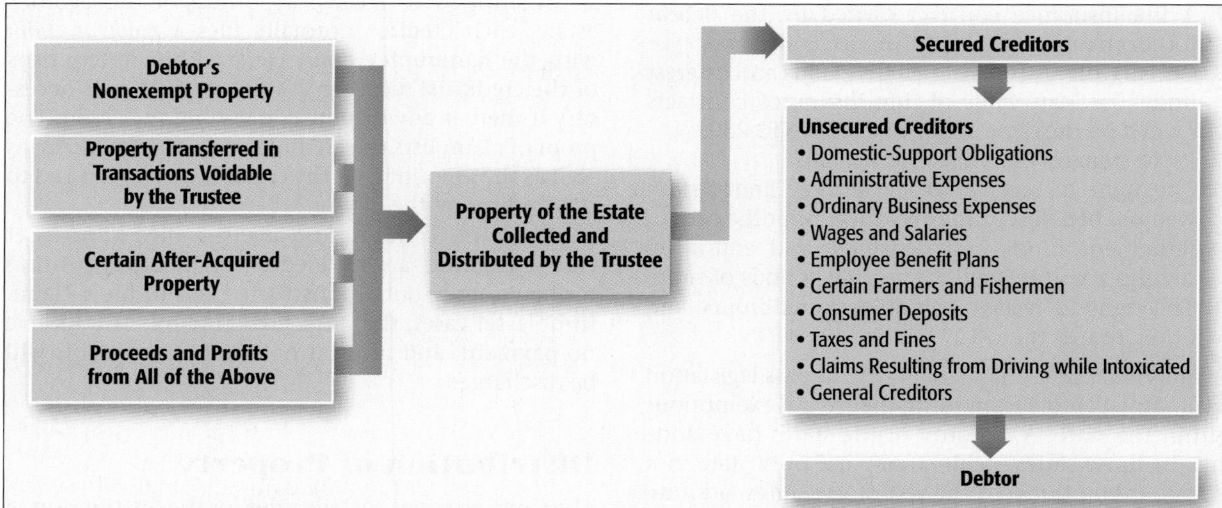

debts owed to *unsecured* creditors, and they are paid in the order of their priority. Each class must be fully paid before the next class is entitled to any of the remaining proceeds.

If there are insufficient proceeds to pay fully all the creditors in a class, the proceeds are distributed *proportionately* to the creditors in that class, and classes lower in priority receive nothing.

In almost all Chapter 7 bankruptcies, the funds will be insufficient to pay all creditors. The order of priority among classes of unsecured creditors is as follows (some of these classes involve cases against bankrupt businesses):

1. Claims for domestic-support obligations, such as child support and alimony.
2. Administrative expenses, including court costs, trustee fees, and attorneys' fees.
3. In an involuntary bankruptcy, expenses incurred by the debtor in the ordinary course of business.
4. Unpaid wages, salaries, and commissions earned within ninety days of the filing of the petition. The amount is capped for each claimant.
5. Unsecured claims for contributions to be made to employee benefit plans. The amount is capped for each claimant.
6. Consumer deposits given to the debtor before the petition was filed. The amount is capped for each claimant.
7. Certain taxes and penalties due to government units, such as income and property taxes.
8. Claims for death or personal injury resulting from the unlawful operation of a motor vehicle.
9. Claims of general creditors.

If any amount remains after the priority classes of creditors have been satisfied, it is turned over to the debtor.

Discharge

From the debtor's point of view, the primary purpose of liquidation is to obtain a fresh start through a discharge of debts. Certain debts, however, are not dischargeable in bankruptcy. Also, certain debtors may not qualify to have all debts discharged in bankruptcy. These situations are discussed next.

EXCEPTIONS TO DISCHARGE Claims that are not dischargeable in bankruptcy include the following:

1. Claims for back taxes accruing within two years prior to bankruptcy.
2. Claims for amounts borrowed by the debtor to pay federal taxes or any nondischargeable taxes.[17]
3. Claims against property or funds obtained by the debtor under false pretenses or by false representations.

17. Taxes accruing within three years prior to bankruptcy are nondischargeable, including federal and state income taxes, employment taxes, taxes on gross receipts, property taxes, excise taxes, customs duties, and any other taxes for which the government claims the debtor is liable in some capacity. See 11 U.S.C. Sections 507(a)(8) and 523(a)(1).

4. Claims by creditors who were not notified of the bankruptcy. These claims did not appear on the schedules the debtor was required to file.
5. Claims based on fraud[18] or misuse of funds by the debtor while acting in a fiduciary capacity or claims involving the debtor's embezzlement or larceny.
6. Domestic-support obligations and property settlements as provided for in a separation agreement or divorce decree.
7. Claims for amounts due on a retirement account loan.
8. Claims based on willful or malicious conduct by the debtor toward another or the property of another.
9. Certain government fines and penalties.
10. Student loans, unless payment of the loans imposes an undue hardship on the debtor and the debtor's dependents. (For an example of what constitutes undue hardship, see *Case in Point 16.13* below.)
11. Consumer debts of more than $650 for luxury goods or services owed to a single creditor incurred within ninety days of the order for relief.
12. Cash advances totaling more than $925 that are extensions of open-end consumer credit obtained by the debtor within seventy days of the order for relief.
13. Judgments against a debtor as a result of the debtor's operation of a motor vehicle while intoxicated.
14. Fees or assessments arising from property in a homeowners' association, as long as the debtor retained an interest in the property.
15. Taxes with respect to which the debtor failed to provide required or requested tax documents.

▶ **Case in Point 16.13** Keldric Mosley incurred student loans while attending Alcorn State University and then joined the U.S. Army Reserve Officers' Training Corps. He was injured during training and resigned from the Corps because of medical problems related to his injuries. Mosley worked briefly for several employers, but depressed and physically limited by his injuries, he was unable to keep any of the jobs. A federal bankruptcy court granted him a discharge under Chapter 7, but it did not include the student loans.

Mosley became homeless and had a monthly income of only $210 in disability benefits, but he still owed $45,000 in student loans. He asked the bankruptcy court to reopen his case and discharge his student loans based on undue hardship. The court held that Mosley's medical problems, lack of skills, and "dire living conditions" made it unlikely that he would be able to hold a job and repay the loans. The court therefore discharged the debt, reasoning that Mosley could not maintain a minimal standard of living if forced to repay the loans.[19] ◀

OBJECTIONS TO DISCHARGE In addition to the exceptions to discharge previously discussed, a bankruptcy court may also deny the discharge based on the debtor's *conduct.* Grounds for denial of discharge of the debtor include the following:

1. The debtor's concealment or destruction of property with the intent to hinder, delay, or defraud a creditor.
2. The debtor's fraudulent concealment or destruction of financial records.
3. The grant of a discharge to the debtor within eight years before the petition was filed.
4. The debtor's failure to complete the required consumer education course.
5. Proceedings in which the debtor could be found guilty of a felony (basically, a court may not discharge any debt until the completion of felony proceedings against the debtor).

When a discharge is denied under any of these circumstances, the debtor's assets are still distributed to the creditors. After the bankruptcy proceeding, however, the debtor remains liable for the unpaid portion of all claims.

EFFECT OF A DISCHARGE The primary effect of a discharge is to void, or set aside, any judgment on a discharged debt and prohibit any action to collect a discharged debt. A discharge does not affect the liability of a co-debtor.

REVOCATION OF DISCHARGE A discharge may be revoked (taken back) within one year if it is discovered that the debtor acted fraudulently or dishonestly during the bankruptcy proceeding. If revocation occurs, a creditor whose claim was not satisfied in the distribution of the debtor's property can proceed with his or her claim against the debtor.

Reaffirmation of Debt

An agreement to pay a debt dischargeable in bankruptcy is called a **reaffirmation agreement.** A debtor may wish to pay a debt—for instance, a debt owed to a family member, physician, bank, or some other creditor—even

18. Even if a debtor who is sued for fraud settles the lawsuit, the settlement agreement may not be discharged in bankruptcy because of the underlying fraud. See *Archer v. Warner,* 538 U.S. 314, 123 S.Ct. 1462, 155 L.Ed.2d 454 (2003).

19. *In re Mosley,* 494 F.3d 1320 (11th Cir. 2007).

though the debt could be discharged in bankruptcy. Also, as noted previously, a debtor cannot retain secured property while continuing to pay without entering into a reaffirmation agreement.

PROCEDURES To be enforceable, reaffirmation agreements must be made before the debtor is granted a discharge. The agreement must be signed and filed with the court. Court approval is required unless the debtor is represented by an attorney during the negotiation of the reaffirmation and submits the proper documents and certifications. Even when the debtor is represented by an attorney, court approval may be required if it appears that the reaffirmation will result in undue hardship to the debtor.

When court approval is required, a separate hearing will take place. The court will approve the reaffirmation only if it finds that the agreement will not result in undue hardship to the debtor and that the reaffirmation is consistent with the debtor's best interests.

REQUIRED DISCLOSURES To discourage creditors from engaging in abusive reaffirmation practices, the law provides specific language for disclosures that must be given to debtors entering into reaffirmation agreements. Among other things, these disclosures explain that the debtor is not required to reaffirm any debt. They also inform the debtor that liens on secured property, such as mortgages and cars, will remain in effect even if the debt is not reaffirmed.

The reaffirmation agreement must disclose the amount of the debt reaffirmed, the rate of interest, the date payments begin, and the right to rescind. The disclosures also caution the debtor: "Only agree to reaffirm a debt if it is in your best interest. Be sure you can afford the payments you agree to make."

The original disclosure documents must be signed by the debtor, certified by the debtor's attorney, and filed with the court at the same time as the reaffirmation agreement. A reaffirmation agreement that is not accompanied by the original signed disclosures will not be effective.

SECTION 7

REORGANIZATIONS

The type of bankruptcy proceeding most commonly used by corporate debtors is the Chapter 11 *reorganization.* In a reorganization, the creditors and the debtor formulate a plan under which the debtor pays a portion of the debts and is discharged of the remainder. The debtor is allowed to continue in business. Although this type of bankruptcy is generally a corporate reorganization, any debtor (except a stockbroker or a commodities broker) who is eligible for Chapter 7 relief is eligible for relief under Chapter 11. Railroads are also eligible.

Congress has established a "fast-track" Chapter 11 procedure for small-business debtors whose liabilities do not exceed $2.49 million and who do not own or manage real estate. The fast track enables a debtor to avoid the appointment of a creditors' committee and also shortens the filing periods and relaxes certain other requirements. Because the process is shorter and simpler, it is less costly.

The same principles that govern the filing of a liquidation (Chapter 7) petition apply to reorganization (Chapter 11) proceedings. The case may be brought either voluntarily or involuntarily. The automatic-stay provisions and its exceptions (such as substantial abuse), as well as the adequate protection doctrine, apply in reorganizations.

Workouts

In some instances, to avoid bankruptcy proceedings, creditors may prefer private, negotiated adjustments of creditor-debtor relations, also known as **workouts.** Often, these out-of-court workouts are much more flexible and thus more conducive to a speedy settlement. Speed is critical because delay is one of the most costly elements in any bankruptcy proceeding. Another advantage of workouts is that they avoid the various administrative costs of bankruptcy proceedings.

Best Interests of the Creditors

Once a petition for Chapter 11 bankruptcy has been filed, a bankruptcy court, after notice and a hearing, can dismiss or suspend all proceedings at any time if dismissal or suspension would better serve the interests of the creditors. The Code also allows a court, after notice and a hearing, to dismiss a case under reorganization "for cause" when there is no reasonable likelihood of rehabilitation. Similarly, a court can dismiss when there is an inability to effect a plan or an unreasonable delay by the debtor that may harm the interests of creditors. A debtor whose petition is dismissed for these reasons can file a subsequent Chapter 11 petition in the future, however.

Debtor in Possession

On entry of the order for relief, the debtor generally continues to operate the business as a **debtor in possession (DIP).** The court, however, may appoint a trustee (often referred to as a *receiver*) to operate the debtor's business if gross mismanagement of the business is shown or if appointing a trustee is in the best interests of the estate.

The DIP's role is similar to that of a trustee in a liquidation. The DIP is entitled to avoid preferential payments made to creditors and fraudulent transfers of assets. The DIP has the power to decide whether to cancel or assume obligations under prepetition executory contracts (those that are not yet performed) or unexpired leases. The DIP can also exercise a trustee's strong-arm powers.

Creditors' Committees

As soon as practicable after the entry of the order for relief, a creditors' committee of unsecured creditors is appointed.[20] This committee is often composed of the biggest suppliers to the business. The committee may consult with the trustee or the DIP concerning the administration of the case or the formulation of the plan. Additional creditors' committees may be appointed to represent special interest creditors.

Generally, no orders affecting the estate will be entered without the consent of the committee or after a hearing in which the judge is informed of the committee's position. As mentioned earlier, businesses with debts of less than $2.49 million that do not own or manage real estate can avoid creditors' committees. In these cases, orders can be entered without a committee's consent.

The Reorganization Plan

A reorganization plan to rehabilitate the debtor is a plan to conserve and administer the debtor's assets in the hope of an eventual return to successful operation and solvency. The plan must be fair and equitable and must do the following:

1. Designate classes of claims and interests.
2. Specify the treatment to be afforded to the classes of creditors. (The plan must provide the same treatment for all claims in a particular class.)
3. Provide an adequate means for the plan's execution. (Individual debtors are required to utilize postpetition assets as necessary to execute the plan.)
4. Provide for payment of tax claims over a five-year period.

FILING THE PLAN Only the debtor may file a plan within the first 120 days after the date of the order for relief. This period may be extended, but not beyond eighteen months from the date of the order for relief. If the debtor does not meet the 120-day deadline or obtain an extension, and if the debtor fails to procure the required creditor consent (discussed next) within 180 days, any party may propose a plan. If a small-business debtor chooses to avoid a creditors' committee, the time for the debtor's filing is 180 days.

ACCEPTANCE OF THE PLAN Once the plan has been developed, it is submitted to each class of creditors for acceptance. For the plan to be adopted, each class must accept it. A class has accepted the plan when a majority of the creditors, representing two-thirds of the amount of the total claim, vote to approve it.

The plan need not provide for full repayment to unsecured creditors. Instead, creditors receive a percentage of each dollar owed to them by the debtor.

CONFIRMATION OF THE PLAN Confirmation is conditioned on the debtor's certifying that all postpetition domestic-support obligations have been paid in full. Even when all classes of creditors accept the plan, the court may refuse to confirm it if it is not "in the best interests of the creditors." For small-business debtors, if the plan meets the listed requirements, the court must confirm the plan within forty-five days (unless this period is extended).

The plan can be modified on the request of the debtor, the DIP, the trustee, the U.S. trustee, or a holder of an unsecured claim. If an unsecured creditor objects to the plan, specific rules apply to the value of property to be distributed under the plan. Tax claims must be paid over a five-year period.

Even if only one class of creditors has accepted the plan, the court may still confirm the plan under the Code's so-called **cram-down provision.** In other words, the court may confirm the plan over the objections of a class of creditors. Before the court can exercise this right of cram-down confirmation,

20. If the debtor has filed a reorganization plan accepted by the creditors, the trustee may decide not to call a meeting of the creditors.

it must be demonstrated that the plan does not discriminate unfairly against any creditors and is fair and equitable.

DISCHARGE The plan is binding on confirmation. Nevertheless, the law provides that confirmation of a plan does not discharge an individual debtor. *For individual debtors, the plan must be completed before discharge will be granted,* unless the court orders otherwise. For all other debtors, the court may order discharge at any time after the plan is confirmed.

The debtor is given a reorganization discharge from all claims not protected under the plan. This discharge does not apply to any claims that would be denied discharge under liquidation.

SECTION 8

BANKRUPTCY RELIEF UNDER CHAPTER 13 AND CHAPTER 12

In addition to bankruptcy relief through liquidation and reorganization, the Code also provides for individuals' repayment plans (Chapter 13) and family-farmer and family-fisherman debt adjustments (Chapter 12).

Individuals' Repayment Plans

Chapter 13 of the Bankruptcy Code provides for "Adjustment of Debts of an Individual with Regular Income." Individuals (not partnerships or corporations) with regular income who owe fixed (liquidated) unsecured debts of less than $383,175 or fixed secured debts of less than $1,149,525 may take advantage of bankruptcy repayment plans.

Among those eligible are salaried employees and sole proprietors, as well as individuals who live on welfare, Social Security, fixed pensions, or investment income. Many small-business debtors have a choice of filing under either Chapter 11 or Chapter 13. Repayment plans offer some advantages because they are less expensive and less complicated than reorganization or liquidation proceedings.

FILING THE PETITION A Chapter 13 repayment plan case can be initiated only by the debtor's filing of a voluntary petition or by court conversion of a Chapter 7 petition (because of a finding of substantial abuse under the means test, for instance). Certain liquidation and reorganization cases may be converted to repayment plan cases with the consent of the debtor.[21]

A trustee, who will make payments under the plan, must be appointed. On the filing of a repayment plan petition, the automatic stay previously discussed takes effect. Although the stay applies to all or part of the debtor's consumer debt, it does not apply to any business debt incurred by the debtor or to any domestic-support obligations.

GOOD FAITH REQUIREMENT The Bankruptcy Code imposes the requirement of good faith on a debtor at both the time of the filing of the petition and the time of the filing of the plan. The Code does not define good faith, but if the circumstances on the whole indicate bad faith, a court can dismiss a debtor's Chapter 13 petition.

▶ **Case in Point 16.14** Roger and Pauline Buis formed an air show business, Otto Airshows, that included a helicopter decorated as "Otto the Clown." After a competitor won a defamation lawsuit against the Buises and Otto Airshows, the Buises stopped doing business as Otto Airshows.

The Buises formed a new firm, Prop and Rotor Aviation, Inc., and leased the Otto equipment to it. Within a month, they filed a bankruptcy petition under Chapter 13. The plan and the schedules failed to mention the lawsuit, the equipment lease, and several other items. The court therefore dismissed the Buises' petition due to bad faith. The debtors had not included all of their assets and liabilities on their initial petition, and they had timed its filing to avoid payment on the defamation judgment.[22] ◀

In determining whether a Chapter 13 plan was proposed in good faith, should the bankruptcy court consider whether the debtor included his Social Security income in the amount of disposable income available for payment of unsecured creditors? That was the issue in the following case.

21. A Chapter 13 repayment plan may be converted to a Chapter 7 liquidation at the request of the debtor or, under certain circumstances, by a creditor "for cause." A Chapter 13 case may be converted to a Chapter 11 case after a hearing.

22. *In re Buis,* 337 Bankr. 243 (N.D.Fla. 2006).

CASE ANALYSIS

Case 16.3 In re Welsh

United States Court of Appeals, Ninth Circuit, 711 F.3d 1120 (2013).

IN THE LANGUAGE OF THE COURT

RIPPLE, Senior Circuit Judge:

* * * *

[David and Sharon Welsh] filed a voluntary Chapter 13 petition [in a federal bankruptcy court]. Their required schedules revealed the following assets: a home in Missoula, Montana, valued at $400,000, encumbered by a secured claim of $330,593.66; a Ford F-250 valued at $10,000, encumbered by a secured claim of $18,959; a 2006 Subaru Outback valued at of $9,500, encumbered by a secured claim of $12,211; a 2005 Toyota Matrix valued at $2,200, encumbered by a secured claim of $1,996; a 2005 Airstream trailer valued at $23,000, encumbered by a secured claim of $39,000; and two 2007 Honda ATVs each valued at $2,700, encumbered by secured claims of $3,065 and $4,500. In addition to their secured debts, the schedules revealed unsecured claims totaling approximately $180,500, the largest of which were their daughter's student loan debt in the amount of $60,000 and a joint debt owed to Bank of America on a line of credit in the amount of $50,000.

Mrs. Welsh is employed as a nurse and reported on Schedule I a monthly income of $6,975.40. She also draws a pension of $1,100 per month. Mr. Welsh is retired, but listed a monthly income of $358.03 from wages, salary and commissions, as well as Social Security income in the amount of $1,165.

Because their income exceeds the median for the state of Montana, the debtors calculated their disposable income according to the means test. * * * They listed their current monthly income as $8,116.31; their current monthly income did not include Mr. Welsh's Social Security income of $1,165 because Social Security income is excluded from the current monthly income calculation. After deducting future payments on secured claims, the debtors were left with a disposable income of $218.12 per month.

The Welshes proposed a plan that provided for payments of $125 per month to unsecured creditors for the first thirty months of the plan. After their vehicle loans were paid, the payments would increase to $500 per month for the last thirty months of the plan. The proposed plan would pay off approximately $14,700 of the debtors' $180,500 unsecured debt.

The [Bankruptcy] Trustee objected on the ground that the debtors had not proposed their plan in good faith * * * because [they failed] to commit one hundred percent of their disposable income to the plan.

* * * *

The bankruptcy court * * * rejected the Trustee's argument.

[On the Trustee's appeal] the [Bankruptcy Appellate Panel (BAP) for the Ninth Circuit] affirmed the bankruptcy court's judgment.

* * * *

In this appeal, the Trustee * * * maintains that, in determining whether the Welshes proposed their Chapter 13 plan in good faith, the bankruptcy court * * * should have considered Mr. Welsh's Social Security income.

* * * *

In 2005, Congress * * * enacted the Bankruptcy Abuse Prevention and Consumer Protection Act ("BAPCPA"). The good faith requirement * * * remained the same, but there were significant changes with respect to the calculation of disposable income. Before the BAPCPA, bankruptcy judges had authority to determine a debtor's ability to pay based on the individual circumstances of each case and each debtor. Congress replaced this discretion with a detailed, mechanical means test, which requires debtors with above-median income to calculate their "disposable income" by subtracting specific expenses from "current monthly income," as defined by the Bankruptcy Code. For our purposes, several elements of this calculation are important. *The debtor begins with his "current monthly income," which, by definition, explicitly "excludes benefits received under the Social Security Act."* The debtor then subtracts living expenses based on the Internal Revenue Service's "Collection Financial Standards," a detailed series of averages for living expenses that the Service uses to calculate necessary expenditures for delinquent taxpayers. The debtor also subtracts his averaged payments to secured creditors due during the following sixty months. [Emphasis added.]

As is the case here, the manner in which the means test calculates "disposable income" may underestimate the amount of actual funds that a taxpayer has available to pay unsecured creditors. A debtor who receives Social Security income * * * does not have to account for that income when calculating "disposable income" according to the means test. * * * The result may be that * * * little "disposable income," as that figure is calculated, remains to pay unsecured creditors.

* * * *

Here, the Trustee does not contend, of course, that the calculation

CASE 16.3 CONTINUES ➧

CASE 16.3 CONTINUED

of disposable income should have incorporated Social Security income; the statutory language is clearly to the contrary. Instead, he concedes that disposable income was calculated correctly under the BAPCPA, but nevertheless maintains that the Welshes' failure to dedicate Mr. Welsh's Social Security income to the payment of unsecured creditors requires a conclusion that the plan was not proposed in good faith * * * . We cannot conclude, however, that a plan prepared completely in accordance with the very detailed calculations that Congress set forth is not proposed in good faith. To hold otherwise would be to allow the bankruptcy court to substitute its judgment of how much and what kind of income should be dedicated to the payment of unsecured creditors for the judgment of Congress. Such an approach would not only flout the express language of Congress, but also one of Congress's purposes in enacting the BAPCPA, namely to reduce the amount of discretion that bankruptcy courts previously had over the calculation of an above-median debtor's income and expenses.

* * * *

We conclude that Congress's adoption of the BAPCPA forecloses a court's consideration of a debtor's Social Security income * * * as part of the inquiry into good faith * * * . We therefore affirm the judgment of the BAP.

LEGAL REASONING QUESTIONS

1. What Bankruptcy Code requirements were at the center of this case?
2. On what ground did the trustee contend that the debtors had not proposed their Chapter 13 plan in good faith?
3. How did the court rule with respect to the trustee's argument? Why?
4. In evaluating a debtor's petition, what factors should be part of a good faith analysis? Should consideration of the calculation of disposable income play a role? Why or why not?

THE REPAYMENT PLAN A plan of rehabilitation by repayment must provide for the following:

1. The turning over to the trustee of such future earnings or income of the debtor as is necessary for execution of the plan.
2. Full payment through deferred cash payments of all claims entitled to priority, such as taxes.[23]
3. Identical treatment of all claims within a particular class. (The Code permits the debtor to list co-debtors, such as guarantors or sureties, as a separate class.)

The repayment plan may provide either for payment of all obligations in full or for payment of a lesser amount. The debtor must begin making payments under the proposed plan within thirty days after the plan has been filed and must continue to make "timely" payments from her or his disposable income. If the debtor fails to make timely payments or to commence payments within the thirty-day period, the court can convert the case to a liquidation (Chapter 7) bankruptcy or dismiss the petition.

Length of the Plan. The length of the payment plan can be three or five years, depending on the debtor's family income. If the debtor's family income is greater than the median family income in the relevant geographic area under the means test, the term of the proposed plan must be for five years.[24] The term may not exceed five years.

Confirmation of the Plan. After the plan is filed, the court holds a confirmation hearing, at which interested parties (such as creditors) may object to the plan. The hearing must be held at least twenty days, but no more than forty-five days, after the meeting of the creditors. The debtor must have filed all prepetition tax returns and paid all postpetition domestic-support obligations before a court will confirm any plan.

The court will confirm a plan with respect to each claim of a secured creditor under any of the following circumstances:

1. If the secured creditors have accepted the plan.

23. As with a Chapter 11 reorganization plan, full repayment of all claims is not always required.

24. See 11 U.S.C. Section 1322(d) for details on when the court will find that the Chapter 13 plan should extend to a five-year period.

2. If the plan provides that secured creditors retain their liens until there is payment in full or until the debtor receives a discharge.
3. If the debtor surrenders the property securing the claims to the creditors.

In addition, for a motor vehicle purchased within 910 days before the petition is filed, the plan must provide that a creditor who extended credit for part or all of the purchase price retains its lien until the entire debt is paid.

DISCHARGE After the debtor has completed all payments, the court grants a discharge of all debts provided for by the repayment plan. Generally, all debts are dischargeable except the following:

1. Allowed claims not provided for by the plan.
2. Certain long-term debts provided for by the plan.
3. Certain tax claims and payments on retirement accounts.
4. Claims for domestic-support obligations.
5. Debts related to injury or property damage caused while driving under the influence of alcohol or drugs.

Family Farmers and Fishermen

To help relieve economic pressure on small farmers, Congress created Chapter 12 of the Bankruptcy Code. In 2005, Congress extended this protection to family fishermen, modified its provisions somewhat, and made it a permanent chapter in the Bankruptcy Code (previously, the statutes authorizing Chapter 12 had to be periodically renewed by Congress).

DEFINITIONS For purposes of Chapter 12, a *family farmer* is one whose gross income is at least 50 percent farm dependent and whose debts are at least 50 percent farm related. The total debt for a family farmer must not exceed $4,031,575. A partnership or close corporation (see Chapter 19) at least 50 percent owned by the farm family can also qualify as a family farmer.[25]

A *family fisherman* is defined as one whose gross income is at least 50 percent dependent on commercial fishing operations[26] and whose debts are at least 80 percent related to commercial fishing. The total debt for a family fisherman must not exceed $1,868,200. As with family farmers, a partnership or closely held corporation can also qualify.

FILING THE PETITION The procedure for filing a family-farmer or family-fisherman bankruptcy plan is very similar to the procedure for filing a repayment plan under Chapter 13. The debtor must file a plan not later than ninety days after the order for relief. The filing of the petition acts as an automatic stay against creditors' and co-obligors' actions against the estate.

A farmer or fisherman who has already filed a reorganization or repayment plan may convert it to a Chapter 12 plan. The debtor may also convert a Chapter 12 plan to a liquidation plan.

CONTENT AND CONFIRMATION OF THE PLAN The content of a plan under Chapter 12 is basically the same as that of a Chapter 13 repayment plan. Generally, the plan must be confirmed or denied within forty-five days of filing.

Court confirmation of the plan is the same as for a repayment plan. The plan must provide for payment of secured debts at the value of the collateral. If the secured debt exceeds the value of the collateral, the remaining debt is unsecured.

For unsecured debtors, the plan must be confirmed if either (1) the value of the property to be distributed under the plan equals the amount of the claim or (2) the plan provides that all of the debtor's disposable income to be received in a three-year period (or longer, by court approval) will be applied to making payments. Disposable income is all income received less amounts needed to support the farmer or fisherman and his or her family and to continue the farming or commercial fishing operation. Completion of payments under the plan discharges all debts provided for by the plan.

See *Concept Summary 16.2* on the following page for a comparison of bankruptcy procedures under Chapters 7, 11, 12, and 13.

25. Note that for a corporation or partnership to qualify under Chapter 12, at least 80 percent of the value of the firm's assets must consist of assets related to the farming operation.

26. Commercial fishing operations include catching, harvesting, or raising fish, shrimp, lobsters, urchins, seaweed, shellfish, or other aquatic species or products.

CONCEPT SUMMARY 16.2

Forms of Bankruptcy Relief Compared

ISSUE	CHAPTER 7	CHAPTER 11	CHAPTERS 12 AND 13
Purpose	Liquidation.	Reorganization.	Adjustment.
Who Can Petition	Debtor (voluntary) or creditors (involuntary).	Debtor (voluntary) or creditors (involuntary).	Debtor (voluntary) only.
Who Can Be a Debtor	Any "person" (including partnerships, corporations, and municipalities) except railroads, insurance companies, banks, savings and loan institutions, investment companies licensed by the Small Business Administration, and credit unions. Farmers and charitable institutions cannot be involuntarily petitioned. If the court finds the petition to be a substantial abuse of the use of Chapter 7, the debtor may be required to convert to a Chapter 13 repayment plan.	Any debtor eligible for Chapter 7 relief. Railroads are also eligible. Individuals have specific rules and limitations.	*Chapter 12*—Any family farmer (one whose gross income is at least 50 percent farm dependent and whose debts are at least 50 percent farm related) or family fisherman (one whose gross income is at least 50 percent dependent on commercial fishing operations and whose debts are at least 80 percent related to commercial fishing) or any partnership or close corporation at least 50 percent owned by a family farmer or fisherman, when total debt does not exceed a specified amount ($4,031,575 for farmers and $1,868,200 for fishermen). *Chapter 13*—Any individual (not partnerships or corporations) with regular income who owes fixed (liquidated) unsecured debts of less than $383,175 or fixed secured debts of less than $1,149,525.
Procedure Leading to Discharge	Nonexempt property is sold, and the proceeds are distributed (in order) to priority groups. Dischargeable debts are terminated.	Plan is submitted. If the plan is approved and followed, debts are discharged.	Plan is submitted and must be approved if the value of the property to be distributed equals the amount of the claims or if the debtor turns over disposable income for a three-year or five-year period. If the plan is followed, debts are discharged.
Advantages	On liquidation and distribution, most debts are discharged, and the debtor has an opportunity for a fresh start.	Debtor continues in business. Creditors can either accept the plan, or it can be "crammed down" on them. The plan allows for the reorganization and liquidation of debts over the plan period.	Debtor continues in business or possession of assets. If the plan is approved, most debts are discharged after the plan period.

Reviewing: Creditor-Debtor Relations and Bankruptcy

Three months ago, Janet Hart's husband of twenty years died of cancer. Although he had medical insurance, he left Janet with outstanding medical bills of more than $50,000. Janet has worked at the local library for the past ten years, earning $1,500 per month. Since her husband's death, Janet also receives $1,500 in Social Security benefits and $1,100 in life insurance proceeds every month, for a total monthly income of $4,300. After she pays the mortgage payment of $1,500 and the amounts due on other debts, Janet has barely enough left to buy groceries for her family (she has two teenage daughters at home). She decides to file for Chapter 7 bankruptcy, hoping for a fresh start. Using the information presented in the chapter, answer the following questions.

1. What must Janet do *before* filing a petition for relief under Chapter 7?
2. How much time does Janet have after filing the bankruptcy petition to submit the required schedules? What happens if Janet does not meet the deadline?
3. Assume that Janet files a petition under Chapter 7. Further assume that the median family income in the geographic area in which Janet lives is $49,300. What steps would a court take to determine whether Janet's petition is presumed to be "substantial abuse" using the means test?
4. Suppose that the court determines that no *presumption* of substantial abuse applies in Janet's case. Nevertheless, the court finds that Janet does have the ability to pay at least a portion of the medical bills out of her disposable income. What would the court likely order in that situation?

DEBATE THIS . . . *Rather than being allowed to file Chapter 7 bankruptcy petitions, individuals and couples should always be forced to make an effort to pay off their debts through Chapter 13.*

Terms and Concepts

ExamPrep

Issue Spotters

1. Jorge contracts with Larry of Midwest Roofing to fix Jorge's roof. Jorge pays half of the contract price in advance. Larry and Midwest complete the job, but Jorge refuses to pay the rest of the price. What can Larry and Midwest do? **(See page 358.)**

2. After graduating from college, Tina works briefly as a salesperson before filing for bankruptcy. Tina's petition states that her only debts are student loans, taxes accruing within the last year, and a claim against her based on her misuse of customers' funds during her employment. Are these debts dischargeable in bankruptcy? Explain. **(See page 376.)**

- **Check your answers to the Issue Spotters against the answers provided in Appendix E at the end of this text.**

Before the Test

Go to **www.cengagebrain.com**, enter the ISBN 9781285428949, and click on "Find" to locate this textbook's Web site. Then, click on "Access Now" under "Study Tools," and select Chapter 16 at the top. There, you will find an Interactive Quiz that you can take to assess your mastery of the concepts in this chapter, as well as Flashcards and a Glossary of important terms.

Business Scenarios

16–1. Liens. Nabil is the owner of a relatively old home valued at $105,000. The home's electrical system is failing and the wiring needs to be replaced. He contracts with Kandhari Electrical to replace the electrical system. Kandhari performs the repairs, and on June 1 submits a bill of $10,000 to Nabil. Because of financial difficulties, Nabil does not pay the bill. Nabil's only asset is his home, but his state's homestead exemption is $60,000. Discuss fully Kandhari's remedies in this situation. **(See page 358.)**

16–2. Voluntary versus Involuntary Bankruptcy. Burke has been a rancher all her life, raising cattle and crops. Her ranch is valued at $500,000, almost all of which is exempt under state law. Burke has eight creditors and a total indebtedness of $70,000. Two of her largest creditors are Oman ($30,000 owed) and Sneed ($25,000 owed). The other six creditors have claims of less than $5,000 each. A drought has ruined all of Burke's crops and forced her to sell many of her cattle at a loss. She cannot pay off her creditors. **(See page 370.)**

(a) Under the Bankruptcy Code, can Burke, with a $500,000 ranch, voluntarily petition herself into bankruptcy? Explain.

(b) Could either Oman or Sneed force Burke into involuntary bankruptcy? Explain.

Business Case Problems

16–3. Guaranty. Majestic Group Korea, Ltd., borrowed $1.5 million from Overseas Private Investment Corp. (OPIC) to finance a Ruby Tuesday's restaurant. Nam Koo Kim, the sole owner of Majestic, and his spouse, Hee Sun Kim, signed personal guaranties for full payment of the loan. Majestic defaulted. OPIC filed a suit against the Kims to recover. Hee claimed that she did not understand the extent of her liability when she signed the guaranty. Was Hee liable for the debt? Explain. [*Overseas Private Investment Corp. v. Kim,* 69 A.D.3d 1185, 895 N.Y.S.2d 217 (2010)] **(See page 364.)**

16–4. Foreclosure on Mortgages and Liens. LaSalle Bank loaned $8 million to Cypress Creek 1, LP, to build an apartment complex. The loan was secured by a mortgage. Cypress Creek hired contractors to provide concrete work, plumbing, carpentry, and other construction services. Cypress Creek went bankrupt, owing LaSalle $3 million. The contractors recorded mechanic's liens when they did not get paid for their work. The property was sold to LaSalle at a sheriff's sale for $1.3 million. The contractors claimed that they should be paid the amounts they were owed out of the $1.3 million and that the mechanic's liens should be satisfied before any funds were distributed to LaSalle for its mortgage. The trial court distributed the $1.3 million primarily to LaSalle, with only a small fraction going to the contractors. Do the liens come before the mortgage in priority of payment? Discuss. [*LaSalle Bank National Association v. Cypress Creek 1, LP,* 242 Ill.2d 231, 950 N.E.2d 1109 (2011)] **(See page 361.)**

16–5. Discharge in Bankruptcy. Monica Sexton filed a petition for Chapter 13 reorganization. One of her creditors was Friedman's Jewelers. Her petition misclassified Friedman's claim as $800 of unsecured debt. Within days, Friedman's filed proof of a secured claim for $300 and an unsecured claim for $462. Eventually, Friedman's was sent payments of about $300 by check. None of the checks were cashed. By then, Friedman's had filed its own petition under Chapter 11, Bankruptcy Receivables Management (BRM) had bought Friedman's unpaid accounts, and the checks had not been forwarded. Sexton received a discharge on the completion of her plan. BRM was not notified. BRM wrote to Sexton's attorney to ask about the status of her case, but received no response. BRM demanded that Sexton surrender the collateral on its claim. Sexton asked the court to impose sanctions on BRM for violating the discharge order. Was Sexton's debt to Friedman's dischargeable? Should BRM be sanctioned? Discuss. [*In re Sexton,* __ Bankr. __ (E.D.N.C. 2011)] **(See page 377.)**

16–6. BUSINESS CASE PROBLEM WITH SAMPLE ANSWER: Automatic Stay.

Michelle Gholston leased a Chevy Impala from EZ Auto Van Rentals. In November 2011, Gholston filed for bankruptcy. Around November 21, the bankruptcy court notified EZ Auto of Gholston's

*bankruptcy and the imposition of an automatic stay. Nevertheless, because Gholston had fallen behind on her payments, EZ Auto repossessed the vehicle on November 28. Gholston's attorney then reminded EZ Auto about the automatic stay, but the company failed to return the car. As a result of the car's repossession, Gholston suffered damages that included emotional distress, lost wages, attorneys' fees, and car rental expenses. Can Gholston recover from EZ Auto? Why or why not? [*In re Gholston, *___ Bankr. ___, 2012 WL 639288 (M.D.Fla. 2012)]* **(See page 372.)**

- **For a sample answer to Problem 16–6, go to Appendix F at the end of this text.**

16–7. Guaranty. Timothy Martinez, owner of Koenig & Vits, Inc. (K&V), guaranteed K&V's debt to Community Bank & Trust. The guaranty stated that the bank was not required to seek payment of the debt from any other source before enforcing the guaranty. K&V defaulted. Through a Wisconsin state court, the bank sought payment of $536,739.40, plus interest at the contract rate of 7.5 percent, from Martinez. Martinez argued that the bank could not enforce his guaranty while other funds were available to satisfy K&V's debt. For example, the debt might be paid out of the proceeds of a sale of corporate assets. Is this an effective defense to a guaranty? Why or why not? [*Community Bank & Trust v. Koenig & Vits, Inc.,* 346 Wis.2d 279 (Wis.App. 2013)] **(See page 364.)**

16–8. Discharge in Bankruptcy. Like many students, Barbara Hann financed her education partially through loans. These loans included three federally insured Stafford Loans of $7,500 each ($22,500 in total). Hann believed that she repaid the loans, but when later, she filed a Chapter 13 petition, Educational Credit Management Corp. (ECMC) filed an unsecured proof of claim based on the loans. Hann objected. At a hearing at which ECMC failed to appear, Hann submitted correspondence from the lender that indicated the loans had been paid. The court entered an order sustaining Hann's objection. Despite the order, can ECMC resume its effort to collect on Hann's loans? Explain. [*In re Hann,* 711 F.3d 235 (1st Cir. 2013)] **(See page 377.)**

16–9. A QUESTION OF ETHICS: Guaranty.

*73-75 Main Avenue, LLC, agreed to lease a portion of the commercial property at 73 Main Avenue, Norwalk, Connecticut, to PP Door Enterprise, Inc. Nan Zhang, as manager of PP Door, signed the lease agreement. The lessor required the principal officers of PP Door to execute personal guaranties. In addition, the principal officers agreed to provide the lessor with credit information. Apparently, both the lessor and the principals of PP Door signed the lease and guaranty agreements that were sent to PP Door's office. When PP Door failed to make monthly payments, 73-75 Main Avenue filed a suit against PP Door and its owner Li. At trial, Li testified that she was the sole owner of PP Door but denied that Zhang was its manager. She also denied signing the guaranty agreement. She claimed that she had signed the credit authorization form because Zhang had told her he was too young to have good credit. Li claimed to have no knowledge of the lease agreement. She did admit, however, that she had paid the rent. She claimed that Zhang had been in a car accident and had asked her to help pay his bills, including the rent at 73 Main Avenue. Li further testified that she did not see the name PP Door on the storefront of the leased location. [*73-75 Main Avenue, LLC v. PP Door Enterprise Inc., *120 Conn.App. 150, 991 A.2d 650 (2010)]* **(See page 364.)**

(a) Li argued that she was not liable on the lease agreement because Zhang was not authorized to bind her to the lease. Do the facts support Li? Why or why not?

(b) Li claimed that the guaranty for rent was not enforceable against her. Why might the court agree?

Legal Reasoning Group Activity

16–10. Discharge in Bankruptcy. Cathy Coleman took out loans to complete her college education. After graduation, Coleman was irregularly employed as a teacher before filing a petition in a federal bankruptcy court under Chapter 13. The court confirmed a five-year plan under which Coleman was required to commit all of her disposable income to paying the student loans. Less than a year later, when Coleman was laid off, she still owed more than $100,000 to Educational Credit Management Corp. Coleman asked the court to discharge the debt on the ground that it would be an undue hardship for her to pay it. **(See page 376.)**

(a) The first group will determine when a debtor normally is entitled to a discharge under Chapter 13.

(b) The second group will discuss whether student loans are dischargeable, and when "undue hardship" is a legitimate ground for an exception.

(c) The third group will outline the goals of bankruptcy law and make an argument, based on these facts and principles, in support of Coleman's request.

UNIT THREE Focus on Ethics

Ethics and the Commercial Environment

Many aspects of the commercial environment lend themselves to ethical analysis. Businesspersons certainly face ethical questions when they deal with the application of black-letter law to contracts. *(Black-letter law* is an informal term for the principles of law that courts usually accept or that are embodied in statutes.) Courts, for example, generally will not inquire into the adequacy of the consideration given in a contract. In other words, a court will not reevaluate a contract to determine whether what each party gave is equivalent to what that party received.

Ethical questions are also at the core of many principles of the law of sales. Many of the provisions of the Uniform Commercial Code (UCC), such as good faith and commercial reasonableness, though designed to meet the practical needs of business dealings, express ethical standards as well. Product liability also involves ethics. Many of the principles of product liability are based on principles designed to aid individuals injured, without extensive inquiry into issues of fault.

The areas of law covered in the previous unit constitute an important part of the legal environment of business. In each of these areas, new legal (and ethical) challenges have emerged as a result of developments in technology. In this *Focus on Ethics* feature, we look at the ethical dimensions of selected topics discussed in the preceding chapters, including some issues that are unique to the cyber age.

Freedom of Contract and Freedom from Contract

Suppose that your neighbor puts a "For sale" sign on her car and offers to sell it for $6,000. You learn that she is moving to another state and needs the extra cash to help finance the move. You know that she could easily get $10,000 for the car, and you consider purchasing it and then reselling it at a profit. But you also discover that your neighbor is completely unaware that she has priced the car significantly below its *Blue Book* value. Are you ethically obligated to tell her that she is essentially giving away $4,000 if she sells you the car for only $6,000?

This kind of situation, transplanted into the world of commercial transactions, raises an obvious question: At what point should the sophisticated businessperson cease looking after his or her own economic welfare and become "his or her brother's keeper," so to speak?

The answer to the question just raised is not simple. On the one hand, a common ethical assumption in our society is that individuals should be held responsible for the consequences of their own actions, including their contractual promises. This principle is expressed in the legal concept of freedom of contract. On the other hand, another common assumption in our society is that individuals should not harm one another by their actions. This is the basis of both tort law and criminal law.

In the area of contract law, ethical behavior often involves balancing these principles. In the above example, if you purchased the car and your neighbor later learned its true value and sued you for the difference, very likely no court of law would find that the contract should be rescinded. At times, however, courts will hold that the principle of freedom *of* contract should give way to the principle of freedom *from* contract, a doctrine based on the assumption that people should not be harmed by the actions of others. We look next at some examples of situations in which parties to contracts may be excused from performance under their contracts to prevent injustice.

Impossibility of Performance The doctrine of impossibility of performance is based to some extent on the ethical question of whether one party should suffer economic loss when it is impossible to perform a contract. The rule that one is "bound by his or her contracts" is not followed when performance becomes impossible.

The doctrine, however, is applied only when the parties themselves did not consciously assume the risk of the events that rendered performance impossible. Furthermore, this doctrine rests on the assumption that the party claiming the defense of impossibility has acted ethically.

A contract is discharged, for example, if it calls for the delivery of a particular car and, through no fault of either party, this car is stolen and completely demolished in an accident. Yet the doctrine would not excuse performance if the party who agreed to sell the car caused its destruction by her or his negligence.

Before the late nineteenth century, courts were reluctant to discharge a contract even when performance was literally impossible. Just as society's ethics changes with the passage of time, however, the law also changes to reflect society's new perceptions of ethical behavior.[1]

Today, courts are much more willing to discharge a contract when its performance has become literally impossible. Holding a party in breach of contract, when performance has become impossible through no fault of that party, no longer coincides with society's notions of fairness.

LEGAL REASONING

1. *Suppose that you contract to purchase steel at a fixed price per ton. Before the contract is performed, a lengthy steelworkers' strike causes the price of steel to triple from the price specified in the contract. If you demand that the supplier fulfill the contract, the supplier will go out of business. What are your ethical obligations in this situation? What are your legal rights?*

Unconscionability The doctrine of unconscionability is a good example of how the law attempts to enforce ethical behavior. Under this doctrine, a contract may be deemed to be so unfair to one party as to be unenforceable—even though that party voluntarily agreed to the contract's terms. Uncon-

1. A leading English case in which the court held that a defendant was discharged from the duty to perform due to impossibility of performance is *Taylor v. Caldwell,* 122 Eng.Rep. 309 (K.B. [King's Bench] 1863).

scionable action, like unethical action, defies precise definition. Information about the particular facts and specific circumstances surrounding the contract is essential. For example, a court might find that a contract made with a marginally literate consumer was unfair and unenforceable but might uphold the same contract made with a major business firm.

Section 2–302 of the Uniform Commercial Code (to be discussed in Chapter 11), incorporates the common law concept of unconscionability. Similarly, it does not define the concept with any precision. Rather, it leaves it to the courts to determine when a contract is so one sided and unfair to one party as to be unconscionable and thus unenforceable.

Usually, courts will do all that they can to save contracts rather than render them unenforceable. Only in extreme situations, as when a contract or clause is so one sided as to "shock the conscience" of the court, will a court hold a contract or contractual clause unconscionable.

Exculpatory Clauses In some situations, courts have also refused to enforce exculpatory clauses on the ground that they are unconscionable or contrary to public policy. An *exculpatory clause* attempts to excuse a party from liability in the event of monetary or physical injury, no matter who is at fault. In some situations, such clauses are upheld.

Nonessential Services. Generally, the law permits parties to assume, by express agreement, the risks inherent in certain nonessential activities. For example, a health club can require its members to sign a clause releasing the club from any liability for injuries the members might incur while using the club's equipment and facilities. Likewise, an exculpatory clause releasing a ski resort from liability for skiing accidents would likely be enforced.[2] In such situations, exculpatory clauses make it possible for a firm's owner to stay in business—by shifting some of the liability risks from the business to the customer.

Disparities in Bargaining Power. Nonetheless, some jurisdictions take a dubious view of exculpatory clauses, particularly when the agreement is between parties with unequal bargaining power, such as a landlord and a tenant or an employer and an employee. Frequently, courts will hold that an exculpatory clause that attempts to exempt an employer from *all* liability for negligence toward its employees is against public policy and thus void.[3]

The courts reason that disparity in bargaining power and economic necessity force the employee to accept the employer's terms. Also, if a plaintiff can prove that an exculpatory clause is ambiguous, the courts generally will not enforce the clause.[4]

2. *Myers v. Lutsen Mountains Corp.*, 587 F.3d 891 (8th Cir. 2009).
3. See, for example, *Wallace v. Busch Entertainment Corp., City of Santa Barbara v. Superior Court*, 62 Cal.Rptr.3d 527, 161 P.3d 1095 (2007).
4. See, for example, *Tatman v. Space Coast Kennel Club, Inc.*, 27 So.3d 108 (Fla.App. 5 Dist., 2010).

LEGAL REASONING

2. *In determining whether an exculpatory clause should be enforced, why does it matter whether the contract containing the clause involves essential services (such as transportation) or nonessential services (such as skiing or other leisure-time activities)?*

Covenants Not to Compete

In today's complicated, technological business world, knowledge learned on the job, including trade secrets, has become a valuable commodity. To prevent this knowledge from falling into the hands of competitors, more and more employers are requiring their employees to sign covenants not to compete. The increasing number of lawsuits over noncompete clauses in employment contracts has caused many courts to reconsider the reasonableness of these covenants.

Generally, the courts have few problems with enforcing a covenant not to compete that is ancillary to the sale of a business as long as the covenant's terms are reasonable. After all, part of what is being sold is the business's reputation and goodwill. If, after the sale, the seller opens a competing business nearby, the value of the original business to the purchaser could be greatly diminished.

More difficult for the courts is determining whether covenants not to compete in the employment context should be enforced. Often, this determination involves balancing the interests of the employer against the interests of the employee. Employers have a legitimate interest in protecting their trade secrets and customer lists. At the same time, employees should not be unreasonably restricted in their ability to work in their chosen profession or trade.

Jurisdictional Differences in Enforcement Jurisdictions vary in their approach to covenants not to compete. Many jurisdictions will enforce noncompete covenants in the employment context if both of the following are true.

1. The limitations placed on an employee are reasonable as to time and geographic area.
2. The limitations do not impose a greater restraint than necessary to protect the goodwill or other business interests of the employer.[5]

In a number of jurisdictions, if a court finds that a restraint in a noncompete covenant is not reasonable in light of the circumstances, it will reform the unreasonable provision and then enforce it. A court might, for instance, rewrite an unreasonable restriction by reducing the time period during which a former employee cannot compete

5. See *Drummond American, LLC v. Share Corp.*, 692 F.Supp.2d 650 (E.D.Tex., 2010); and *TEKsystems, Inc. v. Bolton*, 2010 WL 447782 (D.Md. 2010).

FOCUS ON ETHICS CONTINUES

from three years to one year. The court would then enforce the reformed agreement.[6]

Other jurisdictions are not so "employer friendly" and refuse to enforce unreasonable covenants. Under California law, covenants not to compete are illegal, as are a number of other types of agreements that have a similar effect.[7] Other western states also tend to regard noncompete covenants with suspicion. For example, courts in Washington State refuse to reform noncompete covenants that are unreasonable and lacking in consideration.[8] Courts in Arizona and Texas have reached similar conclusions.[9]

Do Noncompete Covenants Stifle Innovation? One of the reasons that the courts usually look closely at covenants not to compete and evaluate them on a case-by-case basis is the strong public policy favoring competition in this country. Some scholars claim that covenants not to compete, regardless of how reasonable they are, may stifle competition and innovation.

Consider, for example, the argument put forth some years ago by Ronald Gilson, a Stanford University professor of law and business. He contended that California's prohibition on covenants not to compete helped to explain why technological innovation and economic growth skyrocketed in California's Silicon Valley in the late 1990s, while technological development along Massachusetts's Route 128 languished during the same time period. According to Gilson, the different legal rules regarding covenants not to compete in California and Massachusetts were a "critical" factor in explaining why one area saw so much innovation and transfer of technology knowledge and the other area did not.[10]

LEGAL REASONING

3. *Employers often include covenants not to compete in employment contracts to protect their trade secrets. What effect, if any, will the growth in e-commerce have on the reasonableness of covenants not to compete?*

Do Gun Makers Have a Duty to Warn?

One of the big issues in today's legal environment is how tort law principles apply to harms (injury or death) caused by guns. Many negligence lawsuits have been filed across the nation against gun manufacturers. Plaintiffs often claim that gun makers have a duty to warn users of their products of the dangers associated with gun use. Would it be fair to impose such a requirement on gun manufacturers? Some say no, because such dangers are open and obvious. (Recall from Chapter 12 that, generally, there is no duty to warn of open and obvious dangers.) Others contend that warnings could prevent numerous gun accidents.

State courts addressing this issue have generally ruled that manufacturers have no duty to warn users of the obvious risks associated with gun use. For example, New York's highest court held that a gun manufacturer's duty of care does not extend to those who are injured by the illegal use of handguns.[11] Some courts, however, have held that gun makers whose marketing or sales practices cause a large influx of guns into the illegal secondary market could be liable under a public nuisance theory.[12] Other courts have allowed plaintiffs to sue for negligence when guns are sold to a straw purchaser (a person pretending to be a legitimate buyer) and then distributed to criminals.[13]

LEGAL REASONING

4. *In your opinion, should gun manufacturers have a duty to warn gun users of the dangers of using guns? Would such a warning be effective in preventing gun-related violence? Discuss.*

Trademark Protection versus Free Speech Rights

Another legal issue pits the rights of trademark owners against the right to free speech. The question is whether a company's ownership rights in a trademark used as a domain name outweigh the free speech rights of those who use a similar domain name to criticize or parody the company. A common tactic of those critical of a company's goods or services is to add the word *sucks* or *stinks* (or some other disparaging term) to the trademark owner's domain name.

A number of companies have sued the owners of such sites for trademark infringement in the hope that a court or an arbitrating panel will order the site owner to cease using the domain name. To date, though, companies have had little success pursuing this alternative. After all, one of the primary reasons trademarks are protected under U.S. law is to prevent customers from becoming confused about the origin of the

6. See, for example, *Estee Lauder Companies v. Batra,* 430 F.Supp.2d 158 (S.D.N.Y. 2006).
7. See, for example, *SriCom, Inc. v. Ebis Logic, Inc.,* 2012 WL 4051222 (N.D.Ca l. 2012); and *Thomas Weisel Partners, LLC v. BNP Paribas,* 2010 WL 1267744(N.D.Cal. 2010).]
8. See, for example, *International Paper Co. v. Stuit,* 2012 WL 187143 (W.D.Wash. 2012); and *EEOC v. Fry's Electronics, Inc.,* 2011 WL 666328 (W.D.Wash. 2011).
9. *Philipello v. Taylor,* 2012 WL 1435171 (Tex.App.—Waco 2012); and *Varsity Gold, Inc. v. Porzio,* 202 Ariz. 355, 45 P.3d 352 (2002).
10. Ronald J. Gilson, "The Legal Infrastructure of High Technology Industrial Districts: Silicon Valley, Route 128, and Covenants Not to Compete," *New York University Law Review* (June 1999): 575–579.
11. *Hamilton v. Beretta U.S.A. Corp.,* 96 N.Y.2d 222, 750 N.E.2d 1055, 727 N.Y.S.2d 7 (2001). See also, *Williams v. Beesmiller, Inc.,* 962 N.Y.S.2d 834, 103 A.D.3d 1191 (2013).
12. *City of New York v. Beretta U.S.A. Corp.,* 524 F.3d 384 (2d Cir. 2008); *Gilland v. Sportsmen's Outpost, Inc.,* 2011 WL 2479693 (Conn.Super. 2011); and *Illeto v. Glock, Inc.,* 349 F.3d 1191 (9th Cir. 2003).
13. *Williams v. Beemiller, Inc.,* 962 N.Y.S.2d 834, 103 A.D.3d 1191 (2013); and *Smith v. Atlantic Gun & Tackle, Inc.,* 376 F.Supp.2d 291 (E.D.N.Y. 2005).

goods for sale—and a "sucks" site certainly does not create such confusion.

Furthermore, U.S. courts and arbitrators give extensive protection to free speech rights, including the right to express opinions about companies and their products. Even international arbitration panels, when hearing disputes between U.S. parties, give significant weight to U.S. constitutional law protecting speech.[14]

Trade Secrets versus Free Speech Rights

Another ongoing issue with ethical dimensions involves the point at which free speech rights come into conflict with the right of copyright holders to protect their property by using encryption technology. This issue came before the California Supreme Court in the case of *DVD Copy Control Association v. Bunner.*[15]

Trade associations in the movie industry sued an Internet Web site operator who had posted the code of a computer program that cracked technology used to encrypt DVDs. This posed a significant threat to the movie industry because, by using the code-cracking software, users would be able to duplicate the copyrighted movies stored on the DVDs.

In their suit, the trade associations claimed that the Web site operator had misappropriated trade secrets. The defendant argued that software programs designed to break encryption programs were a form of constitutionally protected speech. When the case reached the California Supreme Court, the court held that although the First Amendment applies to computer code, computer code is not a form of "pure speech," and the courts can therefore protect it to a lesser extent. The court reinstated a trial court order that enjoined (prevented) the Web site operator from continuing to post the code.

14. See, for example, *Sutherland Institute v. Continuative, LLC, WIPO Arbitration and Mediation Center,* Case No. D2009-0893.
15. 31 Cal.4th 864, 4 Cal.Rptr.3d 69 (2003). See also *VI 4D, LLP v. Crucians in Focus, Inc.,* 2012 WL 6757243 (VI Super. 2012).

LEGAL REASONING

5. *Generally, do you believe that the law has struck a fair balance between the rights of intellectual property owners and the rights of the public? Why or why not?*

Ethics and Bankruptcy

As discussed in Chapter 16, the first goal of bankruptcy law is to provide relief and protection to debtors. Society generally has concluded that everyone should be given the chance to start over. But how far should society go in allowing debtors to avoid obligations that they voluntarily incurred?

Consider the concept of bankruptcy from the creditor's perspective. The creditor has transferred purchasing power from herself or himself to the debtor. That transfer of purchasing power represents a transfer of an asset for an asset. The debtor obtains the asset of funds, goods, or services, and the creditor obtains the asset of a *secured* or *unsecured* legal obligation to repay.

Once the debtor is in bankruptcy, voluntarily or involuntarily, the creditor's asset generally has a diminished value. Indeed, in many circumstances, that asset has no value. Yet the easier it becomes for debtors to discharge their debts under bankruptcy laws, the greater will be the incentive for debtors to use such laws to avoid paying amounts that are legally owed.

Clearly, bankruptcy law is a balancing act between providing a second chance for debtors and ensuring that creditors are given reasonable protection. Understandably, ethical issues arise in the process.

LEGAL REASONING

6. *Is it unethical to avoid paying one's debts by going into bankruptcy? Does a person have a moral responsibility to pay his or her debts? Discuss.*

Unit Four

The Business Environment

Contents

CHAPTER 17
SMALL BUSINESS ORGANIZATIONS

One of the goals of many business students is to become an **entrepreneur,** one who initiates and assumes the financial risk of a new business enterprise and undertakes to provide or control its management. One of the first decisions an entrepreneur must make is which form of business organization will be most appropriate for the new endeavor.

In selecting an organizational form, the entrepreneur will consider a number of factors, including (1) ease of creation, (2) the liability of the owners, (3) tax considerations, and (4) the ability to raise capital. Keep these factors in mind as you read this unit and learn about the various forms of business organization. You may find it helpful to refer to Exhibit 19–3 in Chapter 19, which compares the major business forms in use today. Remember, too, in considering these business forms that the primary motive of an entrepreneur is to make profits.

Traditionally, entrepreneurs have used three major business forms—the sole proprietorship, the partnership, and the corporation. In this chapter, we examine sole proprietorships and also look at franchises. Although the franchise is not strictly speaking a business organizational form, it is widely used today by entrepreneurs.

SECTION 1
SOLE PROPRIETORSHIPS

The simplest form of business is a **sole proprietorship.** In this form, the owner is the business. Thus, anyone who does business without creating a separate business organization has a sole proprietorship. More than two-thirds of all U.S. businesses are sole proprietorships. They are usually small enterprises—about 99 percent of the sole proprietorships in the United States have revenues of less than $1 million per year. Sole proprietors can own and manage any type of business from an informal, home-office or Web-based undertaking to a large restaurant or construction firm.

Advantages of the Sole Proprietorship

A major advantage of the sole proprietorship is that the proprietor owns the entire business and receives all of the profits (because she or he assumes all of the risk). In addition, starting a sole proprietorship is often easier and less costly than starting any other kind of business, as few legal formalities are required. Generally, no documents need to be filed with the government to start a sole proprietorship.[1]

FLEXIBILITY This form of business organization also offers more flexibility than does a partnership or a corporation. The sole proprietor is free to make any decision he or she wishes concerning the business—such as whom to hire, when to take a vacation, and what kind of business to pursue.

The sole proprietor can sell or transfer all or part of the business to another party at any time and does not need approval from anyone else. (In contrast, approval is typically required from partners in a partnership and from shareholders in a corporation.)

Sometimes, a sole proprietor can even benefit in a lawsuit from the fact that the business is indistinguishable from the owner. ▶ **Case in Point 17.1** James Ferguson operated "Jim's 11-E Auto Sales" as a sole proprietorship and obtained insurance from Consumers Insurance Company. The policy was issued to "Jim Ferguson, Jim's 11-E Auto Sales." Later,

1. Although starting a sole proprietorship involves fewer legal formalities than other business organizational forms, even a small sole proprietorship may need to comply with zoning requirements, obtain a state business license, and the like.

Ferguson bought a motorcycle in his own name, intending to repair and sell it through his dealership. One day when he was riding the motorcycle, he was struck by a car and seriously injured.

When Ferguson sued Consumers Insurance, the insurer argued that because Ferguson bought the motorcycle in his own name and was riding it at the time of the accident, it was his personal vehicle and was not covered under the dealership's policy. The court, however, held that the policy covered Ferguson's injuries. "Because the business is operated as a sole proprietorship, Jim Ferguson and 'Jim's 11-E Auto Sales' are one and the same."[2] ◀

TAXES A sole proprietor pays only personal income taxes (including Social Security and Medicare taxes—see Chapter 21) on the business's profits, which are reported as personal income on the proprietor's personal income tax return. Sole proprietors are also allowed to establish certain retirement accounts that are tax-exempt until the funds are withdrawn.

2. *Ferguson v. Jenkins*, 204 S.W.3d 779 (Tenn.App. 2006).

Disadvantages of the Sole Proprietorship

The major disadvantage of the sole proprietorship is that the proprietor alone bears the burden of any losses or liabilities incurred by the business enterprise. In other words, the sole proprietor has unlimited liability, or legal responsibility, for all obligations that arise in doing business. Any lawsuit against the business or its employees can lead to unlimited personal liability for the owner of a sole proprietorship.

The personal liability of the owner of a sole proprietorship was at issue in the following case.

CASE 17.1

Quality Car & Truck Leasing, Inc. v. Sark

Court of Appeals of Ohio, Fourth District, 2013 -Ohio- 44, 2013 WL 139359 (2013).

BACKGROUND AND FACTS Michael Sark operated a logging business as a sole proprietorship. To acquire equipment for the business, Sark and his wife, Paula, borrowed funds from Quality Car & Truck Leasing, Inc. When his business encountered financial difficulties, Sark became unable to pay his creditors, including Quality. The Sarks sold their house (valued at $203,500) to their son, Michael, Jr., for one dollar but continued to live in it. Three months later, Quality obtained a judgment in an Ohio state court against the Sarks for $150,481.85 and then filed a claim to set aside the transfer of the house to Michael, Jr., as a fraudulent conveyance. From a decision in Quality's favor, the Sarks appealed, arguing that they did not intend to defraud Quality and that they were not actually Quality's debtors.

IN THE LANGUAGE OF THE COURT
KLINE, J. [Judge]

* * * *

The trial court found that summary judgment was proper under [Ohio Revised Code (R.C.) Section] 1336.04(A)(2)(a). That statute provides as follows:

> A transfer made or an obligation incurred by a debtor is fraudulent as to a creditor, whether the claim of the creditor arose before or after the transfer was made or the obligation was incurred, if the debtor made the transfer or incurred the obligation * * * without receiving a reasonably equivalent value in exchange for the transfer or obligation, and * * * the debtor was engaged or was about to engage in a business or a transaction for which the remaining assets of the debtor were unreasonably small in relation to the business or transaction.

The trial court found "that Michael Senior and Paula made a transfer without the exchange of reasonably equivalent value and that the debtor was engaged or was about to engage in a business * * * transaction for which the remaining assets of the debtor were unreasonably small in relation to the business or transaction."

* * * The Sarks argue that summary judgment was not proper because there is a genuine issue of material fact regarding whether they intended to defraud Quality Leasing. The Sarks'

CASE 17.1 CONTINUES ➡

CASE 17.1 CONTINUED

argument fails because intent is not relevant to an analysis under R.C. Section 1336.04(A)(2)(a). *A creditor does not need to show that a transfer was made with intent to defraud in order to prevail under R.C. Section 1336.04(A)(2)(a). Thus, the Sarks cannot defeat summary judgment by showing that they did not act with fraudulent intent when Michael Senior and Paula transferred the Property to Michael Junior.* [Emphasis added.]

The Sarks also claim that summary judgment was improper because there is an issue of fact regarding whether Michael Senior and Paula are actually Quality Leasing's debtors. Michael Senior apparently returned the equipment that secured the debts owed to Quality Leasing. According to the Sarks, Quality Leasing's appraisals of the equipment showed that the value of the equipment would be enough to satisfy the debts.

The Sarks' argument, however, does not address the fact that they are clearly judgment debtors to Quality Leasing and that the judgment has not been satisfied. * * * The Sarks have not challenged the validity of the judgment against them nor have they shown that the judgment has been satisfied. Thus, there is no genuine issue of material fact regarding whether Paula and Michael Senior are debtors to Quality Leasing.

In conclusion, there is no genuine issue as to any material fact. Quality Leasing is entitled to judgment as a matter of law.

DECISION AND REMEDY *A state intermediate appellate court affirmed the lower court's judgment in Quality's favor. "Reasonable minds can come to only one conclusion, and that conclusion is adverse to the Sarks," said the court. The Sarks "are clearly judgment debtors to Quality Leasing and . . . the judgment has not been satisfied."*

THE ECONOMIC DIMENSION *What might the Sarks have done to avoid this dispute, as well as the loss of their home and their apparently declining business?*

THE ETHICAL DIMENSION *Why did the Sarks take the unethical step of fraudulently conveying their home to their son? What should they have done instead?*

PERSONAL ASSETS AT RISK Creditors can pursue the owner's personal assets to satisfy any business debts. Although sole proprietors may obtain insurance to protect the business, liability can easily exceed policy limits. This unlimited liability is a major factor to be considered in choosing a business form.

▶ **Example 17.2** Sheila Fowler operates a golf shop near a world-class golf course as a sole proprietorship. One of Fowler's employees fails to secure a display of golf clubs. They fall on Dean Maheesh, a professional golfer, and seriously injure him. If Maheesh sues Fowler's shop and wins, Fowler's personal liability could easily exceed the limits of her insurance policy. Fowler could lose not only her business, but also her house, car, and any other personal assets that can be attached to pay the judgment. ◀

LACK OF CONTINUITY The sole proprietorship also has the disadvantage of lacking continuity after the death of the proprietor. When the owner dies, so does the business—it is automatically dissolved. Another disadvantage is that in raising capital, the proprietor is limited to his or her personal funds and funds from any loans that he or she can obtain for the business.

SECTION 2

PARTNERSHIPS

A *partnership* arises from an agreement, express or implied, between two or more persons to carry on a business for a profit. Partners are co-owners of the business and have joint control over its operation and the right to share in its profits. Partnerships are governed both by common law concepts—in particular, those relating to agency—and by statutory law. As in so many other areas of business law, the National Conference of Commissioners on Uniform State Laws has drafted uniform laws for partnerships, and these have been widely adopted by the states.

Agency Concepts and Partnership Law

When two or more persons agree to do business as partners, they enter into a special relationship with one another. To an extent, their relationship is similar to an agency relationship because each partner is deemed to be the agent of the other partners and of the partnership. The agency concepts that you will read about in Chapter 20 thus apply—specifically, the imputation of knowledge of, and responsibility for, acts carried out within the scope of the partnership relationship. In their relationships with one another, partners, like agents, are bound by fiduciary ties.

In one important way, however, partnership law differs from agency law. The partners in a partnership agree to commit funds or other assets, labor, and skills to the business with the understanding that profits and losses will be shared. Thus, each partner has an *ownership interest* in the firm. In a nonpartnership agency relationship, the agent usually does not have an ownership interest in the business and is not obligated to bear a portion of ordinary business losses.

The Uniform Partnership Act

The Uniform Partnership Act (UPA) governs the operation of partnerships *in the absence of express agreement* and has done much to reduce controversies in the law relating to partnerships. A majority of the states have enacted the most recent version of the UPA (as amended in 1997) to provide limited liability for partners in a limited liability partnership.[3] We therefore base our discussion of the UPA in this chapter on the 1997 version of the act and refer to older versions of the UPA in footnotes when appropriate.

Definition of a Partnership

The UPA defines a **partnership** as "an association of two or more persons to carry on as co-owners a business for profit" [UPA 101(6)]. Note that the UPA's definition of *person* includes corporations, so a corporation can be a partner in a partnership [UPA 101(10)]. The *intent* to associate is a key element of a partnership, and one cannot join a partnership unless all other partners consent [UPA 401(i)].

Essential Elements of a Partnership

Conflicts sometimes arise over whether a business enterprise is a legal partnership, especially when there is no formal, written partnership agreement. To determine whether a partnership exists, courts usually look for the following three essential elements, which are implicit in the UPA's definition:

1. A sharing of profits or losses.
2. A joint ownership of the business.
3. An equal right to be involved in the management of the business.

If the evidence in a particular case is insufficient to establish all three factors, the UPA provides a set of guidelines to be used.

THE SHARING OF PROFITS AND LOSSES The sharing of both profits and losses from a business creates a presumption (legal inference) that a partnership exists. **▶ Example 17.3** Syd and Drake start a business that sells fruit smoothies near a college campus. They open a joint bank account from which they pay for supplies and expenses, and they share the proceeds (and losses) that the smoothie stand generates. If a conflict arises as to their business relationship, a court will assume that a partnership exists unless the parties prove otherwise. ◀

A court will not presume that a partnership exists, however, if shared profits were received as payment of any of the following [UPA 202(c)(3)]:

1. A debt by installments or interest on a loan.
2. Wages of an employee or for the services of an independent contractor.
3. Rent to a landlord.
4. An annuity to a surviving spouse or representative of a deceased partner.
5. A sale of the **goodwill** (the valuable reputation of a business viewed as an intangible asset) of a business or property.

▶ Example 17.4 Mason Snopel owes a creditor, Alice Burns, $5,000 on an unsecured debt. They agree that Mason will pay 10 percent of his monthly business profits to Alice until the loan with interest has been repaid. Although Mason and Alice are sharing profits from the business, they are not presumed to be partners. ◀

JOINT PROPERTY OWNERSHIP Joint ownership of property does not in and of itself create a partnership [UPA 202(c)(1) and (2)]. The parties' intentions are key. **▶ Example 17.5** Chiang and Burke jointly own farmland and lease it to a farmer for a share of the profits from the farming operation in lieu of fixed rental payments. This arrangement normally would not make Chiang, Burke, and the farmer partners. ◀

Entity versus Aggregate

At common law, a partnership was treated only as an aggregate of individuals and never as a separate legal entity. Thus, at common law a lawsuit could never be

3. At the time this book went to press, more than two-thirds of the states, as well as the District of Columbia, Puerto Rico, and the U.S. Virgin Islands, had adopted the UPA with the 1997 amendments.

brought by or against the firm in its own name. Each individual partner had to sue or be sued.

Today, in contrast, a majority of the states follow the UPA and treat a partnership as an entity for most purposes. For instance, a partnership usually can sue or be sued, collect judgments, and have all accounting performed in the name of the partnership entity [UPA 201, 307(a)].

As an entity, a partnership may hold the title to real or personal property in its name rather than in the names of the individual partners. Additionally, federal procedural laws permit the partnership to be treated as an entity in suits in federal courts and bankruptcy proceedings.

Tax Treatment of Partnerships

Modern law does treat a partnership as an aggregate of the individual partners rather than a separate legal entity in one situation—for federal income tax purposes. The partnership is a pass-through entity and not a taxpaying entity. A **pass-through entity** is a business entity that has no tax liability—the entity's income is passed through to the owners of the entity, who pay income taxes on it.

Thus, the income or losses the partnership incurs are "passed through" the entity framework and attributed to the partners on their individual tax returns. The partnership itself pays no taxes and is responsible only for filing an **information return** with the Internal Revenue Service.

A partner's profit from the partnership (whether distributed or not) is taxed as individual income to the individual partner. Similarly, partners can deduct a share of the partnership's losses on their individual tax returns (in proportion to their partnership interests).

Partnership Formation

As a general rule, agreements to form a partnership can be *oral, written,* or *implied by conduct.* Some partnership agreements, however, such as one authorizing partners to transfer interests in real property, must be in writing (or in an electronic record) to be legally enforceable (see Chapter 9).

A partnership agreement, also known as **articles of partnership,** can include almost any terms that the parties wish, unless they are illegal or contrary to public policy or statute [UPA 103]. The terms commonly included in a partnership agreement are listed in Exhibit 17–1 on the facing page.

The rights and duties of partners are governed largely by the specific terms of their partnership agreement. In the absence of provisions to the contrary in the partnership agreement, the law imposes certain rights and duties, as discussed in the following subsections. The character and nature of the partnership business generally influence the application of these rights and duties.

DURATION OF THE PARTNERSHIP The partnership agreement can specify the duration of the partnership by stating that it will continue until a designated date or until the completion of a particular project. This is called a *partnership for a term.* Generally, withdrawal from a partnership for a term prematurely (before the expiration date) constitutes a breach of the agreement, and the responsible partner can be held liable for any resulting losses [UPA 602(b)(2)]. If no fixed duration is specified, the partnership is a *partnership at will,* which means that the partnership can be dissolved at any time.

PARTNERSHIP BY ESTOPPEL Occasionally, persons who are not partners nevertheless hold themselves out as partners and make representations that third parties rely on in dealing with them.

Liability Imposed. When a third person has reasonably and detrimentally relied on the representation that a nonpartner was part of a partnership, a court may conclude that a **partnership by estoppel** exists and impose liability—but not partnership *rights*—on the alleged partner. Similarly, a partnership by estoppel may be imposed when a partner represents, expressly or impliedly, that a nonpartner is a member of the firm.

Nonpartner Agents. When a partnership by estoppel is deemed to exist, the nonpartner is regarded as an agent whose acts are binding on the partnership [UPA 308].

▶ **Case in Point 17.6** Jackson Paper Manufacturing Company makes paper that is used by Stonewall Packaging, LLC. Jackson and Stonewall have officers and directors in common, and they share employees, property, and equipment. In reliance on Jackson's business reputation, Best Cartage, Inc., agreed to provide transportation services for Stonewall and bought thirty-seven tractor-trailers to use in fulfilling the contract. Best provided the services until Stonewall terminated the agreement.

Best filed a suit for breach of contract against Stonewall and Jackson, seeking $500,678 in unpaid invoices and consequential damages of $1,315,336

EXHIBIT 17–1 Common Terms Included in a Partnership Agreement

Term	Description
Basic Structure	1. Name of the partnership. 2. Names of the partners. 3. Location of the business and the state law under which the partnership is organized. 4. Purpose of the partnership. 5. Duration of the partnership.
Capital Contributions	1. Amount of capital that each partner is contributing. 2. The agreed-on value of any real or personal property that is contributed instead of cash. 3. How losses and gains on contributed capital will be allocated, and whether contributions will earn interest.
Sharing of Profits and Losses	1. Percentage of the profits and losses of the business that each partner will receive. 2. When distributions of profit will be made and how net profit will be calculated.
Management and Control	1. How management responsibilities will be divided among the partners. 2. Name(s) of the managing partner or partners, and whether other partners have voting rights.
Accounting and Partnership Records	1. Name of the bank in which the partnership will maintain its business and checking accounts. 2. Statement that an accounting of partnership records will be maintained and that any partner or her or his agent can review these records at any time. 3. The dates of the partnership's fiscal year (if used) and when the annual audit of the books will take place.
Dissociation and Dissolution	1. Events that will cause the dissociation of a partner or dissolve the partnership, such as the retirement, death, or incapacity of any partner. 2. How partnership property will be valued and apportioned on dissociation and dissolution. 3. Whether an arbitrator will determine the value of partnership property on dissociation and dissolution and whether that determination will be binding.
Arbitration	1. Whether arbitration is required for any dispute relating to the partnership agreement.

for the tractor-trailers it had purchased. Best argued that Stonewall and Jackson had a partnership by estoppel. The court agreed, finding that "defendants combined labor, skills, and property to advance their alleged business partnership." Jackson had negotiated the agreement on Stonewall's behalf, and a news release stated that Jackson had sought tax incentives for Stonewall. Jackson also had bought real estate, equipment, and general supplies for Stonewall with no expectation of payment from Stonewall to Jackson. This was sufficient to prove a partnership by estoppel.[4] ◀

Rights of Partners

The rights of partners in a partnership relate to the following areas: management, interest in the partnership, compensation, inspection of books, accounting, and property.

4. *Best Cartage, Inc. v. Stonewall Packaging, LLC*, 727 S.E.2d 291 (N.C.App. 2012).

MANAGEMENT RIGHTS In a general partnership, all partners have equal rights in managing the partnership [UPA 401(f)]. Unless the partners agree otherwise, each partner has one vote in management matters *regardless of the proportional size of his or her interest in the firm.* In a large partnership, partners often agree to delegate daily management responsibilities to a management committee made up of one or more of the partners.

For Ordinary Decisions. The majority rule controls decisions on ordinary matters connected with partnership business, unless otherwise specified in the agreement. Decisions that significantly affect the nature of the partnership or that are outside the ordinary course of the partnership business, however, require the *unanimous* consent of the partners [UPA 301(2), 401(i), 401(j)].

When Unanimous Consent May Be Required. Unanimous consent is likely to be required for any decision to:

1. Alter the essential nature of the firm's business as expressed in the partnership agreement.

2. Change the capital structure of the partnership.
3. Amend the terms of the partnership agreement.
4. Admit a new partner.
5. Engage in a completely new business.
6. Assign partnership property to a trust for the benefit of creditors, or allow a creditor to enter a judgment against the partnership, for an agreed sum, without the use of legal proceedings.
7. Dispose of the partnership's *goodwill* (defined on page 397).
8. Submit partnership claims to arbitration.
9. Undertake any act that would make further conduct of the partnership business impossible.

INTEREST IN THE PARTNERSHIP Each partner is entitled to the proportion of business profits and losses that is specified in the partnership agreement. If the agreement does not apportion profits (indicate how the profits will be shared), the UPA provides that profits will be shared equally. If the agreement does not apportion losses, losses will be shared in the same ratio as profits [UPA 401(b)].

▶ **Example 17.7** Rimi and Brett form a partnership. The partnership agreement provides for capital contributions of $60,000 from Rimi and $40,000 from Brett, but it is silent as to how they will share profits or losses. In this situation, they will share both profits and losses equally. If their partnership agreement had provided that they would share profits in the same ratio as capital contributions, however, 60 percent of the profits would go to Rimi, and 40 percent would go to Brett. If the agreement was silent as to losses, losses would be shared in the same ratio as profits (60 percent and 40 percent, respectively). ◀

COMPENSATION Devoting time, skill, and energy to partnership business is a partner's duty and generally is not a compensable service. Rather, as mentioned, a partner's income from the partnership takes the form of a distribution of profits according to the partner's share in the business.

Partners can, of course, agree otherwise. For instance, the managing partner of a law firm often receives a salary—in addition to her or his share of profits—for performing special administrative or managerial duties.

INSPECTION OF THE BOOKS Partnership books and records must be kept accessible to all partners. Each partner has the right to receive (and the corresponding duty to produce) full and complete information concerning the conduct of all aspects of partnership business [UPA 403]. Each firm retains books for recording and securing such information. Partners contribute the information, and a bookkeeper typically has the duty to preserve it.

The partnership books must be kept at the firm's principal business office (unless the partners agree otherwise). Every partner is entitled to inspect all books and records on demand and can make copies of the materials. The personal representative of a deceased partner's estate has the same right of access to partnership books and records that the decedent would have had [UPA 403].

ACCOUNTING OF PARTNERSHIP ASSETS OR PROFITS An accounting of partnership assets or profits is required to determine the value of each partner's share in the partnership. An accounting can be performed voluntarily, or it can be compelled by court order. Under UPA 405(b), a partner has the right to bring an action for an accounting during the term of the partnership, as well as on the partnership's dissolution and winding up.

PROPERTY RIGHTS Property acquired *by* a partnership is the property of the partnership and not of the partners individually [UPA 203]. Partnership property includes all property that was originally contributed to the partnership and anything later purchased by the partnership or in the partnership's name (except in rare circumstances) [UPA 204].

A partner may use or possess partnership property only on behalf of the partnership [UPA 401(g)]. A partner is *not* a co-owner of partnership property and has no right to sell, mortgage, or transfer partnership property to another [UPA 501].[5]

In other words, partnership property is owned by the partnership as an entity and not by the individual partners. Thus, partnership property cannot be used to satisfy the personal debt of an individual partner. That partner's creditor, however, can petition a court for a **charging order** to attach the partner's *interest* in the partnership to satisfy the partner's obligation [UPA 502]. A partner's interest in the partnership includes her or his proportionate share of the profits and losses and the right to receive distributions. (A partner can also assign her or his right to a share of the partnership profits to another to satisfy a debt.)

---

5. Under the previous version of the UPA, partners were *tenants in partnership*. This meant that every partner was a co-owner with all other partners of the partnership property. The current UPA does not recognize this concept.

Duties and Liabilities of Partners

The duties and liabilities of partners are derived from agency law. Each partner is an agent of every other partner and acts as both a principal and an agent in any business transaction within the scope of the partnership agreement.

Each partner is also a general agent of the partnership in carrying out the usual business of the firm "or business of the kind carried on by the partnership" [UPA 301(1)]. Thus, every act of a partner concerning partnership business and "business of the kind" and every contract signed in the partnership's name bind the firm.

FIDUCIARY DUTIES The fiduciary duties that a partner owes to the partnership and to the other partners are the duty of care and the duty of loyalty [UPA 404(a)]. Under the UPA, a partner's *duty of care* is limited to refraining from "grossly negligent or reckless conduct, intentional misconduct, or a knowing violation of law" [UPA 404(c)].[6] A partner is not liable to the partnership for simple negligence or honest errors in judgment in conducting partnership business.

The *duty of loyalty* requires a partner to account to the partnership for "any property, profit, or benefit" derived by the partner in the conduct of the partnership's business or from the use of its property. A partner must also refrain from competing with the partnership in business or dealing with the firm as an adverse party [UPA 404(b)].

The duty of loyalty can be breached by self-dealing, misusing partnership property, disclosing trade secrets, or usurping a partnership business opportunity.

BREACH AND WAIVER OF FIDUCIARY DUTIES A partner's fiduciary duties may not be waived or eliminated in the partnership agreement. In fulfilling them, each partner must act consistently with the obligation of good faith and fair dealing [UPA 103(b), 404(d)]. The agreement can specify acts that the partners agree will violate a fiduciary duty.

Note that a partner may pursue his or her own interests without automatically violating these duties [UPA 404(e)]. The key is whether the partner has disclosed the interest to the other partners. ▶ **Example 17.8** Jayne Trell, a partner at Jacoby & Meyers, owns a shopping mall. Trell may vote against a partnership proposal to open a competing mall, provided that she has fully disclosed her interest in the existing shopping mall to the other partners at the firm. ◀ A partner cannot make secret profits or put self-interest before his or her duty to the interest of the partnership, however.

AUTHORITY OF PARTNERS The UPA affirms general principles of agency law that pertain to a partner's authority to bind a partnership in contract. A partner may also subject the partnership to tort liability under agency principles. When a partner is carrying on partnership business with third parties in the usual way, apparent authority exists, and both the partner and the firm share liability.

If a partner acts within the scope of her or his authority, the partnership is legally bound to honor the partner's commitments to third parties. The partnership will not be liable, however, if the third parties *know* that the partner has no such authority.

Limitations on Authority. A partnership may limit a partner's capacity to act as the firm's agent or transfer property on its behalf by filing a "statement of partnership authority" in a designated state office [UPA 105, 303]. Such limits on a partner's authority normally are effective only with respect to third parties who are notified of the limitation. (An exception is made in real estate transactions when the statement has been recorded with the appropriate state office—see Chapter 26.)

The Scope of Implied Powers. The agency concepts relating to apparent authority, actual authority, and ratification that will be discussed in Chapter 20 also apply to partnerships. The extent of *implied authority generally is broader for partners than for ordinary agents,* however.

In an ordinary partnership, the partners can exercise all implied powers reasonably necessary and customary to carry on that particular business. Some customarily implied powers include the authority to make warranties on goods in the sales business and the power to enter into contracts consistent with the firm's regular course of business.

▶ **Example 17.9** Jamie Schwab is a partner in a firm that operates a retail tire store. He regularly promises that "each tire will be warranted for normal wear for 40,000 miles." Because Schwab has authority to make warranties, the partnership is bound to honor the warranty. Schwab would not, however, have the authority to sell the partnership's office equipment or other property without the consent of all of the other partners. ◀

6. The previous version of the UPA touched only briefly on the duty of loyalty and left the details of the partners' fiduciary duties to be developed under the law of agency.

LIABILITY OF PARTNERS One significant disadvantage associated with a traditional partnership is that the partners are *personally* liable for the debts of the partnership. Moreover, in most states, the liability is essentially unlimited because the acts of one partner in the ordinary course of business subject the other partners to personal liability [UPA 305].

Joint Liability. At one time, each partner in a partnership generally was jointly liable for the partnership's obligations. **Joint liability** means that a third party must sue all of the partners as a group, but each partner can be held liable for the full amount.[7]

If, for instance, a third party sues one partner on a partnership contract, that partner has the right to demand that the other partners be sued with her or him. In fact, if the third party does not name all of the partners in the lawsuit, the assets of the partnership cannot be used to satisfy the judgment. With joint liability, the partnership's assets must be exhausted before creditors can reach the partners' individual assets.[8]

Joint and Several Liability. In the majority of the states, under UPA 306(a), partners are both jointly and severally (separately, or individually) liable for all partnership obligations, including contracts, torts, and breaches of trust. **Joint and several liability** means that a third party has the option of suing all of the partners together (jointly) or one or more of the partners separately (severally).

All partners in a partnership can be held liable even if a particular partner did not participate in, know about, or ratify the conduct that gave rise to the cause of action. Normally, though, the partnership's assets must be exhausted before a creditor can enforce a judgment against a partner's separate assets [UPA 307(d)].

A judgment against one partner severally (separately) does not extinguish the others' liability. (Similarly, a release of one partner does not discharge the partners' several liability.) Those not sued in the first action normally may be sued subsequently, unless the court in the first action held that the partnership was in no way liable. If a plaintiff is successful in a suit against a partner or partners, he or she may collect on the judgment only against the assets of those partners named as defendants.

7. Under the prior version of the UPA, which is still in effect in a few states, partners were subject to joint liability on partnership debts and contracts, but not on partnership debts arising from torts.

8. For a case applying joint liability to a partnership, see *Shar's Cars, LLC v. Elder*, 97 P.3d 724 (Utah App. 2004).

Indemnification. With joint and several liability, a partner who commits a tort can be required to indemnify (reimburse) the partnership for any damages it pays. Indemnification will typically be granted *unless* the tort was committed in the ordinary course of the partnership's business.

▶ **Case in Point 17.10** Nicole Moren was a partner in Jax Restaurant. After work one day, Moren was called back to the restaurant to help in the kitchen. She brought her two-year-old son, Remington, and placed him on the kitchen counter. While she was making pizzas, Remington reached into the dough press. His hand was crushed, causing permanent injuries. Through his father, Remington filed a suit against the partnership for negligence.

The partnership filed a complaint against Moren, arguing that it was entitled to indemnification from her for her negligence. The court held in favor of Moren and ordered the partnership to pay damages to Remington. Moren was not required to indemnify the partnership because her negligence occurred in the ordinary course of the partnership's business.[9] ◀

Liability of Incoming Partners. A partner newly admitted to an existing partnership is not personally liable for any partnership obligations incurred before the person became a partner [UPA 306(b)]. In other words, the new partner's liability to existing creditors of the partnership is limited to her or his capital contribution to the firm.

▶ **Example 17.11** Smartclub, an existing partnership with four members, admits a new partner, Alex Jaff. He contributes $100,000 to the partnership. Smartclub has debts amounting to $600,000 at the time Jaff joins the firm. Although Jaff's capital contribution of $100,000 can be used to satisfy Smartclub's obligations, Jaff is not personally liable for partnership debts incurred before he became a partner. Thus, his personal assets cannot be used to satisfy the partnership's preexisting debt.

If, however, the partnership incurs additional debts after Jaff becomes a partner, he will be personally liable for those amounts, along with all the other partners. ◀

Dissociation of a Partner

Dissociation occurs when a partner ceases to be associated in the carrying on of the partnership business. Although a partner always has the *power* to dis-

9. *Moren v. Jax Restaurant*, 679 N.W.2d 165 (Minn.App. 2004).

sociate from the firm, he or she may not have the *right* to dissociate.

Dissociation normally entitles the partner to have his or her interest purchased by the partnership. It also terminates the partner's actual authority to act for the partnership and to participate in running its business. The partnership may continue to do business without the dissociated partner.[10]

EVENTS THAT CAUSE DISSOCIATION Under UPA 601, a partner can be dissociated from a partnership in any of the following ways:

1. By the partner's voluntarily giving notice of an "express will to withdraw." (When a partner gives notice of intent to withdraw, the remaining partners must decide whether to continue the partnership business. If they decide not to continue, the voluntary dissociation of a partner will dissolve the firm [UPA 801(1)].)
2. By the occurrence of an event specified in the partnership agreement.
3. By a unanimous vote of the other partners under certain circumstances, such as when a partner transfers substantially all of her or his interest in the partnership, or when it becomes unlawful to carry on partnership business with that partner.
4. By order of a court or arbitrator if the partner has engaged in wrongful conduct that affects the partnership business. The court may order dissociation if a partner breached the partnership agreement, violated a duty owed to the partnership or to the other partners, or engaged in conduct that makes it "not reasonably practicable to carry on the business in partnership with the partner" [UPA 601(5)].
5. By the partner's declaring bankruptcy, assigning his or her interest in the partnership for the benefit of creditors, or becoming physically or mentally incapacitated, or by the partner's death.

WRONGFUL DISSOCIATION As mentioned, a partner has the power to dissociate from a partnership at any time, but if she or he lacks the right to dissociate, then the dissociation is considered wrongful under the law [UPA 602]. When a partner's dissociation breaches a partnership agreement, for instance, it is wrongful.

▶ **Example 17.12** Jenkins & Whalen's partnership agreement states that it is a breach of the agreement for any partner to assign partnership property to a creditor without the consent of the other partners. If Kenzie, a partner, makes such an assignment, she has not only breached the agreement but has also wrongfully dissociated from the partnership. ◀

A partner who wrongfully dissociates is liable to the partnership and to the other partners for damages caused by the dissociation. This liability is in addition to any other obligation of the partner to the partnership or to the other partners.

EFFECTS OF DISSOCIATION Dissociation (rightful or wrongful) terminates some of the rights of the dissociated partner, requires that the partnership purchase his or her interest, and alters the liability of the parties to third parties.

Rights and Duties. On a partner's dissociation, his or her right to participate in the management and conduct of the partnership business terminates [UPA 603]. The partner's duty of loyalty also ends. A partner's duty of care continues only with respect to events that occurred before dissociation, unless the partner participates in winding up the partnership's business (discussed shortly).

Buyouts. After a partner's dissociation, his or her interest in the partnership must be purchased according to the rules in UPA 701. The **buyout price** is based on the amount that would have been distributed to the partner if the partnership had been wound up on the date of dissociation. Offset against the price are amounts owed by the partner to the partnership, including damages for wrongful dissociation.

▶ **Case in Point 17.13** Wilbur and Dee Warnick and their son Randall bought a ranch for $335,000 and formed a partnership to operate it. The partners' initial capital contributions totaled $60,000, of which Randall paid 34 percent. Over the next twenty years, each partner contributed funds to the operation and received cash distributions from the partnership. In 1999, Randall dissociated from the partnership.

When the parties could not agree on a buyout price, Randall filed a lawsuit. The court awarded Randall $115,783.13—the amount of his cash contributions, plus 34 percent of the increase in the value of the partnership's assets above all partners' cash contributions. Randall's parents appealed, arguing that $50,000 should be deducted from the appraised value of the assets for the estimated expenses of selling

10. Under the previous version of the UPA, when a partner withdrew from a partnership, the partnership was considered dissolved, and the business had to end. The new UPA dramatically changed the law governing partnership breakups by no longer requiring that a partnership end if one partner dissociates.

them. The court affirmed the buyout price, however, because "purely hypothetical costs of sale are not a required deduction in valuing partnership assets" to determine a buyout price.[11] ◀

Liability to Third Parties. For two years after a partner dissociates from a continuing partnership, the partnership may be bound by the acts of the dissociated partner based on apparent authority [UPA 702]. In other words, if a third party reasonably believed at the time of a transaction that the dissociated partner was still a partner, the partnership may be liable. Also, a dissociated partner may be liable for partnership obligations entered into during a two-year period following dissociation [UPA 703].

To avoid this possible liability, a partnership should notify its creditors, customers, and clients of a partner's dissociation. In addition, either the partnership or the dissociated partner can file a statement of dissociation in the appropriate state office to limit the dissociated partner's authority to ninety days after the filing [UPA 704]. Filing this statement helps to minimize the firm's potential liability for the former partner and vice versa.

Partnership Termination

The same events that cause dissociation can result in the end of the partnership if the remaining partners no longer wish to (or are unable to) continue the partnership business. Only certain departures of a partner will end the partnership, though, and generally the partnership can continue if the remaining partners consent [UPA 801].

The termination of a partnership is referred to as **dissolution,** which essentially means the commencement of the winding up process. **Winding up** is the actual process of collecting, liquidating, and distributing the partnership assets.

DISSOLUTION Dissolution of a partnership generally can be brought about by acts of the partners, by operation of law, or by judicial decree [UPA 801]. Any partnership (including one for a fixed term) can be dissolved by the partners' agreement.

If the partnership agreement states that it will dissolve on a certain event, such as a partner's death or bankruptcy, then the occurrence of that event will dissolve the partnership. A partnership for a fixed term or a particular undertaking is dissolved by operation of law at the expiration of the term or on the completion of the undertaking.

Illegality or Impracticality. Any event that makes it unlawful for the partnership to continue its business will result in dissolution [UPA 801(4)]. Under the UPA, a court may order dissolution when it becomes obviously impractical for the firm to continue—for instance, if the business can only be operated at a loss [UPA 801(5)]. Even when one partner has brought a court action seeking to dissolve a partnership, the partnership continues to exist until it is legally dissolved by the court or by the parties' agreement.[12]

Good Faith. Each partner must exercise good faith when dissolving a partnership. Some state statutes allow partners injured by another partner's bad faith to file a tort claim for wrongful dissolution of a partnership.

▶ **Case in Point 17.14** Attorneys Randall Jordan and Mary Helen Moses formed a two-member partnership. Although the partnership was for an indefinite term, Jordan ended the partnership three years later and asked the court for declarations concerning the partners' financial obligations. Moses, who had objected to ending the partnership, filed a claim against Jordan for wrongful dissolution and for appropriating $180,000 in fees that should have gone to the partnership. Ultimately, the court held in favor of Moses.

A claim for wrongful dissolution of a partnership may be based on the excluded partner's loss of "an existing, or continuing, business opportunity" or of income and material assets. Because Jordan had attempted to appropriate partnership assets through dissolution, Moses could sue for wrongful dissolution.[13] ◀

WINDING UP AND DISTRIBUTION OF ASSETS After dissolution, the partnership continues for the limited purpose of winding up the business. The partners cannot create new obligations on behalf of the partnership. They have authority only to complete transactions begun but not finished at the time of dissolution and to wind up the business of the partnership [UPA 803, 804(1)].

Duties and Compensation. *Winding up* includes collecting and preserving partnership assets, discharging liabilities (paying debts), and accounting to each part-

11. *Warnick v. Warnick,* 2006 WY 58, 133 P.3d 997 (2006).

12. See, for example, *Curley v. Kaiser,* 112 Conn.App. 213, 962 A.2d 167 (2009).

13. *Jordan v. Moses,* 291 Ga. 39, 727 S.E.2d 469 (2012).

ner for the value of his or her interest in the partnership. Partners continue to have fiduciary duties to one another and to the firm during this process.

UPA 401(h) provides that a partner is entitled to compensation for services in winding up partnership affairs above and apart from his or her share in the partnership profits. A partner may also receive reimbursement for expenses incurred in the process.

Creditors' Claims. Both creditors of the partnership and creditors of the individual partners can make claims on the partnership's assets. In general, partnership creditors share proportionately with the partners' individual creditors in the partners' assets, which include their interests in the partnership. A partnership's assets are distributed according to the following priorities [UPA 807]:

1. Payment of debts, including those owed to partner and nonpartner creditors.
2. Return of capital contributions and distribution of profits to partners.[14]

If the partnership's liabilities are greater than its assets, the partners bear the losses—in the absence of a contrary agreement—in the same proportion in which they shared the profits (rather than, for example, in proportion to their contributions to the partnership's capital).

14. Under the previous version of the UPA, creditors of the partnership had priority over creditors of the individual partners. Also, in distributing partnership assets, third party creditors were paid before partner creditors, and capital contributions were returned before profits.

Partnership Buy-Sell Agreements

Before entering into a partnership, partners should agree on how the assets will be valued and divided in the event that the partnership dissolves. A **buy-sell agreement,** sometimes called simply a *buy-out agreement,* provides for one or more partners to buy out the other or others, should the situation warrant.

Agreeing beforehand on who buys what, under what circumstances, and, if possible, at what price may eliminate costly negotiations or litigation later. Alternatively, the agreement may specify that one or more partners will determine the value of the interest being sold and that the other or others will decide whether to buy or sell.

Under UPA 701(a), if a partner's dissociation does not result in a dissolution of the partnership, a buyout of the partner's interest is mandatory. The UPA contains an extensive set of buyout rules that apply when the partners do not have a buyout agreement. Basically, a withdrawing partner receives the same amount through a buyout that he or she would receive if the business were winding up [UPA 701(b)].

In the following case, one of the three partners in an agricultural partnership died. Despite provisions in the partnership agreement that required its dissolution on a certain date or on a partner's death, whichever came first, the remaining partners did not dissolve the firm and did not liquidate the assets.

CASE ANALYSIS

Case 17.2 Estate of Webster v. Thomas

Appellate Court of Illinois, Fifth District, 2013 IL App (5th) 120121-U, 2013 WL 164041 (2013).

IN THE LANGUAGE OF THE COURT

Justice *WEXSTTEN* delivered the opinion of the court:

* * * *

Clyde L. Webster, Jr., who formed T & T Agri-Partners Company with partners [James] Theis and [Larry] Thomas, died September 18, 2002. The T & T Agri-Partners Company owns approximately 180 acres of farmland in Christian County [Illinois] subject to mortgage liability to the Rochester State Bank and/or Farm Credit Services of Central Illinois. This farmland constitutes T & T Agri-Partners Company's only asset.

The September 1, 1997, partnership agreement executed by Clyde, Theis, and Thomas * * * issued 180 partnership units, with Thomas holding 40 (22.2%), Theis holding 80 (44.5%), and Clyde holding 60 (33.3%). The partnership agreement further provided as follows: * * *

> Unless extended by the written consent of those Partners whose combined ownership interest equals at least one hundred twenty (120) Partnership units, the Partnership shall continue until the first to

CASE 17.2 CONTINUES

CASE 17.2 CONTINUED

occur of January 31, 2010 A.D., or the earlier dissolution of the Partnership.

* * * *

* * * If a Partner dies, the Partnership will be dissolved, unless those Partners owning at least one hundred twenty (120) Partnership units including the personal representative of the deceased Partner's estate * * * vote to continue the Partnership within one hundred twenty (120) days of the date of the deceased Partner's death.

Upon dissolution, the assets of the Partnership shall be liquidated and distributed.

Any Partner who shall violate any of the terms of this Agreement * * * shall indemnify and hold harmless the Partnership, and all other Partners from any and all * * * losses, * * * including but not limited to attorneys' fees.

On October 14, 2008, [the Estate of Webster through its personal representative Joseph Webster (the plaintiff)] filed its complaint [in an Illinois state circuit court] against [Theis, Thomas, and the partnership (the defendants)]. The plaintiff's complaint sought a declaratory judgment ordering the partnership assets to be distributed based upon the then-current value of the acreage.

* * * *

On December 9, 2009, the circuit court entered an order granting summary judgment on * * * the plaintiff's complaint. [But the defendants did not liquidate the partnership, and the case went to trial.]

* * * *

On September 2, 2011, after the * * * trial, the circuit court entered its order, finding that the partnership expired by its terms on January 31, 2010, and despite demand by the plaintiff, the partnership had failed and refused to liquidate the assets and disburse funds to the plaintiff according to * * * the partnership agreement. The circuit court thereby ordered the defendants to liquidate the partnership.

* * * *

The circuit court further * * * ordered [the defendants to pay] reasonable attorney fees and costs incurred by the plaintiff.

* * * On March 8, 2012, the defendants filed a notice of appeal [arguing that the circuit court erred in ordering them to pay the plaintiff's attorney fees].

* * * *

The partnership agreement clearly provided that upon Clyde's death and the partners' failure to vote to continue the partnership, the partnership dissolved. Pursuant to the plain language of the partnership agreement, the assets upon dissolution were to be liquidated and distributed by paying the partners in proportion to their capital accounts. Yet, the defendants failed to do so. [Emphasis added.]

On December 9, 2009, seven years after Clyde's death, the circuit court entered summary judgment on * * * the plaintiff's complaint and construed the partnership agreement by determining that upon dissolution, which occurred at Clyde's death on September 18, 2002, and as a result of the remaining partners not agreeing to continue partnership, the assets of the partnership were to be liquidated and distributed * * * . Again, however, despite the agreement's language and despite the circuit court's order, the defendants failed to liquidate the partnership assets. In failing to do so, they violated the partnership agreement and were liable for the plaintiff's attorney fees pursuant to the same agreement.

* * * *

* * * The judgment of the * * * court of Christian County is affirmed.

LEGAL REASONING QUESTIONS

1. What did the partnership agreement at the center of this case require on the death of a partner and the dissolution of the firm?
2. What conduct by which parties triggered this litigation?
3. On what did the court base its order regarding attorneys' fees?
4. What might the defendants have done to avoid the dispute that arose from the circumstances of this case?

SECTION 3

FRANCHISES

Instead of setting up a sole proprietorship to market their own products or services, many entrepreneurs opt to purchase a franchise. A **franchise** is an arrangement in which the owner of intellectual property—such as a trademark, a trade name, or a copyright—licenses others to use it in the selling of goods or services. A **franchisee** (a purchaser of a franchise) is generally legally independent of the **franchisor** (the seller of the franchise). At the same time, the franchisee is economically dependent on the franchisor's integrated business system.

In other words, a franchisee can operate as an independent businessperson but still obtain the advantages of a regional or national organization. Today, franchising companies and their franchisees account for a significant portion of all retail sales in this country. Well-known franchises include McDonald's, 7-Eleven, and Holiday Inn. Franchising has also become a popular way for businesses to expand their operations internationally without violating the legal restrictions that many nations impose on foreign ownership of businesses.

Types of Franchises

Many different kinds of businesses now sell franchises, and numerous types of franchises are available. Generally, though, franchises fall into one of three classifications: distributorships, chain-style business operations, and manufacturing arrangements.

DISTRIBUTORSHIP In a *distributorship,* a manufacturer (the franchisor) licenses a dealer (the franchisee) to sell its product. Often, a distributorship covers an exclusive territory. Automobile dealerships and beer distributorships are common examples.

▶ **Example 17.15** Black Butte Beer Company distributes its brands of beer through a network of authorized wholesale distributors, each with an assigned territory. Marik signs a distributorship contract for the area from Gainesville to Ocala, Florida. If the contract states that Marik is the exclusive distributor in that area, then no other franchisee may distribute Black Butte beer in that region. ◀

CHAIN-STYLE BUSINESS OPERATION In a *chain-style business operation,* a franchise operates under a franchisor's trade name and is identified as a member of a select group of dealers that engage in the franchisor's business. The franchisee is generally required to follow standardized or prescribed methods of operation. Often, the franchisor insists that the franchisee maintain certain standards of performance.

In addition, the franchisee may be required to obtain materials and supplies exclusively from the franchisor. McDonald's and most other fast-food chains are examples of this type of franchise. Chain-style franchises are also common in service-related businesses, including real estate brokerage firms, such as Century 21, and tax-preparing services, such as H&R Block, Inc.

MANUFACTURING ARRANGEMENT In a *manufacturing,* or *processing-plant, arrangement,* the franchisor transmits to the franchisee the essential ingredients or formula to make a particular product. The franchisee then markets the product either at wholesale or at retail in accordance with the franchisor's standards. Examples of this type of franchise include Pepsi-Cola and other soft-drink bottling companies.

Laws Governing Franchising

Because a franchise relationship is primarily a contractual relationship, it is governed by contract law. If the franchise exists primarily for the sale of products manufactured by the franchisor, the law governing sales contracts as expressed in Article 2 of the Uniform Commercial Code applies (see Chapter 11).

Additionally, the federal government and most states have enacted laws governing certain aspects of franchising. Generally, these laws are designed to protect prospective franchisees from dishonest franchisors and to prevent franchisors from terminating franchises without good cause.

FEDERAL REGULATION OF FRANCHISES The federal government regulates franchising through laws that apply to specific industries and through the Franchise Rule, created by the Federal Trade Commission (FTC).

Industry-Specific Standards. Congress has enacted laws that protect franchisees in certain industries, such as automobile dealerships and service stations. These laws protect the franchisee from unreasonable demands and bad faith terminations of the franchise by the franchisor.

An automobile manufacturer–franchisor cannot make unreasonable demands of dealer-franchisees or set unrealistically high sales quotas. If an automobile manufacturer–franchisor terminates a franchise because of a dealer-franchisee's failure to comply with unreasonable demands, the manufacturer may be liable for damages.[15]

Similarly, federal law prescribes the conditions under which a franchisor of service stations can terminate the franchise.[16] Federal antitrust laws (discussed in Chapter 27) also apply in certain circumstances to prohibit certain types of anticompetitive agreements.

15. Automobile Dealers' Franchise Act of 1965, also known as the Automobile Dealers' Day in Court Act, 15 U.S.C. Sections 1221 *et seq.*
16. Petroleum Marketing Practices Act (PMPA) of 1979, 15 U.S.C. Sections 2801 *et seq.*

The Franchise Rule. The FTC's Franchise Rule requires franchisors to disclose certain material facts that a prospective franchisee needs in order to make an informed decision concerning the purchase of a franchise.[17] The Franchise Rule requires the following:

1. *Written (or electronically recorded) disclosures.* The franchisor must make numerous disclosures, such as the range of goods and services included and the value and estimated profitability of the franchise. Disclosures can be in writing or done electronically online. Prospective franchisees must be able to download or save all electronic disclosure documents.
2. *Reasonable basis for any representations.* To prevent deception, all representations made to a prospective franchisee must have a reasonable basis at the time they are made.
3. *Projected earnings figures.* If a franchisor provides projected earnings figures, the franchisor must indicate whether the figures are based on actual data or hypothetical examples. (The Franchise Rule does not require franchisors to provide potential earnings figures, however, as discussed in the *Insight into Ethics* feature on the next page.)
4. *Actual data.* If a franchisor makes sales or earnings projections based on actual data for a specific franchise location, the franchisor must disclose the number and percentage of its existing franchises that have achieved this result.
5. *Explanation of terms.* Franchisors are also required to explain termination, cancellation, and renewal provisions of the franchise contract to potential franchisees before the agreement is signed.

Those who violate the Franchise Rule are subject to substantial civil penalties, and the FTC can sue on behalf of injured parties to recover damages.

STATE REGULATION OF FRANCHISING State legislation varies but often is aimed at protecting franchisees from unfair practices and bad faith terminations by franchisors.

State Disclosures. Approximately fifteen states have laws similar to the federal rules that require franchisors to provide presale disclosures to prospective franchisees.[18] Many state laws also require that a disclosure document (known as the Franchise Disclosure Document, or FDD) be registered or filed with a state official. State laws may also require that a franchisor submit advertising aimed at prospective franchisees to the state for approval.

To protect franchisees, a state law might require the disclosure of information such as the actual costs of operation, recurring expenses, and profits earned, along with facts substantiating these figures. State deceptive trade practices acts (see Chapter 24) may also apply and prohibit certain types of actions by franchisors.

May Require Good Cause to Terminate the Franchise. To protect franchisees against arbitrary or bad faith terminations, state law may prohibit termination without "good cause" or require that certain procedures be followed in terminating a franchise. ▶ **Case in Point 17.16** FMS, Inc., entered into a franchise agreement with Samsung Construction Equipment North America to become an authorized dealership selling Samsung construction equipment. Then Samsung sold its equipment business to Volvo Construction Equipment North America, Inc., which was to continue selling Samsung brand equipment.

Later, Volvo rebranded the construction equipment under its own name and canceled FMS's franchise. FMS sued, claiming Volvo had terminated the franchise without "good cause" in violation of state law. Because Volvo was no longer manufacturing the Samsung brand equipment, however, the court found that Volvo had good cause to terminate FMS's franchise. If Volvo had continued making the Samsung equipment, though, it could not have terminated the franchise.[19] ◀

The Franchise Contract

The franchise relationship is defined by the contract between the franchisor and the franchisee. The franchise contract specifies the terms and conditions of the franchise and spells out the rights and duties of the franchisor and the franchisee.

If either party fails to perform its contractual duties, that party may be subject to a lawsuit for breach of contract. Furthermore, if a franchisee is induced to enter into a franchise contract by the franchisor's fraudulent misrepresentation, the franchisor may be liable for damages. Generally, statutes and the case law governing franchising tend to emphasize the

17. 16 C.F.R. Section 436.1.
18. These states include California, Hawaii, Illinois, Indiana, Maryland, Michigan, Minnesota, New York, North Dakota, Oregon, Rhode Island, South Dakota, Virginia, Washington, and Wisconsin.
19. *FMS, Inc. v. Volvo Construction Equipment North America, Inc.,* 557 F.3d 758 (7th Cir. 2009).

INSIGHT INTO ETHICS

Should Franchisors Have to Give Prospective Franchisees Information about Potential Earnings?

Entrepreneurs who are thinking about investing in a franchise almost invariably ask, "How much will I make?" Surprisingly, current law does not require franchisors to provide any information about the earnings potential of a franchise.

Voluntary Disclosure of Earnings Data

Franchisors can voluntarily choose to provide projected earnings in their disclosures but are not required to do so. If franchisors do include earnings data, they must indicate whether these figures are actual or hypothetical and have a reasonable basis for these claims. About 75 percent of franchisors choose *not* to provide information about earnings potential.

Franchisee Complaints

The failure of the FTC's Franchise Rule to require disclosure of earnings potential has led to many complaints from franchisees. After all, some franchisees invest their life savings in franchises that ultimately fail because of unrealistic earnings expectations. Moreover, the franchisee may be legally obliged to continue paying the franchisor even when the business is not turning a profit.

For instance, Thomas Anderson asked the franchisor, Rocky Mountain Chocolate Factory, Inc. (RMCF), and five of its franchisees for earnings information before he entered into a franchise agreement, but he did not receive any data. Although his chocolate franchise failed to become profitable, a court ordered Anderson and his partner to pay $33,109 in past due royalties and interest to RMCF (plus court costs and expenses).[a]

LEGAL CRITICAL THINKING

INSIGHT INTO THE BUSINESS ENVIRONMENT

If the law required franchisors to provide estimates of potential earnings, would there be more or less growth in the number of franchises? Explain your answer.

a. *Rocky Mountain Chocolate Factory, Inc. v. SDMS, Inc.*, 2009 WL 579516 (D.Colo. 2009).

importance of good faith and fair dealing in franchise relationships.

Because each type of franchise relationship has its own characteristics, franchise contracts tend to differ. Nonetheless, certain major issues typically are addressed in a franchise contract. We look at some of them next.

PAYMENT FOR THE FRANCHISE The franchisee ordinarily pays an initial fee or lump-sum price for the franchise license (the privilege of being granted a franchise). This fee is separate from the various products that the franchisee purchases from or through the franchisor. The franchise agreement may also require the franchisee to pay a percentage of the franchisor's advertising costs and certain administrative expenses.

In some industries, the franchisor relies heavily on the initial sale of the franchise for realizing a profit. In other industries, the continued dealing between the parties brings profit to both. Generally, the franchisor receives a stated percentage of the annual (or monthly) sales or volume of business done by the franchisee.

BUSINESS PREMISES The franchise agreement may specify whether the premises for the business must be leased or purchased outright. Sometimes, a building must be constructed to meet the terms of the agreement. The agreement will specify whether the franchisor or the franchisee is responsible for supplying equipment and furnishings for the premises.

LOCATION OF THE FRANCHISE Typically, the franchisor determines the territory to be served. Some franchise contracts give the franchisee exclusive rights, or "territorial rights," to a certain geographic area. Other franchise contracts, while defining the territory allotted to a particular franchise, either specifically state that the franchise is nonexclusive or are silent on the issue of territorial rights.

Many franchise cases involve disputes over territorial rights, and the implied covenant of good faith and fair dealing often comes into play in this area of franchising. If the franchise contract does not grant the franchisee exclusive territorial rights and the franchisor allows a competing franchise to be established nearby, the franchisee may suffer a significant loss in profits. In this situation, a court may hold that the franchisor breached an implied covenant of good faith and fair dealing.

BUSINESS ORGANIZATION The franchisor may require that the business use a particular organizational form and capital structure. The franchise agreement may also set out standards such as sales quotas and record-keeping requirements. Additionally, a franchisor may retain stringent control over the training of personnel involved in the operation and over administrative aspects of the business.

QUALITY CONTROL The day-to-day operation of the franchise business normally is left up to the franchisee. Nonetheless, the franchise agreement may specify that the franchisor will provide some degree of supervision and control so that it can protect the franchise's name and reputation.

Means of Control. When the franchise prepares a product, such as food, or provides a service, such as motel accommodations, the contract often states that the franchisor will establish certain standards for the facility. Typically, the contract will state that the franchisor is permitted to make periodic inspections to ensure that the standards are being maintained.

As a means of controlling quality, franchise agreements also typically limit the franchisee's ability to sell the franchise to another party. ▶ **Example 17.17** Mark Keller, Inc., an authorized Jaguar franchise, contracts to sell its dealership to Henrique Autos West. A Jaguar franchise generally cannot be sold without Jaguar Cars' permission. Prospective franchisees must meet Jaguar's customer satisfaction standards. If Henrique Autos fails to meet those standards, Jaguar can refuse to allow the sale and can terminate the franchise.[20] ◀

Degree of Control. As a general rule, the validity of a provision permitting the franchisor to establish and enforce certain quality standards is unquestioned. The franchisor has a legitimate interest in maintaining the quality of the product or service to protect its name and reputation.

If a franchisor exercises too much control over the operations of its franchisees, however, the franchisor risks potential liability. A franchisor may occasionally be held liable—under the doctrine of *respondeat superior* (see Chapter 20)—for the tortious acts of the franchisees' employees.

PRICING ARRANGEMENTS Franchises provide the franchisor with an outlet for the firm's goods and services. Depending on the nature of the business, the franchisor may require the franchisee to purchase certain supplies from the franchisor at an established price.[21] A franchisor cannot, however, set the prices at which the franchisee will resell the goods because such price setting may be a violation of state or federal antitrust laws, or both. A franchisor can suggest retail prices but cannot mandate them.

Franchise Termination

The duration of the franchise is a matter to be determined between the parties. Sometimes, a franchise relationship starts with a short trial period, such as a year, so that the franchisee and the franchisor can determine whether they want to stay in business with each another. Other times, the duration of the franchise contract correlates with the term of the lease for the business premises, and both are renewable at the end of that period.

GROUNDS FOR TERMINATION SET BY FRANCHISE CONTRACT Usually, the franchise agreement specifies that termination must be "for cause" and then defines the grounds for termination. Cause might include, for instance, the death or disability of the franchisee, insolvency of the franchisee, breach of the franchise agreement, or failure to meet specified sales quotas.

Notice Requirements. Most franchise contracts provide that notice of termination must be given. If no set time for termination is specified, then a reasonable time, with notice, is implied. A franchisee must be given reasonable time to wind up the business—that is, to do the accounting and return the copyright or trademark or any other property of the franchisor.

Opportunity to Cure a Breach. A franchise agreement may state that the franchisee may attempt to cure an ordinary, curable breach within a certain period of time after notice so as to postpone, or even avoid, the termination of the contract. Even when a contract contains a notice-and-cure provision, however, a

20. For example, see *Midwest Automotive III, LLC v. Iowa Department of Transportation,* 646 N.W.2d 417 (Iowa 2002).

21. Although a franchisor can require franchisees to purchase supplies from it, requiring a franchisee to purchase exclusively from the franchisor may violate federal antitrust laws (see Chapter 27).

franchisee's breach of the duty of honesty and fidelity may be enough to allow the franchisor to terminate the franchise.

▶ **Case in Point 17.18** Pilot Air Freight Corporation is a franchisor that moves freight through its network of operations at airports and other sites. LJL Transportation, Inc., was a franchisee. The franchise agreement required LJL to assign all shipments to the Pilot network. The agreement also provided that "Pilot shall allow Franchisee an opportunity to cure a default within ninety (90) days of receipt of written notice."

After eight years as a Pilot franchisee, LJL began to divert shipments to Northeast Transportation, a competing service owned by LJL's owners. Pilot then terminated the franchise agreement. LJL filed a lawsuit claiming that it should be allowed to cure its breach, but the court ruled in favor of Pilot. A franchise agreement may be terminated immediately when there is a material breach so serious that it goes directly to the heart and essence of the contract.[22] ◀

WRONGFUL TERMINATION Because a franchisor's termination of a franchise often has adverse consequences for the franchisee, much franchise litigation involves claims of wrongful termination. Generally, the termination provisions of contracts are more favorable to the franchisor than to the franchisee. This means that the franchisee, who normally invests a substantial amount of time and financial resources in making the franchise operation successful, may receive little or nothing for the business on termination. The franchisor owns the trademark and hence the business.

It is in this area that statutory and case law become important. The federal and state laws discussed earlier attempt, among other things, to protect franchisees from the arbitrary or unfair termination of their franchises by the franchisors.

THE IMPORTANCE OF GOOD FAITH AND FAIR DEALING Generally, both statutory law and case law emphasize the importance of good faith and fair dealing in terminating a franchise relationship. In determining whether a franchisor has acted in good faith when terminating a franchise agreement, the courts usually try to balance the rights of both parties.

If a court perceives that a franchisor has arbitrarily or unfairly terminated a franchise, the franchisee will be provided with a remedy for wrongful termination. If a franchisor's decision to terminate a franchise was made in the normal course of business, however, and reasonable notice of termination was given, a court will be less likely to consider the termination wrongful. The importance of good faith and fair dealing in a franchise relationship is underscored by the consequences of the franchisor's acts in the following case.

22. *LJL Transportation, Inc. v. Pilot Air Freight Corp.*, 599 Pa. 546, 962 A.2d 639 (Pa.Sup.Ct. 2009).

SPOTLIGHT on Holiday Inns

Case 17.3 Holiday Inn Franchising, Inc. v. Hotel Associates, Inc.

Court of Appeals of Arkansas, 2011 Ark.App. 147, 382 S.W.3d 6 (2011).

BACKGROUND AND FACTS Buddy House was in the construction business in Arkansas and Texas. For decades, he collaborated on projects with Holiday Inn Franchising, Inc. Their relationship was characterized by good faith—many projects were undertaken without written contracts. At Holiday Inn's request, House inspected a hotel in Wichita Falls, Texas, to estimate the cost of getting it into shape. Holiday Inn wanted House to renovate the hotel and operate it as a Holiday Inn. House estimated that recovering the cost of renovation would take him more than ten years, so he asked for a franchise term longer than Holiday Inn's usual ten years. Holiday Inn refused, but said that if the hotel was run "appropriately," the term would be extended at the end of ten years. House bought the hotel, renovated it, and operated it as Hotel Associates, Inc. (HAI), generating substantial profits. He refused offers to sell it for as much as $15 million.

Before the ten years had passed, Greg Aden, a Holiday Inn executive, developed a plan to license a different local hotel as a Holiday Inn instead of renewing House's franchise license. Aden stood to earn a

CASE 17.3 CONTINUES ➧

CASE 17.3 CONTINUED

commission from licensing the other hotel. No one informed House of Aden's plan. When the time came, HAI applied for an extension of its franchise, and Holiday Inn asked for major renovations. HAI spent $3 million to comply with this request. Holiday Inn did not renew HAI's license, however, but instead granted a franchise to the other hotel. HAI sold its hotel for $5 million and filed a suit in an Arkansas state court against Holiday Inn, asserting fraud. The court awarded HAI compensatory and punitive damages. Holiday Inn appealed.

IN THE LANGUAGE OF THE COURT
Raymond R. *ABRAMSON*, Judge.

* * * *

Generally, a mere failure to volunteer information does not constitute fraud. But *silence can amount to actionable fraud in some circumstances where the parties have a relation of trust or confidence, where there is inequality of condition and knowledge, or where there are other attendant circumstances*. [Emphasis added.]

In this case, substantial evidence supports the existence of a duty on Holiday Inn's part to disclose the Aden [plan] to HAI. Buddy House had a long-term relationship with Holiday Inn characterized by honesty, trust, and the free flow of pertinent information. He testified that [Holiday Inn's] assurances at the onset of licensure [the granting of the license] led him to believe that he would be relicensed after ten years if the hotel was operated appropriately. Yet, despite Holiday Inn's having provided such an assurance to House, it failed to apprise House of an internal business plan * * * that advocated licensure of another facility instead of the renewal of his license. *A duty of disclosure may exist where information is peculiarly within the knowledge of one party and is of such a nature that the other party is justified in assuming its nonexistence*. Given House's history with Holiday Inn and the assurance he received, we are convinced he was justified in assuming that no obstacles had arisen that jeopardized his relicensure. [Emphasis added.]

Holiday Inn asserts that it would have provided Buddy House with the Aden [plan] if he had asked for it. But, Holiday Inn cannot satisfactorily explain why House should have been charged with the responsibility of inquiring about a plan that he did not know existed. Moreover, several Holiday Inn personnel testified that Buddy House in fact should have been provided with the Aden plan. Aden himself stated that * * * House should have been given the plan. * * * In light of these circumstances, we see no ground for reversal on this aspect of HAI's cause of action for fraud.

DECISION AND REMEDY *The state intermediate appellate court affirmed the lower court's judgment and its award of compensatory damages. The appellate court increased the amount of punitive damages, however, citing Holiday Inn's "degree of reprehensibility."*

THE LEGAL ENVIRONMENT DIMENSION *Why should House and HAI have been advised of Holiday Inn's plan to grant a franchise to a different hotel in their territory?*

THE ECONOMIC DIMENSION *A jury awarded HAI $12 million in punitive damages. The court reduced this award to $1 million, but the appellate court reinstated the original award. What is the purpose of punitive damages? Did Holiday Inn's conduct warrant this award? Explain.*

Reviewing: Small Business Organizations

Grace Tarnavsky and her sons, Manny and Jason, bought a ranch known as the Cowboy Palace in March 2009, and the three verbally agreed to share the business for five years. Grace contributed 50 percent of the investment, and each son contributed 25 percent. Manny agreed to handle the livestock, and Jason agreed to handle the bookkeeping. The Tarnavskys took out joint loans and opened a joint bank account into which they deposited the ranch's proceeds and from which they made payments for property, cattle, equipment, and supplies. In September 2013, Manny severely injured his back while baling hay and became permanently unable to handle livestock. Manny therefore hired additional laborers to tend the livestock, causing the Cowboy Palace to incur significant debt. In September 2014, Al's Feed Barn filed a lawsuit against Jason to collect $32,400 in unpaid debts. Using the information presented in the chapter, answer the following questions.

1. Was this relationship a partnership for a term or a partnership at will?
2. Did Manny have the authority to hire additional laborers to work at the ranch after his injury? Why or why not?
3. Under the current UPA, can Al's Feed Barn bring an action against Jason individually for the Cowboy Palace's debt? Why or why not?
4. Suppose that after his back injury in 2013, Manny sent his mother and brother a notice indicating his intent to withdraw from the partnership. Can he still be held liable for the debt to Al's Feed Barn? Why or why not?

DEBATE THIS . . . *All franchisors should be required by law to provide a comprehensive estimate of the profitability of a prospective franchise based on the experiences of their existing franchisees.*

Terms and Concepts

articles of partnership 398
buyout price 403
buy-sell agreement 405
charging order 400
dissociation 402
dissolution 404
entrepreneur 394
franchise 406
franchisee 406
franchisor 406
goodwill 397
information return 398
joint and several liability 402
joint liability 402
partnership 397
partnership by estoppel 398
pass-through entity 398
sole proprietorship 394
winding up 404

ExamPrep

Issue Spotters

1. Darnell and Eliana are partners in D&E Designs, an architectural firm. When Darnell dies, his widow claims that as Darnell's heir, she is entitled to take his place as Eliana's partner or to receive a share of the firm's assets. Is she right? Why or why not? **(See page 402.)**
2. Anchor Bottling Company and U.S. Beverages, Inc. (USB), enter into a franchise agreement that states the franchise may be terminated at any time "for cause." Anchor fails to meet USB's specified sales quota. Does this constitute "cause" for termination? Why or why not? **(See page 410.)**

- **Check your answers to the Issue Spotters against the answers provided in Appendix E at the end of this text.**

Before the Test

Go to **www.cengagebrain.com**, enter the ISBN 9781285428949, and click on "Find" to locate this textbook's Web site. Then, click on "Access Now" under "Study Tools," and select Chapter 17 at the top. There, you will find an Interactive Quiz that you can take to assess your mastery of the concepts in this chapter, as well as Flashcards and a Glossary of important terms.

Business Scenarios

17–1. Partnership Formation. Daniel is the owner of a chain of shoe stores. He hires Rubya to be the manager of a new store, which is to open in Grand Rapids, Michigan. Daniel, by written contract, agrees to pay Rubya a monthly salary and 20 percent of the profits. Without Daniel's knowledge, Rubya represents himself to Classen as Daniel's partner and shows Classen the agreement to share profits. Classen extends credit to Rubya. Rubya defaults. Discuss whether Classen can hold Daniel liable as a partner. **(See page 398.)**

17–2. Control of a Franchise. National Foods, Inc., sells franchises to its fast-food restaurants, known as Chicky–D's. Under the franchise agreement, franchisees agree to hire and train employees strictly according to Chicky-D's standards. Chicky-D's regional supervisors are required to approve all job candidates before they are hired and all general policies affecting those employees. Chicky-D's reserves the right to terminate a franchise for violating the franchisor's rules. In practice, however, Chicky-D's regional supervisors routinely approve new employees and individual franchisees' policies. After several incidents of racist comments and conduct by Tim, a recently hired assistant manager at a Chicky-D's, Sharon, a counterperson at the restaurant, resigns. Sharon files a suit in a federal district court against National. National files a motion for summary judgment, arguing that it is not liable for harassment by franchise employees. Will the court grant National's motion? Why or why not? **(See page 410.)**

Business Case Problems

17–3. Spotlight on McDonald's—Franchise Termination. J.C., Inc., had a franchise agreement with McDonald's Corp to operate McDonald's restaurants in Lancaster, Ohio. The agreement required J.C. to make monthly payments of certain percentages of the gross sales to McDonald's. If any payment was more than thirty days late, McDonald's had the right to terminate the franchise. The agreement also stated that even if McDonald's accepted a late payment, that would not "constitute a waiver of any subsequent breach." McDonald's sometimes accepted J.C.'s late payments, but when J.C. defaulted on the payments in July 2010, McDonald's gave notice of thirty days to comply or surrender possession of the restaurants. J.C. missed the deadline. McDonald's demanded that J.C. vacate the restaurants, but J.C. refused. McDonald's alleged that J.C. had violated the franchise agreement. J.C. claimed that McDonald's had breached the implied covenant of good faith and fair dealing. Which party should prevail and why? [*McDonald's Corp. v. C.B. Management Co.,*13 F.Supp.2d 705 (N.D.Ill. 1998)] **(See page 410.)**

17–4. Fiduciary Duties of Partners. Karl Horvath, Hein Rüsen, and Carl Thomas formed a partnership, HRT Enterprises, to buy a manufacturing plant. Rüsen and Thomas leased the plant to their own company, Merkur Steel. Merkur then sublet the premises to other companies owned by Rüsen and Thomas. The rent that these companies paid to Merkur was higher than the rent that Merkur paid to HRT. Rüsen and Thomas did not tell Horvath about the subleases. Did Rüsen and Thomas breach their fiduciary duties to HRT and Horvath? Discuss. [*Horvath v. HRT Enterprises,* 489 Mich.App. 992, 800 N.W.2d 595 (2011)] **(See page 401.)**

17–5. Franchise Termination. George Oshana and GTO Investments, Inc., operated a Mobil gas station franchise in Itasca, Illinois. In 2010, Oshana and GTO became involved in a rental dispute with Buchanan Energy, to which Mobil had assigned the lease. In November 2011, Buchanan terminated the franchise because Oshana and GTO had failed to pay the rent. Oshana and GTO, however, alleged that they were "ready, willing, and able to pay the rent" but that Buchanan failed to accept their electronic fund transfer. Have Oshana and GTO stated a claim for wrongful termination of their franchise? Why or why not? [*Oshana v. Buchanan Energy,* 2012 WL 426921 (N.D.Ill. 2012)] **(See page 410.)**

17–6. BUSINESS CASE PROBLEM WITH SAMPLE ANSWER: Partnership Formation.

*Patricia Garcia and Bernardo Lucero were in a romantic relationship. While they were seeing each other, Garcia and Lucero acquired an electronics service center, paying $30,000 apiece. Two years later, they purchased an apartment complex. The property was deeded to Lucero, but neither Garcia nor Lucero made a down payment. The couple considered both properties to be owned "50/50," and they agreed to share profits, losses, and management rights. When the couple's romantic relationship ended, Garcia asked a court to declare that she had a partnership with Lucero. In court, Lucero argued that the couple did not have a written partnership agreement. Did they have a partnership? Why or why not? [*Garcia v. Lucero, *366 S.W.3d 275 (Tex.App. 2012)]* **(See page 398.)**

- **For a sample answer to Problem 17–6, go to Appendix F at the end of this text.**

17–7. Quality Control. JTH Tax, Inc., doing business as Liberty Tax Service, provides tax preparation and related loan services through company-owned and franchised stores. Liberty's agreement with its franchisees reserved the right to control their ads. In operations manuals, Liberty provided step-by-step instructions, directions, and limitations regarding the franchisees' ads and retained the right to unilaterally modify the steps at any time. The California attorney general filed a suit in a California state court against Liberty, alleging that its franchisees had used misleading or deceptive ads regarding refund anticipation loans and e-refund checks. Can Liberty be held liable? Discuss. [*People v. JTH Tax, Inc.*, 212 Cal.App.4th 1219, 151 Cal.Rptr.3d 728 (1 Dist. 2013)] **(See page 410.)**

17–8. Winding Up and Distribution of Assets. Dan and Lori Cole operated a Curves franchise exercise facility in Angola, Indiana, as a partnership. The firm leased commercial space from Flying Cat, LLC, for a renewable three-year term and renewed the lease for a second three-year term. But two years after the renewal, the Coles divorced. By the end of the second term, Flying Cat was owed more than $21,000 on the lease. Without telling the landlord about the divorce, Lori signed another extension. More rent went unpaid. Flying Cat obtained a judgment in an Indiana state court against the partnership for almost $50,000. Can Dan be held liable? Why or why not? [*Curves for Women Angola v. Flying Cat, LLC*, 983 N.E.2d 629 (Ind. App. 2013)] **(See page 404.)**

17–9. A QUESTION OF ETHICS: Wrongful Dissociation.

*Elliot Willensky and Beverly Moran formed a partnership to buy, renovate, and sell a house. Moran agreed to finance the effort, which was to cost no more than $60,000. Willensky agreed to oversee the work, which was to be done in six months. Willensky lived in the house during the renovation. As the project progressed, Willensky incurred excessive and unnecessary expenses, misappropriated funds for his personal use, did not pay bills on time, and did not keep Moran informed of the costs. More than a year later, the renovation was still not completed, and Willensky walked off the project. Moran completed the renovation, which ultimately cost $311,222, and sold the house. Moran then sued to dissolve the partnership and recover damages from Willensky for breach of contract and wrongful dissociation. [*Moran v. Willensky, *395 S.W.3d 651 (Tenn.Ct.App. 2010)]* **(See page 403.)**

(a) Moran alleged that Willensky had wrongfully dissociated from the partnership. When did this dissociation occur? Why was his dissociation wrongful?

(b) Which of Willensky's actions simply represent unethical behavior or bad management, and which constitute a breach of the agreement?

Legal Reasoning Group Activity

17–10. Liability of Partners. At least six months before the Summer Olympic Games in Atlanta, Georgia, Stafford Fontenot and four others agreed to sell Cajun food at the games and began making preparations. On May 19, the group (calling themselves "Prairie Cajun Seafood Catering of Louisiana") applied for a business license from the county health department. Later, Ted Norris sold a mobile kitchen to them for $40,000. They gave Norris an $8,000 check drawn on the "Prairie Cajun Seafood Catering of Louisiana" account and two promissory notes, one for $12,000 and the other for $20,000. The notes, which were dated June 12, listed only Fontenot "d/b/a Prairie Cajun Seafood" as the maker (*d/b/a* is an abbreviation for "doing business as").

On July 31, Fontenot and his friends signed a partnership agreement, which listed specific percentages of profits and losses. They drove the mobile kitchen to Atlanta, but business was "disastrous." When the notes were not paid, Norris filed a suit in a Louisiana state court against Fontenot, seeking payment. **(See page 402.)**

(a) The first group will discuss the elements of a partnership and determine whether a partnership exists among Fontenot and the others.

(b) The second group will determine who can be held liable on the notes and why.

CHAPTER 18
LIMITED LIABILITY BUSINESS FORMS

In the previous chapter, we examined sole proprietorships, franchises, and traditional partnerships. Here, we examine a relatively new form of business organization called the *limited liability company* (LLC). LLCs have become the organizational form of choice among businesspersons. We also examine business forms designed to limit the liability of partners.

This chapter begins with a discussion of the important aspects of an LLC, including its formation, jurisdictional requirements, and the advantages and disadvantages of choosing to do business as an LLC. This is followed by an examination of its management and operation options. We then look at a similar type of entity that is also relatively new—the *limited liability partnership* (LLP). This chapter concludes with a discussion of the *limited partnership* (LP), a special type of partnership in which some of the partners have limited liability, and the *limited liability limited partnership* (LLLP).

SECTION 1 THE LIMITED LIABILITY COMPANY

A **limited liability company (LLC)** is a hybrid that combines the limited liability aspects of a corporation and the tax advantages of a partnership. The LLC has been available for only a few decades, but it has become the preferred structure for many small businesses.

LLCs are governed by state statutes, which vary from state to state. In an attempt to create more uniformity, the National Conference of Commissioners on Uniform State Laws issued the Uniform Limited Liability Company Act (ULLCA). Less than one-fifth of the states have adopted it, though. Thus, the law governing LLCs remains far from uniform.

Some provisions are common to most state statutes, however, and we base our discussion of LLCs in this section on these common elements.

The Nature of the LLC

LLCs share many characteristics with corporations. Like corporations, LLCs must be formed and operated in compliance with state law. Like the shareholders of a corporation, the owners of an LLC, who are called **members,** enjoy limited liability [ULLCA 303].[1]

LIMITED LIABILITY OF MEMBERS Members of LLCs are shielded from personal liability in many situations, even sometimes when sued by employees of the firm. ▶ **Case in Point 18.1** Penny McFarland was the activities director at a retirement community in Virginia that was owned by an LLC. Her supervisor told her to take the residents outside for a walk when the temperature was 95 degrees. McFarland complained to the state health department and was fired from her job. She sued a number of managers and members of the LLC for wrongful discharge.

The court held that under Virginia state law, members, managers, and agents of an LLC are not responsible for its liabilities "solely" by virtue of their status. Only those who "have played a key role in contributing to the company's tortious conduct" can be part of a wrongful discharge claim. The court therefore dismissed the action against all but one defendant.[2] ◀

1. Members of an LLC can also bring derivative actions, which you will read about in Chapter 19, on behalf of the LLC [ULLCA 101]. As with a corporate shareholder's derivative suit, any damages recovered go to the LLC, not to the members personally.
2. *McFarland v. Virginia Retirement Services of Chesterfield, LLC,* 477 F.Supp.2d 727 (2007).

LIABILITY UNDER THE ALTER-EGO THEORY Sometimes, when a corporation is deemed to be merely an "alter ego" of the shareholder-owner, a court will *pierce the corporate veil* and hold the shareholder-owner personally liable (see Chapter 19). A court may apply the alter-ego theory when a shareholder commingles personal and corporate funds or fails to observe required corporate formalities.

Whether the alter-ego theory should be applied to an LLC was at issue in the following case.

CASE ANALYSIS

Case 18.1 ORX Resources, Inc. v. MBW Exploration, LLC

Court of Appeal of Louisiana, Fourth Circuit, 32 So.3d 931 (2010).

IN THE LANGUAGE OF THE COURT
Charles R. *JONES,* Judge.

* * * *

On January 16, 2003, ORX [Resources, Inc.,] entered into the "Clovelly Purchase Agreement" with Coastline Oil & Gas, Inc. Pursuant to this Agreement, ORX purchased certain oil, gas and mineral leases/interests in a tract of land located in Lafourche Parish, known as the "Clovelly Prospect." ORX partnered with other entities, including MBW [Exploration, LLC], to share in the expense and potential profits of the venture to explore and develop the Clovelly Prospect. The partnering parties entered into a Joint Operating Agreement ("JOA") and the Clovelly Prospect Participation Agreement ("Participation Agreement"). Mr. [Mark] Washauer signed these documents in October of 2003 and December of 2004, respectively, on behalf of MBW, in his capacity as a "Managing Member." However, MBW did not come into existence until July of 2005, when its articles of organization were filed with the Louisiana Secretary of State.

The JOA provided that ORX was to serve as the "Operator" drilling a well within the Clovelly Prospect. It further provided that the nonoperating working interest partners, like MBW, would pay their proportionate share of the costs in exchange for a corresponding working interest ownership share in the Clovelly Prospect. The drilled well was governed by the Participation Agreement, which provided that MBW had a working interest in the Clovelly Prospect whereby MBW would share in 2.5% of the costs incurred, and would gain a proportionate share of the returns, if any, produced by the well.

Later, ORX submitted an Authorization for Expenditure ("AFE") to MBW for approval, which Mr. Washauer signed in his own name. Additionally, he paid MBW's participation fee with a check drawn from the account of another entity, MBW Properties, LLC.

In 2006, ORX, as the well Operator, began planning the Allain LeBreton Well No. 2 in the Clovelly Prospect, ("the Well"), which was the "initial well" called for in the Participation Agreement. * * * Mr. Washauer paid the full amount of MBW's share of an ORX cash call invoice of $59,325 with a personal check.

The well proved to be unsuccessful, and was ultimately plugged. MBW's unpaid share of expenses for said project amounted to $84,220.01, for which ORX demanded payment via correspondence, but to no avail. As a result, ORX filed suit for breach of contract against both MBW and Mr. Washauer ("the Appellants").

* * * [The trial court—a state district court—determined that Washauer operated MBW as his alter ego and allowed ORX to pierce the veil of the LLC. The court granted summary judgment in favor of ORX, holding that Washauer and MBW were liable, jointly and severally, to ORX in the amount of $84,220.01.] The Appellants timely filed [an] appeal from this judgment.

* * * *

We first address whether the district court erred in ruling that the alter ego theory of the corporate veil piercing applied to Louisiana limited liability companies.

* * * *

The provisions of La. R.S. [Louisiana Revised Statutes] 12:1320(D) provide for the piercing of an LLC's veil when the situation so warrants.

* * * *

* * * *Piercing the veil of an LLC is justified to prevent the use of the LLC form to defraud creditors.* Under our * * * review, we find that the district court did not err in determining that the alter ego theory of corporate veil piercing applies to a Louisiana limited liability company, under the facts of this case, where it appears that Mr. Washauer used MBW as a shell

CASE 18.1 CONTINUES ➧

CASE 18.1 CONTINUED

and tried to avoid paying a legitimate debt of the LLC. [Emphasis added.]

* * * *

The Louisiana Supreme Court has identified *five nonexclusive factors to be used in determining whether to apply the alter ego doctrine: [commingling of corporate and shareholder funds; failure to follow statutory formalities for incorporating and transacting corporate affairs; undercapitalization; failure to provide separate bank accounts and bookkeeping records; and failure to hold regular shareholder and director meetings].* [Emphasis added.]

* * * *

In applying [these] factors, * * * we find that Mr. Washauer's activities on behalf of MBW do merit the piercing of the veil of this LLC. Commingling of the LLC's funds occurred with the funds of Mr. Washauer and a separate company of his. This commingling occurred because MBW was undercapitalized and did not have a separate bank account to transact its own affairs. Furthermore, at the time MBW began contracting with ORX, it was not yet recognized as an LLC by the Louisiana Secretary of State. Lastly, while LLCs are not bound by corporate laws to hold regular meetings, the fact that MBW has not had a meeting in over a year further evidences that Mr. Washauer was operating MBW at his leisure and direction. Thus, we find that the district court did not err in determining that MBW was being operated as the alter ego of Mr. Washauer under the [above-mentioned] factors, and therefore, he can be held personally liable jointly and solidarily [severally] with MBW.

For the foregoing reasons,* * * the judgment of the district court is affirmed * * * .

LEGAL REASONING QUESTIONS

1. One of the advantages of the LLC is that its members enjoy limited personal liability for the company's obligations. In view of this fact, does the possibility that a court may hold an LLC member personally liable for the LLC's debts reduce the utility of the LLC form of business organization? Explain.
2. What does *jointly* and *severally* mean in terms of liability? Would ORX prefer that Washauer and MBW be held personally liable jointly and severally or that Washauer alone be held personally liable? Explain.
3. How might members of LLCs avoid the liability to which Washauer was subject in this case?
4. MBW appears to have been a one-member LLC. If the firm had had more members, how might that have affected the result in this case?

OTHER SIMILARITIES TO CORPORATIONS Another similarity between corporations and LLCs is that LLCs are legal entities apart from their owners. As a legal person, the LLC can sue or be sued, enter into contracts, and hold title to property [ULLCA 201]. The terminology used to describe LLCs formed in other states or nations is also similar to that used in corporate law. For instance, an LLC formed in one state but doing business in another state is referred to in the second state as a *foreign LLC.*

The Formation of the LLC

LLCs are creatures of statute and thus must follow state statutory requirements. To form an LLC, **articles of organization** must be filed with a central state agency—usually the secretary of state's office [ULLCA 202].[3]

3. In addition to requiring articles of organization to be filed, a few states require that a notice of the intention to form an LLC be published in a local newspaper.

CONTENTS OF THE ARTICLES Typically, the articles of organization must include the name of the business, its principal address, the name and address of a registered agent, the members' names, and how the LLC will be managed [ULLCA 203]. The business's name must include the words *Limited Liability Company* or the initials *LLC* [ULLCA 105(a)]. Although a majority of the states permit one-member LLCs, some states require at least two members.

PREFORMATION CONTRACTS Businesspersons sometimes enter into contracts on behalf of a business organization that is not yet formed. As you will read in Chapter 19, persons who are forming a corporation may enter into contracts during the process of incorporation but before the corporation becomes a legal entity. These contracts are referred to as *preincorporation contracts.* Once the corporation is formed and adopts the preincorporation contracts (by means of a *novation,* discussed in Chapter 10), it can enforce the contract terms.

In dealing with the preorganization contracts of LLCs, courts may apply the well-established principles of corporate law relating to preincorporation contracts. ▶ **Case in Point 18.2** 607 South Park, LLC, entered into an agreement to sell a hotel to 607 Park View Associates, Ltd., which then assigned the rights to the purchase to another company, 02 Development, LLC. At the time, 02 Development did not yet exist—it was legally created several months later. 607 South Park subsequently refused to sell the hotel to 02 Development, and 02 Development sued for breach of the purchase agreement.

A California appellate court ruled that LLCs should be treated the same as corporations with respect to preorganization contracts. Although 02 Development did not exist when the agreement was executed, once it came into existence, it could enforce any preorganization contract made on its behalf.[4] ◀

Jurisdictional Requirements

As we have seen, LLCs and corporations share several characteristics, but a significant difference between these organizational forms involves federal jurisdictional requirements. Under the federal jurisdiction statute, a corporation is deemed to be a citizen of the state where it is incorporated and maintains its principal place of business. The statute does not mention the state citizenship of partnerships, LLCs, and other unincorporated associations, but the courts have tended to regard these entities as citizens of every state of which their members are citizens.

The state citizenship of an LLC may come into play when a party sues the LLC based on diversity of citizenship. Remember from Chapter 2 that when parties to a lawsuit are from different states and the amount in controversy exceeds $75,000, a federal court can exercise diversity jurisdiction. *Total* diversity of citizenship must exist, however.

▶ **Example 18.3** Jen Fong, a citizen of New York, wishes to bring a suit against Skycel, an LLC formed under the laws of Connecticut. One of Skycel's members also lives in New York. Fong will not be able to bring a suit against Skycel in federal court on the basis of diversity jurisdiction because the defendant LLC is also a citizen of New York. The same would be true if Fong was bringing a suit against multiple defendants and one of the defendants lived in New York. ◀

4. *02 Development, LLC v. 607 South Park, LLC,* 159 Cal.App.4th 609, 71 Cal.Rptr.3d 608 (2008).

Advantages of the LLC

The LLC offers many advantages to businesspersons, which is why this form of business organization has become increasingly popular.

LIMITED LIABILITY A key advantage of the LLC is that the liability of members is limited to the amount of their investments. Although the LLC as an entity can be held liable for any loss or injury caused by the wrongful acts or omissions of its members, the members themselves generally are not personally liable.

FLEXIBILITY IN TAXATION Another advantage of the LLC is its flexibility in regard to taxation. An LLC that has *two or more members* can choose to be taxed as either a partnership or a corporation. As will be discussed in Chapter 19, a corporate entity must pay income taxes on its profits, and the shareholders pay personal income taxes on profits distributed as dividends. An LLC that wants to distribute profits to its members may prefer to be taxed as a partnership to avoid the "double taxation" that is characteristic of the corporate entity.

Unless an LLC indicates that it wishes to be taxed as a corporation, the Internal Revenue Service (IRS) automatically taxes it as a partnership. This means that the LLC, as an entity, pays no taxes. Rather, as in a partnership, profits are "passed through" the LLC to the members, who then personally pay taxes on the profits. If an LLC's members want to reinvest profits in the business rather than distribute the profits to members, however, they may prefer to be taxed as a corporation. Corporate income tax rates may be lower than personal tax rates. Part of the attractiveness of the LLC is this flexibility with respect to taxation.

An LLC that has only *one member* cannot be taxed as a partnership. For federal income tax purposes, one-member LLCs are automatically taxed as sole proprietorships unless they indicate that they wish to be taxed as corporations. With respect to state taxes, most states follow the IRS rules.

MANAGEMENT AND FOREIGN INVESTORS Another advantage of the LLC for businesspersons is the flexibility it offers in terms of business operations and management—as will be discussed shortly. Foreign investors are allowed to become LLC members, so organizing as an LLC can enable a business to attract investors from other countries.

Disadvantages of the LLC

The main disadvantage of the LLC is that state LLC statutes are not uniform. Therefore, businesses that operate in more than one state may not receive consistent treatment in these states.

Generally, most states apply to a foreign LLC (an LLC formed in another state) the law of the state where the LLC was formed. Difficulties can arise, though, when one state's court must interpret and apply another state's laws.

SECTION 2

LLC MANAGEMENT AND OPERATION

The members of an LLC have considerable flexibility in managing and operating the business. Here, we discuss management options, fiduciary duties owed, and the operating agreement and general operating procedures of LLCs.

Management of an LLC

Basically, LLC members have two options for managing the firm. It can be either a "member-managed" LLC or a "manager-managed" LLC. Most state LLC statutes and the ULLCA provide that unless the articles of organization specify otherwise, an LLC is assumed to be member managed [ULLCA 203(a)(6)].

In a *member-managed* LLC, all of the members participate in management, and decisions are made by majority vote [ULLCA 404(a)]. In a *manager-managed* LLC, the members designate a group of persons to manage the firm. The management group may consist of only members, both members and nonmembers, or only nonmembers.

Fiduciary Duties

Under the ULLCA, managers in a manager-managed LLC owe fiduciary duties (the duty of loyalty and the duty of care) to the LLC and its members [ULLCA 409(a), 409(h)]. (As you will read in Chapter 19, this same rule applies in corporate law—corporate directors and officers owe fiduciary duties to the corporation and its shareholders.) Because not all states have adopted the ULLCA, though, some state statutes provide that managers owe fiduciary duties only to the LLC and not to the LLC's members. Although to whom the duty is owed may seem insignificant at first glance, it can have a dramatic effect on the outcome of litigation.

In Alabama, where the following case arose, managers owe fiduciary duties to the LLC and to its members.

CASE 18.2

Polk v. Polk

Court of Civil Appeals of Alabama, 70 So.3d 363 (2011).

BACKGROUND AND FACTS Leslie Polk and his children, Yurii and Dusty Polk and Lezanne Proctor, formed Polk Plumbing, LLC, in Alabama. Leslie, Dusty, and Yurii performed commercial plumbing work, and Lezanne, an accountant, maintained the financial records and served as the office manager. After a couple of years, Yurii quit the firm. Eighteen months later, Leslie "fired" Dusty and Lezanne. He denied them access to the LLC's books and offices but continued to operate the business.

Dusty and Lezanne filed a suit in an Alabama state court against Leslie, claiming breach of fiduciary duty. The court submitted the claim to a jury with the instruction that in Alabama employment relationships are "at will" (see Chapter 21). The court also told the jury that it could not consider the plaintiffs' "firing" as part of their claim. The jury awarded Dusty and Lezanne one dollar each in damages. They appealed, arguing that the judge's instructions to the jury were prejudicial—that is, that the instructions had substantially affected the outcome of the trial.

IN THE LANGUAGE OF THE COURT
MOORE, Judge.

* * * *

In this case, Dusty and Lezanne served as managers of the LLC. The LLC's Operating Agreement * * * provided that the Members may elect one or more of the Members to serve as

Managers of the Company for the purpose of handling the day to day details of the Company. * * * The Managers shall serve for a period of one year or until their replacement or recall is voted by a majority of the Members.

Based on the evidence presented at trial showing that the parties continued to act as managers of the LLC after the first year of operation, the foregoing contractual provision guaranteed that Dusty and Lezanne would remain managers until replaced or recalled by a vote of the majority of the members. Hence, their employment as managers of the LLC was not at will and the trial court erred in instructing the jury that it was. [Emphasis added.]

The trial court further erred in not allowing the jury to consider the circumstances of Dusty and Lezanne's "firing" as part of their breach-of-fiduciary-duty claim. * * * The record contains no evidence indicating that a vote was ever held to recall or replace Dusty and Lezanne. Rather, as Leslie testified, he simply acted in disregard of the terms of the Operating Agreement and instead rested on his right as the patriarch of the family to "fire" Dusty and Lezanne for, in his opinion, not working enough. Hence, * * * Leslie did not have the authority under the Operating Agreement to terminate the management positions of Dusty and Lezanne in the manner in which he did.

* * * *

By failing to instruct the jury that it also could consider Leslie's "firing" of Dusty and Lezanne as evidence in support of their breach-of-fiduciary-duty claim, we conclude that the trial court probably injuriously affected substantial rights of Dusty and Lezanne.

* * * *

Had the jury properly considered all the evidence supporting their breach-of-fiduciary-duty claim, it might have concluded that a higher amount of compensatory damages and possibly even punitive damages should have been awarded to Dusty and Lezanne.

DECISION AND REMEDY *A state intermediate appellate court reversed the lower court's judgment on the claim for breach of fiduciary duty and remanded the case for a new trial. The lower court committed reversible error by instructing the jury that Dusty and Lezanne's employment as managers was at will and by failing to instruct the jury that it could consider their "firing" as evidence in support of their claim.*

WHAT IF THE FACTS WERE DIFFERENT? *Suppose that Leslie owned a majority of Polk Plumbing. Could his "firing" of Dusty and Lezanne still be considered as evidence of a breach of fiduciary duty? Explain.*

THE LEGAL ENVIRONMENT DIMENSION *Under what circumstances might the employment-at-will doctrine apply to the members of an LLC?*

The LLC Operating Agreement

The members of an LLC can decide how to operate the various aspects of the business by forming an **operating agreement** [ULLCA 103(a)]. In many states, an operating agreement is not required for an LLC to exist, and if there is one, it need not be in writing. Generally, though, LLC members should protect their interests by creating a written operating agreement.

Operating agreements typically contain provisions relating to the following areas:

1. Management and how future managers will be chosen or removed. (Although most LLC statutes are silent on this issue, the ULLCA provides that members may choose and remove managers by majority vote [ULLCA 404(b)(3)].)
2. How profits will be divided.
3. How membership interests may be transferred.
4. Whether the dissociation of a member, such as by death or departure, will trigger dissolution of the LLC.
5. Whether formal members' meetings will be held.
6. How voting rights will be apportioned. (If the agreement does not cover voting, LLC statutes in most states provide that voting rights are apportioned according to each member's capital contributions.[5] Some states provide that, in the absence of an agreement to the contrary, each member has one vote.)

5. In contrast, partners in a partnership generally have equal rights in management and equal voting rights unless they specify otherwise in their partnership agreement (see Chapter 17).

STATE STATUTES FILL IN GAPS If the agreement does not cover a topic, such as how profits will be divided, the state LLC statute will govern. Most LLC statutes provide that if the members have not specified how profits will be divided, they will be divided equally among the members.

PARTNERSHIP LAW MAY APPLY If a dispute arises and the state's LLC statute does not cover the issue, courts sometimes apply the principles of partnership law. ▶ **Case in Point 18.4** Clifford Kuhn, Jr., and Joseph Tumminelli formed Touch of Class Limousine Service as an LLC. They did not create a written operating agreement but orally agreed that Kuhn would provide the financial backing and that Tumminelli would manage the day-to-day operations. Tumminelli embezzled $283,000 from the company after cashing customers' checks at Quick Cash, Inc., a local check-cashing service.

Kuhn sued Tumminelli and Quick Cash to recover the embezzled funds. He argued that Quick Cash was liable because Tumminelli did not have the authority to cash the company's checks. The court, however, held that in the absence of a written operating agreement to the contrary, a member of an LLC, like a partner in a partnership, has the authority to cash a firm's checks. Therefore, Kuhn's claim against Quick Cash was dismissed.[6] ◀

SECTION 3

DISSOCIATION AND DISSOLUTION OF AN LLC

Recall from Chapter 17 that in a partnership, *dissociation* occurs when a partner ceases to be associated in the carrying on of the partnership business. The same concept applies to LLCs. A member of an LLC has the *power* to dissociate from the LLC at any time, but he or she may not have the *right* to dissociate.

Under the ULLCA, the events that trigger a member's dissociation from an LLC are similar to the events causing a partner to be dissociated under the Uniform Partnership Act (UPA). These include voluntary withdrawal, expulsion by other members or by court order, incompetence, and death. Generally, if a member dies or otherwise dissociates from an LLC, the other members may continue to carry on the LLC business, unless the operating agreement provides otherwise.

Effect of Dissociation

When a member dissociates from an LLC, he or she loses the right to participate in management and the right to act as an agent for the LLC. The member's duty of loyalty to the LLC also terminates, and the duty of care continues only with respect to events that occurred before dissociation.

Generally, the dissociated member also has a right to have his or her interest in the LLC bought out by the other members. The LLC's operating agreement may contain provisions establishing a buyout price, but if it does not, the member's interest is usually purchased at a fair value. In states that have adopted the ULLCA, the LLC must purchase the interest at fair value within 120 days after the dissociation.

If the member's dissociation violates the LLC's operating agreement, it is considered legally wrongful, and the dissociated member can be held liable for damages caused by the dissociation. ▶ **Example 18.5** Chadwick and Barrow are members in an LLC. Chadwick manages the accounts, and Barrow, who has many connections in the community and is a skilled investor, brings in the business. If Barrow wrongfully dissociates from the LLC, the LLC's business will suffer, and Chadwick can hold Barrow liable for the loss of business resulting from her withdrawal. ◀

Dissolution

Regardless of whether a member's dissociation was wrongful or rightful, normally the dissociated member has no right to force the LLC to dissolve. The remaining members can opt either to continue or to dissolve the business.

Members can also stipulate in their operating agreement that certain events will cause dissolution, or they can agree that they have the power to dissolve the LLC by vote. As with partnerships, a court can order an LLC to be dissolved in certain circumstances. For instance, a court might order dissolution when the members have engaged in illegal or oppressive conduct, or when it is no longer feasible to carry on the business.

In the following case, the court had to decide whether an LLC could be dissolved because continuing the business was impracticable.

6. *Kuhn v. Tumminelli,* 366 N.J.Super. 431, 841 A.2d 496 (2004).

CASE 18.3

Venture Sales, LLC v. Perkins

Supreme Court of Mississippi, 86 So.3d 910 (2012).

BACKGROUND AND FACTS Walter Perkins, Gary Fordham, and David Thompson formed Venture Sales, LLC, to develop a subdivision in Petal, Mississippi. All three members contributed land and funds to Venture Sales, resulting in total holdings of 466 acres of land and about $158,000 in cash.

Perkins was an assistant coach for the Cleveland Browns, so he trusted Fordham and Thompson to develop the property. Over a decade later, however, Fordham and Thompson still had not done anything with the property, although they had developed at least two other subdivisions in the area. Fordham and Thompson said that they did not know when they could develop the property and that they had been unable to get the additional $8 million they needed to proceed. Fordham and Thompson suggested selling the property, but Perkins did not agree with the proposed listing price of $3.5 million. Perkins then sought a judicial dissolution of Venture Sales in Mississippi state court. The trial court ordered the company dissolved. Fordham, Thompson, and Venture Sales appealed.

IN THE LANGUAGE OF THE COURT

WALLER, Chief Justice, for the Court.

* * * *

* * * [Under the Mississippi Code, an LLC may be dissolved if it] is not reasonably practicable to carry on the business in conformity with the certificate of formation or the limited liability company agreement * * * .

* * * *

While no definitive, widely accepted test or standard exists for determining "reasonable practicability," it is clear that *when a limited liability company is not meeting the economic purpose for which it was established, dissolution is appropriate. In making this determination, we must first look to the company's operating agreement to determine the purpose for which the company was formed.* [Emphasis added.]

Venture Sales' operating agreement states that the company's purpose is "to initially acquire, *develop and sale* [sic] *commercial and residential properties* near Petal, Forrest County, Mississippi." At trial, Fordham admitted that the company was formed for the purpose of acquiring and developing property. Yet, more than ten years after Venture Sales was formed with Perkins as a member, the property remains completely undeveloped. Fordham and Thompson have offered a number of reasons why development has been delayed to this point. [Emphasis in original.]

* * * *

Despite [the] alleged hindrances, Fordham and Thompson have, during this ten-year period, successfully formed two other LLCs and have developed at least two other subdivisions with around 200 houses, collectively, within twenty-five miles of the subject property. More importantly, though, Fordham and Thompson presented no evidence that Venture Sales would be able to develop the land as intended within the foreseeable future. When asked by the trial court when Venture Sales might be able to begin developing as it had planned, Fordham could not say. Fordham and Thompson admitted that it would take around $8 million to "kick off" construction of the subdivision as planned, and the [trial court] found that Venture Sales was currently unable to get additional bank loans or other funding needed to begin development.

* * * *

Fordham and Thompson claim that Perkins has blocked Venture Sales from taking advantage of certain "business opportunities," such as selling the property at a reduced price of $3.5 million * * * . However, these "business opportunities" were merely ideas from Fordham about how to make use of the property. * * * As discussed above, they presented no evidence that Venture Sales could develop the property, which is the purpose for which the company was formed.

CASE 18.3 CONTINUES ➧

CASE 18.3 CONTINUED

DECISION AND REMEDY *The Mississippi Supreme Court held that Venture Sales could be judicially dissolved. It therefore affirmed the decision of the trial court.*

THE LEGAL ENVIRONMENT DIMENSION *Would dissolution be appropriate if the parties had formed a partnership rather than an LLC? Explain your answer.*

MANAGERIAL IMPLICATIONS *To avoid the type of dispute in which the members of Venture Sales became embroiled, the managers of an LLC or other business organization should take care to act on the firm's "economic purpose" within a reasonable time. To ensure that they will be able to do so, the managers should draw up plans and determine the full cost of the project. They should also ascertain how the needed funds will be obtained. If bank loans or other funding will not be available, as occurred in this case, the LLC should require a higher level of contributions from its members to ensure that there will be sufficient funds to complete the project successfully.*

Winding Up

When an LLC is dissolved, any members who did not wrongfully dissociate may participate in the winding up process. To wind up the business, members must collect, liquidate, and distribute the LLC's assets.

Members may preserve the assets for a reasonable time to optimize their return, and they continue to have the authority to perform reasonable acts in conjunction with winding up. In other words, the LLC will be bound by the reasonable acts of its members during the winding up process.

Once all of the LLC's assets have been sold, the proceeds are distributed to pay off debts to creditors first (including debts owed to members who are creditors of the LLC). The members' capital contributions are returned next, and any remaining amounts are then distributed to members in equal shares or according to their operating agreement.

SECTION 4 LIMITED LIABILITY PARTNERSHIPS

The **limited liability partnership (LLP)** is a hybrid form of business designed mostly for professionals who normally do business as partners in a partnership. Almost all of the states have enacted LLP statutes.

The major advantage of the LLP is that it allows a partnership to continue as a pass-through entity for tax purposes but limits the personal liability of the partners. The LLP is especially attractive for professional service firms and family businesses. All of the "Big Four" accounting firms—the four largest international accountancy and professional services firms—are organized as LLPs, including Ernst & Young, LLP, and PricewaterhouseCoopers, LLP.

Formation of an LLP

LLPs must be formed in compliance with state statutes, which may include provisions of the Uniform Partnership Act (UPA). The appropriate form must be filed with a central state agency, usually the secretary of state's office, and the business's name must include either "Limited Liability Partnership" or "LLP" [UPA 1001, 1002]. An LLP must file an annual report with the state to remain qualified as an LLP in that state [UPA 1003].

In most states, it is relatively easy to convert a traditional partnership into an LLP because the firm's basic organizational structure remains the same. Additionally, all of the statutory and common law rules governing partnerships still apply (apart from those modified by the LLP statute). Normally, LLP statutes are simply amendments to a state's already existing partnership law.

Liability in an LLP

An LLP allows professionals, such as attorneys and accountants, to avoid personal liability for the malpractice of other partners. A partner in an LLP is still liable for her or his own wrongful acts, such as negligence, however. Also liable is the partner who supervised the individual who committed a wrongful act. (This generally is true for all types of partners and partnerships, not just LLPs.)

▶ **Example 18.6** Five lawyers operate a law firm as an LLP. One of the attorneys, Dan Kolcher, is sued for malpractice and loses. The firm's malpractice insurance is insufficient to pay the judgment. If the firm had been organized as a traditional (general) partnership, the personal assets of the other attorneys could be used to satisfy the obligation. Because the firm is organized as an LLP, however, no other partner at the law firm can be held *personally* liable for Kolcher's malpractice, unless she or he acted as Kolcher's supervisor. In the absence of a supervisor, only Kolcher's personal assets can be used to satisfy the judgment. ◀

Although LLP statutes vary from state to state, generally each state statute limits the liability of partners in some way. For instance, Delaware law protects each innocent partner from the "debts and obligations of the partnership arising from negligence, wrongful acts, or misconduct." The UPA more broadly exempts partners from personal liability for any partnership obligation, "whether arising in contract, tort, or otherwise" [UPA 306(c)].

LIABILITY FROM STATE TO STATE When an LLP formed in one state wants to do business in another state, it may be required to register in the second state—for example, by filing a statement of foreign qualification [UPA 1102]. Because state LLP statutes are not uniform, a question sometimes arises as to which law applies if the LLP statutes in the two states provide different liability protection. Most states apply the law of the state in which the LLP was formed, even when the firm does business in another state, which is also the rule under UPA 1101.

SHARING LIABILITY AMONG PARTNERS When more than one partner in an LLP is negligent, there is a question as to how liability should be shared. Some states provide for proportionate liability—that is, for separate determinations of the negligence of the partners.

▶ **Example 18.7** Accountants Zach and Lyla are partners in an LLP, with Zach supervising Lyla. Lyla negligently fails to file a tax return for a client, Centaur Tools. Centaur files a suit against Zach and Lyla. Under a proportionate liability statute, Zach will be liable for no more than his portion of the responsibility for the missed tax deadline. In a state that does not allow for proportionate liability, Zach can be held liable for the entire loss. ◀

Family Limited Liability Partnerships

A **family limited liability partnership (FLLP)** is a limited liability partnership in which the partners are related to each other—for example, as spouses, parents and children, siblings, or cousins. A person acting in a fiduciary capacity for persons so related can also be a partner. All of the partners must be natural persons or persons acting in a fiduciary capacity for the benefit of natural persons.

Probably the most significant use of the FLLP form of business organization is in agriculture. Family-owned farms sometimes find this form to their benefit. The FLLP offers the same advantages as other LLPs with certain additional advantages, such as, in Iowa, an exemption from real estate transfer taxes when partnership real estate is transferred among partners.[7]

SECTION 5

LIMITED PARTNERSHIPS

We now look at a business organizational form that limits the liability of *some* of its owners—the **limited partnership (LP).** Limited partnerships originated in medieval Europe and have been in existence in the United States since the early 1800s. Limited partnerships differ from traditional (general) partnerships in several ways.

A limited partnership consists of at least one **general partner** and one or more **limited partners.** A general partner assumes management responsibility for the partnership and has full responsibility for the partnership and for all its debts. A limited partner contributes cash or other property and owns an interest in the firm but is not involved in management responsibilities and is not personally liable for partnership debts beyond the amount of his or her investment. A limited partner can forfeit limited liability by taking part in the management of the business. A comparison of traditional partnerships (see Chapter 17) and limited partnerships appears in Exhibit 18–1 on the following page.[8]

Most states and the District of Columbia have adopted the Revised Uniform Limited Partnership Act (RULPA), which we refer to in the following discussion. A minority of states have adopted some amendments that were proposed in 2001 to make the RULPA more flexible.

7. Iowa Statutes Section 428A.2.

8. Under the UPA, a general partnership can be converted into a limited partnership and vice versa [UPA 902, 903]. The UPA also provides for the merger of a general partnership with one or more general or limited partnerships [UPA 905].

EXHIBIT 18–1 A Comparison of General Partnerships and Limited Partnerships

Characteristic	General Partnership (UPA)	Limited Partnership (RULPA)
Creation	By agreement of two or more persons to carry on a business as co-owners for profit.	By agreement of two or more persons to carry on a business as co-owners for profit. Must include one or more general partners and one or more limited partners. Filing of a certificate with the secretary of state is required.
Sharing of Profits and Losses	By agreement. In the absence of agreement, profits are shared equally by the partners, and losses are shared in the same ratio as profits.	Profits are shared as required in the certificate agreement, and losses are shared likewise, up to the amount of the limited partners' capital contributions. In the absence of a provision in the certificate agreement, profits and losses are shared on the basis of percentages of capital contributions.
Liability	Unlimited personal liability of all partners.	Unlimited personal liability of all general partners; limited partners liable only to the extent of their capital contributions.
Capital Contribution	No minimum or mandatory amount; set by agreement.	Set by agreement.
Management	By agreement. In the absence of agreement, all partners have an equal voice.	Only the general partner (or the general partners). Limited partners have no voice or else are subject to liability as general partners (but only if a third party has reason to believe that the limited partner is a general partner). A limited partner may act as an agent or employee of the partnership and vote on amending the certificate or on the sale or dissolution of the partnership.
Duration	Terminated by agreement of the partners, but can continue to do business even when a partner dissociates from the partnership.	Terminated by agreement in the certificate or by retirement, death, or mental incompetence of a general partner in the absence of the right of the other general partners to continue the partnership. Death of a limited partner does not terminate the partnership, unless he or she is the only remaining limited partner.
Distribution of Assets on Liquidation—Order of Priorities	1. Payment of debts, including those owed to partner and nonpartner creditors. 2. Return of capital contributions and distribution of profit to partners.	1. Outside creditors and partner creditors. 2. Partners and former partners entitled to distributions of partnership assets. 3. Unless otherwise agreed, return of capital contributions and distribution of profit to partners.

Formation of a Limited Partnership

In contrast to the informal, private, and voluntary agreement that usually suffices for a traditional partnership, the formation of a limited partnership is a public and formal proceeding that must follow statutory requirements. Not only must a limited partnership have at least one general partner and one limited partner, but the partners must also sign a **certificate of limited partnership.**

Like *articles of incorporation* (see Chapter 19), this certificate must include certain information such as the name, mailing address, and capital contribution of each general and limited partner. The certificate must be filed with the designated state official—under the RULPA, the secretary of state. The certificate is usually open to public inspection.

Liabilities of Partners in a Limited Partnership

General partners, unlike limited partners, are personally liable to the partnership's creditors. Thus, at least one general partner is necessary in a limited partnership so that someone has personal liability. This policy can be circumvented in states that allow a corporation to be the general partner in a partnership. Because the corporation has limited liability by virtue of corporation statutes, if a corporation is the general partner, no one in the limited partnership has personal liability.

The liability of a limited partner, as mentioned, is limited to the capital that she or he contributes or agrees to contribute to the partnership [RULPA 502]. Limited partners enjoy this limited liability only so long as they do not participate in management [RULPA 303].

A limited partner who participates in management will be just as liable as a general partner to any creditor who transacts business with the limited partnership. Liability arises when the creditor believes, based on the limited partner's conduct, that the limited partner is a general partner [RULPA 303]. The extent of review and advisement that a limited partner can engage in before being exposed to liability is not always clear, though.

Rights and Duties in a Limited Partnership

With the exception of the right to participate in management, limited partners have essentially the same rights as general partners. Limited partners have a right of access to the partnership's books and to information regarding partnership business.

On dissolution of the partnership, limited partners are entitled to a return of their contributions in accordance with the partnership certificate [RULPA 201(a)(10)]. They can also assign their interests subject to the certificate [RULPA 702, 704]. In addition, limited partners can sue an outside party on behalf of the firm if the general partners with authority to do so have refused to file suit [RULPA 1001].

Dissociation and Dissolution

A general partner has the power to voluntarily dissociate, or withdraw, from a limited partnership unless the partnership agreement specifies otherwise. A limited partner theoretically can withdraw from the partnership by giving six months' notice unless the partnership agreement specifies a term, as most do. Also, some states have passed laws prohibiting the withdrawal of limited partners.

EVENTS THAT CAUSE DISSOCIATION In a limited partnership, a general partner's voluntary dissociation from the firm normally will lead to dissolution *unless* all partners agree to continue the business. Similarly, the bankruptcy, retirement, death, or mental incompetence of a general partner will cause the dissociation of that partner and the dissolution of the limited partnership unless the other members agree to continue the firm [RULPA 801].

Bankruptcy of a limited partner, however, does not dissolve the partnership unless it causes the bankruptcy of the firm. Death or an assignment of the interest of a limited partner does not dissolve a limited partnership [RULPA 702, 704, 705]. A limited partnership can be dissolved by court decree [RULPA 802].

DISTRIBUTION OF ASSETS On dissolution, creditors' claims, including those of partners who are creditors, take first priority. After that, partners and former partners receive unpaid distributions of partnership assets. Unless otherwise agreed, they are also entitled to a return of their contributions in the proportions in which the partners share in distributions [RULPA 804].

VALUATION OF ASSETS Disputes commonly arise about how the partnership's assets should be valued and distributed and whether the business should be sold. ▶ **Case in Point 18.8** Actor Kevin Costner was a limited partner in Midnight Star Enterprises, LP, which runs a casino, bar, and restaurant in South Dakota. There were two other limited partners, Carla and Francis Caneva, who owned a small percentage of the partnership (3.25 units each) and received salaries for managing its operations. Another company owned by Costner, Midnight Star Enterprises, Limited (MSEL), was the general partner. Costner thus controlled a majority of the partnership (93.5 units).

When communications broke down between the partners, MSEL asked a court to dissolve the partnership. MSEL's accountant determined that the firm's fair market value was $3.1 million. The Canevas presented evidence that a competitor would buy the business for $6.2 million. The Canevas wanted the court to force Costner to either buy the business for that price within ten days or sell it on the open market to the highest bidder. Ultimately, the state's highest court held in favor of Costner. A partner cannot force the sale of a limited partnership when the other partners want to continue the business. The court also accepted the $3.1 million buyout price of MSEL's accountant and ordered Costner to pay the Canevas the value of their 6.5 partnership units.[9] ◀

9. *In re Dissolution of Midnight Star Enterprises, LP,* 2006 SD 98, 724 N.W.2d 334 (S.D.Sup.Ct. 2006).

Limited Liability Limited Partnerships

A **limited liability limited partnership (LLLP)** is a type of limited partnership. An LLLP differs from a limited partnership in that a general partner in an LLLP has the same liability as a limited partner in a limited partnership. In other words, the liability of all partners is limited to the amount of their investments in the firm.

A few states provide expressly for LLLPs.[10] In states that do not provide for LLLPs but do allow for limited partnerships and limited liability partnerships, a limited partnership should probably still be able to register with the state as an LLLP.

10. See, for example, Colorado Revised Statutes Annotated Section 7-62-109. Other states that provide for LLLPs include Delaware, Florida, Georgia, Kentucky, Maryland, Nevada, Texas, and Virginia.

Reviewing: Limited Liability Business Forms

The city of Papagos, Arizona, had a deteriorating bridge in need of repair on a prominent public roadway. The city posted notices seeking proposals for an artistic bridge design and reconstruction. Davidson Masonry, LLC, which was owned and managed by Carl Davidson and his wife, Marilyn Rowe, decided to submit a bid to create a decorative concrete structure that incorporated artistic metalwork. They contacted Shana Lafayette, a local sculptor who specialized in large-scale metal creations, to help them design the bridge. The city selected their bridge design and awarded them the contract for a commission of $184,000. Davidson Masonry and Lafayette then agreed to work together on the bridge project. Davidson Masonry agreed to install and pay for concrete and structural work, and Lafayette agreed to install the metalwork at her expense in exchange for 25 percent of the profits. Lafayette designed numerous metal sculptures of trout that were incorporated into colorful decorative concrete forms designed by Rowe, while Davidson performed the structural engineering. Using the information presented in the chapter, answer the following questions.

1. Would Davidson Masonry automatically be taxed as a partnership or a corporation?
2. Is Davidson Masonry member managed or manager managed?
3. Suppose that during construction, Lafayette had entered into an agreement to rent space in a warehouse that was close to the bridge so that she could work on her sculptures near the site where they would eventually be installed. She entered into the contract without the knowledge or consent of Davidson Masonry. In this situation, would a court be likely to hold that Davidson Masonry was bound by the contract that Lafayette entered? Why or why not?
4. Now suppose that Rowe has an argument with her husband and wants to withdraw from being a member of Davidson Masonry. What is the term for such a withdrawal, and what effect would it have on the LLC?

DEBATE THIS . . . *Because LLCs are essentially just partnerships with limited liability for members, all partnership laws should apply.*

Terms and Concepts

articles of organization 418
certificate of limited partnership 426
family limited liability partnership (FLLP) 425
general partner 425
limited liability company (LLC) 416
limited liability limited partnership (LLLP) 428
limited liability partnership (LLP) 424
limited partner 425
limited partnership (LP) 425
member 416
operating agreement 421

ExamPrep

Issue Spotters

1. Gabriel, Harris, and Ida are members of Jeweled Watches, LLC. What are their options with respect to the management of their firm? **(See page 420.)**
2. Dorinda, Luis, and Elizabeth form a limited partnership. Dorinda is a general partner, and Luis and Elizabeth are limited partners. If Elizabeth is petitioned into involuntary bankruptcy, does that constitute a dissolution of the limited partnership. **(See page 427.)**

- **Check your answers to the Issue Spotters against the answers provided in Appendix E at the end of this text.**

Before the Test

Go to **www.cengagebrain.com**, enter the ISBN 9781285428949, and click on "Find" to locate this textbook's Web site. Then, click on "Access Now" under "Study Tools," and select Chapter 18 at the top. There, you will find an Interactive Quiz that you can take to assess your mastery of the concepts in this chapter, as well as Flashcards and a Glossary of important terms.

Business Scenarios

18–1. Limited Liability Companies. John, Lesa, and Tabir form a limited liability company. John contributes 60 percent of the capital, and Lesa and Tabir each contribute 20 percent. Nothing is decided about how profits will be divided. John assumes that he will be entitled to 60 percent of the profits, in accordance with his contribution. Lesa and Tabir, however, assume that the profits will be divided equally. A dispute over the profits arises, and ultimately a court has to decide the issue. What law will the court apply? In most states, what will result? How could this dispute have been avoided in the first place? Discuss fully. **(See page 418.)**

18–2. Diversity Jurisdiction and Limited Liability Companies Joe, a resident of New Jersey, wants to open a restaurant. He asks Kay, his friend, an experienced attorney and a New Yorker, for her business and legal advice in exchange for a 20 percent ownership interest in the restaurant. Kay helps Joe negotiate a lease for the restaurant premises and advises Joe to organize the business as a limited liability company (LLC). Joe forms Café Olé, LLC, and with Kay's help, obtains financing. Then, the night before the restaurant opens, Joe tells Kay that he is "cutting her out of the deal." The restaurant proves to be a success. Kay wants to file a suit in a federal district court against Joe and the LLC. Can a federal court exercise jurisdiction over the parties based on diversity of citizenship? Explain. **(See page 419.)**

Business Case Problems

18–3. Limited Partnership. James Carpenter contracted with Austin Estates, LP, to buy property in Texas. Carpenter asked Sandra McBeth to invest in the deal. He admitted that a dispute had arisen with the city of Austin over water for the property, but he assured her that it would not be a significant obstacle. McBeth agreed to invest $800,000 to hold open the option to buy the property. She became a limited partner in StoneLake Ranch, LP. Carpenter acted as the firm's general partner. Despite his assurances to McBeth, the purchase was delayed due to the water dispute. Unable to complete the purchase in a timely manner, Carpenter paid the $800,000 to Austin Estates without notifying McBeth. Later, Carpenter and others—excluding McBeth—bought the property and sold it at a profit. McBeth filed a suit in a Texas state court against Carpenter. What is the nature of the fiduciary duty that a general partner owes a limited partner? Did Carpenter breach that duty in this case? Explain. [*McBeth v. Carpenter,* 565 F.3d 171 (5th Cir. 2009)] **(See page 425.)**

18–4. Limited Liability Companies. Coco Investments, LLC, and other investors participated in a condominium conversion project to be managed by Zamir Manager River Terrace, LLC. The participants entered into a new LLC agreement for the project. The investors subsequently complained that Zamir had failed to disclose its plans for dramatic changes involving higher-than-expected construction costs and delays, had failed to provide financial information, and had restructured loans in a manner that allowed Zamir representatives to avoid personal liability. The investors sued Zamir on various grounds, including breach of contract and breach of fiduciary duty. Zamir moved for summary judgment. How should the court rule? Explain. [*Coco Investments, LLC v. Zamir Manager River Terrace, LLC,* 26 Misc.3d 1231 (N.Y.Sup. 2010)] **(See page 420.)**

18–5. BUSINESS CASE PROBLEM WITH SAMPLE ANSWER: LLC Operation.

After Hurricane Katrina, James Williford, Patricia Mosser, Marquetta Smith, and Michael Floyd formed Bluewater Logistics, LLC, to bid on construction contracts. Under Mississippi law, every member of a member-managed LLC is entitled to participate in managing the business. The operating agreement provided for a

*"super majority" 75 percent vote to remove a member "under any other circumstances that would jeopardize the company status" as a contractor. After Bluewater had completed more than $5 million in contracts, Smith told Williford that she, Mosser, and Floyd were exercising their "super majority" vote to fire him. No reason was provided. Williford sued Bluewater and the other members. Did Smith, Mosser, and Floyd breach the state LLC statute, their fiduciary duties, or the Bluewater operating agreements? Discuss. [*Bluewater Logistics, LLC v. Williford, *55 So.3d 148 (Miss. 2011)]* **(See page 420.)**

- **For a sample answer to Problem 18–5, go to Appendix F at the end of this text.**

18–6. Jurisdictional Requirements. Fadal Machining Centers, LLC, and MAG Industrial Automation Centers, LLC, sued a New Jersey–based corporation, Mid-Atlantic CNC, Inc., in federal district court. Ten percent of MAG was owned by SP MAG Holdings, a Delaware LLC. SP MAG had six members, including a Delaware limited partnership called Silver Point Capital Fund and a Delaware LLC called SPCP Group III. In turn, Silver Point and SPCP Group had a common member, Robert O'Shea, who was a New Jersey citizen. Assuming that the amount in controversy exceeds $75,000, does the district court have diversity jurisdiction? Why or why not? [*Fadal Machining Centers, LLC v. Mid-Atlantic CNC, Inc.*, 2012 WL 8669 (9th Cir. 2012)] **(See page 419.)**

18–7. A QUESTION OF ETHICS: Limited Liability Companies.

*Blushing Brides, LLC, a publisher of wedding planning magazines in Columbus, Ohio, opened an account with Gray Printing Co. in July 2000. On behalf of Blushing Brides, Louis Zacks, the firm's member-manager, signed a credit agreement that identified the firm as the "purchaser" and required payment within thirty days. Despite the agreement, Blushing Brides typically took up to six months to pay the full amount for its orders. Gray printed and shipped 10,000 copies of a fall/winter 2001 issue for Blushing Brides but had not been paid when the firm ordered 15,000 copies of a spring/summer 2002 issue. Gray refused to print the new order without an assurance of payment. On May 22, Zacks signed a promissory note payable to Gray within thirty days for $14,778, plus interest at 6 percent per year. Gray printed the new order but by October had been paid only $7,500. Gray filed a suit in an Ohio state court against Blushing Brides and Zacks to collect the balance. [*Gray Printing Co. v. Blushing Brides, LLC, *2006 WL 832587 (Ohio App. 2006)]* **(See page 416.)**

(a) Under what circumstances is a member of an LLC liable for the firm's debts? In this case, is Zacks personally liable under the credit agreement for the unpaid amount on Blushing Brides' account? Did Zacks's promissory note affect the parties' liability on the account? Explain.

(b) Should a member of an LLC assume an ethical responsibility to meet the obligations of the firm? Discuss.

(c) Gray shipped only 10,000 copies of the spring/summer 2002 issue of Blushing Brides' magazine, waiting for the publisher to identify a destination for the other 5,000 copies. The magazine had a retail price of $4.50 per copy. Did Gray have a legal or ethical duty to "mitigate the damages" by attempting to sell or otherwise distribute these copies itself? Why or why not?

18–8. SPECIAL CASE ANALYSIS: Limited Liability Companies.

Go to Case Analysis Case 18.1, *ORX Resources, Inc. v. MBW Exploration, LLC*, on pages 417 and 418. Read the excerpt and answer the following questions.

(a) Issue: What was the main issue in this case?

(b) Rule of Law: What rule of law did the court apply?

(c) Applying the Rule of Law: How did the court apply the rule of law to the facts of this case?

(d) Conclusion: What was the court's conclusion?

Legal Reasoning Group Activity

18–9. Fiduciary Duties in LLCs. Newbury Properties Group owns, manages, and develops real property. Jerry Stoker and the Stoker Group, Inc. (the Stokers), also develop real property. Newbury entered into agreements with the Stokers concerning a large tract of property in Georgia. The parties formed Bellemare, LLC, to develop various parcels of the tract for residential purposes. The operating agreement of Bellemare indicated that "no Member shall be accountable to the LLC or to any other Member with respect to any other business or activity even if the business or activity competes with the LLC's business." Later, when the Newbury group contracted with other parties to develop parcels within the tract in competition with Bellemare, LLC, the Stokers sued, alleging breach of fiduciary duty. **(See page 420.)**

(a) The first group will discuss and outline the fiduciary duties that the members of an LLC owe to each other.

(b) The second group will determine whether the terms of an operating agreement can alter these fiduciary duties.

(c) The last group will decide in whose favor the court should rule in this situation.

CORPORATIONS

The corporation is a creature of statute. A corporation is an artificial being, existing only in law and neither tangible nor visible. Its existence generally depends on state law, although some corporations, especially public organizations, are created under federal law. Each state has its own body of corporate law, and these laws are not entirely uniform.

The Model Business Corporation Act (MBCA) is a codification of modern corporation law that has been influential in shaping state corporation statutes. Today, the majority of state statutes are guided by the most recent version of the MBCA, often referred to as the Revised Model Business Corporation Act (RMBCA).

Keep in mind, however, that there is considerable variation among the laws of states that have used the MBCA or the RMBCA as a basis for their statutes. In addition, several states do not follow either act. Consequently, individual state corporation laws should be relied on to determine corporate law rather than the MBCA or RMBCA.

SECTION 1

THE NATURE AND CLASSIFICATION OF CORPORATIONS

A corporation is a legal entity created and recognized by state law. This business entity can have one or more owners (called shareholders), and it operates under a name distinct from the names of its owners. The owners may be individuals, or *natural persons* (as opposed to the artificial *legal person* of the corporation), or other businesses. Although the corporation substitutes itself for its shareholders when conducting corporate business and incurring liability, its authority to act and the liability for its actions are separate and apart from the individuals who own it.

A corporation is recognized as a "person," and it enjoys many of the same rights and privileges under state and federal law that U.S. citizens enjoy. For instance, corporations possess the same right of access to the courts as citizens and can sue or be sued. The constitutional guarantees of due process, free speech, and freedom from unreasonable searches and seizures also apply to corporations.

Corporate Personnel

In a corporation, the responsibility for the overall management of the firm is entrusted to a *board of directors,* whose members are elected by the shareholders. The board of directors makes the policy decisions and hires *corporate officers* and other employees to run the daily business operations.

When an individual purchases a share of stock in a corporation, that person becomes a shareholder and an owner of the corporation. Unlike the partners in a partnership, the body of shareholders can change constantly without affecting the continued existence of the corporation.

A shareholder can sue the corporation, and the corporation can sue a shareholder. Additionally, under certain circumstances, a shareholder can sue on behalf of a corporation. The rights and duties of corporate directors, officers, and shareholders will be discussed later in this chapter.

The Limited Liability of Shareholders

One of the key advantages of the corporate form is the limited liability of its owners. Normally, corporate shareholders are not personally liable for the obligations of the corporation beyond the extent of their investments.

In certain limited situations, however, a court can *pierce the corporate veil* (see page 441) and impose liability on shareholders for the corporation's obligations. Additionally, creditors often will not extend credit to small companies unless the shareholders assume personal liability, as guarantors, for corporate obligations.

Corporate Earnings and Taxation

When a corporation earns profits, it can either pass them on to shareholders in the form of *dividends* (see page 454) or retain them as profits. These **retained earnings,** if invested properly, will yield higher corporate profits in the future and thus cause the price of the company's stock to rise. Individual shareholders can then reap the benefits of these retained earnings in the capital gains that they receive when they sell their stock.

CORPORATE TAXATION Whether a corporation retains its profits or passes them on to the shareholders as dividends, those profits are subject to income tax by various levels of government. Failure to pay taxes can lead to severe consequences. The state can suspend the entity's corporate status until the taxes are paid or even dissolve the corporation for failing to pay taxes. (Businesses today, including corporations, may also be required to collect state sales taxes on goods or services sold via the Internet, as discussed in the *Insight into E-Commerce* feature in Chapter 11.)

Another important aspect of corporate taxation is that corporate profits can be subject to double taxation. The company pays tax on its profits. Then, if the profits are passed on to the shareholders as dividends, the shareholders must also pay income tax on them (unless the dividends represent distributions of capital). The corporation normally does not receive a tax deduction for dividends it distributes. This double-taxation feature is one of the major disadvantages of the corporate form.

HOLDING COMPANIES Some U.S. corporations use holding companies to reduce or defer their U.S. income taxes. At its simplest, a **holding company** (sometimes referred to as a *parent company*) is a company whose business activity consists of holding shares in another company. Typically, the holding company is established in a low-tax or no-tax offshore jurisdiction, such as the Cayman Islands, Dubai, Hong Kong, Luxembourg, Monaco, or Panama.

Sometimes, a U.S. corporation sets up a holding company in a low-tax offshore environment and then transfers its cash, bonds, stocks, and other investments to the holding company. In general, any profits received by the holding company on these investments are taxed at the rate of the offshore jurisdiction where the company is registered. In other words, holding company profits are not taxed at the rates applicable to the parent company or its shareholders in their country of residence. Thus, deposits of cash, for instance, may earn interest that is taxed at only a minimal rate.

Once the profits are brought "onshore," though, they are taxed at the federal corporate income tax rate, and any payments received by the shareholders are also taxable at the full U.S. rates.

Tort Liability

A corporation is liable for the torts committed by its agents or officers within the course and scope of their employment. This principle applies to a corporation exactly as it applies to the ordinary agency relationships that we will discuss in Chapter 20. It follows the doctrine of *respondeat superior.*

The following case arose from a fraudulent scheme perpetrated by the officer of an investment firm through a separate investment fund that the officer controlled and managed. When investors in the fund filed a suit to recover the funds they had lost, the court had to determine whether the corporate employer of the officer could be liable for his actions.

CASE ANALYSIS

Case 19.1 Belmont v. MB Investment Partners, Inc.

United States Court of Appeals, Third Circuit, 708 F.3d 470 (2013).

IN THE LANGUAGE OF THE COURT
JORDAN, Circuit Judge.

* * * *

[Mark] Bloom formed North Hills [L.P.] in 1997, as an enhanced stock index fund based on various stock indices. Bloom was the sole principal and managing member of North Hills Management, LLC, the general partner of North Hills, and he had sole authority over the selection of the

CASE 19.1 CONTINUED

fund's investments. * * * Between 2001 and 2007, Bloom raised approximately $30 million from 40 to 50 investors for the North Hills fund. He claimed that North Hills consistently generated investment returns of 10–15 percent per year without significant risk.

In fact, however, North Hills was a Ponzi scheme that Bloom used to finance his lavish personal lifestyle, and, over time, he diverted at least $20 million from North Hills for his own personal use. Bloom used those funds to acquire multiple apartments and homes, furnishings, luxury cars and boats, and jewelry, and to fund parties and travel.

* * * *

Bloom operated North Hills the entire time that he was an executive of [MB Investment Partners, Inc.] He made no attempt, while working at MB, to conceal his activities related to North Hills. Investments in North Hills were administered by Bloom and other MB personnel, using MB's offices, computers, filing facilities, and office equipment. MB support staff sometimes carried out tasks related to North Hills.

MB officers and directors were aware that Bloom was operating North Hills while he was also working as an investment adviser at MB.

* * * During the period of the North Hills fraud, MB did not have in place basic compliance procedures employed throughout the investment advising industry to identify and prevent fraud and self-dealing by MB employees and affiliates. Compliance weaknesses permitted Bloom to avoid required disclosures to MB about North Hills as a personal investment vehicle. *MB officers and directors failed to make basic inquiries about Bloom's operation of North Hills, and did not collect any information on North Hills or monitor sales of investments in North Hills to MB's own customers.* [Emphasis added.]

* * * *

* * * In 2008, * * * two large investors in North Hills requested a full redemption of their investments. By that time, most of the money that had been invested in North Hills was gone * * * . [Bloom] was arrested on February 25, 2009, and he was terminated by MB that same day.

* * * *

The Investors filed their * * * Complaint in this action on October 28, 2009 * * * , alleging * * * fraud * * * on the part of Bloom * * * and MB.

* * * *

* * * On January 5, 2012, the District Court granted summary judgment to [MB]. * * * On February 17, 2012, the Court entered a default judgment against Bloom and in favor of the Investors in the amount of approximately $5.7 million.

* * * This timely appeal followed.

* * * *

* * * Bloom's violations * * * are beyond dispute, and the Investors argue that those violations may be imputed to MB as his employer.

* * * *The fraud of an officer of a corporation is imputed to the corporation when the officer's fraudulent contact was (1) in the course of his employment, and (2) for the benefit of the corporation.* This is true even if the officer's conduct was unauthorized, effected for his own benefit but clothed with apparent authority of the corporation, or contrary to instructions. The underlying reason is that a corporation can speak and act only through its agents and so must be accountable for any acts committed by one of its agents within his actual or apparent scope of authority and while transacting corporate business. [Emphasis added.]

* * * *

* * * We therefore conclude that imputation may be appropriate in this case, if the Investors can prove that the manner in which Bloom marketed North Hills to them while he was working for MB, and the apparent benefit to MB, made it appear that he marketed North Hills within the scope of his authority as a senior executive of MB.

* * * *

For the foregoing reasons, we * * * will vacate the grant of summary judgment to MB * * * , and we will remand this case for a trial with respect to those claims against MB.

LEGAL REASONING QUESTIONS

1. What is the imputation doctrine? What public-policy reasons support imputing the fraud of a corporate officer to the corporation?
2. What circumstances in this case suggest that MB should be held liable for Bloom's fraud?
3. What conditions did the court place on the application of the imputation doctrine in this case?
4. MB, which was already in financial distress, had to cease operations as a result of Bloom's fraud. How might MB have discovered the fraud before it grew so large as to have such dire effects?

Criminal Acts

Under modern criminal law (see Chapter 7), a corporation may also be held liable for the criminal acts of its agents and employees, provided the punishment is one that can be applied to the corporation. Although corporations cannot be imprisoned, they can be fined. (Of course, corporate directors and officers can be imprisoned, and some have been in recent years.) In addition, under sentencing guidelines for crimes committed by corporate employees (white-collar crimes), corporate lawbreakers can face fines amounting to hundreds of millions of dollars.[1]

▶ **Case in Point 19.1** Brian Gauthier drove a dump truck for Angelo Todesca Corporation. The truck was missing its back-up alarm, but Angelo allowed Gauthier to continue driving it. At a worksite, Gauthier backed up to dump a load and struck and killed a police officer who was directing traffic. The state charged Angelo and Gauthier with the crime of vehicular homicide.

Angelo argued that a corporation could not be guilty of vehicular homicide because it cannot operate a vehicle. The court ruled that if an employee commits a crime "while engaged in corporate business that the employee has been authorized to conduct," the corporation can be held liable for the crime. Hence, the court held that Angelo Todesca Corporation was liable for Gauthier's negligent operation of its truck, which resulted in a person's death.[2] ◀

Classification of Corporations

Corporations can be classified in several ways. The classification of a corporation normally depends on its location, purpose, and ownership characteristics, as described in the following subsections.

DOMESTIC, FOREIGN, AND ALIEN CORPORATIONS A corporation is referred to as a **domestic corporation** by its home state (the state in which it incorporates). A corporation formed in one state but doing business in another is referred to in the second state as a **foreign corporation.** A corporation formed in another country (say, Mexico) but doing business in the United States is referred to in the United States as an **alien corporation.**

A corporation does not have an automatic right to do business in a state other than its state of incorporation. In some instances, it must obtain a *certificate of authority* in any state in which it plans to do business. Once the certificate has been issued, the corporation generally can exercise in that state all of the powers conferred on it by its home state. If a foreign corporation does business in a state without obtaining a certificate of authority, the state can impose substantial fines and sanctions on that corporation.

Note that most state statutes specify certain activities, such as soliciting orders via the Internet, that are not considered "doing business" within the state. Thus, a foreign corporation normally does not need a certificate of authority to sell goods or services via the Internet or by mail.

PUBLIC AND PRIVATE CORPORATIONS A **public corporation** is a corporation formed by the government to meet some political or governmental purpose. Cities and towns that incorporate are common examples. In addition, many federal government organizations, such as the U.S. Postal Service, the Tennessee Valley Authority, and AMTRAK, are public corporations.

Note that a public corporation is not the same as a *publicly held* corporation. A **publicly held corporation** (often called a *public company*) is any corporation whose shares are publicly traded in a securities market, such as the New York Stock Exchange or the NASDAQ (an electronic stock exchange founded by the National Association of Securities Dealers).

In contrast to public corporations (*not* public companies), private corporations are created either wholly or in part for private benefit—that is, for profit. Most corporations are private. Although they may serve a public purpose, as a public electric or gas utility does, they are owned by private persons rather than by a government.[3]

NONPROFIT CORPORATIONS Corporations formed for purposes other than making a profit are called *nonprofit* or *not-for-profit* corporations. Private hospitals, educational institutions, charities, and religious organizations, for example, are frequently organized as nonprofit corporations. The nonprofit corporation is a convenient form of organization that allows various groups to own property and to form contracts without exposing the individual members to personal liability.

CLOSE CORPORATIONS Most corporate enterprises in the United States fall into the category of close corporations. A **close corporation** is one whose shares are held by members of a family or by relatively few persons. Close corporations are also referred to as *closely held, family,* or *privately held* corporations. Usually, the members of the small group constituting the shareholders of a close corporation are personally known to each other. Because the number of shareholders is so small, there is no trading market for the shares.

1. Note that the Sarbanes-Oxley Act of 2002 (see Chapter 4) stiffened the penalties for certain types of corporate crime and ordered the U.S. Sentencing Commission to revise the sentencing guidelines accordingly.
2. *Commonwealth v. Angelo Todesca Corp.*, 446 Mass. 128, 842 N.E.2d 930 (2006).
3. The United States Supreme Court first recognized the property rights of private corporations and clarified the distinction between public and private corporations in the landmark case *Trustees of Dartmouth College v. Woodward,* 17 U.S. (4 Wheaton) 518, 4 L.Ed. 629 (1819).

In practice, a close corporation is often operated like a partnership. Some states have enacted special statutory provisions that apply to these corporations and allow them to depart significantly from certain formalities required by traditional corporation law.[4]

Additionally, the RMBCA gives a close corporation considerable flexibility in determining its rules of operation [RMBCA 7.32]. If all of a corporation's shareholders agree in writing, the corporation can operate without directors and bylaws. In addition, the corporation can operate without annual or special shareholders' or directors' meetings, stock certificates, or formal records of shareholders' or directors' decisions.[5]

Management of Close Corporations. Management of a close corporation resembles that of a sole proprietorship or a partnership, in that a single shareholder or a tightly knit group of shareholders usually hold the positions of directors and officers. As a corporation, however, the firm must meet all specific legal requirements set forth in state statutes.

To prevent a majority shareholder from dominating the company, a close corporation may require that more than a simple majority of the directors approve any action taken by the board. Typically, this would apply only to extraordinary actions, such as changing the amount of dividends or dismissing an employee-shareholder, and not to ordinary business decisions.

Transfer of Shares in Close Corporations. By definition, a close corporation has a small number of shareholders. Thus, the transfer of one shareholder's shares to someone else can cause serious management problems. The other shareholders may find themselves required to share control with someone they do not know or like.

▶ **Example 19.2** Three brothers, Terry, Damon, and Henry Johnson, are the only shareholders of Johnson's Car Wash, Inc. Terry and Damon do not want Henry to sell his shares to an unknown third person. To avoid this situation, the corporation could restrict the transferability of shares to outside persons. Shareholders could be required to offer their shares to the corporation or the other shareholders before selling them to an outside purchaser.

In fact, a few states have statutes that prohibit the transfer of close corporation shares unless certain persons—including shareholders, family members, and the corporation—are first given the opportunity to purchase the shares for the same price. ◀

Shareholder Agreement to Restrict Stock Transfers. Control of a close corporation can also be stabilized through the use of a *shareholder agreement.* A shareholder agreement can provide for proportional control when one of the original shareholders dies. The decedent's shares of stock in the corporation would be divided in such a way that the proportionate holdings of the survivors, and thus their proportionate control, would be maintained.

Agreements between shareholders can also restrict the transfer of a close corporation's stock in other ways. For instance, shareholders might agree that existing shareholders will have an option to purchase stock before it is sold or transferred to an outside party.

Misappropriation of Close Corporation Funds. Sometimes, a majority shareholder in a close corporation takes advantage of his or her position and misappropriates company funds. In such situations, the normal remedy for the injured minority shareholders is to have their shares appraised and to be paid the fair market value for them.

▶ **Case in Point 19.3** John Murray, Stephen Hopkins, and Paul Ryan were the controlling shareholders of Olympic Adhesives, Inc., as well as its officers, directors, and employees. Merek Rubin was a minority shareholder. Murray, Hopkins, and Ryan were paid salaries. Under Olympic's profit-sharing plan, one-third of its net operating income was paid into a fund that was distributed to employees, including Murray, Hopkins, and Ryan.

Twice a year, Murray, Hopkins, and Ryan also paid themselves additional compensation—a percentage of the net profits after profit sharing, allocated according to their stock ownership. Over a fifteen-year period, the percentage grew from 75 percent to between 92 and 98 percent. During this time, the additional compensation totaled nearly $15 million. Rubin filed a suit in a Massachusetts state court against Murray, Hopkins, and Ryan, alleging that they had paid themselves excessive compensation and deprived him of his share of Olympic's profits in violation of their fiduciary duty to him as a minority shareholder. The court ordered the defendants to repay Olympic

4. For example, in some states (such as Maryland), a close corporation need not have a board of directors.
5. Shareholders cannot agree, however, to eliminate certain rights of shareholders, such as the right to inspect corporate books and records or the right to bring *derivative actions* (lawsuits on behalf of the corporation—see page 455).

nearly $6 million to be distributed among its shareholders. The decision was affirmed on appeal.[6] ◀

S CORPORATIONS A close corporation that meets the qualifying requirements specified in Subchapter S of the Internal Revenue Code can choose to operate as an **S corporation.** (A corporation will automatically be taxed under Subchapter C unless it elects S corporation status.) If a corporation has S corporation status, it can avoid the imposition of income taxes at the corporate level while retaining many of the advantages of a corporation, particularly limited liability.

Important Requirements. Among the numerous requirements for S corporation status, the following are the most important:

1. The corporation must be a domestic corporation.
2. The corporation must not be a member of an affiliated group of corporations.
3. The shareholders of the corporation must be individuals, estates, or certain trusts and tax-exempt organizations.
4. The corporation must have no more than one hundred shareholders.
5. The corporation must have only one class of stock, although all shareholders do not need to have the same voting rights.
6. No shareholder of the corporation may be a nonresident alien.

Effect of S Election. An S corporation is treated differently than a regular corporation for tax purposes. An S corporation is taxed like a partnership, so the corporate income passes through to the shareholders, who pay personal income tax on it. This treatment enables the S corporation to avoid the double taxation imposed on regular corporations.

In addition, the shareholders' tax brackets may be lower than the tax bracket that the corporation would have been in if the tax had been imposed at the corporate level. The resulting tax saving is particularly attractive when the corporation wants to accumulate earnings for some future business purpose. If the corporation has losses, the S election allows the shareholders to use the losses to offset other income. Nevertheless, because the limited liability company (see Chapter 18) and the limited liability partnership (see Chapter 17) offer similar tax advantages and greater flexibility, the S corporation has lost much of its appeal.

PROFESSIONAL CORPORATIONS Professionals such as physicians, lawyers, dentists, and accountants can incorporate. Professional corporations are typically identified by the letters *P.C.* (professional corporation), *S.C.* (service corporation), or *P.A.* (professional association).

In general, the laws governing the formation and operation of professional corporations are similar to those governing ordinary business corporations. There are some differences in terms of liability, however, because the shareholder-owners are professionals who are held to a higher standard of conduct.

For liability purposes, some courts treat a professional corporation somewhat like a partnership and hold each professional liable for any malpractice committed within the scope of the business by the others in the firm. With the exception of malpractice or a breach of duty to clients or patients, a shareholder in a professional corporation generally cannot be held liable for the torts committed by other professionals at the firm.

BENEFIT CORPORATIONS A growing number of states have enacted legislation that creates a new corporate form called a *benefit corporation.* A **benefit corporation** is a for-profit corporation that seeks to have a material positive impact on society and the environment. Benefit corporations differ from traditional corporations in the following three ways:

1. *Purpose.* Although the corporation is designed to make a profit, its purpose is to benefit the public as a whole (rather than just to provide long-term shareholder value, as in ordinary corporations). The directors of a benefit corporation must, during the decision-making process, consider the impact of their decisions on society and the environment.
2. *Accountability.* Shareholders of a benefit corporation determine whether the company has achieved a material positive impact. Shareholders also have a right of private action, called a *benefit enforcement proceeding,* enabling them to sue the corporation if it fails to pursue or create public benefit.
3. *Transparency.* A benefit corporation must issue an annual benefit report on its overall social and environmental performance that uses a recognized third party standard to assess its performance. The report must be delivered to the shareholders and posted on a public Web site.

6. *Rubin v. Murray,* 79 Mass.App.Ct. 64, 943 N.E.2d 949 (2011).

SECTION 2
CORPORATE FORMATION

Many Fortune 500 companies started as sole proprietorships or partnerships and then converted to corporate entities as the businesses grew and needed to obtain additional capital by issuing shares of stock. Incorporating a business is much simpler today than it was twenty years ago, and many states allow businesses to incorporate via the Internet. Here, we examine the process by which a corporation comes into existence.

Promotional Activities

In the past, preliminary steps were taken to organize and promote the business prior to incorporating. Contracts were made with investors and others on behalf of the future corporation. Today, due to the relative ease of forming a corporation in most states, persons incorporating their business rarely, if ever, engage in preliminary promotional activities.

Nevertheless, it is important for businesspersons to understand that they are personally liable for all preincorporation contracts made with investors, accountants, or others on behalf of the future corporation. Personal liability continues until the newly formed corporation assumes liability for the preincorporation contracts through a *novation* (see Chapter 10).

▶ **Example 19.4** Jade Sorrel contracts with an accountant, Ray Cooper, to provide tax advice for a proposed corporation, Blackstone, Inc. Cooper provides the services to Sorrel, knowing that the corporation has not yet been formed. Once Blackstone, Inc., is formed, Cooper sends an invoice to the corporation and to Sorrel personally, but the bill is not paid. Because Sorrel is personally liable for the preincorporation contract, Cooper can sue Sorrel for breach of the contract. Cooper cannot seek to hold Blackstone, Inc., liable unless he has entered into a contract with the corporation through a novation. ◀

Incorporation Procedures

Exact procedures for incorporation differ among states, but the basic steps are as follows: (1) select a state of incorporation, (2) secure the corporate name, (3) prepare the articles of incorporation, and (4) file the articles of incorporation with the secretary of state. These steps are discussed in more detail in the following subsections.

SELECT THE STATE OF INCORPORATION The first step in the incorporation process is to select a state in which to incorporate. Because state laws differ, individuals may look for the states that offer the most advantageous tax or incorporation provisions. Another consideration is the fee that a particular state charges to incorporate, as well as the annual fees and the fees for specific transactions (such as stock transfers).

Delaware has historically had the least restrictive laws and provisions that favor corporate management. Consequently, many corporations, including a number of the largest, have incorporated there. Delaware's statutes permit firms to incorporate in that state and conduct business and locate their operating headquarters elsewhere. Most other states now permit this as well.

Note, though, that close corporations, particularly those of a professional nature, generally incorporate in the state where their principal shareholders live and work. For reasons of convenience and cost, businesses often choose to incorporate in the state in which most of the corporation's business will be conducted.

SECURE THE CORPORATE NAME The choice of a corporate name is subject to state approval to ensure against duplication or deception. State statutes usually require that the secretary of state run a check on the proposed name in the state of incorporation.

Some states require that the persons incorporating a firm run a check on the proposed name at their own expense. A check can often be made via the Internet. If a firm is likely to do business in other states—or over the Internet—the incorporators should check existing corporate names in those states as well.

Once cleared, a name can be reserved for a short time, for a fee, pending the completion of the articles of incorporation. All states require the corporation's name to include the word *Corporation (Corp.)*, *Incorporated (Inc.)*, *Company (Co.)*, or *Limited (Ltd.)*.[7]

First Check Available Domain Names. All corporations need to have an online presence to compete effectively

7. Failure to use one of these abbreviations to disclose corporate status may be grounds for holding an individual incorporator liable for corporate contracts under agency law (see Chapter 20).

in today's business climate. The corporate name should be one that can be used as the business's Internet domain name. Therefore, it is advisable to check what domain names are available *before* securing a corporate name with the state.

Incorporators can do this by going to one of the many companies that issue domain names, such as Network Solutions (**www.whois.com/whois**), and finding out if the preferred name is available. If another business is using that name, the incorporators can select an alternative name that can be used as the business's URL, and then seek approval from the state for the name.

Trade Name Disputes. A new corporation's name cannot be the same as (or deceptively similar to) the name of an existing corporation doing business within the same state. If a firm does business under a name that is the same as or deceptively similar to an existing company's name, it may be liable for trade name infringement (see Chapter 14).

▶ **Example 19.5** An existing corporation is named Digital Synergy, Inc. The state is not likely to allow a new corporation to use the name Digital Synergy Company. That name is deceptively similar to the first and could cause confusion. The use of too similar a name could also transfer part of the goodwill established by the first corporate user to the second, thus infringing on the first company's trademark rights. ◀

PREPARE THE ARTICLES OF INCORPORATION The primary document needed to incorporate a business is the **articles of incorporation.** The articles include basic information about the corporation and serve as a primary source of authority for its future organization and business functions. The person or persons who execute (sign) the articles are the *incorporators*.

Generally, the articles of incorporation *must* include the following information [RMBCA 2.02].

1. The name of the corporation.
2. The number of shares the corporation is authorized to issue.
3. The name and street address of the corporation's initial registered agent and registered office.
4. The name and address of each incorporator.

In addition, the articles *may* set forth other information, such as the names and addresses of the initial members of the board of directors, and the duration and purpose of the corporation.

Articles of incorporation vary widely depending on the jurisdiction and the size and type of the corporation. Frequently, the articles do not provide much detail about the firm's operations, which are spelled out in the company's **bylaws** (internal rules of management adopted by the corporation at its first organizational meeting).

Shares of the Corporation. The articles must specify the number of shares of stock the corporation is authorized to issue [RMBCA 2.02(a)]. For instance, a company might state that the aggregate number of shares that the corporation has the authority to issue is five thousand. Large corporations often state a par value for each share, such as $.20 per share, and specify the various types or classes of stock authorized for issuance.

Registered Office and Agent. The corporation must indicate the location and street address of its registered office within the state. Usually, the registered office is also the principal office of the corporation.

The corporation must also give the name and address of a specific person who has been designated as an *agent*. The registered agent is the person who can receive legal documents (such as orders to appear in court) on behalf of the corporation.

Incorporators. Each incorporator must be listed by name and address. The incorporators need not have any interest at all in the corporation, and sometimes signing the articles is their only duty. Many states do not have residency or age requirements for incorporators. It can be as few as one or as many as three. Incorporators frequently participate in the first organizational meeting of the corporation.

Duration and Purpose. A corporation has perpetual existence unless the articles state otherwise. The RMBCA does not require a specific statement of purpose to be included in the articles. A corporation can be formed for any lawful purpose. The articles may indicate that the corporation is organized for "any legal business." By not mentioning specifics, the corporation avoids the need for future amendments to the corporate articles [RMBCA 2.02(b)(2)(i), 3.01].

Internal Management. The articles can describe the corporation's internal management structure, although this usually is included in the bylaws adopted after the corporation is formed. The bylaws typically describe such matters as voting requirements for shareholders, the election of the board of directors, and the methods of replacing directors. Bylaws cannot conflict with the incorporation statute or the articles of incorporation [RMBCA 2.06].

Under the RMBCA, shareholders may amend or repeal the bylaws. The board of directors may also amend or repeal the bylaws unless the articles of incorporation or state statutory provisions reserve this power to the shareholders exclusively [RMBCA 10.20].

FILE THE ARTICLES WITH THE STATE Once the articles of incorporation have been prepared and signed, they are sent to the appropriate state official, usually the secretary of state, along with the required filing fee. In most states, the secretary of state then stamps the articles "Filed" and returns a copy of the articles to the incorporators. Once this occurs, the corporation officially exists.

First Organizational Meeting to Adopt Bylaws

After incorporation, the first organizational meeting must be held. Usually, the most important function of this meeting is the adoption of bylaws, which, as mentioned, are the internal rules of management for the corporation. If the articles of incorporation named the initial board of directors, then the directors, by majority vote, call the meeting to adopt the bylaws and complete the company's organization.

If the articles did not name the directors (as is typical), then the incorporators hold the meeting to elect the directors and adopt bylaws. The incorporators may also complete the routine business of incorporation (such as authorizing the issuance of shares and hiring employees) at this meeting. The business transacted depends on the requirements of the state's corporation statute, the nature of the corporation, the provisions made in the articles, and the desires of the incorporators.

Improper Incorporation

The procedures for incorporation are very specific. If they are not followed precisely, others may be able to challenge the existence of the corporation. Errors in incorporation procedures can become important when, for instance, a third party who is attempting to enforce a contract or bring a suit for a tort injury learns of them.

***DE JURE* CORPORATIONS** If a corporation has substantially complied with all conditions precedent to incorporation, the corporation is said to have *de jure* (rightful and lawful) existence. In most states and under RMBCA 2.03(b), the secretary of state's filing of the articles of incorporation is conclusive proof that all mandatory statutory provisions have been met [RMBCA 2.03(b)].

Sometimes, the incorporators fail to comply with all statutory mandates. If the defect is minor, such as an incorrect address listed on the articles of incorporation, most courts will overlook the defect and find that a corporation (*de jure*) exists.

***DE FACTO* CORPORATIONS** If the defect in formation is substantial, however, such as a corporation's failure to hold an organizational meeting to adopt bylaws, the outcome will vary depending on the jurisdiction. Some states, including Mississippi, New York, Ohio, and Oklahoma, still recognize the common law doctrine of *de facto* corporation.[8] In those states, the courts will treat a corporation as a legal corporation despite the defect in its formation if the following three requirements are met:

1. A state statute exists under which the corporation can be validly incorporated.
2. The parties have made a good faith attempt to comply with the statute.
3. The parties have already undertaken to do business as a corporation.

Many state courts, however, have interpreted their states' version of the RMBCA as abolishing the common law doctrine of *de facto* corporations. These states include Alaska, Arizona, Minnesota, New Mexico, Oregon, South Dakota, Tennessee, Utah, and Washington, as well as the District of Columbia. In those jurisdictions, if there is a substantial defect in complying with the incorporation statute, the corporation does not legally exist, and the incorporators are personally liable.

Corporation by Estoppel

Sometimes, a business association holds itself out to others as being a corporation when it has made no attempt to incorporate. In those situations, the firm normally will be estopped (prevented) from denying corporate status in a lawsuit by a third party. The estoppel doctrine most commonly applies when a

8. See, for example, *In re Hausman*, 13 N.Y.3d 408, 921 N.E.2d 191, 893 N.Y.S.2d 499 (2009).

third party contracts with an entity that claims to be a corporation but has not filed articles of incorporation. It may also apply when a third party contracts with a person claiming to be an agent of a corporation that does not in fact exist.

When justice requires, courts in some states will treat an alleged corporation as if it were an actual corporation for the purpose of determining the rights and liabilities in particular circumstances.[9] Recognition of corporate status does not extend beyond the resolution of the problem at hand.

▶ **Case in Point 19.6** W.P. Media, Inc., entered an agreement with Alabama MBA, Inc., to form a wireless Internet services company. W.P. Media was to create a wireless network, and Alabama MBA was to contribute the capital. Hugh Brown signed the parties' contract on behalf of Alabama MBA as the chair of its board. At the time, however, Alabama MBA's articles of incorporation had not yet been filed. Brown filed the articles of incorporation the following year. Later, Brown and Alabama MBA filed a suit alleging that W.P. Media had breached their contract by not building the wireless network. The Supreme Court of Alabama held that because W.P. Media had treated Alabama MBA as a corporation, W.P. Media was estopped from denying Alabama MBA's corporate existence.[10] ◀

SECTION 3

CORPORATE POWERS

When a corporation is created, the express and implied powers necessary to achieve its purpose also come into existence. The express powers of a corporation are found in its articles of incorporation, in the law of the state of incorporation, and in the state and federal constitutions.

Corporate bylaws and the resolutions of the corporation's board of directors also establish the express powers of the corporation. Because state corporation statutes frequently provide default rules that apply if the company's bylaws are silent on an issue, it is important that the bylaws set forth the specific operating rules of the corporation. In addition, after the bylaws are adopted, the corporation's board of directors will pass resolutions that also grant or restrict corporate powers.

The following order of priority is used if a conflict arises among the various documents involving a corporation:

1. The U.S. Constitution.
2. State constitutions.
3. State statutes.
4. The articles of incorporation.
5. Bylaws.
6. Resolutions of the board of directors.

Implied Powers

When a corporation is created, certain implied powers arise. In the absence of express constitutional, statutory, or other prohibitions, the corporation has the implied power to perform all acts reasonably necessary to accomplish its corporate purposes. For this reason, a corporation has the implied power to borrow funds within certain limits, lend funds, and extend credit to those with whom it has a legal or contractual relationship.

To borrow funds, the corporation acts through its board of directors to authorize the loan. Most often, the president or chief executive officer of the corporation (see page 446) will execute the necessary documents on behalf of the corporation. Corporate officers such as these have the implied power to bind the corporation in matters directly connected with the *ordinary* business affairs of the enterprise.

There is a limit to what a corporate officer can do, though. A corporate officer does not have the authority to bind the corporation to an action that will greatly affect the corporate purpose or undertaking, such as the sale of substantial corporate assets.

Ultra Vires Doctrine

The term ***ultra vires*** means "beyond the power." In corporate law, acts of a corporation that are beyond its express or implied powers are *ultra vires* acts.

WHEN A CORPORATION'S ACTIONS EXCEED ITS STATED PURPOSE In the past, most cases dealing with *ultra vires* acts involved contracts made for unauthorized purposes. Now, however, most private corporations are organized for "any legal business" and do not state a specific purpose, so the *ultra vires* doctrine has declined in importance.

9. Some states have expressly rejected the common law theory of corporation by estoppel, finding that it is inconsistent with their statutory law. Other states have abolished only the doctrines of *de facto* and *de jure* corporations. See, for example, *Stone v. Jetmar Properties, LLC,* 733 N.W.2d 480 (Minn.App. 2007).
10. *Brown v. W.P. Media, Inc.,* 17 So.3d 1167 (2009).

Today, cases that allege *ultra vires* acts usually involve nonprofit corporations or municipal (public) corporations. ▶ **Case in Point 19.7** Four men formed a nonprofit corporation to create the Armenian Genocide Museum & Memorial (AGM&M). The bylaws appointed them as trustees (similar to corporate directors) for life. One of the trustees, Gerard L. Cafesjian, became the chair and president of AGM&M. Eventually, the relationship among the trustees deteriorated, and Cafesjian resigned.

The corporation then brought a suit claiming that Cafesjian had engaged in numerous *ultra vires* acts, self-dealing, and mismanagement. Although the bylaws required an 80 percent affirmative vote of the trustees to take action, Cafesjian had taken many actions without the board's approval. He had also entered into contracts for real estate transactions in which he had a personal interest. Because Cafesjian had taken actions that exceeded his authority and had failed to follow the rules set forth in the bylaws for board meetings, the court ruled that the corporation could go forward with its suit.[11] ◀

REMEDIES FOR *ULTRA VIRES* ACTS Under Section 3.04 of the RMBCA, the shareholders can seek an injunction from a court to prevent (or stop) the corporation from engaging in *ultra vires* acts. The attorney general in the state of incorporation can also bring an action to obtain an injunction against the *ultra vires* transactions or to seek dissolution of the corporation. The corporation or its shareholders (on behalf of the corporation) can seek damages from the officers and directors who were responsible for the *ultra vires* acts.

SECTION 4 PIERCING THE CORPORATE VEIL

Occasionally, the owners use a corporate entity to perpetrate a fraud, circumvent the law, or in some other way accomplish an illegitimate objective. In these situations, the courts will ignore the corporate structure and **pierce the corporate veil,** exposing the shareholders to personal liability [RMBCA 2.04].

Generally, courts pierce the veil when the corporate privilege is abused for personal benefit or when the corporate business is treated so carelessly that it is indistinguishable from that of a controlling shareholder. When the facts show that great injustice would result from the use of a corporation to avoid individual responsibility, a court will look behind the corporate structure to the individual shareholders.

Factors That Lead Courts to Pierce the Corporate Veil

The following are some of the factors that frequently cause the courts to pierce the corporate veil:

1. A party is tricked or misled into dealing with the corporation rather than the individual.
2. The corporation is set up never to make a profit or always to be insolvent, or it is too "thinly" capitalized. That is, it has insufficient capital at the time it is formed to meet its prospective debts or potential liabilities.
3. The corporation is formed to evade an existing legal obligation.
4. Statutory corporate formalities, such as holding required corporation meetings, are not followed.
5. Personal and corporate interests are mixed together, or **commingled,** to such an extent that the corporation has no separate identity.

Although state corporation codes usually do not prohibit a shareholder from lending funds to her or his corporation, courts will scrutinize the transaction closely if the loan comes from an officer, director, or majority shareholder. Loans from persons who control the corporation must be made in good faith and for fair value.

A Potential Problem for Close Corporations

The potential for corporate assets to be used for personal benefit is especially great in a close corporation, in which the shares are held by a single person or by only a few individuals, usually family members. In such a situation, the separate status of the corporate entity and the sole shareholder (or family-member shareholders) must be carefully preserved.

Certain practices invite trouble for the one-person or family-owned (close) corporation, including any of the following:

1. The commingling of corporate and personal funds.

11. *Armenian Assembly of America, Inc. v. Cafesjian*, 692 F.Supp.2d 20 (D.C. 2010).

2. The failure to hold board of directors' meetings and record the minutes.
3. The shareholders' continuous personal use of corporate property (for instance, company-owned vehicles).

In the following case, when a close corporation failed to pay its legal fees, its attorneys sought to hold the shareholders personally liable. The court had to decide whether to pierce the corporate veil.

CASE 19.2

Brennan's, Inc. v. Colbert

Court of Appeal of Louisiana, 85 So.3d 787 (2012).

BACKGROUND AND FACTS Pip, Jimmy, and Theodore Brennan are brothers and shareholders of Brennan's, Inc., which owns and operates New Orleans's famous Brennan's Restaurant. In 1998, the Brennan brothers retained attorney Edward Colbert and his firm, Kenyon & Kenyon, L.L.P., to represent Brennan's, Inc., in a dispute with another family member. All bills were sent to Brennan's, Inc., and the payments came from the company's checking accounts.

As a close corporation, Brennan's, Inc., did not hold formal corporate meetings with agendas and minutes, but it did maintain corporate books, hold corporate bank accounts, and file corporate tax returns. In 2005, Brennan's, Inc., sued Colbert and his law firm for legal malpractice. In its answer, Kenyon & Kenyon demanded unpaid legal fees both from Brennan's, Inc., and from the Brennan brothers personally. The trial court found that the Brennan brothers could not be held personally liable. Kenyon & Kenyon appealed. The law firm argued that the court should pierce the corporate veil because Brennan's, Inc., did not observe corporate formalities and because the Brennan brothers did not honor their promises to pay their legal bills.

IN THE LANGUAGE OF THE COURT
Daniel L. *DYSART,* Judge.

* * * *

As a general rule, a corporation is a distinct legal entity, separate from the individuals who compose it, thus insulating the shareholders from personal liability.

There are limited exceptions where the court may ignore the corporate fiction and find the shareholders personally liable for the debts of a corporation. One of those exceptions is where the corporation is found to be the "alter ego" of the shareholder. It usually involves situations where fraud or deceit has been practiced by the shareholder through the corporation. Another basis is where the shareholders disregard the corporate formalities to the extent that the corporation and the shareholders are no longer distinct entities.

* * * *

Absent fraud, malfeasance or criminal wrongdoing, courts have been reluctant to hold a shareholder personally liable for corporate obligations. When a party seeks to pierce the corporate veil, the totality of the circumstances is determinative. [Emphasis added.]

* * * *

The Kenyon firm was aware of the nature of the operation of Brennan's, Inc., * * * prior to being retained. The client was Brennan's, Inc., bills were sent to Brennan's, Inc., and payments were paid with checks from the Brennan's, Inc., bank accounts. * * * Brennan's, Inc., maintained its own accounting records and filed its own tax returns. * * * The Kenyon firm acknowledged that Brennan's, Inc., *acting through its shareholders,* promised to make good on the debt. [Emphasis in original.]

There is no evidence that the Brennan brothers ever agreed to bind themselves personally for any debt incurred in connection with the legal services provided by the Kenyon firm. There is no written retention agreement between the corporation and the Kenyon firm, nor is there a written guaranty from any of the brothers.

The Kenyon firm admits that there is no requirement for small, [close] corporations to operate with the formality usually expected of larger corporations. The Kenyon firm has failed

CASE 19.2 CONTINUED

to establish that the lack of corporate formalities, particularly meetings, agendas and minutes, is sufficient to pierce the corporation veil. Brennan's, Inc., at all times since its inception has maintained corporate books, corporate bank accounts, and has filed corporate tax returns.

* * * *

The Kenyon firm has not proven that any of the Brennan brothers made promises to pay the firm's bills without the intent to pay them. * * * *If a broken promise to pay was sufficient to establish fraud, then every lawsuit against a corporation for a debt would automatically allow for the piercing of the corporate veil. Clearly, a juridical entity such as a corporation can only speak through its shareholders.* [Emphasis added.]

DECISION AND REMEDY *The Louisiana appellate court held that Kenyon & Kenyon could not hold the Brennan brothers personally liable by piercing the corporate veil. The court therefore affirmed the trial court's judgment for the Brennan brothers.*

THE ETHICAL DIMENSION *Should the Brennan brothers be held personally liable because they misled their attorneys? Why or why not?*

THE ECONOMIC DIMENSION *Do corporations benefit from shareholders' limited liability? If so, how?*

The Alter-Ego Theory

Sometimes, courts pierce the corporate veil under the theory that the corporation was not operated as a separate entity, but was just another side (or alter ego) of the individual or group that actually controlled the corporation. This is called the alter-ego theory, which was discussed in the context of limited liability companies in Chapter 18.

The alter-ego theory is applied when a corporation is so dominated and controlled by an individual or group that the separate identities of the person (or group) and the corporation are no longer distinct. Courts use the alter-ego theory to avoid injustice or fraud that would result if wrongdoers were allowed to hide behind the protection of limited liability. ▶ **Case in Point 19.8** Harvey and Barbara Jacobson owned Aqua Clear Technologies, Inc., which installed and serviced home water-softening systems. The Jacobsons consistently took funds out of the business for their personal expenses, including payments for their home, cars, health-insurance premiums, and credit cards.

Three weeks after Aqua filed a bankruptcy petition, Harvey formed another corporation called Discount Water Services, Inc. Discount appropriated Aqua's equipment and inventory (without buying it) and continued to service water-softening systems for Aqua's customers, even using the same phone number. The trustee appointed to Aqua's bankruptcy case sought to recover Aqua's assets on the ground that Discount was Aqua's alter ego. The court ruled that Discount was simply a continuation of Aqua's business (its alter ego) under a new name, and therefore held Discount liable for the claims asserted against Aqua in bankruptcy (totaling $108,732.64).[12] ◀

SECTION 5

DIRECTORS AND OFFICERS

Corporate directors, officers, and shareholders all play different roles within the corporate entity. Sometimes, actions that may benefit the corporation as a whole do not coincide with the separate interests of the individuals making up the corporation. In such situations, it is important to know the rights and duties of all participants in the corporate enterprise.

The Roles of Directors and Officers

The board of directors is the ultimate authority in every corporation. Directors have responsibility for all policymaking decisions necessary to the management of all corporate affairs. Additionally, the directors must act as a body in carrying out routine corporate

12. *In re Aqua Clear Technologies, Inc.*, 361 Bankr. 567 (S.D.Fla. 2007).

business. The board selects and removes the corporate officers, determines the capital structure of the corporation, and declares dividends. Each director has one vote, and customarily the majority rules. The general areas of responsibility of the board of directors are shown in Exhibit 19–1 below.

Directors are sometimes inappropriately characterized as *agents* because they act on behalf of the corporation. No individual director, however, can act as an agent to bind the corporation. As a group, directors collectively control the corporation in a way that no agent is able to control a principal. In addition, although directors occupy positions of trust and control over the corporation, they are not *trustees* because they do not hold title to property for the use and benefit of others.

Few qualifications are required for directors. Only a handful of states impose minimum age and residency requirements. A director may be a shareholder, but that is not necessary (unless the articles of incorporation or bylaws require ownership interest).

ELECTION OF DIRECTORS Subject to statutory limitations, the number of directors is set forth in the corporation's articles or bylaws. Historically, the minimum number of directors has been three, but today many states permit fewer. Normally, the incorporators appoint the first board of directors at the time the corporation is created, or the directors are named in the articles of incorporation. The initial board serves until the first annual shareholders' meeting. Subsequent directors are elected by a majority vote of the shareholders.

A director usually serves for a term of one year—from annual meeting to annual meeting. Most state statutes permit longer and staggered terms. A common practice is to elect one-third of the board members each year for a three-year term. In this way, there is greater management continuity.

Removal of Directors. A director can be removed *for cause*—that is, for failing to perform a required duty—either as specified in the articles or bylaws or by shareholder action. The board of directors may also have the power to remove a director for cause, subject to shareholder review. In most states, a director cannot be removed without cause unless the shareholders have reserved the right to do so at the time of election.

Vacancies on the Board. Vacancies occur on the board if a director dies or resigns or when a new position is created through amendment of the articles or bylaws. In these situations, either the shareholders or the board itself can fill the vacant position, depending on state law or on the provisions of the bylaws.

Note, however, that even when an election appears to be authorized by the bylaws, a court can invalidate the results if the directors were attempting to manipulate the election in order to reduce the shareholders' influence. ▶ **Case in Point 19.9** The bylaws of Liquid Audio, Inc., authorized a board of five directors. Two directors were elected each year. Another company offered to buy all of Liquid Audio's stock, but the board rejected this offer.

To prevent the shareholders from electing new directors who would allow the sale, the directors amended the bylaws. The amendment increased the number of directors to seven, thereby diminishing the shareholders' influence in the upcoming election. The shareholders filed an action challenging the election. The court ruled that the directors' action was illegal because they had attempted to diminish the

EXHIBIT 19–1 Directors' Management Responsibilities

Authorize Major Corporate Policy Decisions	Select and Remove Corporate Officers and Other Managerial Employees, and Determine Their Compensation	Make Financial Decisions
Examples:	*Examples:*	*Examples:*
• Oversee major contract negotiations and management-labor negotiations. • Initiate negotiations on the sale or lease of corporate assets outside the regular course of business. • Decide whether to pursue new product lines or business opportunities.	• Search for and hire corporate executives and determine the elements of their compensation packages, including stock options. • Supervise managerial employees and make decisions regarding their termination.	• Make decisions regarding the issuance of authorized shares and bonds. • Decide when to declare dividends to be paid to shareholders.

shareholders' right to vote effectively in an election of directors.[13] ◀

COMPENSATION OF DIRECTORS In the past, corporate directors were rarely compensated. Today, directors are often paid at least nominal sums and may receive more substantial compensation in large corporations because of the time, work, effort, and especially risk involved.

Most states permit the corporate articles or bylaws to authorize compensation for directors. In fact, the RMBCA states that unless the articles or bylaws provide otherwise, the board itself may set the directors' compensation [RMBCA 8.11]. Directors also receive indirect benefits, such as business contacts and prestige, and other rewards, such as stock options.

In many corporations, directors are also chief corporate officers (president or chief executive officer, for example) and receive compensation in their managerial positions. A director who is also an officer of the corporation is referred to as an **inside director,** whereas a director who does not hold a management position is an **outside director.** Typically, a corporation's board of directors includes both inside and outside directors.

BOARD OF DIRECTORS' MEETINGS The board of directors conducts business by holding formal meetings with recorded minutes. The dates of regular meetings are usually established in the articles or bylaws or by board resolution, and ordinarily no further notice is required.

Special meetings can be called, with notice sent to all directors. Most states today allow directors to participate in board of directors' meetings from remote locations via telephone, Web conferencing, or Skype, provided that all the directors can simultaneously hear each other during the meeting [RMBCA 8.20].

Quorum of Directors. Unless the articles of incorporation or bylaws specify a greater number, a majority of the board of directors normally constitutes a *quorum* [RMBCA 8.24]. (A **quorum** is the minimum number of members of a body of officials or other group that must be present for business to be validly transacted.) Some state statutes specifically allow corporations to set a quorum at less than a majority but not less than one-third of the directors.[14]

Voting. Once a quorum is present, the directors transact business and vote on issues affecting the corporation. Each director present at the meeting has one vote.[15] Ordinary matters generally require a simple majority vote, but certain extraordinary issues may require a greater-than-majority vote.

COMMITTEES OF THE BOARD OF DIRECTORS When a board of directors has a large number of members and must deal with myriad complex business issues, meetings can become unwieldy. Therefore, the boards of large, publicly held corporations typically create committees of directors and delegate certain tasks to these committees. By focusing on specific subjects, committees can increase the efficiency of the board.

Two common types of committees are the *executive committee* and the *audit committee.* An executive committee handles interim management decisions between board meetings. It is limited to dealing with ordinary business matters, though, and does not have the power to declare dividends, amend the bylaws, or authorize the issuance of stock. The Sarbanes-Oxley Act requires all publicly held corporations to have an audit committee. The audit committee is responsible for the selection, compensation, and oversight of the independent public accountants that audit the firm's financial records.

RIGHTS OF DIRECTORS A corporate director must have certain rights to function properly in that position.

Right to Participation. The *right to participation* means that directors are entitled to participate in all board of directors' meetings and have a right to be notified of these meetings. Because the dates of regular board meetings are usually specified in the bylaws, no notice of these meetings is required. If special meetings are called, however, notice is required unless waived by the director [RMBCA 8.23].

Right of Inspection. A director also has a *right of inspection,* which means that each director can access the corporation's books and records, facilities, and premises. Inspection rights are essential for directors to make informed decisions and to exercise the necessary supervision over corporate officers and employees. This right of inspection is almost absolute and cannot be restricted (by the articles, bylaws, or any act of the board of directors).

13. *MM Companies, Inc. v. Liquid Audio, Inc.,* 813 A.2d 1118 (Del.Sup.Ct. 2003).

14. See, for example, Delaware Code Annotated Title 8, Section 141(b); and New York Business Corporation Law Section 707.

15. Except in Louisiana, which allows a director to vote by proxy under certain circumstances.

Right to Indemnification. When a director becomes involved in litigation by virtue of her or his position or actions, the director may also have a *right to indemnification* (reimbursement) for the legal costs, fees, and damages incurred. Most states allow corporations to indemnify and purchase liability insurance for corporate directors [RMBCA 8.51].

Corporate Officers and Executives

Corporate officers and other executive employees are hired by the board of directors. At a minimum, most corporations have a president, one or more vice presidents, a secretary, and a treasurer. In most states, an individual can hold more than one office, such as president and secretary, and can be both an officer and a director of the corporation.

In addition to carrying out the duties articulated in the bylaws, corporate and managerial officers act as agents of the corporation. Therefore, the ordinary rules of agency (to be discussed in Chapter 20) normally apply to their employment.

Corporate officers and other high-level managers are employees of the company, so their rights are defined by employment contracts. Nevertheless, the board of directors normally can remove a corporate officer at any time with or without cause. If the directors remove an officer in violation of the terms of an employment contract, however, the corporation may be liable for breach of contract.

For a synopsis of the roles of directors and officers, see *Concept Summary 19.1* below.

Duties and Liabilities of Directors and Officers

The duties of corporate directors and officers are similar because both groups are involved in decision making and are in positions of control. Directors and officers are considered to be fiduciaries of the corporation because their relationship with the corporation and its shareholders is one of trust and confidence. As fiduciaries, directors and officers owe ethical—and legal—duties to the corporation and the shareholders as a whole. These fiduciary duties include the duty of care and the duty of loyalty.

DUTY OF CARE Directors and officers must exercise due care in performing their duties. The standard of *due care* has been variously described in judicial deci-

CONCEPT SUMMARY 19.1

Roles of Directors and Officers

ASPECT	DESCRIPTION
Election of Directors	The incorporators usually appoint the first board of directors. Thereafter, shareholders elect the directors. Directors usually serve a one-year term, although the term can be longer. Few qualifications are required. A director can be a shareholder but is not required to be. Compensation usually is specified in the corporate articles or bylaws.
Board of Directors' Meetings	The board of directors conducts business by holding formal meetings with recorded minutes. The dates of regular meetings are usually established in the corporate articles or bylaws. Special meetings can be called, with notice sent to all directors. Usually, a quorum is a majority of the corporate directors. Once a quorum is present, each director has one vote, and the majority normally rules in ordinary matters.
Rights of Directors	Directors' rights include the rights of participation, inspection, compensation, and indemnification.
Board of Directors' Committees	Directors may appoint committees and delegate some of their responsibilities to the committees and to corporate officers and executives. For instance, directors commonly appoint an *executive committee,* which handles ordinary, interim management decisions between board of directors' meetings. Directors may also appoint an *audit committee* to hire and supervise the independent public accountants who audit the corporation's financial records.
Role of Corporate Officers and Executives	The board of directors normally hires the corporate officers and other executive employees. In most states, a person can hold more than one office and can be both an officer and a director of a corporation. The rights of corporate officers and executives are defined by employment contracts.

sions and codified in many state corporation codes. Generally, it requires a director or officer to:

1. Act in good faith (honestly).
2. Exercise the care that an ordinarily prudent (careful) person would exercise in similar circumstances.
3. Do what she or he believes is in the best interests of the corporation [RMBCA 8.30(a), 8.42(a)].

If directors or officers fail to exercise due care and the corporation or its shareholders suffer harm as a result, the directors or officers can be held liable for negligence (unless the *business judgment rule* applies, as will be discussed shortly).

Duty to Make Informed Decisions. Directors and officers are expected to be informed on corporate matters and to conduct a reasonable investigation of the relevant situation before making a decision. This means that they must do what is necessary to be adequately informed—that is, attend meetings and presentations, ask for information from those who have it, read reports, and review other written materials. In other words, directors and officers must investigate, study, and discuss matters and evaluate alternatives before making a decision. They cannot decide on the spur of the moment without adequate research.

Although directors and officers are expected to act in accordance with their own knowledge and training, they are also normally entitled to rely on information given to them by certain other persons. Under the laws of most states and Section 8.30(b) of the RMBCA, such persons include competent officers or employees, professionals such as attorneys and accountants, and committees of the board of directors (on which the director does not serve). The reliance must be in good faith to insulate a director from liability if the information later proves to be inaccurate or unreliable.

Duty to Exercise Reasonable Supervision. Directors are also expected to exercise a reasonable amount of supervision when they delegate work to corporate officers and employees. ▶ **Example 19.10** Dale, a corporate bank director, fails to attend any board of directors' meetings for five years. In addition, Dale never inspects any of the corporate books or records and generally fails to supervise the activities of the bank president and the loan committee. Meanwhile, Brennan, the bank president, who is a corporate officer, makes various improper loans and permits large overdrafts. In this situation, Dale (the corporate director) can be held liable to the corporation for losses resulting from the unsupervised actions of the bank president and the loan committee. ◀

Dissenting Directors. Directors are expected to attend board of directors' meetings, and their votes should be entered into the minutes. Sometimes, an individual director disagrees with the majority's vote (which becomes an act of the board of directors). Unless a dissent is entered in the minutes, the director is presumed to have assented. If the directors are later held liable for mismanagement as a result of a decision, dissenting directors are rarely held individually liable to the corporation. For this reason, a director who is absent from a given meeting sometimes registers a dissent with the secretary of the board regarding actions taken at the meeting.

THE BUSINESS JUDGMENT RULE Directors and officers are expected to exercise due care and to use their best judgment in guiding corporate management, but they are not insurers of business success. Under the **business judgment rule,** a corporate director or officer will not be liable to the corporation or to its shareholders for honest mistakes of judgment and bad business decisions.

Courts give significant deference to the decisions of corporate directors and officers, and consider the reasonableness of a decision at the time it was made, without the benefit of hindsight. Thus, corporate decision makers are not subjected to second-guessing by shareholders or others in the corporation.

When the Rule Applies. The business judgment rule will apply as long as the director or officer:

1. Took reasonable steps to become informed about the matter.
2. Had a rational basis for her or his decision.
3. Did not have a conflict of interest between her or his personal interest and that of the corporation.

Provides Broad Protections. The business judgment rule provides broad protections to corporate decision makers. In fact, unless there is evidence of bad faith, fraud, or a clear breach of fiduciary duties, most courts will apply the rule and protect directors and officers who make bad business decisions from liability for those choices.

▶ **Case in Point 19.11** After a foreign firm announced its intention to acquire Lyondell Chemical Company, Lyondell's directors did nothing to prepare for a possible merger. They failed to research

Lyondell's market value and made no attempt to seek out other potential buyers. The $13 billion cash merger was negotiated and finalized in less than a week—and the directors met for only seven hours to discuss it. Shareholders sued, claiming that the directors had breached their fiduciary duties by failing to maximize the sale price of the corporation. The Delaware Supreme Court ruled that the directors were protected by the business judgment rule.[16] ◀

DUTY OF LOYALTY *Loyalty* can be defined as faithfulness to one's obligations and duties. In the corporate context, the duty of loyalty requires directors and officers to subordinate their personal interests to the welfare of the corporation. For instance, a director should not oppose a transaction that is in the corporation's best interest simply because pursuing it may cost the director his or her position.

16. *Lyondell Chemical Co. v. Ryan,* 970 A.2d 235 (Del.Sup. 2009).

Directors cannot use corporate funds or confidential corporate information for personal advantage and must refrain from self-dealing. Cases dealing with the duty of loyalty typically involve one or more of the following:

1. Competing with the corporation.
2. Usurping (taking personal advantage of) a corporate opportunity.
3. Pursuing an interest that conflicts with that of the corporation.
4. Using information that is not available to the public to make a profit trading securities (see the discussion of *insider trading* in Chapter 28).
5. Authorizing a corporate transaction that is detrimental to minority shareholders.
6. Selling control over the corporation.

The following classic case illustrates the conflict that can arise between a corporate official's personal interest and his or her duty of loyalty.

CLASSIC CASE 19.3

Guth v. Loft, Inc.

Supreme Court of Delaware, 23 Del.Ch. 255, 5 A.2d 503 (1939).

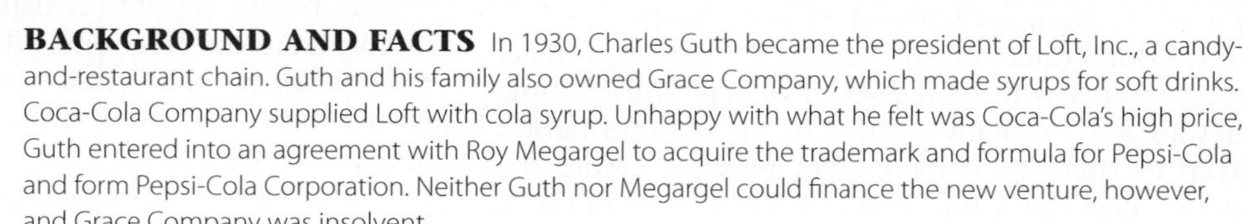

BACKGROUND AND FACTS In 1930, Charles Guth became the president of Loft, Inc., a candy-and-restaurant chain. Guth and his family also owned Grace Company, which made syrups for soft drinks. Coca-Cola Company supplied Loft with cola syrup. Unhappy with what he felt was Coca-Cola's high price, Guth entered into an agreement with Roy Megargel to acquire the trademark and formula for Pepsi-Cola and form Pepsi-Cola Corporation. Neither Guth nor Megargel could finance the new venture, however, and Grace Company was insolvent.

Without the knowledge of Loft's board, Guth used Loft's capital, credit, facilities, and employees to further the Pepsi enterprise. At Guth's direction, a Loft employee made the concentrate for the syrup, which was sent to Grace to add sugar and water. Loft charged Grace for the concentrate but allowed forty months' credit. Grace charged Pepsi for the syrup but also granted substantial credit. Grace sold the syrup to Pepsi's customers, including Loft, which paid on delivery or within thirty days. Loft also paid for Pepsi's advertising. Finally, with profits declining as a result of switching from Coca-Cola, Loft filed a suit in a Delaware state court against Guth, Grace, and Pepsi, seeking their Pepsi stock and an accounting. The court entered a judgment in the plaintiff's favor. The defendants appealed to the Delaware Supreme Court.

IN THE LANGUAGE OF THE COURT
LAYTON, Chief Justice, delivering the opinion of the court:

* * * *

Corporate officers and directors are not permitted to use their position of trust and confidence to further their private interests. * * * They stand in a fiduciary relation to the corporation and its stockholders. A public policy, existing through the years, and derived from a profound knowledge of human characteristics and motives, has established *a rule that demands of a corporate officer or director, peremptorily [not open for debate] and inexorably [unavoidably], the most scrupulous observance of his duty, not only affirmatively to protect the interests of the corporation committed to his charge, but also to refrain from doing anything that would work injury to the corporation* * * * . The rule that requires an undivided and unselfish loyalty to the corporation demands that there shall be no conflict between duty and self-interest. [Emphasis added.]

* * * *

* * * *If there is presented to a corporate officer or director a business opportunity which the corporation is financially able to undertake [that] is * * * in the line of the corporation's business and is of practical advantage to it * * * and, by embracing the opportunity, the self-interest of the officer or director will be brought into conflict with that of his corporation, the law will not permit him to seize the opportunity for himself.* * * * In such circumstances, * * * the corporation may elect to claim all of the benefits of the transaction for itself, and the law will impress a trust in favor of the corporation upon the property, interests and profits so acquired. [Emphasis added.]

* * * *

* * * The appellants contend that no conflict of interest between Guth and Loft resulted from his acquirement and exploitation of the Pepsi-Cola opportunity [and] that the acquisition did not place Guth in competition with Loft * * * . [In this case, however,] Guth was Loft, and Guth was Pepsi. He absolutely controlled Loft. His authority over Pepsi was supreme. As Pepsi, he created and controlled the supply of Pepsi-Cola syrup, and he determined the price and the terms. What he offered, as Pepsi, he had the power, as Loft, to accept. Upon any consideration of human characteristics and motives, he created a conflict between self-interest and duty. He made himself the judge in his own cause. * * * Moreover, a reasonable probability of injury to Loft resulted from the situation forced upon it. Guth was in the same position to impose his terms upon Loft as had been the Coca-Cola Company.

* * * The facts and circumstances demonstrate that Guth's appropriation of the Pepsi-Cola opportunity to himself placed him in a competitive position with Loft with respect to a commodity essential to it, thereby rendering his personal interests incompatible with the superior interests of his corporation; and this situation was accomplished, not openly and with his own resources, but secretly and with the money and facilities of the corporation which was committed to his protection.

DECISION AND REMEDY *The Delaware Supreme Court upheld the judgment of the lower court. The state supreme court was "convinced that the opportunity to acquire the Pepsi-Cola trademark and formula, goodwill and business belonged to [Loft], and that Guth, as its President, had no right to appropriate the opportunity to himself."*

WHAT IF THE FACTS WERE DIFFERENT? *Suppose that Loft's board of directors had approved Pepsi-Cola's use of its personnel and equipment. Would the court's decision have been different? Discuss.*

IMPACT OF THIS CASE ON TODAY'S LAW *This early Delaware decision was one of the first to set forth a test for determining when a corporate officer or director has breached the duty of loyalty. The test has two basic parts: Was the opportunity reasonably related to the corporation's line of business, and was the corporation financially able to undertake the opportunity? The court also considered whether the corporation had an interest or expectancy in the opportunity and recognized that when the corporation had "no interest or expectancy, the officer or director is entitled to treat the opportunity as his own."*

CONFLICTS OF INTEREST Corporate directors often have many business affiliations, and a director may sit on the board of more than one corporation. Of course, directors are precluded from entering into or supporting businesses that operate in direct competition with corporations on whose boards they serve. Their fiduciary duty requires them to make a full disclosure of any potential conflicts of interest that might arise in any corporate transaction [RMBCA 8.60].

Sometimes, a corporation enters into a contract or engages in a transaction in which an officer or director has a personal interest. The director or officer must make a *full disclosure* of the nature of the conflicting interest and all facts pertinent to the transaction, and must abstain from voting on the proposed transaction. Otherwise, directors would be prevented from ever having financial dealings with the corporations they serve.

▶ **Example 19.12** Ballo Corporation needs office space. Stephanie Colson, one of its five directors, owns the building adjoining the corporation's headquarters. Colson can negotiate a lease for the space to Ballo if she fully discloses her conflicting interest and any facts known to her about the proposed transaction to Ballo and the other four directors. If the lease arrangement is fair and reasonable, Colson abstains from voting on it, and the other members of the corporation's board of directors unanimously approve it, the contract is valid. ◀

LIABILITY OF DIRECTORS AND OFFICERS Directors and officers are exposed to liability on many fronts. They can be held liable for negligence in certain circumstances, as previously discussed. They may also be held liable for the crimes and torts committed by themselves or by corporate employees under their supervision. (See this chapter's *Insight into Ethics* below for a discussion of how one federal statute makes lying a crime.)

Additionally, if shareholders perceive that the corporate directors are not acting in the best interests of the corporation, they may sue the directors, in what is called

INSIGHT INTO ETHICS
When Is Lying a Federal Crime?

The federal government defines and prosecutes almost 4,500 crimes. In addition to prosecuting defendants for allegedly committing these crimes, the government can also charge them with lying about their actions. Under Section 1001 of Title 18 of the *United States Code,* any person convicted of knowingly and willfully making "any material false, fictitious or fraudulent statements or misrepresentations" can be fined or imprisoned or both. When prosecutors do not have enough evidence to charge someone with the underlying crime, they may still bring charges under Section 1001 if the person made any false statements in interviews.

A Costly Phone Interview

In 2004, attorney Melissa Ann Mahler was interviewed by phone by an official at the Securities and Exchange Commission. She made a false statement about a securities transaction in her personal brokerage account. Ultimately, a court determined that she had violated Section 1001. The court suspended Mahler's attorney's license, sentenced her to two years on probation, fined her $2,500, and ordered her to perform a hundred hours of community service.[a]

Whistling at a Whale Can Be Dangerous

Nancy Black, a marine biologist who operates a whale-watching boat company in California, also ran afoul of Section 1001. When a humpback whale appeared near one of her boats, the captain of the boat whistled at the whale, hoping that the sound would intrigue the whale and cause it to come closer. Regulators investigated whether the whistling constituted harassment of a whale, which is a federal crime.

Prosecutors have not charged Black with whale harassment. Instead, she has been charged with lying about the incident by supplying the regulators with a video that had been edited to delete material that Black thought was not relevant. In an interview, she commented, "I wasn't charged with anything about the dealings with the humpback. So why would they charge me with lying about it? It makes no sense."[b]

What Constitutes a Lie under Section 1001?

The courts have interpreted Section 1001 as encompassing almost any statement made to a federal official. The statement may be oral or in writing. The person making it need not be under oath, and the government does not have to have warned the person that any falsehood could have very serious consequences.

Although the lie has to be "material," any statement that has a "natural tendency to influence, or [is] capable of influencing, the decision of the decision-making body to which it is addressed" is considered material.[c] In other words, the federal government does not have to show that the falsehood actually influenced or misled anyone.

Consider a not too far-fetched example. Suppose that you fill out your time sheets at work inaccurately by listing more hours than you actually worked and occasionally complete a time sheet for a day that you did not work. If your employer has to submit employees' time sheets to a federal regulatory agency, you could ultimately be held criminally liable for lying.

LEGAL CRITICAL THINKING

INSIGHT INTO THE SOCIAL ENVIRONMENT

Many businesspersons believe that the federal government's power under Section 1001 is almost without limits. What ethical issues are at stake here?

a. *Matter of Mahler,* 94 A.D.3d 114, 939 N.Y.S.2d 900 (2012). See also *In re Simels,* 94 A.D.3d 108, 940 N.Y.S. 2d 577 (2012).

b. "'Lying' Is a Handy Charge for the U.S. Government," *Wall Street Journal,* April 11, 2012.

c. *United States v. Gaudin,* 515 U.S. 506, 115 S.Ct. 2310, 132 L.Ed.2d 444 (1995).

a *shareholder's derivative suit,* on behalf of the corporation. (This type of action will be discussed later in this chapter, in the context of shareholders' rights.) Directors and officers can also be held personally liable under a number of statutes, such as statutes enacted to protect consumers or the environment (see Chapters 24 and 25).

SECTION 6

SHAREHOLDERS

The acquisition of a share of stock makes a person an owner and a shareholder in a corporation. Shareholders thus own the corporation. Although they have no legal title to corporate property, such as buildings and equipment, they do have an equitable (ownership) interest in the firm.

As a general rule, shareholders have no responsibility for the daily management of the corporation, although they are ultimately responsible for choosing the board of directors, which does have such control. Ordinarily, corporate officers and other employees owe no direct duty to individual shareholders (unless some contract or special relationship exists between them in addition to the corporate relationship).

The duty of officers and directors is to act in the best interests of the corporation and its shareholder-owners *as a whole.* In turn, as you will read later in this chapter, controlling shareholders owe a fiduciary duty to minority shareholders.

Shareholders' Powers

Shareholders must approve fundamental changes affecting the corporation before the changes can be implemented. Hence, shareholder approval normally is required to amend the articles of incorporation or bylaws, to conduct a merger or dissolve the corporation, and to sell all or substantially all of the corporation's assets. Some of these powers are subject to prior board approval. Shareholder approval may also be requested (though it is not required) for certain other actions, such as to approve an independent auditor.

Shareholders have the power to vote to elect or remove members of the board of directors. As described earlier, the first board of directors is either named in the articles of incorporation or chosen by the incorporators to serve until the first shareholders' meeting. From that time on, selection and retention of directors are exclusively shareholder functions.

Directors usually serve their full terms. If the shareholders judge them unsatisfactory, they are simply not reelected. Shareholders have the inherent power, however, to remove a director from office *for cause* (breach of duty or misconduct) by a majority vote.[17] As noted earlier in this chapter, some state statutes (and some articles of incorporation) permit removal of directors without cause by the vote of a majority of the shareholders entitled to vote.[18]

Shareholders' Meetings

Shareholders' meetings must occur at least annually. In addition, special meetings can be called to deal with urgent matters.

NOTICE OF MEETINGS A corporation must notify its shareholders of the date, time, and place of an annual or special shareholders' meeting at least ten days, but not more than sixty days, before the meeting date [RMBCA 7.05].[19] (The date and time of the annual meeting can be specified in the bylaws.) Notice of a special meeting must include a statement of the purpose of the meeting, and business transacted at the meeting is limited to that purpose.

The RMBCA does not specify how the notice must be given (such as by mail, e-mail, or social media), but most corporations specify in their bylaws the acceptable methods of notifying shareholders about meetings. Also, some states' incorporation statutes outline the means of notice that a corporation can use in that jurisdiction. For instance, in Alaska, notice may be given in person, by mail, or by fax, e-mail, blog, or Web post—as long as the shareholder has agreed to that electronic method.[20]

PROXIES It usually is not practical for owners of only a few shares of stock of publicly traded corporations to attend a shareholders' meeting. Therefore, the law allows stockholders to appoint another person as their agent to vote their shares at the meeting. The signed appointment form or electronic transmission authorizing an agent to vote the shares is called a **proxy** (from the Latin *procurare,* meaning "to manage or take care of").

17. A director can often demand court review of removal for cause, however.

18. Most states allow *cumulative voting* for directors (described later in the chapter). If cumulative voting is authorized, a director may not be removed if the number of votes against removal would be sufficient to elect a director under cumulative voting. See, for example, California Corporations Code Section 303A. See also Section 8.08(c) of the RMBCA.

19. The shareholder can waive the requirement of notice by signing a waiver form [RMBCA 7.06]. A shareholder who does not receive notice but who learns of the meeting and attends without protesting the lack of notice is said to have waived notice by such conduct.

20. Alaska Statutes Section 10.06.410 Notice of Shareholders' Meetings.

Management often solicits proxies, but any person can do so to concentrate voting power. Groups of shareholders have used proxies as a device for taking over a corporation.

Proxies normally are revocable (can be withdrawn), unless they are specifically designated as irrevocable and coupled with an interest. A proxy is coupled with an interest when, for instance, the person receiving the proxies from shareholders has agreed to buy their shares. Under RMBCA 7.22(c), proxies are valid for eleven months, unless the proxy agreement mandates a longer period.

SHAREHOLDER PROPOSALS When shareholders want to change a company policy, they can put their ideas up for a shareholder vote. They do this by submitting a shareholder proposal to the board of directors and asking the board to include the proposal in the proxy materials that are sent to all shareholders before meetings.

As you will read in Chapter 28, the Securities and Exchange Commission (SEC) regulates the purchase and sale of securities. The SEC has special provisions relating to proxies and shareholder proposals. SEC Rule 14a-8 provides that all shareholders who own stock worth at least $1,000 are eligible to submit proposals for inclusion in corporate proxy materials. The corporation is required to include information on whatever proposals will be considered at the shareholders' meeting along with proxy materials. Only those proposals that relate to significant policy considerations, not ordinary business operations, must be included.

ELECTRONIC PROXY MATERIALS In the past, corporations had to send large packets of paper documents to shareholders, but today, the SEC requires all publicly held companies to distribute electronic proxy (e-proxy) materials.[21] Although the law requires proxy materials to be posted online, public companies may still choose among several options—including paper documents or a DVD sent by mail—for actually delivering the materials to shareholders.

If a company wishes to distribute proxy materials only via the Internet, it can choose the notice-and-access delivery option. Under this model, the corporation posts the proxy materials on a Web site and notifies the shareholders that the proxy materials are available online. If a shareholder requests paper proxy materials, the company must send them within three business days. Shareholders can permanently elect to receive all future proxy materials on paper or by e-mail with electronic links.

Shareholder Voting

Shareholders exercise ownership control through the power of their votes. Corporate business matters are presented in the form of resolutions, which shareholders vote to approve or disapprove. Unless there is a provision to the contrary, each shareholder is entitled to one vote per share, although the voting techniques discussed next enhance the power of the shareholder's vote.

The articles of incorporation can exclude or limit voting rights, particularly for certain classes of shares [RMBCA 7.21]. If a state statute requires specific voting procedures, the corporation's articles or bylaws must be consistent with the statute.

QUORUM REQUIREMENTS For shareholders to act during a meeting, a quorum must be present. Generally, a quorum exists when shareholders holding more than 50 percent of the outstanding shares are present, but state laws often permit the articles of incorporation to set higher or lower quorum requirements. In some states, obtaining the unanimous written consent of shareholders is a permissible alternative to holding a shareholders' meeting [RMBCA 7.25].

Once a quorum is present, voting can proceed. A straight majority vote of the shares represented at the meeting is usually required to pass resolutions. ▶ **Example 19.13** Novo Pictures, Inc., has 10,000 outstanding shares of voting stock. Its articles of incorporation set the quorum at 50 percent of outstanding shares and provide that a majority vote of the shares present is necessary to pass ordinary matters. Therefore, for this firm, a quorum of stockholders representing 5,000 outstanding shares must be present to conduct business at the shareholders' meeting. If exactly 5,000 shares are represented at the meeting, a vote of at least 2,501 of those shares is needed to pass a resolution. If 6,000 shares are represented, a vote of 3,001 will be necessary. ◀

At times, more than a simple majority vote will be required either by statute or by the articles of incorporation. Extraordinary corporate matters, such as a merger, a consolidation, or dissolution of the corporation, require a higher percentage (more than a majority) of all corporate shares entitled to vote [RMBCA 7.27].

VOTING LISTS The corporation prepares the voting list before each shareholders' meeting. Ordinarily, only

21. 17 C.F.R. Parts 240, 249, and 274.

persons whose names appear on the corporation's stockholder records as owners are entitled to vote.[22]

The voting list contains the name and address of each shareholder as shown on the corporate records on a given cutoff date, or *record date*. (Under RMBCA 7.07, the bylaws or board of directors may fix a record date that is as much as seventy days before the meeting.) The voting list also includes the number of voting shares held by each owner. The list is usually kept at the corporate headquarters and must be made available for shareholder inspection [RMBCA 7.20].

CUMULATIVE VOTING Most states permit, and many require, shareholders to elect directors by *cumulative voting,* a voting method designed to allow minority shareholders to be represented on the board of directors.

Formula. With cumulative voting, each shareholder is entitled to a total number of votes equal to the number of board members to be elected multiplied by the number of voting shares that the shareholder owns. The shareholder can cast all of these votes for one candidate or split them among several nominees for director. All nominees stand for election at the same time. When cumulative voting is not required by statute or under the articles, the entire board can be elected by a majority of shares at a shareholders' meeting.

How Cumulative Voting Works. Cumulative voting can best be understood by example. ▶ **Example 19.14** A corporation has 10,000 shares issued and outstanding. The minority shareholders hold 3,000 shares, and the majority shareholders hold the other 7,000 shares. Three members of the board are to be elected. The majority shareholders' nominees are Alvarez, Beasley, and Caravel. The minority shareholders' nominee is Dovrik. Can Dovrik be elected to the board by the minority shareholders?

If cumulative voting is allowed, the answer is yes. The minority shareholders have 9,000 votes among them (the number of directors to be elected times the number of shares, or $3 \times 3{,}000 = 9{,}000$ votes). All of these votes can be cast to elect Dovrik. The majority shareholders have 21,000 votes ($3 \times 7{,}000 = 21{,}000$ votes), but these votes must be distributed among their three nominees.

The principle of cumulative voting is that no matter how the majority shareholders cast their 21,000 votes, they will not be able to elect all three directors if the minority shareholders cast all of their 9,000 votes for Dovrik, as illustrated in Exhibit 19–2 below. ◀

SHAREHOLDER VOTING AGREEMENTS Before a shareholders' meeting, a group of shareholders can create a *shareholder voting agreement* by agreeing in writing to vote their shares together in a specified manner. Such agreements usually are held to be valid and enforceable. Nevertheless, corporate managers must be careful that such agreements do not constitute a breach of their fiduciary duties.

▶ **Case in Point 19.15** Several shareholders of Cryo-Cell International, Inc., mounted a proxy contest in an effort to replace the board of directors. Another stockholder, Andrew Filipowski, agreed to support management in exchange for being included in management's slate of directors. The company's chief executive officer, Mercedes Walton, secretly promised Filipowski that if management's slate won, the board of directors would add another board seat to be filled by a Filipowski designee.

After management won the election, Walton prepared to add Filipowski's designee to the board. When the dissident shareholders challenged the election results, the court held that the board's actions and Walton's secret agreement constituted serious breaches of fiduciary duty that tainted the election. The court therefore ordered a new election to be held.[23] ◀

22. When the legal owner is deceased, bankrupt, mentally incompetent, or in some other way under a legal disability, his or her vote can be cast by a person designated by law to control and manage that owner's property.

23. *Portnoy v. Cryo-Cell International, Inc.*, 940 A.2d 43 (Del.Ch. 2008).

EXHIBIT 19–2 Results of Cumulative Voting

Ballot	Majority Shareholder Votes			Minority Shareholder Votes	Directors Elected
	Alvarez	*Beasley*	*Caravel*	*Dovrik*	
1	10,000	10,000	1,000	9,000	Alvarez, Beasley, Dovrik
2	9,001	9,000	2,999	9,000	Alvarez, Beasley, Dovrik
3	6,000	7,000	8,000	9,000	Beasley, Caravel, Dovrik

VOTING TRUST Another voting technique is for shareholders to enter into a *voting trust.* (A shareholder can also appoint a voting agent and vote by proxy, as mentioned previously.) A **voting trust** is an agreement (a trust contract) under which a shareholder assigns the right to vote his or her shares to a trustee, usually for a specified period of time. The trustee is then responsible for voting the shares on behalf of all the shareholders in the trust. The shareholder retains all rights of ownership (for example, the right to receive dividend payments) except the power to vote the shares [RMBCA 7.30].

Rights of Shareholders

Shareholders possess numerous rights. A significant right—the right to vote their shares—has already been discussed. We look at some additional rights of shareholders in the following subsections.

STOCK CERTIFICATES In the past, corporations commonly issued **stock certificates** that evidenced ownership of a specified number of shares in the corporation. Only a few jurisdictions still require physical stock certificates, and shareholders there have the right to demand that the corporation issue certificates (or replace those that were lost or destroyed). Stock is intangible personal property, however, and the ownership right exists independently of the certificate itself.

In most states and under RMBCA 6.26, a board of directors may provide that shares of stock will be uncertificated, or "paperless"—that is, no actual, physical stock certificates will be issued. When shares are uncertificated, the corporation may be required to send each shareholder a letter or some other form of notice that contains the same information that traditionally appeared on the face of stock certificates. Notice of shareholders' meetings, dividends, and operational and financial reports are all distributed according to the recorded ownership listed in the corporation's books.

PREEMPTIVE RIGHTS Sometimes, the articles of incorporation grant preemptive rights to shareholders. With **preemptive rights,** a shareholder receives a preference over all other purchasers to subscribe to or purchase a prorated share of a new issue of stock. In other words, the shareholder can purchase a percentage of the new shares that is equal to his or her current percentage of ownership in the corporation.

Under RMBCA 6.30, preemptive rights do not exist unless provided for in the articles of incorporation. Generally, preemptive rights apply only to additional, newly issued stock sold for cash, and the preemptive rights must be exercised within a specific time period, which is usually thirty days.

Allow a Shareholder to Maintain Proportionate Interest. Preemptive rights allow each shareholder to maintain her or his proportionate control, voting power, or financial interest in the corporation. ► **Example 19.16** Tron Corporation authorizes and issues 1,000 shares of stock, and Omar Loren purchases 100 shares, making him the owner of 10 percent of the company's stock. Subsequently, Tron, by vote of its shareholders, authorizes the issuance of another 1,000 shares (by amending the articles of incorporation). This increases its capital stock to a total of 2,000 shares.

If preemptive rights have been provided, Loren can purchase one additional share of the new stock being issued for each share he already owns—or 100 additional shares. Thus, he will own 200 of the 2,000 shares outstanding, and his relative position as a shareholder will be maintained. If preemptive rights are not provided, his proportionate control and voting power will be diluted from that of a 10 percent shareholder to that of a 5 percent shareholder because the additional 1,000 shares were issued. ◄

Important in Close Corporations. Preemptive rights are most important in close corporations because each shareholder owns a relatively small number of shares but controls a substantial interest in the corporation. Without preemptive rights, it would be possible for a shareholder to lose his or her proportionate control over the firm. Nevertheless, preemptive rights can hinder a corporation from raising capital from new, outside investors who can provide needed expertise as well as capital.

STOCK WARRANTS **Stock warrants** are rights to buy stock at a stated price by a specified date that are given by the company. Usually, when preemptive rights exist and a corporation is issuing additional shares, it gives its shareholders stock warrants. Warrants are often publicly traded on securities exchanges.

DIVIDENDS As mentioned, a **dividend** is a distribution of corporate profits or income *ordered by the directors* and paid to the shareholders in proportion to their respective shares in the corporation. Dividends can be paid in cash, property, stock of the corporation that is paying the dividends, or stock of other corporations.[24]

24. On one occasion, a distillery declared and paid a dividend in bonded whiskey.

State laws vary, but each state determines the general circumstances and legal requirements under which dividends are paid. State laws also control the sources of revenue to be used. Only certain funds are legally available for paying dividends. Depending on state law, dividends may be paid from the following sources:

1. *Retained earnings.* All states allow dividends to be paid from the undistributed net profits earned by the corporation, including capital gains from the sale of fixed assets. As mentioned earlier, the undistributed net profits are called *retained earnings.*
2. *Net profits.* A few states allow dividends to be issued from current net profits without regard to deficits in prior years.
3. *Surplus.* A number of states allow dividends to be paid out of any kind of surplus. For instance, earned surplus is the sum of a company's net profits over a period of time. It increases by the amount of each year's net income after dividend payments. Earned surplus is not extra cash, but shareholder equity. A company's board of directors may choose to pay dividends from the surplus or to use it for some other corporate purpose (such as for acquisitions).

Illegal Dividends. Sometimes, dividends are improperly paid from an unauthorized account, or their payment causes the corporation to become insolvent. Generally, shareholders must return illegal dividends only if they knew that the dividends were illegal when the payment was received (or if the dividends were paid when the corporation was insolvent). Whenever dividends are illegal or improper, the board of directors can be held personally liable for the amount of the payment.

The Directors' Failure to Declare a Dividend. When directors fail to declare a dividend, shareholders can ask a court to compel the directors to meet and declare a dividend. To succeed, the shareholders must show that the directors have acted so unreasonably in withholding the dividend that their conduct is an abuse of their discretion.

A corporation might accumulate large cash reserves for a legitimate corporate purpose, such as expansion or research. The mere fact that the firm has sufficient earnings or surplus available to pay a dividend normally is not enough to compel the directors to distribute funds that, in the board's opinion, should not be distributed. The courts are reluctant to interfere with corporate operations and will not compel directors to declare dividends unless abuse of discretion is clearly shown.

INSPECTION RIGHTS Shareholders in a corporation enjoy both common law and statutory inspection rights. The RMBCA provides that every shareholder is entitled to examine specified corporate records, including voting lists [RMBCA 7.20, 16.02]. The shareholder may inspect in person, or an attorney, accountant, or other authorized assistant can do so as the shareholder's agent.

A shareholder only has a right to inspect and copy corporate books and records for a *proper purpose,* however, and the request to inspect must be made in advance. A shareholder who is denied the right of inspection can seek a court order to compel the inspection.

The power of inspection is fraught with potential abuses, and the corporation is allowed to protect itself from them. For instance, a shareholder can properly be denied access to corporate records to prevent harassment or to protect trade secrets or other confidential corporate information. In some states, a shareholder must have held her or his shares for a minimum period of time immediately preceding the demand to inspect or must hold a certain percentage of outstanding shares.

TRANSFER OF SHARES Corporate stock represents an ownership right in intangible personal property. The law generally recognizes the right of an owner to transfer property to another person unless there are valid restrictions on its transferability. Restrictions on the transfer of shares in a close corporation usually are valid.

When shares are transferred, a new entry is made in the corporate stock book to indicate the new owner. Until the corporation is notified and the entry is complete, all rights—including voting rights, notice of shareholders' meetings, and the right to dividend distributions—remain with the current record owner.

RIGHTS ON DISSOLUTION When a corporation is dissolved and its outstanding debts and the claims of its creditors have been satisfied, there may be assets remaining. The remaining assets are distributed to the shareholders in proportion to the percentage of shares owned by each shareholder.

The articles of incorporation may provide that certain classes of stock will be given priority. If no class of stock has been given preference in the distribution of assets, all of the stockholders share the remaining assets.

THE SHAREHOLDER'S DERIVATIVE SUIT When the corporation is harmed by the actions of a third party, the directors can bring a lawsuit in the name of the corporation against that party. If the corporate directors fail to bring a lawsuit, shareholders can do so "derivatively" in what is known as a **shareholder's derivative suit.**

Before shareholders can bring a derivative suit, they must submit a written demand to the corporation, asking the board of directors to take appropriate action [RMBCA 7.40]. The directors then have ninety days in which to act. Only if they refuse to do so can the derivative suit go forward.

When Acts of Directors and Officers Cause Harm to the Corporation. The right of shareholders to bring a derivative action is especially important when the wrong suffered by the corporation results from the actions of the corporate directors and officers. For obvious reasons, the directors and officers would probably be unwilling to take any action against themselves.

Nevertheless, a court will dismiss a derivative suit if a majority of the directors or an independent panel determines in good faith that the lawsuit is not in the best interests of the corporation [RMBCA 7.44].

Any Damages Awarded Go to the Corporation. When shareholders bring a derivative suit, they are not pursuing rights or benefits for themselves personally but are acting as guardians of the corporate entity. Therefore, if the suit is successful, any damages recovered normally go into the corporation's treasury, not to the shareholders personally.[25]

Duties and Liabilities of Shareholders

One of the hallmarks of the corporate form of organization is that shareholders are not personally liable for the debts of the corporation. If the corporation fails, the shareholders can lose their investments, but that generally is the limit of their liability. As previously discussed, in certain instances of fraud, undercapitalization, or careless observance of corporate formalities, a court will pierce the corporate veil (disregard the corporate entity) and hold the shareholders individually liable. But these situations are the exception, not the rule.

A shareholder can also be personally liable in certain other rare instances. One relates to illegal dividends, which were discussed previously. Another relates to *watered stock*. Still another concerns the duties majority shareholders owe to minority shareholders.

WATERED STOCK When a corporation issues shares for less than their fair market value, the shares are referred to as **watered stock.**[26] Usually, the shareholder who receives watered stock must pay the difference to the corporation (the shareholder is personally liable). In some states, the shareholder who receives watered stock may be liable to creditors of the corporation for unpaid corporate debts.

▶ **Example 19.17** During the formation of a corporation, Gomez, one of the incorporators, transfers his property, Sunset Beach, to the corporation for 10,000 shares of stock at a par value of $100 per share for a total price of $1 million. After the property is transferred and the shares are issued, Sunset Beach is carried on the corporate books at a value of $1 million.

On appraisal, it is discovered that the market value of the property at the time of transfer was only $500,000. The shares issued to Gomez are therefore watered stock, and he is liable to the corporation for the difference between the value of the shares and the value of the property. ◀

DUTIES OF MAJORITY SHAREHOLDERS In some instances, a majority shareholder is regarded as having a fiduciary duty to the corporation and to the minority shareholders. This duty occurs when a single shareholder (or a few shareholders acting in concert) owns a sufficient number of shares to exercise *de facto* (actual) control over the corporation. In these situations, the majority shareholder owes a fiduciary duty to the minority shareholders.

When a majority shareholder breaches her or his fiduciary duty to a minority shareholder, the minority shareholder can sue for damages. A breach of fiduciary duties by those who control a close corporation normally constitutes what is known as *oppressive conduct.* A common example of a breach of fiduciary duty occurs when the majority shareholders "freeze out" the minority shareholders and exclude them from certain benefits of participating in the firm.

▶ **Case in Point 19.18** Brodie, Jordan, and Barbuto formed a close corporation to operate a machine shop. Each owned one-third of the shares in the company, and all three were directors. Brodie served as the corporate president for twelve years but thereafter met with the other shareholders only a few times a year. After disagreements arose, Brodie asked the company to purchase his shares, but his requests were refused. A few years later, Brodie died, and his wife inherited his shares in the company. Jordan and Barbuto refused to perform a valuation of the company, denied her access to the corporate information she requested, did not declare any dividends, and refused to elect her as a director. In this situation, a court found that the majority shareholders had violated their fiduciary duty to Brodie's wife.[27] ◀

---

25. The shareholders may be entitled to reimbursement for reasonable expenses of the derivative lawsuit, including attorneys' fees.

26. The phrase *watered stock* was originally used to describe cattle that were kept thirsty during a long drive and then were allowed to drink large quantities of water just before their sale. The increased weight of the watered stock allowed the seller to reap a higher profit.

27. *Brodie v. Jordan,* 447 Mass. 866, 857 N.E.2d 1076 (2006).

SECTION 7 MAJOR BUSINESS FORMS COMPARED

As mentioned in Chapter 17, when deciding which form of business organization to choose, businesspersons normally consider several factors, including ease of creation, the liability of the owners, tax considerations, and the ability to raise capital. Each major form of business organization offers distinct advantages and disadvantages with respect to these and other factors.

Exhibit 19–3 below and on the next page summarizes the essential advantages and disadvantages of each of the forms of business organization discussed in Chapters 17 through 19.

EXHIBIT 19–3 Major Forms of Business Compared

Characteristic	Sole Proprietorship	Partnership	Corporation
Method of Creation	Created at will by owner.	Created by agreement of the parties.	Authorized by the state under the state's corporation law.
Legal Position	Not a separate entity; owner is the business.	A general partnership is a separate legal entity in most states.	Always a legal entity separate and distinct from its owners—a legal fiction for the purposes of owning property and being a party to litigation.
Liability	Unlimited liability.	Unlimited liability.	Limited liability of shareholders—shareholders are not liable for the debts of the corporation.
Duration	Determined by owner; automatically dissolved on owner's death.	Terminated by agreement of the partners, but can continue to do business even when a partner dissociates from the partnership.	Can have perpetual existence.
Transferability of Interest	Interest can be transferred, but individual's proprietorship then ends.	Although partnership interest can be assigned, assignee does not have full rights of a partner.	Shares of stock can be transferred.
Management	Completely at owner's discretion.	Each partner has a direct and equal voice in management unless expressly agreed otherwise in the partnership agreement.	Shareholders elect directors, who set policy and appoint officers.
Taxation	Owner pays personal taxes on business income.	Each partner pays pro rata share of income taxes on net profits, whether or not they are distributed.	Double taxation—corporation pays income tax on net profits, with no deduction for dividends, and shareholders pay income tax on disbursed dividends they receive.
Organizational Fees, Annual License Fees, and Annual Reports	None or minimal.	None or minimal.	All required.
Transaction of Business in Other States	Generally no limitation.	Generally no limitation.[a]	Normally must qualify to do business and obtain certificate of authority.

a. A few states have enacted statutes requiring that foreign partnerships qualify to do business there.

Continued

EXHIBIT 19–3 Major Forms of Business Compared—Continued

Charactistic	Limited Partnership	Limited Liability Company	Limited Liability Partnership
Method of Creation	Created by agreement to carry on a business for profit. At least one party must be a general partner and the other(s) limited partner(s). Certificate of limited partnership is filed. Charter must be issued by the state.	Created by an agreement of the member-owners of the company. Articles of organization are filed. Charter must be issued by the state.	Created by agreement of the partners. A statement of qualification for the limited liability partnership is filed.
Legal Position	Treated as a legal entity.	Treated as a legal entity.	Generally, treated same as a general partnership.
Liability	Unlimited liability of all general partners. Limited partners are liable only to the extent of capital contributions.	Member-owners' liability is limited to the amount of capital contributions or investments.	Varies, but under the Uniform Partnership Act, liability of a partner for acts committed by other partners is limited.
Duration	By agreement in certificate, or by termination of the last general partner (retirement, death, and the like) or last limited partner.	Unless a single-member LLC, can have perpetual existence (same as a corporation).	Remains in existence until cancellation or revocation.
Transferability of Interest	Interest can be assigned (same as a general partnership), but if assignee becomes a member with consent of other partners, certificate must be amended.	Member interests are freely transferable.	Interest can be assigned same as in a general partnership.
Management	General partners have equal voice or by agreement. Limited partners may not retain limited liability if they actively participate in management.	Member-owners can fully participate in management or can designate a group of persons to manage on behalf of the members.	Same as a general partnership.
Taxation	Generally taxed as a partnership.	LLC is not taxed, and members are taxed personally on profits "passed through" the LLC.	Same as a general partnership.
Organizational Fees, Annual License Fees, and Annual Reports	Organizational fee required; usually not others.	Organizational fee required. Others vary with states.	Fees are set by each state for filing statements of qualification, statements of foreign qualification, and annual reports.
Transaction of Business in Other States	Generally no limitations.	Generally no limitations, but may vary depending on state.	Must file a statement of foreign qualification before doing business in another state.

Reviewing: Corporations

William Sharp was the sole shareholder and manager of Chickasaw Club, Inc., an S corporation that operated a popular nightclub of the same name in Columbus, Georgia. Sharp maintained a corporate checking account but paid the club's employees, suppliers, and entertainers in cash out of the club's proceeds. Sharp owned the property on which the club was located. He rented it to the club but made mortgage payments out of the club's proceeds and often paid other personal expenses with Chickasaw corporate funds.

At 12:45 A.M. on July 31, eighteen-year-old Aubrey Lynn Pursley, who was already intoxicated, entered the Chickasaw Club. A city ordinance prohibited individuals under the age of twenty-one from entering nightclubs, but Chickasaw employees did not check Pursley's identification to verify her age. Pursley drank more alcohol at Chickasaw and was visibly intoxicated when she left the club at 3:00 A.M. with a beer in her hand. Shortly afterward, Pursley lost control of her car, struck a tree, and was killed. Joseph Dancause, Pursley's stepfather, filed a tort lawsuit in a Georgia state court against Chickasaw Club, Inc., and William Sharp, seeking damages. Using the information presented in the chapter, answer the following questions.

1. Under what theory might the court in this case make an exception to the limited liability of shareholders and hold Sharp personally liable for the damages? What factors would be relevant to the court's decision?
2. Suppose that Chickasaw's articles of incorporation failed to describe the corporation's purpose or management structure as required by state law. Would the court be likely to rule that Sharp is personally liable to Dancause on that basis? Why or why not?
3. Suppose that the club extended credit to its regular patrons in an effort to maintain a loyal clientele, although neither the articles of incorporation nor the corporate bylaws authorized this practice. Would the corporation likely have the power to engage in this activity? Explain.
4. How would the court classify the Chickasaw Club corporation—domestic or foreign, public or private? Why?

DEBATE THIS . . . *The sole shareholder of an S corporation should not be able to avoid liability for the torts of her or his employees.*

Terms and Concepts

alien corporation 434
articles of incorporation 438
benefit corporation 436
business judgment rule 447
bylaws 438
close corporation 434
commingle 441
dividend 454
domestic corporation 434
foreign corporation 434
holding company 432
inside director 445
outside director 445
pierce the corporate veil 441
preemptive rights 454
proxy 451
public corporation 434
publicly held corporation 434
quorum 445
retained earnings 432
S corporation 436
shareholder's derivative suit 455
stock certificate 454
stock warrant 454
ultra vires 440
voting trust 454
watered stock 456

ExamPrep

Issue Spotters

1. Northwest Brands, Inc., is a small business incorporated in Minnesota. Its one class of stock is owned by twelve members of a single family. Ordinarily, corporate income is taxed at the corporate and shareholder levels. Is there a way for Northwest Brands to avoid this double taxation? Explain your answer. **(See page 436.)**
2. Wonder Corporation has an opportunity to buy stock in XL, Inc. The directors decide that instead of Wonder buying the stock, the directors will buy it. Yvon, a Wonder shareholder, learns of the purchase and wants to sue the directors on Wonder's behalf. Can she do it? Explain. **(See page 455.)**

- **Check your answers to the Issue Spotters against the answers provided in Appendix E at the end of this text.**

Before the Test

Go to **www.cengagebrain.com**, enter the ISBN 9781285428949, and click on "Find" to locate this textbook's Web site. Then, click on "Access Now" under

"Study Tools," and select Chapter 19 at the top. There, you will find an Interactive Quiz that you can take to assess your mastery of the concepts in this chapter, as well as Flashcards and a Glossary of important terms.

Business Scenarios

19–1. Preincorporation. Cummings, Okawa, and Taft are recent college graduates who want to form a corporation to manufacture and sell digital tablets. Peterson tells them he will set in motion the formation of their corporation. First, Peterson makes a contract with Owens for the purchase of a piece of land for $20,000. Owens does not know of the prospective corporate formation at the time the contract is signed. Second, Peterson makes a contract with Babcock to build a small plant on the property being purchased. Babcock's contract is conditional on the corporation's formation. Peterson secures all necessary subscription agreements and capitalization, and he files the articles of incorporation. **(See page 437.)**

(a) Discuss whether the newly formed corporation, Peterson, or both are liable on the contracts with Owens and Babcock.

(b) Discuss whether the corporation is automatically liable to Babcock on formation.

19–2. Conflicts of Interest. Oxy Corp. is negotiating with Wick Construction Co. for the renovation of Oxy's corporate headquarters. Wick, the owner of Wick Construction Co., is also one of the five members of Oxy's board of directors. The contract terms are standard for this type of contract. Wick has previously informed two of the other directors of his interest in the construction company. Oxy's board approves the contract by a three-to-two vote, with Wick voting with the majority. Discuss whether this contract is binding on the corporation. **(See page 449.)**

19–3. Liability of Directors. AstroStar, Inc., has approximately five hundred shareholders. Its board of directors consists of three members—Eckhart, Dolan, and Macero. At a regular board meeting, the board selects Galiard as president of the corporation by a two-to-one vote, with Eckhart dissenting. The minutes of the meeting do not register Eckhart's dissenting vote. Later, an audit reveals that Galiard is a former convict and has embezzled $500,000 from the corporation that is not covered by insurance. Can the corporation hold directors Eckhart, Dolan, and Macero personally liable? Discuss. **(See page 450.)**

Business Case Problems

19–4. Spotlight on Smart Inventions—Piercing the Corporate Veil.

Thomas Persson and Jon Nokes founded Smart Inventions, Inc., to market household consumer products. The success of their first product, the Smart Mop, continued with later products, which were sold through infomercials and other means. Persson and Nokes were the firm's officers and equal shareholders. Persson was responsible for product development, and Nokes was in charge of day-to-day operations. By 1998, they had become dissatisfied with each other's efforts. Nokes represented the firm as financially "dying," "in a grim state, . . . worse than ever," and offered to buy all of Persson's shares for $1.6 million. Persson accepted. On the day that they signed the agreement to transfer the shares, Smart Inventions began marketing a new product—the Tap Light. It was an instant success, generating millions of dollars in revenues. In negotiating with Persson, Nokes had intentionally kept the Tap Light a secret. Persson sued Smart Inventions, asserting fraud and other claims. Under what principle might Smart Inventions be liable for Nokes's fraud? Is Smart Inventions liable in this case? Explain. [*Persson v. Smart Inventions, Inc.,* 125 Cal.App.4th 1141, 23 Cal. Rptr.3d 335 (2 Dist. 2005)] **(See page 441.)**

19–5. Close Corporations. Mark Burnett and Kamran Pourgol were the only shareholders in a corporation that built and sold a house. When the buyers discovered that the house exceeded the amount of square footage allowed by the building permit, Pourgol agreed to renovate the house to conform to the permit. No work was done, however, and Burnett filed a suit against Pourgol. Burnett claimed that, without his knowledge, Pourgol had submitted incorrect plans to obtain the building permit, misrepresented the extent of the renovation, and failed to fix the house. Was Pourgol guilty of misconduct? If so, how might it have been avoided? Discuss. [*Burnett v. Pourgol,* 83 A.D.3d 756, 921 N.Y.S.2d 280 (2 Dept. 2011)] **(See page 441.)**

19–6. BUSINESS CASE PROBLEM WITH SAMPLE ANSWER: Rights of Shareholders.

Stanka Woods is the sole member of Hair Ventures, LLC. Hair Ventures owns 3 million shares of stock in Biolustré Inc. For several years, Woods and other Biolustré shareholders did not receive notice of shareholders' meetings or financial reports. On learning that Biolustré planned to issue more stock, Woods, through Hair Ventures, demanded to see Biolustré's books and records.

*Biolustré asserted that the request was not for a proper purpose. Does Woods have a right to inspect Biolustré's books and records? If so, what are the limits? Do any of those limits apply in this case? Explain. [*Biolustré Inc. v. Hair Ventures, LLC, *2011 WL 540054 (Tex.App.—San Antonio 2011)]* **(See page 454.)**

- **For a sample answer to Problem 19–6, go to Appendix F at the end of this text.**

19–7. Piercing the Corporate Veil. In 1997, Leon Greenblatt, Andrew Jahelka, and Richard Nichols incorporated Loop Corp. with only $1,000 of capital. Three years later, Banco Panamericano, Inc., which was run entirely by Greenblatt and owned by a Greenblatt family trust, extended a large line of credit to Loop. Loop's subsidiaries then participated in the credit, giving $3 million to Loop while acquiring a security interest in Loop itself. Loop then opened an account with Wachovia Securities, LLC, to buy stock shares using credit provided by Wachovia. When the stock values plummeted, Loop owed Wachovia $1.89 million. Loop also defaulted on its loan from Banco, but Banco agreed to lend Loop millions of dollars more. Rather than repay Wachovia with the influx of funds, Loop gave the funds to closely related entities and "compensated" Nichols and Jahelka without issuing any W-2 forms (forms reporting compensation to the Internal Revenue Service). The evidence also showed that Loop made loans to other related entities and shared office space, equipment, and telephone and fax numbers with related entities. Loop also moved employees among related entities, failed to file its tax returns on time (or sometimes at all), and failed to follow its own bylaws. In a lawsuit brought by Wachovia, can the court hold Greenblatt, Jahelka, and Nichols personally liable by piercing the corporate veil? Why or why not? [*Wachovia Securities, LLC v. Banco Panamericano, Inc.,* 674 F.3d 743 (9th Cir. 2012)] **(See page 441.)**

19–8. Duty of Loyalty. Kids International Corp. produced children's wear for Wal-mart and other retailers. Gila Dweck was a Kids director and its chief executive officer. Because she felt that she was not paid enough for the company's success, she started Success Apparel to compete with Kids. Success operated out of Kids' premises, used its employees, borrowed on its credit, took advantage of its business opportunities, and capitalized on its customer relationships. As an "administrative fee," Dweck paid Kids 1 percent of Success's total sales. Did Dweck breach any fiduciary duties? Explain. [*Dweck v. Nasser,* 2012 WL 3194069 (Del.Ch. 2012)] **(See page 448.)**

19–9. A QUESTION OF ETHICS: Improper Incorporation.

*Mike Lyons incorporated Lyons Concrete, Inc., in Montana, but did not file its first annual report, so the state involuntarily dissolved the firm in 1996. Unaware of the dissolution, Lyons continued to do business as Lyons Concrete. In 2003, he signed a written contract with William Weimar to form and pour a certain amount of concrete on Weimar's property in Lake County for $19,810. Weimar was in a rush to complete the entire project, and he and Lyons orally agreed to additional work on a time-and-materials basis. When scheduling conflicts arose, Weimar had his own employees set some of the forms, which proved deficient. Weimar also directed Lyons to pour concrete in the rain, which undercut its quality. In mid-project, Lyons submitted an invoice for $14,389, which Weimar paid. After the work was complete, Lyons sent Weimar an invoice for $25,731, but he refused to pay, claiming that the $14,389 covered everything. To recover the unpaid amount, Lyons filed a mechanic's lien as "Mike Lyons d/b/a Lyons Concrete, Inc." against Weimar's property. Weimar filed a suit in a Montana state court to strike the lien, and Lyons filed a counterclaim to reassert it. [*Weimar v. Lyons, *338 Mont. 242, 164 P.3d 922 (2007)]* **(See page 439.)**

(a) Before the trial, Weimar asked for a change of venue on the ground that a sign on the courthouse lawn advertised "Lyons Concrete." How might the sign affect a trial on the parties' dispute? Should the court grant this request? Why or why not?

(b) Weimar asked the court to dismiss the counterclaim on the ground that the state had dissolved Lyons Concrete in 1996. Lyons immediately filed new articles of incorporation for "Lyons Concrete, Inc." Under what doctrine might the court rule that Weimar could not deny the existence of Lyons Concrete? What ethical values underlie this doctrine? Should the court make this ruling? Explain.

(c) At the trial, Weimar argued, in part, that there was no "fixed price" contract between the parties and that even if there were, the poor quality of the work, which required repairs, amounted to a breach, excusing Weimar's further performance. Should the court rule in Weimar's favor on this basis? Why or why not?

Legal Reasoning Group Activity

19–10. Shareholders' Duties. Milena Weintraub and Larry Griffith were shareholders in Grand Casino, Inc., which operated a casino in South Dakota. Griffith owned 51 percent of the stock and Weintraub 49 percent. Weintraub managed the casino, which Griffith typically visited once a week. At the end of 2012, an accounting audit showed that the cash on hand was less than the amount posted in the casino's books. Later, more shortfalls were discovered. In October 2014, Griffith did a complete audit. Weintraub was unable to account for $200,500 in missing cash. Griffith then kept all of the casino's most recent profits, including Weintraub's $90,447.20 share, and, without telling Weintraub, sold the casino for $400,000 and kept all of the proceeds. Weintraub filed a suit against Griffith, asserting a breach of fiduciary duty. Griffith countered with evidence of Weintraub's misappropriation of corporate cash. **(See page 456.)**

(a) The first group will discuss the duties that these parties owed to each other, and determine whether Weintraub or Griffith, or both, breached those duties.

(b) The second group will decide how this dispute should be resolved and who should pay what to whom to reconcile the finances.

(c) A third group will discuss whether Weintraub or Griffin violated any ethical duties to each other or to the corporation.

UNIT FOUR Focus on Ethics

Ethics and the Business Environment

Every now and then, scandals in the business world rock the nation. Certainly, this was true in the first decade of the 2000s when the activities of Enron Corporation, WorldCom, and a number of other companies came to light. Congress responded to public outcry by passing the Sarbanes-Oxley Act, which was mentioned in Chapter 19. That act imposed stricter requirements on corporations with respect to accounting practices and statements made in documents filed with the Securities and Exchange Commission (SEC).

The lesson for the business world is, of course, that if business leaders do not behave ethically (and legally), the government will create new laws and regulations that force them to do so. We offered suggestions on how business decision makers can create an ethical workplace in Chapter 4. Here, we look at selected areas in which the relationships within specific business organizational forms may raise ethical issues.

The Emergence of Corporate Governance

The well-publicized corporate abuses of the last decade provided the impetus for businesspersons to create their own internal rules for corporate governance (which will be discussed in Chapter 28). Examples of these abuses make it clear why such rules are needed. In a few situations, officers have blatantly stolen from the corporation and its shareholders. More frequently, though, officers have received excessive benefits, or "perks," because of their position. To illustrate: Tyco International bought a $6,000 shower curtain and a $15,000 umbrella stand for its chief executive officer's apartment.

Corporate officers may be given numerous benefits, which they may or may not deserve. On several occasions, a leading corporate officer has received compensation of $50 million or more in a year when the company's share price actually declined. Even if corporate officers are scrupulously honest and have modest personal tastes, their behavior may still raise concerns: they may not be good managers, and they may make incompetent corporate decisions. They may be a little lazy and fail to do the hard work necessary to investigate the corporation's alternatives. Sometimes, officers may simply fail to appreciate the concerns of shareholders on certain matters, such as maximizing short-term versus long-term results.

Corporate governance controls are meant to ensure that officers receive only the benefits they earn. Governance monitors the actions taken by officers to make sure they are wise and in the best interests of the company. In this way, the corporation can be confident that it is acting ethically toward its shareholders.

Fiduciary Duties Revisited

The law of agency, which will be outlined in Chapter 20, permeates nearly all relationships within any partnership or corporation. An important duty that arises in the law of agency, and applies to all partners and corporate directors, officers, and management personnel, is the duty of loyalty. As caretakers of the shareholders' wealth, corporate directors and officers also have a fiduciary duty to exercise care when making decisions affecting the corporate enterprise.

The Duty of Loyalty Every individual has personal interests, which may at times conflict with the interests of the partnership or corporation with which he or she is affiliated. In particular, partners or corporate officers and directors may face a conflict between personal interests and the interests of the business entity.

Acquiring Assets. Corporate officers and directors may find themselves in a position to acquire assets that would also benefit the corporation if acquired in the corporation's name. If an officer does purchase the asset without offering the opportunity to the corporation, however, she or he may be liable for usurping a corporate opportunity.[1]

Disclosure. Most courts also hold that a corporate officer or director has a fiduciary duty to disclose improper conduct to the corporation. For example, a leading case on the issue involved Thomas Coughlin, a top executive in theft prevention at Wal-Mart. He had held several other high-level positions prior to becoming a member of the board of directors. When he retired, Coughlin signed an agreement and release of claims with Wal-Mart under which he was to receive millions of dollars in benefits over the years.

Then Wal-Mart discovered that Coughlin, before his retirement, had abused his position of authority. He had conspired with subordinates to misappropriate hundreds of thousands of dollars in property and cash through various fraudulent schemes. Wal-Mart sued Coughlin alleging that he had breached his fiduciary duty of loyalty by failing to disclose his misconduct before entering a self-dealing contract.

Ultimately, the Supreme Court of Arkansas agreed and held that the director's fiduciary duty obligated him to divulge material facts of *past* fraud to the corporation before entering the contract. The court stated, "We are persuaded, in addition, that the majority view is correct, which is that the failure of a fiduciary to disclose material facts of his fraudulent conduct to his corporation prior to entering into a self-dealing contract with that corporation will void that contract."[2]

The Duty of Care In addition to the duty of loyalty, every corporate director or officer owes a duty of care. *Due care* means

1. For a landmark case on this issue, see *Guth v. Loft, Inc.,* 5 A.2d 503 (Del. 1939), presented as Case 19.3 in Chapter 19.
2. *Wal-Mart Stores, Inc. v. Coughlin,* 369 Ark. 365, 255 S.W.3d 424 (2007). See also *Blankenship v. USA Truck, Inc.,* 601 F.3d 852 (8th Cir. 2010), interpreting Arkansas law by applying the *Wal-Mart* case; and *Mazak Corp. v. King,* 2012 WL 3590817 (6th Cir. 2012), in which a federal court recognized that the *Wal-Mart* case stated the rule in the majority of states.

FOCUS ON ETHICS CONTINUES ➧

UNIT FOUR Focus on Ethics

Ethics and the Business Environment, *Continued*

that officers and directors must keep themselves informed and make businesslike judgments. Officers have a duty to disclose material information that shareholders need for competent decision making.

Some courts have even suggested that corporate directors have a duty to detect and "ferret out" wrongdoing within the corporation.[3] In fact, a number of courts applying Delaware law have recognized that directors may be held liable for failing to exercise proper oversight.[4] For example, one Delaware court held that shareholders of Citigroup, Inc., could sue the directors and officers for failure to exercise due care to adequately protect the corporation from exposure to the subprime lending market.[5] Corporate law also creates other structures to protect shareholder interests, such as the right to inspect books and records.

Although traditionally the duty of care did not require directors to monitor the behavior of corporate employees to detect and prevent wrongdoing, the tide may be changing. The corporate sentencing guidelines give courts the power to impose substantial penalties on corporations and corporate directors for criminal wrongdoing. Moreover, since the Sarbanes-Oxley Act required the sentencing commission to revise these guidelines, the penalties for white-collar crimes, such as federal mail and wire fraud, have increased dramatically. The guidelines allow these penalties to be mitigated, though, if a company can show that it has an effective compliance program in place to detect and prevent wrongdoing by corporate personnel.

LEGAL REASONING

1. *Three decades ago, corporations and corporate directors were rarely prosecuted for crimes, and penalties for corporate crimes were relatively light. Today, this is no longer true. Under the corporate sentencing guidelines, corporate wrongdoers can receive substantial penalties. Do these developments mean that corporations are committing more crimes today than in the past? Will stricter laws be effective in curbing corporate criminal activity? How can a company avoid liability for crimes committed by its employees?*

Fiduciary Duties to Creditors It is a long-standing principle that corporate directors ordinarily owe fiduciary duties only to a corporation's shareholders. Directors who have favored the interests of other corporate "stakeholders," such as creditors, over those of the shareholders have been held liable for breaching these duties.

The picture changes, however, when a corporation approaches insolvency. At this point, the shareholders' equity interests in the corporation may be worthless, while the interests of creditors become paramount. In this situation, do the fiduciary duties of loyalty and care extend to the corporation's creditors as well as to the shareholders?

The answer to this question, according to some courts, is yes. In one case, a Delaware court held that when a corporation is on the brink of insolvency, the directors assume a fiduciary duty to other stakeholders that sustain the corporate entity, including creditors.[6] When a corporation is insolvent, courts may require directors to consider the best interests of the whole corporate enterprise, including all its constituent groups, and not to give preference to the interests of any one group.[7]

LEGAL REASONING

2. *Do you agree that when a corporation is approaching insolvency, the directors' fiduciary obligations should extend to the corporation's creditors as well as to the shareholders? Why or why not?*

Franchise Relationships

Franchise relationships can create significant ethical issues. One issue has to do with the franchisor's quality control over the franchisee's activities. On the one hand, if the franchisor ignores the problem of quality control, the reputation of the franchisor's business may suffer. On the other hand, if a franchisor's control over the operations of the franchisee is too extensive, the franchisor may be liable for the torts of the franchisee's employees under agency theory (see Chapter 20). Even when an independent business entity purchases a franchise and the franchise agreement specifies that no agency relationship exists, the courts may find otherwise.

LEGAL REASONING

3. *As explained, if a franchisor exercises "too much control" over a franchisee's business operations, a court may deem the franchisor to be liable as an employer for the torts committed by the franchisee's employees. How can holding franchisors liable in such circumstances be squared with the doctrine of freedom of contract (see page 388)?*

3. *In re China Agritech, Inc. Shareholder Derivative Litigation,* 2013 WL 2181514 (Del.Ch. 2013); and *In re Caremark International, Inc. Derivative Litigation,* 698 A.2d 959 (Del.Ch. 1996).
4. See, for example, *McCall v. Scott,* 239 F.3d 808 (6th Cir. 2001); *Guttman v. Huang,* 823 A.2d 492 (Del.Ch. 2003); *Landy v. D'Alessandro,* 316 F.Supp.2d 49 (D.Mass. 2004); and *Miller v. U.S. Foodservice, Inc.,* 361 F.Supp.2d 470 (D.Md. 2005).
5. *In re Citigroup, Inc. Shareholder Derivative Litigation,* 964 A.2d 106 (Del.Ch. 2009).
6. *Credit Lyonnais Bank Nederland N.V. v. Pathe Communications Corp.,* 1991 WL 277613 (Del.Ch. 1991). See also *Production Resources Group, LLC v. NCT Group, Inc.,* 863 A.2d 772 (Del.Ch. 2004); and *In re USDigital, Inc.,* 443 Bankr. 22 (D.Del. 2011).
7. See *Berg & Berg Enterprises, LLC v. Boyle,* 178 Cal.App.4th 1020, 100 Cal.Rptr.3d 875 (2009); *In re Moeller,* 466 Bankr. 525 (S.D.Cal. 2012); and *Scouler & Co., LLC v. Schwartz,* 2012 WL 1502762 (N.D.Cal. 2012).

UNIT FIVE

THE EMPLOYMENT ENVIRONMENT

CONTENTS

CHAPTER 20
AGENCY

One of the most common, important, and pervasive legal relationships is that of **agency.** In an agency relationship involving two parties, one of the parties, called the *agent,* agrees to represent or act for the other, called the *principal.* The principal has the right to control the agent's conduct in matters entrusted to the agent. By using agents, a principal can conduct multiple business operations simultaneously in various locations. Thus, for example, contracts that bind the principal can be made at different places with different persons at the same time.

A familiar example of an agent is a corporate officer who serves in a representative capacity for the owners of the corporation. In this capacity, the officer has the authority to bind the principal (the corporation) to a contract. In fact, agency law is essential to the existence and operation of a corporate entity because only through its agents can a corporation function and enter into contracts.

Most employees are also considered to be agents of their employers. Thus, some of the concepts of employment law that you will learn about in Chapters 21 and 22 are based on agency law. Indeed, agency relationships permeate the business world. For that reason, an understanding of the law of agency is crucial to understanding business law.

SECTION 1
AGENCY RELATIONSHIPS

Section 1(1) of the *Restatement (Third) of Agency*[1] defines *agency* as "the fiduciary relation [that] results from the manifestation of consent by one person to another that the other shall act in his [or her] behalf and subject to his [or her] control, and consent by the other so to act." In other words, in a principal-agent relationship, the parties have agreed that the agent will act *on behalf and instead of* the principal in negotiating and transacting business with third parties.

The term **fiduciary** is at the heart of agency law. This term can be used both as a noun and as an adjective. When used as a noun, it refers to a person having a duty created by his or her undertaking to act primarily for another's benefit in matters connected with the undertaking. When used as an adjective, as in the phrase *fiduciary relationship,* it means that the relationship involves trust and confidence.

Agency relationships commonly exist between employers and employees. Agency relationships may sometimes also exist between employers and independent contractors who are hired to perform special tasks or services.

Employer-Employee Relationships

Normally, all employees who deal with third parties are deemed to be agents. A salesperson in a department store, for instance, is an agent of the store's owner (the principal) and acts on the owner's behalf. Any sale of goods made by the salesperson to a customer is binding on the principal. Similarly, most representations of fact made by the salesperson with respect to the goods sold are binding on the principal.

Because employees who deal with third parties generally are deemed to be agents of their employers, agency law and employment law overlap considerably. Agency relationships, though, as will become apparent, can exist outside an employer-employee relationship, and thus agency law has a broader reach than employment law does.

Employment laws (state and federal) apply only to the employer-employee relationship. Thus, statutes that govern Social Security, withholding taxes, workers' compensation, unemployment compensation, and workplace safety apply only when an employer-

1. The *Restatement (Third) of Agency* is an authoritative summary of the law of agency and is often referred to by judges in their decisions and opinions.

employee relationship exists (see Chapter 21). Similarly, laws that prohibit employment discrimination (see Chapter 22) apply only to employers and employees. *These laws do not apply to an independent contractor.*

Employer–Independent Contractor Relationships

Independent contractors are not employees because, by definition, those who hire them have no control over the details of their work performance. Section 2 of the *Restatement (Third) of Agency* defines an **independent contractor** as follows:

> [An independent contractor is] a person who contracts with another to do something for him [or her] but who is not controlled by the other nor subject to the other's right to control with respect to his [or her] physical conduct in the performance of the undertaking. He [or she] may or may not be an agent.

Building contractors and subcontractors are independent contractors. A property owner who hires a contractor and subcontractors to complete a project does not control the details of the way they perform their work. Truck drivers who own their vehicles and hire out on a per-job basis are independent contractors, but truck drivers who drive company trucks on a regular basis usually are employees.

The relationship between a principal and an independent contractor may or may not involve an agency relationship. To illustrate: A homeowner who hires a real estate broker to sell her house has not only contracted with an independent contractor (the broker) but also established an agency relationship for the specific purpose of selling the property. Another example is an insurance agent, who is both an independent contractor and an agent of the insurance company for which he sells policies. (Note that an insurance *broker,* in contrast, normally is an agent of the person obtaining insurance and not of the insurance company.)

Determination of Employee Status

The courts are frequently asked to determine whether a particular worker is an employee or an independent contractor. How a court decides this issue can have a significant effect on the rights and liabilities of the parties. For instance, employers are required to pay certain taxes, such as Social Security and unemployment taxes, for employees but not for independent contractors.

CRITERIA USED BY THE COURTS In deciding whether a worker is categorized as an employee or an independent contractor, courts often consider the following questions:

1. *How much control does the employer exercise over the details of the work?* If the employer exercises considerable control over the details of the work and the day-to-day activities of the worker, this indicates employee status. This is perhaps the most important factor weighed by the courts in determining employee status.
2. *Is the worker engaged in an occupation or business distinct from that of the employer?* If so, this points to independent-contractor, not employee, status.
3. *Is the work usually done under the employer's direction or by a specialist without supervision?* If the work is usually done under the employer's direction, this indicates employee status.
4. *Does the employer supply the tools at the place of work?* If so, this indicates employee status.
5. *For how long is the person employed?* If the person is employed for a long period of time, this indicates employee status.
6. *What is the method of payment—by time period or at the completion of the job?* Payment by time period, such as once every two weeks or once a month, indicates employee status.
7. *What degree of skill is required of the worker?* If a great degree of skill is required, this may indicate that the person is an independent contractor hired for a specialized job and not an employee.

Disputes Involving Employment Law. Sometimes, workers may benefit from having employee status—for tax purposes and to be protected under certain employment laws, for example. As mentioned earlier, federal statutes governing employment discrimination apply only when an employer-employee relationship exists. Protection under employment-discrimination statutes provides a significant incentive for workers to claim that they are employees rather than independent contractors.

▶ **Case in Point 20.1** A Puerto Rican television station, WIPR, contracted with Victoria Alberty-Vélez to cohost a television show. Alberty signed a new contract for each episode and was committed to work for WIPR only during the filming of the episodes. WIPR paid her a lump sum for each contract and did not withhold any taxes.

When Alberty became pregnant, WIPR stopped contracting with her. She filed a lawsuit claiming that WIPR was discriminating against her in violation of federal antidiscrimination laws, but the court found in favor of WIPR. Because the parties had used repeated fixed-length contracts and had described Alberty as an independent contractor on tax documents, she could not maintain an employment-discrimination suit.[2] ◀

Disputes Involving Tort Liability. Whether a worker is an employee or an independent contractor can also affect the employer's liability for the worker's actions. ▶ **Case in Point 20.2** El Palmar Taxi, Inc., requires its drivers to supply their own cabs, which must display El Palmar's logo. The drivers pay gas, maintenance, and insurance costs, and a fee to El Palmar. They are expected to comply with the law, including licensing regulations, but they can work when they want for as long as they want. Mario Julaju drove a taxi under a contract with El Palmar that described him as an independent contractor.

El Palmar sent Julaju to pick up Maria Lopez and her children. During the ride, Julaju's cab collided with a truck. To recover for their injuries, the Lopezes sued El Palmar. The employer argued that it was not liable because Julaju was an independent contractor. The court held in favor of El Palmar. An employer normally is not responsible for the actions of an independent contractor with whom the employer contracts. Here, the employment contract had clearly specified that Julaju was an independent contractor, and there were no facts indicating that he was an employee (or that the employer controlled his activities).[3] ◀

In the following case, the court had to determine the status of an auto service company and its tow truck driver who assaulted the passenger of a vehicle the company had been hired to tow.

2. *Alberty-Vélez v. Corporación de Puerto Rico para la Difusión Pública,* 361 F.3d 1 (1st Cir. 2004).

3. *Lopez v. El Palmar Taxi, Inc.,* 297 Ga.App. 121, 676 S.E.2d 460 (2009).

CASE 20.1

Coker v. Pershad

Superior Court of New Jersey, Appellate Division, 2013 WL 1296271 (2013).

BACKGROUND AND FACTS AAA North Jersey, Inc., contracted with Five Star Auto Service to perform towing and auto repair services for AAA. Terence Pershad, the driver of a tow truck for Five Star, responded to a call to AAA for assistance by the driver of a car involved in an accident in Hoboken, New Jersey. Pershad got into a fight with Nicholas Coker, a passenger in the car, and assaulted Coker with a knife. Coker filed a suit in a New Jersey state court against Pershad, Five Star, and AAA. The court determined that Pershad was Five Star's employee and that Five Star was an independent contractor, not AAA's employee. Thus, AAA was "not responsible for the alleged negligence of its independent contractor, defendant Five Star, in hiring Mr. Pershad." Five Star entered into a settlement with Coker. Coker appealed the ruling in AAA's favor.

IN THE LANGUAGE OF THE COURT
PER CURIAM.

* * * *

The important difference between an employee and an independent contractor is that one who hires an independent contractor has no right of control over the manner in which the work is to be done. [Emphasis added.]

* * * *

* * * Plaintiff [Coker] argues AAA controlled the means and method of the work performed by Five Star. * * * Factors * * * [that] determine whether a principal maintains the right of control over an individual or a corporation claimed to be an independent contractor [include]:

(a) the extent of control which, by the agreement, the master may exercise over the details of the work;
(b) whether or not the one employed is engaged in a distinct occupation or business;
(c) the kind of occupation, with reference to whether, in the locality, the work is usually done under the direction of the employer or by a specialist without supervision;

CASE 20.1 CONTINUED

(d) the skill required in the particular occupation;
(e) whether the employer or the workman supplies the * * * tools * * * ;
(f) the length of time for which the person is employed * * * .

Applying these factors to the facts of this case, it is clear AAA did not control the manner and means of Five Star's work. The Agreement specifically stated Five Star was an independent contractor. Five Star purchased its own trucks and any other necessary equipment. AAA assigned jobs to Five Star and Five Star completed the work without any further supervision by AAA. Five Star chose the employees to send on towing calls and the trucks and equipment the employees would use.

Five Star was also in business for itself and performed auto repair services for principals and customers other than AAA. Five Star hired and fired its own employees * * * .

* * * *

Plaintiff also argues Five Star should be considered to be controlled by AAA because "providing towing and other roadside assistance is arguably the focus of the regular business of AAA." * * * [But] AAA is an automobile club that provides a wide variety of services to its members. It contracts with numerous service providers, such as gas stations, motels and other businesses, to provide these services. Thus, AAA is not solely in the towing business.

* * * AAA had used Five Star to provide towing services for approximately eight years and there is nothing in the record to demonstrate it lacked the skill needed to provide these services.

DECISION AND REMEDY *A state intermediate appellate court affirmed the lower court's ruling. AAA could not be held liable for the actions of Five Star, its independent contractor, because "AAA did not control the manner and means of Five Star's work."*

THE LEGAL ENVIRONMENT DIMENSION *Five Star's contract with AAA required Five Star to be available to provide service for AAA members. Does this support Coker's argument that Five Star was AAA's employee? Why or why not?*

MANAGERIAL IMPLICATIONS *When an employment contract clearly designates one party as an independent contractor, the relationship between the parties is presumed to be that of employer and independent contractor. But this is only a presumption. Evidence can be introduced to show that the employer exercised sufficient control to establish the other party as an employee. The Internal Revenue Service is increasingly pursuing employers that it claims have wrongly classified employees as independent contractors. Thus, from a tax perspective, business managers need to ensure that all independent contractors fully control their own work.*

CRITERIA USED BY THE IRS The Internal Revenue Service (IRS) has established its own criteria for determining whether a worker is an independent contractor or an employee. The most important factor is the degree of control the business exercises over the worker.

The IRS tends to closely scrutinize a firm's classification of its workers because, as mentioned, employers can avoid certain tax liabilities by hiring independent contractors instead of employees. Even when a firm has classified a worker as an independent contractor, the IRS may decide that the worker is actually an employee.

If the IRS decides that an employee is misclassified, the employer will be responsible for paying any applicable Social Security, withholding, and unemployment taxes. Microsoft Corporation, for instance, was once ordered to pay back payroll taxes for hundreds of temporary workers who had contractually agreed to work for Microsoft as independent contractors.[4]

EMPLOYEE STATUS AND "WORKS FOR HIRE" Under the Copyright Act, any copyrighted work created by an employee within the scope of her or his employment at the request of the employer is a "work for hire." The employer owns the copyright to the work. In contrast, when an employer hires an independent contractor—a freelance artist, writer, or computer programmer, for example—the independent contractor normally owns the copyright. An exception is made if the parties agree in writing that the work is a "work

4. *Vizcaino v. U.S. District Court for the Western District of Washington,* 173 F.3d 713 (9th Cir. 1999).

for hire" and the work falls into one of nine specific categories, including audiovisual and other works.

▶ **Case in Point 20.3** Artisan House, Inc., hired a professional photographer, Steven H. Lindner, owner of SHL Imaging, Inc., to take pictures of its products for the creation of color slides to be used by Artisan's sales force. Lindner controlled his own work and carefully chose the lighting and angles used in the photographs. When Artisan published the photographs in a catalogue and brochures without Lindner's permission, SHL filed a lawsuit for copyright infringement. Artisan claimed that its publication of the photographs was authorized because they were works for hire. The court, however, decided that SHL was an independent contractor and owned the copyright to the photographs. Because SHL had not given Artisan permission (a license) to reproduce the photographs in other publications, Artisan was liable for copyright infringement.[5] ◀

SECTION 2

FORMATION OF THE AGENCY RELATIONSHIP

Agency relationships normally are *consensual*—that is, they come about by voluntary consent and agreement between the parties. Generally, the agreement need not be in writing,[6] and consideration is not required.

A person must have contractual capacity to be a principal.[7] Those who cannot legally enter into contracts directly should not be allowed to do so indirectly through an agent. Any person can be an agent, however, regardless of whether he or she has the capacity to contract (including minors).

An agency relationship can be created for any legal purpose. An agency relationship created for a purpose that is illegal or contrary to public policy is unenforceable. ▶ **Example 20.4** Archer (as principal) contracts with Burke (as agent) to sell illegal narcotics. The agency relationship is unenforceable because selling illegal narcotics is a felony and is contrary to public policy. If Burke sells the narcotics and keeps the profits, Archer cannot sue to enforce the agency agreement. ◀

An agency relationship can arise in four ways: by agreement of the parties, by ratification, by estoppel, and by operation of law.

Agency by Agreement

Most agency relationships are based on an express or implied agreement that the agent will act for the principal and that the principal agrees to have the agent so act.

An agency agreement can take the form of an express written contract or be created by an oral agreement. ▶ **Example 20.5** Rees asks Grace, a gardener, to contract with others for the care of his lawn on a regular basis. If Grace agrees, an agency relationship exists between Reese and Grace for the lawn care. ◀

An agency agreement can also be implied by conduct. ▶ **Case in Point 20.6** Gilbert Bishop was admitted to Laurel Creek Health Care Center suffering from various physical ailments. During an examination, Bishop told Laurel Creek staff that he could not use his hands well enough to write or hold a pencil, but he was otherwise found to be mentally competent. Bishop's sister, Rachel Combs, offered to sign the admissions forms, but it was Laurel Creek's policy to have the patient's spouse sign the admissions papers if the patient was unable to do so. Therefore, Gilbert asked Combs to get his wife, Anna, so that she could sign his admissions papers.

Combs then brought Anna to the hospital, and Anna signed the admissions paperwork, which contained a provision for mandatory arbitration. Later, the Bishops sued the hospital for negligence, and Laurel Creek sought to compel arbitration. The Bishops argued that Anna was not Bishop's agent and had no legal authority to make decisions for him, but the court concluded that an agency relationship between Bishop and his wife, Anna, had been formed by conduct.[8] ◀

Agency by Ratification

On occasion, a person who is in fact not an agent (or who is an agent acting outside the scope of her or his authority) may make a contract on behalf of another (a principal). If the principal approves or affirms that contract by word or by action, an agency relationship

5. *SHL Imaging, Inc. v. Artisan House, Inc.*, 117 F.Supp.2d 301 (S.D.N.Y. 2000).
6. There are two main exceptions to the statement that agency agreements need not be in writing: (1) Under the *equal dignity rule* (discussed later in this chapter), an agreement must be in writing if it empowers the agent to enter into a contract that the Statute of Frauds requires to be in writing. (2) An agreement that gives an agent power of attorney must also be in writing.
7. Note that some states allow a minor to be a principal. When a minor is permitted to be a principal, any resulting contracts will be voidable by the minor principal but *not* by the adult third party.
8. *Laurel Creek Health Care Center v. Bishop*, 2010 WL 985299 (Ky.App. 2010).

is created by *ratification*. Ratification involves a question of intent, and intent can be expressed by either words or conduct. The basic requirements for ratification will be discussed later in this chapter.

Agency by Estoppel

Sometimes, a principal causes a third person to believe that another person is the principal's agent, and the third person acts to his or her detriment in reasonable reliance on that belief. When this occurs, the principal is "estopped to deny" (prevented from denying) the agency relationship. An agency by estoppel arises when the principal's actions have created the *appearance* of an agency that does not in fact exist.

The third person must prove that he or she *reasonably* believed that an agency relationship existed, however. Facts and circumstances must show that an ordinary, prudent person familiar with business practice and custom would have been justified in concluding that the agent had authority.

▶ **Case in Point 20.7** Francis Azur was president and chief executive officer of ATM Corporation of America. Michelle Vanek, Azur's personal assistant at ATM, reviewed his credit-card statements, among other duties. For seven years, Vanek took unauthorized cash advances from Azur's credit-card account with Chase Bank. The charges appeared on at least sixty-five monthly statements. When Azur discovered Vanek's fraud, he fired her and closed the account. He filed a suit against Chase, arguing that the bank should not have allowed Vanek to take cash advances. The court concluded that Azur (the principal) had given the bank reason to believe that Vanek (the agent) had authority. Therefore, Azur was estopped (prevented) from denying Vanek's authority.[9] ◀

Note that the acts or declarations of a purported *agent* in and of themselves do not create an agency by estoppel. Rather, it is the deeds or statements of the *principal* that create an agency by estoppel.

Agency by Operation of Law

The courts may find an agency relationship in the absence of a formal agreement in other situations as well. This may occur in family relationships, such as when one spouse purchases certain basic necessaries and charges them to the other spouse's account. The courts often rule that a spouse is liable for payment for the necessaries because of either a social policy or a legal duty to supply necessaries to family members.

Agency by operation of law may also occur in emergency situations. If an agent cannot contact the principal and failure to act would cause the principal substantial loss, the agent may take steps beyond the scope of her or his authority. For example, a railroad engineer may contract on behalf of his or her employer for medical care for an injured motorist hit by the train.

Concept Summary 20.1 below reviews the various ways that agencies are formed.

9. *Azur v. Chase Bank, USA, N.A.*, 601 F.3d 212 (3d Cir. 2010).

CONCEPT SUMMARY 20.1

Formation of the Agency Relationship

METHOD OF FORMATION	DESCRIPTION
By Agreement	The agency relationship is formed through express consent (oral or written) or implied by conduct.
By Ratification	The principal either by act or by agreement ratifies the conduct of a person who is not in fact an agent.
By Estoppel	The principal causes a third person to believe that another person is the principal's agent, and the third person acts to his or her detriment in reasonable reliance on that belief.
By Operation of Law	The agency relationship is based on a social or legal duty (such as the need to support family members) or formed in emergency situations when the agent is unable to contact the principal and failure to act outside the scope of the agent's authority would cause the principal substantial loss.

SECTION 3

DUTIES OF AGENTS AND PRINCIPALS

Once the principal-agent relationship has been created, both parties have duties that govern their conduct. As discussed previously, the principal-agent relationship is *fiduciary*—based on trust. In a fiduciary relationship, each party owes the other the duty to act with the utmost good faith. In this section, we examine the various duties of agents and principals.

Agent's Duties to the Principal

Generally, the agent owes the principal five duties—performance, notification, loyalty, obedience, and accounting.

PERFORMANCE An implied condition in every agency contract is the agent's agreement to use reasonable diligence and skill in performing the work. When an agent fails to perform his or her duties, liability for breach of contract may result.

Standard of Care. The degree of skill or care required of an agent is usually that expected of a reasonable person under similar circumstances. Generally, this is interpreted to mean ordinary care. If an agent has represented herself or himself as possessing special skills, however, the agent is expected to exercise the degree of skill claimed. Failure to do so constitutes a breach of the agent's duty.

Gratuitous Agents. Not all agency relationships are based on contract. In some situations, an agent acts gratuitously—that is, without payment. A gratuitous agent cannot be liable for breach of contract because there is no contract. He or she is subject only to tort liability. Once a gratuitous agent has begun to act in an agency capacity, he or she has the duty to continue to perform in that capacity. A gratuitous agent must perform in an acceptable manner and is subject to the same standards of care and duty to perform as other agents.

▶ **Example 20.8** Bower's friend Alcott is a real estate broker. Alcott offers to sell Bower's vacation home at no charge. If Alcott never attempts to sell the home, Bower has no legal cause of action to force her to do so. If Alcott does attempt to sell the home to Friedman, but then performs so negligently that the sale falls through, Bower can sue Alcott for negligence. ◀

NOTIFICATION An agent is required to notify the principal of all matters that come to her or his attention concerning the subject matter of the agency. This is the *duty of notification,* or the duty to inform.

▶ **Example 20.9** Perez, an artist, is about to negotiate a contract to sell a series of paintings to Barber's Art Gallery for $25,000. Perez's agent learns that Barber is insolvent and will be unable to pay for the paintings. The agent has a duty to inform Perez of Barber's insolvency because it is relevant to the subject matter of the agency, which is the sale of Perez's paintings. ◀

Generally, the law assumes that the principal is aware of any information acquired by the agent that is relevant to the agency—regardless of whether the agent actually passes on this information to the principal. It is a basic tenet of agency law that notice to the agent is notice to the principal.

LOYALTY Loyalty is one of the most fundamental duties in a fiduciary relationship. Basically, the agent has the duty to act *solely for the benefit of his or her principal* and not in the interest of the agent or a third party. For instance, an agent cannot represent two principals in the same transaction unless both know of the dual capacity and consent to it.

The duty of loyalty also means that any information or knowledge acquired through the agency relationship is confidential. It is a breach of loyalty to disclose such information either during the agency relationship or after its termination. Typical examples of confidential information are trade secrets and customer lists compiled by the principal.

The agent's loyalty must be undivided. The agent's actions must be strictly for the benefit of the principal and must not result in any secret profit for the agent.

OBEDIENCE When acting on behalf of the principal, an agent has a duty to follow all lawful and clearly stated instructions of the principal. Any deviation from such instructions is a violation of this duty.

During emergency situations, however, when the principal cannot be consulted, the agent may deviate from the instructions without violating this duty. Whenever instructions are not clearly stated, the agent can fulfill the duty of obedience by acting in good faith and in a manner reasonable under the circumstances.

ACCOUNTING Unless the agent and principal agree otherwise, the agent must keep and make available to the principal an account of all property and funds received and paid out on the principal's behalf. This includes gifts from third parties in connection with the agency. For instance, a gift from a customer to a salesperson for prompt deliveries made by the salesperson's firm, in the absence of a company policy to the contrary, belongs to the firm.

The agent has a duty to maintain a separate account for the principal's funds and must not intermingle these funds with the agent's personal funds. If a licensed professional (such as an attorney) violates this duty, he or she may be subject to disciplinary proceedings carried out by the appropriate regulatory institution (such as the state bar association). Of course, the professional will also be liable to the principal (the professional's client) for failure to account.

Principal's Duties to the Agent

The principal also has certain duties to the agent. These duties relate to compensation, reimbursement and indemnification, cooperation, and safe working conditions.

COMPENSATION In general, when a principal requests certain services from an agent, the agent reasonably expects payment. The principal therefore has a duty to pay the agent for services rendered. For instance, when an accountant or an attorney is asked to act as an agent, an agreement to compensate the agent for this service is implied.

The principal also has a duty to pay that compensation in a timely manner. Unless the agency relationship is gratuitous and the agent does not act in exchange for payment, the principal must pay the agreed-on value for the agent's services. If no amount has been expressly agreed on, then the principal owes the agent the customary compensation for such services.

REIMBURSEMENT AND INDEMNIFICATION The principal has a duty to reimburse the agent for any funds disbursed at the principal's request. The principal must also reimburse the agent for any necessary expenses incurred in the course of the reasonable performance of her or his agency duties.[10] Agents cannot recover for expenses incurred as a result of their own misconduct or negligence, though.

Subject to the terms of the agency agreement, the principal has the duty to *indemnify* (compensate) an agent for liabilities incurred because of authorized and lawful acts and transactions. For instance, if the agent, on the principal's behalf, forms a contract with a third party, and the principal fails to perform the contract, the third party may sue the agent for damages. In this situation, the principal is obligated to compensate the agent for any costs incurred by the agent as a result of the principal's failure to perform the contract.

Additionally, the principal must indemnify the agent for the value of benefits that the agent confers on the principal. The amount of indemnification usually is specified in the agency contract. If it is not, the courts will look to the nature of the business and the type of loss to determine the amount. Note that this rule applies to acts by gratuitous agents as well.

COOPERATION A principal has a duty to cooperate with the agent and to assist the agent in performing his or her duties. The principal must do nothing to prevent that performance.

For instance, when a principal grants an agent an exclusive territory, the principal creates an **exclusive agency,** in which the principal cannot compete with the agent or appoint or allow another agent to compete. If the principal does so, he or she violates the exclusive agency and is exposed to liability for the agent's lost profits.

▶ **Example 20.10** River City Times Company (the principal) grants Emir (the agent) the right to sell its newspapers at a busy downtown intersection to the exclusion of all other vendors. This creates an exclusive territory within which only Emir has the right to sell those newspapers. If River City Times allows another vendor to sell its papers on another corner of the same intersection, Emir can sue for lost profits. ◀

SAFE WORKING CONDITIONS The common law requires the principal to provide safe working premises, equipment, and conditions for all agents and employees. The principal has a duty to inspect working areas and to warn agents and employees about any unsafe situations. When the agent is an employee, the employer's liability is frequently covered by state workers' compensation insurance. In addition, federal and state statutes often require the employer to meet certain safety standards (see Chapter 21).

Rights and Remedies of Agents and Principals

In general, for every duty of the principal, the agent has a corresponding right, and vice versa. When one party

10. This principle applies to acts by gratuitous agents as well. If a finder of a dog that becomes sick takes the dog to a veterinarian and pays the veterinarian's fees, the gratuitous agent is entitled to be reimbursed by the dog's owner.

to the agency relationship violates his or her duty to the other party, the remedies available to the nonbreaching party arise out of contract and tort law. These remedies include monetary damages, termination of the agency relationship, an injunction, and required accountings.

The agent has the right to be compensated, to be reimbursed and indemnified, and to have a safe working environment. An agent also has the right to perform agency duties without interference by the principal. An agent can also withhold further performance and demand that the principal give an accounting.

A principal has contract remedies for an agent's breach of fiduciary duties. The principal also has tort remedies if the agent engages in misrepresentation, negligence, deceit, libel, slander, or trespass. In addition, any breach of a fiduciary duty by an agent may justify the principal's termination of the agency.

SECTION 4 SCOPE OF AGENT'S AUTHORITY

The liability of a principal to third parties with whom an agent contracts depends on whether the agent had the authority to enter into legally binding contracts on the principal's behalf. An agent's authority can be either *actual* (express or implied) or *apparent*. If an agent contracts outside the scope of his or her authority, the principal may still become liable by ratifying the contract.

Express Authority

Express authority is authority declared in clear, direct, and definite terms. Express authority can be given orally or in writing.

THE EQUAL DIGNITY RULE In most states, the **equal dignity rule** requires that if the contract being executed is or must be in writing, then the agent's authority must also be in writing. Failure to comply with the equal dignity rule can make a contract voidable *at the option of the principal*. The law regards the contract at that point as a mere offer. If the principal decides to accept the offer, the acceptance must be ratified, or affirmed, in writing (or in an electronic record).

▶ **Example 20.11** Paloma (the principal) orally asks Austin (the agent) to sell a ranch that Paloma owns. Austin finds a buyer and signs a sales contract (a contract for an interest in realty must be in writing) on behalf of Paloma to sell the ranch. The buyer cannot enforce the contract unless Paloma subsequently ratifies Austin's agency status *in writing*. Once the sales contract is ratified, either party can enforce rights under the contract. ◀

Modern business practice allows several exceptions to the equal dignity rule:

1. An executive officer of a corporation normally can conduct *ordinary* business transactions without obtaining written authority from the corporation (see Chapter 19).
2. When the agent acts in the presence of the principal, the rule does not apply.
3. When the agent's act of signing is merely a formality, then the agent does not need written authority to sign. ▶ **Example 20.12** Sandra Healy (the principal) negotiates a contract but is called out of town the day it is to be signed. If Healy orally authorizes Santini to sign, the oral authorization is sufficient. ◀

POWER OF ATTORNEY Giving an agent a **power of attorney** confers express authority.[11] A power of attorney is a written document and is usually notarized. (A document is notarized when a **notary public**—a public official authorized to attest to the authenticity of signatures—signs and dates the document and imprints it with her or his seal of authority.) Most states have statutory provisions for creating a power of attorney.

A power of attorney can be *special* (permitting the agent to perform specified acts only), or it can be *general* (permitting the agent to transact all business for the principal). Because of the extensive authority granted to an agent by a general power of attorney, it should be used with great caution and usually only in exceptional circumstances. Ordinarily, a power of attorney terminates on the incapacity or death of the person giving the power.[12]

Implied Authority

An agent has the **implied authority** to do what is reasonably necessary to carry out express authority and accomplish the objectives of the agency.

11. An agent who holds a power of attorney is called an *attorney-in-fact* for the principal. The holder does not have to be an attorney-at-law (and often is not).

12. A *durable* power of attorney, however, continues to be effective despite the principal's incapacity. An elderly person, for example, might grant a durable power of attorney to provide for the handling of property and investments or specific health-care needs should he or she become incompetent.

Authority can also be implied by custom or inferred from the position the agent occupies. (For a discussion of what happens when an employee-agent makes unauthorized use of the employer's computer data, see this chapter's *Insight into Ethics* feature below.)

▶ **Example 20.13** Archer is employed by Packard Grocery to manage one of its stores. Packard has not expressly stated that Archer has authority to contract with third persons. Nevertheless, authority to manage a business implies authority to do what is reasonably required (as is customary or can be inferred from a manager's position) to operate the business. It is reasonable to imply the authority to form contracts to hire employees, to buy merchandise and equipment, and to advertise the products sold in the store. ◀

Note, however, that an agent's implied authority cannot contradict his or her express authority. Thus, if a principal has limited an agent's express authority, then the fact that the agent customarily would have such authority is irrelevant. ▶ **Example 20.14** Juanita Alvarez is the owner of six Baja Tacos restaurants. Alvarez (the principal) strictly forbids the managers (agents) of her taco shops from entering into contracts to hire additional workers. Therefore, the fact that managers customarily would have authority to hire employees is immaterial. ◀

INSIGHT INTO ETHICS

The Ethical and Legal Implications of Breaching Company Policy on the Use of Electronic Data

Suppose that an employee-agent who is authorized to access company trade secrets contained in computer files takes those secrets to a competitor for whom the employee is about to begin working. Clearly, the agent has violated the ethical—and legal—duty of loyalty to the principal. Does this breach of loyalty mean that the employee's act of accessing the trade secrets was unauthorized?

The question has significant implications for both parties. If the action was unauthorized, the employee will be subject to state and federal laws prohibiting unauthorized access to computer information and data, including the Computer Fraud and Abuse Act (CFAA, discussed in Chapter 7). If the action was authorized, these laws will not apply.

Does Exceeding Authorized Access to a Company's Database Violate the Law?

David Nosal once worked for Korn/Ferry and had access to the company's confidential database. When he left, he encouraged several former colleagues who still worked there to join him in starting a competing firm. He asked them to access Korn/Ferry's database and download source lists, names, and client contact information before they quit. The employees had authority to access the database, but Korn/Ferry's policy forbade disclosure of confidential information.

The government filed charges against Nosal and his colleagues for violating the CFAA, among other things.

A Court Rules That Violating an Employer's Use Restrictions Is Not a Crime

The U.S. Court of Appeals for the Ninth Circuit refused to find that the defendants had violated the CFAA. The court ruled that the phrase "exceed authorized access" in the CFAA refers to restrictions on access, not restrictions on use. The court reasoned that Congress's intent in enacting the CFAA was to prohibit people from hacking into computers without authorization.

The court also stated that the CFAA should not be used to criminally prosecute persons who use data in an unauthorized or unethical way. The court pointed out that "adopting the government's interpretation would turn vast numbers of teens and pre-teens into juvenile delinquents—and their parents and teachers into delinquency contributors." Furthermore, "the effect this broad construction of the CFAA has on workplace conduct pales by comparison with its effect on everyone else who uses a computer, smart-phone, iPad, Kindle, Nook, X-box, Blu-Ray player or any other Internet-enabled device."[a]

LEGAL CRITICAL THINKING

INSIGHT INTO THE LEGAL ENVIRONMENT

If an employee accesses Facebook at work even though personal use of a workplace computer is against the employer's stated policies, can the employee be criminally prosecuted? Why or why not?

a. *United States. v. Nosal*, 675 F.3d 854 (9th Cir. 2012).

Apparent Authority

Actual authority (express or implied) arises from what the principal makes clear *to the agent.* Apparent authority, in contrast, arises from what the principal causes a third party to believe. An agent has **apparent authority** when the principal, by either word or action, causes a *third party* reasonably to believe that the agent has authority to act, even though the agent has no express or implied authority.

Apparent authority usually comes into existence through a principal's pattern of conduct over time. ▶ **Example 20.15** Bailey is a traveling salesperson with the authority to solicit orders for the goods of Carlon Industries (the principal). Because she does not carry any goods with her, she normally would not have the implied authority to collect payments from customers on Carlon's behalf.

Suppose that Bailey does accept payments from Jayco Enterprises, however, and submits them to Carlon's accounting department for processing. If Carlon does nothing to stop Bailey from continuing this practice, a pattern develops over time. Thus, the principal confers apparent authority on Bailey to accept payments from Jayco. ◀

At issue in the following *Spotlight Case* was whether the manager of a horse breeding operation had the authority to bind the farm's owner in a contract guaranteeing breeding rights.

SPOTLIGHT on Apparent Authority

Case 20.2 Lundberg v. Church Farm, Inc.

Court of Appeals of Illinois, 151 Ill.App.3d 452, 502 N.E.2d 806, (1986).

BACKGROUND AND FACTS Gilbert Church owned a horse breeding farm managed by Herb Bagley. Advertisements for the breeding rights to one of Church Farm's stallions, Imperial Guard, directed all inquiries to "Herb Bagley, Manager." Vern and Gail Lundberg bred Thoroughbred horses. The Lundbergs contacted Bagley and executed a preprinted contract giving them breeding rights to Imperial Guard "at Imperial Guard's location," subject to approval of the mares by Church. Bagley handwrote a statement on the contract that guaranteed the Lundbergs "six live foals in the first two years." He then signed it "Gilbert G. Church by H. Bagley."

The Lundbergs bred four mares, which resulted in one live foal. Church then moved Imperial Guard from Illinois to Oklahoma. The Lundbergs sued Church for breaching the contract by moving the horse. Church claimed that Bagley was not authorized to sign contracts for Church or to change or add terms, but only to present preprinted contracts to potential buyers. Church testified that although Bagley was his farm manager and the contact person for breeding rights, Bagley had never before modified the preprinted forms or signed Church's name on these contracts. The jury found in favor of the Lundbergs and awarded $147,000 in damages. Church appealed.

IN THE LANGUAGE OF THE COURT
Justice *UNVERZAGT* delivered the opinion of the court.

* * * *

* * * Defendant contends that plaintiffs have failed to establish that Bagley had apparent authority to negotiate and sign the Lundberg contract for Church Farm * * *.

*The party asserting an agency has the burden of proving its existence * * * but may do so by inference and circumstantial evidence. * * * Additionally, an agent may bind his principal by acts which the principal has not given him actual authority to perform, but which he appears authorized to perform.* * * * An agent's apparent authority is that authority which "the principal knowingly permits the agent to assume or which he holds his agent out as possessing. It is the authority that a reasonably prudent man, exercising diligence and discretion, in view of the principal's conduct, would naturally suppose the agent to possess." [Emphasis added.]

Plaintiffs produced evidence at trial that Gil Church approved the Imperial Guard advertisement listing Herb Bagley as Church Farm's manager, and directing all inquiries to him. Church also permitted Bagley to live on the farm and to handle its daily operations. Bagley was the only person available to visitors to the farm. Bagley answered Church Farm's phone calls, and there was a preprinted signature line for him on the breeding rights package.

The conclusion is inescapable that Gil Church affirmatively placed Bagley in a managerial position giving him complete control of Church Farm and its dealings with the public. We believe that this is just the sort of "holding out" of an agent by a principal that justifies a third person's reliance on the agent's authority.

We cannot accept defendant's contention that the Lundbergs were affirmatively obligated to seek out Church to ascertain the actual extent of Bagley's authority. Where an agent has apparent authority to act, the principal will be liable in spite of any undisclosed limitations the principal has placed on that authority.

DECISION AND REMEDY *The state appellate court affirmed the lower court's judgment in favor of the Lundbergs for $147,000. Because Church allowed circumstances to lead the Lundbergs to believe Bagley had the authority, Church was bound by Bagley's actions.*

THE LEGAL ENVIRONMENT DIMENSION *The court held that Church had allowed the Lundbergs to believe that Bagley was his agent. What steps could Church have taken to protect himself against a finding of apparent authority?*

THE ETHICAL DIMENSION *Does a principal have an ethical responsibility to inform an unaware third party that an apparent agent does not in fact have the authority to act on the principal's behalf?*

Emergency Powers

When an unforeseen emergency demands action by the agent to protect or preserve the property and rights of the principal, but the agent is unable to communicate with the principal, the agent has emergency power. ▶ **Example 20.16** Rob Fulsom is an engineer for Pacific Drilling Company. While Fulsom is acting within the scope of his employment, he is severely injured in an accident at an oil rig many miles from home.

Acosta, the rig supervisor, directs Thompson, a physician, to give medical aid to Fulsom and to charge Pacific for the medical services. Acosta, an agent, has no express or implied authority to bind the principal, Pacific Drilling, for Thompson's medical services. Because of the emergency situation, however, the law recognizes Acosta as having authority to act appropriately under the circumstances. ◀

Ratification

Ratification occurs when the principal affirms, or accepts responsibility for, an agent's *unauthorized* act. When ratification occurs, the principal is bound to the agent's act, and the act is treated as if it had been authorized by the principal *from the outset*. Ratification can be either express or implied.

If the principal does not ratify the contract, the principal is not bound, and the third party's agreement with the agent is viewed as merely an unaccepted offer. Because the third party's agreement is an unaccepted offer, the third party can revoke it at any time, without liability, before the principal ratifies the contract. The agent, however, may be liable to the third party for misrepresenting her or his authority.

The requirements for ratification can be summarized as follows:

1. The agent must have acted on behalf of an identified principal who subsequently ratifies the action.
2. The principal must know all of the material facts involved in the transaction. If a principal ratifies a contract without knowing all of the facts, the principal can rescind (cancel) the contract.[13]
3. The principal must affirm the agent's act in its entirety.
4. The principal must have the legal capacity to authorize the transaction at the time the agent engages in the act and at the time the principal ratifies. The third party must also have the legal capacity to engage in the transaction.
5. The principal's affirmation (ratification) must occur before the third party withdraws from the transaction.
6. The principal must observe the same formalities when ratifying the act as would have been required to authorize it initially.

13. If the third party has changed position in reliance on the apparent contract, however, the principal can rescind but must reimburse the third party for any costs.

Concept Summary 20.2 below summarizes the rules concerning an agent's authority to bind the principal and a third party.

SECTION 5

LIABILITY FOR CONTRACTS

Liability for contracts formed by an agent depends on how the principal is classified and on whether the actions of the agent were authorized or unauthorized. Principals are classified as disclosed, partially disclosed, or undisclosed.[14]

1. A **disclosed principal** is a principal whose identity is known by the third party at the time the contract is made by the agent.
2. A **partially disclosed principal** is a principal whose identity is not known by the third party. Nevertheless, the third party knows that the agent is or *may* be acting for a principal at the time the contract is made. ▶ **Example 20.17** Eileen has contracted with a real estate agent to sell certain property. She wishes to keep her identity a secret, but the agent makes it clear to potential buyers of the property that the agent is acting in an agency capacity. In this situation, Eileen is a partially disclosed principal. ◀
3. An **undisclosed principal** is a principal whose identity is totally unknown by the third party. In addition, the third party has no knowledge that the agent is acting in an agency capacity at the time the contract is made.

Authorized Acts

If an agent acts within the scope of her or his authority, normally the principal is obligated to perform the contract regardless of whether the principal was disclosed, partially disclosed, or undisclosed.

Whether the *agent may also be held liable* under the contract, however, depends on the disclosed, partially disclosed, or undisclosed status of the principal.

DISCLOSED OR PARTIALLY DISCLOSED PRINCIPAL A disclosed or partially disclosed principal is liable to a third party for a contract made by the agent. If the principal is disclosed, the agent has no contractual liability for the nonperformance of the principal or the third party. If the principal is partially disclosed, in most states the agent is also treated as a party to the contract, and the third party can hold the agent liable for contractual nonperformance.[15]

▶ **Case in Point 20.18** Walgreens leased commercial property at a mall owned by Kedzie Plaza Associates.

14. *Restatement (Third) of Agency,* Section 1.04(2).

15. *Restatement (Third) of Agency,* Section 6.02.

CONCEPT SUMMARY 20.2

Authority of an Agent to Bind the Principal and a Third Party

AUTHORITY OF AGENT	DEFINITION	EFFECT ON PRINCIPAL AND THIRD PARTY
Express Authority	Authority expressly given by the principal to the agent.	Principal and third party are bound in contract.
Implied Authority	Authority implied (1) by custom, (2) from the position in which the principal has placed the agent, or (3) because such authority is necessary if the agent is to carry out expressly authorized duties and responsibilities.	Principal and third party are bound in contract.
Apparent Authority	Authority created when the conduct of the principal leads a third party to believe that the principal's agent has authority.	Principal and third party are bound in contract.
Unauthorized Acts	Acts committed by an agent that are outside the scope of his or her express, implied, or apparent authority.	Principal and third party are not bound in contract—*unless* the principal ratifies prior to the third party's withdrawal.

Kedzie used Taxman Corporation, a property management company. Taxman signed the lease with Walgreens on behalf of the principal, Kedzie. The lease required the landlord to keep the sidewalks free of snow and ice. Therefore, Taxman, on behalf of Kedzie, contracted with another company to remove ice and snow from the sidewalks surrounding the Walgreens store.

When a Walgreens employee slipped on ice outside the store and was injured, she sued Taxman, among others, for negligence. Because the identity of the principal (Kedzie) was fully disclosed in the snow-removal contract, however, the court ruled that the agent, Taxman, could not be held liable. Taxman did not assume a contractual obligation to remove the snow but merely retained a contractor to do so on behalf of the owner.[16] ◀

UNDISCLOSED PRINCIPAL When neither the fact of an agency relationship nor the identity of the principal is disclosed, the undisclosed principal is bound to perform just as if the principal had been fully disclosed at the time the contract was made.

When a principal's identity is undisclosed and the agent is forced to pay the third party, the agent is entitled to be *indemnified* (compensated) by the principal. The principal had a duty to perform, even though his or her identity was undisclosed, and failure to do so will make the principal ultimately liable. Once the undisclosed principal's identity is revealed, the third party generally can elect to hold either the principal or the agent liable on the contract.

Conversely, the undisclosed principal can require the third party to fulfill the contract, *unless* one of the following is true:

1. The undisclosed principal was expressly excluded as a party in the written contract.
2. The contract is a negotiable instrument signed by the agent with no indication of signing in a representative capacity.[17]
3. The performance of the agent is personal to the contract, thus allowing the third party to refuse the principal's performance.

Unauthorized Acts

If an agent has no authority but nevertheless contracts with a third party, the *principal* cannot be held liable on the contract. It does not matter whether the principal was disclosed, partially disclosed, or undisclosed. The *agent* is liable, however.

▶ **Example 20.19** Chu signs a contract for the purchase of a truck, purportedly acting as an agent under authority granted by Navarro. In fact, Navarro has not given Chu any such authority. Navarro refuses to pay for the truck, claiming that Chu had no authority to purchase it. The seller of the truck is entitled to hold Chu liable for payment. ◀

IMPLIED WARRANTY If the principal is disclosed or partially disclosed, and the agent contracts with a third party without authorization, the agent is liable to the third party who relied on the agency status. The agent's liability here is based on his or her breach of the *implied warranty of authority,* not on the breach of the contract itself.[18] An agent impliedly warrants that he or she has the authority to enter a contract on behalf of the principal.

THIRD PARTY'S KNOWLEDGE Note that if the third party knows at the time the contract is made that the agent does not have authority, then the agent is not liable. Similarly, if the agent expressed to the third party *uncertainty* as to the extent of her or his authority, the agent is not personally liable.

Actions by E-Agents

Although in the past standard agency principles applied only to *human* agents, today these same agency principles also apply to e-agents. An electronic agent, or **e-agent,** is a semiautonomous computer program that is capable of executing specific tasks. For instance, software that can search through many databases and retrieve only relevant information for the user is an e-agent.

The Uniform Electronic Transactions Act (UETA), which was discussed in Chapter 9, sets forth provisions relating to the principal's liability for the actions of e-agents. According to Section 15 of the UETA, e-agents can enter into binding agreements on behalf of their principals—at least, in those states that have adopted the act. Thus, if consumers place an order over the Internet, and the company (principal) takes the order via an e-agent, the company cannot later claim that it did not receive the order.

16. *McBride v. Taxman Corp.,* 327 Ill.App.3d 992, 765 N.E.2d 51 (2002).
17. Under the Uniform Commercial Code (UCC), only the agent is liable if the instrument neither names the principal nor shows that the agent signed in a representative capacity [UCC 3–402(b)(2)].
18. The agent is not liable on the contract because the agent was never intended personally to be a party to the contract.

The UETA also stipulates that if an e-agent does not provide an opportunity to prevent errors at the time of the transaction, the other party to the transaction can avoid the transaction. Therefore, if an e-agent fails to provide an on-screen confirmation of a purchase or sale, the other party can avoid the effect of any errors. ▶ **Example 20.20** Bigelow wants to purchase three copies of three different books (a total of nine items). The e-agent mistakenly records an order for thirty-three of a single book and does not provide an on-screen verification of the order. If thirty-three books are then sent to Bigelow, he can avoid the contract to purchase them. ◀

SECTION 6
LIABILITY FOR TORTS AND CRIMES

Obviously, any person, including an agent, is liable for his or her own torts and crimes. Whether a principal can also be held liable for an agent's torts and crimes depends on several factors, which we examine here. In some situations, a principal may be held liable not only for the torts of an agent but also for torts committed by an independent contractor.

Principal's Tortious Conduct

A principal who acts through an agent may be liable for harm resulting from the principal's own negligence or recklessness. Thus, a principal may be liable if he or she gives improper instructions, authorizes the use of improper materials or tools, or establishes improper rules that result in the agent's committing a tort.

▶ **Example 20.21** Parker knows that Audrey's driver's license has been suspended but nevertheless tells her to use the company truck to deliver some equipment to a customer. If someone is injured as a result, Parker will be liable for his own negligence in instructing Audrey to drive without a valid license. ◀

Principal's Authorization of Agent's Tortious Conduct

Similarly, a principal who authorizes an agent to commit a tort may be liable to persons or property injured thereby, because the act is considered to be the principal's. ▶ **Example 20.22** Pedro directs his agent, Andy, to cut the corn on specific acreage, which neither of them has the right to do. The harvest is therefore a trespass (a tort), and Pedro is liable to the owner of the corn. ◀

Note that an agent acting at the principal's direction can be liable as a *tortfeasor* (one who commits a wrong, or tort), along with the principal, for committing the tortious act even if the agent was unaware that the act was wrong. Assume in *Example 20.22* that Andy, the agent, did not know that Pedro lacked the right to harvest the corn. Andy can still be held liable to the owner of the field for damages, along with Pedro, the principal.

Liability for Agent's Misrepresentation

A principal is exposed to tort liability whenever a third person sustains a loss due to the agent's misrepresentation. The principal's liability depends on whether the agent was actually or apparently authorized to make representations and whether the representations were made within the scope of the agency. The principal is always directly responsible for an agent's misrepresentation made within the scope of the agent's authority.

▶ **Example 20.23** Ainsley is a demonstrator for Pavlovich's products. Pavlovich sends Ainsley to a home show to demonstrate the products and to answer questions from consumers. Pavlovich has given Ainsley authority to make statements about the products. If Ainsley makes only true representations, all is fine. But if he makes false claims, Pavlovich will be liable for any injuries or damages sustained by third parties in reliance on Ainsley's false representations. ◀

APPARENT IMPLIED AUTHORITY When a principal has placed an agent in a position of apparent authority—making it possible for the agent to defraud a third party—the principal may also be liable for the agent's fraudulent acts. For instance, partners in a partnership generally have the apparent implied authority to act as agents of the firm, as was discussed in Chapter 17. Thus, if one of the partners commits a tort or a crime, the partnership itself—and often the other partners personally—can be held liable for the loss.

INNOCENT MISREPRESENTATION Tort liability based on fraud requires proof that a material misstatement was made knowingly and with the intent to deceive. An agent's *innocent* misstatements in a contract or warranty transaction can also provide grounds for the third party's rescission of the contract and the award of damages. Justice dictates that when a principal knows that an agent is not accurately advised of facts but does not correct either the agent's or the third party's impressions, the principal is responsible. The point is that the principal is always directly responsible for an agent's misrepresentation made within the scope of authority.

Liability for Agent's Negligence

Under the doctrine of ***respondeat superior*** (a Latin term meaning "let the master respond),"[19] a principal may also be liable for harm that his or her agent causes to a third party. This doctrine imposes **vicarious liability,** or indirect liability, on an employer that is similar to strict liability (see Chapter 13), in that both are imposed regardless of fault. Under this doctrine, the employer is liable for torts committed by an employee acting within the course or scope of employment. (Of course, the employee is also liable for any torts that she or he commits.)

Third parties injured through the negligence of an employee can sue either that employee or the employer, if the employee's negligent conduct occurred while the employee was acting within the scope of employment. ▶ **Case in Point 20.24** Aegis Communications hired Southwest Desert Images (SDI) to provide landscaping services for its property. An herbicide sprayed by SDI employee David Hoggatt entered the Aegis building through the air-conditioning system and caused Catherine Warner, an Aegis employee, to suffer a heart attack. Warner sued SDI and Hoggatt for negligence, but the lower court dismissed the suit against Hoggatt. On appeal, the court found that Hoggatt was also liable. An agent is not excused from responsibility for tortious conduct just because he is working for a principal. Both the agent and the principal are liable.[20] ◀

THE DOCTRINE OF *RESPONDEAT SUPERIOR* At early common law, a servant (employee) was viewed as the master's (employer's) property. The master was deemed to have absolute control over the servant's acts and was held strictly liable for them, no matter how carefully the master supervised the servant. Although employers today are not masters of their employees, control is still a central concept to liability.

Underlying Rationale. The rationale for the doctrine of *respondeat superior* is based on the social duty that requires every person to manage his or her affairs so as not to injure another. This duty applies even when a person acts through an agent (controls the conduct of another).

Public Policy. Generally, public policy requires that an injured person be afforded effective relief, and a business enterprise is usually better able to provide that relief than is an individual employee. Employers normally carry liability insurance to cover any damages awarded as a result of such lawsuits. They are also able to spread the cost of risk over the entire business enterprise.

The courts have applied the doctrine of *respondeat superior* for nearly two centuries. It continues to have practical implications in all situations involving principal-agent (employer-employee) relationships. Today, the small-town grocer with one clerk and the multinational corporation with thousands of employees are equally subject to the doctrine. (Keep this principle in mind when you read Chapters 21 and 22.)

DETERMINING THE SCOPE OF EMPLOYMENT The key to determining whether a principal may be liable for the torts of an agent under the doctrine of *respondeat superior* is whether the torts are committed within the scope of the agency or employment. Courts may consider the following factors in determining whether a particular act occurred within the course and scope of employment:

1. Whether the employee's act was authorized by the employer.
2. The time, place, and purpose of the act.
3. Whether the act was one commonly performed by employees on behalf of their employers.
4. The extent to which the employer's interest was advanced by the act.
5. The extent to which the private interests of the employee were involved.
6. Whether the employer furnished the means or instrumentality (for example, a truck or a machine) by which an injury was inflicted.
7. Whether the employer had reason to know that the employee would perform the act in question and whether the employee had done it before.

---

19. Pronounced ree-*spahn*-dee-uht soo-*peer*-ee-your. The doctrine of *respondeat superior* applies not only to employer-employee relationships but also to other principal-agent relationships in which the principal has the right of control over the agent.
20. *Warner v. Southwest Desert Images, LLC,* 218 Ariz. 121, 180 P.3d 986 (2008).

8. Whether the act involved the commission of a serious crime.

Whether a real estate salesperson's actions in connection with certain real estate transactions fell within the salesperson's scope of employment was at issue in the following case.

CASE ANALYSIS

Case 20.3 Auer v. Paliath

Court of Appeals of Ohio, Second District, 2013 -Ohio- 391, 986 N.E.2d 1052 (2013).

IN THE LANGUAGE OF THE COURT

FROELICH, J. [Judge]

* * * *

Torri Auer [a California resident] brought suit [in an Ohio state court] against real estate salesperson Jamie Paliath, real estate broker Keller Williams Home Town Realty, and others based on alleged fraud by Paliath in the sale of several rental properties [in Dayton, Ohio] to Auer * * * . After a jury trial * * * , Paliath was found liable to Torri Auer in the amount of $135,200 for fraud in the inducement of Auer's purchases of the properties. * * * The jury also awarded $135,200 to Auer from Home Town Realty, based on the broker's vicarious liability for Paliath's actions in connection with Auer's purchases of the properties.

Home Town Realty appeals from the trial court's judgment.

* * * *

* * * Under [Ohio Revised Code (R.C.) Section 4735.01] the term "real estate broker" includes "any person, partnership, association, limited liability company, limited liability partnership, or corporation * * * who for another * * * and who for a fee, commission, or other valuable consideration" engages in various activities regarding real estate, including selling, purchasing, leasing, renting, listing, auctioning, buying, managing, and advertising real estate. A real estate salesperson generally means "any person associated with a licensed real estate broker to do or to deal with any acts or transactions set out or comprehended by the definition of a real estate broker, for compensation or otherwise."

Under R.C. Section 4735.21, no real estate salesperson may collect any money in connection with any real estate transaction, except as in the name of and with the consent of the licensed real estate broker under whom the salesperson is licensed.

* * * *

* * * *A real estate broker will be held vicariously liable for intentional torts committed by salesmen acting within the scope of their authority. Vicarious liability is appropriate because a real estate salesman has no independent status or right to conclude a sale and can only function through the broker with whom he is associated. A salesman is required to be under the supervision of a licensed broker in all of his activities related to real estate transactions.* [Emphasis added.]

* * * *

* * * When a real estate salesperson acts in the name of a real estate broker in connection with the type of real estate transaction for which he or she was hired and the broker collects a commission for the transaction, the salesperson's actions in connection with that real estate transaction are within the scope of the salesperson's employment, as a matter of law.

In this case, Paliath contracted with Home Town Realty as a real estate salesperson to assist clients with the purchase and sale of real estate. Paliath advised and assisted Auer in the purchase of the * * * properties, and her fraudulent conduct involved misrepresentations regarding those properties.

Reviewing the properties separately, the evidence at trial established that Home Town Realty was listed as the real estate broker on the purchase contract, the agency disclosure statement, and the settlement statement for the Belton Street sale. Home Town Realty received a commission check of $180 from the title company that conducted the closing. Based on this evidence, it was established, as a matter of law, that Paliath acted within the scope of her employment as a real estate salesperson with Home Town Realty in relation to Auer's purchase of the Belton property.

Similarly, Paliath's actions with respect to the 1111–1115 Richmond Avenue properties were taken as a real estate salesperson assisting Auer with the purchase of the properties. Home Town was listed as a broker on the purchase contract, the agency disclosure statement, and the settlement statement for 1111 Richmond Avenue, and it received a commission of $2,400 following the closing. * * * The evidence thus demonstrated, as a matter of law, that Paliath was acting in the scope of her employment regarding the sale of 1111 Richmond Avenue.

* * * *

* * * The trial court's judgment will be affirmed.

CASE 20.3 CONTINUED

LEGAL REASONING QUESTIONS

1. What conduct was at the center of the dispute in this case?
2. Who did the plaintiff allege was liable for this conduct? Which of these parties was the principal, and which was the agent?
3. What factors did the court apply to determine liability in this case?
4. How did the court rule on the question of vicarious liability?

THE DISTINCTION BETWEEN A "DETOUR" AND A "FROLIC" A useful insight into the concept of "scope of employment" may be gained from Judge Baron Parke's classic distinction between a "detour" and a "frolic" in the case of *Joel v. Morison* (1834).[21] In this case, the English court held that if a servant merely took a detour from his master's business, the master will be responsible. If, however, the servant was on a "frolic of his own" and not in any way "on his master's business," the master will not be liable.

▶ **Example 20.25** Mandel, a traveling salesperson, while driving his employer's vehicle to call on a customer, decides to stop at the post office—which is one block off his route—to mail a personal letter. As Mandel approaches the post office, he negligently runs into a parked vehicle owned by Chan. In this situation, because Mandel's detour from the employer's business is not substantial, he is still acting within the scope of employment, and the employer is liable.

The result would be different, though, if Mandel had decided to pick up a few friends for drinks in another city and in the process had negligently run his vehicle into Chan's. In that circumstance, the departure from the employer's business would be substantial, and the employer normally would not be liable to Chan for damages. Mandel would be considered to have been on a "frolic" of his own. ◀

EMPLOYEE TRAVEL TIME An employee going to and from work or to and from meals usually is considered to be outside the scope of employment. In contrast, all travel time of traveling salespersons or others whose jobs require travel is normally considered to be within the scope of employment for the duration of the business trip, including the return trip home.

21. 6 Car. & P. 501, 172 Eng.Rep. 1338 (1834).

NOTICE OF DANGEROUS CONDITIONS The employer is charged with knowledge of any dangerous conditions discovered by an employee and pertinent to the employment situation. ▶ **Example 20.26** Brad, a maintenance employee in an apartment building, notices a lead pipe protruding from the ground in the building's courtyard. Brad neglects either to fix the pipe or to inform his employer of the danger. John trips on the pipe and is injured.

The employer is charged with knowledge of the dangerous condition regardless of whether Brad actually informed the employer. That knowledge is imputed to the employer by virtue of the employment relationship. ◀

Liability for Agent's Intentional Torts

Most intentional torts that individuals commit have no relation to their employment, and their employers will not be held liable. Nevertheless, under the doctrine of *respondeat superior,* the employer can be liable for intentional torts that an employee commits within the course and scope of employment. For instance, an employer is liable when an employee (such as a "bouncer" at a nightclub or a security guard at a department store) commits the tort of assault and battery or false imprisonment while acting within the scope of employment.

In addition, an employer who knows or should know that an employee has a propensity for committing tortious acts is liable for the employee's acts even if they would not ordinarily be considered within the scope of employment. ▶ **Example 20.27** Chaz, the owner of the Comedy Club, hires Alec as a bouncer for the club even though he knows that Alec has a history of arrests for criminal assault and battery. In this situation, Chaz may be liable if Alec viciously attacks a customer in the parking lot after hours. ◀ An employer is also liable for permitting an employee to engage in reckless actions that can injure others, such as smoking next to highly flammable liquids.

Liability for Independent Contractor's Torts

Generally, an employer is not liable for physical harm caused to a third person by the negligent act of an independent contractor in the performance of the contract. This is because the employer does not have *the right to control* the details of an independent contractor's performance.

Courts make an exception to this rule when the contract involves unusually hazardous activities, such as blasting operations, the transportation of highly volatile chemicals, or the use of poisonous gases. In these situations, strict liability (discussed in Chapter 13) is imposed, so an employer cannot be shielded from liability merely by using an independent contractor.

Liability for Agent's Crimes

An agent is liable for his or her own crimes. A principal or employer normally is *not* liable for an agent's crime even if the crime was committed within the scope of authority or employment. An exception to this rule is made when the principal or employer participated in the crime by conspiracy or other action.

Also, in some jurisdictions, a principal may be liable under specific statutes if an agent, in the course and scope of employment, violates certain regulations. For instance, a principal might be liable for an agent's violation of sanitation rules or regulations governing prices, weights, and the sale of liquor.

SECTION 7

TERMINATION OF AN AGENCY

Agency law is similar to contract law in that both an agency and a contract may be terminated *by an act of the parties or by operation of law.* Once the relationship between the principal and the agent has ended, the agent no longer has the right (*actual* authority) to bind the principal. For an agent's *apparent* authority to be terminated, though, third persons may also need to be notified that the agency has been terminated.

Termination by Act of the Parties

An agency relationship may be terminated by act of the parties in any of the following ways:

1. *Lapse of time.* When an agency agreement specifies the time period during which the agency relationship will exist, the agency ends when that time period expires. If no definite time is stated, then the agency continues for a reasonable time and can be terminated at will by either party. What constitutes a reasonable time depends on the circumstances and the nature of the agency relationship.
2. *Purpose achieved.* If an agent is employed to accomplish a particular objective, such as the purchase of breeding stock for a cattle rancher, the agency automatically ends after the cattle have been purchased. If more than one agent is employed to accomplish the same purpose, such as the sale of real estate, the first agent to complete the sale automatically terminates the agency relationship for all the others.
3. *Occurrence of a specific event.* When an agency relationship is to terminate on the happening of a certain event, the agency automatically ends when the event occurs. ▶ **Example 20.28** If Posner appoints Rubik to handle her business affairs while she is away, the agency automatically terminates when Posner returns. ◀
4. *Mutual agreement.* The parties to an agency can cancel (rescind) their contract by mutually agreeing to terminate the agency relationship, even if it was for a specific (longer) duration.
5. *Termination by one party.* As a general rule, either party can terminate the agency relationship. The act of termination is called *revocation* if done by the principal and *renunciation* if done by the agent. Although both parties may have the *power* to terminate the agency, they may not possess the right and therefore may be liable for breach of contract or *wrongful termination.*

WRONGFUL TERMINATION Wrongful termination can subject the canceling party to a lawsuit for breach of contract. ▶ **Example 20.29** Rawlins has a one-year employment contract with Munro to act as agent in return for $65,000. Although Munro has the *power* to discharge Rawlins before the contract period expires, if he does so, he can be sued for breaching the contract because he had no *right* to terminate the agency. ◀

Even in an agency at will—in which either party may terminate at any time—the principal who wishes to terminate must give the agent *reasonable* notice. The notice must be at least sufficient to allow the agent to recoup his or her expenses and, in some situations, to make a normal profit.

AGENCY COUPLED WITH AN INTEREST A special rule applies to an *agency coupled with an interest.* In an **agency coupled with an interest,** the agent has some legal right to (an interest in) the property that is the subject of the agency. For instance, a principal might provide inventory for the agent to sell and then to keep the profits. Because the agent has an additional interest in the property beyond the normal commission for selling it, the agent's position cannot be terminated until the agent's interest ends.

This type of agency is not an agency in the usual sense because it is created for the agent's benefit instead of for the principal's benefit. ▶ **Example 20.30** Julie borrows $5,000 from Rob, giving Rob some of her jewelry and signing a letter authorizing him to sell the jewelry as her agent if she fails to repay the loan. After Julie receives the $5,000 from Rob, she attempts to revoke his authority to sell the jewelry as her agent. Julie will not succeed in this attempt because a principal cannot revoke an agency created for the agent's benefit. ◀

An agency coupled with an interest should not be confused with a situation in which the agent merely derives proceeds or profits from the sale of the subject matter. Many agents are paid a commission for their services, but the agency relationship involved does not constitute an agency coupled with an interest. For instance, a real estate agent who merely receives a commission from the sale of real property does not have a beneficial interest in the property itself.

NOTICE OF TERMINATION When the parties terminate an agency, it is the principal's duty to inform any third parties who know of the existence of the agency that it has been terminated. No particular form is required for notice of termination of the principal-agent relationship to be effective. The principal can personally notify the agent, or the agent can learn of the termination through some other means.

Although an agent's actual authority ends when the agency is terminated, an agent's *apparent authority* continues until the third party receives notice (from any source) that such authority has been terminated. ▶ **Example 20.31** Manning bids on a shipment of steel, and Stone is hired as an agent to arrange transportation for the shipment. When Stone learns that Manning has lost the bid, Stone's authority to make the transportation arrangement terminates. ◀

If the principal knows that a third party has dealt with the agent, the principal is expected to notify that person *directly.* For third parties who have heard about the agency but have not yet dealt with the agent, *constructive notice* is sufficient.[22] If the agent's authority is written, however, normally it must be revoked in writing (unless the written document contained an expiration date).

Termination by Operation of Law

Certain events terminate agency authority automatically because their occurrence makes it impossible for the agent to perform or improbable that the principal would continue to want performance. We look at these events here. Note that when an agency terminates by operation of law, there is no duty to notify third persons—unless the agent's authority is coupled with an interest.

1. *Death or insanity.* The general rule is that the death or insanity of either the principal or the agent automatically and immediately terminates an ordinary agency relationship.[23] Knowledge of the death or insanity is not required. ▶ **Example 20.32** Grey sends Bosley to Japan to purchase a rare book. Before Bosley makes the purchase, Grey dies. Bosley's agent status is terminated at the moment of Grey's death, even though Bosley does not know that Grey has died. ◀

   (Some states, however, have enacted statutes that change the common law rule to require an agent's knowledge of the principal's death before termination.)
2. *Impossibility.* When the specific subject matter of an agency is destroyed or lost, the agency terminates. ▶ **Example 20.33** Tsang employs Arnez to sell Tsang's house. Prior to any sale, the house is destroyed by fire. Arnez's agency and authority to sell the house terminate. ◀ Similarly, when it is impossible for the agent to perform the agency lawfully because of a change in the law, the agency terminates.

22. With *constructive notice* of a fact, knowledge of the fact is imputed by law to a person if he or she could have discovered the fact by proper diligence. Constructive notice is often accomplished by publication in a newspaper.
23. An exception to this rule exists in the bank-customer relationship. A bank, as agent, can continue to exercise specific types of authority even after the customer's death or insanity, and can continue to pay checks drawn by the customer for ten days after death.

3. *Changed circumstances*. Sometimes, an event occurs that has such an unusual effect on the subject matter of the agency that the agent can reasonably infer that the principal will not want the agency to continue. In such situations, the agency terminates. ▶ **Example 20.34** Baird hires Joslen to sell a tract of land for $40,000. Subsequently, Joslen learns that there is oil under the land and that the land is therefore worth $1 million. The agency and Joslen's authority to sell the land for $40,000 are terminated. ◀
4. *Bankruptcy*. If either the principal or the agent petitions for bankruptcy, the agency is *usually* terminated. In certain circumstances, such as when the agent's financial status is irrelevant to the purpose of the agency, the agency relationship may continue. *Insolvency* (the inability to pay debts when they come due or when liabilities exceed assets), as distinguished from bankruptcy, does not necessarily terminate the relationship.
5. *War*. When the principal's country and the agent's country are at war with each other, the agency is terminated. In this situation, the agency is automatically suspended or terminated because there is no way to enforce the legal rights and obligations of the parties.

See *Concept Summary 20.3* below for a synopsis of the rules governing the termination of an agency.

CONCEPT SUMMARY 20.3
Termination of an Agency

METHOD OF TERMINATION	RULES	TERMINATION OF AGENT'S AUTHORITY
Act of the Parties		
1. Lapse of time.	Automatic at end of the stated time.	**Notice to Third Parties Required—** 1. Direct to those who have dealt with agency. 2. Constructive to all others.
2. Purpose achieved.	Automatic on the completion of the purpose.	
3. Occurrence of a specific event.	Normally automatic on the happening of the event.	
4. Mutual agreement.	Mutual consent required.	
5. At the option of one party (revocation, if by principal, renunciation, if by agent).	Either party normally has a right to terminate the agency but may lack the power to do so, which can lead to liability for breach of contract.	
Operation of Law		
1. Death or insanity.	Automatic on the death or insanity of either the principal or the agent (except when the agency is coupled with an interest).	**No Notice Required—** Automatic on the happening of the event.
2. Impossibility—destruction of the specific subject matter.	Applies any time the agency cannot be performed because of an event beyond the parties' control.	
3. Changed circumstances.	Events so unusual that it would be inequitable to allow the agency to continue to exist.	
4. Bankruptcy.	Bankruptcy petition (not mere insolvency) usually terminates the agency.	
5. War between principal's country and agent's country.	Automatically suspends or terminates agency—no way to enforce legal rights.	

Reviewing: Agency

Lynne Meyer, on her way to a business meeting and in a hurry, stopped at a Buy-Mart store for a new car charger for her smartphone. There was a long line at one of the checkout counters, but a cashier, Valerie Watts, opened another counter and began loading the cash drawer. Meyer told Watts that she was in a hurry and asked Watts to work faster. Instead, Watts slowed her pace. At this point, Meyer hit Watts.

It is not clear whether Meyer hit Watts intentionally or, in an attempt to retrieve the car charger, hit her inadvertently. In response, Watts grabbed Meyer by the hair and hit her repeatedly in the back of the head, while Meyer screamed for help. Management personnel separated the two women and questioned them about the incident. Watts was immediately fired for violating the store's no-fighting policy. Meyer subsequently sued Buy-Mart, alleging that the store was liable for the tort (assault and battery) committed by its employee. Using the information presented in the chapter, answer the following questions.

1. Under what doctrine discussed in this chapter might Buy-Mart be held liable for the tort committed by Watts?
2. What is the key factor in determining whether Buy-Mart is liable under this doctrine?
3. How is Buy-Mart's potential liability affected by whether Watts's behavior constituted an intentional tort or a tort of negligence?
4. Suppose that when Watts applied for the job at Buy-Mart, she disclosed in her application that she had previously been convicted of felony assault and battery. Nevertheless, Buy-Mart hired Watts as a cashier. How might this fact affect Buy-Mart's liability for Watts's actions?

DEBATE THIS . . . *The doctrine of* respondeat superior *should be modified to make agents solely liable for their tortious (wrongful) acts committed within the scope of employment.*

Terms and Concepts

agency 466
agency coupled with an interest 485
apparent authority 476
disclosed principal 478
e-agent 479
equal dignity rule 474
exclusive agency 473
express authority 474
fiduciary 466
implied authority 474
independent contractor 467
notary public 474
partially disclosed principal 478
power of attorney 474
ratification 477
respondeat superior 481
undisclosed principal 478
vicarious liability 481

ExamPrep

Issue Spotters

1. Dimka Corporation wants to build a new mall on a specific tract of land. Dimka contracts with Nadine to buy the property. When Nadine learns of the difference between the price that Dimka is willing to pay and the price at which the owner is willing to sell, she wants to buy the land and sell it to Dimka herself. Can she do this? Discuss. **(See page 472.)**
2. Davis contracts with Estee to buy a certain horse on her behalf. Estee asks Davis not to reveal her identity. Davis makes a deal with Farmland Stables, the owner of the horse, and makes a down payment. Estee does not pay the rest of the price. Farmland Stables sues Davis for breach of contract. Can Davis hold Estee liable for whatever damages he has to pay? Why or why not? **(See page 479.)**

- **Check your answers to the Issue Spotters against the answers provided in Appendix E at the end of this text.**

Before the Test

Go to **www.cengagebrain.com**, enter the ISBN 9781285428949, and click on "Find" to locate this textbook's Web site. Then, click on "Access Now" under "Study Tools," and select Chapter 20 at the top. There, you will find an Interactive Quiz that you can take to assess your mastery of the concepts in this chapter, as well as Flashcards and a Glossary of important terms.

Business Scenarios

20–1. Duty of Loyalty. Peter hires Alice as an agent to sell a piece of property he owns. The price is to be at least $30,000. Alice discovers that the fair market value of Peter's property is actually at least $45,000 and could be higher because a shopping mall is going to be built nearby. Alice forms a real estate partnership with her cousin Carl. Then she prepares for Peter's signature a contract for the sale of the property to Carl for $32,000. Peter signs the contract. Just before closing and passage of title, Peter learns about the shopping mall and the increased fair market value of his property. Peter refuses to deed the property to Carl. Carl claims that Alice, as Peter's agent, solicited a price above that agreed on when the agency was created and that the contract is therefore binding and enforceable. Discuss fully whether Peter is bound to this contract. **(See page 472.)**

20–2. *Respondeat Superior.* ABC Tire Corp. hires Arnez as a traveling salesperson and assigns him a geographic area and time schedule in which to solicit orders and service customers. Arnez is given a company car to use in covering the territory. One day, Arnez decides to take his personal car to cover part of his territory. It is 11:00 A.M., and Arnez has just finished calling on all customers in the city of Tarrytown. His next appointment is at 2:00 P.M. in the city of Austex, twenty miles down the road. Arnez starts out for Austex, but halfway there he decides to visit a former college roommate who runs a farm ten miles off the main highway. Arnez is enjoying his visit with his former roommate when he realizes that it is 1:45 P.M. and that he will be late for the appointment in Austex. Driving at a high speed down the country road to reach the main highway, Arnez crashes his car into a tractor, severely injuring Thomas, the driver of the tractor. Thomas claims that he can hold ABC Tire Corp. liable for his injuries. Discuss fully ABC's liability in this situation. **(See page 481.)**

Business Case Problems

20–3. Spotlight on Agency—Independent Contractors. Frank

Frausto delivered newspapers under a renewable six-month contract called a "Delivery Agent Agreement." The agreement identified Frausto as an independent contractor. The company collected payment from customers and took complaints about delivery. Frausto was given the route for his paper delivery and was required to deliver the paper within a certain time period each day. Frausto delivered the papers using his own vehicle and had to provide proof of insurance to the company. The company provided health and disability insurance but did not withhold taxes from Frausto's weekly income. One morning, Frausto was delivering papers and collided with Santiago on his motorcycle. Santiago filed a negligence action against Frausto and the newspaper company. The newspaper company argued that it should not be liable because Frausto was an independent contractor. What was the result? Why? [*Santiago v. Phoenix Newspapers, Inc.*, 794 P.2d 138 (Ariz. 1990)] **(See page 467.)**

20–4. Disclosed Principal. To display desserts in restaurants, Mario Sclafani ordered refrigeration units from Felix Storch, Inc. Felix faxed a credit application to Sclafani. The application was faxed back with a signature that appeared to be Sclafani's. Felix delivered the units. When they were not paid for, Felix filed a suit against Sclafani to collect. Sclafani denied that he had seen the application or signed it. He testified that he referred all credit questions to "the girl in the office." Who was the principal? Who was the agent? Who is liable on the contract? Explain. [*Felix Storch, Inc. v. Martinucci Desserts USA, Inc.*, 30 Misc.2d 1217, 924 N.Y.S.2d 308 (Suffolk Co. 2011)] **(See page 478.)**

20–5. Employment Relationships. William Moore owned Moore Enterprises, a wholesale tire business. William's son, Jonathan, worked as a Moore Enterprises employee while he was in high school. Later, Jonathan started his own business, called Morecedes Tire. Morecedes regrooved tires and sold them to businesses, including Moore Enterprises. A decade after Jonathan started Morecedes, William offered him work with Moore Enterprises. On the first day, William told Jonathan to load certain tires on a trailer but did not tell him how to do it. Was Jonathan an independent contractor? Discuss. [*Moore v. Moore*, 152 Idaho 245, 269 P.3d 802 (2011)] **(See page 467.)**

20–6. BUSINESS CASE PROBLEM WITH SAMPLE ANSWER: Liability for Contracts.

Thomas Huskin and his wife entered into a contract to have their home remodeled by House Medic Handyman Service. Todd Hall signed the contract as an authorized representative of House Medic. It turned out that House Medic was a fictitious name for Hall Hauling, Ltd. The contract did not indicate this, however, and Hall did not inform the Huskins about Hall Hauling. When a contract dispute later arose, the Huskins sued Todd Hall per-

sonally for breach of contract. Can Hall be held personally liable? Why or why not? [Huskin v. Hall, *2012 WL 553136 (Ohio Ct.App. 2012)]* **(See page 478.)**

- **For a sample answer to Problem 20–6, go to Appendix F at the end of this text.**

20–7. Agent's Duties to Principal. William and Maxine Miller were shareholders of Claimsco International, Inc. They filed a suit against the other shareholders, Michael Harris and Kenneth Hoxie, and the accountant who worked for all of them—John Verchota. The Millers alleged that Verchota had breached a duty that he owed them. They claimed that at Harris's instruction, Verchota had adjusted Claimsco's books to maximize the Millers' financial liabilities, falsely reflect income to them without actually transferring that income, and unfairly disadvantage them compared to the other shareholders. Which duty are the Millers referring to? If the allegations can be proved, did Verchota breach this duty? Explain. [*Miller v. Harris,* 2013 IL App (2d) 120512, 985 N.E.2d 671 (Ill.App. 2 Dist. 2013)] **(See page 472.)**

20–8. Agent's Authority. Basic Research, L.L.C., advertised its products on television networks owned by Rainbow Media Holdings, Inc., through an ad agency, Icebox Advertising, Inc. As Basic's agent, Icebox had the express authority to buy ads from Rainbow on Basic's behalf, but the authority was limited to buying ads with cash in advance. Despite this limit, Rainbow sold ads to Basic through Icebox on credit. Basic paid Icebox for the ads, but Icebox did not pass all of the payments on to Rainbow. Icebox filed for bankruptcy. Can Rainbow recoup the unpaid amounts from Basic? Explain. [*American Movie Classics v. Rainbow Media Holdings,* 2013 WL 323229 (10th Cir. 2013)] **(See page 474.)**

20–9. A QUESTION OF ETHICS: Agency Formation and Duties.

Western Fire Truck, Inc., contracted with Emergency One, Inc. (EO), to be its exclusive dealer in Colorado and Wyoming through December 2003. James Costello, a Western salesperson, was authorized to order EO vehicles for his customers. Without informing Western, Costello e-mailed EO about Western's difficulties in obtaining cash to fund its operations. He asked about the viability of Western's contract and his possible employment with EO. On EO's request, and in disregard of Western's instructions, Costello sent some payments for EO vehicles directly to EO. In addition, Costello, with EO's help, sent a competing bid to a potential Western customer. EO's representative e-mailed Costello, "You have my permission to kick [Western's] ass." In April 2002, EO terminated its contract with Western, and, after reviewing Costello's e-mail, fired Costello. Western filed a suit in a Colorado state court, alleging that Costello breached his duty as an agent and that EO aided and abetted the breach. [Western Fire Truck, Inc. v. Emergency One, Inc., *134 P.3d 570 (Colo. App. 2006)]* **(See page 470.)**

(a) Was there an agency relationship between Western and Costello? Western required monthly reports from its sales staff, but Costello did not report regularly. Does this indicate that Costello was not Western's agent? In determining whether an agency relationship exists, is the right to control or the fact of control more important? Explain.

(b) Did Costello owe Western a duty? If so, what was the duty? Did Costello breach it? If so, how?

(c) A Colorado state statute allows a court to award punitive damages in "circumstances of fraud, malice, or willful and wanton conduct." Did any of these circumstances exist in this case? Should punitive damages be assessed against either defendant? Why or why not?

Legal Reasoning Group Activity

20–10. Liability for Independent Contractor's Torts. Dean Brothers Corp. owns and operates a steel drum manufacturing plant. Lowell Wyden, the plant superintendent, hired Best Security Patrol, Inc. (BSP), a security company, to guard Dean property and "deter thieves and vandals." Some BSP security guards, as Wyden knew, carried firearms. Pete Sidell, a BSP security guard, was not certified as an armed guard but nevertheless came to work with his gun (in a briefcase).

While working at the Dean plant on October 31, 2014, Sidell fired his gun at Tyrone Gaines, in the belief that Gaines was an intruder. The bullet struck and killed Gaines. Gaines's mother filed a lawsuit claiming that her son's death was the result of BSP's negligence, for which Dean was responsible. **(See page 480.)**

(a) The first group will determine what the plaintiff's best argument is to establish that Dean is responsible for BSP's actions.

(b) The second group will discuss Dean's best defense and formulate arguments in support of it.

CHAPTER 21
EMPLOYMENT RELATIONSHIPS

Until the early 1900s, most employer-employee relationships were governed by the common law. Even today, under the common law *employment-at-will doctrine,* private employers have considerable freedom to hire and fire workers at will, regardless of the employees' performance.

In addition, however, numerous statutes and administrative agency regulations now govern the workplace. Thus, to a large extent, statutory law has displaced common law doctrines. In this chapter and the next two chapters, we look at the most significant laws regulating employment relationships.

In this chapter, we discuss federal statutes that regulate various aspects of the workplace, including employee wages, hours, medical leave, safety, and pension and health plans. We consider employee privacy rights and such issues as the use of electronic monitoring by employers and drug testing.

We deal with other important laws regulating the workplace—those that prohibit employment discrimination, restrict immigration, and regulate labor unions—in Chapters 22 and 23.

SECTION 1

EMPLOYMENT AT WILL

Employment relationships have traditionally been governed by the common law doctrine of **employment at will.** Under this doctrine, either party may terminate the employment relationship at any time and for any reason, unless doing so violates an employee's statutory or contractual rights.

Today, the majority of U.S. workers continue to have the legal status of "employees at will." In other words, this common law doctrine is still in widespread use, and only one state (Montana) does not apply it.

Nonetheless, federal and state statutes governing employment relationships prevent the doctrine from being applied in a number of circumstances. An employer may not fire an employee if doing so would violate a federal or state statute, such as one prohibiting employment discrimination (see Chapter 22).

Note that the distinction made under agency law (discussed in Chapter 20) between employee status and independent-contractor status is important here. The employment laws that will be discussed in this chapter and in Chapters 22 and 23 apply only to the employer-employee relationship. They do not apply to independent contractors.

Exceptions to the Employment-at-Will Doctrine

Because of the harsh effects of the employment-at-will doctrine for employees, courts have carved out various exceptions to it. These exceptions are based on contract theory, tort theory, and public policy.

EXCEPTIONS BASED ON CONTRACT THEORY Some courts have held that an *implied* employment contract exists between the employer and the employee. If the employee is fired outside the terms o6f the implied contract, he or she may succeed in an action for breach of contract even though no written employment contract exists.

▶ **Example 21.1** BDI Enterprise's employment manual and personnel bulletin both state that, as a matter of policy, workers will be dismissed only for good cause. Jing Chin is an employee at BDI. If Chin reasonably expects BDI to follow this policy, a court may find that there is an implied contract based on the terms stated in the manual and bulletin. ◀ Generally, the key consideration in determining whether an employment manual creates an implied contractual obligation is the employee's reasonable expectations.

Courts in a few states have gone further and held that all employment contracts contain an implied covenant of good faith. This means that both sides promise to abide by the contract in good faith. If an employer fires an employee for an arbitrary or unjustified reason, the employee can claim that the employer breached the covenant of good faith and violated the contract.

In the following case, an employment contract that explicitly stated that the employment was "at will" also contained provisions relating to the contract's renewal under certain circumstances. Was this an at-will contract, or was the employer bound by the renewal provisions? That was the issue before the court.

CASE ANALYSIS

Case 21.1 Ellis v. BlueSky Charter School

Court of Appeals of Minnesota, 2010 WL 1541352 (2010).

IN THE LANGUAGE OF THE COURT

CRIPPEN, Judge.

Challenging his termination as director of respondent BlueSky Charter School, relator[a] Thomas Ellis argues that the termination breached his contract with respondent.

In November 2008, the parties signed an employment agreement providing that relator was to serve as the director of the school for the 2008–09 school year. The title of the agreement states the dates "July 01/2008–June 30/2009."

The first sentence of the agreement lists the administrative positions to which the agreement applies and states, "This is a general **at will agreement.**" [Emphasis in original.] Yet the agreement provides that "positions will automatically renew for one year after one year of service unless specific actions are taken by the board before April 15th of each year." It defines the work year as 220 days from July 1 to June 30 * * * .

Respondent terminated relator's contract at a meeting of its board of directors on May 7, 2009.

a. A *relator* is a private person at whose prompting or complaint an action against a public office or organization is undertaken.

* * * *

Relator argues that, under his contract, because his contract was terminated after April 15, 2009, respondent was obligated to employ him for the remainder of the 2008–09 school year and through the 2009–10 school year. He seeks damages for pay he was owed as of May 2009 and thereafter through the school year ending in 2010. He also seeks future damages for lost benefits and diminution in value of retirement benefits, as well as severance pay and other amounts associated with termination.

* * * *

In Minnesota, an employment contract of indefinite duration is generally interpreted to be a contract for employment at will, which may be terminated at any time without cause. Conversely, an employment agreement for a fixed term is generally interpreted as terminable only for cause. Express language may override these general rules of interpretation. [Emphasis added.]

The employment agreement of the parties unambiguously declared "at will" employment. Without qualification or limitation, the first line of the agreement states that it is a "general at will agreement covering the [listed] positions." The words "at will agreement" are the only terms that appear in bold type in the text of the contract.

* * * *

The agreement refers to a work year from July 1, 2008 to June 30, 2009. * * * Relator argues that these references establish a fixed-term contract. Although the contract is not expressly declared an agreement for a set term, the references to start and end dates, standing alone, would likely be sufficient to establish a term contract terminable only for cause. But * * * the general rule for construing indefinite contracts is overcome by express terms in a contract. The plain language of the "at will" phrase overrides the general rule for construing a fixed-term contract, expressly replacing any implication that might have been drawn from the reference to start and end dates.

* * * *

To the extent the damages relator seeks are based on a breach of his employment agreement, he is not entitled to recover because his position was at-will.

* * * *

Affirmed; motion denied.

LEGAL REASONING QUESTIONS

1. Why did Ellis, the relator, believe that his employment was not at will but based on an employment contract?
2. What was Ellis seeking as damages in this lawsuit?

CASE 21.1 CONTINUES ➧

CASE 21.1 CONTINUED

3. According to the court, was Ellis an at-will employee?
4. What reasons did the court give to support its conclusion?

EXCEPTIONS BASED ON TORT THEORY In some situations, the discharge of an employee may give rise to an action for wrongful discharge under tort theories. Abusive discharge procedures may result in a lawsuit for intentional infliction of emotional distress or defamation.

In addition, some courts have permitted workers to sue under the tort theory of fraud when an employer made false promises to a prospective employee. ▶ **Example 21.2** Goldfinch Consulting, Inc., induces Brianna to leave a lucrative job and move to another state by offering her "a long-term job with a thriving business." In fact, Goldfinch is not only having significant financial problems but is also planning a merger that will result in the elimination of the position offered to Brianna. If she takes the job in reliance on Goldfinch's representations and is fired shortly thereafter, Brianna may be able to bring an action against the employer for fraud. ◀

EXCEPTIONS BASED ON PUBLIC POLICY The most common exception to the employment-at-will doctrine is made on the basis that the employer's reason for firing the employee violates a fundamental public policy of the jurisdiction. Generally, the courts require that the public policy involved be expressed clearly in the statutory law governing the jurisdiction.

The public-policy exception may apply to an employee who is discharged for **whistleblowing**—that is, telling government authorities, upper-level managers, or the media that her or his employer is engaged in some unsafe or illegal activity.

▶ **Case in Point 21.3** Rebecca Wendeln was the staff coordinator at a nursing home. She discovered that a patient at the home had been improperly moved and had been injured as a result. Wendeln reported the incident to state authorities, as she was required to do by state law. Her supervisor was angry about the report, and Wendeln was fired shortly thereafter. When Wendeln sued, the court held that although she was an employee at will, she was protected in this instance from retaliatory firing because a clear mandate of public policy had been violated.[1] ◀ (Normally, whistleblowers seek protection from retaliatory discharge under federal and state statutes, such as the Whistleblower Protection Act of 1989.[2])

In the following case, an employer fired an employee after he complained about how his supervisor performed her job. The court had to decide whether the employee was protected by the employer's whistleblower policy even though it was implemented after he was hired.

1. *Wendeln v. The Beatrice Manor, Inc.*, 271 Neb. 373, 712 N.W.2d 226 (2006).
2. 5 U.S.C. Section 1201.

CASE 21.2

Waddell v. Boyce Thompson Institute for Plant Research, Inc.

Supreme Court of New York, Appellate Division, 92 A.D.3d 1172, 940 N.Y.S.2d 331 (2012).

BACKGROUND AND FACTS Donald Waddell worked as a business office supervisor for the Boyce Thompson Institute for Plant Research. Waddell did not have an employment contract for a fixed term. The Institute's employee manual said that his job was "terminable at the will of either the employee or [the Institute], at any time, with or without cause." Several months after hiring Waddell, the Institute implemented a whistleblower policy designed to encourage "the highest standards of financial reporting and lawful and ethical behavior." The whistleblower policy stated that the Institute would not retaliate against an employee for making a complaint "in good faith pursuant to this policy."

Beginning in May 2010, Waddell repeatedly complained that his supervisor, Sophia Darling, needed to file certain financial documents more promptly. In August 2010, Darling fired Waddell, telling him that his disrespectful and insubordinate conduct violated the Institute's Code of Conduct. Waddell then sued the Institute, and the trial court held that he failed to state a proper claim for breach of an implied contract. Waddell appealed.

CASE 21.2 CONTINUED

IN THE LANGUAGE OF THE COURT
PETERS, J.P. [Justice Presiding]

* * * *

* * * *It is well settled that, "absent an agreement establishing a fixed duration, an employment relationship is presumed to be a hiring at will, terminable at any time by either party."* This presumption may be rebutted by proof establishing that "the employer made the employee aware of its express written policy limiting its right of discharge and that the employee detrimentally relied on that policy in accepting the employment." Notably, "the requirements for such an implied contract of employment have been strictly construed, and the successful plaintiff must sustain an 'explicit and difficult pleading burden.' " [Emphasis added.]

* * * We find that plaintiff has failed to state a cause of action for breach of an implied contract. It is undisputed that the Whistleblower Policy had not been implemented until several months after plaintiff began employment with defendant. As such, [the trial court] correctly found that the essential element of detrimental reliance in accepting employment was lacking. Further, plaintiff did not allege that he forsook any other employment opportunities in reliance upon defendant's Whistleblower Policy or because of what he believed to be defendant's termination policy. Nor is the quality of plaintiff's service relevant in determining whether the presumption of at-will employment has been overcome. * * * Accordingly, plaintiff's claim for breach of an implied employment contract was properly dismissed.

DECISION AND REMEDY *The New York appellate court found that Waddell did not state a proper claim for breach of contract. It therefore affirmed the judgment for the Institute.*

THE LEGAL ENVIRONMENT DIMENSION *If Waddell had been allowed to bring a claim for breach of contract, how might his supervisor, Sophia Darling, have defended her conduct? Explain your answer.*

THE ETHICAL DIMENSION *Is the at-will employment doctrine fair to employees? Why or why not?*

Wrongful Discharge

Whenever an employer discharges an employee in violation of an employment contract or a statutory law protecting employees, the employee may bring an action for **wrongful discharge.** Even if an employer's actions do not violate any express employment contract or statute, the employer may still be subject to liability under a common law doctrine, such as a tort theory or agency. For instance, if an employer discharges a female employee while publicly disclosing private facts about her sex life to her co-workers, the employee could bring a wrongful discharge suit based on an invasion of privacy (see Chapter 12).

SECTION 2

WAGES, HOURS, AND LAYOFFS

In the 1930s, Congress enacted several laws to regulate the wages and working hours of employees, including the following:

1. The Davis-Bacon Act[3] requires contractors and subcontractors working on federal government construction projects to pay "prevailing wages" to their employees.
2. The Walsh-Healey Act[4] applies to U.S. government contracts. It requires that a minimum wage, as well as overtime pay at 1.5 times regular pay rates, be paid to employees of manufacturers or suppliers entering into contracts with agencies of the federal government.
3. The Fair Labor Standards Act (FLSA)[5] extended wage-hour requirements to cover all employers engaged in interstate commerce or in producing goods for interstate commerce, plus selected other types of businesses. The FLSA, as amended, provides the most comprehensive federal regulation of wages and hours today.

Child Labor

The FLSA prohibits oppressive child labor. Children under fourteen years of age are allowed to do only certain types of work, such as deliver newspapers, work for their parents, and be employed in entertainment and (with some exceptions) agriculture. Children

3. 40 U.S.C. Sections 276a–276a-5.
4. 41 U.S.C. Sections 35–45.
5. 29 U.S.C. Sections 201–260.

aged fourteen and fifteen are allowed to work, but not in hazardous occupations. There are also numerous restrictions on how many hours per day and per week children can work.

Working times and hours are not restricted for persons between the ages of sixteen and eighteen, but they cannot be employed in hazardous jobs. None of these restrictions apply to those over the age of eighteen.

Minimum Wages

The FLSA provides that a **minimum wage** of $7.25 per hour must be paid to employees in covered industries (by the time you read this text, the minimum wage may be higher). Congress periodically revises this minimum wage. Additionally, many states have minimum wages. When the state minimum wage is greater than the federal minimum wage, the employee is entitled to the higher wage.

When an employee receives tips while on the job, the employer is required to pay only $2.13 an hour in direct wages—if that amount, plus the tips received, equals at least the federal minimum wage. If an employee's tips and direct wages do not equal the federal minimum wage, the employer must make up the difference. If employers pay at least the federal minimum wage, the FLSA allows them to take employee tips and make other arrangements for their distribution.

Overtime Provisions and Exemptions

Under the FLSA, any employee who works more than forty hours per week must be paid no less than 1.5 times her or his regular pay for all hours over forty. The FLSA overtime provisions apply only after an employee has worked more than forty hours per *week,* so employees who work ten hours a day, four days per week, are not entitled to overtime pay.

Certain employees—usually administrative, executive, and professional employees, as well as outside salespersons and computer programmers—are exempt from the FLSA's overtime provisions. Employers are not required to pay overtime wages to exempt employees. An employer can voluntarily pay overtime to ineligible employees but cannot waive or reduce the overtime requirements of the FLSA.

EXECUTIVE EMPLOYEES An executive employee is one whose primary duty is management. An employee's primary duty is determined by what he or she does that is of principal value to the employer, not by how much time the employee spends doing particular tasks. An employer cannot deny overtime wages based only on an employee's job title, however, and must be able to show that the employee's primary duty qualifies her or him for an exemption.[6]

▶ **Case in Point 21.4** Kevin Keevican, a manager at a Starbucks store, worked seventy hours a week for $650 to $800, a 10 to 20 percent bonus, and paid sick leave. Keevican (and other former managers) filed a claim against Starbucks for unpaid overtime. Keevican claimed that he had spent 70 to 80 percent of his time waiting on customers and thus was not an executive employee. The court, however, found that Keevican was "the single highest-ranking employee" in his particular store. He was responsible on site for that store's day-to-day overall operations. Because his primary duty was managerial, Starbucks was not required to pay overtime.[7] ◀

ADMINISTRATIVE EMPLOYEES To qualify under the administrative employee exemption, the employee must be paid a salary, not hourly wages, and have a primary duty directly related to management or the employer's general business operations. In addition, the employee's primary duty must include the exercise of discretion and independent judgment with respect to matters of significance.

▶ **Case in Point 21.5** Patty Lee Smith was a pharmaceutical sales representative at Johnson and Johnson (J&J). She traveled to ten physicians' offices a day to promote the benefits of J&J's drug Concerta. Smith's work was unsupervised, she controlled her own schedule, and she received a salary of $66,000. When she filed a claim for overtime pay, the court held that she was an administrative employee and therefore exempt from the FLSA's overtime provisions.[8] ◀

Layoffs

During the latest economic recession, millions of workers were laid off from their jobs as companies reduced costs by restructuring their operations and downsizing their workforces. In this section, we discuss the laws pertaining to employee layoffs, an area that is increasingly the subject of litigation.

THE WORKER ADJUSTMENT AND RETRAINING NOTIFICATION ACT The Worker Adjustment and Retraining Notification (WARN) Act[9] applies to

6. See, for example, *Slusser v. Vantage Builders, Inc.,* 576 F.Supp.2d 1207 (D.N.M. 2008).
7. *Mims v. Starbucks Corp.,* 2007 WL 10369 (S.D.Tex. 2007).
8. *Smith v. Johnson and Johnson,* 593 F.3d 280 (3d Cir. 2010).
9. 29 U.S.C. Sections 2101 *et seq.*

employers with at least one hundred full-time employees. It requires an employer to provide sixty days' notice before implementing a mass layoff or closing a plant that employs more than fifty full-time workers. A mass layoff is a layoff of at least one-third of the full-time employees at a particular job site.

Notification Requirements. Employers must provide advance notice of the layoff to the affected workers *or* their representative (if the workers are members of a labor union). Employers must also notify state and local government authorities so that they can provide resources, such as job training, to displaced workers. Any part-time and seasonal employees who are being laid off must be notified, even though these workers do not count in determining whether the act's provisions are triggered. Even companies that anticipate filing for bankruptcy normally must provide notice under the WARN Act before implementing a mass layoff.

Remedies for Violations. If sued, an employer that orders a mass layoff or plant closing in violation of the WARN Act can be fined up to $500 for each day of the violation. Employees can recover back pay for each day of the violation (up to sixty days), plus reasonable attorneys' fees. An employee can also recover benefits under an employee benefit plan, including the cost of medical expenses that would have been covered by the plan.

Because the WARN Act applies to large employers that lay off thousands of workers, lawsuits can be expensive. The amount that an employer must pay grows larger each day and is multiplied by the number of employees involved in the suit.

STATE LAWS MAY ALSO REQUIRE LAYOFF NOTICES Many states also have statutes requiring employers to provide notice before initiating mass layoffs. These laws may have requirements different from and even stricter than those in the WARN Act. In New York, for instance, companies with fifty or more employees must provide ninety days' notice before any layoff that affects twenty-five or more full-time employees.

SECTION 3

FAMILY AND MEDICAL LEAVE

In 1993, Congress passed the Family and Medical Leave Act (FMLA)[10] to allow employees to take time off work for family or medical reasons. A majority of the states also have legislation allowing for family or medical leave. Many employers voluntarily choose to maintain family-leave plans for their workers. The FMLA does not supersede any state or local law that provides more generous family- or medical-leave protection. Additional categories of FMLA leave were created in 2009 for military caregivers and for qualifying exigencies that arise due to military service.

Coverage and Application

The FMLA requires employers that have fifty or more employees to provide an employee with up to twelve weeks of unpaid family or medical leave during any twelve-month period. The FMLA expressly covers private and public (government) employees who have worked for their employers for at least a year.

An eligible employee may take up to *twelve weeks of leave* within a twelve-month period for any of the following reasons:

1. To care for a newborn baby within one year of birth.
2. To care for an adopted or foster child within one year of the time the child is placed with the employee.
3. To care for the employee's spouse, child, or parent who has a serious health condition.
4. If the employee suffers from a serious health condition and is unable to perform the essential functions of her or his job.
5. For any qualifying exigency (nonmedical emergency) arising out of the fact that the employee's spouse, son, daughter, or parent is a covered military member on active duty.[11] For instance, an employee can take leave to arrange for child care or to deal with financial or legal matters when a spouse is being deployed to Korea.

In addition, an employee may take up to *twenty-six weeks of military caregiver leave* within a twelve-month period to care for a family member with a serious injury or illness incurred as a result of military duty.[12]

Benefits and Protections

When an employee takes FMLA leave, the employer must continue the worker's health-care coverage on the same terms as if the employee had continued to

10. 29 U.S.C. Sections 2601, 2611–2619, 2651–2654.

11. 29 C.F.R. Section 825.126.
12. 29 C.F.R. Section 825.200.

work. On returning from FMLA leave, most employees must be restored to their original position or to a comparable position (with nearly equivalent pay and benefits, for example). An important exception allows the employer to avoid reinstating a *key employee*—defined as an employee whose pay falls within the top 10 percent of the firm's workforce.

Violations

An employer that violates the FMLA can be required to provide various remedies, including the following:

1. Damages to compensate the employee for lost wages and benefits, denied compensation, and actual monetary losses (such as the cost of providing for care of a family member). Compensatory damages are available up to an amount equivalent to the employee's wages for twelve weeks.
2. Job reinstatement.
3. Promotion, if a promotion has been denied.

A successful plaintiff is also entitled to court costs and attorneys' fees. If bad faith on the part of the employer is shown, the plaintiff can receive twice the amount of damages awarded by the judge or jury. Supervisors can also be held personally liable, as employers, for violations of the act.

Employers generally are required to notify employees when an absence will be counted against FMLA leave. If an employer fails to provide such notice, and the employee consequently incurs costs or is otherwise harmed because he or she did not receive notice, the employer may be sanctioned.[13]

SECTION 4

WORKER HEALTH AND SAFETY

Under the common law, employees who were injured on the job had to file lawsuits against their employers to obtain recovery. Today, numerous state and federal statutes protect employees from the risk of accidental injury, death, or disease resulting from their employment.

The Occupational Safety and Health Act

At the federal level, the primary legislation protecting employees' health and safety is the Occupational Safety and Health Act,[14] which is administered by the Occupational Safety and Health Administration (OSHA). The act imposes on employers a general duty to keep the workplace safe.

To this end, OSHA has established specific safety standards that employers must follow depending on the industry. For instance, OSHA regulations require the use of safety guards on certain mechanical equipment and set maximum levels of exposure to substances in the workplace that may be harmful to a worker's health.

NOTICES, RECORDS, AND REPORTS The act requires that employers post certain notices in the workplace, maintain specific records, and submit reports. Employers with eleven or more employees are required to keep occupational injury and illness records for each employee. Each record must be made available for inspection when requested by an OSHA compliance officer.

Whenever a work-related injury or disease occurs, employers must make reports directly to OSHA. If an employee dies or three or more employees are hospitalized because of a work-related incident, the employer must notify OSHA within eight hours. A company that fails to do so will be fined. Following the incident, a complete inspection of the premises is mandatory.

INSPECTIONS OSHA compliance officers may enter and inspect the facilities of any establishment covered by the Occupational Safety and Health Act. Employees may also file complaints of violations. Under the act, an employer cannot discharge an employee who files a complaint or who, in good faith, refuses to work in a high-risk area if bodily harm or death might result.

State Workers' Compensation Laws

State **workers' compensation laws** establish an administrative procedure for compensating workers injured on the job. Instead of suing, an injured worker files a claim with the state agency or board that administers local workers' compensation claims.

Most workers' compensation statutes are similar. No state covers all employees. Typically, domestic workers, agricultural workers, temporary employees, and employees of common carriers (companies that provide transportation services to the public) are excluded, but minors are covered.

13. *Ragsdale v. Wolverine World Wide, Inc.*, 535 U.S. 81, 122 S.Ct. 1155, 152 L.Ed.2d 167 (2002).

14. 29 U.S.C. Sections 553, 651–678.

Usually, the statutes allow employers to purchase insurance from a private insurer or a state fund to pay workers' compensation benefits in the event of a claim. Most states also allow employers to be *self-insured*—that is, employers that show an ability to pay claims do not need to buy insurance.

WORKERS' COMPENSATION REQUIREMENTS In general, the only requirements to recover benefits under state workers' compensation laws are:

1. The existence of an employment relationship.
2. An *accidental* injury that *occurred on the job or in the course of employment,* regardless of fault. (An injury that occurs while an employee is commuting to or from work usually is not covered because it did not occur on the job or in the course of employment.)

An injured employee must notify her or his employer promptly (usually within thirty days of the accident). Generally, an employee must also file a workers' compensation claim within a certain period (sixty days to two years) from the time the injury is first noticed, rather than from the time of the accident.

WORKERS' COMPENSATION VERSUS LITIGATION If an employee accepts workers' compensation benefits, he or she may not sue for injuries caused by the employer's negligence. By barring lawsuits for negligence, workers' compensation laws also prevent employers from avoiding liability by using defenses, such as contributory negligence or assumption of risk. A worker may sue an employer who *intentionally* injures the worker, however.

SECTION 5 INCOME SECURITY

Federal and state governments participate in insurance programs designed to protect employees and their families from the financial impact of retirement, disability, death, hospitalization, and unemployment. The key federal law on this subject is the Social Security Act.[15]

Social Security

The Social Security Act provides for old-age (retirement), survivors', and disability insurance. The act is therefore often referred to as OASDI. Both employers and employees must "contribute" under the Federal Insurance Contributions Act (FICA)[16] to help pay for benefits that will partially make up for the employees' loss of income on retirement.

The basis for the employee's and the employer's contribution is the employee's annual wage base—the maximum amount of the employee's wages that is subject to the tax. The employer withholds the employee's FICA contribution from the employee's wages and then matches this contribution.

The annual wage base is adjusted each year as needed to take into account the rising cost of living. In 2013, employers were required to withhold 6.2 percent of each employee's wages, up to a maximum wage base of $113,700, and to match this contribution.

Retired workers are eligible to receive monthly payments from the Social Security Administration, which administers the Social Security Act. Social Security benefits are fixed by statute but increase automatically with increases in the cost of living.

Medicare

Medicare is a federal government health-insurance program administered by the Social Security Administration for people sixty-five years of age and older and for some under age sixty-five who are disabled. It originally had two parts, one pertaining to hospital costs and the other to nonhospital medical costs, such as visits to physicians' offices.

ADDITIONAL COVERAGE OPTIONS Medicare now offers additional coverage options and a prescription-drug plan. People who have Medicare hospital insurance can obtain additional federal medical insurance if they pay small monthly premiums.

TAX CONTRIBUTIONS Like Social Security, Medicare is funded by "contributions" from the employer and the employee, but there is no cap on the amount of wages subject to the Medicare tax. In 2013, both the employer and the employee were required to pay 1.45 percent of *all* wages and salaries to finance Medicare.

Thus, for Social Security and Medicare together, in 2013 the employer and employee each paid 7.65 percent of the first $113,700 of income (6.2 percent for Social Security + 1.45 percent for Medicare), for a combined total of 15.3 percent. In addition, all wages and salaries above $113,700 were taxed at a

15. 42 U.S.C. Sections 301–1397e.

16. 26 U.S.C. Sections 3101–3125.

combined (employer and employee) rate of 2.9 percent for Medicare.[17] Self-employed persons pay both the employer and the employee portions of the Social Security and Medicare taxes.

In addition, as of 2013, a Medicare tax of 3.8 percent is applied to all investment income for single wage earners making more than $200,000 and married couples making more than $250,000.

Private Pension Plans

The major federal statute that regulates employee retirement plans is the Employee Retirement Income Security Act (ERISA).[18] Its provisions governing employers who have private pension funds for their employees are enforced by the U.S. Department of Labor.

ERISA created the Pension Benefit Guaranty Corporation (PBGC), an independent federal agency, to provide timely and uninterrupted payment of voluntary private pension benefits. The pension plans pay annual insurance premiums (at set rates adjusted for inflation) to the PBGC, which then pays benefits to participants in the event that a plan is unable to do so.

ERISA does *not* require an employer to establish a pension plan. When a plan exists, however, ERISA provides standards for its management. ERISA also imposes detailed record-keeping and reporting requirements.

VESTING A key provision of ERISA concerns vesting. **Vesting** gives an employee a legal right to receive pension benefits at some future date when she or he stops working. Before ERISA was enacted, some employees who had worked for companies for as long as thirty years received no pension benefits when their employment terminated because those benefits had not vested.

ERISA establishes complex vesting rules. Generally, however, all of an employee's contributions to a pension plan vest immediately, and the employee's rights to the employer's contributions vest after five years of employment.

INVESTMENT OF PENSION FUNDS In an attempt to prevent mismanagement of pension funds, ERISA established rules on how they must be invested. Managers must choose investments cautiously and must diversify the plan's investments to minimize the risk of large losses.

17. As a result of the Health Care and Education Reconciliation Act of 2010, Medicare tax rates will rise, and the applicable compensation base will include more than just salary incomes.

18. 29 U.S.C. Sections 1001 *et seq.*

Unemployment Insurance

The Federal Unemployment Tax Act (FUTA)[19] created a state-administered system that provides unemployment compensation to eligible individuals who have lost their jobs. The FUTA and state laws require employers that fall under the provisions of the act to pay unemployment taxes at regular intervals. The proceeds from these taxes are then paid out to qualified unemployed workers.

To be eligible for unemployment compensation, a worker must be willing and able to work. Workers who have been fired for misconduct or who have voluntarily left their jobs are not eligible for benefits. Normally, workers must be actively seeking employment to continue receiving benefits. Temporary measures recently enacted in response to persistent high unemployment rates also allow some jobless persons to retain unemployment benefits while pursuing additional education and training.

COBRA

Federal law also enables employees to continue health-care coverage after their jobs have been terminated and they are no longer eligible for group health-insurance plans. The Consolidated Omnibus Budget Reconciliation Act (COBRA)[20] prohibits an employer from eliminating a worker's medical, vision, or dental insurance on the voluntary or involuntary termination of the worker's employment.

Employers, with some exceptions, must inform employees of COBRA's provisions when they face termination or a reduction of hours that would affect their eligibility for coverage under the plan. Only workers fired for gross misconduct are excluded. An employer that does not comply with COBRA risks substantial penalties, such as a tax of up to 10 percent of the annual cost of the group plan or $500,000, whichever is less.

PROCEDURES A worker has sixty days (from the date that the group coverage would stop) to decide whether to continue with the employer's group insurance plan. If the worker chooses to discontinue the coverage, the employer has no further obligation.

If the worker chooses to continue coverage, the employer is obligated to keep the policy active for up to eighteen months (twenty-nine months if the worker is disabled). The coverage must be the same as that provided to the worker prior to the termination

19. 26 U.S.C. Sections 3301–3310.

20. 29 U.S.C. Sections 1161–1169.

or reduction of work. If family members were originally included, COBRA prohibits their exclusion.

PAYMENT Generally, an employer can require the employee to pay all of the premiums, plus a 2 percent administrative charge. If the worker fails to pay the premiums, becomes eligible for Medicare, or obtains coverage under another plan (or if the employer completely eliminates its group plan), the employer is relieved of further responsibility.

Employer-Sponsored Group Health Plans

The Health Insurance Portability and Accountability Act (HIPAA),[21] discussed in Chapter 5, also affects employer-sponsored group health plans. HIPAA does not require employers to provide health insurance, but it does establish requirements for those that do. Under HIPAA, employers must give credit to employees for previous health coverage (including COBRA coverage) to decrease any waiting period before their coverage becomes effective.

In addition, HIPAA restricts the manner in which employers collect, use, and disclose the health information of employees and their families. Employers must train employees, designate privacy officials, and distribute privacy notices to ensure that employees' health information is not disclosed to unauthorized parties.

Failure to comply with HIPAA regulations can result in civil penalties of up to $100 per person per violation (with a cap of $25,000 per year). The employer is also subject to criminal prosecution for certain types of HIPAA violations and can face up to $250,000 in criminal fines and imprisonment for up to ten years if convicted.

Affordable Care Act

Under the Affordable Care Act[22] (ACA, commonly referred to as Obamacare), most employers with fifty or more full-time employees are required to offer health-insurance benefits. There is no requirement to provide health benefits if fewer than fifty people are employed. Any business offering health benefits to its employees (even if not legally required to do so) may be eligible for tax credits of up to 35 percent to offset the costs.

An employer who fails to provide health benefits as required under the statute can be fined up to $2,000 for each employee after the first thirty people. (This is known as the 50/30 rule: employers with fifty employees must provide insurance, and those failing to do so will be fined for each employee after the first thirty.) An employer who offers a plan that costs an employee more than 9.5 percent of the employee's income may receive a penalty of $3,000.

Employers will be fined for failing to provide benefits only if one of their employees receives a federal subsidy to buy health insurance through a health-insurance exchange. The act provided for these exchanges to establish marketplaces where business owners and individuals can compare premiums and purchase policies.

SECTION 6

EMPLOYEE PRIVACY RIGHTS

In the last thirty years, concerns about the privacy rights of employees have arisen as employers purportedly use invasive tactics to monitor and screen workers. Perhaps the greatest privacy concern in employment today involves electronic monitoring of employees' activities.

Electronic Monitoring

More than half of employers engage in some form of electronic monitoring of their employees. Many employers review employees' e-mail, blogs, instant messages, and tweets, as well as their social media, smartphone, and Internet use. Employers may also video their employees at work, record and listen to their telephone conversations and voice mail, and read their text messages and social media posts.

EMPLOYEE PRIVACY PROTECTION Employees of private (nongovernment) employers have some privacy protection under tort law (see Chapter 12) and state constitutions. In addition, state and federal statutes may limit an employer's conduct in certain respects. For instance, as discussed in Chapter 15, the Electronic Communications Privacy Act prohibits employers from intercepting an employee's personal electronic communications unless they are made on devices and systems furnished by the employer. Nonetheless, employers do have considerable leeway to monitor employees in the workplace.

21. 29 U.S.C. Sections 1181 *et seq.*

22. Pub. L. No. 111-148, 124 Stat. 119, March 23, 2010, codified in various sections of 42 U.S.C.

Private employers generally are free to use filtering software (discussed in Chapter 5) to block access to certain Web sites, such as sites containing sexually explicit images. The First Amendment's protection of free speech prevents only *government employers* from restraining speech by blocking Web sites.

WAS THERE A REASONABLE EXPECTATION OF PRIVACY? When determining whether an employer should be held liable for violating an employee's privacy rights, the courts generally weigh the employer's interests against the employee's reasonable expectation of privacy. Normally, if employees have been informed that their communications are being monitored, they cannot reasonably expect those interactions to be private. Also, if the employer provided the e-mail system or blog that the employee used for communications, a court will typically hold that the employee did not have a reasonable expectation of privacy.

If employees are *not* informed that certain communications are being monitored, however, the employer may be held liable for invading their privacy. Most employers that engage in electronic monitoring notify their employees about the monitoring. Nevertheless, a general policy may not sufficiently protect an employer who monitors forms of communications that the policy fails to mention. For instance, notifying employees that their e-mails and phone calls may be monitored does not necessarily protect an employer who monitors social media posts or text messages.

Other Types of Monitoring

In addition to monitoring their employees' online activities, employers also engage in other types of employee screening and monitoring. The practices discussed next have often been challenged as violations of employee privacy rights.

LIE-DETECTOR TESTS At one time, many employers required employees or job applicants to take polygraph examinations (lie-detector tests). Today, the Employee Polygraph Protection Act[23] generally prohibits employers from requiring employees or job applicants to take lie-detector tests or suggesting or requesting that they do so. The act also restricts employers' ability to use or ask about the results of any lie-detector test or to take any negative employment action based on the results.

Certain employers are exempt from these prohibitions. Federal, state, and local government employers, and certain security service firms, may conduct polygraph tests. In addition, companies that manufacture and distribute controlled substances may perform lie-detector tests. Other employers may use polygraph tests when investigating losses attributable to theft, including embezzlement and the theft of trade secrets.

DRUG TESTING In the interests of public safety and to reduce unnecessary costs, many employers, including the government, require their employees to submit to drug testing.

Public Employers. Government (public) employers are constrained in drug testing by the Fourth Amendment to the U.S. Constitution, which prohibits unreasonable searches and seizures (see Chapter 5). Drug testing of public employees is allowed by statute for transportation workers. Courts normally uphold drug testing of certain employees when drug use in a particular job may threaten public safety. Also, when there is a reasonable basis for suspecting public employees of drug use, courts often find that drug testing does not violate the Fourth Amendment.

Private Employers. The Fourth Amendment does not apply to drug testing conducted by private employers. Hence, the privacy rights and drug testing of private-sector employees are governed by state law, which varies from state to state. Many states have statutes that allow drug testing by private employers but put restrictions on when and how the testing may be performed. A collective bargaining agreement (to be discussed in Chapter 23) may also provide protection against (or authorize) drug testing.

The permissibility of a private employee's drug test often hinges on whether the employer's testing was reasonable. Random drug tests and even "zero-tolerance" policies (which deny a "second chance" to employees who test positive for drugs) have been held to be reasonable.[24]

Many workers at U.S. government facilities are employees of private contractors, not of the government. Until recently, these workers generally were not subject to the drug testing and background checks that are applied to federal government employees. In the following case, several contract workers claimed that their privacy rights had been violated by new standards that required them to submit to background checks.

23. 29 U.S.C. Sections 2001 *et seq.*

24. See *CITGO Asphalt Refining Co. v. Paper, Allied-Industrial, Chemical, and Energy Workers International Union Local No. 2-991*, 385 F.3d 809 (3d Cir. 2004).

CASE 21.3

National Aeronautics and Space Administration v. Nelson

Supreme Court of the United States, __ U.S. __, 131 S.Ct. 746, 178 L.Ed.2d 667 (2011).

COMPANY PROFILE The National Aeronautics and Space Administration (NASA) is an independent federal agency charged with planning and conducting "space activities." One of NASA's facilities is the Jet Propulsion Laboratory (JPL), which develops and runs most U.S. unmanned space missions—from the Explorer 1 satellite in 1958 to the Mars rovers of this century. The JPL is owned by NASA but is operated by the California Institute of Technology and is staffed exclusively by contract employees.

BACKGROUND AND FACTS In 2007, under newly implemented standards, contract employees with long-term access to federal facilities were ordered to complete a standard background check. The National Agency Check with Inquiries (NACI) performs background checks for the government. The NACI is designed to obtain information on such issues as counseling and treatment, as well as mental and financial stability. Robert Nelson and other JPL employees filed a lawsuit in a federal district court against NASA, claiming that the NACI violated their privacy rights. The court denied the plaintiffs' request to prohibit use of the NACI, but the U.S. Court of Appeals for the Ninth Circuit reversed this decision. NASA appealed to the United States Supreme Court, arguing that the Privacy Act of 1974 provides sufficient protection for employees' privacy. This act allows the government to retain information only for "relevant and necessary" purposes, requires written consent before the information may be disclosed, and imposes criminal liability for violations.

IN THE LANGUAGE OF THE COURT
Justice *ALITO* delivered the opinion of the Court.

Respondents in this case, federal contract employees at a Government laboratory, claim that two parts of a standard employment background investigation violate their rights * * * . Respondents challenge a section of a form questionnaire that asks employees about treatment or counseling for recent illegal-drug use. They also object to certain open-ended questions on a form sent to employees' designated references.

* * * *

*We will assume for present purposes that the Government's challenged inquiries implicate a privacy interest of constitutional significance. We hold, however, that, whatever the scope of this interest, it does not prevent the Government from asking reasonable questions * * * in an employment background investigation that is subject to the Privacy Act's safeguards against public disclosure.* [Emphasis added.]

* * * *

* * * The questions challenged by respondents are part of a standard employment background check of the sort used by millions of private employers. The Government itself has been conducting employment investigations since the earliest days of the Republic. Since 1871, the President has enjoyed statutory authority to ascertain the fitness of applicants for the civil service as to age, health, character, knowledge and ability for the employment sought and that [statute] appears to have been regarded as a codification of established practice. Standard background investigations similar to those at issue here became mandatory for all candidates for the federal civil service in 1953. And the particular investigations challenged in this case arose from a decision to extend that requirement to federal contract employees requiring long-term access to federal facilities.

As this long history suggests, the Government has an interest in conducting basic employment background checks. Reasonable investigations of applicants and employees aid the Government in ensuring the security of its facilities and in employing a competent, reliable workforce.

DECISION AND REMEDY *The United States Supreme Court reversed the judgment of the lower court and remanded the case. The NACI does not violate an individual's right to privacy because its inquiries are reasonable and the Privacy Act protects against the disclosure of private information.*

CASE 21.3 CONTINUES ➧

CASE 21.3 CONTINUED

WHAT IF THE FACTS WERE DIFFERENT? *Suppose that after the decision in this case, a JPL employee refused to cooperate in an NACI background check. What would be the most likely consequences?*

THE LEGAL ENVIRONMENT DIMENSION *The U.S. Constitution does not explicitly mention a general right to privacy. From what sources does the Court infer this right? (Hint: See the section on "Privacy Rights" in Chapter 5.)*

GENETIC TESTING A serious privacy issue arose when some employers began conducting genetic testing of employees or prospective employees in an effort to identify individuals who might develop significant health problems in the future. To prevent the improper use of genetic information by employers and health-insurance providers, in 2008 Congress passed the Genetic Information Nondiscrimination Act (GINA).[25]

Under GINA, employers cannot make decisions about hiring, firing, job placement, or promotion based on the results of genetic testing. GINA also prohibits group health plans and insurers from denying coverage or charging higher premiums based solely on a genetic predisposition to develop a disease in the future.

25. 26 U.S.C. Section 9834; 42 U.S.C. Sections 300gg-53, 1320d-9, 2000ff-1 to 2000ff-11.

Reviewing: Employment Relationships

Rick Saldona began working as a traveling salesperson for Aimer Winery in 2008. Sales constituted 90 percent of Saldona's work time. Saldona worked an average of fifty hours per week but received no overtime pay. In June 2014, Saldona's new supervisor, Caesar Braxton, claimed that Saldona had been inflating his reported sales calls and required Saldona to submit to a polygraph test. Saldona reported Braxton to the U.S. Department of Labor, which prohibited Aimer from requiring Saldona to take a polygraph test for this purpose.

In August 2014, Saldona's wife, Venita, fell from a ladder and sustained a head injury while employed as a full-time agricultural harvester. Saldona presented Aimer's Human Resources Department with a letter from his wife's physician indicating that she would need daily care for several months, and Saldona took leave until December 2014. Aimer had sixty-three employees at that time. When Saldona returned to Aimer, he was informed that his position had been eliminated because his sales territory had been combined with an adjacent territory. Using the information presented in the chapter, answer the following questions.

1. Would Saldona have been legally entitled to receive overtime pay at a higher rate? Why or why not?
2. What is the maximum length of time Saldona would have been allowed to take leave to care for his injured spouse?
3. Under what circumstances would Aimer have been allowed to require an employee to take a polygraph test?
4. Would Aimer likely be able to avoid reinstating Saldona under the *key employee* exception? Why or why not?

DEBATE THIS . . . *The U.S. labor market is highly competitive, so state and federal laws that require overtime pay are unnecessary and should be abolished.*

Terms and Concepts

employment at will 490
minimum wage 494
vesting 498
whistleblowing 492
workers' compensation law 496
wrongful discharge 493

ExamPrep

Issue Spotters

1. American Manufacturing Company (AMC) issues an employee handbook that states that employees will be discharged only for good cause. One day, Greg, an AMC supervisor, says to Larry, "I don't like your looks. You're fired." Can AMC be held liable for breach of contract? If so, why? If not, why? **(See page 490.)**
2. Erin, an employee of Fine Print Shop, is injured on the job. For Erin to obtain workers' compensation, does her injury have to have been caused by Fine Print's negligence? Does it matter whether the action causing the injury was intentional? Explain. **(See page 496.)**

- **Check your answers to the Issue Spotters against the answers provided in Appendix E at the end of this text.**

Before the Test

Go to **www.cengagebrain.com**, enter the ISBN 9781285428949, and click on "Find" to locate this textbook's Web site. Then, click on "Access Now" under "Study Tools," and select Chapter 21 at the top. There, you will find an Interactive Quiz that you can take to assess your mastery of the concepts in this chapter, as well as Flashcards and a Glossary of important terms.

Business Scenarios

21–1. Wrongful Discharge. Denton and Carlo were employed at an appliance plant. Their job required them to perform occasional maintenance work while standing on a wire mesh twenty feet above the plant floor. Other employees had fallen through the mesh, and one of them had been killed by the fall. When their supervisor told them to perform tasks that would likely involve walking on the mesh, Denton and Carlo refused because they feared they might suffer bodily injury or death. Because they refused to do the requested work, the two employees were fired from their jobs. Was their discharge wrongful? If so, under what federal employment law? To what federal agency or department should they turn for assistance? **(See page 493.)**

21–2. Family and Medical Leave Act. Serge worked for Service Attendant Corporation (SAC). He requested time off under the Family and Medical Leave Act (FMLA) from April 29 through May 31 to undergo treatment for alcoholism. For the month of May, he was hospitalized as part of the treatment. When he did not return to work on June 1, SAC fired him. Did SAC violate Serge's rights under the FMLA? Explain your answer. **(See page 495.)**

Business Case Problems

21–3. Spotlight on Coca Cola—Family and Medical Leave Act.

Jennifer Willis worked for Coca Cola Enterprises, Inc. (CCE), in Louisiana as a senior account manager. On a Monday in May 2003, Willis called her supervisor to tell him that she was sick and would not be able to work that day. She also said that she was pregnant, but she did not say she was sick because of the pregnancy. On Tuesday, she called to ask where to report to work and was told that she could not return without a doctor's release. She said that she had a doctor's appointment on "Wednesday," which her supervisor understood to be the next day. Willis meant the following Wednesday. For more than a week, Willis did not contact CCE. When she returned to work, she was told that she had violated CCE's "No Call/No Show" policy. Under this policy "an employee absent from work for three consecutive days without notifying the supervisor during that period will be considered to have voluntarily resigned." She was fired. Willis filed a suit in a federal district court against CCE under the Family and Medical Leave Act (FMLA). To be eligible for FMLA leave, an employee must inform an employer of the reason for the leave. Did Willis meet this requirement? Did CCE's response to Willis's absence violate the FMLA? Explain. [*Willis v. Coca Cola Enterprises, Inc.*, 445 F.3d 413 (5th Cir. 2006)] **(See page 495.)**

21–4. Minimum Wage. Misty Cumbie worked as a waitress at the Vita Café in Portland, Oregon. The café was owned and operated by Woody Woo, Inc. Woody Woo paid its servers an hourly wage that was higher than the state's minimum wage, but the servers were required to contribute their tips to a "tip pool." Approximately one-third of the tip-pool funds went to the servers, and the rest was distributed to kitchen staff members, who otherwise rarely received tips for their services. Did this tip-pooling arrangement violate the minimum wage provisions of the Fair Labor Standards Act? Explain. [*Cumbie v. Woody Woo, Inc.*, 596 F.3d 577 (9th Cir. 2010)] **(See page 494.)**

21–5. BUSINESS CASE PROBLEM WITH SAMPLE ANSWER: Workers' Compensation.

As a safety measure, Dynea USA, Inc., required an employee, Tony Fairbanks, to wear steel-toed boots. One of the boots caused a sore on Fairbanks's leg. The skin over the sore broke, and within a week, Fairbanks was hospitalized with a methicillin-resistant staphylococcus aureus (MRSA) infection. He filed a

*workers' compensation claim. Dynea argued that the MRSA bacteria that caused the infection had been on Fairbanks's skin before he came to work. What are the requirements to recover workers' compensation benefits? Does this claim qualify? Explain. [*Dynea USA, Inc. v. Fairbanks, *241 Or.App. 311, 250 P.3d 389 (2011)]* **(See page 496.)**

- **For a sample answer to Problem 21–5, go to Appendix F at the end of this text.**

21–6. Exceptions to the Employment-at-Will Doctrine. Li Li worked for Packard Bioscience, and Mark Schmeizl was her supervisor. In March 2000, Schmeizl told Li to call Packard's competitors, pretend to be a potential customer, and request "pricing information and literature." Li refused to perform the assignment. She told Schmeizl that she thought the work was illegal and recommended that he contact Packard's legal department. Although a lawyer recommended against the practice, Schmeizl insisted that Li perform the calls. Moreover, he later wrote negative performance reviews because she was unable to get the requested information when she called competitors and identified herself as a Packard employee. On June 1, 2000, Li was terminated on Schmeizl's recommendation. Can Li bring a claim for wrongful discharge? Why or why not? [*Li v. Canberra Industries,* 39 A.3d 789 (Conn.App. 2012)] **(See page 490.)**

21–7. A QUESTION OF ETHICS: Workers' Compensation Law.

*In 1999, after working for Atchison Leather Products, Inc., in Kansas for ten years, Beverly Tull began to complain of hand, wrist, and shoulder pain. Atchison recommended that she contact a certain physician, who in April 2000 diagnosed the condition as carpal tunnel syndrome "severe enough" for surgery. In August, Tull filed a claim with the state workers' compensation board. Because Atchison changed workers' compensation insurance companies every year, a dispute arose as to which company should pay Tull's claim. Fearing liability, no insurer would authorize treatment, and Tull was forced to delay surgery until December. The board granted her temporary total disability benefits for the subsequent six weeks that she missed work. On April 23, 2002, Berger Co. bought Atchison. The new employer adjusted Tull's work so that it was less demanding and stressful, but she continued to suffer pain. In July, a physician diagnosed her condition as permanent. The board granted her permanent partial disability benefits. By May 2005, the bickering over the financial responsibility for Tull's claim involved five insurers—four of which had each covered Atchison for a single year and one of which covered Berger. [*Tull v. Atchison Leather Products, Inc., *37 Kan.App.2d 87, 150 P.3d 316 (2007)]* **(See page 496.)**

(a) When an injured employee files a claim for workers' compensation, a proceeding is held to assess the injury and determine the amount of compensation. Should a dispute between insurers over the payment of the claim be resolved in the same proceeding? Why or why not?

(b) The board designated April 23, 2002, as the date of Tull's injury. What is the reason for determining the date of a worker's injury? Should the board in this case have selected this date or a different date? Why?

(c) How should the board assess liability for the payment of Tull's medical expenses and disability benefits? Would it be appropriate to impose joint and several liability on the insurers (holding each of them responsible for the full amount of damages), or should the individual liability of each of them be determined? Explain.

Legal Reasoning Group Activity

21–8. Wrongful Discharge. Stefan Sorril, a health teacher at Madison Middle School and a triathlete, appeared shirtless and showed off his "ripped" body as an extra on an episode of a new reality TV show. A week after the show aired, school officials called him into the district office and asked for his resignation. Sorril later claimed that he was pressured and coerced into resigning. He said the school officials had informed him that—as a result of his appearance on the show—he would no longer be offered tenure (a senior academic's contractual right not to be terminated without just cause). Sorril subsequently sued for wrongful discharge. **(See page 493.)**

(a) The first group will discuss whether Sorril was an employee at will and how that status would affect his claim.

(b) The second group will determine if Sorril can assert any of the exceptions to the employment-at-will doctrine.

(c) The third group will decide whether the school district should be held liable for wrongful discharge, and explain their reasoning.

CHAPTER 22
EMPLOYMENT DISCRIMINATION

Out of the 1960s civil rights movement to end racial and other forms of discrimination grew a body of law protecting employees against discrimination in the workplace. Legislation, judicial decisions, and administrative agency actions restrict employers from discriminating against workers on the basis of race, color, religion, national origin, gender, age, or disability. A class of persons defined by one or more of these criteria is known as a **protected class.**

Several federal statutes prohibit **employment discrimination** against members of protected classes. The most important statute is Title VII of the Civil Rights Act of 1964.[1] Title VII prohibits employment discrimination on the basis of race, color, religion, national origin, and gender. The Age Discrimination in Employment Act of 1967[2] and the Americans with Disabilities Act of 1990[3] prohibit discrimination on the basis of age and disability, respectively. The protections afforded under these laws also extend to U.S. citizens who are working abroad for U.S. firms or for companies that are controlled by U.S. firms (see Chapter 8).

This chapter focuses on the kinds of discrimination prohibited by these federal statutes. Note, however, that discrimination against employees on the basis of any of the above-mentioned criteria may also violate state human rights statutes or other state laws prohibiting discrimination. By encouraging employment of members of protected classes, these laws also promote diversity in the workplace.

1. 42 U.S.C. Sections 2000e–2000e-17.
2. 29 U.S.C. Sections 621–634.
3. 42 U.S.C. Sections 12102–12118.

SECTION 1

TITLE VII OF THE CIVIL RIGHTS ACT OF 1964

Title VII of the Civil Rights Act of 1964 and its amendments prohibit job discrimination against employees, applicants, and union members on the basis of race, color, national origin, religion, and gender at any stage of employment. It prohibits discrimination in the hiring process, discipline procedures, discharge, promotion, and benefits.

Title VII applies to employers with fifteen or more employees, labor unions with fifteen or more members, labor unions that operate hiring halls (to which members go regularly to be assigned jobs as they become available), employment agencies, and state and local governing units or agencies. The United States Supreme Court has ruled that an employer with fewer than fifteen employees is not automatically shielded from a lawsuit filed under Title VII.[4] In addition, the act prohibits discrimination in most federal government employment. When Title VII applies to the employer, any employee—including an undocumented (alien) worker—can bring an action for employment discrimination.

The Equal Employment Opportunity Commission

The Equal Employment Opportunity Commission (EEOC) monitors compliance with Title VII. An employee alleging discrimination must file a claim with the EEOC before a lawsuit can be brought against the employer. The EEOC may investigate the dispute and attempt to obtain the parties' voluntary consent to an out-of-court settlement. If a voluntary

4. *Arbaugh v. Y&H Corp.*, 546 U.S. 500, 126 S.Ct. 1235, 163 L.Ed.2d 1097 (2006).

agreement cannot be reached, the EEOC may file a suit against the employer on the employee's behalf.

The EEOC does not investigate every claim of employment discrimination. Generally, it takes only "priority cases," such as cases that affect many workers and those involving retaliatory discharge (firing an employee in retaliation for submitting a claim to the EEOC). If the EEOC decides not to investigate a claim, the employee may bring his or her own lawsuit against the employer.

Limitations on Class Actions

In 2011, the United States Supreme Court limited the rights of employees to bring discrimination claims against their employer as a group, or class. The decision did not affect the rights of individual employees to sue under Title VII, however.

▶ **Case in Point 22.1** A group of female employees sued Wal-Mart, the nation's largest private employer. The employees alleged that store managers who had discretion over pay and promotions were biased against women and disproportionately favored men. The Supreme Court ruled in favor of Wal-Mart, effectively blocking the class action (a lawsuit in which a small number of plaintiffs sue on behalf of a larger group). The Court held that the women had failed to prove a company-wide policy of discrimination that had a common effect on all women included in the class. Therefore, they could not maintain a class action.[5] ◀

Intentional and Unintentional Discrimination

Title VII of the Civil Rights Act of 1964 prohibits both intentional and unintentional discrimination.

5. *Wal-Mart Stores, Inc. v. Dukes*, ___ U.S. ___, 131 S.Ct. 2541, 180 L.Ed.2d 374 (2011).

INTENTIONAL DISCRIMINATION Intentional discrimination by an employer against an employee is known as **disparate-treatment discrimination.** Because intent may sometimes be difficult to prove, courts have established certain procedures for resolving disparate-treatment cases.

▶ **Example 22.2** Samantha applies for employment with a construction firm and is rejected. If she sues on the basis of disparate-treatment discrimination in hiring, she must show that:

1. She is a member of a protected class.
2. She applied and was qualified for the job in question.
3. She was rejected by the employer.
4. The employer continued to seek applicants for the position or filled the position with a person not in a protected class.

If Samantha can meet these relatively easy requirements, she has made out a ***prima facie* case** of illegal discrimination. This means that she has met her initial burden of proof and will win unless the employer can present a legally acceptable defense. (Defenses to claims of employment discrimination will be discussed later in this chapter.)

The burden then shifts to the employer-defendant, who must articulate a legal reason for not hiring the plaintiff. For instance, the employer might say that Samantha was not hired because she lacked sufficient experience or training. To prevail, the plaintiff must then show that the employer's reason is a *pretext* (not the true reason) and that discriminatory intent actually motivated the employer's decision. ◀

In the following case, the trial court assumed that the plaintiff had established a *prima facie* case of discrimination before considering the defendant's evidence of a nondiscriminatory reason for its decision to discharge the plaintiff. The reviewing court had to consider whether to uphold the trial court's finding.

CASE ANALYSIS

Case 22.1 Dees v. United Rentals North America, Inc.

United States Court of Appeals, Ninth Circuit, 2013 WL 28405 (2013).

COMPANY PROFILE *United Rentals North America, Inc., rents, sells, and services equipment for underground construction, temporary power, climate control, disaster recovery, and more. Since its founding in 1997, United Rentals has grown to become the world's largest rental equipment provider, with more than $7 billion of inventory available at more than 830 locations and online. The company's customer base includes construction and industrial companies, government agencies, local governments, and individual homeowners.*

CASE 22.1 CONTINUED

IN THE LANGUAGE OF THE COURT

PER CURIAM. [By the Whole Court]

* * * *

In * * * 2006 [Ellis Dees, an African American, applied] to United Rentals for employment at its Gulfport, Mississippi location, and was offered a service technician position in St. Rose, Louisiana. Branch Manager Mike Sauve made the decision to make the offer, which Dees accepted.

Although the first two years of Dees' employment in St. Rose went smoothly, United Rentals contends that his attitude and work performance deteriorated beginning in 2009. Specifically, it alleges that he began, with increasing frequency, to mark equipment as fit to be rented even though it was not in working order. Dees' managers—Sauve and Lee Vincent—coached him when these incidents occurred, and noted them in his 2009 mid-year and full-year performance reviews. Dees was also given written warnings in August 2009, October 2009, February 2010, and March 2010. Dees was given a "final written warning" on March 4, 2010, advising him that "the next incident will result in immediate termination." Following a further incident six days later, Sauve and Vincent told Dees that he was fired. Dees was sixty-two years old at the time.

Dees filed a charge with the Equal Employment Opportunity Commission, alleging employment discrimination based on his race and age [in violation of Title VII of the Civil Rights Act and the Age Discrimination in Employment Act (ADEA)]. After receiving a "right to sue" notice, he filed suit in [a federal district court]. United Rentals filed a motion for summary judgment, which the district court granted * * * . Dees timely appealed.

* * * *

* * * [Under Title VII or the ADEA] Dees first must make a *prima facie* case of discrimination based on age or race. To establish a *prima facie* case, Dees must show that he: (1) was a member of a protected group; (2) qualified for the position in question; (3) was subjected to an adverse employment action; and (4) received less favorable treatment due to his membership in the protected class than did other similarly situated employees who were not members of the protected class, under nearly identical circumstances.

If Dees makes a prima facie *case, the burden then shifts to United Rentals to articulate a legitimate, nondiscriminatory reason for firing him.* If it does so, Dees must, as to his Title VII claim, offer sufficient evidence to create a genuine issue of material fact either (1) that United Rentals' reason is not true, but is instead a pretext for discrimination * * * ; or (2) that United Rentals' reason, while true, is only one of the reasons for its conduct, and another motivating factor is Dees' protected characteristic. [Emphasis added.]

* * * *

The district court assumed, without deciding, that Dees established a *prima facie* case of discrimination under Title VII and the ADEA. The district court * * * determined that United Rentals had provided extensive evidence of a legitimate, non-discriminatory reason for Dees' termination—namely, unsatisfactory job performance. * * * The burden shifted back to Dees to produce evidence that United Rentals' reason was a pretext for discrimination. The district court concluded that Dees had only made conclusory [conclusive] allegations that he was discriminated against.

* * * *

His termination notice states that he was terminated for failing to follow United Rentals' policy of ensuring that the batteries in rental equipment were in good working order prior to delivery of the equipment.

* * * Dees has presented nothing to tie United Rentals' final termination decision to a discriminatory motive. * * * Dees himself describes United Rentals as motivated by an "I ain't missing no rents" philosophy that encouraged renting out equipment regardless of its readiness. No evidence shows that United Rentals' philosophy also included discriminating against African Americans or senior workers. Similarly, no evidence demonstrates that United Rentals' decision to discharge Dees was motivated by his race or age. * * * Dees' subjective belief that United Rentals discriminated against him is clearly insufficient to demonstrate pretext.

* * * *

For the reasons set forth above, we AFFIRM the district court's grant of summary judgment in United Rentals' favor.

LEGAL REASONING QUESTIONS

1. How did the court treat Dees's attempt to establish a *prima facie* case of employment discrimination?
2. On what did both the trial court and the appellate court focus their analysis?
3. What did the plaintiff fail to do in submitting his side of the case? How did this failure affect his claims?
4. If Dees had been laid off due to a reduction in force of all workers whose performance did not meet the defendant's standards, would the result in this case have been different? Explain.

UNINTENTIONAL DISCRIMINATION Employers often use interviews and tests to choose from among a large number of applicants for job openings. Minimum educational requirements are also common. Some employer practices, such as those involving educational requirements, may have an unintended discriminatory impact on a protected class.

Disparate-impact discrimination occurs when a protected group of people is adversely affected by an employer's practices, procedures, or tests, even though they do not appear to be discriminatory. In a disparate-impact discrimination case, the complaining party must first show statistically (using the methods discussed next) that the employer's practices, procedures, or tests are discriminatory in effect. Once the plaintiff has made out a *prima facie* case, the burden of proof shifts to the employer to show that the practices or procedures in question were justified.

There are two ways of proving that disparate-impact discrimination exists.

Pool of Applicants. A plaintiff can prove a disparate impact by comparing the employer's workforce to the pool of qualified individuals available in the local labor market. The plaintiff must show that (1) as a result of educational or other job requirements or hiring procedures, (2) the percentage of nonwhites, women, or members of other protected classes in the employer's workforce (3) does not reflect the percentage of that group in the pool of qualified applicants. If the plaintiff can show a connection between the practice and the disparity, he or she has made out a *prima facie* case and need not provide evidence of discriminatory intent.

Rate of Hiring. A plaintiff can also prove disparate-impact discrimination by comparing the *selection rates* of whites and nonwhites (or members of another protected class), regardless of the racial balance in the employer's workforce. When an educational or other job requirement or hiring procedure excludes members of a protected class from an employer's workforce at a substantially higher rate than for nonmembers, discrimination occurs.

Under EEOC guidelines, a selection rate for a protected class that is less than four-fifths, or 80 percent, of the rate for the group with the highest rate of hiring generally will be regarded as evidence of disparate impact. ▶ **Example 22.3** One hundred white applicants take an employment test, and fifty pass the test and are hired. One hundred minority group applicants take the test, and twenty pass the employment test and are hired. Because twenty is less than four-fifths (80 percent) of fifty, the test would be considered discriminatory under the EEOC guidelines. ◀

Discrimination Based on Race, Color, and National Origin

Title VII prohibits employers from discriminating against employees or job applicants on the basis of race, color, or national origin. Race is interpreted broadly to apply to the ancestry or ethnic characteristics of a group of persons, such as Native Americans. National origin refers to discrimination based on a person's birth in another country or his or her ancestry or culture, such as Hispanic. (For a discussion of whether employers can legally discriminate against employees based on their appearance, see this chapter's *Insight into Ethics* on the facing page.)

If an employer's standards or policies for selecting or promoting employees have a discriminatory effect on employees or job applicants in these protected classes, then a presumption of illegal discrimination arises. To avoid liability, the employer must show that its standards or policies have a substantial, demonstrable relationship to realistic qualifications for the job in question.

▶ **Case in Point 22.4** Jiann Min Chang was an instructor at Alabama Agricultural and Mechanical University (AAMU). When AAMU terminated his employment, Chang filed a lawsuit claiming discrimination based on national origin. Chang established a *prima facie* case because he (1) was a member of a protected class, (2) was qualified for the job, (3) suffered an adverse employment action, and (4) was replaced by someone outside his protected class (a non-Asian instructor). When the burden of proof shifted to the employer, however, AAMU showed that Chang had argued with a vice president and refused to comply with her instructions. The court ruled that the university had not renewed Chang's contract for a legitimate reason—insubordination—and therefore was not liable for unlawful discrimination.[6] ◀

REVERSE DISCRIMINATION Note that Title VII also protects against *reverse discrimination*—that is, discrimination against majority group individuals, such as white males. ▶ **Case in Point 22.5** An African American woman fired four white men from their

6. *Jiann Min Chang v. Alabama Agricultural and Mechanical University*, 2009 WL 3403180 (11th Cir. 2009).

INSIGHT INTO ETHICS
Appearance-Based Discrimination

Research has shown that short men make statistically less income than tall men. It has also shown that compared with attractive individuals, less attractive people generally receive poorer performance reviews, lower salaries, and smaller damages awards if they win lawsuits. Should something be done about this?

Can "Lookism" Be Prohibited?

Although there is certainly evidence that appearance-based discrimination exists in the workplace and elsewhere, it is not so clear that it can be prohibited. In the 1970s, Michigan decided to do something about "lookism" and passed a law barring various kinds of appearance-based discrimination.[a] Whether because of the cost or the difficulty of proving this type of discrimination, however, only a few lawsuits based on the law have been filed each year. At least six cities have similar laws, but these laws also have not given rise to many lawsuits.

Federal and state laws prohibit discrimination against people who are clinically obese, but discrimination against those who are merely overweight is usually not illegal. Given that one study found that more than 40 percent of overweight women felt stigmatized by their employers, this remains a serious problem.

a. Michigan Compiled Laws Section 37.2202.

A Double Standard for Grooming

Women sometimes complain that they are held to different grooming standards in the workplace than their male counterparts. A female bartender at a casino in Nevada brought a lawsuit after she was fired for not complying with rules that required her to wear makeup and teased hair while male bartenders were just told to "look neat." The court ruled, however, that these allegations were not enough to outweigh an at-will employment contract.[b]

At the same time, women in senior management positions find that they can look "too sexy." A few years ago, a Citibank employee made headlines when she claimed that she was fired for her excessive sexiness, which supposedly distracted her male co-workers.

LEGAL CRITICAL THINKING

INSIGHT INTO SOCIAL MEDIA

The majority of workers today post photographs of themselves, their families, and their friends on Facebook and other social media. How might this practice affect appearance-based discrimination in the workplace?

b. *Jespersen v. Harrah's Operating Co.*, 444 F.3d 1104 (9th Cir. 2006).

management positions at a school district. She claimed that the terminations were part of a reorganization plan to cut costs in the department. The men sued for (reverse) racial discrimination and won. They were awarded nearly $3 million in damages.[7] ◀

In 2009, the United States Supreme Court issued a decision that has had a significant impact on disparate-impact and reverse discrimination litigation. ▶ **Case in Point 22.6** The fire department in New Haven, Connecticut, administered a test to identify which firefighters were eligible for promotions. No African Americans and only two Hispanic firefighters passed the test. Fearing that it would be sued for racial discrimination if it used the test results for promotions, the city refused to use the results.

The white firefighters (and one Hispanic) who had passed the test then sued the city, claiming reverse discrimination. The Supreme Court held that the city's actions were not justified. Mere fear of litigation was not a sufficient reason for the city to discard its test results.[8] The city subsequently certified the test results and promoted all the firefighters involved in the lawsuit. ◀

POTENTIAL SECTION 1981 CLAIMS Victims of racial or ethnic discrimination may also have a cause of action under 42 U.S.C. Section 1981. This section, which was enacted as part of the Civil Rights Act of 1866 to protect the rights of freed slaves, prohibits discrimination on the basis of race or ethnicity in the formation

7. *Johnston v. School District of Philadelphia*, 2006 WL 999966 (E.D.Pa. 2006). The damages awarded by a jury were reduced slighted by the appellate court.

8. *Ricci v. DeStefano*, 557 U.S. 557, 129 S.Ct. 2658, 174 L.Ed.2d 490 (2009).

or enforcement of contracts. Because employment is often a contractual relationship, Section 1981 can provide an alternative basis for a plaintiff's action and is potentially advantageous because it does not place a cap on damages.

Discrimination Based on Religion

Title VII of the Civil Rights Act of 1964 also prohibits government employers, private employers, and unions from discriminating against persons because of their religion. Employers cannot treat their employees more or less favorably based on their religious beliefs or practices and cannot require employees to participate in any religious activity (or forbid them from participating in one).

▶ **Example 22.7** Jason Sewell claims that his employer, a car dealership, fired him for not attending the weekly prayer meetings of dealership employees. If the dealership does require its employees to attend prayer gatherings and fired Sewell for not attending, he has a valid claim of religious discrimination. ◀

REASONABLE ACCOMMODATION An employer must "reasonably accommodate" the religious practices of its employees, unless to do so would cause undue hardship to the employer's business. An employee's religion might prohibit her or him from working on a certain day of the week, for instance, or at a certain type of job. The employer must make a reasonable attempt to accommodate the employee's sincerely held religious belief. Reasonable accommodation is required even if the belief is not based on the doctrines of a traditionally recognized religion, such as Christianity or Judaism, or of a denomination, such as Baptist.

UNDUE HARDSHIP A reasonable attempt to accommodate does not necessarily require the employer to make every change an employee requests or to make a permanent change for an employee's benefit. An employer is not required to make an accommodation that would cause the employer undue hardship.

▶ **Case in Point 22.8** Miguel Sánchez-Rodríguez sold cell phones at kiosks in shopping malls for AT&T in Puerto Rico. After six years, Sánchez informed his supervisors that he had become a Seventh Day Adventist and could no longer work on Saturdays for religious reasons. AT&T responded that his position required rotating Saturday shifts and that his inability to work on Saturdays would cause it hardship.

As a reasonable accommodation, the company suggested that Sánchez swap schedules with others and offered him two other positions that would not require work on Saturdays. Sánchez was unable to find workers to swap shifts with him, however, and declined the other jobs because they would result in less income (no commissions). He began missing work on Saturdays. After a time, AT&T indicated that it would discipline him for any additional Saturdays that he missed. Eventually, he was placed on active disciplinary status. Sánchez resigned and filed a religious discrimination lawsuit. The court found in favor of AT&T, and a federal appellate court affirmed. The company had made adequate efforts at accommodation by allowing Sánchez to swap shifts and offering him other positions that did not require work on Saturdays.[9] ◀

Discrimination Based on Gender

Under Title VII and other federal acts, employers are forbidden from discriminating against employees on the basis of gender. Employers are prohibited from classifying or advertising jobs as male or female unless the employer can prove that the gender of the applicant is essential to the job. Employers also cannot have separate male and female seniority lists or refuse to promote employees based on their gender.

GENDER MUST BE A DETERMINING FACTOR Generally, to succeed in a suit for gender discrimination, a plaintiff must demonstrate that gender was a determining factor in the employer's decision to hire, fire, or promote him or her. Typically, this involves looking at all of the surrounding circumstances.

▶ **Case in Point 22.9** Wanda Collier worked for Turner Industries Group, LLC, in the maintenance department. She complained to her supervisor that Jack Daniell, the head of the department, treated her unfairly. Her supervisor told her that Daniell had a problem with her gender and was harder on women. The supervisor talked to Daniell about Collier's complaint, but did not take any disciplinary action.

A month later, Daniell confronted Collier, pushing her up against a wall and berating her. After this incident, Collier filed a formal complaint and kept a male co-worker with her at all times. A month later, she was fired. She subsequently filed a lawsuit alleging gender discrimination. The court allowed Collier's clam to go to a jury because there was suf-

9. *Sánchez-Rodríguez v. AT&T Mobility Puerto Rico, Inc.*, 673 F.3d 1 (1st Cir. 2012).

ficient evidence that gender was a determining factor in Daniell's conduct.[10] ◀

PREGNANCY DISCRIMINATION The Pregnancy Discrimination Act[11] amended Title VII and expanded the definition of gender discrimination to include discrimination based on pregnancy. Women affected by pregnancy, childbirth, or related medical conditions must be treated—for all employment-related purposes, including the receipt of benefits under employee benefit programs—the same as other persons not so affected but similar in ability to work.

WAGE DISCRIMINATION Several laws prohibit employers from engaging in gender-based wage discrimination. The Equal Pay Act[12] requires equal pay for male and female employees working at the same establishment doing similar work (a barber and a hair stylist, for example).

To determine whether the Equal Pay Act has been violated, a court will look to the primary duties of the two jobs—the job content rather than the job description controls.[13] If a court finds that the wage differential is due to "any factor other than gender," such as a seniority or merit system, then it does not violate the Equal Pay Act.

In 2009, Congress enacted the Lilly Ledbetter Fair Pay Act, which made discriminatory wages actionable under federal law regardless of when the discrimination began.[14] This act countered a previous decision by the United States Supreme Court that had limited the time period in which plaintiffs could file a wage-discrimination complaint to 180 days after the employer's decision.[15] Today, if a plaintiff continues to work for the employer while receiving discriminatory wages, the time period for filing a complaint is practically unlimited.

Constructive Discharge

The majority of Title VII complaints involve unlawful discrimination in decisions to hire or fire employees. In some situations, however, employees who leave their jobs voluntarily can claim that they were "constructively discharged" by the employer. **Constructive discharge** occurs when the employer causes the employee's working conditions to be so intolerable that a reasonable person in the employee's position would feel compelled to quit.

PROVING CONSTRUCTIVE DISCHARGE The employee must present objective proof of intolerable working conditions, which the employer knew or had reason to know about yet failed to correct within a reasonable time period. Courts generally also require the employee to show causation—that the employer's unlawful discrimination caused the working conditions to be intolerable. Put a different way, the employee's resignation must be a foreseeable result of the employer's discriminatory action. Courts weigh the facts on a case-by-case basis.

Employee demotion is one of the most frequently cited reasons for a finding of constructive discharge, particularly when the employee was subjected to humiliation. ▶ **Example 22.10** Khalil's employer humiliates him by informing him in front of his co-workers that he is being demoted to an inferior position. Khalil's co-workers then continually insult him, harass him, and make derogatory remarks to him about his national origin (he is from Iran). The employer is aware of this discriminatory treatment but does nothing to remedy the situation, despite repeated complaints from Khalil. After several months, Khalil quits his job and files a Title VII claim. In this situation, Khalil would likely have sufficient evidence to maintain an action for constructive discharge in violation of Title VII. ◀

APPLIES TO ALL TITLE VII DISCRIMINATION Plaintiffs can use constructive discharge to establish any type of discrimination claims under Title VII, including race, color, national origin, religion, gender, and pregnancy, but it is most commonly asserted in cases involving sexual harassment. Constructive discharge may also be used in cases involving discrimination based on age or disability (discussed later in this chapter).

When constructive discharge is claimed, the employee can pursue damages for loss of income, including back pay. These damages ordinarily are not available to an employee who left a job voluntarily.

Sexual Harassment

Title VII also protects employees against **sexual harassment** in the workplace. Sexual harassment can take two forms:

---

10. *Collier v. Turner Industries Group, LLC,* 797 F.Supp.2d 1029 (D. Idaho 2011).
11. 42 U.S.C. Section 2000e(k).
12. 29 U.S.C. Section 206(d).
13. For an illustration of the factors courts consider in wage-discrimination claims under the Equal Pay Act, see *Beck-Wilson v. Principi,* 441 F.3d 353 (6th Cir. 2006).
14. Pub. L. No. 111-2, 123 Stat. 5 (January 5, 2009), amending 42 U.S.C. Section 2000e-5[e].
15. *Ledbetter v. Goodyear Tire Co.,* 550 U.S. 618, 127 S.Ct. 2162, 167 L.Ed.2d 982 (2007).

1. *Quid pro quo* harassment occurs when sexual favors are demanded in return for job opportunities, promotions, salary increases, or other benefits. *Quid pro quo* is a Latin phrase that is often translated as "something in exchange for something else."
2. *Hostile-environment* harassment occurs when a pattern of sexually offensive conduct runs throughout the workplace and the employer has not taken steps to prevent or discourage it. In the words of the United States Supreme Court, hostile-environment harassment exists when "the workplace is permeated with discriminatory intimidation, ridicule, and insult, that is sufficiently severe or pervasive to alter the conditions of the victim's employment and create an abusive working environment."[16]

The courts determine whether the sexually offensive conduct was sufficiently severe or pervasive to create a hostile environment on a case-by-case basis. Typically, a single incident of sexually offensive conduct is not enough to permeate the work environment (although there have been exceptions when the conduct was particularly objectionable).[17]

If the employee who is alleging sexual harassment has signed an employment contract containing an arbitration clause (see Chapter 3), she or he will most likely be required to arbitrate the claim.[18] In other words, the dispute will not be litigated in court.

HARASSMENT BY SUPERVISORS For an employer to be held liable for a supervisor's sexual harassment, the supervisor normally must have taken a *tangible employment action* against the employee. A **tangible employment action** is a significant change in employment status or benefits, such as when an employee is fired, refused a promotion, demoted, or reassigned to a position with significantly different responsibilities. Only a supervisor, or another person acting with the authority of the employer, can cause this sort of harm. A constructive discharge also qualifies as a tangible employment action.[19]

THE *ELLERTH/FARAGHER* AFFIRMATIVE DEFENSE In 1998, the United States Supreme Court issued several important rulings that have had a lasting impact on cases involving alleged sexual harassment by supervisors.[20] The Court held that an employer (a city) was liable for a supervisor's harassment of employees even though the employer was unaware of the behavior. Although the city had a written policy against sexual harassment, it had not distributed the policy to its employees and had not established any complaint procedures for employees who felt that they had been sexually harassed. In another case, the Court held that an employer can be liable for a supervisor's sexual harassment even though the employee does not suffer adverse job consequences.

The Court's decisions in these cases established what has become known as the *Ellerth/Faragher* affirmative defense to charges of sexual harassment. The defense has two elements:

1. The employer must have taken reasonable care to prevent and promptly correct any sexually harassing behavior (by establishing effective harassment policies and complaint procedures, for instance).
2. The plaintiff-employee must have unreasonably failed to take advantage of preventive or corrective opportunities provided by the employer to avoid harm.

An employer that can prove both elements normally will not be liable for a supervisor's harassment.

RETALIATION BY EMPLOYERS Employers sometimes retaliate against employees who complain about sexual harassment or other Title VII violations. Retaliation can take many forms. An employer might demote or fire the person, or otherwise change the terms, conditions, and benefits of employment. Title VII prohibits retaliation, and employees can sue their employers when it occurs.

In a *retaliation claim,* an individual asserts that she or he has suffered harm as a result of making a charge, testifying, or participating in a Title VII investigation or proceeding. Plaintiffs do not have to prove that the challenged action adversely affected their workplace or employment. Instead, plaintiffs must show that the action would likely have dissuaded a reasonable worker from making or supporting a charge of discrimination.

Title VII's retaliation protection extends to an employee who speaks out about discrimination

16. *Harris v. Forklift Systems,* 510 U.S. 17, 114 S.Ct. 367, 126 L.Ed.2d 295 (1993). See also *Baker v. Via Christi Regional Medical Center,* 491 F.Supp.2d 1040 (D.Kan. 2007).
17. See, for example, *Pomales v. Celulares Telefonica, Inc.,* 447 F.3d 79 (1st Cir. 2006); and *Fontanez-Nunez v. Janssen Ortho, LLC,* 447 F.3d 50 (1st Cir. 2006).
18. See, for example, *EEOC v. Cheesecake Factory, Inc.,* 2009 WL 1259359 (D.Ariz. 2009).
19. See, for example, *Pennsylvania State Police v. Suders,* 542 U.S. 129, 124 S.Ct. 2342, 159 L.Ed.2d 204 (2004).
20. *Burlington Industries, Inc. v. Ellerth,* 524 U.S. 742, 118 S.Ct. 2257, 141 L.Ed.2d 633 (1998); and *Faragher v. City of Boca Raton,* 524 U.S. 775, 118 S.Ct. 2275, 141 L.Ed.2d 662 (1998).

against another employee during an employer's internal investigation.[21] The Supreme Court has also held that Title VII protected an employee who was fired after his fiancée filed a gender discrimination claim against their employer.[22]

21. *Crawford v. Metropolitan Government of Nashville and Davidson County, Tennessee,* 555 U.S. 271, 129 S.Ct. 846, 172 L.Ed.2d 650 (2009).
22. See *Thompson v. North American Stainless, LP,* ___ U.S. ___, 131 S.Ct. 863, 178 L.Ed.2d 694 (2011).

In the following case, a law professor lost her job after she complained about comments made by her dean and colleagues. The court had to decide whether she had been retaliated against for engaging in protected conduct.

CASE 22.2

Morales-Cruz v. University of Puerto Rico

United States Court of Appeals, First Circuit, 676 F.3d 220 (2012).

BACKGROUND AND FACTS In 2003, Myrta Morales-Cruz began a tenure-track teaching position at the University of Puerto Rico School of Law. During Morales-Cruz's probationary period, one of her colleagues in a law school clinic had an affair with one of their students that resulted in a pregnancy. In 2008, Morales-Cruz wanted the university's administrative committee to approve a one-year extension for her tenure review. The law school's dean asked Morales-Cruz about her colleague's affair and criticized her for failing to report it. He later recommended granting the extension but called Morales-Cruz "insecure," "immature," and "fragile." Similarly, a law school committee recommended granting the extension. Nevertheless, a dissenting professor commented that in dealing with her colleague's affair, Morales-Cruz had shown poor judgment, exhibited "personality flaws," and demonstrated that she had trouble with "complex and sensitive" situations.

Morales-Cruz soon learned about the dean's and the dissenting professor's comments and complained in writing to the university's chancellor. As a result, the dean then recommended denying the one-year extension, and the administrative committee ultimately did just that. When her employment was terminated, Morales-Cruz sued the university under Title VII. Among other things, she asserted that the dean had retaliated against her for complaining to the chancellor. The district court found that Morales-Cruz had not stated a proper retaliation claim under Title VII.

IN THE LANGUAGE OF THE COURT
SELYA, Circuit Judge.

* * * *

The amended complaint alleges that various officials described the plaintiff as "fragile," "immature," "unable to handle complex and sensitive issues," * * * and exhibiting "lack of judgment." These descriptors are admittedly unflattering—but they are without exception gender-neutral. All of them apply equally to persons of either gender * * * .

* * * *

* * * Title VII makes it unlawful for an employer to take materially adverse action against an employee "because he has opposed any practice made an unlawful employment practice by this subchapter." *To state a cause of action under this portion of the statute, the pleading must contain plausible allegations indicating that the plaintiff opposed a practice prohibited by Title VII and suffered an adverse employment action as a result of that opposition.* [Emphasis added.]

The plaintiff alleges that she was retaliated against for writing to the Chancellor to complain about the "discriminatory" comments made in the course of her request for an extension. In support of this allegation, she points out that after she sent her letter the Dean reversed his position on her extension. This construct suffers from a fatal flaw: her factual allegations do not support a reasonable inference that she was engaging in protected conduct when she opposed the remarks made.

CASE 22.2 CONTINUES ➧

CASE 22.2 CONTINUED

* * * The facts alleged * * * provide no reasonable basis for inferring that the comments cited reflected gender-based discrimination. Those comments were unarguably gender-neutral and do not afford an objectively reasonable foundation for a retaliation action.

DECISION AND REMEDY *The appellate court held that Morales-Cruz could not bring a retaliation claim under Title VII. It therefore affirmed the district court's judgment for the University of Puerto Rico.*

THE ETHICAL DIMENSION *Could Morales-Cruz's dean have had legitimate reasons for changing his mind about the one-year extension? If so, what might they have been?*

THE LEGAL ENVIRONMENT DIMENSION *What steps should employers take to reduce the likelihood that supervisors will retaliate against employees who make or support discrimination claims?*

HARASSMENT BY CO-WORKERS AND OTHERS When the harassment of co-workers, rather than supervisors, creates a hostile working environment, an employee may still have a cause of action against the employer. Normally, though, the employer will be held liable only if it knew or should have known about the harassment and failed to take immediate remedial action.

Occasionally, a court may also hold an employer liable for harassment by *nonemployees* if the employer knew about the harassment and failed to take corrective action. ▶ **Example 22.11** Jordan, who owns and manages a Great Bites restaurant, knows that one of his regular customers, Dean, repeatedly harasses Kaylia, a waitress. If Jordan does nothing and permits the harassment to continue, he may be liable under Title VII even though Dean is not an employee of the restaurant. ◀

SAME-GENDER HARASSMENT In *Oncale v. Sundowner Offshore Services, Inc.*,[23] the United States Supreme Court held that Title VII protection extends to individuals who are sexually harassed by members of the same gender. Proving that the harassment in same-gender cases is "based on sex" can be difficult, though. It is easier to establish a case of same-gender harassment when the harasser is homosexual.[24]

SEXUAL ORIENTATION HARASSMENT Federal law (Title VII) does not prohibit discrimination or harassment based on a person's sexual orientation. Nonetheless, a growing number of states have enacted laws that prohibit sexual orientation discrimination in private employment.[25] Some states, such as Michigan, explicitly prohibit discrimination based on a person's gender identity or expression. Many companies have also voluntarily established nondiscrimination policies that include sexual orientation.

Online Harassment

Employees' online activities can create a hostile working environment in many ways. Racial jokes, ethnic slurs, or other comments contained in e-mail, texts, blogs, and social media can lead to a claim of hostile-environment harassment or other forms of discrimination. A worker who regularly sees sexually explicit images on a co-worker's computer screen may find the images offensive and claim that they create a hostile working environment.

Nevertheless, employers may be able to avoid liability for online harassment by taking prompt remedial action.

Remedies under Title VII

Employer liability under Title VII may be extensive. If the plaintiff successfully proves that unlawful discrimination occurred, he or she may be awarded reinstatement, back pay, retroactive promotions, and damages.

Compensatory damages are available only in cases of intentional discrimination. Punitive damages may be recovered against a private employer only if the employer acted with malice or reckless indifference to an individual's rights. The statute limits the total amount of compensatory and punitive damages that plaintiffs can recover from specific employers,

23. 523 U.S. 75, 118 S.Ct. 998, 140 L.Ed.2d 207 (1998).
24. See, for example, *Tepperwien v. Entergy Nuclear Operations, Inc.*, 606 F.Supp.2d 427 (S.D.N.Y. 2009).
25. See, for example, 775 Illinois Compiled Statutes 5/1–103.

depending on the size of the employer. For instance, there is a $50,000 cap on damages from employers with one hundred or fewer employees.

SECTION 2

DISCRIMINATION BASED ON AGE

Age discrimination is potentially the most widespread form of discrimination because anyone—regardless of race, color, national origin, or gender—could be a victim at some point in life. The Age Discrimination in Employment Act[26] (ADEA), as amended, prohibits employment discrimination on the basis of age against individuals forty years of age or older. The act also prohibits mandatory retirement for nonmanagerial workers.

The United States Supreme Court has ruled that the ADEA encompasses not only claims of age discrimination, but also claims of retaliation for complaining about age discrimination.[27] Thus, the ADEA protects federal and private-sector employees from retaliation based on age-related complaints.

For the act to apply, an employer must have twenty or more employees, and the employer's business activities must affect interstate commerce. The EEOC administers the ADEA, but the act also permits private causes of action against employers for age discrimination.

26. 29 U.S.C. Sections 621–634.

27. *Gomez-Perez v. Potter*, 553 U.S. 474, 128 S.Ct. 1931, 170 L.Ed.2d 887 (2008).

Procedures under the ADEA

The burden-shifting procedure under the ADEA differs from the procedure under Title VII as a result of a 2009 United States Supreme Court decision, which dramatically changed the burden of proof in age discrimination cases.[28] As explained earlier, if the plaintiff in a Title VII case can show that the employer was motivated, at least in part, by unlawful discrimination, the burden of proof shifts to the employer to articulate a legitimate nondiscriminatory reason for the challenged action. Thus, in cases in which the employer has a "mixed motive" for discharging an employee, the employer has the burden of proving its reason was legitimate.

Under the ADEA, in contrast, a plaintiff must show that the unlawful discrimination was not just *a* reason but *the* reason for the adverse employment action. In other words, the employee has the burden of establishing *but for* causation—that is, "but for" the employee's age, the action would not have been taken.

Thus, to establish a *prima facie* case, the plaintiff must show that she or he (1) was a member of the protected age group, (2) was qualified for the position from which she or he was discharged, and (3) was discharged because of age discrimination. Then the burden shifts to the employer. If the employer offers a legitimate reason for its action, the plaintiff must show that the stated reason is only a pretext for the employer's decision. The following case illustrates this process.

28. *Gross v. FBL Financial Services, Inc.*, 557 U.S. 167, 129 S.Ct. 2343, 174 L.Ed.2d 119 (2009).

CASE 22.3

Mora v. Jackson Memorial Foundation, Inc.

United States Court of Appeals, Eleventh Circuit, 597 F.3d 1201 (2010).

BACKGROUND AND FACTS Josephine Mora, a fund-raiser for Jackson Memorial Foundation, Inc., was sixty-two years old when the foundation's chief executive officer (CEO) fired her, citing errors and issues with professionalism. Mora filed a suit against the foundation, alleging age discrimination. She asserted that when she was fired, the CEO told her, "I need someone younger I can pay less." She had a witness who heard that statement and also heard the CEO say that Mora was "too old to be working here anyway." The foundation moved for summary judgment, arguing that Mora was fired chiefly because she was incompetent. The district court granted the motion, and Mora appealed.

IN THE LANGUAGE OF THE COURT

PER CURIAM. [By the Whole Court]

* * * *

CASE 22.3 CONTINUES ➧

CASE 22.3 CONTINUED

After Plaintiff [Mora] appealed, the Supreme Court, in *Gross v. FBL Financial Services, Inc.*,[a] clarified the nature of ADEA claims. The Supreme Court concluded that ADEA claims are not subject to the burden-shifting protocol set forth for Title VII suits in *Price Waterhouse v. Hopkins*.[b] The ADEA requires that "age [be] the reason that the employer decided to act." *Because an ADEA plaintiff must establish "but for" causality, no "same decision" affirmative defense [the argument that the same decision—to fire someone, for example—would have been made regardless of the alleged discrimination] can exist: the employer either acted "because of" the plaintiff's age or it did not.* [Emphasis added.]

Because the Supreme Court has excluded the whole idea of a "mixed motive" ADEA claim—and the corresponding "same decision" defense—we need not consider the district court's analysis of Defendant's [the foundation's] affirmative defense. Instead, * * * we look to determine whether a material factual question exists on this record about whether Defendant discriminated against her. We say "Yes."

* * * *

A plaintiff in an ADEA claim may "establish a claim of illegal age discrimination through either direct evidence or circumstantial evidence." Plaintiff's testimony that Rodriguez [the CEO] fired her because she was "too old" was substantiated by the affidavits of two other employees of Defendant. Rodriguez and Quevedo [another employee] testified that no such comments were made * * * .

The resolution of this case depends on whose account of the pertinent conversations a jury would credit. We conclude that a reasonable juror could accept that Rodriguez made the discriminatory-sounding remarks and that the remarks are sufficient evidence of a discriminatory motive which was the "but for" cause of Plaintiff's dismissal. Summary judgment for Defendant was therefore incorrect.

We have considered cases factually similar to Plaintiff's. In [one case], we concluded that statements from a county official who "didn't want to hire any old pilots" were direct evidence of discrimination * * * . In [another case], we likewise concluded that an employer's statement that he wanted "aggressive, young men like himself to be promoted" was circumstantial evidence of discrimination.

While these cases were litigated under the now-defunct ADEA mixed motive theory, they remain instructive. Plaintiff's situation is similar. A reasonable juror could find that Rodriguez's statements should be taken at face value and that he fired Plaintiff because of her age.

DECISION AND REMEDY *The U.S. Court of Appeals for the Eleventh Circuit vacated (set aside) the decision of the trial court and remanded the case for further proceedings. Because there was a "disputed question of material fact" as to whether the plaintiff had been fired because of her age, the defendant was not entitled to summary judgment.*

THE ETHICAL DIMENSION *Is the court's decision in this case fair to employers? Why or why not?*

MANAGERIAL IMPLICATIONS *Business owners and supervisory personnel should be careful to avoid statements regarding an employee's age that may sound discriminatory. If the employee later has to be dismissed due to poor performance, comments about his or her age may become the basis for an age discrimination lawsuit.*

a. 557 U.S. 167, 129 S.Ct. 2343, 174 L.Ed.2d 119 (2009).
b. 490 U.S. 228, 109 S.Ct. 1775, 104 L.Ed.2d 268 (1989).

Replacing Older Workers with Younger Workers

Numerous age discrimination cases have been brought against employers who, to cut costs, replaced older, higher-salaried employees with younger, lower-salaried workers. Whether a firing is discriminatory or simply part of a rational business decision to prune the company's ranks is not always clear.

A plaintiff must prove that the discharge was motivated by age bias. The plaintiff does not need to prove that she or he was replaced by a person "outside the protected class" (under the age of forty years), as long as the replacement worker is younger than the plaintiff. Nevertheless, the bigger the age gap, the more likely the plaintiff will succeed in showing age discrimination.

State Employees Not Covered by the ADEA

Generally, the states are immune under the Eleventh Amendment from lawsuits brought by private individuals in federal court—unless a state consents to the suit. This immunity stems from the United States Supreme Court's interpretation of the Eleventh Amendment (see Appendix B).

State immunity under the Eleventh Amendment is not absolute, however. In some situations, such as when fundamental rights are at stake, Congress has the power to abrogate (abolish) state immunity to private suits through legislation that unequivocally shows Congress's intent to subject states to private suits.[29]

Generally, though, the Court has found that state employers are immune from private suits brought by employees under the ADEA (for age discrimination), the Americans with Disabilities Act (for disability-based discrimination),[30] and the Fair Labor Standards Act.[31] State employers are not immune from the requirements of the Family and Medical Leave Act, however.[32]

SECTION 3

DISCRIMINATION BASED ON DISABILITY

The Americans with Disabilities Act (ADA) of 1990[33] prohibits disability-based discrimination in all workplaces with fifteen or more workers. An exception is state government employers, who are generally immune under the Eleventh Amendment, as just discussed. Basically, the ADA requires that employers "reasonably accommodate" the needs of persons with disabilities unless to do so would cause the employer to suffer an "undue hardship." The ADA Amendments Act[34] broadened the coverage of the ADA's protections, as discussed shortly.

Procedures under the ADA

To prevail on a claim under the ADA, a plaintiff must show that he or she (1) has a disability, (2) is otherwise qualified for the employment in question, and (3) was excluded from the employment solely because of the disability. As in Title VII cases, the plaintiff must pursue the claim through the EEOC before filing an action in court for a violation of the ADA.

The EEOC may decide to investigate and perhaps even sue the employer on behalf of the employee. The EEOC can bring a suit on behalf of the employee under the ADA even if the employee signed an arbitration agreement with the employer.[35] If the EEOC decides not to sue, then the employee may do so.

Plaintiffs in lawsuits brought under the ADA may seek many of the same remedies that are available under Title VII. These include reinstatement, back pay, a limited amount of compensatory and punitive damages (for intentional discrimination), and certain other forms of relief. Repeat violators may be ordered to pay fines of up to $100,000.

What Is a Disability?

The ADA is broadly drafted to cover persons with physical or mental impairments that "substantially limit" their everyday activities. Specifically, the ADA defines a *disability* as including any of the following:

1. A physical or mental impairment that substantially limits one or more of the major life activities of the affected individual.
2. A record of having such an impairment.
3. Being regarded as having such an impairment.

TYPES OF DISABILITY Health conditions that have been considered disabilities under federal law include blindness, alcoholism, heart disease, cancer, muscular dystrophy, cerebral palsy, paraplegia, diabetes, acquired immune deficiency syndrome (AIDS), testing positive for the human immunodeficiency virus

29. *Tennessee v. Lane,* 541 U.S. 509, 124 S.Ct. 1978, 158 L.Ed.2d 820 (2004).
30 *Board of Trustees of the University of Alabama v. Garrett,* 531 U.S. 356, 121 S.Ct. 955, 148 L.Ed.2d 866 (2001).
31. *Alden v. Maine,* 527 U.S. 706, 119 S.Ct. 2240, 144 L.Ed.2d 636 (1999).
32. *Nevada Department of Human Resources v. Hibbs,* 538 U.S. 721, 123 S.Ct. 1972, 155 L.Ed.2d 953 (2003).
33. 42 U.S.C. Sections 12103–12118.
34. 42 U.S.C. Sections 12103 and 12205a.
35. This was the Supreme Court's ruling in *EEOC v. Waffle House, Inc.,* 534 U.S. 279, 122 S.Ct. 754, 151 L.Ed.2d 755 (2002).

(HIV, the virus that causes AIDS), and morbid obesity (which exists when an individual's weight is twice the normal weight for his or her height).

The ADA includes a separate provision that prevents employers from taking adverse employment actions based on stereotypes or assumptions about individuals who associate with people who have disabilities.[36] An employer cannot, for instance, refuse to hire the parent of a child with a disability based on the assumption that the person will miss work too often or be unreliable.[37]

CORRECTABLE CONDITIONS At one time, the courts focused on whether a person had a disability *after* the use of corrective devices or medication. A person with severe myopia (nearsightedness), which can be corrected with lenses, for instance, did not qualify as having a disability because that individual's major life activities were not substantially impaired.

In 2008, Congress amended the ADA to strengthen its protections and prohibit employers from considering mitigating measures or medications when determining if an individual has a disability. Disability is now determined on a case-by-case basis. A condition may fit the definition of disability in one set of circumstances, but not in another.

Reasonable Accommodation

The ADA does not require that employers accommodate the needs of job applicants or employees with disabilities who are not otherwise qualified for the work. If a job applicant or an employee with a disability, with reasonable accommodation, can perform essential job functions, however, the employer must make the accommodation.

Required modifications may include installing ramps for a wheelchair, establishing flexible working hours, creating or modifying job assignments, and designing or improving training materials and procedures. Generally, employers should give primary consideration to employees' preferences in deciding what accommodations should be made.

UNDUE HARDSHIP Employers who do not accommodate the needs of persons with disabilities must demonstrate that the accommodations would cause *undue hardship* in terms of being significantly difficult or expensive for the employer. Usually, the courts decide whether an accommodation constitutes an undue hardship on a case-by-case basis.

► **Example 22.12** Bryan Lockhart, who uses a wheelchair, works for a cell phone company that provides parking for its employees. Lockhart informs his supervisor that the parking spaces are so narrow that he is unable to extend the ramp on his van that allows him to get in and out of the vehicle. Lockhart therefore requests that the company reasonably accommodate his needs by paying a monthly fee for him to use a larger parking space in an adjacent lot. In this situation, a court would likely find that it would *not* be an undue hardship for the employer to pay for additional parking for Lockhart. ◄

JOB APPLICATIONS AND PHYSICAL EXAMS Employers must modify their job-application and selection process so that those with disabilities can compete for jobs with those who do not have disabilities. For instance, a job announcement might be modified to allow applicants to respond by e-mail or letter, as well as by telephone, so that it does not discriminate against potential applicants with hearing impairments.

Employers are restricted in the kinds of questions they may ask on job-application forms and during preemployment interviews. In addition, employers cannot require persons with disabilities to submit to preemployment physicals unless such exams are required of all other applicants. An employer can disqualify the applicant only if the medical problems discovered during a preemployment physical would make it impossible for the applicant to perform the job.

► **Example 22.13** Abba Freight Systems runs a trucking operation. When filling the position of delivery truck driver, Abba cannot screen out all applicants who are unable to meet the U.S. Department of Transportation's hearing standard. Abba would first have to prove that drivers who are deaf are not qualified to perform the essential job function of driving safely and pose a higher risk of accidents than drivers who are not deaf.[38] ◄

SUBSTANCE ABUSERS Drug addiction is considered a disability under the ADA because it is a substantially limiting impairment. The act does not protect individuals who are actually using illegal drugs, however. Instead, the ADA protects only persons with *former* drug addictions—those who have completed or are now in a supervised drug-rehabilitation program.

36. 42 U.S.C. Section 12112(b)(4).
37. See, for example, *Francin v. Mosby, Inc.*, 248 S.W.3d 619 (Mo. 2008).
38. See, for example, *Bates v. United Parcel Service, Inc.*, 465 F.3d 1069 (9th Cir. 2006).

Individuals who have used drugs casually in the past also are not protected under the act. They are not considered addicts and therefore do not have a disability (addiction).

People suffering from alcoholism are protected by the ADA. Employers cannot legally discriminate against employees simply because they suffer from alcoholism. Of course, employers can prohibit the use of alcohol in the workplace and require that employees not be under the influence of alcohol while working. Employers can also fire or refuse to hire a person who is an alcoholic if (1) he or she poses a *substantial risk of harm* either to himself or herself or to others, and (2) the risk cannot be reduced by reasonable accommodation.

HEALTH-INSURANCE PLANS Workers with disabilities must be given equal access to any health insurance provided to other employees. An employer can put a limit, or cap, on health-care payments under its group health policy, however, as long as the cap is applied equally to all insured employees and does not discriminate on the basis of disability. Whenever a group health-care plan makes a disability-based distinction in its benefits, the plan violates the ADA. (An exception exists if the employer can justify its actions under the business necessity defense, as discussed in the next section).

SECTION 4

DEFENSES TO EMPLOYMENT DISCRIMINATION

The first line of defense for an employer charged with employment discrimination is to assert that the plaintiff has failed to meet his or her initial burden of proving that discrimination occurred. As noted, plaintiffs bringing age discrimination claims may find it difficult to meet this initial burden because they must prove that age discrimination was the reason for their employer's decision.

Once a plaintiff succeeds in proving that discrimination occurred, the burden shifts to the employer to justify the discriminatory practice. Possible justifications include that the discrimination was the result of a business necessity, a bona fide occupational qualification, or a seniority system. In some situations, as noted earlier, an effective antiharassment policy and prompt remedial action when harassment occurs may shield employers from liability for sexual harassment under Title VII.

Business Necessity

An employer may defend against a claim of disparate-impact (unintentional) discrimination by asserting that a practice that has a discriminatory effect is a **business necessity.** ▶ **Example 22.14** Jiffy Mart requires its employees to have a high school diploma. If this requirement is shown to have a discriminatory effect, Jiffy might argue that a high school education is necessary for workers to perform the job at a required level of competence. If Jiffy can demonstrate to the court's satisfaction that a definite connection exists between a high school education and job performance, then Jiffy normally will succeed in this business necessity defense. ◀

Bona Fide Occupational Qualification

Another defense applies when discrimination against a protected class is essential to a job—that is, when a particular trait is a **bona fide occupational qualification (BFOQ).** Race, color, and national origin, however, can never be BFOQs.

Generally, courts have restricted the BFOQ defense to instances in which the employee's gender or religion is essential to the job. ▶ **Example 22.15** Urban Minx, a women's clothing store, might legitimately hire only female salespersons if part of a salesperson's job involves assisting clients in the store's dressing rooms. Similarly, the Federal Aviation Administration can legitimately impose age limits for airline pilots—but an airline cannot impose weight limits only on female flight attendants. ◀

Seniority Systems

An employer with a history of discrimination may have no members of protected classes in upper-level positions. Even if the employer now seeks to be unbiased, it may face a lawsuit from members of protected classes claiming that they should be promoted ahead of schedule to compensate for past discrimination. If no present intent to discriminate is shown, however, and if promotions or other job benefits are distributed according to a fair **seniority system** (in which workers with more years of service are promoted first or laid off last), the employer normally has a good defense against the suit.

According to the United States Supreme Court, this defense may also apply to claims of discrimination under the ADA. ▶ **Case in Point 22.16** A baggage handler who had injured his back requested an assignment to a mailroom position at U.S. Airways, Inc. The airline refused to give the employee the position because another employee had seniority. The Court sided with U.S. Airways. If an employee with a disability requests an accommodation that conflicts with an employer's seniority system, the accommodation generally will not be considered "reasonable" under the ADA.[39] ◀

After-Acquired Evidence of Employee Misconduct

In some situations, employers have attempted to avoid liability for employment discrimination on the basis of "after-acquired evidence"—that is, evidence that the employer discovers after a lawsuit is filed—of an employee's misconduct. ▶ **Example 22.17** An employer fires a worker, Ravi, who then sues the employer for employment discrimination. During pretrial investigation, the employer learns that Ravi made material misrepresentations on his employment application—misrepresentations that, had the employer known about them, would have served as a ground to fire the individual. ◀

According to the United States Supreme Court, after-acquired evidence of wrongdoing cannot be used to shield an employer entirely from liability for employment discrimination. It may, however, be used to limit the amount of damages for which the employer is liable.[40]

SECTION 5

AFFIRMATIVE ACTION

Federal statutes and regulations providing for equal opportunity in the workplace were designed to reduce or eliminate discriminatory practices with respect to hiring, retaining, and promoting employees. **Affirmative action** programs go a step further and attempt to "make up" for past patterns of discrimination by giving members of protected classes preferential treatment in hiring or promotion.

These programs also promote diversity in schools and workplaces. During the 1960s, all federal and state government agencies, private companies that contracted to do business with the federal government, and institutions that received federal funding were required to implement affirmative action policies.

Title VII of the Civil Rights Act of 1964 neither requires nor prohibits affirmative action. Thus, most private companies and organizations have not been required to implement affirmative action policies, though many have done so voluntarily. Affirmative action programs have been controversial, however, particularly when they result in reverse discrimination against members of a majority group, such as white males.

Constitutionality of Affirmative Action Programs

Because of their inherently discriminatory nature, affirmative action programs may violate the equal protection clause of the Fourteenth Amendment to the U.S. Constitution. The United States Supreme Court has held that any federal, state, or local government affirmative action program that uses racial or ethnic classifications as the basis for making decisions is subject to strict scrutiny by the courts.[41] Recall from Chapter 5 that strict scrutiny is the highest standard, which means that most programs do not survive a court's analysis under this test.

Today, an affirmative action program normally is constitutional only if it attempts to remedy past discrimination and does not make use of quotas or preferences. Furthermore, once such a program has succeeded in the goal of remedying past discrimination, it must be changed or dropped.

Affirmative Action in Schools

Most of the affirmative action cases that have reached the United States Supreme Court in the last twenty years have involved university admissions programs and schools, rather than business employers.

RACE AS A "PLUS" FACTOR Generally, the Court has found that a school admissions policy that *automatically* awards minority group applicants a specified number of points violates the equal protection clause.[42] A school can, however, "consider race or ethnicity more flexibly as a 'plus' factor in the context of individualized consideration of each and every applicant."[43] In other words, it is unconstitutional for schools to

39. *U.S. Airways, Inc. v. Barnett,* 535 U.S. 391, 122 S.Ct. 1516, 152 L.Ed.2d 589 (2002).
40. *McKennon v. Nashville Banner Publishing Co.,* 513 U.S. 352, 115 S.Ct. 879, 130 L.Ed.2d 852 (1995). See also *EEOC v. Dial Corp.,* 469 F.3d 735 (8th Cir. 2006).
41. See the landmark decision in *Adarand Constructors, Inc. v. Peña,* 515 U.S. 200, 115 S.Ct. 2097, 132 L.Ed.2d 158 (1995).
42. *Gratz v. Bollinger,* 539 U.S. 244, 123 S.Ct. 2411, 156 L.Ed.2d 257 (2003).
43. *Grutter v. Bollinger,* 539 U.S. 306, 123 S.Ct. 2325, 156 L.Ed.2d 304 (2003).

apply a mechanical formula that gives "diversity bonuses" based on race or ethnicity.

▶ **Case in Point 22.18** School districts in Seattle, Washington, and Jefferson County, Kentucky, adopted plans that relied on race to assign certain children to schools. The Seattle plan classified children as "white" or "nonwhite" and used racial classifications as a "tie-breaker" to determine which school students would attend. The school district in Jefferson County classified students as "black" or "other" to assign children to elementary schools.

Parent groups filed lawsuits claiming that the racial preferences violated the equal protection clause. The United States Supreme Court held that the school districts had failed to show that the use of racial classifications in their student assignment plans was necessary to achieve their stated goal of racial diversity. Hence, the affirmative action programs of both school districts were unconstitutional.[44] ◀

44. The Court consolidated the two cases and issued one opinion for both. See *Parents Involved in Community Schools v. Seattle School District No. 1,* 551 U.S. 701, 127 S.Ct. 2738, 168 L.Ed.2d 508 (2007).

A 2013 CHALLENGE TO RACE-CONSCIOUS POLICIES

In 2013, the Supreme Court issued a ruling in the case of *Fisher v. University of Texas.*[45] The case involved Abigail Fisher, a white woman who claimed that her rights to equal protection had been violated when she was denied admission to the University of Texas. The university's affirmative action program followed the guidelines previously set forth by the Court and considered race merely as a plus factor. Although many thought that the Supreme Court would use this case to invalidate race-conscious affirmative action programs, that did not occur. Instead, the Court held that the lower court had applied the wrong standard when it did not hold the university to the demanding burden of strict scrutiny articulated in the Court's prior decisions. The case was therefore remanded for further proceedings.

45. ___ U.S. ___, 133 S.Ct. 2411, 186 L.Ed.2d 474 (2013).

Reviewing: Employment Discrimination

Amaani Lyle, an African American woman, was hired by Warner Brothers Television Productions to be a scriptwriters' assistant for the writers of *Friends,* a popular, adult-oriented television series. One of her essential job duties was to type detailed notes for the scriptwriters during brainstorming sessions in which they discussed jokes, dialogue, and story lines. The writers then combed through Lyle's notes after the meetings for script material. During these meetings, the three male scriptwriters told lewd and vulgar jokes and made sexually explicit comments and gestures. They often talked about their personal sexual experiences and fantasies, and some of these conversations were then used in episodes of *Friends.*

During the meetings, Lyle never complained that she found the writers' conduct offensive. After four months, Lyle was fired because she could not type fast enough to keep up with the writers' conversations during the meetings. She filed a suit against Warner Brothers, alleging sexual harassment and claiming that her termination was based on racial discrimination. Using the information presented in the chapter, answer the following questions.

1. Would Lyle's claim of racial discrimination be for intentional (disparate-treatment) or unintentional (disparate-impact) discrimination? Explain.
2. Can Lyle establish a *prima facie* case of racial discrimination? Why or why not?
3. When Lyle was hired, she was told that typing speed was extremely important to the position. At the time, she maintained that she could type eighty words per minute, so she was not given a typing test. It later turned out that Lyle could type only fifty words per minute. What impact might typing speed have on Lyle's lawsuit?
4. Lyle's sexual-harassment claim is based on the hostile working environment created by the writers' sexually offensive conduct at meetings that she was required to attend. The writers, however, argue that their behavior was essential to the "creative process" of writing for *Friends,* a show that routinely

Continued

contained sexual innuendos and adult humor. Which defense discussed in the chapter might Warner Brothers assert using this argument?

DEBATE THIS . . . *Members of minority groups and women have made enough economic progress in the last several decades that they no longer need special legislation to protect them.*

Terms and Concepts

affirmative action 520
bona fide occupational qualification (BFOQ) 519
business necessity 519
constructive discharge 511
disparate-impact discrimination 508
disparate-treatment discrimination 506
employment discrimination 505
prima facie case 506
protected class 505
seniority system 519
sexual harassment 511
tangible employment action 512

ExamPrep

Issue Spotters

1. Ruth is a supervisor for a Subs & Suds restaurant. Tim is a Subs & Suds employee. The owner announces that some employees will be discharged. Ruth tells Tim that if he has sex with her, he can keep his job. Is this sexual harassment? Why or why not? **(See page 511.)**
2. Koko, a person with a disability, applies for a job at Lively Sales Corporation for which she is well qualified, but she is rejected. Lively continues to seek applicants and eventually fills the position with a person who does not have a disability. Could Koko succeed in a suit against Lively for discrimination? Explain. **(See page 517.)**

- **Check your answers to the Issue Spotters against the answers provided in Appendix E at the end of this text.**

Before the Test

Go to **www.cengagebrain.com**, enter the ISBN 9781285428949, and click on "Find" to locate this textbook's Web site. Then, click on "Access Now" under "Study Tools," and select Chapter 22 at the top. There, you will find an Interactive Quiz that you can take to assess your mastery of the concepts in this chapter, as well as Flashcards and a Glossary of important terms.

Business Scenarios

22–1. Title VII Violations. Discuss fully whether either of the following actions would constitute a violation of Title VII of the 1964 Civil Rights Act, as amended: **(See page 505.)**

(a) Tennington, Inc., is a consulting firm and has ten employees. These employees travel on consulting jobs in seven states. Tennington has an employment record of hiring only white males.

(b) Novo Films is making a movie about Africa and needs to employ approximately one hundred extras for this picture. To hire these extras, Novo advertises in all major newspapers in Southern California. The ad states that only African Americans need apply.

22–2. Religious Discrimination. Gina Gomez, a devout Roman Catholic, worked for Sam's Department Stores, Inc., in Phoenix, Arizona. Sam's considered Gomez a productive employee because her sales exceeded $200,000 per year. At the time, the store gave its managers the discretion to grant unpaid leave to employees but prohibited vacations or leave during the holiday season—October through December. Gomez felt that she had a "calling" to go on a "pilgrimage" in October to Bosnia where some persons claimed to have had visions of the Virgin Mary. The Catholic Church had not designated the site an official pilgrimage site, the visions were not expected to be stronger in October, and tours were available at other times. The store managers denied Gomez's request for leave, but she had a nonrefundable ticket and left anyway. Sam's terminated her employment, and she could not find another job. Can Gomez establish a *prima facie* case of religious discrimination? Explain. **(See page 510.)**

Business Case Problems

22–3. Spotlight on Title VII of the Civil Rights Act of 1964—Discrimination Based on Gender.

Burlington Coat Factory Warehouse, Inc., had a dress code that required male salesclerks to wear business attire consisting of slacks, shirt, and a necktie. Female salesclerks, by contrast, were required to wear a smock so that customers could readily identify them. Karen O'Donnell and other female employees refused to wear the smock. Instead they reported to work in business attire and were suspended. After numerous suspensions, the female employees were fired for violating Burlington's dress code policy. All other conditions of employment, including salary, hours, and benefits, were the same for female and male employees. Was the dress code policy discriminatory? Why or why not? [*O'Donnell v. Burlington Coat Factory Warehouse, Inc.,* 656 F.Supp. 263 (S.D. Ohio 1987)] **(See page 510.)**

22–4. Discrimination Based on Gender. Brenda Lewis had been employed for two years at Heartland Inns of America, LLC, and gradually worked her way up the management ladder. Lewis, who described herself as a tomboy, was commended for her good work. When she moved to a different Heartland hotel, the director of operations, Barbara Cullinan, told one of the owners that Lewis was not a "good fit" for the front desk because she was not feminine enough. Cullinan told various people that the hotel wanted "pretty" girls at the front desk. Cullinan then informed Lewis that her hiring had not been done properly and that she would need to undergo another interview. Soon after the interview, Cullinan fired Lewis. The reason given in a letter was that Lewis was hostile during the interview. Lewis sued Heartland for gender discrimination based on unlawful gender stereotyping. The district court dismissed the suit. Lewis appealed. Does her claim fall under Title VII's prohibition against discrimination based on gender? Why or why not? [*Lewis v. Heartland Inns of America, LLC,* 591 F.3d 1033 (8th Cir. 2010)] **(See page 510.)**

22–5. BUSINESS CASE PROBLEM WITH SAMPLE ANSWER: Retaliation by Employers.

*Entek International hired Shane Dawson, a male homosexual. Some of Dawson's co-workers, including his supervisor, made derogatory comments about his sexual orientation. Dawson's work deteriorated. He filed a complaint with Entek's human resources department. Two days later, he was fired. State law made it unlawful for an employer to discriminate against an individual based on sexual orientation. Could Dawson establish a claim for retaliation? Explain. [*Dawson v. Entek International,* 630 F.3d 928 (9th Cir. 2011)]* **(See page 512.)**

- **For a sample answer to Problem 22–5, go to Appendix F at the end of this text.**

22–6. Sexual Harassment by Co-Worker. Billie Bradford worked for the Kentucky Department of Community Based Services (DCBS). One of Bradford's co-workers, Lisa Stander, routinely engaged in extreme sexual behavior (such as touching herself and making crude comments) in Bradford's presence. Bradford and others regularly complained about Stander's conduct to their supervisor, Angie Taylor. Rather than resolve the problem, Taylor nonchalantly told Stander to stop, encouraged Bradford to talk to Stander, and suggested that Stander was just having fun. Assuming that Bradford was subjected to a hostile work environment, could DCBS be liable? Why or why not? [*Bradford v. Department of Community Based Services,* 2012 WL 360032 (E.D.Ky. 2012)] **(See page 511.)**

22–7. Age Discrimination. Beginning in 1986, Paul Rangel was a sales professional for the pharmaceutical company sanofi-aventis U.S. LLC (S-A). Rangel had satisfactory performance reviews until 2006, when S-A issued new "Expectations" guidelines with sales call quotas and other standards that he failed to meet. After two years of negative performance reviews, Rangel—who was then more than forty years old—was terminated as part of a nationwide reduction in force of all sales professionals who had not met the "Expectations" guidelines, including younger workers. Did S-A engage in age discrimination? Discuss. [*Rangel v. sanofi aventis U.S. LLC,* 2013 WL 142040 (10th Cir. 2013)] **(See page 515.)**

22–8. SPECIAL CASE ANALYSIS: Employment Discrimination.

Go to Case Analysis Case 22.1, *Dees v. United Rentals North America, Inc.,* on pages 506 and 507. Read the excerpt and answer the following questions.

- **(a) Issue:** What conduct on the part of the plaintiff and what action on the part of the defendant were at the center of the dispute in this case?
- **(b) Rule of Law:** Once a *prima facie* case of employment discrimination has been established, as the case moves forward, who must prove what, and who must respond with evidence of what else?
- **(c) Applying the Rule of Law:** What was the court's evaluation of the parties' allegations and evidence in this case?
- **(d) Conclusion:** In whose favor did the court rule? Why?

22–9. A QUESTION OF ETHICS: Discrimination Based on Disability.

Titan Distribution, Inc., employed Quintak, Inc., to run its tire mounting and distribution operation in Des Moines, Iowa. Robert Chalfant worked for Quintak as a second shift supervisor at Titan. He suffered a heart attack in 1992 and underwent heart bypass surgery in 1997. He also had arthritis. In July 2002, Titan

*decided to fire Quintak. Chalfant applied to work at Titan. On his application, he described himself as disabled. After a physical exam, Titan's physician concluded that Chalfant could work in his current capacity, and he was notified that he would be hired. Despite the notice, Nadis Barucic, a Titan employee, wrote "not pass px" at the top of Chalfant's application, and he was not hired. He took a job with AMPCO Systems, a parking ramp management company. This work involved walking up to five miles a day and lifting more weight than he had at Titan. In September, Titan eliminated its second shift. Chalfant filed a suit in a federal district court against Titan, in part, under the Americans with Disabilities Act (ADA). Titan argued that it had not hired Chalfant because he did not pass the physical, but no one—including Barucic—could explain why she had written "not pass px" on his application. Later, Titan claimed that Chalfant was not hired because the entire second shift was going to be eliminated. [*Chalfant v. Titan Distribution, Inc., *475 F.3d 982 (8th Cir. 2007)]* **(See page 517.)**

(a) What must Chalfant establish to make his case under the ADA? Can he meet these requirements? Explain.

(b) In employment-discrimination cases, punitive damages can be appropriate when an employer acts with malice or reckless indifference toward an employee's protected rights. Would an award of punitive damages to Chalfant be appropriate in this case? Discuss.

Legal Reasoning Group Activity

22–10. Racial Discrimination. Two African American plaintiffs sued the producers of the reality television series *The Bachelor* and *The Bachelorette* for racial discrimination. The plaintiffs claimed that the shows have never featured persons of color in the lead roles. The plaintiffs also alleged that the producers failed to provide people of color who auditioned for the lead roles with the same opportunities to compete as white people who auditioned. **(See page 506.)**

(a) The first group will assess whether the plaintiffs can establish a *prima facie* case of disparate-treatment (intentional) discrimination.

(b) The second group will consider whether the plaintiffs can establish disparate-impact discrimination.

(c) The third group will assume that the plaintiffs established a *prima facie* case and that the burden has shifted to the employer to articulate a legal reason for not hiring the plaintiffs. What legitimate reasons might the employer assert for not hiring the plaintiffs in this situation? Should the law require television producers to hire persons of color for lead roles in reality television shows? Discuss.

ANTITRUST LAW

After the Civil War (1861–1865), the American public became increasingly concerned about declining competition in the marketplace. Large corporate enterprises were attempting to reduce or eliminate competition by legally tying themselves together in contracts to create *business trusts* (unincorporated organizations with limited liability).

The most famous trust was the Standard Oil trust of the late 1800s. Its participants transferred their stock to a trustee who then fixed prices, controlled production, and established exclusive geographic markets for all of the oil companies that were members of the trust. Some observers began to argue that the trust wielded so much economic power that corporations outside the trust could not compete effectively.

Eventually, legislation began to be enacted at both the state and the federal level to rein in the trusts. Hence, the laws that regulate economic competition in the United States today are still referred to as **antitrust laws.** At the national level, antitrust legislation began when Congress passed the Interstate Commerce Act[1] in 1887, followed by the Sherman Antitrust Act[2] in 1890. In 1914, Congress passed the Clayton Act[3] and the Federal Trade Commission Act[4] to further curb anticompetitive or unfair business practices. This chapter examines these major antitrust statutes, focusing particularly on the Sherman Act and the Clayton Act, as amended, and the types of activities they prohibit.

As you read the chapter, remember that the purpose of antitrust legislation was—and still is—to foster competition. Behind the laws lies our society's belief that competition leads to lower prices, better products, a wider selection of goods, and more product information. This is why the U.S. government became concerned about the pricing of e-books, as you will read later in this chapter.

1. 49 U.S.C. Sections 501–526
2. 15 U.S.C. Sections 1–7.
3. 15 U.S.C. Sections 12–27.
4. 15 U.S.C. Sections 41–58a.

SECTION 1
THE SHERMAN ANTITRUST ACT

The author of the Sherman Antitrust Act of 1890, Senator John Sherman, was the brother of the famed Civil War general and a recognized financial authority. He had been concerned for years about what he saw as diminishing competition within U.S. industry and the emergence of monopolies. He told Congress that the Sherman Act "does not announce a new principle of law, but applies old and well-recognized principles of the common law."[5]

Indeed, not only the legislation that Sherman proposed but subsequent antitrust laws as well were the direct descendants of common law actions intended to limit **restraints of trade** (agreements between firms that have the effect of reducing competition in the marketplace). The common law was not always consistent, however, and had not been effective in curbing the trusts. Therefore, in 1890 Congress passed "An Act to Protect Trade and Commerce against Unlawful Restraints and Monopolies"—more commonly referred to as the Sherman Antitrust Act, or simply the Sherman Act.

5. 21 *Congressional Record* 2456 (1890).

Major Provisions of the Sherman Act

Sections 1 and 2 contain the main provisions of the Sherman Act:

1. Every contract, combination in the form of trust or otherwise, or conspiracy, in restraint of trade

or commerce among the several States, or with foreign nations, is hereby declared to be illegal [and is a felony punishable by fine and/or imprisonment].

2. Every person who shall monopolize, or attempt to monopolize, or combine or conspire with any other person or persons, to monopolize any part of the trade or commerce among the several States, or with foreign nations, shall be deemed guilty of a felony [and is similarly punishable].

Differences between Section 1 and Section 2

These two sections of the Sherman Act are quite different. Section 1 requires two or more persons, as a person cannot contract, combine, or conspire alone. Thus, the essence of the illegal activity is *the act of joining together.* Section 2, though, can apply either to one person or to two or more persons because it refers to "every person." Thus, unilateral conduct can result in a violation of Section 2.

The cases brought to the courts under Section 1 of the Sherman Act differ from those brought under Section 2. Section 1 cases are often concerned with whether an agreement (written or oral) leads to a restraint of trade. Section 2 cases deal with the structure of a monopoly that exists in the marketplace. The term **monopoly** generally is used to describe a market in which there is a single seller or a very limited number of sellers. Whereas Section 1 focuses on agreements that are restrictive—that is, agreements that have a wrongful purpose—Section 2 looks at the so-called misuse of **monopoly power** in the marketplace.

Monopoly power exists when a firm has an extreme amount of **market power**—the ability to affect the market price of its product. Both Section 1 and Section 2 seek to curtail market practices that result in undesired monopoly pricing and output behavior. For a case to be brought under Section 2, however, the "threshold" or "necessary" amount of monopoly power must already exist.

Jurisdictional Requirements

The Sherman Act applies only to restraints that have a significant impact on interstate commerce. Courts have generally held that any activity that substantially affects interstate commerce falls within the scope of the Sherman Act. As will be discussed later in this chapter, the Sherman Act also extends to U.S. nationals abroad that are engaged in activities that affect U.S. foreign commerce.

Federal courts have exclusive jurisdiction over antitrust cases brought under the Sherman Act. State laws regulate local restraints on competition, and state courts can decide claims brought under those laws.

SECTION 2

SECTION 1 OF THE SHERMAN ACT

The underlying assumption of Section 1 of the Sherman Act is that society's welfare is harmed if rival firms are permitted to join in an agreement that consolidates their market power or otherwise restrains competition. The types of trade restraints that Section 1 of the Sherman Act prohibits generally fall into two broad categories: *horizontal restraints* and *vertical restraints,* both of which will be discussed shortly. First, though, we look at the rules that the courts may apply when assessing the anticompetitive impact of alleged restraints of trade.

Per Se Violations versus the Rule of Reason

Some restraints are so substantially anticompetitive that they are deemed ***per se* violations**—illegal *per se* (inherently)—under Section 1. Other agreements, however, even though they result in enhanced market power, do not *unreasonably* restrain trade and are therefore lawful. Using the **rule of reason,** the courts analyze anticompetitive agreements that allegedly violate Section 1 of the Sherman Act to determine whether they actually constitute reasonable restraints of trade.

RATIONALE FOR THE RULE OF REASON The need for a rule-of-reason analysis of some agreements in restraint of trade is obvious. If the rule of reason had not been developed, almost any business agreement could conceivably be held to violate the Sherman Act.

FACTORS THAT COURTS CONSIDER When analyzing an alleged Section 1 violation under the rule of reason, a court will consider the following factors:

1. The purpose of the agreement.
2. The parties' ability to implement the agreement to achieve that purpose.

3. The effect or potential effect of the agreement on competition.
4. Whether the parties could have relied on less restrictive means to achieve their purpose.

▶ **Case in Point 27.1** The National Football League (NFL) includes thirty-two separately owned professional football teams. Each team has its own name, colors, and logo, and owns related intellectual property that it markets through National Football League Properties (NFLP). Until 2000, the NFLP granted nonexclusive licenses to a number of vendors, permitting them to manufacture and sell apparel bearing NFL team insignias. American Needle, Inc., was one of those licensees.

In late 2000, the teams authorized the NFLP to grant exclusive licenses. The NFLP granted Reebok International, Ltd., an exclusive ten-year license to manufacture and sell trademarked headwear for all thirty-two teams. It then declined to renew American Needle's nonexclusive license.

American Needle sued, claiming that the NFL teams, the NFLP, and Reebok had violated Section 1 of the Sherman Act. The United States Supreme Court agreed. The Court concluded that the agreement among the NFL teams to license their intellectual property exclusively through the NFLP to Reebok constituted concerted activity.[6] ◀

Horizontal Restraints

The term **horizontal restraint** is encountered frequently in antitrust law. A horizontal restraint is any agreement that in some way restrains competition between rival firms competing in the same market. Horizontal restraints may include price fixing, group boycotts, market divisions, and trade associations.

PRICE FIXING Any **price-fixing agreement**—an agreement among competitors to fix prices—constitutes a *per se* violation of Section 1. The agreement on price need not be explicit. As long as it restricts output or artificially fixes price, it violates the law.

▶ **Case in Point 27.2** Independent oil producers in Texas and Louisiana were caught between falling demand due to the Great Depression of the 1930s and increasing supply from newly discovered oil fields in the region. In response to these conditions, a group of the major refining companies agreed to buy "distress" gasoline (excess supplies) from the independents so as to dispose of it in an "orderly manner." Although there was no explicit agreement as to price, it was clear that the purpose of the agreement was to limit the supply of gasoline on the market and thereby raise prices.

There may have been good reasons for the agreement. Nonetheless, the United States Supreme Court recognized the potentially adverse effects that such an agreement could have on open and free competition. The Court held that the reasonableness of a price-fixing agreement is never a defense. Any agreement that restricts output or artificially fixes price is a *per se* violation of Section 1.[7] ◀

Price Fixing and E-Books. The U.S. government actively pursues companies that it suspects of being involved in price-fixing cartels (groups). ▶ **Case in Point 27.3** In 2012, the U.S. Justice Department filed a lawsuit against five major book publishers and Apple, Inc., charging that they had conspired to fix the prices of e-books. Increased competition among e-book sellers—such as Amazon—had reduced e-book prices to $9.99 per e-book, which cut into the retail profit margins of the five publishers and Apple. The companies allegedly responded by working together to raise retail e-book prices and eliminate price competition—and the price of e-books did go up. All five of the book publishers subsequently settled with the Justice Department, but Apple proceeded to trial and lost. The court ruled that compelling evidence showed that Apple had conspired to fix prices in violation of the Sherman Act.[8] ◀

Price Fixing and Drug Manufacturers. Price-fixing accusations are also frequently made against drug manufacturers. ▶ **Case in Point 27.4** The manufacturer of the prescription drug Cardizem CD, which can help prevent heart attacks, was about to lose its patent on the drug. Another company had developed a generic version in anticipation of the patent's expiration. After the two firms became involved in litigation over the patent, the original manufacturer agreed to pay the second company $40 million per year not to market the generic version until their dispute was resolved. This agreement was held to be a *per se* violation of the Sherman Act because it restrained competition between rival firms and delayed the entry of generic versions of Cardizem into the market.[9] ◀

6. *American Needle, Inc. v. National Football League,* 560 U.S. 183, 130 S.Ct. 2201, 176 L.Ed.2d 947 (2010).

7. *United States v. Socony-Vacuum Oil Co.,* 310 U.S. 150, 60 S.Ct. 811, 84 L.Ed. 1129 (1940).
8. *United States v. Apple, Inc.,* ___ F.Supp.2d ___, 2013 WL 3454986 (S.D.N.Y. 2013).
9. *In re Cardizem CD Antitrust Litigation,* 332 F.3d 896 (6th Cir. 2003).

GROUP BOYCOTTS A **group boycott** is an agreement by two or more sellers to refuse to deal with (boycott) a particular person or firm. Because they involve concerted action, group boycotts have been held to constitute *per se* violations of Section 1 of the Sherman Act.

To prove a violation of Section 1, the plaintiff must demonstrate that the boycott or joint refusal to deal was undertaken with the intention of eliminating competition or preventing entry into a given market. Although most boycotts are illegal, a few, such as group boycotts against a supplier for political reasons, may be protected under the First Amendment right to freedom of expression.

HORIZONTAL MARKET DIVISION It is a *per se* violation of Section 1 of the Sherman Act for competitors to divide up territories or customers. ▶ **Example 27.5** Alred Office Supply, Belmont Business, and Carlson's, Inc., compete against each other in the states of Kansas, Nebraska, and Oklahoma. They agree that Alred will sell products only in Kansas, Belmont will sell only in Nebraska, and Carlson's will sell only in Oklahoma. This concerted action reduces the firms' marketing costs and allows all three (assuming there is no other competition) to raise the price of the goods sold in their respective states—a *per se* violation of Section 1.

The same violation would take place if the three firms agreed to divide up their territories by customers. For example, Alred might sell only to institutional purchasers (such as governments and schools) in all three states, Belmont only to wholesalers, and Carlson only to retailers. ◀

TRADE ASSOCIATIONS Businesses in the same general industry or profession frequently organize trade associations to pursue common interests. A trade association may engage in various joint activities, such as exchanging information, representing the members' business interests before governmental bodies, and conducting advertising campaigns. Trade associations also frequently are involved in setting regulatory standards to govern the industry or profession.

Generally, the rule of reason is applied to many of these horizontal actions. If a court finds that a trade association practice or agreement that restrains trade is nonetheless sufficiently beneficial both to the association and to the public, it may deem the restraint reasonable.

In *concentrated industries,* however, trade associations can be, and have been, used as a means to facilitate anticompetitive actions, such as fixing prices or allocating markets. A **concentrated industry** is one in which either a single firm or a small number of firms control a large percentage of market sales. When trade association agreements have substantially anticompetitive effects, a court will consider them to be in violation of Section 1 of the Sherman Act.

Vertical Restraints

A **vertical restraint** of trade results from an agreement between firms at different levels in the manufacturing and distribution process. In contrast to horizontal relationships, which occur at the same level of operation, vertical relationships encompass the entire chain of production.

The chain of production normally includes the purchase of inventory, basic manufacturing, distribution to wholesalers, and eventual sale of a product at the retail level. For some products, these distinct phases are carried on by different firms. In other instances, a single firm carries out two or more of the separate functional phases. Such enterprises are said to be **vertically integrated firms.**

Even though firms operating at different functional levels are not in direct competition with one another, they are in competition with other firms. Thus, agreements between firms standing in a vertical relationship may affect competition. Some vertical restraints are *per se* violations of Section 1. Others are judged under the rule of reason.

TERRITORIAL OR CUSTOMER RESTRICTIONS In arranging for the distribution of its products, a manufacturing firm often wishes to insulate dealers from direct competition with other dealers selling its products. To do so, the manufacturer may institute territorial restrictions or attempt to prohibit wholesalers or retailers from reselling the products to certain classes of buyers, such as competing retailers.

May Have Legitimate Purpose. A firm may have legitimate reasons for imposing such territorial or customer restrictions. For instance, an electronics manufacturer may wish to prevent a dealer from reducing costs and undercutting rivals by offering its products without promotion or customer service. The manufacturer legitimately seeks to prevent the cost-cutting dealer from reaping the benefits (sales of the product) paid for by other dealers who undertake promotion and provide customer service. By not offering customer service (and relying on a nearby dealer to provide these services), the cost-cutting dealer may also harm the manufacturer's reputation.

Judged under the Rule of Reason. Territorial and customer restrictions were once considered *per se* violations of Section 1,[10] but in 1977, the United States Supreme Court held that they should be judged under the rule of reason. ▶ **Case in Point 27.6** GTE Sylvania, Inc., a manufacturer of television sets, limited the number of retail franchises that it granted in any given geographic area. It also required each franchisee to sell only Sylvania products from the location at which it was franchised. Sylvania retained sole discretion to increase the number of retailers in an area.

When Sylvania decided to open a new franchise, it terminated the franchise of Continental T.V., Inc., an existing franchisee in that area that would have been in competition with the new franchise. Continental filed a lawsuit claiming that Sylvania's vertically restrictive franchise system violated Section 1 of the Sherman Act. The United States Supreme Court found that "vertical restrictions promote interbrand competition by allowing the manufacturer to achieve certain efficiencies in the distribution of his products." Therefore, Sylvania's vertical system, which was not price restrictive, did not constitute a *per se* violation of Section 1 of the Sherman Act.[11] ◀

The decision in the *Continental* case marked a definite shift from rigid characterization of territorial and customer restrictions to a more flexible, economic analysis of these vertical restraints under the rule of reason. This rule is still applied in most vertical restraint cases.

RESALE PRICE MAINTENANCE AGREEMENTS An agreement between a manufacturer and a distributor or retailer in which the manufacturer specifies what the retail prices of its products must be is known as a **resale price maintenance agreement.** Such agreements were once considered to be *per se* violations of Section 1 of the Sherman Act. In 1997, however, the United States Supreme Court ruled that *maximum* resale price maintenance agreements should be judged under the rule of reason.[12] The setting of a maximum price that retailers and distributors can charge for a manufacturer's products may sometimes increase competition and benefit consumers.

The question before the United States Supreme Court in the following case was whether *minimum* resale price maintenance agreements should be treated as *per se* violations.

10. See *United States v. Arnold, Schwinn & Co.*, 388 U.S. 365, 87 S.Ct. 1856, 18 L.Ed.2d 1249 (1967).

11. *Continental T.V., Inc. v. GTE Sylvania, Inc.*, 433 U.S. 36, 97 S.Ct. 2549, 53 L.Ed.2d 568 (1977).

12. *State Oil Co. v. Khan*, 522 U.S. 3, 118 S.Ct. 275, 139 L.Ed.2d 199 (1997).

CASE ANALYSIS

Case 27.1 Leegin Creative Leather Products, Inc. v. PSKS, Inc.

Supreme Court of the United States, 551 U.S. 877, 127 S.Ct. 2705, 168 L.Ed.2d 623 (2007).

IN THE LANGUAGE OF THE COURT

Justice *KENNEDY* delivered the opinion of the Court.

* * * *

Petitioner, Leegin Creative Leather Products, Inc. (Leegin), designs, manufactures, and distributes leather goods and accessories. In 1991, Leegin began to sell [products] under the brand name "Brighton."

Respondent, PSKS, Inc. (PSKS), operates Kay's Kloset, a women's apparel store in Lewisville, Texas. * * * It first started purchasing Brighton goods from Leegin in 1995.

* * * *

In December 2002, Leegin discovered Kay's Kloset had been marking down Brighton's entire line by 20 percent. * * * Leegin stopped selling [Brighton products] to the store.

PSKS sued Leegin in the United States District Court for the Eastern District of Texas. It alleged, among other claims, that Leegin had violated the antitrust laws by "enter[ing] into agreements with retailers to charge only those prices fixed by Leegin." * * * [The court] entered judgment against Leegin in the amount of $3,975,000.80.

The [U.S.] Court of Appeals for the Fifth Circuit affirmed. * * * We granted *certiorari* * * * .

* * * *

The rule of reason is the accepted standard for testing whether a practice restrains trade in violation of [Section] 1 [of the Sherman Act].

* * * *

*Resort to per se rules is confined to restraints * * * that would always or almost always tend to restrict competition and decrease output. To justify a per se prohibition a restraint must have manifestly anticompetitive effects,*

CASE 27.1 CONTINUES ➧

CASE 27.1 CONTINUED

*and lack * * * any redeeming virtue.* [Emphasis added.]

As a consequence, the *per se* rule is appropriate only after courts have had considerable experience with the type of restraint at issue, and only if courts can predict with confidence that it would be invalidated in all or almost all instances under the rule of reason.

* * * *

The reasoning of the Court's more recent jurisprudence has rejected the rationales on which [the application of the *per se* rule to minimum resale price maintenance agreements] was based. * * * [These rationales were] based on formalistic legal doctrine rather than demonstrable economic effect.

* * * Furthermore [the Court] treated vertical agreements a manufacturer makes with its distributors as analogous to a horizontal combination among competing distributors. * * * Our recent cases formulate antitrust principles in accordance with the appreciated differences in economic effect between vertical and horizontal agreements * * * .

* * * *

The justifications for vertical price restraints are similar to those for other vertical restraints. *Minimum resale price maintenance can stimulate interbrand competition * * * by reducing intrabrand competition* * * * . The promotion of interbrand competition is important because the primary purpose of the antitrust laws is to protect this type of competition. * * * *Resale price maintenance also has the potential to give consumers more options so that they can choose among low-price, low-service brands; high-price, high-service brands; and brands that fall in between.* [Emphasis added.]

* * * *

While vertical agreements setting minimum resale prices can have procompetitive justifications, they may have anticompetitive effects in other cases; and unlawful price fixing, designed solely to obtain monopoly profits, is an ever present temptation.

* * * *

Notwithstanding the risks of unlawful conduct, it cannot be stated with any degree of confidence that resale price maintenance always or almost always tends to restrict competition and decrease output. Vertical agreements establishing minimum resale prices can have either procompetitive or anticompetitive effects, depending upon the circumstances in which they are formed. * * * As the *[per se]* rule would proscribe a significant amount of procompetitive conduct, these agreements appear ill suited for *per se* condemnation.

* * * *

The judgment of the Court of Appeals is reversed, and the case is remanded for proceedings consistent with this opinion.

LEGAL REASONING QUESTIONS

1. Should the Court have applied the doctrine of *stare decisis* to hold that minimum resale price maintenance agreements are still subject to the *per se* rule? Why or why not?
2. What factors might the courts consider in applying the rule of reason to minimum resale price maintenance agreements?
3. In what ways do minimum resale price maintenance agreements facilitate interbrand competition?
4. In general, how are the interests of manufacturers, retailers, and consumers aligned—and in conflict—with respect to a product's profit margin? (A product's profit margin is the difference between the price a manufacturer charges retailers and the price retailers charge consumers.)

SECTION 3

SECTION 2 OF THE SHERMAN ACT

Section 1 of the Sherman Act proscribes certain concerted, or joint, activities that restrain trade. In contrast, Section 2 condemns "every person who shall monopolize, or attempt to monopolize." Thus, two distinct types of behavior are subject to sanction under Section 2: *monopolization* and *attempts to monopolize.*

One tactic that may be involved in either offense is predatory pricing. **Predatory pricing** occurs when one firm (the predator) attempts to drive its competitors from the market by selling its product at prices substantially *below* the normal costs of production. Once the competitors are eliminated, the predator presumably will raise its prices far above their competitive levels to recapture its losses and earn higher profits.

Monopolization

The United States Supreme Court has defined **monopolization** as involving the following two elements:

1. The possession of monopoly power in the relevant market.
2. "The willful acquisition or maintenance of the power as distinguished from growth or development as a consequence of a superior product, business acumen, or historic accident."[13]

To establish a violation of Section 2, a plaintiff must prove both of these elements—monopoly power and an *intent* to monopolize.

MONOPOLY POWER The Sherman Act does not define *monopoly.* In economic theory, monopoly refers to control of a specific market by a single entity. It is well established in antitrust law, however, that a firm may be a monopolist even though it is not the sole seller in a market.

Additionally, size alone does not determine whether a firm is a monopoly. ▶ **Example 27.7** A "mom and pop" grocery located in the isolated town of Happy Camp, Idaho, is a monopolist if it is the only grocery serving that particular market. Size in relation to the market is what matters because monopoly involves the power to affect prices. ◀

Monopoly power may be proved by direct evidence that the firm used its power to control prices and restrict output.[14] Usually, though, there is not enough evidence to show that the firm intentionally controlled prices, so the plaintiff has to offer indirect, or circumstantial, evidence of monopoly power. To prove monopoly power indirectly, the plaintiff must show that the firm has a dominant share of the relevant market and that there are significant barriers for new competitors entering that market.

In the following case, the court had to decide whether there was sufficient evidence to show that a company possessed monopoly power in the relevant market.

13. *United States v. Grinnell Corp.,* 384 U.S. 563, 86 S.Ct. 1698, 16 L.Ed.2d 778 (1966).

14. See, for example, *Broadcom Corp. v. Qualcomm, Inc.,* 501 F.3d 297 (3d Cir. 2007).

CASE 27.2

E.I. DuPont de Nemours and Co. v. Kolon Industries

United States Court of Appeals, Fourth Circuit, 637 F.3d 435 (2011).

COMPANY PROFILE DuPont was founded in 1802 as a gunpowder manufacturer. Today, it operates in ninety countries in the fields of agriculture, apparel, communications, electronics, home construction, nutrition, and transportation. It recently made a major investment in a biodegradable ingredient used in cosmetics, liquid detergents, and antifreeze.

BACKGROUND AND FACTS DuPont manufactures and sells para-aramid fiber, which is a complex synthetic fiber used to make body armor, fiber-optic cables, and tires, among other things. Although several companies around the world manufacture this fiber, only three sell into the U.S. market—DuPont (based in the United States), Teijin (based in the Netherlands), and Kolon Industries, Inc. (based in Korea). DuPont is the industry leader, producing more than 70 percent of all para-aramid fibers purchased in the United States. In 2009, DuPont brought a lawsuit against Kolon for misappropriation of trade secrets.

Kolon counterclaimed that DuPont had monopolized and attempted to monopolize the para-aramid market in violation of Section 2 of the Sherman Act. Kolon claimed that DuPont had illegally used multiyear supply agreements for all of its high-volume para-aramid fiber customers. Under the agreements, the customers were required to purchase between 80 and 100 percent of their para-aramid needs from DuPont. Kolon alleged that those agreements removed substantial commercial opportunities from competition and limited other para-aramid fiber producers' ability to compete. On DuPont's motion, a federal district court dismissed Kolon's counterclaim, finding that Kolon had failed to sufficiently plead (demonstrate) unlawful exclusionary conduct. Kolon appealed to the U.S. Court of Appeals for the Fourth Circuit.

IN THE LANGUAGE OF THE COURT

James *WYNN,* United States Circuit Judge.

* * * *

* * * *To prove a Section 2 monopolization offense, a plaintiff must establish two elements: (1) the possession of monopoly power; and (2) willful acquisition or maintenance of that power—as*

CASE 27.2 CONTINUES ➧

CASE 27.2 CONTINUED

opposed to simply superior products or historic accidents. An attempted monopolization offense consists of: (1) the use of anticompetitive conduct; (2) with specific intent to monopolize; and (3) a dangerous probability of success. [Emphasis added.]

* * * *

* * * To run afoul of Section 2, a defendant must be guilty of illegal conduct "to foreclose competition, to gain a competitive advantage, or to destroy a competitor." Conduct that might otherwise be lawful may be impermissibly exclusionary under antitrust law when practiced by a monopolist. Indeed, "a monopolist is not free to take certain actions that a company in a competitive * * * market may take, because there is no market constraint on a monopolist's behavior." And although not *per se* illegal, exclusive dealing arrangements can constitute an improper means of acquiring or maintaining a monopoly.

* * * *

Here, the district court assumed that Kolon adequately pled possession of monopoly power. That assumption was correct, given that Kolon pled, among other things, that: numerous barriers to entry into the U.S. para-aramid fiber market exist and supply is low; DuPont has long dominated the U.S. para-aramid fiber market; and DuPont currently controls over 70 percent of that market, [that is,] that "DuPont's market share remains greater than 70% of all sales by purchase volume of para-aramid fiber in the United States."

* * * *

* * * Kolon complained that "because DuPont's supply contracts severely restricted access to customers and preclude effective competition, DuPont's conduct has had a direct, substantial, and adverse effect on competition. And DuPont's anticompetitive conduct has allowed it to control output and increase prices for para-aramid fiber in the United States." And "by precluding Kolon from competition for these customers when demand for para-aramid fibers has significantly increased and supply is low, DuPont's conduct has constrained the only potential entrant to the United States in decades from effectively entering the market, reducing if not practically eliminating additional competition, as well as preserving and growing DuPont's monopoly position." These allegations are sufficient to withstand a motion to dismiss.

DECISION AND REMEDY *The federal appellate court reversed the district court's decision. The appellate court found that Kolon had alleged sufficient facts to show that DuPont's behavior violated the prohibition against monopolization and attempted monopolization in Section 2 of the Sherman Act.*

WHAT IF THE FACTS WERE DIFFERENT? *Suppose that DuPont had 45 percent of the market and Kolon and numerous other competitors had the remaining 55 percent. Would the appellate court have ruled the same way? Why or why not?*

MANAGERIAL IMPLICATIONS *Kolon's success in raising antitrust issues against a major supplier of a particular product in the United States can give some hope to other companies that are attempting to expand their market share against a dominant competitor. In other words, managers who see competitive opportunities, even though their companies have only a very small market share, may be able to resort to the courts to prevent the dominant company or companies from acting in anticompetitive ways.*

RELEVANT MARKET Before a court can determine whether a firm has a dominant market share, it must define the relevant market. The relevant market consists of two elements: (1) a relevant product market and (2) a relevant geographic market.

Relevant Product Market. The relevant product market includes all products that, although produced by different firms, have identical attributes, such as sugar. It also includes products that are reasonably interchangeable for the purpose for which they are produced. Products will be considered reasonably interchangeable if consumers treat them as acceptable substitutes.

Establishing the relevant product market is often the key issue in monopolization cases because the way the market is defined may determine whether a firm has monopoly power. By defining the product market narrowly, the degree of a firm's market power is enhanced.

▶ **Case in Point 27.8** Whole Foods Market, Inc., wished to acquire Wild Oats Markets, Inc., its main competitor in nationwide high-end organic food supermarkets. The Federal Trade Commission (FTC) filed a Section 2 claim against Whole Foods to prevent the merger. The FTC argued that the relevant product market consisted of only "premium natural and organic supermarkets" rather than all supermarkets, as Whole Foods maintained. An appellate court accepted the FTC's narrow definition of the relevant market and remanded the case to the lower court to decide what remedies were appropriate, as the merger had already taken place. Whole Foods later entered into a settlement with the FTC under which it was required to divest (sell or give up control over) thirteen stores, most of which were formerly Wild Oats outlets.[15] ◀

Relevant Geographic Market. The second component of the relevant market is the geographic extent of the market in which the firm and its competitors sell the product or services. For products that are sold nationwide, the geographic boundaries of the market can encompass the entire United States.

If transportation costs are significant or a producer and its competitors sell in only a limited area (one in which customers have no access to other sources of the product), then the geographic market is limited to that area. A national firm may thus compete in several distinct areas and have monopoly power in one geographic area but not in another.

Generally, the geographic market is that section of the country within which a firm can increase its price a bit without attracting new sellers or without losing many customers to alternative suppliers outside that area. Of course, the Internet is changing perceptions of the size and limits of a geographic market. Indeed, it has become difficult to show that a geographic market is strictly local, except for products that are not easily transported, such as concrete.

THE INTENT REQUIREMENT Monopoly power, in and of itself, does not constitute the offense of monopolization under Section 2 of the Sherman Act. The offense also requires an *intent* to monopolize.

Why Intent Is Required. A dominant market share may be the result of good business judgment or the development of a superior product. It may simply be the result of a historical accident. In these situations, the acquisition of monopoly power is not an antitrust violation. It would not be in society's interest to condemn every firm that acquired a position of power because it was well managed and efficient and marketed a product desired by consumers.

Inferred from Anticompetitive Conduct. If a firm possesses market power as a result of carrying out some purposeful act to acquire or maintain that power through anticompetitive means, then it is in violation of Section 2. In most monopolization cases, intent may be inferred from evidence that the firm had monopoly power and engaged in anticompetitive behavior.

▶ **Case in Point 27.9** When Navigator, the first popular graphical Internet browser, was introduced, Microsoft perceived a threat to its dominance of the operating-system market. Microsoft developed a competing browser, Internet Explorer (IE), and then began to require computer makers that wanted to install the Windows operating system to install IE and exclude Navigator. Microsoft included codes in Windows that would cripple the operating system if IE was deleted and paid Internet service providers to distribute IE and exclude Navigator.

Because of this pattern of exclusionary conduct, a court found that Microsoft was guilty of monopolization. The court reasoned that Microsoft's pattern of conduct could be rational only if the firm knew that it possessed monopoly power.[16] ◀

UNILATERAL REFUSALS TO DEAL As discussed previously, joint refusals to deal (group boycotts) are subject to close scrutiny under Section 1 of the Sherman Act. A single manufacturer acting unilaterally, though, normally is free to deal, or not to deal, with whomever it wishes.[17]

Nevertheless, in some instances, a unilateral refusal to deal will violate Section 2 of the Sherman Act. These instances occur only if (1) the firm refusing to deal has—or is likely to acquire—monopoly power and (2) the refusal is likely to have an anticompetitive effect on a particular market.

15. *Federal Trade Commission v. Whole Foods Market, Inc.*, 548 F.3d 1028 (D.C.Cir. 2008); and 592 F.Supp.2d 107 (D.D.C. 2009).

16. *United States v. Microsoft Corp.*, 253 F.3d 34 (D.C.Cir. 2001). Microsoft has faced numerous antitrust claims and has settled a number of lawsuits in which it was accused of antitrust violations and anticompetitive tactics.

17. For a classic case in this area, see *United States v. Colgate & Co.*, 250 U.S. 300, 39 S.Ct. 465, 63 L.Ed. 992 (1919). See also *Pacific Bell Telephone Co. v. Linkline Communications, Inc.*, 555 U.S. 438, 129 S.Ct. 1109, 172 L.Ed.2d 836 (2009).

▶ **Case in Point 27.10** Aspen Skiing Company, the owner of three of the four major ski areas in Aspen, Colorado, refused to continue its participation in a jointly offered "all Aspen" lift ticket. The United States Supreme Court ruled that the owner's refusal to cooperate with its smaller competitor was a violation of Section 2 of the Sherman Act. Because the company owned three-fourths of the local ski areas, it had monopoly power, and thus its unilateral refusal had an anticompetitive effect on the market.[18] ◀

Attempts to Monopolize

Section 2 also prohibits **attempted monopolization** of a market, which requires proof of the following three elements:

1. Anticompetitive conduct.
2. The specific intent to exclude competitors and garner monopoly power.
3. A "dangerous" probability of success in achieving monopoly power. The probability cannot be dangerous unless the alleged offender possesses some degree of market power.[19]

As mentioned earlier, predatory pricing is a form of anticompetitive conduct that, in theory, could be used by firms that are attempting to monopolize. (Predatory pricing may also lead to claims of price discrimination, to be discussed shortly.)

Predatory bidding involves the acquisition and use of *monopsony power,* which is market power on the *buy* side of a market. This may occur when a buyer bids up the price of an input too high for its competitors to pay, causing them to leave the market. The predatory bidder may then attempt to drive down input prices so that it can reap above-competitive profits and recoup any losses it suffered in bidding up the prices. The United States Supreme Court has held that the antitrust test that applies to claims of predatory pricing also applies to claims of predatory bidding.[20]

18. *Aspen Skiing Co. v. Aspen Highlands Skiing Corp.,* 472 U.S. 585, 105 S.Ct. 2847, 86 L.Ed.2d 467 (1985). See also *America Channel, LLC v. Time Warner Cable, Inc.,* 2007 WL 142173 (D.Minn. 2007).
19. See, for example, *Nobody in Particular Presents, Inc. v. Clear Channel Communications, Inc.,* 311 F.Supp.2d 1048 (D.Colo. 2004); and *City of Moundridge, Kansas v. Exxon Mobil Corp.,* 471 F.Supp.2d 20 (D.D.C. 2007).
20. *Weyerhaeuser Co. v. Ross-Simmons Hardwood Lumber Co.,* 549 U.S. 312, 127 S.Ct. 1069, 166 L.Ed.2d 911 (2007).

SECTION 4
THE CLAYTON ACT

In 1914, Congress enacted the Clayton Act. The act was aimed at specific anticompetitive or monopolistic practices that the Sherman Act did not cover. The substantive provisions of the act—set out in Sections 2, 3, 7, and 8—deal with four distinct forms of business behavior, which are declared illegal but not criminal. For each provision, the act states that the behavior is *illegal only if it tends to substantially lessen competition or to create monopoly power.*

Section 2—Price Discrimination

Section 2 of the Clayton Act prohibits **price discrimination,** which occurs when a seller charges different prices to competing buyers for identical goods or services. Congress strengthened this section by amending it with the passage of the Robinson-Patman Act in 1936.

As amended, Section 2 prohibits price discrimination that cannot be justified by differences in production costs, transportation costs, or cost differences due to other reasons. In short, a seller is prohibited from charging one buyer a lower price than it charges that buyer's competitor.

REQUIRED ELEMENTS To violate Section 2, the seller must be engaged in interstate commerce, the goods must be of like grade and quality, and the goods must have been sold to two or more purchasers. In addition, the effect of the price discrimination must be to substantially lessen competition, tend to create a monopoly, or otherwise injure competition. Without proof of an actual injury resulting from the price discrimination, the plaintiff cannot recover damages.

Note that price discrimination claims can arise from discounts, offsets, rebates, or allowances given to one buyer over another. Moreover, giving favorable credit terms, delivery, or freight charges to some buyers, but not others, can also lead to allegations of price discrimination. For example, when a seller offers goods to different customers at the same price but includes free delivery for certain buyers, it may violate Section 2 in some circumstances.

DEFENSES There are several statutory defenses to liability for price discrimination.

1. *Cost justification.* If the seller can justify the price reduction by demonstrating that a particular buyer's purchases saved the seller costs in producing and selling the goods, the seller will not be liable for price discrimination.
2. *Meeting a competitor's prices.* If the seller charged the lower price in a good faith attempt to meet an equally low price of a competitor, the seller will not be liable for price discrimination. ▶ **Case in Point 27.11** Water Craft was a retail dealership of Mercury Marine outboard motors. On discovering that Mercury was selling its outboard motors at a substantial discount to Water Craft's largest competitor, Water Craft filed a price discrimination lawsuit against Mercury. Mercury Marine was able to show that the discounts were made in good faith to meet the low price charged by another manufacturer of marine motors. Therefore, the court found that the "meeting competition defense" applied.[21] ◀
3. *Changing market conditions.* A seller may lower its price on an item in response to changing conditions affecting the market for or the marketability of the goods concerned. Sellers are allowed to readjust their prices to meet the realities of the market without liability for price discrimination. Thus, if an advance in technology makes a particular product less marketable than it was previously, a seller can lower the product's price.

Section 3—Exclusionary Practices

Under Section 3 of the Clayton Act, sellers or lessors cannot sell or lease goods "on the condition, agreement or understanding that the . . . purchaser or lessee thereof shall not use or deal in the goods . . . of a competitor or competitors of the seller." In effect, this section prohibits two types of vertical agreements involving exclusionary practices—exclusive-dealing contracts and tying arrangements.

EXCLUSIVE-DEALING CONTRACTS A contract under which a seller forbids a buyer to purchase products from the seller's competitors is called an **exclusive-dealing contract.** A seller is prohibited from making an exclusive-dealing contract under Section 3 if the effect of the contract is "to substantially lessen competition or tend to create a monopoly."

In the past, courts were more inclined than courts today to find that exclusive-dealing contracts substantially lessened competition. ▶ **Case in Point 27.12** In one classic case, Standard Oil Company, the largest gasoline seller in the nation in the late 1940s, made exclusive-dealing contracts with independent stations in seven western states. The contracts involved 16 percent of all retail outlets, whose sales were approximately 7 percent of all retail sales in that market. The United States Supreme Court ruled that the market was substantially concentrated because the seven largest gasoline suppliers all used exclusive-dealing contracts with their independent retailers and together controlled 65 percent of the market.

Looking at market conditions after the arrangements were instituted, the Court found that market shares were extremely stable and that entry into the market was apparently restricted. Thus, the Court held that the Clayton Act had been violated because competition was "foreclosed in a substantial share" of the relevant market.[22] ◀

In recent years, however, a number of decisions have called into doubt the Supreme Court's holding in *Case in Point 27.12.* Today, it is clear that to violate antitrust law, an exclusive-dealing agreement (or a tying arrangement, discussed next) must qualitatively and substantially harm competition. To prevail, a plaintiff must present affirmative evidence that the performance of the agreement will foreclose competition and harm consumers.

TYING ARRANGEMENTS When a seller conditions the sale of a product (the tying product) on the buyer's agreement to purchase another product (the tied product) produced or distributed by the same seller, a **tying arrangement** results. The legality of a tying arrangement (or *tie-in sales agreement*) depends on several factors, such as the purpose of the agreement. Courts also focus on the agreement's likely effect on competition in the relevant markets (the market for the tying product and the market for the tied product).

▶ **Example 27.13** Morshigi Precision, Inc., manufactures laptop hardware and provides repair service for the hardware. Morshigi also makes and markets software, but the company will provide support for buyers of the software only if they also buy its hardware service. This is a tying arrangement. Depending on the purpose of the agreement and the effect of the

21. *Water Craft Management, LLC v. Mercury Marine,* 457 F.3d 484 (5th Cir. 2006).

22. *Standard Oil Co. of California v. United States,* 337 U.S. 293, 69 S.Ct. 1051, 93 L.Ed. 1371 (1949).

agreement on competition in the market for the two products, the agreement may be illegal. ◀

Section 3 of the Clayton Act has been held to apply only to commodities, not to services. Tying arrangements, however, can also be considered agreements that restrain trade in violation of Section 1 of the Sherman Act. Thus, cases involving tying arrangements of services have been brought under Section 1 of the Sherman Act. Although earlier cases condemned tying arrangements as illegal *per se,* courts now evaluate tying agreements under the rule of reason.[23]

Section 7—Mergers

Under Section 7 of the Clayton Act, a person or business organization cannot hold stock or assets in more than one business when "the effect . . . may be to substantially lessen competition." Section 7 is the statutory authority for preventing mergers that could result in monopoly power or a substantial lessening of competition in the marketplace. Section 7 applies to both horizontal and vertical mergers, as discussed in the following subsections.

A crucial consideration in most merger cases is **market concentration.** Determining market concentration involves allocating percentage market shares among the various companies in the relevant market. When a small number of companies share a large part of the market, the market is concentrated. ▶ **Example 27.14** If the four largest grocery stores in Chicago accounted for 80 percent of all retail food sales, the market clearly would be concentrated in those four firms. If one of these stores absorbed the assets and liabilities of another, so the other ceased to exist, the resulting merger would further concentrate the market and possibly diminish competition. ◀

Competition is not necessarily diminished solely as a result of market concentration, however. Courts will consider other factors in determining if a merger violates Section 7. One factor of particular importance is whether the merger will make it more difficult for *potential* competitors to enter the relevant market.

HORIZONTAL MERGERS Mergers between firms that compete with each other in the same market are called **horizontal mergers.** If a horizontal merger creates an entity with a significant market share, the merger may be considered illegal because it increases market concentration. The Federal Trade Commission (FTC) and the U.S. Department of Justice (DOJ) have established guidelines for determining which mergers will be challenged.[24]

When analyzing the legality of a horizontal merger, the courts consider three additional factors. The first factor is the overall concentration of the relevant market. The second is the relevant market's history of tending toward concentration. The final factor is whether the merger is apparently designed to establish market power or restrict competition.

VERTICAL MERGERS A **vertical merger** occurs when a company at one stage of production acquires a company at a higher or lower stage of production. An example of a vertical merger is a company merging with one of its suppliers or retailers. Whether a vertical merger will be deemed illegal generally depends on several factors, such as whether the merger creates a single firm that controls an undue percentage share of the relevant market.

The courts also analyze whether the merger results in a significant increase in the concentration of firms in that market, barriers to entry into the market, and the apparent intent of the merging parties. If a merger does not prevent competitors of either of the merging firms from competing in a segment of the market, the merger will not be condemned as foreclosing competition and thus is legal.

Section 8—Interlocking Directorates

Section 8 of the Clayton Act deals with *interlocking directorates*—that is, the practice of having individuals serve as directors on the boards of two or more competing companies simultaneously. Specifically, no person may be a director for two or more competing corporations at the same time if either of the corporations has capital, surplus, or undivided profits aggregating more than $28,883,000 or competitive sales of $2,888,300 or more. The Federal Trade Commission adjusts these threshold amounts each year. (The amounts given here are those announced by the commission in 2013.)

23. The United States Supreme Court held that the rule of reason applies to tying arrangements in *Illinois Tool Works, Inc. v. Independent Ink, Inc.,* 547 U.S. 28, 126 S.Ct. 1281, 164 L.Ed.2d 26 (2006). This decision was the first time the Court recognized that tying arrangements can have legitimate business justifications.

24. These guidelines include a formula for assessing the degree of concentration in the relevant market called the *Herfindahl-Hirschman Index* (HHI). The HHI was revised in 2010 and is available at www.justice.gov/atr/public/guidelines/hmg-2010.html.

SECTION 5

ENFORCEMENT AND EXEMPTIONS

The federal agencies that enforce the federal antitrust laws are the U.S. Department of Justice (DOJ) and the Federal Trade Commission (FTC), which was established by the Federal Trade Commission Act of 1914. Section 5 of that act condemns all forms of anticompetitive behavior that are not covered under other federal antitrust laws.

Agency Actions

Only the DOJ can prosecute violations of the Sherman Act, which can be either criminal or civil offenses. Violations of the Clayton Act are not crimes, but the act can be enforced by either the DOJ or the FTC through civil proceedings.

The DOJ or the FTC may ask the courts to impose various remedies, including **divestiture** (making a company give up one or more of its operations) and dissolution. A meatpacking firm, for instance, might be forced to divest itself of control or ownership of butcher shops.

The FTC has sole authority to enforce violations of Section 5 of the Federal Trade Commission Act. FTC actions are effected through administrative orders, but if a firm violates an FTC order, the FTC can seek court sanctions for the violation.

The president, of course, plays a role in establishing enforcement policies at the agencies. The Obama administration—much like the European Union—has vigorously enforced antitrust regulations in recent years.

Private Actions

A private party who has been injured as a result of a violation of the Sherman Act or the Clayton Act can sue for **treble damages** (three times the actual damages suffered) and attorneys' fees. In some instances, private parties may also seek injunctive relief to prevent antitrust violations.

REQUIRED ELEMENTS A party wishing to sue under the Sherman Act must prove that:

1. The antitrust violation either caused or was a substantial factor in causing the injury that was suffered.
2. The unlawful actions of the accused party affected business activities of the plaintiff that were protected by the antitrust laws.

PROOF OF ILLEGALITY Additionally, the United States Supreme Court has held that to pursue antitrust lawsuits, private parties must present some evidence suggesting that an illegal agreement was made. ▶ **Case in Point 27.15** A group of subscribers to local telephone and high-speed Internet services filed a class-action lawsuit against several regional telecommunication companies (including Bell Atlantic). The plaintiffs claimed that the companies had conspired with one another and engaged in *parallel conduct*—offering similar services and pricing—over a period of years to prevent other companies from entering the market and competing.

The United States Supreme Court dismissed the case, finding that "without more, parallel conduct does not suggest conspiracy." A bare assertion of conspiracy is not enough to allow an antitrust lawsuit to go forward. The Court noted that more specificity is necessary to avoid potentially "massive" discovery costs, which are especially likely to occur when the suit is brought by a large class of plaintiffs.[25] ◀

Exemptions from Antitrust Laws

There are many legislative and constitutional limitations on antitrust enforcement. Most of the statutory and judicially created exemptions to the antitrust laws apply in such areas as labor, insurance, and foreign trade (see Exhibit 27–1 on the following page).

One of the most significant exemptions covers joint efforts by businesspersons to obtain legislative, judicial, or executive action. Under this exemption, for example, Blu-ray producers can jointly lobby Congress to change the copyright laws without being held liable for attempting to restrain trade. Another exemption covers professional baseball teams.

SECTION 6

U.S. ANTITRUST LAWS IN THE GLOBAL CONTEXT

U.S. antitrust laws have a broad application. Not only may persons in foreign nations be subject to their provisions, but the laws may also be applied to protect

25. *Bell Atlantic Corp. v. Twombly,* 550 U.S. 544, 127 S.Ct. 1955, 167 L.Ed.2d 929 (2007).

EXHIBIT 27–1 Exemptions to Antitrust Enforcement

Exemption	Source and Scope
Labor	Clayton Act—Permits unions to organize and bargain without violating antitrust laws and specifies that strikes and other labor activities normally do not violate any federal law.
Agricultural associations	Clayton Act and Capper-Volstead Act—Allow agricultural cooperatives to set prices.
Fisheries	Fisheries Cooperative Marketing Act—Allows the fishing industry to set prices.
Insurance companies	McCarran-Ferguson Act—Exempts the insurance business in states in which the industry is regulated.
Exporters	Webb-Pomerene Act—Allows U.S. exporters to engage in cooperative activity to compete with similar foreign associations. Export Trading Company Act—Permits the U.S. Department of Justice to exempt certain exporters.
Professional baseball	The United States Supreme Court has held that professional baseball is exempt because it is not "interstate commerce."[a]
Oil marketing	Interstate Oil Compact—Allows states to set quotas on oil to be marketed in interstate commerce.
Defense activities	Defense Production Act—Allows the president to approve, and thereby exempt, certain activities to further the military defense of the United States.
Small businesses' cooperative research	Small Business Administration Act—Allows small firms to undertake cooperative research.
State actions	The United States Supreme Court has held that actions by a state are exempt if the state clearly articulates and actively supervises the policy behind its action.[b]
Regulated industries	Industries (such as airlines) are exempt when a federal administrative agency (such as the Federal Aviation Administration) has primary regulatory authority.
Businesspersons' joint efforts to seek government action	Cooperative efforts by businesspersons to obtain legislative, judicial, or executive action are exempt unless it is clear that an effort is "objectively baseless" and is an attempt to make anticompetitive use of government processes.[c]

a. *Federal Baseball Club of Baltimore, Inc. v. National League of Professional Baseball Clubs,* 259 U.S. 200, 42 S.Ct. 465, 66 L.Ed. 898 (1922). A federal district court has held that this exemption applies only to the game's reserve system. (Under the reserve system, teams hold players' contracts for the players' entire careers. The reserve system generally is being replaced by the free agency system.) See *Piazza v. Major League Baseball,* 831 F.Supp. 420 (E.D.Pa. 1993).

b. See *Parker v. Brown,* 317 U.S. 341, 63 S.Ct. 307, 87 L.Ed. 315 (1943).

c. *Eastern Railroad Presidents Conference v. Noerr Motor Freight, Inc.,* 365 U.S. 127, 81 S.Ct. 523, 5 L.Ed.2d 464 (1961); and *United Mine Workers of America v. Pennington,* 381 U.S. 657, 89 S.Ct. 1585, 14 L.Ed.2d 626 (1965). These two cases established the exception often referred to as the *Noerr-Pennington* doctrine.

foreign consumers and competitors from violations committed by U.S. business firms. Consequently, *foreign persons,* a term that by definition includes foreign governments, may sue under U.S. antitrust laws in U.S. courts.

The Extraterritorial Application of U.S. Antitrust Laws

Section 1 of the Sherman Act provides for the extraterritorial effect of the U.S. antitrust laws. The United States is a major proponent of free competition in the global economy, and thus any conspiracy that has a *substantial effect* on U.S. commerce is within the reach of the Sherman Act. The violation may even occur outside the United States, and foreign governments as well as individuals can be sued for violation of U.S. antitrust laws.

Before U.S. courts will exercise jurisdiction and apply antitrust laws, it must be shown that the alleged violation had a substantial effect on U.S. commerce. U.S. jurisdiction is automatically invoked, however, when a *per se* violation occurs.

If a domestic firm, for example, joins a foreign cartel to control the production, price, or distribution of goods, and this cartel has a *substantial effect* on U.S. commerce, a *per se* violation may exist. Hence, both the domestic firm and the foreign cartel could be sued for violation of the U.S. antitrust laws. Likewise, if a foreign firm doing business in the United States enters into a price-fixing or other anticompetitive agreement to control a portion of U.S. markets, a *per se* violation may exist.

In the following case, the court had to decide whether an alleged anticompetitive conspiracy had a substantial effect on U.S. commerce.

CASE 27.3

Carrier Corp. v. Outokumpu Oyj

United States Court of Appeals, Sixth Circuit, 673 F.3d 430 (2012).

BACKGROUND AND FACTS Carrier Corporation is a U.S. firm that manufactures air-conditioning and refrigeration (ACR) equipment. To make these products, Carrier uses ACR copper tubing bought from Outokumpu Oyj, a Finnish company. Carrier is one of the world's largest purchasers of ACR copper tubing. The Commission of the European Communities (EC) found that Outokumpu had conspired with other companies to fix ACR tubing prices in Europe. Carrier then filed a suit in a U.S. court, alleging that the cartel had also conspired to fix prices in the United States by agreeing that only Outokumpu would sell ACR tubing in the U.S. market. The district court dismissed Carrier's claim for lack of jurisdiction. Carrier appealed.

IN THE LANGUAGE OF THE COURT
Karen Nelson *MOORE,* Circuit Judge.

* * * *

Carrier's complaint describes, in some detail, an elaborate worldwide conspiracy in which the U.S. market for ACR copper tubing was assigned to Outokumpu. Furthermore, *Carrier alleges that this conspiracy caused the price of goods purchased within the United States to increase, which in turn caused a direct antitrust injury.* In support of these allegations, the complaint references numerous specific dates during which the * * * cartel met and the various agreements its members entered into. *Assuming that these allegations are true, as we must, we conclude that Carrier has met any applicable requirement that it allege a [substantial] effect on U.S. commerce.* [Emphasis added.]

Outokumpu, which attached the full EC decision to its motion to dismiss, counters that many of the details contained in the complaint are drawn from [an] EC * * * decision that found no evidence that the cartel's focus extended beyond Europe. * * * As a consequence, Outokumpu argues that any details regarding specific meetings and agreements occurring during the [cartel] meetings are of no assistance to Carrier because they relate only to a European conspiracy.

We are [not] persuaded by this argument. * * * The EC * * * decision clearly states that "insofar as the activities of the cartel relate to sales in countries that are not members of the Community * * * they lie outside the scope of this Decision." Thus, any silence on the part of the EC decision as to U.S. markets may simply reflect the limited scope of the decision.

* * * *

Furthermore, Carrier offers additional circumstantial allegations that corroborate its claim that the market-allocation scheme extended to the United States. Although Carrier's complaint provides numerous circumstantial allegations, of particular interest is its claim that [Outokumpu's competitors] initially refrained from aggressively competing for Carrier's U.S. business until 2003, and then suddenly began doing so at that time. It is true that the mere fact that competitors do not intrude upon one another's markets does not necessarily mean that an illegal market-allocation scheme is taking place. When two companies refrain from entering a market and then suddenly do so after a cartel dissolves, however, there are good grounds for suspicion.

CASE 27.3 CONTINUES ➧

CASE 27.3 CONTINUED

DECISION AND REMEDY *The federal appellate court found that the district court had jurisdiction over Carrier's Sherman Act claims. It therefore reversed the district court's judgment for the defendants.*

THE LEGAL ENVIRONMENT DIMENSION *When this case proceeds, should the district court apply the rule of reason? Why or why not?*

WHAT IF THE FACTS WERE DIFFERENT? *Suppose that Carrier had engaged in anticompetitive conduct that affected Outokumpu. Discuss fully whether the foreign firm would be protected from illegal competition by the U.S. firm.*

The Application of Foreign Antitrust Laws

Large U.S. companies increasingly need to worry about the application of foreign antitrust laws as well. The European Union (EU), in particular, has stepped up its enforcement actions against antitrust violators in recent years.

EUROPEAN UNION ENFORCEMENT The EU's laws promoting competition are stricter in many respects than those of the United States and define more conduct as anticompetitive. The EU actively pursues antitrust violators, especially individual companies and cartels that allegedly engage in monopolistic conduct. ▶ **Example 27.16** The EU fined Intel, Inc., the world's largest semiconductor chip maker, $1.44 billion in an antitrust case. According to European regulators, Intel offered computer manufacturers and retailers price discounts and marketing subsidies if they agreed to buy Intel's chips rather than the chips produced by Intel's main competitor in Europe. The EU has also fined Microsoft Corporation more than $2 billion in the last ten years for anticompetitive conduct. ◀

INCREASED ENFORCEMENT IN ASIA AND LATIN AMERICA Many other nations also have laws that promote competition and prohibit trade restraints. For instance, Japanese antitrust laws forbid unfair trade practices, monopolization, and restrictions that unreasonably restrain trade. China's antitrust rules restrict monopolization and price fixing (although the Chinese government may set prices on exported goods without violating these rules). Indonesia, Malaysia, South Korea, and Vietnam all have statutes protecting competition. Argentina, Brazil, Chile, Peru, and several other Latin American countries have adopted modern antitrust laws as well.

Most of the antitrust laws apply extraterritorially, as U.S. antitrust laws do. This means that a U.S. company may be subject to another nation's antitrust laws if the company's conduct has a substantial effect on that nation's commerce. For instance, South Korea once fined Intel $25 million for antitrust violations, and Japan settled an antitrust case against Intel.

Reviewing: Antitrust Law

The Internet Corporation for Assigned Names and Numbers (ICANN) is a nonprofit entity that organizes Internet domain names. It is governed by a board of directors elected by various groups with commercial interests in the Internet. One of ICANN's functions is to authorize an entity to serve as a registry for certain "Top-Level Domains" (TLDs). ICANN and VeriSign entered into an agreement that authorized VeriSign to serve as a registry for the ".com" TLD and provide registry services in accordance with ICANN's specifications. VeriSign complained that ICANN was restricting the services that it could make available as a registrar and blocking new services, imposing unnecessary conditions on those services, and setting the prices at which the services were offered. VeriSign claimed that ICANN's control of the registry services for domain names violated Section 1 of the Sherman Act. Using the information presented in the chapter, answer the following questions.

1. Should ICANN's actions be judged under the rule of reason or be deemed *per se* violations of Section 1 of the Sherman Act? Why?
2. Should ICANN's actions be viewed as a horizontal or a vertical restraint of trade? Why?
3. Does it matter that ICANN's directors are chosen by groups with a commercial interest in the Internet? Explain.
4. If the dispute is judged under the rule of reason, what might be ICANN's defense for having a standardized set of registry services that must be used?

DEBATE THIS . . . *The Internet and the rise of e-commerce have rendered our current antitrust concepts and laws obsolete.*

Terms and Concepts

antitrust law 599
attempted monopolization 608
concentrated industry 602
divestiture 611
exclusive-dealing contract 609
group boycott 602
horizontal merger 610
horizontal restraint 601
market concentration 610
market power 600
monopolization 604
monopoly 600
monopoly power 600
***per se* violation 600**
predatory pricing 604
price discrimination 608
price-fixing agreement 601
resale price maintenance agreement 603
restraint of trade 599
rule of reason 600
treble damages 611
tying arrangement 609
vertical merger 610
vertical restraint 602
vertically integrated firm 602

ExamPrep

Issue Spotters

1. Under what circumstances would Pop's Market, a small store in a small, isolated town, be considered a monopolist? If Pop's is a monopolist, is it in violation of Section 2 of the Sherman Act? Why or why not? **(See page 604.)**
2. Maple Corporation conditions the sale of its syrup on the buyer's agreement to buy Maple's pancake mix. What factors would a court consider to decide whether this arrangement violates the Clayton Act? **(See page 609.)**

- **Check your answers to the Issue Spotters against the answers provided in Appendix E at the end of this text.**

Before the Test

Go to **www.cengagebrain.com**, enter the ISBN 9781285428949, and click on "Find" to locate this textbook's Web site. Then, click on "Access Now" under "Study Tools," and select Chapter 27 at the top. There, you will find an Interactive Quiz that you can take to assess your mastery of the concepts in this chapter, as well as Flashcards and a Glossary of important terms.

Business Scenarios

27–1. Group Boycott. Jorge's Appliance Corp. was a new retail seller of appliances in Sunrise City. Because of its innovative sales techniques and financing, Jorge's caused the appliance department of No-Glow Department Store, a large chain store with a great deal of buying power, to lose a substantial amount of sales. No-Glow told a number of appliance manufacturers from whom it made large-volume purchases that if they continued to sell to Jorge's, No-Glow would stop buying from them. The manufacturers immediately stopped selling appliances to Jorge's. Jorge's filed a suit against No-Glow and the manufacturers, claiming that their actions constituted an antitrust violation. No-Glow and the manufacturers were able to prove that Jorge's was a small retailer with a small market share. They claimed that because the relevant market was not substantially affected, they were not guilty of restraint of trade. Discuss fully whether there was an antitrust violation. **(See page 602.)**

27–2. Antitrust Laws. Allitron, Inc., and Donovan, Ltd., are interstate competitors selling similar appliances, principally in the states of Illinois, Indiana, Kentucky, and Ohio. Allitron and Donovan agree that Allitron will no longer sell in Indiana and Ohio and that Donovan will no longer sell in Illinois and Kentucky. Have Allitron and Donovan violated any antitrust laws? If so, which law? Explain. **(See page 602.)**

Business Case Problems

27–3. Tying Arrangement. John Sheridan owned a Marathon gas station franchise. He sued Marathon Petroleum Co. under Section 1 of the Sherman Act and Section 3 of the Clayton Act, charging it with illegally tying the processing of credit-card sales to the gas station. As a condition of obtaining a Marathon dealership, dealers had to agree to let the franchisor process credit cards. They could not shop around to see if credit-card processing could be obtained at a lower price from another source. The district court dismissed the case for failure to state a claim. Sheridan appealed. Is there a tying arrangement? If so, does it violate the law? Explain. [*Sheridan v. Marathon Petroleum Co.*, 530 F.3d 590 (7th Cir. 2008)] **(See page 608.)**

27–4. Monopolization. When Deer Valley Resort Co. (DVRC) was developing its ski resort in the Wasatch Mountains near Park City, Utah, it sold parcels of land in the resort village to third parties. Each sales contract reserved the right of approval over the conduct of certain businesses on the property, including ski rentals. For fifteen years, DVRC permitted Christy Sports, LLC, to rent skis in competition with DVRC's ski rental outlet. When DVRC opened a new midmountain ski rental outlet, it revoked Christy's permission to rent skis. This meant that most skiers who flew into Salt Lake City and shuttled to Deer Valley had few choices: they could carry their ski equipment with them on their flights, take a shuttle into Park City and look for cheaper ski rentals there, or rent from DVRC. Christy filed a suit in a federal district court against DVRC. Was DVRC's action an attempt to monopolize in violation of Section 2 of the Sherman Act? Why or why not? [*Christy Sports, LLC v. Deer Valley Resort Co.*, 555 F.3d 1188 (10th Cir. 2009)] **(See page 604.)**

27–5. Price Fixing. Together, EMI, Sony BMG Music Entertainment, Universal Music Group Recordings, Inc., and Warner Music Group Corp. produced, licensed, and distributed 80 percent of the digital music sold in the United States. The companies formed MusicNet to sell music to online services that sold the songs to consumers. MusicNet required all of the services to sell the songs at the same price and subject to the same restrictions. Digitization of music became cheaper, but MusicNet did not change its prices. Did MusicNet violate the antitrust laws? Explain. [*Starr v. Sony BMG Music Entertainment*, 592 F.3d 314 (2d Cir. 2010)] **(See page 601.)**

27–6. BUSINESS CASE PROBLEM WITH SAMPLE ANSWER: Price Discrimination.

Dayton Superior Corp. sells its products in interstate commerce to several companies, including Spa Steel Products, Inc. The purchasers often compete directly with each other for customers. From 2005 to 2007, one of Spa Steel's customers purchased Dayton Superior's products from two of Spa Steel's competitors. According to the customer, Spa Steel's prices were always 10 to 15 percent higher for the same products. As a result, Spa Steel lost sales to at least that customer and perhaps others. Spa Steel wants to sue Dayton Superior for price discrimination. Which requirements for such a claim under Section 2 of the Clayton Act does Spa Steel satisfy? What additional facts will it need to prove? [Dayton Superior Corp. v. Spa Steel Products, Inc., *2012 WL 113663 (N.D.N.Y. 2012)*] **(See page 608.)**

- **For a sample answer to Problem 27–6, go to Appendix F at the end of this text.**

27–7. SPECIAL CASE ANALYSIS: Resale Price Maintenance Agreements.

Go to Case Analysis Case 27.1, *Leegin Creative Leather Products, Inc. v. PSKS, Inc.*, on pages 603 and 604. Read the excerpt and answer the following questions.

(a) **Issue:** The dispute in this case was between which parties and turned on what legal issue?

(b) **Rule of Law:** In resolving this dispute, what common law rule did the Court overturn, and what rule did the Court create to replace this rejected precedent?

(c) **Applying the Rule of Law:** What reasons did the Court give to justify its change in the law, and how did the new rule apply in this case?

(d) **Conclusion:** In whose favor did the Court rule and why?

27–8. A QUESTION OF ETHICS: Section 1 of the Sherman Act.

In the 1990s, DuCoa, L.P., made choline chloride, a B-complex vitamin essential for the growth and development of animals. DuCoa, Bioproducts, Inc., and Chinook Group, Ltd., each had one-third of the U.S. market for choline chloride. To stabilize the market and keep the price of the vitamin higher than it would otherwise have been, the companies agreed to fix the price and allocate market share by deciding which of them would offer the lowest price to

*each customer. At times, however, the companies disregarded the agreement. During an increase in competitive activity in August 1997, Daniel Rose became president of DuCoa. The next month, a subordinate advised him of the conspiracy. By February 1998, Rose had begun to implement a strategy to persuade DuCoa's competitors to rejoin the conspiracy. By April, the three companies had reallocated their market shares and increased their prices. In June, the U.S. Department of Justice began to investigate allegations of price fixing in the vitamin market. Ultimately, a federal district court convicted Rose of conspiracy to violate Section 1 of the Sherman Act. [*United States v. Rose, *449 F.3d 627 (5th Cir. 2006)]* **(See page 600.)**

(a) The court "enhanced" Rose's sentence to thirty months' imprisonment, one year of supervised release, and a $20,000 fine based, among other things, on his role as "a manager or supervisor" in the conspiracy. Rose appealed this enhancement to the U.S. Court of Appeals for the Fifth Circuit. Was it fair to increase Rose's sentence on this ground? Why or why not?

(b) Was Rose's participation in the conspiracy unethical? If so, how might Rose have behaved ethically instead? If not, could any of the participants' conduct be considered unethical? Explain.

Legal Reasoning Group Activity

27–9. Antitrust Violations. Residents of the city of Madison, Wisconsin, became concerned about overconsumption of liquor near the campus of the University of Wisconsin (UW). The city initiated a new policy, imposing conditions on area bars to discourage reduced-price "specials" that were believed to encourage high-volume and dangerous drinking. In 2012, the city began to draft an ordinance to ban all drink specials. Bar owners responded by announcing that they had "voluntarily" agreed to discontinue drink specials on Friday and Saturday nights after 8:00 P.M. The city put its ordinance on hold. Several UW students filed a lawsuit against the local bar owners association, alleging violations of antitrust law. **(See page 601.)**

(a) The first group will identify the grounds on which the plaintiffs might base their claim for relief and formulate an argument on behalf of the plaintiffs.

(b) The second group will determine whether the defendants are exempt from the antitrust laws.

(c) The third group will decide how the court should rule in this dispute and provide reasons for the ruling.

CHAPTER 28

INVESTOR PROTECTION AND CORPORATE GOVERNANCE

After the stock market crash of October 29, 1929, and the ensuing economic depression, Congress enacted legislation to regulate securities markets. The result was the Securities Act of 1933[1] and the Securities Exchange Act of 1934.[2] Both acts were designed to provide investors with more information to help them make buying and selling decisions about securities and to prohibit deceptive, unfair, and manipulative practices.

Securities generally include any instruments evidencing corporate ownership (stock) or debts (bonds).

Today, the sale and transfer of securities are heavily regulated by federal and state statutes and by government agencies. Moreover, the Securities and Exchange Commission has implemented new regulations since Congress passed the Dodd-Frank Wall Street Reform and Consumer Protection Act[3] in reaction to the latest economic recession. This chapter discusses the nature of federal securities regulation and its effect on the business world.

We also discuss corporate governance and the Sarbanes-Oxley Act, which significantly affects certain types of securities transactions. In the concluding pages of this chapter, we look at how securities laws are being adapted to the online environment.

1. 15 U.S.C. Sections 77a–77aa.
2. 15 U.S.C. Sections 78a–78mm.
3. Pub. L. No. 111-203, July 21, 2010, 124 Stat. 1376; 12 U.S.C. Sections 5301 *et seq.*

SECTION 1

THE SECURITIES AND EXCHANGE COMMISSION

The Securities Exchange Act of 1934 created the Securities and Exchange Commission (SEC) as an independent regulatory agency. The SEC administers the Securities Act of 1933 and the 1934 act. The SEC also plays a key role in interpreting the provisions of these acts (and their amendments) and in creating regulations governing the purchase and sale of securities. The basic functions of the SEC are as follows:

1. Interprets federal securities laws and investigates securities law violations.
2. Issues new rules and amends existing rules.
3. Oversees the inspection of securities firms, brokers, investment advisers, and ratings agencies.
4. Oversees private regulatory organizations in the securities, accounting, and auditing fields.
5. Coordinates U.S. securities regulation with federal, state, and foreign authorities.

Updating the Regulatory Process

The SEC is working to make the regulatory process more efficient and more relevant to today's securities trading practices. To this end, the SEC has embraced modern technology and communications methods, especially the Internet, more completely than many other federal agencies have. For instance, the agency requires companies to file certain information electronically so that it can be posted on the SEC's EDGAR (Electronic Data Gathering, Analysis, and Retrieval) database.

In addition, the SEC now requires companies to make disclosures about the potential impacts of climate change on their future profitability.[4] For instance, companies should disclose estimates for any material capital expenditures for pollution-control facilities and risk factors relating to existing or pending environmental legislation.

4. 17 C.F.R. Parts 211, 231, and 241.

The SEC's Expanding Regulatory Powers

Since the SEC's creation, its regulatory functions have gradually been increased by legislation granting it authority in different areas. For instance, to further curb securities fraud, Congress enacted the Securities Enforcement Remedies and Penny Stock Reform Act of 1990.[5] This act expanded the SEC's enforcement options and allowed SEC administrative law judges to hear cases involving more types of alleged securities law violations, such as fraudulent financial reporting and financial fraud. The Securities Acts Amendments of 1990 authorized the SEC to seek sanctions against those who violate foreign securities laws.[6]

The National Securities Markets Improvement Act of 1996 expanded the power of the SEC to exempt persons, securities, and transactions from the requirements of the securities laws.[7] The Sarbanes-Oxley Act of 2002, which you will read about later in this chapter, further expanded the authority of the SEC and required the SEC to adopt new rules.

SECTION 2

THE SECURITIES ACT OF 1933

The Securities Act of 1933 governs initial sales of stock by businesses. The act was designed to prohibit various forms of fraud and to stabilize the securities industry by requiring that investors receive financial and other significant information concerning the securities being offered for public sale. Basically, the purpose of this act is to require disclosure. The 1933 act provides that all securities transactions must be registered with the SEC unless they are specifically exempt from the registration requirements.

What Is a Security?

Section 2(1) of the Securities Act of 1933 contains a broad definition of securities, which generally include the following:[8]

1. Instruments commonly known as securities, such as preferred and common stocks, treasury stocks, bonds, debentures, and stock warrants.
2. Any interests commonly known as securities, such as stock options, puts, calls, or other types of privilege on a security or on the right to purchase a security or a group of securities in a national security exchange.
3. Notes, instruments, or other evidence of indebtedness, including certificates of interest in a profit-sharing agreement and certificates of deposit.
4. Any fractional undivided interest in oil, gas, or other mineral rights.
5. Investment contracts, which include interests in limited partnerships and other investment schemes.

THE *HOWEY* TEST In interpreting the 1933 act, the United States Supreme Court has held that an **investment contract** is any transaction in which a person (1) invests (2) in a common enterprise (3) reasonably expecting profits (4) derived *primarily* or *substantially* from others' managerial or entrepreneurial efforts. Known as the *Howey* test, this definition continues to guide the determination of what types of contracts can be considered securities.[9]

▶ **Case in Point 28.1** Alpha Telcom sold, installed, and maintained pay-phone systems. The company guaranteed buyers of the systems a 14 percent annual return. Alpha was operating at a net loss, however, and continually borrowed funds to pay investors the fixed rate of return it had promised. Eventually, the company filed for bankruptcy, and the SEC brought an action alleging that Alpha had violated the Securities Act of 1933. A federal court concluded that the pay-phone program was a security because it involved an investment contract.[10] ◀

MANY TYPES OF SECURITIES For our purposes, it is convenient to think of securities in their most common form—stocks and bonds issued by corporations. Bear in mind, though, that securities can take many forms, including interests in whiskey, cosmetics, worms, beavers, boats, vacuum cleaners, muskrats, and cemetery lots. Almost any stake in the ownership or debt of a company can be considered a security. Investment contracts in condominiums, franchises, limited partnerships in real estate, and oil or gas or other mineral rights have qualified as securities.

5. 15 U.S.C. Section 77g.
6. 15 U.S.C. Section 78a.
7. 15 U.S.C. Sections 77z-3, 78mm.
8. 15 U.S.C. Section 77b(1). Amendments in 1982 added stock options.
9. *SEC v. W. J. Howey Co.*, 328 U.S. 293, 66 S.Ct. 1100, 90 L.Ed. 1244 (1946).
10. *SEC v. Alpha Telcom, Inc.*, 187 F.Supp.2d 1250 (2002). See also *SEC v. Edwards*, 540 U.S. 389, 124 S.Ct. 892, 157 L.Ed.2d 813 (2004), in which the United States Supreme Court held that an investment scheme offering contractual entitlement to a fixed rate of return can be an investment contract and therefore can be considered a security under federal law.

Registration Statement

Section 5 of the Securities Act of 1933 broadly provides that if a security does not qualify for an exemption, that security must be *registered* before it is offered to the public. Issuing corporations must file a *registration statement* with the SEC and must provide all investors with a *prospectus*.

A **prospectus** is a disclosure document that describes the security being sold, the financial operations of the issuing corporation, and the investment or risk attaching to the security. The prospectus also serves as a selling tool for the issuing corporation.

The SEC now allows an issuer to deliver its prospectus to investors electronically via the Internet.[11] In principle, the registration statement and the prospectus supply sufficient information to enable unsophisticated investors to evaluate the financial risk involved.

CONTENTS OF THE REGISTRATION STATEMENT The registration statement must be written in plain English and fully describe the following:

1. The securities being offered for sale, including their relationship to the registrant's other capital securities.
2. The corporation's properties and business (including a financial statement certified by an independent public accounting firm).
3. The management of the corporation, including managerial compensation, stock options, pensions, and other benefits. Any interests of directors or officers in any material transactions with the corporation must be disclosed.
4. How the corporation intends to use the proceeds of the sale.
5. Any pending lawsuits or special risk factors.

All companies, both domestic and foreign, must file their registration statements electronically so that they can be posted on the SEC's EDGAR database (mentioned previously) and investors can access the information via the Internet. The EDGAR database includes material on *initial public offerings* (IPOs), proxy statements, corporations' annual reports, registration statements, and other documents that have been filed with the SEC.

REGISTRATION PROCESS The registration statement does not become effective until it has been reviewed and approved by the SEC (unless it is filed by a *well-known seasoned issuer,* as will be discussed shortly). The 1933 act restricts the types of activities that an issuer can engage in at each stage of the registration process. If an issuer violates these restrictions, investors can rescind their contracts to purchase the securities.

Prefiling Period. During the *prefiling period* (before the registration statement is filed), the issuer normally cannot sell or offer to sell the securities. Once the registration statement has been filed, a waiting period begins while the SEC reviews the registration statement for completeness.[12]

Waiting Period. During the waiting period, the securities can be offered for sale but cannot be sold by the issuing corporation. Only certain types of offers are allowed. All issuers can distribute a *preliminary prospectus,*[13] which contains most of the information that will be included in the final prospectus but often does not include a price.

Most issuers can also use a *free-writing prospectus* during this period (although some inexperienced issuers will need to file a preliminary prospectus first). A **free-writing prospectus** is any type of written, electronic, or graphic offer that describes the issuer or its securities and includes a legend indicating that the investor may obtain the prospectus at the SEC's Web site.

Posteffective Period. Once the SEC has reviewed and approved the registration statement and the waiting period is over, the registration is effective, and the *posteffective period* begins. The issuer can now offer and sell the securities without restrictions.

If the company issued a preliminary or free-writing prospectus to investors, it must provide those investors with a final prospectus either before or at the time they purchase the securities. The issuer can require investors to download the final prospectus from a Web site if it notifies them of the appropriate Internet address.

---

11. Basically, an electronic prospectus must meet the same requirements as a printed prospectus. The SEC rules address situations in which the graphics, images, or audio files in or accompanying a printed prospectus cannot be reproduced in an electronic form. 17 C.F.R. Section 232.304.

12. The waiting period must last at least twenty days but always extends much longer because the SEC inevitably requires numerous changes and additions to the registration statement.

13. A preliminary prospectus may also be called a *red herring prospectus*. The name comes from the legend printed in red across the prospectus stating that the registration has been filed but has not become effective.

Well-Known Seasoned Issuers

A *well-known seasoned issuer* (WKSI) is a firm that has issued at least $1 billion in securities in the last three years or has at least $700 million of value of outstanding stock in the hands of the public. WKSIs can file registration statements the day they announce a new offering and are not required to wait for SEC review and approval. They can also use a free-writing prospectus at any time, even during the prefiling period.

Exempt Securities and Transactions

Certain types of securities are exempt from the registration requirements of the Securities Act of 1933. These securities—which generally can also be resold without being registered—are summarized under the heading "Exempt Securities" in Exhibit 28–1 on the following page.[14] The exhibit also lists and describes certain transactions that are exempt from registration requirements under various SEC regulations.

The transaction exemptions are the most important because they are very broad and can enable an issuer to avoid the high cost and complicated procedures associated with registration. Because the coverage of the exemptions overlaps somewhat, an offering may qualify for more than one. Therefore, many sales occur without registration.

Even when a transaction is exempt from the registration requirements, the offering is still subject to the antifraud provisions of the 1933 act (as well as those of the 1934 act, to be discussed later in this chapter).

REGULATION A OFFERINGS An exemption from registration is available for an issuer's offerings that do not exceed $5 million in securities during any twelve-month period.[15] Under Regulation A,[16] the issuer must file with the SEC a notice of the issue and an offering circular, which must also be provided to investors before the sale. This process is much less expensive than the procedures associated with full registration.

Testing the Waters. Companies are allowed to "test the waters" for potential interest before preparing the offering circular. To *test the waters* means to determine potential interest without actually selling any securities or requiring any commitment from those who express interest. Small-business issuers can also use an integrated registration and reporting system that requires simpler forms than the full registration system.

Using the Internet. Some companies have sold their securities via the Internet using Regulation A. ▶ **Example 28.2** The Spring Street Brewing Company was the first company to sell securities via an online initial public offering (IPO). Spring Street raised about $1.6 million—without having to pay any commissions to brokers or underwriters. ◀

Such online IPOs are particularly attractive to small companies and start-up ventures that may find it difficult to raise capital from institutional investors or through underwriters. By making the offering online, the company can avoid both commissions and the costly and time-consuming filings required for a traditional IPO under federal and state law.

SMALL OFFERINGS—REGULATION D The SEC's Regulation D contains several exemptions from registration requirements (Rules 504, 504a, 505, and 506) for offers that either involve a small dollar amount or are made in a limited manner.

Rule 504. Rule 504 is the exemption used by most small businesses. It provides that noninvestment company offerings up to $1 million in any twelve-month period are exempt.[17] Noninvestment companies are firms that are not engaged primarily in the business of investing or trading in securities. (In contrast, an **investment company** is a firm that buys a large portfolio of securities and professionally manages it on behalf of many smaller shareholders/owners. A **mutual fund** is a well-known type of investment company.)

▶ **Example 28.3** Zeta Enterprises is a limited partnership that develops commercial property. Zeta intends to offer $600,000 of its limited partnership interests for sale between June 1 and May 31 of the next year. The buyers will become limited partners in Zeta. Because an interest in a limited partnership meets the definition of a security (discussed earlier in this chapter), this offering would be subject to the registration and prospectus requirements of the Securities Act of 1933.

---

14. 15 U.S.C. Section 77c.
15. 15 U.S.C. Section 77c(b).
16. 17 C.F.R. Sections 230.251–230.263.
17. 17 C.F.R. Section 230.504. Small businesses in California may also be exempt under SEC Rule 1001. California's rule permits limited offerings of up to $5 million *per transaction*, if they satisfy certain conditions.

EXHIBIT 28–1 Exemptions for Securities Offerings under the 1933 Securities Act

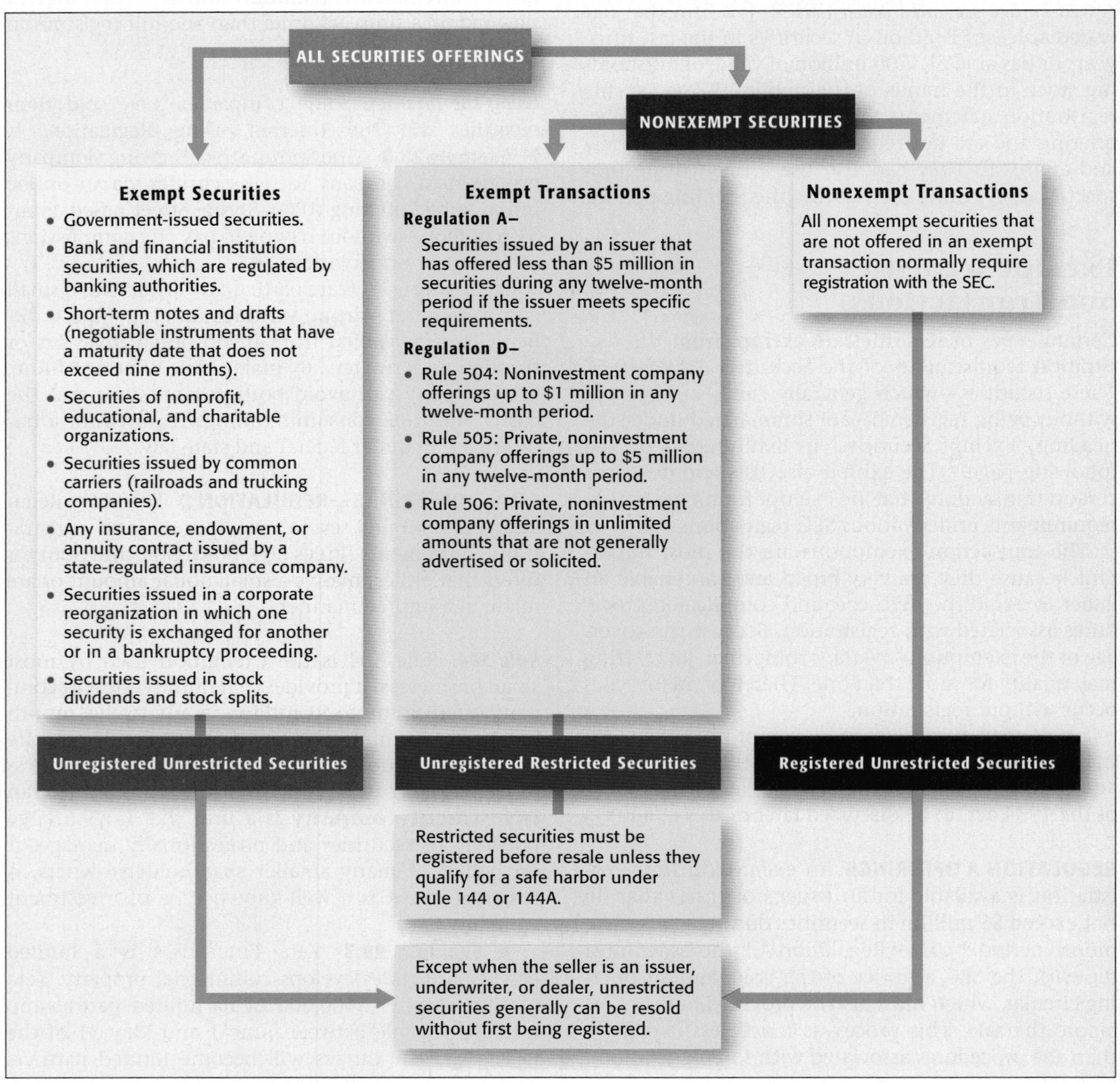

Under Rule 504, however, the sales of Zeta's interests are exempt from these requirements because Zeta is a noninvestment company making an offering of less than $1 million in a given twelve-month period. Therefore, Zeta can sell its interests without filing a registration statement with the SEC or issuing a prospectus to any investor. ◀

Rule 505. Another exemption is available under Rule 505 for private, noninvestment company offerings up to $5 million in any twelve-month period. Under this exemption, the offer may be made to an unlimited number of *accredited investors* and up to thirty-five unaccredited investors. **Accredited investors** include banks, insurance companies, investment companies, employee benefit plans, the issuer's executive officers and directors, and persons whose income or net worth exceeds a certain threshold.

The SEC must be notified of the sales, and precautions must be taken because these *restricted securities* may be resold only by registration or in an exempt transaction. No general solicitation or advertising is allowed. The issuer must provide any unaccredited investors with disclosure documents that generally are the same as those used in registered offerings.

Rule 506—Private Placement Exemption. Rule 506 exempts private, noninvestment company offerings in unlimited amounts that are not generally solicited or advertised. This exemption is often referred to as the *private placement exemption* because it exempts "transactions not involving any public offering."[18] There can be an unlimited number of accredited investors and up to thirty-five unaccredited investors. To qualify for the exemption, the issuer must believe that each unaccredited investor has sufficient knowledge or experience in financial matters to be capable of evaluating the investment's merits and risks.[19]

The private placement exemption is perhaps the most important exemption for firms that want to raise funds through the sale of securities without registering them. ▶ **Example 28.4** Citco Corporation needs to raise capital to expand its operations. Citco decides to make a private $10 million offering of its common stock directly to two hundred accredited investors and a group of thirty highly sophisticated, but unaccredited, investors. Citco provides all of these investors with a prospectus and material information about the firm, including its most recent financial statements.

As long as Citco notifies the SEC of the sale, this offering will likely qualify as an exempt transaction under Rule 506. The offering is nonpublic and not generally advertised. There are fewer than thirty-five unaccredited investors, and each of them possesses sufficient knowledge and experience to evaluate the risks involved. The issuer has provided all purchasers with the material information. Thus, Citco will *not* be required to comply with the registration requirements of the Securities Act of 1933. ◀

RESALES AND SAFE HARBOR RULES Most securities can be resold without registration. The Securities Act of 1933 provides exemptions for resales by most persons other than issuers or underwriters. The average investor who sells shares of stock need not file a registration statement with the SEC.

Resales of restricted securities acquired under Rule 505 or Rule 506, however, trigger the registration requirements *unless the party selling them complies with Rule 144 or Rule 144A*. These rules are sometimes referred to as safe harbors.

Rule 144. Rule 144 exempts restricted securities from registration on resale if all of the following conditions are met:

1. There is adequate current public information about the issuer. ("Adequate current public information" refers to the reports that certain companies are required to file under the Securities Exchange Act of 1934.)
2. The person selling the securities has owned them for at least six months if the issuer is subject to the reporting requirements of the 1934 act.[20] If the issuer is not subject to the 1934 act's reporting requirements, the seller must have owned the securities for at least one year.
3. The securities are sold in certain limited amounts in unsolicited brokers' transactions.
4. The SEC is notified of the resale.[21]

Rule 144A. Securities that at the time of issue were not of the same class as securities listed on a national securities exchange or quoted in a U.S. automated interdealer quotation system may be resold under Rule 144A.[22] They may be sold only to a qualified institutional buyer (an institution, such as an insurance company or a bank, that owns and invests at least $100 million in securities). The seller must take reasonable steps to ensure that the buyer knows that the seller is relying on the exemption under Rule 144A.

Violations of the 1933 Act

It is a violation of the Securities Act of 1933 to intentionally defraud investors by misrepresenting or omitting facts in a registration statement or prospectus. Liability is also imposed on those who are negligent

18. 15 U.S.C. Section 77d(2).
19. 17 C.F.R. Section 230.506.
20. Before 2008, when amendments to Rule 144 became effective, the holding period for restricted securities was one year if the issuer was subject to the reporting requirements of the 1934 act. See the revised SEC Rules and Regulations at 72 Federal Rules 71546-01, 2007 WL 4368599, Release No. 33-8869. This reduced holding period allows nonpublic issuers to raise capital electronically from private and overseas sources more quickly.
21. 17 C.F.R. Section 230.144.
22. 17 C.F.R. Section 230.144A.

in not discovering the fraud. Selling securities before the effective date of the registration statement or under an exemption for which the securities do not qualify results in liability.

REMEDIES Criminal violations are prosecuted by the U.S. Department of Justice. Violators may be fined up to $10,000, imprisoned for up to five years, or both.

The SEC is authorized to impose civil sanctions against those who willfully violate the 1933 act. It can request an injunction to prevent further sales of the securities involved or ask a court to grant other relief, such as ordering a violator to refund profits. Private parties who purchase securities and suffer harm as a result of false or omitted statements or other violations may bring a suit in a federal court to recover their losses and additional damages.

DEFENSES There are three basic defenses to charges of violations under the 1933 act. A defendant can avoid liability by proving any of the following:

1. The statement or omission was not material.
2. The plaintiff knew about the misrepresentation at the time the stock was purchased.
3. The defendant exercised *due diligence* in preparing the registration and reasonably believed at the time that the statements were true.

The due diligence defense is the most important because it can be asserted by any defendant, except the issuer of the stock. The defendant must prove that she or he reasonably believed, at the time the registration statement became effective, that the statements in it were true and there were no omissions of material facts.

The following case involved allegations of omissions of material information from an issuing company's registration statement. The defendants contended that the omissions were not material.

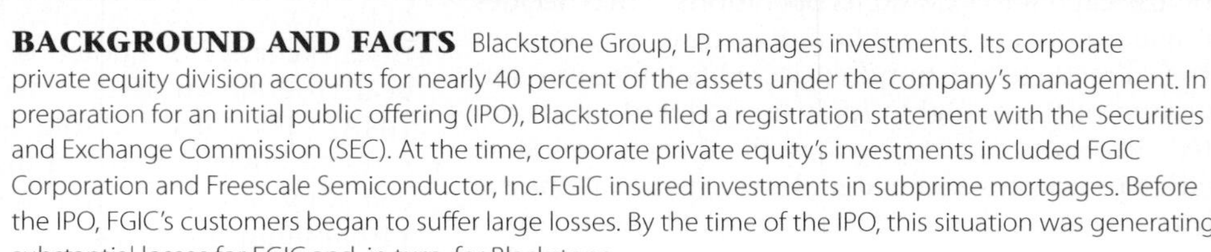

CASE 28.1

Litwin v. Blackstone Group, LP

United States Court of Appeals, Second Circuit, 634 F.3d 706 (2011).

BACKGROUND AND FACTS Blackstone Group, LP, manages investments. Its corporate private equity division accounts for nearly 40 percent of the assets under the company's management. In preparation for an initial public offering (IPO), Blackstone filed a registration statement with the Securities and Exchange Commission (SEC). At the time, corporate private equity's investments included FGIC Corporation and Freescale Semiconductor, Inc. FGIC insured investments in subprime mortgages. Before the IPO, FGIC's customers began to suffer large losses. By the time of the IPO, this situation was generating substantial losses for FGIC and, in turn, for Blackstone.

Meanwhile, Freescale had recently lost an exclusive contract to make wireless 3G chipsets for Motorola, Inc. (its largest customer). Blackstone's registration statement did not mention the impact on its revenue of the investments in FGIC and Freescale. Martin Litwin and others who invested in the IPO filed a suit in a federal district court against Blackstone and its officers, alleging material omissions from the statement. Blackstone filed a motion to dismiss, which the court granted. The plaintiffs appealed.

IN THE LANGUAGE OF THE COURT
STRAUB, Circuit Judge:

* * * *

Materiality is an inherently fact-specific finding that is satisfied when a plaintiff alleges a statement or omission that a reasonable investor would have considered significant in making investment decisions. * * * However, it is not necessary to assert that the investor would have acted differently if an accurate disclosure was made. Rather, when a district court is presented with a motion [to dismiss,] a complaint may not properly be dismissed on the ground that the alleged misstatements or omissions are not material unless they are so obviously unimportant to a reasonable investor that reasonable minds could not differ on the question of their importance. [Emphasis added.]

In this case, the key information that plaintiffs assert should have been disclosed is whether, and to what extent, the particular known trend, event, or uncertainty might have

CASE 28.1 CONTINUED

been reasonably expected to materially affect Blackstone's investments. * * * Plaintiffs are not seeking the disclosure of the mere fact of Blackstone's investment in FGIC, of the downward trend in the real estate market, or of Freescale's loss of its exclusive contract with Motorola. Rather, plaintiffs claim that Blackstone was required to disclose the manner in which those then-known trends, events, or uncertainties might reasonably be expected to materially impact Blackstone's future revenues.

* * * The question, of course, is not whether a loss in a particular investment's value will merely affect revenues, because * * * it will almost certainly have some effect. *The relevant question is whether Blackstone reasonably expects the impact to be material.* [Emphasis added.]

* * * Because Blackstone's Corporate Private Equity segment plays such an important role in Blackstone's business and provides value to all of its other asset management and financial advisory services, a reasonable investor would almost certainly want to know information related to that segment that Blackstone reasonably expects will have a material adverse effect on its future revenues. Therefore, the alleged * * * omissions relating to FGIC and Freescale were plausibly material.

DECISION AND REMEDY *The U.S. Court of Appeals for the Second Circuit vacated the lower court's dismissal and remanded the case. The plaintiffs had provided sufficient allegations that Blackstone had omitted material information that it was required to disclose under the securities laws for the case to go to trial.*

THE LEGAL ENVIRONMENT DIMENSION *Litwin alleged that Blackstone had negligently omitted material information from the registration statement. What will he and the others have to show to prove their case?*

THE ECONOMIC DIMENSION *Blackstone raised more than $4.5 billion through the IPO. Blackstone officers received nearly all of the net proceeds. If the company had disclosed the omitted information in its registration statement, how might these results have been different?*

SECTION 3

THE SECURITIES EXCHANGE ACT OF 1934

The Securities Exchange Act of 1934 provides for the regulation and registration of securities exchanges, brokers, dealers, and national securities associations, such as the National Association of Securities Dealers (NASD). Unlike the 1933 act, which is a one-time disclosure law, the 1934 act provides for continuous periodic disclosures by publicly held corporations to enable the SEC to regulate subsequent trading.

The Securities Exchange Act of 1934 applies to companies that have assets in excess of $10 million and five hundred or more shareholders. These corporations are referred to as *Section 12 companies* because they are required to register their securities under Section 12 of the 1934 act. Section 12 companies are required to file reports with the SEC annually and quarterly, and sometimes even monthly if specified events occur (such as a merger).

The act also authorizes the SEC to engage in market surveillance to deter undesirable market practices such as fraud, market manipulation, and misrepresentation. In addition, the act provides for the SEC's regulation of proxy solicitations for voting (discussed in Chapter 19).

Section 10(b), SEC Rule 10b-5, and Insider Trading

Section 10(b) is one of the more important sections of the Securities Exchange Act of 1934. This section prohibits the use of any manipulative or deceptive mechanism in violation of SEC rules and regulations. Among the rules that the SEC has promulgated pursuant to the 1934 act is **SEC Rule 10b-5,** which prohibits the commission of fraud in connection with the purchase or sale of any security.

SEC Rule 10b-5 applies to almost all cases concerning the trading of securities, whether on organized exchanges, in over-the-counter markets, or in private transactions. Generally, the rule covers just about any form of security. The securities need not be registered under the 1933 act for the 1934 act to apply.

Private parties can sue for securities fraud under the 1934 act and SEC rules. The basic elements of a securities fraud action are as follows:

1. A *material misrepresentation* (or omission) in connection with the purchase and sale of securities.
2. *Scienter* (a wrongful state of mind).
3. *Reliance* by the plaintiff on the material misrepresentation.
4. An *economic loss.*
5. *Causation,* meaning that there is a causal connection between the misrepresentation and the loss.

INSIDER TRADING One of the major goals of Section 10(b) and SEC Rule 10b-5 is to prevent **insider trading,** which occurs when persons buy or sell securities on the basis of information that is not available to the public. Corporate directors, officers, and others, such as majority shareholders, often have advance inside information that can affect the future market value of the corporate stock. Obviously, if they act on this information, their positions give them a trading advantage over the general public and other shareholders.

The 1934 Securities Exchange Act defines inside information. It also extends liability to those who take advantage of such information in their personal transactions when they know that the information is unavailable to those with whom they are dealing. Section 10(b) of the 1934 act and SEC Rule 10b-5 apply to anyone who has access to or receives information of a nonpublic nature on which trading is based—not just to corporate "insiders."

DISCLOSURE UNDER SEC RULE 10B-5 Any material omission or misrepresentation of material facts in connection with the purchase or sale of a security may violate Section 10(b) of the 1934 act and SEC Rule 10b-5. The key to liability (which can be civil or criminal) is whether the information omitted or misrepresented is *material.*

The following are some examples of material facts calling for disclosure under SEC Rule 10b-5:

1. Fraudulent trading in the company stock by a broker-dealer.
2. A dividend change (whether up or down).
3. A contract for the sale of corporate assets.
4. A new discovery, a new process, or a new product.
5. A significant change in the firm's financial condition.
6. Potential litigation against the company.

Note that any one of these facts, by itself, is not automatically considered material. Rather, it will be regarded as a material fact only if it is significant enough that it would likely affect an investor's decision as to whether to purchase or sell the company's securities.

▶ **Example 28.5** Zilotek, Inc., is the defendant in a class-action product liability suit that its attorney believes the company will lose. The attorney has advised Zilotek's directors, officers, and accountants that the company will likely have to pay a substantial damages award. Zilotek plans to make a $5 million offering of newly issued stock before the date when the trial is expected to end. Zilotek's potential liability and the financial consequences to the firm are material facts that must be disclosed because they are significant enough to affect an investor's decision as to whether to purchase the stock. ◀

The case that follows is a classic decision interpreting materiality under SEC Rule 10b-5.

CLASSIC CASE 28.2

SEC v. Texas Gulf Sulphur Co.

United States Court of Appeals, Second Circuit, 401 F.2d 833 (1968).

BACKGROUND AND FACTS Texas Gulf Sulphur Company (TGS) conducted aerial geophysical surveys over more than 15,000 square miles of eastern Canada. The operations indicated concentrations of commercially exploitable minerals. At one site near Timmins, Ontario, TGS drilled a hole that appeared to yield a core with an exceedingly high mineral content. The company did not disclose the results of the core sample to the public. After learning of the sample, TGS officers and employees made substantial purchases of TGS's stock or accepted stock options (rights to purchase stock). Further drilling, however, was necessary to establish whether there was enough ore to be mined commercially. Several months later, TGS

CASE 28.2 CONTINUED

announced that the strike was expected to yield at least 25 million tons of ore. Subsequently, the price of TGS stock rose substantially. The Securities and Exchange Commission (SEC) brought a suit against the officers and employees of TGS for violating SEC Rule 10b-5. The officers and employees argued that the information on which they had traded had not been material at the time of their trades because the mine had not then been commercially proved. The trial court held that most of the defendants had not violated SEC Rule 10b-5, and the SEC appealed.

IN THE LANGUAGE OF THE COURT

WATERMAN, Circuit Judge.

* * * *

* * * Whether facts are material within Rule 10b-5 when the facts relate to a particular event and are undisclosed by those persons who are knowledgeable thereof *will depend at any given time upon a balancing of both the indicated probability that the event will occur and the anticipated magnitude of the event in light of the totality of the company activity.* Here, * * * knowledge of the possibility, which surely was more than marginal, of the existence of a mine of the vast magnitude indicated by the remarkably rich drill core located rather close to the surface (suggesting mineability by the less expensive openpit method) within the confines of a large anomaly (suggesting an extensive region of mineralization) might well have affected the price of TGS stock and would certainly have been an important fact to a reasonable, if speculative, investor in deciding whether he should buy, sell, or hold. [Emphasis added.]

* * * *

* * * A major factor in determining whether the * * * discovery was a material fact is the importance attached to the drilling results by those who knew about it. * * * The timing by those who knew of it of their stock purchases * * *—purchases in some cases by individuals who had never before purchased * * * TGS stock—virtually compels the inference that the insiders were influenced by the drilling results.

DECISION AND REMEDY *The appellate court ruled in favor of the SEC. All of the trading by insiders who knew of the mineral find before its true extent had been publicly announced violated SEC Rule 10b-5.*

WHAT IF THE FACTS WERE DIFFERENT? *Suppose that further drilling had revealed that there was not enough ore at this site for it to be mined commercially. Would the defendants still have been liable for violating SEC Rule 10b-5? Why or why not?*

IMPACT OF THIS CASE ON TODAY'S LAW *This landmark case affirmed the principle that the test of whether information is "material," for SEC Rule 10b-5 purposes, is whether it would affect the judgment of reasonable investors. The corporate insiders' purchases of stock and stock options indicated that they were influenced by the drilling results and that the information about the drilling results was material. The courts continue to cite this case when applying SEC Rule 10b-5 to cases of alleged insider trading.*

OUTSIDERS AND SEC RULE 10B-5 The traditional insider-trading case involves true insiders—corporate officers, directors, and majority shareholders who have access to (and trade on) inside information. Increasingly, however, liability under Section 10(b) of the 1934 act and SEC Rule 10b-5 has been extended to include certain "outsiders"—those who trade on inside information acquired indirectly. Two theories have been developed under which outsiders may be held liable for insider trading: the *tipper/tippee theory* and the *misappropriation theory.*

Tipper/Tippee Theory. Anyone who acquires inside information as a result of a corporate insider's breach of his or her fiduciary duty can be liable under SEC Rule 10b-5. This liability extends to **tippees** (those who receive "tips" from insiders) and even remote tippees (tippees of tippees).

The key to liability under this theory is that the inside information must be obtained as a result of someone's breach of a fiduciary duty to the corporation whose shares are traded. The tippee is liable only if the following requirements are met:

1. There is a breach of a duty not to disclose inside information.
2. The disclosure is made in exchange for personal benefit.
3. The tippee knows (or should know) of this breach and benefits from it.[23]

Misappropriation Theory. Liability for insider trading may also be established under the misappropriation theory. This theory holds liable an individual who wrongfully obtains (misappropriates) inside information and trades on it for her or his personal gain because the individual basically stole information rightfully belonging to another.

The misappropriation theory has been controversial because it significantly extends the reach of SEC Rule 10b-5 to outsiders who ordinarily would *not* be deemed fiduciaries of the corporations in whose stock they trade. It is not always wrong to disclose material, nonpublic information about a company to a person who would not otherwise be privy to it. Nevertheless, a person who obtains the information and trades securities on it can be held liable.

▶ **Case in Point 28.6** Patricia Rocklage was the wife of Scott Rocklage, the CEO of Cubist Pharmaceuticals, Inc. Scott had sometimes disclosed material, nonpublic information about Cubist to Patricia. She had always kept the information confidential. When Scott told Patricia that one of Cubist's key drugs had failed its clinical trial, however, Patricia informed her brother, William Beaver, who owned Cubist stock. Beaver sold his Cubist shares and tipped his friend David Jones, who sold his shares. When Cubist publicly announced the trial results, the price of its stock dropped. Beaver and Jones avoided significant losses by selling when they did. The SEC filed a lawsuit against Patricia, Beaver, and Jones. The court found all three defendants guilty of insider trading under the misappropriation theory.[24] ◀

Insider Reporting and Trading—Section 16(b)

Section 16(b) of the 1934 act provides for the recapture by the corporation of all profits realized by certain insiders on any purchase and sale or sale and purchase of the corporation's stock within any six-month period. It is irrelevant whether the insider actually uses inside information—*all such short-swing profits must be returned to the corporation.*

In this context, insiders means officers, directors, and large stockholders of Section 12 corporations (those owning 10 percent of the class of equity securities registered under Section 12 of the 1934 act).[25] To discourage such insiders from using nonpublic information about their companies to their personal benefit in the stock market, they must file reports with the SEC concerning their ownership and trading of the corporation's securities.

Section 16(b) applies not only to stock but also to warrants, options, and securities convertible into stock. In addition, the courts have fashioned complex rules for determining profits. Note that the SEC exempts a number of transactions under Rule 16b-3.[26] For all of these reasons, corporate insiders should seek the advice of competent counsel before trading in the corporation's stock. Exhibit 28–2 on the facing page compares the effects of SEC Rule 10b-5 and Section 16(b).

The Private Securities Litigation Reform Act

The disclosure requirements of SEC Rule 10b-5 had the unintended effect of deterring the disclosure of forward-looking information. To understand why, consider the following situation. ▶ **Example 28.7** QT Company announces that it projects that its earnings in a future time period will be a certain amount, but the forecast turns out to be wrong. The earnings are in fact much lower, and the price of the company's stock is affected—negatively. The shareholders then bring a class-action suit against the company, alleging that the directors violated SEC Rule 10b-5 by disclosing misleading financial information. ◀

In an attempt to rectify this problem and promote disclosure, in 1995 Congress passed the Private Securities Litigation Reform Act (PSLRA). Among other things, the PSLRA provides a "safe harbor" for publicly held companies that make forward-looking statements, such as financial forecasts. Those who make such statements are protected against liability for securities fraud if they include "meaningful cautionary statements identifying important factors that

23. See, for example, *Chiarella v. United States,* 445 U.S. 222, 100 S.Ct. 1108, 63 L.Ed.2d 348 (1980); and *Dirks v. SEC,* 463 U.S. 646, 103 S.Ct. 3255, 77 L.Ed.2d 911 (1983).
24. *SEC v. Rocklage,* 470 F.3d 1 (1st Cir. 2006).
25. 15 U.S.C. Section 78*l*. Note that Section 403 of the Sarbanes-Oxley Act shortened the reporting deadlines specified in Section 16(b).
26. 17 C.F.R. Section 240.16b-3.

EXHIBIT 28–2 Comparison of Coverage, Application, and Liability under SEC Rule 10b-5 and Section 16(b)

Area of Comparison	SEC Rule 10b-5	Section 16(b)
What is the subject matter of the transaction?	Any security (does not have to be registered).	Any security (does not have to be registered).
What transactions are covered?	Purchase or sale.	Short-swing purchase and sale or short-swing sale and purchase.
Who is subject to liability?	Almost anyone with inside information under a duty to disclose—including officers, directors, controlling shareholders, and tippees.	Officers, directors, and certain shareholders who own 10 percent or more.
Is omission or misrepresentation necessary for liability?	Yes.	No.
Are there any exempt transactions?	No.	Yes, there are a number of exemptions.
Who may bring an action?	A person transacting with an insider, the SEC, or a purchaser or seller damaged by a wrongful act.	A corporation or a shareholder by derivative action.

could cause actual results to differ materially from those in the forward-looking statement."[27]

The PSLRA also affected the level of detail required in securities fraud complaints. Plaintiffs must specify each misleading statement and say how it led them to a mistaken belief.

Regulation of Proxy Statements

Section 14(a) of the Securities Exchange Act of 1934 regulates the solicitation of proxies (see Chapter 19) from shareholders of Section 12 companies. The SEC regulates the content of proxy statements. Whoever solicits a proxy must fully and accurately disclose in the proxy statement all of the facts that are pertinent to the matter on which the shareholders are to vote. SEC Rule 14a-9 is similar to the antifraud provisions of SEC Rule 10b-5. Remedies for violations are extensive, ranging from injunctions to prevent a vote from being taken to monetary damages.

Violations of the 1934 Act

As mentioned earlier, violations of Section 10(b) of the Securities Exchange Act of 1934 and SEC Rule 10b-5, including insider trading, may lead to both criminal and civil liability.

SCIENTER REQUIREMENT For either criminal or civil sanctions to be imposed, however, *scienter* must exist—that is, the violator must have had an intent to defraud or knowledge of his or her misconduct. *Scienter* can be proved if it is shown that the defendant made false statements or wrongfully failed to disclose material facts.

In some situations, *scienter* can even be proved by showing that the defendant was consciously reckless as to the truth or falsity of his or her statements. **Case in Point 28.8** Alvin Gebhart and Jack Archer started a business venture purchasing mobile home parks (MHPs) from owners and converting them to resident ownership. They formed MHP Conversions, LP, to facilitate the conversion process and issue promissory notes that were sold to investors to raise funds for the purchases.

Archer ran the MHP program, and Gebhart sold the promissory notes. Gebhart sold nearly $2.4 million in MHP promissory notes to clients, who bought the notes based on Gebhart's positive statements about the investment. During the time Gebhart was selling the notes, however, he never actually looked into the finances of the MHP program. He relied entirely on information that Archer gave him, some of which was not true. When Gebhart was later sued for securities fraud, a federal appellate court concluded that there was sufficient evidence of *scienter*. Gebhart knew that he had no knowledge of the financial affairs of MHP, and he had been consciously

27. 15 U.S.C. Sections 77z-2, 78u-5.

reckless as to the truth or falsity of his statements about investing in MHP.[28] ◀

In the complaint, the plaintiff must state facts giving rise to an inference of *scienter* at least as likely as any plausible opposing inference. Opposing inferences and their proof were at issue in the following case.

28. *Gebhart v. SEC,* 595 F.3d 1034 (9th Cir. 2010).

CASE ANALYSIS

Case 28.3 City of Livonia Employees' Retirement System and Local 295/Local 851 v. Boeing Co.

United States Court of Appeals, Seventh Circuit, 711 F.3d 754 (2013).

IN THE LANGUAGE OF THE COURT

POSNER, Circuit Judge.

* * * *

* * * On April 21 [2009] Boeing [Company] performed a stress test on the wings of its new 787-8 Dreamliner, a plane that had not yet flown. The wings failed the test * * * . Yet Boeing announced on May 3 that "all structural tests required on the static airframe prior to first flight are complete" and that "the initial results of the test are positive" * * * . The implication was that the plane was on track for its "First Flight," which had been scheduled for June 30.

In mid-May, after making some changes in the design * * * , Boeing conducted another test. Although the plane failed that test too, [Boeing's chief executive officer James] McNerney stated publicly that he thought the plane would fly in June. Later [the head of Boeing's commercial aircraft division Scott] Carson told [the media] that the Dreamliner "definitely will fly" this month (June).

* * * Yet on June 23, * * * Boeing announced that the First Flight of the Dreamliner had been canceled because, Carson explained, of an "anomaly" revealed by the * * * tests. He said that Boeing had hoped to be able to solve the problem in time for a First Flight in June, but had been unable to do so. In fact the First Flight did not take place until December 2009.

When Boeing announced the cancellation of the First Flight, it also announced that the cancellation would cause a delay of unspecified length in the delivery of the Dreamliner, which many airlines had already ordered. In the two days after these announcements, Boeing's stock price dropped by more than 10 percent. * * * Persons who bought Boeing stock between the tests and the announcements of the cancellation and of the delay in delivery and who therefore lost money when the price dropped [filed a suit in a federal district court against Boeing and its officers, alleging violations of Section 10(b) and Rule 10b-5].

The district judge dismissed the * * * complaint. [The plaintiffs appealed.]

There is no securities fraud by hindsight. The law does not require public disclosure of mere risks of failure. No prediction—even a prediction that the sun will rise tomorrow—has a 100 percent probability of being correct. The future is shrouded in uncertainty. If a mistaken prediction is deemed a fraud, there will be few predictions, including ones that are well grounded, as no one wants to be held hostage to an unknown future. [Emphasis added.]

Any sophisticated purchaser of a product that is still on the drawing boards knows, moreover, that its market debut may be delayed, or indeed that the project may be abandoned before it yields salable product. The purchasers of the Dreamliner protected themselves against the possibility of delay in delivery by reserving the right to cancel their orders; there are no allegations regarding cancellation penalties, or for that matter penalties imposed on Boeing for delivery delays. And therefore * * * the defendants * * * had, so far as appears, little incentive to delay the announcement of the postponement.

Without a motive to commit securities fraud, businessmen are unlikely to commit it. A more plausible inference than that of fraud is that the defendants, unsure whether they could fix the problem by the end of June, were reluctant to tell the world "we have a problem and maybe it will cause us to delay the First Flight and maybe not, but we're working on the problem and we hope we can fix it in time to prevent any significant delay, but we can't be sure, so stay tuned." There is a difference * * * between a duty of truthfulness and a duty of candor, or between a lie and reticence [uncommunicativeness]. There is no duty of total corporate transparency—no rule that every hitch or glitch, every pratfall [embarrassing mistake], in a company's operations must be disclosed in real time, forming a running commentary, a baring of the corporate innards, day and night. [Emphasis added.]

* * * *

* * * The * * * complaint alleged [that] what McNerney and Carson knew about the likely postponement of the First Flight * * * was confirmed by "internal e-mails" of Boeing. The reference to internal e-mails implied that someone inside Boeing was aiding the plaintiffs. But as no such

CASE 28.3 CONTINUED

person was identified, the judge could not determine whether such e-mails * * * existed.

Allegations * * * merely implying unnamed confidential sources of damaging information require a heavy discount. The sources may be ill-informed, may be acting from spite rather than knowledge, may be misrepresented, may even be nonexistent * * * . The district judge therefore rightly refused to give any weight to the "internal e-mails" to which the complaint referred.

* * * *

The judgment dismissing the suit is affirmed.

LEGAL REASONING QUESTIONS

1. Which *pleading* (a document filed with the court—see Chapter 2) was at the center of the dispute in this case?
2. What must this pleading state in a suit alleging violations of Section 10(b) and Rule 10b-5?
3. Did the court conclude that the pleading here met this requirement? Why or why not?
4. If a pleading does not meet this requirement, should the court impose sanctions on the lawyers who filed it? Discuss.

***SCIENTER* NOT REQUIRED FOR SECTION 16(B) VIOLATIONS** Violations of Section 16(b) include the sale by insiders of stock acquired less than six months before the time of sale (or less than six months after the sale, if selling short—that is, selling securities that one does not yet own). These violations are subject to civil sanctions. Liability under Section 16(b) is strict liability. Neither *scienter* nor negligence is required.

CRIMINAL PENALTIES For violations of Section 10(b) and Rule 10b-5, an individual may be fined up to $5 million, imprisoned for up to twenty years, or both. A partnership or a corporation may be fined up to $25 million. Under Section 807 of the Sarbanes-Oxley Act of 2002, for a *willful* violation of the 1934 act the violator can be imprisoned for up to twenty-five years (in addition to being subject to a fine).

For a defendant to be convicted in a criminal prosecution under the securities laws, there can be no reasonable doubt that the defendant knew he or she was acting wrongfully. In other words, a jury is not allowed merely to speculate that the defendant may have acted willfully. ▶ **Case in Point 28.9** Martha Stewart, founder of a well-known media and homemaking empire, was charged with intentionally deceiving investors based on statements she made at a conference. In 2001, Stewart's stockbroker allegedly informed Stewart that the head of ImClone Systems, Inc., was selling his shares in that company. Stewart then sold her ImClone shares. The next day, ImClone announced that the U.S. Food and Drug Administration had failed to approve Erbitux, the company's greatly anticipated medication.

After the government began investigating Stewart's ImClone trades, she publicly stated that she had previously instructed her stockbroker to sell her ImClone stock if the price fell to $60 per share. The government prosecutor claimed that Stewart's statement showed she had the intent to deceive investors. The court, however, acquitted Stewart on this charge because "to find the essential element of criminal intent beyond a reasonable doubt, a rational juror would have to speculate."[29] ◀

CIVIL SANCTIONS The SEC can also bring a civil action against anyone who purchases or sells a security while in the possession of material nonpublic information in violation of the 1934 act or SEC rules.[30] The violation must occur through the use of a national securities exchange or a broker or dealer.[31]

A court can assess a penalty amounting to as much as triple the profits gained or the loss avoided by the guilty party.[32] The Insider Trading and Securities Fraud Enforcement Act enlarged the class of persons who may be subject to civil liability for insider trading. This act also gave the SEC authority to offer monetary rewards to informants.[33]

Private parties may also sue violators of Section 10(b) and Rule 10b-5. A private party can obtain rescission (cancellation) of a contract to buy securities or damages to the extent of the violator's illegal profits. Those found liable have a right to seek contribution from those who share responsibility for the violations,

29. *United States v. Stewart,* 305 F.Supp.2d 368 (S.D.N.Y. 2004). (Stewart was later convicted on other charges relating to her ImClone trading that did not require proof of intent.)
30. 15 U.S.C. Section 78u(d)(2)(A).
31. Transactions pursuant to a public offering by an issuer of securities are excepted.
32. 15 U.S.C. Section 78u(d)(2)(C).
33. 15 U.S.C. Section 78u-1.

including accountants, attorneys, and corporations. For violations of Section 16(b), a corporation can bring an action to recover the short-swing profits.

SECTION 4

STATE SECURITIES LAWS

Today, every state has its own corporate securities laws, or **blue sky laws,** that regulate the offer and sale of securities within its borders. (The phrase *blue sky laws* comes from a 1917 United States Supreme Court decision. The Court stated that the purpose of such laws was to prevent "speculative schemes which have no more basis than so many feet of 'blue sky.'")[34] Article 8 of the Uniform Commercial Code also imposes various requirements relating to the purchase and sale of securities.

Requirements

Typically, state laws have disclosure requirements and antifraud provisions, many of which are patterned after Section 10(b) of the Securities Exchange Act of 1934 and SEC Rule 10b-5. State laws also provide for the registration of securities offered or issued for sale within the state and impose disclosure requirements.

Methods of registration, required disclosures, and exemptions from registration vary among states. Unless an exemption from registration is applicable, issuers must register or qualify their stock with the appropriate state official, often called a *corporations commissioner.* Additionally, most state securities laws regulate securities brokers and dealers.

Concurrent Regulation

State securities laws apply mainly to intrastate transactions. Since the adoption of the 1933 and 1934 federal securities acts, the state and federal governments have regulated securities concurrently. Issuers must comply with both federal and state securities laws, and exemptions from federal law are not exemptions from state laws.

The dual federal and state system has not always worked well, particularly during the early 1990s, when the securities markets underwent considerable expansion. Today, many of the duplicate regulations have been eliminated, and the SEC has exclusive power to regulate most national securities activities. The National Conference of Commissioners on Uniform State Laws also substantially revised the Uniform Securities Act in 2002 to coordinate state and federal securities regulation and enforcement efforts. Seventeen states have adopted the most recent version of the Uniform Securities Act.[35]

SECTION 5

CORPORATE GOVERNANCE

Corporate governance can be narrowly defined as the relationship between a corporation and its shareholders. Defined more broadly, corporate governance specifies the rights and responsibilities among different corporate participants (including stakeholders) and spells out the rules and procedures for making decisions on corporate affairs. Regardless of the way it is defined, effective corporate governance requires more than just compliance with laws and regulations.

Effective corporate governance is essential in large corporations because corporate ownership (by shareholders) is separated from corporate control (by officers and managers). Under these circumstances, officers and managers may attempt to advance their own interests at the expense of the shareholders. The well-publicized corporate scandals in the early 2000s clearly illustrate the reasons for concern about managerial opportunism. Indeed, corporate governance has become an issue of concern for corporate entities around the world. With the globalization of business, a corporation's bad acts (or lack of control systems) can have far-reaching consequences.

Attempts at Aligning the Interests of Officers with Those of Shareholders

Some corporations have sought to align the financial interests of their officers with those of the company's shareholders by providing the officers with **stock options,** which enable them to purchase shares of the corporation's stock at a set price. When the market price rises above that level, the officers can sell their

34. *Hall v. Geiger-Jones Co.,* 242 U.S. 539, 37 S.Ct. 217, 61 L.Ed. 480 (1917).

35. At the time this book went to press, the Uniform Securities Act had been adopted in Georgia, Hawaii, Idaho, Indiana, Iowa, Kansas, Maine, Michigan, Minnesota, Mississippi, Missouri, New Mexico, Oklahoma, South Carolina, South Dakota, Vermont, and Wisconsin, as well as in the U.S. Virgin Islands. You can find current information on state adoptions at www.uniformlaws.org.

shares for a profit. Because a stock's market price generally increases as the corporation prospers, the options give the officers a financial stake in the corporation's well-being and supposedly encourage them to work hard for the benefit of the shareholders.

Options have turned out to be an imperfect device for providing effective governance, however. Executives in some companies have "cooked" the company's books in order to keep share prices high so that they could sell their stock for a profit. Executives in other corporations have experienced no losses when share prices dropped because their options were "repriced" so that they did not suffer from the share price decline. Thus, although stock options theoretically can motivate officers to protect shareholder interests, stock option plans have sometimes become a way for officers to take advantage of shareholders.

With stock options generally failing to work as planned, there has been an outcry for more "outside" directors (those with no formal employment affiliation with the company). The theory is that independent directors will more closely monitor the actions of corporate officers. Hence, today we see more boards with outside directors. Note, though, that outside directors may not be truly independent of corporate officers. They may be friends or business associates of the leading officers.

The Goal Is to Promote Accountability

Effective corporate governance standards are designed to address problems such as those briefly discussed above and to motivate officers to make decisions that promote the financial interests of the company's shareholders. Generally, corporate governance entails corporate decision-making structures that monitor employees (particularly officers) to ensure that they are acting for the benefit of the shareholders. Thus, corporate governance involves, at a minimum:

1. The audited reporting of financial conditions at the corporation so that managers can be evaluated.
2. Legal protections for shareholders so that violators of the law who attempt to take advantage of shareholders can be punished for misbehavior and victims can recover damages for any associated losses.

THE COMPANY BENEFITS Effective corporate governance can have considerable practical significance. Firms that are more accountable to shareholders typically report higher profits, higher sales growth, higher firm value, and other economic advantages. Thus, a corporation with better corporate governance and greater accountability to investors may also have a higher valuation than a corporation that is less concerned about governance. Corporations that promote diversity in the workplace, and especially in management, may similarly experience increased profits, growth, and value.

GOVERNANCE AND CORPORATE LAW State corporation statutes set up the legal framework for corporate governance. Under the corporate law of Delaware, where most major companies incorporate, all corporations must have certain structures of corporate governance in place. The most important structure, of course, is the board of directors because the board makes the major decisions about the future of the corporation.

THE BOARD OF DIRECTORS Under corporate law, a corporation must have a board of directors elected by the shareholders. Almost anyone can become a director, though some organizations, such as the New York Stock Exchange, require certain standards of service for directors of their listed corporations.

Directors are responsible for ensuring that the corporation's officers are operating wisely and in the exclusive interest of shareholders. Directors receive reports from the officers and give them managerial directions. In reality, though, corporate directors devote a relatively small amount of time to monitoring officers.

Ideally, shareholders would monitor the directors' supervision of the officers. In practice, however, it can be difficult for shareholders to monitor directors and hold them responsible for corporate failings. Although the directors can be sued if they fail to do their jobs effectively, directors are rarely held personally liable.

THE COMPENSATION COMMITTEE An important committee of the board of directors is the *compensation committee,* which determines the compensation to be paid to the company's officers. As part of this process, the committee must assess the officers' performance and design a compensation system that will best align the officers' interests with those of the shareholders.

The Sarbanes-Oxley Act

In 2002, Congress passed the Sarbanes-Oxley Act (introduced in Chapter 4) in response to a series of corporate scandals. The act addresses certain issues relating to corporate governance. Generally, the act attempts to increase corporate accountability by imposing strict disclosure requirements and harsh penalties for violations of securities laws. Among other things, the act requires chief corporate executives to take personal responsibility for the accuracy of financial statements and reports that are filed with the SEC.

Additionally, the act requires that certain financial and stock-transaction reports be filed with the SEC earlier than was required under the previous rules. The act also created a new entity, called the Public Company Accounting Oversight Board, which regulates and oversees public accounting firms. Other provisions of the act established private civil actions and expanded the SEC's remedies in administrative and civil actions.

Because of the importance of this act for corporate leaders and for those dealing with securities transactions, we present excerpts and explanatory comments in Appendix D at the end of this text. We also highlight some of its key provisions relating to corporate accountability in Exhibit 28–3 on the next page.

MORE INTERNAL CONTROLS AND ACCOUNTABILITY The Sarbanes-Oxley Act also introduced direct *federal* corporate governance requirements for public companies (companies whose shares are traded in the public securities markets). The law addressed many of the corporate governance procedures just discussed and created new requirements in an attempt to make the system work more effectively. The requirements deal with independent monitoring of company officers by both the board of directors and auditors.

Sections 302 and 404 of the Sarbanes-Oxley Act require high-level managers (the most senior officers) to establish and maintain an effective system of internal controls. Moreover, senior management must reassess the system's effectiveness annually. Some companies had to take expensive steps to bring their internal controls up to the new federal standards. These include "disclosure controls and procedures" to ensure that company financial reports are accurate and timely and to document financial results prior to reporting. After the act was passed, hundreds of companies reported that they had identified and corrected shortcomings in their internal control systems.

EXEMPTIONS FOR SMALLER COMPANIES The act initially required all public companies to have an independent auditor file a report with the SEC on management's assessment of internal controls. Congress, however, enacted an exemption for smaller companies in 2010 in an effort to reduce compliance costs. Public companies with a market capitalization, or public float, of less than $75 million no longer need to have an auditor report on management's assessment of internal controls.

CERTIFICATION AND MONITORING REQUIREMENTS Section 906 of the Sarbanes-Oxley Act requires that chief executive officers and chief financial officers certify the accuracy of the information in the corporate financial statements. These corporate officers are subject to both civil and criminal penalties for violations of this section. This requirement makes the officers directly accountable for the accuracy of their financial reporting and precludes any "ignorance defense" if shortcomings are later discovered.

The act also includes requirements to improve directors' monitoring of officers' activities. All members of a publicly traded corporation's audit committee, which oversees the corporation's accounting and financial reporting processes, must be outside directors. (The New York Stock Exchange has a similar rule that also extends to the board's compensation committee, which monitors and determines the compensation of the company's officers.)

The audit committee must have a written charter that sets out its duties and provides for performance appraisal. At least one "financial expert" must serve on the audit committee, which must hold executive meetings without company officers being present. The audit committee must also establish procedures to encourage whistleblowers (see Chapter 21) to report violations. In addition to reviewing the internal controls, the committee also monitors the actions of the outside auditor.

SECTION 6
ONLINE SECURITIES FRAUD

A major problem facing the SEC today is how to enforce the antifraud provisions of the securities laws in the online environment. In 1999, in the first cases involving illegal online securities offerings, the SEC filed suit against three individuals for illegally offering securities on an Internet auction site.[36] In essence, all three indicated that their companies would soon go public and attempted to sell unregistered securities via the Web auction site. All of these actions were in violation of Sections 5, 17(a)(1), and 17(a)(3) of the 1933 Securities Act.

Since then, the SEC has brought a variety of Internet-related fraud cases and regularly issues interpretive releases to explain how securities laws apply in the online environment.

---

36. *In re Davis,* SEC Administrative File N.o. 3-10080 (October 20, 1999); *In re Haas,* SEC Administrative File No. 3-10081 (October 20, 1999); and *In re Sitaras,* SEC Administrative File No. 3-10082 (October 20, 1999).

EXHIBIT 28–3 Some Key Provisions of the Sarbanes-Oxley Act Relating to Corporate Accountability

Certification Requirements—Under Section 906 of the Sarbanes-Oxley Act, the chief executive officers (CEOs) and chief financial officers (CFOs) of most major companies listed on public stock exchanges must certify financial statements that are filed with the SEC. CEOs and CFOs have to certify that filed financial reports "fully comply" with SEC requirements and that all of the information reported "fairly represents in all material respects, the financial conditions and results of operations of the issuer."

Under Section 302 of the act, CEOs and CFOs of reporting companies are required to certify that a signing officer reviewed each quarterly and annual filing with the SEC and that none contained untrue statements of material fact. Also, the signing officer or officers must certify that they have established an internal control system to identify all material information and that any deficiencies in the system were disclosed to the auditors.

Effectiveness of Internal Controls on Financial Reporting—Under Section 404(a), all public companies are required to assess the effectiveness of their internal control over financial reporting. Section 404(b) requires independent auditors to report on management's assessment of internal controls, but companies with a public float of less than $75 million are exempted from this requirement.

Loans to Directors and Officers—Section 402 prohibits any reporting company, as well as any private company that is filing an initial public offering, from making personal loans to directors and executive officers (with a few limited exceptions, such as for certain consumer and housing loans).

Protection for Whistleblowers—Section 806 protects "whistleblowers"—employees who report ("blow the whistle" on) securities violations by their employers—from being fired or in any way discriminated against by their employers.

Blackout Periods—Section 306 prohibits certain types of securities transactions during "blackout periods"—periods during which the issuer's ability to purchase, sell, or otherwise transfer funds in individual account plans (such as pension funds) is suspended.

Enhanced Penalties for—

- ***Violations of Section 906 Certification Requirements***—A CEO or CFO who certifies a financial report or statement filed with the SEC knowing that the report or statement does not fulfill all of the requirements of Section 906 will be subject to criminal penalties of up to $1 million in fines, ten years in prison, or both. *Willful* violators of the certification requirements may be subject to $5 million in fines, twenty years in prison, or both.
- ***Violations of the Securities Exchange Act of 1934***—Penalties for securities fraud under the 1934 act were also increased (as discussed earlier in this chapter). Individual violators may be fined up to $5 million, imprisoned for up to twenty years, or both. *Willful* violators may be imprisoned for up to twenty-five years in addition to being fined.
- ***Destruction or Alteration of Documents***—Anyone who alters, destroys, or conceals documents or otherwise obstructs any official proceeding will be subject to fines, imprisonment for up to twenty years, or both.
- ***Other Forms of White-Collar Crime***—The act stiffened the penalties for certain criminal violations, such as federal mail and wire fraud, and ordered the U.S. Sentencing Commission to revise the sentencing guidelines for white-collar crimes (see Chapter 7).

Statute of Limitations for Securities Fraud—Section 804 provides that a private right of action for securities fraud may be brought no later than two years after the discovery of the violation or five years after the violation, whichever is earlier.

Online Investment Scams

As discussed in Chapter 7, the Internet has created a new vehicle for criminals to use to commit fraud and provided them with new ways of targeting innocent investors. The criminally inclined can use spam, online newsletters and bulletin boards, chat rooms, blogs, social media, and tweets to spread false information and perpetrate fraud. For a relatively small cost, criminals can even build sophisticated Web pages to facilitate their investment scams.

FRAUDULENT E-MAIL There are countless variations of investment scams, but they almost always promise spectacular returns for small investments. A person might receive spam e-mail that falsely claims that a home business can "turn $5 into $60,000 in just three to six weeks." Although most people today are dubious of the bogus claims made in spam messages, such offers can appear more attractive during times of economic recession. Often, investment scams are simply the electronic version of pyramid schemes in which the participants attempt to profit solely by recruiting new participants.

ONLINE INVESTMENT NEWSLETTERS AND FORUMS Hundreds of online investment newsletters provide free information on stocks. Legitimate online newsletters can help investors gather valuable information, but some online newsletters are used for fraud.

The law allows companies to pay people who write these newsletters to tout their securities, but the newsletters are required to disclose who paid for the advertising. Many fraudsters either fail to disclose or lie about who paid them. Thus, an investor reading an online newsletter may believe that the information is unbiased, when in fact the fraudsters will directly profit by convincing investors to buy or sell particular stocks.

The same deceptive tactics can be used on online bulletin boards (such as newsgroups and usenet groups), blogs, and social networking sites, including Twitter. While hiding their true identity, fraudsters may falsely pump up a company or reveal some "inside" information about a new product or lucrative contract to convince people to invest. By using multiple aliases on an online forum, a single person can easily create the illusion of widespread interest in a small stock.

Ponzi Schemes

Although securities fraud is increasingly occurring online, schemes conducted primarily offline have not disappeared. In recent years, the SEC has filed an increasing number of enforcement actions against perpetrators of *Ponzi schemes* (see Chapter 7).

Since 2010, the SEC has brought more than a hundred enforcement actions against nearly two hundred individuals and two hundred and fifty entities for carrying out Ponzi schemes. It has also barred more than sixty-five persons from working in the securities industry.

OFFSHORE FRAUD Ponzi schemes sometimes target U.S. residents and convince them to invest in offshore companies or banks. ▶ **Case in Point 28.10** In 2012, Texas billionaire R. Allen Stanford, of the Stanford Financial Group, was convicted for orchestrating a $7 billion scheme to defraud more than five thousand investors. Stanford had advised clients to buy certificates of deposit with improbably high interest rates from his Antigua-based Stanford International Bank. Although some early investors were paid returns from the funds provided by later investors, Stanford used $1.6 billion of the funds for personal purchases. He also falsified financial statements that were filed with the SEC and reportedly paid more than $100,000 in bribes to an Antigua official to ensure that the bank would not be audited.[37] ◀

"RISK-FREE" FRAUD Another type of online fraud scheme offers risk-free or low-risk investments to lure investors. ▶ **Case in Point 28.11** Michael C. Regan used his firm, Regan & Company, to fraudulently obtain at least $15.9 million from dozens of investors by selling securities in his River Stream Fund. Regan told investors that he had a "proven track record" of successful securities trading. He showed them false account statements and tax returns that listed artificially high account balances.

In reality, Regan was not a registered investment adviser, had not traded any securities for several years, and had suffered substantial losses on investments he did make. Regan promised investors returns averaging 20 percent with minimal risk to their principal and claimed to be using an investment strategy based on "short-term price trends." He used less than half of the funds entrusted to him for trading purposes and spent at least $2.4 million for his personal and family expenses. In 2009, the SEC filed a complaint alleging that Regan and his company had engaged in a multimillion-dollar Ponzi scheme. Regan agreed to settle the case and return more than $8.7 million (plus interest) of the wrongfully acquired funds.[38] ◀

37. *United States v. Stanford,* 860 F.Supp.2d 371 (S.D.Tex. 2012).
38. You can read the SEC's complaint against Regan at www.sec.gov/litigation/complaints/2009/comp21102.pdf.

Reviewing: Investor Protection and Corporate Governance

Dale Emerson served as the chief financial officer for Reliant Electric Company, a distributor of electricity serving portions of Montana and North Dakota. Reliant was in the final stages of planning a takeover of Dakota Gasworks, Inc., a natural gas distributor that operated solely within North Dakota. Emerson went on a weekend fishing trip with his uncle, Ernest Wallace. Emerson mentioned to Wallace that he had been putting in a lot of extra hours at the office planning a takeover of Dakota Gasworks. When he returned from the fishing trip, Wallace purchased $20,000 worth of Reliant stock. Three weeks later, Reliant made a tender offer to Dakota Gasworks stockholders and purchased 57 percent of Dakota Gasworks stock. Over the next two weeks, the price of Reliant stock rose 72 percent before leveling out. Wallace then sold his Reliant stock for a gross profit of $14,400. Using the information presented in the chapter, answer the following questions.

1. Would registration with the SEC be required for Dakota Gasworks securities? Why or why not?
2. Did Emerson violate Section 10(b) of the Securities Exchange Act of 1934 and SEC Rule 10b-5? Why or why not?
3. What theory or theories might a court use to hold Wallace liable for insider trading?
4. Under the Sarbanes-Oxley Act of 2002, who would be required to certify the accuracy of the financial statements Reliant filed with the SEC?

DEBATE THIS . . . *Insider trading should be legalized.*

Terms and Concepts

accredited investor 622
blue sky laws 632
corporate governance 632
free-writing prospectus 620
insider trading 626
investment company 621
investment contract 619
mutual fund 621
prospectus 620
SEC Rule 10b-5 625
securities 618
stock option 632
tippee 627

ExamPrep

Issue Spotters

1. When a corporation wishes to issue certain securities, it must provide sufficient information for an unsophisticated investor to evaluate the financial risk involved. Specifically, the law imposes liability for making a false statement or omission that is "material." What sort of information would an investor consider material? **(See page 626.)**
2. Lee is an officer of Magma Oil, Inc. Lee knows that a Magma geologist has just discovered a new deposit of oil. Can Lee take advantage of this information to buy and sell Magma stock? Why or why not? **(See page 626.)**

- **Check your answers to the Issue Spotters against the answers provided in Appendix E at the end of this text.**

Before the Test

Go to **www.cengagebrain.com**, enter the ISBN 9781285428949, and click on "Find" to locate this textbook's Web site. Then, click on "Access Now" under "Study Tools," and select Chapter 28 at the top. There, you will find an Interactive Quiz that you can take to assess your mastery of the concepts in this chapter, as well as Flashcards and a Glossary of important terms.

Business Scenarios

28–1. Registration Requirements. Estrada Hermanos, Inc., a corporation incorporated and doing business in Florida, decides to sell $1 million worth of its common stock to the public. The stock will be sold only within the state of Florida. José Estrada, the chair of the board, says the offering need not be registered with the Securities and Exchange Commission. His brother, Gustavo, disagrees. Who is right? Explain. **(See page 620.)**

28–2. Registration Requirements. Huron Corp. has 300,000 common shares outstanding. The owners of these outstanding shares live in several different states. Huron has decided to split the 300,000 shares two for one. Will

Huron Corp. have to file a registration statement and prospectus on the 300,000 new shares to be issued as a result of the split? Explain. **(See page 620.)**

28–3. Insider Trading. David Gain was the chief executive officer (CEO) of Forest Media Corp., which became interested in acquiring RS Communications, Inc. To initiate negotiations, Gain met with RS's CEO, Gill Raz, on Friday, July 12. Two days later, Gain phoned his brother Mark, who bought 3,800 shares of RS stock on the following Monday. Mark discussed the deal with their father, Jordan, who bought 20,000 RS shares on Thursday. On July 25, the day before the RS bid was due, Gain phoned his parents' home, and Mark bought another 3,200 RS shares. The same routine was followed over the next few days, with Gain periodically phoning Mark or Jordan, both of whom continued to buy RS shares. Forest's bid was refused, but on August 5, RS announced its merger with another company. The price of RS stock rose 30 percent, increasing the value of Mark and Jordan's shares by $664,024 and $412,875, respectively. Did Gain engage in insider trading? What is required to impose sanctions for this offense? Could a court hold Gain liable? Why or why not? **(See page 626.)**

Business Case Problems

28–4. Violations of the 1934 Act. To comply with accounting principles, a company that engages in software development must either "expense" the cost (record it immediately on the company's financial statement) or "capitalize" it (record it as a cost incurred in increments over time). If the project is in the pre- or post-development stage, the cost must be expensed. Otherwise it may be capitalized. Capitalizing a cost makes a company look more profitable in the short term. Digimarc Corp., which provides secure personal identification documents, announced that it had improperly capitalized software development costs over at least the previous eighteen months. The errors resulted in $2.7 million in overstated earnings, requiring a restatement of prior financial statements. Zucco Partners, LLC, which had bought Digimarc stock within the relevant period, filed a suit in a federal district court against the firm. Zucco claimed that it could show that there had been disagreements within Digimarc over its accounting. Is this sufficient to establish a violation of SEC Rule 10b-5? Why or why not? [*Zucco Partners, LLC v. Digimarc Corp.*, 552 F.3d 981 (9th Cir. 2009)] **(See page 629.)**

28–5. Insider Trading. Jabil Circuit, Inc., is a publicly traded electronics and technology company headquartered in St. Petersburg, Florida. In 2008, a group of shareholders who had owned Jabil stock from 2001 to 2007 sued the company and its auditors, directors, and officers for insider trading. Jabil's compensation for executives included stock options. Some stock options were backdated to a point in time when the stock price was lower, making the options worth more to certain company executives. Backdating is legal as long as it is reported, but Jabil did not report that backdating had occurred. Thus, expenses were understated and net income was overstated by millions of dollars. The shareholders claimed that by rigging the value of the stock options by backdating, the executives had engaged in insider trading. The shareholders also asserted that there was a pattern of stock sales by executives before unfavorable news about the company was reported to the public. The shareholders, however, had no specific information about these stock trades or when (or even if) a particular executive was aware of any accounting errors related to backdating. Were the shareholders' allegations sufficient to assert that insider trading had occurred under SEC Rule 10b-5? Why or why not? [*Edward J. Goodman Life Income Trust v. Jabil Circuit, Inc.*, 594 F.3d 783 (11th Cir. 2010)] **(See page 626.)**

28–6. BUSINESS CASE PROBLEM WITH SAMPLE ANSWER: Violations of the 1934 Act.

Matrixx Initiatives, Inc., makes and sells over-the-counter pharmaceutical products. Its core brand is Zicam, which accounts for 70 percent of its sales. Matrixx received reports that some consumers had lost their sense of smell (a condition called anosmia*) after using Zicam Cold Remedy. Four product liability suits were filed against Matrixx, seeking damages for anosmia. In public statements relating to revenues and product safety, however, Matrixx did not reveal this information. James Siracusano and other Matrixx investors filed a suit in a federal district court against the company and its executives under Section 10(b) of the Securities Exchange Act of 1934 and SEC Rule 10b-5, claiming that the statements were misleading because they did not disclose the information regarding the product liability suits. Matrixx argued that to be material, information must consist of a statistically significant number of adverse events that require disclosure. Because Siracusano's claim did not allege that Matrixx knew of a statistically significant number of adverse events, the company contended that the claim should be dismissed. What is the standard for materiality in this context? Should Siracusano's claim be dismissed? Explain. [*Matrixx Initiatives, Inc. v. Siracusano*, __ U.S. __, 131 S.Ct. 1309, 179 L.Ed.2d 398 (2011)]* **(See page 629.)**

- **For a sample answer to Problem 28–6, go to Appendix F at the end of this text.**

28–7. Disclosure under SEC Rule 10b-5. Dodona I, LLC, invested $4 million in two securities offerings from Goldman, Sachs & Co. The investments were in collateralized debt obligations (CDOs). Their value depended on residential mortgage-backed securities (RMBS), whose value in turn depended on the performance of subprime residential mortgages. Before marketing the CDOs, Goldman had noticed several "red flags" relating to investments in the subprime market, in which it had invested heavily. To limit its risk, Goldman began betting against subprime mortgages, RMBS, and CDOs, including the CDOs it had sold to Dodona. In an internal e-mail, one Goldman official commented that the company had managed to "make some lemonade from some big old lemons." Nevertheless, Goldman's marketing materials provided only boilerplate statements about the risks of investing in the securities. The CDOs were later downgraded to junk status, and Dodona suffered a major loss while Goldman profited. Assuming that Goldman did not affirmatively misrepresent any facts about the CDOs, can Dodona still recover under SEC Rule 10b-5? If so, how? [*Dodona I, LLC v. Goldman, Sachs & Co.*, 847 F.Supp.2d 624 (S.D.N.Y. 2012)] **(See page 625.)**

28–8. A QUESTION OF ETHICS: Violations of the 1934 Act.

*Melvin Lyttle told John Montana and Paul Knight about a "Trading Program" that purportedly would buy and sell securities in deals that were fully insured, as well as monitored and controlled by the Federal Reserve. Without checking the details or even verifying whether the Program existed, Montana and Knight, with Lyttle's help, began to sell interests in the Program to investors. For a minimum investment of $1 million, the investors were promised extraordinary rates of return—from 10 percent to as much as 100 percent per week—without risk. They were told, among other things, that the Program would "utilize banks that can ensure full bank integrity of The Transaction whose undertaking[s] are in complete harmony with international banking rules and protocol and who guarantee maximum security of a Funder's Capital Placement Amount." Nothing was required but the investors' funds and their silence—the Program was to be kept secret. Over a four-month period in 1999, Montana raised approximately $23 million from twenty-two investors. The promised gains did not accrue, however. Instead, Montana, Lyttle, and Knight depleted investors' funds in high-risk trades or spent the funds on themselves. [*SEC v. Montana, *464 F.Supp.2d 772 (S.D.Ind. 2006)]* **(See page 629.)**

(a) The Securities and Exchange Commission (SEC) filed a suit in a federal district court against Montana and the others, seeking an injunction, civil penalties, and refund of profits with interest. The SEC alleged, among other things, violations of Section 10(b) of the Securities Exchange Act of 1934 and SEC Rule 10b-5. What is required to establish such violations? Describe how and why the facts in this case meet, or fail to meet, these requirements.

(b) It is often remarked, "There's a sucker born every minute!" Does that phrase describe the Program's investors? Ultimately, about half of the investors recouped the amount they invested. Should the others be considered at least partly responsible for their own losses? Why or why not?

Legal Reasoning Group Activity

28–9. Violations of Securities Laws. Karel Svoboda, a credit officer for Rogue Bank, evaluated and approved his employer's extensions of credit to clients. These responsibilities gave Svoboda access to nonpublic information about the clients' earnings, performance, acquisitions, and business plans from confidential memos, e-mail, and other sources. Svoboda devised a scheme with Alena Robles, an independent accountant, to use this information to trade securities. Pursuant to their scheme, Robles traded in the securities of more than twenty different companies and profited by more than $2 million. Svoboda also executed trades for his own profit of more than $800,000, despite their agreement that Robles would do all of the trading. Aware that their scheme violated Rogue Bank's policy, they attempted to conduct their trades to avoid suspicion. When the bank questioned Svoboda about his actions, he lied, refused to cooperate, and was fired. **(See page 626.)**

(a) The first group will determine whether Svoboda or Robles committed any crimes.

(b) The second group will decide whether Svoboda or Robles is subject to civil liability. If so, who could file a suit and on what ground? What are the possible sanctions?

(c) A third group will identify any defenses that Svoboda or Robles could raise and determine their likelihood of success.

UNIT SIX Focus on Ethics

Ethics and the Regulatory Environment

If this text had been written a hundred years ago, it would have had little to say about federal government regulation. Today, in contrast, just about every area of economic activity is regulated by the government. Ethical issues in government regulation arise because regulation, by its very nature, means that some traditional rights and freedoms must be given up to ensure that other rights and freedoms are protected.

Essentially, government regulation brings two ethical principles into conflict. On the one hand, deeply embedded in American culture is the idea that the government should play a limited role in directing our lives. On the other hand, one of the basic functions of government is to protect the welfare of individuals and the environment in which they live.

Ultimately, nearly every law or rule regulating business represents a decision to give up certain rights in order to protect other perceived rights. In this *Focus on Ethics* feature, we look at some of the ethical aspects of government regulation.

Television Programmers and Antitrust Law

When consumers want cable or satellite television programming, they can choose among various cable and satellite providers, or distributors, but each distributor will offer multichannel packages. In other words, a consumer cannot order just the channels that she or he watches regularly. All of the multichannel packages include some very popular channels and some other channels that have very low viewership. Thus, consumers are forced to pay for some unwanted channels in order to get the ones they do want.

A group of consumers sued NBC Universal, the Walt Disney Company, and other programmers, as well as cable and satellite distributors. The consumers claimed that the defendants, because of their full or partial ownership of broadcast channels and their ownership or control of multiple cable or satellite channels, had a higher degree of market power vis-à-vis all distributors. They also claimed that the programmers had exploited this power by requiring the "bundling" of numerous channels in each multichannel package offered to consumers.

The U.S. Court of Appeals for the Ninth Circuit disagreed. The court pointed out that the Sherman Act applies to actions that diminish competition and, in this instance, there was still competition among programmers and distributors.[1]

LEGAL REASONING

1. *Should TV programmers and distributors be held in violation of the Sherman Act for requiring consumers to buy multichannel packages? Why or why not?*

Privacy Concerns and the Fair Debt Collection Practices Act

Debt-collection practices have often raised privacy concerns. There have been many lawsuits against collection agencies over voice messages or voice mails left by debt collectors. The Fair Debt Collection Practices Act (FDCPA) prohibits disclosures about a debt to third parties.

Does leaving a voice message regarding a debt collection on an answering machine constitute such a disclosure? That depends on the jurisdiction and the situation. In one case, a Florida court ruled in favor of the debtor. It stated that if a collection agency leaves a voice message for a consumer on an answering machine—even at home—other people (third parties) could hear the message.[2] In another case, a federal district court in California held that a debt-collection company had violated the FDCPA by leaving a voice message for the debtor. The message announcing that the debtor had failed to pay his auto insurance was overheard by his mother.[3]

In contrast, a federal court in Minnesota held that leaving voice messages on a debtor's cell phone did not violate the FDCPA, even though the debtor's children listened to them. Because the messages did not identify the debtor or the debt, the court reasoned that "they conveyed no more information than would have been obvious in caller ID." The suit against the debt collector was dismissed.[4]

LEGAL REASONING

2. *Do you think that debt collectors should be able to leave voice messages regarding the debt on a debtor's phone? Why or why not? Does the fact that many people today only have cell phones affect your answer? Explain.*

Environmental Law

Questions of fairness inevitably arise in regard to environmental law. Has the government gone too far—or not far enough—in regulating businesses in the interest of protecting the environment? At what point do the costs of environmental regulations become too burdensome for society to bear? Consider the problem of toxic waste. Although everybody is in favor of cleaning up America's toxic waste dumps, nobody knows what this task will ultimately cost. Moreover, there is no agreed-on standard as to how clean a site must be before it no longer poses any threat. Must 100 percent of the contamination be removed, or would removal of some lesser amount achieve a reasonable degree of environmental quality?

Concerns over Pharmaceuticals in Drinking Water

The amount of pharmaceuticals used by the U.S. public and in agriculture (antibiotics and hormones given to livestock) has grown substantially in recent years. Widespread trace amounts of many drugs have been detected in our nation's water supply. The drinking water of at least 41 million Americans

1. *Brantley v. NBC Universal, Inc.*, 675 F.3d 1192 (9th Cir. 2012).
2. *Berg v. Merchants Association Collection Division, Inc.*, 586 F.Supp.2d 1336 (S.D.Fla. 2008).
3. *Branco v. Credit Collection Services, Inc.*, 2011 WL 3684503 (E.D.Cal. 2011).
4. *Zortman v. J.C. Christensen & Associates, Inc.*, 2012 WL 1563918 (D.Minn. 2012).

in twenty-four regions across the country has been found to contain small amounts of prescription drugs.

Some of these trace amounts came from unmetabolized drugs that had passed through the humans and animals that ingested them, but the rest had been flushed down the toilet. For many years, pharmacists, physicians, and the federal government have recommended that people dispose of unused medications by flushing them away. This prevents children from accidentally ingesting the drugs and keeps controlled substances such as the painkillers oxycodone and morphine from falling into the hands of people who might abuse them. At the time, no one considered the long-term effect on the environment of adding pharmaceuticals to the water supply.

The quantities present in water now are far below medicinal doses, but no one knows how long-term exposure to random combinations of drugs will affect humans or wildlife. As yet, there is little scientific evidence about the long-term effects. The federal government does not require drinking water to be tested for drugs, so Americans do not know whether their drinking water is contaminated. Requiring that water be tested and that all traces of drugs be filtered from it would be enormously expensive.

LEGAL REASONING

3. *Should the government wait until there is scientific proof of the harmful effects on humans and wildlife before attempting to regulate pharmaceuticals in drinking water? Or should the government enact legislation to address the problem now—before it becomes worse? Discuss fully.*

Land-Use Regulations and the "Takings Clause"

When property owners claim that a "regulatory taking" has occurred, the courts decide the issue on a case-by-case basis. In other words, there is no general rule that indicates whether a specific situation will be deemed a taking. In a case decided in 2010, a group of Florida beachfront property owners challenged the constitutionality of the state's decision to add seventy-five feet of sand to the shoreline.

Under Florida law, the boundary between private beachfront property and state-owned land is ordinarily the average high-water line. The state owns any land submerged beneath the ocean or other navigable waters. It is common for storms to cause some fluctuation in the shoreline, however, as sand is deposited or washed away by waves. A change that occurs gradually and imperceptibly over time is called an *accretion,* whereas a sudden change is called an *avulsion.* If an accretion deposits more sand on the shore, the owners of private beachfront property automatically acquire ownership rights to more land—to the new high-water line. If an avulsion occurs, however, the property owners' boundaries remain the same, so the state owns the land abutting the water's edge.

As a result of several hurricanes, 6.9 miles of beach were eroded (an avulsion) in the city of Destin and Walton County. The state therefore requested and received a permit from the Florida Department of Environmental Protection to add seventy-five feet of dry sand on its side (the seaward side) of the high-water line. Owners of the private beachfront property in the area formed a nonprofit corporation to fight the proposed addition of sand, but they lost at an administrative hearing. They then filed a lawsuit claiming that the state's action constituted an unlawful taking of their beachfront property.

The Courts Disagree A Florida appellate court agreed with the property owners that the state had taken their rights to receive accretions and to have their property remain in contact with the water. The Florida Supreme Court reversed, and the United States Supreme Court granted *certiorari.*

The United States Supreme Court held that Florida had not engaged in an unconstitutional taking. According to the Court, there was no taking because the property owners did not show that their rights to future accretions and to contact with the water were superior to Florida's right to fill in its submerged land.

The state did not relocate the property line to take private property, but simply added sand to property that it already owned (on the side toward the water). Therefore, the state had a right to restore the beach even though the addition of sand interfered with the property owners' rights to have their property touch the water.[5] Although a majority of the Supreme Court justices concurred in the result, there were substantial differences in their reasoning.

A Question of Fairness The question of whether private landowners should be compensated when their land is essentially "taken" for public use by environmental and land-use regulations clearly involves issues of fairness. On the one hand, states, cities, and other local governments want to preserve their natural resources and need some authority to regulate land use to achieve this goal.

On the other hand, private property owners complain that they alone should not have to bear the costs of creating a benefit—such as more sandy beaches for recreation or environmental preservation. These are benefits that all members of the public enjoy. In addition, as a different group of Florida beachfront property owners complained in 2013, if the state adds sand to beaches in front of their property, it may lower the property's value.

LEGAL REASONING

4. *Is it fair for courts to decide whether a regulatory taking has occurred on a case-by-case basis, rather than articulating a general rule on which landowners can rely? Why or why not?*

5. *Stop the Beach Renourishment, Inc. v. Florida Department of Environmental Protection,* ___ U.S. ___, 130 S.Ct. 2592, 177 L.Ed.2d 184 (2010).

FOCUS ON ETHICS CONTINUES ➧

UNIT SIX Focus on Ethics

Ethics and the Regulatory Environment, *Continued*

Corporate Blogs and Tweets and Securities Fraud

In the fast-paced world of securities trading, there is a great demand for the latest information about companies, earnings, and market conditions. Corporations have adapted to technology by establishing Web sites and blogs, and by using other social and online media, such as Twitter and online shareholder forums. Nearly 20 percent of Fortune 500 companies sponsor blogs. Corporations that use the Internet to distribute information about the company to investors, however, need to make sure that they comply with the regulations issued by the SEC. The SEC treats statements by employees in online media, such as blogs and Twitter, the same as any other company statements for purposes of federal securities laws.

"Tweets" That Contain Financial Information Some corporate blogs include links to corporate employees' Twitter accounts so that readers can communicate directly with, and get updates from, the individual who posted the information. For example, when eBay, Inc., launched its corporate blog, it hired Richard Brewer-Hay, a seasoned blogger, to report online. He began tweeting about eBay's quarterly earnings and what took place at Silicon Valley technology conferences.

Brewer-Hay's tweets won him a following, but then eBay's lawyers required him to include a regulatory disclaimer with certain posts to avoid problems with the SEC. Many of his followers were disappointed by the company's oversight, which put an end to his spontaneous, personal, and informal style. Brewer-Hay's tweets on financial matters became much more reserved and often simply repeated eBay executives' statements verbatim.[6]

The SEC Provides Guidance The reaction of eBay's lawyers to Brewer-Hay's tweets was prompted in part by an interpretive release that the SEC issued in August 2008. The SEC generally embraces new technology and encourages companies to use electronic communication methods. The SEC noted that "the use of the Internet has grown such that, for some companies in certain circumstances, posting of the information on the company's Web site, in and of itself, may be a sufficient method of public disclosure."

The release also addressed company-sponsored blogs, electronic shareholders' forums, and other "interactive Web site features." The SEC acknowledged that blogs and other interactive Web features are a useful means of ongoing communications among companies, their clients, investors, shareholders, and stakeholders.

The SEC cautioned, though, that all communications made by or on behalf of a company are subject to the antifraud provisions of federal securities laws. "While blogs or forums can be informal and conversational in nature, statements made there . . . will not be treated differently from other company statements." In addition, the release stated that companies cannot require investors to waive protections under federal securities laws as a condition of participating in a blog or forum. (The release also cautioned companies that they can, in some situations, be liable for providing hyperlinks to third party information or inaccurate summaries of financial information on their Web sites.)[7]

LEGAL REASONING

5. *When a company's executives offer opinions about the firm's financial status and future business prospects through blogs, social media, and other Internet forums, the SEC can hold the company liable for violating securities laws. Is this fair to investors who want to hear the straight scoop from the firm's executives? What arguments can you make in favor of this restriction? What arguments can you make against it?*

6. Cari Tuna, "Corporate Blogs and 'Tweets' Must Keep SEC in Mind," *online.wsj.com*, April 27, 2009.

7. SEC Release Nos. 34–58288, IC–28351, File No.S7–23–08. Commission Guidance on the Use of Company Web Sites.

How to Brief Cases

To fully understand the law with respect to business, you need to be able to read and understand court decisions. To make this task easier, you can use a method of case analysis that is called *briefing*. There is a fairly standard procedure that you can follow when you "brief" any court case. You must first read the case opinion carefully. When you feel you understand the case, you can prepare a brief of it.

Although the format of the brief may vary, typically it will present the essentials of the case under headings such as those listed below.

1. **Citation.** Give the full citation for the case, including the name of the case, the date it was decided, and the court that decided it.
2. **Facts.** Briefly indicate (a) the reasons for the lawsuit; (b) the identity and arguments of the plaintiff(s) and defendant(s), respectively; and (c) the lower court's decision—if appropriate.
3. **Issue.** Concisely phrase, in the form of a question, the essential issue before the court. (If more than one issue is involved, you may have two—or even more—questions here.)
4. **Decision.** Indicate here—with a "yes" or "no," if possible—the court's answer to the question (or questions) in the *Issue* section above.
5. **Reason.** Summarize as briefly as possible the reasons given by the court for its decision (or decisions) and the case or statutory law relied on by the court in arriving at its decision.

An Example of a Briefed Sample Court Case

As an example of the format used in briefing cases, we present here a briefed version of the sample court case that was presented in Chapter 1 in Exhibit 1–6.

APPLE, INC. v. AMAZON.COM, INC.
United States District Court, Northern District of California, __ F.Supp.2d __, 2013 WL 11896 (2013).

FACTS In July 2008, Apple, Inc. began to sell applications for its mobile devices through its APP STORE service. In March 2011, Amazon.com, Inc., launched the Amazon Appstore for Android. Apple filed a suit in a federal district court against Amazon in the same month, asserting false advertising. Apple alleged that that by using the word "Appstore" in the name of Amazon's store, Amazon implied that its store was affiliated with or sponsored by Apple. Apple argued that Amazon's service did not have the characteristics and qualities that the public had come to expect from the name APP STORE. For this reason, Apple contended, Amazon's use of "Appstore" misled the public. Amazon filed a motion for summary judgment.

ISSUE Can a vendor use the term "Appstore" to designate a site for buying apps without representing that the nature, characteristics, or quality of the site is the same as that of another vendor's "APP STORE"?

DECISION Yes. The court granted Amazon's motion for summary judgment.

REASON The court pointed out that a false advertising claim requires either a false statement of fact in an ad or evidence showing "exactly what message was conveyed that was sufficient to constitute false advertising." Here, Apple failed to show that Amazon made any false statement and presented no evidence that consumers were misled. Apple did not show that consumers understood "app store" to include specific qualities, characteristics, or attributes of the Apple APP STORE or were otherwise misled by Amazon's use of the term. Nothing indicated that a consumer would expect the two sites to be identical—especially considering that Apple sold apps solely for Apple devices and Amazon sold apps solely for Android and Kindle devices. Apple did not make clear how Amazon's use of Appstore constituted a "statement" that implied something false about Apple's APP STORE. Apple "made no showing that such (implied) statement deceived or had a tendency to deceive users of Amazon's Appstore."

Review of Sample Court Case

Here we provide a review of the briefed version to indicate the kind of information that is contained in each section.

CITATION The name of the case is *Apple, Inc. v. Amazon.com, Inc.* Apple is the plaintiff. Amazon is the defendant. The U.S. District Court for the Northern District of California (a trial court) decided this case in 2013. The citation states that this case can be found in volume ___ of the *Federal Supplement, Second Series,* on page ___, and on Westlaw® at 2013 WL 11896.

FACTS The *Facts* section identifies the plaintiff and the defendant, describes the events leading up to this suit and the allegations made by the plaintiff in the suit. If this case were a decision of one of the U.S. courts of appeals, the lower court's ruling, the party appealing, and the appellant's contention on appeal would also be included here.

ISSUE The *Issue* section presents the central issue (or issues) decided by the court. This case involves a false advertising claim. The court considers whether a vendor can use the term "Appstore" to designate a site for buying apps without representing that the nature, characteristics, or quality of the site is the same as that of another vendor's "APP STORE."

DECISION The *Decision* section includes the court's decision on the issues before it. The decision reflects the opinion of the judge or justice hearing the case. Here, the court determined that consumers were not deceived by the two vendors' use of the same term. There was no evidence that consumers understood "app store" to include specific qualities, characteristics, or attributes or were otherwise misled by the use of the term. Decisions by appellate courts are frequently phrased in reference to the lower court's decision. That is, the appellate court may "affirm" the lower court's ruling or "reverse" it.

REASON The *Reason* section includes references to the relevant laws and legal principles that were applied in coming to the conclusion arrived at in the case before the court. The relevant law here included the principle that a false advertising claim requires either a false statement of fact in an ad or evidence showing "exactly what message was conveyed that was sufficient to constitute false advertising." This section also explains the court's application of the law to the facts in this case.

Analyzing Case Problems

In addition to learning how to brief cases, students of business law and the legal environment also find it helpful to know how to analyze case problems. Part of the study of business law and the legal environment usually involves analyzing case problems, such as those included in this text at the end of each chapter.

For each case problem in this book, we provide the relevant background and facts of the lawsuit and the issue before the court. When you are assigned one of these problems, your job will be to determine how the court should decide the issue, and why. In other words, you will need to engage in legal analysis and reasoning. Here, we offer some suggestions on how to make this task less daunting. We begin by presenting a sample problem:

> While Janet Lawson, a famous pianist, was shopping in Quality Market, she slipped and fell on a wet floor in one of the aisles. The floor had recently been mopped by one of the store's employees, but there were no signs warning customers that the floor in that area was wet. As a result of the fall, Lawson injured her right arm and was unable to perform piano concerts for the next six months. Had she been able to perform the scheduled concerts, she would have earned approximately $60,000 over that period of time. Lawson sued Quality Market for this amount, plus another $10,000 in medical expenses. She claimed that the store's failure to warn customers of the wet floor constituted negligence and therefore the market was liable for her injuries. Will the court agree with Lawson? Discuss.

Understand the Facts

This may sound obvious, but before you can analyze or apply the relevant law to a specific set of facts, you must clearly understand those facts. In other words, you should read through the case problem carefully—more than once, if necessary—to make sure you understand the identity of the plaintiff(s) and defendant(s) in the case and the progression of events that led to the lawsuit.

In the sample case problem just given, the identity of the parties is fairly obvious. Janet Lawson is the one bringing the suit—therefore, she is the plaintiff. Quality Market, against whom she is bringing the suit, is the defendant. Some of the case problems you may work on have multiple plaintiffs or defendants. Often, it is helpful to use abbreviations for the parties. To indicate a reference to a plaintiff, for example, the *pi* symbol—π—is often used, and a defendant is denoted by a *delta*—Δ—a triangle.

The events leading to the lawsuit are also fairly straightforward. Lawson slipped and fell on a wet floor, and she contends that Quality Market should be liable for her injuries because it was negligent in not posting a sign warning customers of the wet floor.

When you are working on case problems, realize that the facts should be accepted as they are given. For example, in our sample problem, it should be accepted that the floor was wet and that there was no sign. In other words, avoid making conjectures, such as "Maybe the floor wasn't too wet," or "Maybe an employee was getting a sign to put up," or "Maybe someone stole the sign." Questioning the facts as they are presented only adds confusion to your analysis.

Legal Analysis and Reasoning

Once you understand the facts given in the case problem, you can begin to analyze the case. Recall from Chapter 1 that the IRAC method is a helpful tool to use in the legal analysis and reasoning process. IRAC is an acronym for Issue, Rule, Application, Conclusion. Applying this method to our sample problem would involve the following steps:

1. First, you need to decide what legal **issue** is involved in the case. In our sample case, the basic issue is whether Quality Market's failure to warn customers of the wet floor constituted negligence. As discussed in Chapter 12, negligence is a *tort*—a civil wrong. In a tort lawsuit, the plaintiff seeks to be compensated for another's wrongful act. A defendant will be deemed negligent if he or she breached a duty of care owed to the plaintiff and the breach of that duty caused the plaintiff to suffer harm.
2. Once you have identified the issue, the next step is to determine what **rule of law** applies to the issue. To make this determination, you will want to review carefully the text of the chapter in which the relevant rule of law for the problem appears. Our sample case problem involves the tort of

negligence, which is covered in Chapter 12. The applicable rule of law is the tort law principle that business owners owe a duty to exercise reasonable care to protect their customers ("business invitees"). Reasonable care, in this context, includes either removing—or warning customers of—*foreseeable* risks about which the owner *knew* or *should have known.* Business owners need not warn customers of "open and obvious" risks, however. If a business owner breaches this duty of care (fails to exercise the appropriate degree of care toward customers), and the breach of duty causes a customer to be injured, the business owner will be liable to the customer for the customer's injuries.

3. The next—and usually the most difficult—step in analyzing case problems is the **application** of the relevant rule of law to the specific facts of the case you are studying. In our sample problem, applying the tort law principle just discussed presents few difficulties. An employee of the store had mopped the floor in the aisle where Lawson slipped and fell, but no sign was present indicating that the floor was wet. That a customer might fall on a wet floor is clearly a foreseeable risk. Therefore, the failure to warn customers about the wet floor was a breach of the duty of care owed by the business owner to the store's customers.
4. Once you have completed Step 3 in the IRAC method, you should be ready to draw your **conclusion.** In our sample problem, Quality Market is liable to Lawson for her injuries, because the market's breach of its duty of care caused Lawson's injuries.

The fact patterns in the case problems presented in this text are not always as simple as those presented in our sample problem. Often, for example, a case has more than one plaintiff or defendant. A case may also involve more than one issue and have more than one applicable rule of law. Furthermore, in some case problems the facts may indicate that the general rule of law should not apply. For example, suppose that a store employee advised Lawson not to walk on the floor in the aisle because it was wet, but Lawson decided to walk on it anyway. This fact could alter the outcome of the case because the store could then raise the defense of assumption of risk (see Chapter 12). Nonetheless, a careful review of the chapter should always provide you with the knowledge you need to analyze the problem thoroughly and arrive at accurate conclusions.

Preamble

We the People of the United States, in Order to form a more perfect Union, establish Justice, insure domestic Tranquility, provide for the common defence, promote the general Welfare, and secure the Blessings of Liberty to ourselves and our Posterity, do ordain and establish this Constitution for the United States of America.

Article I

Section 1. All legislative Powers herein granted shall be vested in a Congress of the United States, which shall consist of a Senate and House of Representatives.

Section 2. The House of Representatives shall be composed of Members chosen every second Year by the People of the several States, and the Electors in each State shall have the Qualifications requisite for Electors of the most numerous Branch of the State Legislature.

No Person shall be a Representative who shall not have attained to the Age of twenty five Years, and been seven Years a Citizen of the United States, and who shall not, when elected, be an Inhabitant of that State in which he shall be chosen.

Representatives and direct Taxes shall be apportioned among the several States which may be included within this Union, according to their respective Numbers, which shall be determined by adding to the whole Number of free Persons, including those bound to Service for a Term of Years, and excluding Indians not taxed, three fifths of all other Persons. The actual Enumeration shall be made within three Years after the first Meeting of the Congress of the United States, and within every subsequent Term of ten Years, in such Manner as they shall by Law direct. The Number of Representatives shall not exceed one for every thirty Thousand, but each State shall have at Least one Representative; and until such enumeration shall be made, the State of New Hampshire shall be entitled to chuse three, Massachusetts eight, Rhode Island and Providence Plantations one, Connecticut five, New York six, New Jersey four, Pennsylvania eight, Delaware one, Maryland six, Virginia ten, North Carolina five, South Carolina five, and Georgia three.

When vacancies happen in the Representation from any State, the Executive Authority thereof shall issue Writs of Election to fill such Vacancies.

The House of Representatives shall chuse their Speaker and other Officers; and shall have the sole Power of Impeachment.

Section 3. The Senate of the United States shall be composed of two Senators from each State, chosen by the Legislature thereof, for six Years; and each Senator shall have one Vote.

Immediately after they shall be assembled in Consequence of the first Election, they shall be divided as equally as may be into three Classes. The Seats of the Senators of the first Class shall be vacated at the Expiration of the second Year, of the second Class at the Expiration of the fourth Year, and of the third Class at the Expiration of the sixth Year, so that one third may be chosen every second Year; and if Vacancies happen by Resignation, or otherwise, during the Recess of the Legislature of any State, the Executive thereof may make temporary Appointments until the next Meeting of the Legislature, which shall then fill such Vacancies.

No Person shall be a Senator who shall not have attained to the Age of thirty Years, and been nine Years a Citizen of the United States, and who shall not, when elected, be an Inhabitant of that State for which he shall be chosen.

The Vice President of the United States shall be President of the Senate, but shall have no Vote, unless they be equally divided.

The Senate shall chuse their other Officers, and also a President pro tempore, in the Absence of the Vice President, or when he shall exercise the Office of President of the United States.

The Senate shall have the sole Power to try all Impeachments. When sitting for that Purpose, they shall be on Oath or Affirmation. When the President of the United States is tried, the Chief Justice shall preside: And no Person shall be convicted without the Concurrence of two thirds of the Members present.

Judgment in Cases of Impeachment shall not extend further than to removal from Office, and disqualification to hold and enjoy any Office of honor, Trust, or Profit under the United States: but the Party convicted shall nevertheless be liable and subject to Indictment, Trial, Judgment, and Punishment, according to Law.

Section 4. The Times, Places and Manner of holding Elections for Senators and Representatives, shall be prescribed in each State by the Legislature thereof; but the Congress may at any time by Law make or alter such Regulations, except as to the Places of chusing Senators.

The Congress shall assemble at least once in every Year, and such Meeting shall be on the first Monday in December, unless they shall by Law appoint a different Day.

Section 5. Each House shall be the Judge of the Elections, Returns, and Qualifications of its own Members, and a Majority of each shall constitute a Quorum to do Business; but a smaller Number may adjourn from day to day, and may be authorized to compel the Attendance of absent Members, in such Manner, and under such Penalties as each House may provide.

Each House may determine the Rules of its Proceedings, punish its Members for disorderly Behavior, and, with the Concurrence of two thirds, expel a Member.

Each House shall keep a Journal of its Proceedings, and from time to time publish the same, excepting such Parts as may in their Judgment require Secrecy; and the Yeas and Nays of the Members of either House on any question shall, at the Desire of one fifth of those Present, be entered on the Journal.

Neither House, during the Session of Congress, shall, without the Consent of the other, adjourn for more than three days, nor to any other Place than that in which the two Houses shall be sitting.

Section 6. The Senators and Representatives shall receive a Compensation for their Services, to be ascertained by Law, and paid out of the Treasury of the United States. They shall in all Cases, except Treason, Felony and Breach of the Peace, be privileged from Arrest during their Attendance at the Session of their respective Houses, and in going to and returning from the same; and for any Speech or Debate in either House, they shall not be questioned in any other Place.

No Senator or Representative shall, during the Time for which he was elected, be appointed to any civil Office under the Authority of the United States, which shall have been created, or the Emoluments whereof shall have been increased during such time; and no Person holding any Office under the United States, shall be a Member of either House during his Continuance in Office.

Section 7. All Bills for raising Revenue shall originate in the House of Representatives; but \the Senate may propose or concur with Amendments as on other Bills.

Every Bill which shall have passed the House of Representatives and the Senate, shall, before it become a Law, be presented to the President of the United States; If he approve he shall sign it, but if not he shall return it, with his Objections to the House in which it shall have originated, who shall enter the Objections at large on their Journal, and proceed to reconsider it. If after such Reconsideration two thirds of that House shall agree to pass the Bill, it shall be sent together with the Objections, to the other House, by which it shall likewise be reconsidered, and if approved by two thirds of that House, it shall become a Law. But in all such Cases the Votes of both Houses shall be determined by Yeas and Nays, and the Names of the Persons voting for and against the Bill shall be entered on the Journal of each House respectively. If any Bill shall not be returned by the President within ten Days (Sundays excepted) after it shall have been presented to him, the Same shall be a Law, in like Manner as if he had signed it, unless the Congress by their Adjournment prevent its Return in which Case it shall not be a Law.

Every Order, Resolution, or Vote, to which the Concurrence of the Senate and House of Representatives may be necessary (except on a question of Adjournment) shall be presented to the President of the United States; and before the Same shall take Effect, shall be approved by him, or being disapproved by him, shall be repassed by two thirds of the Senate and House of Representatives, according to the Rules and Limitations prescribed in the Case of a Bill.

Section 8. The Congress shall have Power To lay and collect Taxes, Duties, Imposts and Excises, to pay the Debts and provide for the common Defence and general Welfare of the United States; but all Duties, Imposts and Excises shall be uniform throughout the United States;

To borrow Money on the credit of the United States;

To regulate Commerce with foreign Nations, and among the several States, and with the Indian Tribes;

To establish an uniform Rule of Naturalization, and uniform Laws on the subject of Bankruptcies throughout the United States;

To coin Money, regulate the Value thereof, and of foreign Coin, and fix the Standard of Weights and Measures;

To provide for the Punishment of counterfeiting the Securities and current Coin of the United States;

To establish Post Offices and post Roads;

To promote the Progress of Science and useful Arts, by securing for limited Times to Authors and Inventors the exclusive Right to their respective Writings and Discoveries;

To constitute Tribunals inferior to the supreme Court;

To define and punish Piracies and Felonies committed on the high Seas, and Offenses against the Law of Nations;

To declare War, grant Letters of Marque and Reprisal, and make Rules concerning Captures on Land and Water;

To raise and support Armies, but no Appropriation of Money to that Use shall be for a longer Term than two Years;

To provide and maintain a Navy;

To make Rules for the Government and Regulation of the land and naval Forces;

To provide for calling forth the Militia to execute the Laws of the Union, suppress Insurrections and repel Invasions;

To provide for organizing, arming, and disciplining, the Militia, and for governing such Part of them as may be employed in the Service of the United States, reserving to the States respectively, the Appointment of the Officers, and the Authority of training the Militia according to the discipline prescribed by Congress;

To exercise exclusive Legislation in all Cases whatsoever, over such District (not exceeding ten Miles square) as may, by Cession of particular States, and the Acceptance of Congress, become the Seat of the Government of the United States, and to exercise like Authority over all Places purchased by the Consent of the Legislature of the State in which the Same shall be, for the Erection of Forts, Magazines, Arsenals, dock-Yards, and other needful Buildings;—And

To make all Laws which shall be necessary and proper for carrying into Execution the foregoing Powers, and all other Powers vested by this Constitution in the Government of the United States, or in any Department or Officer thereof.

Section 9. The Migration or Importation of such Persons as any of the States now existing shall think proper to admit, shall not be prohibited by the Congress prior to the Year one thousand eight hundred and eight, but a Tax or duty may be imposed on such Importation, not exceeding ten dollars for each Person.

The privilege of the Writ of Habeas Corpus shall not be suspended, unless when in Cases of Rebellion or Invasion the public Safety may require it.

No Bill of Attainder or ex post facto Law shall be passed.

No Capitation, or other direct, Tax shall be laid, unless in Proportion to the Census or Enumeration herein before directed to be taken.

No Tax or Duty shall be laid on Articles exported from any State.

No Preference shall be given by any Regulation of Commerce or Revenue to the Ports of one State over those of another: nor shall Vessels bound to, or from, one State be obliged to enter, clear, or pay Duties in another.

No Money shall be drawn from the Treasury, but in Consequence of Appropriations made by Law; and a regular Statement and Account of the Receipts and Expenditures of all public Money shall be published from time to time.

No Title of Nobility shall be granted by the United States: And no Person holding any Office of Profit or Trust under them, shall, without the Consent of the Congress, accept of any present, Emolument, Office, or Title, of any kind whatever, from any King, Prince, or foreign State.

Section 10. No State shall enter into any Treaty, Alliance, or Confederation; grant Letters of Marque and Reprisal; coin Money; emit Bills of Credit; make any Thing but gold and silver Coin a Tender in Payment of Debts; pass any Bill of Attainder, ex post facto Law, or Law impairing the Obligation of Contracts, or grant any Title of Nobility.

No State shall, without the Consent of the Congress, lay any Imposts or Duties on Imports or Exports, except what may be absolutely necessary for executing its inspection Laws: and the net Produce of all Duties and Imposts, laid by any State on Imports or Exports, shall be for the Use of the Treasury of the United States; and all such Laws shall be subject to the Revision and Controul of the Congress.

No State shall, without the Consent of Congress, lay any Duty of Tonnage, keep Troops, or Ships of War in time of Peace, enter into any Agreement or Compact with another State, or with a foreign Power, or engage in War, unless actually invaded, or in such imminent Danger as will not admit of delay.

Article II

Section 1. The executive Power shall be vested in a President of the United States of America. He shall hold his Office during the Term of four Years, and, together with the Vice President, chosen for the same Term, be elected, as follows:

Each State shall appoint, in such Manner as the Legislature thereof may direct, a Number of Electors, equal to the whole Number of Senators and Representatives to which the State may be entitled in the Congress; but no Senator or Representative, or Person holding an Office of Trust or Profit under the United States, shall be appointed an Elector.

The Electors shall meet in their respective States, and vote by Ballot for two Persons, of whom one at least shall not be an Inhabitant of the same State with themselves. And they shall make a List of all the Persons voted for, and of the Number of Votes for each; which List they shall sign and certify, and transmit sealed to the Seat of the Government of the United States, directed to the President of the Senate. The President of the Senate shall, in the Presence of the Senate and House of Representatives, open all the Certificates, and the Votes shall then be counted. The Person having the greatest Number of Votes shall be the President, if such Number be a Majority of the whole Number of Electors appointed; and if there be more than one who have such Majority, and have an equal Number of Votes, then the House of Representatives shall immediately chuse by Ballot one of them for President; and if no Person have a Majority, then from the five highest on the List the said House shall in like Manner chuse the President. But in chusing the President, the Votes shall be taken by States, the Representation from each State having one Vote; A quorum for this Purpose shall consist of a Member or Members from two thirds of the States, and a Majority of all the States shall be necessary to a Choice. In every Case, after the Choice of the President, the Person having the greater Number of Votes of the Electors shall be the Vice President. But if there should remain two or more who have equal Votes, the Senate shall chuse from them by Ballot the Vice President.

The Congress may determine the Time of chusing the Electors, and the Day on which they shall give their Votes; which Day shall be the same throughout the United States.

No person except a natural born Citizen, or a Citizen of the United States, at the time of the Adoption of this Constitution, shall be eligible to the Office of President; neither shall any Person be eligible to that Office who shall not have attained to the Age of thirty five Years, and been fourteen Years a Resident within the United States.

In Case of the Removal of the President from Office, or of his Death, Resignation or Inability to discharge the Powers and Duties of the said Office, the same shall devolve on the Vice President, and the Congress may by Law provide for the Case of Removal, Death, Resignation or Inability, both of the President and Vice President, declaring what Officer shall then act as President, and such Officer shall act accordingly, until the Disability be removed, or a President shall be elected.

The President shall, at stated Times, receive for his Services, a Compensation, which shall neither be increased nor diminished during the Period for which he shall have been elected, and he shall not receive within that Period any other Emolument from the United States, or any of them.

Before he enter on the Execution of his Office, he shall take the following Oath or Affirmation: "I do solemnly swear (or affirm) that I will faithfully execute the Office of President of the United States, and will to the best of my Ability, preserve, protect and defend the Constitution of the United States."

Section 2. The President shall be Commander in Chief of the Army and Navy of the United States, and of the Militia of the several States, when called into the actual Service of the United States; he may require the Opinion, in writing, of the principal Officer in each of the executive Departments, upon any Subject relating to the Duties of their respective Offices, and he shall have Power to grant Reprieves and Pardons for Offenses against the United States, except in Cases of Impeachment.

He shall have Power, by and with the Advice and Consent of the Senate to make Treaties, provided two thirds of the Senators present concur; and he shall nominate, and by and with the Advice and Consent of the Senate, shall appoint

Ambassadors, other public Ministers and Consuls, Judges of the supreme Court, and all other Officers of the United States, whose Appointments are not herein otherwise provided for, and which shall be established by Law; but the Congress may by Law vest the Appointment of such inferior Officers, as they think proper, in the President alone, in the Courts of Law, or in the Heads of Departments.

The President shall have Power to fill up all Vacancies that may happen during the Recess of the Senate, by granting Commissions which shall expire at the End of their next Session.

Section 3. He shall from time to time give to the Congress Information of the State of the Union, and recommend to their Consideration such Measures as he shall judge necessary and expedient; he may, on extraordinary Occasions, convene both Houses, or either of them, and in Case of Disagreement between them, with Respect to the Time of Adjournment, he may adjourn them to such Time as he shall think proper; he shall receive Ambassadors and other public Ministers; he shall take Care that the Laws be faithfully executed, and shall Commission all the Officers of the United States.

Section 4. The President, Vice President and all civil Officers of the United States, shall be removed from Office on Impeachment for, and Conviction of, Treason, Bribery, or other high Crimes and Misdemeanors.

Article III

Section 1. The judicial Power of the United States, shall be vested in one supreme Court, and in such inferior Courts as the Congress may from time to time ordain and establish. The Judges, both of the supreme and inferior Courts, shall hold their Offices during good Behaviour, and shall, at stated Times, receive for their Services a Compensation, which shall not be diminished during their Continuance in Office.

Section 2. The judicial Power shall extend to all Cases, in Law and Equity, arising under this Constitution, the Laws of the United States, and Treaties made, or which shall be made, under their Authority;—to all Cases affecting Ambassadors, other public Ministers and Consuls;—to all Cases of admiralty and maritime Jurisdiction;—to Controversies to which the United States shall be a Party;—to Controversies between two or more States;—between a State and Citizens of another State;—between Citizens of different States;—between Citizens of the same State claiming Lands under Grants of different States, and between a State, or the Citizens thereof, and foreign States, Citizens or Subjects.

In all Cases affecting Ambassadors, other public Ministers and Consuls, and those in which a State shall be a Party, the supreme Court shall have original Jurisdiction. In all the other Cases before mentioned, the supreme Court shall have appellate Jurisdiction, both as to Law and Fact, with such Exceptions, and under such Regulations as the Congress shall make.

The Trial of all Crimes, except in Cases of Impeachment, shall be by Jury; and such Trial shall be held in the State where the said Crimes shall have been committed; but when not committed within any State, the Trial shall be at such Place or Places as the Congress may by Law have directed.

Section 3. Treason against the United States, shall consist only in levying War against them, or, in adhering to their Enemies, giving them Aid and Comfort. No Person shall be convicted of Treason unless on the Testimony of two Witnesses to the same overt Act, or on Confession in open Court.

The Congress shall have Power to declare the Punishment of Treason, but no Attainder of Treason shall work Corruption of Blood, or Forfeiture except during the Life of the Person attainted.

Article IV

Section 1. Full Faith and Credit shall be given in each State to the public Acts, Records, and judicial Proceedings of every other State. And the Congress may by general Laws prescribe the Manner in which such Acts, Records and Proceedings shall be proved, and the Effect thereof.

Section 2. The Citizens of each State shall be entitled to all Privileges and I2mmunities of Citizens in the several States.

A Person charged in any State with Treason, Felony, or other Crime, who shall flee from Justice, and be found in another State, shall on Demand of the executive Authority of the State from which he fled, be delivered up, to be removed to the State having Jurisdiction of the Crime.

No Person held to Service or Labour in one State, under the Laws thereof, escaping into another, shall, in Consequence of any Law or Regulation therein, be discharged from such Service or Labour, but shall be delivered up on Claim of the Party to whom such Service or Labour may be due.

Section 3. New States may be admitted by the Congress into this Union; but no new State shall be formed or erected within the Jurisdiction of any other State; nor any State be formed by the Junction of two or more States, or Parts of States, without the Consent of the Legislatures of the States concerned as well as of the Congress.

The Congress shall have Power to dispose of and make all needful Rules and Regulations respecting the Territory or other Property belonging to the United States; and nothing in this Constitution shall be so construed as to Prejudice any Claims of the United States, or of any particular State.

Section 4. The United States shall guarantee to every State in this Union a Republican Form of Government, and shall protect each of them against Invasion; and on Application of the Legislature, or of the Executive (when the Legislature cannot be convened) against domestic Violence.

Article V

The Congress, whenever two thirds of both Houses shall deem it necessary, shall propose Amendments to this Constitution, or, on the Application of the Legislatures of two thirds of the several States, shall call a Convention for proposing Amendments, which, in either Case, shall be valid to all Intents and Purposes, as part of this Constitution, when ratified by the Legislatures of three fourths of the several States, or by Conventions in three fourths thereof, as the one or the other Mode of Ratification may be proposed by the Congress; Provided that no Amendment which may be made prior to the Year One thousand eight hundred and eight shall in any Manner affect the first and fourth Clauses in the Ninth Section of the first Article; and that no State, without its Consent, shall be deprived of its equal Suffrage in the Senate.

Article VI

All Debts contracted and Engagements entered into, before the Adoption of this Constitution shall be as valid against the United States under this Constitution, as under the Confederation.

This Constitution, and the Laws of the United States which shall be made in Pursuance thereof; and all Treaties made, or which shall be made, under the Authority of the United States, shall be the supreme Law of the Land; and the Judges in every State shall be bound thereby, any Thing in the Constitution or Laws of any State to the Contrary notwithstanding.

The Senators and Representatives before mentioned, and the Members of the several State Legislatures, and all executive and judicial Officers, both of the United States and of the several States, shall be bound by Oath or Affirmation, to support this Constitution; but no religious Test shall ever be required as a Qualification to any Office or public Trust under the United States.

Article VII

The Ratification of the Conventions of nine States shall be sufficient for the Establishment of this Constitution between the States so ratifying the Same.

Amendment I [1791]

Congress shall make no law respecting an establishment of religion, or prohibiting the free exercise thereof; or abridging the freedom of speech, or of the press; or the right of the people peaceably to assembly, and to petition the Government for a redress of grievances.

Amendment II [1791]

A well regulated Militia, being necessary to the security of a free State, the right of the people to keep and bear Arms, shall not be infringed.

Amendment III [1791]

No Soldier shall, in time of peace be quartered in any house, without the consent of the Owner, nor in time of war, but in a manner to be prescribed by law.

Amendment IV [1791]

The right of the people to be secure in their persons, houses, papers, and effects, against unreasonable searches and seizures, shall not be violated, and no Warrants shall issue, but upon probable cause, supported by Oath or affirmation, and particularly describing the place to be searched, and the persons or things to be seized.

Amendment V [1791]

No person shall be held to answer for a capital, or otherwise infamous crime, unless on a presentment or indictment of a Grand Jury, except in cases arising in the land or naval forces, or in the Militia, when in actual service in time of War or public danger; nor shall any person be subject for the same offence to be twice put in jeopardy of life or limb; nor shall be compelled in any criminal case to be a witness against himself, nor be deprived of life, liberty, or property, without due process of law; nor shall private property be taken for public use, without just compensation.

Amendment VI [1791]

In all criminal prosecutions, the accused shall enjoy the right to a speedy and public trial, by an impartial jury of the State and district wherein the crime shall have been committed, which district shall have been previously ascertained by law, and to be informed of the nature and cause of the accusation; to be confronted with the witnesses against him; to have compulsory process for obtaining witnesses in his favor, and to have the Assistance of Counsel for his defence.

Amendment VII [1791]

In Suits at common law, where the value in controversy shall exceed twenty dollars, the right of trial by jury shall be preserved, and no fact tried by jury, shall be otherwise re-examined in any Court of the United States, than according to the rules of the common law.

Amendment VIII [1791]

Excessive bail shall not be required, nor excessive fines imposed, nor cruel and unusual punishments inflicted.

Amendment IX [1791]

The enumeration in the Constitution, of certain rights, shall not be construed to deny or disparage others retained by the people.

Amendment X [1791]

The powers not delegated to the United States by the Constitution, nor prohibited by it to the States, are reserved to the States respectively, or to the people.

Amendment XI [1798]

The Judicial power of the United States shall not be construed to extend to any suit in law or equity, commenced or prosecuted against one of the United States by Citizens of another State, or by Citizens or Subjects of any Foreign State.

Amendment XII [1804]

The Electors shall meet in their respective states, and vote by ballot for President and Vice-President, one of whom, at least, shall not be an inhabitant of the same state with themselves; they shall name in their ballots the person voted for as President, and in distinct ballots the person voted for as Vice-President, and they shall make distinct lists of all persons voted for as President, and of all persons voted for as Vice-President, and of the number of votes for each, which lists they shall sign and certify, and transmit sealed to the seat of the government of the United States, directed to the President of the Senate;—The President of the Senate shall, in the presence of the Senate and House of Representatives, open all the certificates and the votes shall then be counted;—The person having the greatest number of votes for President, shall be the President, if such number be a majority of the whole number of Electors appointed; and if no person have such majority, then from the persons having the highest numbers not exceeding three on the list of those voted for as President, the House of Representatives shall choose immediately, by ballot, the President. But in choosing the President, the votes shall be taken by states, the representation from each state having one vote; a quorum for this purpose shall consist of a member or members from two-thirds of the states, and a majority of all states shall be necessary to a choice. And if the House of Representatives shall not choose a President whenever the right of choice shall devolve upon them, before the fourth day of March next following, then the Vice-President shall act as President, as in the case of the death or other constitutional disability of the President.—The person having the greatest number of votes as Vice-President, shall be the Vice-President, if such number be a majority of the whole number of Electors appointed, and if no person have a majority, then from the two highest numbers on the list, the Senate shall choose the Vice-President; a quorum for the purpose shall consist of two-thirds of the whole number of Senators, and a majority of the whole number shall be necessary to a choice. But no person constitutionally ineligible to the office of President shall be eligible to that of Vice-President of the United States.

Amendment XIII [1865]

Section 1. Neither slavery nor involuntary servitude, except as a punishment for crime whereof the party shall have been duly convicted, shall exist within the United States, or any place subject to their jurisdiction.

Section 2. Congress shall have power to enforce this article by appropriate legislation.

Amendment XIV [1868]

Section 1. All persons born or naturalized in the United States, and subject to the jurisdiction thereof, are citizens of the United States and of the State wherein they reside. No State shall make or enforce any law which shall abridge the privileges or immunities of citizens of the United States; nor shall any State deprive any person of life, liberty, or property, without due process of law; nor deny to any person within its jurisdiction the equal protection of the laws.

Section 2. Representatives shall be apportioned among the several States according to their respective numbers, counting the whole number of persons in each State, excluding Indians not taxed. But when the right to vote at any election for the choice of electors for President and Vice President of the United States, Representatives in Congress, the Executive and Judicial officers of a State, or the members of the Legislature thereof, is denied to any of the male inhabitants of such State, being twenty-one years of age, and citizens of the United States, or in any way abridged, except for participation in rebellion, or other crime, the basis of representation therein shall be reduced in the proportion which the number of such male citizens shall bear to the whole number of male citizens twenty-one years of age in such State.

Section 3. No person shall be a Senator or Representative in Congress, or elector of President and Vice President, or hold any office, civil or military, under the United States, or under any State, who having previously taken an oath, as a member of Congress, or as an officer of the United States, or as a member of any State legislature, or as an executive or judicial officer of any State, to support the Constitution of the United States, shall have engaged in insurrection or rebellion against the same, or given aid or comfort to the enemies thereof. But Congress may by a vote of two-thirds of each House, remove such disability.

Section 4. The validity of the public debt of the United States, authorized by law, including debts incurred for payment of pensions and bounties for services in suppressing insurrection or rebellion, shall not be questioned. But neither the United States nor any State shall assume or pay any debt or obligation incurred in aid of insurrection or rebellion against the United States, or any claim for the loss or emancipation of any slave; but all such debts, obligations and claims shall be held illegal and void.

Section 5. The Congress shall have power to enforce, by appropriate legislation, the provisions of this article.

Amendment XV [1870]

Section 1. The right of citizens of the United States to vote shall not be denied or abridged by the United States or by any State on account of race, color, or previous condition of servitude.

Section 2. The Congress shall have power to enforce this article by appropriate legislation.

Amendment XVI [1913]

The Congress shall have power to lay and collect taxes on incomes, from whatever source derived, without apportionment among the several States, and without regard to any census or enumeration.

Amendment XVII [1913]

Section 1. The Senate of the United States shall be composed of two Senators from each State, elected by the people thereof, for six years; and each Senator shall have one vote. The electors in each State shall have the qualifications requisite for electors of the most numerous branch of the State legislatures.

Section 2. When vacancies happen in the representation of any State in the Senate, the executive authority of such State shall issue writs of election to fill such vacancies: *Provided,* That the legislature of any State may empower the executive thereof to make temporary appointments until the people fill the vacancies by election as the legislature may direct.

Section 3. This amendment shall not be so construed as to affect the election or term of any Senator chosen before it becomes valid as part of the Constitution.

Amendment XVIII [1919]

Section 1. After one year from the ratification of this article the manufacture, sale, or transportation of intoxicating liquors within, the importation thereof into, or the exportation thereof from the United States and all territory subject to the jurisdiction thereof for beverage purposes is hereby prohibited.

Section 2. The Congress and the several States shall have concurrent power to enforce this article by appropriate legislation.

Section 3. This article shall be inoperative unless it shall have been ratified as an amendment to the Constitution by the legislatures of the several States, as provided in the Constitution, within seven years from the date of the submission hereof to the States by the Congress.

Amendment XIX [1920]

Section 1. The right of citizens of the United States to vote shall not be denied or abridged by the United States or by any State on account of sex.

Section 2. Congress shall have power to enforce this article by appropriate legislation.

Amendment XX [1933]

Section 1. The terms of the President and Vice President shall end at noon on the 20th day of January, and the terms of Senators and Representatives at noon on the 3d day of January, of the years in which such terms would have ended if this article had not been ratified; and the terms of their successors shall then begin.

Section 2. The Congress shall assemble at least once in every year, and such meeting shall begin at noon on the 3d day of January, unless they shall by law appoint a different day.

Section 3. If, at the time fixed for the beginning of the term of the President, the President elect shall have died, the Vice President elect shall become President. If the President shall not have been chosen before the time fixed for the beginning of his term, or if the President elect shall have failed to qualify, then the Vice President elect shall act as President until a President shall have qualified; and the Congress may by law provide for the case wherein neither a President elect nor a Vice President elect shall have qualified, declaring who shall then act as President, or the manner in which one who is to act shall be selected, and such person shall act accordingly until a President or Vice President shall have qualified.

Section 4. The Congress may by law provide for the case of the death of any of the persons from whom the House of Representatives may choose a President whenever the right of choice shall have devolved upon them, and for the case of the death of any of the persons from whom the Senate may choose a Vice President whenever the right of choice shall have devolved upon them.

Section 5. Sections 1 and 2 shall take effect on the 15th day of October following the ratification of this article.

Section 6. This article shall be inoperative unless it shall have been ratified as an amendment to the Constitution by the legislatures of three-fourths of the several States within seven years from the date of its submission.

Amendment XXI [1933]

Section 1. The eighteenth article of amendment to the Constitution of the United States is hereby repealed.

Section 2. The transportation or importation into any State, Territory, or possession of the United States for delivery or use therein of intoxicating liquors, in violation of the laws thereof, is hereby prohibited.

Section 3. This article shall be inoperative unless it shall have been ratified as an amendment to the Constitution by conventions in the several States, as provided in the Constitution, within seven years from the date of the submission hereof to the States by the Congress.

Amendment XXII [1951]

Section 1. No person shall be elected to the office of the President more than twice, and no person who has held the office of President, or acted as President, for more than two years of a term to which some other person was elected President shall be elected to the office of President more than once. But this Article shall not apply to any person holding the office of President when this Article was proposed by the Congress, and shall not prevent any person who may be holding the office of President, or acting as President, during the term within which this Article becomes operative from holding the office of President or acting as President during the remainder of such term.

Section 2. This article shall be inoperative unless it shall have been ratified as an amendment to the Constitution by the legislatures of three-fourths of the several States within seven years from the date of its submission to the States by the Congress.

Amendment XXIII [1961]

Section 1. The District constituting the seat of Government of the United States shall appoint in such manner as the Congress may direct:

A number of electors of President and Vice President equal to the whole number of Senators and Representatives in Congress to which the District would be entitled if it were a State, but in no event more than the least populous state; they shall be in addition to those appointed by the states, but they shall be considered, for the purposes of the election of President and Vice President, to be electors appointed by a state; and they shall meet in the District and perform such duties as provided by the twelfth article of amendment.

Section 2. The Congress shall have power to enforce this article by appropriate legislation.

Amendment XXIV [1964]

Section 1. The right of citizens of the United States to vote in any primary or other election for President or Vice President, for electors for President or Vice President, or for Senator or Representative in Congress, shall not be denied or abridged by the United States, or any State by reason of failure to pay any poll tax or other tax.

Section 2. The Congress shall have power to enforce this article by appropriate legislation.

Amendment XXV [1967]

Section 1. In case of the removal of the President from office or of his death or resignation, the Vice President shall become President.

Section 2. Whenever there is a vacancy in the office of the Vice President, the President shall nominate a Vice President who shall take office upon confirmation by a majority vote of both Houses of Congress.

Section 3. Whenever the President transmits to the President pro tempore of the Senate and the Speaker of the House of Representatives his written declaration that he is unable to discharge the powers and duties of his office, and until he transmits to them a written declaration to the contrary, such powers and duties shall be discharged by the Vice President as Acting President.

Section 4. Whenever the Vice President and a majority of either the principal officers of the executive departments or of such other body as Congress may by law provide, transmit to the President pro tempore of the Senate and the Speaker of the House of Representatives their written declaration that the President is unable to discharge the powers and duties of his office, the Vice President shall immediately assume the powers and duties of the office as Acting President.

Thereafter, when the President transmits to the President pro tempore of the Senate and the Speaker of the House of Representatives his written declaration that no inability exists, he shall resume the powers and duties of his office unless the Vice President and a majority of either the principal officers of the executive department or of such other body as Congress may by law provide, transmit within four days to the President pro tempore of the Senate and the Speaker of the House of Representatives their written declaration that the President is unable to discharge the powers and duties of his office. Thereupon Congress shall decide the issue, assembling within forty-eight hours for that purpose if not in session. If the Congress, within twenty-one days after receipt of the latter written declaration, or, if Congress is not in session, within twenty-one days after Congress is required to assemble, determines by two-thirds vote of both Houses that the President is unable to discharge the powers and duties of his office, the Vice President shall continue to discharge the same as Acting President; otherwise, the President shall resume the powers and duties of his office.

Amendment XXVI [1971]

Section 1. The right of citizens of the United States, who are eighteen years of age or older, to vote shall not be denied or abridged by the United States or by any State on account of age.

Section 2. The Congress shall have power to enforce this article by appropriate legislation.

Amendment XXVII [1992]

No law, varying the compensation for the services of the Senators and Representatives, shall take effect, until an election of Representatives shall have intervened.

Articles 2 and 2A of the Uniform Commercial Code

(Adopted in fifty-two jurisdictions—all fifty States, although Louisiana has adopted only Articles 1, 3, 4, 7, 8, and 9; the District of Columbia; and the Virgin Islands.)

The Code consists of the following articles:

Article

1. General Provisions
2. Sales
2A. Leases
3. Negotiable Instruments
4. Bank Deposits and Collections
4A. Funds Transfers
5. Letters of Credit
6. Repealer of Article 6—Bulk Transfers and [Revised] Article 6—Bulk Sales
7. Warehouse Receipts, Bills of Lading and Other Documents of Title
8. Investment Securities
9. Secured Transactions
10. Effective Date and Repealer
11. Effective Date and Transition Provisions

ARTICLE 1: GENERAL PROVISIONS

Part 1—General Provisions

§ 1–101. Short Titles.

(a) This [Act] may be cited as Uniform Commercial Code.
(b) This article may be cited as Uniform Commercial Code-Uniform Provisions.

§ 1–102. Scope of Article.

This article applies to a transaction to the extent that it is governed by another article of [the Uniform Commercial Code].

§ 1–103. Construction of [Uniform Commercial Code] to Promote Its Purpose and Policies; Applicability of Supplemental Principles of Law.

(a) [The Uniform Commercial Code] must be liberally construed and applied to promote its underlying purposes and policies, which are:

(1) to simplify, clarify, and modernize the law governing commercial transactions;
(2) to permit the continued expansion of commercial practices through custom, usage, and agreement of the parties; and
(3) to make uniform the law among the various jurisdictions.

(b) Unless displaced by the particular provisions of [the Uniform Commercial Code], the principles of law and equity, including the law merchant and the law relative to capacity to contract, principal and agent, estoppel, fraud, misrepresentation, duress, coercion, mistake, bankruptcy, and other validating or invalidating cause, supplement its provisions.

§ 1–104. Construction Against Implicit Repeal.

This Act being a general act intended as a unified coverage of its subject matter, no part of it shall be deemed to be impliedly repealed by subsequent legislation if such construction can reasonably be avoided.

§ 1–105. Severability.

If any provision or clause of [the Uniform Commercial Code] or its application to any person or circumstance is held invalid, the invalidity does not affect other provisions or applications of [the Uniform Commercial Code] which can be given effect without the invalid provision or application, and to this end the provisions of [the Uniform Commercial Code] are severable.

§ 1–106. Use of Singular and Plural; Gender.

In [the Uniform Commercial Code], unless the statutory context otherwise requires:
(1) words in the singular number include the plural, and those in the plural include the singular; and
(2) words of any gender also refer to any other gender.

§ 1–107. Section Captions.

Section captions are part of [the Uniform Commercial Code].

§ 1–108. Relation to Electronic Signatures in Global and National Commerce Act.

This article modifies, limits, and supersedes the Federal Electronic Signatures in Global and National Commerce Act, 15 U.S.C. Sections 7001 *et seq.*, except that nothing in this article modifies, limits, or supersedes Section 7001(c) of that act or authorizes electronic delivery of any of the notices described in Section 7003(b) of that Act.

Part 2—General Definitions and Principles of Interpretation

§ 1–201. General Definitions.

Subject to additional definitions contained in the subsequent Articles of this Act which are applicable to specific Articles or Parts thereof, and unless the context otherwise requires, in this Act:
(1) "Action", in the sense of a judicial proceeding, includes recoupment, counterclaim, set-off, suit in equity, and any other proceedings in which rights are determined.
(2) "Aggrieved party" means a party entitled to resort to a remedy.
(3) "Agreement", as distinguished from "contract", means the bargain of the parties in fact, as found in their language or by implication from other circumstances, including course of performance, course of dealing, or usage of trade as provided in Section 1–303.
(4) "Bank" means a person engaged in the business of banking and includes a savings bank, savings and loan association, credit union, and trust company.

(5) "Bearer" means a person in control of a negotiable electronic document of title or a person in possession of a negotiable instrument, negotiable tangible document of title, or certificated security that is payable to bearer or indorsed in blank.

(6) "Bill of lading" means a document of title evidencing the receipt of goods for shipment issued by a person engaged in the business of directly or indirectly transporting or forwarding goods. The term does not include a warehouse receipt.

(7) "Branch" includes a separately incorporated foreign branch of a bank.

(8) "Burden of establishing" a fact means the burden of persuading the trier of fact that the existence of the fact is more probable than its nonexistence.

(9) "Buyer in ordinary course of business" means a person that buys goods in good faith, without knowledge that the sale violates the rights of another person in the goods, and in the ordinary course from a person, other than a pawnbroker, in the business of selling goods of that kind. A person buys goods in the ordinary course if the sale to the person comports with the usual or customary practices in the kind of business in which the seller is engaged or with the seller's own usual or customary practices. A person that sells oil, gas, or other minerals at the wellhead or minehead is a person in the business of selling goods of that kind. A buyer in ordinary course of business may buy for cash, by exchange of other property, or on secured or unsecured credit, and may acquire goods or documents of title under a pre-existing contract for sale. Only a buyer that takes possession of the goods or has a right to recover the goods from the seller under Article 2 may be a buyer in ordinary course of business. A person that acquires goods in a transfer in bulk or as security for or in total or partial satisfaction of a money debt is not a buyer in ordinary course of business.

(10) "Conspicuous", with reference to a term, means so written, displayed, or presented that a reasonable person against which it is to operate ought to have noticed it. Whether a term is "conspicuous" or not is a decision for the court. Conspicuous terms include the following:

- **(A)** a heading in capitals equal to or greater in size than the surrounding text, or in contrasting type, font, or color to the surrounding text of the same or lesser size; and
- **(B)** language in the body of a record or display in larger type than the surrounding text, or in contrasting type, font, or color to the surrounding text of the same size, or set off from surrounding text of the same size by symbols or other marks that call attention to the language.

(11) "Consumer" means an individual who enters into a transaction primarily for personal, family, or household purposes.

(12) "Contract", as distinguished from "agreement", means the total legal obligation that results from the parties' agreement as determined by [the Uniform Commercial Code] as supplemented by any other laws.

(13) "Creditor" includes a general creditor, a secured creditor, a lien creditor and any representative of creditors, including an assignee for the benefit of creditors, a trustee in bankruptcy, a receiver in equity and an executor or administrator of an insolvent debtor's or assignor's estate.

(14) "Defendant" includes a person in the position of defendant in a counterclaim, cross-action, or third-party claim.

(15) "Delivery" with respect to an electronic document of title means voluntary transfer of control and with respect to an instrument, a tangible document of title, or chattel paper means voluntary transfer of possession.

(16) "Document of title" means a record (i) that in regular course of business or financing is treated as adequately evidencing that the person in possession or control of the record is entitled to receive, control, hold, and dispose of the record and the goods the record covers and (ii) that purports to be issued by or addressed to a bailee and to cover goods in the bailee's possession which are either identified or are fungible portions of an identified mass. The term includes a bill of lading, transport document, dock warrant, dock receipt, warehouse receipt, and order for delivery of goods. An electronic document of title means a document of title evidenced by a record consisting of information stored in an electronic medium. A tangible document of title means a document of title evidenced by a record consisting of information that is inscribed on a tangible medium.

(17) "Fault" means a default, breach, or wrongful act or omission.

(18) "Fungible goods" means:

- **(A)** goods of which any unit, by nature or usage of trade, is the equivalent of any other like unit; or
- **(B)** goods that by agreement are treated as equivalent.

(19) "Genuine" means free of forgery or counterfeiting.

(20) "Good faith," except as otherwise provided in Article 5, means honesty in fact and the observance of reasonable commercial standards of fair dealing.

(21) "Holder" means:

- **(A)** the person in possession of a negotiable instrument that is payable either to bearer or to an identified person that is the person in possession;
- **(B)** the person in possession of a negotiable tangible document of title if the goods are deliverable either to bearer or to the order of the person in possession; or
- **(C)** the person in control of a negotiable electronic document of title.

(22) "Insolvency proceeding" includes an assignment for the benefit of creditors or other proceeding intended to liquidate or rehabilitate the estate of the person involved.

(23) "Insolvent" means:

- **(A)** having generally ceased to pay debts in the ordinary course of business other than as a result of bona fide dispute;
- **(B)** being unable to pay debts as they become due; or
- **(C)** being insolvent within the meaning of federal bankruptcy law.

(24) "Money" means a medium of exchange currently authorized or adopted by a domestic or foreign government. The term includes a monetary unit of account established by an intergovernmental organization or by agreement between two or more countries.

(25) "Organization" means a person other than an individual.

(26) "Party", as distinguished from "third party", means a person that has engaged in a transaction or made an agreement subject to [the Uniform Commercial Code].

(27) "Person" means an individual, corporation, business trust, estate, trust, partnership, limited liability company, association, joint venture, government, governmental subdivision, agency, or instrumentality, public corporation, or any other legal or commercial entity.

(28) "Present value" means the amount as of a date certain of one or more sums payable in the future, discounted to the date certain by use of either an interest rate specified by the parties if that rate is not manifestly unreasonable at the time the transaction is entered into or, if an interest rate is not so specified, a commercially reasonable rate that takes into account the facts and circumstances at the time the transaction is entered into.

(29) "Purchase" means taking by sale, lease, discount, negotiation, mortgage, pledge, lien, security interest, issue or reissue, gift, or any other voluntary transaction creating an interest in property.

(30) "Purchaser" means a person that takes by purchase.

(31) "Record" means information that is inscribed on a tangible medium or that is stored in an electronic or other medium and is retrievable in perceivable form.

(32) "Remedy" means any remedial right to which an aggrieved party is entitled with or without resort to a tribunal.

(33) "Representative" means a person empowered to act for another, including an agent, an officer of a corporation or association, and a trustee, executor, or administrator of an estate.

(34) "Right" includes remedy.

(35) "Security interest" means an interest in personal property or fixtures which secures payment or performance of an obligation. "Security interest" includes any interest of a consignor and a buyer of accounts, chattel paper, a payment intangible, or a promissory note in a transaction that is subject to Article 9. "Security interest" does not include the special property interest of a buyer of goods on identification of those goods to a contract for sale under Section 2–401, but a buyer may also acquire a "security interest" by complying with Article 9. Except as otherwise provided in Section 2–505, the right of a seller or lessor of goods under Article 2 or 2A to retain or acquire possession of the goods is not a "security interest", but a seller or lessor may also acquire a "security interest" by complying with Article 9. The retention or reservation of title by a seller of goods notwithstanding shipment or delivery to the buyer under Section 2–401 is limited in effect to a reservation of a "security interest." Whether a transaction in the form of a lease creates a "security interest" is determined pursuant to Section 1–203.

(36) "Send" in connection with a writing, record, or notice means:

> **(A)** to deposit in the mail or deliver for transmission by any other usual means of communication with postage or cost of transmission provided for and properly addressed and, in the case of an instrument, to an address specified thereon or otherwise agreed, or if there be none to any address reasonable under the circumstances; or
>
> **(B)** in any other way to cause to be received any record or notice within the time it would have arrived if properly sent.

(37) "Signed" includes using any symbol executed or adopted with present intention to adopt or accept a writing.

(38) "State" means a State of the United States, the District of Columbia, Puerto Rico, the United States Virgin Islands, or any territory or insular possession subject to the jurisdiction of the United States.

(39) "Surety" includes a guarantor or other secondary obligor.

(40) "Term" means a portion of an agreement that relates to a particular matter.

(41) "Unauthorized signature" means a signature made without actual, implied, or apparent authority. The term includes a forgery.

(42) "Warehouse receipt" means a document of title issued by a person engaged in the business of storing goods for hire.

(43) "Writing" includes printing, typewriting, or any other intentional reduction to tangible form. "Written" has a corresponding meaning.

As amended in 2003.

§ 1–202. Notice; Knowledge.

(a) Subject to subsection (f), a person has "notice" of a fact if the person:

> **(1)** has actual knowledge of it;
>
> **(2)** has received a notice or notification of it; or
>
> **(3)** from all the facts and circumstances known to the person at the time in question, has reason to know that it exists.

(b) "Knowledge" means actual knowledge. "Knows" has a corresponding meaning.

(c) "Discover", "learn", or words of similar import refer to knowledge rather than to reason to know.

(d) A person "notifies" or "gives" a notice or notification to another person by taking such steps as may be reasonably required to inform the other person in ordinary course, whether or not the other person actually comes to know of it.

(e) Subject to subsection (f), a person "receives" a notice or notification when:

> **(1)** it comes to that person's attention; or
>
> **(2)** it is duly delivered in a form reasonable under the circumstances at the place of business through which the contract was made or at another location held out by that person as the place for receipt of such communications.

(f) Notice, knowledge, or a notice or notification received by an organization is effective for a particular transaction from the time it is brought to the attention of the individual conducting that transaction and, in any event, from the time it would have been brought to the individual's attention if the organization had exercised due diligence. An organization exercises due diligence if it maintains reasonable routines for communicating significant information to the person conducting the transaction and there is reasonable compliance with the routines. Due diligence does not require an individual acting for the organization to communicate information unless the communication is part of the individual's regular duties or the individual has reason to know of the transaction and that the transaction would be materially affected by the information.

§ 1–203. Lease Distinguished from Security Interest.

(a) Whether a transaction in the form of a lease creates a lease or security interest is determined by the facts of each case.

(b) A transaction in the form of a lease creates a security interest if the consideration that the lessee is to pay the lessor for the right to possession and use of the goods is an obligation for the term of the lease and is not subject to termination by the lessee, and:

(1) the original term of the lease is equal to or greater than the remaining economic life of the goods;

(2) the lessee is bound to renew the lease for the remaining economic life of the goods or is bound to become the owner of the goods;

(3) the lessee has an option to renew the lease for the remaining economic life of the goods for no additional consideration or for nominal additional consideration upon compliance with the lease agreement; or

(4) the lessee has an option to become the owner of the goods for no additional consideration or for nominal additional consideration upon compliance with the lease agreement.

(c) A transaction in the form of a lease does not create a security interest merely because:

(1) the present value of the consideration the lessee is obligated to pay the lessor for the right to possession and use of the goods is substantially equal to or is greater than the fair market value of the goods at the time the lease is entered into;

(2) the lessee assumes risk of loss of the goods;

(3) the lessee agrees to pay, with respect to the goods, taxes, insurance, filing, recording, or registration fees, or service or maintenance costs;

(4) the lessee has an option to renew the lease or to become the owner of the goods;

(5) the lessee has an option to renew the lease for a fixed rent that is equal to or greater than the reasonably predictable fair market rent for the use of the goods for the term of the renewal at the time the option is to be performed; or

(6) the lessee has an option to become the owner of the goods for a fixed price that is equal to or greater than the reasonably predictable fair market value of the goods at the time the option is to be performed.

(d) Additional consideration is nominal if it is less than the lessee's reasonably predictable cost of performing under the lease agreement if the option is not exercised. Additional consideration is not nominal if:

(1) when the option to renew the lease is granted to the lessee, the rent is stated to be the fair market rent for the use of the goods for the term of the renewal determined at the time the option is to be performed; or

(2) when the option to become the owner of the goods is granted to the lessee, the price is stated to be the fair market value of the goods determined at the time the option is to be performed.

(e) The "remaining economic life of the goods" and "reasonably predictable" fair market rent, fair market value, or cost of performing under the lease agreement must be determined with reference to the facts and circumstances at the time the transaction is entered into.

§ 1–204. Value.

Except as otherwise provided in Articles 3, 4, [and] 5, [and 6], a person gives value for rights if the person acquires them:

(1) in return for a binding commitment to extend credit or for the extension of immediately available credit, whether or not drawn upon and whether or not a charge-back is provided for in the event of difficulties in collection;

(2) as security for, or in total or partial satisfaction of, a preexisting claim;

(3) by accepting delivery under a preexisting contract for purchase; or

(4) in return for any consideration sufficient to support a simple contract.

§ 1–205. Reasonable Time; Seasonableness.

(a) Whether a time for taking an action required by [the Uniform Commercial Code] is reasonable depends on the nature, purpose, and circumstances of the action.

(b) An action is taken seasonably if it is taken at or within the time agreed or, if no time is agreed, at or within a reasonable time.

§ 1–206. Presumptions.

Whenever [the Uniform Commercial Code] creates a "presumption" with respect to a fact, or provides that a fact is "presumed," the trier of fact must find the existence of the fact unless and until evidence is introduced that supports a finding of its nonexistence.

Part 3—Territorial Applicability and General Rules

§ 1–301. Territorial Applicability; Parties' Power to Choose Applicable Law.

(a) In this section:

(1) "Domestic transaction" means a transaction other than an international transaction.

(2) "International transaction" means a transaction that bears a reasonable relation to a country other than the United States.

(b) This section applies to a transaction to the extent that it is governed by another article of the [Uniform Commercial Code].

(c) Except as otherwise provided in this section:

(1) an agreement by parties to a domestic transaction that any or all of their rights and obligations are to be determined by the law of this State or of another State is effective, whether or not the transaction bears a relation to the State designated; and

(2) an agreement by parties to an international transaction that any or all of their rights and obligations are to be determined by the law of this State or of another State or country is effective, whether or not the transaction bears a relation to the State or country designated.

(d) In the absence of an agreement effective under subsection (c), and except as provided in subsections (e) and (g), the rights and obligations of the parties are determined by the law that would be selected by application of this State's conflict of laws principles.

(e) If one of the parties to a transaction is a consumer, the following rules apply:

(1) An agreement referred to in subsection (c) is not effective unless the transaction bears a reasonable relation to the State or country designated.

(2) Application of the law of the State or country determined pursuant to subsection (c) or (d) may not deprive the consumer of the protection of any rule of law governing a matter within the scope of this section, which both is protective of consumers and may not be varied by agreement: (A) of the State or country in which the consumer principally resides, unless subparagraph (B) applies; or (B) if the transaction is a sale of goods, of the State or country in which the consumer both makes the contract and take delivery of those goods, if such State or country is not the State or country in which the consumer principally resides.

(f) An agreement otherwise effective under subsection (c) is not effective to the extent that application of the law of the State or country designated would be contrary to a fundamental policy of the State or country whose law would govern in the absence of agreement under subsection (d).

(g) To the extent that [the Uniform Commercial Code] governs a transaction, if one of the following provisions of [the Uniform Commercial Code] specifies the applicable law, that provision governs and a contrary agreement is effective only to the extent permitted by the law so specified: (1) Section 2–402; (2) Sections 2A–105 and 2A–106; (3) Section 4–102; (4) Section 4A–507; (5) Section 5–116; [(6) Section 6–103;] (7) Section 8–110; (8) Sections 9–301 through 9–307.

§ 1–302. Variation by Agreement.

(a) Except as otherwise provided in subsection (b) or elsewhere in [the Uniform Commercial Code], the effect of provisions of [the Uniform Commercial Code] may be varied by agreement.

(b) The obligations of good faith, diligence, reasonableness, and care prescribed by [the Uniform Commercial Code] may not be disclaimed by agreement. The parties, by agreement, may determine the standards by which the performance of those obligations is to be measured if those standards are not manifestly unreasonable. Whenever [the Uniform Commercial Code] requires an action to be taken within a reasonable time, a time that is not manifestly unreasonable may be fixed by agreement.

(c) The presence in certain provisions of [the Uniform Commercial Code] of the phrase "unless otherwise agreed", or words of similar import, does not imply that the effect of other provisions may not be varied by agreement under this section.

§ 1–303. Course of Performance, Course of Dealing, and Usage of Trade.

(a) A "course of performance" is a sequence of conduct between the parties to a particular transaction that exists if:

(1) the agreement of the parties with respect to the transaction involves repeated occasions for performance by a party; and

(2) the other party, with knowledge of the nature of the performance and opportunity for objection to it, accepts the performance or acquiesces in it without objection.

(b) A "course of dealing" is a sequence of conduct concerning previous transactions between the parties to a particular transaction that is fairly to be regarded as establishing a common basis of understanding for interpreting their expressions and other conduct.

(c) A "usage of trade" is any practice or method of dealing having such regularity of observance in a place, vocation, or trade as to justify an expectation that it will be observed with respect to the transaction in question. The existence and scope of such a usage must be proved as facts. If it is established that such a usage is embodied in a trade code or similar record, the interpretation of the record is a question of law.

(d) A course of performance or course of dealing between the parties or usage of trade in the vocation or trade in which they are engaged or of which they are or should be aware is relevant in ascertaining the meaning of the parties' agreement, may give particular meaning to specific terms of the agreement, and may supplement or qualify the terms of the agreement. A usage of trade applicable in the place in which part of the performance under the agreement is to occur may be so utilized as to that part of the performance.

(e) Except as otherwise provided in subsection (f), the express terms of an agreement and any applicable course of performance, course of dealing, or usage of trade must be construed whenever reasonable as consistent with each other. If such a construction is unreasonable:

(1) express terms prevail over course of performance, course of dealing, and usage of trade;

(2) course of performance prevails over course of dealing and usage of trade; and

(3) course of dealing prevails over usage of trade.

(f) Subject to Section 2–209 and Section 2A–208, a course of performance is relevant to show a waiver or modification of any term inconsistent with the course of performance.

(g) Evidence of a relevant usage of trade offered by one party is not admissible unless that party has given the other party notice that the court finds sufficient to prevent unfair surprise to the other party.

§ 1–304. Obligation of Good Faith.

Every contract or duty within [the Uniform Commercial Code] imposes an obligation of good faith in its performance and enforcement.

§ 1–305. Remedies to be Liberally Administered.

(a) The remedies provided by [the Uniform Commercial Code] must be liberally administered to the end that the aggrieved party may be put in as good a position as if the other party had fully performed but neither consequential or special damages nor penal damages may be had except as specifically provided in [the Uniform Commercial Code] or by other rule of law.

(b) Any right or obligation declared by [the Uniform Commercial Code] is enforceable by action unless the provision declaring it specifies a different and limited effect.

§ 1–306. Waiver or Renunciation of Claim or Right After Breach.

A claim or right arising out of an alleged breach may be discharged in whole or in part without consideration by agreement of the aggrieved party in an authenticated record.

§ 1–307. *Prima Facie* Evidence by Third-Party Documents.

A document in due form purporting to be a bill of lading, policy or certificate of insurance, official weigher's or inspector's certificate, consular invoice, or any other document authorized or required by the contract to be issued by a third party is *prima facie* evidence of its own authenticity and genuineness and of the facts stated in the document by the third party.

§ 1–308. Performance or Acceptance Under Reservation of Rights.

(a) A party that with explicit reservation of rights performs or promises performance or assents to performance in a manner demanded or offered by the other party does not thereby prejudice the rights reserved. Such words as "without prejudice," "under protest," or the like are sufficient.

(b) Subsection (a) does not apply to an accord and satisfaction.

§ 1–309. Option to Accelerate at Will.

A term providing that one party or that party's successor in interest may accelerate payment or performance or require collateral or additional collateral "at will" or when the party "deems itself insecure," or words of similar import, means that the party has power to do so only if that party in good faith believes that the prospect of payment or performance is impaired. The burden of establishing lack of good faith is on the party against which the power has been exercised.

§ 1–310. Subordinated Obligations.

An obligation may be issued as subordinated to performance of another obligation of the person obligated, or a creditor may subordinate its right to performance of an obligation by agreement with either the person obligated or another creditor of the person obligated. Subordination does not create a security interest as against either the common debtor or a subordinated creditor.

ARTICLE 2: SALES

Part 1—Short Title, General Construction and Subject Matter

§ 2–101. Short Title.

This Article shall be known and may be cited as Uniform Commercial Code—Sales.

§ 2–102. Scope; Certain Security and Other Transactions Excluded From This Article.

Unless the context otherwise requires, this Article applies to transactions in goods; it does not apply to any transaction which although in the form of an unconditional contract to sell or present sale is intended to operate only as a security transaction nor does this Article impair or repeal any statute regulating sales to consumers, farmers or other specified classes of buyers.

§ 2–103. Definitions and Index of Definitions.

(1) In this Article unless the context otherwise requires

(a) "Buyer" means a person who buys or contracts to buy goods.

(b) "Good faith" in the case of a merchant means honesty in fact and the observance of reasonable commercial standards of fair dealing in the trade.

(c) "Receipt" of goods means taking physical possession of them.

(d) "Seller" means a person who sells or contracts to sell goods.

(2) Other definitions applying to this Article or to specified Parts thereof, and the sections in which they appear are:

"Acceptance". Section 2–606.
"Banker's credit". Section 2–325.
"Between merchants". Section 2–104.
"Cancellation". Section 2–106(4).
"Commercial unit". Section 2–105.
"Confirmed credit". Section 2–325.
"Conforming to contract". Section 2–106.
"Contract for sale". Section 2–106.
"Cover". Section 2–712.
"Entrusting". Section 2–403.
"Financing agency". Section 2–104.
"Future goods". Section 2–105.
"Goods". Section 2–105.
"Identification". Section 2–501.
"Installment contract". Section 2–612.
"Letter of Credit". Section 2–325.
"Lot". Section 2–105.
"Merchant". Section 2–104.
"Overseas". Section 2–323.
"Person in position of seller". Section 2–707.
"Present sale". Section 2–106.
"Sale". Section 2–106.
"Sale on approval". Section 2–326.
"Sale or return". Section 2–326.
"Termination". Section 2–106.

(3) The following definitions in other Articles apply to this Article:

"Check". Section 3–104.
"Consignee". Section 7–102.
"Consignor". Section 7–102.
"Consumer goods". Section 9–109.
"Dishonor". Section 3–507.
"Draft". Section 3–104.

(4) In addition Article 1 contains general definitions and principles of construction and interpretation applicable throughout this Article.

As amended in 1994 and 1999.

§ 2–104. Definitions: "Merchant"; "Between Merchants"; "Financing Agency".

(1) "Merchant" means a person who deals in goods of the kind or otherwise by his occupation holds himself out as having knowledge or skill peculiar to the practices or goods involved in the transaction or to whom such knowledge or skill may be attributed by his employment of an agent or broker or other intermediary who by his occupation holds himself out as having such knowledge or skill.

(2) "Financing agency" means a bank, finance company or other person who in the ordinary course of business makes advances against goods or documents of title or who by arrangement with either the seller or the buyer intervenes in ordinary course to make or collect payment due or claimed under the contract for sale, as by purchasing or paying the seller's draft or making advances against it or by merely taking it for collection whether or not documents of title accompany the draft. "Financing agency" includes also a bank or other person who similarly intervenes between persons who are in the position of seller and buyer in respect to the goods (Section 2–707).

(3) "Between merchants" means in any transaction with respect to which both parties are chargeable with the knowledge or skill of merchants.

§ 2–105. Definitions: Transferability; "Goods"; "Future" Goods; "Lot"; "Commercial Unit".

(1) "Goods" means all things (including specially manufactured goods) which are movable at the time of identification to the contract for sale other than the money in which the price is to be paid, investment securities (Article 8) and things in action. "Goods" also includes the unborn young of animals and growing crops and other identified things attached to realty as described in the section on goods to be severed from realty (Section 2–107).
(2) Goods must be both existing and identified before any interest in them can pass. Goods which are not both existing and identified are "future" goods. A purported present sale of future goods or of any interest therein operates as a contract to sell.
(3) There may be a sale of a part interest in existing identified goods.
(4) An undivided share in an identified bulk of fungible goods is sufficiently identified to be sold although the quantity of the bulk is not determined. Any agreed proportion of such a bulk or any quantity thereof agreed upon by number, weight or other measure may to the extent of the seller's interest in the bulk be sold to the buyer who then becomes an owner in common.
(5) "Lot" means a parcel or a single article which is the subject matter of a separate sale or delivery, whether or not it is sufficient to perform the contract.
(6) "Commercial unit" means such a unit of goods as by commercial usage is a single whole for purposes of sale and division of which materially impairs its character or value on the market or in use. A commercial unit may be a single article (as a machine) or a set of articles (as a suite of furniture or an assortment of sizes) or a quantity (as a bale, gross, or carload) or any other unit treated in use or in the relevant market as a single whole.

§ 2–106. Definitions: "Contract"; "Agreement"; "Contract for Sale"; "Sale"; "Present Sale"; "Conforming" to Contract; "Termination"; "Cancellation".

(1) In this Article unless the context otherwise requires "contract" and "agreement" are limited to those relating to the present or future sale of goods. "Contract for sale" includes both a present sale of goods and a contract to sell goods at a future time. A "sale" consists in the passing of title from the seller to the buyer for a price (Section 2–401). A "present sale" means a sale which is accomplished by the making of the contract.
(2) Goods or conduct including any part of a performance are "conforming" or conform to the contract when they are in accordance with the obligations under the contract.
(3) "Termination" occurs when either party pursuant to a power created by agreement or law puts an end to the contract otherwise than for its breach. On "termination" all obligations which are still executory on both sides are discharged but any right based on prior breach or performance survives.
(4) "Cancellation" occurs when either party puts an end to the contract for breach by the other and its effect is the same as that of "termination" except that the cancelling party also retains any remedy for breach of the whole contract or any unperformed balance.

§ 2–107. Goods to Be Severed From Realty: Recording.

(1) A contract for the sale of minerals or the like (including oil and gas) or a structure or its materials to be removed from realty is a contract for the sale of goods within this Article if they are to be severed by the seller but until severance a purported present sale thereof which is not effective as a transfer of an interest in land is effective only as a contract to sell.
(2) A contract for the sale apart from the land of growing crops or other things attached to realty and capable of severance without material harm thereto but not described in subsection (1) or of timber to be cut is a contract for the sale of goods within this Article whether the subject matter is to be severed by the buyer or by the seller even though it forms part of the realty at the time of contracting, and the parties can by identification effect a present sale before severance.
(3) The provisions of this section are subject to any third party rights provided by the law relating to realty records, and the contract for sale may be executed and recorded as a document transferring an interest in land and shall then constitute notice to third parties of the buyer's rights under the contract for sale.
As amended in 1972.

Part 2—Form, Formation and Readjustment of Contract

§ 2–201. Formal Requirements; Statute of Frauds.

(1) Except as otherwise provided in this section a contract for the sale of goods for the price of $500 or more is not enforceable by way of action or defense unless there is some writing sufficient to indicate that a contract for sale has been made between the parties and signed by the party against whom enforcement is sought or by his authorized agent or broker. A writing is not insufficient because it omits or incorrectly states a term agreed upon but the contract is not enforceable under this paragraph beyond the quantity of goods shown in such writing.
(2) Between merchants if within a reasonable time a writing in confirmation of the contract and sufficient against the sender is received and the party receiving it has reason to know its contents, its satisfies the requirements of subsection (1) against such party unless written notice of objection to its contents is given within ten days after it is received.
(3) A contract which does not satisfy the requirements of subsection (1) but which is valid in other respects is enforceable

(a) if the goods are to be specially manufactured for the buyer and are not suitable for sale to others in the ordinary course of the seller's business and the seller, before notice of repudiation is received and under circumstances which reasonably indicate that the goods are for the buyer, has made either a substantial beginning of their manufacture or commitments for their procurement; or
(b) if the party against whom enforcement is sought admits in his pleading, testimony or otherwise in court that a contract for sale was made, but the contract is not enforceable under this provision beyond the quantity of goods admitted; or
(c) with respect to goods for which payment has been made and accepted or which have been received and accepted (Sec. 2–606).

§ 2–202. Final Written Expression: Parol or Extrinsic Evidence.

Terms with respect to which the confirmatory memoranda of the parties agree or which are otherwise set forth in a writing intended by the parties as a final expression of their agreement with respect to such terms as are included therein may not be contradicted by evidence of any prior agreement or of a contemporaneous oral agreement but may be explained or supplemented

(a) by course of dealing or usage of trade (Section 1–205) or by course of performance (Section 2–208); and

(b) by evidence of consistent additional terms unless the court finds the writing to have been intended also as a complete and exclusive statement of the terms of the agreement.

§ 2–203. Seals Inoperative.

The affixing of a seal to a writing evidencing a contract for sale or an offer to buy or sell goods does not constitute the writing a sealed instrument and the law with respect to sealed instruments does not apply to such a contract or offer.

§ 2–204. Formation in General.

(1) A contract for sale of goods may be made in any manner sufficient to show agreement, including conduct by both parties which recognizes the existence of such a contract.

(2) An agreement sufficient to constitute a contract for sale may be found even though the moment of its making is undetermined.

(3) Even though one or more terms are left open a contract for sale does not fail for indefiniteness if the parties have intended to make a contract and there is a reasonably certain basis for giving an appropriate remedy.

§ 2–205. Firm Offers.

An offer by a merchant to buy or sell goods in a signed writing which by its terms gives assurance that it will be held open is not revocable, for lack of consideration, during the time stated or if no time is stated for a reasonable time, but in no event may such period of irrevocability exceed three months; but any such term of assurance on a form supplied by the offeree must be separately signed by the offeror.

§ 2–206. Offer and Acceptance in Formation of Contract.

(1) Unless other unambiguously indicated by the language or circumstances

(a) an offer to make a contract shall be construed as inviting acceptance in any manner and by any medium reasonable in the circumstances;

(b) an order or other offer to buy goods for prompt or current shipment shall be construed as inviting acceptance either by a prompt promise to ship or by the prompt or current shipment of conforming or nonconforming goods, but such a shipment of non-conforming goods does not constitute an acceptance if the seller seasonably notifies the buyer that the shipment is offered only as an accommodation to the buyer.

(2) Where the beginning of a requested performance is a reasonable mode of acceptance an offeror who is not notified of acceptance within a reasonable time may treat the offer as having lapsed before acceptance.

§ 2–207. Additional Terms in Acceptance or Confirmation.

(1) A definite and seasonable expression of acceptance or a written confirmation which is sent within a reasonable time operates as an acceptance even though it states terms additional to or different from those offered or agreed upon, unless acceptance is expressly made conditional on assent to the additional or different terms.

(2) The additional terms are to be construed as proposals for addition to the contract. Between merchants such terms become part of the contract unless:

(a) the offer expressly limits acceptance to the terms of the offer;

(b) they materially alter it; or

(c) notification of objection to them has already been given or is given within a reasonable time after notice of them is received.

(3) Conduct by both parties which recognizes the existence of a contract is sufficient to establish a contract for sale although the writings of the parties do not otherwise establish a contract. In such case the terms of the particular contract consist of those terms on which the writings of the parties agree, together with any supplementary terms incorporated under any other provisions of this Act.

§ 2–208. Course of Performance or Practical Construction.

(1) Where the contract for sale involves repeated occasions for performance by either party with knowledge of the nature of the performance and opportunity for objection to it by the other, any course of performance accepted or acquiesced in without objection shall be relevant to determine the meaning of the agreement.

(2) The express terms of the agreement and any such course of performance, as well as any course of dealing and usage of trade, shall be construed whenever reasonable as consistent with each other; but when such construction is unreasonable, express terms shall control course of performance and course of performance shall control both course of dealing and usage of trade (Section 1–205).

(3) Subject to the provisions of the next section on modification and waiver, such course of performance shall be relevant to show a waiver or modification of any term inconsistent with such course of performance.

§ 2–209. Modification, Rescission and Waiver.

(1) An agreement modifying a contract within this Article needs no consideration to be binding.

(2) A signed agreement which excludes modification or rescission except by a signed writing cannot be otherwise modified or rescinded, but except as between merchants such a requirement on a form supplied by the merchant must be separately signed by the other party.

(3) The requirements of the statute of frauds section of this Article (Section 2–201) must be satisfied if the contract as modified is within its provisions.

(4) Although an attempt at modification or rescission does not satisfy the requirements of subsection (2) or (3) it can operate as a waiver.

(5) A party who has made a waiver affecting an executory portion of the contract may retract the waiver by reasonable notification received by the other party that strict performance will be required of any term waived, unless the retraction would be unjust in view of a material change of position in reliance on the waiver.

§ 2–210. Delegation of Performance; Assignment of Rights.

(1) A party may perform his duty through a delegate unless otherwise agreed or unless the other party has a substantial interest in having his original promisor perform or control the acts required by the contract. No delegation of performance relieves the party delegating of any duty to perform or any liability for breach.

(2) Except as otherwise provided in Section 9–406, unless otherwise agreed, all rights of either seller or buyer can be assigned except where the assignment would materially change the duty of the other party, or increase materially the burden or risk imposed on him by his contract, or impair materially his chance of obtaining return performance. A right to damages for breach of the whole contract or a right arising out of the assignor's due performance of his entire obligation can be assigned despite agreement otherwise.

(3) The creation, attachment, perfection, or enforcement of a security interest in the seller's interest under a contract is not a transfer that materially changes the duty of or increases materially the burden or risk imposed on the buyer or impairs materially the buyer's chance of obtaining return performance within the purview of subsection (2) unless, and then only to the extent that, enforcement actually results in a delegation of material performance of the seller. Even in that event, the creation, attachment, perfection, and enforcement of the security interest remain effective, but (i) the seller is liable to the buyer for damages caused by the delegation to the extent that the damages could not reasonably by prevented by the buyer, and (ii) a court having jurisdiction may grant other appropriate relief, including cancellation of the contract for sale or an injunction against enforcement of the security interest or consummation of the enforcement.

(4) Unless the circumstances indicate the contrary a prohibition of assignment of "the contract" is to be construed as barring only the delegation to the assignee of the assignor's performance.

(5) An assignment of "the contract" or of "all my rights under the contract" or an assignment in similar general terms is an assignment of rights and unless the language or the circumstances (as in an assignment for security) indicate the contrary, it is a delegation of performance of the duties of the assignor and its acceptance by the assignee constitutes a promise by him to perform those duties. This promise is enforceable by either the assignor or the other party to the original contract.

(6) The other party may treat any assignment which delegates performance as creating reasonable grounds for insecurity and may without prejudice to his rights against the assignor demand assurances from the assignee (Section 2–609).

As amended in 1999.

Part 3—General Obligation and Construction of Contract

§ 2–301. General Obligations of Parties.

The obligation of the seller is to transfer and deliver and that of the buyer is to accept and pay in accordance with the contract.

§ 2–302. Unconscionable Contract or Clause.

(1) If the court as a matter of law finds the contract or any clause of the contract to have been unconscionable at the time it was made the court may refuse to enforce the contract, or it may enforce the remainder of the contract without the unconscionable clause, or it may so limit the application of any unconscionable clause as to avoid any unconscionable result.

(2) When it is claimed or appears to the court that the contract or any clause thereof may be unconscionable the parties shall be afforded a reasonable opportunity to present evidence as to its commercial setting, purpose and effect to aid the court in making the determination.

§ 2–303. Allocations or Division of Risks.

Where this Article allocates a risk or a burden as between the parties "unless otherwise agreed", the agreement may not only shift the allocation but may also divide the risk or burden.

§ 2–304. Price Payable in Money, Goods, Realty, or Otherwise.

(1) The price can be made payable in money or otherwise. If it is payable in whole or in part in goods each party is a seller of the goods which he is to transfer.

(2) Even though all or part of the price is payable in an interest in realty the transfer of the goods and the seller's obligations with reference to them are subject to this Article, but not the transfer of the interest in realty or the transferor's obligations in connection therewith.

§ 2–305. Open Price Term.

(1) The parties if they so intend can conclude a contract for sale even though the price is not settled. In such a case the price is a reasonable price at the time for delivery if

(a) nothing is said as to price; or

(b) the price is left to be agreed by the parties and they fail to agree; or

(c) the price is to be fixed in terms of some agreed market or other standard as set or recorded by a third person or agency and it is not so set or recorded.

(2) A price to be fixed by the seller or by the buyer means a price for him to fix in good faith.

(3) When a price left to be fixed otherwise than by agreement of the parties fails to be fixed through fault of one party the other may at his option treat the contract as cancelled or himself fix a reasonable price.

(4) Where, however, the parties intend not to be bound unless the price be fixed or agreed and it is not fixed or agreed there is no contract. In such a case the buyer must return any goods already received or if unable so to do must pay their reasonable value at the time of delivery and the seller must return any portion of the price paid on account.

§ 2–306. Output, Requirements and Exclusive Dealings.

(1) A term which measures the quantity by the output of the seller or the requirements of the buyer means such actual output or requirements as may occur in good faith, except that no quantity unreasonably disproportionate to any stated estimate or in the absence of a stated estimate to any normal or otherwise comparable prior output or requirements may be tendered or demanded.

(2) A lawful agreement by either the seller or the buyer for exclusive dealing in the kind of goods concerned imposes unless otherwise agreed an obligation by the seller to use best efforts to supply the goods and by the buyer to use best efforts to promote their sale.

§ 2–307. Delivery in Single Lot or Several Lots.
Unless otherwise agreed all goods called for by a contract for sale must be tendered in a single delivery and payment is due only on such tender but where the circumstances give either party the right to make or demand delivery in lots the price if it can be apportioned may be demanded for each lot.

§ 2–308. Absence of Specified Place for Delivery.
Unless otherwise agreed

(a) the place for delivery of goods is the seller's place of business or if he has none his residence; but

(b) in a contract for sale of identified goods which to the knowledge of the parties at the time of contracting are in some other place, that place is the place for their delivery; and

(c) documents of title may be delivered through customary banking channels.

§ 2–309. Absence of Specific Time Provisions; Notice of Termination.

(1) The time for shipment or delivery or any other action under a contract if not provided in this Article or agreed upon shall be a reasonable time.

(2) Where the contract provides for successive performances but is indefinite in duration it is valid for a reasonable time but unless otherwise agreed may be terminated at any time by either party.

(3) Termination of a contract by one party except on the happening of an agreed event requires that reasonable notification be received by the other party and an agreement dispensing with notification is invalid if its operation would be unconscionable.

§ 2–310. Open Time for Payment or Running of Credit; Authority to Ship Under Reservation.
Unless otherwise agreed

(a) payment is due at the time and place at which the buyer is to receive the goods even though the place of shipment is the place of delivery; and

(b) if the seller is authorized to send the goods he may ship them under reservation, and may tender the documents of title, but the buyer may inspect the goods after their arrival before payment is due unless such inspection is inconsistent with the terms of the contract (Section 2–513); and

(c) if delivery is authorized and made by way of documents of title otherwise than by subsection (b) then payment is due at the time and place at which the buyer is to receive the documents regardless of where the goods are to be received; and

(d) where the seller is required or authorized to ship the goods on credit the credit period runs from the time of shipment but post-dating the invoice or delaying its dispatch will correspondingly delay the starting of the credit period.

§ 2–311. Options and Cooperation Respecting Performance.

(1) An agreement for sale which is otherwise sufficiently definite (subsection (3) of Section 2–204) to be a contract is not made invalid by the fact that it leaves particulars of performance to be specified by one of the parties. Any such specification must be made in good faith and within limits set by commercial reasonableness.

(2) Unless otherwise agreed specifications relating to assortment of the goods are at the buyer's option and except as otherwise provided in subsections (1)(c) and (3) of Section 2–319 specifications or arrangements relating to shipment are at the seller's option.

(3) Where such specification would materially affect the other party's performance but is not seasonably made or where one party's cooperation is necessary to the agreed performance of the other but is not seasonably forthcoming, the other party in addition to all other remedies

(a) is excused for any resulting delay in his own performance; and

(b) may also either proceed to perform in any reasonable manner or after the time for a material part of his own performance treat the failure to specify or to cooperate as a breach by failure to deliver or accept the goods.

§ 2–312. Warranty of Title and Against Infringement; Buyer's Obligation Against Infringement.

(1) Subject to subsection (2) there is in a contract for sale a warranty by the seller that

(a) the title conveyed shall be good, and its transfer rightful; and

(b) the goods shall be delivered free from any security interest or other lien or encumbrance of which the buyer at the time of contracting has no knowledge.

(2) A warranty under subsection (1) will be excluded or modified only by specific language or by circumstances which give the buyer reason to know that the person selling does not claim title in himself or that he is purporting to sell only such right or title as he or a third person may have.

(3) Unless otherwise agreed a seller who is a merchant regularly dealing in goods of the kind warrants that the goods shall be delivered free of the rightful claim of any third person by way of infringement or the like but a buyer who furnishes specifications to the seller must hold the seller harmless against any such claim which arises out of compliance with the specifications.

§ 2–313. Express Warranties by Affirmation, Promise, Description, Sample.

(1) Express warranties by the seller are created as follows:

(a) Any affirmation of fact or promise made by the seller to the buyer which relates to the goods and becomes part of the basis of the bargain creates an express warranty that the goods shall conform to the affirmation or promise.

(b) Any description of the goods which is made part of the basis of the bargain creates an express warranty that the goods shall conform to the description.

(c) Any sample or model which is made part of the basis of the bargain creates an express warranty that the whole of the goods shall conform to the sample or model.

(2) It is not necessary to the creation of an express warranty that the seller use formal words such as "warrant" or "guarantee" or that he have a specific intention to make a warranty, but an affirmation merely of the value of the goods or a statement purporting to be merely the seller's opinion or commendation of the goods does not create a warranty.

§ 2–314. Implied Warranty: Merchantability; Usage of Trade.

(1) Unless excluded or modified (Section 2–316), a warranty that the goods shall be merchantable is implied in a contract for their sale if the seller is a merchant with respect to goods of that kind. Under this section the serving for value of food or drink to be consumed either on the premises or elsewhere is a sale.

(2) Goods to be merchantable must be at least such as

(a) pass without objection in the trade under the contract description; and

(b) in the case of fungible goods, are of fair average quality within the description; and

(c) are fit for the ordinary purposes for which such goods are used; and

(d) run, within the variations permitted by the agreement, of even kind, quality and quantity within each unit and among all units involved; and

(e) are adequately contained, packaged, and labeled as the agreement may require; and

(f) conform to the promises or affirmations of fact made on the container or label if any.

(3) Unless excluded or modified (Section 2–316) other implied warranties may arise from course of dealing or usage of trade.

§ 2–315. Implied Warranty: Fitness for Particular Purpose.

Where the seller at the time of contracting has reason to know any particular purpose for which the goods are required and that the buyer is relying on the seller's skill or judgment to select or furnish suitable goods, there is unless excluded or modified under the next section an implied warranty that the goods shall be fit for such purpose.

§ 2–316. Exclusion or Modification of Warranties.

(1) Words or conduct relevant to the creation of an express warranty and words or conduct tending to negate or limit warranty shall be construed wherever reasonable as consistent with each other; but subject to the provisions of this Article on parol or extrinsic evidence (Section 2–202) negation or limitation is inoperative to the extent that such construction is unreasonable.

(2) Subject to subsection (3), to exclude or modify the implied warranty of merchantability or any part of it the language must mention merchantability and in case of a writing must be conspicuous, and to exclude or modify any implied warranty of fitness the exclusion must be by a writing and conspicuous. Language to exclude all implied warranties of fitness is sufficient if it states, for example, that "There are no warranties which extend beyond the description on the face hereof."

(3) Notwithstanding subsection (2)

(a) unless the circumstances indicate otherwise, all implied warranties are excluded by expressions like "as is", "with all faults" or other language which in common understanding calls the buyer's attention to the exclusion of warranties and makes plain that there is no implied warranty; and

(b) when the buyer before entering into the contract has examined the goods or the sample or model as fully as he desired or has refused to examine the goods there is no implied warranty with regard to defects which an examination ought in the circumstances to have revealed to him; and

(c) an implied warranty can also be excluded or modified by course of dealing or course of performance or usage of trade.

(4) Remedies for breach of warranty can be limited in accordance with the provisions of this Article on liquidation or limitation of damages and on contractual modification of remedy (Sections 2–718 and 2–719).

§ 2–317. Cumulation and Conflict of Warranties Express or Implied.

Warranties whether express or implied shall be construed as consistent with each other and as cumulative, but if such construction is unreasonable the intention of the parties shall determine which warranty is dominant. In ascertaining that intention the following rules apply:

(a) Exact or technical specifications displace an inconsistent sample or model or general language of description.

(b) A sample from an existing bulk displaces inconsistent general language of description.

(c) Express warranties displace inconsistent implied warranties other than an implied warranty of fitness for a particular purpose.

§ 2–318. Third Party Beneficiaries of Warranties Express or Implied.

Note: If this Act is introduced in the Congress of the United States this section should be omitted. (States to select one alternative.)

Alternative A

A seller's warranty whether express or implied extends to any natural person who is in the family or household of his buyer or who is a guest in his home if it is reasonable to expect that such person may use, consume or be affected by the goods and who is injured in person by breach of the warranty. A seller may not exclude or limit the operation of this section.

Alternative B

A seller's warranty whether express or implied extends to any natural person who may reasonably be expected to use, consume or be affected by the goods and who is injured in person by breach of the warranty. A seller may not exclude or limit the operation of this section.

Alternative C

A seller's warranty whether express or implied extends to any person who may reasonably be expected to use, consume or be affected by the goods and who is injured by breach of the warranty. A seller may not exclude or limit the operation of this section with respect to injury to the person of an individual to whom the warranty extends.

As amended 1966.

§ 2–319. F.O.B. and F.A.S. Terms.

(1) Unless otherwise agreed the term F.O.B. (which means "free on board") at a named place, even though used only in connection with the stated price, is a delivery term under which

(a) when the term is F.O.B. the place of shipment, the seller must at that place ship the goods in the manner provided in this Article (Section 2–504) and bear the expense and risk of putting them into the possession of the carrier; or

(b) when the term is F.O.B. the place of destination, the seller must at his own expense and risk transport the goods to that place and there tender delivery of them in the manner provided in this Article (Section 2–503);

(c) when under either (a) or (b) the term is also F.O.B. vessel, car or other vehicle, the seller must in addition at his own expense and risk load the goods on board. If the term is F.O.B. vessel the buyer must name the vessel and in an appropriate case the seller must comply with the provisions of this Article on the form of bill of lading (Section 2–323).

(2) Unless otherwise agreed the term F.A.S. vessel (which means "free alongside") at a named port, even though used only in connection with the stated price, is a delivery term under which the seller must

(a) at his own expense and risk deliver the goods alongside the vessel in the manner usual in that port or on a dock designated and provided by the buyer; and

(b) obtain and tender a receipt for the goods in exchange for which the carrier is under a duty to issue a bill of lading.

(3) Unless otherwise agreed in any case falling within subsection (1)(a) or (c) or subsection (2) the buyer must seasonably give any needed instructions for making delivery, including when the term is F.A.S. or F.O.B. the loading berth of the vessel and in an appropriate case its name and sailing date. The seller may treat the failure of needed instructions as a failure of cooperation under this Article (Section 2–311). He may also at his option move the goods in any reasonable manner preparatory to delivery or shipment.

(4) Under the term F.O.B. vessel or F.A.S. unless otherwise agreed the buyer must make payment against tender of the required documents and the seller may not tender nor the buyer demand delivery of the goods in substitution for the documents.

§ 2–320. C.I.F. and C. & F. Terms.

(1) The term C.I.F. means that the price includes in a lump sum the cost of the goods and the insurance and freight to the named destination. The term C. & F. or C.F. means that the price so includes cost and freight to the named destination.

(2) Unless otherwise agreed and even though used only in connection with the stated price and destination, the term C.I.F. destination or its equivalent requires the seller at his own expense and risk to

(a) put the goods into the possession of a carrier at the port for shipment and obtain a negotiable bill or bills of lading covering the entire transportation to the named destination; and

(b) load the goods and obtain a receipt from the carrier (which may be contained in the bill of lading) showing that the freight has been paid or provided for; and

(c) obtain a policy or certificate of insurance, including any war risk insurance, of a kind and on terms then current at the port of shipment in the usual amount, in the currency of the contract, shown to cover the same goods covered by the bill of lading and providing for payment of loss to the order of the buyer or for the account of whom it may concern; but the seller may add to the price the amount of the premium for any such war risk insurance; and

(d) prepare an invoice of the goods and procure any other documents required to effect shipment or to comply with the contract; and

(e) forward and tender with commercial promptness all the documents in due form and with any indorsement necessary to perfect the buyer's rights.

(3) Unless otherwise agreed the term C. & F. or its equivalent has the same effect and imposes upon the seller the same obligations and risks as a C.I.F. term except the obligation as to insurance.

(4) Under the term C.I.F. or C. & F. unless otherwise agreed the buyer must make payment against tender of the required documents and the seller may not tender nor the buyer demand delivery of the goods in substitution for the documents.

§ 2–321. C.I.F. or C. & F.: "Net Landed Weights"; "Payment on Arrival"; Warranty of Condition on Arrival.

Under a contract containing a term C.I.F. or C. & F.

(1) Where the price is based on or is to be adjusted according to "net landed weights", "delivered weights", "out turn" quantity or quality or the like, unless otherwise agreed the seller must reasonably estimate the price. The payment due on tender of the documents called for by the contract is the amount so estimated, but after final adjustment of the price a settlement must be made with commercial promptness.

(2) An agreement described in subsection (1) or any warranty of quality or condition of the goods on arrival places upon the seller the risk of ordinary deterioration, shrinkage and the like in transportation but has no effect on the place or time of identification to the contract for sale or delivery or on the passing of the risk of loss.

(3) Unless otherwise agreed where the contract provides for payment on or after arrival of the goods the seller must before payment allow such preliminary inspection as is feasible; but if the goods are lost delivery of the documents and payment are due when the goods should have arrived.

§ 2–322. Delivery "Ex-Ship".

(1) Unless otherwise agreed a term for delivery of goods "ex-ship" (which means from the carrying vessel) or in equivalent language is not restricted to a particular ship and requires delivery from a ship which has reached a place at the named port of destination where goods of the kind are usually discharged.

(2) Under such a term unless otherwise agreed

(a) the seller must discharge all liens arising out of the carriage and furnish the buyer with a direction which puts the carrier under a duty to deliver the goods; and

(b) the risk of loss does not pass to the buyer until the goods leave the ship's tackle or are otherwise properly unloaded.

§ 2–323. Form of Bill of Lading Required in Overseas Shipment; "Overseas".

(1) Where the contract contemplates overseas shipment and contains a term C.I.F. or C. & F. or F.O.B. vessel, the seller unless otherwise agreed must obtain a negotiable bill of lading stating that the goods have been loaded on board or, in the case of a term C.I.F. or C. & F., received for shipment.

(2) Where in a case within subsection (1) a bill of lading has been issued in a set of parts, unless otherwise agreed if the documents are not to be sent from abroad the buyer may demand tender of the full set; otherwise only one part of the bill of lading need be tendered. Even if the agreement expressly requires a full set

(a) due tender of a single part is acceptable within the provisions of this Article on cure of improper delivery (subsection (1) of Section 2–508); and

(b) even though the full set is demanded, if the documents are sent from abroad the person tendering an incomplete set may nevertheless require payment upon furnishing an indemnity which the buyer in good faith deems adequate.

(3) A shipment by water or by air or a contract contemplating such shipment is "overseas" insofar as by usage of trade or agreement it is subject to the commercial, financing or shipping practices characteristic of international deep water commerce.

§ 2–324. "No Arrival, No Sale" Term.

Under a term "no arrival, no sale" or terms of like meaning, unless otherwise agreed,

(a) the seller must properly ship conforming goods and if they arrive by any means he must tender them on arrival but he assumes no obligation that the goods will arrive unless he has caused the non-arrival; and

(b) where without fault of the seller the goods are in part lost or have so deteriorated as no longer to conform to the contract or arrive after the contract time, the buyer may proceed as if there had been casualty to identified goods (Section 2–613).

§ 2–325. "Letter of Credit" Term; "Confirmed Credit".

(1) Failure of the buyer seasonably to furnish an agreed letter of credit is a breach of the contract for sale.

(2) The delivery to seller of a proper letter of credit suspends the buyer's obligation to pay. If the letter of credit is dishonored, the seller may on seasonable notification to the buyer require payment directly from him.

(3) Unless otherwise agreed the term "letter of credit" or "banker's credit" in a contract for sale means an irrevocable credit issued by a financing agency of good repute and, where the shipment is overseas, of good international repute. The term "confirmed credit" means that the credit must also carry the direct obligation of such an agency which does business in the seller's financial market.

§ 2–326. Sale on Approval and Sale or Return; Rights of Creditors.

(1) Unless otherwise agreed, if delivered goods may be returned by the buyer even though they conform to the contract, the transaction is

(a) a "sale on approval" if the goods are delivered primarily for use, and

(b) a "sale or return" if the goods are delivered primarily for resale.

(2) Goods held on approval are not subject to the claims of the buyer's creditors until acceptance; goods held on sale or return are subject to such claims while in the buyer's possession.

(3) Any "or return" term of a contract for sale is to be treated as a separate contract for sale within the statute of frauds section of this Article (Section 2–201) and as contradicting the sale aspect of the contract within the provisions of this Article or on parol or extrinsic evidence (Section 2–202).

As amended in 1999.

§ 2–327. Special Incidents of Sale on Approval and Sale or Return.

(1) Under a sale on approval unless otherwise agreed

(a) although the goods are identified to the contract the risk of loss and the title do not pass to the buyer until acceptance; and

(b) use of the goods consistent with the purpose of trial is not acceptance but failure seasonably to notify the seller of election to return the goods is acceptance, and if the goods conform to the contract acceptance of any part is acceptance of the whole; and

(c) after due notification of election to return, the return is at the seller's risk and expense but a merchant buyer must follow any reasonable instructions.

(2) Under a sale or return unless otherwise agreed

(a) the option to return extends to the whole or any commercial unit of the goods while in substantially their original condition, but must be exercised seasonably; and

(b) the return is at the buyer's risk and expense.

§ 2–328. Sale by Auction.

(1) In a sale by auction if goods are put up in lots each lot is the subject of a separate sale.

(2) A sale by auction is complete when the auctioneer so announces by the fall of the hammer or in other customary manner. Where a bid is made while the hammer is falling in acceptance of a prior bid the auctioneer may in his discretion reopen the bidding or declare the goods sold under the bid on which the hammer was falling.

(3) Such a sale is with reserve unless the goods are in explicit terms put up without reserve. In an auction with reserve the auctioneer may withdraw the goods at any time until he announces completion of the sale. In an auction without reserve, after the auctioneer calls for bids on an article or lot, that article or lot cannot be withdrawn unless no bid is made within a reasonable time. In either case a bidder may retract his bid until the auctioneer's announcement of completion of the sale, but a bidder's retraction does not revive any previous bid.

(4) If the auctioneer knowingly receives a bid on the seller's behalf or the seller makes or procures such as bid, and notice has not been given that liberty for such bidding is reserved, the buyer may at his option avoid the sale or take the goods at the price of the last good faith bid prior to the completion of the sale. This subsection shall not apply to any bid at a forced sale.

Part 4—Title, Creditors and Good Faith Purchasers

§ 2–401. Passing of Title; Reservation for Security; Limited Application of This Section.

Each provision of this Article with regard to the rights, obligations and remedies of the seller, the buyer, purchasers or other third parties applies irrespective of title to the goods except where the provision refers to such title. Insofar as situations are not covered by the other provisions of this Article and matters concerning title became material the following rules apply:

(1) Title to goods cannot pass under a contract for sale prior to their identification to the contract (Section 2–501), and unless otherwise explicitly agreed the buyer acquires by their identification a special property as limited by this Act. Any retention or reservation by the seller of the title (property) in goods shipped or delivered to the buyer is limited in effect to a reservation of a security interest. Subject to these provisions and to the provisions of the Article on Secured Transactions (Article 9), title to goods passes from the seller to the buyer in any manner and on any conditions explicitly agreed on by the parties.

(2) Unless otherwise explicitly agreed title passes to the buyer at the time and place at which the seller completes his performance with reference to the physical delivery of the goods, despite any reservation of a security interest and even though a document of title is to be delivered at a different time or place; and in particular and despite any reservation of a security interest by the bill of lading

(a) if the contract requires or authorizes the seller to send the goods to the buyer but does not require him to deliver them at destination, title passes to the buyer at the time and place of shipment; but

(b) if the contract requires delivery at destination, title passes on tender there.

(3) Unless otherwise explicitly agreed where delivery is to be made without moving the goods,

(a) if the seller is to deliver a document of title, title passes at the time when and the place where he delivers such documents; or

(b) if the goods are at the time of contracting already identified and no documents are to be delivered, title passes at the time and place of contracting.

(4) A rejection or other refusal by the buyer to receive or retain the goods, whether or not justified, or a justified revocation of acceptance revests title to the goods in the seller. Such revesting occurs by operation of law and is not a "sale".

§ 2–402. Rights of Seller's Creditors Against Sold Goods.

(1) Except as provided in subsections (2) and (3), rights of unsecured creditors of the seller with respect to goods which have been identified to a contract for sale are subject to the buyer's rights to recover the goods under this Article (Sections 2–502 and 2–716).

(2) A creditor of the seller may treat a sale or an identification of goods to a contract for sale as void if as against him a retention of possession by the seller is fraudulent under any rule of law of the state where the goods are situated, except that retention of possession in good faith and current course of trade by a merchant-seller for a commercially reasonable time after a sale or identification is not fraudulent.

(3) Nothing in this Article shall be deemed to impair the rights of creditors of the seller

(a) under the provisions of the Article on Secured Transactions (Article 9); or

(b) where identification to the contract or delivery is made not in current course of trade but in satisfaction of or as security for a pre-existing claim for money, security or the like and is made under circumstances which under any rule of law of the state where the goods are situated would apart from this Article constitute the transaction a fraudulent transfer or voidable preference.

§ 2–403. Power to Transfer; Good Faith Purchase of Goods; "Entrusting".

(1) A purchaser of goods acquires all title which his transferor had or had power to transfer except that a purchaser of a limited interest acquires rights only to the extent of the interest purchased. A person with voidable title has power to transfer a good title to a good faith purchaser for value. When goods have been delivered under a transaction of purchase the purchaser has such power even though

(a) the transferor was deceived as to the identity of the purchaser, or

(b) the delivery was in exchange for a check which is later dishonored, or

(c) it was agreed that the transaction was to be a "cash sale", or

(d) the delivery was procured through fraud punishable as larcenous under the criminal law.

(2) Any entrusting of possession of goods to a merchant who deals in goods of that kind gives him power to transfer all rights of the entruster to a buyer in ordinary course of business.

(3) "Entrusting" includes any delivery and any acquiescence in retention of possession regardless of any condition expressed between the parties to the delivery or acquiescence and regardless of whether the procurement of the entrusting or the possessor's disposition of the goods have been such as to be larcenous under the criminal law.

(4) The rights of other purchasers of goods and of lien creditors are governed by the Articles on Secured Transactions (Article 9), Bulk Transfers (Article 6) and Documents of Title (Article 7). As amended in 1988.

Part 5—Performance

§ 2–501. Insurable Interest in Goods; Manner of Identification of Goods.

(1) The buyer obtains a special property and an insurable interest in goods by identification of existing goods as goods to which the contract refers even though the goods so identified are non-conforming and he has an option to return or reject them. Such identification can be made at any time and in any manner explicitly agreed to by the parties. In the absence of explicit agreement identification occurs

(a) when the contract is made if it is for the sale of goods already existing and identified;

(b) if the contract is for the sale of future goods other than those described in paragraph (c), when goods are shipped, marked or otherwise designated by the seller as goods to which the contract refers;

(c) when the crops are planted or otherwise become growing crops or the young are conceived if the contract is for the sale of unborn young to be born within twelve months after contracting or for the sale of crops to be harvested within twelve months or the next normal harvest season after contracting whichever is longer.

(2) The seller retains an insurable interest in goods so long as title to or any security interest in the goods remains in him and where the identification is by the seller alone he may until default or insolvency or notification to the buyer that the identification is final substitute other goods for those identified.

(3) Nothing in this section impairs any insurable interest recognized under any other statute or rule of law.

§ 2–502. Buyer's Right to Goods on Seller's Insolvency.

(1) Subject to subsections (2) and (3) and even though the goods have not been shipped a buyer who has paid a part or all of the price of goods in which he has a special property under the provisions of the immediately preceding section may on making and keeping good a tender of any unpaid portion of their price recover them from the seller if:

(a) in the case of goods bought for personal, family, or household purposes, the seller repudiates or fails to deliver as required by the contract; or

(b) in all cases, the seller becomes insolvent within ten days after receipt of the first installment on their price.

(2) The buyer's right to recover the goods under subsection (1)(a) vests upon acquisition of a special property, even if the seller had not then repudiated or failed to deliver.

(3) If the identification creating his special property has been made by the buyer he acquires the right to recover the goods only if they conform to the contract for sale.

As amended in 1999.

§ 2–503. Manner of Seller's Tender of Delivery.

(1) Tender of delivery requires that the seller put and hold conforming goods at the buyer's disposition and give the buyer any notification reasonably necessary to enable him to take delivery. The manner, time and place for tender are determined by the agreement and this Article, and in particular

(a) tender must be at a reasonable hour, and if it is of goods they must be kept available for the period reasonably necessary to enable the buyer to take possession; but

(b) unless otherwise agreed the buyer must furnish facilities reasonably suited to the receipt of the goods.

(2) Where the case is within the next section respecting shipment tender requires that the seller comply with its provisions.

(3) Where the seller is required to deliver at a particular destination tender requires that he comply with subsection (1) and also in any appropriate case tender documents as described in subsections (4) and (5) of this section.

(4) Where goods are in the possession of a bailee and are to be delivered without being moved

(a) tender requires that the seller either tender a negotiable document of title covering such goods or procure acknowledgment by the bailee of the buyer's right to possession of the goods; but

(b) tender to the buyer of a non-negotiable document of title or of a written direction to the bailee to deliver is sufficient tender unless the buyer seasonably objects, and receipt by the bailee of notification of the buyer's rights fixes those rights as against the bailee and all third persons; but risk of loss of the goods and of any failure by the bailee to honor the non-negotiable document of title or to obey the direction remains on the seller until the buyer has had a reasonable time to present the document or direction, and a refusal by the bailee to honor the document or to obey the direction defeats the tender.

(5) Where the contract requires the seller to deliver documents

(a) he must tender all such documents in correct form, except as provided in this Article with respect to bills of lading in a set (subsection (2) of Section 2–323); and

(b) tender through customary banking channels is sufficient and dishonor of a draft accompanying the documents constitutes non-acceptance or rejection.

§ 2–504. Shipment by Seller.

Where the seller is required or authorized to send the goods to the buyer and the contract does not require him to deliver them at a particular destination, then unless otherwise agreed he must

(a) put the goods in the possession of such a carrier and make such a contract for their transportation as may be reasonable having regard to the nature of the goods and other circumstances of the case; and

(b) obtain and promptly deliver or tender in due form any document necessary to enable the buyer to obtain possession of the goods or otherwise required by the agreement or by usage of trade; and

(c) promptly notify the buyer of the shipment.

Failure to notify the buyer under paragraph (c) or to make a proper contract under paragraph (a) is a ground for rejection only if material delay or loss ensues.

§ 2–505. Seller's Shipment under Reservation.

(1) Where the seller has identified goods to the contract by or before shipment:

(a) his procurement of a negotiable bill of lading to his own order or otherwise reserves in him a security interest in the goods. His procurement of the bill to the order of a financing agency or of the buyer indicates in addition only the seller's expectation of transferring that interest to the person named.

(b) a non-negotiable bill of lading to himself or his nominee reserves possession of the goods as security but except in a case of conditional delivery (subsection (2) of Section 2–507) a non-negotiable bill of lading naming the buyer as consignee reserves no security interest even though the seller retains possession of the bill of lading.

(2) When shipment by the seller with reservation of a security interest is in violation of the contract for sale it constitutes an improper contract for transportation within the preceding section but impairs neither the rights given to the buyer by shipment and identification of the goods to the contract nor the seller's powers as a holder of a negotiable document.

§ 2–506. Rights of Financing Agency.

(1) A financing agency by paying or purchasing for value a draft which relates to a shipment of goods acquires to the extent of the payment or purchase and in addition to its own rights under the draft and any document of title securing it any rights of the shipper in the goods including the right to stop delivery and the shipper's right to have the draft honored by the buyer.

(2) The right to reimbursement of a financing agency which has in good faith honored or purchased the draft under commitment to or authority from the buyer is not impaired by subsequent discovery of defects with reference to any relevant document which was apparently regular on its face.

§ 2–507. Effect of Seller's Tender; Delivery on Condition.

(1) Tender of delivery is a condition to the buyer's duty to accept the goods and, unless otherwise agreed, to his duty to pay for them. Tender entitles the seller to acceptance of the goods and to payment according to the contract.

(2) Where payment is due and demanded on the delivery to the buyer of goods or documents of title, his right as against the seller to retain or dispose of them is conditional upon his making the payment due.

§ 2–508. Cure by Seller of Improper Tender or Delivery; Replacement.

(1) Where any tender or delivery by the seller is rejected because non-conforming and the time for performance has not yet expired, the seller may seasonably notify the buyer of his intention to cure and may then within the contract time make a conforming delivery.

(2) Where the buyer rejects a non-conforming tender which the seller had reasonable grounds to believe would be acceptable with or without money allowance the seller may if he seasonably notifies the buyer have a further reasonable time to substitute a conforming tender.

§ 2–509. Risk of Loss in the Absence of Breach.

(1) Where the contract requires or authorizes the seller to ship the goods by carrier

(a) if it does not require him to deliver them at a particular destination, the risk of loss passes to the buyer when the goods are duly delivered to the carrier even though the shipment is under reservation (Section 2–505); but

(b) if it does require him to deliver them at a particular destination and the goods are there duly tendered while in the possession of the carrier, the risk of loss passes to the buyer when the goods are there duly so tendered as to enable the buyer to take delivery.

(2) Where the goods are held by a bailee to be delivered without being moved, the risk of loss passes to the buyer

(a) on his receipt of a negotiable document of title covering the goods; or

(b) on acknowledgment by the bailee of the buyer's right to possession of the goods; or

(c) after his receipt of a non-negotiable document of title or other written direction to deliver, as provided in subsection (4)(b) of Section 2–503.

(3) In any case not within subsection (1) or (2), the risk of loss passes to the buyer on his receipt of the goods if the seller is a merchant; otherwise the risk passes to the buyer on tender of delivery.

(4) The provisions of this section are subject to contrary agreement of the parties and to the provisions of this Article on sale on approval (Section 2–327) and on effect of breach on risk of loss (Section 2–510).

§ 2–510. Effect of Breach on Risk of Loss.

(1) Where a tender or delivery of goods so fails to conform to the contract as to give a right of rejection the risk of their loss remains on the seller until cure or acceptance.

(2) Where the buyer rightfully revokes acceptance he may to the extent of any deficiency in his effective insurance coverage treat the risk of loss as having rested on the seller from the beginning.

(3) Where the buyer as to conforming goods already identified to the contract for sale repudiates or is otherwise in breach before risk of their loss has passed to him, the seller may to the extent of any deficiency in his effective insurance coverage treat the risk of loss as resting on the buyer for a commercially reasonable time.

§ 2–511. Tender of Payment by Buyer; Payment by Check.

(1) Unless otherwise agreed tender of payment is a condition to the seller's duty to tender and complete any delivery.

(2) Tender of payment is sufficient when made by any means or in any manner current in the ordinary course of business unless the seller demands payment in legal tender and gives any extension of time reasonably necessary to procure it.

(3) Subject to the provisions of this Act on the effect of an instrument on an obligation (Section 3–310), payment by check is conditional and is defeated as between the parties by dishonor of the check on due presentment.

As amended in 1994.

§ 2–512. Payment by Buyer Before Inspection.

(1) Where the contract requires payment before inspection non-conformity of the goods does not excuse the buyer from so making payment unless

(a) the non-conformity appears without inspection; or

(b) despite tender of the required documents the circumstances would justify injunction against honor under this Act (Section 5–109(b)).

(2) Payment pursuant to subsection (1) does not constitute an acceptance of goods or impair the buyer's right to inspect or any of his remedies.

As amended in 1995.

§ 2–513. Buyer's Right to Inspection of Goods.

(1) Unless otherwise agreed and subject to subsection (3), where goods are tendered or delivered or identified to the contract for sale, the buyer has a right before payment or acceptance to inspect them at any reasonable place and time and in any reasonable manner. When the seller is required or authorized to send the goods to the buyer, the inspection may be after their arrival.

(2) Expenses of inspection must be borne by the buyer but may be recovered from the seller if the goods do not conform and are rejected.

(3) Unless otherwise agreed and subject to the provisions of this Article on C.I.F. contracts (subsection (3) of Section 2–321), the buyer is not entitled to inspect the goods before payment of the price when the contract provides

(a) for delivery "C.O.D." or on other like terms; or

(b) for payment against documents of title, except where such payment is due only after the goods are to become available for inspection.

(4) A place or method of inspection fixed by the parties is presumed to be exclusive but unless otherwise expressly agreed it does not postpone identification or shift the place for delivery or for passing the risk of loss. If compliance becomes impossible, inspection shall be as provided in this section unless the place or method fixed was clearly intended as an indispensable condition failure of which avoids the contract.

§ 2–514. When Documents Deliverable on Acceptance; When on Payment.

Unless otherwise agreed documents against which a draft is drawn are to be delivered to the drawee on acceptance of the draft if it is payable more than three days after presentment; otherwise, only on payment.

§ 2–515. Preserving Evidence of Goods in Dispute.

In furtherance of the adjustment of any claim or dispute

(a) either party on reasonable notification to the other and for the purpose of ascertaining the facts and preserving evidence has the right to inspect, test and sample the goods including such of them as may be in the possession or control of the other; and

(b) the parties may agree to a third party inspection or survey to determine the conformity or condition of the goods and may agree that the findings shall be binding upon them in any subsequent litigation or adjustment.

Part 6—Breach, Repudiation and Excuse

§ 2–601. Buyer's Rights on Improper Delivery.

Subject to the provisions of this Article on breach in installment contracts (Section 2–612) and unless otherwise agreed under the sections on contractual limitations of remedy (Sections 2–718 and 2–719), if the goods or the tender of delivery fail in any respect to conform to the contract, the buyer may

(a) reject the whole; or

(b) accept the whole; or

(c) accept any commercial unit or units and reject the rest.

§ 2–602. Manner and Effect of Rightful Rejection.

(1) Rejection of goods must be within a reasonable time after their delivery or tender. It is ineffective unless the buyer seasonably notifies the seller.

(2) Subject to the provisions of the two following sections on rejected goods (Sections 2–603 and 2–604),

(a) after rejection any exercise of ownership by the buyer with respect to any commercial unit is wrongful as against the seller; and

(b) if the buyer has before rejection taken physical possession of goods in which he does not have a security interest under the provisions of this Article (subsection (3) of Section 2–711), he is under a duty after rejection to hold them with reasonable care at the seller's disposition for a time sufficient to permit the seller to remove them; but

(c) the buyer has no further obligations with regard to goods rightfully rejected.

(3) The seller's rights with respect to goods wrongfully rejected are governed by the provisions of this Article on Seller's remedies in general (Section 2–703).

§ 2–603. Merchant Buyer's Duties as to Rightfully Rejected Goods.

(1) Subject to any security interest in the buyer (subsection (3) of Section 2–711), when the seller has no agent or place of business at the market of rejection a merchant buyer is under a duty after rejection of goods in his possession or control to follow any reasonable instructions received from the seller with respect to the goods and in the absence of such instructions to make reasonable efforts to sell them for the seller's account if they are perishable or threaten to decline in value speedily. Instructions are not reasonable if on demand indemnity for expenses is not forthcoming.

(2) When the buyer sells goods under subsection (1), he is entitled to reimbursement from the seller or out of the proceeds for reasonable expenses of caring for and selling them, and if the expenses include no selling commission then to such commission as is usual in the trade or if there is none to a reasonable sum not exceeding ten per cent on the gross proceeds.

(3) In complying with this section the buyer is held only to good faith and good faith conduct hereunder is neither acceptance nor conversion nor the basis of an action for damages.

§ 2–604. Buyer's Options as to Salvage of Rightfully Rejected Goods.

Subject to the provisions of the immediately preceding section on perishables if the seller gives no instructions within a reasonable time after notification of rejection the buyer may store the rejected goods for the seller's account or reship them to him or resell them for the seller's account with reimbursement as provided in the preceding section. Such action is not acceptance or conversion.

§ 2–605. Waiver of Buyer's Objections by Failure to Particularize.

(1) The buyer's failure to state in connection with rejection a particular defect which is ascertainable by reasonable inspection precludes him from relying on the unstated defect to justify rejection or to establish breach

(a) where the seller could have cured it if stated seasonably; or

(b) between merchants when the seller has after rejection made a request in writing for a full and final written statement of all defects on which the buyer proposes to rely.

(2) Payment against documents made without reservation of rights precludes recovery of the payment for defects apparent on the face of the documents.

§ 2–606. What Constitutes Acceptance of Goods.

(1) Acceptance of goods occurs when the buyer

(a) after a reasonable opportunity to inspect the goods signifies to the seller that the goods are conforming or that he will take or retain them in spite of their nonconformity; or

(b) fails to make an effective rejection (subsection (1) of Section 2–602), but such acceptance does not occur until the buyer has had a reasonable opportunity to inspect them; or

(c) does any act inconsistent with the seller's ownership; but if such act is wrongful as against the seller it is an acceptance only if ratified by him.

(2) Acceptance of a part of any commercial unit is acceptance of that entire unit.

§ 2–607. Effect of Acceptance; Notice of Breach; Burden of Establishing Breach After Acceptance; Notice of Claim or Litigation to Person Answerable Over.

(1) The buyer must pay at the contract rate for any goods accepted.

(2) Acceptance of goods by the buyer precludes rejection of the goods accepted and if made with knowledge of a non-conformity cannot be revoked because of it unless the acceptance was on the reasonable assumption that the non-conformity would be seasonably cured but acceptance does not of itself impair any other remedy provided by this Article for non-conformity.

(3) Where a tender has been accepted

(a) the buyer must within a reasonable time after he discovers or should have discovered any breach notify the seller of breach or be barred from any remedy; and

(b) if the claim is one for infringement or the like (subsection (3) of Section 2–312) and the buyer is sued as a result of such a breach he must so notify the seller within a reasonable time after he receives notice of the litigation or be barred from any remedy over for liability established by the litigation.

(4) The burden is on the buyer to establish any breach with respect to the goods accepted.

(5) Where the buyer is sued for breach of a warranty or other obligation for which his seller is answerable over

(a) he may give his seller written notice of the litigation. If the notice states that the seller may come in and defend and that if the seller does not do so he will be bound in any action against him by his buyer by any determination of fact common to the two litigations, then unless the seller after seasonable receipt of the notice does come in and defend he is so bound.

(b) if the claim is one for infringement or the like (subsection (3) of Section 2–312) the original seller may demand in writing that his buyer turn over to him control of the litigation including settlement or else be barred from any remedy over and if he also agrees to bear all expense and to satisfy any adverse judgment, then unless the buyer after seasonable receipt of the demand does turn over control the buyer is so barred.

(6) The provisions of subsections (3), (4) and (5) apply to any obligation of a buyer to hold the seller harmless against infringement or the like (subsection (3) of Section 2–312).

§ 2–608. Revocation of Acceptance in Whole or in Part.

(1) The buyer may revoke his acceptance of a lot or commercial unit whose non-conformity substantially impairs its value to him if he has accepted it

(a) on the reasonable assumption that its nonconformity would be cured and it has not been seasonably cured; or

(b) without discovery of such non-conformity if his acceptance was reasonably induced either by the difficulty of discovery before acceptance or by the seller's assurances.

(2) Revocation of acceptance must occur within a reasonable time after the buyer discovers or should have discovered the ground for it and before any substantial change in condition of the goods which is not caused by their own defects. It is not effective until the buyer notifies the seller of it.

(3) A buyer who so revokes has the same rights and duties with regard to the goods involved as if he had rejected them.

§ 2–609. Right to Adequate Assurance of Performance.

(1) A contract for sale imposes an obligation on each party that the other's expectation of receiving due performance will not be impaired. When reasonable grounds for insecurity arise with respect to the performance of either party the other may in writing demand adequate assurance of due performance and until he receives such assurance may if commercially reasonable suspend any performance for which he has not already received the agreed return.

(2) Between merchants the reasonableness of grounds for insecurity and the adequacy of any assurance offered shall be determined according to commercial standards.

(3) Acceptance of any improper delivery or payment does not prejudice the party's right to demand adequate assurance of future performance.

(4) After receipt of a justified demand failure to provide within a reasonable time not exceeding thirty days such assurance of due performance as is adequate under the circumstances of the particular case is a repudiation of the contract.

§ 2–610. Anticipatory Repudiation.

When either party repudiates the contract with respect to a performance not yet due the loss of which will substantially impair the value of the contract to the other, the aggrieved party may

(a) for a commercially reasonable time await performance by the repudiating party; or

(b) resort to any remedy for breach (Section 2–703 or Section 2–711), even though he has notified the repudiating party that he would await the latter's performance and has urged retraction; and

(c) in either case suspend his own performance or proceed in accordance with the provisions of this Article on the seller's right to identify goods to the contract notwithstanding breach or to salvage unfinished goods (Section 2–704).

§ 2–611. Retraction of Anticipatory Repudiation.

(1) Until the repudiating party's next performance is due he can retract his repudiation unless the aggrieved party has since the repudiation cancelled or materially changed his position or otherwise indicated that he considers the repudiation final.

(2) Retraction may be by any method which clearly indicates to the aggrieved party that the repudiating party intends to perform, but must include any assurance justifiably demanded under the provisions of this Article (Section 2–609).

(3) Retraction reinstates the repudiating party's rights under the contract with due excuse and allowance to the aggrieved party for any delay occasioned by the repudiation.

§ 2–612. "Installment Contract"; Breach.

(1) An "installment contract" is one which requires or authorizes the delivery of goods in separate lots to be separately accepted, even though the contract contains a clause "each delivery is a separate contract" or its equivalent.

(2) The buyer may reject any installment which is non-conforming if the non-conformity substantially impairs the value of that installment and cannot be cured or if the non-conformity is a defect in the required documents; but if the non-conformity does not fall within subsection (3) and the seller gives adequate assurance of its cure the buyer must accept that installment.

(3) Whenever non-conformity or default with respect to one or more installments substantially impairs the value of the whole contract there is a breach of the whole. But the aggrieved party reinstates the contract if he accepts a non-conforming installment without seasonably notifying of cancellation or if he brings an action with respect only to past installments or demands performance as to future installments.

§ 2–613. Casualty to Identified Goods.

Where the contract requires for its performance goods identified when the contract is made, and the goods suffer casualty without fault of either party before the risk of loss passes to the buyer, or in a proper case under a "no arrival, no sale" term (Section 2–324) then

(a) if the loss is total the contract is avoided; and

(b) if the loss is partial or the goods have so deteriorated as no longer to conform to the contract the buyer may nevertheless demand inspection and at his option either treat the contract as voided or accept the goods with due allowance from the contract price for the deterioration or the deficiency in quantity but without further right against the seller.

§ 2–614. Substituted Performance.

(1) Where without fault of either party the agreed berthing, loading, or unloading facilities fail or an agreed type of carrier becomes unavailable or the agreed manner of delivery otherwise becomes commercially impracticable but a commercially reasonable substitute is available, such substitute performance must be tendered and accepted.

(2) If the agreed means or manner of payment fails because of domestic or foreign governmental regulation, the seller may withhold or stop delivery unless the buyer provides a means or manner of payment which is commercially a substantial equivalent. If delivery has already been taken, payment by the means or in the manner provided by the regulation discharges the buyer's obligation unless the regulation is discriminatory, oppressive or predatory.

§ 2–615. Excuse by Failure of Presupposed Conditions.

Except so far as a seller may have assumed a greater obligation and subject to the preceding section on substituted performance:

(a) Delay in delivery or non-delivery in whole or in part by a seller who complies with paragraphs (b) and (c) is not a breach of his duty under a contract for sale if performance as agreed has been made impracticable by the occurrence of a contingency the nonoccurrence of which was a basic assumption on which the contract was made or by compliance in good faith with any applicable foreign or domestic governmental regulation or order whether or not it later proves to be invalid.

(b) Where the causes mentioned in paragraph (a) affect only a part of the seller's capacity to perform, he must allocate production and deliveries among his customers but may at his option include regular customers not then under contract as well as his own requirements for further manufacture. He may so allocate in any manner which is fair and reasonable.

(c) The seller must notify the buyer seasonably that there will be delay or non-delivery and, when allocation is required under paragraph (b), of the estimated quota thus made available for the buyer.

§ 2–616. Procedure on Notice Claiming Excuse.

(1) Where the buyer receives notification of a material or indefinite delay or an allocation justified under the preceding section he may by written notification to the seller as to any delivery concerned, and where the prospective deficiency substantially impairs the value of the whole contract under the provisions of this Article relating to breach of installment contracts (Section 2–612), then also as to the whole,

(a) terminate and thereby discharge any unexecuted portion of the contract; or

(b) modify the contract by agreeing to take his available quota in substitution.

(2) If after receipt of such notification from the seller the buyer fails so to modify the contract within a reasonable time not exceeding thirty days the contract lapses with respect to any deliveries affected.

(3) The provisions of this section may not be negated by agreement except in so far as the seller has assumed a greater obligation under the preceding section.

Part 7—Remedies

§ 2–701. Remedies for Breach of Collateral Contracts Not Impaired.

Remedies for breach of any obligation or promise collateral or ancillary to a contract for sale are not impaired by the provisions of this Article.

§ 2–702. Seller's Remedies on Discovery of Buyer's Insolvency.

(1) Where the seller discovers the buyer to be insolvent he may refuse delivery except for cash including payment for all goods theretofore delivered under the contract, and stop delivery under this Article (Section 2–705).

(2) Where the seller discovers that the buyer has received goods on credit while insolvent he may reclaim the goods upon demand made within ten days after the receipt, but if misrepresentation of solvency has been made to the particular seller in writing within three months before delivery the ten day limitation does not apply. Except as provided in this subsection the seller may not base a right to reclaim goods on the buyer's fraudulent or innocent misrepresentation of solvency or of intent to pay.

(3) The seller's right to reclaim under subsection (2) is subject to the rights of a buyer in ordinary course or other good faith purchaser under this Article (Section 2–403). Successful reclamation of goods excludes all other remedies with respect to them.

§ 2–703. Seller's Remedies in General.

Where the buyer wrongfully rejects or revokes acceptance of goods or fails to make a payment due on or before delivery or repudiates with respect to a part or the whole, then with respect to any goods directly affected and, if the breach is of the whole contract (Section 2–612), then also with respect to the whole undelivered balance, the aggrieved seller may

(a) withhold delivery of such goods;

(b) stop delivery by any bailee as hereafter provided (Section 2–705);

(c) proceed under the next section respecting goods still unidentified to the contract;

(d) resell and recover damages as hereafter provided (Section 2–706);

(e) recover damages for non-acceptance (Section 2–708) or in a proper case the price (Section 2–709);

(f) cancel.

§ 2–704. Seller's Right to Identify Goods to the Contract Notwithstanding Breach or to Salvage Unfinished Goods.

(1) An aggrieved seller under the preceding section may

(a) identify to the contract conforming goods not already identified if at the time he learned of the breach they are in his possession or control;

(b) treat as the subject of resale goods which have demonstrably been intended for the particular contract even though those goods are unfinished.

(2) Where the goods are unfinished an aggrieved seller may in the exercise of reasonable commercial judgment for the purposes of avoiding loss and of effective realization either complete the manufacture and wholly identify the goods to the contract or cease manufacture and resell for scrap or salvage value or proceed in any other reasonable manner.

§ 2–705. Seller's Stoppage of Delivery in Transit or Otherwise.

(1) The seller may stop delivery of goods in the possession of a carrier or other bailee when he discovers the buyer to be insolvent (Section 2–702) and may stop delivery of carload, truckload, planeload or larger shipments of express or freight when the buyer repudiates or fails to make a payment due before delivery or if for any other reason the seller has a right to withhold or reclaim the goods.

(2) As against such buyer the seller may stop delivery until

(a) receipt of the goods by the buyer; or

(b) acknowledgment to the buyer by any bailee of the goods except a carrier that the bailee holds the goods for the buyer; or

(c) such acknowledgment to the buyer by a carrier by reshipment or as warehouseman; or

(d) negotiation to the buyer of any negotiable document of title covering the goods.

(3) (a) To stop delivery the seller must so notify as to enable the bailee by reasonable diligence to prevent delivery of the goods.

(b) After such notification the bailee must hold and deliver the goods according to the directions of the seller but the seller is liable to the bailee for any ensuing charges or damages.

(c) If a negotiable document of title has been issued for goods the bailee is not obliged to obey a notification to stop until surrender of the document.

(d) A carrier who has issued a non-negotiable bill of lading is not obliged to obey a notification to stop received from a person other than the consignor.

§ 2–706. Seller's Resale Including Contract for Resale.

(1) Under the conditions stated in Section 2–703 on seller's remedies, the seller may resell the goods concerned or the undelivered balance thereof. Where the resale is made in good faith and in a commercially reasonable manner the seller may recover the difference between the resale price and the contract price together with any incidental damages allowed under the provisions of this Article (Section 2–710), but less expenses saved in consequence of the buyer's breach.

(2) Except as otherwise provided in subsection (3) or unless otherwise agreed resale may be at public or private sale including sale by way of one or more contracts to sell or of identification to an existing contract of the seller. Sale may be as a unit or in parcels and at any time and place and on any terms but every aspect of the sale including the method, manner, time, place and terms must be commercially reasonable. The resale must be reasonably identified as referring to the broken contract, but it is not necessary that the goods be in existence or that any or all of them have been identified to the contract before the breach.

(3) Where the resale is at private sale the seller must give the buyer reasonable notification of his intention to resell.

(4) Where the resale is at public sale

(a) only identified goods can be sold except where there is a recognized market for a public sale of futures in goods of the kind; and

(b) it must be made at a usual place or market for public sale if one is reasonably available and except in the case of goods which are perishable or threaten to decline in value speedily the seller must give the buyer reasonable notice of the time and place of the resale; and

(c) if the goods are not to be within the view of those attending the sale the notification of sale must state the place where the goods are located and provide for their reasonable inspection by prospective bidders; and

(d) the seller may buy.

(5) A purchaser who buys in good faith at a resale takes the goods free of any rights of the original buyer even though the seller fails to comply with one or more of the requirements of this section.

(6) The seller is not accountable to the buyer for any profit made on any resale. A person in the position of a seller (Section 2–707) or a buyer who has rightfully rejected or justifiably revoked acceptance must account for any excess over the amount of his security interest, as hereinafter defined (subsection (3) of Section 2–711).

§ 2–707. "Person in the Position of a Seller".

(1) A "person in the position of a seller" includes as against a principal an agent who has paid or become responsible for the price of goods on behalf of his principal or anyone who otherwise holds a security interest or other right in goods similar to that of a seller.

(2) A person in the position of a seller may as provided in this Article withhold or stop delivery (Section 2–705) and resell (Section 2–706) and recover incidental damages (Section 2–710).

§ 2–708. Seller's Damages for Non-Acceptance or Repudiation.

(1) Subject to subsection (2) and to the provisions of this Article with respect to proof of market price (Section 2–723), the measure of damages for non-acceptance or repudiation by the buyer is the difference between the market price at the time and place for tender and the unpaid contract price together with any incidental damages provided in this Article (Section 2–710), but less expenses saved in consequence of the buyer's breach.

(2) If the measure of damages provided in subsection (1) is inadequate to put the seller in as good a position as performance would have done then the measure of damages is the profit (including reasonable overhead) which the seller would have made from full performance by the buyer, together with any incidental damages provided in this Article (Section 2–710), due allowance for costs reasonably incurred and due credit for payments or proceeds of resale.

§ 2–709. Action for the Price.

(1) When the buyer fails to pay the price as it becomes due the seller may recover, together with any incidental damages under the next section, the price

(a) of goods accepted or of conforming goods lost or damaged within a commercially reasonable time after risk of their loss has passed to the buyer; and

(b) of goods identified to the contract if the seller is unable after reasonable effort to resell them at a reasonable price or the circumstances reasonably indicate that such effort will be unavailing.

(2) Where the seller sues for the price he must hold for the buyer any goods which have been identified to the contract and are still in his control except that if resale becomes possible he may resell them at any time prior to the collection of the judgment. The net proceeds of any such resale must be credited to the buyer and payment of the judgment entitles him to any goods not resold.

(3) After the buyer has wrongfully rejected or revoked acceptance of the goods or has failed to make a payment due or has repudiated (Section 2–610), a seller who is held not entitled to the price under this section shall nevertheless be awarded damages for non-acceptance under the preceding section.

§ 2–710. Seller's Incidental Damages.

Incidental damages to an aggrieved seller include any commercially reasonable charges, expenses or commissions incurred in stopping delivery, in the transportation, care and custody of goods after the buyer's breach, in connection with return or resale of the goods or otherwise resulting from the breach.

§ 2–711. Buyer's Remedies in General; Buyer's Security Interest in Rejected Goods.

(1) Where the seller fails to make delivery or repudiates or the buyer rightfully rejects or justifiably revokes acceptance then with respect to any goods involved, and with respect to the whole if the breach goes to the whole contract (Section 2–612), the buyer may cancel and whether or not he has done so may in addition to recovering so much of the price as has been paid

(a) "cover" and have damages under the next section as to all the goods affected whether or not they have been identified to the contract; or

(b) recover damages for non-delivery as provided in this Article (Section 2–713).

(2) Where the seller fails to deliver or repudiates the buyer may also

(a) if the goods have been identified recover them as provided in this Article (Section 2–502); or

(b) in a proper case obtain specific performance or replevy the goods as provided in this Article (Section 2–716).

(3) On rightful rejection or justifiable revocation of acceptance a buyer has a security interest in goods in his possession or control for any payments made on their price and any expenses reasonably incurred in their inspection, receipt, transportation, care and custody and may hold such goods and resell them in like manner as an aggrieved seller (Section 2–706).

§ 2–712. "Cover"; Buyer's Procurement of Substitute Goods.

(1) After a breach within the preceding section the buyer may "cover" by making in good faith and without unreasonable delay any reasonable purchase of or contract to purchase goods in substitution for those due from the seller.

(2) The buyer may recover from the seller as damages the difference between the cost of cover and the contract price together with any incidental or consequential damages as hereinafter defined (Section 2–715), but less expenses saved in consequence of the seller's breach.

(3) Failure of the buyer to effect cover within this section does not bar him from any other remedy.

§ 2–713. Buyer's Damages for Non-Delivery or Repudiation.

(1) Subject to the provisions of this Article with respect to proof of market price (Section 2–723), the measure of damages for non-delivery or repudiation by the seller is the difference between the market price at the time when the buyer learned of the breach and the contract price together with any incidental and consequential damages provided in this Article (Section 2–715), but less expenses saved in consequence of the seller's breach.

(2) Market price is to be determined as of the place for tender or, in cases of rejection after arrival or revocation of acceptance, as of the place of arrival.

§ 2–714. Buyer's Damages for Breach in Regard to Accepted Goods.

(1) Where the buyer has accepted goods and given notification (subsection (3) of Section 2–607) he may recover as damages for any non-conformity of tender the loss resulting in the ordinary course of events from the seller's breach as determined in any manner which is reasonable.

(2) The measure of damages for breach of warranty is the difference at the time and place of acceptance between the value

of the goods accepted and the value they would have had if they had been as warranted, unless special circumstances show proximate damages of a different amount.
(3) In a proper case any incidental and consequential damages under the next section may also be recovered.

§ 2–715. Buyer's Incidental and Consequential Damages.

(1) Incidental damages resulting from the seller's breach include expenses reasonably incurred in inspection, receipt, transportation and care and custody of goods rightfully rejected, any commercially reasonable charges, expenses or commissions in connection with effecting cover and any other reasonable expense incident to the delay or other breach.
(2) Consequential damages resulting from the seller's breach include
(a) any loss resulting from general or particular requirements and needs of which the seller at the time of contracting had reason to know and which could not reasonably be prevented by cover or otherwise; and
(b) injury to person or property proximately resulting from any breach of warranty.

§ 2–716. Buyer's Right to Specific Performance or Replevin.

(1) Specific performance may be decreed where the goods are unique or in other proper circumstances.
(2) The decree for specific performance may include such terms and conditions as to payment of the price, damages, or other relief as the court may deem just.
(3) The buyer has a right of replevin for goods identified to the contract if after reasonable effort he is unable to effect cover for such goods or the circumstances reasonably indicate that such effort will be unavailing or if the goods have been shipped under reservation and satisfaction of the security interest in them has been made or tendered. In the case of goods bought for personal, family, or household purposes, the buyer's right of replevin vests upon acquisition of a special property, even if the seller had not then repudiated or failed to deliver.
As amended in 1999.

§ 2–717. Deduction of Damages From the Price.

The buyer on notifying the seller of his intention to do so may deduct all or any part of the damages resulting from any breach of the contract from any part of the price still due under the same contract.

§ 2–718. Liquidation or Limitation of Damages; Deposits.

(1) Damages for breach by either party may be liquidated in the agreement but only at an amount which is reasonable in the light of the anticipated or actual harm caused by the breach, the difficulties of proof of loss, and the inconvenience or nonfeasibility of otherwise obtaining an adequate remedy. A term fixing unreasonably large liquidated damages is void as a penalty.
(2) Where the seller justifiably withholds delivery of goods because of the buyer's breach, the buyer is entitled to restitution of any amount by which the sum of his payments exceeds
(a) the amount to which the seller is entitled by virtue of terms liquidating the seller's damages in accordance with subsection (1), or
(b) in the absence of such terms, twenty per cent of the value of the total performance for which the buyer is obligated under the contract or $500, whichever is smaller.
(3) The buyer's right to restitution under subsection (2) is subject to offset to the extent that the seller establishes
(a) a right to recover damages under the provisions of this Article other than subsection (1), and
(b) the amount or value of any benefits received by the buyer directly or indirectly by reason of the contract.
(4) Where a seller has received payment in goods their reasonable value or the proceeds of their resale shall be treated as payments for the purposes of subsection (2); but if the seller has notice of the buyer's breach before reselling goods received in part performance, his resale is subject to the conditions laid down in this Article on resale by an aggrieved seller (Section 2–706).

§ 2–719. Contractual Modification or Limitation of Remedy.

(1) Subject to the provisions of subsections (2) and (3) of this section and of the preceding section on liquidation and limitation of damages,
(a) the agreement may provide for remedies in addition to or in substitution for those provided in this Article and may limit or alter the measure of damages recoverable under this Article, as by limiting the buyer's remedies to return of the goods and repayment of the price or to repair and replacement of nonconforming goods or parts; and
(b) resort to a remedy as provided is optional unless the remedy is expressly agreed to be exclusive, in which case it is the sole remedy.
(2) Where circumstances cause an exclusive or limited remedy to fail of its essential purpose, remedy may be had as provided in this Act.
(3) Consequential damages may be limited or excluded unless the limitation or exclusion is unconscionable. Limitation of consequential damages for injury to the person in the case of consumer goods is *prima facie* unconscionable but limitation of damages where the loss is commercial is not.

§ 2–720. Effect of "Cancellation" or "Rescission" on Claims for Antecedent Breach.

Unless the contrary intention clearly appears, expressions of "cancellation" or "rescission" of the contract or the like shall not be construed as a renunciation or discharge of any claim in damages for an antecedent breach.

§ 2–721. Remedies for Fraud.

Remedies for material misrepresentation or fraud include all remedies available under this Article for non-fraudulent breach. Neither rescission or a claim for rescission of the contract for sale nor rejection or return of the goods shall bar or be deemed inconsistent with a claim for damages or other remedy.

§ 2–722. Who Can Sue Third Parties for Injury to Goods.
Where a third party so deals with goods which have been identified to a contract for sale as to cause actionable injury to a party to that contract

(a) a right of action against the third party is in either party to the contract for sale who has title to or a security interest or a special property or an insurable interest in the goods; and if the goods have been destroyed or converted a right of action is also in the party who either bore the risk of loss under the contract for sale or has since the injury assumed that risk as against the other;

(b) if at the time of the injury the party plaintiff did not bear the risk of loss as against the other party to the contract for sale and there is no arrangement between them for disposition of the recovery, his suit or settlement is, subject to his own interest, as a fiduciary for the other party to the contract;

(c) either party may with the consent of the other sue for the benefit of whom it may concern.

§ 2–723. Proof of Market Price: Time and Place.
(1) If an action based on anticipatory repudiation comes to trial before the time for performance with respect to some or all of the goods, any damages based on market price (Section 2–708 or Section 2–713) shall be determined according to the price of such goods prevailing at the time when the aggrieved party learned of the repudiation.

(2) If evidence of a price prevailing at the times or places described in this Article is not readily available the price prevailing within any reasonable time before or after the time described or at any other place which in commercial judgment or under usage of trade would serve as a reasonable substitute for the one described may be used, making any proper allowance for the cost of transporting the goods to or from such other place.

(3) Evidence of a relevant price prevailing at a time or place other than the one described in this Article offered by one party is not admissible unless and until he has given the other party such notice as the court finds sufficient to prevent unfair surprise.

§ 2–724. Admissibility of Market Quotations.
Whenever the prevailing price or value of any goods regularly bought and sold in any established commodity market is in issue, reports in official publications or trade journals or in newspapers or periodicals of general circulation published as the reports of such market shall be admissible in evidence. The circumstances of the preparation of such a report may be shown to affect its weight but not its admissibility.

§ 2–725. Statute of Limitations in Contracts for Sale.
(1) An action for breach of any contract for sale must be commenced within four years after the cause of action has accrued. By the original agreement the parties may reduce the period of limitation to not less than one year but may not extend it.

(2) A cause of action accrues when the breach occurs, regardless of the aggrieved party's lack of knowledge of the breach. A breach of warranty occurs when tender of delivery is made, except that where a warranty explicitly extends to future performance of the goods and discovery of the breach must await the time of such performance the cause of action accrues when the breach is or should have been discovered.

(3) Where an action commenced within the time limited by subsection (1) is so terminated as to leave available a remedy by another action for the same breach such other action may be commenced after the expiration of the time limited and within six months after the termination of the first action unless the termination resulted from voluntary discontinuance or from dismissal for failure or neglect to prosecute.

(4) This section does not alter the law on tolling of the statute of limitations nor does it apply to causes of action which have accrued before this Act becomes effective.

ARTICLE 2A: LEASES

Part 1—General Provisions

§ 2A–101. Short Title.
This Article shall be known and may be cited as the Uniform Commercial Code—Leases.

§ 2A–102. Scope.
This Article applies to any transaction, regardless of form, that creates a lease.

§ 2A–103. Definitions and Index of Definitions.
(1) In this Article unless the context otherwise requires:

(a) "Buyer in ordinary course of business" means a person who in good faith and without knowledge that the sale to him [or her] is in violation of the ownership rights or security interest or leasehold interest of a third party in the goods buys in ordinary course from a person in the business of selling goods of that kind but does not include a pawnbroker. "Buying" may be for cash or by exchange of other property or on secured or unsecured credit and includes receiving goods or documents of title under a pre-existing contract for sale but does not include a transfer in bulk or as security for or in total or partial satisfaction of a money debt.

(b) "Cancellation" occurs when either party puts an end to the lease contract for default by the other party.

(c) "Commercial unit" means such a unit of goods as by commercial usage is a single whole for purposes of lease and division of which materially impairs its character or value on the market or in use. A commercial unit may be a single article, as a machine, or a set of articles, as a suite of furniture or a line of machinery, or a quantity, as a gross or carload, or any other unit treated in use or in the relevant market as a single whole.

(d) "Conforming" goods or performance under a lease contract means goods or performance that are in accordance with the obligations under the lease contract.

(e) "Consumer lease" means a lease that a lessor regularly engaged in the business of leasing or selling makes to a lessee who is an individual and who takes under the lease primarily for a personal, family, or household purpose [, if the total payments to be made under the lease contract, excluding payments for options to renew or buy, do not exceed $______].

(f) "Fault" means wrongful act, omission, breach, or default.

(g) "Finance lease" means a lease with respect to which:

(i) the lessor does not select, manufacture or supply the goods;

(ii) the lessor acquires the goods or the right to possession and use of the goods in connection with the lease; and

(iii) one of the following occurs:

(A) the lessee receives a copy of the contract by which the lessor acquired the goods or the right to possession and use of the goods before signing the lease contract;

(B) the lessee's approval of the contract by which the lessor acquired the goods or the right to possession and use of the goods is a condition to effectiveness of the lease contract;

(C) the lessee, before signing the lease contract, receives an accurate and complete statement designating the promises and warranties, and any disclaimers of warranties, limitations or modifications of remedies, or liquidated damages, including those of a third party, such as the manufacturer of the goods, provided to the lessor by the person supplying the goods in connection with or as part of the contract by which the lessor acquired the goods or the right to possession and use of the goods; or

(D) if the lease is not a consumer lease, the lessor, before the lessee signs the lease contract, informs the lessee in writing (a) of the identity of the person supplying the goods to the lessor, unless the lessee has selected that person and directed the lessor to acquire the goods or the right to possession and use of the goods from that person, (b) that the lessee is entitled under this Article to any promises and warranties, including those of any third party, provided to the lessor by the person supplying the goods in connection with or as part of the contract by which the lessor acquired the goods or the right to possession and use of the goods, and (c) that the lessee may communicate with the person supplying the goods to the lessor and receive an accurate and complete statement of those promises and warranties, including any disclaimers and limitations of them or of remedies.

(h) "Goods" means all things that are movable at the time of identification to the lease contract, or are fixtures (Section 2A–309), but the term does not include money, documents, instruments, accounts, chattel paper, general intangibles, or minerals or the like, including oil and gas, before extraction. The term also includes the unborn young of animals.

(i) "Installment lease contract" means a lease contract that authorizes or requires the delivery of goods in separate lots to be separately accepted, even though the lease contract contains a clause "each delivery is a separate lease" or its equivalent.

(j) "Lease" means a transfer of the right to possession and use of goods for a term in return for consideration, but a sale, including a sale on approval or a sale or return, or retention or creation of a security interest is not a lease. Unless the context clearly indicates otherwise, the term includes a sublease.

(k) "Lease agreement" means the bargain, with respect to the lease, of the lessor and the lessee in fact as found in their language or by implication from other circumstances including course of dealing or usage of trade or course of performance as provided in this Article. Unless the context clearly indicates otherwise, the term includes a sublease agreement.

(l) "Lease contract" means the total legal obligation that results from the lease agreement as affected by this Article and any other applicable rules of law. Unless the context clearly indicates otherwise, the term includes a sublease contract.

(m) "Leasehold interest" means the interest of the lessor or the lessee under a lease contract.

(n) "Lessee" means a person who acquires the right to possession and use of goods under a lease. Unless the context clearly indicates otherwise, the term includes a sublessee.

(o) "Lessee in ordinary course of business" means a person who in good faith and without knowledge that the lease to him [or her] is in violation of the ownership rights or security interest or leasehold interest of a third party in the goods, leases in ordinary course from a person in the business of selling or leasing goods of that kind but does not include a pawnbroker. "Leasing" may be for cash or by exchange of other property or on secured or unsecured credit and includes receiving goods or documents of title under a pre-existing lease contract but does not include a transfer in bulk or as security for or in total or partial satisfaction of a money debt.

(p) "Lessor" means a person who transfers the right to possession and use of goods under a lease. Unless the context clearly indicates otherwise, the term includes a sublessor.

(q) "Lessor's residual interest" means the lessor's interest in the goods after expiration, termination, or cancellation of the lease contract.

(r) "Lien" means a charge against or interest in goods to secure payment of a debt or performance of an obligation, but the term does not include a security interest.

(s) "Lot" means a parcel or a single article that is the subject matter of a separate lease or delivery, whether or not it is sufficient to perform the lease contract.

(t) "Merchant lessee" means a lessee that is a merchant with respect to goods of the kind subject to the lease.

(u) "Present value" means the amount as of a date certain of one or more sums payable in the future, discounted to the date certain. The discount is determined by the interest rate specified by the parties if the rate was not manifestly unreasonable at the time the transaction was entered into; otherwise, the discount is determined by a commercially reasonable rate that takes into account the facts and circumstances of each case at the time the transaction was entered into.

(v) "Purchase" includes taking by sale, lease, mortgage, security interest, pledge, gift, or any other voluntary transaction creating an interest in goods.

(w) "Sublease" means a lease of goods the right to possession and use of which was acquired by the lessor as a lessee under an existing lease.

(x) "Supplier" means a person from whom a lessor buys or leases goods to be leased under a finance lease.

(y) "Supply contract" means a contract under which a lessor buys or leases goods to be leased.

(z) "Termination" occurs when either party pursuant to a power created by agreement or law puts an end to the lease contract otherwise than for default.

(2) Other definitions applying to this Article and the sections in which they appear are:

"Accessions". Section 2A–310(1).
"Construction mortgage". Section 2A–309(1)(d).
"Encumbrance". Section 2A–309(1)(e).
"Fixtures". Section 2A–309(1)(a).
"Fixture filing". Section 2A–309(1)(b).
"Purchase money lease". Section 2A–309(1)(c).

(3) The following definitions in other Articles apply to this Article:

"Accounts". Section 9–106.
"Between merchants". Section 2–104(3).
"Buyer". Section 2–103(1)(a).
"Chattel paper". Section 9–105(1)(b).
"Consumer goods". Section 9–109(1).
"Document". Section 9–105(1)(f).
"Entrusting". Section 2–403(3).
"General intangibles". Section 9–106.
"Good faith". Section 2–103(1)(b).
"Instrument". Section 9–105(1)(i).
"Merchant". Section 2–104(1).
"Mortgage". Section 9–105(1)(j).
"Pursuant to commitment". Section 9–105(1)(k).
"Receipt". Section 2–103(1)(c).
"Sale". Section 2–106(1).
"Sale on approval". Section 2–326.
"Sale or return". Section 2–326.
"Seller". Section 2–103(1)(d).

(4) In addition Article 1 contains general definitions and principles of construction and interpretation applicable throughout this Article.
As amended in 1990 and 1999.

§ 2A–104. Leases Subject to Other Law.

(1) A lease, although subject to this Article, is also subject to any applicable:

(a) certificate of title statute of this State: (list any certificate of title statutes covering automobiles, trailers, mobile homes, boats, farm tractors, and the like);

(b) certificate of title statute of another jurisdiction (Section 2A–105); or

(c) consumer protection statute of this State, or final consumer protection decision of a court of this State existing on the effective date of this Article.

(2) In case of conflict between this Article, other than Sections 2A–105, 2A–304(3), and 2A–305(3), and a statute or decision referred to in subsection (1), the statute or decision controls.

(3) Failure to comply with an applicable law has only the effect specified therein.
As amended in 1990.

§ 2A–105. Territorial Application of Article to Goods Covered by Certificate of Title.

Subject to the provisions of Sections 2A–304(3) and 2A–305(3), with respect to goods covered by a certificate of title issued under a statute of this State or of another jurisdiction, compliance and the effect of compliance or noncompliance with a certificate of title statute are governed by the law (including the conflict of laws rules) of the jurisdiction issuing the certificate until the earlier of (a) surrender of the certificate, or (b) four months after the goods are removed from that jurisdiction and thereafter until a new certificate of title is issued by another jurisdiction.

§ 2A–106. Limitation on Power of Parties to Consumer Lease to Choose Applicable Law and Judicial Forum.

(1) If the law chosen by the parties to a consumer lease is that of a jurisdiction other than a jurisdiction in which the lessee resides at the time the lease agreement becomes enforceable or within 30 days thereafter or in which the goods are to be used, the choice is not enforceable.

(2) If the judicial forum chosen by the parties to a consumer lease is a forum that would not otherwise have jurisdiction over the lessee, the choice is not enforceable.

§ 2A–107. Waiver or Renunciation of Claim or Right After Default.

Any claim or right arising out of an alleged default or breach of warranty may be discharged in whole or in part without consideration by a written waiver or renunciation signed and delivered by the aggrieved party.

§ 2A–108. Unconscionability.

(1) If the court as a matter of law finds a lease contract or any clause of a lease contract to have been unconscionable at the time it was made the court may refuse to enforce the lease contract, or it may enforce the remainder of the lease contract without the unconscionable clause, or it may so limit the application of any unconscionable clause as to avoid any unconscionable result.

(2) With respect to a consumer lease, if the court as a matter of law finds that a lease contract or any clause of a lease contract has been induced by unconscionable conduct or that unconscionable conduct has occurred in the collection of a claim arising from a lease contract, the court may grant appropriate relief.

(3) Before making a finding of unconscionability under subsection (1) or (2), the court, on its own motion or that of a party, shall afford the parties a reasonable opportunity to present evidence as to the setting, purpose, and effect of the lease contract or clause thereof, or of the conduct.

(4) In an action in which the lessee claims unconscionability with respect to a consumer lease:

(a) If the court finds unconscionability under subsection (1) or (2), the court shall award reasonable attorney's fees to the lessee.

(b) If the court does not find unconscionability and the lessee claiming unconscionability has brought or maintained an action he [or she] knew to be groundless, the court shall award reasonable attorney's fees to the party against whom the claim is made.

(c) In determining attorney's fees, the amount of the recovery on behalf of the claimant under subsections (1) and (2) is not controlling.

§ 2A–109. Option to Accelerate at Will.

(1) A term providing that one party or his [or her] successor in interest may accelerate payment or performance or require collateral or additional collateral "at will" or "when he [or she] deems himself [or herself] insecure" or in words of similar import must be construed to mean that he [or she] has power to do so only if he [or she] in good faith believes that the prospect of payment or performance is impaired.

(2) With respect to a consumer lease, the burden of establishing good faith under subsection (1) is on the party who exercised the power; otherwise the burden of establishing lack of good faith is on the party against whom the power has been exercised.

Part 2—Formation and Construction of Lease Contract

§ 2A–201. Statute of Frauds.

(1) A lease contract is not enforceable by way of action or defense unless:

(a) the total payments to be made under the lease contract, excluding payments for options to renew or buy, are less than $1,000; or

(b) there is a writing, signed by the party against whom enforcement is sought or by that party's authorized agent, sufficient to indicate that a lease contract has been made between the parties and to describe the goods leased and the lease term.

(2) Any description of leased goods or of the lease term is sufficient and satisfies subsection (1)(b), whether or not it is specific, if it reasonably identifies what is described.

(3) A writing is not insufficient because it omits or incorrectly states a term agreed upon, but the lease contract is not enforceable under subsection (1)(b) beyond the lease term and the quantity of goods shown in the writing.

(4) A lease contract that does not satisfy the requirements of subsection (1), but which is valid in other respects, is enforceable:

(a) if the goods are to be specially manufactured or obtained for the lessee and are not suitable for lease or sale to others in the ordinary course of the lessor's business, and the lessor, before notice of repudiation is received and under circumstances that reasonably indicate that the goods are for the lessee, has made either a substantial beginning of their manufacture or commitments for their procurement;

(b) if the party against whom enforcement is sought admits in that party's pleading, testimony or otherwise in court that a lease contract was made, but the lease contract is not enforceable under this provision beyond the quantity of goods admitted; or

(c) with respect to goods that have been received and accepted by the lessee.

(5) The lease term under a lease contract referred to in subsection (4) is:

(a) if there is a writing signed by the party against whom enforcement is sought or by that party's authorized agent specifying the lease term, the term so specified;

(b) if the party against whom enforcement is sought admits in that party's pleading, testimony, or otherwise in court a lease term, the term so admitted; or

(c) a reasonable lease term.

§ 2A–202. Final Written Expression: Parol or Extrinsic Evidence.

Terms with respect to which the confirmatory memoranda of the parties agree or which are otherwise set forth in a writing intended by the parties as a final expression of their agreement with respect to such terms as are included therein may not be contradicted by evidence of any prior agreement or of a contemporaneous oral agreement but may be explained or supplemented:

(a) by course of dealing or usage of trade or by course of performance; and

(b) by evidence of consistent additional terms unless the court finds the writing to have been intended also as a complete and exclusive statement of the terms of the agreement.

§ 2A–203. Seals Inoperative.

The affixing of a seal to a writing evidencing a lease contract or an offer to enter into a lease contract does not render the writing a sealed instrument and the law with respect to sealed instruments does not apply to the lease contract or offer.

§ 2A–204. Formation in General.

(1) A lease contract may be made in any manner sufficient to show agreement, including conduct by both parties which recognizes the existence of a lease contract.

(2) An agreement sufficient to constitute a lease contract may be found although the moment of its making is undetermined.

(3) Although one or more terms are left open, a lease contract does not fail for indefiniteness if the parties have intended to make a lease contract and there is a reasonably certain basis for giving an appropriate remedy.

§ 2A–205. Firm Offers.

An offer by a merchant to lease goods to or from another person in a signed writing that by its terms gives assurance it will be held open is not revocable, for lack of consideration, during the time stated or, if no time is stated, for a reasonable time, but in no event may the period of irrevocability exceed 3 months. Any such term of assurance on a form supplied by the offeree must be separately signed by the offeror.

§ 2A–206. Offer and Acceptance in Formation of Lease Contract.

(1) Unless otherwise unambiguously indicated by the language or circumstances, an offer to make a lease contract must be construed as inviting acceptance in any manner and by any medium reasonable in the circumstances.

(2) If the beginning of a requested performance is a reasonable mode of acceptance, an offeror who is not notified of acceptance within a reasonable time may treat the offer as having lapsed before acceptance.

§ 2A–207. Course of Performance or Practical Construction.

(1) If a lease contract involves repeated occasions for performance by either party with knowledge of the nature of the performance and opportunity for objection to it by the other, any course of performance accepted or acquiesced in without objection is relevant to determine the meaning of the lease agreement.

(2) The express terms of a lease agreement and any course of performance, as well as any course of dealing and usage of trade, must be construed whenever reasonable as consistent with each other; but if that construction is unreasonable, express terms control course of performance, course of performance controls both course of dealing and usage of trade, and course of dealing controls usage of trade.

(3) Subject to the provisions of Section 2A–208 on modification and waiver, course of performance is relevant to show a waiver or modification of any term inconsistent with the course of performance.

§ 2A–208. Modification, Rescission and Waiver.

(1) An agreement modifying a lease contract needs no consideration to be binding.

(2) A signed lease agreement that excludes modification or rescission except by a signed writing may not be otherwise modified or rescinded, but, except as between merchants, such a requirement on a form supplied by a merchant must be separately signed by the other party.

(3) Although an attempt at modification or rescission does not satisfy the requirements of subsection (2), it may operate as a waiver.

(4) A party who has made a waiver affecting an executory portion of a lease contract may retract the waiver by reasonable notification received by the other party that strict performance will be required of any term waived, unless the retraction would be unjust in view of a material change of position in reliance on the waiver.

§ 2A–209. Lessee under Finance Lease as Beneficiary of Supply Contract.

(1) The benefit of the supplier's promises to the lessor under the supply contract and of all warranties, whether express or implied, including those of any third party provided in connection with or as part of the supply contract, extends to the lessee to the extent of the lessee's leasehold interest under a finance lease related to the supply contract, but is subject to the terms warranty and of the supply contract and all defenses or claims arising therefrom.

(2) The extension of the benefit of supplier's promises and of warranties to the lessee (Section 2A–209(1)) does not: (i) modify the rights and obligations of the parties to the supply contract, whether arising therefrom or otherwise, or (ii) impose any duty or liability under the supply contract on the lessee.

(3) Any modification or rescission of the supply contract by the supplier and the lessor is effective between the supplier and the lessee unless, before the modification or rescission, the supplier has received notice that the lessee has entered into a finance lease related to the supply contract. If the modification or rescission is effective between the supplier and the lessee, the lessor is deemed to have assumed, in addition to the obligations of the lessor to the lessee under the lease contract, promises of the supplier to the lessor and warranties that were so modified or rescinded as they existed and were available to the lessee before modification or rescission.

(4) In addition to the extension of the benefit of the supplier's promises and of warranties to the lessee under subsection (1), the lessee retains all rights that the lessee may have against the supplier which arise from an agreement between the lessee and the supplier or under other law.

As amended in 1990.

§ 2A–210. Express Warranties.

(1) Express warranties by the lessor are created as follows:

(a) Any affirmation of fact or promise made by the lessor to the lessee which relates to the goods and becomes part of the basis of the bargain creates an express warranty that the goods will conform to the affirmation or promise.

(b) Any description of the goods which is made part of the basis of the bargain creates an express warranty that the goods will conform to the description.

(c) Any sample or model that is made part of the basis of the bargain creates an express warranty that the whole of the goods will conform to the sample or model.

(2) It is not necessary to the creation of an express warranty that the lessor use formal words, such as "warrant" or "guarantee," or that the lessor have a specific intention to make a warranty, but an affirmation merely of the value of the goods or a statement purporting to be merely the lessor's opinion or commendation of the goods does not create a warranty.

§ 2A–211. Warranties Against Interference and Against Infringement; Lessee's Obligation Against Infringement.

(1) There is in a lease contract a warranty that for the lease term no person holds a claim to or interest in the goods that arose from an act or omission of the lessor, other than a claim by way of infringement or the like, which will interfere with the lessee's enjoyment of its leasehold interest.

(2) Except in a finance lease there is in a lease contract by a lessor who is a merchant regularly dealing in goods of the kind a warranty that the goods are delivered free of the rightful claim of any person by way of infringement or the like.

(3) A lessee who furnishes specifications to a lessor or a supplier shall hold the lessor and the supplier harmless against any claim by way of infringement or the like that arises out of compliance with the specifications.

§ 2A–212. Implied Warranty of Merchantability.

(1) Except in a finance lease, a warranty that the goods will be merchantable is implied in a lease contract if the lessor is a merchant with respect to goods of that kind.

(2) Goods to be merchantable must be at least such as

(a) pass without objection in the trade under the description in the lease agreement;

(b) in the case of fungible goods, are of fair average quality within the description;

(c) are fit for the ordinary purposes for which goods of that type are used;

(d) run, within the variation permitted by the lease agreement, of even kind, quality, and quantity within each unit and among all units involved;

(e) are adequately contained, packaged, and labeled as the lease agreement may require; and
(f) conform to any promises or affirmations of fact made on the container or label.
(3) Other implied warranties may arise from course of dealing or usage of trade.

§ 2A–213. Implied Warranty of Fitness for Particular Purpose.

Except in a finance of lease, if the lessor at the time the lease contract is made has reason to know of any particular purpose for which the goods are required and that the lessee is relying on the lessor's skill or judgment to select or furnish suitable goods, there is in the lease contract an implied warranty that the goods will be fit for that purpose.

§ 2A–214. Exclusion or Modification of Warranties.

(1) Words or conduct relevant to the creation of an express warranty and words or conduct tending to negate or limit a warranty must be construed wherever reasonable as consistent with each other; but, subject to the provisions of Section 2A–202 on parol or extrinsic evidence, negation or limitation is inoperative to the extent that the construction is unreasonable.
(2) Subject to subsection (3), to exclude or modify the implied warranty of merchantability or any part of it the language must mention "merchantability", be by a writing, and be conspicuous. Subject to subsection (3), to exclude or modify any implied warranty of fitness the exclusion must be by a writing and be conspicuous. Language to exclude all implied warranties of fitness is sufficient if it is in writing, is conspicuous and states, for example, "There is no warranty that the goods will be fit for a particular purpose".
(3) Notwithstanding subsection (2), but subject to subsection (4),
(a) unless the circumstances indicate otherwise, all implied warranties are excluded by expressions like "as is" or "with all faults" or by other language that in common understanding calls the lessee's attention to the exclusion of warranties and makes plain that there is no implied warranty, if in writing and conspicuous;
(b) if the lessee before entering into the lease contract has examined the goods or the sample or model as fully as desired or has refused to examine the goods, there is no implied warranty with regard to defects that an examination ought in the circumstances to have revealed; and
(c) an implied warranty may also be excluded or modified by course of dealing, course of performance, or usage of trade.
(4) To exclude or modify a warranty against interference or against infringement (Section 2A–211) or any part of it, the language must be specific, be by a writing, and be conspicuous, unless the circumstances, including course of performance, course of dealing, or usage of trade, give the lessee reason to know that the goods are being leased subject to a claim or interest of any person.

§ 2A–215. Cumulation and Conflict of Warranties Express or Implied.

Warranties, whether express or implied, must be construed as consistent with each other and as cumulative, but if that construction is unreasonable, the intention of the parties determines which warranty is dominant. In ascertaining that intention the following rules apply:
(a) Exact or technical specifications displace an inconsistent sample or model or general language of description.
(b) A sample from an existing bulk displaces inconsistent general language of description.
(c) Express warranties displace inconsistent implied warranties other than an implied warranty of fitness for a particular purpose.

§ 2A–216. Third-Party Beneficiaries of Express and Implied Warranties.

Alternative A

A warranty to or for the benefit of a lessee under this Article, whether express or implied, extends to any natural person who is in the family or household of the lessee or who is a guest in the lessee's home if it is reasonable to expect that such person may use, consume, or be affected by the goods and who is injured in person by breach of the warranty. This section does not displace principles of law and equity that extend a warranty to or for the benefit of a lessee to other persons. The operation of this section may not be excluded, modified, or limited, but an exclusion, modification, or limitation of the warranty, including any with respect to rights and remedies, effective against the lessee is also effective against any beneficiary designated under this section.

Alternative B

A warranty to or for the benefit of a lessee under this Article, whether express or implied, extends to any natural person who may reasonably be expected to use, consume, or be affected by the goods and who is injured in person by breach of the warranty. This section does not displace principles of law and equity that extend a warranty to or for the benefit of a lessee to other persons. The operation of this section may not be excluded, modified, or limited, but an exclusion, modification, or limitation of the warranty, including any with respect to rights and remedies, effective against the lessee is also effective against the beneficiary designated under this section.

Alternative C

A warranty to or for the benefit of a lessee under this Article, whether express or implied, extends to any person who may reasonably be expected to use, consume, or be affected by the goods and who is injured by breach of the warranty. The operation of this section may not be excluded, modified, or limited with respect to injury to the person of an individual to whom the warranty extends, but an exclusion, modification, or limitation of the warranty, including any with respect to rights and remedies, effective against the lessee is also effective against the beneficiary designated under this section.

§ 2A–217. Identification.

Identification of goods as goods to which a lease contract refers may be made at any time and in any manner explicitly agreed to by the parties. In the absence of explicit agreement, identification occurs:
(a) when the lease contract is made if the lease contract is for a lease of goods that are existing and identified;

(b) when the goods are shipped, marked, or otherwise designated by the lessor as goods to which the lease contract refers, if the lease contract is for a lease of goods that are not existing and identified; or
(c) when the young are conceived, if the lease contract is for a lease of unborn young of animals.

§ 2A–218. Insurance and Proceeds.

(1) A lessee obtains an insurable interest when existing goods are identified to the lease contract even though the goods identified are nonconforming and the lessee has an option to reject them.
(2) If a lessee has an insurable interest only by reason of the lessor's identification of the goods, the lessor, until default or insolvency or notification to the lessee that identification is final, may substitute other goods for those identified.
(3) Notwithstanding a lessee's insurable interest under subsections (1) and (2), the lessor retains an insurable interest until an option to buy has been exercised by the lessee and risk of loss has passed to the lessee.
(4) Nothing in this section impairs any insurable interest recognized under any other statute or rule of law.
(5) The parties by agreement may determine that one or more parties have an obligation to obtain and pay for insurance covering the goods and by agreement may determine the beneficiary of the proceeds of the insurance.

§ 2A–219. Risk of Loss.

(1) Except in the case of a finance lease, risk of loss is retained by the lessor and does not pass to the lessee. In the case of a finance lease, risk of loss passes to the lessee.
(2) Subject to the provisions of this Article on the effect of default on risk of loss (Section 2A–220), if risk of loss is to pass to the lessee and the time of passage is not stated, the following rules apply:

(a) If the lease contract requires or authorizes the goods to be shipped by carrier

(i) and it does not require delivery at a particular destination, the risk of loss passes to the lessee when the goods are duly delivered to the carrier; but
(ii) if it does require delivery at a particular destination and the goods are there duly tendered while in the possession of the carrier, the risk of loss passes to the lessee when the goods are there duly so tendered as to enable the lessee to take delivery.

(b) If the goods are held by a bailee to be delivered without being moved, the risk of loss passes to the lessee on acknowledgment by the bailee of the lessee's right to possession of the goods.
(c) In any case not within subsection (a) or (b), the risk of loss passes to the lessee on the lessee's receipt of the goods if the lessor, or, in the case of a finance lease, the supplier, is a merchant; otherwise the risk passes to the lessee on tender of delivery.

§ 2A–220. Effect of Default on Risk of Loss.

(1) Where risk of loss is to pass to the lessee and the time of passage is not stated:

(a) If a tender or delivery of goods so fails to conform to the lease contract as to give a right of rejection, the risk of their loss remains with the lessor, or, in the case of a finance lease, the supplier, until cure or acceptance.
(b) If the lessee rightfully revokes acceptance, he [or she], to the extent of any deficiency in his [or her] effective insurance coverage, may treat the risk of loss as having remained with the lessor from the beginning.

(2) Whether or not risk of loss is to pass to the lessee, if the lessee as to conforming goods already identified to a lease contract repudiates or is otherwise in default under the lease contract, the lessor, or, in the case of a finance lease, the supplier, to the extent of any deficiency in his [or her] effective insurance coverage may treat the risk of loss as resting on the lessee for a commercially reasonable time.

§ 2A–221. Casualty to Identified Goods.

If a lease contract requires goods identified when the lease contract is made, and the goods suffer casualty without fault of the lessee, the lessor or the supplier before delivery, or the goods suffer casualty before risk of loss passes to the lessee pursuant to the lease agreement or Section 2A–219, then:
(a) if the loss is total, the lease contract is avoided; and
(b) if the loss is partial or the goods have so deteriorated as to no longer conform to the lease contract, the lessee may nevertheless demand inspection and at his [or her] option either treat the lease contract as avoided or, except in a finance lease that is not a consumer lease, accept the goods with due allowance from the rent payable for the balance of the lease term for the deterioration or the deficiency in quantity but without further right against the lessor.

Part 3—Effect of Lease Contract

§ 2A–301. Enforceability of Lease Contract.

Except as otherwise provided in this Article, a lease contract is effective and enforceable according to its terms between the parties, against purchasers of the goods and against creditors of the parties.

§ 2A–302. Title to and Possession of Goods.

Except as otherwise provided in this Article, each provision of this Article applies whether the lessor or a third party has title to the goods, and whether the lessor, the lessee, or a third party has possession of the goods, notwithstanding any statute or rule of law that possession or the absence of possession is fraudulent.

§ 2A–303. Alienability of Party's Interest Under Lease Contract or of Lessor's Residual Interest in Goods; Delegation of Performance; Transfer of Rights.

(1) As used in this section, "creation of a security interest" includes the sale of a lease contract that is subject to Article 9, Secured Transactions, by reason of Section 9–109(a)(3).
(2) Except as provided in subsections (3) and Section 9–407, a provision in a lease agreement which (i) prohibits the voluntary or involuntary transfer, including a transfer by sale, sublease, creation or enforcement of a security interest, or attachment, levy, or other judicial process, of an interest of a party under the lease contract or of the lessor's residual interest in the goods, or (ii) makes such a transfer an event of default, gives rise to the rights and remedies provided in subsection (4),

but a transfer that is prohibited or is an event of default under the lease agreement is otherwise effective.

(3) A provision in a lease agreement which (i) prohibits a transfer of a right to damages for default with respect to the whole lease contract or of a right to payment arising out of the transferor's due performance of the transferor's entire obligation, or (ii) makes such a transfer an event of default, is not enforceable, and such a transfer is not a transfer that materially impairs the propsect of obtaining return performance by, materially changes the duty of, or materially increases the burden or risk imposed on, the other party to the lease contract within the purview of subsection (4).

(4) Subject to subsection (3) and Section 9–407:

(a) if a transfer is made which is made an event of default under a lease agreement, the party to the lease contract not making the transfer, unless that party waives the default or otherwise agrees, has the rights and remedies described in Section 2A–501(2);

(b) if paragraph (a) is not applicable and if a transfer is made that (i) is prohibited under a lease agreement or (ii) materially impairs the prospect of obtaining return performance by, materially changes the duty of, or materially increases the burden or risk imposed on, the other party to the lease contract, unless the party not making the transfer agrees at any time to the transfer in the lease contract or otherwise, then, except as limited by contract, (i) the transferor is liable to the party not making the transfer for damages caused by the transfer to the extent that the damages could not reasonably be prevented by the party not making the transfer and (ii) a court having jurisdiction may grant other appropriate relief, including cancellation of the lease contract or an injunction against the transfer.

(5) A transfer of "the lease" or of "all my rights under the lease", or a transfer in similar general terms, is a transfer of rights and, unless the language or the circumstances, as in a transfer for security, indicate the contrary, the transfer is a delegation of duties by the transferor to the transferee. Acceptance by the transferee constitutes a promise by the transferee to perform those duties. The promise is enforceable by either the transferor or the other party to the lease contract.

(6) Unless otherwise agreed by the lessor and the lessee, a delegation of performance does not relieve the transferor as against the other party of any duty to perform or of any liability for default.

(7) In a consumer lease, to prohibit the transfer of an interest of a party under the lease contract or to make a transfer an event of default, the language must be specific, by a writing, and conspicuous.

As amended in 1990 and 1999.

§ 2A–304. Subsequent Lease of Goods by Lessor.

(1) Subject to Section 2A–303, a subsequent lessee from a lessor of goods under an existing lease contract obtains, to the extent of the leasehold interest transferred, the leasehold interest in the goods that the lessor had or had power to transfer, and except as provided in subsection (2) and Section 2A–527(4), takes subject to the existing lease contract. A lessor with voidable title has power to transfer a good leasehold interest to a good faith subsequent lessee for value, but only to the extent set forth in the preceding sentence. If goods have been delivered under a transaction of purchase the lessor has that power even though:

(a) the lessor's transferor was deceived as to the identity of the lessor;

(b) the delivery was in exchange for a check which is later dishonored;

(c) it was agreed that the transaction was to be a "cash sale"; or

(d) the delivery was procured through fraud punishable as larcenous under the criminal law.

(2) A subsequent lessee in the ordinary course of business from a lessor who is a merchant dealing in goods of that kind to whom the goods were entrusted by the existing lessee of that lessor before the interest of the subsequent lessee became enforceable against that lessor obtains, to the extent of the leasehold interest transferred, all of that lessor's and the existing lessee's rights to the goods, and takes free of the existing lease contract.

(3) A subsequent lessee from the lessor of goods that are subject to an existing lease contract and are covered by a certificate of title issued under a statute of this State or of another jurisdiction takes no greater rights than those provided both by this section and by the certificate of title statute.

As amended in 1990.

§ 2A–305. Sale or Sublease of Goods by Lessee.

(1) Subject to the provisions of Section 2A–303, a buyer or sublessee from the lessee of goods under an existing lease contract obtains, to the extent of the interest transferred, the leasehold interest in the goods that the lessee had or had power to transfer, and except as provided in subsection (2) and Section 2A–511(4), takes subject to the existing lease contract. A lessee with a voidable leasehold interest has power to transfer a good leasehold interest to a good faith buyer for value or a good faith sublessee for value, but only to the extent set forth in the preceding sentence. When goods have been delivered under a transaction of lease the lessee has that power even though:

(a) the lessor was deceived as to the identity of the lessee;

(b) the delivery was in exchange for a check which is later dishonored; or

(c) the delivery was procured through fraud punishable as larcenous under the criminal law.

(2) A buyer in the ordinary course of business or a sublessee in the ordinary course of business from a lessee who is a merchant dealing in goods of that kind to whom the goods were entrusted by the lessor obtains, to the extent of the interest transferred, all of the lessor's and lessee's rights to the goods, and takes free of the existing lease contract.

(3) A buyer or sublessee from the lessee of goods that are subject to an existing lease contract and are covered by a certificate of title issued under a statute of this State or of another jurisdiction takes no greater rights than those provided both by this section and by the certificate of title statute.

§ 2A–306. Priority of Certain Liens Arising by Operation of Law.

If a person in the ordinary course of his [or her] business furnishes services or materials with respect to goods subject to a lease contract, a lien upon those goods in the possession of that person given by statute or rule of law for those materials or services takes priority over any interest of the lessor or lessee under the lease contract or this Article unless the lien is created by statute and the statute provides otherwise or unless the lien is created by rule of law and the rule of law provides otherwise.

§ 2A–307. Priority of Liens Arising by Attachment or Levy on, Security Interests in, and Other Claims to Goods.

(1) Except as otherwise provided in Section 2A–306, a creditor of a lessee takes subject to the lease contract.

(2) Except as otherwise provided in subsection (3) and in Sections 2A–306 and 2A–308, a creditor of a lessor takes subject to the lease contract unless the creditor holds a lien that attached to the goods before the lease contract became enforceable.

(3) Except as otherwise provided in Sections 9–317, 9–321, and 9–323, a lessee takes a leasehold interest subject to a security interest held by a creditor of the lessor.

As amended in 1990 and 1999.

§ 2A–308. Special Rights of Creditors.

(1) A creditor of a lessor in possession of goods subject to a lease contract may treat the lease contract as void if as against the creditor retention of possession by the lessor is fraudulent under any statute or rule of law, but retention of possession in good faith and current course of trade by the lessor for a commercially reasonable time after the lease contract becomes enforceable is not fraudulent.

(2) Nothing in this Article impairs the rights of creditors of a lessor if the lease contract (a) becomes enforceable, not in current course of trade but in satisfaction of or as security for a pre-existing claim for money, security, or the like, and (b) is made under circumstances which under any statute or rule of law apart from this Article would constitute the transaction a fraudulent transfer or voidable preference.

(3) A creditor of a seller may treat a sale or an identification of goods to a contract for sale as void if as against the creditor retention of possession by the seller is fraudulent under any statute or rule of law, but retention of possession of the goods pursuant to a lease contract entered into by the seller as lessee and the buyer as lessor in connection with the sale or identification of the goods is not fraudulent if the buyer bought for value and in good faith.

§ 2A–309. Lessor's and Lessee's Rights When Goods Become Fixtures.

(1) In this section:

(a) goods are "fixtures" when they become so related to particular real estate that an interest in them arises under real estate law;

(b) a "fixture filing" is the filing, in the office where a mortgage on the real estate would be filed or recorded, of a financing statement covering goods that are or are to become fixtures and conforming to the requirements of Section 9–502(a) and (b);

(c) a lease is a "purchase money lease" unless the lessee has possession or use of the goods or the right to possession or use of the goods before the lease agreement is enforceable;

(d) a mortgage is a "construction mortgage" to the extent it secures an obligation incurred for the construction of an improvement on land including the acquisition cost of the land, if the recorded writing so indicates; and

(e) "encumbrance" includes real estate mortgages and other liens on real estate and all other rights in real estate that are not ownership interests.

(2) Under this Article a lease may be of goods that are fixtures or may continue in goods that become fixtures, but no lease exists under this Article of ordinary building materials incorporated into an improvement on land.

(3) This Article does not prevent creation of a lease of fixtures pursuant to real estate law.

(4) The perfected interest of a lessor of fixtures has priority over a conflicting interest of an encumbrancer or owner of the real estate if:

(a) the lease is a purchase money lease, the conflicting interest of the encumbrancer or owner arises before the goods become fixtures, the interest of the lessor is perfected by a fixture filing before the goods become fixtures or within ten days thereafter, and the lessee has an interest of record in the real estate or is in possession of the real estate; or

(b) the interest of the lessor is perfected by a fixture filing before the interest of the encumbrancer or owner is of record, the lessor's interest has priority over any conflicting interest of a predecessor in title of the encumbrancer or owner, and the lessee has an interest of record in the real estate or is in possession of the real estate.

(5) The interest of a lessor of fixtures, whether or not perfected, has priority over the conflicting interest of an encumbrancer or owner of the real estate if:

(a) the fixtures are readily removable factory or office machines, readily removable equipment that is not primarily used or leased for use in the operation of the real estate, or readily removable replacements of domestic appliances that are goods subject to a consumer lease, and before the goods become fixtures the lease contract is enforceable; or

(b) the conflicting interest is a lien on the real estate obtained by legal or equitable proceedings after the lease contract is enforceable; or

(c) the encumbrancer or owner has consented in writing to the lease or has disclaimed an interest in the goods as fixtures; or

(d) the lessee has a right to remove the goods as against the encumbrancer or owner. If the lessee's right to remove terminates, the priority of the interest of the lessor continues for a reasonable time.

(6) Notwithstanding paragraph (4)(a) but otherwise subject to subsections (4) and (5), the interest of a lessor of fixtures, including the lessor's residual interest, is subordinate to the conflicting interest of an encumbrancer of the real estate under a construction mortgage recorded before the goods become fixtures if the goods become fixtures before the completion of the construction. To the extent given to refinance a construction mortgage, the conflicting interest of an encumbrancer of the real estate under a mortgage has this priority to the same extent as the encumbrancer of the real estate under the construction mortgage.

(7) In cases not within the preceding subsections, priority between the interest of a lessor of fixtures, including the lessor's residual interest, and the conflicting interest of an encumbrancer or owner of the real estate who is not the lessee is determined by the priority rules governing conflicting interests in real estate.
(8) If the interest of a lessor of fixtures, including the lessor's residual interest, has priority over all conflicting interests of all owners and encumbrancers of the real estate, the lessor or the lessee may (i) on default, expiration, termination, or cancellation of the lease agreement but subject to the agreement and this Article, or (ii) if necessary to enforce other rights and remedies of the lessor or lessee under this Article, remove the goods from the real estate, free and clear of all conflicting interests of all owners and encumbrancers of the real estate, but the lessor or lessee must reimburse any encumbrancer or owner of the real estate who is not the lessee and who has not otherwise agreed for the cost of repair of any physical injury, but not for any diminution in value of the real estate caused by the absence of the goods removed or by any necessity of replacing them. A person entitled to reimbursement may refuse permission to remove until the party seeking removal gives adequate security for the performance of this obligation.
(9) Even though the lease agreement does not create a security interest, the interest of a lessor of fixtures, including the lessor's residual interest, is perfected by filing a financing statement as a fixture filing for leased goods that are or are to become fixtures in accordance with the relevant provisions of the Article on Secured Transactions (Article 9).
As amended in 1990 and 1999.

§ 2A–310. Lessor's and Lessee's Rights When Goods Become Accessions.

(1) Goods are "accessions" when they are installed in or affixed to other goods.
(2) The interest of a lessor or a lessee under a lease contract entered into before the goods became accessions is superior to all interests in the whole except as stated in subsection (4).
(3) The interest of a lessor or a lessee under a lease contract entered into at the time or after the goods became accessions is superior to all subsequently acquired interests in the whole except as stated in subsection (4) but is subordinate to interests in the whole existing at the time the lease contract was made unless the holders of such interests in the whole have in writing consented to the lease or disclaimed an interest in the goods as part of the whole.
(4) The interest of a lessor or a lessee under a lease contract described in subsection (2) or (3) is subordinate to the interest of

(a) a buyer in the ordinary course of business or a lessee in the ordinary course of business of any interest in the whole acquired after the goods became accessions; or
(b) a creditor with a security interest in the whole perfected before the lease contract was made to the extent that the creditor makes subsequent advances without knowledge of the lease contract.

(5) When under subsections (2) or (3) and (4) a lessor or a lessee of accessions holds an interest that is superior to all interests in the whole, the lessor or the lessee may (a) on default, expiration, termination, or cancellation of the lease contract by the other party but subject to the provisions of the lease contract and this Article, or (b) if necessary to enforce his [or her] other rights and remedies under this Article, remove the goods from the whole, free and clear of all interests in the whole, but he [or she] must reimburse any holder of an interest in the whole who is not the lessee and who has not otherwise agreed for the cost of repair of any physical injury but not for any diminution in value of the whole caused by the absence of the goods removed or by any necessity for replacing them. A person entitled to reimbursement may refuse permission to remove until the party seeking removal gives adequate security for the performance of this obligation.

§ 2A–311. Priority Subject to Subordination.

Nothing in this Article prevents subordination by agreement by any person entitled to priority.
As added in 1990.

Part 4—Performance of Lease Contract: Repudiated, Substituted and Excused

§ 2A–401. Insecurity: Adequate Assurance of Performance.

(1) A lease contract imposes an obligation on each party that the other's expectation of receiving due performance will not be impaired.
(2) If reasonable grounds for insecurity arise with respect to the performance of either party, the insecure party may demand in writing adequate assurance of due performance. Until the insecure party receives that assurance, if commercially reasonable the insecure party may suspend any performance for which he [or she] has not already received the agreed return.
(3) A repudiation of the lease contract occurs if assurance of due performance adequate under the circumstances of the particular case is not provided to the insecure party within a reasonable time, not to exceed 30 days after receipt of a demand by the other party.
(4) Between merchants, the reasonableness of grounds for insecurity and the adequacy of any assurance offered must be determined according to commercial standards.
(5) Acceptance of any nonconforming delivery or payment does not prejudice the aggrieved party's right to demand adequate assurance of future performance.

§ 2A–402. Anticipatory Repudiation.

If either party repudiates a lease contract with respect to a performance not yet due under the lease contract, the loss of which performance will substantially impair the value of the lease contract to the other, the aggrieved party may:
(a) for a commercially reasonable time, await retraction of repudiation and performance by the repudiating party;
(b) make demand pursuant to Section 2A–401 and await assurance of future performance adequate under the circumstances of the particular case; or
(c) resort to any right or remedy upon default under the lease contract or this Article, even though the aggrieved party has notified the repudiating party that the aggrieved party would await the repudiating party's performance and assurance and has urged retraction. In addition, whether or not the aggrieved

party is pursuing one of the foregoing remedies, the aggrieved party may suspend performance or, if the aggrieved party is the lessor, proceed in accordance with the provisions of this Article on the lessor's right to identify goods to the lease contract notwithstanding default or to salvage unfinished goods (Section 2A–524).

§ 2A–403. Retraction of Anticipatory Repudiation.

(1) Until the repudiating party's next performance is due, the repudiating party can retract the repudiation unless, since the repudiation, the aggrieved party has cancelled the lease contract or materially changed the aggrieved party's position or otherwise indicated that the aggrieved party considers the repudiation final.

(2) Retraction may be by any method that clearly indicates to the aggrieved party that the repudiating party intends to perform under the lease contract and includes any assurance demanded under Section 2A–401.

(3) Retraction reinstates a repudiating party's rights under a lease contract with due excuse and allowance to the aggrieved party for any delay occasioned by the repudiation.

§ 2A–404. Substituted Performance.

(1) If without fault of the lessee, the lessor and the supplier, the agreed berthing, loading, or unloading facilities fail or the agreed type of carrier becomes unavailable or the agreed manner of delivery otherwise becomes commercially impracticable, but a commercially reasonable substitute is available, the substitute performance must be tendered and accepted.

(2) If the agreed means or manner of payment fails because of domestic or foreign governmental regulation:

(a) the lessor may withhold or stop delivery or cause the supplier to withhold or stop delivery unless the lessee provides a means or manner of payment that is commercially a substantial equivalent; and

(b) if delivery has already been taken, payment by the means or in the manner provided by the regulation discharges the lessee's obligation unless the regulation is discriminatory, oppressive, or predatory.

§ 2A–405. Excused Performance.

Subject to Section 2A–404 on substituted performance, the following rules apply:

(a) Delay in delivery or nondelivery in whole or in part by a lessor or a supplier who complies with paragraphs (b) and (c) is not a default under the lease contract if performance as agreed has been made impracticable by the occurrence of a contingency the nonoccurrence of which was a basic assumption on which the lease contract was made or by compliance in good faith with any applicable foreign or domestic governmental regulation or order, whether or not the regulation or order later proves to be invalid.

(b) If the causes mentioned in paragraph (a) affect only part of the lessor's or the supplier's capacity to perform, he [or she] shall allocate production and deliveries among his [or her] customers but at his [or her] option may include regular customers not then under contract for sale or lease as well as his [or her] own requirements for further manufacture. He [or she] may so allocate in any manner that is fair and reasonable.

(c) The lessor seasonably shall notify the lessee and in the case of a finance lease the supplier seasonably shall notify the lessor and the lessee, if known, that there will be delay or nondelivery and, if allocation is required under paragraph (b), of the estimated quota thus made available for the lessee.

§ 2A–406. Procedure on Excused Performance.

(1) If the lessee receives notification of a material or indefinite delay or an allocation justified under Section 2A–405, the lessee may by written notification to the lessor as to any goods involved, and with respect to all of the goods if under an installment lease contract the value of the whole lease contract is substantially impaired (Section 2A–510):

(a) terminate the lease contract (Section 2A–505(2)); or

(b) except in a finance lease that is not a consumer lease, modify the lease contract by accepting the available quota in substitution, with due allowance from the rent payable for the balance of the lease term for the deficiency but without further right against the lessor.

(2) If, after receipt of a notification from the lessor under Section 2A–405, the lessee fails so to modify the lease agreement within a reasonable time not exceeding 30 days, the lease contract lapses with respect to any deliveries affected.

§ 2A–407. Irrevocable Promises: Finance Leases.

(1) In the case of a finance lease that is not a consumer lease the lessee's promises under the lease contract become irrevocable and independent upon the lessee's acceptance of the goods.

(2) A promise that has become irrevocable and independent under subsection (1):

(a) is effective and enforceable between the parties, and by or against third parties including assignees of the parties, and

(b) is not subject to cancellation, termination, modification, repudiation, excuse, or substitution without the consent of the party to whom the promise runs.

(3) This section does not affect the validity under any other law of a covenant in any lease contract making the lessee's promises irrevocable and independent upon the lessee's acceptance of the goods.

As amended in 1990.

Part 5—Default

A. In General

§ 2A–501. Default: Procedure.

(1) Whether the lessor or the lessee is in default under a lease contract is determined by the lease agreement and this Article.

(2) If the lessor or the lessee is in default under the lease contract, the party seeking enforcement has rights and remedies as provided in this Article and, except as limited by this Article, as provided in the lease agreement.

(3) If the lessor or the lessee is in default under the lease contract, the party seeking enforcement may reduce the party's claim to judgment, or otherwise enforce the lease contract by self-help or any available judicial procedure or nonjudicial procedure, including administrative proceeding, arbitration, or the like, in accordance with this Article.

(4) Except as otherwise provided in Section 1–106(1) or this Article or the lease agreement, the rights and remedies referred to in subsections (2) and (3) are cumulative.
(5) If the lease agreement covers both real property and goods, the party seeking enforcement may proceed under this Part as to the goods, or under other applicable law as to both the real property and the goods in accordance with that party's rights and remedies in respect of the real property, in which case this Part does not apply.
As amended in 1990.

§ 2A–502. Notice After Default.

Except as otherwise provided in this Article or the lease agreement, the lessor or lessee in default under the lease contract is not entitled to notice of default or notice of enforcement from the other party to the lease agreement.

§ 2A–503. Modification or Impairment of Rights and Remedies.

(1) Except as otherwise provided in this Article, the lease agreement may include rights and remedies for default in addition to or in substitution for those provided in this Article and may limit or alter the measure of damages recoverable under this Article.
(2) Resort to a remedy provided under this Article or in the lease agreement is optional unless the remedy is expressly agreed to be exclusive. If circumstances cause an exclusive or limited remedy to fail of its essential purpose, or provision for an exclusive remedy is unconscionable, remedy may be had as provided in this Article.
(3) Consequential damages may be liquidated under Section 2A–504, or may otherwise be limited, altered, or excluded unless the limitation, alteration, or exclusion is unconscionable. Limitation, alteration, or exclusion of consequential damages for injury to the person in the case of consumer goods is *prima facie* unconscionable but limitation, alteration, or exclusion of damages where the loss is commercial is not *prima facie* unconscionable.
(4) Rights and remedies on default by the lessor or the lessee with respect to any obligation or promise collateral or ancillary to the lease contract are not impaired by this Article.
As amended in 1990.

§ 2A–504. Liquidation of Damages.

(1) Damages payable by either party for default, or any other act or omission, including indemnity for loss or diminution of anticipated tax benefits or loss or damage to lessor's residual interest, may be liquidated in the lease agreement but only at an amount or by a formula that is reasonable in light of the then anticipated harm caused by the default or other act or omission.
(2) If the lease agreement provides for liquidation of damages, and such provision does not comply with subsection (1), or such provision is an exclusive or limited remedy that circumstances cause to fail of its essential purpose, remedy may be had as provided in this Article.
(3) If the lessor justifiably withholds or stops delivery of goods because of the lessee's default or insolvency (Section 2A–525 or 2A–526), the lessee is entitled to restitution of any amount by which the sum of his [or her] payments exceeds:

(a) the amount to which the lessor is entitled by virtue of terms liquidating the lessor's damages in accordance with subsection (1); or
(b) in the absence of those terms, 20 percent of the then present value of the total rent the lessee was obligated to pay for the balance of the lease term, or, in the case of a consumer lease, the lesser of such amount or $500.

(4) A lessee's right to restitution under subsection (3) is subject to offset to the extent the lessor establishes:

(a) a right to recover damages under the provisions of this Article other than subsection (1); and
(b) the amount or value of any benefits received by the lessee directly or indirectly by reason of the lease contract.

§ 2A–505. Cancellation and Termination and Effect of Cancellation, Termination, Rescission, or Fraud on Rights and Remedies.

(1) On cancellation of the lease contract, all obligations that are still executory on both sides are discharged, but any right based on prior default or performance survives, and the cancelling party also retains any remedy for default of the whole lease contract or any unperformed balance.
(2) On termination of the lease contract, all obligations that are still executory on both sides are discharged but any right based on prior default or performance survives.
(3) Unless the contrary intention clearly appears, expressions of "cancellation," "rescission," or the like of the lease contract may not be construed as a renunciation or discharge of any claim in damages for an antecedent default.
(4) Rights and remedies for material misrepresentation or fraud include all rights and remedies available under this Article for default.
(5) Neither rescission nor a claim for rescission of the lease contract nor rejection or return of the goods may bar or be deemed inconsistent with a claim for damages or other right or remedy.

§ 2A–506. Statute of Limitations.

(1) An action for default under a lease contract, including breach of warranty or indemnity, must be commenced within 4 years after the cause of action accrued. By the original lease contract the parties may reduce the period of limitation to not less than one year.
(2) A cause of action for default accrues when the act or omission on which the default or breach of warranty is based is or should have been discovered by the aggrieved party, or when the default occurs, whichever is later. A cause of action for indemnity accrues when the act or omission on which the claim for indemnity is based is or should have been discovered by the indemnified party, whichever is later.
(3) If an action commenced within the time limited by subsection (1) is so terminated as to leave available a remedy by another action for the same default or breach of warranty or indemnity, the other action may be commenced after the expiration of the time limited and within 6 months after the termination of the first action unless the termination resulted from voluntary discontinuance or from dismissal for failure or neglect to prosecute.
(4) This section does not alter the law on tolling of the statute of limitations nor does it apply to causes of action that have accrued before this Article becomes effective.

§ 2A–507. Proof of Market Rent: Time and Place.

(1) Damages based on market rent (Section 2A–519 or 2A–528) are determined according to the rent for the use of the goods concerned for a lease term identical to the remaining lease term of the original lease agreement and prevailing at the times specified in Sections 2A–519 and 2A–528.

(2) If evidence of rent for the use of the goods concerned for a lease term identical to the remaining lease term of the original lease agreement and prevailing at the times or places described in this Article is not readily available, the rent prevailing within any reasonable time before or after the time described or at any other place or for a different lease term which in commercial judgment or under usage of trade would serve as a reasonable substitute for the one described may be used, making any proper allowance for the difference, including the cost of transporting the goods to or from the other place.

(3) Evidence of a relevant rent prevailing at a time or place or for a lease term other than the one described in this Article offered by one party is not admissible unless and until he [or she] has given the other party notice the court finds sufficient to prevent unfair surprise.

(4) If the prevailing rent or value of any goods regularly leased in any established market is in issue, reports in official publications or trade journals or in newspapers or periodicals of general circulation published as the reports of that market are admissible in evidence. The circumstances of the preparation of the report may be shown to affect its weight but not its admissibility.

As amended in 1990.

B. Default by Lessor

§ 2A–508. Lessee's Remedies.

(1) If a lessor fails to deliver the goods in conformity to the lease contract (Section 2A–509) or repudiates the lease contract (Section 2A–402), or a lessee rightfully rejects the goods (Section 2A–509) or justifiably revokes acceptance of the goods (Section 2A–517), then with respect to any goods involved, and with respect to all of the goods if under an installment lease contract the value of the whole lease contract is substantially impaired (Section 2A–510), the lessor is in default under the lease contract and the lessee may:

- **(a)** cancel the lease contract (Section 2A–505(1));
- **(b)** recover so much of the rent and security as has been paid and is just under the circumstances;
- **(c)** cover and recover damages as to all goods affected whether or not they have been identified to the lease contract (Sections 2A–518 and 2A–520), or recover damages for nondelivery (Sections 2A–519 and 2A–520);
- **(d)** exercise any other rights or pursue any other remedies provided in the lease contract.

(2) If a lessor fails to deliver the goods in conformity to the lease contract or repudiates the lease contract, the lessee may also:

- **(a)** if the goods have been identified, recover them (Section 2A–522); or
- **(b)** in a proper case, obtain specific performance or replevy the goods (Section 2A–521).

(3) If a lessor is otherwise in default under a lease contract, the lessee may exercise the rights and pursue the remedies provided in the lease contract, which may include a right to cancel the lease, and in Section 2A–519(3).

(4) If a lessor has breached a warranty, whether express or implied, the lessee may recover damages (Section 2A–519(4)).

(5) On rightful rejection or justifiable revocation of acceptance, a lessee has a security interest in goods in the lessee's possession or control for any rent and security that has been paid and any expenses reasonably incurred in their inspection, receipt, transportation, and care and custody and may hold those goods and dispose of them in good faith and in a commercially reasonable manner, subject to Section 2A–527(5).

(6) Subject to the provisions of Section 2A–407, a lessee, on notifying the lessor of the lessee's intention to do so, may deduct all or any part of the damages resulting from any default under the lease contract from any part of the rent still due under the same lease contract.

As amended in 1990.

§ 2A–509. Lessee's Rights on Improper Delivery; Rightful Rejection.

(1) Subject to the provisions of Section 2A–510 on default in installment lease contracts, if the goods or the tender or delivery fail in any respect to conform to the lease contract, the lessee may reject or accept the goods or accept any commercial unit or units and reject the rest of the goods.

(2) Rejection of goods is ineffective unless it is within a reasonable time after tender or delivery of the goods and the lessee seasonably notifies the lessor.

§ 2A–510. Installment Lease Contracts: Rejection and Default.

(1) Under an installment lease contract a lessee may reject any delivery that is nonconforming if the nonconformity substantially impairs the value of that delivery and cannot be cured or the nonconformity is a defect in the required documents; but if the nonconformity does not fall within subsection (2) and the lessor or the supplier gives adequate assurance of its cure, the lessee must accept that delivery.

(2) Whenever nonconformity or default with respect to one or more deliveries substantially impairs the value of the installment lease contract as a whole there is a default with respect to the whole. But, the aggrieved party reinstates the installment lease contract as a whole if the aggrieved party accepts a nonconforming delivery without seasonably notifying of cancellation or brings an action with respect only to past deliveries or demands performance as to future deliveries.

§ 2A–511. Merchant Lessee's Duties as to Rightfully Rejected Goods.

(1) Subject to any security interest of a lessee (Section 2A–508(5)), if a lessor or a supplier has no agent or place of business at the market of rejection, a merchant lessee, after rejection of goods in his [or her] possession or control, shall follow any reasonable instructions received from the lessor or the supplier with respect to the goods. In the absence of those instructions, a merchant lessee shall make reasonable efforts to sell, lease, or otherwise dispose of the goods for the lessor's account if they threaten to decline in value speedily. Instructions are not reasonable if on demand indemnity for expenses is not forthcoming.

(2) If a merchant lessee (subsection (1)) or any other lessee (Section 2A–512) disposes of goods, he [or she] is entitled to reimbursement either from the lessor or the supplier or out of the proceeds for reasonable expenses of caring for and disposing of the goods and, if the expenses include no disposition commission, to such commission as is usual in the trade, or if there is none, to a reasonable sum not exceeding 10 percent of the gross proceeds.
(3) In complying with this section or Section 2A–512, the lessee is held only to good faith. Good faith conduct hereunder is neither acceptance or conversion nor the basis of an action for damages.
(4) A purchaser who purchases in good faith from a lessee pursuant to this section or Section 2A–512 takes the goods free of any rights of the lessor and the supplier even though the lessee fails to comply with one or more of the requirements of this Article.

§ 2A–512. Lessee's Duties as to Rightfully Rejected Goods.

(1) Except as otherwise provided with respect to goods that threaten to decline in value speedily (Section 2A–511) and subject to any security interest of a lessee (Section 2A–508(5)):

(a) the lessee, after rejection of goods in the lessee's possession, shall hold them with reasonable care at the lessor's or the supplier's disposition for a reasonable time after the lessee's seasonable notification of rejection;
(b) if the lessor or the supplier gives no instructions within a reasonable time after notification of rejection, the lessee may store the rejected goods for the lessor's or the supplier's account or ship them to the lessor or the supplier or dispose of them for the lessor's or the supplier's account with reimbursement in the manner provided in Section 2A–511; but
(c) the lessee has no further obligations with regard to goods rightfully rejected.

(2) Action by the lessee pursuant to subsection (1) is not acceptance or conversion.

§ 2A–513. Cure by Lessor of Improper Tender or Delivery; Replacement.

(1) If any tender or delivery by the lessor or the supplier is rejected because nonconforming and the time for performance has not yet expired, the lessor or the supplier may seasonably notify the lessee of the lessor's or the supplier's intention to cure and may then make a conforming delivery within the time provided in the lease contract.
(2) If the lessee rejects a nonconforming tender that the lessor or the supplier had reasonable grounds to believe would be acceptable with or without money allowance, the lessor or the supplier may have a further reasonable time to substitute a conforming tender if he [or she] seasonably notifies the lessee.

§ 2A–514. Waiver of Lessee's Objections.

(1) In rejecting goods, a lessee's failure to state a particular defect that is ascertainable by reasonable inspection precludes the lessee from relying on the defect to justify rejection or to establish default:

(a) if, stated seasonably, the lessor or the supplier could have cured it (Section 2A–513); or
(b) between merchants if the lessor or the supplier after rejection has made a request in writing for a full and final written statement of all defects on which the lessee proposes to rely.

(2) A lessee's failure to reserve rights when paying rent or other consideration against documents precludes recovery of the payment for defects apparent on the face of the documents.

§ 2A–515. Acceptance of Goods.

(1) Acceptance of goods occurs after the lessee has had a reasonable opportunity to inspect the goods and

(a) the lessee signifies or acts with respect to the goods in a manner that signifies to the lessor or the supplier that the goods are conforming or that the lessee will take or retain them in spite of their nonconformity; or
(b) the lessee fails to make an effective rejection of the goods (Section 2A–509(2)).

(2) Acceptance of a part of any commercial unit is acceptance of that entire unit.

§ 2A–516. Effect of Acceptance of Goods; Notice of Default; Burden of Establishing Default after Acceptance; Notice of Claim or Litigation to Person Answerable Over.

(1) A lessee must pay rent for any goods accepted in accordance with the lease contract, with due allowance for goods rightfully rejected or not delivered.
(2) A lessee's acceptance of goods precludes rejection of the goods accepted. In the case of a finance lease, if made with knowledge of a nonconformity, acceptance cannot be revoked because of it. In any other case, if made with knowledge of a nonconformity, acceptance cannot be revoked because of it unless the acceptance was on the reasonable assumption that the nonconformity would be seasonably cured. Acceptance does not of itself impair any other remedy provided by this Article or the lease agreement for nonconformity.
(3) If a tender has been accepted:

(a) within a reasonable time after the lessee discovers or should have discovered any default, the lessee shall notify the lessor and the supplier, if any, or be barred from any remedy against the party notified;
(b) except in the case of a consumer lease, within a reasonable time after the lessee receives notice of litigation for infringement or the like (Section 2A–211) the lessee shall notify the lessor or be barred from any remedy over for liability established by the litigation; and
(c) the burden is on the lessee to establish any default.

(4) If a lessee is sued for breach of a warranty or other obligation for which a lessor or a supplier is answerable over the following apply:

(a) The lessee may give the lessor or the supplier, or both, written notice of the litigation. If the notice states that the person notified may come in and defend and that if the person notified does not do so that person will be bound in any action against that person by the lessee by any determination of fact common to the two litigations, then unless the person notified after seasonable receipt of the notice does come in and defend that person is so bound.

(b) The lessor or the supplier may demand in writing that the lessee turn over control of the litigation including settlement if the claim is one for infringement or the like (Section 2A–211) or else be barred from any remedy over. If the demand states that the lessor or the supplier agrees to bear all expense and to satisfy any adverse judgment, then unless the lessee after seasonable receipt of the demand does turn over control the lessee is so barred.

(5) Subsections (3) and (4) apply to any obligation of a lessee to hold the lessor or the supplier harmless against infringement or the like (Section 2A–211).
As amended in 1990.

§ 2A–517. Revocation of Acceptance of Goods.

(1) A lessee may revoke acceptance of a lot or commercial unit whose nonconformity substantially impairs its value to the lessee if the lessee has accepted it:

(a) except in the case of a finance lease, on the reasonable assumption that its nonconformity would be cured and it has not been seasonably cured; or

(b) without discovery of the nonconformity if the lessee's acceptance was reasonably induced either by the lessor's assurances or, except in the case of a finance lease, by the difficulty of discovery before acceptance.

(2) Except in the case of a finance lease that is not a consumer lease, a lessee may revoke acceptance of a lot or commercial unit if the lessor defaults under the lease contract and the default substantially impairs the value of that lot or commercial unit to the lessee.

(3) If the lease agreement so provides, the lessee may revoke acceptance of a lot or commercial unit because of other defaults by the lessor.

(4) Revocation of acceptance must occur within a reasonable time after the lessee discovers or should have discovered the ground for it and before any substantial change in condition of the goods which is not caused by the nonconformity. Revocation is not effective until the lessee notifies the lessor.

(5) A lessee who so revokes has the same rights and duties with regard to the goods involved as if the lessee had rejected them.
As amended in 1990.

§ 2A–518. Cover; Substitute Goods.

(1) After a default by a lessor under the lease contract of the type described in Section 2A–508(1), or, if agreed, after other default by the lessor, the lessee may cover by making any purchase or lease of or contract to purchase or lease goods in substitution for those due from the lessor.

(2) Except as otherwise provided with respect to damages liquidated in the lease agreement (Section 2A–504) or otherwise determined pursuant to agreement of the parties (Sections 1–102(3) and 2A–503), if a lessee's cover is by lease agreement substantially similar to the original lease agreement and the new lease agreement is made in good faith and in a commercially reasonable manner, the lessee may recover from the lessor as damages (i) the present value, as of the date of the commencement of the term of the new lease agreement, of the rent under the new lease agreement applicable to that period of the new lease term which is comparable to the then remaining term of the original lease agreement minus the present value as of the same date of the total rent for the then remaining lease term of the original lease agreement, and (ii) any incidental or consequential damages, less expenses saved in consequence of the lessor's default.

(3) If a lessee's cover is by lease agreement that for any reason does not qualify for treatment under subsection (2), or is by purchase or otherwise, the lessee may recover from the lessor as if the lessee had elected not to cover and Section 2A–519 governs.
As amended in 1990.

§ 2A–519. Lessee's Damages for Non-Delivery, Repudiation, Default, and Breach of Warranty in Regard to Accepted Goods.

(1) Except as otherwise provided with respect to damages liquidated in the lease agreement (Section 2A–504) or otherwise determined pursuant to agreement of the parties (Sections 1–102(3) and 2A–503), if a lessee elects not to cover or a lessee elects to cover and the cover is by lease agreement that for any reason does not qualify for treatment under Section 2A–518(2), or is by purchase or otherwise, the measure of damages for non-delivery or repudiation by the lessor or for rejection or revocation of acceptance by the lessee is the present value, as of the date of the default, of the then market rent minus the present value as of the same date of the original rent, computed for the remaining lease term of the original lease agreement, together with incidental and consequential damages, less expenses saved in consequence of the lessor's default.

(2) Market rent is to be determined as of the place for tender or, in cases of rejection after arrival or revocation of acceptance, as of the place of arrival.

(3) Except as otherwise agreed, if the lessee has accepted goods and given notification (Section 2A–516(3)), the measure of damages for non-conforming tender or delivery or other default by a lessor is the loss resulting in the ordinary course of events from the lessor's default as determined in any manner that is reasonable together with incidental and consequential damages, less expenses saved in consequence of the lessor's default.

(4) Except as otherwise agreed, the measure of damages for breach of warranty is the present value at the time and place of acceptance of the difference between the value of the use of the goods accepted and the value if they had been as warranted for the lease term, unless special circumstances show proximate damages of a different amount, together with incidental and consequential damages, less expenses saved in consequence of the lessor's default or breach of warranty.
As amended in 1990.

§ 2A–520. Lessee's Incidental and Consequential Damages.

(1) Incidental damages resulting from a lessor's default include expenses reasonably incurred in inspection, receipt, transportation, and care and custody of goods rightfully rejected or goods the acceptance of which is justifiably revoked, any commercially reasonable charges, expenses or commissions in connection with effecting cover, and any other reasonable expense incident to the default.

(2) Consequential damages resulting from a lessor's default include:

(a) any loss resulting from general or particular requirements and needs of which the lessor at the time of contracting had reason to know and which could not reasonably be prevented by cover or otherwise; and

(b) injury to person or property proximately resulting from any breach of warranty.

§ 2A–521. Lessee's Right to Specific Performance or Replevin.

(1) Specific performance may be decreed if the goods are unique or in other proper circumstances.

(2) A decree for specific performance may include any terms and conditions as to payment of the rent, damages, or other relief that the court deems just.

(3) A lessee has a right of replevin, detinue, sequestration, claim and delivery, or the like for goods identified to the lease contract if after reasonable effort the lessee is unable to effect cover for those goods or the circumstances reasonably indicate that the effort will be unavailing.

§ 2A–522. Lessee's Right to Goods on Lessor's Insolvency.

(1) Subject to subsection (2) and even though the goods have not been shipped, a lessee who has paid a part or all of the rent and security for goods identified to a lease contract (Section 2A–217) on making and keeping good a tender of any unpaid portion of the rent and security due under the lease contract may recover the goods identified from the lessor if the lessor becomes insolvent within 10 days after receipt of the first installment of rent and security.

(2) A lessee acquires the right to recover goods identified to a lease contract only if they conform to the lease contract.

C. Default by Lessee

§ 2A–523. Lessor's Remedies.

(1) If a lessee wrongfully rejects or revokes acceptance of goods or fails to make a payment when due or repudiates with respect to a part or the whole, then, with respect to any goods involved, and with respect to all of the goods if under an installment lease contract the value of the whole lease contract is substantially impaired (Section 2A–510), the lessee is in default under the lease contract and the lessor may:

(a) cancel the lease contract (Section 2A–505(1));

(b) proceed respecting goods not identified to the lease contract (Section 2A–524);

(c) withhold delivery of the goods and take possession of goods previously delivered (Section 2A–525);

(d) stop delivery of the goods by any bailee (Section 2A–526);

(e) dispose of the goods and recover damages (Section 2A–527), or retain the goods and recover damages (Section 2A–528), or in a proper case recover rent (Section 2A–529)

(f) exercise any other rights or pursue any other remedies provided in the lease contract.

(2) If a lessor does not fully exercise a right or obtain a remedy to which the lessor is entitled under subsection (1), the lessor may recover the loss resulting in the ordinary course of events from the lessee's default as determined in any reasonable manner, together with incidental damages, less expenses saved in consequence of the lessee's default.

(3) If a lessee is otherwise in default under a lease contract, the lessor may exercise the rights and pursue the remedies provided in the lease contract, which may include a right to cancel the lease. In addition, unless otherwise provided in the lease contract:

(a) if the default substantially impairs the value of the lease contract to the lessor, the lessor may exercise the rights and pursue the remedies provided in subsections (1) or (2); or

(b) if the default does not substantially impair the value of the lease contract to the lessor, the lessor may recover as provided in subsection (2).

As amended in 1990.

§ 2A–524. Lessor's Right to Identify Goods to Lease Contract.

(1) After default by the lessee under the lease contract of the type described in Section 2A–523(1) or 2A–523(3)(a) or, if agreed, after other default by the lessee, the lessor may:

(a) identify to the lease contract conforming goods not already identified if at the time the lessor learned of the default they were in the lessor's or the supplier's possession or control; and

(b) dispose of goods (Section 2A–527(1)) that demonstrably have been intended for the particular lease contract even though those goods are unfinished.

(2) If the goods are unfinished, in the exercise of reasonable commercial judgment for the purposes of avoiding loss and of effective realization, an aggrieved lessor or the supplier may either complete manufacture and wholly identify the goods to the lease contract or cease manufacture and lease, sell, or otherwise dispose of the goods for scrap or salvage value or proceed in any other reasonable manner.

As amended in 1990.

§ 2A–525. Lessor's Right to Possession of Goods.

(1) If a lessor discovers the lessee to be insolvent, the lessor may refuse to deliver the goods.

(2) After a default by the lessee under the lease contract of the type described in Section 2A–523(1) or 2A–523(3)(a) or, if agreed, after other default by the lessee, the lessor has the right to take possession of the goods. If the lease contract so provides, the lessor may require the lessee to assemble the goods and make them available to the lessor at a place to be designated by the lessor which is reasonably convenient to both parties. Without removal, the lessor may render unusable any goods employed in trade or business, and may dispose of goods on the lessee's premises (Section 2A–527).

(3) The lessor may proceed under subsection (2) without judicial process if that can be done without breach of the peace or the lessor may proceed by action.

As amended in 1990.

§ 2A–526. Lessor's Stoppage of Delivery in Transit or Otherwise.

(1) A lessor may stop delivery of goods in the possession of a carrier or other bailee if the lessor discovers the lessee to be insolvent and may stop delivery of carload, truckload, planeload, or larger shipments of express or freight if the lessee repudiates or fails to make a payment due before delivery, whether for rent, security or otherwise under the lease contract, or for any other reason the lessor has a right to withhold or take possession of the goods.

(2) In pursuing its remedies under subsection (1), the lessor may stop delivery until

(a) receipt of the goods by the lessee;

(b) acknowledgment to the lessee by any bailee of the goods, except a carrier, that the bailee holds the goods for the lessee; or

(c) such an acknowledgment to the lessee by a carrier via reshipment or as warehouseman.

(3) **(a)** To stop delivery, a lessor shall so notify as to enable the bailee by reasonable diligence to prevent delivery of the goods.

(b) After notification, the bailee shall hold and deliver the goods according to the directions of the lessor, but the lessor is liable to the bailee for any ensuing charges or damages.

(c) A carrier who has issued a nonnegotiable bill of lading is not obliged to obey a notification to stop received from a person other than the consignor.

§ 2A–527. Lessor's Rights to Dispose of Goods.

(1) After a default by a lessee under the lease contract of the type described in Section 2A–523(1) or 2A–523(3)(a) or after the lessor refuses to deliver or takes possession of goods (Section 2A–525 or 2A–526), or, if agreed, after other default by a lessee, the lessor may dispose of the goods concerned or the undelivered balance thereof by lease, sale, or otherwise.

(2) Except as otherwise provided with respect to damages liquidated in the lease agreement (Section 2A–504) or otherwise determined pursuant to agreement of the parties (Sections 1–102(3) and 2A–503), if the disposition is by lease agreement substantially similar to the original lease agreement and the new lease agreement is made in good faith and in a commercially reasonable manner, the lessor may recover from the lessee as damages (i) accrued and unpaid rent as of the date of the commencement of the term of the new lease agreement, (ii) the present value, as of the same date, of the total rent for the then remaining lease term of the original lease agreement minus the present value, as of the same date, of the rent under the new lease agreement applicable to that period of the new lease term which is comparable to the then remaining term of the original lease agreement, and (iii) any incidental damages allowed under Section 2A–530, less expenses saved in consequence of the lessee's default.

(3) If the lessor's disposition is by lease agreement that for any reason does not qualify for treatment under subsection (2), or is by sale or otherwise, the lessor may recover from the lessee as if the lessor had elected not to dispose of the goods and Section 2A–528 governs.

(4) A subsequent buyer or lessee who buys or leases from the lessor in good faith for value as a result of a disposition under this section takes the goods free of the original lease contract and any rights of the original lessee even though the lessor fails to comply with one or more of the requirements of this Article.

(5) The lessor is not accountable to the lessee for any profit made on any disposition. A lessee who has rightfully rejected or justifiably revoked acceptance shall account to the lessor for any excess over the amount of the lessee's security interest (Section 2A–508(5)).

As amended in 1990.

§ 2A–528. Lessor's Damages for Non-acceptance, Failure to Pay, Repudiation, or Other Default.

(1) Except as otherwise provided with respect to damages liquidated in the lease agreement (Section 2A–504) or otherwise determined pursuant to agreement of the parties (Section 1–102(3) and 2A–503), if a lessor elects to retain the goods or a lessor elects to dispose of the goods and the disposition is by lease agreement that for any reason does not qualify for treatment under Section 2A–527(2), or is by sale or otherwise, the lessor may recover from the lessee as damages for a default of the type described in Section 2A–523(1) or 2A–523(3)(a), or if agreed, for other default of the lessee, (i) accrued and unpaid rent as of the date of the default if the lessee has never taken possession of the goods, or, if the lessee has taken possession of the goods, as of the date the lessor repossesses the goods or an earlier date on which the lessee makes a tender of the goods to the lessor, (ii) the present value as of the date determined under clause (i) of the total rent for the then remaining lease term of the original lease agreement minus the present value as of the same date of the market rent as the place where the goods are located computed for the same lease term, and (iii) any incidental damages allowed under Section 2A–530, less expenses saved in consequence of the lessee's default.

(2) If the measure of damages provided in subsection (1) is inadequate to put a lessor in as good a position as performance would have, the measure of damages is the present value of the profit, including reasonable overhead, the lessor would have made from full performance by the lessee, together with any incidental damages allowed under Section 2A–530, due allowance for costs reasonably incurred and due credit for payments or proceeds of disposition.

As amended in 1990.

§ 2A–529. Lessor's Action for the Rent.

(1) After default by the lessee under the lease contract of the type described in Section 2A–523(1) or 2A–523(3)(a) or, if agreed, after other default by the lessee, if the lessor complies with subsection (2), the lessor may recover from the lessee as damages:

(a) for goods accepted by the lessee and not repossessed by or tendered to the lessor, and for conforming goods lost or damaged within a commercially reasonable time after risk of loss passes to the lessee (Section 2A–219), (i) accrued and unpaid rent as of the date of entry of judgment in favor of the lessor (ii) the present value as of the same date of the rent for the then remaining lease term of the lease agreement, and (iii) any incidental damages allowed under Section 2A–530, less expenses saved in consequence of the lessee's default; and

(b) for goods identified to the lease contract if the lessor is unable after reasonable effort to dispose of them at a reasonable price or the circumstances reasonably indicate that effort will be unavailing, (i) accrued and unpaid rent as of the date of entry of judgment in favor of the lessor, (ii) the present value as of the same date of the rent for the then remaining lease term of the lease agreement, and (iii) any incidental damages allowed under Section 2A–530, less expenses saved in consequence of the lessee's default.

(2) Except as provided in subsection (3), the lessor shall hold for the lessee for the remaining lease term of the lease agreement any goods that have been identified to the lease contract and are in the lessor's control.

(3) The lessor may dispose of the goods at any time before collection of the judgment for damages obtained pursuant to subsection (1). If the disposition is before the end of the remaining lease term of the lease agreement, the lessor's recovery against the lessee for damages is governed by Section 2A–527 or Section 2A–528, and the lessor will cause an appropriate credit to be provided against a judgment for damages to the extent that the amount of the judgment exceeds the recovery available pursuant to Section 2A–527 or 2A–528.

(4) Payment of the judgment for damages obtained pursuant to subsection (1) entitles the lessee to the use and possession of the goods not then disposed of for the remaining lease term of and in accordance with the lease agreement.

(5) After default by the lessee under the lease contract of the type described in Section 2A–523(1) or Section 2A–523(3)(a) or, if agreed, after other default by the lessee, a lessor who is held not entitled to rent under this section must nevertheless be awarded damages for non-acceptance under Sections 2A–527 and 2A–528.

As amended in 1990.

§ 2A–530. Lessor's Incidental Damages.

Incidental damages to an aggrieved lessor include any commercially reasonable charges, expenses, or commissions incurred in stopping delivery, in the transportation, care and custody of goods after the lessee's default, in connection with return or disposition of the goods, or otherwise resulting from the default.

§ 2A–531. Standing to Sue Third Parties for Injury to Goods.

(1) If a third party so deals with goods that have been identified to a lease contract as to cause actionable injury to a party to the lease contract (a) the lessor has a right of action against the third party, and (b) the lessee also has a right of action against the third party if the lessee:

(i) has a security interest in the goods;

(ii) has an insurable interest in the goods; or

(iii) bears the risk of loss under the lease contract or has since the injury assumed that risk as against the lessor and the goods have been converted or destroyed.

(2) If at the time of the injury the party plaintiff did not bear the risk of loss as against the other party to the lease contract and there is no arrangement between them for disposition of the recovery, his [or her] suit or settlement, subject to his [or her] own interest, is as a fiduciary for the other party to the lease contract.

(3) Either party with the consent of the other may sue for the benefit of whom it may concern.

§ 2A–532. Lessor's Rights to Residual Interest.

In addition to any other recovery permitted by this Article or other law, the lessor may recover from the lessee an amount that will fully compensate the lessor for any loss of or damage to the lessor's residual interest in the goods caused by the default of the lessee.

As added in 1990.

THE SARBANES-OXLEY ACT (EXCERPTS AND EXPLANATORY COMMENTS)

Note: The author's explanatory comments appear in italics following the excerpt from each section.

SECTION 302
Corporate responsibility for financial reports[1]

(a) Regulations required

The Commission shall, by rule, require, for each company filing periodic reports under section 13(a) or 15(d) of the Securities Exchange Act of 1934 (15 U.S.C. 78m, 78o(d)), that the principal executive officer or officers and the principal financial officer or officers, or persons performing similar functions, certify in each annual or quarterly report filed or submitted under either such section of such Act that—

(1) the signing officer has reviewed the report;

(2) based on the officer's knowledge, the report does not contain any untrue statement of a material fact or omit to state a material fact necessary in order to make the statements made, in light of the circumstances under which such statements were made, not misleading;

(3) based on such officer's knowledge, the financial statements, and other financial information included in the report, fairly present in all material respects the financial condition and results of operations of the issuer as of, and for, the periods presented in the report;

(4) the signing officers—

(A) are responsible for establishing and maintaining internal controls;

(B) have designed such internal controls to ensure that material information relating to the issuer and its consolidated subsidiaries is made known to such officers by others within those entities, particularly during the period in which the periodic reports are being prepared;

(C) have evaluated the effectiveness of the issuer's internal controls as of a date within 90 days prior to the report; and

(D) have presented in the report their conclusions about the effectiveness of their internal controls based on their evaluation as of that date;

(5) the signing officers have disclosed to the issuer's auditors and the audit committee of the board of directors (or persons fulfilling the equivalent function)—

(A) all significant deficiencies in the design or operation of internal controls which could adversely affect the issuer's ability to record, process, summarize, and report financial data and have identified for the issuer's auditors any material weaknesses in internal controls; and

(B) any fraud, whether or not material, that involves management or other employees who have a significant role in the issuer's internal controls; and

(6) the signing officers have indicated in the report whether or not there were significant changes in internal controls or in other factors that could significantly affect internal controls subsequent to the date of their evaluation, including any corrective actions with regard to significant deficiencies and material weaknesses.

(b) Foreign reincorporations have no effect

Nothing in this section shall be interpreted or applied in any way to allow any issuer to lessen the legal force of the statement required under this section, by an issuer having reincorporated or having engaged in any other transaction that resulted in the transfer of the corporate domicile or offices of the issuer from inside the United States to outside of the United States.

(c) Deadline

The rules required by subsection (a) of this section shall be effective not later than 30 days after July 30, 2002.

* * * *

Explanatory Comments:

Section 302 requires the chief executive officer (CEO) and chief financial officer (CFO) of each public company to certify that they have reviewed the company's quarterly and annual reports to be filed with the Securities and Exchange Commission (SEC). The CEO and CFO must certify that, based on their knowledge, the reports do not contain any untrue statement of a material fact or any half-truth that would make the report misleading, and that the information contained in the reports fairly presents the company's financial condition.

In addition, this section also requires the CEO and CFO to certify that they have created and designed an internal control system for their company and have recently evaluated that system to ensure that it is effectively providing them with relevant and accurate financial information. If the signing officers have found any significant deficiencies or weaknesses in the company's system or have discovered any evidence of fraud, they must have reported the situation, and any corrective actions they have taken, to the auditors and the audit committee.

SECTION 306
Insider trades during pension fund blackout periods[2]

(a) Prohibition of insider trading during pension fund blackout periods

(1) In general

Except to the extent otherwise provided by rule of the Commission pursuant to paragraph (3), it shall be unlawful for any director or executive officer of an issuer of any

1. This section of the Sarbanes-Oxley Act is codified at 15 U.S.C. Section 7241.

2. Codified at 15 U.S.C. Section 7244.

equity security (other than an exempted security), directly or indirectly, to purchase, sell, or otherwise acquire or transfer any equity security of the issuer (other than an exempted security) during any blackout period with respect to such equity security if such director or officer acquires such equity security in connection with his or her service or employment as a director or executive officer.

(2) Remedy

(A) In general

Any profit realized by a director or executive officer referred to in paragraph (1) from any purchase, sale, or other acquisition or transfer in violation of this subsection shall inure to and be recoverable by the issuer, irrespective of any intention on the part of such director or executive officer in entering into the transaction.

(B) Actions to recover profits

An action to recover profits in accordance with this subsection may be instituted at law or in equity in any court of competent jurisdiction by the issuer, or by the owner of any security of the issuer in the name and in behalf of the issuer if the issuer fails or refuses to bring such action within 60 days after the date of request, or fails diligently to prosecute the action thereafter, except that no such suit shall be brought more than 2 years after the date on which such profit was realized.

(3) Rulemaking authorized

The Commission shall, in consultation with the Secretary of Labor, issue rules to clarify the application of this subsection and to prevent evasion thereof. Such rules shall provide for the application of the requirements of paragraph (1) with respect to entities treated as a single employer with respect to an issuer under section 414(b), (c), (m), or (o) of Title 26 to the extent necessary to clarify the application of such requirements and to prevent evasion thereof. Such rules may also provide for appropriate exceptions from the requirements of this subsection, including exceptions for purchases pursuant to an automatic dividend reinvestment program or purchases or sales made pursuant to an advance election.

(4) Blackout period

For purposes of this subsection, the term "blackout period", with respect to the equity securities of any issuer—

(A) means any period of more than 3 consecutive business days during which the ability of not fewer than 50 percent of the participants or beneficiaries under all individual account plans maintained by the issuer to purchase, sell, or otherwise acquire or transfer an interest in any equity of such issuer held in such an individual account plan is temporarily suspended by the issuer or by a fiduciary of the plan; and

(B) does not include, under regulations which shall be prescribed by the Commission—

(i) a regularly scheduled period in which the participants and beneficiaries may not purchase, sell, or otherwise acquire or transfer an interest in any equity of such issuer, if such period is—

(I) incorporated into the individual account plan; and

(II) timely disclosed to employees before becoming participants under the individual account plan or as a subsequent amendment to the plan; or

(ii) any suspension described in subparagraph (A) that is imposed solely in connection with persons becoming participants or beneficiaries, or ceasing to be participants or beneficiaries, in an individual account plan by reason of a corporate merger, acquisition, divestiture, or similar transaction involving the plan or plan sponsor.

(5) Individual account plan

For purposes of this subsection, the term "individual account plan" has the meaning provided in section 1002(34) of Title 29, except that such term shall not include a one-participant retirement plan (within the meaning of section 1021(i)(8)(B) of Title 29).

(6) Notice to directors, executive officers, and the Commission

In any case in which a director or executive officer is subject to the requirements of this subsection in connection with a blackout period (as defined in paragraph (4)) with respect to any equity securities, the issuer of such equity securities shall timely notify such director or officer and the Securities and Exchange Commission of such blackout period.

* * * *

Explanatory Comments:

Corporate pension funds typically prohibit employees from trading shares of the corporation during periods when the pension fund is undergoing significant change. Before 2002, however, these blackout periods did not affect the corporation's executives, who frequently received shares of the corporate stock as part of their compensation. Section 306 was Congress's solution to the basic unfairness of this situation. This section of the act required the SEC to issue rules that prohibit any director or executive officer from trading during pension fund blackout periods. (The SEC later issued these rules, entitled Regulation Blackout Trading Restriction, or Reg BTR.)

Section 306 also provided shareholders with a right to file a shareholder's derivative suit against officers and directors who have profited from trading during these blackout periods (provided that the corporation has failed to bring a suit). The officer or director can be forced to return to the corporation any profits received, regardless of whether the director or officer acted with bad intent.

SECTION 402
Periodical and other reports[3]

* * * *

(i) Accuracy of financial reports

Each financial report that contains financial statements, and that is required to be prepared in accordance with (or reconciled to) generally accepted accounting principles under this chapter and filed with the Commission shall reflect all material correcting adjustments that have been identified by a registered

3. This section of the Sarbanes-Oxley Act amended some of the provisions of the 1934 Securities Exchange Act and added the paragraphs reproduced here at 15 U.S.C. Section 78m.

public accounting firm in accordance with generally accepted accounting principles and the rules and regulations of the Commission.

(j) Off-balance sheet transactions

Not later than 180 days after July 30, 2002, the Commission shall issue final rules providing that each annual and quarterly financial report required to be filed with the Commission shall disclose all material off-balance sheet transactions, arrangements, obligations (including contingent obligations), and other relationships of the issuer with unconsolidated entities or other persons, that may have a material current or future effect on financial condition, changes in financial condition, results of operations, liquidity, capital expenditures, capital resources, or significant components of revenues or expenses.

(k) Prohibition on personal loans to executives

(1) In general

It shall be unlawful for any issuer (as defined in section 7201 of this title), directly or indirectly, including through any subsidiary, to extend or maintain credit, to arrange for the extension of credit, or to renew an extension of credit, in the form of a personal loan to or for any director or executive officer (or equivalent thereof) of that issuer. An extension of credit maintained by the issuer on July 30, 2002, shall not be subject to the provisions of this subsection, provided that there is no material modification to any term of any such extension of credit or any renewal of any such extension of credit on or after July 30, 2002.

(2) Limitation

Paragraph (1) does not preclude any home improvement and manufactured home loans (as that term is defined in section 1464 of Title 12), consumer credit (as defined in section 1602 of this title), or any extension of credit under an open end credit plan (as defined in section 1602 of this title), or a charge card (as defined in section 1637(c)(4)(e) of this title), or any extension of credit by a broker or dealer registered under section 78o of this title to an employee of that broker or dealer to buy, trade, or carry securities, that is permitted under rules or regulations of the Board of Governors of the Federal Reserve System pursuant to section 78g of this title (other than an extension of credit that would be used to purchase the stock of that issuer), that is—

(A) made or provided in the ordinary course of the consumer credit business of such issuer;

(B) of a type that is generally made available by such issuer to the public; and

(C) made by such issuer on market terms, or terms that are no more favorable than those offered by the issuer to the general public for such extensions of credit.

(3) Rule of construction for certain loans

Paragraph (1) does not apply to any loan made or maintained by an insured depository institution (as defined in section 1813 of Title 12), if the loan is subject to the insider lending restrictions of section 375b of Title 12.

(l) Real time issuer disclosures

Each issuer reporting under subsection (a) of this section or section 78o(d) of this title shall disclose to the public on a rapid and current basis such additional information concerning material changes in the financial condition or operations of the issuer, in plain English, which may include trend and qualitative information and graphic presentations, as the Commission determines, by rule, is necessary or useful for the protection of investors and in the public interest.

Explanatory Comments:

Before this act, many corporate executives typically received extremely large salaries, significant bonuses, and abundant stock options, even when the companies for which they worked were suffering. Executives were also routinely given personal loans from corporate funds, many of which were never paid back. The average large company during that period loaned almost $1 million a year to top executives, and some companies loaned hundreds of millions of dollars to their executives every year. Section 402 amended the 1934 Securities Exchange Act to prohibit public companies from making personal loans to executive officers and directors.

There are a few exceptions to this prohibition, such as home-improvement loans made in the ordinary course of business. Note also that while loans are forbidden, outright gifts are not. A corporation is free to give gifts to its executives, including cash, provided that these gifts are disclosed on its financial reports. The idea is that corporate directors will be deterred from making substantial gifts to their executives by the disclosure requirement—particularly if the corporation's financial condition is questionable—because making such gifts could be perceived as abusing their authority.

SECTION 403
Directors, officers, and principal stockholders[4]

(a) Disclosures required

(1) Directors, officers, and principal stockholders required to file

Every person who is directly or indirectly the beneficial owner of more than 10 percent of any class of any equity security (other than an exempted security) which is registered pursuant to section 78l of this title, or who is a director or an officer of the issuer of such security, shall file the statements required by this subsection with the Commission (and, if such security is registered on a national securities exchange, also with the exchange).

(2) Time of filing

The statements required by this subsection shall be filed—

(A) at the time of the registration of such security on a national securities exchange or by the effective date of a registration statement filed pursuant to section 78l(g) of this title;

(B) within 10 days after he or she becomes such beneficial owner, director, or officer;

(C) if there has been a change in such ownership, or if such person shall have purchased or sold a security-based swap agreement (as defined in section 206(b) of the Gramm-Leach-Bliley Act (15 U.S.C. 78c note)) involving such equity security, before the end of the second business day following the day on which the subject transaction has been executed, or at such other

4. This section of the Sarbanes-Oxley Act amended the disclosure provisions of the 1934 Securities Exchange Act, at 15 U.S.C. Section 78p.

time as the Commission shall establish, by rule, in any case in which the Commission determines that such 2-day period is not feasible.

(3) Contents of statements

A statement filed—

(A) under subparagraph (A) or (B) of paragraph (2) shall contain a statement of the amount of all equity securities of such issuer of which the filing person is the beneficial owner; and

(B) under subparagraph (C) of such paragraph shall indicate ownership by the filing person at the date of filing, any such changes in such ownership, and such purchases and sales of the security-based swap agreements as have occurred since the most recent such filing under such subparagraph.

(4) Electronic filing and availability

Beginning not later than 1 year after July 30, 2002—

(A) a statement filed under subparagraph (C) of paragraph (2) shall be filed electronically;

(B) the Commission shall provide each such statement on a publicly accessible Internet site not later than the end of the business day following that filing; and

(C) the issuer (if the issuer maintains a corporate website) shall provide that statement on that corporate website, not later than the end of the business day following that filing.

* * * *

Explanatory Comments:

This section dramatically shortens the time period provided in the Securities Exchange Act of 1934 for disclosing transactions by insiders. The prior law stated that most transactions had to be reported within ten days of the beginning of the following month, although certain transactions did not have to be reported until the following fiscal year (within the first forty-five days).

In several instances, some insider trading was not disclosed (and was therefore not discovered) until long after the transactions. So Congress added this section to reduce the time period for making disclosures. Under Section 403, most transactions by insiders must be electronically filed with the SEC within two business days.

Also, any company that maintains a Web site must post these SEC filings on its site by the end of the next business day. Congress enacted this section in the belief that if insiders are required to file reports of their transactions promptly with the SEC, companies will do more to police themselves and prevent insider trading.

SECTION 404
Management assessment of internal controls[5]

(a) Rules required

The Commission shall prescribe rules requiring each annual report required by section 78m(a) or 78o(d) of this title to contain an internal control report, which shall—

(1) state the responsibility of management for establishing and maintaining an adequate internal control structure and procedures for financial reporting; and

(2) contain an assessment, as of the end of the most recent fiscal year of the issuer, of the effectiveness of the internal control structure and procedures of the issuer for financial reporting.

(b) Internal control evaluation and reporting

With respect to the internal control assessment required by subsection (a) of this section, each registered public accounting firm that prepares or issues the audit report for the issuer shall attest to, and report on, the assessment made by the management of the issuer. An attestation made under this subsection shall be made in accordance with standards for attestation engagements issued or adopted by the Board. Any such attestation shall not be the subject of a separate engagement.

* * * *

Explanatory Comments:

This section was enacted to prevent corporate executives from claiming they were ignorant of significant errors in their companies' financial reports. For instance, several CEOs testified before Congress that they simply had no idea that the corporations' financial statements were off by billions of dollars. Congress therefore passed Section 404, which requires each annual report to contain a description and assessment of the company's internal control structure and financial reporting procedures. The section also requires that an audit be conducted of the internal control assessment, as well as the financial statements contained in the report. This section goes hand in hand with Section 302 (which, as discussed previously, requires various certifications attesting to the accuracy of the information in financial reports).

Section 404 has been one of the more controversial and expensive provisions in the Sarbanes-Oxley Act because it requires companies to assess their own internal financial controls to make sure that their financial statements are reliable and accurate. A corporation might need to set up a disclosure committee and a coordinator, establish codes of conduct for accounting and financial personnel, create documentation procedures, provide training, and outline the individuals who are responsible for performing each of the procedures. Companies that were already well managed have not experienced substantial difficulty complying with this section. Other companies, however, have spent millions of dollars setting up, documenting, and evaluating their internal financial control systems. Although initially creating the internal financial control system is a one-time-only expense, the costs of maintaining and evaluating it are ongoing. Some corporations that spent considerable sums complying with Section 404 have been able to offset these costs by discovering and correcting inefficiencies or frauds within their systems. Nevertheless, it is unlikely that any corporation will find compliance with this section to be inexpensive.

SECTION 802(A)
Destruction, alteration, or falsification of records in Federal investigations and bankruptcy[6]

Whoever knowingly alters, destroys, mutilates, conceals, covers up, falsifies, or makes a false entry in any record, document, or tangible object with the intent to impede, obstruct, or influence the investigation or proper administration of any matter within the jurisdiction of any department or agency of the United States or any case filed under title 11, or in relation to or

5. Codified at 15 U.S.C. Section 7262.

6. Codified at 15 U.S.C. Section 1519.

contemplation of any such matter or case, shall be fined under this title, imprisoned not more than 20 years, or both.

Destruction of corporate audit records[7]

(a) **(1)** Any accountant who conducts an audit of an issuer of securities to which section 10A(a) of the Securities Exchange Act of 1934 (15 U.S.C. 78j-1(a)) applies, shall maintain all audit or review workpapers for a period of 5 years from the end of the fiscal period in which the audit or review was concluded.

(2) The Securities and Exchange Commission shall promulgate, within 180 days, after adequate notice and an opportunity for comment, such rules and regulations, as are reasonably necessary, relating to the retention of relevant records such as workpapers, documents that form the basis of an audit or review, memoranda, correspondence, communications, other documents, and records (including electronic records) which are created, sent, or received in connection with an audit or review and contain conclusions, opinions, analyses, or financial data relating to such an audit or review, which is conducted by any accountant who conducts an audit of an issuer of securities to which section 10A(a) of the Securities Exchange Act of 1934 (15 U.S.C. 78j-1(a)) applies. The Commission may, from time to time, amend or supplement the rules and regulations that it is required to promulgate under this section, after adequate notice and an opportunity for comment, in order to ensure that such rules and regulations adequately comport with the purposes of this section.

(b) Whoever knowingly and willfully violates subsection (a)(1), or any rule or regulation promulgated by the Securities and Exchange Commission under subsection (a)(2), shall be fined under this title, imprisoned not more than 10 years, or both.

(c) Nothing in this section shall be deemed to diminish or relieve any person of any other duty or obligation imposed by Federal or State law or regulation to maintain, or refrain from destroying, any document.

* * * *

Explanatory Comments:

Section 802(a) enacted two new statutes that punish those who alter or destroy documents. The first statute is not specifically limited to securities fraud cases. It provides that anyone who alters, destroys, or falsifies records in federal investigations or bankruptcy may be criminally prosecuted and sentenced to a fine or to up to twenty years in prison, or both. The second statute requires auditors of public companies to keep all audit or review working papers for five years but expressly allows the SEC to amend or supplement these requirements as it sees fit. The SEC has, in fact, amended this section by issuing a rule that requires auditors who audit reporting companies to retain working papers for seven years from the conclusion of the review. Section 802(a) further provides that anyone who knowingly and willfully violates this statute is subject to criminal prosecution and can be sentenced to a fine, imprisoned for up to ten years, or both if convicted.

This portion of the Sarbanes-Oxley Act implicitly recognizes that persons who are under investigation often are tempted to respond by destroying or falsifying documents that might prove their complicity in wrongdoing. The severity of the punishment should provide a strong incentive for these individuals to resist the temptation.

SECTION 804
Time limitations on the commencement of civil actions arising under Acts of Congress[8]

(a) Except as otherwise provided by law, a civil action arising under an Act of Congress enacted after the date of the enactment of this section may not be commenced later than 4 years after the cause of action accrues.

(b) Notwithstanding subsection (a), a private right of action that involves a claim of fraud, deceit, manipulation, or contrivance in contravention of a regulatory requirement concerning the securities laws, as defined in section 3(a)(47) of the Securities Exchange Act of 1934 (15 U.S.C. 78c(a)(47)), may be brought not later than the earlier of—

(1) 2 years after the discovery of the facts constituting the violation; or

(2) 5 years after such violation.

* * * *

Explanatory Comments:

Before the enactment of this section, Section 10(b) of the Securities Exchange Act of 1934 had no express statute of limitations. The courts generally required plaintiffs to have filed suit within one year from the date that they should (using due diligence) have discovered that a fraud had been committed but no later than three years after the fraud occurred. Section 804 extends this period by specifying that plaintiffs must file a lawsuit within two years after they discover (or should have discovered) a fraud but no later than five years after the fraud's occurrence. This provision has prevented the courts from dismissing numerous securities fraud lawsuits.

SECTION 806
Civil action to protect against retaliation in fraud cases[9]

(a) Whistleblower protection for employees of publicly traded companies.—

No company with a class of securities registered under section 12 of the Securities Exchange Act of 1934 (15 U.S.C. 78l), or that is required to file reports under section 15(d) of the Securities Exchange Act of 1934 (15 U.S.C. 78o(d)), or any officer, employee, contractor, subcontractor, or agent of such company, may discharge, demote, suspend, threaten, harass, or in any other manner discriminate against an employee in the terms and conditions of employment because of any lawful act done by the employee—

(1) to provide information, cause information to be provided, or otherwise assist in an investigation regarding any conduct which the employee reasonably believes constitutes a violation of section 1341, 1343, 1344, or 1348, any rule or regulation of the Securities and Exchange Commission, or any provision of Federal law relating to fraud against shareholders, when the information or assistance is provided to or the investigation is conducted by—

---

7. Codified at 15 U.S.C. Section 1520.

8. Codified at 28 U.S.C. Section 1658.

9. Codified at 18 U.S.C. Section 1514A.

(A) a Federal regulatory or law enforcement agency;

(B) any Member of Congress or any committee of Congress; or

(C) a person with supervisory authority over the employee (or such other person working for the employer who has the authority to investigate, discover, or terminate misconduct); or

(2) to file, cause to be filed, testify, participate in, or otherwise assist in a proceeding filed or about to be filed (with any knowledge of the employer) relating to an alleged violation of section 1341, 1343, 1344, or 1348, any rule or regulation of the Securities and Exchange Commission, or any provision of Federal law relating to fraud against shareholders.

(b) Enforcement action.—

(1) In general.—A person who alleges discharge or other discrimination by any person in violation of subsection (a) may seek relief under subsection (c), by—

(A) filing a complaint with the Secretary of Labor; or

(B) if the Secretary has not issued a final decision within 180 days of the filing of the complaint and there is no showing that such delay is due to the bad faith of the claimant, bringing an action at law or equity for de novo review in the appropriate district court of the United States, which shall have jurisdiction over such an action without regard to the amount in controversy.

(2) Procedure.—

(A) In general.—An action under paragraph (1)(A) shall be governed under the rules and procedures set forth in section 42121(b) of title 49, United States Code.

(B) Exception.—Notification made under section 42121(b)(1) of title 49, United States Code, shall be made to the person named in the complaint and to the employer.

(C) Burdens of proof.—An action brought under paragraph (1)(B) shall be governed by the legal burdens of proof set forth in section 42121(b) of title 49, United States Code.

(D) Statute of limitations.—An action under paragraph (1) shall be commenced not later than 90 days after the date on which the violation occurs.

(c) Remedies.—

(1) In general.—An employee prevailing in any action under subsection (b)(1) shall be entitled to all relief necessary to make the employee whole.

(2) Compensatory damages.—Relief for any action under paragraph (1) shall include—

(A) reinstatement with the same seniority status that the employee would have had, but for the discrimination;

(B) the amount of back pay, with interest; and

(C) compensation for any special damages sustained as a result of the discrimination, including litigation costs, expert witness fees, and reasonable attorney fees.

(d) Rights retained by employee.—Nothing in this section shall be deemed to diminish the rights, privileges, or remedies of any employee under any Federal or State law, or under any collective bargaining agreement.

Explanatory Comments:
Section 806 is one of several provisions that were included in the Sarbanes-Oxley Act to encourage and protect whistleblowers—that is, employees who report their employer's alleged violations of securities law to the authorities. This section applies to employees, agents, and independent contractors who work for publicly traded companies or testify about such a company during an investigation. It sets up an administrative procedure at the U.S. Department of Labor for individuals who claim that their employer retaliated against them (fired or demoted them, for example) for blowing the whistle on the employer's wrongful conduct. It also allows the award of civil damages—including back pay, reinstatement, special damages, attorneys' fees, and court costs—to employees who prove that they suffered retaliation. Since this provision was enacted, whistleblowers have filed numerous complaints with the U.S. Department of Labor under this section.

SECTION 807
Securities fraud[10]

Whoever knowingly executes, or attempts to execute, a scheme or artifice—

(1) to defraud any person in connection with any security of an issuer with a class of securities registered under section 12 of the Securities Exchange Act of 1934 (15 U.S.C. 78l) or that is required to file reports under section 15(d) of the Securities Exchange Act of 1934 (15 U.S.C. 78o(d)); or

(2) to obtain, by means of false or fraudulent pretenses, representations, or promises, any money or property in connection with the purchase or sale of any security of an issuer with a class of securities registered under section 12 of the Securities Exchange Act of 1934 (15 U.S.C. 78l) or that is required to file reports under section 15(d) of the Securities Exchange Act of 1934 (15 U.S.C. 78o(d)); shall be fined under this title, or imprisoned not more than 25 years, or both.

* * * *

Explanatory Comments:
Section 807 adds a new provision to the federal criminal code that addresses securities fraud. Before 2002, federal securities law had already made it a crime—under Section 10(b) of the Securities Exchange Act of 1934 and SEC Rule 10b-5, both of which were discussed in Chapter 28—to intentionally defraud someone in connection with a purchase or sale of securities, but the offense was not listed in the federal criminal code.

Also, paragraph 2 of Section 807 goes beyond what is prohibited under securities law by making it a crime to obtain by means of false or fraudulent pretenses any money or property from the purchase or sale of securities. This new provision allows violators to be punished by up to twenty-five years in prison, a fine, or both.

SECTION 906
Failure of corporate officers to certify financial reports[11]

(a) Certification of periodic financial reports.—Each periodic report containing financial statements filed by an issuer with the Securities Exchange Commission pursuant to section 13(a)

10. Codified at 18 U.S.C. Section 1348.

11. Codified at 18 U.S.C. Section 1350.

or 15(d) of the Securities Exchange Act of 1934 (15 U.S.C. 78m(a) or 78o(d)) shall be accompanied by a written statement by the chief executive officer and chief financial officer (or equivalent thereof) of the issuer.

(b) Content.—The statement required under subsection (a) shall certify that the periodic report containing the financial statements fully complies with the requirements of section 13(a) or 15(d) of the Securities Exchange Act of 1934 (15 U.S.C. 78m or 78o(d)) and that information contained in the periodic report fairly presents, in all material respects, the financial condition and results of operations of the issuer.

(c) Criminal penalties.—Whoever—

(1) certifies any statement as set forth in subsections (a) and (b) of this section knowing that the periodic report accompanying the statement does not comport with all the requirements set forth in this section shall be fined not more than $1,000,000 or imprisoned not more than 10 years, or both; or

(2) willfully certifies any statement as set forth in subsections (a) and (b) of this section knowing that the periodic report accompanying the statement does not comport with all the requirements set forth in this section shall be fined not more than $5,000,000, or imprisoned not more than 20 years, or both.

Explanatory Comments:

As previously discussed, under Section 302 a corporation's CEO and CFO are required to certify that they believe the quarterly and annual reports their company files with the SEC are accurate and fairly present the company's financial condition. Section 906 adds "teeth" to these requirements by authorizing criminal penalties for those officers who intentionally certify inaccurate SEC filings.

Knowing violations of the requirements are punishable by a fine of up to $1 million, ten years' imprisonment, or both. Willful violators may be fined up to $5 million, sentenced to up to twenty years' imprisonment, or both. Although the difference between a knowing and a willful violation is not entirely clear, the section is obviously intended to remind corporate officers of the serious consequences of certifying inaccurate reports to the SEC.

CHAPTER 1

1. *Under what circumstances might a judge rely on case law to determine the intent and purpose of a statute?* Case law includes courts' interpretations of statutes, as well as constitutional provisions and administrative rules. Statutes often codify common law rules. For these reasons, a judge might rely on the common law as a guide to the intent and purpose of a statute.

2. *Assuming that these convicted war criminals had not disobeyed any law of their country and had merely been following their government's orders, what law had they violated? Explain.* At the time of the Nuremberg trials, "crimes against humanity" were new international crimes. The laws criminalized such acts as murder, extermination, enslavement, deportation, and other inhumane acts committed against any civilian population. These international laws derived their legitimacy from "natural law."

Natural law, which is the oldest and one of the most significant schools of jurisprudence, holds that governments and legal systems should reflect the moral and ethical ideals that are inherent in human nature. Because natural law is universal and discoverable by reason, its adherents believe that all other law is derived from natural law. Natural law therefore supersedes laws created by humans (national, or "positive," law), and in a conflict between the two, national or positive law loses its legitimacy.

The defendants asserted that they had been acting in accordance with German law. The judges dismissed these claims, reasoning that the defendants' acts were commonly regarded as crimes and that the accused must have known that the acts would be considered criminal. The judges clearly believed the tenets of natural law and expected that the defendants, too, should have been able to realize that their acts ran afoul of it. The fact that the "positivist law" of Germany at the time required them to commit these acts is irrelevant. Under natural law theory, the international court was justified in finding the defendants guilty of crimes against humanity.

CHAPTER 2

1. *Does the court in Sue's state have jurisdiction over Tipton? What factors will the court consider?* A corporation normally is subject to personal jurisdiction in the state in which it is incorporated, has its principal office, and/or is doing business. Under the authority of a state long arm statute, a court can exercise personal jurisdiction over certain out-of-state defendants based on activities that took place within the state. Before a court can exercise jurisdiction, though, it must be demonstrated that the defendant had minimum contacts with the state to justify the jurisdiction.

The minimum-contacts requirement is usually met if the corporation advertises or sells its products within the state, or places its goods into the "stream of commerce" with the intent that the goods be sold in the state. Therefore, a court will consider whether Tipton advertised or sold its product within Sue's state. The court may also look at whether the contract between Sue and Tipton was negotiated or signed within the state.

2. *Tom can call his first witness. What else might he do?* Tom could file a motion for a directed verdict. This motion asks the judge to direct a verdict for Tom on the ground that Sue presented no evidence that would justify granting Jan relief. The judge grants the motion if there is insufficient evidence to raise an issue of fact.

CHAPTER 3

1. *If a dispute arises, is the arbitration clause enforceable? Why or why not?* Maybe not. The Federal Arbitration Act (FAA) promotes enforcement of arbitration clauses in contracts involving interstate commerce, which would include contracts with smartphone providers. Nevertheless, because this agreement was presented on a take-it-or-leave it basis to a consumer, it is an adhesion contract that might be deemed unconscionable. Sue, the consumer, had no opportunity to negotiate the terms of this consumer arbitration agreement. Moreover, the smartphone provider's terms required the consumer (Sue) to pay two-thirds of the costs of arbitration, which seems unfair. Therefore, a court may conclude that the contract was unconscionable and refuse to enforce it (and the dispute would be litigated in court).

2. *If the dispute is not resolved, or if either party disagrees with the decision of the mediator or arbitrator, will a court hear the case? Explain.* Yes. Submission of the dispute to mediation or nonbinding arbitration is mandatory, but compliance with a decision of the mediator or arbitrator is voluntary.

CHAPTER 4

1. *Are there ethical concerns about putting traumatized children on the news immediately after an event like this? Why or why not?* In determining whether it is ethical to interview these children soon after a tragic event, it is important to analyze the competing interests and reasons behind the interviews. The interviews may generate more viewers, which may lead to higher ratings and more advertising revenue for the company and its shareholders. Alternatively, the value of the interview to the public or to any investigation may be minimal. The children may not have accurate information and may be further traumatized by the interview process.

2. ***Is it ethical for Johnny to take a performance-enhancing drug that has not been banned? Why or why not?*** Maybe. Individuals and businesses often face ethical dilemmas when the letter of the law seems clear but alternatives exist that may violate what is known as the spirit of the law or the purpose for the law. In this case, the restrictions exist to stop athletes from performing better than they would naturally because of a foreign substance. The list of banned substances may not be able to keep up with the advances in technology and science in developing performance enhancing drugs.

Some might argue that it is ethical for him to take anything that is not formally banned and that all competitors have the same ability to access and take those substances and therefore any advantage is eliminated. Because there seems to be no unfair advantage, the purpose of the restriction is not frustrated. There is an implicit assumption, however, that all performers have the connections and the resources to obtain the non-banned substance. Because this assumption is not necessarily true, it is more likely an ethical violation to take the non-banned performance enhancing drugs, even if it is not technically against the rules.

CHAPTER 5

1. ***Can a state, in the interest of energy conservation, ban all advertising by power utilities if conservation could be accomplished by less restrictive means? Why or why not?*** No. Even if commercial speech is not related to illegal activities nor misleading, it may be restricted if a state has a substantial interest that cannot be achieved by less restrictive means. In this case, the interest in energy conservation is substantial, but it could be achieved by less restrictive means. That would be the utilities' defense against the enforcement of this state law.

2. ***Is this a violation of equal protection if the only reason for the tax is to protect the local firms from out-of-state competition? Explain.*** Yes. The tax would limit the liberty of some persons (out of state businesses), so it is subject to a review under the equal protection clause. Protecting local businesses from out-of-state competition is not a legitimate government objective. Thus, such a tax would violate the equal protection clause.

CHAPTER 6

1. ***What safeguards promote the ALJ's fairness?*** Under the Administrative Procedure Act (APA), the administrative law judge (ALJ) must be separate from the agency's investigative and prosecutorial staff. *Ex parte* communications between the ALJ and a party to a proceeding are prohibited. Under the APA, an ALJ is exempt from agency discipline except on a showing of good cause.

2. ***Does the firm have any opportunity to express its opinion about the pending rule? Explain.*** Yes. Administrative rulemaking starts with the publication of a notice of the rulemaking in the *Federal Register*. A public hearing is held at which proponents and opponents can offer evidence and question witnesses. After the hearing, the agency considers what was presented at the hearing and drafts the final rule.

CHAPTER 7

1. ***With respect to the gas station, has she committed a crime? If so, what is it?*** Yes. With respect to the gas station, she has obtained goods by false pretenses. She might also be charged with larceny and forgery, and most states have special statutes covering illegal use of credit cards.

2. ***Has Ben committed a crime? If so, what is it?*** Yes. The Counterfeit Access Device and Computer Fraud and Abuse Act provides that a person who accesses a computer online, without permission, to obtain classified data—such as consumer credit files in a credit agency's database—is subject to criminal prosecution. The crime has two elements: accessing the computer without permission and taking data. It is a felony if done for private financial gain. Penalties include fines and imprisonment for up to twenty years. The victim of the theft can also bring a civil suit against the criminal to obtain damages and other relief.

CHAPTER 8

1. ***Under what circumstances would a U.S. court enforce the judgment of the Ecuadoran court?*** Under the principle of comity, a U.S court would defer and give effect to foreign laws and judicial decrees that are consistent with U.S. law and public policy.

2. ***How can this attempt to undersell U.S. businesses be defeated?*** The practice described in this problem is known as dumping, which is regarded as an unfair international trade practice. Dumping is the sale of imported goods at "less than fair value." Based on the price of those goods in the exporting country, an extra tariff—known as an antidumping duty—can be imposed on the imports.

CHAPTER 9

1. ***What standard determines whether these parties have a contract?*** Under the objective theory of contracts, if a reasonable person would have thought that Joli had accepted Kerin's offer when she signed and returned the letter, then a contract was made, and Joli is obligated to buy the book. This depends, in part, on what was said in the letter and what was said in response. For instance, did the letter contain a valid offer, and did the response constitute a valid acceptance? Under any circumstances, the issue is not whether either party subjectively believed that they did, or did not, have a contract.

2. ***Can Ed recover? Why or why not?*** No. This contract, although not fully executed, is for an illegal purpose and therefore is void. A void contract gives rise to no legal obligation on the part of any party. A contract that is void is no contract. There is nothing to enforce.

CHAPTER 10

1. *Is the contract enforceable? Why or why not?* No, the contract can be avoided because Simmons and Jenson have made a bilateral mistake. The issue is whether the mistake involves the identity of the stone (quartz versus diamond) or the value of the stone ($10 versus $1,000). Because both parties were mistaken as to the true character of the subject matter, the contract can be rescinded by either. Had either party known that the stone was some type of gem, then even though its exact nature was unknown (diamond), the mistake would be one of value, not fact, and the contract would not be rescindable.

2. *If Haney sues Greg, what would be the measure of recovery?* A nonbreaching party is entitled to his or her benefit of the bargain under the contract. Here, the innocent party is entitled to be put in the position she would have been in if the contract had been fully performed. The measure of the benefit is the cost to complete the work ($500). These are compensatory damages.

CHAPTER 11

1. *Is this an acceptance of the offer or a counteroffer? If it is an acceptance, is it a breach of the contract? What if Fav-O-Rite told E-Design it was sending the printer stands as "an accommodation"?* A shipment of nonconforming goods constitutes an acceptance of the offer and a breach, unless the seller seasonably notifies the buyer that the nonconforming shipment does not constitute an acceptance and is offered only as an accommodation. Thus, since there was no notification here, the shipment was both an acceptance and a breach. If, however, Fav-O-Rite had notified E-Design that it was sending the printer stands as an accommodation, the shipment would not constitute an acceptance and Fav-O-Rite would not be in breach.

2. *Can Poster Planet sue Brite without waiting until May 1? Why or why not?* Yes. When anticipatory repudiation occurs, a buyer (or lessee) can resort to any remedy for breach even if the buyer tells the seller (the repudiating party in this problem) that the buyer will wait for the seller's performance.

CHAPTER 12

1. *Can Lou recover from Jana? Why or why not?* Probably. To recover on the basis of negligence, the injured party as a plaintiff must show that the truck's owner owed the plaintiff a duty of care, that the owner breached that duty, that the plaintiff was injured, and that the breach caused the injury.

In this situation, the owner's actions breached the duty of reasonable care. The billboard falling on the plaintiff was the direct cause of the injury, not the plaintiff's own negligence. Thus, liability turns on whether the plaintiff can connect the breach of duty to the injury. This involves the test of proximate cause—the question of foreseeability. The consequences to the injured party must have been a foreseeable result of the owner's carelessness.

2. *What might the firm successfully claim in defense?* The company might defend against this electrician's claim by asserting that the electrician should have known of the risk and, therefore, the company had no duty to warn. According to the problem, the danger is common knowledge in the electrician's field and should have been apparent to this electrician, given his years of training and experience. In other words, the company most likely had no need to warn the electrician of the risk.

The firm could also raise comparative negligence. Both parties' negligence, if any, could be weighed and the liability distributed proportionately. The defendant could also assert assumption of risk, claiming that the electrician voluntarily entered into a dangerous situation, knowing the risk involved.

CHAPTER 13

1. *Is Superior Vehicles liable? Explain your answer.* Yes. The manufacturer is liable for the injuries to the user of the product. A manufacturer is liable for its failure to exercise due care to any person who sustains an injury proximately caused by a negligently made (defective) product.

2. *If Real, Sweet, and Tasty were not negligent, can they be liable for the injury? Why or why not?* Yes. Under the doctrine of strict liability, persons may be liable for the results of their acts regardless of their intentions or their exercise of reasonable care (that is, regardless of fault).

CHAPTER 14

1. *Has Roslyn violated any of the intellectual property rights discussed in this chapter? Explain.* Yes, Roslyn has committed theft of trade secrets. Lists of suppliers and customers cannot be patented, copyrighted, or trademarked, but the information they contain is protected against appropriation by others as trade secrets. And most likely, Roslyn signed a contract, agreeing not to use this information outside her employment by Organic. But even without this contract, Organic could have made a convincing case against its ex-employee for a theft of trade secrets.

2. *Is this patent infringement? If so, how might Global save the cost of suing World for infringement and at the same time profit from World's sales?* This is patent infringement. A software maker in this situation might best protect its product, save litigation costs, and profit from its patent by the use of a license. In the context of this problem, a license would grant permission to sell a patented item. (A license can be limited to certain purposes and to the licensee only.)

CHAPTER 15

1. *Has Karl done anything wrong? Explain.* Karl may have committed trademark infringement. Search engines compile their results by looking through Web sites' key-word fields. Key words, or meta tags, increase the likelihood that a site will be included in search engine results, even if the words have no connection to the site.

A site that appropriates the key words of other sites with more frequent hits will appear in the same search engine results as the more popular sites. But using another's trademark as a key word without the owner's permission normally constitutes trademark infringement. Of course, some uses of another's trademark as a meta tag may be permissible if the use is reasonably necessary and does not suggest that the owner authorized or sponsored the use.

2. ***Can Eagle Corporation stop this use of eagle? If so, what must the company show? Explain.*** Yes. This may be an instance of trademark dilution. Dilution occurs when a trademark is used, without permission, in a way that diminishes the distinctive quality of the mark. Dilution does not require proof that consumers are likely to be confused by the use of the unauthorized mark. The products involved do not have to be similar. Dilution does require, however, that a mark be famous when the dilution occurs.

CHAPTER 16

1. ***What can Larry and Midwest do?*** Each of the parties can place a mechanic's lien on the debtor's property. If the debtor does not pay what is owed, the property can be sold to satisfy the debt. The only requirements are that the lien be filed within a specific time from the time of the work, depending on the state statute, and notice of the foreclosure and sale must be given to the debtor in advance.

2. ***Are these debts dischargeable in bankruptcy? Explain.*** No. Besides the claims listed in this problem, the debts that cannot be discharged in bankruptcy include amounts borrowed to pay back taxes, goods obtained by fraud, debts that were not listed in the petition, domestic support obligations, certain cash advances, and others.

CHAPTER 17

1. ***When Darnell dies, his widow claims that as Darnell's heir, she is entitled to take his place as Eliana's partner or to receive a share of the firm's assets. Is she right? Why or why not?*** No. A widow (or widower) has no right to take a dead partner's place. A partner's death causes dissociation after which the partnership must purchase the dissociated partner's partnership interest. Therefore, the surviving partners must pay the decedent's estate (for his widow) the value of the deceased partner's interest in the partnership.

2. ***Does this constitute "cause" for termination? Why or why not?*** Yes. Failing to meet a specified sales quota can constitute a breach of a franchise agreement. If the franchisor is acting in good faith, "cause" may also include the death or disability of the franchisee, the insolvency of the franchisee, and a breach of another term of the franchise agreement.

CHAPTER 18

1. ***What are their options with respect to the management of their firm?*** The members of a limited liability company (LLC) may designate a group to run their firm, in which situation the firm would be considered a manager-managed LLC. The group may include only members, only nonmembers, or members and nonmembers. If instead, all members participate in management, the firm would be a member-managed LLC. In fact, unless the members agree otherwise, all members are considered to participate in the management of the firm.

2. ***If Elizabeth is petitioned into involuntary bankruptcy, does that constitute a dissolution of the limited partnership?*** Bankruptcy of the limited partnership itself causes dissolution, but bankruptcy of one of the limited partners does not dissolve the partnership unless it causes the bankruptcy of the firm. Therefore, Elizabeth's involuntary bankruptcy would not dissolve the firm.

CHAPTER 19

1. ***Is there a way for Northwest Brands to avoid this double taxation? Explain your answer.*** Yes. Small businesses that meet certain requirements can qualify as S corporations, created specifically to permit small businesses to avoid double taxation. The six requirements of an S corporation are (1) the firm must be a domestic corporation, (2) the firm must not be a member of an affiliated group of corporations, (3) the firm must have less than a certain number of shareholders, (4) the shareholders must be individuals, estates, or qualified trusts (or corporations in some cases), (5) there can be only one class of stock, and (6) no shareholder can be a nonresident alien.

2. ***Yvon, a Wonder shareholder, learns of the purchase and wants to sue the directors on Wonder's behalf. Can she do it? Explain.*** Yes. A shareholder can bring a derivative suit on behalf of a corporation, if some wrong is done to the corporation. Normally, any damages recovered go into the corporate treasury.

CHAPTER 20

1. ***When Nadine learns the difference between the price that Dimka is willing to pay and the price at which the owner is willing to sell, she wants to buy the land and sell it to Dimka herself. Can she do this? Discuss.*** No. Nadine, as an agent, is prohibited from taking advantage of the agency relationship to obtain property that the principal (Dimka Corporation) wants to purchase. This is the duty of loyalty that arises with every agency relationship.

2. ***Can Davis hold Estee liable for whatever damages he has to pay? Why or why not?*** Yes. A principal has a duty to indemnify an agent for liabilities incurred because of authorized and lawful acts and transactions and for losses suffered because of the principal's failure to perform his or her duties.

CHAPTER 21

1. ***Can AMC be held liable for breach of contract? If so, why? If not, why not?*** Yes. Some courts have held that an implied employment contract exists between employer and employee when an employee handbook states that employees

will be dismissed only for good cause. An employer who fires a worker contrary to this promise can be held liable for breach of contract.

2. *For Erin to obtain workers' compensation, does her injury have to have been caused by Fine Print's negligence? Does it matter whether the action causing the injury was intentional? Explain.* Workers' compensation laws establish a procedure for compensating workers who are injured on the job. Instead of suing to collect benefits, an injured worker notifies the employer of an injury and files a claim with the appropriate state agency.

The right to recover is normally determined without regard to negligence or fault, but intentionally inflicted injuries are not covered. Unlike the potential for recovery in a lawsuit based on negligence or fault, recovery under a workers' compensation statute is limited to the specific amount designated in the statute for the employee's injury.

CHAPTER 22

1. *Is this sexual harassment? Why or why not?* Yes. One type of sexual harassment occurs when a request for sexual favors is a condition of employment, and the person making the request is a supervisor or acts with the authority of the employer. A tangible employment action, such as continued employment, may also lead to the employer's liability for the supervisor's conduct. That the injured employee is a male and the supervisor a female, instead of the other way around, would not affect the outcome. Same-gender harassment is also actionable.

2. *Could Koko succeed in a suit against Lively for discrimination? Explain.* Yes, if she can show that she was not hired solely because of her disability. The other elements for a discrimination suit based on a disability are that the plaintiff (1) has a disability and (2) is otherwise qualified for the job. Both of these elements appear to be satisfied in this problem.

CHAPTER 23

1. *What must Gara do under the Immigration Act to hire foreign employees for Skytech?* To hire a foreign individual to work in the U.S., an employer must submit a petition to U.S. Citizenship and Immigration Services, which determines whether the job candidate meets the legal standards. Each visa is for a specific job. In this situation, because Gara is looking for persons with specialized skills, he needs to show the individual qualifies for an H-1B visa. To qualify, the person must have highly specialized knowledge and a bachelor's degree or higher. Because only sixty-five thousand H-1B visas are set aside each year for immigrants, Gara must be prepared and file the application within the first few weeks of the year.

2. *Are these conditions legal? Why or why not?* No. A closed shop (a company that requires union membership as a condition of employment) is illegal. A union shop (a company that does not require union membership as a condition of employment but requires workers to join the union after a certain time on the job) is illegal in a state with a right-to-work law, which makes it illegal to require union membership for continued employment.

CHAPTER 24

1. *To market the drug, what must United prove to the Food and Drug Administration?* Under an extensive set of procedures established by the U.S. Food and Drug Administration, which administers the federal Food, Drug, and Cosmetic Act, drugs must be shown to be effective as well as safe before they may be marketed to the public. In general, manufacturers are responsible for ensuring that the drugs they offer for sale are free of any substances that could injure consumers.

2. *What can Gert do?* Under the Truth-in-Lending Act, a buyer who wishes to withhold payment for a faulty product purchased with a credit card must follow specific procedures to settle the dispute. The credit card issuer then must intervene and attempt to settle the dispute.

CHAPTER 25

1. *Are there any reasons that the court might refuse to issue an injunction against Resource's operation? Explain.* Yes. On the ground that the hardships that would be imposed on the polluter and on the community are greater than the hardships suffered by the residents, the court might deny an injunction. If the plant is the core of the local economy, for instance, the residents may be awarded only damages.

2. *If the Environmental Protection Agency cleans up the site, from whom can it recover the cost?* The Comprehensive Environmental Response, Compensation, and Liability Act of 1980 regulates the clean-up of hazardous waste disposal sites. Any potentially responsible party can be charged with the entire cost of cleaning up a site. Potentially responsible parties include the person that generated the waste (ChemCorp) the person that transported the waste to the site (Disposal), the person that owned or operated the site at the time of the disposal (Eliminators), and the current owner or operator of the site (Fluid). A party held responsible for the entire cost may be able to recoup some of it in a lawsuit against other potentially responsible parties.

CHAPTER 26

1. *Delmira wants to have Consuela evicted from the property. What can Consuela do?* This is a breach of the warranty deed's covenant of quiet enjoyment. The buyer can sue the seller and recover the purchase price of the house, plus any damages.

2. *Can Haven transfer possession for even less time to Idyll Company? Explain.* Yes. An owner of a fee simple has the most rights possible—he or she can give the property away, sell it, transfer it by will, use it for almost any purpose, possess it to the exclusion of all the world, or as in this case, transfer possession for any period of time. The party to whom possession is transferred can also transfer his or her interest (usually only with the owner's permission) for any lesser period of time.

CHAPTER 27

1. *If Pop's is a monopolist, is it in violation of Section 2 of the Sherman Act? Why or why not?* Size alone does not determine whether a firm is a monopoly—size in relation to the market is what matters. A small store in a small, isolated town is a monopolist if it is the only store serving that market. Monopoly involves the power to affect prices and output. If a firm has sufficient market power to control prices and exclude competition, that firm has monopoly power. Monopoly power in itself is not a violation of Section 2 of the Sherman Act. The offense also requires that the defendant intended to acquire or maintain that power through anticompetitive means.

2. *What factors would a court consider to decide whether this arrangement violates the Clayton Act?* This agreement is a tying arrangement. The legality of a tying arrangement depends the purpose of the agreement, the agreement's likely effect on competition in the relevant markets (the market for the tying product and the market for the tied product), and other factors. Tying arrangements for commodities are subject to Section 3 of the Clayton Act. Tying arrangements for services can be agreements in restraint of trade in violation of Section 1 of the Sherman Act.

CHAPTER 28

1. *What sort of information would an investor consider material?* The average investor is not concerned with minor inaccuracies but with facts that if disclosed would tend to deter him or her from buying the securities. This would include facts that have an important bearing on the condition of the issuer and its business—liabilities, loans to officers and directors, customer delinquencies, and pending lawsuits.

2. *Can Lee take advantage of this information to buy and sell Magma stock? Why or why not?* No. The Securities Exchange Act of 1934 extends liability to officers and directors in their personal transactions for taking advantage of inside information when they know it is unavailable to the persons with whom they are dealing.

APPENDIX F
SAMPLE ANSWERS FOR BUSINESS CASE PROBLEMS WITH SAMPLE ANSWER

PROBLEM 1–6. *Reading Citations.* The court's opinion in this case—*United States v. Yi,* 704 F.3d 800 (9th Cir. 2013)—can be found in volume 704 of West's *Federal Reporter, Third Series,* on page 800. The United States Court of Appeals for the Ninth Circuit issued this opinion in 2013.

PROBLEM 2–8. *Discovery.* Yes, the items that were deleted from a Facebook page can be recovered. Normally, a party must hire an expert to recover material in an electronic format, and this can be time consuming and expensive.

Electronic evidence, or e-evidence, consists of all computer-generated or electronically recorded information, such as posts on Facebook and other social media sites. The effect that e-evidence can have in a case depends on its relevance and what it reveals. In the facts presented in this problem, Isaiah should be sanctioned—he should be required to cover Allied's cost of hiring the recovery expert and attorneys' fees for confronting the misconduct. In a jury trial, the court might also instruct the jury to presume that any missing items are harmful to Isaiah's case. If all of the material is retrieved and presented at the trial, any prejudice to Allied's case might thereby be mitigated. If not, the court might go so far as to order a new trial.

In the actual case on which this problem is based, Allied hired an expert, who determined that Isaiah had in fact removed some photos and other items from his Facebook page. After the expert testified about the missing material, Isaiah provided Allied with all of it, including the photos that he had deleted. Allied requested a retrial, but the court instead reduced the amount of damages awarded to Isaiah by the amount that it cost Allied to address his "misconduct."

PROBLEM 3–4. *Arbitration Clause.* Based on a recent holding by the Washington state supreme court, the federal appeals court held that the arbitration provision was unconscionable and therefore invalid. Because it was invalid, the restriction on class-action suits was also invalid.

The state court held that placing class-action restrictions in arbitration agreements with consumers improperly stripped consumers of rights they would normally have to attack certain industry practices. Class-action suits are often brought in cases alleging deceptive or unfair industry practices when the losses suffered by the individual consumer are too small to warrant the consumer bringing suit. In other words, the supposed added cell phone fees were so small that no individual consumer would be likely to litigate or arbitrate the matter due to the expenses involved. Therefore, the clause in the arbitration agreement preventing consumers from joining together in a class-action suit violates public policy and is void and unenforceable.

PROBLEM 4–5. *Online Privacy.* Facebook created a program that makes decisions for users. Many believe that privacy is an extremely important right that should be fiercely protected. Thus, using duty-based ethics, any program that has a default setting of giving out information is unethical. Facebook should create the program as an opt-in program.

In addition, under the Kantian categorical imperative, if every company used opt-out programs that allowed the disclosure of potentially personal information, privacy might become merely theoretical. If privacy were reduced or eliminated, the world might not be a better place. From a utilitarian or outcome-based approach, an opt-out program might offer the benefits of being easy to created and start, as well as making it easy to recruit partner programs. On the negative side, the program would eliminate users' ability to chose whether to disclose information about themselves. An opt-in program would maintain that user control but might entail higher start-up costs because it would require more marketing to users up front to persuade them to opt in.

PROBLEM 5–6. *Establishment Clause.* The establishment clause prohibits the government from passing laws or taking actions that promote religion or show a preference for one religion over another. In assessing a government action, the courts look at the predominant purpose of the action and ask whether the action has the effect of endorsing religion.

Although here DeWeese claimed to have a nonreligious purpose for displaying the poster of the Ten Commandments in a courtroom, his own statements showed a religious purpose. These statements reflected his views about "warring" legal philosophies and his belief that "our legal system is based on moral absolutes from divine law handed down by God through the Ten Commandments." This plainly constitutes a religious purpose that violates the establishment clause because it has the effect of endorsing Judaism or Christianity over other religions. In the case on which this problem is based, the court ruled in favor of the American Civil Liberties Union.

PROBLEM 6–5. *Agency Powers.* The United States Supreme Court held that greenhouse gases fit within the Clean Air Act's (CAA's) definition of "air pollutant." Thus, the Environmental Protection Agency (EPA) has the authority under that statute to regulate the emission of such gases from new motor vehicles. According to the Court, the definition, which includes "any" air pollutant, embraces all airborne compounds "of whatever stripe."

The EPA's focus on Congress's 1990 amendments (or their lack) does not indicate the original intent behind the statute (and its amendments before 1990). Nothing in the statute suggests that Congress meant to curtail the agency's power to treat greenhouse gases as air pollutants. In other words, the agency has a preexisting mandate to regulate "any air pollutant" that may endanger the public welfare.

The EPA also argued that, even if it had the authority to regulate greenhouse gases, the agency would not exercise that authority because any regulation would conflict with other administration priorities. The Court acknowledged that the CAA conditions EPA action on the agency's formation of a "judgment," but explained that judgment must relate to whether a pollutant "cause[s], or contribute[s] to, air pollution which may reasonably be anticipated to endanger public health or welfare."

Thus, the EPA can avoid issuing regulations only if the agency determines that greenhouse gases do not contribute to climate change (or if the agency reasonably explains why it cannot or will not determine whether they do). The EPA's refusal to regulate was thus "arbitrary, capricious, or otherwise not in accordance with law." The Court remanded the case for the EPA to "ground its reasons for action or inaction in the statute."

PROBLEM 7–8. *Criminal Liability.* Yes, Green exhibited the required mental state to establish criminal liability. A wrongful mental state *(mens rea)* is one of the elements typically required to establish criminal liability. The required mental state, or intent, is indicated in an applicable statute or law. For example, for murder, the required mental state is the intent to take another's life. A court can also find that the required mental state is present when a defendant's acts are reckless or criminally negligent. A defendant is criminally reckless if he or she consciously disregards a substantial and unjustifiable risk.

In this problem, Green was clearly aware of the danger to which he was exposing people on the street below, but he did not indicate that he specifically intended to harm anyone. The risk of death created by his conduct, however, was obvious. He must have known what was likely to happen if a bottle or plate thrown from the height of twenty-six stories hit a pedestrian or the windshield of an occupied motor vehicle on the street below. Despite his claim that he was intoxicated, he was sufficiently aware to stop throwing things from the balcony when he saw police in the area, and he later recalled what he had done and what had happened.

In the actual case on which this problem is based, after a jury trial, Green was convicted of reckless endangerment. On appeal, a state intermediate appellate court affirmed the conviction, based in part on the reasoning stated above.

PROBLEM 8–6. *Sovereign Immunity.* The doctrine of sovereign immunity exempts foreign nations from the jurisdiction of U.S. courts, subject to certain conditions. The Foreign Sovereign Immunities Act (FSIA) of 1976 codifies this doctrine and exclusively governs the circumstances in which an action may be brought in a U.S. court against a foreign nation.

A foreign state is not immune from the jurisdiction of U.S. courts when the state (a) waives immunity, (b) engages in commercial activity, or (c) commits a tort in the United States or violates certain international laws. Under the FSIA, a foreign state includes its political subdivisions and "instrumentalities"—departments and agencies. A commercial activity is a regular course of commercial conduct, transaction, or act that is carried out by the foreign state within the United States or has a direct effect in the United States.

The details of what constitutes a commercial activity are left to the courts. But it seems clear that a foreign government can be considered to engage in commercial activity when, instead of regulating a market, the government participates in it. In other words, when a foreign state, or its political subdivisions or instrumentalities, performs the type of actions in which a private party engages in commerce, the state's actions are likewise commercial.

In the facts of this problem, Iran engaged in commercial activity outside the United States by making and marketing its counterfeit versions of Bell's Model 206 Series helicopters. This activity caused a direct effect in the United States by the consumer confusion that will likely result from Iran's unauthorized use of Bell's trade dress. Thus, the court can exercise jurisdiction in these circumstances, and Iran may be as liable as a private party would be for the same acts.

In the actual case on which this problem is based, Iran did not respond to Bell's complaint. The court held that it had jurisdiction under the FSIA's commercial activity exception, as explained above. The court entered a default judgment against Iran and awarded damages and an injunction to Bell.

PROBLEM 9–4. *Offer and Acceptance.* No, a contract was not formed in this case. As the Iowa Supreme Court pointed out, the parties must voluntarily agree to enter into a contract. Courts determine whether an offer has been made objectively—not subjectively.

Under the *Restatement of Contracts (Second),* "the test for an offer is whether it induces a reasonable belief in the recipient that [the recipient] can, by accepting, bind the sender." The offeror may decide to whom to extend the offer. According to the *Restatement,* an offer may create a power of acceptance in a specified person or in one or more of a specified group or class of persons, acting separately or together.

The court hearing this case explained: "In this situation, Prairie Meadows is the offeror. It makes an offer to its patrons that, if accepted by wagering an amount and the patron wins, it will pay off the wager. Simply stated, the issue is whether Prairie Meadows made an offer to Blackford. Because Prairie Meadows has the ability to determine the class of individuals to whom the offer is made, it may also exclude certain individuals. Blackford had been banned for life from the casino. . . . Under an objective test, unless the ban had been lifted, Blackford could not have reasonably believed he was among the class of individuals invited to accept Prairie Meadows's offer."

In the actual case on which this problem is based, the jury found that the ban against Blackford had not been lifted and, therefore, Prairie Meadows had not extended him an offer to wager. Because there was no offer to him, no contract could result. The state supreme court therefore reversed the decision of the state appellate court and affirmed the trial court's judgment.

PROBLEM 10–5. *Consequential Damages.* Simard is liable only for the losses and expenses related to the first resale. Simard could reasonably anticipate that his breach would require another sale and that the sales price might be less than what he agreed to pay. Therefore, he should be liable for the difference between his sales price and the first resale price ($29,000), plus any expenses arising from the first resale. Simard is not liable, however, for any expenses and losses related to the second resale. After all, Simard did not cause the second purchaser's default, and he could not reasonably foresee that default as a probable result of his breach.

PROBLEM 11–5. *Nonconforming Goods.* Padma Paper Mills notified Universal Exports about its breach, so Padma has two ways to recover even though it accepted the goods.

Padma's first option is to argue that it revoked its acceptance, giving it the right to reject the goods. To revoke acceptance, Padma would have to show that (a) the nonconformity substantially impaired the value of the shipment, (b) it predicated its acceptance on a reasonable assumption that Universal Exports would cure the nonconformity, and (c) Universal Exports did not cure the nonconformity within a reasonable time.

Padma's second option is to keep the goods and recover for the damages caused by Universal Exports' breach. Under this option, Padma could recover at least the difference between the value of the goods as promised and their value as accepted.

PROBLEM 12–8. *Negligence.* Negligence requires proof that (a) the defendant owed a duty of care to the plaintiff, (b) the defendant breached that duty, (c) the defendant's breach caused the plaintiff's injury, and (d) the plaintiff suffered a legally recognizable injury. With respect to the duty of care, a business owner has a duty to use reasonable care to protect business invitees. This duty includes an obligation to discover and correct or warn of unreasonably dangerous conditions that the owner of the premises should reasonably foresee might endanger an invitee. Some risks are so obvious that an owner need not warn of them. But even if a risk is obvious, a business owner may not be excused from the duty to protect its customers from foreseeable harm.

Because Lucario was the Weatherford's business invitee, the hotel owed her a duty of reasonable care to make its premises safe for her use. The balcony ran nearly the entire width of the window in Lucario's room. She could have reasonably believed that the window was a means of access to the balcony. The window/balcony configuration was dangerous, however, because the window opened wide enough for an adult to climb out, but the twelve-inch gap between one side of the window and the balcony was unprotected. This unprotected gap opened to a drop of more than three stories to a concrete surface below.

Should the hotel have anticipated the potential harm to a guest opening the window in Room 59 and attempting to access the balcony? The hotel encouraged guests to "step out onto the balcony" to smoke. The dangerous window/balcony configuration could have been remedied at a minimal cost. These circumstances could be perceived as creating an "unreasonably dangerous" condition. And it could be concluded that the hotel created or knew of the condition and failed to take reasonable steps to warn of it or correct it. Of course, the Weatherford might argue that the window/balcony configuration was so obvious that the hotel was not liable for Lucario's fall.

In the actual case on which this problem is based, the court concluded that the Weatherford did not breach its duty of care to Lucario. On McMurtry's appeal, a state intermediate appellate court held that this conclusion was in error, vacated the lower court's judgment in favor of the hotel on this issue, and remanded the case.

PROBLEM 13–8. *Product Liability.* Here, the accident was caused by Jett's inattention, not by the texting device in the cab of his truck. In a product liability case based on a design defect, the plaintiff has to prove that the product was defective at the time it left the hands of the seller or lessor. The plaintiff must also show that this defective condition made the product "unreasonably dangerous" to the user or consumer. If the product was delivered in a safe condition and subsequent mishandling made it harmful to the user, the seller or lessor normally is not liable. To successfully assert a design defect, a plaintiff has to show that a reasonable alternative design was available and that the defendant failed to use it.

The plaintiffs could contend that the defendant manufacturer of the texting device owed them a duty of care because injuries to vehicle drivers and passengers, and others on the roads, were reasonably foreseeable due to the product's design that (a) required the driver to divert his eyes from the road to view an incoming text from the dispatcher and (b) permitted the receipt of texts while the vehicle was moving. But manufacturers are not required to design a product incapable of distracting a driver. The duty owed by a manufacturer to the user or consumer of a product does not require guarding against hazards that are commonly known or obvious or protecting against injuries that result from a user's careless conduct. That is what happened here.

In the actual case on which this problem is based, the court reached the same conclusion, based on the reasoning stated above, and an intermediate appellate court affirmed the judgment.

PROBLEM 14–5. *Trade Secrets.* Some business information that cannot be protected by trademark, patent, or copyright law is protected against appropriation by competitors as trade secrets. Trade secrets consist of anything that makes a company unique and that would have value to a competitor—customer lists, plans, research and development, pricing information, marketing techniques, and production techniques, for example. Theft of trade secrets is a federal crime.

In this problem, the documents in the boxes in the car could constitute trade secrets. But a number of factors suggest that a finding of theft and imposition of liability would not be appropriate. The boxes were not marked in any way that would indicate they contained confidential information. The boxes were stored in an employee's car. The alleged thief was the employee's spouse, not a CPR competitor, and she apparently had no idea what was in the boxes. Leaving trade secrets so accessible does not show an effort to protect the information.

In the case on which this problem is based, the court dismissed Jones's claim, in part on the reasoning stated above.

PROBLEM 15–6. *Privacy.* No, Rolfe did not have a privacy interest in the information obtained by the subpoenas issued to Midcontinent Communications. The courts have held that the right to privacy is guaranteed by the U.S. Constitution's Bill of Rights, and some state constitutions contain an explicit guarantee of the right. A person must have a reasonable expectation of privacy, though, to maintain a suit or to assert a successful defense for an invasion of privacy.

People clearly have a reasonable expectation of privacy when they enter their personal banking or credit-card information online. They also have a reasonable expectation that online companies will follow their own privacy policies. But people do not a reasonable expectation of privacy in statements made on Twitter and other data that they publicly disseminate. In other words, there is no violation of a subscriber's right to privacy when a third party Internet service provider receives a subpoena and discloses the subscriber's information.

Here, Rolfe supplied his e-mail address and other personal information, including his Internet protocol address, to Midcontinent. In other words, Rolfe publicly disseminated this information. Law enforcement officers obtained this information from Midcontinent through the subpoenas issued by the South Dakota state court. Rolfe provided his information to Midcontinent—he has no legitimate expectation of privacy in that information.

In the actual case on which this problem is based, Rolfe was charged with, and convicted of, possessing, manufacturing, and distributing child pornography, as well as other crimes. As part of the proceedings, the court found that Rolfe had no expectation of privacy in the information that he made available to Midcontinent. On appeal, the South Dakota Supreme Court upheld the conviction.

PROBLEM 16–6. *Automatic Stay.* Gholston can recover damages because EZ Auto willfully violated the automatic stay. EZ Auto repossessed the car even though it received notice of the automatic stay from the bankruptcy court. Moreover, EZ Auto retained the car even after it was reminded of the stay by Gholston's attorney. Thus, EZ Auto knew about the automatic stay and violated it intentionally. Because Gholston suffered direct damages as a result, she can recover from EZ Auto.

PROBLEM 17–6. *Partnership Formation.* Garcia and Lucero probably satisfied all three requirements for forming a partnership. They owned the two properties equally, agreed to share both profits and losses, and enjoyed equal management rights. Moreover, it is immaterial that they lacked a written partnership agreement. The writing requirement (Statute of Frauds) does not apply to these facts, and a partnership agreement can be oral or implied by the parties' conduct.

PROBLEM 18–5. *LLC Operation.* No. One Bluewater member could not unilaterally "fire" another member without providing a reason. Part of the attractiveness of the limited liability company (LLC) as a form of business enterprise is its flexibility. The members can decide how to operate the business through an operating agreement. For example, the agreement can set forth procedures for choosing or removing members or managers.

Here, the Bluewater operating agreement provided for a "super majority" vote to remove a member under circumstances that would jeopardize the firm's contractor status. Thus, one Bluewater member could not unilaterally "fire" another member without providing a reason. In fact, a majority of the members could not terminate the other's interest in the firm without providing a reason. Moreover, the only acceptable reason would be a circumstance that undercut the firm's status as a contractor.

The flexibility of the LLC business form relates to its framework, not to its members' capacity to violate its operating agreement. In the actual case on which this problem is based, Smith attempted to "fire" Williford without providing a reason. In Williford's suit, the court issued a judgment in his favor.

PROBLEM 19–6. *Rights of Shareholders.* Yes. Woods has a right to inspect Biolustré's books and records. Every shareholder is entitled to examine corporate records. A shareholder can inspect the books in person or through an agent such as an attorney, accountant, or other authorized assistant.

The right of inspection is limited to the inspection and copying of corporate books and records for a proper purpose. This is because the power of inspection is fraught with potential for abuse—for example, it can involve the disclosure of trade secrets and other confidential information. Thus, a corporation is allowed to protect itself.

Here, Woods, through Hair Ventures, has the right to inspect Biolustré's books and records. She has a proper purpose for the inspection—to obtain information about Biolustré's financial situation. She, and other shareholders, had not received notice of shareholders' meetings or corporate financial reports for years, or notice of Biolustré's plan to issue additional stock. Hair Ventures had a substantial investment in the company. In the actual case on which this problem is based, the court ordered Biolustré to produce its books and records for Hair Ventures' inspection.

PROBLEM 20–6. *Liability for Contracts.* Hall may be held personally liable. Hall could not be an agent for House Medic because it was a fictitious name and not a real entity. Moreover, when the contract was formed, Hall did not disclose his true principal, which was Hall Hauling, Ltd. Thus, Hall may be held personally liable as a party to the contract.

PROBLEM 21–5. *Workers' Compensation.* Fairbanks's claim qualifies for workers' compensation benefits. To recover benefits under state workers' compensation laws, the requirements are that the injury (a) was accidental and (b) occurred on the job or in the course of employment. Fault is not an issue. The employee must file a claim with the appropriate state agency or board that administers local workers' compensation claims.

In this problem, Fairbanks's claim for workers' compensation benefits appears to have been timely filed with the appropriate state agency. The focus of the dispute is on the second requirement listed above—an accidental injury that occurred on the job or in the course of employment. Dynea required its employees to wear certain boots as a safety measure. One of the boots caused a sore on Fairbanks's leg. The sore developed into a pustule and broke into a lesion. Within a week, Fairbanks was hospitalized with an MRSA infection.

Dynea argued that the bacteria were on Fairbanks's skin before he came to work. Even if this were true, however, it was the rubbing of the boot that caused the sore through which the bacteria entered his body. This fact fulfills the second requirement for the recovery of workers' compensation benefits.

In the actual case on which this problem is based, the court issued a decision in favor of Fairbanks's claim for benefits.

PROBLEM 22–5. *Retaliation by Employers.* Yes. Dawson could establish a claim for retaliation. Title VII prohibits retaliation. In a retaliation claim, an individual asserts that she or he suffered harm as a result of making a charge, testifying, or participating in a Title VII investigation or proceeding. To prove retaliation, a plaintiff must show that the challenged action was one that would likely have dissuaded a reasonable worker from making or supporting a charge of discrimination.

In this problem, under applicable state law, it was unlawful for an employer to discriminate against an individual based on sexual orientation. Dawson was subjected to derision on the part of co-workers, including his supervisor, based on his sexual orientation. He filed a complaint with his employer's human resources department. Two days later, he was fired. The proximity in time and the other circumstances, especially the supervisor's conduct, would support a retaliation claim. Also, the discharge would likely have dissuaded Dawson, or any reasonable worker, from making a claim of discrimination. In the actual case on which this problem is based, the court held that Dawson offered enough evidence that "a reasonable trier of fact could find in favor of Dawson on his retaliation claim."

PROBLEM 23–5. *Unfair Labor Practices.* Yes. The NLRB has consistently been suspicious of companies that grant added benefits during election campaigns. These benefits will be considered as an unfair labor practice that biases elections, unless the employer can demonstrate that the benefits were unrelated to the unionization. Therefore, the union's conduct of persuading the employer to fire Stone for resisting paying union dues is an unfair labor practice.

PROBLEM 24–7. *Fair Debt-Collection Practices.* Engler may recover under the Fair Debt Collection Practices Act (FDCPA). Atlantic is subject to the FDCPA because it is a debt-collection agency, and it was attempting to collect a debt on behalf of Bank of America. Atlantic also used offensive tactics to collect from Engler. After all, Atlantic gave Engler's employer the false impression that Engler was a criminal, had a pending case, and was about to be arrested. Finally, Engler suffered harm because he experienced discomfort, embarrassment, and distress as a result of Atlantic's abusive conduct. Engler may recover actual damages, statutory damages, and attorneys' fees from Atlantic.

PROBLEM 25–5. *Environmental Impact Statement.* When an agency acts in an arbitrary and capricious manner, then the court has grounds for intervention. Otherwise, the court defers to the expertise of the agency, as revealed in the record.

Here, the environmental impact statement (EIS) was comprehensive, and the National Park Service (NPS) had credible reason to believe that the use of rafts on the river did not damage the wilderness status of portions of the park. Since the NPS acted within its statutory guidelines and followed proper procedure in its decision making, the court would not intervene in the agency's decision. The appellate court found that the plaintiffs had failed to establish that the NPS acted in an arbitrary and capricious manner when it adopted the plan.

PROBLEM 26–7. *Adverse Possession.* The McKeags satisfied the first three requirements for adverse possession:

(a) Their possession was actual and exclusive because they used the beach and prevented others from doing so, including the Finleys,

(b) Their possession was open, visible, and notorious because they made improvements to the beach and regularly kept their belongings there.

(c) Their possession was continuous and peaceable for the required ten years. They possessed the property for more than four decades, and they even kept a large float there during the winter months.

Nevertheless, the McKeags' possession was *not* hostile and adverse, which is the fourth requirement. The Finleys had substantial evidence that they gave the McKeags permission to use the beach. Rather than reject the Finleys' permission as unnecessary, the McKeags sometimes said nothing and other times seemingly affirmed that the property belonged to the Finleys. Thus, because the McKeags did not satisfy all four requirements, they cannot establish adverse possession.

PROBLEM 27–6. *Price Discrimination.* Spa Steel satisfies most of the requirements for a price discrimination claim under Section 2 of the Clayton Act. Dayton Superior is engaged in interstate commerce, and it sells goods of like grade and quality to at least three purchasers. Moreover, Spa Steel can show that, because it sells Dayton Superior's products at a higher price, it lost business and thus suffered an injury.

To recover, however, Spa Steel will also need to prove that Dayton Superior charged Spa Steel's competitors a lower price for the same product. Spa Steel cannot recover if its prices were higher for reasons related to its own business, such as having a higher overhead or seeking a larger profit.

PROBLEM 28–6. *Violations of the 1934 Act.* An omission or misrepresentation of a material fact in connection with the purchase or sale of a security may violate Section 10(b) of the Securities Exchange Act of 1934 and SEC Rule 10b-5. The key question is whether the omitted or misrepresented information is material. A fact, by itself, is not automatically material.

A fact will be regarded as material only if it is significant enough that it would likely affect an investor's decision as to whether to buy or sell the company's securities. For example, a company's potential liability in a product liability suit and the financial consequences to the firm are material facts that must be disclosed because they affect an investor's decision to buy stock in the company.

In this case, the plaintiffs' claim should not be dismissed. To prevail on their claim that the defendants made material omissions in violation of Section 10(b) and SEC Rule 10-5, the plaintiffs must prove that the omission was material. Their complaint alleged the omission of information linking Zicam and anosmia (loss of the sense of smell) and plausibly suggested that reasonable investors would have viewed this information as material. Zicam products account for 70 percent of Matrixx's sales. Matrixx received reports of consumers who suffered anosmia after using Zicam Cold Remedy.

In public statements discussing revenues and product safety, Matrixx did not disclose this information. But the information was significant enough to likely affect a consumer's decision to use the product, and this would affect the company's revenue and ultimately the commercial viability of the product. The information was therefore significant enough to likely affect an investor's decision whether to buy or sell Matrixx's stock, and this would affect the stock price. Thus, the plaintiffs' allegations were sufficient. Contrary to the defendants' assertion, statistical sampling is not required to show materiality—reasonable investors could view reports of adverse events as material even if the reports did not provide statistically significant evidence.

GLOSSARY

A

Acceptance In contract law, the offeree's notification to the offeror that the offeree agrees to be bound by the terms of the offeror's proposal. Although historically the terms of acceptance had to be the mirror image of the terms of the offer, the Uniform Commercial Code provides that even modified terms of the offer in a definite expression of acceptance constitute a contract.

Accredited investors In the context of securities offerings, "sophisticated" investors, such as banks, insurance companies, investment companies, the issuer's executive officers and directors, and persons whose income or net worth exceeds certain limits.

Acquittal A certification or declaration following a trial that the individual accused of a crime is innocent, or free from guilt, and is thus absolved of the charges.

Act of state doctrine A doctrine that provides that the judicial branch of one country will not examine the validity of public acts committed by a recognized foreign government within its own territory.

Actionable Capable of serving as the basis of a lawsuit.

Actual authority Authority of an agent that is express or implied.

Actual malice A condition that exists when a person makes a statement with either knowledge of its falsity or a reckless disregard for the truth. In a defamation suit, a statement made about a public figure normally must be made with actual malice for liability to be incurred.

Actus reus (pronounced *ak*-tus *ray*-uhs) A guilty (prohibited) act. The commission of a prohibited act is one of the two essential elements required for criminal liability, the other element being the intent to commit a crime.

Adequate protection doctrine In bankruptcy law, a doctrine that protects secured creditors from losing their security as a result of an automatic stay on legal proceedings by creditors against the debtor once the debtor petitions for bankruptcy relief. In certain circumstances, the bankruptcy court may provide adequate protection by requiring the debtor or trustee to pay the creditor or provide additional guaranties to protect the creditor against the losses suffered by the creditor as a result of the stay.

Adhesion contract A "standard-form" contract, such as that between a large retailer and a consumer, in which the stronger party dictates the terms.

Adjudication The process of resolving a dispute by presenting evidence and arguments before a neutral third party decision maker in a court or an administrative law proceeding.

Adjustable-rate mortgage (ARM) A mortgage in which the rate of interest paid by the borrower changes periodically, often with reference to a predetermined government interest rate (the index). Usually, the interest rate for ARMs is initially low and increases over time, but there is a cap on the amount that the rate can increase during any adjustment period.

Administrative agency A federal, state, or local government agency established to perform a specific function. Administrative agencies are authorized by legislative acts to make and enforce rules to administer and enforce the acts.

Administrative law The body of law created by administrative agencies (in the form of rules, regulations, orders, and decisions) in order to carry out their duties and responsibilities.

Administrative law judge (ALJ) One who presides over an administrative agency hearing and who has the power to administer oaths, take testimony, rule on questions of evidence, and make determinations of fact.

Administrative process The procedure used by administrative agencies in the administration of law.

Adverse possession The acquisition of title to real property by occupying it openly, without the consent of the owner, for a period of time specified by a state statute. The occupation must be actual, open, notorious, exclusive, and in opposition to all others, including the owner.

Affidavit A written or printed voluntary statement of facts, confirmed by the oath or affirmation of the party making it and made before a person having the authority to administer the oath or affirmation.

Affirm To validate; to give legal force to. *See also* Ratification

Affirmative action Job-hiring policies that give special consideration to members of protected classes in an effort to overcome present effects of past discrimination.

Affirmative defense A response to a plaintiff's claim that does not deny the plaintiff's facts but attacks the plaintiff's legal right to bring an action. An example is the running of the statute of limitations.

After-acquired evidence A type of evidence submitted in support of an affirmative defense in employment discrimination cases. Evidence that, prior to the employer's discriminatory act, the employee engaged in misconduct sufficient to warrant dismissal had the employer known of it earlier.

Agency A relationship between two parties in which one party (the agent) agrees to represent or act for the other (the principal).

Agency by estoppel An agency that arises when a principal negligently allows an agent to exercise powers not granted to the agent, thus justifying others in believing that the agent possesses the requisite agency authority.

Agency coupled with an interest An agency relationship in which the agent has some legal right to (an interest in) the property that is the subject of the agency, and thus the agency is created for the agent's benefit instead of the principal's. Because the agent has an additional interest in the property beyond the normal commission for selling it, the agent's position cannot be terminated until the agent's interest ends.

Agent A person who agrees to represent or act for another, called the principal.

Agreement A meeting of two or more minds in regard to the terms of a contract. Agreement is usually broken down into two events—an offer by one party to form a contract, and an acceptance of the offer by the person to whom the offer is made.

Alien corporation A designation in the United States for a corporation formed in another country but doing business in the United States.

Allegation A statement, claim, or assertion.

Allege To state, recite, assert, or charge.

Alternative dispute resolution (ADR) The resolution of disputes in ways other than those involved in the traditional judicial process. Negotiation, mediation, and arbitration are forms of ADR.

Amend To change through a formal procedure.

American Arbitration Association (AAA) The major organization offering arbitration services in the United States.

Answer Procedurally, a defendant's response to the plaintiff's complaint.

Antecedent claim A preexisting claim.

Anticipatory repudiation An assertion or action by a party indicating that he or she will not perform an obligation that the party is contractually obligated to perform at a future time.

Antitrust law The body of federal and state laws and statutes protecting trade and commerce from unlawful restraints, price discrimination, price fixing, and monopolies. The principal federal antitrust statues are the Sherman Act of 1890, the Clayton Act of 1914, and the Federal Trade Commission Act of 1914.

Apparent authority Authority that is only apparent, not real. In agency law, a person may be deemed to have had the power to act as an agent for another party if the other party's manifestations to a third party led the third party to believe that an agency existed when, in fact, it did not.

Appeal Resort to a superior court, such as an appellate court, to review the decision of an inferior court, such as a trial court or an administrative agency.

Appellant The party who takes an appeal from one court to another.

Appellate court A court having appellate jurisdiction.

Appellate jurisdiction Courts having appellate jurisdiction act as reviewing courts, or appellate courts. Generally, cases can be brought before appellate courts only on appeal from an order or a judgment of a trial court or other lower court.

Appellee The party against whom an appeal is taken—that is, the party who opposes setting aside or reversing the judgment.

Appropriation In tort law, the use by one person of another person's name, likeness, or other identifying characteristic without permission and for the benefit of the user.

Arbitrary and capricious test A court reviewing an informal administrative agency action applies this test to determine whether or not that action was in clear error. The court gives wide discretion to the expertise of the agency and decides if the agency had sufficient factual information on which to base its action. If no clear error was made, then the agency's action stands.

Arbitration The settling of a dispute by submitting it to a disinterested third party (other than a court), who renders a decision. The decision may or may not be legally binding.

Arbitration clause A clause in a contract that provides that, in the event of a dispute, the parties will submit the dispute to arbitration rather than litigate the dispute in court.

Arbitrator A neutral third party or panel of experts that hear a dispute in arbitration.

Arraignment A procedure in which an accused person is brought before the court to answer criminal charges. The charge is read to the person, and he or she is asked to enter a plea—such as "guilty" or "not guilty."

Arson The malicious burning of another's dwelling. Some statutes have expanded this to include any real property regardless of ownership and the destruction of property by other means—for example, by explosion.

Articles of incorporation The document filed with the appropriate governmental agency, usually the secretary of state, when a business is incorporated. State statutes usually prescribe what kind of information must be contained in the articles of incorporation.

Articles of organization The document filed with a designated state official by which a limited liability company is formed.

Articles of partnership A written agreement that sets forth each partner's rights and obligations with respect to the partnership.

Artisan's lien A possessory lien given to a person who has made improvements and added value to another person's personal property as security for payment for services performed.

Assault Any word or action intended to make another person fearful of immediate physical harm; a reasonably believable threat.

Assignee The person to whom contract rights are assigned.

Assignment The act of transferring to another all or part of one's rights arising under a contract.

Assignor The person who assigns contract rights.

Assumption of risk A defense against negligence that can be used when the plaintiff was aware of a danger and voluntarily assumed the risk of injury from that danger.

Attachment (1) In the context of secured transactions, the process by which a security interest in the property of another becomes enforceable. (2) In the context of judicial liens, a court-ordered seizure and taking into custody of property prior to the securing of a judgment for a past-due debt.

Attempted monopolization Any actions by a firm to eliminate competition and gain monopoly power.

Authenticate To sign a record, or with the intent to sign a record, to execute or to adopt an electronic sound, symbol, or the like to link with the record. A *record* is retrievable information inscribed on a tangible medium or stored in an electronic or other medium.

Authority In agency law, the agent's permission to act on behalf of the principal. An agent's authority may be actual (express or implied) or apparent. *See also* Actual authority; Apparent authority

Authorization card A card signed by an employee that gives a union permission to act on his or her behalf in negotiations with management. Unions typically use authorization cards as evidence of employee support during union organization.

Authorized means In contract law, the means of acceptance authorized by the offeror.

Automatic stay In bankruptcy proceedings, the suspension of almost all litigation and other action by creditors against the debtor or the debtor's property. The stay is effective the moment the debtor files a petition in bankruptcy.

Award In the context of litigation, the amount of money awarded to a plaintiff in a civil lawsuit as damages. In the context of arbitration, the arbitrator's decision.

B

Bailment A situation in which the personal property of one person (a bailor) is entrusted to another (a bailee), who is obligated to return the bailed property to the bailor or dispose of it as directed.

Bait-and-switch advertising Advertising a product at a very attractive price (the bait) and then informing the consumer, once he or she is in the store, that the advertised product is either not available or is of poor quality. The customer is then urged to purchase (switched to) a more expensive item.

Bankruptcy court A federal court of limited jurisdiction that handles only bankruptcy proceedings. Bankruptcy proceedings are governed by federal bankruptcy law.

Bankruptcy trustee A person who is either appointed by the U.S. Department of Justice or by creditors in bankruptcy cases. In all bankruptcies under Chapters 7, 12, or 13, a trustee is appointed by the U.S. Trustee, who is an officer of the Department of Justice. Chapter 11 bankruptcies allow the debtor to continue to manage the property as a "debtor in possession," but this person can be replaced for cause with a bankruptcy trustee.

Battery The unprivileged, intentional touching of another.

Benefit corporation A for-profit corporation that seeks to have a material positive impact on society and the environment. This new business form is available by statute in a growing number of states.

Beyond a reasonable doubt The standard used to determine the guilt or innocence of a person criminally charged. To be guilty of a crime, one must be proved guilty "beyond and to the exclusion of every reasonable doubt." A reasonable doubt is one that would cause a prudent person to hesitate before acting in matters important to him or her.

Bilateral contract A type of contract that arises when a promise is given in exchange for a return promise.

Bill of lading A document that serves both as evidence of the receipt of goods for shipment and as documentary evidence of title to the goods.

Bill of Rights The first ten amendments to the U.S. Constitution.

Binding authority Any source of law that a court must follow when deciding a case. Binding authorities include constitutions, statutes, and regulations that govern the issue being decided, as well as court decisions that are controlling precedents within the jurisdiction.

Blue sky laws State laws that regulate the offer and sale of securities.

Bona fide Good faith. A bona fide obligation is one made in good faith—that is, sincerely and honestly.

Bona fide occupational qualification (BFOQ) Identifiable characteristics reasonably necessary to the normal operation of a particular business. These characteristics can include gender, national origin, and religion, but not race.

Botnet Short for *robot network*—a group of computers that run an application that is controlled and manipulated only by the software source. Although the network is sometimes legitimate, usually this term is reserved for a group of computers that have been infected by malicious robot software. In a botnet, each connected computer becomes a zombie, or drone.

Boycott A concerted refusal to do business with a particular person or entity in order to obtain concessions or to express displeasure with certain acts or practices of that person or business. *See also* Secondary boycott

Breach To violate a law, by an act or an omission, or to break a legal obligation that one owes to another person or to society.

Breach of contract The failure, without legal excuse, of a promisor to perform the obligations of a contract.

Bribery The offering, giving, receiving, or soliciting of anything of value with the aim of influencing an official action or an official's discharge of a legal or public duty or (with respect to commercial bribery) a business decision.

Brief A formal legal document submitted by the attorney for the appellant—or the appellee (in answer to the appellant's brief)—to an appellate court when a case is appealed. The appellant's brief outlines the facts and issues of the case, the judge's rulings or jury's findings that should be reversed or modified, the applicable law, and the arguments on the client's behalf.

Browse-wrap terms Terms and conditions of use that are presented to an Internet user at the time certain products, such as software, are being downloaded but that need not be agreed to (by clicking "I agree," for example) before being able to install or use the product.

Bureaucracy A large organization that is structured hierarchically to carry out specific functions.

Burglary The unlawful entry into a building with the intent to commit a felony. (Some state statutes expand this to include the intent to commit any crime.)

Business ethics Ethics in a business context; a consensus of what constitutes right or wrong behavior in the world of business and the application of moral principles to situations that arise in a business setting.

Business invitees Those people, such as customers or clients, who are invited onto business premises by the owner of those premises for business purposes.

Business judgment rule A rule that immunizes corporate management from liability for actions that result in corporate losses or damages if the actions are undertaken in good faith and are within both the power of the corporation and the authority of management to make.

Business necessity A defense to allegations of employment discrimination in which the employer demonstrates that an employment practice that discriminates against members of a protected class is related to job performance.

Business tort Wrongful interference with the business rights of another.

Buyout price The amount payable to a partner on his or her dissociation from a partnership, based on the amount distributable to that partner if the firm were wound up on that date, and offset by any damages for wrongful dissociation.

Buy-sell agreement In the context of partnerships, an express agreement made at the time of partnership formation for one or more of the partners to buy out the other or others should the situation warrant—and thus provide for the smooth dissolution of the partnership.

Bylaws A set of governing rules adopted by a corporation or other association.

Bystander A spectator, witness, or person who was standing nearby when an event occurred and who did not engage in the business or act leading to the event.

C

C.I.F. or C.&F. Cost, insurance, and freight—or just cost and freight. A pricing term in a contract for the sale of goods requiring, among other things, that the seller place the goods in the possession of a carrier before risk passes to the buyer.

Case law The rules of law announced in court decisions. Case law includes the aggregate of reported cases that interpret judicial precedents, statutes, regulations, and constitutional provisions.

Case on point A previous case involving factual circumstances and issues that are similar to those in the case before the court.

Categorical imperative A concept developed by the philosopher Immanuel Kant as an ethical guideline for behavior. In deciding whether an action is right or wrong, or desirable or undesirable, a person should evaluate the action in terms of what would happen if everybody else in the same situation, or category, acted the same way.

Causation in fact An act or omission without ("but for") which an event would not have occurred.

Cause of action A situation or set of facts sufficient to justify a right to sue.

Cease-and-desist order An administrative or judicial order prohibiting a person or business firm from conducting activities that an agency or court has deemed illegal.

Certificate of limited partnership The basic document filed with a designated state official by which a limited partnership is formed.

Certification mark A mark used by one or more persons, other than the owner, to certify the region, materials, mode of manufacture, quality, or accuracy of the owner's goods or services. When used by members of a cooperative, association, or other organization, such a mark is referred to as a collective mark. Examples of certification marks include the "Good Housekeeping Seal of Approval" and "UL Tested."

Certiorari *See* Writ of *certiorari*

Chain-style business franchise A franchise that operates under a franchisor's trade name and that is identified as a member of a select group of dealers that engage in the franchisor's business. The franchisee is generally required to follow standardized or prescribed methods of operation. Examples of this type of franchise are McDonald's and most other fast-food chains.

Chancellor An adviser to the king at the time of the early king's courts of England. Individuals petitioned the king for relief when they could not obtain an adequate remedy in a court of law, and these petitions were decided by the chancellor.

Charging order In partnership law, an order granted by a court to a judgment creditor that entitles the creditor to attach profits or assets of a partner on dissolution of the partnership.

Checks and balances The system by which each of the three branches of the national government (executive, legislative, and judicial) exercises checks on the powers of the other branches.

Choice-of-language clause A clause in a contract designating the official language by which the contract will be interpreted in the event of a future disagreement over the contract's terms.

Choice-of-law clause A clause in a contract designating the law (such as the law of a particular state or nation) that will govern the contract.

Citation A reference to a publication in which a legal authority—such as a statute or a court decision—or other source can be found.

Civil law The branch of law dealing with the definition and enforcement of all private or public rights, as opposed to criminal matters.

Civil law system A system of law derived from that of the Roman Empire and based on a code rather than case law. The predominant system of law in the nations of continental Europe and the nations that were once their colonies. In the United States, Louisiana is the only state that has a civil law system.

Click-on agreement An agreement that arises when a buyer, engaging in a transaction on a computer, indicates his or her assent to be bound by the terms of an offer by clicking on a button that says, for example, "I agree"; sometimes referred to as a *click-on license* or a *click-wrap agreement.*

Close corporation A corporation whose shareholders are limited to a small group of persons, often only family members. The rights of shareholders of a close corporation usually are restricted regarding the transfer of shares to others. Close corporations are also referred to as *closely held, family,* or *privately held* corporations.

Closed shop A firm that requires union membership by its workers as a condition of employment. The closed shop was made illegal by the Labor-Management Relations Act of 1947.

Closing The final step in the sale of real estate—also called *settlement* or *closing escrow.* The escrow agent coordinates the closing with the recording of deeds, the obtaining of title insurance, and other concurrent closing activities. A number of costs must be paid, in cash, at the time of closing, and they can range from several hundred to several thousand dollars, depending on the amount of the mortgage loan and other conditions of the sale.

Closing argument An argument made after the plaintiff and defendant have rested their cases. Closing arguments are made prior to the jury charges.

Cloud computing The delivery to users of on-demand services from third-party servers over a network. Cloud computing is a delivery model. The most widely used cloud computing services are Software as a Service (SaaS), which offers companies a cheaper way to buy and use packaged applications that are no longer run on servers in house.

Collateral Under Article 9 of the Uniform Commercial Code, the property subject to a security interest.

Collateral promise A secondary promise that is ancillary (subsidiary) to a principal transaction or primary contractual relationship, such as a promise made by one person to pay the debts of another if the latter fails to perform. A collateral promise normally must be in writing to be enforceable.

Collective bargaining The process by which labor and management negotiate the terms and conditions of employment, including working hours and workplace conditions.

Collective mark A mark used by members of a cooperative, association, or other organization to certify the region, materials, mode of manufacture, quality, or accuracy of the specific goods or services. Examples of collective marks include the labor union marks found on tags of certain products and the credits of movies, which indicate the various associations and organizations that participated in the making of the movies.

Comity A deference by which one nation gives effect to the laws and judicial decrees of another nation. This recognition is based primarily on respect.

Comment period A period of time following an administrative agency's publication or a notice of a proposed rule during which private parties may comment in writing on the agency proposal in an effort to influence agency policy. The agency takes any comments received into consideration when drafting the final version of the regulation.

Commerce clause The provision in Article I, Section 8, of the U.S. Constitution that gives Congress the power to regulate interstate commerce.

Commercial impracticability A doctrine under which a seller may be excused from performing a contract when (1) a contingency occurs, (2) the contingency's occurrence makes performance impracticable, and (3) the nonoccurrence of the contingency was a basic assumption on which the contract was made. Despite the fact that UCC 2–615 expressly frees only sellers under this doctrine, courts have not distinguished between buyers and sellers in applying it.

Commercial use Use of land for business activities only; sometimes called *business use.*

Commingle To put funds or goods together into one mass so that the funds or goods are so mixed that they no longer have separate identities. In corporate law, if personal and corporate interests are commingled to the extent that the corporation has no separate identity, a court may "pierce the corporate veil" and expose the shareholders to personal liability.

Common carrier A carrier that transfers people or goods for hire to the general public.

Common law That body of law developed from custom or judicial decisions in English and U.S. courts, not attributable to a legislature.

Common stock Shares of ownership in a corporation that give the owner of the stock a proportionate interest in the corporation with regard to control, earnings, and net assets. Shares of common stock are lowest in priority with respect to payment of dividends and distribution of the corporation's assets on dissolution.

Community property A form of concurrent ownership of property in which each spouse technically owns an undivided one-half interest in property acquired during the marriage. This form of joint ownership occurs in only a minority of states and Puerto Rico.

Comparative negligence A theory in tort law under which the liability for injuries resulting from negligent acts is shared by all parties who were negligent (including the injured party), on the basis of each person's proportionate negligence.

Compelling government interest A test of constitutionality that requires the government to have compelling reasons for passing any law that restricts fundamental rights, such as free speech, or distinguishes between people based on a suspect trait.

Compensatory damages A money award equivalent to the actual value of injuries or damages sustained by the aggrieved party.

Complaint The pleading made by a plaintiff alleging wrongdoing on the part of the defendant; the document that, when filed with a court, initiates a lawsuit.

Complete performance Performance of a contract strictly in accordance with the contract's terms.

Computer crime Any violation of criminal law that involves knowledge of computer technology for its perpetration, investigation, or prosecution.

Concentrated industry An industry in which a large percentage of market sales is controlled by either a single firm or a small number of firms.

Concurrent jurisdiction Jurisdiction that exists when two different courts have the power to hear a case. For example, some cases can be heard in either a federal or a state court.

Concurrent ownership Joint ownership.

Concurring opinion A written opinion outlining the views of a judge or justice to make or emphasize a point that was not made or emphasized in the majority opinion.

Condemnation The process of taking private property for public use through the government's power of eminent domain.

Condition A possible future event, the occurrence or nonoccurrence of which will trigger the performance of a legal obligation or terminate an existing obligation under a contract.

Condition precedent A condition in a contract that must be met before a party's promise becomes absolute.

Confiscation A government's taking of privately owned business or personal property without a proper public purpose or an award of just compensation.

Conforming goods Goods that conform to contract specifications.

Consent Voluntary agreement to a proposition or an act of another. A concurrence of wills.

Consequential damages Special damages that compensate for a loss that is not direct or immediate (for example, lost profits). The special damages must have been reasonably foreseeable at the time the breach or injury occurred in order for the plaintiff to collect them.

Consideration Generally, the value given in return for a promise or a performance. The consideration, which must be present to make the contract legally binding, must be something of legally sufficient value and bargained for.

Constitutional law Law that is based on the U.S. Constitution and the constitutions of the various states.

Constructive delivery An act equivalent to the actual, physical delivery of property that cannot be physically delivered because of difficulty or impossibility. For example, the transfer of a key to a safe constructively delivers the contents of the safe.

Constructive discharge A termination of employment brought about by making an employee's working conditions so intolerable that the employee reasonably feels compelled to leave.

Consumer credit Credit extended primarily for personal or household use.

Consumer-debtor An individual whose debts are primarily consumer debts (debts for purchases made primarily for personal or household use).

Consumer goods Goods that are primarily for personal or household use.

Consumer law The body of statutes, agency rules, and judicial decisions protecting consumers of goods and services from dangerous manufacturing techniques, mislabeling, unfair credit practices, deceptive advertising, and so on. Consumer laws provide remedies and protections that are not ordinarily available to merchants or to businesses.

Contract An agreement that can be enforced in court; formed by two or more parties, each of whom agrees to perform or to refrain from performing some act now or in the future.

Contractual capacity The legal ability to enter into contracts. The threshold mental capacity required by law for a party who enters into a contract to be bound by that contract.

Contributory negligence A theory in tort law under which a complaining party's own negligence contributed to or caused his or her injuries. Contributory negligence is an absolute bar to recovery in a minority of jurisdictions.

Conversion The wrongful taking, using, or retaining possession of personal property that belongs to another.

Conveyance The transfer of a title to land from one person to another by deed; a document (such as a deed) by which an interest in land is transferred from one person to another.

Conviction The outcome of a criminal trial in which the defendant has been found guilty of the crime.

"Cooling-off" laws A set of federal and state laws designed to protect purchasers and lessees of goods or property. For example, the Federal Trade Commission's cooling-off period is three business days for purchases of goods or services from door-to-door salespersons. Cooling-off periods vary for loans, mortgages, leases, etc.

Co-ownership Joint ownership.

Copyright The exclusive right of authors to publish, print, or sell an intellectual production for a statutory period of time. A copyright has the same monopolistic nature as a patent or trademark, but it differs in that it applies exclusively to works of art, literature, and other works of authorship, including computer programs.

Corporate governance The relationship between a corporation and its shareholders—specifically, a system that details the distribution of rights and responsibilities of those within the corporation and spells out the rules and procedures for making corporate decisions.

Corporate social responsibility The concept that corporations can and should act ethically and be accountable to society for their actions.

Corporation A legal entity formed in compliance with statutory requirements. The entity is distinct from its shareholders-owners.

Cosign The act of signing a document (such as a note promising to pay another in return for a loan or other benefit) jointly with another person and thereby assuming liability for performing what was promised in the document.

Cost-benefit analysis A decision-making technique that involves weighing the costs of a given action against the benefits of the action.

Co-surety A joint surety. One who assumes liability jointly with another surety for the payment of an obligation.

Counteradvertising New advertising that is undertaken pursuant to a Federal Trade Commission order for the purpose of correcting earlier false claims that were made about a product.

Counterclaim A claim made by a defendant in a civil lawsuit that in effect sues the plaintiff.

Counteroffer An offeree's response to an offer in which the offeree rejects the original offer and at the same time makes a new offer.

Course of dealing Prior conduct between parties to a contract that establishes a common basis for their understanding.

Course of performance The conduct that occurs under the terms of a particular agreement. Such conduct indicates what the parties to an agreement intended it to mean.

Court of equity A court that decides controversies and administers justice according to the rules, principles, and precedents of equity.

Court of law A court in which the only remedies that could be granted were things of value, such as money damages. In the early English king's courts, courts of law were distinct from courts of equity.

Covenant not to compete A contractual promise to refrain from competing with another party for a certain period of time and within a certain geographic area. Although covenants not to compete restrain trade, they are commonly found in partnership agreements, business sale agreements, and employment contracts. If they are ancillary to such agreements, covenants not to compete will normally be enforced by the courts unless the time period or geographic area is deemed unreasonable.

Cover A buyer or lessee's purchase on the open market of goods to substitute for those promised but never delivered by the seller. Under the Uniform Commercial Code, if the cost of cover exceeds the cost of the contract goods, the buyer or lessee can recover the difference, plus incidental and consequential damages.

Cram-down provision A provision of the Bankruptcy Code that allows a court to confirm a debtor's Chapter 11 reorganization plan even though only one class of creditors has accepted it. To exercise the court's right under this provision, the court must demonstrate that the plan does not discriminate unfairly against any creditors and is fair and equitable.

Creditor A person to whom a debt is owed by another person (the debtor).

Creditors' composition agreement An agreement formed between a debtor and his or her creditors in which the creditors agree to accept a lesser sum than that owed by the debtor in full satisfaction of the debt.

Crime A wrong against society proclaimed in a statute and punishable by society through fines and/or imprisonment—or, in some cases, death.

Criminal act *See Actus reus*

Criminal intent *See Mens rea*

Criminal law Law that defines and governs actions that constitute crimes. Generally, criminal law has to do with wrongful actions committed against society for which society demands redress.

Cross-examination The questioning of an opposing witness during a trial.

Cumulative voting A method of shareholder voting designed to allow minority shareholders to be represented on the board of directors. With cumulative voting, the number of members of the board to be elected is multiplied by the total number of voting shares held. The result equals the number of votes a shareholder has, and this total can be cast for one or more nominees for director.

Cure Under the Uniform Commercial Code, the right of a party who tenders nonconforming performance to correct his or her performance within the contract period.

Cyber crime A crime that occurs online, in the virtual community of the Internet, as opposed to the physical world.

Cyber fraud Fraud that involves the online theft of credit-card information, banking details, and other information for criminal use.

Cyber mark A trademark in cyberspace.

Cyber tort A tort committed via the Internet.

Cyberlaw An informal term used to refer to all laws governing electronic communications and transactions, particularly those conducted via the Internet.

Cybersquatting The act of registering a domain name that is the same as, or confusingly similar to, the trademark of another and then offering to sell that domain name back to the trademark owner.

D

Damages Money sought as a remedy for a breach of contract or for a tortious act.

Debtor in possession (DIP) In Chapter 11 bankruptcy proceedings, a debtor who is allowed to continue in possession of the estate in property (the business) and to continue business operations.

Deceptive advertising Advertising that misleads consumers, either by making unjustified claims concerning a product's performance or by omitting a material fact concerning the product's composition or performance.

Declaratory judgment A court's judgment on a justiciable controversy when the plaintiff is in doubt as to his or her legal rights.

Decree The judgment of a court of equity.

Deed A document by which title to property (usually real property) is passed.

Defamation Any published or publicly spoken false statement that causes injury to another's good name, reputation, or character.

Default When a debtor fails to pay as promised.

Default judgment A judgment entered by a court against a defendant who has failed to appear in court to answer or defend against the plaintiff's claim.

Defendant One against whom a lawsuit is brought or the accused person in a criminal proceeding.

Defense Reasons that a defendant offers in an action or suit as to why the plaintiff should not obtain what he or she is seeking.

Delegation The transfer of a contractual duty to a third party. The party delegating the duty (the delegator) to the third party (the delegatee) is still obliged to perform on the contract should the delegatee fail to perform.

Delegation doctrine A doctrine based on Article I, Section 8, of the U.S. Constitution, which has been construed to allow Congress to delegate some of its power to make and implement laws to administrative agencies. The delegation is considered to be proper as long as Congress sets standards outlining the scope of the agency's authority.

Deposition The testimony of a party to a lawsuit or a witness taken under oath before a trial.

Destination contract A contract in which the seller is required to ship the goods by carrier and deliver them at a particular destination. The seller assumes liability for any losses or damage to the goods until they are tendered at the destination specified in the contract.

Dilution With respect to trademarks, a doctrine under which distinctive or famous trademarks are protected from certain unauthorized uses of the marks regardless of a showing of competition or a likelihood of confusion. Congress created a federal cause of action for dilution in 1995 with the passage of the Federal Trademark Dilution Act.

Direct examination The examination of a witness by the attorney who calls the witness to the stand to testify on behalf of the attorney's client.

Disaffirmance The legal avoidance, or setting aside, of a contractual obligation.

Discharge The termination of an obligation. (1) In contract law, discharge occurs when the parties have fully performed their contractual obligations or when events, conduct of the parties, or operation of law releases the parties from performance. (2) In bankruptcy proceedings, the extinction of the debtor's dischargeable debts.

Discharge in bankruptcy The release of a debtor from all debts that are provable, except those specifically excepted from discharge by statute.

Disclosed principal A principal whose identity is known to a third party at the time the agent makes a contract with the third party.

Discovery A phase in the litigation process during which the opposing parties may obtain information from each other and from third parties prior to trial.

Disparagement of property An economically injurious false statement made about another's product or property. A general term for torts that are more specifically referred to as *slander of quality* or *slander of title.*

Disparate-impact discrimination A form of employment discrimination that results from certain employer practices or procedures that, although not discriminatory on their face, have a discriminatory effect.

Disparate-treatment discrimination A form of employment discrimination that results when an employer intentionally discriminates against employees who are members of protected classes.

Dissenting opinion A written opinion by a judge or justice who disagrees with the majority opinion.

Dissociation The severance of the relationship between a partner and a partnership when the partner ceases to be associated with the carrying on of the partnership business.

Dissolution The formal disbanding of a partnership or a corporation. It can take place by (1) acts of the partners or, in a corporation, of the shareholders and board of directors; (2) the death of a partner; (3) the expiration of a time period stated in a partnership agreement or a certificate of incorporation; or (4) judicial decree.

Distributed network A network that can be used by persons located (distributed) around the country or the globe to share computer files.

Distribution agreement A contract between a seller and a distributor of the seller's products setting out the terms and conditions of the distributorship.

Distributorship A business arrangement that is established when a manufacturer licenses a dealer to sell its product. An example of a distributorship is an automobile dealership.

Diversity of citizenship Under Article III, Section 2, of the Constitution, a basis for federal court jurisdiction over a lawsuit between (1) citizens of different states, (2) a foreign country and citizens of a state or of different states, or (3) citizens of a state and citizens or subjects of a foreign country. The amount in controversy must be more than $75,000 before a federal court can take jurisdiction in such cases.

Divestiture The act of selling one or more of a company's parts, such as a subsidiary or plant; often mandated by the courts in merger or monopolization cases.

Dividend A distribution to corporate shareholders of corporate profits or income, disbursed in proportion to the number of shares held.

Docket The list of cases entered on a court's calendar and thus scheduled to be heard by the court.

Document of title Paper exchanged in the regular course of business that evidences the right to possession of goods (for example, a bill of lading or a warehouse receipt).

Domain name The series of letters and symbols used to identify site operators on the Internet; Internet "addresses."

Domestic corporation In a given state, a corporation that does business in, and is organized under the laws of, that state.

Double jeopardy A situation occurring when a person is tried twice for the same criminal offense; prohibited by the Fifth Amendment to the Constitution.

Double taxation A feature (and disadvantage) of the corporate form of business. Because a corporation is a separate legal entity, corporate profits are taxed by state and federal governments. Dividends are again taxable as ordinary income to the shareholders receiving them.

Down payment The part of the purchase price of real property that is paid in cash up front, reducing the amount of the loan or mortgage.

Dram shop act A state statute that imposes liability on the owners of bars and taverns, as well as those who serve alcoholic drinks to the public, for injuries resulting from accidents caused by intoxicated persons when the sellers or servers of alcoholic drinks contributed to the intoxication.

Due process clause The provisions of the Fifth and Fourteenth Amendments to the Constitution that guarantee that no person shall be deprived of life, liberty, or property without due process of law. Similar clauses are found in most state constitutions.

Dumping The selling of goods in a foreign country at a price below the price charged for the same goods in the domestic market.

Duress Unlawful pressure brought to bear on a person, causing the person to perform an act that he or she would not otherwise perform.

Duty-based ethics An ethical philosophy rooted in the idea that every person has certain duties to others, including both humans and the planet. Those duties may be derived from religious principles or from other philosophical reasoning.

Duty of care The duty of all persons, as established by tort law, to exercise a reasonable amount of care in their dealings with others. Failure to exercise due care, which is normally determined by the "reasonable person standard," constitutes the tort of negligence.

E

E-agent A semiautonomous computer program that is capable of executing specific tasks.

E-commerce Business transacted in cyberspace.

E-contract A contract that is entered into in cyberspace and is evidenced only by electronic impulses (such as those that make up a computer's memory), rather than, for example, a typewritten form.

E-evidence A type of evidence that consists of computer-generated or electronically recorded information, including e-mail, voice mail, spreadsheets, word-processing documents, and other data.

E-signature As defined by the Uniform Electronic Transactions Act, "an electronic sound, symbol, or process attached to or logically associated with a record and executed or adopted by a person with the intent to sign the record."

Early neutral case evaluation A form of alternative dispute resolution in which a neutral third party evaluates the strengths and weakness of the disputing parties' positions. The evaluator's opinion forms the basis for negotiating a settlement.

Easement A nonpossessory right to use another's property in a manner established by either express or implied agreement.

Embezzlement The fraudulent appropriation of funds or other property by a person to whom the funds or property has been entrusted.

Eminent domain The power of a government to take land for public use from private citizens for just compensation.

Employee A person who works for an employer for a salary or for wages.

Employer An individual or business entity that hires employees, pays them salaries or wages, and exercises control over their work.

Employment at will A common law doctrine under which either party may terminate an employment relationship at any time for any reason, unless a contract specifies otherwise.

Employment discrimination Treating employees or job applicants unequally on the basis of race, color, national origin, religion, gender, age, or disability; prohibited by federal statutes.

Enabling legislation A statute enacted by Congress that authorizes the creation of an administrative agency and specifies the name, composition, purpose, and powers of the agency being created.

Encryption The process by which a message (plaintext) is transformed into something (ciphertext) that the sender and receiver intend third parties not to understand.

Entrapment In criminal law, a defense in which the defendant claims that he or she was induced by a public official—usually an undercover agent or police officer—to commit a crime that he or she would otherwise not have committed.

Entrepreneur One who initiates and assumes the financial risks of a new enterprise and who undertakes to provide or control its management.

Environmental impact statement (EIS) A statement required by the National Environmental Policy Act for any major federal action that will significantly affect the quality of the environment. The statement must analyze the action's impact on the environment and explore alternative actions that might be taken.

Environmental law The body of statutory, regulatory, and common law relating to the protection of the environment.

Equal dignity rule In most states, a rule stating that express authority given to an agent must be in writing if the contract to be made on behalf of the principal is required to be in writing.

Equal protection clause The provision in the Fourteenth Amendment to the Constitution that guarantees that no state will "deny to any person within its jurisdiction the equal protection of the laws." This clause mandates that state governments treat similarly situated individuals in a similar manner.

Equitable maxims General propositions or principles of law that have to do with fairness (equity).

Escrow account An account that is generally held in the name of the depositor and escrow agent. The funds in the account are paid to a third person only on fulfillment of the escrow condition.

Establishment clause The provision in the First Amendment to the U.S. Constitution that prohibits Congress from creating any law "respecting an establishment of religion."

Ethical reasoning A reasoning process in which an individual links his or her moral convictions or ethical standards to the particular situation at hand.

Ethics Moral principles and values applied to social behavior.

Evidence Proof offered at trial—in the form of testimony, documents, records, exhibits, objects, and so on—for the purpose of convincing the court or jury of the truth of a contention.

Exclusionary rule In criminal procedure, a rule under which any evidence that is obtained in violation of the accused's constitutional rights guaranteed by the Fourth, Fifth, and Sixth Amendments, as well as any evidence derived from illegally obtained evidence, will not be admissible in court.

Exclusive agency An agency in which a principal grants an agent an exclusive territory and does not allow another agent to compete in that territory.

Exclusive jurisdiction Jurisdiction that exists when a case can be heard only in a particular court or type of court, such as a federal court or a state court.

Exclusive-dealing contract An agreement under which a seller forbids a buyer to purchase products from the seller's competitors.

Exculpatory clause A clause that releases a contractual party from liability in the event of monetary or physical injury, no matter who is at fault.

Executed contract A contract that has been completely performed by both parties.

Executive agency An administrative agency within the executive branch of government. At the federal level, executive agencies are those within the cabinet departments.

Executory contract A contract that has not as yet been fully performed.

Export To sell products to buyers located in other countries.

Express authority Authority expressly given by one party to another. In agency law, an agent has express authority to act for a principal if both parties agree, orally or in writing, that an agency relationship exists in which the agent had the power (authority) to act in the place of, and on behalf of, the principal.

Express contract A contract in which the terms of the agreement are fully and explicitly stated in words, oral or written.

Express warranty A seller's or lessor's oral or written promise, ancillary to an underlying sales or lease agreement, as to the quality, description, or performance of the goods being sold or leased.

Expropriation The seizure by a government of privately owned business or personal property for a proper public purpose and with just compensation.

Extrinsic evidence Evidence that relates to a contract but is not contained within the document itself, such as the testimony of parties and witnesses, or additional agreements or communications. A court may consider extrinsic evidence only when a contract term is ambiguous and the evidence does not contradict the express terms of the contract.

F

F.A.S. Free alongside. A contract term that requires the seller, at his or her own expense and risk, to deliver the goods alongside the ship before risk passes to the buyer.

F.O.B. Free on board. A contract term that indicates that the selling price of the goods includes transportation costs (and that the seller carries the risk of loss) to the specific F.O.B. place named in the contract. The place can be either the place of initial shipment (for example, the seller's city or place of business) or the place of destination (for example, the buyer's city or place of business).

Family limited liability partnership (FLLP) A limited liability partnership (LLP) in which the majority of the partners are persons related to each other, essentially as spouses, parents, grandparents, siblings, cousins, nephews, or nieces. A person acting in a fiduciary capacity for persons so related could also be a partner. All of the partners must be natural persons or persons acting in a fiduciary capacity for the benefit of natural persons.

Federal form of government A system of government in which the states form a union and the sovereign power is divided between a central government and the member states.

Federal question A question that pertains to the U.S. Constitution, acts of Congress, or treaties. A federal question provides a basis for federal jurisdiction.

Federal Rules of Civil Procedure (FRCP) The rules controlling procedural matters in civil trials brought before the federal district courts.

Fee simple absolute An ownership interest in land in which the owner has the greatest possible aggregation of rights, privileges, and power. The owner can use, possess, or dispose of the property as he or she chooses during his or her lifetime. On death, the interest in the property passes to the owner's heirs.

Felony A crime—such as arson, murder, rape, or robbery—that carries the most severe sanctions, usually ranging from one year in a state or federal prison to the forfeiture of one's life.

Fiduciary As a noun, a person having a duty created by his or her undertaking to act primarily for another's benefit in matters connected with the undertaking. As an adjective, a relationship founded on trust and confidence.

Fiduciary duty The duty, imposed on a fiduciary by virtue of his or her position, to act primarily for another's benefit.

Filtering software A computer program that includes a pattern through which data are passed. When designed to block access to certain Web sites, the pattern blocks the retrieval of a site whose URL or key words are on a list within the program.

Final order The final decision of an administrative agency on an issue. If no appeal is taken, or if the case is not reviewed or considered anew by the agency commission, the administrative law judge's initial order becomes the final order of the agency.

Firm offer An offer (by a merchant) that is irrevocable without consideration for a period of time (not longer than three months). A firm offer by a merchant must be in writing and must be signed by the offeror.

Fixed-rate mortgage A standard mortgage with a fixed, or unchanging, rate of interest. The loan payments on these mortgages remain the same for the duration of the loan, which ranges between fifteen and forty years.

Fixed-term tenancy A type of tenancy under which property is leased for a specified period of time, such as a month, a year, or a period of years; also called a *tenancy for years.*

Forbearance The act of refraining from exercising a legal right. An agreement between the lender and the borrower in which the lender agrees to temporarily cease requiring mortgage payments, to delay foreclosure, or to accept smaller payments than previously scheduled.

Force majeure (pronounced mah-*zhure*) **clause** A provision in a contract stipulating that certain unforeseen events—such as war, political upheavals, acts of God, or other events—will excuse a party from liability for nonperformance of contractual obligations.

Foreclosure A proceeding in which a mortgagee either takes title to or forces the sale of the mortgagor's property in satisfaction of a debt.

Foreign corporation In a given state, a corporation that does business in the state without being incorporated therein.

Foreseeable risk In negligence law, the risk of harm or injury to another that a person of ordinary intelligence and prudence should have reasonably anticipated or foreseen when undertaking an action or refraining from undertaking an action.

Forgery The fraudulent making or altering of any writing in a way that changes the legal rights and liabilities of another.

Formal contract A contract that by law requires a specific form, such as being executed under seal, to be valid.

Forum A jurisdiction, court, or place in which disputes are litigated and legal remedies are sought.

Forum-selection clause A provision in a contract designating the court, jurisdiction, or tribunal that will decide any disputes arising under the contract.

Franchise Any arrangement in which the owner of a trademark, trade name, or copyright licenses another to use that trademark, trade name, or copyright, under specified conditions or limitations, in the selling of goods and services.

Franchise tax A state or local government tax on the right and privilege of carrying on a business in the form of a corporation.

Franchisee One receiving a license to use another's (the franchisor's) trademark, trade name, or copyright in the sale of goods and services.

Franchisor One licensing another (the franchisee) to use his or her trademark, trade name, or copyright in the sale of goods or services.

Fraudulent misrepresentation (fraud) Any misrepresentation, either by misstatement or omission of a material fact, knowingly made with the intention of deceiving another and on which a reasonable person would and does rely to his or her detriment.

Free exercise clause The provision in the First Amendment to the U.S. Constitution that prohibits Congress from making any law "prohibiting the free exercise" of religion.

Free-writing prospectus Any type of written, electronic, or graphic offer of securities that describes the issuing corporation or its securities and includes a legend indicating that the investor may obtain the prospectus at the SEC's Web site.

Frustration of purpose A court-created doctrine under which a party to a contract will be relieved of his or her duty to perform when the objective purpose for performance no longer exists (due to reasons beyond that party's control).

Full faith and credit clause A clause in Article IV, Section 1, of the Constitution that provides that "Full Faith and Credit shall be given in each State to the public Acts, Records, and Judicial Proceedings of every other State." The clause ensures that rights established under deeds, wills, contracts, and the like in one state will be honored by the other states and that any judicial decision with respect to such property rights will be honored and enforced in all states.

G

Garnishment A legal process used by a creditor to collect a debt by seizing property of the debtor (such as wages) that is being held by a third party (such as the debtor's employer).

General jurisdiction Exists when a court's subject-matter jurisdiction is not restricted. A court of general jurisdiction normally can hear any type of case.

General partner In a limited partnership, a partner who assumes responsibility for the management of the partnership and liability for all partnership debts.

Good faith Under the Uniform Commercial Code, good faith means honesty in fact. With regard to merchants, good faith means honesty in fact *and* the observance of reasonable commercial standards of fair dealing in the trade.

Good Samaritan statute A state statute that provides that persons who rescue or provide emergency services to others in peril—unless they do so recklessly, thus causing further harm—cannot be sued for negligence.

Goodwill In the business context, the valuable reputation of a business viewed as an intangible asset.

Grand jury A group of citizens called to decide, after hearing the state's evidence, whether a reasonable basis (probable cause) exists for believing that a crime has been committed and whether a trial ought to be held.

Grant deed A deed that simply recites words of consideration and conveyance. Under statute, a grant deed may impliedly warrant that at least the grantor has not conveyed the property's title to someone else.

Grantee One to whom a grant (of land or property, for example) is made.

Grantor A person who makes a grant, such as a transferor of property or the creator of a trust.

Group boycott The refusal to deal with a particular person or firm by a group of competitors; prohibited by the Sherman Act.

Guarantor A person who agrees to satisfy the debt of another (the debtor) only after the principal debtor defaults. A guarantor's liability is thus secondary.

H

Hacker A person who uses one computer to break into another. Professional computer programmers refer to such persons as "crackers."

Hearsay An oral or written statement made out of court that is later offered in court by a witness (not the person who made the statement) to prove the truth of the matter asserted in the statement. Hearsay is generally inadmissible as evidence.

Herfindahl-Hirschman Index (HHI) An index measuring market concentration for purposes of antitrust enforcement. It is calculated by summing the squares of the percentage market shares held by the respective firms.

Historical school A school of legal thought that emphasizes the evolutionary process of law and that looks to the past to discover what the principles of contemporary law should be.

Holding company A company whose business activity is holding shares in another company.

Homestead exemption A law permitting a debtor to retain the family home, either in its entirety or up to a specified dollar amount, free from the claims of unsecured creditors or trustees in bankruptcy.

Horizontal merger A merger between two firms that are competing in the same market.

Horizontal restraint Any agreement that in some way restrains competition between rival firms competing in the same market.

Hot-cargo agreement An agreement in which employers voluntarily agree with unions not to handle, use, or deal in nonunion-produced goods of other employers. A type of secondary boycott explicitly prohibited by the Labor-Management Reporting and Disclosure Act of 1959.

I

I-551 Alien Registration Receipt Proof that a noncitizen has obtained permanent residency in the United States; the so-called green card.

I-9 verification A form from the Department of Homeland Security, U.S. Citizenship and Immigration Services, used for employment eligibility verification; a form that documents that each new employee is authorized to work in the United States

Identification In a sale of goods, the express designation of the specific goods provided for in the contract.

Identity theft The act of stealing another's identifying information—such as a name, date of birth, or Social Security number—and using that information to access the victim's financial resources.

Impeach To challenge the credibility of a person's testimony or attempt to discredit a party or witness.

Implication A way of creating an easement or profit in real property when it is reasonable to imply its existence from the circumstances surrounding the division of the property.

Implied authority Authority that is created not by an explicit oral or written agreement but by implication. In agency law, implied authority (of the agent) can be conferred by custom, inferred from the position the agent occupies, or implied by virtue of being reasonably necessary to carry out express authority.

Implied contract A contract formed in whole or in part from the conduct of the parties (as opposed to an express contract). Also known as *implied-in-fact* contract.

Implied warranty A warranty that the law derives by implication or inference from the nature of the transaction or the relative situation or circumstances of the parties.

Implied warranty of fitness for a particular purpose A warranty that goods sold or leased are fit for a particular purpose. The warranty arises when any seller or lessor knows the particular purpose for which a buyer or lessee will use the goods and knows that the buyer or lessee is relying on the skill and judgment of the seller or lessor to select suitable goods.

Implied warranty of habitability An implied promise by a landlord that rented residential premises are fit for human habitation—that is, in a condition that is safe and suitable for people to live in.

Implied warranty of merchantability A warranty that goods being sold or leased are reasonably fit for the ordinary purpose for which they are sold or leased, are properly packaged and labeled, and are of fair quality. The warranty automatically arises in every sale or lease of goods made by a merchant who deals in goods of the kind sold or leased.

Impossibility of performance A doctrine under which a party to a contract is relieved of his or her duty to perform when performance becomes impossible or totally impracticable (through no fault of either party).

***In personam* jurisdiction** Court jurisdiction over the "person" involved in a legal action; personal jurisdiction.

***In rem* jurisdiction** Court jurisdiction over a defendant's property.

Incidental damages Expenses that are caused directly by a breach of contract, such as those incurred to obtain performance from another source.

Indemnify To compensate or reimburse another for losses or expenses incurred.

Independent contractor One who works for, and receives payment from, an employer but whose working conditions and methods are not controlled by the employer. An independent contractor is not an employee but may be an agent.

Independent regulatory agency An administrative agency that is not considered part of the government's executive branch and is not subject to the authority of the president. Independent agency officials cannot be removed without cause.

Indictment (pronounced in-*dyte*-ment) A charge by a grand jury that a reasonable basis (probable cause) exists for believing that a crime has been committed and that a trial should be held.

Industrial use Land use for light or heavy manufacturing, shipping, or heavy transportation.

Informal contract A contract that does not require a specified form or formality in order to be valid.

Information A formal accusation or complaint (without an indictment) issued in certain types of actions (usually criminal actions involving lesser crimes) by a law officer, such as a magistrate.

Information return A tax return submitted by a partnership that reports the income earned by the business. The partnership as an entity does not pay taxes on the income received by the partnership. A partner's profit from the partnership (whether distributed or not) is taxed as individual income to the individual partner.

Infringement A violation of another's legally recognized right. The term is commonly used with reference to the invasion by one party of another party's rights in a patent, trademark, or copyright.

Initial order In the context of administrative law, an agency's disposition in a matter other than a rulemaking. An administrative law judge's initial order becomes final unless it is appealed.

Injunction A court decree ordering a person to do or refrain from doing a certain act or activity.

Inside director A person on the board of directors who is also an officer of the corporation.

Insider A corporate director or officer, or other employee or agent, with access to confidential information and a duty not to disclose that information in violation of insider-trading laws.

Insider trading The purchase or sale of securities on the basis of "inside information" (information that has not been made available to the public) in violation of a duty owed to the company whose stock is being traded.

Insolvent Under the Uniform Commercial Code, a term describing a person who ceases to pay "his debts in the ordinary course of business or cannot pay his debts as they become due or is insolvent within the meaning of federal bankruptcy law" [UCC 1–201(23)].

Insurable interest An interest either in a person's life or well-being or in property that is sufficiently substantial that insuring against injury to (or the death of) the person or against damage to the property does not amount to a mere wagering (betting) contract.

Insurance A contract in which, for a stipulated consideration, one party agrees to compensate the other for loss on a specific subject by a specified peril.

Intangible property Property that is incapable of being apprehended by the senses (such as by sight or touch). Intellectual property is an example of intangible property.

Intellectual property Property resulting from intellectual, creative processes. Patents, trademarks, and copyrights are examples of intellectual property.

Intended beneficiary A third party for whose benefit a contract is formed. An intended beneficiary can sue the promisor if such a contract is breached.

Intentional tort A wrongful act knowingly committed.

International law The law that governs relations among nations. International customs and treaties are generally considered to be two of the most important sources of international law.

International organization In international law, a term that generally refers to an organization composed mainly of nations and usually established by treaty. The United States is a member of more than one hundred multilateral and bilateral organizations, including at least twenty through the United Nations.

Internet service provider (ISP) A business or organization that offers users access to the Internet and related services.

Interpretive rule An administrative agency rule that simply declares a policy or explains the agency's position and does not establish any legal rights or obligations.

Interrogatories A series of written questions for which written answers are prepared and then signed under oath by a party to a lawsuit, usually with the assistance of the party's attorney.

Inverse condemnation The taking of private property by the government without payment of just compensation as required by the U.S. Constitution. The owner must sue the government to recover just compensation.

Investment company A company that acts on behalf of many smaller shareholder-owners by buying a large portfolio of securities and professionally managing that portfolio.

Investment contract In securities law, a transaction in which a person invests in a common enterprise reasonably expecting profits that are derived primarily from the efforts of others.

Irrevocable offer An offer that cannot be revoked or recalled by the offeror without liability. A merchant's firm offer is an example of an irrevocable offer.

J

Joint and several liability In partnership law, a doctrine under which a plaintiff may sue, and collect a judgment from, one or more of the partners separately (severally, or individually) or all of the partners together (jointly). This is true even if one of the partners sued did not participate in, ratify, or know about whatever gave rise to the cause of action.

Joint liability Shared liability. In partnership law, partners incur joint liability for partnership obligations and debts. For example, if a third party sues a partner on a partnership debt, the partner has the right to insist that the other partners be sued with him or her.

Joint tenancy The joint ownership of property by two or more co-owners in which each co-owner owns an undivided portion of the property. On the death of one of the joint tenants, his or her interest automatically passes to the surviving joint tenants.

Judgment The final order or decision resulting from a legal action.

Judicial lien A lien on property created by a court order.

Judicial process The procedures relating to, or connected with, the administration of justice through the judicial system.

Judicial review The process by which courts decide on the constitutionality of legislative enactments and actions of the executive branch.

Junior lienholder A person or business that holds a lien that is subordinate to one or more other liens on the same property.

Jurisdiction The authority of a court to hear and decide a specific action.

Jurisprudence The science or philosophy of law.

Justiciable controversy A controversy that is not hypothetical or academic but real and substantial. A requirement that must be satisfied before a court will hear a case.

K

King's court A medieval English court. The king's courts, or *curiae regis,* were established by the Norman conquerors of England. The body of law that developed in these courts was common to the entire English realm and thus became known as the common law.

L

Laches The equitable doctrine that bars a party's right to legal action if the party has neglected for an unreasonable length of time to act on his or her rights.

Larceny The wrongful taking and carrying away of another person's personal property with the intent to permanently deprive the owner of the property. Some states classify larceny as either grand or petit, depending on the property's value.

Latent defects A defect that is not obvious or cannot readily be ascertained.

Law A body of enforceable rules governing relationships among individuals and between individuals and their society.

Lease In real property law, a contract by which the owner of real property (the landlord, or lessor) grants to a person (the tenant, or lessee) an exclusive right to use and possess the property, usually for a specified period of time, in return for rent or some other form of payment.

Lease agreement In regard to the lease of goods, an agreement in which one person (the lessor) agrees to transfer the right to the possession and use of property to another person (the lessee) in exchange for rental payments.

Leasehold estate An estate in realty held by a tenant under a lease. In every leasehold estate, the tenant has a qualified right to possess and/or use the land.

Legal positivism A school of legal thought centered on the assumption that there is no law higher than the laws created by a national government. Laws must be obeyed, even if they are unjust, to prevent anarchy.

Legal realism A school of legal thought that was popular in the 1920s and 1930s and that challenged many existing jurisprudential assumptions, particularly the assumption that subjective elements play no part in judicial reasoning. Legal realists generally advocated a less abstract and more pragmatic approach to the law, an approach that would take into account customary practices and the circumstances in which transactions take place. The school left a lasting imprint on American jurisprudence.

Legal reasoning The process of reasoning by which a judge harmonizes his or her decision with the judicial decisions of previous cases.

Legislative rule An administrative agency rule that affects substantive legal rights and carries the same weight as a congressionally enacted statute.

Lessee One who acquires the right to possess and use goods under the Uniform Commercial Code or real property under a lease.

Lessor One who transfers the right to possess and use goods (or real property) to another under a lease.

Letter of credit A written instrument, usually issued by a bank on behalf of a customer or other person, in which the issuer promises to honor drafts or other demands for payment by third persons in accordance with the terms of the instrument.

Liability Any actual or potential legal obligation, duty, debt, or responsibility.

Libel Defamation in writing or other form (such as in a digital recording) having the quality of permanence.

License In the context of intellectual property, a contract permitting the use of a trademark, copyright, patent, or trade secret for certain purposes. In the context of real property, a revocable right or privilege of a person to come on another person's land.

Licensee One who receives a license to use, or enter onto, another's property.

Lien (pronounced *leen*) A claim against specific property to satisfy a debt.

Life estate An interest in land that exists only for the duration of the life of some person, usually the holder of the estate.

Limited jurisdiction Exists when a court's subject-matter jurisdiction is limited. Bankruptcy courts and probate courts are examples of courts with limited jurisdiction.

Limited liability company (LLC) A hybrid form of business enterprise that offers the limited liability of the corporation but the tax advantages of a partnership.

Limited liability limited partnership (LLLP) A type of limited partnership. The difference between a limited partnership and an LLLP is that the liability of the general partner in an LLLP is the same as the liability of the limited partner. That is, the liability of all partners is limited to the amount of their investments in the firm.

Limited liability partnership (LLP) A form of partnership that allows professionals to enjoy the tax benefits of a partnership while limiting their personal liability for the malpractice of other partners.

Limited partner In a limited partnership, a partner who contributes capital to the partnership but has no right to participate in the management and operation of the business. The limited partner assumes no liability for partnership debts beyond the capital contributed.

Limited partnership (LP) A partnership consisting of one or more general partners (who manage the business and are liable to the full extent of their personal assets for debts of the partnership) and one or more limited partners (who contribute only assets and are liable only to the extent of their contributions).

Liquidated damages An amount, stipulated in the contract, that the parties to a contract believe to be a reasonable estimation of the damages that will occur in the event of a breach.

Liquidated debt A debt that is due and certain in amount.

Liquidation (1) In regard to bankruptcy, the sale of all of the nonexempt assets of a debtor and the distribution of the proceeds to the debtor's creditors. Chapter 7 of the Bankruptcy Code provides for liquidation bankruptcy proceedings. (2) In regard to corporations, the process by which corporate assets are converted into cash and distributed among creditors and shareholders according to specific rules of preference.

Litigant A party to a lawsuit.

Litigation The process of resolving a dispute through the court system.

Lockout Occurs when an employer shuts down to prevent employees from working typically because it cannot reach a collective bargaining agreement with the union.

Long arm statute A state statute that permits a state to obtain personal jurisdiction over nonresident defendants. A defendant must have "minimum contacts" with that state for the statute to apply.

M

Mailbox rule A rule providing that an acceptance of an offer becomes effective on dispatch. Acceptance takes effect, thus completing formation of the contract, at the time the offeree sends or delivers the communication via the mode expressly or impliedly authorized by the offeror.

Main purpose rule A rule of contract law under which an exception to the Statute of Frauds is made if the main purpose in accepting secondary liability under a contract is to secure a personal benefit. If this situation exists, the contract need not be in writing to be enforceable.

Majority opinion A court's written opinion, outlining the views of the majority of the judges or justices deciding the case.

Malpractice Professional misconduct or the failure to exercise the requisite degree of skill as a professional. Negligence—the failure to exercise due care—on the part of a professional, such as a physician or an attorney, is commonly referred to as malpractice.

Malware Malicious software programs designed to disrupt or harm a computer, network, smartphone, or other device.

Market concentration A situation that exists when a small number of firms share the market for a particular good or service. For example, if the four largest grocery stores in Chicago accounted for 80 percent of all retail food sales, the market clearly would be concentrated in those four firms.

Market power The power of a firm to control the market price of its product. A monopoly has the greatest degree of market power.

Marketable title Title to real estate that is reasonably free from encumbrances, defects in the chain of title, and other matters that affect title, such as adverse possession.

Market-share liability A theory of product liability under which a court can hold each manufacturer of a harmful product responsible for a percentage of a plaintiff's damages that is equal to the percentage of its market share.

Material fact A fact to which a reasonable person would attach importance in determining his or her course of action.

Mechanic's lien A statutory lien on the real property of another, created to ensure payment for work performed and materials furnished in the repair or improvement of real property, such as a building.

Mediation A method of settling disputes outside of court by using the services of a neutral third party, called a mediator. The mediator acts as a communicating agent between the parties and suggests ways in which the parties can resolve their dispute.

Mediator A neutral third party that hears disputes in mediation.

Member The term used to designate a person who has an ownership interest in a limited liability company.

Mens rea (pronounced *mehns ray*-uh) Criminal intent. A wrongful mental state, which is as necessary as a wrongful act, to establish criminal liability. What constitutes a guilty mental state varies according to the wrongful action. Thus, for murder, the *mens rea* is the intent to take a life. For theft, the *mens rea* must involve both the knowledge that the property belongs to another and the intent to deprive the owner of it.

Merchant A person who is engaged in the purchase and sale of goods. Under the Uniform Commercial Code, a person who deals in goods of the kind involved in the sales contract; for further definitions, see UCC 2–104.

Meta tags Words inserted into a Web site's keywords field to increase the site's appearance in search engine results.

Metadata Data that are automatically recorded by electronic devices and provide information about who created a file and when, and who accessed, modified, or transmitted it on their hard drives. Can be described as data about data.

Minimum-contacts requirement The requirement that before a state court can exercise jurisdiction over a foreign corporation, the foreign corporation must have sufficient contacts with the state. A foreign corporation that has its home office in the state or that has manufacturing plants in the state meets this requirement.

Minimum wage The lowest wage, either by government regulation or union contract, that an employer may pay an hourly worker.

Mini-trial A private proceeding in which each party to a dispute argues its position before the other side and vice versa. A neutral third party may be present and act as an adviser if the parties fail to reach an agreement.

Mirror image rule A common law rule that requires, for a valid contractual agreement, that the terms of the offeree's acceptance adhere exactly to the terms of the offeror's offer.

Misdemeanor A lesser crime than a felony, punishable by a fine or imprisonment for up to one year in other than a state or federal penitentiary.

Mitigation of damages A rule requiring a plaintiff to have done whatever was reasonable to minimize the damages caused by the defendant.

Money laundering Falsely reporting income that has been obtained through criminal activity as income obtained through a legitimate business enterprise—in effect, "laundering" the "dirty money."

Monopolization The possession of monopoly power in the relevant market and the willful acquisition or maintenance of that power, as distinguished from growth or development as a consequence of a superior product, business acumen, or historic accident.

Monopoly A term generally used to describe a market in which there is a single seller or a limited number of sellers.

Monopoly power The ability of a monopoly to dictate what takes place in a given market.

Moral minimum The minimum degree of ethical behavior expected of a business firm, which is usually defined as compliance with the law.

Mortgage A written instrument that gives a creditor (the mortgagee) an interest in, or lien on, the debtor's (mortgagor's) real property as security for a debt. If the debt is not paid, the property can be sold by the creditor and the proceeds used to pay the debt.

Motion A procedural request or application presented by an attorney to the court on behalf of a client.

Motion for a directed verdict In a state court, a party's request that the judge enter a judgment in her or his favor before the case is submitted to a jury because the other party has not presented sufficient evidence to support the claim. The federal courts refer to this request as a *motion for judgment as a matter of law.*

Motion for a new trial A motion asserting that the trial was so fundamentally flawed (because of error, newly discovered evidence, prejudice, or other reason) that a new trial is necessary to prevent a miscarriage of justice.

Motion for judgment as a matter of law In a federal court, a party's request that the judge enter a judgment in her or his favor before the case is submitted to a jury because the other party has not presented sufficient evidence to support the claim. The state courts refer to this request as a *motion for a directed verdict.*

Motion for judgment *n.o.v.* A motion requesting the court to grant judgment in favor of the party making the motion on the ground that the jury verdict against him or her was unreasonable and erroneous.

Motion for judgment on the pleadings A motion by either party to a lawsuit at the close of the pleadings requesting the court to decide the issue solely on the pleadings without proceeding to trial. The motion will be granted only if no facts are in dispute.

Motion for summary judgment A motion requesting the court to enter a judgment without proceeding to trial. The motion can be based on evidence outside the pleadings and will be granted only if no facts are in dispute.

Motion to dismiss A pleading in which a defendant asserts that the plaintiff's claim fails to state a cause of action (that is, has no basis in law) or that there are other grounds on which a suit should be dismissed.

Multiple product order An order issued by the Federal Trade Commission to a firm that has engaged in deceptive advertising by which the firm is required to cease and desist from false advertising not only in regard to the product that was the subject of the action but also in regard to all the firm's other products.

Municipal court A city or community court with criminal jurisdiction over traffic violations and, less frequently, with civil jurisdiction over other minor matters.

Mutual assent The element of agreement in the formation of a contract. The manifestation of contract parties' mutual assent to the same bargain is required to establish a contract.

Mutual fund A specific type of investment company that continually buys or sells to investors shares of ownership in a portfolio.

Mutual rescission An agreement between the parties to cancel their contract, releasing the parties from further obligations under the contract. The object of the agreement is to restore the parties to the positions they would have occupied had no contract ever been formed. *See also* Rescission

N

National law Law that pertains to a particular nation (as opposed to international law).

Natural law The belief that government and the legal system should reflect universal moral and ethical principles that are inherent in human nature. The natural law school is the oldest and one of the most significant schools of legal thought.

Necessity In criminal law, a defense against liability. Under Section 3.02 of the Model Penal Code, this defense is justifiable if "the harm or evil sought to be avoided" by a given action "is greater than that sought to be prevented by the law defining the offense charged."

Negligence The failure to exercise the standard of care that a reasonable person would exercise in similar circumstances.

Negligence *per se* An act (or failure to act) in violation of a statutory requirement.

Negotiation In regard to dispute settlement, a process in which parties attempt to settle their dispute without going to court, with or without attorneys to represent them.

Nominal damages A small monetary award (often one dollar) granted to a plaintiff when no actual damage was suffered or when the plaintiff is unable to show such loss with sufficient certainty.

Nonconforming goods Goods that do not conform to contract specifications.

Normal trade relations (NTR) status A status granted through an international treaty by which each member nation must treat other members at least as well as it treats the country that receives its most favorable treatment. This status was formerly known as most-favored-nation status.

Notary public A public official authorized to attest to the authenticity of signatures.

Notice-and-comment rulemaking An administrative rulemaking procedure that involves the publication of a notice of a proposed rulemaking in the *Federal Register,* a comment period for interested parties to express their views on the proposed rule, and the publication of the agency's final rule in the *Federal Register.*

Novation The substitution, by agreement, of a new contract for an old one, with the rights under the old one being terminated. Typically, there is a substitution of a new person who is responsible for the contract and the removal of an original party's rights and duties under the contract.

Nuisance A common law doctrine under which persons may be held liable for using their property in a manner that unreasonably interferes with others' rights to use or enjoy their own property.

O

Objective theory of contracts A theory under which the intent to form a contract will be judged by outward, objective facts (what the party said when entering into the contract, how the party acted or appeared, and the circumstances surrounding the transaction) as interpreted by a reasonable person, rather than by the party's own secret, subjective intentions.

Offer A promise or commitment to perform or refrain from performing some specified act in the future.

Offeree A person to whom an offer is made.

Offeror A person who makes an offer.

Online dispute resolution (ODR) The resolution of disputes with the assistance of organizations that offer dispute-resolution services via the Internet.

Opening statement A statement made to the jury at the beginning of a trial by a party's attorney, prior to the presentation of evidence. The attorney briefly outlines the evidence that will be offered and the legal theory that will be pursued.

Operating agreement In a limited liability company, an agreement in which the members set forth the details of how the business will be managed and operated.

Opinion A statement by the court expressing the reasons for its decision in a case.

Option contract A contract under which the offeror cannot revoke his or her offer for a stipulated time period and the offeree can accept or reject the offer during this period without fear that the offer will be made to another person. The offeree must give consideration for the option (the irrevocable offer) to be enforceable.

Order for relief A court's grant of assistance to a complainant. In bankruptcy proceedings, the order relieves the debtor of the immediate obligation to pay the debts listed in the bankruptcy petition.

Ordinance A law passed by a local governing unit, such as a municipality or a county.

Original jurisdiction Courts having original jurisdiction are courts of the first instance, or trial courts—that is, courts in which lawsuits begin, trials take place, and evidence is presented.

Outcome-based ethics An ethical philosophy that focuses on the impacts of a decision on society or on key stakeholders.

Output contract An agreement in which a seller agrees to sell and a buyer agrees to buy all or up to a stated amount of what the seller produces.

Outside director A person on the board of directors who does not hold a management position at the corporation.

P

Partially disclosed principal A principal whose identity is unknown by a third person, but the third person knows that the agent is or may be acting for a principal at the time the agent and the third person form a contract.

Partner A co-owner of a partnership.

Partnership An agreement by two or more persons to carry on, as co-owners, a business for profit.

Partnership by estoppel A judicially created partnership that may, at the court's discretion, be imposed for purposes of fairness. The court can prevent those who present themselves as partners (but who are not) from escaping liability if a third person relies on an alleged partnership in good faith and is harmed as a result.

Pass-through entity Any entity that does not have its income taxed at the level of that entity. Examples are partnerships, S corporations, and limited liability companies.

Past consideration Something given or some act done in the past, which cannot ordinarily be consideration for a later bargain.

Patent A government grant that gives an inventor the exclusive right or privilege to make, use, or sell his or her invention for a limited time period. The word *patent* usually refers to some invention and designates either the instrument by which patent rights are evidenced or the patent itself.

Peer-to-peer (P2P) networking The sharing of resources (such as files, hard drives, and processing styles) among multiple computers without necessarily requiring a central network server.

Penalty A sum inserted into a contract, not as a measure of compensation for its breach but rather as punishment for a default. The agreement as to the amount will not be enforced, and recovery will be limited to actual damages.

***Per curiam* opinion** By the whole court; a court opinion written by the court as a whole instead of being authored by a judge or justice.

Per se A Latin term meaning "in itself" or "by itself."

***Per se* violation** A type of anticompetitive agreement—such as a horizontal price-fixing agreement—

that is considered to be so injurious to the public that there is no need to determine whether it actually injures market competition. Rather, it is in itself (*per se*) a violation of the Sherman Act.

Perfect tender rule A common law rule under which a seller was required to deliver to the buyer goods that conformed perfectly to the requirements stipulated in the sales contract. A tender of nonconforming goods would automatically constitute a breach of contract. Under the Uniform Commercial Code, the rule has been greatly modified.

Performance In contract law, the fulfillment of one's duties arising under a contract with another; the normal way of discharging one's contractual obligations.

Periodic tenancy A lease interest in land for an indefinite period involving payment of rent at fixed intervals, such as week to week, month to month, or year to year.

Persuasive authority Any legal authority or source of law that a court may look to for guidance but need not follow when making its decision.

Petition in bankruptcy The document that is filed with a bankruptcy court to initiate bankruptcy proceedings. The official forms required for a petition in bankruptcy must be completed accurately, sworn to under oath, and signed by the debtor.

Petitioner In equity practice, a party that initiates a lawsuit.

Petty offense In criminal law, the least serious kind of criminal offense, such as a traffic or building-code violation.

Phishing Online fraud in which criminals pretend to be legitimate companies by using e-mails or malicious Web sites that trick individuals and companies into providing useful information, such as bank account numbers, Social Security numbers, and credit-card numbers.

Pierce the corporate veil To disregard the corporate entity, which limits the liability of shareholders, and hold the shareholders personally liable for a corporate obligation.

Plaintiff One who initiates a lawsuit.

Plea In criminal law, a defendant's allegation, in response to the charges brought against him or her, of guilt or innocence.

Plea bargaining The process by which a criminal defendant and the prosecutor in a criminal case work out a mutually satisfactory disposition of the case, subject to court approval. It usually involves the defendant's pleading guilty to a lesser offense in return for a lighter sentence.

Pleadings Statements made by the plaintiff and the defendant in a lawsuit that detail the facts, charges, and defenses involved in the litigation. The complaint and answer are part of the pleadings.

Plurality opinion A court opinion that is joined by the largest number of the judges or justices hearing the case, but less than half of the total number.

Police powers Powers possessed by states as part of their inherent sovereignty. These powers may be exercised to protect or promote the public order, health, safety, morals, and general welfare.

Possessory lien A lien that allows one person to retain possession of another's property as security for a debt or obligation owed by the owner of the property to the lienholder. An example of a possessory lien is an artisan's lien.

Potentially responsible party (PRP) A potentially liable party under the Comprehensive Environmental Response, Compensation and Liability Act (CERCLA). Any person who generated the hazardous waste, transported the waste, owned or operated the site at the time of disposal, or currently owns or operates the site may be responsible for some or all of the clean-up costs involved.

Power of attorney A written document, which is usually notarized, authorizing another to act as one's agent; can be special (permitting the agent to do specified acts only) or general (permitting the agent to transact all business for the principal).

Precedent A court decision that furnishes an example or authority for deciding subsequent cases involving identical or similar facts.

Predatory pricing The pricing of a product below cost with the intent to drive competitors out of the market.

Predominant-factor test A test courts use to determine whether a contract is primarily for the sale of goods or for the sale of services.

Preemption A doctrine under which certain federal laws preempt, or take precedence over, conflicting state or local laws.

Preemptive rights Rights held by shareholders that entitle them to purchase newly issued shares of a corporation's stock, equal in percentage to shares already held, before the stock is offered to any outside buyers. Preemptive rights enable shareholders to maintain their proportionate ownership and voice in the corporation.

Preference In bankruptcy proceedings, property transfers or payments made by the debtor that favor (give preference to) one creditor over others. The bankruptcy trustee is allowed to recover payments made both voluntarily and involuntarily to one creditor in preference over another.

Preferred creditor One who has received a preferential transfer from a debtor.

Preferred stock Classes of stock that have priority over common stock as to payment of dividends and distribution of assets on the corporation's dissolution.

Prepayment penalty A provision in a mortgage loan contract that requires the borrower to pay a penalty if the mortgage is repaid in full within a certain period.

Preponderance of the evidence A standard in civil law cases under which the plaintiff must convince the court that, based on the evidence presented by both parties, it is more likely than not that the plaintiff's allegation is true.

Prescription A way of creating an easement or profit in real property by openly using the property, without the true owner's consent, for the required period of time (similar to adverse possession).

Pretrial conference A conference, scheduled before the trial begins, between the judge and the attorneys litigating the suit. The parties may settle the dispute, clarify the issues, schedule discovery, and so on during the conference.

Pretrial motion A written or oral application to a court for a ruling or order, made before trial.

Price discrimination Setting prices in such a way that two competing buyers pay two different prices for an identical product or service.

Price-fixing agreement An agreement between competitors in which the competitors agree to fix the prices of products or services at a certain level; prohibited by the Sherman Act.

***Prima facie* case** A case in which the plaintiff has produced sufficient evidence of his or her conclusion that the case can go to a jury; a case in which the evidence compels the plaintiff's conclusion if the defendant produces no evidence to disprove it.

Principal In agency law, a person who agrees to have another, called the agent, act on his or her behalf.

Principle of rights The principle that human beings have certain fundamental rights (to life, freedom, and the pursuit of happiness, for example). Those who adhere to this "rights theory" believe that a key factor in determining whether a business decision is ethical is how that decision affects the rights of others. These others include the firm's owners, its employees, the consumers of its products or services, its suppliers, the community in which it does business, and society as a whole.

Privilege In tort law, the ability to act contrary to another person's right without that person's having legal redress for such acts. Privilege may be raised as a defense to defamation.

Privileges and immunities clause Article IV, Section 2, of the Constitution requires states not to discriminate against one another's citizens. A resident of one state cannot be treated as an alien when in another state. He or she may not be denied such privileges and immunities as legal protection, access to courts, travel rights, and property rights.

Privity of contract The relationship that exists between the promisor and the promisee of a contract.

Pro rata Proportionately; in proportion.

Probable cause Reasonable grounds to believe the existence of facts warranting certain actions, such as the search or arrest of a person.

Probate court A state court of limited jurisdiction that conducts proceedings relating to the settlement of a deceased person's estate.

Procedural due process The requirement that any government decision to take life, liberty, or property must be made fairly. For example, fair procedures must be used in determining whether a person will be subjected to punishment or have some burden imposed on him or her.

Procedural law Rules that define the manner in which the rights and duties of individuals may be enforced.

Procedural unconscionability Occurs when one contractual party lacks knowledge or understanding of the contract terms, often due to inconspicuous print or the lack of an opportunity to read the contract or to ask questions about its meaning. Procedural unconscionability often involves an *adhesion contract,* which is a contract drafted by the dominant party and then presented to the other—the adhering party—on a take-it-or-leave-it basis.

Product liability The legal liability of manufacturers, sellers, and lessors of goods to consumers, users, and bystanders for injuries or damages that are caused by the goods.

Product misuse A defense against product liability that may be raised when the plaintiff used a product in a manner not intended by the manufacturer. If the misuse is reasonably foreseeable, the seller will not escape liability unless measures were taken to guard against the harm that could result from the misuse.

Profit In real property law, the right to enter onto and remove things from the property of another (for example, the right to enter onto a person's land and remove sand and gravel therefrom).

Promise A person's assurance that he or she will or will not do something.

Promissory estoppel A doctrine that applies when a promisor makes a clear and definite promise on which the promisee justifiably relies. Such a promise is binding if justice will be better served by the enforcement of the promise.

Prospectus A document required by federal or state securities laws that describes the financial operations of a corporation, thus allowing investors to make informed decisions.

Protected class A class of persons with identifiable characteristics who historically have been victimized by discriminatory treatment for certain purposes. Depending on the context, these characteristics include age, color, gender, national origin, race, and religion.

Proximate cause Legal cause; exists when the connection between an act and an injury is strong enough to justify imposing liability.

Proxy In corporation law, a written agreement between a stockholder and another under which the stockholder authorizes the other to vote the stockholder's shares in a certain manner.

Proxy fight A conflict between an individual, group, or firm attempting to take control of a corporation and the corporation's management for the votes of the shareholders.

Public corporation A corporation owned by a federal, state, or municipal government—not to be confused with a publicly held corporation.

Public figures Individuals who are thrust into the public limelight. Public figures include government officials and politicians, movie stars, well-known businesspersons, and generally anybody who becomes known to the public because of his or her position or activities.

Public policy A government policy based on widely held societal values and (usually) expressed or implied in laws or regulations.

Publicly held corporation A corporation for which shares of stock have been sold to the public.

Puffery A salesperson's exaggerated claims concerning the quality of goods offered for sale. Such claims involve opinions rather than facts and are not considered to be legally binding promises or warranties.

Punitive damages Money damages that may be awarded to a plaintiff to punish the defendant and deter future similar conduct.

Purchase-money security interest (PMSI) A security interest that arises when a seller or lender extends credit for part or all of the purchase price of goods purchased by a buyer.

Q

Quantum meruit (pronounced *kwahn*-tuhm *mehr*-oo-wuht) Literally, "as much as he deserves"—an expression describing the extent of liability on a contract implied in law (quasi contract). An equitable doctrine based on the concept that one who benefits from another's labor and materials should not be unjustly enriched thereby but should be required to pay a reasonable amount for the benefits received, even absent a contract.

Quasi contract A fictional contract imposed on parties by a court in the interests of fairness and justice. Usually, quasi contracts are imposed to avoid the unjust enrichment of one party at the expense of another.

Question of fact In a lawsuit, an issue involving a factual dispute that can only be decided by a judge (or, in a jury trial, a jury).

Question of law In a lawsuit, an issue involving the application or interpretation of a law. Therefore, the judge, and not the jury, decides the issue.

Quitclaim deed A deed intended to pass any title, interest, or claim that the grantor may have in the property but not warranting that such title is valid. A quitclaim deed offers the least amount of protection against defects in the title.

Quorum The number of members of a decision-making body that must be present before business may be transacted.

Quota An assigned import limit on goods.

R

Ratification The act of accepting and giving legal force to an obligation that previously was not enforceable.

Reaffirmation agreement An agreement between a debtor and a creditor in which the debtor reaffirms, or promises to pay, a debt dischargeable in bankruptcy. To be enforceable, the agreement must be made prior to the discharge of the debt by the bankruptcy court.

Real property Land and everything attached to it, such as foliage and buildings.

Reasonable person standard The standard of behavior expected of a hypothetical "reasonable person." The standard against which negligence is measured and that must be observed to avoid liability for negligence.

Rebuttal The refutation of evidence introduced by an adverse party's attorney.

Receiver In a corporate dissolution, a court-appointed person who winds up corporate affairs and liquidates corporate assets.

Record According to the Uniform Electronic Transactions Act, information that is either inscribed on a tangible medium or stored in an electronic or other medium and that is retrievable. The Uniform Computer Information Transactions Act uses the term *record* instead of *writing*.

Recording statutes Statutes that allow deeds, mortgages, and other real property transactions to be recorded so as to provide notice to future purchasers or creditors of an existing claim on the property.

Redemption A repurchase, or buying back.

Reformation A court-ordered correction of a written contract so that it reflects the true intentions of the parties.

Regulation Z A set of rules promulgated by the Federal Reserve Board to implement the provisions of the Truth-in-Lending Act.

Rejection In contract law, an offeree's express or implied manifestation not to accept an offer. In the law governing contracts for the sale of goods, a buyer's manifest refusal to accept goods on the ground that they do not conform to contract specifications.

Rejoinder The defendant's answer to the plaintiff's rebuttal.

Release A contract in which one party forfeits the right to pursue a legal claim against the other party.

Relevant evidence Evidence tending to make a fact at issue in the case more or less probable than it would be without the evidence. Only relevant evidence is admissible in court.

Remanded Sent back. If an appellate court disagrees with a lower court's judgment, the case may be remanded to the lower court for further proceedings in which the lower court's decision should be consistent with the appellate court's opinion on the matter.

Remedy The relief given to an innocent party to enforce a right or compensate for the violation of a right.

Remedy at law A remedy available in a court of law. Money damages are awarded as a remedy at law.

Remedy in equity A remedy allowed by courts in situations where remedies at law are not appropriate. Remedies in equity are based on settled rules of fairness, justice, and honesty, and include injunction, specific performance, rescission and restitution, and reformation.

Replevin (pronounced rih-*pleh*-vin) An action to recover specific goods in the hands of a party who is wrongfully withholding them from the other party.

Reply Procedurally, a plaintiff's response to a defendant's answer.

Reporter A publication in which court cases are published, or reported.

Requirements contract An agreement in which a buyer agrees to purchase and the seller agrees to sell all or up to a stated amount of what the buyer needs or requires.

Res ipsa loquitur (pronounced *rehs ehp*-suh *low*-quuh-tuhr) A doctrine under which negligence may be inferred simply because an event occurred, if it is the type of event that would not occur in the absence of negligence. Literally, the term means "the facts speak for themselves."

Resale price maintenance agreement An agreement between a manufacturer and a retailer in which the manufacturer specifies the minimum retail price of its products. Resale price maintenance agreements are illegal *per se* under the Sherman Act.

Rescind (pronounced rih-*sihnd*) To cancel. *See also* Rescission

Rescission (pronounced rih-*sih*-zhen) A remedy whereby a contract is canceled and the parties are returned to the positions they occupied before the contract was made; may be effected through the mutual consent of the parties, by their conduct, or by court decree.

Residential use Use of land for construction of buildings for human habitation only.

Respondeat superior (pronounced ree-*spahn*-dee-uht soo-*peer*-ee-your) In Latin, "Let the master respond." A doctrine under which a principal or an employer is held liable for the wrongful acts committed by agents or employees while acting within the course and scope of their agency or employment.

Respondent In equity practice, the party who answers a bill or other proceeding.

Restitution An equitable remedy under which a person is restored to his or her original position prior to loss or injury, or placed in the position he or she would have been in had the breach not occurred.

Restraint of trade Any contract or combination that tends to eliminate or reduce competition, effect a monopoly, artificially maintain prices, or otherwise hamper the course of trade and commerce as it would be carried on if left to the control of natural economic forces.

Restrictive covenant A private restriction on the use of land. If its benefit or obligation passes with the land's ownership, it is said to "run with the land."

Retained earnings The portion of a corporation's profits that has not been paid out as dividends to shareholders.

Retainer An advance payment made by a client to a law firm to cover part of the legal fees and/or costs that will be incurred on that client's behalf.

Reverse To reject or overrule a court's judgment. An appellate court, for example, might reverse a lower court's judgment on an issue if it feels that the lower court committed an error during the trial or that the jury was improperly instructed.

Reverse discrimination Discrimination against majority groups, such as white males, that results from affirmative action programs, in which preferences are given to minority members and women.

Reversible error An error by a lower court that is sufficiently substantial to justify an appellate court's reversal of the lower court's decision.

Revocation In contract law, the withdrawal of an offer by an offeror. Unless an offer is irrevocable, it can be revoked at any time prior to acceptance without liability.

Right of contribution The right of a co-surety who pays more than his or her proportionate share on a debtor's default to recover the excess paid from other co-sureties.

Right of first refusal The right to purchase personal or real property—such as corporate shares or real estate—before the property is offered for sale to others.

Right of redemption The right of a defaulting borrower to redeem property before a foreclosure sale by paying the full amount of the debt, plus any interest and costs that have accrued.

Right of reimbursement The legal right of a person to be restored, repaid, or indemnified for costs, expenses, or losses incurred or expended on behalf of another.

Right of subrogation The right of a person to stand in the place of (be substituted for) another, giving the substituted party the same legal rights that the original party had.

Right-to-work law A state law providing that employees are not to be required to join a union as a condition of obtaining or retaining employment.

Robbery The act of forcefully and unlawfully taking personal property of any value from another. Force or intimidation is usually necessary for an act of theft to be considered a robbery.

Rule of four A rule of the United States Supreme Court under which the Court will not issue a writ of *certiorari* unless at least four justices approve of the decision to issue the writ.

Rule of reason A test by which a court balances the positive effects (such as economic efficiency) of an agreement against its potentially anticompetitive effects. In antitrust litigation, many practices are analyzed under the rule of reason.

Rulemaking The process undertaken by an administrative agency when formally adopting a new regulation or amending an old one. Rulemaking involves notifying the public of a proposed rule or change and receiving and considering the public's comments.

Rules of evidence Rules governing the admissibility of evidence in trial courts.

S

S corporation A close business corporation that has met certain requirements as set out by the Internal

Revenue Code and thus qualifies for special income tax treatment. Essentially, an S corporation is taxed the same as a partnership, but its owners enjoy the privilege of limited liability.

Sale The passing of title (evidence of ownership rights) from the seller to the buyer for a price.

Sales contract A contract for the sale of goods under which the ownership of goods is transferred from a seller to a buyer for a price.

Scienter (pronounced *sy-en*-ter) Knowledge by the misrepresenting party that material facts have been falsely represented or omitted with an intent to deceive.

Search warrant An order granted by a public authority, such as a judge, that authorizes law enforcement personnel to search particular premises or property.

Seasonably Within a specified time period. If no period is specified, within a reasonable time.

SEC Rule 10b-5 A rule of the Securities and Exchange Commission that makes it unlawful, in connection with the purchase or sale of any security, to make any untrue statement of a material fact or to omit a material fact if such omission causes the statement to be misleading.

Secondary boycott A union's refusal to work for, purchase from, or handle the products of a secondary employer, with whom the union has no dispute, for the purpose of forcing that employer to stop doing business with the primary employer, with whom the union has a labor dispute.

Securities Generally, corporate stocks and bonds. A security may also be a note, debenture, stock warrant, or any document given as evidence of an ownership interest in a corporation or as a promise of repayment by a corporation.

Self-defense The legally recognized privilege to protect one's self or property against injury by another. The privilege of self-defense protects only acts that are reasonably necessary to protect one's self or property.

Self-incrimination The act of implicating oneself in a crime or exposing oneself to criminal prosecution. The Fifth Amendment to the U.S. Constitution protects persons from being compelled to incriminate themselves.

Seniority system In regard to employment relationships, a system in which those who have worked longest for the company are first in line for promotions, salary increases, and other benefits. They are also the last to be laid off if the workforce must be reduced.

Service mark A mark used in the sale or the advertising of services, such as to distinguish the services of one person from the services of others. Titles, character names, and other distinctive features of radio and television programs may be registered as service marks.

Service of process The delivery of the complaint and summons to a defendant.

Sexual harassment In the employment context, the granting of job promotions or other benefits in return for sexual favors or conduct that is so sexually offensive that it creates a hostile working environment.

Share A unit of stock. *See also* Stock

Shareholder One who purchases shares of a corporation's stock, thus acquiring an equity interest in the corporation.

Shareholder's derivative suit A suit brought by a shareholder to enforce a corporate cause of action against a third person.

Sharia Civil law principles of some Middle Eastern countries that are based on the Islamic directives that follow the teachings of the prophet Muhammad.

Shipment contract A contract in which the seller is required to ship the goods by carrier. The buyer assumes liability for any losses or damage to the goods after they are delivered to the carrier. Generally, all contracts are assumed to be shipment contracts if nothing to the contrary is stated in the contract.

Short sale A sale of real property for an amount that is less than the balance owed on the mortgage loan, usually due to financial hardship. Both the lender and the borrower must consent to a short sale. Following a short sale, the borrower still owes the balance of the mortgage debt (after the sale proceeds are applied) to the lender unless the lender agrees to forgive the remaining debt.

Short-swing profits Profits made by officers, directors, and certain large stockholders resulting from the use of nonpublic (inside) information about their companies; prohibited by Section 12 of the 1934 Securities Exchange Act.

Shrink-wrap agreement An agreement whose terms are expressed in a document located inside a box in which goods (usually software) are packaged; sometimes called a *shrink-wrap license.*

Signature Under the Uniform Commercial Code, "any symbol executed or adopted by a party with a present intention to authenticate a writing."

Slander Defamation in oral form.

Slander of quality The publication of false information about another's product, alleging that it is not what its seller claims.

Slander of title The publication of a statement that denies or casts doubt on another's legal ownership of any property, causing financial loss to that property's owner. Also called *trade libel.*

Small claims courts Special courts in which parties may litigate small claims (usually, claims involving $2,500 or less). Attorneys are not required in small claims courts, and in many states attorneys are not allowed to represent the parties.

Social media The means by which people can create, share, and exchange ideas and comments via the Internet.

Sociological school A school of legal thought that views the law as a tool for promoting justice in society.

Sole proprietorship The simplest form of business, in which the owner is the business. The owner reports business income on his or her personal income tax return and is legally responsible for all debts and obligations incurred by the business.

Sovereign immunity A doctrine that immunizes foreign nations from the jurisdiction of U.S. courts when certain conditions are satisfied.

Sovereignty The quality of having independent authority over a geographic area. For instance, state governments have the authority to regulate affairs within their border.

Spam Bulk, unsolicited (junk) e-mail.

Special-use permit A permit that allows for a specific exemption to zoning regulations for a particular piece of land in a location that has a particular zoning characteristic. Local zoning authorities grant special-use permits.

Specific performance An equitable remedy requiring the breaching party to perform as promised under the contract; usually granted only when money damages would be an inadequate remedy and the subject matter of the contract is unique (for example, real property).

Spot zoning A zoning classification granted to a parcel of land that is different from the classification given to other land in the immediate area.

Stakeholders Groups, other than the company's shareholders, that are affected by corporate decisions. Stakeholders include employees, customers, creditors, suppliers, and the community in which the corporation operates.

Standing to sue The requirement that an individual must have a sufficient stake in a controversy before he or she can bring a lawsuit. The plaintiff must demonstrate that he or she either has been injured or has been threatened with injury.

Stare decisis (pronounced *ster*-ay dih-*si*-ses) A common law doctrine under which judges are obligated to follow the precedents established in prior decisions.

Statute of Frauds A state statute under which certain types of contracts must be in writing to be enforceable.

Statute of limitations A federal or state statute setting the maximum time period during which a certain action can be brought or certain rights enforced.

Statute of repose Basically, a statute of limitations that is not dependent on the happening of a cause of action. Statutes of repose generally begin to run at an earlier date and run for a longer period of time than statutes of limitations.

Statutory law The body of law enacted by legislative bodies (as opposed to constitutional law, administrative law, or case law).

Stock An equity (ownership) interest in a corporation, measured in units of shares.

Stock buyback Sometimes, publicly held companies use funds from their own treasuries to repurchase their own stock. The result is that the price of the stock usually goes up.

Stock certificate A certificate issued by a corporation evidencing the ownership of a specified number of shares in the corporation.

Stock option *See* Stock warrant

Stock warrant A certificate that grants the owner the option to buy a given number of shares of stock, usually within a set time period.

Strict liability Liability regardless of fault. In tort law, strict liability may be imposed on defendants in cases involving abnormally dangerous activities, dangerous animals, or defective products.

Strike An extreme action undertaken by unionized workers when collective bargaining fails. The workers leave their jobs, refuse to work, and (typically) picket the employer's workplace.

Subject-matter jurisdiction Jurisdiction over the subject matter of a lawsuit.

Submission The act of referring a dispute to an arbitrator.

Subpoena A document commanding a person to appear at a certain time and place or give testimony concerning a certain matter.

Substantial performance Performance that does not vary greatly from the performance promised in a contract. The performance must create substantially the same benefits as those promised in the contract.

Substantive due process A requirement that focuses on the content, or substance, of legislation. If a law or other governmental action limits a fundamental right, such as the right to travel or to vote, it will be held to violate substantive due process unless it promotes a compelling or overriding state interest.

Substantive law Law that defines the rights and duties of individuals with respect to each other, as opposed to procedural law, which defines the manner in which these rights and duties may be enforced.

Substantive unconscionability Occurs when contracts, or portions of contracts, are oppressive or overly harsh. Courts generally focus on provisions that deprive one party of the benefits of the agreement or leave that party without remedy for nonperformance by the other. An example of substantive unconscionability is the agreement by a welfare recipient with a fourth-grade education to purchase a refrigerator for $2,000 under an installment contract.

Suit *See* Litigation

Summary jury trial (SJT) A method of settling disputes in which a trial is held, but the jury's verdict is not binding. The verdict acts only as a guide to both sides in reaching an agreement during the mandatory negotiations that immediately follow the summary jury trial.

Summons A document informing a defendant that a legal action has been commenced against him or her and that the defendant must appear in court on a certain date to answer the plaintiff's complaint. The document is delivered by a sheriff or any other person so authorized.

Superseding cause An intervening force or event that breaks the connection between a wrongful act and an injury to another; in negligence law, a defense to liability.

Supremacy clause The provision in Article VI of the Constitution that provides that the Constitution, laws, and treaties of the United States are "the supreme Law of the Land." Under this clause, state and local laws that directly conflict with federal law will be rendered invalid.

Surety A person, such as a cosigner on a note, who agrees to be primarily responsible for the debt of another.

Suretyship An express contract in which a third party to a debtor-creditor relationship (the surety) promises to be primarily responsible for the debtor's obligation.

Symbolic speech Nonverbal conduct that expresses opinions or thoughts about a subject. Symbolic speech is protected under the First Amendment's guarantee of freedom of speech.

T

Taking The taking of private property by the government for public use. Under the Fifth Amendment to the Constitution, the government may not take private property for public use without "just compensation."

Tangible employment action A significant change in employment status, such as firing or failing to promote an employee, reassigning the employee to a position with significantly different responsibilities, or effecting a significant change in employment benefits.

Tangible property Property that has physical existence and can be distinguished by the senses of touch, sight, and so on. A car is tangible property. A patent right is intangible property.

Tariff A tax on imported goods.

Technology licensing Allowing another to use and profit from intellectual property (patents, copyrights, trademarks, innovative products or processes, and so on) for consideration. In the context of international business transactions, technology licensing is sometimes an attractive alternative to the establishment of foreign production facilities.

Tenancy at sufferance A type of tenancy under which one who, after rightfully being in possession of leased premises, continues (wrongfully) to occupy the property after the lease has been terminated. The tenant has no rights to possess the property and occupies it only because the person entitled to evict the tenant has not done so.

Tenancy at will A type of tenancy under which either party can terminate the tenancy without notice; usually arises when a tenant who has been under a tenancy for years retains possession, with the landlord's consent, after the tenancy for years has terminated.

Tenancy by the entirety The joint ownership of property by a husband and wife. Neither party can transfer his or her interest in the property without the consent of the other.

Tenancy in common Co-ownership of property in which each party owns an undivided interest that passes to his or her heirs at death.

Tenant One who has the temporary use and occupation of real property owned by another person, called the landlord. The duration and terms of the tenancy are usually established by a lease.

Tender An unconditional offer to perform an obligation by a person who is ready, willing, and able to do so.

Tender of delivery Under the Uniform Commercial Code, a seller's or lessor's act of placing conforming goods at the disposal of the buyer or lessee and giving the buyer or lessee whatever notification is reasonably necessary to enable the buyer or lessee to take delivery.

Third party beneficiary One for whose benefit a promise is made in a contract but who is not a party to the contract.

Tippee A person who receives inside information.

Title insurance Insurance commonly purchased by a purchaser of real property to protect against loss in the event that the title to the property is not free from liens or superior ownership claims.

Tolling Temporary suspension of the running of a prescribed period (such as a statute of limitations). For instance, a statute of limitations may be tolled until the party suffering an injury has discovered it or should have discovered it.

Tombstone ad An advertisement, historically in a format resembling a tombstone, of a securities offering. The ad informs potential investors of where and how they may obtain a prospectus.

Tort A civil wrong not arising from a breach of contract. A breach of a legal duty that proximately causes harm or injury to another.

Tortfeasor One who commits a tort.

Toxic tort A personal injury caused by exposure to a toxic substance, such as asbestos or hazardous waste. Victims can sue for medical expenses, lost wages, and pain and suffering.

Trade dress The image and overall appearance of a product—for example, the distinctive decor, menu, layout, and style of service of a particular restaurant. Basically, trade dress is subject to the same protection as trademarks.

Trade libel The publication of false information about another's product, alleging it is not what its seller claims; also referred to as *slander of quality.*

Trade name A term that is used to indicate part or all of a business's name and that is directly related to the business's reputation and goodwill. Trade names are protected under the common law (and under trademark law, if the name is the same as the firm's trademark).

Trade secret Information or a process that gives a business an advantage over competitors who do not know the information or process.

Trademark A distinctive mark, motto, device, or implement that a manufacturer stamps, prints, or otherwise affixes to the goods it produces so that they may be identified on the market and their origins made known. Once a trademark is established (under the common law or through registration), the owner is entitled to its exclusive use.

Transferred intent A legal principle under which a person who intends to harm one individual, but unintentionally harms a second person, can be liable to the second victim for an intentional tort. The law transfers the required intent to the second victim.

Treaty An agreement formed between two or more independent nations.

Treble damages Damages consisting of three times the amount of damages determined by a jury in certain cases as required by statute.

Trespass to land The entry onto, above, or below the surface of land owned by another without the owner's permission or legal authorization.

Trespass to personal property The unlawful taking or harming of another's personal property; interference with another's right to the exclusive possession of his or her personal property.

Trespasser One who commits the tort of trespass in one of its forms.

Trial court A court in which trials are held and testimony taken.

Triple bottom line The idea that investors and others should consider not only corporate profits, but also the corporation's impact on people and on the planet in assessing the firm. (The bottom line is people, planet, and profits.)

Tying arrangement An agreement between a buyer and a seller in which the buyer of a specific product or service becomes obligated to purchase additional products or services from the seller.

Typosquatting A form of cybersquatting that relies on mistakes, such as typographical errors, made by Internet users when inputting information into a Web browser.

U

U.S. trustee A government official who performs certain administrative tasks that a bankruptcy judge would otherwise have to perform.

Ultra vires (pronounced *uhl*-trah *vye*-reez) A Latin term meaning "beyond the powers"; in corporate law, acts of a corporation that are beyond its express and implied powers to undertake.

Unanimous opinion A court opinion in which all of the judges or justices of the court agree to the court's decision.

Unconscionable (pronounced un-*kon*-shun-uh-bul) A contract or clause that is void on the basis of public policy because one party, as a result of his or her disproportionate bargaining power, is forced to accept terms that are unfairly burdensome and that unfairly benefit the dominating party. *See also* Procedural unconscionability; Substantive unconscionability

Undisclosed principal A principal whose identity is unknown by a third person, and the third person has no knowledge that the agent is acting for a principal at the time the agent and the third person form a contract.

Unenforceable contract A valid contract rendered unenforceable by some statute or law.

Uniform law A model law created by the National Conference of Commissioners on Uniform State Laws and/or the American Law Institute for the states to consider adopting. If the state adopts the law, it becomes statutory law in that state. Each state has the option of adopting or rejecting all or part of a uniform law.

Unilateral contract A contract that results when an offer can only be accepted by the offeree's performance.

Union shop A place of employment in which all workers, once employed, must become union members within a specified period of time as a condition of their continued employment.

Unliquidated debt A debt that is uncertain in amount.

Unreasonably dangerous product In product liability, a product that is defective to the point of threatening a consumer's health and safety. A product will be considered unreasonably dangerous if it is dangerous beyond the expectation of the ordinary consumer or if a less dangerous alternative was economically feasible for the manufacturer, but the manufacturer failed to produce it.

Usage of trade Any practice or method of dealing having such regularity of observance in a place, vocation, or trade as to justify an expectation that it will be observed with respect to the transaction in question.

Usury Charging an illegal rate of interest.

Utilitarianism An approach to ethical reasoning in which ethically correct behavior is related to an evaluation of the consequences of a given action on those who will be affected by it. In utilitarian reasoning, a "good" decision is one that results in the greatest good for the greatest number of people affected by the decision.

V

Valid contract A contract that results when elements necessary for contract formation (agreement, consideration, legal purpose, and contractual capacity) are present.

Validation notice An initial notice to a debtor from a collection agency informing the debtor that he or she has thirty days to challenge the debt and request verification.

Variance A form of relief or exception from zoning and other laws that is granted to a property owner.

Venue (pronounced *ven*-yoo) The geographical district in which an action is tried and from which the jury is selected.

Verdict A formal decision made by a jury.

Vertical merger The acquisition by a company at one stage of production of a company at a higher or lower stage of production (such as its supplier or retailer).

Vertical restraint Any restraint on trade created by agreements between firms at different levels in the manufacturing and distribution process.

Vertically integrated firm A firm that carries out two or more functional phases—such as manufacture, distribution, retailing—of a product.

Vesting Under the Employee Retirement Income Security Act of 1974, a pension plan becomes vested when an employee has a legal right to the benefits purchased with the employer's contributions, even if the employee is no longer working for this employer.

Vicarious liability Legal responsibility placed on one person for the acts of another.

Virus A type of malware that is transmitted between computers and attempts to do deliberate damage to systems and data.

Void contract A contract having no legal force or binding effect.

Voidable contract A contract that may be legally avoided (canceled, or annulled) at the option of one of the parties.

Voidable preference In bankruptcy law, a preference that may be avoided, or set aside, by the trustee.

Voir dire (pronounced *vwahr deehr*) A French phrase meaning, literally, "to see, to speak." In jury trials, the phrase refers to the process in which the attorneys question prospective jurors to determine whether they are biased or have any connection with a party to the action or with a prospective witness.

Voting trust An agreement (trust contract) under which legal title to shares of corporate stock is transferred to a trustee who is authorized by the shareholders to vote the shares on their behalf.

W

Waiver An intentional, knowing relinquishment of a legal right.

Warranty A promise that certain facts are truly as they are represented to be.

Warranty deed A deed in which the grantor guarantees to the grantee that the grantor has title to the property conveyed in the deed, that there are no encumbrances on the property other than what the grantor has represented, and that the grantee will enjoy quiet possession of the property; a deed that provides the greatest amount of protection for the grantee.

Warranty disclaimer A seller's or lessor's negation or qualification of a warranty.

Waste The abuse or destructive use of real property by one who is in rightful possession of the property but who does not have title to it. Waste does not include ordinary depreciation due to age and normal use.

Watered stock Shares of stock issued by a corporation for which the corporation receives, as payment, less than the fair market value of the shares.

Wetlands Areas of land designated by government agencies (such as the Army Corps of Engineers or the Environmental Protection Agency) as protected areas that support wildlife and that therefore cannot be filled in or dredged by private contractors or parties.

Whistleblowing An employee's disclosure to government, the press, or upper-management authorities that the employer is engaged in unsafe or illegal activities.

White-collar crime Nonviolent crime committed by individuals or corporations to obtain a personal or business advantage.

Winding up The second of two stages involved in the termination of a partnership or corporation. Once the firm is dissolved, it continues to exist legally until the process of winding up all business affairs (collecting and distributing the firm's assets) is complete.

Workers' compensation laws State statutes establishing an administrative procedure for compensating workers' injuries that arise out of—or in the course of—their employment, regardless of fault.

Workout A formal contract between a debtor and his or her creditors in which the parties agree to negotiate a payment plan for the amount due on the loan instead of proceeding to foreclosure.

Worm A type of malware that is designed to copy itself from one computer to another without human interaction. A worm can copy itself automatically and can replicate in great volume and with great speed. Worms, for example, can send out copies of themselves to every contact in your e-mail address book.

Writ of attachment A court's order, prior to a trial to collect a debt, directing the sheriff or other officer to seize nonexempt property of the debtor. If the creditor prevails at trial, the seized property can be sold to satisfy the judgment.

Writ of *certiorari* (pronounced sur-shee-uh-*rah*-ree) A writ from a higher court asking the lower court for the record of a case.

Writ of execution A court's order, after a judgment has been entered against the debtor, directing the sheriff to seize (levy) and sell any of the debtor's nonexempt real or personal property. The proceeds of the sale are used to pay off the judgment, accrued interest, and costs of the sale. Any surplus is paid to the debtor.

Wrongful discharge An employer's termination of an employee's employment in violation of an employment contract or laws that protect employees.

Z

Zoning The division of a city by legislative regulation into districts and the application in each district of regulations having to do with structural and architectural designs of buildings and prescribing the use to which buildings within designated districts may be put.

Zoning laws The rules and regulations that collectively manage the development and use of land.

TABLE OF CASES

Following is a list of all the cases mentioned in this text, including those within the footnotes, features, and case problems. Any case that was an excerpted case for a chapter is given special emphasis by having its title **boldfaced.**

A

B

C

D

E

F

G

H

T

U

V

W

Y

Z

B

C

D

E

F

J

K

L

N

O

P

U

V

W

Y

Z

ADDITIONAL CASES

EXTENDED CASE 9.3 Baer v. Chase

United States Court of Appeals, Third Circuit, 2004. 392 F.3d 609.

***GREENBERG,* Circuit Judge.**

* * * *

[David] Chase, who originally was from New Jersey, but relocated to Los Angeles in 1971, is the creator, producer, writer and director of *The Sopranos*. Chase has numerous credits for other television productions as well. * * * Chase had worked on a number of projects involving organized crime activities based in New Jersey, including a script for "a mob boss in therapy," a concept that, in part, would become the basis for *The Sopranos*.

In 1995, Chase was producing and directing a *Rockford Files* "movie-of-the-week" when he met Joseph Urbancyk who was working on the set as a camera operator and temporary director of photography.

[Through Urbancyk, Chase met Robert] Baer, * * * a New Jersey attorney [who] recently had left his employment in the Union County Prosecutor's Office in Elizabeth, New Jersey, where he had worked for the previous six years.

* * * *

Chase, Urbancyk, and Baer met for lunch on June 20, 1995 * * * , with Baer describing his experience as a prosecutor. Baer also pitched the idea to shoot "a film or television shows about the New Jersey Mafia." At that time Baer was unaware of Chase's previous work involving mob activity premised in New Jersey. At the lunch there was no reference to any payment that Chase might make to Baer for the latter's services * * * .

In October 1995, Chase visited New Jersey for three days. During this "research visit" Baer arranged meetings for Chase with Detective Thomas Koczur, Detective Robert A. Jones, and Tony Spirito who provided Chase with information, material, and personal stories about their experiences with organized crime. * * * Baer does not dispute that virtually all of the ideas and locations that he "contributed" to Chase existed in the public record.

After returning to Los Angeles, Chase sent Baer a copy of a draft of a *Sopranos* screenplay that he had written, which was dated December 20, 1995. Baer asserts that after he read it he called Chase and made various comments with regard to it. Baer claims that the two spoke at least four times during the following year and that he sent a letter to Chase dated February 10, 1997, discussing *The Sopranos* script.

* * * *

Baer asserts that he and Chase orally agreed on three separate occasions that if the show became a success, Chase would "take care of" Baer, and "remunerate Baer in a manner commensurate to the true value of his services."

Baer claims that on each of these occasions the parties had the same conversation in which Chase offered to pay Baer, stating "you help me; I pay you." Baer always rejected Chase's offer, reasoning that Chase would be unable to pay him "for the true value of the services Baer was rendering." Each time Baer rejected Chase's offer he did so with a counteroffer, "that I would perform the services while assuming the risk that if the show failed Chase would owe me nothing. If, however, the show succeeded he would remunerate me in a manner commensurate to the true value of my services." Baer acknowledges that this counteroffer * * * always was oral and did not include any fixed term of duration or price. * * * In fact, Chase has not paid Baer for his services.

On or about May 15, 2002, Baer filed a * * * complaint against Chase in [a federal] district court * * * [claiming among other things] * * * breach of implied contract. Eventually Chase brought a motion for summary judgment * * * . Chase claimed that the alleged contract * * * [was] too vague, ambiguous and lacking in essential terms to be enforced * * * .

The district court granted Chase's motion * * * .

* * * *

Baer predicates [bases] his contract claim on this appeal on an implied-in-fact contract * * * . The issue with respect to the implied-in-fact contract claim concerns whether Chase and Baer entered into an enforceable contract for services Baer rendered that aided in the creation and production of *The Sopranos*.

* * * *

* * * A contract arises from offer and acceptance, and must be sufficiently definite so that

the performance to be rendered by each party can be ascertained with reasonable certainty. Therefore parties create an enforceable contract when they agree on its essential terms and manifest an intent that the terms bind them. *If parties to an agreement do not agree on one or more essential terms of the purported agreement, courts generally hold it to be unenforceable.* [Emphasis added.]

* * * *

* * * [The] law deems the price term, i.e., the amount of compensation, an essential term of any contract. An agreement lacking definiteness of price, however, is not unenforceable if the parties specify a practicable method by which they can determine the amount. However, *in the absence of an agreement as to the manner or method of determining compensation the purported agreement is invalid.* Additionally, *the duration of the contract is deemed an essential term and therefore any agreement must be sufficiently definitive to allow a court to determine the agreed upon length of the contractual relationship.* [Emphasis added.]

* * * *

The * * * question with respect to Baer's contract claim, therefore, is whether his contract is enforceable in light of the traditional requirement of definitiveness * * * . A contract may be expressed in writing, or orally, or in acts, or partly in one of these ways and partly in others. There is a point, however, at which interpretation becomes alteration. In this case, even when all of the parties' verbal and non-verbal actions are aggregated and viewed most favorably to Baer, we cannot find a contract that is distinct and definitive enough to be enforceable.

Nothing in the record indicates that the parties agreed on how, how much, where, or for what period Chase would compensate Baer. The parties did not discuss who would determine the "true value" of Baer's services, when the "true value" would be calculated, or what variables would go into such a calculation. There was no discussion or agreement as to the meaning of "success" of *The Sopranos.* There was no discussion how "profits" were to be defined. There was no contemplation of dates of commencement or termination of the contract. And again, nothing in Baer's or Chase's conduct, or the surrounding circumstances of the relationship, shed light on, or answers, any of these questions. The district court was correct in its description of the contract between the parties: "The contract as articulated by the Plaintiff lacks essential terms, and is vague, indefinite and uncertain; no version of the alleged agreement contains sufficiently precise terms to constitute an enforceable contract." We therefore will affirm the district court's rejection of Baer's claim to recover under a theory of implied-in-fact contract.

QUESTIONS

1. Why must the terms of a contract be "sufficiently definite" before a court will enforce the contract?
2. What might a court consider when looking for a "sufficiently definite meaning" to make a contract term enforceable?

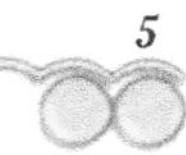

CASE 10.3 Hadley v. Baxendale

Court of Exchequer, 1854. 156 Eng.Rep. 145.

Background and Facts The Hadleys (the plaintiffs) ran a flour mill in Gloucester. The crankshaft attached to the steam engine in the mill broke, causing the mill to shut down. The shaft had to be sent to a foundry located in Greenwich so that the new shaft could be made to fit the other parts of the engine. Baxendale, the defendant, was a common carrier that transported the shaft from Gloucester to Greenwich. The freight charges were collected in advance, and Baxendale promised to deliver the shaft the following day. It was not delivered for a number of days, however. As a consequence, the mill was closed for several days. The Hadleys sued to recover the profits lost during that time. Baxendale contended that the loss of profits was "too remote" to be recoverable. The court held for the plaintiffs, and the jury was allowed to take into consideration the lost profits. The defendant appealed.

IN THE LANGUAGE OF THE COURT
***ALDERSON*, B. [Baron]**

* * * *

* * * Where two parties have made a contract which one of them has broken, the damages which the other party ought to receive in respect of such breach of contract should be such as may fairly and reasonably be considered either arising naturally, *i.e.*, according to the usual course of things, from such breach of contract itself, or such as may reasonably be supposed to have been in the contemplation of both parties, at the time they made the contract, as the probable result of the breach of it. Now, if the special circumstances under which the contract was actually made were communicated by the plaintiffs to the defendants, and thus known to both parties, the damages resulting from the breach of such a contract, *which they would reasonably contemplate*, would be the amount of injury which would ordinarily follow from a breach of contract under these special circumstances so known and communicated. * * * Now, in the present case, if we are to apply the principles above laid down, we find that the only circumstances here communicated by the plaintiffs to the defendants at the time the contract was made, were, that the article to be carried was the broken shaft of a mill, and that the plaintiffs were the millers of that mill. * * * Special circumstances were here never communicated by the plaintiffs to the defendants. It follows, therefore, that the loss of profits here cannot reasonably be considered such a consequence of the breach of contract as could have been fairly and reasonably contemplated by both the parties when they made this contract. [Emphasis added.]

Decision and Remedy *The Court of Exchequer ordered a new trial. According to the court, to collect consequential damages, the plaintiffs would have to have given express notice of the special circumstances that caused the loss of profits.*

Impact of This Case on Today's Law *This case established the rule that when damages are awarded, compensation is given only for those injuries that the defendant could reasonably have foreseen as a probable result of the usual course of events following a breach. Today, the rule enunciated by the court in this case still applies. To recover consequential damages, the plaintiff must show that the defendant had reason to know or foresee that a particular loss or injury would occur.*

The E-Commerce Dimension *If a Web merchant loses business due to a computer system's failure that can be attributed to malfunctioning software, can the merchant recover the lost profits from the software maker? Explain.*

CASE 13.1 Jarvis v. Ford Motor Co.

United States Court of Appeals, Second Circuit, 2002. 283 F.3d 33.

• **Company Profile** Henry Ford founded the Ford Motor Company (**www.ford.com**) in Dearborn, Michigan, in 1903 to design and make a mass-produced automobile. Five years later, Ford introduced the Model T, which was made affordable by the company's efficient use of assembly lines. By 1920, 60 percent of all of the vehicles on the road were made by Ford. Today, Ford is the world's largest maker of pickup trucks and the second-largest producer of cars. Ford brand names include Aston Martin, Jaguar, Lincoln, Mercury, and Volvo. Its most popular models are Ford Taurus cars and F-Series pickup trucks. Ford also makes the Aerostar minivan.

• **Background and Facts** In 1991, Kathleen Jarvis bought a new Aerostar. Six days later, she started the van in the driveway of her home in Woodstock, New York. After she turned on the ignition, the engine suddenly revved and the vehicle took off. Jarvis pumped the brake with both feet, but the van would not stop. She steered to avoid people walking in the road before the van entered a ditch and turned over. As a result of the accident, Jarvis suffered a head injury and could not return to her job. She filed a suit in a federal district court against Ford, asserting product liability based, in part, on negligence. Jarvis alleged that a defect in the van had caused the sudden acceleration. Her proof included her testimony, the testimony of other Aerostar owners who had experienced similar problems, and evidence that hundreds of additional Aerostar owners had experienced sudden acceleration. She also presented an expert who theorized that the van's cruise control had malfunctioned and who proposed an inexpensive remedy for this problem. Ford argued that Jarvis had failed to prove the defect that caused the cruise control to malfunction. A jury issued a verdict in Jarvis's favor, but the court granted Ford's motion for judgment as a matter of law. Jarvis appealed to the U.S. Court of Appeals for the Second Circuit.

IN THE LANGUAGE OF THE COURT

***SOTOMAYOR,* Circuit Judge.**

* * * *

* * * A plaintiff's failure to prove why a product malfunctioned does not necessarily prevent a plaintiff from showing that the product was defective. * * * While the burden is upon the plaintiff to prove that the product was defective and that the defect existed while the product was in the manufacturer's possession, [the] plaintiff is not required to prove the specific defect, especially where the product is complicated in nature. *Proof of necessary facts may be circumstantial. Though the happening of the accident is not proof of a defective condition, a defect may be inferred from proof that the product did not perform as intended by the manufacturer* * * *. [Emphasis added.]

* * * *

The district court erred in requiring proof of a specific defect in the Aerostar's cruise control and in not considering Jarvis's circumstantial evidence of a defect. The malfunction in the design of the Aerostar that Jarvis has alleged is that it suddenly accelerated, opening full throttle without Jarvis depressing the accelerator pedal, and that her efforts to stop the vehicle by pumping the brakes were unavailing. If Jarvis's six-day-old Aerostar performed in this manner, a jury could reasonably conclude that it was defective when put on the market by Ford, and that the defect made it reasonably certain that the vehicle would be dangerous when put to normal use, as required [in a cause of action based on] negligent design. Although Ford argued that the accident was caused instead by driver error, this theory would have been rejected if the jury had believed Jarvis's testimony that she had her feet on the brake and not on the accelerator, as Ford claimed. * * * Construing the evidence in Jarvis's favor and crediting her version of events, a reasonable jury could find that Ford breached its duty of care. Even accepting as true that sudden acceleration in the 1991 Aerostar would occur, at most, very infrequently when measured against all Aerostar ignition starts [as Ford claimed], the consequences of sudden acceleration could easily be catastrophic, the design of which Jarvis complains has no particular utility to balance its potential for harm, and, according to Jarvis's expert, the malfunction in the cruise control could be avoided by an inexpensive switch that would shut off power to the cruise control when not in use.

CASE CONTINUES

CASE 13.1 CONTINUED

• **Decision and Remedy** *The U.S. Court of Appeals for the Second Circuit vacated (set aside, voided) the judgment of the lower court and remanded the case with instructions to reinstate the jury's verdict that Ford was negligent in the design of the cruise control mechanism in the 1991 Aerostar. A plaintiff in a product liability action based on negligence is not required to prove a specific defect when a defect may be inferred from proof that the product did not perform as the manufacturer intended.*[a]

• **The Legal Environment Dimension** *If plaintiffs were required to prove the specific defect that caused their injury, as the trial court in this case had ruled, what impact would this have on product liability claims based on negligence? Would there be more or fewer of these types of lawsuits filed?*

• **The Global Dimension** *Assume that other nations do not have laws concerning product liability based on negligence. Can a U.S. manufacturer sell a negligently designed product in a foreign market without risk of liability? Should it? Why or why not?*

a. This is also the principle in a strict product liability action, according to the *Restatement (Third) of Torts: Products Liability*, which will be discussed later in this chapter.

EXTENDED CASE 13.3 Crosswhite v. Jumpking, Inc.

United States District Court, District of Oregon, 2006. 411 F.Supp.2d 1228.

***AIKEN*, J. [Judge]**

* * * *

On May 11, 2002, plaintiff, Gary Crosswhite, was jumping on a trampoline with another boy. The trampoline was owned by Jack and Misty Urbach * * *. The 14-foot round-shaped "backyard" trampoline was manufactured by defendant * * *, Jumpking [Inc.], and purchased by the Urbachs from Costco, Inc. sometime in 1999.

While on the trampoline, plaintiff attempted to execute a back-flip and accidentally landed on his head and neck. The force of the fall caused a fracture in plaintiff's cervical spine resulting in paraplegia. Plaintiff was sixteen years old at the time of his injury. Plaintiff alleges that his injuries were caused by * * * inadequate warnings and instructions [among other things]. Plaintiff brings this lawsuit [in a federal district court] against Jumpking alleging * * * strict liability [and other product liability claims].

Plaintiff, represented by counsel, filed this lawsuit on September 1, 2004. Over one year later, on November 10, 2005, defendant filed the summary judgment motion at bar.

* * * *

* * * *A product is not in a defective condition when it is safe for normal handling.* * * * *If the injury results from abnormal handling* * * * *the seller is not liable. Where, however, the seller has reason to anticipate that danger may result from a particular use,* * * * *the seller may be required to give adequate warning of the danger* * * * *and a product sold without such warning is in a defective condition.* [Emphasis added.]

* * * To prevent the product from being unreasonably dangerous, the seller may be required to give directions or warning, on the container, as to its use. However, where warning is given, the seller may reasonably assume that it will be read and heeded; and a product bearing such a warning is not in a defective condition, nor is it unreasonably dangerous.

Defendant's trampoline is manufactured with nine warning labels that are affixed to various trampoline components. In addition to these nine warning labels, defendant also provides a large laminated warning placard that is designed to be attached by the consumer to the metal frame near the ladder upon which jumpers mount the trampoline. Defendant further provides consumers with a detailed *User Manual* and a videotape that instructs both users and supervisors about safe and responsible trampoline use.

Uniform trampoline safety standards are published by the American Society for Testing and Materials (ASTM). The ASTM standard sets forth specific warning language to accompany trampolines. The record supports defendant's allegation that the trampoline at issue, including the warning that accompanied it, complied with all ASTM standards relevant at the time. Moreover, the ASTM standards at that time did not require warnings against users performing somersaults (flips) and/or jumping with multiple people to appear on the trampoline itself, however, defendant did affix those warnings to the trampoline as well as on a large warning placard attached to the trampoline at the point of entry or mounting. Specifically, one warning attached to the trampoline frame leg stated:

! WARNING
Do not land on head or neck.
Paralysis or death can result, even if you
land in the middle of the trampoline mat (bed).
To reduce the chance of landing on your head or neck, do not do flips.

Accompanying these warning labels is a "stick-figure" drawing of an individual landing on his head. The drawing is located above the warning language and is enclosed in a circular "x-ed" or "crossed-out" notation, commonly understood to mean that the conduct described should be avoided.

Another pair of warning labels affixed to the trampoline legs read:

CASE CONTINUES

CASE 13.3 CONTINUED

! WARNING
Only one person at a time on the trampoline. Multiple jumpers increase the chances of loss of control, collision, and falling off. This can result in broken head, neck, back or leg.

Accompanying these warnings and placed above the warning language is a drawing of two individuals jumping on a single trampoline, which is also enclosed in a "crossed-out" or "x-ed" notation. These same warning labels warning users against performing flips or somersaults and against jumping with multiple people were also on the trampoline frame pad, the large 8" × 11" warning placard framed by the colors orange and yellow and attached to the trampoline frame at the point of entry, and in various places throughout the *User Manual.* The court notes that these warnings went beyond what was required by the ASTM safety standards.

Further, Jack Urbach testified that the warning placard, which specifically warns against both multiple jumping and performing flips or somersaults and the risk of paralysis, was included in the trampoline he purchased, and that he attached the placard to the trampoline upon its initial assembly. Urbach further testified that he had his entire family watch the safety video provided by defendant prior to assembling and using the trampoline.

* * * [D]efendant is entitled to assume that its many warnings will be read, watched and heeded. *The fact that plaintiff may not have seen the many warnings defendant provided prior to his accident does not create a material issue of fact as to whether the warnings rendered the trampoline defective and unreasonably dangerous.* Defendant's summary judgment motion is granted as to plaintiff's claim that the trampoline's warnings were inadequate. I find that defendant's warnings were adequate as a matter of law. [Emphasis added.]

* * * *

IT IS SO ORDERED.

QUESTIONS

1. If Crosswhite had proved that he had not seen, before his accident, the warnings that Jumpking provided, would the court have considered the trampoline defective or unreasonably dangerous? Why or why not?
2. Is the danger from jumping on a trampoline so obvious that even if Jumpking's product had lacked warnings, the manufacturer should not be held liable for a user's injuries? Explain.

EXTENDED CASE 15.2 Hebbring v. U.S. Trustee

United States Court of Appeals, Ninth Circuit, 2006. 463 F.3d 902.

***WARDLAW*, Circuit Judge.**

* * * *

Lisa Hebbring filed a Chapter 7 bankruptcy petition in the United States Bankruptcy Court for the District of Nevada on June 5, 2003, seeking relief from $11,124 in consumer credit card debt. Her petition and accompanying schedules show that Hebbring owns a single-family home in Reno, Nevada valued at $160,000, on which she owes $154,103; a 2001 Volkswagen Beetle valued at $14,000, on which she owes $18,839; and miscellaneous personal property valued at $1,775. Hebbring earns approximately $49,000 per year as a customer service representative for SBC Nevada. Her petition reports monthly net income of $2,813 and monthly expenditures of $2,897, for a monthly deficit of $84. In calculating her income, Hebbring excluded a $232 monthly pre-tax deduction for a 401(k) plan and an $81 monthly after-tax deduction for a retirement savings bond. When she filed for bankruptcy Hebbring was thirty-three years old and had accumulated $6,289 in retirement savings.

The United States Trustee ("Trustee") moved to dismiss Hebbring's petition for substantial abuse, see 11 U.S.C. [Section] 707(b), arguing that she should not be allowed to deduct voluntary retirement contributions from her income and that her recent paystubs showed that her gross income was higher than she had claimed. As a result, the Trustee contended, Hebbring's monthly net income was actually $3,512, leaving her $615 per month in disposable income, sufficient to repay 100% of her unsecured debt over three years.

* * * *

The bankruptcy court granted the Trustee's motion to dismiss * * * [and ultimately Hebbring appealed the dismissal to the U.S. Court of Appeals for the Ninth Circuit].

* * * *

* * * In determining whether a petition constitutes a substantial abuse of Chapter 7, we examine the totality of the circumstances, focusing principally on whether the debtor will have sufficient future disposable income to fund a Chapter 13 plan that would pay a substantial portion of his unsecured debt. To calculate a debtor's disposable income, we begin with current monthly income and subtract amounts reasonably necessary to be expended * * * for the maintenance or support of the debtor or a dependent of the debtor.

* * * [Some] courts * * * have adopted a case-by-case approach, under which contributions to a retirement plan may be found reasonably necessary depending on the debtor's circumstances.

We believe this * * * approach better comports [is consistent] with Congress's intent, as expressed in the language, purpose, and structure of the Bankruptcy Code. By not defining the phrase "reasonably necessary" or providing any examples of expenses that categorically are or are not reasonably necessary, the Code suggests courts should examine each debtor's specific circumstances to determine whether a claimed expense is reasonably necessary for that debtor's maintenance or support. We find no evidence that Congress intended courts to employ a *per se* rule against retirement contributions, which may be crucial for debtors' support upon retirement, particularly for older debtors who have little or no savings. Where Congress intended courts to use a *per se* rule rather than a case-by-case approach in classifying financial interests or obligations under the Bankruptcy Code, it has explicitly communicated its intent. *Congress's decision not to categorically exclude any specific expense, including retirement contributions, from being considered reasonably necessary is probative* [an indication] *of its intent.* [Emphasis added.]

Requiring a fact-specific analysis to determine whether an expense is reasonably necessary is sound policy because it comports with the Code's approach to identifying substantial abuse of the Chapter 7 relief provisions. * * * Congress chose [not] to define "substantial abuse" * * * . Congress thus left a flexible standard enabling courts to address each petition on its own merit. That Congress granted courts the discretion to identify substantial abuse necessarily suggests it intended courts to have the discretion to answer the subsidiary question of whether particular expenses are reasonably necessary.

In light of these considerations, and in the absence of any indication that Congress sought to prohibit debtors from voluntarily contributing to retirement plans *per se,* we conclude that bankruptcy courts have discretion to determine whether retirement contributions are a reasonably nec-

CASE CONTINUES

essary expense for a particular debtor based on the facts of each individual case. In making this fact-intensive determination, courts should consider a number of factors, including but not limited to: the debtor's age, income, overall budget, expected date of retirement, existing retirement savings, and amount of contributions; the likelihood that stopping contributions will jeopardize the debtor's fresh start by forcing the debtor to make up lost contributions after emerging from bankruptcy; and the needs of the debtor's dependents. *Courts must allow debtors to seek bankruptcy protection while voluntarily saving for retirement if such savings appear reasonably necessary for the maintenance or support of the debtor or the debtor's dependents.* [Emphasis added.]

* * * *

Here, the bankruptcy court * * * found * * * that Hebbring's retirement contributions are not a reasonably necessary expense based on her age and specific financial circumstances. * * * When she filed her bankruptcy petition, Hebbring was only thirty-three years old and was contributing approximately 8% of her gross income toward her retirement. Although Hebbring had accumulated only $6,289 in retirement savings, she was earning $49,000 per year and making mortgage payments on a house. In light of these circumstances, the bankruptcy court's conclusion that Hebbring's retirement contributions are not a reasonably necessary expense is not clearly erroneous.

* * * *

For the foregoing reasons, the district court's order affirming the bankruptcy court's order dismissing this case is AFFIRMED.

QUESTIONS

1. Is it fair for the court to treat retirement contributions differently depending on a person's age?
2. Is it likely to have made a difference to the result in this case that the debtor's retirement contributions were automatically and electronically deducted from her pay? Explain.

CASE 19.1 Alberty-Vélez v. Corporación de Puerto Rico para la Difusión Pública

United States Court of Appeals, First Circuit, 2004. 361 F.3d 1.
www.ca1.uscourts.gov[a]

• **Background and Facts** In July 1993, Victoria Lis Alberty-Vélez (Alberty) began to co-host a new television show, *Desde Mi Pueblo,* on WIPR, a television station in Puerto Rico. The show profiled Puerto Rican cities and towns. Instead of signing a single contract, Alberty signed a new contract for each episode. Each contract obligated her to work a certain number of days. She was not obliged to do other work for WIPR, and WIPR was not obliged to contract with her for other work. During the filming, Alberty was responsible for providing her own clothing, shoes, accessories, hairstylist, and other services and materials. She was paid a lump sum, ranging from $400 to $550, for each episode. WIPR did not withhold income or Social Security taxes and did not provide health insurance, life insurance, a retirement plan, paid sick leave, maternity leave, or vacation pay. Alberty became pregnant, and after November 1994, WIPR stopped contracting with her. She filed a suit in a federal district court against WIPR's owner, Corporación de Puerto Rico para la Difusión Pública, alleging, among other things, discrimination on the basis of her pregnancy in violation of a federal statute. The court issued a judgment in the defendant's favor. Alberty appealed to the U.S. Court of Appeals for the First Circuit.

IN THE LANGUAGE OF THE COURT
***HOWARD,* Circuit Judge.**

* * * *

* * * We * * * will apply the common law test to determine whether Alberty was WIPR's employee or an independent contractor.

Under the common law test, a court must consider * * * *the hiring party's right to control the manner and means by which the product is accomplished.* Among other factors relevant to this inquiry are the skills required; the source of the instrumentalities [means] and tools; the location of the work; the duration of the relationship between the parties; whether the hiring party has the right to assign additional projects to the hired party; the extent of the hired party's discretion over when and how long to work; the method of payment; * * * whether the work is part of the regular business of the hiring party; whether the hiring party is in business; the provision of employee benefits; and the tax treatment of the hired party. [Emphasis added.]

* * * *

Several factors favor classifying Alberty as an independent contractor. First, a television actress is a skilled position requiring talent and training not available on-the-job. In this regard, Alberty possesses a master's degree in public communications and journalism; is trained in dance, singing, and modeling; taught within the drama department at the University of Puerto Rico; and acted in several theater and television productions prior to her affiliation with "Desde Mi Pueblo."

Second, Alberty provided the tools and instrumentalities necessary for her to perform. Specifically, she provided, or obtained sponsors to provide, the costumes, jewelry, and other image-related supplies and services necessary for her appearance.

Third, WIPR could not assign Alberty work in addition to filming "Desde Mi Pueblo."

Fourth, the method of payment favors independent-contractor status. Alberty received a lump sum fee for each episode. Her compensation was based on completing the filming, not the time consumed. If she did not film an episode she did not get paid.

Fifth, WIPR did not provide Alberty with benefits.

Sixth, Alberty's tax treatment suggests independent-contractor status.

Despite these factors favoring independent-contractor status, Alberty argues that she was WIPR's employee because WIPR controlled the manner of her work by directing her during filming, dictated the location of her work by selecting the filming sites, and determined the hours of her work * * * . *While "control" over the manner, location, and hours of work is often critical to the independent contractor/employee analysis, it must be considered in light of the work performed and the industry at issue.* Considering the tasks that an actor performs, we do not believe that the sort of control identified by Alberty necessarily indicates employee status. [Emphasis added.]

* * * *

a. In the right-hand column, click on "Opinions." When that page opens, under "General Search," type "02-2187" in the "Opinion Number begins with" box and click on "Submit Query." In the result, click on the appropriate link to access the opinion. The U.S. Court of Appeals for the First Circuit maintains this Web site.

CASE 19.1 CONTINUED

* * * Alberty's work on "Desde Mi Pueblo" required her to film at the featured sites at the required times and to follow the instructions of the director. WIPR could only achieve its goal of producing its program by having Alberty follow these directions. Just as an orchestra musician is subject to the control of the conductor during concerts and rehearsals, an actor is subject to the control of the director during filming.

* * * *

While no one factor is dispositive [determines the outcome], it is clear, based on the parties' entire relationship, that a reasonable fact finder could only conclude that Alberty was an independent contractor. * * * Accordingly, we conclude that Alberty was an independent contractor as a matter of law and therefore cannot maintain [this] action against WIPR.

• **Decision and Remedy** *The U.S. Court of Appeals for the First Circuit affirmed the lower court's judgment in WIPR's favor. The court stated, "The parties structured their relationship through the use of set length contracts that permitted Alberty the freedom to pursue other opportunities and assured WIPR that it would not have to pay Alberty for the weeks that it was not filming. Further, the lack of benefits, the method of payment, and the parties' own description of their relationship in tax documents all indicate independent-contractor status."*

• **What If the Facts Were Different?** *Suppose that Alberty had been a full-time, hourly worker and that such status was common among television hosts, but WIPR had manipulated the benefits and tax withholdings to favor independent-contractor status. How might the result have been different?*

• **The Global Dimension** *Would Alberty have been defined as an employee if she had been a foreign correspondent who reported on stories from international locations and WIPR had paid her travel and related expenses? Explain.*

CASE 20.2 Mims v. Starbucks Corp.

United States District Court, Southern District of Texas, 2007. __ F.Supp.2d __.

• Company Profile Starbucks Corporation (**www.starbucks.com**) is the largest and best-known purveyor of specialty coffees and coffee products in North America. Named after the first mate in Herman Melville's *Moby Dick*, Starbucks does business in more than 10,000 retail locations in the United States and forty-one foreign countries and territories. Starbucks also supplies premium, fresh-roasted coffee to bookstores, grocery stores, restaurants, airlines, sports and entertainment venues, movie theaters, hotels, and cruise ship lines throughout the world. Starbucks' success is predicated on the consistently high quality of its coffees and the other products and services it provides. Starbucks has a reputation for excellence and is recognized for its knowledgeable staff and service.

• Background and Facts In Starbucks Corporation's stores, baristas wait on customers, make drinks for customers, serve customers, operate the cash register, clean the store, and maintain its equipment. In each store, a manager supervises and motivates six to thirty employees, including baristas, shift supervisors, and assistant managers. The manager oversees customer service and processes employee records, payrolls, and inventory counts. He or she also develops strategies to increase revenues, control costs, and comply with corporate policies. Kevin Keevican was hired as a barista in March 2000. Keevican was subsequently promoted to shift supervisor, assistant manager, and, in November 2001, manager. During his tenure, Keevican doubled pastry sales at one store, nearly tripled revenues at another, and won sales awards at both. As a manager, Keevican worked seventy hours a week for $650 to $800, a 10 to 20 percent bonus, and fringe benefits that were not available to baristas, such as paid sick leave. Keevican resigned in 2004. He and other former managers, including Kathleen Mims, filed a suit in a federal district court against Starbucks, seeking unpaid overtime and other amounts. The plaintiffs admitted that they performed many managerial tasks, but argued that they spent 70 to 80 percent of their time on barista chores. Starbucks filed a motion for summary judgment.

IN THE LANGUAGE OF THE COURT
***EWING WERLEIN, JR.*, United States District Judge.**

* * * *

* * * An employee's primary duty is usually what the employee does that is of principal value to the employer, not the collateral tasks that she may also perform, even if they consume more than half her time.

* * * *

Where an employee spends less than 50 percent of his time on management, as both Plaintiffs claim they did, management may still be the employee's primary duty if certain pertinent factors support such a conclusion. *The four factors ordinarily considered are: (1) the relative importance of managerial duties compared to other duties; (2) the frequency with which the employee makes discretionary decisions; (3) the employee's relative freedom from supervision; and (4) the relationship between the employee's salary and the wages paid to employees who perform relevant nonexempt work.* * * * [Emphasis added.]

* * * *

The uncontroverted [not put into question] * * * record establishes that Plaintiffs' significant managerial functions—such as ordering and controlling inventory; deciding whom to interview and hire for barista positions; training and scheduling employees; special marketing promotions; and monitoring labor costs—were critical to the successes of their respective stores. If Plaintiffs while each managing a store with annual sales exceeding $1 million were able to spend 70 or 80 percent of their time pouring coffee and performing other barista chores that six to 30 subordinates also performed, those activities of the manager quite obviously were of minor importance to Defendant when compared to the significant management responsibilities performed during the other 20 to 30 percent of their time, management responsibilities that directly influenced the ultimate commercial and financial success or failure of the store.

* * * *

It is uncontroverted that Plaintiffs, as the highest-ranking employees in their stores, made decisions on matters such as deciding whom to interview and hire as a barista, whom to assign to train

CASE 20.2 CONTINUED new hires, when to discipline employees, whom to deploy in certain positions, what promotions to run, and the amount of product to order for efficient inventory control. Plaintiffs argue, however, that they infrequently exercised discretion because they worked under the "ultimate managing authority" of their district managers, who had authority to hire more senior employees, approve changes to Plaintiffs' work schedules, set rates of pay for newly-hired employees if the pay exceeded Starbucks's guidelines, and establish guidelines for Plaintiffs when completing performance reviews. *However, the manager of a local store in a modern multi-store organization has management as his or her primary duty even though the discretion usually associated with management may be limited by the company's desire for standardization and uniformity.* * * * [Emphasis added.]

Plaintiffs also contend that they were not relatively free from supervision because their district managers spent "substantial amounts of time" in Plaintiffs' stores. * * * On the other hand, it is uncontroverted that each Plaintiff as store manager was the single highest-ranking employee in his particular store and was responsible on site for that store's day-to-day overall operations. Indeed, department and assistant managers have been held exempt under the executive exemption even when their superiors worked in close proximity to them at the same location. Viewing the evidence in the light most favorable to Plaintiffs, Plaintiffs still were vested with enough discretionary power and freedom from supervision to qualify for the executive exemption.

* * * *

The final factor is the relationship between Plaintiffs' salary and the wages paid to non-exempt employees. Plaintiffs argue, with no supporting evidence, that their compensation "approximated that received by some assistant store managers." It is undisputed, however, that Plaintiffs received nearly twice the total annual compensation received by their highest-paid shift supervisors, and Plaintiffs received bonuses and benefits not available to other employees (including assistant managers). This marked disparity in pay and benefits between Plaintiffs and the non-exempt employees is a hallmark of exempt status.

- **Decision and Remedy** *The court issued a summary judgment in Starbucks' favor and dismissed the claims of the plaintiffs, who were exempt from the FLSA's overtime provisions as executive employees. The court concluded that during their employment the plaintiffs' "primary duty" was management.*

- **What If the Facts Were Different?** *Suppose that Keevican's job title had been "glorified barista" instead of "manager." Would the result have been different? Explain.*

- **The Legal Environment Dimension** *What might the court have concluded if the store could have operated successfully without the plaintiffs' performing their "managerial" functions?*

CASE 16.3 Moren v. Jax Restaurant

Minnesota Court of Appeals, 2004. 679 N.W.2d 165.
www.lawlibrary.state.mn.us/archive/cap1st.html[a]

• Background and Facts "Jax Restaurant" is a partnership that operates Jax Restaurant in Foley, Minnesota. One afternoon in October 2000, Nicole Moren, one of the partners, finished her shift at the restaurant at 4:00 P.M. and picked up her two-year-old son, Remington, from day care. About 5:30 P.M., Moren returned to the restaurant with Remington after Amy Benedetti, the other partner and Moren's sister, asked for help. Moren's husband offered to pick up Remington in twenty minutes. Because Moren did not want Remington running around the restaurant, she brought him into the kitchen with her, set him on top of the counter, and began rolling out pizza dough using a dough-pressing machine. While she was making pizzas, Remington reached his hand into the dough press. His hand was crushed, causing permanent injuries. Through his father, Remington filed a suit in a Minnesota state court against the partnership, alleging negligence. The partnership filed a complaint against Moren, arguing that it was entitled to indemnity (compensation or reimbursement) from Moren for her negligence. The court issued a summary judgment in favor of Moren on the complaint. The partnership appealed this judgment to a state intermediate appellate court.

IN THE LANGUAGE OF THE COURT
***CRIPPEN*, Judge.**

* * * *

Under Minnesota's Uniform Partnership Act [the most recent version of the UPA], a partnership is an entity distinct from its partners, and as such, a partnership may sue and be sued in the name of the partnership. [Under the UPA] *"[a] partnership is liable for loss or injury caused to a person * * * as a result of a wrongful act or omission, or other actionable conduct, of a partner acting in the ordinary course of business of the partnership or with authority of the partnership."* Accordingly, a "partnership shall * * * indemnify [reimburse]a partner for liabilities incurred by the partner in the ordinary course of the business of the partnership * * * ." Stated conversely, an "act of a partner which is not apparently for carrying on in the ordinary course the partnership business or business of the kind carried on by the partnership binds the partnership only if the act was authorized by the other partners." Thus, under the plain language of the UPA, *a partner has a right to indemnity from the partnership, but the partnership's claim of indemnity from a partner is not authorized or required.* [Emphasis added.]

The [lower] court correctly concluded that Nicole Moren's conduct was in the ordinary course of business of the partnership and, as a result, indemnity by the partner to the partnership was inappropriate. It is undisputed that one of the cooks scheduled to work that evening did not come in, and that Moren's partner asked her to help in the kitchen. It also is undisputed that Moren was making pizzas for the partnership when her son was injured. Because her conduct at the time of the injury was in the ordinary course of business of the partnership, under the UPA, her conduct bound the partnership and it owes indemnity to her for her negligence.

* * * *

Appellant * * * claims that because Nicole Moren's action of bringing Remington into the kitchen was partly motivated by personal reasons, her conduct was outside the ordinary course of business. Because it has not been previously addressed, there is no Minnesota authority regarding this issue. * * * We conclude that the conduct of Nicole Moren was no less in the ordinary course of business because it also served personal purposes. It is undisputed that Moren was acting for the benefit of the partnership by making pizzas when her son was injured, and even though she was simultaneously acting in her role as a mother, her conduct remained in the ordinary course of the partnership business.

• Decision and Remedy *The state intermediate appellate court affirmed the lower court's judgment. "Minnesota law requires a partnership to indemnify its partners for the result of their negligence." The appellate court also reasoned that "the conduct of a partner may be partly motivated by personal reasons and still occur in the ordinary course of business of the partnership." Thus "liability for Nicole Moren's negligence rested with the partnership, even if the partner's conduct partly served her personal interests."*

---

a. In the "Published" section, click on "M–O." On that page, scroll to the name of the case and click on the docket number to access the opinion. The Minnesota State Law Library maintains this Web site.

CASE 16.3 CONTINUED

• **What If the Facts Were Different?** *Suppose that Moren's predominant motive in bringing her son to the restaurant had been to benefit herself by feeding him free pizza. Would the result have been different? Why or why not?*

• **The Legal Environment Dimension** *What seems to have occurred in this case that might have served as an alternative basis for imposing liability on the partnership? (Hint: Who besides Moren had the authority to act on behalf of the partnership?)*

CASE 12.1
Trustees of University of District of Columbia v. Vossoughi

District of Columbia Court of Appeals, 963 A.2d 1162 (2009).

BACKGROUND AND FACTS • Jafar Vossoughi is an expert in applied mechanics and experimental biomechanics, which encompasses the testing of mechanical theories and the creation and use of experimental devices for biomechanical research. In the 1990s, while teaching at the University of the District of Columbia (UDC), Vossoughi set up a laboratory to conduct research. When his employment contract expired, he remained on campus and continued his research. In 2000, without Vossoughi's knowledge, UDC cleaned out the laboratory and threw away most of its contents. Vossoughi filed a suit in a District of Columbia court against UDC, seeking damages for the loss of his course materials, unpublished research data, unique scientific instruments, and other items. He personally testified as to the "replacement cost." A jury found UDC liable for conversion (the wrongful taking of someone's personal property) and awarded Vossoughi $1.65 million. UDC appealed.

IN THE LANGUAGE OF THE COURT

GLICKMAN, Associate Judge:

* * * *

The usual and traditional measure of damages for conversion of property is the fair market value of the property at the time of the conversion. * * * But fair market value is not always the test. Sometimes fair market value cannot be determined, or would be inadequate, as when, for example, the article destroyed was unique or possessed qualities the special nature of which could only be appreciated by the owner. Accordingly, *for purposes of awarding adequate compensation for the destruction of property, value means exchange value or the value to the owner if this is greater than the exchange value.* In general, therefore, a person tortiously deprived of property is entitled to damages based upon its special value to him if that is greater than its market value. Where the lost property in such cases is replaceable, it is appropriate to measure damages for its loss by the cost of replacement. [Emphasis added.]

* * * Dr. Vossoughi's course materials, unpublished research and fabricated instruments * * * had great use value to Dr. Vossoughi but no comparable (if any) market value.

* * * *

* * * Dr. Vossoughi based his estimates of the value of the property on the time it would take him to replicate it. This was a conceptually reasonable approach * * * . UDC complains of the vagueness of Dr. Vossoughi's testimony: for example, his estimates were rough approximations, and he did not specify exactly how he valued his or others' time * * * . But our cases have held that an owner is qualified to estimate the value of his property based on his familiarity with its quality and condition * * * . In this case, Dr. Vossoughi certainly had the requisite [necessary] familiarity, and given his experience as a fabricator of instruments, a teacher, a researcher, and a grant recipient, he also had considerable expertise to draw on. His opinions clearly were informed ones. There is nothing to show that his estimates were unrealistic; on the contrary, they were corroborated [substantiated] by [Vossoughi's expert witnesses] Dr. Conway and Dr. Saha.

UDC further argues that Dr. Vossoughi's valuation of his course materials was flawed in [two] respects. First, Dr. Vossoughi admitted his course materials were not salable ("Nobody would buy somebody else's [teaching] notes. It's useless [except] for that particular class."). But * * * the absence of an exchange value does not mean the course materials had no compensable use value to Dr. Vossoughi. Second, Dr. Vossoughi acknowledged having been compensated by * * * UDC from his teaching salary to prepare the course materials and teach the courses. But this fact does not diminish the value of his course materials to Dr. Vossoughi; if anything, it confirms their value.

DECISION AND REMEDY • *The District of Columbia Court of Appeals affirmed the award. Vossoughi's evidence was "not speculative and unreliable." His lost property was difficult to value, but the evidence allowed the jury to make a fair estimate of its worth.*

CASE 12.1 CONTINUED ➧ **THE LEGAL ENVIRONMENT DIMENSION** • *Should plaintiffs be required to prove the amount of their damages with certainty and exactitude? Why or why not?*

THE ETHICAL DIMENSION • *Did Vossoughi have an ethical duty to reduce the amount of his damages by, for example, retrieving from the trash as much of his property as he could? Discuss.*

EXTENDED CASE 27.1
Clarett v. National Football League

United States Court of Appeals, Second Circuit, 369 F.3d 124 (2004).

IN THE LANGUAGE OF THE COURT

SOTOMAYOR, Circuit Judge.

* * * *

[Maurice] Clarett, former running back for Ohio State University ("OSU") and Big Ten Freshman of the Year, is an accomplished and talented amateur football player. After gaining national attention as a high school player, Clarett became the first college freshman since 1943 to open as a starter at the position of running back for OSU. He led that team through an undefeated season, even scoring the winning touchdown in a double-overtime victory in the 2003 Fiesta Bowl to claim the national championship. * * * Clarett is now interested in turning professional by entering the [National Football League ("NFL" or "the League")] draft. Clarett is precluded from so doing, however, under the NFL's current rules governing draft eligibility.

* * * The eligibility rules * * * permit a player to enter the draft three full seasons after that player's high school graduation.

Clarett graduated high school on December 11, 2001, two-thirds of the way through the 2001 NFL season and is a season shy of the three necessary to qualify under the draft's eligibility rules. Unwilling to forgo the prospect of a year of lucrative professional play or run the risk of a career-compromising injury were his entry into the draft delayed until next year, Clarett filed this suit [in a federal district court] alleging that the NFL's draft eligibility rules are an unreasonable restraint of trade in violation of Section 1 of the Sherman Act and Section 4 of the Clayton Act.

* * * The major source of the parties' * * * disputes is the relationship between the challenged eligibility rules and the current collective bargaining agreement governing the terms and conditions of employment for NFL players * * *. The current collective bargaining agreement between the NFL and its players union was negotiated between the NFL Management Council ("NFLMC"), which is the NFL member clubs' multi-employer bargaining unit, and the NFL Players Association ("NFLPA"), the NFL players' exclusive bargaining representative.

* * * *

* * * On February 5, 2004, the district court granted summary judgment in favor of Clarett and ordered him eligible to enter this year's draft. * * * [The NFL appealed to this court.]

* * * *

* * * *To accommodate the collective bargaining process, certain concerted activity among and between labor and employers [is] held to be beyond the reach of the antitrust laws.* [Emphasis added.]

* * * *

Although the NFL has maintained draft eligibility rules in one form or another for much of its history, the inception of a collective bargaining relationship between the NFL and its players union some thirty years ago irrevocably altered the governing legal regime. * * *Prospective players no longer have the right to negotiate directly with the NFL teams over the terms and conditions of their employment. That responsibility is instead committed to the NFL and the players union to accomplish through the collective bargaining process, and throughout that process the NFL and the players union are to have the freedom to craft creative solutions to their differences in light of the economic imperatives of their industry. Furthermore, the NFL teams are permitted to engage in joint conduct with respect to the terms and conditions of players' employment as a multi-employer bargaining unit without risking antitrust liability.

* * * *

Clarett's argument that antitrust law should permit him to circumvent this scheme established by federal labor law starts with the contention that the eligibility rules do not constitute a mandatory subject of collective bargaining and thus cannot fall within the protection of the * * * exemption. * * * However, we find that the eligibility rules are mandatory bargaining subjects. Though tailored to the unique circumstance of a professional sports league, the eligibility rules for the draft represent a quite literal condition for initial employment and for that reason alone might constitute a mandatory bargaining subject. But moreover, the eligibility rules constitute a mandatory bargaining subject because they have tangible effects on the wages and working conditions of current NFL players. Because the unusual economic imperatives of professional sports raise numerous problems with little or no precedent in standard industrial relations, * * * many of the arrangements in professional sports that, at first glance, might not appear to deal with wages or working conditions are indeed mandatory bargaining subjects.

Furthermore, by reducing competition in the market for entering players, the eligibility rules also affect the job security of veteran players. Because the size of NFL teams is capped, the eligibility rules diminish a veteran player's risk of being replaced by either a drafted

EXTENDED CASE CONTINUES

EXTENDED CASE 27.1 CONTINUED

rookie or a player who enters the draft and, though not drafted, is then hired as a rookie free agent. Consequently, * * * we find that to regard the NFL's eligibility rules as merely permissive bargaining subjects would ignore the reality of collective bargaining in sports.

* * * *

For the foregoing reasons, the judgment of the district court is REVERSED and the case REMANDED with instructions to enter judgment in favor of the NFL. The order of the district court designating Clarett eligible to enter this year's NFL draft is VACATED.

QUESTIONS

1. Why are the NFL's member clubs permitted to agree that a player will not be hired until three full football seasons after the player's high school graduation?
2. Why couldn't the NFL's eligibility rules be eliminated from the list of mandatory subjects for the parties' collective bargaining agreement?

CASE 29.1
SEC v. Texas Gulf Sulphur Co.

United States Court of Appeals, Second Circuit, 401 F.2d 833 (1968).

BACKGROUND AND FACTS • Texas Gulf Sulphur Company (TGS) conducted aerial geophysical surveys over more than 15,000 square miles of eastern Canada. The operations indicated concentrations of commercially exploitable minerals. At one site near Timmins, Ontario, TGS drilled a hole that appeared to yield a core with an exceedingly high mineral content. TGS kept secret the results of the core sample. Officers and employees of the company made substantial purchases of TGS's stock or accepted stock options (rights to purchase stock) after learning of the ore discovery, even though further drilling was necessary to establish whether there was enough ore to be mined commercially. Several months later, TGS announced that the strike was expected to yield at least 25 million tons of ore. Subsequently, the price of TGS stock rose substantially. The Securities and Exchange Commission (SEC) brought a suit against the officers and employees of TGS for violating SEC Rule 10b-5. The officers and employees argued that the information on which they had traded had not been material at the time of their trades because the mine had not then been commercially proved. The trial court held that most of the defendants had not violated SEC Rule 10b-5, and the SEC appealed.

IN THE LANGUAGE OF THE COURT

WATERMAN, Circuit Judge.

* * * *

* * * Whether facts are material within Rule 10b-5 when the facts relate to a particular event and are undisclosed by those persons who are knowledgeable thereof *will depend at any given time upon a balancing of both the indicated probability that the event will occur and the anticipated magnitude of the event in light of the totality of the company activity.* Here, * * * knowledge of the possibility, which surely was more than marginal, of the existence of a mine of the vast magnitude indicated by the remarkably rich drill core located rather close to the surface (suggesting mineability by the less expensive openpit method) within the confines of a large anomaly (suggesting an extensive region of mineralization) might well have affected the price of TGS stock and would certainly have been an important fact to a reasonable, if speculative, investor in deciding whether he should buy, sell, or hold. [Emphasis added.]

* * * *

* * * A major factor in determining whether the * * * discovery was a material fact is the importance attached to the drilling results by those who knew about it. * * * The timing by those who knew of it of their stock purchases * * *—purchases in some cases by individuals who had never before purchased * * * TGS stock—virtually compels the inference that the insiders were influenced by the drilling results.

DECISION AND REMEDY • *The appellate court ruled in favor of the SEC. All of the trading by insiders who knew of the mineral find before its true extent had been publicly announced violated SEC Rule 10b-5.*

IMPACT OF THIS CASE ON TODAY'S LAW • *This landmark case affirmed the principle that the test of whether information is "material," for SEC Rule 10b-5 purposes, is whether it would affect the judgment of reasonable investors. The corporate insiders' purchases of stock and stock options indicated that they were influenced by the drilling results and that the information about the drilling results was material. The courts continue to cite this case when applying SEC Rule 10b-5 to cases of alleged insider trading.*

WHAT IF THE FACTS WERE DIFFERENT? • *Suppose that further drilling had revealed that there was not enough ore at this site for it to be mined commercially. Would the defendants still have been liable for violating SEC Rule 10b-5? Why or why not?*

The Private Securities Litigation Reform Act. One of the unintended effects of SEC Rule 10b-5 was to deter disclosure of forward-looking information. To understand why, consider an example. A company announces that its projected earnings in a certain time period will be $15 million. It turns out that the forecast is wrong. The earnings are in fact much lower, and the price of the company's stock is affected—negatively. The shareholders then bring a class-action suit against the company, alleging that the directors violated SEC Rule 10b-5 by disclosing misleading financial information.

In an attempt to rectify this problem and promote disclosure, Congress passed the Private Securities Litigation Reform Act (PSLRA) of 1995. Among other things, the PSLRA provides a "safe harbor" for publicly held companies that make forward-looking statements, such as financial forecasts. Those who make such statements are protected against liability for securities fraud as long as the statements are accompanied by "meaningful cautionary statements identifying important factors that could cause actual results to differ materially from those in the forward-looking statement."[24]

The Securities Litigation Uniform Standards Act. After the PSLRA was passed, a number of class-action suits involving securities were filed in state courts to skirt its requirements. In response to this problem, Congress passed the Securities Litigation Uniform Standards Act (SLUSA) of 1998.[25] This act placed stringent limits on the ability of plaintiffs to bring class-action suits in state courts against firms whose securities are traded on national stock exchanges. The SLUSA not only prevents the purchasers and sellers of securities from bringing class-action fraud claims under state securities laws, but it also applies to investors who are fraudulently induced to hold on to their securities.[26]